Oxford
School
Thesaurus

Editor: Robert Allen
Literacy Consultant: John Mannion

OXFORD
UNIVERSITY PRESS

OXFORD
UNIVERSITY PRESS

Great Clarendon Street, Oxford OX2 6DP

Oxford University Press is a department of the University of Oxford.
It furthers the University's objective of excellence in research,
scholarship, and education by publishing worldwide in

Oxford New York

Auckland Cape Town Dar es Salaam Hong Kong Karachi
Kuala Lumpur Madrid Melbourne Mexico City Nairobi
New Delhi Shanghai Taipei Toronto

With offices in

Argentina Austria Brazil Chile Czech Republic France Greece
Guatemala Hungary Italy Japan Poland Portugal Singapore
South Korea Switzerland Thailand Turkey Ukraine Vietnam

Oxford is a registered trade mark of Oxford University Press
in the UK and in certain other countries

First published 2005
Second edition 2007
This edition 2012

British Library Cataloguing in Publication Data
Data available

ISBN: 978 0 19 275690 9 (hardback)

ISBN: 978 0 19 275694 7 (paperback)

10 9 8 7 6 5 4 3 2

Printed in China

Paper used in the production of this book is a natural, recyclable product made from wood grown in
sustainable forests. The manufacturing process conforms to the environmental regulations of the
country of origin.

Contents

Preface

The *Oxford School Thesaurus* has been specially written for students aged 10 and above. It is particularly useful for students who are about to start secondary school and who need an up-to-date, student-friendly reference tool that they can consult at home and at school.

This thesaurus is easy to use and understand. The vocabulary has been carefully selected and covers school curriculum topics ranging from English Language, Science and Technology, to Sports and Music in order to support students in their writing assignments and homework.

The *Oxford School Thesaurus* gives all the information that students need for exam success in a simple and accessible format. Use of the thesaurus will help students develop the best English language skills, and equip them with excellent writing and speaking skills for years to come.

The *Oxford School Thesaurus* can also be used very effectively in conjunction with the *Oxford School Dictionary*, which offers further support with reading, writing, and vocabulary building.

The publisher and editors are indebted to all the advisers, consultants, and teachers who were involved in planning and compiling this thesaurus.

Introduction

How a thesaurus can help you

A thesaurus gives you alternatives—often more interesting and colourful ones—to the words you already know and use; these are known as **synonyms**. In some cases it also gives you the opposites of words, which are known as **antonyms.** Using a thesaurus regularly will extend your vocabulary and help you to be more accurate and imaginative in the way you express yourself.

When you are speaking, you often don't have time to choose the exact or most appropriate word, but when you are writing and redrafting, a thesaurus can be very useful in helping you to avoid such things as overused words or words that are too general to have any impact. For example, *nice* is a perfectly acceptable word in conversation, but a thesaurus will allow you to replace it with more interesting words like *pleasant, agreeable, enjoyable, likeable,* or *friendly.*

When you are speaking, you generally know your audience and have a good idea about which words are appropriate. In writing, you need to think about such things as whether your language should be formal or colloquial. A word that is 'right' for one audience might not be for another. An important role for a thesaurus is to provide you with more choices of words for different situations. For example, *kill* is a word for general use, whereas *slay* is mostly found in stories and dramas; *little* is a much more affectionate and intimate word than its more neutral synonym *small* (compare *a little child* and *a small child*). In this thesaurus you will find guidance on whether a particular word or expression is formal or informal and whether it is used in a disapproving manner.

The difference between a dictionary and a thesaurus

Dictionaries and thesauruses help you in different ways with using language. A dictionary tells you mostly about what words mean, whereas a thesaurus helps you to find alternative words to the ones you know and so helps you to put more words into use.

For instance, all of the following words have the same meaning in a dictionary: 'a place where people live'.

house, home, dwelling, abode, residence

A thesaurus gives you a chance to choose which of these words you want to use.

Abode would be a good choice in a very formal piece of writing.

House will be good for most occasions.

Home gives an idea of warmth and friendliness.

When you are writing you might look up a word in a dictionary to check its exact meaning or spelling, but you use a thesaurus when you want to find a **better** or **more interesting** or **more exact** way of expressing your ideas. You will also find that thesauruses organize words around key ideas and that looking up a word can give you **further ideas** for writing.

Finding a better word

When you are writing a first draft you quite often put down the first appropriate word that comes to mind. This gets the idea down, but is it the best way of saying it? For example, the sentence

The new school uniform rules made me angry.

is an acceptable sentence that captures an idea, but is it the best one? Using the thesaurus you might come up with

The new school uniform rules made me see red.
The new school uniform rules made me lose my temper.
The new school uniform rules made me freak out.

The three new sentences mean the same as the original, but they will have a different impact on the reader. One is more formal, one is less formal, and one uses a metaphor. Which sentence is the best for you will depend on the purpose of your writing.

Finding a more interesting word

There are nearly always different ways of expressing the same idea. In your writing you will often need to think of different ways to say the same thing when you are writing a long piece on a single topic.

For example, suppose you are writing a letter of complaint about the non-stop noise at a nightclub near you. You can say *non-stop* the first time you mention the idea, but the thesaurus will help you describe the noise as

continuous, constant, endless, uninterrupted, unending, never-ending, or *ceaseless.*

Finding a more exact word

Research has shown that students who get the best exam grades tend to make exact choices of words. They do not say 'A bird made a noise in the tree' but 'An owl hooted in the oak tree'. An exact choice of words, particularly of nouns and verbs, helps your reader to imagine what you are describing.

For example, a simple sentence like

I walked home.

can, with the help of the thesaurus, become

I *hiked* home or I *trudged* home or I *traipsed* home.

Just by changing one word you can give the reader a better idea of the nature and difficulty of the walk.

Further ideas

One of the advantages of a paper-based thesaurus over an electronic one is that when you look up a word you do not just see that word, you also see the ones around it. (This is quite apart from the interesting words that you might see on the way to the word you want.)

For instance, if you were writing about *beginnings* you would also see on the same page entries for *begin* and *beginner*. Ideas often cluster in this way, and by exploring the words around the one you are interested in, you might find useful and interesting pointers that will help in your writing.

Thesaurus features

headwords are in blue to find words easily

giant ADJECTIVE
The thrust from the four giant engines pushed him back in his seat.
► huge, enormous, gigantic, colossal, immense, massive, mighty, vast, large, elephantine, gargantuan, mammoth, monstrous, prodigious, titanic, (*more informal*) whopping, (*more informal*) jumbo, (*more informal*) king-size
OPPOSITES ARE tiny, miniature

over 100,000 synonyms are given to select from

labels encourage accurate use of language

opposites are given to extend vocabulary further

words classes (parts of speech) are given to build grammatical skills

glance VERB
1 *She glanced at her watch.*
► look, peek, peep, take a look at
2 **glance at** or **through** *I only had time to glance at the article.*
► scan, skim, read quickly, run your eye over

up-to-date example sentences and phrases show how words are used in context

panels highlight overused words and give alternatives

go VERB This word is often overused. Here are some alternatives:
1 *She started to go towards the entrance.*
► move, advance, proceed, walk, make your way, progress
2 *We are going to London on Friday.*
► travel, journey, make a trip

Topic panels list words in 'families' or groups of words with related meanings

different meanings are clearly numbered

insect NOUN
Some insects are disguised as a leaf or a twig.
► bug, pest, (*more informal*) creepy-crawly
SOME COMMON INSECTS
flies: fly, blackfly, bluebottle, gadfly, gnat, horsefly, housefly, hoverfly, midge, mosquito, sandfly, tsetse fly.

Usage panels provide extra information on how to use the headword correctly

List of panels

Topic panels

General
anniversary
clothes
coats
computer
crockery
dwelling
engineering
entertainment
family
fish
film
games
gems
languages
rooms
restaurants
shapes
shops
sounds

Art
jewellery
painting
pictures

Design & Technology
cereal
cheese
coffee
colours
food
fruit
herbs
meals
nuts

pasta
tools
vegetables
wood

English
collective nouns
fiction
non-fiction
poems
reference
stories
theatre
writers

Geography
coasts
habitats
roads
rocks
transport
weather

History
dinosaurs
disasters
rulers

Music
music
keyboard
singer
songs
voice

PSHE
communication

crime
government

RE
festivals
priest
religions
sacred texts
worship, places of

PE
dance
sail
sports
teams

Science
acid
animals
birds
body
bones
chemical elements
doctors
insects
measurement
metal
mineral
phobias
planets
plants
reptiles
rodents
science
snakes
young animals

Overused words

all right	fat	hit	new	short
bad	get	laugh	nice	small
big	go	like	old	strong
bit	good	little	put	thin
cry	great	look	run	very
eat	happy	lovely	sad	walk
end	hard	move	say	

Aa

aback ADVERB
taken aback *Mrs Diggory looked taken aback for a moment.*
► surprised, shocked, astonished, startled, disconcerted, nonplussed, dumbfounded

abandon VERB
1 *The children had been abandoned in the war.*
► desert, leave behind, leave stranded, strand, forsake, leave in the lurch, maroon, wash your hands of
2 *The car was abandoned near the motorway.*
► leave, (*more informal*) dump, (*more informal*) ditch
3 *The entire project had to be abandoned.*
► cancel, drop, discontinue, (*more informal*) give up, (*more informal*) scrap, (*very informal*) ditch
4 *The company abandoned its claims to the money*
► drop, give up, renounce, waive, (*more formal*) relinquish

abbreviate VERB
The medium is known as a digital video disc, usually abbreviated to DVD.
► shorten, reduce, abridge

abduct VERB
The woman had been abducted by two men and held for several days.
► kidnap, seize, carry off, capture

abhorrent ADJECTIVE
Racial abuse is abhorrent to most people.
► hateful, loathsome, detested (by), detestable, repugnant, repellent, obnoxious, odious, offensive, horrifying, repulsive, revolting, abominable, disgusting, distasteful, execrable, horrible, horrid, nauseating

abide VERB
1 *I cannot abide grown men walking around in trainers.*
► bear, stand, endure, tolerate, (*more informal*) stomach, (*more informal*) put up with
2 **abide by** *The company expects its employees to abide by its rules.*
► obey, observe, follow, accept, keep to, carry out, conform to, stick to, adhere to, act in accordance with, stand by, submit to

ability NOUN
1 *An unexpected inheritance gave him the ability to travel the world.*
► power, resources, capability, capacity, means, opportunity, potential, wherewithal
2 *Jane's new employers had received good reports of her ability.*
► capability, competence, aptitude, expertise, proficiency, (*more informal*) know-how
3 *You have the ability to do well in life.*
► capacity, talent, intelligence, skill, aptitude, flair
4 *He has many unusual abilities.*
► talent, skill, accomplishment, gift, qualification

able ADJECTIVE
1 *a group of the most able students*
► talented, accomplished, proficient, efficient, gifted, capable, clever, skilled, competent, intelligent, effective
AN OPPOSITE IS incompetent
2 **able to** *Are you able to come?*
► allowed to, free to, prepared to, in a position to, (*more informal*) up to (coming)

abnormal ADJECTIVE
1 *The tests produced some abnormal results.*
► unusual, untypical, uncommon, extraordinary, exceptional, unrepresentative, aberrant, anomalous, freak
2 *He was surprised by her abnormal beliefs and behaviour.*
► strange, peculiar, odd, weird, curious, eccentric, wayward, perverse, erratic, queer, bizarre
AN OPPOSITE IS normal

abnormality NOUN
1 *The study gave evidence of some abnormality.*
► strangeness, peculiarity, irregularity, oddity, oddness, aberration, anomaly, deviation, eccentricity, idiosyncrasy, waywardness, singularity
2 *The baby was born with several abnormalities.*
► deformity, malformation

abolish VERB
a decision to abolish the community charge
► end, cancel, put an end to, (*more informal*) get rid of, (*more informal*) do away with, (*technical*) abrogate, annul, repeal, remove, rescind, revoke, quash, suppress, terminate, eliminate, eradicate, overturn, withdraw
AN OPPOSITE IS create

abominable ADJECTIVE
The revolt was suppressed with abominable cruelty.
► atrocious, appalling, detestable, hateful, odious, vile, obnoxious, brutal, dreadful, abhorrent, diabolical, disgusting, repellent, horrifying
AN OPPOSITE IS humane

abort VERB
1 *The treatment caused the foetus to abort.*
► miscarry
2 *The pilot had reached a speed at which the take-off could not be aborted.*
► terminate, cancel, discontinue, stop, end, halt, call off

abortion NOUN
She decided against an abortion.
► termination (of pregnancy)

abortive ADJECTIVE
There had been several abortive attempts to assassinate the president.
► failed, vain, unsuccessful, fruitless, futile, ineffective, ineffectual, useless, pointless, unproductive
AN OPPOSITE IS successful

A

about-turn NOUN
The change in policy amounted to a complete about-turn.
▶ reversal, U-turn, volte face, change of direction, change of course, change of mind, sea change

abrasive ADJECTIVE
Charles had a manner that some thought abrasive.
▶ harsh, curt, brusque, caustic, acerbic, abrupt, grating, biting, vitriolic, rough, insensitive
OPPOSITES ARE kind, gentle

abridge VERB
The editor may want to abridge letters for publication.
▶ shorten, reduce, cut, truncate, edit, trim, condense, abbreviate
OPPOSITES ARE expand, lengthen

abridged ADJECTIVE
For the exam you can read an abridged version of the novel.
▶ shortened, reduced, cut, cut down, condensed, edited, censored, *(more informal)* potted

abridgement NOUN
In 1676 he published an abridgement of the Book of Martyrs.
▶ short version, condensation, summary, synopsis, digest, precis

abrupt ADJECTIVE
1 *She gave a cry and came to an abrupt halt.*
▶ sudden, hurried, unexpected, quick, hasty, rapid, swift, precipitate, unforeseen, unpredicted
2 *Beyond the cliff edge they could see an abrupt drop.*
▶ sheer, sharp, steep, precipitous
AN OPPOSITE IS gradual
3 *He had a decidedly abrupt manner.*
▶ blunt, harsh, curt, terse, gruff, rude, offhand, brusque, insensitive, outspoken, plain-spoken
OPPOSITES ARE polite, courteous

absent ADJECTIVE
1 *The man had been absent from work all week.*
▶ away, off, missing, *(more informal)* skiving
AN OPPOSITE IS present
2 *Her eyes had an absent look.*
▶ distracted, dreamy, far-away, absorbed, inattentive, preoccupied absent-minded
OPPOSITES ARE attentive, alert

absent-minded ADJECTIVE
Stephen looked absent-minded as he hurried off.
▶ forgetful, distracted, preoccupied, inattentive, absorbed, scatterbrained
OPPOSITES ARE attentive, alert

absolute ADJECTIVE
1 *The house was an absolute mess.*
▶ complete, total, utter, sheer, perfect, downright, unmitigated
2 *The venture had been an absolute success.*
▶ complete, total, outright, categorical, out-and-out, unqualified
3 *Speak only the absolute truth.*
▶ definite, positive, categorical, undoubted, unquestioned

4 *The country had known only absolute rulers.*
▶ autocratic, despotic, dictatorial, tyrannical, omnipotent, sovereign, totalitarian, unrestricted, undemocratic

absolutely ADVERB
You are absolutely right.
▶ completely, totally, utterly, perfectly, quite, unquestionably, unreservedly

absorb VERB
1 *Wood absorbs wetness and expands.*
▶ soak up, suck up, assimilate, take in
AN OPPOSITE IS emit
2 *It is difficult to absorb so much information at once.*
▶ assimilate, take in, soak up, digest, comprehend
3 *Getting through the day absorbed all her energies.*
▶ consume, drain, exhaust, use up, take up, swallow up
4 *Special buffers absorb the impact.*
▶ cushion, deaden, soften, reduce, lessen
5 *The children were absorbed by their game.*
▶ preoccupy, engross, captivate, occupy, enthral, fascinate, interest, involve, rivet

absorbent ADJECTIVE
Line the cage with a good layer of absorbent paper.
▶ porous, spongy, absorptive, permeable
AN OPPOSITE IS impervious

abstain VERB
abstain from *They agreed to abstain from violent action for the time being.*
▶ go without, give up, forgo, refrain from, eschew, avoid, reject, renounce, deny yourself, desist from
AN OPPOSITE IS indulge (yourself)

abstemious ADJECTIVE
They lead an abstemious life.
▶ frugal, temperate, austere, ascetic, restrained, sparing, puritanical, strict, spartan, sober
AN OPPOSITE IS self-indulgent

abstract ADJECTIVE
1 *Abstract concepts are hard to define.*
▶ theoretical, conceptual, hypothetical, academic, notional, metaphysical, philosophical, intangible, intellectual, indefinite
AN OPPOSITE IS concrete
2 *The pieces are stitched together to form a large abstract design.*
▶ symbolic, non-pictorial, non-representational
AN OPPOSITE IS representational

abstract NOUN
An abstract of the lecture was circulated in advance.
▶ summary, precis, résumé, outline

abstruse ADJECTIVE
He had spent a lifetime poring over abstruse codes.
▶ obscure, cryptic, complex, difficult, hard, puzzling, incomprehensible, perplexing, mysterious, unfathomable
AN OPPOSITE IS obvious

absurd ADJECTIVE
It was an absurd suggestion.
▶ ridiculous, preposterous, ludicrous, unreasonable, nonsensical, incredible, irrational, senseless, insane, mad, anomalous, silly, stupid, illogical, incongruous, meaningless, paradoxical, untenable, laughable, (*more informal*) crazy, (*more informal*) daft, (*more informal*) barmy, (*more informal*) zany
OPPOSITES ARE reasonable, sensible

abundant ADJECTIVE
Luckily, there was an abundant supply of things to do.
▶ plentiful, copious, ample, liberal, profuse, generous, lavish, rich, bountiful, prolific, inexhaustible
OPPOSITES ARE scarce, sparse

abuse NOUN
1 *The action amounted to a serious abuse of authority.*
▶ misuse, misapplication
2 *No society can tolerate the abuse of children.*
▶ maltreatment, mistreatment, ill-treatment, misuse, (sexual) assault, molestation
3 *A group of mothers yelled abuse.*
▶ insults, invective, obscenities, curses, slanders

abuse VERB
1 *Players on both sides were abusing the referee.*
▶ insult, be rude to, curse, swear at, call someone names, malign, revile, defame, slander
2 *He was accused of abusing children.*
▶ mistreat, maltreat, ill-treat, (sexually) assault, molest, interfere with, batter, harm, hurt
3 *The judge had abused his authority in his directions to the jury.*
▶ misuse, misapply, exploit

abusive ADJECTIVE
He was thrown out of the hall for yelling abusive remarks.
▶ insulting, derogatory, rude, offensive, opprobrious, pejorative, defamatory, disparaging, scathing, hurtful, impolite, libellous, obscene, scurrilous, slanderous, vituperative
OPPOSITES ARE friendly, polite

abysmal ADJECTIVE
1 *The service was abysmal.*
▶ poor, very bad, awful, appalling, dreadful, disgraceful, terrible, worthless
2 *the abysmal ignorance of science in Britain*
▶ profound, extreme, utter, complete, deep, unfathomable, immeasurable, incalculable, infinite

abyss NOUN
There is still a deep abyss to be crossed.
▶ chasm, pit, void, gulf, crater, fissure, gap, hole, opening, rift

academic ADJECTIVE
1 *She had spent her entire life in an academic environment.*
▶ educational, scholastic, scholarly, pedagogical
2 *They are academic historians and not writers for the popular market.*
▶ scholarly, studious, learned, intellectual, erudite, educated, cultured, bookish, clever, highbrow, intelligent, well-read, (*more informal*) brainy
3 *The point is of more than academic interest.*
▶ theoretical, notional, conceptual, conjectural, hypothetical, speculative
AN OPPOSITE IS practical

academic NOUN
a group of visiting academics
▶ scholar, intellectual, professor, lecturer, thinker, (*more informal*) egghead, (*more informal*) highbrow

academy NOUN
The students of the academy were involved in a project to catalogue the papers.
▶ college, educational institution, training establishment, conservatory, conservatoire, university, institute

accede VERB
accede to *He acceded to all her demands.*
▶ agree to, consent to, accept, grant, comply with, concur with

accelerate VERB
1 *The vehicle accelerated sharply.*
▶ go faster, speed up, pick up speed, quicken speed
OPPOSITES ARE decelerate, slow down
2 *The oil-producing countries have agreed to accelerate production.*
▶ increase, step up, stimulate, expedite, promote, spur on

accent NOUN
1 *She spoke with a distinct Welsh accent.*
▶ pronunciation, intonation, inflection, tone, cadence, enunciation
2 *There is an accent on the first syllable.*
▶ stress, emphasis, accentuation, force
3 *The accent is on economy.*
▶ emphasis, stress

accept VERB
1 *I decided to accept the offer.*
▶ receive, take, get, welcome, (*more informal*) jump at
2 *The council does not accept responsibility*
▶ admit, acknowledge, bear, assume, undertake
3 *Reluctantly, he had to accept the decision.*
▶ agree to, go along with, accede to, acquiesce in, defer to, comply with, consent to, concur with, abide by, acknowledge, be reconciled to, recognize, resign yourself to, submit to, yield to
AN OPPOSITE IS reject

acceptable ADJECTIVE
1 *The agreement was acceptable to the majority.*
▶ welcome, agreeable, appreciated, gratifying, pleasant, pleasing, worthwhile
2 *The courses fell below an acceptable standard.*
▶ adequate, satisfactory, reasonable, tolerable, admissible, appropriate, passable, suitable
AN OPPOSITE IS unacceptable

a
b
c
d
e
f
g
h
i
j
k
l
m
n
o
p
q
r
s
t
u
v
w
x
y
z

acceptance NOUN

1 *The plan found wide acceptance.*
▶ approval, consent, acquiescence, agreement, welcome
AN OPPOSITE IS refusal
2 *Their acceptance of the explanation came as some relief.*
▶ belief (in), confidence (in)

accepted ADJECTIVE

These artists question accepted notions of taste and beauty.
▶ recognized, acknowledged, agreed, undisputed, indisputable, standard, unquestioned, undeniable
AN OPPOSITE IS controversial

access NOUN

1 *The away fans could not gain access to that end of the stadium.*
▶ entry, admission, admittance, right of entry
2 *The building has no access at the front.*
▶ entrance, entry, way in, approach

accessible ADJECTIVE

1 *The library has been made accessible for wheelchairs.*
▶ reachable, within reach, at hand, available, convenient, (*more informal*) get-at-able, (*more informal*) handy
AN OPPOSITE IS inaccessible
2 *Ministers want to be more accessible.*
▶ approachable, available, informal, welcoming

accessory NOUN

1 *Accessories include a remote control.*
▶ attachment, fitting, extra, addition, appendage, extension
2 *He might be charged with being an accessory to the crime.*
▶ accomplice, associate, collaborator (in)

accident NOUN

1 *He died in an accident while working on his boat.*
▶ misfortune, mishap, disaster, calamity, catastrophe, misadventure
2 *She had witnessed a traffic accident.*
▶ collision, smash, (*more informal*) pile-up
3 *It was pure accident that we met that day.*
▶ chance, luck, coincidence, fate, a fluke
by accident *I found it by accident.*
▶ by chance, accidentally, fortuitously, unwittingly, coincidentally

accidental ADJECTIVE

Make sure you avoid accidental erasure of the tape.
▶ unintentional, chance, coincidental, fortuitous, inadvertent, unintended, adventitious, arbitrary, casual, lucky, random
AN OPPOSITE IS intentional

accidentally ADVERB

We met accidentally.
▶ by accident, by chance, fortuitously, unintentionally, unwittingly
AN OPPOSITE IS intentionally

acclaim VERB

The film has been widely acclaimed in the press.
▶ praise, applaud, commend, cheer, congratulate, celebrate

acclimatize VERB

They soon became acclimatized to their new surroundings.
▶ accustom, adjust, familiarize

accolade NOUN

He received the accolade of a knighthood.
▶ praise, honour, tribute, recognition, admiration, acclamation, plaudits

accommodate VERB

1 *We will do our best to accommodate your wishes.*
▶ serve, help, aid, assist, supply, oblige, provide
2 *The lodge accommodates nine residents.*
▶ house, lodge, provide for, cater for, shelter, board, take in, hold, (*more informal*) put up

accommodating ADJECTIVE

The local tourist office is very accommodating
▶ helpful, obliging, cooperative, considerate

accommodation NOUN

The cost includes three days' accommodation in Bruges.
▶ board, lodging, shelter, housing, rooms

accompany VERB

1 *She regularly accompanied groups of her students.*
▶ go with, escort, travel with, attend, follow, chaperon, look after, partner, (*more informal*) tag along with
2 *A note accompanied the flowers.*
▶ go with, occur with, coincide with, be present with, coexist with, complement, belong with, supplement

accomplice NOUN

An accomplice stood at the door on lookout.
▶ associate, partner, accessory, abetter, confederate, collaborator, co-conspirator

accomplish VERB

Brady believes his side can accomplish the awesome task.
▶ achieve, fulfil, succeed in, realize, complete, conclude, bring off, carry out, discharge, attain, effect, execute, finish, perform

accomplished ADJECTIVE

Diana is an accomplished pianist.
▶ expert, talented, able, skilled, gifted, capable, clever, competent, proficient

accomplishment NOUN

This was quite an accomplishment and she was duly rewarded.
▶ achievement, attainment, ability, talent, skill, gift

accord VERB

accord with *The theory accords with all the known facts.*
▶ correspond to, agree with, concur with, be compatible with, (*more informal*) square with

accost VERB
A police officer accosted me in the street.
▶ stop, approach, detain, waylay, apprehend

account NOUN
1 *Write down a full account of what you saw.*
▶ description, report, statement, record, explanation, narrative, version, commentary, (*more informal*) write-up
2 *An account for the work has come in the post.*
▶ invoice, statement, bill
3 *The damage done to the vehicles is of little account.*
▶ importance, significance, consequence, concern, moment, interest, worth, value, use
on account of *They stayed indoors on account of the bad weather.*
▶ because of, in view of, owing to, due to, as a result of, as a consequence of, considering

account VERB
account for *It is difficult to account for such a sudden change in their attitude.*
▶ explain, justify, clarify, elucidate, answer for, give reasons for, excuse, make excuses for, rationalize, vindicate

accountable ADJECTIVE
The Minister is accountable to Parliament
▶ responsible, answerable, subject, liable

accrue VERB
The honour that is supposed to accrue from being unpaid.
▶ result, follow, ensue, arise, stem, spring, emanate, be produced

accumulate VERB
1 *He accumulated information from different sources.*
▶ gather, collect, amass, assemble, bring together, heap up, mass, pile up, hoard, store up, (*more informal*) stash away
AN OPPOSITE IS disperse
2 *Leaves tend to accumulate in the gullies.*
▶ build up, increase, multiply, grow, accrue
AN OPPOSITE IS decrease

accumulation NOUN
The book is an accumulation of work by many scholars.
▶ collection, build-up, mass, store, supply, heap, pile, hoard, stock, conglomeration

accuracy NOUN
Can we trust the accuracy of these figures?
▶ precision, correctness, exactness, validity, reliability

accurate ADJECTIVE
1 *It was an accurate account of what had happened.*
▶ faithful, factual, authentic, true, truthful, close, exact, precise, reliable
2 *She took accurate notes during the meeting.*
▶ exact, precise, correct, careful, faultless, errorless, error-free, meticulous, minute, perfect, scrupulous
3 *His aim was steady and accurate.*
▶ certain, unerring, sure, (*more informal*) spot-on
AN OPPOSITE IS inaccurate

accursed ADJECTIVE
She was determined to leave the accursed house that very night.
▶ hateful, loathsome, detestable, damnable, damned, diabolical, evil
AN OPPOSITE IS holy

accusation NOUN
There had been several accusations of cheating.
▶ allegation, charge, complaint, indictment, alleged offence

accuse VERB
1 **accuse of** *The men were accused of disorderly behaviour.*
▶ charge with, blame for, put on trial for, take to court for, indict for
2 **accuse of** *The banks are accused of creating confusion among customers.*
▶ blame for, hold responsible for, criticize for condemn for, denounce for
AN OPPOSITE IS defend

accustomed ADJECTIVE
Wars remove whole populations from their accustomed ways of life.
▶ normal, customary, familiar, habitual, established, usual, common, conventional, traditional, ordinary, regular, routine, set
become or **get accustomed to** *The family soon became accustomed to life in the country.*
▶ get used to, adapt to, adjust to, acclimatize to, become conditioned to, become inured to, familiarize yourself with, (*more informal*) feel at home in

ache NOUN
A nagging stomach ache spoiled the evening.
▶ pain, pang, soreness, hurt, discomfort, twinge

ache VERB
His tooth was beginning to ache.
▶ hurt, smart, be painful, be sore, throb, sting

achieve VERB
1 *Students who achieve their goals will be promised jobs.*
▶ succeed in, accomplish, fulfil, complete, carry out, attain, manage, bring about, bring off
2 *They worked hard to achieve success.*
▶ acquire, win, gain, earn, get, obtain, procure, reach, score

achievement NOUN
1 *They are proud of their achievement.*
▶ accomplishment, attainment, success, deed, exploit
2 *We hoped for the achievement of all our aims.*
▶ attainment, realization, accomplishment, fulfilment, reaching, gaining, winning, conclusion

acid NOUN
TYPES OF ACID
monobasic acid, dibasic acid, tribasic acid, amino acid, carbolic acid, fatty acid, Lewis acid, mineral acid, nucleic acid, organic acid.

a
b
c
d
e
f
g
h
i
j
k
l
m
n
o
p
q
r
s
t
u
v
w
x
y
z

A

acid ADJECTIVE

1 *The fruit had an acid taste.*
▶ sour, sharp, bitter, tart, tangy, vinegary
AN OPPOSITE IS sweet

2 *They had to put up with acid comments from their supervisors.*
▶ sharp, sarcastic, scathing, caustic, acerbic, cutting, bitter, spiteful, vicious, abrasive

acknowledge VERB

1 *They acknowledged their obligation to their predecessors.*
▶ admit, concede, accept, grant, recognize, allow
AN OPPOSITE IS deny

2 *No one has acknowledged my letter.*
▶ answer, reply to, respond to, react to, notice

3 *She acknowledged him with a nod.*
▶ greet, salute, hail, recognize, respond to, (*more informal*) say hallo to

acknowledgement NOUN

1 *There was an acknowledgement of a need for action.*
▶ admission, acceptance, agreement, realization, concession

2 *Tom gave a smile of acknowledgement.*
▶ greeting, recognition, welcome, (*more formal*) salutation

acquaint VERB

be acquainted with *Lorna is acquainted with several European languages.*
▶ be familiar with, be conversant with, be versed in, be informed about
AN OPPOSITE IS be ignorant of

acquaintance NOUN

Philip was just a business acquaintance.
▶ associate, colleague, contact

acquiesce VERB

acquiesce in *We found it difficult to acquiesce in such a foolish scheme.*
▶ consent to, agree to, allow, permit, concur with, cooperate with, (*more informal*) go along with, (*more informal*) okay

acquire VERB

His father had acquired some shares in a freight company.
▶ obtain, get, receive, come by, gain, appropriate

acquisition NOUN

There will be a display of the museum's new acquisitions.
▶ accession, addition, purchase, (*more informal*) buy, gain, possession

acquisitive ADJECTIVE

You are acquisitive, like a magpie.
▶ hoarding, possessive, avaricious, grasping, mercenary

acquit VERB

The jury acquitted all three of the accused.
▶ absolve, clear, exonerate, find innocent, find not guilty, free, discharge, excuse, (*more informal*) let off

acquit yourself *The youngsters acquitted themselves with distinction.*
▶ perform, conduct yourself, behave, act, operate, work

acrid ADJECTIVE

People were choking on the acrid fumes.
▶ pungent, sharp, bitter, caustic, harsh, unpleasant

acrimonious ADJECTIVE

The meetings were acrimonious and badly managed.
▶ bitter, hostile, abusive, peevish, acerbic, caustic, angry, petulant, bad-tempered, ill-tempered, ill-natured, venomous, biting, sharp
AN OPPOSITE IS peaceable

acrobat NOUN

An acrobat performed a back somersault.
▶ gymnast, tumbler, contortionist

act NOUN

1 *It needed an act of great courage.*
▶ deed, feat, action, exploit, undertaking, effort, enterprise, operation, proceeding

2 *The next act will be a juggler.*
▶ item, turn, performance, routine, sketch

put on an act
▶ pretend, dissemble, play a part

act VERB

1 *Jim was beginning to act strangely.*
▶ behave, conduct yourself

2 *The large table also acted as a work area. The medicine will soon begin to act.*
▶ function, operate, serve, work, take effect, have an effect

3 *He has always wanted to act the role of a villain.*
▶ play, portray, appear (as), perform, represent, assume the character of, characterize, enact, impersonate

4 *It was obvious that they were only acting.*
▶ pretend, sham, fake, pose, (*more informal*) kid

acting ADJECTIVE

Henry will be acting captain.
▶ deputy, interim, temporary, substitute, stand-by, provisional, stopgap

action NOUN

1 *It was a decisive action and very effective.*
▶ act, deed, step, feat, exploit, endeavour, enterprise, proceeding, effort, measure, performance, process, undertaking

2 *Write a story with plenty of action.*
▶ activity, drama, excitement, vitality, movement, energy, liveliness, vigour

3 *The action of the play is set in medieval France.*
▶ story, plot, events, happenings, incidents

4 *The clock has a mechanical action.*
▶ working, works, mechanism, functioning, operation

5 *McLeish led his troops into action.*
▶ battle, engagement

activate VERB
The smaller button activates the reboot function.
▶ operate, start, initiate, mobilize, actuate, trigger off, set in motion

active ADJECTIVE
1 *They were having an active time.*
▶ busy, lively, eventful, energetic, vivacious
OPPOSITES ARE inactive, uneventful
2 *She is very active for her age.*
▶ energetic, agile, sprightly, lively, spry, frisky, (*more informal*) on the go, (*more informal*) full of beans
OPPOSITES ARE inactive, lethargic
3 *Yvonne is an active member of the society.*
▶ diligent, hard-working, dedicated, enthusiastic, assiduous, industrious, committed, devoted, staunch, zealous
OPPOSITES ARE inactive, unenthusiastic
4 *Part of the old factory was still active.*
▶ functional, functioning, operative, working, in operation
OPPOSITES ARE inactive, defunct

activity NOUN
1 *At weekends the house is always a scene of great activity.*
▶ liveliness, action, commotion, bustle, life, hustle, animation, movement, excitement, hurly-burly, industry, stir
2 *Marketing is an activity in which all staff can be involved.*
▶ job, task, venture, enterprise, undertaking, project, scheme
3 *She enjoyed many leisure activities.*
▶ interest, pursuit, hobby, pastime, occupation

actor NOUNS
He was the actor who played James Bond.
▶ player, performer, stage performer, artist, (*female*) actress, (*female*) artiste

actual ADJECTIVE
Have you seen the actual damage done?
▶ real, true, physical, genuine, definite, certain, concrete
OPPOSITES ARE imaginary, supposed, notional, non-existent

acute ADJECTIVE
1 *The pain was acute.*
▶ sharp, severe, stabbing, burning, intense, piercing, fierce
AN OPPOSITE IS mild
2 *There is an acute shortage of teachers.*
▶ severe, drastic, extreme, serious, dire, grave
AN OPPOSITE IS continual
3 *He was suffering from an acute illness.*
▶ critical, sudden
4 *Jenna has an acute mind.*
▶ sharp, keen, astute, shrewd, penetrating, perceptive, quick, discerning
OPPOSITES ARE dull, stupid

adamant ADJECTIVE
They were adamant that we should come.
▶ determined, insistent, resolved, resolute
AN OPPOSITE IS hesitant

adapt VERB
1 **adapt to** *The children have adapted well to their new surroundings.*
▶ adjust to, acclimatize yourself to, get used to, reconcile yourself to
2 *The vans are all adapted to carry dangerous substances.*
▶ modify, alter, convert, change, rearrange, reorganize, reconstruct, customize, tailor, prepare, transform
3 *The story has been adapted for television.*
▶ edit, modify, prepare, alter

adaptable ADJECTIVE
1 *The tool is adaptable to many tasks.*
▶ adjustable, versatile, convertible
2 *Michael is always willing and very adaptable.*
▶ flexible, versatile, resilient, amenable

add VERB
1 *Add all the numbers in the first column*
▶ add up, count, count up, calculate, total, find the sum of, work out, (*more informal*) tot up
OPPOSITES ARE deduct, subtract
2 *A conservatory was added in the 1930s.*
▶ build on, attach, add on, integrate, join, (*more informal*) tack on
OPPOSITES ARE remove, demolish
3 **add to** *Our shouts only added to the confusion.*
▶ increase, intensify, amplify, augment, enlarge, supplement

add up
1 *It was time to add up the scores.*
▶ count, count up, calculate, total, find the sum of, work out, (*more informal*) tot up
2 (*more informal*) *The story didn't add up.*
▶ make sense, be convincing, be reasonable, (*more informal*) hold water, (*more informal*) ring true
add up to *The costs added up to many thousands.*
▶ total, amount to, come to, make

addict NOUN
1 *a drug addict*
▶ abuser, (*more informal*) user, (*more informal*) dope fiend, (*more informal*) junkie
2 *a football addict*
▶ enthusiast, devotee

addiction NOUN
An addiction to crisps was putting cellulite on her thighs.
▶ dependence, compulsion, craving, fixation, habit, obsession

addition NOUN
1 *I'm not very good at addition.*
▶ adding, adding up, counting, calculating, totalling
2 *The porch is a nineteenth-century addition.*
▶ supplement, appendage, extension, attachment, afterthought, (*more informal*) add-on

A

additional ADJECTIVE
The railways need additional resources.
▶ extra, added, further, supplementary, increased, more, new, other, spare

address NOUN
1 *They live at a smart address in town.*
▶ residence, location, locality, home, abode
2 *The president gave a short address to the press.*
▶ speech, talk, discourse, lecture, monologue, (*more formal*) oration, (*more formal*) disquisition

address VERB
A man came up and addressed me.
▶ greet, hail, salute, speak to, talk to, accost, approach, engage in conversation, (*more informal*) buttonhole
address yourself to (*formal*) *Let us address ourselves to the task in hand.*
▶ concentrate on, devote yourself to, apply yourself to, attend to, engage in, focus on, settle down to, get involved in, tackle, undertake

adept ADJECTIVE
Becoming an adept interviewer is an invaluable skill.
▶ skilled, skilful, expert, accomplished, proficient, talented, gifted, competent, deft

adequate ADJECTIVE
1 *The work must be of an adequate standard.*
▶ satisfactory, acceptable, sufficient, suitable, tolerable, competent, fair, good enough, passable, presentable, respectable
AN OPPOSITE IS inadequate
2 *The hospital lacks adequate resources.*
▶ sufficient, enough, suitable, appropriate

adhere VERB
1 *A piece of fluff adhered to his collar.*
▶ stick, cling, be fixed, be fastened
2 adhere to *We must adhere to our principles.*
▶ maintain, observe, follow, respect, stick to, abide by, stand by, comply with

adherent NOUN
an adherent of a single currency
▶ supporter, follower, advocate, defender, upholder, devotee, enthusiast, (*more informal*) fan

adhesive ADJECTIVE
a substance with adhesive properties
▶ sticky, tacky, gluey

adhesive NOUN
Fix the handle with some adhesive.
▶ glue, paste, gum, cement, (*more informal*) sticky stuff

adjacent ADJECTIVE
adjacent to *the area adjacent to the fire station*
▶ adjoining, bordering, abutting, neighbouring, alongside, touching, next to, close by, nextdoor to, (*more formal*) contiguous with

adjoin VERB
The house adjoins an old warehouse.
▶ be next to, abut, border on, connect with, link up with, be next door to, touch, (*more formal*) be contiguous with

adjourn VERB
The meeting was adjourned for a week.
▶ suspend, break off, discontinue, defer, dissolve, postpone, interrupt, put off

adjournment NOUN
The reason for the adjournment of the meeting will become clear in time.
▶ suspension, postponement, putting off, break (in), pause (in), interruption, discontinuation, deferment

adjust VERB
1 *You need to adjust the picture.*
▶ modify, alter, regulate, rectify, tune, vary, change, balance, amend, arrange, position, put right
2 adjust to *The workforce have had to adjust to new procedures.*
▶ adapt to, acclimatize yourself to, accommodate yourself to, familiarize yourself with, get used to, reconcile yourself to, harmonize yourself with

adjustable ADJECTIVE
The driver has an adjustable seat.
▶ modifiable, adaptable, variable, alterable, changeable, flexible, movable
AN OPPOSITE IS fixed

ad-lib ADJECTIVE
The chairperson made a few ad-lib remarks.
▶ impromptu, extempore, improvised, spontaneous, unplanned, unprepared, unrehearsed, made-up, (*more informal*) off the cuff, (*more informal*) off the top of your head

ad-lib VERB
She ad-libbed a large part of her speech.
▶ improvise, extemporize, make it up, (*more informal*) play it by ear

administer VERB
1 *The director administers an organization of two hundred people.*
▶ regulate, run, manage, direct, preside over, conduct the affairs of, control, supervise, govern, head, lead, look after, command, organize, oversee
2 *A nurse administered medicines throughout the ward.*
▶ dispense, hand out, deal out, give, provide, supply, apply, distribute, dole out, measure out, mete out (a punishment)

admirable ADJECTIVE
Their aims are admirable but will be difficult to achieve.
▶ laudable, praiseworthy, worthy, fine, commendable, creditable, estimable, excellent, pleasing, exemplary, honourable, wonderful, marvellous, enjoyable, likeable
AN OPPOSITE IS deplorable

admiration NOUN
Their achievement won much admiration.
▶ esteem, acclaim, commendation, high regard, honour, praise, respect, appreciation, approval
AN OPPOSITE IS contempt

admire VERB
1 *Jill is much admired for her efficiency.*
▶ applaud, approve of, respect, praise, revere, esteem, value, look up to, marvel at, think highly of, (*more formal*) laud
AN OPPOSITE IS despise
2 *Come and admire the view.*
▶ enjoy, appreciate, be delighted by

admirer NOUN
He is a great admirer of Napoleon.
▶ fan, devotee, supporter, adherent, enthusiast

admissible ADJECTIVE
The court ruled that a claim for damages is admissible.
▶ allowable, permissible, permitted, acceptable, tolerable, legitimate, justifiable
AN OPPOSITE IS inadmissible

admission NOUN
1 *Admission to the gallery is free.*
▶ entrance, entry, admittance, access
2 *The statement sounded like an admission of guilt.*
▶ confession, declaration, acknowledgement, profession, revelation, affirmation, avowal, acceptance
AN OPPOSITE IS denial

admit VERB
1 *Some of the people were not admitted to the house.*
▶ let in, allow in, grant access, receive, take in
AN OPPOSITE IS exclude
2 *She admitted she had been to the house that morning.*
▶ acknowledge, concede, confess, reveal, declare, disclose, divulge, agree, grant, accept, allow, own up, profess, recognize
AN OPPOSITE IS deny

adolescence NOUN
The problems are the normal ones of adolescence and will pass in time.
▶ puberty, teens, youth, boyhood, girlhood, growing up

adolescent ADJECTIVE
Two adolescent girls were standing arm in arm.
▶ teenage, boyish, girlish, youthful, juvenile, immature, puerile
USAGE These words, and especially the last three, are often used in a way that disapproves of young people's behaviour.

adolescent NOUN
The highest sugar consumers are male adolescents.
▶ teenager, youth, juvenile, minor, youngster

adopt VERB
1 *The blue shirt was adopted as the official uniform in the 1930s. He asked them to adopt a more professional approach.*
▶ take up, choose, support, follow, accept, approve, back, embrace, espouse, endorse, (*more informal*) go for
2 *She already knew that she had been adopted.*
▶ foster, take in

adorable ADJECTIVE
What an adorable little cat!
▶ lovable, delightful, charming, appealing, enchanting

adore VERB
1 *Neil obviously still adores you.*
▶ love, be fond of, dote on, idolize, worship, cherish, admire, glorify, revere, venerate, (*more informal*) think the world of
2 *We all adore shopping.*
▶ love, like
OPPOSITES ARE hate, detest

adorn VERB
The room was adorned with tapestries.
▶ decorate, embellish, enhance, beautify, furnish, trim

adornment NOUN
The room was stark and without adornment.
▶ embellishment, decoration, enhancement

adult ADJECTIVE
a medical problem associated with adult males
▶ grown-up, of age, fully grown, full-grown, developed, mature
AN OPPOSITE IS immature

adulterate VERB
The brewery was accused of adulterating its beer.
▶ contaminate, pollute, taint, dilute, thin down, water down, weaken, (*more informal*) doctor

advance NOUN
There has been a considerable advance in cancer treatments.
▶ progress, development, improvement, headway, step, stride

advance VERB
1 *The column of soldiers began to advance.*
▶ move forward, go forward, proceed, press ahead, press on, progress, approach, come near, gain ground, forge ahead, make headway, make progress, (*more informal*) make strides, (*more informal*) push on
AN OPPOSITE IS retreat
2 *Computer technology has advanced in the last few years.*
▶ develop, evolve, improve, increase, grow, thrive
AN OPPOSITE IS regress
3 *Good qualifications will advance your career.*
▶ benefit, boost, further, promote, foster, assist, expedite, facilitate, accelerate
AN OPPOSITE IS hinder
4 *The Bank has agreed to advance the money.*
▶ lend, loan, pay in advance, provide, supply
5 *He advanced some interesting ideas.*
▶ present, propose, submit, suggest, adduce, cite, furnish, give

A

advanced ADJECTIVE
1 *Advanced techniques have solved many of these problems.*
▶ progressive, leading, modern, sophisticated, up-to-date, forward, latest
AN OPPOSITE IS obsolete
2 *Their ideas were very advanced for the time.*
▶ forward-looking, innovative, pioneering, progressive, revolutionary, trend-setting, leading, futuristic, avant-garde, new, novel, original
AN OPPOSITE IS old- fashioned
3 *a course in advanced mathematics*
▶ higher, complex, complicated, difficult, hard
AN OPPOSITE IS elementary
4 *Jamie appears quite advanced for his age.*
▶ mature, grown-up, sophisticated, well-developed

advantage NOUN
There is an advantage in having a bank account.
▶ benefit, asset, help, assistance, aid, blessing, convenience, boon, favour, gain, use, service
take advantage of *His friends all took advantage of him.*
▶ exploit, make use of, utilize, profit by, manipulate

advantageous ADJECTIVE
An element of surprise can be advantageous.
▶ beneficial, helpful, useful, fruitful, worthwhile, favourable, profitable, valuable

advent NOUN
the advent of the personal computer
▶ arrival, appearance, emergence, coming

adventure NOUN
1 *His adventures had already turned him into a local hero.*
▶ exploit, escapade, venture, enterprise, undertaking, deed, feat
2 *They travelled the world together in search of adventure.*
▶ excitement, danger, interesting times, fun, stimulation

adventurous ADJECTIVE
1 *an adventurous child*
▶ daring, enterprising, bold, venturesome, heroic, intrepid, valiant
2 *an adventurous time*
▶ eventful, exciting, challenging, dangerous, perilous, risky
AN OPPOSITE IS unadventurous

adverse ADJECTIVE
1 *The request brought an adverse response.*
▶ hostile, unfriendly, unfavourable, critical, antagonistic, negative, uncomplimentary, derogatory, disapproving, censorious
2 *The treatment can produce adverse side effects.*
▶ harmful, unfavourable, disadvantageous, unfortunate, inauspicious, uncongenial, unpropitious, contrary
AN OPPOSITE IS favourable

adversity NOUN
Peter showed he was stable in adversity.
▶ misfortune, bad luck, hardship, difficulty, affliction, tribulation, suffering, sorrow, misery, hard times

advertise VERB
The job will be advertised in national newspapers.
▶ publicize, promote, make known, market, announce, broadcast, display, flaunt, show off, (*more informal*) push, (*more informal*) spotlight, (*more informal*) tout, (*more informal*) plug

advertisement NOUN
1 *There are far more advertisements on television now.*
▶ commercial, (*more informal*) ad, (*more informal*) advert
2 *Let's put an advertisement in the local newsagent.*
▶ announcement, notice, (*more informal*) ad, (*more informal*) advert
3 *There are advertisements all along the main road.*
▶ hoarding, placard

advice NOUN
I could do with some advice.
▶ guidance, counselling, counsel, directions, suggestions, recommendations, tips, pointers

advisable ADJECTIVE
It is advisable to arrive early.
▶ wise, sensible, prudent, desirable, a good idea, recommended
AN OPPOSITE IS inadvisable

advise VERB
1 *He advised her to go to the police.*
▶ recommend, counsel, instruct, encourage, admonish, caution, warn, (*more formal*) enjoin, (*more formal*) exhort
2 *The doctor advised a period of rest.*
▶ suggest, prescribe, urge, advocate
3 *Visitors are advised that the house will close at six o'clock.*
▶ inform, notify, warn

adviser NOUN
a personal adviser to the Queen
▶ counsellor, consultant, counsel, confidant

advocate NOUN
1 *an advocate of political and economic reform*
▶ supporter, champion, exponent, proponent, upholder
2 *a legal advocate*
▶ lawyer, barrister, counsel

advocate VERB
They advocated sweeping changes.
▶ recommend, prescribe, advise

affair NOUN
1 *The meeting was an odd affair.*
▶ incident, event, happening, episode, occurrence, circumstance, occasion, (*more informal*) business
2 *She suspected her husband was having an affair.*
▶ relationship, love affair, romance, (*more informal*) fling

3 affairs *They need to put their financial affairs in order.*
▶ business, activities, concerns, transactions, operations, undertakings, interests, matters

affect VERB
1 *Alcohol affects women and men differently.*
▶ have an effect on, have an impact on, influence, impinge on, modify, act on, alter, attack, change, transform, (*more informal*) hit
2 *The sad news affected all of us.*
▶ upset, disturb, trouble, concern, move, perturb, sadden, distress, agitate, grieve, impress, stir, touch
3 *The man affects a Glasgow accent.*
▶ assume, feign, put on

affectation NOUN
His accent is an affectation.
▶ pretence, mannerism, sham, insincerity

affected ADJECTIVE
He assumed an affected voice, as though coming from God.
▶ artificial, sham, insincere, pretentious, assumed, (*more informal*) put on

affection NOUN
The friends show obvious affection for one another.
▶ fondness, friendship, friendliness, attachment, devotion, tenderness, warmth, feeling, liking, love, (*more informal*) soft spot
AN OPPOSITE IS hatred

affectionate ADJECTIVE
an affectionate smile
▶ fond, loving, devoted, tender, friendly, kind, kind-hearted, warm-hearted, sympathetic

affiliate VERB
a political group affiliated to an international organization.
▶ associate (with), join, ally, connect (with), federate, unite

affirm VERB
The government affirmed their intention to reduce taxation.
▶ declare, confirm, assert, pronounce

affirmative ADJECTIVE
The answer was affirmative.
▶ positive, agreeing, consenting, assenting, concurring, confirming
AN OPPOSITE IS negative

afflict VERB
The family has been afflicted by illness.
▶ trouble, bother, torment, beset, burden, strike, distress, oppress, harass, vex, plague

affliction NOUN
He bore his affliction with great dignity.
▶ suffering, distress, misfortune, hardship, misery, torment, ordeal, pain, trouble, tribulation, adversity

affluence NOUN
In recent years the country has shown signs of greater affluence.
▶ wealth, prosperity, opulence, fortune, richness

affluent ADJECTIVE
The more affluent houses had compost heaps in their large gardens.
▶ prosperous, rich, well-off, wealthy, opulent, (*more informal*) flush
OPPOSITES ARE poor, impoverished

afford VERB
1 *We can't afford a holiday this year.*
▶ have enough money for, pay for, manage
2 *The area affords many beautiful walks.*
▶ provide, offer, present, furnish, give, render, produce

afraid ADJECTIVE
1 *The younger children were afraid of the dark.*
▶ frightened, scared, terrified, alarmed (at, by), fearful, intimidated (by), anxious, nervous
OPPOSITES ARE unafraid, brave, bold, confident
2 *I'm afraid all the food has gone.*
▶ sorry, regretful, unhappy
3 *Don't be afraid to ask.*
▶ reluctant, hesitant, shy, slow, chary (of)

aftermath NOUN
There were several important tasks awaiting him in the aftermath of his election victory.
▶ consequences, repercussions, results, effects, outcome

age NOUN
1 *The grandparents were showing signs of age.*
▶ old age, senility, elderliness, decrepitude, dotage, decline
AN OPPOSITE IS youth
2 *the Elizabethan age*
▶ era, period, epoch, days, generation, time, years
3 (*more informal*) *It's an age since you were last here. We've had to wait for ages.*
▶ lifetime, long time, aeon

age VERB
1 *Frank had aged in the last few years.*
▶ decline, degenerate, look older, fade
2 *A good wine needs to age.*
▶ mature, mellow, ripen, develop, grow older

aged ADJECTIVE
an aged relative
▶ elderly, old, senile

agency NOUN
a recruitment agency
▶ office, business, department, service, bureau

agenda NOUN
The meeting had no fixed agenda.
▶ list of items, schedule, plan, programme, timetable

agent NOUN
When she became a writer she needed an agent.
▶ representative, mediator, intermediary, broker, delegate, emissary, go-between, middleman, negotiator, trustee

A

aggravate VERB
1 *The delays only aggravated the situation.*
▶ worsen, exacerbate, increase, intensify, magnify, add to, make more serious, make worse, augment, compound, heighten, inflame, exaggerate
AN OPPOSITE IS alleviate
2 (*informal*) *Their flippant remarks aggravated us.*
▶ annoy, irritate, bother, exasperate, incense, vex, irk, anger, nettle, provoke, trouble, (*more informal*) needle, (*more informal*) peeve

aggravation NOUN
It's not worth all the aggravation.
▶ bother, annoyance, nuisance, trouble, hassle, irritation, difficulty

aggression NOUN
an act of aggression
▶ hostility, aggressiveness, provocation, militancy, violence

aggressive ADJECTIVE
Lily was in one of her aggressive moods.
▶ hostile, provocative, pugnacious, antagonistic, militant, belligerent, bellicose, argumentative, quarrelsome, attacking, violent, warlike, assertive, bullying, (*more informal*) pushy, (*more informal*) macho
AN OPPOSITE IS friendly

aggrieved ADJECTIVE
He sounded aggrieved and astonished.
▶ offended, indignant, resentful, wronged, distressed, discontented, piqued, riled

aghast ADJECTIVE
They were aghast at the news.
▶ horrified, appalled, shocked, dismayed, astounded, astonished, amazed

agile ADJECTIVE
The child was as agile as a monkey.
▶ nimble, lithe, spry, deft, graceful, fleet, adroit, sprightly, supple, lively, acrobatic, active, limber, lissom, mobile, quick-moving, swift
OPPOSITES ARE clumsy, slow

agitate VERB
1 *A special device agitates the clothes.*
▶ stir, disturb, shake, ruffle, stimulate, beat, churn, convulse, toss
2 *Her remark seemed to agitate her guest.*
▶ upset, alarm, rouse, unsettle, disquiet, disturb, excite, worry, confuse, trouble, disconcert, fluster, perturb, stir up
AN OPPOSITE IS calm

agitated ADJECTIVE
She became agitated when they did not appear.
▶ upset, unsettled, anxious, confused, disturbed, ruffled, edgy, excited, distraught, flustered, nervous, restive, restless, fidgety, feverish, (*more informal*) in a tizzy
OPPOSITES ARE calm, relaxed

agonize VERB
We agonized for hours over the decision.
▶ worry, fret, fuss, struggle, labour, suffer, wrestle, be anxious

agonizing ADJECTIVE
an agonizing pain
▶ excruciating, acute, intense, severe, extreme, piercing, painful

agony NOUN
The victims died in agony.
▶ pain, torment, torture, suffering, anguish, distress, suffering

agree VERB
1 *I'll have a word with your father, and I'm sure he'll agree.*
▶ approve, consent, be willing
2 *You must agree to take six books in the first year of membership.*
▶ be willing, consent, undertake, promise
3 *I think we all agree on the action needed.*
▶ concur, be unanimous, be united, (*more informal*) see eye to eye
4 *No two versions of the story seem to agree.*
▶ match, accord, correspond, tally, coincide, conform, harmonize, fit
OPPOSITES ARE disagree, conflict
agree on *We should agree on a price.*
▶ fix, settle, decide on, establish, choose
agree to *He agreed to their requests.*
▶ accept, consent to, acquiesce in, accede to, assent to, grant, allow
agree with *I don't agree with the decision to go to war.*
▶ support, advocate, defend, argue for, (*more informal*) back

agreeable ADJECTIVE
I spent an agreeable day with their family.
▶ pleasant, likeable, pleasing, delightful, congenial, appealing
OPPOSITES ARE disagreeable, unpleasant

agreement NOUN
1 *There's a large measure of agreement between them.*
▶ accord, concord, concurrence, unanimity, consensus, harmony, unity, affinity, similarity, sympathy, conformity, consistency, correspondence
AN OPPOSITE IS disagreement
2 *The two sides reached an agreement.*
▶ settlement, deal, compact, accord, pact, understanding, pledge, arrangement

aid NOUN
The project was largely financed from foreign aid.
▶ help, support, assistance, relief, favour, patronage

aid VERB
1 *an agreement to aid the poorest countries*
▶ help, assist, support, sustain, relieve, subsidize
2 *These measures will aid the process.*
▶ encourage, support, promote, facilitate, expedite

aim NOUN

Our aim is to win the championship.
▶ ambition, goal, objective, object, aspiration, plan, purpose, intention, target, wish, end, dream, hope, desire, design

aim VERB

1 *He aimed a gun at her.*
▶ point, direct, level, train, focus

2 *We aim to meet our targets in full next year.*
▶ intend, aspire, resolve, want, wish, seek, plan, strive, try, endeavour, attempt

aimless ADJECTIVE

an aimless existence
▶ pointless, purposeless, undirected, haphazard, random, meaningless, senseless, fruitless

air NOUN

1 *the air around us*
▶ sky, atmosphere, ether, heavens, airspace

2 *Open the window and let some air in.*
▶ breeze, draught, breath of air, oxygen, waft, wind

3 *She showed an air of defiance.*
▶ appearance, look, aura, manner, impression, bearing, aspect, ambience, character, demeanour, effect, feeling

air VERB

1 *You will need to air the room.*
▶ ventilate, aerate, freshen

2 *an opportunity to air your opinions*
▶ express , voice, utter, disclose, divulge, vent, declare, make known

airy ADJECTIVE

1 *The room was light and airy.*
▶ fresh, well ventilated, spacious, roomy, breezy
OPPOSITES ARE stuffy, airless, close, oppressive

2 *He looked at them with an airy confidence.*
▶ cheerful, cheery, light-hearted, nonchalant, lively
OPPOSITES ARE serious, solemn

aisle NOUN

The cinema had several aisles.
▶ gangway, passage, passageway, corridor, lane

alarm NOUN

1 *The woman looked round in alarm.*
▶ fear, fright, panic, terror, trepidation, apprehension, consternation, dismay, anxiety, distress, nervousness, uneasiness

2 *Suddenly the alarm sounded.*
▶ signal, alarm signal, warning signal, distress signal, siren

alarm VERB

The news had alarmed us
▶ frighten, scare, startle, unnerve, agitate, shock, disturb, fluster, surprise, terrify, upset, daunt, dismay, distress, panic, (more informal) put the wind up
AN OPPOSITE IS reassure

alcohol NOUN

I don't touch alcohol.
▶ liquor, drink, strong drink, (more informal) booze

alcoholic ADJECTIVE

Certain religions may prohibit alcoholic drink.
▶ intoxicating, distilled, fermented, brewed, potent, (more informal) hard, (more informal) strong

alcove NOUN

There was an alcove with several rows of shelves.
▶ recess, niche, bay, nook, opening

alert ADJECTIVE

1 *We need to stay alert driving in the dark.*
▶ attentive, vigilant, watchful, aware, circumspect, wide awake, on the lookout, on the ball, on your guard, (more informal) on the qui vive
AN OPPOSITE IS inattentive

2 *mentally alert*
▶ sharp, quick-witted, alive, active, acute

alert VERB

We alerted them to the problem.
▶ warn (of), notify (of), tip off (about), inform (about)

alias NOUN

Jack was not his real name, only an alias.
▶ pseudonym, false name, assumed name, (said of a writer) pen name, (said of an actor) stage name

alibi NOUN

She has a cast-iron alibi for that evening.
▶ excuse, pretext, story, defence, explanation

alien ADJECTIVE

1 *an alien landscape*
▶ strange, unfamiliar, outlandish, exotic, foreign, remote

2 *alien beings*
▶ foreign, extra-terrestrial, remote

alien NOUN

illegal aliens
▶ foreigner, immigrant, stranger, outsider

alienate VERB

She managed to alienate all her friends.
▶ antagonize, estrange, drive away, turn away, isolate, distance

alight ADJECTIVE

The house was well and truly alight.
▶ on fire, ablaze, burning, blazing, in flames, ignited, lit up

alight VERB

1 *Three passengers alighted from the train.*
▶ get off, get down, descend, disembark, dismount

2 *The bird alighted on a branch.*
▶ land, settle, perch, come to rest, touch down, come down

A

align VERB
1 *The shelves are aligned in rows.*
▶ place in line, arrange in line, line up, straighten up
2 *He aligns himself with the workers.*
▶ associate, affiliate, side, sympathize, agree, ally, cooperate, join

alike ADJECTIVE
All the houses looked alike.
▶ similar, identical, indistinguishable, the same, uniform, comparable, interchangeable

alive ADJECTIVE
1 *She was last seen alive a week ago.*
▶ living, live, breathing, animate, existing
AN OPPOSITE IS dead
2 *Many of the old customs of the country are kept alive.*
▶ active, in existence, current, functioning, flourishing, surviving
OPPOSITES ARE obsolete, inactive
3 *The company is alive to recent developments.*
▶ alert, sensitive, aware (of), conscious (of), apprised (of), cognizant (of)

allay VERB
The report had a decisive effect in allaying public fears.
▶ reduce, lessen, alleviate, assuage, alleviate, relieve, calm, ease, quell
OPPOSITES ARE increase, stimulate

allegation NOUN
There were the usual allegations of police brutality.
▶ accusation, charge, claim, assertion, declaration, statement, testimony

allege VERB
She alleged that he had attacked her.
▶ assert, affirm, maintain, claim, contend, declare, insist, state

allegiance NOUN
an oath of allegiance to the king
▶ loyalty, fidelity, obedience, devotion, duty, faithfulness, (*historical*) fealty

allergic ADJECTIVE
1 *If you are allergic to foods, you'll know what these are.*
▶ sensitive
2 (*more informal*) *I think I must be allergic to hard work.*
▶ averse, opposed, hostile, resistant, disinclined, antagonistic, unsympathetic, antipathetic

alleviate VERB
Medicines can help alleviate the pain.
▶ ease, relieve, calm, soothe, diminish, reduce, lessen, dull, assuage, moderate
AN OPPOSITE IS aggravate

alliance NOUN
1 *a political alliance*
▶ association, confederation, federation, compact, league, bloc, treaty, pact
2 *a business alliance*
▶ partnership, relationship, consortium, affiliation

allocate VERB
Funds are allocated to each project.
▶ allot, assign, apportion, grant, award, distribute, set aside (for), allow, dispense, give out, share out

allot VERB
An extra three billion pounds were allotted to transport.
▶ allocate, assign, apportion, grant, award, distribute, set aside (for), allow, dispense, give out, share out

allow VERB
1 *Smoking is only allowed in certain parts of the hotel.*
▶ permit, approve, authorize, tolerate, bear, (*more informal*) put up with
AN OPPOSITE IS forbid
2 *The teacher allowed him to go home..*
▶ permit, let, authorize, give permission, enable
3 *We need to allow more time for the journey.*
▶ provide, set aside, grant, allot, allocate, give
4 *I will allow that you are right about that.*
▶ admit, concede, acknowledge, agree, grant, accept

allowance NOUN
1 *A weekly allowance is provided for each prisoner.*
▶ allocation, portion, measure, quota, ration, share, amount
2 *He received an allowance from his father.*
▶ remittance, payment, pocket money, subsistence, annuity, grant, stipend, pension
3 *The shop will offer you an allowance for your old appliance.*
▶ discount, rebate, reduction, deduction
make allowances for *You have to make allowances for possible delays on the journey.*
▶ take into account, consider, bear in mind, keep in mind, remember, have regard for

alloy NOUN
an alloy of two metals
▶ blend, combination, composite, compound, amalgam, fusion, mixture

all right ADJECTIVE This word is often overused. Here are some alternatives:
1 *She seemed all right.*
▶ well, unhurt, unharmed, uninjured, in good health, safe, secure
2 *The food's all right, though not very exciting.*
▶ satisfactory, acceptable, adequate, reasonable, tolerable, passable
OPPOSITES ARE unsatisfactory, unacceptable

allude VERB
allude to *Several speakers alluded to the problem.*
▶ refer to, hint at, make an allusion to, mention, touch on, speak of, suggest

allure VERB
allured by the smell of food
▶ attract, entice, lure, tempt, coax, draw

alluring ADJECTIVE
She wore a stunning dress and an alluring perfume.
▶ attractive, enticing, appealing, tempting, beguiling, seductive

allusion NOUN
The 'twins' are an allusion to the legendary founders of Rome, Romulus and Remus.
▶ reference, mention (of), hint (of), suggestion (of), intimation (of)

ally NOUN
a political ally
▶ associate, colleague, collaborator, partner, companion, confederate, supporter, friend, helper, accomplice, helpmate
AN OPPOSITE IS enemy

ally VERB
Bruce again allied himself with the English.
▶ unite, join, band together, join forces, side, team up, form an alliance, make common cause

almighty ADJECTIVE
1 *Almighty God*
▶ all-powerful, omnipotent, supreme, pre-eminent
2 *an almighty explosion*
▶ huge, enormous, tremendous, mighty, overpowering, overwhelming, big

almost ADVERB
The riders had almost reached her He was earning almost a million a year by now I was almost tempted to ask why they had come.
▶ nearly, not quite, practically, virtually, about, just about, all but, around, as good as, approximately

alone ADJECTIVE
1 *The man was alone in the house at the time.*
▶ on your own, by yourself, solitary, single, unaccompanied, apart, separate, solo
2 *She said she often felt very alone.*
▶ lonely, isolated, lonesome, solitary, friendless, forlorn, desolate

aloof ADJECTIVE
Michele seemed aloof and oddly tense.
▶ distant, remote, haughty, supercilious, forbidding, cold, unfriendly, reserved, standoffish, austere, scornful, unsympathetic, unforthcoming, inaccessible, detached
OPPOSITES ARE friendly, approachable

aloud ADVERB
Madge read the letter aloud.
▶ out loud, audibly, clearly, distinctly, plainly, loudly
AN OPPOSITE IS silently

also ADVERB
His married sister also lives nearby.
▶ too, additionally, in addition, as well, besides, furthermore, moreover

alter VERB
The text of the speech had been altered to take account of the recent events.
▶ change, adjust, modify, vary, adapt, convert, transform, amend, re-form

alteration NOUN
After a few alterations the typescript was ready for publication.
▶ change, modification, variation, adaptation, adjustment, amendment, reorganization, transformation

alternate VERB
In a democratic system political parties alternate in office.
▶ take turns, interchange, act alternately, swap round, replace each other, rotate

alternative NOUN
There is no alternative.
▶ choice, option, other possibility, substitute, replacement

altitude NOUN
an altitude of 35,000 feet
▶ height, elevation

altogether ADVERB
We are not altogether satisfied.
▶ completely, entirely, fully, wholly, totally, perfectly, absolutely, quite, thoroughly, utterly

always ADVERB
1 *You are always late.*
▶ every time, constantly, repeatedly, habitually, invariably, regularly
2 *He is always complaining.*
▶ forever, constantly, incessantly, endlessly
3 *I will always remember you.*
▶ for ever, permanently, perpetually, evermore

amalgamate VERB
The two departments amalgamated. We amalgamated the two departments.
▶ combine, merge, integrate, unite, join together, consolidate, fuse, link up

amass VERB
The family amassed a huge art collection.
▶ gather, collect, accumulate, assemble, hoard

amateur ADJECTIVE
The band was made up entirely of amateur musicians.
▶ unpaid, unqualified, untrained, inexperienced
AN OPPOSITE IS professional

amateur NOUN
The players were all amateurs.
▶ non-professional, layman, layperson, enthusiast, devotee, dabbler
AN OPPOSITE IS professional

amateurish ADJECTIVE
There are some very poor amateurish productions around.
▶ unskilful, incompetent, inept, inexpert, crude, bumbling, amateur
AN OPPOSITE IS skilled

a
b
c
d
e
f
g
h
i
j
k
l
m
n
o
p
q
r
s
t
u
v
w
x
y
z

A

amaze VERB
It always amazes me how dirty the place is.
▶ astonish, astound, surprise, stagger, startle, disconcert, dumbfound, shock, flabbergast, perplex, stun, stupefy, bewilder, confound

amazed ADJECTIVE
The girl stood there looking amazed.
▶ astonished, astounded, surprised, staggered, startled, disconcerted, dumbfounded, speechless, shocked, flabbergasted, perplexed, stunned, stupefied, bewildered, (*more informal*) thunderstruck

amazing ADJECTIVE
an amazing sight
▶ astonishing, astounding, extraordinary, remarkable, staggering, startling, stunning, breathtaking, fantastic, wonderful, magnificent, phenomenal, incredible
AN OPPOSITE IS unimpressive

ambiguous ADJECTIVE
The replies were ambiguous and misleading.
▶ confusing, obscure, enigmatic, ambivalent, uncertain, unclear, equivocal, indefinite, indeterminate, puzzling, vague, woolly
AN OPPOSITE IS definite

ambition NOUN
1 *young people with a lot of ambition*
▶ drive, enthusiasm, enterprise, self-assertion, zeal, (*more informal*) push
2 *Her ambition is to become a model.*
▶ aim, dream, hope, goal, aspiration, objective, object, target, wish, desire, ideal, intention

ambitious ADJECTIVE
1 *an ambitious politician*
▶ aspiring, assertive, determined, enthusiastic, (*more informal*) go-ahead, (*more informal*) pushy
AN OPPOSITE IS apathetic.
2 *ambitious ideas*
▶ grand, grandiose, large-scale, big, far-reaching, unrealistic
OPPOSITES ARE modest, realistic

ambivalent ADJECTIVE
an ambivalent attitude towards the new technology
▶ equivocal, uncertain, hesitant, fluctuating, contradictory, inconsistent, vacillating, wavering, ambiguous, confused, muddled

amble VERB
He ambled up the road to the local post office.
▶ stroll, saunter, ramble, wander, meander, drift, dawdle

ambush NOUN
The fighters set up an ambush.
▶ surprise attack, trap, snare, ambuscade

ambush VERB
The gang specialized in ambushing unsuspecting passers-by.
▶ waylay, pounce on, surprise, swoop on, trap, entrap, ensnare, intercept, attack

amenable ADJECTIVE
an amenable child
▶ compliant, accommodating, agreeable, biddable, responsive, acquiescent, manageable
OPPOSITES ARE obstinate, stubborn

amend VERB
Some parts of the law need amending.
▶ alter, revise, modify, change, rectify, adapt, adjust, put right, reform, remedy, correct, improve

amends NOUN
make amends to *It's not too late to make amends to them for the trouble you caused.*
▶ recompense, compensate, make it up to

amenity NOUN
an old house with few amenities
▶ facility, service, benefit, provision

amiable ADJECTIVE
an amiable old fellow
▶ friendly, amicable, agreeable, affable, likeable, pleasant, congenial

ammunition NOUN
1 *The house was full of ammunition.*
▶ bullets, cartridges, shells, bombs, missiles, shrapnel
2 *The blunder provided ammunition for the opposition.*
▶ evidence, arguments, material, information

amnesty NOUN
The new government granted an amnesty.
▶ pardon, reprieve, release, discharge, dispensation, indulgence

amok, amuck ADVERB
run amok *Some of the animals had broken loose and run amok.*
▶ go berserk, go on the rampage, run riot, go out of control, go crazy

amoral ADJECTIVE
Guy was greedy, amoral, and obsessed with power.
▶ unprincipled, loose, lax, unethical
AN OPPOSITE IS moral.

amorous ADJECTIVE
Her employer had made amorous advances.
▶ sexual, romantic, lustful, erotic, carnal, passionate, impassioned
OPPOSITES ARE unloving, frigid

amorphous ADJECTIVE
an amorphous mass of cells
▶ shapeless, formless, indeterminate, nebulous, unformed

amount NOUN
1 *He wrote out a cheque for the whole amount.*
▶ quantity, sum, total, lot, whole
2 *The program needs a large amount of computer memory.*
▶ quantity, volume, bulk, lot, mass, expanse, extent, measure, supply

amount VERB

amount to *The cost amounted to several thousands.*
▶ add up to, come to, total, aggregate, be equivalent to, equal, make

ample ADJECTIVE

1 *an ample supply of books and magazines*
▶ plentiful, abundant, copious, lavish, generous, liberal, rich
AN OPPOSITE IS meagre

2 *ample space for several cars*
▶ enough, adequate, sufficient, plenty of
OPPOSITES ARE inadequate, insufficient

amplify VERB

1 *A good acoustic will amplify the sound.*
▶ louden, magnify, boost, intensify, heighten, increase, make louder, raise the volume of
AN OPPOSITE IS decrease

2 *The following notes amplify the position.*
▶ expand, enlarge on, elaborate on, develop, supplement, augment, add to, flesh out, broaden
AN OPPOSITE IS condense

amputate VERB

The injured leg had to be amputated.
▶ cut off, sever, chop off, remove, truncate, separate

amuse VERB

Their comments amused him.
▶ entertain, delight, divert, enliven, gladden, cheer up, make laugh, raise a smile, (*more informal*) tickle
amuse yourself *He amused himself by writing postcards.*
▶ occupy yourself, pass the time, engage yourself, interest yourself, immerse yourself (in)

amusement NOUN

1 *We read the article with amusement.*
▶ mirth, hilarity, delight, merriment, enjoyment, laughter

2 *A theme park with a wide range of amusements for all the family.*
▶ entertainment, activity, leisure activity, recreation, diversion, interest, delight, distraction, enjoyment, game, hobby, pastime, sport

amusing ADJECTIVE

an amusing story
▶ entertaining, enjoyable, witty, funny, diverting, pleasing

anaemic ADJECTIVE

Her complexion looked anaemic.
▶ colourless, bloodless, pale, pallid, pasty, sallow, sickly, insipid, wan, weak, feeble, frail

analogy NOUN

There is an analogy between the human brain and a computer.
▶ similarity, parallel, resemblance, comparison, likeness, correspondence, correlation

analyse VERB

1 *You need to analyse your motives.*
▶ examine, evaluate, review, scrutinize, consider, study, interpret, investigate

2 *The substance can be analysed by several methods.*
▶ break down, resolve, separate, separate out, dissect

analysis NOUN

An analysis of the unemployment figures.
▶ examination, breakdown, evaluation, study, scrutiny, research (into), enquiry (into), interpretation, investigation, test

analytical ADJECTIVE

an analytical approach to the problem
▶ systematic, logical, methodical, rational, critical, rigorous, searching, inquiring, investigative, penetrating, questioning
AN OPPOSITE IS unsystematic

anarchist NOUN

a trashy novel about spies and anarchists
▶ rebel, revolutionary, agitator, terrorist

anarchy NOUN

The country is threatened with anarchy.
▶ lawlessness, disorder, bedlam, disorganization, insurrection, chaos, confusion, misgovernment, misrule, mutiny, pandemonium, riot

ancestor NOUN

We can trace our ancestors back to the Stuarts.
▶ forebear, forefather, antecedent, predecessor, progenitor
AN OPPOSITE IS descendant
RELATED ADJECTIVE atavistic

ancestry NOUN

The family has a Spanish ancestry.
▶ lineage, origin, pedigree, roots, stock, parentage, ancestors, forebears

anchor VERB

1 *Several ships had anchored in the harbour.*
▶ berth, moor, tie up, make fast

2 *The lid was anchored to the sides with screws.*
▶ fasten, attach, fix

ancient ADJECTIVE

1 *the ancient buildings at Pompeii*
▶ old, historic, early, classical

2 *ancient civilizations*
▶ early, old, historic, prehistoric (= before the time of written records), archaic, bygone
AN OPPOSITE IS modern

anecdote NOUN

an anecdote about an elopement
▶ story, tale, narrative, reminiscence, (*more informal*) yarn

angel NOUN

1 *a depiction of angels with wings and beautiful faces*
▶ archangel, divine messenger, cherub, seraph

2 *She was an absolute angel during my illness.*
▶ dear, darling, treasure, gem, (*more informal*) brick

A

angelic ADJECTIVE

1 *angelic beings*
▶ heavenly, celestial, divine, ethereal

2 *an angelic expression*
▶ beautiful, lovely, heavenly, enchanting

3 *angelic behaviour*
▶ innocent, virtuous, exemplary, pure, saintly, pious, unworldly
AN OPPOSITE IS devilish.

anger NOUN

Anger surged through him.
▶ annoyance, irritation, crossness, exasperation, displeasure, fury, rage, indignation, temper, vexation, bitterness, hostility, outrage, resentment, passion, pique, (*more formal*) rancour, (*literary*) wrath, (*literary*) ire

anger VERB

Their rudeness angered all of us.
▶ enrage, annoy, irritate, infuriate, exasperate, incense, vex, madden, aggravate, antagonize, displease, incite, inflame, make angry, (*more informal*) needle, (*more informal*) rile, (*more informal*) bug, (*more informal*) rub up the wrong way
OPPOSITES ARE pacify, placate, appease

angle NOUN

1 *a cupboard built into the angle of the two walls*
▶ corner, intersection, recess

2 *We need to look at the problem from another angle.*
▶ perspective, point of view, standpoint, viewpoint, position, slant, approach, outlook

angle VERB

Angle the light towards the ceiling.
▶ slant, turn, direct, point, tilt, twist, bend

angry ADJECTIVE

John looked angry and started to shout. She gave us all an angry look.
▶ annoyed, enraged, angered, cross, displeased, furious, irritated, irate, infuriated, incensed, indignant, outraged
OPPOSITES ARE pleased, calm

become angry *Eventually the witch became angry.*
▶ lose your temper, go into a rage, fly into a rage, flare up, (*more informal*) see red, (*more informal*) fly off the handle, (*more informal*) hit the roof, (*more informal*) go off the deep end, (*very informal*) freak out, (*very informal*) go ballistic

anguish NOUN

a cry of anguish
▶ agony, pain, distress, torment, torture, sorrow, suffering, anxiety, grief, misery, tribulation, heartache, (*literary*) woe

anguished ADJECTIVE

an anguished look
▶ agonized, distressed, tormented, tortured, despairing, wretched, heart-broken

animal NOUN

1 *Like many animals they hibernate in winter.*
▶ living being, creature, beast, being, brute

2 **animals**
▶ wildlife

WORDS FOR TYPES OF ANIMAL

vertebrates (animals with skeleton and backbone): mammals (warm-blooded, have hair or fur, feed young on milk, e.g. humans, elephants, rats, mice, horses, cattle, deer, whales); birds (warm-blooded, have feathers and wings, lay eggs, e.g. sparrows, larks, thrushes, ostriches); reptiles (cold-blooded, have scaly skin, most lay eggs, e.g. snakes, lizards, crocodiles, tortoises, turtles); amphibians (cold-blooded, have thin, moist skin, young breathe with gills, adults breathe with lungs, lay eggs with tadpole or larval stage, e.g. frogs, toads and newts); fish (cold-blooded, have scaly skin, breathe with gills, most lay eggs, e.g. salmon, plaice, shark, catfish);.

invertebrates (animals with no backbone): arthropods (segmented bodies, hard external skeleton, jointed legs, e.g. spiders, insects, crabs, lobsters); echinoderms (spiny skin, sucker feet with a five-rayed body, e.g. starfish, sea urchin); molluscs (soft body, most with shells, e.g. snails, slugs, octopuses, squid); worms (flatworms, roundworms, segmented worms); jellyfish (body with an opening surrounded by tentacles); sponges (body like a bag with only one opening).

animal ADJECTIVE

1 *animal passions*
▶ carnal, bodily, physical, sensual
AN OPPOSITE IS spiritual

2 *animal behaviour*
▶ bestial, brutish, inhuman, savage, wild, coarse, crude

animate ADJECTIVE

an animate being
▶ live, living, alive, breathing, conscious, feeling, sentient
AN OPPOSITE IS inanimate

animate VERB

A feeling of excitement animated the whole team.
▶ invigorate, enliven, vitalize, revitalize, energize, stimulate, hearten, activate, revive, liven up, excite, encourage, exhilarate, fire, inspire, arouse, rejuvenate, galvanize, (*more informal*) buck up, (*more informal*) pep up, (*more informal*) give a buzz

animated ADJECTIVE

There was a sound of animated conversation in the next room.
▶ lively, spirited, excited, enthusiastic, exuberant,

heated, vivacious, high-spirited, passionate, impassioned
OPPOSITES ARE lethargic, lifeless

animation NOUN
They arrived full of animation and determination.
▶ liveliness, energy, vitality, spirit, enthusiasm, excitement, activity
OPPOSITES ARE lethargy, inertia

animosity NOUN
There was a strong animosity between the two brothers.
▶ hostility, ill-feeling, antagonism, enmity, acrimony, antipathy, rancour, bitterness, hate, hatred, loathing, venom
OPPOSITES ARE goodwill, rapport, friendship

annex VERB
The king annexed further territory during each campaign.
▶ occupy, seize, appropriate, usurp, acquire, conquer, take over

annexe NOUN
the hospital annexe
▶ extension, wing, addition, attached building

annihilate VERB
The army set about annihilating the whole population.
▶ destroy, wipe out, eliminate, eradicate, exterminate, extinguish, obliterate, slaughter, raze, abolish, erase, liquidate, (*more formal*) extirpate, (*more informal*) kill off

---

anniversary NOUN
SPECIAL ANNIVERSARIES
centenary (100 years), sesquicentenary (150 years), bicentenary (200 years), tercentenary (300 years), quatercentenary (400 years), quincentenary (500 years), sexcentenary (600 years), septcentenary (700 years), octocentenary (800 years), millenary (1,000 years).
USAGE The names for anniversaries from 300 years to 900 years are not often used in ordinary writing. It is more normal to write, e.g., 'the four- hundredth anniversary'. There is no word in ordinary use for a nine- hundredth anniversary. Note that the fifth name in the list is spelt *quater-* (from Latin *quater* = four times) and not *quarter-*.
SPECIAL WEDDING ANNIVERSARIES ARE
paper (first), wood (fifth), tin (tenth), crystal (fifteenth), china (twentieth), silver (twenty-fifth), pearl (thirtieth), coral (thirty-fifth), ruby (fortieth), sapphire (forty-fifth), golden (fiftieth), emerald (fifty-fifth), diamond (sixtieth), platinum (seventieth).

---

announce VERB
1 *The government will announce its plans next week.*
▶ make public, make known, declare, reveal, disclose, divulge, publish, publicize, broadcast, advertise
OPPOSITES ARE conceal, suppress
2 *The presenter announced the next act.*
▶ introduce, present

announcement NOUN
1 *There will be an announcement from the Palace this afternoon.*
▶ statement, declaration, communiqué, pronouncement, proclamation, bulletin, dispatch
2 *We are still waiting for an announcement of the decision.*
▶ declaration, notification, intimation, disclosure

announcer NOUN
The announcer gave details of the programme changes.
▶ presenter, anchorman, anchorwoman, newscaster, newsreader, broadcaster, commentator, compère, master of ceremonies

annoy VERB
The comments had clearly annoyed her.
▶ irritate, displease, anger, infuriate, enrage, exasperate, incense, vex, madden, aggravate, nettle, antagonize, inflame, make angry, (*more informal*) needle, (*more informal*) rile, (*more informal*) bug, (*more informal*) rub up the wrong way
OPPOSITES ARE please, gratify

annoyance NOUN
1 *Much to her annoyance, Mike had taken the car.*
▶ irritation, indignation, displeasure, exasperation, pique, chagrin, vexation
2 *The animals in the road proved quite an annoyance.*
▶ irritant, irritation, nuisance, bother, worry, (*more informal*) aggravation

annoyed ADJECTIVE
His mother was beginning to look annoyed.
▶ irritated, angry, cross, displeased, vexed, peeved, infuriated, incensed, enraged, (*more informal*) miffed, (*more informal*) put out
AN OPPOSITE IS pleased

annoying ADJECTIVE
His mouth curled into an annoying smile.
▶ irritating, infuriating, exasperating, maddening, irksome, bothersome, tiresome
OPPOSITES ARE pleasant, agreeable

anonymous ADJECTIVE
1 *The author was anonymous.*
▶ unnamed, nameless, incognito, unacknowledged, unidentified, unknown, unspecified, (*literary*) unsung
2 *an anonymous letter*
▶ unattributed, unsigned
3 *an anonymous way of writing*
▶ impersonal, nondescript, characterless, faceless, unremarkable

a
b
c
d
e
f
g
h
i
j
k
l
m
n
o
p
q
r
s
t
u
v
w
x
y
z

answer NOUN

1 *Our letter brought a quick answer.*
▶ reply, response, reaction, acknowledgement, riposte

2 *The answer to the question was far from clear.*
▶ solution, explanation

3 *Violence is no answer.*
▶ solution, remedy, way out

4 *his answer to the charge*
▶ defence, plea, vindication

answer VERB

1 *Please answer my question. Will nobody answer me?*
▶ reply to, respond to, acknowledge, give an answer to, react to

2 *"I'm not feeling well," she answered.*
▶ rejoin, reply, respond, retort, return

3 *A good encyclopedia will answer your problem.*
▶ resolve, solve, explain

4 *The accused could answer all but one of the charges.*
▶ refute, rebut, defend yourself against

5 *We have enough money to answer our present needs.*
▶ satisfy, serve, fulfil, meet, correspond to, echo, fit, match up to, suffice, suit

6 *The police have arrested a man answering the description.*
▶ match, fit, correspond to, conform to

answer someone back *It was unwise to answer back in those days, however it provoked you felt.*
▶ talk back to, be impertinent to, be cheeky to, contradict, (*more informal*) cheek

answerable ADJECTIVE

Ministers are answerable to Parliament.
▶ responsible, accountable, subject

antagonism NOUN

She was pleased, despite her antagonism to him.
▶ hostility, ill-feeling, animosity, enmity, acrimony, antipathy, rancour, bitterness, hate, hatred, loathing, venom
OPPOSITES ARE goodwill, rapport, friendship

antagonist NOUN

Old friends and old antagonists came across one another again.
▶ opponent, adversary, enemy, rival, competitor, contender

antagonistic ADJECTIVE

The march threatened to attract an antagonistic rival mob.
▶ hostile, opposed, ill-disposed, antipathetic

antagonize VERB

They seem to be trying to antagonize us.
▶ alienate, provoke, make an enemy of, offend, anger, annoy, embitter, estrange, irritate, upset
OPPOSITES ARE pacify, placate

anthem NOUN

The choir sang an anthem.
▶ hymn, song, song of praise, chorale, paean, psalm, canticle, chant

anthology NOUN

an anthology of short stories
▶ collection, selection, treasury, compilation, compendium, miscellany, digest

anticipate VERB

1 *It was impossible to anticipate all the possible moves.*
▶ forestall, pre-empt, intercept, prevent

2 *I anticipate that the result will be a draw.*
▶ expect, foresee, predict, forecast, foretell, hope

anticlimax NOUN

After all the excitement, the journey proved to be rather an anticlimax.
▶ let-down, comedown, disappointment

antics NOUN

He was reminded of his childhood antics.
▶ foolery, tricks, capers, buffoonery, tomfoolery, clowning, escapades, fooling, pranks, (*more informal*) larking about, (*more informal*) skylarking

antidote NOUN

The poison has no known antidote.
▶ antitoxin, cure, remedy, neutralizing agent

antipathy NOUN

He expressed his antipathy to institutions of any kind.
▶ hostility, ill-feeling, animosity, enmity, acrimony, antagonism, rancour, bitterness, hate, hatred, loathing, venom
OPPOSITES ARE fondness, goodwill, liking

antiquated ADJECTIVE

Their ideas seem antiquated these days. an antiquated typewriter
▶ old-fashioned, out-dated, outmoded, out-of-date, obsolete, ancient, antediluvian, antique, archaic, dated, anachronistic, old, passé, (*more informal*) past it, (*more informal*) prehistoric, primitive, quaint, (*humorous*) superannuated, unfashionable
OPPOSITES ARE up to date, modern, current, new

antique ADJECTIVE

Amanda has an eye for good antique furniture.
▶ old, ancient, antiquarian, antiquated, historic, old-fashioned, traditional, veteran (car), vintage (car)
OPPOSITES ARE modern, new

antique NOUN

a sale of antiques
▶ collector's item, curio, curiosity, rarity

antiquity NOUN

1 *The place had been a harbour in antiquity.*
▶ ancient times, the ancient past, past times

2 *a site of great antiquity*
▶ age, oldness, elderliness

antiseptic ADJECTIVE

1 *an antiseptic dressing*
▶ aseptic, germfree, disinfected, medicated, sanitized, sterile, sterilized, hygienic, clean, unpolluted

2 *antiseptic cream*
▶ disinfectant, germicidal, sterilizing

antisocial ADJECTIVE
Most people show some signs of antisocial behaviour.
► asocial, unsociable, unacceptable, objectionable, undisciplined, offensive, disorderly, disruptive, obnoxious, uncooperative, unfriendly, troublesome, unruly, alienated, anarchic, disagreeable, nasty, rebellious, rude
OPPOSITES ARE friendly, sociable

anxiety NOUN
1 *anxiety about money*
► concern, apprehension, unease, worry, disquiet, foreboding, nervousness, tension, distress, doubt, dread, fear, fretfulness, misgiving, qualm, scruple, strain, stress, uncertainty
AN OPPOSITE IS calmness
2 *She showed a strong anxiety to please.*
► eagerness, enthusiasm, desire, keenness, impatience, willingness
OPPOSITES ARE reluctance, unwillingness

anxious ADJECTIVE
1 *Anxious relatives were waiting for further news. Everyone is anxious about the next few weeks.*
► worried, concerned, nervous, apprehensive, fearful, uneasy, troubled, distressed, agitated, tense, restless
AN OPPOSITE IS calm
2 *She always seems anxious to please.*
► eager, keen, enthusiastic, willing, impatient
be anxious *He was anxious about his work.*
► worry, fret

apart ADVERB
Their parents are now living apart.
► separately, independently, on your own
apart from *Everyone came apart from him.*
► except (for), but for, aside from, besides, excepting, excluding

apartment NOUN
an apartment in the centre of town
► flat, set of rooms

apathetic ADJECTIVE
They seem apathetic about the whole idea.
► uninterested (in), indifferent (to), unconcerned, unenthusiastic, uncommitted, unfeeling, uninvolved, unmotivated (by)
OPPOSITES ARE enthusiastic, eager, keen (on)

apathy NOUN
At the general election the voters showed more than usual apathy.
► indifference, coolness, lack of interest, unconcern, lassitude, lethargy, listlessness, passivity, inertia, inactivity
AN OPPOSITE IS enthusiasm

aperture NOUN
There was a strange window-like aperture in one wall.
► opening, hole, gap, slit, vent, fissure, (technical) orifice

apex NOUN
1 *Two poles cross at the apex of the tent.*
► tip, top, peak, summit, pinnacle, crest, crown, head, point, vertex
OPPOSITES ARE bottom, base
2 *Her career had reached its apex.*
► climax, acme, pinnacle, peak, high point, culmination, height, zenith, apogee, consummation, crowning moment
OPPOSITES ARE nadir, low point

apologetic ADJECTIVE
They don't sound too apologetic considering it was their fault.
► regretful, repentant, sorry, contrite, penitent, remorseful, rueful
OPPOSITES ARE unrepentant, defiant

apologize VERB
He apologized for his mistake.
► say sorry, express regret, ask for forgiveness, be penitent, make an apology, repent

apology NOUN
We all owe you an apology.
► expression of regret, acknowledgement, confession, explanation, justification, defence, excuse, plea

apostle NOUN
a Christian apostle
► evangelist, proselytizer, preacher, teacher
the Apostles
► Christ's disciples, Christ's followers

appal VERB
The level of violence appals most people.
► horrify, shock, alarm, outrage, dismay, scandalize, repel, offend, disgust, sicken, revolt

appalling ADJECTIVE
1 *Their attitude was appalling in its callousness.*
► horrifying, horrific, shocking, outrageous, revolting, repellent, repulsive, terrifying, terrible, dreadful, awful, unnerving, sickening, nauseating, horrible
2 *an appalling piece of work*
► dreadful, awful, terrible, atrocious, abysmal

apparatus NOUN
1 *an apparatus for processing sea water*
► device, appliance, gadget, instrument, machine, mechanism, system, tool, (usually disapproving) contraption, (more informal) setup
2 *Laboratory apparatus can be extremely expensive.*
► equipment, implements, materials, machinery, (more informal) tackle, (more informal) gear

apparent ADJECTIVE
There was no apparent motive for the crime. A sense of relief was all too apparent.
► evident, discernible, ostensible, perceptible, recognizable, noticeable, observable, obvious, clear, manifest, conspicuous, detectable, overt, patent, visible, self-explanatory
OPPOSITES ARE obscure, hidden, concealed

apparently ADVERB
Apparently satisfied, the man leaned back.
▶ seemingly, evidently, ostensibly

apparition NOUN
The white apparition turned out to be a dead swan.
▶ ghost, spectre, phantom, hallucination, illusion, manifestation, phantasm, presence, shade, spirit, chimera, vision, wraith, (*more informal*) spook

appeal NOUN
1 *The radio station broadcast an appeal for calm.*
▶ call, request, cry, entreaty, petition, supplication, prayer
2 *Packaging is an important part of a product's appeal.*
▶ attraction, attractiveness, charm, allure, charisma, seductiveness, (*more informal*) pull

appeal VERB
1 **appeal for** *Detectives are appealing for information about the incident.*
▶ call for, cry out for, beg for, plead for, ask earnestly for, request, solicit
2 **appeal to** *Hoskins said that at first the film role didn't appeal to him.*
▶ attract, interest, please, entice, tempt

appealing ADJECTIVE
The prospect of a whole day with Jemima was rather appealing.
▶ attractive, agreeable, engaging, captivating, charming, delightful, lovely, enchanting
OPPOSITES ARE unappealing, disagreeable

appear VERB
1 *A large building appeared in the distance.*
▶ come into view, come into sight, be seen, arise, loom up
OPPOSITES ARE disappear, vanish
2 *By lunchtime the twins still hadn't appeared.*
▶ arrive, come, make an appearance, put in an appearance, (*more informal*) show your face, (*more informal*) show up, (*more informal*) turn up
3 *A few problems have appeared since we last met.*
▶ emerge, arise, develop, come to light, materialize, occur, (*more informal*) crop up, (*more informal*) turn up
4 *The road did not appear to lead anywhere.*
▶ seem, look, turn out
5 *Jake's sister was appearing in the school play for the first time.*
▶ perform, take part, act

appearance NOUN
1 *His scruffy appearance took us by surprise.*
▶ look, looks, aspect, bearing, demeanour, impression
2 *an appearance of friendliness*
▶ semblance, air, pretence, illusion, facade, guise, veneer

appease VERB
The gift was an attempt to appease him.
▶ placate, calm, win over, assuage, mollify, pacify, conciliate, propitiate, reconcile, soothe, quiet, (*more informal*) sweeten
AN OPPOSITE IS anger

appendix NOUN
an appendix to a book
▶ addendum, supplement, addition, annexe, postscript, rider

appetite NOUN
1 *A long walk will sharpen our appetites.*
▶ hunger, need for food, taste buds
2 *Her appetite for information was phenomenal.*
▶ craving, longing, yearning, eagerness, hankering (after), desire, passion, thirst, relish, zest, demand

appetizing ADJECTIVE
The woman brought in a large appetizing meal.
▶ tasty, delicious, inviting, palatable, (*more informal*) mouth-watering

applaud VERB
1 *The audience applauded loudly.*
▶ clap, cheer, give an ovation, acclaim, show your approval, (*more informal*) bring the house down
OPPOSITES ARE boo, hiss
2 *They were watching and applauding the youngsters' efforts.*
▶ acclaim, commend, praise, salute, congratulate, compliment, eulogize, extol, (*more formal*) laud
AN OPPOSITE IS criticize

applause NOUN
1 *There was a great round of applause when the dance ended.*
▶ clapping, cheering, acclamation, (an) ovation, plaudits, approval
2 *The author wins universal applause from his followers.*
▶ praise, acclaim, approval, acclamation, plaudits, accolades, admiration

appliance NOUN
There's no reason why you shouldn't use individual heating appliances.
▶ device, apparatus, gadget, instrument, machine, mechanism, system, tool, (*usually disapproving*) contraption, (*more informal*) setup

applicable ADJECTIVE
The law is not applicable in all cases.
▶ appropriate , relevant, pertinent, apposite, germane

applicant NOUN
The best applicant was a female graduate with fresh ideas.
▶ candidate, contender, interviewee, competitor, entrant, participant, aspirant

application NOUN
1 *an application for a grant*
▶ request, appeal, claim
2 *the application of new solutions to old problems*
▶ implementation, employment, use, exercise
3 *A degree is a sign that you have the application needed to hold down a job.*
▶ diligence, conscientiousness, industry, dedication, commitment, perseverance, endurance, stamina

apply VERB
1 *Apply antiseptic cream to the cut.*
▶ administer, bring into contact, lay on, put on, spread
2 *Contestants will need to apply all their skill and experience.*
▶ employ, exercise, use, utilize, bring into use, implement, practise
apply for *More than a hundred people have applied for the job.*
▶ put in an application for, seek, request, (*more informal*) put in for
apply to *The rules only apply to England and Wales.*
▶ be relevant to, pertain to, refer to, relate to, appertain to, concern, affect, involve
apply yourself
▶ concentrate, exert yourself, be diligent, be assiduous, be industrious, work hard, make an effort, persevere, (*more informal*) buckle down

appoint VERB
Amanda had been appointed store manager.
▶ name, nominate, designate, choose (to be), engage (as), take on (as), install (as)

appointment NOUN
1 *June had to rush to keep her five o'clock appointment.*
▶ engagement, assignation, arrangement, consultation, session, date, fixture, meeting, rendezvous, (*in poetry*) tryst
2 *the appointment of new members of staff*
▶ nomination, selection, choice, choosing, commissioning, election, naming
3 *Frank held an appointment at the University.*
▶ position, post, job, situation, office, place

appraisal NOUN
The article is an honest appraisal of the problems.
▶ assessment, evaluation, estimation, valuation, review, rating, consideration, appreciation

appraise VERB
They stood back to appraise the work they had done.
▶ assess, evaluate, estimate, review, consider, (*more informal*) size up

appreciable ADJECTIVE
an appreciable sum of money
▶ considerable, substantial, significant, sizeable, large, (*more informal*) tidy

appreciate VERB
1 *I'd appreciate any help you can give me.*
▶ be grateful for, value, welcome, prize, regard highly, esteem
OPPOSITES ARE think little of, despise, disparage
2 *We appreciate good music.*
▶ enjoy, value, cherish, respect, treasure, like, think highly of
OPPOSITES ARE despise, dislike
3 *I appreciate that you cannot stay long.*
▶ recognize, realize, understand, acknowledge, comprehend, know, apprehend, see
OPPOSITES ARE be unaware of, disregard

4 *Most properties in the area have appreciated in value.*
▶ increase, gain, rise, go up, grow, improve, build up, escalate, mount, soar, strengthen
OPPOSITES ARE depreciate, decrease, fall, go down, weaken

appreciation NOUN
1 *They showed their appreciation by taking us out to dinner.*
▶ gratitude, indebtedness, thanks, obligation, thankfulness
2 *an appreciation of good literature*
▶ enjoyment, understanding

appreciative ADJECTIVE
We are appreciative of all your efforts.
▶ grateful (for), thankful (for), indebted (for)
OPPOSITES ARE unappreciative, ungrateful

apprehension NOUN
A run of bad luck left him with great apprehension about the future.
▶ anxiety, concern, unease, worry, disquiet, foreboding, nervousness, tension, distress, doubt, dread, fear, fretfulness, misgiving, uncertainty

apprehensive ADJECTIVE
Polly was apprehensive about going back up on deck.
▶ anxious, worried, concerned, nervous, fearful, uneasy, troubled, distressed, agitated, tense, restless

apprentice NOUN
James joined his uncle's engineering firm as an apprentice.
▶ trainee, learner, novice, beginner, probationer, pupil, starter, (*humorous*) tiro

apprise VERB
He promised to apprise them fully of any developments.
▶ inform, notify, advise, enlighten (about), keep posted (about), update (on)

approach NOUN
1 *Flowers in the park announced the approach of spring.*
▶ arrival, coming, advance, appearance, nearing, imminence, advent
OPPOSITES ARE retreat, departure
2 *The most beautiful approach to the city is from the south.*
▶ access, passage, road, way in, entry, entrance, drive
3 *His approach was to try out new ideas on other people.*
▶ method, procedure, technique, way, system, course, manner, means, style, mode
4 *We need an international approach to problems such as global warming.*
▶ attitude, perspective, policy (for, regarding), outlook (on), point of view (on), viewpoint (on)
5 *I made an informal approach to the bank manager*
▶ appeal, application, invitation, offer, overture, proposal, proposition

A

approach VERB

1 *A grinning dark-haired youth approached them, holding out his hand.*
▶ move towards, proceed towards, come towards, go towards, come near, draw near, advance on, bear down on, near

2 *The committee approached its task with determination.*
▶ set about, tackle, embark on, make a start on, begin, undertake, get down to

3 *Should we approach the bank manager about a loan?*
▶ contact, speak to, sound out, appeal to

4 *The likely cost was now approaching several millions.*
▶ border on, get near, get close to, verge on, approximate, (*more informal*) get on for

approachable ADJECTIVE

She looked younger and more approachable.
▶ friendly, welcoming, well-disposed, congenial, cordial, agreeable, pleasant, obliging, communicative, accessible, affable, informal, kind, open, sociable, sympathetic, (*more informal*) unstuffy, (*more informal*) matey
OPPOSITES ARE aloof, formal

appropriate ADJECTIVE

1 *This isn't an appropriate time to ask questions.*
▶ suitable, fitting, proper, apt

2 *The form should be completed with any appropriate comments.*
▶ relevant, apposite, pertinent, applicable, germane
OPPOSITES ARE inappropriate, irrelevant

approval NOUN

1 *Jane looked at them with approval.*
▶ favour, approbation, admiration, support, appreciation, commendation, acclaim, acclamation, applause, respect, regard, esteem, liking
OPPOSITES ARE disapproval, disfavour

2 *Congress had given final approval to the bill in October.*
▶ consent, assent, support, agreement, endorsement, acceptance, authorization, acquiescence, (*more informal*) blessing, (*more informal*) (the) go-ahead, (*more informal*) (the) green light, (*more informal*) OK, (*more informal*) thumbs up
OPPOSITES ARE refusal, veto

approve VERB

1 *Some members are thought to have approved the plan.*
▶ support, accept, agree to, assent to, consent to, acquiesce in, accede to, endorse, back, subscribe to, authorize
OPPOSITES ARE refuse, veto

2 **approve of** *Some parents and teachers still do not approve of the use of calculators.*
▶ welcome, favour, endorse, advocate, support, hold with, countenance, tolerate, recommend, (*more informal*) go along with
OPPOSITES ARE disapprove of, condemn, reject

approximate ADJECTIVE

All measurements are approximate.
▶ rough, estimated, close, inexact, near
AN OPPOSITE IS exact

approximately ADVERB

Homework should last approximately an hour.
▶ roughly, about, round about, around, more or less, nearly, in the region of, in the order of, approaching, (*more informal*) something like, (*more informal*) ... or so, (*more informal*) ... or thereabouts, (*much more informal*) pushing, (*literary*) nigh on

apt ADJECTIVE

1 *He tried to think of an apt reply.*
▶ appropriate, suitable, fitting, proper

2 *The old man is apt to fall asleep in the evening.*
▶ inclined, liable, prone, likely

aptitude NOUN

an aptitude for dancing
▶ talent, gift, flair, ability, genius, faculty, capacity

arable ADJECTIVE

arable land
▶ cultivated, cultivable, cultivatable, productive
AN OPPOSITE IS infertile

arbitrary ADJECTIVE

1 *Decisions can appear arbitrary without all the information.*
▶ random, irrational, indiscriminate, capricious, unreasonable, unpredictable, whimsical, wilful, casual, chance, fanciful, illogical, subjective
OPPOSITES ARE methodical, rational

2 *the exercise of arbitrary power*
▶ autocratic, despotic, dictatorial, absolute, unrestrained, high-handed, oppressive, repressive, imperious, summary, tyrannical, tyrannous

arbitrate VERB

The ambassador offered to arbitrate in the dispute.
▶ adjudicate, judge, intercede, mediate, negotiate, pass judgement, referee, umpire, settle, make peace, decide the outcome

arbitration NOUN

The county court will automatically refer the matter to arbitration.
▶ mediation, negotiation, conciliation, adjudication, judgement, settlement

arbitrator NOUN

An independent arbitrator will review all the facts of the case.
▶ adjudicator, mediator, arbiter, intermediary, judge, go-between, negotiator, ombudsman, peacemaker, referee, umpire, (*more informal*) troubleshooter

arch NOUN

The entrance consists of a high stone arch.
▶ archway, arc, bridge, vault, curve

arch VERB

The cat arched its back
▶ curve, arc, bend, bow

archaic ADJECTIVE

1 *archaic Greek sculpture*
▶ ancient, old, primitive
2 *He arrived in a top hat and morning coat, already a somewhat achaic form of working dress.*
▶ old-fashioned, antiquated, outmoded, obsolete

architect NOUN

Ictinus, architect of the Parthenon
▶ builder, master builder, designer, planner

archives NOUN

Bernard said he would go to the archives and read the files for himself.
▶ records, annals, chronicles, documents, libraries, papers

ardent ADJECTIVE

ardent admirers of good music
▶ passionate, avid, fervent, zealous, eager, keen, enthusiastic

ardour NOUN

She spoke about her travels with all the ardour of youth.
▶ fervour, eagerness, intensity, enthusiasm, excitement, passion, vigour, energy, spirit, keenness, zeal, warmth

arduous ADJECTIVE

an arduous journey over the hills
▶ exhausting, tiring, punishing, onerous, demanding, daunting, rigorous, tough
OPPOSITES ARE easy, effortless

area NOUN

1 *They came to an open area of land.*
▶ expanse, extent, stretch, patch, tract, sector, sheet, space, surface, width, breadth
2 *More money is needed for deprived urban areas.*
▶ district, region, sector, locality, neighbourhood, precinct, vicinity, zone, environment, environs, province, territory
3 *an area of study*
▶ field, domain, sphere, subject

arena NOUN

1 *A new sports arena will be built in time for the games.*
▶ stadium, ground, park, pitch, field, playing area, ring, rink, amphitheatre
2 *She wanted to be more active in the political arena.*
▶ scene, sphere, domain, realm

arguable ADJECTIVE

It is arguable that the official figures exaggerate the unemployment problem.
▶ possible, conceivable, tenable, credible, defensible

argue VERB

1 *The children do seem to argue a lot.*
▶ quarrel, squabble, wrangle, bicker, row
2 *The group argued late into the night.*
▶ deliberate, discuss, debate, dispute
3 *Some people argue that all ownership is theft.*
▶ contend, maintain, postulate, assert, claim, submit, suggest, reason, insist, show, demonstrate, prove

argument NOUN

1 *A fierce argument followed.*
▶ quarrel, disagreement, squabble, row, wrangle, altercation, difference, dispute, dissension, clash, controversy, feud, fight, remonstration, expostulation, (*more informal*) set-to
2 *a long argument about politics*
▶ discussion, debate, consultation, deliberation
3 *No convincing argument has been offered.*
▶ case, line of reasoning, demonstration, hypothesis, defence, gist, idea, summary, synopsis, view
4 *the principal argument of the book*
▶ thesis, contention, theme, topic, plot

argumentative ADJECTIVE

He could be difficult and argumentative at times.
▶ quarrelsome, combative, contentious, disputatious, truculent, aggressive

arid ADJECTIVE

an arid landscape
▶ barren, parched, desert, dry, waste, waterless, infertile, lifeless, sterile, torrid, unproductive
OPPOSITES ARE fertile, lush

arise VERB

1 *If any problems arise go and see your doctor.*
▶ emerge, develop, appear, come to light, materialize, occur, (*more informal*) crop up, (*more informal*) turn up
2 *The misunderstanding arose from poor communications.*
▶ result, originate, stem, derive, spring, follow, ensue, proceed
3 (*more formal*) *The animal arose and began to walk.*
▶ rise, stand up, get up, spring up, jump up, get to your feet

aristocrat NOUN

an aristocrat from an old family
▶ noble, nobleman, noblewoman, lord, lady, peer, peeress, patrician, grandee, titled person, (*more informal*) toff, (*more informal*) nob

aristocratic ADJECTIVE

a member of an aristocratic family
▶ noble, upper-class, high-born, titled, patrician, blue-blooded, lordly, princely, royal, courtly, élite, thoroughbred

arm NOUN

the political arm of the movement
▶ branch, section, division, wing, offshoot

arm VERB

The woman had gone downstairs, armed with an empty bottle.
▶ equip, provide, protect, supply, fortify, furnish

A

armada NOUN

an armada of heavily-armed warships
▶ fleet, flotilla, navy, squadron, task force

armistice NOUN

Fighting ended with an armistice.
▶ ceasefire, suspension of hostilities, cessation of hostilities, truce, agreement, peace, treaty, peace treaty

armour NOUN

1 *a knight in armour*
▶ chain mail, mail

2 *an animal's armour*
▶ protective covering, sheathing, shield, protection

armoury NOUN

an armoury of weapons
▶ arsenal, arms depot, depot, ordnance depot, magazine, stockpile, ammunition dump

army NOUN

1 *The king raised an army of ten thousand foot soldiers.*
▶ armed force, fighting force, force, militia, horde
RELATED ADJECTIVE military

2 *an army of tourists*
▶ crowd, swarm, throng, horde, stream, mass, herd, host, multitude

aroma NOUN

an aroma of fresh coffee
▶ smell, fragrance, odour, bouquet, perfume, scent, (*more informal*) whiff

arouse VERB

The proposals aroused strong public hostility.
▶ rouse, cause, kindle, prompt, provoke, instigate, spark off, stimulate, stir up, (*more informal*) whip up
AN OPPOSITE IS allay

arrange VERB

1 *It was time to arrange the seating for dinner.*
▶ organize, set out, lay out, sort out, put in order, plan, fix, order, spread out, dispose

2 *We hope to arrange an outing for next week.*
▶ organize, fix, fix up, plan, set up, make arrangements for, devise, schedule, contrive, coordinate, manage, prepare, see to, settle

3 *Ravel arranged the music for an orchestra.*
▶ adapt, score, set, harmonize, orchestrate

arrangement NOUN

1 *They've changed the arrangement of the furniture.*
▶ positioning, layout, placing, planning, spacing, disposition, distribution, organization, setting out, alignment, display, grouping, design

2 *an arrangement to share the costs*
▶ agreement, understanding, settlement, compact, contract, deal, pact, scheme, terms

3 *a musical arrangement*
▶ adaptation, setting, harmonization, orchestration, version

array NOUN

a gleaming array of vintage cars
▶ arrangement, display, presentation, show, exhibition, parade, collection, muster, (*more informal*) line-up

array VERB

1 *A picnic was arrayed on rugs on the ground.*
▶ arrange, lay out, spread out, display, assemble

2 *We were arrayed in our best clothes.*
▶ dress, attire, clothe, deck out, adorn, fit out, garb, robe, wrap, decorate, (*more informal*) get up, (*more informal*) rig out

arrest VERB

1 *Police arrested him for shoplifting.*
▶ apprehend, detain, take into custody, take in, (*more informal*) book, (*more informal*) pull in, (*more informal*) pick up, (*more informal*) nick, (*more informal*) nab

2 *Recent measures have arrested the spread of disease.*
▶ check, stop, end, halt, prevent, retard, slow, stem, impede, slow down, block, inhibit, interrupt, delay, hinder, obstruct

arrival NOUN

1 *A crowd awaited the Queen's arrival.*
▶ coming, appearance, approach, entrance, homecoming, landing, return, touchdown

2 *Pretty girls greeted the new arrivals.*
▶ comer, caller, newcomer, visitor

arrive VERB

1 *Guests started to arrive at around six o'clock.*
▶ come, come along, appear, enter, present yourself, (*more informal*) turn up, (*more informal*) roll up, (*more informal*) show up

2 (*informal*) *When they got the invitation they knew they had arrived.*
▶ succeed, be successful, reach the top, break through, (*more informal*) make it

arrive at *We arrived at the bus station.*
▶ reach, come to, get to, (*more informal*) make

arrogance NOUN

His arrogance took her breath away.
▶ haughtiness, conceit, self-importance, high-handedness, condescension, disdain, insolence

arrogant ADJECTIVE

He was proud, and had an arrogant manner.
▶ haughty, conceited, self-important, high-handed, lordly, overbearing, boastful, scornful, condescending, supercilious, superior, bumptious, disdainful, cavalier, imperious, insolent, pompous, presumptuous, proud, snobbish, vain, (*more informal*) hoity-toity, (*more informal*) cocky, (*more informal*) high and mighty, (*more informal*) stuck-up
AN OPPOSITE IS modest

arsenal NOUN
Both countries have arsenals of nuclear weapons.
▶ armoury, arms depot, depot, ordnance depot, magazine, stockpile, ammunition dump

art NOUN
1 *She had done an art course.*
▶ fine art, painting, sculpture, drawing, artistry, artwork, craft, craftsmanship, draughtsmanship
2 *the art of writing*
▶ skill, craft, talent, technique, aptitude, gift, knack, expertise, facility, knack, proficiency, trick, cleverness, dexterity

article NOUN
1 *various household articles*
▶ object, item, thing, commodity, product, (*in plural*) goods
2 *I read an article on the subject.*
▶ essay, report, paper, study, feature, review, account, piece

articulate ADJECTIVE
a most articulate speaker
▶ eloquent, fluent, lucid, expressive, intelligible, clear, coherent, comprehensible, distinct
OPPOSITES ARE inarticulate, unintelligible

articulate VERB
It is not easy to articulate your feelings.
▶ express, voice, state, speak, say, communicate, utter, declare, set forth, pronounce

artificial ADJECTIVE
1 *artificial light   artificial trees*
▶ synthetic, imitation, simulated, unnatural, man-made, manufactured, false, fake, substitute
AN OPPOSITE IS natural
2 *an artificial smile*
▶ false, spurious, affected, fake, feigned, assumed, pretended, bogus, contrived, counterfeit, factitious, pseudo, sham, simulated, unreal, (*more informal*) phoney, (*more informal*) put on
AN OPPOSITE IS genuine

artist NOUN
1 *The artist used a wide range of colour.*
▶ painter, sculptor, craftsman, craftswoman, designer
2 *a music-hall artist*
▶ performer

artistic ADJECTIVE
Desktop publishing requires artistic skills. The designs looked very artistic.
▶ creative, imaginative, aesthetic, decorative, ornamental, tasteful, stylish, elegant, beautiful, attractive, cultured
OPPOSITES ARE crude, ugly

ascend VERB
1 *He ascended the stairs.*
▶ climb, climb up, go up, come up, mount, move up, scale
2 *The little plane began slowly to ascend.*
▶ rise, soar, take off, lift off, fly up

3 *An unmade road ascends to the church.*
▶ climb, slope up
AN OPPOSITE IS descend

ascent NOUN
A gradual ascent made the walk more arduous.
▶ rise, slope, gradient, hill, incline, climb, elevation, ramp
AN OPPOSITE IS descent

ascertain VERB
The police had to ascertain whether Darren had actually entered the room.
▶ find out, establish, confirm, determine, discover, learn, make certain, make sure, settle, verify, identify

ascribe VERB
The inquest ascribed his death to natural causes.
▶ attribute, assign, put down, blame (on), connect (with), associate (with)

ash NOUN
Ash from a fire lay in the hearth.
▶ cinders, clinker, embers, burnt remains

ashamed ADJECTIVE
1 *She was ashamed of her outburst of bad temper.*
▶ sorry (for), apologetic (about), remorseful (about), contrite (about), repentant (about), shamefaced (about), abashed (about), penitent (about), embarrassed (about), distressed (about), upset (about), conscience-stricken (about), discomfited (about), mortified (about), red-faced (about), chastened (about), rueful (about)
OPPOSITES ARE unrepentant, unabashed
2 *He seemed too ashamed to admit his mistake.*
▶ reticent, reluctant, loath, unwilling, bashful, shy, diffident, hesitant, embarrassed, modest, prudish, self-conscious, sheepish
OPPOSITES ARE proud, shameless

ask VERB
1 *I'll ask him what he means.*
▶ enquire (of somebody), quiz (somebody about)
2 *They want to ask a few questions.*
▶ pose, put, raise, submit
3 *Ask them to fetch help.*
▶ entreat, request, implore, beg, solicit, exhort, urge, plead with, (*literary*) beseech, (*literary*) enjoin
4 *We could ask them to dinner.*
▶ invite, summon, (*more formal*) request the pleasure of the company of
ask for *Don't hesitate to ask for anything you need.*
▶ request, demand, seek
ask for *The remarks were asking for trouble.*
▶ look for, provoke, invite, attract, court, incite, tempt, cause, encourage, generate, (*more informal*) stir up

asleep ADJECTIVE
The girls were asleep in bed.
▶ sleeping, slumbering, dozing, napping, (*more informal*) out like a light, (*more informal*) dead to the world

A

aspect NOUN

1 *The article describes every aspect of life in deprived areas.*
▶ feature, facet, characteristic, side, angle, respect, particular, circumstance, detail, standpoint

2 *Dark stone gave the facade a grim aspect.*
▶ appearance, look, air

3 *The house has a southern aspect*
▶ outlook, view, prospect, exposure, orientation, direction, position, situation

aspersions NOUN

cast aspersions on *The remarks are not intended to cast any aspersions on your honesty.*
▶ criticize, disparage, denigrate, belittle, vilify, deprecate, poor scorn on, decry, condemn, malign, discredit, stigmatize, denounce

aspiration NOUN

Giotto, the artist who Matisse said was the peak of his aspiration.
▶ ambition, hope, desire, wish, longing, purpose, aim, goal, target, objective, object, dream

aspire VERB

aspire to *They aspired to be back in the city to which they belonged. We can aspire to a higher and fuller life.*
▶ aim to or for, wish to or for, want, yearn to or for, strive (after), seek (to), long to or for, desire to, crave to or for, dream of, hope to or for, pursue, set your sights on, have ambitions to or for

aspiring ADJECTIVE

aspiring young writers
▶ would-be, intending, aspirant, budding, hopeful, eager, potential

assault VERB

He was prosecuted for assaulting a police officer.
▶ attack , hit, strike, set upon, beat up, fall on, molest, (*more informal*) rough up

assault NOUN

an assault on the enemy position
▶ attack , onslaught, strike, offensive, raid, foray, sortie, charge

assemble VERB

1 *A crowd began to assemble.*
▶ gather, congregate, come together, collect, converge, convene, crowd together, rally, rally round, meet, flock together, join up, swarm, muster, throng round, accumulate

2 *We assembled our belongings in the hall. The general assembled his forces.*
▶ gather, collect together, bring together, amass, convene, get together, round up, marshal, mobilize, muster, pile up, rally
OPPOSITES ARE disperse, scatter

3 *Few cars are now assembled in Britain.*
▶ build, construct, manufacture, produce, put together, erect, fabricate, fit together, make, piece together
AN OPPOSITE IS dismantle

assembly NOUN

1 *a political assembly   an assembly of bishops*
▶ gathering, meeting, congress, convocation, assemblage, council, synod (church)

2 *An assembly of spectators waited at the gates.*
▶ crowd , gathering, throng, rally, meeting, (*literary*) multitude

3 *The special glue is used in the assembly of model aircraft.*
▶ construction, building, making, putting together, manufacture, erection (of buildings)

assent NOUN

Parents need to give their assent to attendance on field trips.
▶ agreement, approval, consent, permission, authorization, blessing, (*more informal*) go-ahead
AN OPPOSITE IS refusal

assert VERB

1 *She asserted that multinational companies should not be blamed for damage to the environment.*
▶ declare, maintain, contend, submit, insist, argue, proclaim, profess, claim, emphasize, affirm, allege, protest, state, stress

2 *It is not always easy for people to assert their rights.*
▶ insist on, claim, stand up for, make use of, uphold

assert yourself *Some of the newer committee members began to assert themselves at meetings.*
▶ be assertive, behave confidently, be resolute, make yourself felt, exert your influence, make demands, persist, stand firm, (*more informal*) stick to your guns

assertive ADJECTIVE

You will need to be assertive in this job.
▶ forceful, determined, resolute, confident, decisive, firm, assured, self-assured, authoritative, strong-willed, bold, positive, aggressive, domineering, strong, (*usually disapproving*) pushy
OPPOSITES ARE submissive, reticent, retiring

assess VERB

1 *The hospital used a scanner to assess the extent of their head injuries.*
▶ evaluate, gauge, judge, determine, review, reckon, estimate, appraise, calculate, work out, value

2 *All pupils are assessed and graded at the end of their first term.*
▶ rate, judge, appraise, check, review

asset NOUN

1 *A good sense of humour can be an asset.*
▶ benefit, advantage, blessing, boon, strength, virtue, help, aid, support, good, (*more informal*) plus, (*more informal*) godsend

2 **assets** *The family's assets were reckoned at over two million dollars.*
▶ capital, resources, possessions, reserves, property, estate, funds, goods, holdings, means, money, savings, securities, wealth, (*more informal*) worldly goods

assign VERB
1 *Tasks are assigned on the basis of experience.*
► allocate, distribute, allot, apportion, dispense, give out, hand over, share out
2 *Kathryn was told she would be assigned to the case.*
► appoint, consign, delegate, designate, nominate, put down, choose (for), select (for)

assignment NOUN
1 *I have a difficult assignment to finish.*
► task, piece of work, exercise, project, job, duty
2 *the assignment of responsibilities*
► allocation, issuing, granting

assist VERB
Could you assist us for a while?
► help, aid, support, give a hand to, lend a (helping) hand to, oblige
OPPOSITES ARE hinder, impede

assistance NOUN
They said they would not need any assistance.
► help, support, aid, encouragement, reinforcement, backing, collaboration, cooperation, contribution, patronage, sponsorship, subsidy
AN OPPOSITE IS hindrance

assistant NOUN
The team leader has three assistants.
► helper, subordinate, supporter, associate, deputy, colleague, underling, junior, ancillary, collaborator

associate VERB
1 *Stephen had been associating with dropouts and oddballs.*
► mix, keep company, go about, consort, socialize, fraternize, mingle, (*more informal*) hang about
AN OPPOSITE IS dissociate
2 *Patience was not a quality I associated at all with him.*
► connect, link, identify, equate, relate (to)

association NOUN
1 *They enjoyed several years of friendly association.*
► relationship, connection, link, bond, ties, friendship, attachment, union
2 *an association of sports clubs*
► organization, confederation, federation, coalition, society, league, partnership, alliance, syndicate, group

assorted ADJECTIVE
a collection of assorted objects
► miscellaneous, mixed, different, sundry, varied, various, differing, diverse, diversified, heterogeneous, manifold, motley, multifarious, several, (*old-fashioned*) divers

assortment NOUN
an assortment of dog-eared paperbacks
► mixture, selection, collection, variety, array, miscellany, choice, diversity, medley, mélange

assume VERB
1 *I assumed the book was a gift.*
► presume, suppose, infer, deduce, take for granted, surmise, conjecture, reckon, imagine, come to the conclusion, guess, suspect, believe, imagine, deduce, expect, think, understand, (*more informal*) have a hunch
2 *The children should be encouraged to assume responsibilities.*
► take on, undertake, accept, embrace
3 *To play the part she had to assume a Scottish accent.*
► adopt, put on, feign, acquire

assumed ADJECTIVE
She writes under an assumed name.
► false, fictitious, invented, adopted, made-up, bogus, fake, spurious

assumption NOUN
The assumption is that prices will stay the same.
► supposition, presumption, conjecture, expectation, belief, guess, hypothesis, premise, surmise, theory

assurance NOUN
She had an air of complete assurance.
► confidence, composure, self-confidence, poise, aplomb, level-headedness, self-possession, self-reliance

assure VERB
1 *He assured me he would arrive in time.*
► promise, reassure, convince, persuade, satisfy
2 *The win assured them a place in the finals.*
► ensure, secure, guarantee, make certain, confirm, establish

assured ADJECTIVE
an assured manner
► confident, self-confident, self-assured, positive, assertive, composed, collected, calm, level-headed

astonish VERB
We were astonished at how much the place had changed.
► amaze, astound, surprise, stagger, startle, disconcert, dumbfound, shock, flabbergast, perplex, stun, stupefy, bewilder

astonishing ADJECTIVE
The results were astonishing.
► amazing, astounding, staggering, extraordinary, startling, stunning, breathtaking, fantastic, wonderful, phenomenal, incredible

astound VERB
His arrogance astounded her.
► astonish, amaze, surprise, stagger, startle, disconcert, dumbfound, shock, flabbergast, perplex, stun, stupefy, bewilder

astounding ADJECTIVE
an astounding statement
► amazing, astonishing, staggering, extraordinary, startling, stunning, breathtaking, fantastic, wonderful, phenomenal, incredible

astray ADVERB
Several missiles had gone astray and hit civilian targets.
► off course, adrift, amiss, awry, lost, wide of the mark

astute ADJECTIVE
an astute manager   some astute remarks
▶ shrewd, sharp, acute, canny, prudent, clever, intelligent, quick-witted, perceptive, discerning, crafty, wily
AN OPPOSITE IS stupid

asylum NOUN
Spain refused to hand over four men who had sought asylum in their embassy.
▶ haven, shelter, refuge, retreat, safety, sanctuary

athletic ADJECTIVE
an athletic physique
▶ muscular, fit, well-built, powerful, strong, sturdy, acrobatic, active, energetic, robust, sinewy, vigorous, wiry, (*more informal*) sporty, (*more informal*) strapping
OPPOSITES ARE frail, weak

atmosphere NOUN
1 *Harmful gases are escaping into the atmosphere.*
▶ air, sky, ether, (*literary*) heavens
2 *the warm cosy atmosphere of the kitchen*
▶ ambience, aura, environment, surroundings, quality, character, climate, mood, feeling, (*more informal*) vibes

atom NOUN
There is not an atom of truth in the story.
▶ scrap, speck, spot, trace, morsel, bit, crumb, grain, iota, jot, molecule, particle

atrocious ADJECTIVE
They were guilty of atrocious brutality.
▶ abominable, appalling, brutal, vicious, detestable, hateful, odious, vile, obnoxious, dreadful, abhorrent, diabolical, disgusting, repellent, horrifying
AN OPPOSITE IS humane

atrocity NOUN
Further atrocities have been reported.
▶ outrage, enormity, cruelty, act of brutality

attach VERB
1 *The brackets are attached to the wall with a pair of small screws.*
▶ fix, fasten, secure, affix, join, link, stick, bond, couple, anchor, connect, tie, add, append
OPPOSITES ARE detach, remove
2 *We attach great importance to punctuality.*
▶ attribute, ascribe, assign, apply, put (on), place (on), associate (with), impute

attached ADJECTIVE
attached to *The sisters seem very attached to each other.*
▶ fond of, close to, devoted to, dear to, affectionate to or towards, friendly to or towards, loving to or towards, loyal to or towards, warm to or towards

attack NOUN
1 *An attack on the enemy was planned for the next day.*
▶ assault, onslaught, strike, offensive, raid, charge, ambush, foray, sortie, rush, blitz, bombardment, broadside, cannonade, counter-attack

2 *Their attack on her honesty upset her very much.*
▶ criticism (of), tirade (against), outburst (against), vilification (of), abuse (of), censure (of), denunciation (of), diatribe (against), revilement (of), invective (against)
3 *an attack of coughing*
▶ fit, bout, spasm, convulsion, outbreak, paroxysm, seizure, stroke, (*more informal*) turn

attack VERB
1 *We attack the enemy position at dawn.*
▶ charge, bombard, assault, ambush, raid, rush, descend on, storm, strike at, (*more informal*) blast, (*more informal*) pitch into, (*more informal*) wade into
2 *A bunch of youths attacked him in the street on his way home.*
▶ assault, mob, mug, pounce on, ambush, set about, set on, jump on, (*more informal*) beat up, (*more informal*) do over, (*more informal*) lay into
3 *The clergy regularly attack government policy.*
▶ criticize, find fault with, censure, denounce, condemn, impugn, vilify, inveigh against, malign, round on, snipe at
AN OPPOSITE IS defend
4 *We need to attack the problem of poverty.*
▶ confront, address, focus on, attend to, apply yourself to, deal with, (*more informal*) have a go at

attacker NOUN
1 *The little force fought bravely against its attackers.*
▶ aggressor, assailant, invader, opponent, raider, enemy
2 *The attacker ran off empty-handed.*
▶ assailant, mugger, aggressor, intruder, rapist
3 *The journal agreed to publish a defence against her attackers.*
▶ critic, detractor, persecutor, opponent, enemy

attain VERB
He did not attain this honour until the reign of Queen Victoria.
▶ achieve, accomplish, obtain, gain, win, earn, get, acquire, secure, reach, (*more informal*) clinch, (*more informal*) carry off, (*more informal*) pull off

attainment NOUN
many exceptional attainments
▶ achievement, accomplishment, success, deed, exploit

attempt NOUN
a brave attempt
▶ try, effort, endeavour, venture, (*more informal*) shot

attempt VERB
1 *We attempted to visit all three sites in one day.*
▶ try, endeavour, aim, aspire, strive, undertake, set out, make an effort or every effort, do your best, do your utmost, venture, seek, (*more informal*) have a go (at), (*more informal*) have a stab (at), (*more informal*) bend over backwards
2 *Candidates should attempt three questions.*
▶ undertake, try, choose, answer

attend VERB

1 *Frances had to attend an interview the following week.*
▶ go to or for, present yourself at, appear at, be present at
2 *The bride was attended by two bridesmaids.*
▶ escort, assist, accompany, chaperon, follow, guard, usher, wait on
3 **attend to** *A nurse attended to the injured.*
▶ look after, care for, tend, treat, help, deal with, (*more formal*) minister to
4 **attend to** *Frank said he would attend to the details of the trip.*
▶ deal with, take care of, look after, see to, manage, organize, make arrangements for, take responsibility for
5 **attend to** *Please attend to what I say.*
▶ listen to, pay attention to, heed, mark, mind, concentrate on, follow carefully, hear, note, notice, observe, think about

attendant NOUN

The Queen had three attendants.
▶ assistant, aide, retainer, companion, escort, equerry, servant, bodyguard

attention NOUN

Please give the matter your full attention.
▶ concentration, observation, regard, consideration, scrutiny, notice, thought, concern, care, diligence, heed, recognition

attentive ADJECTIVE

1 *Julian was standing silent and attentive in the shadows.*
▶ alert, vigilant, watchful, aware, circumspect, wide awake, on the lookout, on the ball, on your guard, (*more informal*) on the qui vive
2 *Helen was patient and attentive, holding my hand to calm me.*
▶ thoughtful, considerate, kind, caring, understanding, tender, devoted

attitude NOUN

a positive, joyful attitude
▶ outlook, approach, air, manner, demeanour, disposition, inclination, position, bearing, frame of mind, mien, mood, posture, stance, behaviour

attract VERB

1 *The recent lecture attracted a good turnout.*
▶ draw, bring, bring in, produce, cause, generate
2 *They were attracted by the beauty of the place.*
▶ enchant, entrance, excite, captivate, lure, entice, allure, tempt, charm, fascinate, beguile, bewitch
AN OPPOSITE IS repel

attractive ADJECTIVE

1 *an attractive young woman*
▶ good-looking, nice-looking, pretty, striking, fetching, beautiful, gorgeous, lovely, charming, engaging, appealing, delightful, glamorous, stunning
AN OPPOSITE IS repulsive

2 *an attractive offer*
▶ appealing, agreeable, tempting, interesting, difficult to resist or refuse

attribute VERB

A cool head is not the first quality I would attribute to the colonel.
▶ ascribe, associate (with), connect (with), assign, put down, blame (on)

audacious ADJECTIVE

an audacious decision
▶ bold, daring, brave, courageous, adventurous, enterprising

audacity NOUN

1 *His sheer audacity was enough to carry the day.*
▶ bravery, daring, boldness, courage, enterprise
2 (*usually disapproving*) *Then they had the audacity to ask for money.*
▶ effrontery, cheek, nerve, boldness, temerity, impertinence, impudence, insolence, presumptuousness, shamelessness, (*more informal*) sauce

audible ADJECTIVE

Her words were hardly audible above the noise of the traffic.
▶ perceptible, discernible, recognizable, clear, distinct, detectable, high, loud, noisy, strong
AN OPPOSITE IS inaudible

audience NOUN

There was a more lively audience on the Saturday.
▶ spectators, onlookers, crowd, gathering, turnout, (*television*) viewers, (*radio*) listeners

audit NOUN

an audit of the company's accounts
▶ inspection, examination, scrutiny, investigation, vetting, survey, study, analysis

auditorium NOUN

It was difficult to see the performers from the back of the packed auditorium.
▶ theatre, concert hall, hall, assembly room

auspicious ADJECTIVE

an auspicious day for a picnic
▶ favourable, hopeful, positive, promising, propitious

austere ADJECTIVE

1 *Their lives tended to be short and austere.*
▶ severe, sober, frugal, strict, spartan, restrained, abstemious, ascetic, temperate, simple, chaste
OPPOSITES ARE indulgent, elaborate
2 *She seemed austere but had a great deal of charm, once you got to know her.*
▶ stern, severe, strict, grave, solemn, forbidding, dour, formal, remote, distant, aloof
AN OPPOSITE IS genial
3 *Dark windows gave the house an austere appearance.*
▶ stark, grim, bleak, forbidding
OPPOSITES ARE bright, ornate

A

authentic ADJECTIVE

1 *an authentic painting by Rembrandt*
► actual, bona fide, certain, genuine, legitimate, original, real, true, valid
AN OPPOSITE IS fake

2 *an authentic story*
► accurate, authoritative, dependable, factual, honest, reliable, truthful, veracious
AN OPPOSITE IS false

authenticate VERB

The claim has still to be authenticated.
► validate, substantiate, verify, corroborate, confirm, certify, support, back up

author NOUN

1 *modern American authors*
► writer, novelist, dramatist, composer, creator, playwright, poet, scriptwriter

2 *the author of the plan*
► originator, creator, initiator, instigator, architect, producer, begetter, designer, inventor

authoritarian ADJECTIVE

an authoritarian regime
► dictatorial, autocratic, tyrannical, despotic, oppressive, harsh, disciplinarian

authoritative ADJECTIVE

1 *an authoritative edition of the text*
► definitive, authorized, classic, standard

2 *an authoritative source of information*
► reliable, dependable, sound, authentic, trustworthy

authority NOUN

1 *The salesperson does not always have the authority to deal with a complaint.*
► authorization, power, right, prerogative, consent, licence, mandate, permission

2 *I was convinced that she would never accept a challenge to her authority.*
► power, sovereignty, control, jurisdiction, domination, supremacy, charge, command, force, influence, might, prerogative, right, sway, weight

3 *He is the world's foremost authority on the subject.*
► expert, specialist, pundit, boffin, connoisseur (of)

the authorities *The matter was reported to the authorities.*
► officials, officialdom, government, management, administration, people in charge, (*more informal*) the powers that be

authorize VERB

The government has authorized a further billion pounds of spending on health .
► approve, permit, allow, agree to, enable, sanction, back, accede to, consent to, (*more informal*) OK, ratify, (*more informal*) rubber-stamp, (*more informal*) give the go-ahead for

autobiography NOUN

She began her autobiography in middle age.
► memoirs, reminiscences, life history

autocrat NOUN

The new king acted like an autocrat.
► despot, dictator, tyrant, absolute ruler

autocratic ADJECTIVE

an autocratic ruler
► dictatorial, authoritarian, tyrannical, despotic, oppressive, harsh, disciplinarian

automatic ADJECTIVE

1 *His reaction was automatic.*
► instinctive, spontaneous, involuntary, unconscious, reflex, unthinking, unintentional, natural, mechanical, habitual, impulsive

2 *automatic windows*
► mechanical, automated, computerized, programmed, robotic, self-regulating, unmanned

autonomous ADJECTIVE

an autonomous nation
► independent, self-governing, sovereign, free, self-ruling, self-determining
AN OPPOSITE IS subject

auxiliary ADJECTIVE

an auxiliary power supply
► supplementary, additional, ancillary, reserve, secondary, spare, subsidiary, emergency, extra, (*more informal*) back-up

available ADJECTIVE

Camping facilities will be available on site.
► obtainable, accessible, procurable, ready, at or on or to hand, to be had, usable, disposable
AN OPPOSITE IS unavailable

avenge VERB

We shall avenge their deaths a thousand times.
► take revenge for, take vengeance for, punish, exact punishment for, exact retribution for, repay, (*more informal*) get your own back for

avenue NOUN

The house was separated from the field by an avenue of trees.
► row, broadway, boulevard, thoroughfare, road

average ADJECTIVE

1 *Few of us have any idea how much water we use on an average day.*
► typical, normal, ordinary, usual, regular, standard

2 *He is only an average golfer.*
► mediocre, undistinguished, unremarkable, indifferent, unexceptional, run-of-the-mill, second-rate, passable, tolerable, mainstream
OPPOSITES ARE exceptional, outstanding

3 *The average summer temperature is 18 degrees.*
► mean, medial, standard

average NOUN

Prices of new cars will rise by an average of 3 per cent.
► mean, median, mid-point

averse ADJECTIVE
averse to She is not averse to bribery.
▶ opposed to, against, hostile to, resistant to, antagonistic to or towards, unfavourably disposed to or towards
AN OPPOSITE IS keen (on)

aversion NOUN
He had an obvious aversion to work of any kind.
▶ opposition, hostility, loathing (of), distaste (for), disgust (for), revulsion (for or towards), repugnance (for or towards), abhorrence (of)

avert VERB
1 *The outbreak of war helped avert a financial crisis.*
▶ prevent, avoid, forestall, (*more informal*) nip in the bud
2 *She was sitting still with her head partly averted.*
▶ turn away, turn aside
3 *It was difficult to avert the blow.*
▶ deflect, avoid, parry, stave off

avid ADJECTIVE
avid fans of the movies
▶ keen, eager, enthusiastic, ardent, passionate, fervent, devoted, dedicated, zealous
OPPOSITES ARE uninterested, apathetic

avoid VERB
1 *I try to avoid arguments.*
▶ refrain from, stay clear of, steer clear of, eschew, circumvent
OPPOSITES ARE seek, confront
2 *You cannot avoid responsibility for the decision.*
▶ evade, escape, dodge, shirk, sidestep, (*more informal*) get out of, (*more informal*) duck
AN OPPOSITE IS face up to
3 *She had to swerve to avoid a collision.*
▶ prevent, avert, circumvent
4 *There was a woman at the party he was anxious to avoid.*
▶ ignore, shun, keep away from, hide from, stay clear of, steer clear of
AN OPPOSITE IS seek out
5 *Women should avoid alcohol during pregnancy.*
▶ refrain from, desist from, abstain from, eschew
AN OPPOSITE IS indulge in

await VERB
Relatives of the victims continued to await news.
▶ wait for, hope for, expect, look out for, be ready for, lie in wait for

awake ADJECTIVE
They are often not awake until ten or eleven. She felt too awake to go back to sleep again.
▶ conscious, alert, sleepless, wakeful, wide awake, lively, restless
AN OPPOSITE IS asleep

awake VERB
1 *The alarm awoke her at six.*
▶ wake (up), waken, awaken, rouse, arouse
2 *James awoke with a start.*
▶ wake (up), waken, awaken, stir, come to

3 *The accident awoke old fears about passenger safety.*
▶ awaken, waken, rouse, arouse, stir up, revive, stimulate, trigger, bring back
USAGE The normal word to use for the main meanings is *wake* or *wake up*. There are three other words, *awake, awaken*, and *waken*, but you cannot use *up* with any of these. All four words can be transitive (i.e. can take an object, as in the first example in this entry) or intransitive (i.e. can have no object, as in the second example). *Awaken* and *waken* are rather more formal or literary in effect than *awake* and *wake*.

awaken VERB
1 *The noise outside awakened us. We awakened early.*
▶ wake (up), waken, awake, stir, come to
2 *The incident awakened strong feelings in her.*
▶ awake, waken, rouse, arouse, stir up, revive, stimulate, trigger, bring back

award NOUN
1 *By his third year he had won three awards.*
▶ prize, trophy, decoration, medal
2 *an award of £5,000*
▶ payment, grant, subsidy, subvention, bursary
3 *the award of an honour*
▶ granting, bestowal, conferment, conferral

award VERB
1 *MPs plan to award themselves a four-per-cent pay rise. Referee Hart did not even award a free kick.*
▶ grant, give, present, accord, allot, assign
2 *The college awarded her a scholarship.*
▶ grant, present, (*more formal*) endow, (*more formal*) confer, (*more formal*) bestow
USAGE If you use *present* or *endow*, you say *The college presented* (or *endowed*) *her with a scholarship*. If you use *bestow* or *confer*, you say *They bestowed* (or *conferred*) *a scholarship on her*. These words are much more formal in effect and are mainly used in official language.

aware ADJECTIVE
aware of The children were aware of the dangers.
▶ conscious of, acquainted with, alive to, appreciative of, mindful of, informed about, knowledgeable about, sensitive to, familiar with, attentive to, conversant with, heedful of, observant of, responsive to
OPPOSITES ARE unaware, ignorant, insensitive (to)

awe NOUN
He regarded her with awe.
▶ wonder, wonderment, amazement, admiration, astonishment, respect, reverence, veneration, dread, fear, terror

awe-inspiring ADJECTIVE
The stained-glass windows were awe-inspiring in gold and blue.
▶ awesome, breathtaking, dramatic, stunning, stupendous, spectacular, astonishing, grand, imposing, impressive, magnificent, amazing,

marvellous, overwhelming, wonderful, fearsome,
(*poetic*) wondrous
OPPOSITES ARE insignificant, unimpressive

awful ADJECTIVE

1 *awful weather*
► bad, terrible, dreadful, atrocious, appalling,
frightful, poor, (*more informal*) lousy
OPPOSITES ARE wonderful, lovely

2 *an awful smell*
► unpleasant, disgusting, nasty, dreadful, terrible,
horrible, horrid, foul, frightful, obnoxious
OPPOSITES ARE pleasant, lovely

3 *awful news an awful illness*
► grave, serious, bad, terrible, dreadful
AN OPPOSITE IS excellent

4 *I felt awful for losing my temper.*
► guilty, remorseful, regretful, ashamed, sorry

awkward ADJECTIVE

1 *The case was an awkward object to carry.*
► cumbersome, bulky, unmanageable, unwieldy,
inconvenient
AN OPPOSITE IS convenient

2 *He ran with awkward movements.*
► clumsy, ungainly, inept, inexpert, unskilful,
uncoordinated, graceless, blundering, bungling,
gauche, gawky, ham-fisted, maladroit
OPPOSITES ARE skilful, dexterous, adroit

3 *This is an awkward situation to be in.*
► difficult, troublesome, trying, vexatious, vexing,
annoying, perplexing
AN OPPOSITE IS straightforward

4 *There was an awkward pause in the conversation.*
► embarrassing, uncomfortable, uneasy, delicate,
tricky, unwelcome
AN OPPOSITE IS comfortable

5 *He thought she was being extremely awkward.*
► unreasonable, unhelpful, uncooperative,
stubborn, obstinate, perverse, tiresome,
exasperating, wayward, (*more informal*)
bloody-minded, (*more informal*) bolshie
OPPOSITES ARE cooperative, obliging, amenable

axe NOUN

*Daniel was walking towards the tree carrying a large
axe.*
► hatchet, chopper, cleaver, battleaxe, tomahawk

axe VERB

The company will axe thousands of jobs.
► terminate, discontinue, eliminate, cut, cancel,
drop, get rid of, remove, withdraw

axis NOUN

The earth spins on its axis once a day.
► centre line, central line, pivot

axle NOUN

Something had broken the car's back axle.
► rod, shaft, spindle

Bb

baby NOUN

1 *The woman was holding a baby.*
► babe, infant, toddler, child
2 *a baby car*
► miniature, mini, small-scale, midget, diminutive

babyish ADJECTIVE

Older children are usually told that it is babyish to cry.
► childish, juvenile, puerile, immature, infantile
AN OPPOSITE IS mature

back NOUN

1 *a person's back*
► spine, backbone, spinal column
RELATED ADJECTIVE dorsal (upper side of an animal),
lumbar (lower back)
2 *the back of the vehicle*
► end, rear, tail-end
AN OPPOSITE IS front
3 *the back of the building*
► rear, rear side
OPPOSITES ARE front, facade
4 *the back of the ship*
► stern
OPPOSITES ARE front, bow
5 *the back of an envelope*
► reverse, verso
AN OPPOSITE IS front
6 *the back of an animal*
► rear, tail, hindquarters, posterior
AN OPPOSITE IS front

back ADJECTIVE

1 *the back door*
► rear
AN OPPOSITE IS front
2 *an animal's back legs*
► rear, hind, hindmost
AN OPPOSITE IS front
3 *the back row of the hall*
► end, rearmost
AN OPPOSITE IS front
4 *a bird's back feathers the back fin of a fish*
► (*technical*) dorsal
5 *back issues of a journal*
► past, previous
OPPOSITES ARE forthcoming, future

back VERB

1 *He decided to back his van into the space. The car
backed slowly up the drive.*
► reverse, go backwards, move back
2 *We would like them to back our plan.*
► support, endorse, approve of, stand behind,
sponsor, patronize
3 *He backed a horse at 3-1.*
► bet on, place a bet on, put money on
back down *The government has had to back down on
tax increases.*
► withdraw, concede, yield, give way, retreat,

change your mind, (*more informal*) do a U-turn
back out of *Mr James wanted to back out of the deal.*
▶ withdraw from, give up, pull out of

backbone NOUN

1 *She has an injured backbone.*
▶ spine, spinal column, vertebrae
RELATED ADJECTIVE spinal

2 *The backbone of a good team is a good manager.*
▶ mainstay, foundation, cornerstone, chief support

3 *Drivers need to have some backbone to sustain pole position.*
▶ courage, nerve, spirit, mettle, determination, strength of character, firmness of purpose

backfire VERB

The plan backfired.
▶ miscarry, misfire, fail, flop, rebound

background NOUN

1 *You can see a steeple in the background.*
▶ distance, (on the) horizon
AN OPPOSITE IS foreground

2 *the background to the war*
▶ circumstances (of), context (of), history, (*informal*) lead-up

3 *students from different backgrounds*
▶ environment, social circumstances, breeding, culture, (*formal*) milieu, tradition, upbringing

backing NOUN

1 *We need the backing of the unions.*
▶ support, agreement, endorsement, assistance, encouragement, help

2 *financial backing*
▶ support, funding, patronage, subsidy, sponsorship

3 *a musical backing*
▶ accompaniment, orchestration, scoring

backlash NOUN

The announcement provoked a violent backlash.
▶ reaction, response, repercussion, retaliation

backlog NOUN

a backlog of work
▶ arrears, accumulation, mountain

backward ADJECTIVE

1 *a backward movement*
▶ reverse, rearward, regressive, retrograde, retrogressive
AN OPPOSITE IS forward

2 *Don't be backward if you need to ask for help.*
▶ reticent, bashful, coy, diffident, shy, timid, unforthcoming, hesitant, inhibited, afraid, modest, reluctant, reserved, self-effacing
AN OPPOSITE IS confident

3 *The decision was a backward step.*
▶ retrograde, regressive, negative

4 *a backward learner*
▶ subnormal, (*offensive*) retarded

bad ADJECTIVE This word is often overused. Here are some alternatives:

1 *bad work*
▶ poor, inferior, substandard, second-rate, unsatisfactory, inadequate, deficient, awful, terrible, dreadful, (*more informal*) shoddy, (*more informal*) ropy
OPPOSITES ARE excellent, outstanding, good

2 *a bad driver*
▶ incompetent, poor, awful, terrible, dreadful

3 *a bad effect*
▶ harmful, damaging, detrimental, injurious, undesirable
OPPOSITES ARE beneficial, good

4 *leading a bad life*
▶ wicked, sinful, immoral, depraved, degenerate, dissolute
OPPOSITES ARE virtuous, good

5 *a bad child*
▶ naughty, badly behaved, disobedient, mischievous
OPPOSITES ARE well behaved, good

6 *bad language*
▶ vulgar, crude, foul, coarse, indecent, offensive, profane, blasphemous

7 *bad news*
▶ unpleasant, disagreeable, unwelcome
OPPOSITES ARE good, welcome

8 *a bad time to buy a house*
▶ unsuitable, inappropriate, difficult, unfavourable, unfortunate, inauspicious
OPPOSITES ARE favourable, suitable, good

9 *a bad accident   a bad toothache*
▶ serious, severe, acute, grave, critical
OPPOSITES ARE minor, slight

10 *the meat is bad*
▶ rotten, off, putrid, decomposing, decomposed, mouldy, contaminated, sour (milk), rancid (butter)
AN OPPOSITE IS fresh

11 *feeling bad*
▶ unwell, ill, sick
OPPOSITES ARE well, healthy

12 *a bad leg*
▶ injured, wounded, diseased

13 *I felt bad after losing my temper.*
▶ guilty, remorseful, ashamed, conscience-stricken
OPPOSITES ARE proud, unrepentant

badge NOUN

a police officer's badge
▶ identification, insignia, shield, emblem, sign

badger VERB

Stop badgering me.
▶ harass, bother, pester, annoy

bad-tempered ADJECTIVE

She was a thoroughly selfish, bad-tempered little girl.
▶ irritable, irascible, grumpy, testy, grouchy, touchy, crotchety, cantankerous, peevish, fractious,

B

cross, (*more informal*) stroppy, (*more informal*) shirty
OPPOSITES ARE good- tempered, good- humoured,
affable

baffle VERB
Her answer baffled him.
▶ perplex, bewilder, puzzle, mystify, confuse,
bemuse, disconcert, confound, fox, (*more informal*)
flummox, (*more informal*) floor

baffling ADJECTIVE
a baffling response
▶ puzzling, bewildering, perplexing, confusing,
mystifying, mysterious, inexplicable, inscrutable,
insoluble, unfathomable, extraordinary, frustrating
OPPOSITES ARE clear, straightforward,
comprehensible

bag NOUN
1 *I'll put these things in a bag.*
▶ container, carrier bag, carrier
2 *We'd better go and pack our bags*
▶ case, suitcase
3 *She always carried a bag.*
▶ handbag, shoulder bag
4 *The walkers had bags on their backs.*
▶ backpack, rucksack

bag VERB
1 *You need to get there early and bag a good seat.*
▶ secure, obtain, reserve, acquire, get
2 *He bagged four pheasants.*
▶ catch, shoot, kill, capture

baggage NOUN
She put her baggage in and climbed aboard.
▶ luggage, bags, cases, suitcases, trunks,
belongings, paraphernalia, (*informal*) gear, (*informal*)
stuff

baggy ADJECTIVE
baggy trousers
▶ loose, loose-fitting, roomy

bait NOUN
The offer was meant to be a bait.
▶ enticement, inducement, lure, bribe, allurement,
attraction

bait VERB
The boys wouldn't stop baiting her.
▶ tease, torment, annoy, goad, persecute, pester,
provoke, hound, jeer at, (*more informal*) needle

bake VERB
The hot sun was baking the earth.
▶ scorch, burn, parch, sear

balance NOUN
1 *You can weigh the fruit in the balance.*
▶ scales, weighing machine
2 *It is easy to stumble and lose your balance.*
▶ equilibrium, stability, equipoise, poise, steadiness
3 *a balance between fairness and firmness*
▶ parity, correspondence, symmetry, evenness,
equality, equivalence

4 *a sense of personal balance*
▶ composure, self-assurance, equanimity,
self-possession
5 *The balance of the payment is due in July.*
▶ remainder, difference, rest, residue
on balance *On balance it is a good scheme.*
▶ overall, all in all, by and large

balance VERB
1 *If I carry one bag in each hand, they balance each
other*
▶ counteract, counterbalance, neutralize, offset,
equalize, match, stabilize, steady
2 *He tried to eat by balancing a plate on his knee.*
▶ support, keep, keep balanced, steady
3 *You have to balance the advantages and
disadvantages*
▶ weigh, weigh up, compare, assess, appraise,
consider, estimate

balanced ADJECTIVE
1 *a balanced view of the issues*
▶ fair, objective, impartial, equitable, even-handed,
impartial, disinterested
OPPOSITES ARE partial, biased
2 *a balanced individual*
▶ level-headed, equable, sensible, sane, stable,
practical
OPPOSITES ARE unbalanced, neurotic
3 *a balanced diet*
▶ mixed, varied, well-planned, healthy
OPPOSITES ARE unbalanced, unhealthy

bald ADJECTIVE
1 *a bald man*
▶ bald-headed, hairless, (*euphemistic*) thin on top
2 *bald tyres*
▶ bare, smooth
3 *a bald statement*
▶ plain, direct, forthright, plain, simple, stark,
straightforward, unadorned, uncompromising

bale NOUN
huge bales of firewood
▶ bundle, pack, pack, load, parcel, truss, bunch

ball NOUN
1 *a ball of string   The little animal curled itself into a
ball.*
▶ sphere, globe, globule, orb, shot, spheroid
2 *a ball of food*
▶ pellet, globule, slug
3 *a fancy- dress ball*
▶ dance, party, disco, social

balloon NOUN
across the ocean in a balloon
▶ hot-air balloon, airship, dirigible

balloon VERB
The curtains ballooned out into the room.
▶ billow, blow, puff, swell, bulge

ballot NOUN
a ballot for the party leadership
▶ election, vote, poll, plebiscite, referendum

ban NOUN
a ban on smoking
▶ embargo, prohibition, bar, moratorium, veto

ban VERB
The government wants to ban some blood sports.
▶ prohibit, forbid, bar, disallow, proscribe, suppress, make illegal, stop, restrict
OPPOSITES ARE permit, allow

banal ADJECTIVE
a banal image of the perfect married couple
▶ trite, hackneyed, commonplace, stereotypical, stock, humdrum, clichéd, dull, unimaginative, tired, boring, tedious, (*more informal*) corny
OPPOSITES ARE original, interesting

band NOUN
1 *red with a blue band along the top*
▶ strip, stripe, streak, belt, line, loop, ribbon, ring
2 *a band of followers*
▶ troop, body, company, group, gang, horde, party, association, clique, club, crew, flock, herd, society
3 *A band was playing.*
▶ orchestra, ensemble, group

band VERB
band together *The village banded together to repel their attackers.*
▶ gather, group, unite, cooperate, join together, work together, fight together, collaborate

bandage NOUN
The nurse put a bandage on his wound.
▶ dressing, plaster, gauze, lint

bandit NOUN
The camp was attacked by bandits.
▶ robber, brigand, thief, outlaw, desperado, gangster, gunman, marauder, highwayman, pirate, hijacker

bandy ADJECTIVE
All ducks are bandy. They waddle.
▶ bow-legged, bandy-legged, bowed

bandy VERB
bandy about *Several prices are being bandied about.*
▶ put about, discuss, circulate, spread about or around, pass about or around, exchange, interchange, swap, toss about or around

bane NOUN
Tight deadlines continue to be the bane of journalists' lives.
▶ ruin, curse, death, misfortune

bang NOUN
1 *He had got a bang on the head.*
▶ blow, hit, smack, knock, thump, rap, clout, punch, whack, cuff, bump, collision, slam, stroke, (*more informal*) wallop
2 *Suddenly there was a loud bang.*
▶ blast, report, boom, crack, thud, thump, explosion, clap, crash, pop

bang VERB
He banged the table with his fist.
▶ hit, thump, strike, whack, (*more informal*) bash, (*more informal*) clout

banish VERB
1 *The authorities banished him as a traitor.*
▶ exile, expel, deport, send away, eject, evict, expatriate, outlaw, ship away, transport
2 *Her look banished any remainng fears.*
▶ dispel, remove, dismiss, disperse, allay, scatter, dissipate, drive away or out

bank NOUN
1 *a grassy bank*
▶ slope, rise, incline, earthwork, embankment, mound, ridge, dike, rampart
2 *the bank of the lake*
▶ edge, border, margin, shore, side, brink
3 *a steep bank on the curve*
▶ camber, gradient, incline, slope, tilt, ramp, rise, (*formal*) declivity
4 *a bank of dials and switches*
▶ array, row, panel, tier, console, collection, series, display, file, group, line
5 *a blood bank*
▶ store, reserve, stock, supply, fund, depository

bank VERB
1 *The little plane banked to the left.*
▶ tilt, lean, slant, pitch, tip, incline, cant, heel, list, slope
2 *Bank the cheque immediately.*
▶ deposit, pay in

bankrupt ADJECTIVE
1 *The business was soon bankrupt.*
▶ insolvent, failed, ruined, in liquidation, (*more informal*) bust
AN OPPOSITE IS solvent
2 *By the end of the day Ken was bankrupt.*
▶ broke, penniless, destitute, (*more formal*) impecunious, (*more informal*) skint
OPPOSITES ARE wealthy, flush

banner NOUN
A banner was flying from a tall building.
▶ flag, pennant, pennon, standard, streamer, ensign, colours (*plural*)

banquet NOUN
The conference ended with a sumptuous banquet.
▶ feast, dinner, (*literary*) repast, (*more informal*) blowout

banter NOUN
good-humoured banter
▶ joking, jesting, repartee, badinage, raillery, ribbing, jocularity, teasing, word play, chaffing, pleasantry

bar NOUN
1 *an iron bar*
▶ rod, pole, stake, shaft, batten, stick, strut, beam, girder, rail, railing

bar

2 *a bar of chocolate   a bar of soap*
► block, slab, cake, tablet, chunk, wedge, piece, hunk, ingot, lump, nugget

3 *a bar to progress*
► obstacle, barrier, obstruction, hindrance, impediment, block, hurdle, check, deterrent, barricade

4 *eating and drinking at bars*
► pub, public house, saloon, cafe, tavern

bar VERB

1 *The people were barred from entering the country.*
► ban, prohibit, forbid, exclude, debar, forbid to enter, prevent from entering, keep out

2 *An angry crowd barred the way.*
► block, obstruct, hinder, impede, check, halt, prevent, stop, thwart

barbarian NOUN

attacked by barbarians
► savage, vandal, brute, ruffian, hooligan, heathen, hun, philistine

barbaric ADJECTIVE

a barbaric attack
► barbarous, brutal, cruel, cold-blooded, inhuman, primitive, savage, uncivilized, wild
OPPOSITES ARE civilized, humane

bare ADJECTIVE

1 *bare flesh*
► naked, unclothed, uncovered, nude, stark-naked, exposed, stripped, unclad, undressed, bald
OPPOSITES ARE clothed, covered

2 *a bare landscape*
► barren, bleak, desolate, exposed, featureless, treeless, stark, empty, open, windswept
OPPOSITES ARE lush, fertile

3 *bare trees*
► leafless, defoliated
AN OPPOSITE IS leafy

4 *a bare room*
► empty, unfurnished, vacant, cleared, plain, simple, austere

5 *a bare wall*
► blank, clean, uncovered, unadorned, undecorated, unmarked, stripped

6 *the bare facts*
► straightforward, plain, simple, basic, pure, essential, fundamental, hard, bald, literal, unadorned, unambiguous, unembellished, unconcealed, undisguised

7 *the bare necessities*
► basic, essential, minimum, mere, just adequate, just sufficient

bare VERB

She bared her arm for the injection.
► uncover, expose, unclothe, strip

barefaced ADJECTIVE

a barefaced lie
► shameless, flagrant, blatant, glaring, undisguised, patent

bargain NOUN

1 *The government has made a bargain with the other parties.*
► agreement, deal, understanding, arrangement, pact, pledge, compact, contract, negotiation, promise, settlement, transaction, treaty

2 *a bargain at £12.99*
► good buy, good value, (*more informal*) snip, (*more informal*) steal

into the bargain *They were half an hour late into the bargain.*
► in addition, furthermore, as well, besides, moreover, what is more

bargain VERB

The union is trying to bargain with the employers.
► negotiate, do a deal, barter, discuss terms, hold talks, argue, haggle

bargain on or **for** *The crush at the doors was something I hadn't bargained for.*
► expect, foresee, imagine, plan for, allow for, reckon on, anticipate, be prepared for, contemplate, consider

bark VERB

1 *The dog barked.*
► woof, yap, yelp

2 *The sergeant barked an order.*
► shout, snap, growl, snarl

bark NOUN

the dog's bark
► woof, yap, yelp

barmy ADJECTIVE

(*informal*) *You must be barmy.   a barmy idea*
► mad, crazy, foolish

barn NOUN

The farm vehicles were kept in a barn.
► shed, outbuilding

barrage NOUN

1 *a barrage across a river*
► dam, barrier, embankment, wall

2 *a barrage of gunfire*
► bombardment, salvo, battery, cannonade, fusillade, storm, volley, assault, attack, onslaught

3 *a barrage of criticism*
► stream, deluge, flood, onslaught, torrent, shower, mass

barrel NOUN

a barrel of beer
► cask, butt, keg, tub, tun, drum, canister, hogshead, water-butt

barren ADJECTIVE

1 *barren desert*
► infertile, lifeless, arid, parched, desert, dry, waste, waterless, sterile, torrid, unproductive
OPPOSITES ARE fertile, lush

2 *a barren woman*
► infertile, sterile, childless, sterilized
AN OPPOSITE IS fertile

barricade NOUN
barricades across the road
▶ barrier, obstruction, obstacle, blockade, bulwark, fence, palisade, stockade

barrier NOUN
1 *Police put up barriers to keep out the crowd.*
▶ barricade, fence, obstacle, obstruction, railing, fencing, wall, bar, hurdle
2 *a barrier to progress*
▶ obstacle, hindrance, impediment, check, drawback, handicap, limitation, restriction, stumbling block

barter VERB
1 *You can barter with the shopkeepers for souvenirs.*
▶ bargain, haggle, negotiate, deal
2 *The peasants were able to barter any surplus food for equipment.*
▶ trade, exchange, swap, traffic

base ADJECTIVE
base motives
▶ immoral, dishonourable, depraved, low, evil, shameful, sordid, vile, wicked

base NOUN
1 *the base of the tower*
▶ foot, bottom, foundation, pedestal
2 *The hut was used as a base for the expedition.*
▶ headquarters, centre, station, camp, depot, post

base VERB
1 *The company is based in Paris.*
▶ locate, establish, set up, station
2 *Base your story on events in the news.*
▶ build, construct, establish, found, ground

basement NOUN
They stored old papers in the basement.
▶ cellar, crypt, vault

bash VERB
She could hardly avoid bashing him in the stomach.
▶ hit, strike, knock, smack, clout, (*more informal*) biff
bash into *The car bashed into a lamp post.*
▶ collide with, crash into, run into, bang into, bump into

bashful ADJECTIVE
Men tend to be bashful about their feelings.
▶ shy, coy, reserved, diffident, embarrassed, inhibited, modest, self-conscious, hesitant, timid, reserved, retiring
OPPOSITES ARE assertive, forward, bold, confident

basic ADJECTIVE
1 *You must first learn the basic principles of the subject.*
▶ fundamental, chief, main, key, crucial, principal, central, primary, elementary
AN OPPOSITE IS secondary
2 *Washing facilities at the camp are very basic.*
▶ plain, simple, crude, modest, stark, sparse, spartan, unsophisticated
OPPOSITES ARE elaborate, sophisticated

basin NOUN
She poured some water into the basin.
▶ bowl, dish, sink, stoup

basis NOUN
The accusations had no factual basis.
▶ foundation, justification, support, rationale, base

bask VERB
basking in the sunshine
▶ laze, relax, lounge, wallow, sunbathe, bathe
bask in *basking in the glory of their success*
▶ revel in, wallow in, delight in, glory in, relish, enjoy

basket NOUN
a basket of fruit
▶ hamper, pannier, creel, punnet, trug

bass ADJECTIVE
a bass note
▶ low, deep, bottom

batch NOUN
a batch of cakes
▶ consignment, group, quantity, assortment, lot, set

bath NOUN
I'm going to have a bath.
▶ wash, douche, jacuzzi, sauna, shower, (*more informal*) soak

bathe VERB
1 *Holidaymakers were bathing in the sea.*
▶ swim, paddle, plunge, splash about, (*more informal*) take a dip
2 *The wound must be carefully bathed.*
▶ cleanse, clean, wash, rinse, immerse, moisten, soak, steep, swill

batter VERB
1 *Someone battered on the door.*
▶ pound, beat, knock
2 *Winds were battering the waterfront.*
▶ pound, buffet, lash, pummel
3 *He was battered into submission.*
▶ beat, pummel, thump

battered ADJECTIVE
help for battered wives
▶ beaten, abused, assaulted, maltreated, victimized

battle NOUN
1 *The battle took place a few miles north of the city.*
▶ fight, engagement, action, clash, encounter, conflict
2 *a legal battle for ownership of the club*
▶ conflict, struggle, dispute
3 *a battle to save the library from closure*
▶ campaign, crusade

battle VERB
They battled to control the fire.
▶ fight, struggle, strive

baulk VERB
baulk at *Some farmers baulk at using pesticides.*
▶ resist, (*more formal*) eschew, be reluctant to

bawdy ADJECTIVE
bawdy stories
▶ rude, indecent, crude, ribald, naughty, improper, risqué, lewd, vulgar, obscene

bawl VERB
1 *The child sat on its bed bawling.*
▶ cry, sob, weep, blubber
2 *'Get out,' she bawled.*
▶ yell, shout, roar, bellow, shriek, scream

bay NOUN
1 *a large bay on the coast*
▶ cove, inlet, gulf, bight
2 *a loading bay*
▶ recess, alcove, booth, compartment, niche, nook, opening

bazaar NOUN
the church bazaar
▶ sale, fair, fete, jumble sale, car boot sale, bring-and-buy, market, auction

be VERB
1 *There was a young family next door.*
▶ exist, live
2 *After he'd been there a while he ordered a drink.*
▶ remain, stay, wait, linger, (*more informal*) hang on
3 *The next performance of the play will be tomorrow.*
▶ take place, occur, happen, come about

beach NOUN
a picnic on the beach
▶ shore, sand, sands, seashore, coast, (*poetic*) strand

beacon NOUN
a beacon on the hill
▶ flare, signal, bonfire, beam

bead NOUN
beads of sweat
▶ drop, droplet, globule, blob, drip, pearl

beaker NOUN
a beaker of water
▶ mug, tumbler, goblet, cup, glass, jar, tankard

beam NOUN
1 *a house with wooden beams*
▶ timber, joist, girder, spar, bar, plank, post, rafter, support, stanchion, boom
2 *a beam of light*
▶ ray, shaft, gleam, stream

beam VERB
1 *Satellites beam radio waves to rooftop aerials.*
▶ broadcast, transmit, direct, emit, radiate, send out, aim
2 *Daphne beamed happily.*
▶ smile, grin
OPPOSITES ARE glower, frown

bear VERB
1 *The rope would no longer bear his weight.*
▶ support, carry, hold, sustain, prop up, take
2 *The document bore a signature.*
▶ display, possess, show, exhibit, have

3 *The postman arrived, bearing a large parcel.*
▶ carry, bring, convey, transport, deliver, fetch, move, take, transfer
4 *I cannot bear pain. We found the noise hard to bear.*
▶ put up with, endure, tolerate, stand, stomach, abide, accept, cope with, live with, suffer, sustain, undergo, brook
5 *The woman bore a child.*
▶ give birth to, produce, mother, bring forth
bear down on *A huge vehicle was bearing down on them.*
▶ approach, advance on, close in on
bear out *The report bears out what I was saying.*
▶ confirm, endorse, corroborate

bearable ADJECTIVE
The pain was only just bearable.
▶ tolerable, endurable, acceptable

bearing NOUN
1 *The Baroness had a regal bearing.*
▶ demeanour, air, manner, look, appearance, behaviour, presence, carriage, deportment, mien, poise, posture, style
2 *The discovery could have some bearing on the mystery.*
▶ connection (with), relevance (to), significance (for), import (for), pertinence (to), reference (to), relationship (with)

bearings PLURAL NOUN
When it got dark we began to lose our bearings.
▶ sense of direction, orientation, whereabouts, position, situation, way

beast NOUN
1 *the roars of wild beasts*
▶ animal , creature, brute
2 *Her husband was a beast.*
▶ brute, monster, fiend, demon
RELATED ADJECTIVE bestial

beastly ADJECTIVE
Derek had been beastly to them.
▶ unkind, cruel, mean, nasty, horrible, spiteful

beat NOUN
1 *music with a strong beat*
▶ rhythm, pulse, throb, accent, stress
2 *a policeman's beat*
▶ circuit, rounds, route, itinerary, journey, path, way

beat VERB
1 *The man was beating a dog with a stick.*
▶ hit, strike, thrash, whip, attack, assault, (*more informal*) wallop, (*more informal*) whack
2 *Molly was beating eggs for her omelette.*
▶ whip, agitate, blend, froth up, mix, stir
3 *His heart was beating faster.*
▶ pound, pulsate, race, thump, flutter, palpitate
4 *William of Normandy beat the English at the Battle of Hastings. The visitors beat the home team decisively.*

► defeat, overcome, conquer, vanquish, subdue, crush, overpower, overwhelm, rout, trounce, win against, get the better of, (*more informal*) thrash

beat about the bush *Let's not beat about the bush.*
► prevaricate, vacillate, hedge, (*more informal*) flannel

beat up *They went into town and got beaten up.*
► assault, attack

beautiful ADJECTIVE
a beautiful young woman   a beautiful garden
► attractive, pretty, good-looking, nice-looking, lovely, glamorous, gorgeous, stunning
AN OPPOSITE IS ugly

beauty NOUN
the beauty of the scene
► attractiveness, prettiness, loveliness, charm, allure, magnificence, radiance, splendour, appeal, glamour, glory, grace, handsomeness
AN OPPOSITE IS ugliness
RELATED ADJECTIVE aesthetic

beaver VERB
beaver away *She beavered away at her homework.*
► work hard, toil, labour, slave

because CONJUNCTION
because of *He missed most of the season because of injury.*
► on account of, owing to, due to, as a result of, as a consequence of, in view of

beckon VERB
She beckoned him to go over to her.
► signal, gesture, motion, gesticulate, invite

become VERB
1 *Caterpillars become butterflies.*
► grow into, turn into, change into, develop into
2 *The family soon became rich.*
► grow, come to be, turn
3 *She wants to become the second woman prime minister.*
► be appointed, be elected, be chosen, be made
4 *Dark colours become you.*
► suit, flatter, befit, grace, set off, enhance, harmonize with

becoming ADJECTIVE
The dress is very becoming.
► attractive, elegant, fetching, pretty, comely

bed NOUN
1 *A cat lay on the bed.*
► divan, bunk, couch
2 *a flower bed*
► plot, patch, area
3 *the bed of a river*
► bottom, floor, course
4 *posts set in a bed of concrete*
► base, foundation, support, setting

bedraggled ADJECTIVE
The heavy rain had left him looking bedraggled.
► dishevelled, unkempt, untidy, sodden, messy, scruffy, dirty, soiled, stained, wet
OPPOSITES ARE neat, clean, spruce

bee NOUN
Bees hovered round the flowers.
► drone, worker, bumblebee, honeybee, queen

a bee in your bonnet *He had a bee in his bonnet about queues.*
► obsession, preoccupation, fixation, compulsion, (*more informal*) hang-up

beefy ADJECTIVE
A beefy man sat at the bar.
► muscular, brawny, burly, hefty, stocky, fat, portly

befitting ADJECTIVE
Wear clothes befitting the occasion.
► suitable for, appropriate to, fitting

before ADVERB
She had called the day before.
► earlier, in advance, previously, sooner

befriend VERB
He had tried to befriend the new boy.
► make friends with, get to know, look after, stand by, help, support, take under your wing

beg VERB
1 *A man on the pavement was begging.*
► ask for money, solicit money, (*more informal*) cadge, (*more informal*) scrounge
2 *Do we have to beg for a favour?*
► plead, entreat, implore, ask, beseech, crave, importune, petition, pray, request, (*formal*) supplicate

beggar NOUN
He always gave money to beggars he met in the street.
► tramp, vagrant, destitute person, down-and-out, homeless person, (*more formal*) mendicant, pauper, poor person

begin VERB
1 *We will begin work tomorrow.*
► start, embark on, set about, get down to, (*more formal*) commence
AN OPPOSITE IS finish
2 *The interviewer began with a few quick questions.*
► start, start off, open, lead off, get going
AN OPPOSITE IS conclude
3 *Where did the rumour begin?*
► start, originate, spring up, emerge, (*more formal*) commence
AN OPPOSITE IS end
RELATED ADJECTIVE incipient

beginner NOUN
The course is for beginners.
► novice, initiate, learner, starter, new recruit, trainee, apprentice, tiro

beginning NOUN
1 *the beginning of a new era*
▶ birth, dawn, start, starting point, inception, establishment, origin, onset, emergence
2 *She had been opposed to the idea from the beginning*
▶ outset, start
3 *the beginning of the story*
▶ opening, start, prelude

begrudge VERB
Kate didn't seem to begrudge Harry all his wealth.
▶ resent, grudge, mind, object to, be bitter about, covet, envy, be jealous of, be envious of

behave VERB
The children worked hard and behaved well.
▶ conduct yourself, act, react, respond, run, acquit yourself
behave yourself *Try to behave yourself.*
▶ be good, act correctly, be on your best behaviour

behaviour NOUN
Their behaviour was disgusting.
▶ conduct, manners, attitude, demeanour, deportment, bearing

behead VERB
The king was beheaded.
▶ decapitate, execute, guillotine

being NOUN
1 *She loves him with all her being.*
▶ existence, soul, spirit, essence, actuality, life, living, reality, solidity, substance
2 *a mortal being*
▶ person, creature, individual, animal, entity

belated ADJECTIVE
belated birthday greetings
▶ late, tardy, overdue
OPPOSITES ARE timely, opportune

belch VERB
1 *Laurence belched behind his hand.*
▶ burp, emit wind
2 *The vehicle was belching black smoke.*
▶ emit, give out, discharge, send out, smoke, spew out, erupt, fume, gush

belief NOUN
1 *She had a strong belief that he was innocent.*
▶ conviction, confidence, opinion, certainty, credence, sureness
OPPOSITES ARE disbelief, doubt
2 *a belief in the benefits of a good diet*
▶ trust, reliance (on), credence
3 *religious belief*
▶ faith, ideology, principle, creed, dogma
AN OPPOSITE IS scepticism

believe VERB
1 *I find that hard to believe.*
▶ accept, be certain about, be convinced by, regard as true, (*more informal*) swallow
AN OPPOSITE IS disbelieve
RELATED ADJECTIVE credible

2 *I believe several people have cheated.*
▶ think, consider, maintain, conclude, be of the opinion, think it likely, feel, imagine, judge, suppose, take it for granted

believer NOUN
a religious believer
▶ devotee, disciple, follower, adherent, fanatic, proselyte, supporter, upholder, zealot
OPPOSITES ARE sceptic, agnostic, atheist

belittle VERB
There is a tendency to belittle or ignore old people.
▶ ridicule, dismiss, decry, undervalue, run down, disparage, criticize, denigrate, depreciate, (*more informal*) rubbish

bell NOUN
I can hear the bell.
▶ chime, gong, alarm, carillon, knell, peal, signal

belligerent ADJECTIVE
1 *She stared in a belligerent manner.*
▶ aggressive, hostile, antagonistic, confrontational, argumentative, quarrelsome, militant, combative, provocative, contentious, pugnacious
2 *a belligerent nation*
▶ warlike, bellicose, militant, militaristic, violent
AN OPPOSITE IS peaceable

bellow VERB
He bellowed something in her ear.
▶ shout, yell, bawl, roar, boom, shriek

belly NOUN
He stood scratching his belly.
▶ stomach, abdomen, middle, (*usually disapproving*) paunch, (*more informal*) tummy, (*much more informal*) tum

belong VERB
1 **belong to** *The house belongs to his mother.*
▶ be owned by, be the property of
2 **belong to** *I belong to a sports club.*
▶ be a member of, be affiliated with, be connected with
3 *They felt they did not belong there.*
▶ feel welcome, have a place, be at home
4 *The book belongs on the top shelf.*
▶ be located, have a place, go

belongings NOUN
Remember to take all your belongings with you.
▶ possessions, property, personal effects, (*more informal*) stuff

beloved ADJECTIVE
her beloved father
▶ dear, dearest, darling, loved, much loved, cherished

belt NOUN
1 *a raincoat tied with a belt*
▶ girdle, sash, strap, waistband, (*of a man's evening suit*) cummerbund
2 *a spindle driven by a belt*
▶ band, loop, circle

3 *a belt of woodland*
▶ strip, stretch, area, tract, zone, region, district, line, swathe

belt VERB
belt along (*informal*) *They all belted along to the bus station.*
▶ hurry, rush, speed

bemused ADJECTIVE
She sat there with a bemused expression.
▶ bewildered, confused, distracted, puzzled, muddled, baffled, perplexed

bench NOUN
The children sat in a row on a bench.
▶ pew, long seat, form, stall

bend NOUN
We came to a bend in the road.
▶ curve, turn, angle, corner, twist, zigzag

bend VERB
1 *You can bend the pipe round the tank.*
▶ curve, curl, angle, turn
2 *The road bends ahead.*
▶ curve, turn, veer, deviate, twist
bend down *He bent down to pick up the piece of paper.*
▶ stoop, bow, crouch, duck, kneel, lean

benefactor NOUN
An anonymous benefactor paid for my trip
▶ patron, supporter, backer, donor, promoter, sponsor, philanthropist, well-wisher

beneficial ADJECTIVE
A good diet is beneficial to health.
▶ good (for), advantageous, favourable, useful, valuable, helpful, salutary, wholesome
AN OPPOSITE IS harmful

benefit NOUN
1 *the benefits of a healthy diet*
▶ advantage, reward, strength, blessing, convenience, gain, asset, service
AN OPPOSITE IS disadvantage
2 *We are doing it for your benefit.*
▶ good, sake, interest, welfare, advantage
3 *the unemployed who are on benefit*
▶ social security, welfare, assistance, allowance, income support

benefit VERB
The tax cuts will benefit those on a low income.
▶ help, advantage, assist, aid, advance, be beneficial to, do good to, profit, serve
AN OPPOSITE IS hinder

benevolence NOUN
The hospital is dependent on the benevolence of local businesses.
▶ kindness, generosity, goodness, goodwill, consideration, charity, magnanimity

benevolent ADJECTIVE
She smiled a benevolent smile.
▶ kind, generous, helpful, caring, benign, friendly, magnanimous, sympathetic, considerate, philanthropic
AN OPPOSITE IS unkind

benign ADJECTIVE
1 *a benign smile*
▶ friendly, kind, benevolent
2 *a benign influence*
▶ favourable, beneficial, advantageous, propitious

bent ADJECTIVE
1 *a bent nail*
▶ crooked, twisted, misshapen, angled, buckled, distorted, folded, looped, warped
AN OPPOSITE IS straight
2 *a man with a bent back*
▶ crooked, hunched, arched, bowed, curved
3 (*informal*) *bent politicians*
▶ corrupt, criminal, dishonest, fraudulent, immoral, untrustworthy, wicked
AN OPPOSITE IS honest

bequeath VERB
He bequeathed his estate to his grandchildren.
▶ will, leave, settle (on), endow, hand down, pass on

bequest NOUN
She received a bequest under her aunt's will.
▶ legacy, inheritance, settlement, endowment, gift

bereavement NOUN
a bereavement in the family
▶ death, loss, deprivation

bereft ADJECTIVE
bereft of *bereft of intelligence*
▶ lacking, deprived of, wanting, destitute of, devoid of, robbed of, in need of

berserk ADJECTIVE
go berserk *reports of a man who went berserk in the street and was hit by a car*
▶ go crazy, go mad, become demented, become frantic, become hysterical, go out of your mind, rave, become deranged, run amok, (*more informal*) freak out

berth NOUN
a berth for a ship
▶ mooring, anchorage, quay, dock, wharf
give a wide berth to *After that she gave Gerald a wide berth.*
▶ avoid, shun, keep away from, steer clear of

berth VERB
The ship berthed at Hull.
▶ dock, moor, tie up, drop anchor, anchor, land

beseech VERB
She beseeched him to stay.
▶ beg, implore, entreat, ask

b

besiege VERB

1 *Alexander besieged the city for two years.*
▶ lay siege to, blockade, surround, encircle, confine, beleaguer, (*old use*) invest

2 *She spent a whole day besieged by reporters outside her London home.*
▶ surround, mob, plague, harass, pester, overwhelm

best ADJECTIVE

1 *one of the best bookshops in London*
▶ foremost, leading, top, finest, pre-eminent, supreme, premier, optimum, outstanding, unsurpassed, unequalled, unrivalled
AN OPPOSITE IS worst

2 *Do whatever you think best.*
▶ most suitable, most appropriate, most fitting, most sensible

bestow VERB

The college bestowed a scholarship on her.
▶ award, confer, endow, (*less formal*) present, (*less formal*) give

USAGE If you use *award*, you say *The college awarded her a scholarship.* This is a much less formal and more ordinary word. If you use *present* or *endow*, you say *The college presented (or endowed) her with a scholarship.* If you use *confer*, you say *The college conferred a scholarship on her.*

bet NOUN

1 *a £10 bet*
▶ gamble, wager, (*informal*) punt

2 *My bet is they won't come.*
▶ opinion, forecast, prediction, feeling, hunch

bet VERB

1 *She bet all her savings and won.*
▶ wager, gamble, stake, risk

2 (*informal*) *I bet I'm right.*
▶ (*less informal*) be sure, (*less informal*) be confident, (*less informal*) be convinced, (*less informal*) expect

betray VERB

1 *We trusted him and he betrayed us.*
▶ let down, break your promise to, be unfaithful to, double-cross, deceive

2 *They were betrayed to the authorities.*
▶ inform on, denounce

3 *Please don't betray my secret. He found it hard not to betray his feelings.*
▶ reveal, give away, manifest, show, indicate, disclose, divulge, expose, let out, let slip, tell

betrothed ADJECTIVE

His elder son was betrothed to Mark's sister.
▶ engaged, pledged

better ADJECTIVE

1 *We are looking for better facilities.*
▶ superior, finer, preferable

2 *Are you feeling better?*
▶ healthier, fitter, stronger, recovered, (*more informal*) on the mend

better VERB

The idea cannot be bettered.
▶ improve on, surpass, outdo

beware VERB

1 *There are landmines in the fields so beware.*
▶ watch out, look out, be careful, take care, be on the lookout, be on the alert

2 *Beware of the dog.*
▶ watch out for, mind, avoid, steer clear of

bewilder VERB

His remarks had bewildered her.
▶ puzzle, perplex, baffle, mystify, confuse, bemuse, disconcert, confound, (*more informal*) flummox, (*more informal*) floor

bewildered ADJECTIVE

Harry looked quite bewildered.
▶ puzzled, perplexed, baffled, mystified, confused, bemused, disconcerted, (*more informal*) flummoxed

bewitch VERB

We were bewitched by the beauty of the place.
▶ captivate, charm, enchant, entrance, enthral, delight, mesmerize
AN OPPOSITE IS repel

bewitching ADJECTIVE

a bewitching sight
▶ captivating, charming, enchanting, entrancing, enthralling, attractive

bias NOUN

The management was accused of bias.
▶ prejudice, partiality, discrimination, unfairness, injustice, partisanship, favouritism, bigotry, intolerance, chauvinism, racism, sexism

biased ADJECTIVE

a biased attitude   The judge was clearly biased.
▶ prejudiced, partial, one-sided, partisan, subjective, bigoted, chauvinistic, racist, sexist
OPPOSITES ARE unbiased, impartial

bicker VERB

I don't want to stand here all day bickering about it.
▶ quarrel, squabble, wrangle, argue, scrap, row

bid NOUN

1 *a bid of £5,000*
▶ offer, tender, proposal, price, proposition

2 *a bid to discover the truth*
▶ attempt, effort, endeavour, try (at), (*informal*) go (at), (*informal*) crack (at)

bid VERB

A buyer bid a record price at the auction.
▶ offer, make an offer of, put in a bid of, tender, proffer, propose

biff VERB

He had biffed her by mistake.
▶ hit, strike, knock, smack, bash, clout

big ADJECTIVE This word is often overused. Here are some alternatives:
1 *a big house*   *The bill was very big.*
▶ large, great, huge, enormous, colossal, immense
2 *a big difference*
▶ significant, important, substantial, considerable, sizeable
3 *big ideas*
▶ ambitious, grand, grandiose, far-reaching
4 *That was big of you.*
▶ generous, considerate, magnanimous, kind, gracious

bigoted ADJECTIVE
He disliked people who held such bigoted views.
▶ prejudiced, biased, partial, intolerant, narrow-minded
USAGE Note that *bigoted* is a much stronger word than the alternatives given here.

bilious ADJECTIVE
He woke up feeling bilious.
▶ sick, nauseous, liverish, queasy, ill

bill NOUN
1 *The bill came to over a thousand pounds.*
▶ account, invoice, statement, list of charges
2 *a bill advertising a sale*
▶ poster, notice, advertisement, placard, sheet, leaflet, broadsheet, circular, handout, bulletin
3 *a bill in parliament*
▶ draft law, proposed law

billow VERB
1 *Her dress billowed out in the wind.*
▶ balloon, blow, puff, swell, bulge
2 *Smoke billowed from the chimney.*
▶ pour, swirl, spiral

bin NOUN
a row of storage bins
▶ container, canister, receptacle, drum

bind VERB
1 *I'll bind the two pieces with string.*
▶ fasten, tie, secure, attach, clamp, stick, connect, join, lash, link, rope, strap, truss, hitch
2 *A nurse bound their wounds.*
▶ bandage, dress, cover, wrap, swathe
3 *They were bound by a solemn oath not to reveal their secret.*
▶ oblige, require, compel, constrain, force, necessitate
4 *Their sufferings had bound them together.*
▶ unite, join, draw, hold

binding ADJECTIVE
a binding agreement
▶ irrevocable, obligatory, mandatory, compulsory, permanent
AN OPPOSITE IS informal

biography NOUN
He read biographies of his great heroes.
▶ life-story, life, memoirs, recollections, autobiography (= a biography written by its subject)

bird NOUN
WORDS FOR TYPES OF BIRD
passerine (perching) birds: sparrow, thrush, blackbird, robin, starling, bluetit, linnet, chaffinch, greenfinch, swallow, wren, martin, jay, swift, skylark, crow, raven, magpie, jackdaw, jay, pigeon, dove, nightingale, woodpecker.
waterbirds: duck, goose, swan, grebe, heron, flamingo, stork, pelican, kingfisher, mallard, moorhen, coot, dipper, crane.
sea birds: gull, guillemot, tern, albatross, gannet, cormorant, shag, auk, penguin, puffin.
owls and birds of prey: eagle, hawk, falcon, kite, merlin, kestrel, buzzard, osprey, vulture, condor, tawny owl, barn owl, little owl, eagle owl, snowy owl.
game birds: pheasant, grouse, partridge, quail, gamebird.
flightless or running birds: emu, ostrich, rhea, kiwi, cassowary, penguin.
cage birds: canary, budgerigar ((*informal*) budgie), lovebird, parrot, parakeet, cockatoo, cockatiel, myna bird, macaw, toucan.
domesticated birds: chicken, hen, turkey, duck, goose, guinea fowl.

birth NOUN
1 *the birth of a child*
▶ delivery, childbirth, (*technical*) parturition
RELATED ADJECTIVE natal
2 *of noble birth*
▶ ancestry, descent, origin, parentage, lineage, pedigree, breeding, background, blood, extraction, family, genealogy, line, race, stock, strain
3 *the birth of socialism*
▶ beginning, origin, emergence, advent, dawn

bit NOUN This word is often overused. Here are some alternatives:
a bit of chocolate   *a bit of stone*
▶ piece, portion, chunk, lump, hunk, fragment, morsel, particle, slice
a bit *That was a bit hard.*
▶ rather, fairly, slightly, somewhat, a little, (*more informal*) pretty
a bit of *a bit of a shame*
▶ rather
bit by bit *Bit by bit she began to understand.*
▶ gradually, slowly, little by little

bitchy ADJECTIVE
(*informal*) *bitchy remarks*
▶ spiteful, vindictive, malicious, backbiting, nasty, mean

a
b
c
d
e
f
g
h
i
j
k
l
m
n
o
p
q
r
s
t
u
v
w
x
y
z

B

bite NOUN
1 *a bite on the arm*
► nip, sting, pinch, wound
2 *a bite to eat*
► mouthful, snack, morsel, bit, nibble, piece, taste

bite VERB
1 *He bit a chunk out of an apple.*
► munch, nibble, chew, crunch, gnaw, nip, champ, (*formal*) masticate
2 *She had been bitten by an insect.*
► sting, pierce
3 *Tax increases will begin to bite in the new tax year.*
► take effect, have an effect, take hold
4 **bite into** *Acid starts to bite into the metal.*
► eat into, corrode, erode, wear away

biting ADJECTIVE
1 *a biting wind*
► bitterly cold, bitter, freezing, icy, raw, piercing, perishing, arctic
2 *a biting remark*
► caustic, harsh, cutting, incisive, bitter, penetrating, stinging, hurtful, cruel, sharp

bitter ADJECTIVE
1 *a bitter taste*
► sour, sharp, acid, acrid, tart, harsh
OPPOSITES ARE mild, sweet
2 *The decision was seen as a bitter disappointment.*
► cruel, distressing, painful, unpleasant
3 *bitter remarks*
► harsh, cutting, caustic, incisive, biting, penetrating, stinging, hurtful, cruel, sharp
4 *She felt bitter about what had happened.*
► resentful, embittered, cynical, aggrieved, disgruntled
5 *a bitter quarrel*
► acrimonious, rancorous, angry, vitriolic
6 *a bitter wind*
► biting, freezing, icy, raw, piercing, perishing, bitterly cold, arctic
AN OPPOSITE IS gentle

bizarre ADJECTIVE
a bizarre story of survival in wartime
► strange, weird, odd, extraordinary, eccentric, peculiar, curious, queer, unusual, grotesque
AN OPPOSITE IS ordinary

black ADJECTIVE
1 *black ink*
► jet-black, coal-black
2 *a black night*
► dark, unlit, moonless, starless, gloomy
3 *hands black from mending the mower*
► filthy, dirty, grimy, grubby, soiled
AN OPPOSITE IS spotless
4 *in a black mood*
► melancholy, miserable, glum, wretched, unhappy, despondent

black VERB
I blacked my shoes.
► blacken, polish

blacken VERB
She decided to blacken her hair.
► darken, make black

blackmail NOUN
He was always vulnerable to blackmail.
► extortion, intimidation

blame NOUN
1 *They were cleared of all blame.*
► responsibility, guilt, liability, culpability
2 *Who got the blame for it?*
► criticism, censure, condemnation, (*more informal*) rap

blame VERB
The report blamed the driver for the accident.
► hold responsible, hold accountable, condemn, censure, criticize, reprove, reprimand, accuse (of), charge (with)
AN OPPOSITE IS excuse

blameless ADJECTIVE
a blameless life
► innocent, guiltless, faultless, exemplary, irreproachable, upright, virtuous, unblemished
OPPOSITES ARE blameworthy, guilty

bland ADJECTIVE
1 *a bland taste*
► insipid, uninteresting, dull, weak, nondescript, watery, mild, boring, flat
OPPOSITES ARE sharp, strong
2 *a bland personality bland remarks*
► dull, tedious, uninteresting, unexciting, monotonous, drab, dreary, feeble, vapid, weak, (*informal*) wishy-washy
OPPOSITES ARE interesting, stimulating

blank ADJECTIVE
1 *a blank page*
► empty, unused, unfilled, clear, bare, void, unmarked
AN OPPOSITE IS used
2 *a blank look*
► expressionless, featureless, impassive, vacant, deadpan, inscrutable, unresponsive
AN OPPOSITE IS expressive

blanket NOUN
a blanket of fog
► covering, layer, film, shroud, cloak, mantle, mask, sheet, cover

blare VERB
Sirens were blaring.
► blast, resound, screech, shriek

blasé ADJECTIVE
He had become blasé about the dangers.
► nonchalant, indifferent, unconcerned, apathetic

blaspheme VERB
How dare you blaspheme before your own father!
► curse, swear, profane

blasphemous ADJECTIVE
blasphemous language
► sacrilegious, profane, irreverent, irreligious, godless, impious, ungodly, disrespectful
AN OPPOSITE IS reverent

blast NOUN
1 *a blast of cold air*
► gust, rush, blow, draught, squall
2 *Hundreds were injured in the blast.*
► explosion, discharge, shock

blast VERB
1 *A series of missiles blasted the building*
► blow up, bomb, demolish, raze
2 *radios blasting out rock music*
► blare, boom, roar, thunder, bellow

blatant ADJECTIVE
a blatant lie
► flagrant, brazen, barefaced, glaring, shameless, unconcealed
AN OPPOSITE IS inconspicuous

blaze NOUN
1 *It took firefighters all night to control the blaze.*
► fire, flames
2 *a blaze of light*
► burst, flash, gleam, streak, beam, glitter

blaze VERB
1 *The fire began to blaze.*
► burn, flare up, be alight
2 *Lights blazed from the top floor.*
► shine, beam, flare, flash, gleam, glitter

bleach VERB
The blinds were bleached in the sun.
► turn white, whiten, fade, blanch

bleak ADJECTIVE
a bleak landscape
► bare, barren, desolate, exposed, featureless, treeless, stark, empty, open, windswept

bleary ADJECTIVE
bleary eyes   bleary vision
► blurred, blurry, unfocused, clouded, cloudy, fogged, foggy, hazy, murky
AN OPPOSITE IS clear

bleed VERB
The wound began to bleed.
► lose blood, haemorrhage, weep, seep

blemish NOUN
a beautiful rose bloom without a single blemish.
► imperfection, flaw, fault, defect, spot, mark, stain, speck, taint

blend NOUN
a blend of several ingredients
► mixture, mix, combination, mingling, amalgam, fusion, synthesis

blend VERB
1 *Blend the ingredients carefully.*
► mix, combine, mingle, merge, stir together, beat, fold in, integrate, whip, whisk

2 *The colours blend well.*
► harmonize, match, fit

bless VERB
The couple were blessed with a child.
► favour, grace, endow

blessed ADJECTIVE
a blessed place
► holy, sacred, sanctified, adored, divine, hallowed, revered

blessing NOUN
1 *The priest gave a blessing*
► benediction, grace, prayer
2 *The manager gave the scheme his blessing.*
► approval, backing, support, consent, approbation, leave, permission
AN OPPOSITE IS disapproval
3 *Central heating is a blessing in the winter*
► benefit, advantage, asset, boon, comfort, convenience, godsend, help
AN OPPOSITE IS affliction

blight NOUN
1 *potato blight*
► disease, rot, decay, (*more formal*) infestation
2 *the blight of traffic noise*
► affliction, curse, plague, menace, nuisance, tribulation, trial, misfortune
AN OPPOSITE IS blessing

blight VERB
Their lives were blighted by troublesome neighbours.
► ruin, wreck, spoil, afflict, shatter, disrupt

blind ADJECTIVE
1 *She had been blind from birth.*
► sightless, unsighted, visually impaired, partially sighted, unseeing
2 *blind to all dangers*
► oblivious, imperceptive, heedless (of), unaware (of), inattentive, indifferent, insensible, insensitive, ignorant (of), blinkered (from)
OPPOSITES ARE aware, perceptive
3 *showing a blind acceptance of criticism*
► uncritical, reckless, impulsive, indiscriminate, unreasoning, mindless
4 *a blind corner*
► concealed, hidden, obscure, obstructed

blind NOUN
She pulled down a blind.
► screen, shade, cover, curtain, shutter

blind VERB
1 *The light blinded her for a few moments.*
► dazzle
2 *They are trying to blind us all with science.*
► confuse, deceive, overawe, intimidate, disconcert, unsettle, (*more informal*) put off

blink VERB
A light on the control panel began to blink.
► flash, wink, flicker, twinkle, flutter, gleam, glimmer

B

bliss NOUN
a life of bliss
▶ joy, delight, pleasure, rapture, ecstasy, euphoria, felicity, gladness, happiness, heaven, paradise
AN OPPOSITE IS misery

blissful ADJECTIVE
They spent a blissful week together.
▶ ecstatic, joyful, rapturous, euphoric, elated, happy
AN OPPOSITE IS miserable

blizzard NOUN
They were kept indoors by blizzards.
▶ snowstorm, squall

bloated ADJECTIVE
a bloated stomach
▶ swollen, dilated, distended, enlarged, inflated
OPPOSITES ARE shrunken, shrivelled

blob NOUN
a blob of ice cream
▶ drop, droplet, globule, lump

bloc NOUN
the former communist bloc
▶ alliance, association, federation, union

block NOUN
1 *a block of chocolate a block of stone*
▶ chunk, hunk, slab, bar, brick, cake, lump, mass, piece
2 *The pipe had a block in it.*
▶ blockage, obstruction, stoppage
3 *Lack of funds proved a block to progress.*
▶ barrier, hindrance, impediment, obstacle

block VERB
1 *(informal) The drain was blocked with leaves*
▶ bung up, choke, clog, close, congest, constrict, dam, fill, jam, obstruct, plug, stop up
2 *A parked van was blocking access to the house.*
▶ obstruct, bar, impede, inhibit, restrict, limit
3 *The scheme was blocked by the directors.*
▶ stop, prevent, halt, thwart

blockade NOUN
a blockade of the city
▶ siege, encirclement, investment

blockage NOUN
The drain has a blockage.
▶ obstruction, stoppage, block, constriction, jam, obstacle, resistance, barrier, bottleneck, congestion

bloke NOUN
(informal) He's a funny bloke, isn't he?
▶ chap, fellow, guy, man, boy, individual

blond, blonde ADJECTIVE
blond hair
▶ fair, flaxen, golden, light, yellow, bleached

blood NOUN
a person of noble blood
▶ ancestry, descent, origin, parentage, lineage, pedigree, breeding, background, birth, extraction, family, genealogy, line, race, stock, strain

bloodcurdling ADJECTIVE
a bloodcurdling scream
▶ terrifying, frightening, horrifying, fearful, spine-chilling, hair-raising

bloodshed NOUN
The government were anxious to avoid further bloodshed.
▶ killing, slaughter, carnage, butchery, violence

bloodthirsty ADJECTIVE
bloodthirsty attackers
▶ brutal, murderous, cruel, barbaric, savage, vicious, violent, warlike, bloody, ferocious, fierce

bloody ADJECTIVE
1 *a bloody wound*
▶ bleeding, bloodstained, raw, gaping
2 *a bloody battle*
▶ fierce, gory, bloodthirsty, violent

bloom NOUN
1 *rose blooms*
▶ blossom, flower, bud
2 *the bloom of youth*
▶ prime, peak, glow, flush, acme

bloom VERB
1 *The roses have all bloomed now.*
▶ blossom, flower, open
AN OPPOSITE IS fade
2 *The children had bloomed in the country air.*
▶ flourish, thrive, prosper, blossom, develop

blossom NOUN
apple blossom
▶ blooms, buds, florets, flowers

blossom VERB
1 *The trees have started to blossom.*
▶ bloom, flower, open
AN OPPOSITE IS fade
2 *The scheme can blossom with the right support.*
▶ flourish, thrive, prosper, bloom, develop

blot NOUN
1 *a blot of ink*
▶ spot, blotch, mark, smear, smudge, stain, splodge, blob
2 *a blot on the landscape*
▶ eyesore, blemish, defect, fault, flaw

blot VERB
Ink blotted the page.
▶ smudge, mark, spoil, spot, stain, bespatter, mar
blot out *A tall building blotted out the view*
▶ conceal, hide, mask, obliterate, obscure, cover, delete, eclipse, erase, expunge, rub out, wipe out, cancel

blotch NOUN
The walls had damp blotches down them.
▶ patch, smudge, speck, speckle, blot, mark

blotchy ADJECTIVE
a blotchy skin
▶ spotty, spotted, blemished, marked, patchy, smudged, uneven

blow NOUN

1 *a blow on the head*
▶ knock, bang, hit, thump, smack
2 *The news was a terrible blow.*
▶ shock, surprise, reverse, setback, upset, disappointment, calamity, disaster

blow VERB

1 *The storm blew the ship on the rocks.*
▶ drive, sweep, force, blast, fling, whisk
2 *Leaves were blowing across the drive.*
▶ drift, flutter, whirl, stream
blow out *The heater blows out hot air.*
▶ puff out, blast out, exhale, breathe, fan, waft
blow up
1 *I'll blow up the tyres.*
▶ inflate, pump up, fill, dilate, expand
OPPOSITES ARE let down, deflate
2 *The photograph can be blown up.*
▶ enlarge
3 *A bomb blew up the building.*
▶ bomb, blast, detonate, dynamite, explode
4 (*informal*) *When he heard what we had done he blew up.*
▶ grow angry, lose your temper, rage

blue ADJECTIVE

1 *a pretty blue colour*
▶ sky-blue, turquoise, ultramarine, aquamarine, azure, cerulean, cobalt, indigo, navy, sapphire
2 *a blue movie*
▶ indecent, coarse, obscene, salacious, risqué
3 (*informal*) *Jake was feeling blue that day.*
▶ sad, depressed, dejected

blueprint NOUN

1 *blueprints of the new aircraft*
▶ design, plan, drawing, draft, outline, pattern, layout, prototype
2 *a blueprint for political reform*
▶ model, plan, scheme, framework, basis, pattern, guide, proposal

blues NOUN

the blues *I woke up with the blues just like you did.*
▶ depression, sadness, melancholy, dejection, despondency, low spirits, misery, gloom

bluff NOUN

The offer is regarded as a crude bluff.
▶ deception, subterfuge, sham, pretence, fake, fraud, ruse, artifice, trick

bluff VERB

1 *We think they must be bluffing us.*
▶ deceive, delude, mislead, hoodwink, trick
2 *I am sure they are only bluffing.*
▶ pretend, sham, put on an act, lie, (*more informal*) kid

blunder NOUN

Harry shook his head at his own blunder.
▶ mistake, error, gaffe, slip, faux pas, (*more informal*) howler, (*much more informal*) cock-up

blunder VERB

The security officer had blundered by letting the men into the building.
▶ make a mistake, bungle, err, be in error, misjudge, miscalculate, slip up, (*more informal*) put your foot in it, (*more informal*) goof, (*much more informal*) screw up, (*much more informal*) cock up

blunt ADJECTIVE

1 *a blunt knife*
▶ dull, rounded, thick, unpointed, unsharpened
AN OPPOSITE IS sharp
2 *a blunt reply*
▶ abrupt, harsh, curt, terse, gruff, rude, offhand, brusque, insensitive, outspoken, plain-spoken
OPPOSITES ARE polite, tactful

blunt VERB

A series of snacks blunted my appetite.
▶ dull, reduce, dampen, take the edge off, weaken
OPPOSITES ARE sharpen, intensify

blur VERB

The steam had blurred her glasses.
▶ cloud, fog, mask, obscure, befog, blear, dim, smear

blurred ADJECTIVE

When he lifted his head everything looked blurred.
▶ indistinct, blurry, bleary, fuzzy, hazy, misty

blurt VERB

blurt out *She had blurted out the first thing that came into her head.*
▶ come out with, exclaim, cry out, disclose, divulge, let out, let slip, reveal

blush VERB

She blushed as he kissed her hand.
▶ go red, flush, glow, colour

blustery ADJECTIVE

a wet blustery day
▶ gusty, squally, windy

board NOUN

1 *a wooden board*
▶ plank, panel, beam, length of timber, lath
2 *the board of directors*
▶ committee, council, panel

board VERB

1 *Passengers may now board the aircraft.*
▶ get on, go on board, enter, embark, ascend
2 *His wife boarded students in a spare room.*
▶ accommodate, house, lodge, put up, billet, quarter

boast VERB

His mother had been boasting about how clever he was.
▶ brag, crow, bluster, swank, show off, gloat, sing someone's praises, (*more informal*) talk big

boastful ADJECTIVE

(*informal*) *He was constantly boastful of all his achievements.*
▶ bragging, conceited, big-headed, bumptious,

B

proud, puffed up, swaggering, swollen-headed, vain, egotistical, (*informal*) cocky, (*informal*) swanky
AN OPPOSITE IS modest

boat NOUN
boats in the little harbour
▶ craft, vessel, ship

bob VERB
Little boats were bobbing in the water.
▶ bounce, move up and down, dance, toss about, skip about, oscillate
bob up *A woman at the back bobbed up to ask a question.*
▶ jump up, leap up, spring up, rise (up), appear

bode VERB
This incident did not bode well for his future as a film director.
▶ augur, promise, signal, forebode, herald, portend

bodily ADJECTIVE
bodily contact
▶ physical, corporeal

---

body NOUN
1 *the human body*
▶ frame, figure, form, physique, shape, anatomy, being, build
RELATED ADJECTIVES corporal, somatic
2 *a blow to the body*
▶ trunk, torso
3 *a body floating in the river*
▶ corpse, cadaver, carcass, mortal remains, (*more informal*) stiff
4 *the managing body*
▶ committee, company, association, corporation, society, band
5 *a large body of evidence*
▶ quantity, collection, volume, mass, accumulation, agglomeration, corpus

WORDS FOR PARTS OF THE BODY

the skin: skin, pores.

the head: head, scalp, face; jaw, chin, cheek, eye, ear, forehead, nose, nostril; mouth, lip, tooth, tongue, gum; neck, throat.

the limbs: limb; arm, elbow, funny bone, wrist, hand, finger, fingernail, thumb, knuckle; leg, foot, toe, toenail, ankle, heel, shin, calf, thigh, knee, kneecap, hip.

the torso: torso, trunk; buttocks, bottom; waist, abdomen, belly, chest, navel, breast, nipple, shoulder, shoulder blade.

main internal parts: skeleton, backbone, vertebra, spine, spinal cord, bone; blood, artery, vein, capillary, gland, marrow, muscle, nerve, ovary, oviduct; adrenals, saliva; hormones; brain, tonsils, adenoids, windpipe; heart, lung, liver, appendix, bladder, bowels, colon, gall bladder, gullet, gut, intestines, kidney, pancreas, pelvis, penis, stomach, testis, uterus or womb; rectum, anus. ▶▶

---

bodily systems: blood system, digestive system, endocrine system (hormone production), excretory system, nervous system, reproductive system, respiratory system (breathing), skeletal system (bones and muscles).

---

bodyguard NOUN
He could not travel anywhere without a bodyguard.
▶ guard, minder, protector

boffin NOUN
the boffins who invented radar
▶ expert, specialist, scientist

bog NOUN
The ground became wetter, and eventually they were on the edge of a bog.
▶ marsh, marshland, swamp, mire, morass, fen, quicksands, mudflats, quagmire
bogged down *bogged down with all the work*
▶ encumbered, hindered, impeded, slowed down, in difficulties, stuck, sunk

bogus ADJECTIVE
The man had given a bogus address.
▶ fake, false, spurious, fraudulent, counterfeit, pretended

bogy NOUN
bogies and other beings of the night
▶ evil spirit, ghost, spectre, phantom

boil NOUN
a boil on the skin
▶ swelling, pustule, pimple, abscess, blister, spot, tumour

boil VERB
1 *Boil the potatoes in water.*
▶ bring to boiling point, bring to the boil, cook, heat, simmer
2 *The water was beginning to boil.*
▶ bubble, effervesce, foam, seethe, steam
3 *She was boiling with anger.*
▶ seethe, be angry, lose your temper, go into a rage, fly into a rage, flare up, (*more informal*) see red

boisterous ADJECTIVE
a boisterous beach game
▶ lively, spirited, animated, exuberant, rough, rowdy
OPPOSITES ARE restrained, calm

bold ADJECTIVE
1 *a bold move   a bold traveller*
▶ brave, courageous, daring, adventurous, audacious, confident, dauntless, enterprising, fearless, forceful, gallant, heroic, intrepid, self-confident, valiant, valorous, venturesome, (*more informal*) plucky
AN OPPOSITE IS cowardly

2 *bold remarks*
▶ brazen, forward, cheeky, brash, impertinent, impudent, insolent, presumptuous, fresh, pert, rude, saucy, shameless, unashamed
OPPOSITES ARE polite, reticent
3 *a bold pattern bold colours*
▶ striking, strong, bright, clear, conspicuous, eye-catching, prominent, pronounced, showy, vivid
AN OPPOSITE IS inconspicuous

boldness NOUN
Their boldness took everyone by surprise.
▶ bravery, daring, audacity

bolt NOUN
1 *The door bolt was stuck.*
▶ catch, bar, latch, lock, fastening
2 *Put a nut on the bolt.*
▶ pin, rivet, rod, screw
a bolt from the blue
▶ shock, surprise, (*more informal*) bombshell

bolt VERB
1 *We'd better bolt the door.*
▶ fasten, latch, lock, secure, bar
2 *She bolted from the room.*
▶ dash, dart, flee, fly, rush, hurry, sprint, run, escape
3 *He was in such a rush he had to bolt his food.*
▶ gobble, gulp, wolf, guzzle, stuff, scoff down

bomb NOUN
The building was destroyed by bombs.
▶ explosive, missile

bomb VERB
The city was bombed for days on end.
▶ bombard, drop bombs on, shell

bombard VERB
1 *Offshore ships bombarded the city all night.*
▶ shell, pound, blast, strafe, assault, attack, beset, bomb, fire at, pelt, shoot at, assail
2 *The speaker was bombarded with questions.*
▶ overwhelm, inundate, swamp, flood, deluge, pester, plague

bombardment NOUN
The city was practically demolished by the bombardment.
▶ barrage, blast, shelling, attack, cannonade, discharge, fusillade, hail, salvo, volley

bond NOUN
1 *There was a close bond between the two brothers.*
▶ attachment, connection, tie, link, relationship, affinity, unity, affiliation
2 *By running away he had broken his bond*
▶ promise, pledge, word, agreement, compact, contract, covenant, guarantee
3 bonds *The prisoner struggled to undo his bonds.*
▶ chains, fetters, manacles, shackles, restraints, fastenings

bond VERB
The fitting is bonded to the wall with strong glue.
▶ stick, fix, attach, fasten

bondage NOUN
The slaves were released from years of bondage.
▶ slavery, servitude, enslavement, subjection, captivity, imprisonment, incarceration

---

bone NOUN

THE BONES OF THE HUMAN BODY INCLUDE

in the head: cranium (skull), mandible (jaw), orbit (eye socket), maxilla (upper jaw), mandible (lower jaw).

in the upper body and trunk: scapula (shoulderblade), clavicle (collarbone), ribs, sternum (breastbone), thoracic vertebrae (supporting the ribs), lumbar vertebrae (in the lower back), sacrum (at the base of the spine), coccyx, pelvis (or pelvic girdle, consisting of ilium, pubis, and ischium).

in the arms: humerus (in the upper arm), radius (on the side where the thumb is), ulna (on the side where the little finger is), carpus (wrist bones, consisting of carpals), metacarpus (hand bones, consisting of metacarpals), phalanx (plural phalanges), bones of the fingers.

in the legs: femur (thighbone), patella (kneebone), tibia (shinbone), fibula, tarsus (ankle, consisting of tarsal bones), metatarsus (foot, consisting of metatarsals), phalanx (plural phalanges), bones of the toes.

---

bonny ADJECTIVE
a bonny baby
▶ beautiful, attractive, pretty, sweet, cute

bonus NOUN
1 *no Christmas bonus this year*
▶ extra payment, handout, reward
2 *A meal out was an unexpected bonus.*
▶ benefit, extra, addition, advantage, (*informal*) plus

bony ADJECTIVE
a bony figure
▶ thin, angular, gawky, lanky, gaunt, emaciated, gangling, lean, scraggy, scrawny, skinny
AN OPPOSITE IS plump

book NOUN
a book to read and enjoy
▶ volume, tome, publication, tract, booklet

book VERB
1 *On his way to the hospital he was booked for speeding.*
▶ arrest, take your name, write down details
2 *We booked tickets for the concert.*
▶ reserve, order, arrange for, prearrange, buy
3 *Will you book a disco for the party?*
▶ engage, organize, sign up, arrange

booklet NOUN
a booklet of travel advice
▶ pamphlet, brochure, leaflet, paperback

boom NOUN
1 *Suddenly there was the boom of the one o'clock gun.*
▶ bang, reverberation, roar, sound, blast

B

2 *a boom in trade*
▶ upturn, upsurge, upswing, boost, growth, improvement, expansion, increase, spurt
AN OPPOSITE IS slump

boom VERB
1 *The guns began to boom.*
▶ rumble, thunder, crash, reverberate, resound, echo
2 *Business is booming.*
▶ thrive, prosper, flourish, do well, (*more informal*) pick up
OPPOSITES ARE decline, slump

boon NOUN
Cheap travel is such a boon.
▶ benefit, blessing, help, asset, advantage, (*more informal*) piece of luck

boost NOUN
1 *a boost to morale*
▶ impetus, stimulus, lift, uplift, (*more informal*) shot in the arm
2 *a boost in sales*
▶ increase, expansion, growth, improvement, boom, upturn, upsurge, upswing, spurt
OPPOSITES ARE decrease, decline

boost VERB
The award boosted everyone's morale.
▶ raise, uplift, heighten, stimulate, bolster, increase, enhance
OPPOSITES ARE depress, hinder

boot NOUN
He had lost his left boot in the mud.
▶ gumboot, wellington, (*more informal*) welly

booth NOUN
a telephone booth   a voting booth
▶ cubicle, kiosk, stall, compartment, enclosure, carrel, hut, stand

booty NOUN
The gang arranged to meet and divide the booty.
▶ loot, plunder, haul, pillage, spoils

booze NOUN
Lunch had to include lots of booze (informal).
▶ alcohol, drink, alcoholic drink, liquor, spirits

booze VERB
They had been boozing all night (informal).
▶ drink, have a drink, indulge, imbibe, (*also informal*) tipple

border NOUN
1 *the border of a tablecloth   the border of a lake*
▶ edge, margin, perimeter, fringe, verge
2 *the border between Italy and Slovenia*
▶ frontier, boundary, borderline

border VERB
border on *The park borders a housing estate.*
▶ skirt, adjoin, be adjacent to, be alongside, abut on, join, share a border with, touch

borderline ADJECTIVE
a borderline case
▶ marginal, indeterminate, uncertain, ambivalent

bore VERB
1 *You need to bore a hole in the wall.*
▶ drill, punch, cut, pierce, sink
2 *Long films tend to bore him.*
▶ weary, tire, (*more informal*) turn off
OPPOSITES ARE interest, entertain

bore NOUN
What a bore to have to wait another hour.
▶ nuisance, bother, annoyance, (*more informal*) drag (*more informal*) pain, (*more informal*) pest

boring ADJECTIVE
What a boring book.   The work turned out to be very boring.
▶ tedious, dull, monotonous, dreary, humdrum, routine, uninteresting, unexciting, insipid, vapid, jejune
OPPOSITES ARE interesting, stimulating

born ADJECTIVE
a born comic
▶ natural, untaught, instinctive, genuine

borrow VERB
I need to borrow a pen.
▶ loan, have use of, obtain, acquire, (*more informal*) cadge, (*more informal*) scrounge
AN OPPOSITE IS lend

bosom NOUN
1 *The dress was cut high over her bosom.*
▶ bust, chest, breasts
2 *The family took her into its bosom.*
▶ care, protection, shelter

boss NOUN
(informal) The boss would be away all that week.
▶ head, chief, manager, leader

boss VERB
You have no right to boss me about like this.
▶ order, dictate to, push around, lord it over, bully, domineer

bossy ADJECTIVE
Why do you treat us in such a bossy manner?
▶ domineering, officious, overbearing, high-handed, imperious, dictatorial, authoritarian, autocratic, aggressive, bullying, despotic, lordly, oppressive, peremptory, tyrannical
AN OPPOSITE IS submissive

botch VERB
They managed to botch the next job as well.
▶ bungle, make a mess of, mismanage, mishandle, do badly, spoil, mess up, (*more informal*) screw up
AN OPPOSITE IS succeed in

bother NOUN
1 *There was some bother at the disco.*
▶ disorder, trouble, disturbance, difficulty, fuss, (*more informal*) hassle, (*more informal*) aggro

2 *It was a bother to keep the food hot.*
► nuisance, annoyance, irritation, inconvenience, palaver, pest, trouble, worry, trial, job

bother VERB
1 *We found a quiet spot where no one would be able to bother us.*
► disturb, trouble, pester, molest, annoy, vex, worry, concern, dismay, exasperate, harass, (*informal*) hassle, inconvenience, irk, irritate, nag, plague, upset
2 *The accident was too minor to bother about.*
► concern yourself, be concerned, be worried, care, mind

bottle NOUN
1 *a bottle of wine   water in bottles*
► flask, carafe, decanter, flagon, jar, pitcher
2 (*informal*) *She had bottle to stand up to him, they had to admit.*
► courage, nerve, pluck, spirit, mettle, daring, audacity, boldness, bravery

bottle VERB
bottle up *He had bottled up his problems for too long.*
► suppress, repress, hold in, keep in, stifle

bottleneck NOUN
There was a bottleneck ahead at the old bridge.
► blockage, hold-up, traffic jam, tailback

bottom ADJECTIVE
1 *the bottom rung of a ladder*
► deepest, lowest
AN OPPOSITE IS top
2 *bottom marks*
► least, minimum
AN OPPOSITE IS top

bottom NOUN
1 *the bottom of the stairs*
► foot, base
AN OPPOSITE IS top
2 *the bottom of the wall*
► foot, base, foundation
AN OPPOSITE IS top
3 *the bottom of the car*
► underside, underneath
AN OPPOSITE IS topside
4 *the bottom of the sea*
► bed, depths, floor
AN OPPOSITE IS surface
5 *They were at the bottom of their fortunes*
► lowest point, nadir
AN OPPOSITE IS peak
6 *It is very hard to get to the bottom of the problem.*
► origin, root, source, heart, essence, grounds
7 *She said she had a tattoo on her bottom.*
► buttocks, rear, rump, seat, (*more informal*) behind, (*more informal*) backside, (*more informal*) bum, (*humorous*) sit-upon, (*formal or humorous*) posterior

bottomless ADJECTIVE
a bottomless pit
► deep, profound, fathomless, boundless, immeasurable

bounce VERB
The ball hit the ground and bounced up.
► rebound, spring up, bob up, bound, leap up, recoil, ricochet

bounce NOUN
She was exhausted and had lost much of her bounce.
► vitality, energy, vigour, liveliness, vivacity, verve, exuberance

bound ADJECTIVE
1 *Our friends are bound to help.*
► certain, sure, very likely, liable, obliged, destined, fated
2 *bound by an oath*
► obligated, committed, obliged, duty-bound, pledged, compelled
3 *His wrists and ankles were bound with rope.*
► tied, tied up, shackled, fettered, secured, trussed up, strapped
4 **bound for** *a train bound for the north*
► going to, heading for, making for, off to, travelling towards

bound VERB
A dog bounded across the lawn
► leap, jump, skip, spring, bounce, gambol, bob, caper, frisk

boundary NOUN
1 *A wire fence marks the boundary.*
► border, frontier, borderline, dividing line
2 *the boundary of the estate*
► bounds, confines, circumference, perimeter, extremity, outer edge, fringe, limit, margin

boundless ADJECTIVE
The boys seemed to have boundless energy.
► unlimited, limitless, unbounded, untold, endless, immeasurable, incalculable, inexhaustible, infinite, unflagging, vast
AN OPPOSITE IS limited

bouquet NOUN
1 *a bouquet of flowers*
► bunch, spray, posy, sprig, nosegay, corsage, garland
2 *The white wine had a sweet bouquet.*
► aroma, fragrance, nose, scent

bourgeois ADJECTIVE
a bourgeois family
► middle-class, suburban, conventional, traditional, conservative

bout NOUN
1 *a bout of coughing*
► attack, fit, spasm, outburst, burst, convulsion
2 *a boxing bout*
► contest, match, round, fight, encounter, engagement, struggle, combat, competition

B

bow VERB (rhymes with *cow*)
1 *The man bowed his head.*
▶ incline, lower, bend
2 *In the end they had to bow to pressure.*
▶ yield, succumb, submit, surrender, give way, give in

bow NOUN (rhymes with *cow*)
the bow of a ship
▶ front, prow, fore-end

bow NOUN (rhymes with *no*)
She tied the ribbon into a neat bow.
▶ loop, knot

bowl NOUN
a bowl of soup
▶ dish, basin, tureen, vessel

bowl VERB
He bowled three fast balls in a row.
▶ throw, toss, fling, hurl, pitch, lob

box NOUN
a box of coloured pencils
▶ carton, pack, packet, case, casket, chest

boy NOUN
He had loved reading as a boy.
▶ lad, youngster, (*more informal*) kid, (*more informal*) nipper

boycott NOUN
a boycott of imported goods
▶ ban, bar, embargo, moratorium, prohibition, blacklist

boycott VERB
Palestinian leaders threatened to boycott the talks.
▶ shun, spurn, avoid, stay away from, ignore, cold-shoulder

boyish ADJECTIVE
He had a boyish sense of fun.
▶ youthful, childlike, young, (*disapproving*) childish, (*disapproving*) puerile
OPPOSITES ARE manly, mature, adult

bracing ADJECTIVE
The sea air is very bracing.
▶ invigorating, stimulating, refreshing, exhilarating, fortifying
AN OPPOSITE IS debilitating

bracket NOUN
The shelf is fixed to the wall with a pair of brackets.
▶ support, prop

brag VERB
He was bragging about all the friends he had (*informal*).
▶ boast, crow, bluster, swank, show off, gloat, sing someone's praises, (*more informal*) talk big

brain NOUN
1 *You need brains to succeed in this job.*
▶ intelligence, intellect, sense, common sense, understanding, a good mind, a good head, (*informal*) grey matter, (*informal*) nous

2 *the brains of the family*
▶ intellectual, clever one, clever person, mastermind, (*more informal*) egghead
RELATED ADJECTIVE cerebral

brainwash VERB
He likes to brainwash people into thinking they need help.
▶ indoctrinate, condition, re-educate

brainy ADJECTIVE
a brainy child
▶ intelligent, clever, bright, gifted, brilliant, intellectual, highbrow, (*more informal*) smart
OPPOSITES ARE stupid, unintelligent

brake VERB
She saw a child step out and braked quickly.
▶ slow down, reduce speed, put on the brakes, (*more formal*) decelerate
AN OPPOSITE IS accelerate

branch NOUN
1 *a branch of a tree*
▶ bough, limb, arm, offshoot, sprig
2 *the executive branch of government*
▶ department, section, division, subdivision, wing, part
3 *The firm has closed several overseas branches.*
▶ office, bureau, agency

branch VERB
The road branches ahead.
▶ divide, fork
branch out *She wanted to branch out into another career.*
▶ diversify, develop, expand, extend, enlarge, broaden out

brand NOUN
a new brand of margarine
▶ make, kind, type, variety, brand-name, trademark, label, line, sort

brand VERB
1 *The cattle are branded with hot irons.*
▶ mark, stamp, burn, identify, label, scar
2 *The men are all branded as troublemakers.*
▶ stigmatize, vilify, censure, denounce, discredit, disgrace, taint, give (someone) the reputation of

brandish VERB
a woman brandishing an umbrella
▶ flourish, wield, flaunt, wave

brash ADJECTIVE
a group of brash youths
▶ brazen, forward, insolent, (*more informal*) cocky
OPPOSITES ARE meek, shy

bravado NOUN
With great bravado, she attacked her pile of work.
▶ boldness, swagger, bluster, bombast, show, pretence

brave ADJECTIVE
He was a good fighter and a brave man. They put up a brave fight.
▶ courageous, valiant, daring, audacious, spirited, intrepid, plucky, adventurous, fearless
AN OPPOSITE IS cowardly

bravery NOUN
Everyone praised their bravery.
▶ courage, audacity, boldness, daring, nerve, gallantry, determination, fearlessness, fortitude, heroism, (*more informal*) bottle, (*more informal*) grit, (*more informal*) guts, (*more informal*) pluck, (*much more informal*) spunk
AN OPPOSITE IS cowardice

brawl NOUN
The argument rapidly grew into a drunken brawl.
▶ fight , affray, melee, wrangle, altercation, fracas, clash, fray, scrap, scuffle, tussle, (*informal*) punch-up, (*more informal*) set-to, (*more informal*) bust-up

brawl VERB
grown men brawling in the street
▶ fight, scuffle, scrap, tussle, wrestle, exchange blows

brawny ADJECTIVE
a brawny wrestler
▶ muscular, sinewy, athletic, burly, beefy, strong
OPPOSITES ARE puny, scrawny

brazen ADJECTIVE
a brazen lie
▶ blatant, barefaced, flagrant, shameless, unashamed, unabashed, audacious, cheeky, defiant, impertinent, impudent, insolent, rude
OPPOSITES ARE modest, shamefaced

breach NOUN
1 *a breach of the rules*
▶ breaking, infringement, violation, contravention, offence (against), transgression
2 *a breach between the king and his chancellor*
▶ rift, break, split, difference, disagreement, drifting apart, estrangement, quarrel, separation, alienation
3 *a breach in the sea wall*
▶ break, split, fissure, gap, crack, fracture, rupture, aperture, chasm, hole, opening

bread NOUN
She was responsible for keeping a roof over their heads and bread in their mouths.
▶ food, nourishment, sustenance, subsistence

break NOUN
1 *a break in a pipe*
▶ breach, split, fissure, gap, crack, fracture, rupture, aperture, chasm, hole, opening
2 *a break in work*
▶ pause, respite, rest, breathing space, intermission, interval, hiatus, interlude, (*informal*) let-up, lull, (*informal*) breather
3 *He had listened to thirty new songs without a break.*
▶ interruption, disruption, halt, stop, lapse, suspension

break VERB
1 *The cup fell to the floor and broke.*
▶ shatter, smash, crack, split, fragment, splinter, (*more informal*) bust
2 *He broke the stick into three pieces.*
▶ split, cut, divide, sever, (*more informal*) bust
OPPOSITES ARE repair, mend
3 *It would be unwise to break the law.*
▶ contravene, violate, disobey, flout, infringe
OPPOSITES ARE obey, respect, abide by
4 *Let's break for lunch.*
▶ pause, stop, take a break, (*more informal*) knock off
5 *She was determined to break the power of the unions.*
▶ subdue, tame, defeat, crush, smash, suppress, undermine

break down
1 *The car broke down near the border.*
▶ stop working, go wrong, (*more informal*) pack up, (*more informal*) conk out
2 *Negotiations broke down without an agreement.*
▶ fail, collapse, fall through, come to nothing

break in
1 *His mother then broke in with a question about the arrangements.*
▶ interrupt, butt in, intrude
2 *Thieves had broken in during the night.*
▶ commit burglary, force your way in, make a raid

break off *It was hard to break off before finishing the chapter.*
▶ discontinue, pause, stop

break out of *Several prisoners were able to break out of the detention centre.*
▶ escape from, abscond from, break loose from

break up
1 *A dump where they break up old cars.*
▶ demolish, dismantle, take apart
2 *The meeting broke up after several hours.*
▶ adjourn, finish, end, come to an end, (*more formal*) terminate
3 *The crowd began to break up.*
▶ disperse, scatter, disband, go their separate ways
4 *Jane and her boyfriend had recently broken up.*
▶ separate, split up, stop living together, get divorced

breakdown NOUN
1 *The system has experienced a complete breakdown.*
▶ malfunction, failure, collapse
2 *A breakdown in the peace talks*
▶ failure, collapse
3 *a breakdown of the figures*
▶ analysis, classification, itemization

break-in NOUN
a break-in at the bank
▶ burglary, robbery, theft, raid

breakneck ADJECTIVE
driving at breakneck speed
▶ headlong, dangerous, reckless, fast , hasty, suicidal

breakthrough NOUN
a breakthrough in the search for a cure
▶ advance, leap forward, discovery, development, revolution, progress, find, improvement, innovation, invention, success

breakwater NOUN
A breakwater sheltered them from the wind.
▶ sea wall, embankment, sea-defence, jetty, mole, pier, groyne

breast NOUN
a woman's breast
▶ bosom(s), bust, chest, front
RELATED ADJECTIVE mammary

breath NOUN
1 *Take a deep breath.*
▶ gulp of air, (*technical*) inhalation
2 *a breath of wind*
▶ puff, waft, whiff, whisper, breeze, sigh

breathe VERB
1 *It is lovely to breathe fresh air again.*
▶ inhale, exhale, respire, puff, pant
2 *Try not to breathe a word of what happened.*
▶ speak, whisper, hint, let out

breathless ADJECTIVE
They arrived breathless and red in the face.
▶ out of breath, gasping, panting, puffing, tired out, wheezy, exhausted

breathtaking ADJECTIVE
The view was breathtaking.
▶ spectacular, magnificent, stunning, amazing, astonishing, astounding, staggering, startling, fantastic, wonderful, phenomenal
AN OPPOSITE IS unimpressive

breed NOUN
1 *a rare breed of dog*
▶ variety, type, kind, sort, strain, family, pedigree
2 *a new breed of writer*
▶ type, kind, sort, class, variety, genre, order

breed VERB
1 *Rabbits have a reputation for breeding rapidly.*
▶ reproduce, produce young, bear young, multiply, procreate, increase
2 *Familiarity breeds contempt*
▶ produce, cause, create, arouse, engender, foster, cultivate, develop, generate, induce, nourish, nurture, occasion

breeze NOUN
A slight breeze made the tall grass tremble.
▶ gentle wind, breath of air, puff of air, flurry

breezy ADJECTIVE
1 *a breezy afternoon*
▶ windy, blowy, fresh, brisk, airy, draughty
OPPOSITES ARE still, windless
2 *She walked in with a breezy air.*
▶ cheerful, jaunty, lively, bright, animated, carefree, light-hearted
OPPOSITES ARE sombre, serious

brevity NOUN
Everyone who had to read it welcomed the brevity of the report.
▶ conciseness, shortness, succinctness, economy, briefness, compression, incisiveness, pithiness, terseness, crispness, curtness
OPPOSITES ARE verbosity, long-windedness

brew NOUN
a strong brew made with fruit juices
▶ mixture, blend, concoction, compound, infusion, potion, preparation, punch, drink, liquor

brew VERB
1 *Southerners just can't brew good beer.*
▶ ferment, make
2 *Christopher and Francis disappeared to brew coffee.*
▶ make, prepare, heat
3 *Someone is brewing mischief for us.*
▶ plot, stir up, foment, threaten, concoct, contrive, hatch, plan, prepare, scheme, (*more informal*) cook up
4 *Trouble is brewing.*
▶ develop, loom, build up, threaten, gather

bribe NOUN
He was accused of accepting bribes.
▶ inducement, enticement, incentive, (*more informal*) sweetener, (*more informal*) backhander, (*more informal*) carrot

bribe VERB
They had tried to bribe an official.
▶ offer a bribe to, buy off, pay off, corrupt, entice, influence, pervert, (*more formal*) suborn

bric-à-brac NOUN
an old shop full of enticing bric-à-brac.
▶ ornaments, odds and ends, oddments, trinkets, curios, antiques, baubles, knick-knacks

brick NOUN
an outhouse made of bricks
▶ block, building block, breeze-block

bridge NOUN
a bridge over the river
▶ viaduct, aqueduct (carrying water), arch, crossing, span, way over

bridge VERB
A footpath bridged the motorway.
▶ span, cross, straddle, traverse, go over, extend across, reach across

brief ADJECTIVE
1 *a brief visit*
▶ short, cursory, fleeting, passing, quick, hasty, limited, little, momentary, sharp, short-lived, temporary, transient
OPPOSITES ARE long, prolonged
2 *a brief account of the incident*
▶ short, concise, succinct, pithy, crisp, incisive, compact, condensed, curt, terse, thumbnail
OPPOSITES ARE wordy, verbose, lengthy

brief NOUN
1 *Here is a detailed brief for the assignment.*
▶ (set of) instructions, (set of) orders, (set of) directions, (set of) guidelines, set of information, outline, plan
2 *a barrister's brief*
▶ case, defence, argument, dossier, summary

brief VERB
Staff will be briefed about the changes.
▶ inform, advise, direct, instruct, prime, apprise of, give the facts, guide, prepare, (*more informal*) fill in, (*more informal*) put in the picture

briefly ADVERB
He paused briefly.
▶ for a moment, for a few moments, momentarily, temporarily

briefs PLURAL NOUN
He stood in the doorway in nothing but briefs.
▶ underpants, pants, knickers, panties, shorts, trunks

brigade NOUN
a brigade of infantry
▶ unit, contingent, division

brigand NOUN
The travellers were robbed by brigands.
▶ bandit, robber, thief, outlaw, desperado, gangster, gunman, marauder, highwayman, footpad, pirate, hijacker

bright ADJECTIVE
1 *bright colours   bright sunshine*
▶ shining, luminous, brilliant, vivid, radiant, dazzling, glaring, blazing, sparkling, twinkling
OPPOSITES ARE dark, dull
2 *a bright morning*
▶ sunny, fine, fair, clear, cloudless
OPPOSITES ARE dull, cloudy
3 *a bright manner*
▶ cheerful, jaunty, lively, breezy, animated
AN OPPOSITE IS subdued
4 *a bright student*
▶ clever, intelligent, gifted, sharp, quick, quick-witted, smart, brilliant
OPPOSITES ARE dull, stupid, unintelligent

brighten VERB
The weather brightened
▶ become sunny, become bright, clear up, lighten
AN OPPOSITE IS darken
brighten up *Some pictures will brighten the place up.*
▶ cheer up, smarten up, embellish, enhance, enliven, gladden, illuminate, light up, revitalize
AN OPPOSITE IS darken

brilliant ADJECTIVE
1 *brilliant light*
▶ blazing, bright, dazzling, glaring, gleaming, glittering, glorious, resplendent, scintillating, shining, showy, sparkling, splendid, vivid
AN OPPOSITE IS dull

2 *a brilliant student*
▶ clever, intelligent, outstanding, gifted, sharp, quick, quick-witted, smart, bright
OPPOSITES ARE dull, stupid
3 (*informal*) *a brilliant game*
▶ excellent, marvellous, wonderful, superb, exceptional

brim NOUN
full to the brim
▶ top, rim, edge, limit, lip, brink, circumference, margin, perimeter, periphery

bring VERB
1 *She brought me a mug of tea.*
▶ fetch, carry, convey, bear, deliver, take, transfer, transport
2 *Bring your friends into the garden.*
▶ escort, accompany, conduct, guide, lead, usher
3 *Their success brought a great deal of attention.*
▶ draw, attract, produce, cause, engender, generate
bring about *The new manager brought about many changes.*
▶ cause, effect, achieve, create, engineer, manage
bring in
1 *The appeal brought in a huge response.*
▶ result in, lead to, realize, yield, earn, gross
2 *The company is bringing in a new product.*
▶ introduce, initiate, start, make available
bring off *It was a difficult play to bring off.*
▶ achieve, accomplish, be successful in, do successfully, succeed in
bring on *The shock brought on his asthma.*
▶ cause, give rise to, induce, trigger, lead to, precipitate, provoke, aggravate
bring out
1 *The publishers are to bring out a new edition.*
▶ publish, release, issue, produce, print
2 *The description brings out the comical side of the story.*
▶ emphasize, accentuate, underline, highlight, stress, dwell on, feature, make obvious, play up, point up, show clearly, spotlight
bring up
1 *As a young child she was brought up in Poland.*
▶ raise, rear, educate, care for, look after, nurture, teach, train
2 *The baby brought up his dinner.*
▶ vomit, sick up
3 *There's a small matter I want to bring up.*
▶ mention, raise, broach, touch on, refer to

brink NOUN
1 *The children stood at the brink staring into the water.*
▶ edge, verge, margin, bank, brim, border
2 *We were on the brink of a major discovery.*
▶ verge, point, threshold, start

brisk ADJECTIVE
1 *walking at a brisk pace*
▶ quick, rapid, fast, lively, energetic, speedy, swift, hurried
OPPOSITES ARE leisurely, slow

2 *brisk exercise*
▶ vigorous, energetic, bracing, refreshing

3 *The hotel was doing a brisk trade.*
▶ busy, bustling, lively, hectic, good
OPPOSITES ARE quiet, slack

bristle NOUN
John rubbed a hand over his bristles.
▶ stubble, facial hair, whisker, prickle, spine, wire

bristle VERB
1 *She bristled at his remarks.*
▶ become angry, get angry, be infuriated, be irritated

2 *The roofs bristled with antennae.*
▶ abound (in), teem, be crowded, be packed

bristly ADJECTIVE
His skin felt bristly.
▶ hairy, whiskery, scratchy, prickly, rough, coarse

brittle ADJECTIVE
brittle bones
▶ breakable, fragile, frail, delicate, splintery, crackly
OPPOSITES ARE flexible, resilient

broach VERB
I was reluctant to broach the subject again.
▶ introduce, mention, bring up, touch on, refer to

broad ADJECTIVE
1 *They were walking along a broad path.*
▶ wide, large, big, ample, capacious, expansive, extensive, great, large, open, roomy, spacious, sweeping, vast
OPPOSITES ARE narrow, small

2 *a broad sweep of countryside*
▶ wide, spacious, ample, extensive, vast, rolling

3 *the broad outline of the story*
▶ general, rough, vague, loose, imprecise, indefinite, inexact, undetailed
OPPOSITES ARE detailed, precise

4 *She had broad tastes in music*
▶ comprehensive, eclectic, catholic, wide-ranging, all-embracing, encyclopaedic, universal
OPPOSITES ARE restricted, limited, narrow

5 *broad humour*
▶ coarse, earthy, racy, ribald, indecent, vulgar, indelicate, bawdy, suggestive, improper, impure, (*more informal*) blue

6 *a broad local accent*
▶ pronounced, strong, marked, noticeable

7 *You'll need to drop a broad hint.*
▶ clear, direct, obvious, unmistakable

broadcast NOUN
a radio broadcast
▶ transmission, relay, programme

broadcast VERB
1 *The concert was broadcast worldwide on televsion.*
▶ transmit, relay, send out, televise, show, (*more informal*) screen, (*more informal*) air

2 *This is sensitive information and should not be broadcast too widely.*
▶ report, publicize, circulate, spread, make known, make public, proclaim, advertise, announce, (*more formal*) disseminate, (*more formal*) promulgate

broadcaster NOUN
a well-known writer and broadcaster
▶ presenter, announcer, linkman, newsreader, commentator, compère, anchorman, anchorwoman, disc jockey, DJ, entertainer

broaden VERB
You need to broaden your interests
▶ expand, extend, develop, increase, open up, spread, widen, branch out (into something), diversify, enlarge, build up

broad-minded ADJECTIVE
Their language would offend the most broad-minded of people.
▶ liberal, tolerant, enlightened, permissive, forbearing, open-minded, unbiased, receptive
OPPOSITES ARE narrow-minded, intolerant

broadside NOUN
The artillery fired broadsides.
▶ salvo, volley, barrage, bombardment

brochure NOUN
a travel brochure
▶ leaflet, prospectus, pamphlet, booklet, circular, folder, handbill, broadsheet, catalogue

broke ADJECTIVE
(*informal*) *He reached home completely broke.*
▶ impoverished, penniless, poor, insolvent, destitute, ruined

broken ADJECTIVE
1 *A waitress was picking up the broken plates.*
▶ smashed, shattered, cracked, split
OPPOSITES ARE whole, unbroken

2 *The television is broken.*
▶ faulty, defective, out of order, not working, (*more formal*) inoperative
OPPOSITES ARE working, fixed

3 *The failure of the company left him a broken man.*
▶ defeated, crushed, beaten, overwhelmed

4 *a broken marriage*
▶ failed, ended

5 *a few hours of broken sleep*
▶ interrupted, disturbed, disrupted, fitful, troubled
OPPOSITES ARE continuous, uninterrupted

broken-down ADJECTIVE
a few broken-down cars by the side of the road
▶ dilapidated, worn-out, out-of-order, ruined

broken-hearted ADJECTIVE
The little girl was broken-hearted at the loss of her doll.
▶ heartbroken, inconsolable, devastated, grief-stricken, desolate, despairing
AN OPPOSITE IS happy

broker NOUN
a city broker
▶ dealer, agent, intermediary

brooch NOUN
Louise was wearing a little opal brooch.
► clasp, breastpin, clip, badge

brood NOUN
1 *a mother hen and her brood*
► young, offspring, clutch, family
2 *Felicity was the eldest of a large brood.*
► family, household

brood VERB
1 *A hen was brooding her eggs.*
► hatch, incubate, sit on
2 *It's a mistake to brood over past mistakes.*
► dwell (on), agonize, muse (on), ponder, reflect (on), think (about), sulk (about), fret, meditate (on), mope, mull over

brook NOUN
a babbling brook
► stream, beck, burn, channel, rivulet, (*poetic*) rill

brother NOUN
Freddie was Margaret's brother.
► sibling
RELATED ADJECTIVE fraternal

brow NOUN
the brow of the hill
► peak, crest, summit, crown, top
OPPOSITES ARE foot, bottom

browbeat VERB
They had tried to browbeat him into changing his story.
► bully, intimidate, badger, coerce, pressurize, harass

brown ADJECTIVE
1 *brown hair*
► brunette, auburn, bronze, chestnut, chocolate-coloured
2 *a brown coat*
► fawn, beige, buff, tan, tawny, biscuit, terracotta, dun, khaki, ochre, russet, sepia, umber

browned off ADJECTIVE
(*informal*) *He was feeling tired and browned off.*
► fed up, dispirited, depressed, peeved, disgruntled, disheartened

browse VERB
1 *I was browsing in a book*
► flick through, leaf through, look through, scan, skim, thumb through, dip in, (*more formal*) peruse
2 *Cattle browsed in a field.*
► graze, pasture, crop grass, feed, eat

bruise NOUN
He had a bruise on his leg.
► swelling, bump, contusion, lesion, discoloration

bruise VERB
The blow bruised her arm.
► mark, discolour, injure, hurt

brunt NOUN
His wife bore the brunt of his temper tantrums.
► force, impact, impetus, thrust, effect, shock, burden

brush NOUN
1 *Use a brush to sweep up.*
► broom, besom
2 *a brush with the law*
► clash, encounter, altercation, quarrel, wrangle

brush VERB
Wait while I brush my hair.
► tidy, comb, groom
brush aside *The minister tried to brush aside the objections.*
► discount, dismiss, disregard, ignore, shrug off, put aside, (*more informal*) pooh-pooh
brush off *He was trying to be friendly but they brushed him off.*
► spurn, rebuff, snub, cold-shoulder, reject, disregard, ignore, slight
brush up *Are you going to brush up your French?*
► revise, improve, read up, go over, refresh your memory of, relearn, study, (*more informal*) swot up

brush-off NOUN
(*informal*) *Be careful you don't get another brush-off.*
► rejection, snub, rebuff, dismissal

brusque ADJECTIVE
The reply seemed a shade brusque.
► curt, abrupt, blunt, terse, discourteous, tactless
OPPOSITES ARE polite, courteous

brutal ADJECTIVE
a brutal attack
► savage, cruel, vicious, fierce, ferocious, barbaric, callous, heartless, cold-blooded, pitiless, ruthless, merciless, vile, sadistic, brutish
OPPOSITES ARE gentle, humane

brutality NOUN
The crime was committed with staggering brutality.
► savagery, cruelty, viciousness, ferocity, barbarity, callousness, heartlessness, cold-bloodedness, ruthlessness
AN OPPOSITE IS gentleness

brutalize VERB
Life in the trenches brutalized many soldiers.
► dehumanize, desensitize, harden, toughen, degrade

brute NOUN
He began behaving like the brute he was.
► beast, animal, monster, fiend, demon

brute ADJECTIVE
brute force
► physical, crude, rough, unthinking

bubble NOUN
1 *bubbles rising to the ceiling*
► globule, ball, blister, hollow, (*more formal*) vesicle
2 *bubbles soap bubbles*
► foam, froth, lather, suds
3 *bubbles bubbles of champagne*
► effervescence, fizz

bubble VERB
The water was bubbling.
► boil, gurgle, seethe, sparkle

a
b
c
d
e
f
g
h
i
j
k
l
m
n
o
p
q
r
s
t
u
v
w
x
y
z

bubbly ADJECTIVE

1 *a bubbly drink*
▶ fizzy, carbonated, foaming, seething, sparkling, effervescent
OPPOSITES ARE still, flat
2 *a bubbly personality*
▶ vivacious, animated, spirited, vibrant, lively
AN OPPOSITE IS dull

buccaneer NOUN

a crew of daring buccaneers
▶ adventurer, brigand, corsair, bandit, marauder, pirate, privateer, robber

buck VERB

The horse began to buck.
▶ jump, leap, prance, bound, jerk, spring
buck up (*informal*)
1 *We'll have to buck up if we're going to catch the train.*
▶ hurry, speed up, get a move on
2 *She did her best to buck me up but I still felt miserable.*
▶ cheer up, encourage, rally, hearten, enliven, inspire, make cheerful, please, revitalize, revive

bucket NOUN

a bucket of water
▶ pail, can, tub, pitcher

buckle NOUN

a belt buckle
▶ clasp, clip, fastener, fastening, hasp, catch

buckle VERB

1 *He quickly buckled his coat.*
▶ fasten, do up, clasp, hook up, secure, clip
2 *The bridge began to buckle under the weight.*
▶ bend, warp, twist, crumple, distort, fold, bulge, collapse, contort, curve, dent

bud NOUN

the buds of flowers
▶ shoot, sprout, floret

bud VERB

The trees are budding early.
▶ shoot, sprout, form buds

budding ADJECTIVE

a budding young singer
▶ promising, aspiring, developing, (*informal*) hopeful, inexperienced, intending, new, potential, (*more informal*) would-be
OPPOSITES ARE established, experienced

budge VERB

1 *The window was stuck and wouldn't budge.*
▶ give way, move, shift, change position
2 *The solution is a compromise but no one will budge.*
▶ change your mind, give way, yield, compromise, influence, move, persuade, propel, push, remove, shift, sway
3 *They are much too stubborn and won't be budged.*
▶ persuade, influence, sway, induce, cajole

budget NOUN

The hospital had not spent all its budget for the year.
▶ allowance, allocation of funds, quota, estimate, resources, funds, means

budget VERB

We will need to budget five thousand pounds for computers next year.
▶ allocate, assign, earmark, put aside, designate

buffer NOUN

a buffer against inflation
▶ cushion, safeguard, shield, protection

buffet NOUN

We went to the buffet for a snack.
▶ cafeteria, counter, snack bar, café, refreshment room, bar

buffet VERB

The sea front was buffeted by the wind and spray.
▶ batter, pound, lash, dash

buffoon NOUN

She thought her cousin was a complete buffoon.
▶ fool, idiot, clown, ass, dolt, blockhead, (*more informal*) prat, (*more informal*) halfwit, (*more informal*) chump

bug NOUN

1 *The plants were covered in tiny bugs.*
▶ insect, pest, mite
2 *a stomach bug*
▶ illness, disease, upset, ailment, complaint, disorder
3 *The computer software developed a bug.*
▶ fault, error, defect, flaw, (*more informal*) gremlin

bug VERB

1 *The telephone had been bugged.*
▶ intercept, tap, interfere with, listen in to
2 (*informal*) *Her constant whining was bugging me.*
▶ annoy, irritate, anger, infuriate, needle, rile

build VERB

There are plans to build a new apartment block on the site.
▶ construct, erect, raise, put up, set up, assemble, fabricate
OPPOSITES ARE demolish, destroy
build up
1 *He has built up a thriving business.*
▶ establish, develop, create, enlarge, expand, raise, accumulate, amass, assemble, begin, bring together, collect
2 *Traffic is building up in the city centre.*
▶ increase, intensify, escalate, grow, mount up, strengthen, rise, augment

build NOUN

a man of slim build
▶ physique, form, frame, body

building NOUN

a large grim building with few windows
▶ structure, construction, premises, erection, establishment, place, piece of architecture, (*more formal*) edifice, (*more informal*) pile

build-up NOUN

a steady military build-up on the border
▶ increase, growth, escalation, expansion, development, accumulation, proliferation

bulge NOUN
There was a strange bulge at the bottom of the bed.
▶ bump, swelling, protuberance, hump, lump, projection, (*more formal*) protrusion

bulge VERB
The sheets bulged in the breeze.
▶ swell, billow, puff out, balloon out, dilate, distend, expand, belly, enlarge, project, protrude, stick out

bulk NOUN
1 *The sheer bulk of the containers was staggering.*
▶ size, volume, dimensions, proportions, extent, magnitude, mass, substance, amplitude, body, immensity, largeness
2 *We did the bulk of the work ourselves*
▶ most, best part, most part, greater part, preponderance, majority

bulky ADJECTIVE
a bulky parcel
▶ sizeable, large, substantial, cumbersome, unwieldy, massive, immense, enormous
OPPOSITES ARE small, compact, manageable

bulletin NOUN
1 *a television news bulletin*
▶ report, statement, announcement, communication, communiqué, dispatch, message, newsflash, notice, proclamation
2 *The club's monthly bulletin*
▶ newsletter, news-sheet, gazette

bully NOUN
the well-known school bullies
▶ tormentor, persecutor, oppressor, thug, tough, (*more informal*) heavy

bully VERB
Some of the other children used to bully him.
▶ persecute, torment, intimidate, oppress, tyrannnize, (*more informal*) push around

bump NOUN
1 *The man fell on the floor with a bump.*
▶ thud, thump, smack, crash, bang, blow, collision, hit, knock, smash
2 *When he got up he had a bump on the head.*
▶ swelling, lump, bulge, (*technical*) contusion, protuberance

bump VERB
1 *Chris bumped his head while snorkelling.*
▶ hit, strike, knock, bang
2 **bump into** *A lorry had bumped into a parked car.*
▶ collide with, run into, crash into, bang into, smash into, knock into, knock, hit, ram, slam, strike
3 *We were bumping up and down on the rough road.*
▶ bounce, shake, jerk, jolt
bump off (*informal*) *He became president by bumping off all his rivals .*
▶ kill, murder, assassinate, eliminate

bumper ADJECTIVE
a bumper harvest
▶ abundant, plentiful, bountiful, copious, ample

bumpy ADJECTIVE
1 *a bumpy ride*
▶ bouncy, rough, jerky, jolting, lurching
2 *a bumpy surface*
▶ uneven, rough, irregular, pitted, knobbly, lumpy
OPPOSITES ARE even, smooth

bunch NOUN
1 *a bunch of carrots   a bunch of keys*
▶ bundle, cluster, clump, collection, heap, batch, set, lot, number, quantity
2 *a bunch of flowers*
▶ bouquet, posy, spray, garland
3 *a friendly bunch of people*
▶ group, set, circle, band, (*more informal*) gang, (*more informal*) crowd

bunch VERB
The friends had bunched together in a corner.
▶ gather, assemble, cluster, huddle, collect, congregate, crowd, flock, group, herd
AN OPPOSITE IS scatter

bundle NOUN
a bundle of papers
▶ bunch, sheaf, carton, collection, pack, package, packet, parcel, bag, bale

bundle VERB
1 *He quickly bundled up the remaining papers.*
▶ tie, bind, wrap, bale, truss, fasten, pack, roll
2 *The kidnappers bundled their victim into the back of the car.*
▶ hustle, jostle, shove, sweep

bung VERB
You'd better bung that in the bin.
▶ throw, chuck, toss, stick, put

bungle VERB
Two prisoners bungled an escape bid after running either side of a lamp post while handcuffed.
▶ mishandle, mismanage, botch, ruin, spoil, fluff, muff, mess up, make a mess of, (*more informal*) make a hash of, (*much more informal*) cock up, (*much more informal*) screw up
OPPOSITES ARE succeed in, bring off

bunk NOUN
do a bunk (*informal*) *He tried to do a bunk while the guard was preoccupied.*
▶ escape, make off, run off, skive off, play truant

buoy VERB
buoy up *Her spirits were buoyed up by knowing her father was in the audience*
▶ cheer, brighten, lift, raise, support, invigorate, hearten, comfort

buoyant ADJECTIVE
1 *a buoyant material*
▶ floating, light
2 *in a buoyant mood*
▶ cheerful, happy, cheery, carefree, light-hearted, lively, optimistic, animated, sunny
OPPOSITES ARE depressed, pessimistic

burden NOUN
1 *donkeys carrying heavy burdens*
▶ load, weight, encumbrance, pack, bundle, cargo
2 *a large financial burden*
▶ responsibility, obligation, liability, duty, onus,
charge, affliction, anxiety, worry, care, handicap,
problem, millstone

burden VERB
For years she was burdened by family worries.
▶ afflict, oppress, bother, beset, torment, distress,
strain, tax, trouble, worry, encumber, hamper,
handicap, load (with), (*informal*) lumber (with),
(*informal*) saddle (with)

bureau NOUN
an information bureau
▶ agency, office, service, department, organization,
counter

bureaucracy NOUN
hampered by regulations and bureaucracy
▶ administration, government, officialdom,
paperwork, (*more informal*) red tape

burglar NOUN
Burglars stole jewellery worth thousands of pounds.
▶ housebreaker, robber, thief, intruder

burglary NOUN
Barry had been convicted of burglary.
▶ housebreaking, breaking and entering, robbery,
theft, forcible entry, larceny, pilfering, stealing,
thieving, break-in

burgle VERB
The house had been burgled several times before.
▶ break into, steal from, thieve from

burial NOUN
a burial service
▶ burying, entombment, funeral, interment,
obsequies

burly ADJECTIVE
a burly figure
▶ hefty, beefy, sturdy, well-built, strapping, brawny,
hulking, muscular, powerful, stocky, stout, athletic,
big, heavy
OPPOSITES ARE slight, thin

burn VERB
1 *The bonfire burned all day*
▶ be alight, be on fire, be ablaze, flare, blaze, flicker,
glow, smoke, smoulder
2 *An incinerator will burn anything.*
▶ ignite, kindle, incinerate, cremate, consume
3 *The heat began to burn our skin.*
▶ scald, scorch, blister, brand, toast, char, sear,
singe, sting

burning ADJECTIVE
1 *a burning building*
▶ blazing, flaming, glowing, ablaze, afire, alight,
incandescent, lit up, on fire, raging, smouldering
2 *a burning pain*
▶ scalding, searing, acute, stinging, biting

3 *a burning desire*
▶ intense, extreme, fervent, passionate, eager,
ardent, profound, consuming
4 *a burning question*
▶ urgent, crucial, vital, essential, pressing,
important, pertinent, relevant

burrow VERB
A rabbit could burrow under the fence.
▶ tunnel, excavate, dig, mine, delve

burst VERB
1 *The impact caused a tyre to burst.*
▶ rupture, split open
2 *Water burst through the hole.*
▶ gush, surge, stream, pour, spurt, cascade
3 *A man suddenly burst into the room*
▶ rush, run, charge, plunge, shove your way

bury VERB
1 *The dog buried its bone in the ground.*
▶ hide, conceal, cover, sink, embed
AN OPPOSITE IS uncover
2 *The dead are buried in the local cemetery.*
▶ inter, lay to rest, entomb
3 *She buried herself in her work.*
▶ absorb, engross, engage, occupy, immerse

bush NOUN
The ball was caught up in a bush.
▶ shrub, hedge, thicket, undergrowth

bushy ADJECTIVE
a bushy beard
▶ thick, shaggy, fuzzy, rough, bristling, bristly,
dense, hairy, tangled, thick-growing, untidy

business NOUN
1 *It proved to be quite a tricky business.*
▶ matter, affair, issue, problem, point, question,
concern
2 *What sort of business do you want to go into?*
▶ work, job, occupation, employment, career, line
of work, profession, pursuit, trade, vocation, calling,
craft, industry
3 *The new supermarket has taken a lot of business from
the local shops.*
▶ trade, trading, buying and selling, selling,
merchandising, transactions, commerce, dealings,
industry, marketing
4 *He wants to run his own business.*
▶ firm, company, establishment, enterprise,
organization, concern, venture, corporation,
practice, (*more informal*) outfit, (*more informal*) set-up

businesslike ADJECTIVE
The office was run in a businesslike way.
▶ efficient, professional, competent, methodical,
well organized, systematic, practical, pragmatic,
orderly

businessman, businesswoman NOUN
a shrewd businesswoman
▶ entrepreneur, executive, industrialist, dealer,
financier, manager, merchant, trader, tycoon,
magnate

B

bust NOUN
a woman's bust
▶ bosom, chest, breast, breasts

bust VERB
Be careful with that or you'll bust it.
▶ break, snap, crack, split, burst

bustle NOUN
The air terminal was full of bustle
▶ activity, hustle, commotion, stir, excitement, flurry, fuss, haste, hurly-burly, hurry, movement, restlessness, scurry, agitation

bustle VERB
People were bustling about looking for their friends.
▶ rush, dash, scurry, scamper, scuttle, hurry, hustle, dart, fuss, move busily, scramble, whirl, hasten, *(more informal)* tear

busy ADJECTIVE
1 *Are you very busy at work?*
▶ active, occupied, hard-pressed, *(more informal)* rushed off your feet
AN OPPOSITE IS idle
2 *She's a very busy person.*
▶ active, energetic, diligent, industrious
OPPOSITES ARE lazy, idle
3 *The manager is busy at the moment but can see you this afternoon.*
▶ engaged, unavailable, occupied, *(more informal)* tied up
AN OPPOSITE IS free
4 *Her mother leads a busy life.*
▶ active, hectic, lively, strenuous, demanding, exacting
5 *The committee members are busy organizing the next conference.*
▶ occupied (with), working (at), engaged (in), hard at work (on), wrapped up (in)
6 *The shopping malls were busy all day.*
▶ crowded, hectic, lively, teeming, bustling, swarming, thronging, frantic, full of people
AN OPPOSITE IS quiet

busybody NOUN
Pry was an inquisitive busybody.
▶ meddler, interferer, gossip, scandalmonger, snooper, eavesdropper, *(more informal)* nosy parker, *(more informal)* gawper

butch ADJECTIVE
(informal) a butch builder
▶ masculine, manly, virile
OPPOSITES ARE effeminate, feminine

butt NOUN
1 *the butt of a rifle*
▶ stock, shaft, shank, handle, hilt, haft
2 *a water butt*
▶ barrel, cask, keg, vat
3 *a cigarette butt*
▶ stub, end, stump, remnant, *(more informal)* fag end
4 *the butt of a joke*
▶ target, victim, object, subject, mark

butt VERB
He butted her playfully with his head.
▶ hit, ram, bump, knock, jab, prod, poke
butt in *Nick didn't want to butt in, so he waited patiently.*
▶ interrupt, break in, cut in, *(more informal)* chip in

buttocks NOUN
He knelt with his heels against his buttocks.
▶ bottom, behind, backside, rear, rump, seat, haunches, hindquarters, *(more informal)* arse, *(more informal)* bum, *(usually humorous)* posterior

buttonhole VERB
I'll try to buttonhole him after the meeting.
▶ catch, accost, intercept, waylay, *(more informal)* get hold of, *(more informal)* nab

buttress NOUN
a stone buttress
▶ support, brace, stay, prop, pier, reinforcement

buy VERB
1 *I will buy the drinks.*
▶ get, pay for, obtain, acquire, *(more formal)* purchase
AN OPPOSITE IS sell
2 *a man who could not be bought*
▶ bribe, buy off, suborn, corrupt

buy NOUN
A well looked-after used car can be a good buy.
▶ acquisition, deal, bargain, *(more formal)* purchase

buyer NOUN
Typical buyers of this product are younger women.
▶ customer, shopper, consumer, *(more informal)* purchaser
AN OPPOSITE IS seller

bypass NOUN
proposals for a new bypass round the town
▶ ring road, relief road

bypass VERB
1 *To speed things up we can bypass the usual checking process.*
▶ ignore, omit, avoid, circumvent, sidestep, neglect, find a way round, get out of, go round, dodge, evade
2 *The road bypasses the viaduct.*
▶ go round, go past, pass round, avoid, make a detour round

by-product NOUN
Temporary deafness was a by-product of her illness.
▶ side effect, consequence, repercussion, result, complement, corollary, *(more informal)* knock-on effect, *(more informal)* spin-off (from), *(more informal)* fallout (from)

bystander NOUN
The man had assaulted a bystander and smashed windows.
▶ onlooker, passer-by, observer, spectator, watcher, witness, eyewitness

Cc

cab NOUN
the driver's cab
▶ compartment, cabin

cabaret NOUN
a cabaret at a nightclub in town
▶ floor show, revue, entertainment

cabin NOUN
1 *a cabin by the river*
▶ hut, lodge, chalet, shack, shanty, shed, shelter
2 *a cabin on the lower deck*
▶ berth, compartment, sleeping quarters
3 *the driver's cabin*
▶ cab, compartment

cabinet NOUN
a glass-fronted cabinet for china
▶ cupboard, dresser, closet, chest

cable NOUN
1 *The ship was moored by means of thick cables.*
▶ rope, cord, hawser, line, chain, mooring
2 *Watch out for the power cable.*
▶ wire, lead, line

cache NOUN
a cache of weapons   a cache of gold
▶ hoard, store, stock, stockpile, depot, dump, repository, storehouse, supply

cadet NOUN
a naval cadet
▶ recruit, trainee, beginner, learner

cadge VERB
Can we cadge a lift to the station?
▶ beg, scrounge, sponge, hitch

cafe NOUN
We could have a snack at a local cafe.
▶ snack bar, cafeteria, coffee bar, coffee shop, tea shop, buffet, canteen, bistro

cage NOUN
an animal's cage
▶ enclosure, pen, pound, coop, hutch
USAGE A large cage for birds is called an *aviary*.

cagey ADJECTIVE
He was being very cagey about what he had been up to.
▶ secretive, guarded, cautious, tight-lipped, reticent, evasive, wary, chary
OPPOSITES ARE open, frank

cajole VERB
cajole into *Tania had been cajoled into giving the party at her house.*
▶ coax into, talk into, wheedle into, persuade to, beguile into, entice into

cake NOUN
1 *There are cakes for tea today.*
▶ bun, gateau

2 *a cake of soap*
▶ bar, tablet, block, lump, piece, slab

cake VERB
Finn's shoes were caked with mud.
▶ cover, coat, clog, encrust

calamity NOUN
Disobedience will bring calamity on the nation.
▶ disaster, catastrophe, tragedy, misfortune, affliction, blow, cataclysm, tribulation, mishap

calculate VERB
Interest on the loan is calculated monthly.
▶ work out, compute, reckon, assess, count, determine, add up

calculated ADJECTIVE
a calculated risk
▶ deliberate, intentional, planned, premeditated, conscious, considered, purposive

calculating ADJECTIVE
Cohen looked around and nodded his head in a calculating manner.
▶ cunning, crafty, sly, devious, wily, scheming, shrewd

calibre NOUN
People of this calibre are not something you come across every day.
▶ quality, ability, distinction, excellence, capacity, standard, talent, stature, character

call VERB
1 *'Come here!' she called.*
▶ cry, cry out, shout, yell, exclaim
2 *I'll call you this evening.*
▶ phone, telephone, ring, ring up, give someone a call
3 *What did they call him?*
▶ baptize, christen, dub, name
4 *Why did you call your cat Albert?*
▶ name
5 *His mother said she would call him early next morning.*
▶ wake, wake up, waken, awaken, get someone up, arouse, rouse
6 *The headteacher called me to her office.*
▶ summon, invite, order
7 *We'd better call the doctor.*
▶ send for, fetch, summon, ask to come
8 *We need to call a meeting.*
▶ convene, organize, gather
9 *Harriet's mother called the next day.*
▶ visit, pay a visit, (*more informal*) drop in, (*more informal*) drop by

call for
1 *The assignment calls for careful planning.*
▶ require, need, demand, necessitate, make necessary, involve, entail, warrant
2 *Shall we call for you about six o'clock?*
▶ fetch, pick up, come for, collect

call off *The barbecue was called off because of bad weather.*

► cancel, abandon, postpone, adjourn, discontinue, drop, end, halt

USAGE You use *cancel* if you mean calling off for good, and *postpone* if you mean calling off until a later date. You often use *abandon* to refer to things that have been started but cannot be completed.

call on *I might call on my friends this afternoon.*
► visit, go and see, (*more informal*) drop in on, (*more informal*) look up

call NOUN

1 *a call for help*
► cry, exclamation, shout, yell, scream

2 *a call for strike action*
► appeal, plea, summons, demand, request

3 *He decided to pay a call on his old father.*
► visit, stop

4 *There's little call for caviar here.*
► demand, market, need

5 *There's no call for that kind of talk.*
► need, necessity, occasion, reason, justification, excuse

calling NOUN

He thought that the law was the right calling.
► profession, career, line of work, occupation, vocation, business, employment, walk of life, job, trade, work

callous ADJECTIVE

a callous remark
► heartless, hard-hearted, unfeeling, uncaring, indifferent, insensitive, cruel, brutal, ruthless
OPPOSITES ARE kind, considerate

calm ADJECTIVE

1 *a calm sunny day*
► still, tranquil, quiet, peaceful, balmy
OPPOSITES ARE stormy, windy

2 *The sea was calm.*
► smooth, tranquil, still, flat, waveless

3 *He remained calm despite the difficulties.*
► composed, collected, self-possessed, cool, poised, dispassionate, unperturbed, imperturbable, unruffled, unflustered, unbothered, untroubled, unemotional, (*more informal*) unflappable, (*more informal*) laid-back
OPPOSITES ARE anxious, upset, excited

4 *a calm temperament*
► serene, placid, phlegmatic, tranquil, relaxed

calm NOUN

1 *the calm of a summer afternoon*
► tranquillity, calmness, quietness, stillness, peace, quiet, quietude
AN OPPOSITE IS storm

2 *I had to admire her calm.*
► composure, calmness, self-possession, equanimity

calm VERB

He was so upset it was impossible to calm him.
► soothe, placate, quieten, mollify, pacify, settle down, sober down, tranquillize, appease, compose, control, cool down, lull
OPPOSITES ARE agitate, upset

camouflage NOUN

1 *The foliage made good camouflage.*
► disguise, concealment, cover, screen, veil, blind, cloak, front, guise, mask

2 *an animal's camouflage*
► protective colouring

3 *Their friendly manner was only camouflage.*
► facade, front, disguise, mask, pretence

camouflage VERB

The vehicle was camouflaged with branches from the trees.
► disguise, hide, mask, conceal, cover up, obscure, screen

camp NOUN

an army camp
► encampment, camping ground, campsite, base

campaign NOUN

1 *a military campaign*
► operation, offensive, action, engagement, advance, battle, push

2 *a campaign to save the environment*
► crusade, movement, drive, effort, struggle, fight, push

campaign VERB

He began campaigning for the Wildlife Trust.
► crusade, fight, work, agitate

can NOUN

a can of orange juice
► tin, canister, jar

canal NOUN

There is a path by the canal.
► channel, watercourse, waterway

cancel VERB

1 *The family had to cancel their holiday.*
► call off, abandon, drop, end, (*more informal*) axe

2 *They agreed to cancel the debt.*
► revoke, annul, nullify, rescind, erase, expunge, set aside, withdraw

cancel out *One small mistake could cancel out all our hard work.*
► counterbalance, neutralize, wipe out, offset, outweigh, make up for, compensate for

cancer NOUN

1 *The problem was diagnosed as cancer*
► malignant growth, tumour, melanoma, lymphoma
RELATED ADJECTIVE carcinogenic

2 *Violent crime is a cancer in our society.*
► evil, blight, scourge, plague, pestilence, poison

candid ADJECTIVE
a candid reply
▶ frank, honest, open, sincere, straightforward, blunt, truthful, outspoken, forthright, unequivocal
OPPOSITES ARE insincere, guarded, devious

candidate NOUN
1 *a candidate for a job*
▶ applicant, contender, aspirant
2 *a candidate in an exam*
▶ entrant, examinee

candour NOUN
He gave his opinion with complete candour.
▶ frankness, honesty, openness, sincerity, directness, forthrightness, bluntness

canny ADJECTIVE
a canny businessman
▶ shrewd, astute, sharp, acute, perceptive, clever, prudent
USAGE Canny is a generally favourable word. Other words that are less favourable, because they imply a kind of dishonesty, are *cunning*, *crafty*, and *wily*..

canopy NOUN
The caravan has a canopy at the side.
▶ awning, shade, cover, covering

cantankerous ADJECTIVE
The heat had made him especially cantankerous.
▶ bad-tempered, irritable, irascible, grumpy, testy, grouchy, touchy, crotchety, peevish, fractious, cross, (*more informal*) stroppy, (*more informal*) shirty
OPPOSITES ARE good-tempered, good-humoured, affable

canteen NOUN
Let's have a quick lunch in the canteen.
▶ snack bar, cafeteria, cafe, coffee bar, coffee shop, tea shop, buffet, bistro

canvass VERB
They are canvassing for the green party.
▶ campaign, electioneer, seek votes

canyon NOUN
The army moved through a deep canyon.
▶ gorge, ravine, defile

cap VERB
The mountains were capped with snow.
▶ cover , top, crown, blanket

capable ADJECTIVE
a capable young woman
▶ competent, able, accomplished, proficient, efficient, talented, gifted, clever, skilled, intelligent, effective
AN OPPOSITE IS incompetent
be capable of *He's capable of doing any of these tasks.*
▶ have the ability (to do), be competent (to do), be adept (at doing), be equal (to doing)
AN OPPOSITE IS be incapable of

capacity NOUN
1 *The tank's capacity is 30 litres.*
▶ size, volume, magnitude, extent, space

2 *You need the capacity to motivate yourself.*
▶ ability, power, potential, capability, competence, aptitude, faculty, skill, talent
3 *He acted in his capacity as commander-in-chief of the army.*
▶ position, function, role, office

cape NOUN
1 *She was wearing a waterproof cape.*
▶ cloak, mantle, shawl, wrap, stole
2 *The ship rounded the cape at dawn.*
▶ headland, promontory, head, point, foreland

caper VERB
The children capered about the room.
▶ skip, bound, dance, leap, cavort, jump, spring, bounce, gambol, bob, frisk

capital ADJECTIVE
1 *a capital city*
▶ chief, principal, leading, main, first, foremost
2 *in capital letters*
▶ upper-case, large, big, block

capital NOUN
1 *Rome is the capital of Italy.*
▶ chief city, first city, seat of government, centre of government
2 *In three years he had enough capital to start his own business.*
▶ funds, finance, money, cash, assets, savings, means, wherewithal

capitalize VERB
capitalize on *The opposition capitalized on the government's mistakes.*
▶ exploit, take advantage of, profit from, make capital out of

capitulate VERB
The enemy capitulated after a siege of ten months.
▶ surrender, give in, submit, succumb, admit defeat, yield, (*more informal*) throw in the towel
OPPOSITES ARE resist, hold out

capricious ADJECTIVE
the capricious nature of the financial markets
▶ changeable, erratic, unstable, variable, volatile, uncertain, unpredictable, inconstant, unreliable, fickle, wayward
OPPOSITES ARE predictable, steady

capsize VERB
Some of the boats capsized.
▶ overturn, tip over, turn over, turn upside down, flip over, keel over, (*more informal*) turn turtle

capsule NOUN
1 *The medicine is taken in the form of capsules.*
▶ pill, tablet, lozenge
2 *a space capsule*
▶ module, craft, pod

captain NOUN
1 *the captain of the winning team*
▶ leader, chief player, head, boss
2 *the ship's captain*
▶ commander, master, officer in charge, skipper

3 *a captain of industry*
► magnate, mogul, tycoon, mandarin, baron

caption NOUN
The poster needed a caption.
► title, legend, heading, label, description, explanation, headline, (*technical*) superscription

captivate VERB
The beauty of the scene captivates all visitors.
► charm, enchant, delight, entrance, enthral, fascinate, bewitch, beguile, engross, excite, mesmerize
OPPOSITES ARE repel, disgust

captivating ADJECTIVE
a captivating young woman
► charming, enchanting, entrancing, delightful, enthralling, bewitching, beguiling

captive ADJECTIVE
1 *captive animals*
► confined, caged, captured, incarcerated, chained, detained, enslaved, ensnared, fettered, gaoled, imprisoned, jailed, restricted, secure, taken prisoner
2 *The men had been held captive for several weeks.*
► locked up, imprisoned, jailed, detained, under lock and key
AN OPPOSITE IS free

captive NOUN
The captives all wore handcuffs.
► prisoner, convict, detainee, inmate, internee, hostage

captivity NOUN
Years of captivity had ruined his health.
► imprisonment, confinement, internment, incarceration, detention, custody
AN OPPOSITE IS freedom

capture VERB
1 *He was captured boarding a ship for France.*
► catch, arrest, apprehend, seize, take prisoner, take into custody, (*more informal*) nab, (*more informal*) pull in, (*much more informal*) nick
2 *The building was captured by stormtroopers.*
► occupy, take, seize, secure

car NOUN
A lot of the students arrived in cars.
► motor car, automobile, motor, vehicle

carcass NOUN
1 *an animal's carcass*
► cadaver, corpse, body, meat, remains
2 *the rusting carcass of an old car*
► hulk, shell, remains, skeleton, framework, structure

card NOUN
1 *a piece of stiff card*
► cardboard, pasteboard, board
2 *Let's play cards.*
► card game, game of cards

USAGE *Card* is often short for *playing card*, *greetings* (or *birthday* or *Christmas*) *card*, and *credit card*.
on the cards (*informal*) *A marriage was always on the cards.*
► possible, a possibility, likely, a likelihood, probable, a probability, in the offing
AN OPPOSITE IS out of the question

cardboard NOUN
a cardboard cutout
► card, pasteboard

care NOUN
1 *We need to proceed with care.*
► caution, carefulness, vigilance, watchfulness, awareness, prudence, circumspection, concentration, attention, concern, diligence, heed
AN OPPOSITE IS carelessness
2 *The job needs to be done with great care.*
► discretion, thought, attention, thoroughness, meticulousness, concentration
3 *You need to escape from all your cares.*
► worry, anxiety, trouble, concern, burden, problem, difficulty, hardship, responsibility, sorrow, stress, tribulation, vexation, woe
AN OPPOSITE IS joy
4 *She left the baby in the care of a minder.*
► charge, safe keeping, keeping, custody, control, supervision, protection

care VERB
1 **care about** *She obviously cares about her staff.*
► interest yourself in, concern yourself about, mind about, bother about, worry about, be troubled by
2 **care for** *The hospice cares for sick children.*
► look after, take care of, tend, attend to, provide for, nurse, supervise, watch over, (*more informal*) keep an eye on
3 **care for** *He cares for his grandchildren.*
► love, be fond of, adore, cherish, hold dear, dote on, think the world of
4 **care for** *I don't really care for those biscuits.*
► like, fancy, feel like, be keen on, enjoy, want

career NOUN
a career in teaching
► profession, occupation, job, calling, position

career VERB
The shopping trolley careered down the slope.
► rush, hurtle, shoot, speed, dash, zoom

carefree ADJECTIVE
1 *a carefree young girl*
► unworried, untroubled, cheerful, cheery, light-hearted, easy-going, casual, relaxed, (*more informal*) laid-back
OPPOSITES ARE anxious, tense
2 *a carefree time*
► relaxing, restful, trouble-free, untroubled, peaceful, quiet
OPPOSITES ARE hectic, nerve-wracking

careful ADJECTIVE

1 *Be careful walking through the park at night.*
▶ alert, vigilant, heedful, attentive, watchful
AN OPPOSITE IS careless

2 *You must be careful with your spending.*
▶ prudent, cautious, circumspect, economical, thrifty, canny
OPPOSITES ARE careless, extravagant, reckless

3 *Such a long journey needs careful planning*
▶ detailed, thorough, meticulous, conscientious, scrupulous

4 *She's a very careful driver.*
▶ attentive, diligent, conscientious
OPPOSITES ARE careless, inattentive

careless ADJECTIVE

1 *a careless driver careless remarks*
▶ inattentive, thoughtless, inconsiderate, negligent, absent-minded, heedless, irresponsible, reckless
OPPOSITES ARE careful, attentive

2 *There is no excuse for careless work.*
▶ slipshod, shoddy, slapdash, slovenly, inaccurate, scrappy, incorrect
OPPOSITES ARE careful, accurate

3 *She has always been rather careless about money.*
▶ extravagant, reckless
OPPOSITES ARE careful, prudent

carelessness NOUN

The accident was caused by carelessness.
▶ inattention, inattentiveness, absent-mindedness, negligence, recklessness, irresponsibility, slovenliness, thoughtlessness, untidiness, haste, (*more informal*) sloppiness
OPPOSITES ARE care, carefulness

caress NOUN

She longed for his gentle caress.
▶ embrace, touch, stroke, cuddle, hug, kiss, pat

caress VERB

He caressed her lovingly.
▶ stroke, embrace, hug, cuddle, touch, fondle, kiss, pet, rub against, smooth

caretaker NOUN

the caretaker at the village hall
▶ janitor, warden, custodian, attendant, keeper, porter, custodian, superintendent, watchman

careworn ADJECTIVE

a face that was old and careworn
▶ haggard, drawn, weary , anxious, worried, strained, harassed

cargo NOUN

a ship's cargo
▶ freight, load, haul, payload, consignment, merchandise, shipment, goods

caricature NOUN

He drew a clever caricature of the President.
▶ cartoon, parody, satire, lampoon, travesty, (*more informal*) send-up, (*more informal*) take-off

caricature VERB

She caricatured the movements of a ballerina.
▶ parody, mimic, imitate, lampoon, mock, ridicule, satirize, burlesque, make fun of, exaggerate, (*more informal*) send up, (*more informal*) take off

caring ADJECTIVE

a caring employer
▶ kind, kind-hearted, considerate, thoughtful, concerned

carnage NOUN

the carnage of the battlefield
▶ slaughter, massacre, bloodshed, bloodbath, butchery

carnival NOUN

the town's annual carnival
▶ festival, gala, jamboree, fiesta, fete, fair, celebration, revelry

carp VERB

Journalists always find something to carp about.
▶ complain, grumble, grouse

carriage NOUN

a railway carriage
▶ coach, wagon

carry VERB

1 *We will have to carry our own luggage.*
▶ convey, take, transfer, bring, fetch, haul, lift, manhandle, move, remove, shoulder, (*more informal*) lug

2 *The channel ships carry passengers and freight.*
▶ transport, convey, handle, ferry, ship

3 *Telegraph wires carry signals.*
▶ communicate, relay, transmit

4 *The bridge would not bear the weight of a large vehicle.*
▶ support, bear, hold up

5 *The job carries many responsibilities.*
▶ demand, entail, involve, require, lead to, result in

carry on

1 *We carried on for as long as we could.*
▶ persevere, persist, continue, go on, keep on, last, remain, stay, (*informal*) stick it out

2 *She has been carrying on her own business for several years.*
▶ run, engage in, maintain, manage, operate, administer

3 (*informal*) *Tell them to stop carrying on like that!*
▶ misbehave, behave badly, cause trouble

carry out *They were just carrying out orders.*
▶ obey, follow, discharge, implement, execute, finish, perform, complete

cart NOUN

The fruit was taken to the barns in carts.
▶ barrow, wheelbarrow, handcart, trolley, truck

cart VERB

(*informal*) *The books were too bulky to cart around.*
▶ carry, move, take, haul, (*informal*) lug

carton NOUN
a carton of ice cream
► box, packet, pack, case, container

cartoon NOUN
1 *The story is in the form of a cartoon.*
► comic strip, drawing, caricature, sketch
2 *a film cartoon*
► animation
3 *a political cartoon*
► caricature, parody, lampoon

cartridge NOUN
1 *a film cartridge   a tape cartridge*
► cassette, canister, capsule, cylinder, tube, case
2 *a cartridge for a rifle*
► magazine, round, shell

carve VERB
1 *It was time to carve the meat.*
► cut, slice, chop
2 *a tool for carving wood*
► chisel, hew, sculpt, fashion, form, shape

carving NOUN
ancient rock carvings
► sculpture, figure, statue, effigy

cascade NOUN
cascades of water down the rock face
► torrent, shower, fall, waterfall, cataract

case NOUN
1 *She hurriedly threw a few clothes into a case.*
► suitcase, bag, travel bag, trunk
2 *The books were still in their packing cases.*
► box, chest, canister, carton, crate, container
3 *The videotape was spilling out of its case.*
► shell, cartridge, cassette, container, capsule, cover
4 *The china was kept in a handsome display case.*
► cabinet, cupboard, showcase, sideboard
5 *a classic case of misunderstanding*
► instance, example, occurrence, occasion, manifestation, illustration
6 *If that's the case we'll have to think of an another way.*
► situation, position, state of affairs, event, circumstances
7 *Police from several forces are involved in the case.*
► investigation, inquiry
8 *The lawyers agreed it was a difficult case.*
► lawsuit, action, legal action, suit, trial

cash NOUN
a purse full of cash
► money, notes, banknotes, coins, change, ready money

cash VERB
I need to cash a cheque.
► exchange, change, get money for, get cash for
cash in on *I don't like to cash in on your bad luck.*
► take advantage of, profit by, exploit

cashier NOUN
Take your payment to one of the cashiers.
► teller, clerk, checkout, banker, treasurer

casing NOUN
The hard disk has its own protective casing.
► case, shell, cover, sheath, housing, sleeve

cask NOUN
a cask of wine
► barrel, keg, butt, vat, tun, hogshead, firkin

casket NOUN
a casket of jewels
► case, box, chest

cast VERB
1 *He cast a coin into the fountain.*
► throw, toss, fling, flip, sling, (more informal) chuck, hurl
2 *The statue is cast entirely in bronze.*
► mould, form, shape, model, sculpture
cast down *They all felt cast down at the news.*
► dejected, depressed, saddened, upset, disheartened

castle NOUN
The castle was heavily fortified.
► fort, fortress, citadel, palace, stronghold, tower, château

casual ADJECTIVE
1 *a casual encounter with an old friend*
► chance, unexpected, unforeseen, unintentional, unplanned, fortuitous, accidental, random
OPPOSITES ARE deliberate, intentional
2 *a casual remark*
► offhand, spontaneous, impromptu, unconsidered, random
OPPOSITES ARE committed, enthusiastic
3 *a casual acquaintance*
► slight, vague
OPPOSITES ARE close, intimate
4 *a casual approach to life*
► relaxed, nonchalant, lackadaisical, indifferent, carefree, easy-going, offhand, apathetic, flippant, (more informal) laid-back
OPPOSITES ARE concerned, serious
5 *He gave her a casual glance*
► cursory, fleeting, passing, hasty, quick, perfunctory
OPPOSITES ARE thorough, careful
6 *casual clothes*
► informal
AN OPPOSITE IS formal

casualty NOUN
The bombing led to many casualties.
► death, fatality, injury, loss, victim, (in plural) dead and wounded

cat NOUN
People thought he was odd for talking to his cat.
► tom, tomcat, tabby, kitten, (more informal) moggy, (more informal) pussy
RELATED ADJECTIVE feline

catalogue NOUN
1 *a library catalogue*
► inventory, list, record, register, directory, index, roll, schedule, table

2 *a catalogue of mistakes*
▶ series, sequence, string, long list

catalogue VERB
It will take a long time to catalogue the whole collection.
▶ index, make an inventory of, record, archive, classify, list, register, log, file

catastrophe NOUN
The floods were a catastrophe for the area.
▶ calamity, tragedy, misfortune, mishap, affliction, cataclysm, blow

catch VERB
1 *Josh caught the ball.*
▶ seize, grab, take hold of, grip, clutch, intercept
2 *They hadn't managed to catch any fish.*
▶ hook, net, land, trap
3 *Do you think they will catch the thief?*
▶ capture, arrest, apprehend
4 *We have a train to catch.*
▶ board, be in time for, get to, reach
5 *He caught a rare virus on a business trip.*
▶ contract, be infected with, develop, get, go down with, become sick with, become ill with
6 *She caught them in the act.*
▶ discover, detect, find, find out, surprise, expose
7 *A trip to Paris caught their fancy.*
▶ capture, attract, appeal to, seize, win, absorb, engross
8 *I didn't catch what you said.*
▶ hear, perceive, discern, make out, recognize
catch up *If we hurry we can catch them up.*
▶ reach, overtake, draw level with

catch NOUN
1 *The fishermen returned with their catch over their shoulders.*
▶ haul, net, bag, booty, prize
2 *The price is so good there must be a catch.*
▶ snag, disadvantage, difficulty, drawback, obstacle, problem, trap, trick
3 *He tried to slip the catch on the window.*
▶ latch, lock, fastener, fastening, bolt, clasp

catching ADJECTIVE
Fortunately the disease is not catching.
▶ infectious, contagious, communicable, transmittable, spreading

catchy ADJECTIVE
a catchy tune
▶ memorable, tuneful, haunting, attractive, popular, singable

categorical ADJECTIVE
a categorical assurance
▶ absolute, unqualified, unconditional, unequivocal, unreserved, outright, complete, definite, express

category NOUN
There is a maximum penalty for each category of offence. Non-fiction books fall into several categories.
▶ class, type, classification, kind, sort, division, group, grade, heading

cater VERB
1 **cater for** *The hotel will cater for vegetarians.*
▶ provide for, make arrangements for, supply, feed, cook for
2 **cater for** *A simple barrow will cater for most of your gardening needs.*
▶ serve, satisfy, answer, provide for, cope with, take care of

catholic ADJECTIVE
Their taste in reading is very catholic.
▶ broad, wide, wide-ranging, varied, diverse, eclectic, comprehensive, broad-based, all-embracing, general, universal, cosmopolitan, liberal

cattle PLURAL NOUN
The farmers need land for grazing their cattle.
▶ livestock, cows, bulls, bullocks, calves, heifers, oxen
RELATED ADJECTIVE bovine

catty ADJECTIVE
(informal) a catty remark
▶ spiteful, malicious, mean, nasty, unkind, hurtful, snide, vindictive, cruel

cause NOUN
1 *Police are still trying to find the cause of the explosion.*
▶ source, origin, root, basis, reason (for), beginning, genesis, grounds, motivation, motive, occasion, spring, stimulus
2 *The older boys were the cause of much of the trouble.*
▶ initiator, instigator, originator, producer, agent
3 *There is no cause for alarm.*
▶ reason, grounds, justification, call, need, necessity, occasion, excuse, pretext
4 *a worthy cause*
▶ purpose, object, end, aim, ideal, undertaking, enterprise

cause VERB
1 *The bad weather has caused many delays.*
▶ bring about, result in, give rise to, lead to, produce, generate, create, precipitate, induce, entail, stimulate
2 *Poor health caused him to give up work.*
▶ force, compel, lead, encourage, induce, make

caustic ADJECTIVE
1 *a caustic substance*
▶ corrosive, acid, astringent, burning
2 *caustic remarks*
▶ sharp, sarcastic, scathing, hurtful, acid, acerbic, cutting, bitter, spiteful, vicious, abrasive

caution NOUN
1 *Drivers were advised to proceed with extreme caution.*
▶ care, alertness, attentiveness, carefulness, wariness, watchfulness, vigilance, restraint, discretion, circumspection, heed, heedfulness, prudence
AN OPPOSITE IS recklessness
2 *A first offender is usually let off with a caution.*
▶ reprimand, warning, admonition

caution VERB
1 *Everyone was cautioned about the dangers of the place.*
▶ warn, advise, alert (to)
2 *The offenders were all cautioned.*
▶ reprimand, give a warning (to), admonish, censure, reprehend

cautious ADJECTIVE
1 *He was a cautious man and avoided risks.*
▶ careful, attentive, vigilant, circumspect, heedful, alert, prudent, scrupulous, watchful
OPPOSITES ARE careless, reckless
2 *Their response was cautious.*
▶ guarded, discreet, wary, chary, tactful
OPPOSITES ARE forthright, impetuous

cave NOUN
There are caves at the foot of the cliffs.
▶ cavern, grotto, hollow, cavity, underground chamber, den, hole, pothole

cave VERB
1 **cave in** *The roof caved in*
▶ collapse, fall in, give way, disintegrate, crumble
2 **cave in** *The government refused to cave in to the protesters' demands.*
▶ yield, surrender, comply (with)

cavernous ADJECTIVE
a cavernous space
▶ vast, huge, large, spacious, immense, capacious, voluminous, gaping

cavity NOUN
a secret cavity in the wall
▶ space, chamber, hollow, hole, pit, cave, crater, dent

cavort VERB
The children cavorted about the room.
▶ skip, bound, dance, leap, caper, jump, spring, bounce, gambol, bob, frisk

cease VERB
Hostilities will cease at midnight. Both armies have ceased military activity.
▶ end, stop, finish, halt, come or bring to an end, conclude, terminate
AN OPPOSITE IS commence

ceasefire NOUN
A ceasefire had been in force for three months.
▶ armistice, suspension of hostilities, cessation of hostilities, truce, agreement, peace, treaty, peace treaty

ceaseless ADJECTIVE
ceaseless activity
▶ continuous, continual, constant, incessant, endless, unceasing, interminable, non-stop
OPPOSITES ARE temporary, intermittent

cede VERB
The treaty required both countries to cede territory won during the fighting.
▶ relinquish, surrender, yield, concede, renounce, hand over

celebrate VERB
1 *They celebrated with a bottle of champagne.*
▶ enjoy yourself, have fun, have a good time, make merry
2 *The couple celebrate their golden wedding this week.*
▶ commemorate, observe, mark, recognize, honour, remember, keep

celebrated ADJECTIVE
a celebrated writer and broadcaster
▶ acclaimed, admired, famous, well-known, prominent, revered, renowned, distinguished, honoured, eminent, exalted, illustrious, notable, noted
OPPOSITES ARE unknown, obscure

celebration NOUN
1 *a birthday celebration*
▶ party, function, festivity, (*more informal*) binge
2 *a cause for celebration*
▶ festivities, jollification, merrymaking, enjoying yourself, partying

celebrity NOUN
1 *a team made up of celebrities*
▶ star, famous person, public figure, dignitary, idol, personality, luminary
2 *The group seemed to be enjoying their celebrity.*
▶ fame, stardom, prominence, popularity, glory, reputation, renown

celestial ADJECTIVE
1 *celestial bodies*
▶ heavenly, extraterrestrial, stellar, universal, cosmic, galactic, interplanetary, interstellar, starry
2 *celestial music*
▶ heavenly, divine, sublime, ethereal, blissful, angelic, godlike

celibacy NOUN
priests who had taken a vow of celibacy
▶ chastity, virginity, self-denial, abstinence, purity, bachelorhood, spinsterhood

celibate ADJECTIVE
a celibate life
▶ chaste, single, unmarried, unwedded, pure, virgin

cell NOUN
1 *a prison cell*
▶ room, cubicle, chamber, compartment, enclosure, unit
2 *cells of a honeycomb*
▶ compartment, cavity, chamber, hollow, section
3 *a terrorist cell*
▶ unit, group, faction, caucus, section, arm, wing

cellar NOUN
Old bottles are kept in the cellar.
▶ basement, crypt, vault

cemetery NOUN
Mourners will want to visit the cemetery.
▶ graveyard, burial ground, churchyard, necropolis (= ancient cemetery)

censor VERB
Parts of the film had to be censored.
▶ cut, edit, expurgate

censure NOUN
Her voice had a note of censure.
▶ criticism, disapproval, reproach, rebuke, condemnation, reproof

censure VERB
The authorities censured people who had not voted.
▶ criticize, reprimand, condemn, rebuke, reproach

central ADJECTIVE
1 *the central chamber of the temple*
▶ innermost, inner, interior, middle, focal
2 *the central issues*
▶ chief, key, main, essential, pivotal, primary, principal, vital, fundamental, crucial, major, overriding, important
AN OPPOSITE IS peripheral

centralize VERB
The processes will be centralized in a business centre.
▶ concentrate, unify, amalgamate, bring together, rationalize, streamline
OPPOSITES ARE devolve, disperse

centre NOUN
1 *the centre of a circle*
▶ middle, mid-point, heart, core, eye, bullseye
2 *the centre of the city*
▶ middle, heart, nucleus

cereal NOUN
farmers who prefer cereal production to livestock
▶ corn, grain

CEREALS INCLUDE

barley, corn, maize, millet, oats, rice, rye, sorghum, sweetcorn, wheat.

ceremonial ADJECTIVE
a ceremonial occasion
▶ formal, official, stately, solemn, ritual, ritualistic
OPPOSITES ARE informal, unofficial

ceremony NOUN
1 *a wedding ceremony*
▶ rite, ritual, service, observance, celebration
2 *a grand occasion with all due ceremony*
▶ formality, pomp, protocol, propriety, ritual, solemnity

certain ADJECTIVE
1 *I was certain they did it.*
▶ sure, confident, positive, convinced, assured, satisfied
OPPOSITES ARE uncertain (whether), doubtful (whether)
2 *It is certain that there will be reprisals.*
▶ definite, undeniable, indubitable, unquestionable, clear, plain, evident, obvious, conclusive
OPPOSITES ARE uncertain (whether), doubtful
3 *She faced certain failure.*
▶ inevitable, assured, inescapable, unavoidable

4 *They are certain to win.*
▶ sure, bound, assured (of winning)
AN OPPOSITE IS unlikely
5 *A certain person has been here.*
▶ particular, specific, definite, unnamed, individual

certainly ADVERB
It was certainly a beautiful building.
▶ undoubtedly, unquestionably, surely, undeniably definitely, without question, without doubt

certainty NOUN
1 *The answers may never be known with certainty.*
▶ assurance, assuredness, confidence, conviction, certitude
OPPOSITES ARE uncertainty, doubt
2 *A high-scoring match seemed a certainty.*
▶ inevitability, certain fact, foregone conclusion, matter of course, necessity, (*more informal*) sure thing
AN OPPOSITE IS impossibility

certificate NOUN
a certificate of airworthiness
▶ guarantee, document, permit, certification, diploma, award, licence, authorization, warrant, proof

certify VERB
You have to sign the form to certify that the information is true.
▶ verify, guarantee, confirm, affirm, testify, warrant, declare, demonstrate

chain NOUN
1 *The prisoners were held in chains.*
▶ fetters, shackles, bonds, irons, manacles, coupling, handcuffs, links
2 *a chain of events*
▶ series, sequence, succession, string, course, train, progression
3 *a chain of supermarkets*
▶ group, firm, series

chain VERB
The bicycle was chained to a fence.
▶ tie, fasten, secure, hitch, tether, manacle, fetter

chairman, chairwoman NOUN
the chairman of a committee
▶ chairperson, chair, president, convener, organizer, director, speaker

challenge VERB
1 *The woman had challenged an intruder.*
▶ accost, confront, take on
2 *It was a job that would challenge their abilities.*
▶ test, tax, try, stretch
3 *He challenged one of the men to a duel.*
▶ dare, summon, invite, defy, provoke
4 *We will have to challenge the decision.*
▶ dispute, oppose, object to, protest against, query, question, disagree with, argue against, dissent from

challenge NOUN
1 *Will you accept the challenge?*
▶ dare, summons

2 *Coping with the extra work proved quite a challenge.*
▶ trial, task, undertaking, problem, difficulty
3 *a challenge to the party leadership*
▶ opposition, confrontation (with), dispute (with)

challenging ADJECTIVE
a challenging task
▶ demanding, testing, taxing, exacting, stimulating
OPPOSITES ARE easy, undemanding

chamber NOUN
1 *a debating chamber*
▶ room, hall
2 *the chambers of the heart*
▶ compartment, cavity, cell, space

champion NOUN
1 *the world champion*
▶ title-holder, victor, conqueror, winner
2 *a champion of reform*
▶ supporter, advocate, defender, upholder, patron, backer, guardian, protector

champion VERB
a charity championing the rights of asylum-seekers
▶ support, promote, uphold, defend, campaign for, fight for, stand up for, advance, espouse, protect

championship NOUN
a golf championship
▶ competition, contest, tournament

chance ADJECTIVE
a chance discovery
▶ accidental, fortuitous, coincidental, casual, incidental, unintentional, unforeseen, random
OPPOSITES ARE intentional, planned

chance NOUN
1 *There is a slight chance of snow.*
▶ possibility, likelihood, probability, prospect, risk, danger
2 *Give them a chance to answer.*
▶ opportunity, time, turn, occasion
3 *We were taking an awful chance.*
▶ risk, gamble
by chance *I found the earring by chance.*
▶ by accident, accidentally, fortuitously, inadvertently, unwittingly

chance VERB
1 *I chanced to be passing at that moment.*
▶ happen
2 *Shall we chance another look?*
▶ risk, venture, hazard, try

chancy ADJECTIVE
(informal) It was chancy taking a shortcut across the meadow in the dark.
▶ risky, dangerous, hazardous, unsafe, precarious, insecure, tricky, uncertain, unpredictable, (more informal) dicey
OPPOSITES ARE safe, predictable

change NOUN
1 *a change of plan*
▶ alteration, modification, variation, revision, amendment (to), replacement (for)

2 *We'd like a change.*
▶ diversion, novelty, innovation, variety
3 *I've got no change for the bus.*
▶ coins, small change, loose change

change VERB
1 *These events have changed the world for ever.*
▶ alter, make different, transform, modify, reshape, refashion, reorder
2 *Things have changed a lot since we were last here.*
▶ alter, become different, develop, fluctuate, (more informal) move on
3 *I need to change my library book.*
▶ exchange, swap, substitute, switch, replace

changeable ADJECTIVE
The weather is very changeable.
▶ variable, unsettled, unpredictable, unreliable, temperamental, volatile

channel NOUN
1 *a water channel*
▶ duct, conduit, gully, gutter, furrow, flume
2 *a channel of communication*
▶ medium, avenue, means, route, path, way
3 *a television channel (informal)*
▶ station, waveband, wavelength

channel VERB
It would be wiser to channel your energies into something new.
▶ direct, guide, devote (to), put

chaos NOUN
When we arrived on the scene there was total chaos.
▶ confusion, disorder, mayhem, muddle, bedlam, pandemonium, anarchy, disorganization, lawlessness, shambles, tumult
AN OPPOSITE IS order

chaotic ADJECTIVE
1 *A good party is a chaotic jumble of noise and movement.*
▶ disorderly, confused, disorganized, disordered, topsy-turvy, uncontrolled, muddled, tumultuous
OPPOSITES ARE organized, orderly
2 *The country was in a chaotic state for years.*
▶ anarchic, lawless, unruly, uncontrolled
AN OPPOSITE IS orderly

chap NOUN
Some chap gave it to me (informal).
▶ man, boy, individual, bloke

chapter NOUN
1 *a chapter of a book*
▶ section, part, division
2 *a new chapter in the nation's history*
▶ stage, phase, period, era, epoch

char VERB
The heat has charred the woodwork.
▶ scorch, sear, singe, blacken, brown, burn, carbonize

character NOUN

1 *Jane has a forceful character.*
▶ personality, temperament, nature, temper
2 *The trees and parks add a special character to the town.*
▶ distinctiveness, individuality, uniqueness, stamp, feature
3 *He was acquitted without a stain on his character.*
▶ reputation, name, standing, stature, position
4 (*informal*) *The new doctor is a charming character.*
▶ person, individual, being, sort, type, fellow, (*more informal*) bloke, (*more informal*) chap
5 (*informal*) *Her father is something of a character.*
▶ eccentric, oddity, (*more informal*) oddball, (*more informal*) case
6 *a woman of character*
▶ integrity, honour, quality
7 *She has played several characters in the same play.*
▶ part, role
8 *The sign was printed in Greek characters.*
▶ letter, figure, symbol

characteristic ADJECTIVE

He spoke with his characteristic eloquence.
▶ typical, distinctive, usual, normal, particular, singular, special, individual, peculiar, recognizable, specific, unique, distinguishing, essential, idiosyncratic

characteristic NOUN

The building has some interesting characteristics.
▶ feature, peculiarity, trait, attribute, distinguishing feature, property, aspect, hallmark, idiosyncrasy

characterize VERB

1 *The film characterizes the king as a cruel dictator.*
▶ portray, depict, represent, describe, categorize, delineate, draw, present
2 *The period after the War was characterized by great social hardship.*
▶ distinguish, mark, identify, set apart, brand, differentiate, individualize, recognize, typify

charade NOUN

The presidential elections had been a shameless charade.
▶ farce, pantomime, fabrication, pretence, sham, mockery, deception, masquerade

charge NOUN

1 *Our charges will increase from next April.*
▶ fee, price, cost, tariff
2 *The children were left in their sister's charge.*
▶ care, protection, custody, keeping, surveillance, command, control, responsibility, safe-keeping, trust
3 *The company's directors face criminal charges.*
▶ accusation, allegation, indictment, imputation
4 *The infantry suffered heavy casualties in the charge.*
▶ assault, attack, onslaught, offensive, rush, sortie, raid

in charge of *He was in charge of the factory during his father's absence.*
▶ responsible for, in control of, managing, running, looking after

charge VERB

1 *What do they charge for a coffee?*
▶ ask for, ask in payment, make you pay, exact, levy, require
2 *They charged him with producing a video of the event.*
▶ entrust, burden, saddle, tax, empower
3 *The witness was later charged with perjury.*
▶ accuse (of), prosecute (for), indict (for), put on trial (for)
4 *The mounted cavalry charged the enemy line.*
▶ attack, storm, rush, assault, assail, fall on, set on

charitable ADJECTIVE

1 *a charitable activity*
▶ philanthropic, humanitarian, benevolent
2 *a charitable attitude*
▶ generous, magnanimous, friendly, liberal, benign, considerate, compassionate, understanding, broad-minded

charity NOUN

1 *Show some charity towards those in need.*
▶ goodwill, generosity, consideration, kindness, sympathy, compassion, fellow feeling
AN OPPOSITE IS selfishness
2 *The church depends on the charity of parishioners.*
▶ financial assistance, generosity, donations, contributions, subsidies, patronage

charm NOUN

1 *As he relaxed, his charm and humour returned.*
▶ attractiveness, appeal, allure, lure, charisma, desirability, fascination, enchantment
2 *magical charms*
▶ spell, incantation
3 *a lucky charm*
▶ trinket, talisman, amulet, mascot, idol

charm VERB

He charmed everyone with his stories.
▶ delight, please, captivate, bewitch, enchant, entrance, enthral, mesmerize
OPPOSITES ARE repel, disgust

charming ADJECTIVE

My mother tells me that I was a charming baby.
▶ delightful, attractive, pleasant, pleasing, endearing, alluring, disarming, likeable

chart NOUN

1 *a flow chart*
▶ diagram, graph, plan, table
2 *a weather chart*
▶ map

charter NOUN

The company was granted a royal charter
▶ privilege, right, permit, licence, authority, authorization, franchise, contract

charter VERB

We can charter an aircraft over the mountains.
▶ hire, lease, rent, commission, employ, engage

chary
75
cheeky

chary ADJECTIVE

She was chary about lending him any more money.
▶ wary, cautious, doubtful, dubious, careful, hesitant, guarded
AN OPPOSITE IS heedless

chase VERB

The farmer chased the intruders across a field.
▶ pursue, run after, track, trail, drive, follow, hound, hunt

chase around *I've been chasing around all morning trying to finish my work.*
▶ rush, hurry, bustle, scamper

chasm NOUN

Below the bridge was a deep chasm
▶ crevasse, ravine, opening, abyss, canyon, gorge, void, drop, fissure, gap, gulf, hollow, rift, pit, hole

chaste ADJECTIVE

leading a chaste life
▶ pure, virtuous, virginal, celibate, innocent
AN OPPOSITE IS immoral

chastise VERB

He was chastised for his rudeness.
▶ punish, discipline, beat, scold, reprimand, admonish, upbraid

chastity NOUN

a life of chastity
▶ celibacy, purity, virginity, innocence, virtue, abstinence

chat VERB

We spent hours chatting about nothing in particular.
▶ talk, gossip, chatter, (*more informal*) jabber, (*more informal*) babble

chat up (*informal*) *He tried to chat Jenny up in the bus queue.*
▶ flirt with, make up to, make advances to

chat NOUN

I needed to have a chat with her.
▶ talk, conversation, chatter, (*more informal*) natter, (*more informal*) chinwag

chatter VERB

Some of the people stayed chattering at one end of the room.
▶ talk, gossip, chat, (*more informal*) jabber, (*more informal*) babble

chatty ADJECTIVE

(*informal*) *She seemed to be in a chatty mood.*
▶ talkative, communicative, effusive, expansive, open, friendly

chauvinism NOUN

1 *His devotion to his country amounted to chauvinism.*
▶ jingoism, excessive patriotism, nationalism
2 *The management were accused of chauvinism.*
▶ sexism, discrimination, prejudice, bigotry

cheap ADJECTIVE

1 *a cheap edition of Shakespeare's works*
▶ inexpensive, economical, low-priced, affordable, reasonable
2 *racks of cheap digital watches*
▶ inferior, second-rate, shoddy, vulgar, tawdry, (*more informal*) tatty, (*more informal*) tacky
3 *cheap tabloid journalism*
▶ mean, despicable, low, contemptible, tasteless
4 *They made us feel cheap.*
▶ ashamed, embarrassed, humiliated, degraded

cheapen VERB

They cheapened themselves with their boastful talk.
▶ demean, belittle, discredit, disgrace, diminish

cheat VERB

Some dealers are cheating their customers.
▶ swindle, defraud, deceive, exploit, hoodwink, short-change, dupe, (*more informal*) con, (*more informal*) rip off

cheat NOUN

1 *He called his brother a cheat.*
▶ swindler, deceiver, fraud, charlatan, impostor, (*more informal*) phoney
2 *The scheme was really a bit of a cheat.*
▶ deception, deceit, fraud, pretence, hoax, trick, (*more informal*) racket, (*more informal*) fiddle

check VERB

1 *Police were checking vehicles at roadblocks.*
▶ examine, inspect, test, look over, scrutinize, scan, investigate
2 *I'll check the answers against this list.*
▶ verify, confirm, test, compare
3 *He checked an impulse to look round.*
▶ resist, control, suppress, restrain, curb, repress, stifle
4 *Extensive flooding checked their progress.*
▶ hinder, obstruct, hamper, impede, restrict, inhibit, frustrate

check NOUN

1 *There will be an official check of documents at the border.*
▶ inspection, examination, scrutiny, perusal, investigation
2 *a check on the abuse of power*
▶ curb, restraint, control

check-up NOUN

The car goes for a check-up next week.
▶ check, inspection, examination, overhaul

cheek NOUN

He had the cheek to tell me to leave (informal).
▶ audacity, effrontery, nerve, temerity, impertinence, impudence, insolence, presumptuousness, shamelessness, (*more informal*) sauce

cheeky ADJECTIVE

A cheeky boy from down the road called after him.
▶ impudent, impertinent, insolent, impolite, disrespectful, brazen, audacious, forward, pert

cheer VERB

1 *We'll be there to cheer our team.*
▶ applaud, acclaim, clap, shout
2 *The good news cheered them a great deal.*
▶ comfort, console, gladden, delight, encourage, uplift, exhilarate, make cheerful, please, solace
AN OPPOSITE IS sadden

cheer up *As I reached home I began to cheer up.*
▶ take heart, become more cheerful, perk up, brighten, rally, revive

cheer NOUN

The spectators gave her a cheer.
▶ hurrah, cry of approval, shout of approval, ovation, acclamation, applause, encouragement

cheerful ADJECTIVE

They arrived looking cheerful. It was a cheerful occasion.
▶ happy, jolly, glad, joyful, joyous, lively, elated, animated, contented, buoyant, good-humoured, light-hearted, chirpy
OPPOSITES ARE sad, dejected

cheerless ADJECTIVE

The town was a nondescript cheerless place.
▶ dreary, dull, gloomy, bleak, dismal, grim, sombre, dingy, drab, stark, desolate
AN OPPOSITE IS cheerful

cheery ADJECTIVE

She answered the phone with a cheery 'Good morning'.
▶ cheerful, jolly, merry, spirited, jaunty, carefree, happy, sunny, joyful, joyous

cheese NOUN

KINDS OF CHEESE
USAGE Many cheeses are named after the place where they were first developed: this is true of most English cheeses and some others, eg Camembert (in Normandy, North-West France), Edam (In the Netherlands), and Parmesan (from Parma in northern Italy). Some cheeses are also produced in countries other than the country of origin; for example, a kind of Brie is also made in Britain. Some names are trademarks: for example, Boursin and Cambozola.

British cheeses: Caerphilly, Cheddar, Cheshire, Colby, Cotswold, crowdie (Scottish), Derby, Double Gloucester, Gloucester, Ilchester, Lancashire, Leicester, Red Leicester, sage Derby, Stilton, Wensleydale, Wiltshire, Windsor, Windsor Red.
Dutch cheeses: Edam, Gouda.
French cheeses: Beaufort, blue brie, Boursin, Brie, Camembert, Cantal, Chaumes, chèvre (goat's-milk cheese), fromage blanc (= 'white cheese'), fromage frais (= 'fresh cheese'), Gervais, Neufchâtel, Port Salut, Roquefort. ▶▶

German cheeses: Cambozola (a cross between Camembert and Gorgonzola), Tilsit.
Italian cheeses: Bel Paese (="fair country'), Dolcelatte (= 'sweet milk'), fontina, Gorgonzola, mascarpone, mozzarella, Parmesan, pecorino (= sheep's-milk cheese), provolone, ricotta (= 'cooked again'), taleggio.
Swiss cheeses: Emmental, Gruyère.
Other European cheeses: feta (Greece, made from sheep's or goat's milk), Limbourger (Belgium).
other types of cheese: cottage cheese, cream cheese, curd cheese, quark (low-fat curd cheese).

chemical elements NOUN

WORDS FOR CHEMICAL ELEMENTS
115 chemical elements have been discovered, but only 90 occur naturally. Elements can be sorted into metals, non-metals and semi-metals. Over three-quarters of all the elements are metals, of which the most important are listed below.

metals: lithium(Li), beryllium (Be), sodium (Na), magnesium (Mg), aluminium (Al), potassium (K), calcium (Ca), scandium (Sc), titanium (Ti), vanadium (V), chromium (Cr), manganese (Mn), iron (Fe), cobalt (Co), nickel (Ni), copper (Cu), zinc (Zn), gallium (Ga), strontium (Sr), zirconium (Zr), molybdenum (Mo), silver (Ag), cadmium (Cd), tin (Sn), barium (Ba), tungsten (W), platinum (Pt), gold (Au), mercury (Hg), lead (Pb), bismuth (Bi), uranium (U).
non-metals: hydrogen (H), helium (He), carbon (C), nitrogen (N), oxygen (O), fluorine (F), neon (Ne), phosophorus (P), sulphur (S), chlorine (Cl), argon (Ar), bromine (Br), krypton (Kr), iodine (I), xenon (Xe), radon (Rn).
semi-metals or metalloids: boron (B), silicon (Si), germanium (Ge), arsenic (As), selenium (Se), antimony (Sb), tellurium (Tb), polonium (Po), astatine (At).

cherish VERB

1 *His friends all cherished him.*
▶ adore, love, be devoted to, be fond of, hold dear, care for, foster, keep safe, look after, nourish, nurse, protect
2 *I shall cherish this gift all my life.*
▶ treasure, value, prize

chest NOUN

1 *The ball hit him in the chest.*
▶ breast, ribcage
RELATED ADJECTIVE pectoral
2 *a large chest of tools*
▶ case, crate, box, casket, coffer, strongbox, trunk

hew VERB

Claire was chewing a piece of bread.
▶ eat, munch, nibble, champ, bite, crunch, gnaw, (*more formal*) masticate

hewy ADJECTIVE

The meat was very chewy.
▶ tough, gristly, leathery, rubbery
AN OPPOSITE IS tender

hic ADJECTIVE

a woman in a chic outfit
▶ stylish, elegant, fashionable, smart, modish
OPPOSITES ARE unfashionable, drab, dowdy

hief ADJECTIVE

1 *Money was the chief problem.*
▶ main, principal, primary, prime, most important, overriding, foremost, fundamental, key, crucial, central, paramount, predominant, basic, essential
2 *the chief cook*
▶ head, senior, principal, leading

hief NOUN

He is the chief of a merchant bank.
▶ head, principal, president, chairman, chief executive

hiefly ADVERB

Dogs were chiefly to blame for the damage.
▶ mainly, mostly, primarily, principally, predominantly, especially, essentially

hild NOUN

1 *She was only a child when I last saw her.*
▶ youngster, girl (or boy), baby, infant, little one, (*more informal*) kid, (*more informal*) nipper, (*more informal*) tot
RELATED ADJECTIVE juvenile
2 *She is the child of Greek parents.*
▶ offspring, progeny, daughter (or son), descendant, heir, issue

childhood NOUN

He has suffered from the illness from childhood.
▶ infancy, youth, boyhood (or girlhood), adolescence, teens

childish ADJECTIVE

It was childish of him to say that.
▶ immature, babyish, puerile, infantile, juvenile, silly, foolish
AN OPPOSITE IS mature

USAGE Note that *childish* is normally an unfavourable word, whereas *childlike* is favourable or neutral in tone.

childlike ADJECTIVE

a world of childlike simplicity
▶ innocent, naive, artless, guileless, ingenuous, trusting
OPPOSITES ARE artful, disingenuous

chill NOUN

1 *We felt a distinct chill in the air.*
▶ coldness, chilliness, coolness, crispness, rawness, bite, nip
2 *She decided to stay at home because of her chill.*
▶ cold, flu

chill VERB

The drinks need to be chilled.
▶ cool, refrigerate, ice, freeze, make cold
AN OPPOSITE IS warm

chilly ADJECTIVE

1 *a chilly evening in March*
▶ cold, crisp, sharp, fresh, cool, frosty, icy, raw, (*more informal*) nippy, (*more informal*) parky
AN OPPOSITE IS warm
2 *You may get a chilly reception.*
▶ unfriendly, cool, lukewarm, unwelcoming, frigid, hostile, unsympathetic, reserved, aloof, (*informal*) standoffish
OPPOSITES ARE warm, friendly, enthusiastic

chime VERB

The church bells began to chime.
▶ sound, strike, ring, peal, toll

china NOUN

Put out the best china.
▶ porcelain, crockery, cups and saucers, earthenware

chink NOUN

1 *a chink in the clouds   a chink in the wall*
▶ opening, gap, hole, space, crack, split, fissure
2 *the chink of glasses*
▶ clink, tinkle, ring

chip NOUN

1 *a chip of wood*
▶ fragment, piece, bit, sliver, splinter, slice, flake, fleck, scrap, shaving
2 *The cup had a chip in it.*
▶ crack, nick, flaw, scratch, gash, notch, snick

chip VERB

Someone had chipped the teapot.
▶ crack, nick, scratch, splinter, notch, damage

chirp VERB

Birds chirped in the trees.
▶ cheep, tweet, chirrup, twitter, sing

chirpy ADJECTIVE

She came in with a chirpy grin.
▶ cheerful, happy, jolly, glad, joyful, joyous, lively, elated

chivalrous ADJECTIVE

He treated everyone in the same chivalrous manner.
▶ gallant, courteous, polite, honorable, considerate, gracious, thoughtful
OPPOSITES ARE dishonourable, rude

chivalry NOUN

Where is your sense of chivalry Roger?
▶ gallantry, courtesy, politeness, consideration, graciousness, thoughtfulness

a
b
c
d
e
f
g
h
i
j
k
l
m
n
o
p
q
r
s
t
u
v
w
x
y
z

choice NOUN

1 *We have no other choice now.*
▶ option, alternative, possibility, answer
2 *the viewers' choice of programmes*
▶ selection, choosing, preference, election
3 *Write in with your choice.*
▶ decision, selection, vote, nomination
4 *a wide choice of good food*
▶ range, variety, selection, array, assortment, display

choice ADJECTIVE

choice vegetables
▶ fine, superior, first-class, first-rate, excellent, prime, select

choir NOUN

Her mother sang in a local choir.
▶ chorus, choral group, choral society, vocal ensemble

choke VERB

1 *The dust was nearly choking them.*
▶ suffocate, asphyxiate, smother, stifle
2 *There was a danger of the necklace choking her to death.*
▶ strangle, throttle, suffocate, asphyxiate
3 *Oliver choked and had to be thumped on the back.*
▶ gag, gasp, retch, suffocate
4 *The motorways are constantly choked with traffic.*
▶ clog, congest, constrict, block, obstruct
choke back *Sandra choked back the tears as she tried to answer.*
▶ stifle, suppress, fight back, hold back

choose VERB

1 *We chose a quiet spot by the river.*
▶ pick, pick out, select, opt for, plump for, go for, settle on, fix on, decide on
2 *Mark chose to go in first.*
▶ decide, elect, make up your mind, determine, prefer, resolve, see fit

choosy ADJECTIVE

choosy about food
▶ fussy, finicky, particular, fastidious, picky

chop VERB

1 *He was in the yard chopping wood.*
▶ cut, hew
2 *Chop the vegetables into small chunks.*
▶ cut up, slice, split, dice
chop down *The tree should be chopped down.*
▶ cut down, fell
chop off *His arm had been chopped off in an accident.*
▶ sever, amputate, detach, lop off

chopper NOUN

He cut up the logs with a chopper.
▶ axe, cleaver

choppy ADJECTIVE

a choppy sea
▶ rough, turbulent, stormy, heavy
OPPOSITES ARE calm, smooth

chore NOUN

I spent the day cooking and doing household chores.
▶ task, job, duty, burden, errand

chorus NOUN

1 *The chorus sang well.*
▶ choir, choral group, choral society, vocal ensemble
2 *Everyone can join in the choruses.*
▶ refrain, response

christen VERB

1 *The church in which Tania was christened.*
▶ baptize, name
2 *His friends christened him 'The King'*
▶ name, dub, style, designate

chronic ADJECTIVE

1 *a chronic illness*
▶ persistent, long-standing, lifelong, lingering, incurable
OPPOSITES ARE acute, temporary
2 *chronic food shortages*
▶ constant, persistent, continuous, continual

chronicle NOUN

a chronicle of events in the region
▶ record, account, history, annals, diary, journal, narrative, story

chronological ADJECTIVE

chronological order
▶ consecutive, sequential

chubby ADJECTIVE

a chubby little baby
▶ plump, tubby, podgy, round, dumpy, portly, rotund, stout, buxom

chuck VERB

(informal) I'll chuck the letter in the bin.
▶ throw, toss, fling, hurl, dump, sling
chuck out *There are a lot of old clothes to chuck out.*
▶ throw away, discard, dispose of, reject, scrap

chuckle VERB

Andrew chuckled as he left the room.
▶ chortle, snigger, giggle, laugh

chunk NOUN

little chunks of cheese on a plate   a chunk of wood
▶ lump, hunk, block, wedge, piece, portion, slab

chunky ADJECTIVE

a chunky lad of twenty
▶ stocky, sturdy, burly, bulky, beefy, dumpy

churlish ADJECTIVE

It seems churlish to complain.
▶ rude, boorish, discourteous, ill-mannered, ungracious, impolite

churn VERB

churn up *The propellers churned up the water.*
▶ agitate, stir up, disturb
churn out *When he was young he churned out poem after poem.*
▶ produce, turn out

circle NOUN
1 *The children stood in a circle*
► ring, round
RELATED ADJECTIVE circular
2 *He has a new circle of friends.*
► group, set, band, body, company, society, association, gang, party

circle VERB
1 *The birds circled over his head.*
► wheel, fly round, spiral
2 *Satellites circle the earth.*
► orbit, go round, circumnavigate, revolve round
3 *The grass was circled by trees.*
► surround, enclose, encircle, ring, skirt, girdle, hem in

circuit NOUN
1 *two circuits of the playing field*
► lap, turn, round, revolution
2 *a racing circuit*
► track, course

circuitous ADJECTIVE
a circuitous route
► roundabout, indirect, meandering, winding, rambling, tortuous
OPPOSITES ARE direct, straight

circular ADJECTIVE
a circular window
► round, disc-shaped, ring-shaped
USAGE You can also use *oval* and *elliptical* to describe a shape that is nearly circular but slightly flattened.

circular NOUN
an advertising circular
► advertisement, leaflet, letter, notice, pamphlet

circulate VERB
We circulated a notice about our sale
► send round, distribute, issue, publicize, publish, spread about, disseminate

circulation NOUN
1 *air circulation*
► flow, motion, movement, course
2 *the circulation of information*
► dissemination, distribution, spread, transmission, broadcasting
3 *a newspaper's circulation*
► distribution, readership, sales figures

circumference NOUN
the circumference of the field
► circuit, perimeter, border, boundary, edge, periphery, rim, limit, margin, outline, outside

circumstances PLURAL NOUN
1 *the right economic circumstances*
► situation, conditions, state of affairs, factors, position, background
2 *The police wanted to know all the circumstances.*
► facts, details, particulars, incidents, events

citadel NOUN
A river passes the citadel walls.
► fortress, stronghold, bastion, castle, keep, tower, fortification, acropolis

cite VERB
1 *You should cite the passage in full.*
► quote, reproduce
2 *She cited the decisions reached in previous cases.*
► refer to, name, quote, mention, adduce, specify, advance, invoke, (*more informal*) bring up

citizen NOUN
1 *a British citizen*
► subject, national, taxpayer, voter
RELATED ADJECTIVES civic, civil, civilian
2 *the citizens of Glasgow*
► inhabitants, resident, native, townsperson, householder

city NOUN
a large city north of the river
► town, metropolis, conurbation
RELATED ADJECTIVES civic, urban

civil ADJECTIVE
1 *I know you don't like her but try to be civil.*
► polite, respectful, well-mannered, courteous, considerate, affable, civilized, refined, obliging
OPPOSITES ARE impolite, rude
2 *a civil wedding*
► secular, non-religious
3 *civil rights*
► social, state, communal, national, public
4 *civil politics*
► domestic, home, internal, national, local

civilization NOUN
1 *ancient civilizations*
► culture, society, people
2 *advances in civilization*
► human development, human achievements, human attainments, enlightenment

civilized ADJECTIVE
1 *a civilized nation*
► advanced, developed, enlightened, cultured, refined
AN OPPOSITE IS uncivilized
2 *civilized behaviour*
► polite, orderly

claim VERB
1 *You can claim a refund at the office.*
► ask for, request, demand, collect, require, take
2 *He claimed the witness had been lying.*
► allege, maintain, contend, assert, avow, protest, insist

claim NOUN
1 *a claim for damages   an insurance claim*
► application, demand, request
2 *Their claim is hardly credible.*
► assertion, allegation, contention, declaration

clairvoyant ADJECTIVE

I didn't know about it and I'm not clairvoyant.
► psychic, telepathic, prophetic, extrasensory, oracular

clairvoyant NOUN

The woman claimed she was a clairvoyant.
► psychic, fortune teller, prophet, oracle, seer, sibyl, soothsayer

clamber VERB

It was dangerous clambering over the rocks.
► scramble, crawl, climb, move awkwardly

clammy ADJECTIVE

1 *They sat waiting with clammy hands for an hour and a half.*
► moist, sticky, sweaty, damp

2 *The atmosphere was cold and clammy.*
► dank, humid, damp, moist, muggy, slimy, sticky

clamp VERB

Each shelf is clamped to three brackets.
► fasten, fix, secure, attach, clip

clamp down on *a plan to clamp down on illegal parking*
► reduce, suppress, end, stop, eradicate, get tough on, crack down on

clan NOUN

a Scottish clan
► family, house, tribe, dynasty

clap NOUN

1 *a clap of thunder*
► crash, crack, boom, bang, thunderclap

2 *a clap on the shoulder*
► slap, thump, smack, blow

clap VERB

1 *The audience clapped her performance.*
► applaud, cheer, acclaim

2 *Someone clapped me on the shoulder.*
► slap, hit, pat, smack

claptrap NOUN

(informal) He was speaking claptrap.
► nonsense, rubbish, gibberish, drivel, (informal) poppycock

clarify VERB

To clarify matters, let us ask some basic questions.
► explain, throw light on, elucidate, make clear, gloss, illuminate, define
AN OPPOSITE IS confuse

clarity NOUN

She explained the problem with great clarity.
► clearness, lucidity, transparency, intelligibility, simplicity, precision, coherence

clash NOUN

1 *There was a metallic clash as the two vehicles came together.*
► crash, striking, bang

2 *Clashes followed between students and riot police.*
► fight, conflict, hostilities, collision

3 *a clash between the president and his secretary of state*
► disagreement, altercation, argument, quarrel, exchange

clash VERB

1 *The cymbals clashed.*
► crash, strike, resound, bang

2 *The violence began outside a chip shop, when rival gangs clashed.*
► disagree, conflict, quarrel, wrangle, fight

3 *The interview clashes with my holiday.*
► coincide, conflict, come at the same time (as)

clasp NOUN

1 *The bracelet needs a strong clasp.*
► fastener, fastening, catch, hook, buckle, clip, hasp, pin

2 *His clasp loosened a bit, but he didn't let her go.*
► hold, grasp, grip, embrace, squeeze, hug, cuddle

clasp VERB

1 *John clasped the woman in his arms.*
► hug, hold, embrace, squeeze, cling to, clutch, enfold, grasp, grip

2 *Before leaving she clasped his hand for a few moments.*
► grasp, hold, grip, clutch

class NOUN

1 *Our hotel is quite good for its class.*
► category, grade, classification, group, section, division, status

2 *a new class of medicine*
► type, kind, sort, genre, species, genus

3 *discrimination on the basis of social class*
► status, standing, position, station, caste, grouping

4 *a history class*
► form, set, group, stream

class VERB

Her performance was classed as a distinction.
► classify, categorize, group, grade, designate, rank, label

classic ADJECTIVE

1 *the classic book on the subject classic works of literature*
► definitive, outstanding, established, best, ideal, time-honoured, abiding, enduring

2 *a classic example of how a good idea has gone wrong*
► typical, characteristic, quintessential, archetypal, perfect

classic NOUN
The film has good points but is certainly not a classic.
▶ masterpiece, masterwork, model

classical ADJECTIVE
1 *classical civilizations*
▶ ancient, Greek and Roman
2 *a classical style*
▶ traditional, simple, pure, restrained, elegant, well-proportioned
3 *classical music classical ballet*
▶ traditional, established, harmonious, highbrow
AN OPPOSITE IS modern

classification NOUN
the classification of volcanoes into active, dormant, and extinct a system of classification
▶ categorization, division, grading, ordering, organization, codification, taxonomy

classify VERB
We can classify the plants according to the shape of their leaves.
▶ categorize, class, group, organize, grade, sort, catalogue, order

classy ADJECTIVE
a classy outfit
▶ stylish, elegant, smart, chic, sophisticated, fashionable, high-class, (*more informal*) posh, (*more informal*) snazzy

clatter VERB
Something in the engine began to clatter.
▶ rattle, clank, clunk

clause NOUN
There is an extra clause in the new contract.
▶ section, article, condition, provision, proviso, subsection, paragraph, item, part, passage

claw NOUN
1 *a bird's claws*
▶ talon, nail
2 *a crab's claw*
▶ pincer, nipper

claw VERB
One soldier lifted his arm and clawed at her face.
▶ scratch, scrabble, scrape, tear

clean ADJECTIVE
1 *She went in to put on clean clothes.*
▶ washed, cleaned, laundered, pristine
2 *Keep the wound clean.*
▶ sterile, sterilized, healthy, uncontaminated
3 *Write your details on a clean sheet of paper.*
▶ blank, unused, empty, plain, fresh, bare
4 *The air is clean in the mountains.*
▶ pure, clear, fresh, untainted
5 *The family all led a clean life.*
▶ virtuous, honest, moral, decent, respectable, exemplary, blameless, upright, pure, innocent
6 *We hope for a clean fight.*
▶ fair, honest, sporting
7 *Make a clean cut with a sharp knife.*
▶ smooth, neat, tidy, straight, accurate

8 *I decided to make a clean break with the place.*
▶ complete, total, thorough, decisive, final

clean VERB
1 *I'll go and clean the car.*
▶ wash, sponge, hose down, shampoo, polish
2 *We'll have to clean the bathroom floor.*
▶ wash, wipe, sponge, scrub, sweep, mop, swab
3 *Put out the clothes you want to be cleaned.*
▶ launder, dry-clean
4 *The whole room needs cleaning.*
▶ dust, brush, spruce up
5 *Make sure you clean the wound.*
▶ cleanse, wash, bathe, disinfect, sanitize, purify

clear ADJECTIVE
1 *clear instructions*
▶ plain, understandable, easy, direct, logical
2 *It was clear we would have to wait. a clear case of discrimination*
▶ evident, obvious, plain, apparent, patent, blatant, glaring, manifest
3 *a pool of clear water*
▶ transparent, translucent, crystalline
4 *a clear blue sky*
▶ bright, cloudless, unclouded, sunny, fair, fine
5 *a clear complexion*
▶ fresh, unblemished
6 *a clear voice*
▶ pure, distinct
7 *The motorway was clear again by the afternoon.*
▶ open, unobstructed, unblocked, unrestricted, passable
8 *a clear conscience*
▶ untroubled, undisturbed, easy, calm, guiltless, blameless
9 *a clear month's notice*
▶ full, whole, entire, complete, total

clear VERB
1 *The weather seemed to be clearing.*
▶ brighten, become brighter, turn fine, lighten
OPPOSITES ARE darken, get worse
2 *Rain will slowly clear from the south.*
▶ disappear, fade out, dwindle, disperse, recede, diminish, peter out, wear off, dry out
3 *We should clear the backlog of work by Friday.*
▶ complete, eliminate, deal with, get rid of
4 *a special tool for clearing drains*
▶ unblock, unclog, free, loosen
AN OPPOSITE IS block
5 *I have cleared most of the weeds.*
▶ tidy, remove, get rid of, eliminate, disentangle
6 *Staff were told to clear the building immediately.*
▶ evacuate, empty, leave
7 *The ball cleared the bar easily.*
▶ go over, pass over, go above

8 *The appeal judges are expected to clear him this week.*
▶ acquit, exonerate, free
AN OPPOSITE IS condemn

clear up
1 *I'll stay here and clear up the mess.*
▶ tidy (up), clean (up)
2 *I'm glad we've cleared up the misunderstanding.*
▶ resolve, explain, straighten out, get to the bottom of

clear-cut ADJECTIVE
It is not always easy to make a clear-cut distinction between the two ideas.
▶ definite, clear, precise, hard and fast, distinct, well defined

clearing NOUN
a clearing in the forest
▶ opening, space, gap, glade

clearly ADVERB
1 *Clearly we will need to make some changes.*
▶ obviously, evidently, surely, plainly, undoubtedly, patently
2 *It is important to write clearly.*
▶ legibly, distinctly, intelligibly

clench VERB
1 *She clenched her hands to stop them shaking.*
▶ squeeze (tightly), press (together)
2 *He looked ridiculous, clenching a rose in his teeth.*
▶ hold, clasp, grasp, grip

clergyman, clergywoman NOUN
an elderly clergyman in a cassock
▶ cleric, churchman, churchwoman, man or woman of God, minister, priest, vicar, pastor, parson, chaplain
USAGE Special ranks of clerics include *canon, curate, deacon, dean, rector.*

clerical ADJECTIVE
1 *There is a good deal of clerical work involved.*
▶ administrative, secretarial, office
2 *To his surprise, she wore a clerical collar.*
▶ ecclesiastical, pastoral

clerk NOUN
One of the clerks turned up for work with a black eye.
▶ office worker, clerical worker, office assistant, filing clerk, administrator
RELATED ADJECTIVE clerical

clever ADJECTIVE
a clever young student It was clever of you to work that out.
▶ intelligent, bright, gifted, brilliant, intellectual, talented, capable, (*more informal*) smart

cleverness NOUN
They made you marvel at their cleverness.
▶ intelligence, ability, talent, sharpness, shrewdness, (*more informal*) brains
AN OPPOSITE IS stupidity

cliché NOUN
The speech was a string of clichés
▶ platitude, commonplace, familiar phrase, hackneyed expression, banality, well-worn phrase

client NOUN
a salesman with about a hundred clients to deal with
▶ customer, buyer, patron, purchaser, user, consumer

cliff NOUN
Tiny figures at the top of the cliff
▶ rock face, bluff, crag, escarpment, precipice

climate NOUN
1 *countries with a temperate climate*
▶ weather, weather conditions, weather pattern
2 *a changed political climate*
▶ atmosphere, mood, spirit, ambience, temper, trend, environment, feeling

climax NOUN
The appointment marked the climax of her career.
▶ peak, summit, acme, zenith, highlight, high point, head
AN OPPOSITE IS nadir

climb VERB
1 *She climbed the stairs.*
▶ ascend, go up, mount, move up, scale, clamber up
2 *The plane climbed to 30,000 feet.*
▶ rise, ascend, fly up, soar
3 *The road climbs steeply into the hills.*
▶ rise, ascend, slope up
4 *They climbed the mountain in three days.*
▶ conquer, reach the top of
climb down *The Government has had to climb down on the issue.*
▶ give way, back down, yield, retreat, capitulate

climb NOUN
a steep climb
▶ ascent, clamber
AN OPPOSITE IS descent

clinch VERB
eager to clinch a deal
▶ conclude, agree, settle, sign, close, ratify, confirm, decide, make certain of, shake hands on, verify

cling VERB
1 **cling to** *Climbing plants cling to the walls.*
▶ adhere to, fasten on, stick to
2 **cling to** *Charles took her hand and clung to it.*
▶ clasp, clutch, embrace, grasp, hug
3 **cling to** *I still cling to the hope that I'm mistaken.*
▶ adhere to, stand by, abide by, have faith in, cherish

clinic NOUN
an appointment at the local clinic
▶ health centre, infirmary, medical centre, surgery

clinical ADJECTIVE
Her attitude seemed surprisingly clinical.
▶ detached, unemotional, uninvolved, impersonal, dispassionate, aloof, distant

clip NOUN
1 *He undid the clip and opened the case.*
▶ fastener, clasp, catch, hook
2 *a clip from a film*
▶ excerpt, extract, section, fragment

clip VERB
1 *It's my job to clip the hedge.*
▶ cut, trim, snip, prune, crop
2 *Clip the coupon and send it to the address below.*
▶ cut out, remove, detach, tear out
3 *She clipped him on the head and made him yell.*
▶ slap, smack, hit, cuff

clique NOUN
a clique of London journalists
▶ circle, group, set, coterie, crowd

cloak NOUN
1 *She threw her cloak over her shoulder.*
▶ cape, wrap, mantle, coat, cope, robe
2 *a cloak of secrecy*
▶ screen, mask, shield, cover, veneer

clog VERB
Wet leaves had clogged the drains.
▶ block, bung up, stop up, obstruct, choke

close ADJECTIVE
1 **close to** *A large proportion of the world's population lives close to rivers.*
▶ near, near to, adjacent to, alongside, not far from, in the vicinity of, within reach of
2 **close to** *He seemed to be close to tears as he told the story.*
▶ near to, on the verge of, on the brink of, on the point of
3 *The house is fairly close.*
▶ near, nearby
4 *At last an agreement seemed close.*
▶ imminent, impending, at hand
5 *It was a very close contest.*
▶ even, level, evenly matched, evenly balanced, hard-fought
6 *The aircraft were flying in a close formation.*
▶ tight, dense, concentrated, compact
7 *They are close friends.*
▶ intimate, dear, devoted, loving, constant
8 *The problem needs our close attention.*
▶ careful, thorough, fixed, concentrated, keen, intense
9 *The weather had become somewhat close.*
▶ humid, muggy, stuffy, airless, heavy, sticky, clammy, oppressive

close VERB
1 *Come in and close the door.*
▶ shut, lock, secure, fasten, bolt
2 *The road was closed at the far end.*
▶ block off, cordon off, bar, barricade, obstruct
3 *The chairman closed the meeting at this point.*
▶ conclude, end, finish, stop, terminate, discontinue, wind up, complete
4 *The hole had been closed with a wad of paper.*
▶ fill, stop, seal, plug, bung

5 *a plan to close the gap between rich and poor*
▶ narrow, reduce, lessen, shorten, fill, make smaller

close NOUN
At the close of polling, the votes are collected in a central area.
▶ end, finish, completion, conclusion, cessation, termination

clot NOUN
1 *a clot of blood* (formal)
▶ lump, mass, (in an artery or vein) embolism, thrombosis
2 *I felt a real clot.* (informal)
▶ fool, idiot

clot VERB
a substance to make the blood clot
▶ coagulate, congeal, set, thicken, solidify, stiffen

cloth NOUN
a length of cloth
▶ fabric, material, textile

clothe VERB
1 *Despite the war she was able to clothe herself well.*
▶ dress, fit out, attire
2 **be clothed in** *He was clothed in a long striped garment.*
▶ be dressed in, be attired in, wear

---

clothes PLURAL NOUN
She wore lovely clothes, beautifully made from fine materials.
▶ clothing, garments, attire, garb, dress, (more informal) gear, wardrobe, outfit
RELATED ADJECTIVE sartorial

NAMES FOR TYPES OF CLOTHES

outdoor coats: coat, overcoat, raincoat, mackintosh, (informal)mac, duffel coat, trench coat, cape.

casual coats: anorak, cagoule, bomber jacket, windcheater, blouson, Barbour jacket, combat jacket, donkey jacket, fleece, wrap, parka, poncho, reefer, safari jacket, shell jacket .

other outdoor clothes: gloves, scarf, muffler.

men's clothes: jacket, blazer, trousers, suit, slacks, jeans, shorts; kilt; shirt, T-shirt, sweatshirt; jersey, jumper, cardigan, waistcoat; underpants, jeans, briefs, boxer shorts, vest; socks; tie, cravat.

women's clothes: dress, suit, blouse, T-shirt, sweatshirt; skirt, miniskirt; sarong; shorts; jersey, jumper; bra, underpants, knickers, panties, petticoat, slip; stockings, tights, pantihose, leggings, leg warmers.

shoes: shoe, boot, bootee, court shoe, brogue; sandal, pump, espadrille, flip-flop, moccasin, mule, slip-on, slipper, sneaker, trainer, plimsoll, gymshoe; galosh, wellington, wader, gumboot.

cloud NOUN

1 *Visibility was affected by cloud.*
▶ haze, vapour, mist
2 *a cloud of steam*
▶ mass, billow, haze, mist, puff

cloud VERB

1 *A light haze clouded the view.*
▶ obscure, shade, hide, conceal, shroud, mist, dim
2 *Anger clouded their judgement.*
▶ confuse, obscure, blur, muddle, obfuscate

cloudy ADJECTIVE

1 *a cloudy sky*
▶ overcast, dull, grey, gloomy, hazy, leaden
OPPOSITES ARE clear, bright
2 *The water went cloudy.*
▶ hazy, milky, murky, muddy
AN OPPOSITE IS clear

clout VERB

His mother clouted him on the ear.
▶ hit, slap, thump, bash, box, smack, cuff, strike

clout NOUN

She threatened him with another clout on the ear.
▶ slap, smack, thump, bash

clown NOUN

They regarded him as the clown of the group.
▶ joker, jester, comedian, comic, fool, funny man orwoman, buffoon

club NOUN

1 *He had been hit with a heavy club.*
▶ cosh, cudgel, bat, bludgeon, truncheon, baton, stick
2 *She belonged to a local book club.*
▶ society, association, circle, group, union, organization, league, set

club VERB

The man had been clubbed almost to death.
▶ beat, batter, cosh, cudgel, hit, strike, (*more informal*) clobber

clue NOUN

1 *Give me a clue what it's all about.*
▶ hint, indication, sign, pointer, inkling, tip, idea, pointer, suggestion, key
2 *Police are looking for clues in the immediate area of the crime.*
▶ piece of evidence, lead, evidence
not have a clue *I didn't have a clue what to do next* (*informal*).
▶ have no idea, be baffled, be completely stuck, be at a loss, (*more informal*) not have the faintest idea

clump NOUN

1 *a clump of trees*
▶ cluster, group, mass, thicket, bunch, bundle, collection
2 *a clump of grass*
▶ tuft, bundle, bunch
3 *a clump of earth*
▶ lump, clod, mass

clumsy ADJECTIVE

1 *She was clumsy and spilt most of the milk.*
▶ inept, bungling, bumbling, blundering, fumbling uncoordinated, unskilful
OPPOSITES ARE careful, adroit
2 *His movements looked clumsy.*
▶ awkward, ungainly, graceless, ungraceful, gawky gangling, fumbling
OPPOSITES ARE graceful, elegant

cluster NOUN

1 *a cluster of buildings*
▶ group, bunch, collection
2 *a cluster of people*
▶ crowd, group, gathering, body, throng, assembly

clutch VERB

They were all clutching beer mugs.
▶ grip, grasp, clasp, hold

clutches PLURAL NOUN

At last he was free from their clutches.
▶ power, control, grasp, clasp, grip, hold, possession

clutter NOUN

It's difficult to work with all this clutter around.
▶ mess, muddle, confusion, untidiness, disorder, jumble, junk, litter, lumber, mix-up, odds and ends, rubbish

clutter VERB

Bits of broken machinery cluttered the yard.
▶ litter, fill, cover, bestrew, mess up

coach NOUN

1 *The coach takes the motorway.*
▶ bus, motor coach
2 *a horse-drawn coach*
▶ carriage, hansom, hackney, trap
3 *a railway coach*
▶ carriage, wagon, van
4 *a sports coach*
▶ trainer, instructor, teacher

coach VERB

Michael coached her to an international standard.
▶ train, instruct, tutor, teach, prepare

coagulate VERB

The warm blood coagulates.
▶ clot, congeal, cake, set, thicken, solidify, stiffen

coalition NOUN

a coalition from the three main political parties
▶ combination, alliance, union, partnership

coarse ADJECTIVE

1 *coarse sand   coarse cloth*
▶ rough, unrefined, unprocessed, lumpy, gritty
OPPOSITES ARE fine, soft
2 *coarse language*
▶ crude, vulgar, offensive, bawdy, lewd, foul, dirty, smutty, indecent, indelicate, improper, obscene, ribald
OPPOSITES ARE refined, polite

coast NOUN

a house by the coast
▶ seaside, seashore, sea, shore, beach, coastline, seaboard

WORDS FOR COASTAL FEATURES

geographical features: bay, beach, cliff, coral reef, current, delta, estuary, fjord, harbour, headland, island, mudbank, port, reef, sandbank, sand-dune, salt marsh, sea cave, shingle ridge, rock pool, stack, strand, strandline, tide, tideline, wave.

structures for coastal protection: breakwater, groyne, sea-wall.

oast VERB

The little car coasted down the slope.
▶ freewheel, cruise, taxi, drift, glide, sail

coat NOUN

1 *Put on a coat if you go out.*
▶ overcoat, jacket
2 *the coat of an animal*
▶ fur, hair, hide, pelt, skin, fleece
3 *a coat of paint*
▶ layer, coating, covering, veneer

KINDS OF COAT

long outdoor coats: overcoat, raincoat, mackintosh, (*informal*) mac, duffel coat, trench coat, cape.

casual outdoor coats: anorak, cagoule, bomber jacket, windcheater, blouson, Barbour jacket, combat jacket, donkey jacket, fleece, wrap, parka, poncho, reefer, safari jacket, shell jacket.

coat VERB

Coat the surface with varnish.
▶ cover, paint, glaze, varnish, laminate, smear

coating NOUN

a thick coating of paint
▶ layer, covering, coat, veneer

coax VERB

It was impossible to coax them back home.
▶ persuade, tempt, cajole, allure, entice, induce, wheedle, beguile, inveigle, woo

cobble VERB

He had two days to cobble together a report.
▶ improvise, contrive, scribble, knock up, put together

cocky ADJECTIVE

He had a cocky look on his face.
▶ arrogant, presumptuous, vain, conceited, self-important, bumptious, superior, disdainful, (*more informal*) pushy
AN OPPOSITE IS modest

code NOUN

1 *a code of conduct   a social code*
▶ system, set of rules, set of principles
2 *The message was written in code.*
▶ cipher, secret language

coerce VERB

He was coerced into signing an agreement.
▶ pressure, pressurize, force (to), compel (to), constrain (to), bully, browbeat, intimidate

coercion NOUN

Some form of coercion is needed to get them to start work.
▶ compulsion, pressure, force, constraint, intimidation, duress, harassment

coffee NOUN

KINDS OF COFFEE

cappuccino (milky with froth), cafe au lait (with milk), cafe noir (black, ie without milk), decaffeinated coffee, espresso (strong black Italian coffee), filter coffee, latte (frothy milk mixed with espresso), mocha (fine coffee with added chocolate), Gaelic coffee (with cream and whisky), Greek coffee (strong black coffee with grounds at the bottom), instant coffee, percolated coffee, Irish coffee (kind of Gaelic coffee), Turkish coffee (like Greek coffee).

coherent ADJECTIVE

a coherent argument
▶ logical, reasonable, rational, lucid, clear, sound, cogent, compelling, persuasive
OPPOSITES ARE incoherent, illogical

coil NOUN

coils of rope
▶ loop, twist, ring, spiral, roll, turn

coil VERB

He coiled her hair round his finger.
▶ curl, wind, twine, loop, roll

coin NOUN

1 *a pile of silver coins*
▶ piece, bit
2 *large quantities of coin*
▶ change, loose change, small change, coppers, silver

coin VERB

1 *The city began to coin silver money at this time.*
▶ mint, make, mould, stamp
RELATED ADJECTIVE numismatic
2 *A Czech writer coined the word 'robot'*
▶ invent, devise, make up, create, originate, think up, conceive

coincide VERB

1 *It was a nuisance that the two programmes coincided.*
▶ come together, occur simultaneously, happen at the same time, overlap, clash

2 coincide with *His life coincides with the decline of the Empire.*
▶ clash, coexist, fall together, happen together, synchronize

3 *Your interests and ours do not always coincide.*
▶ correspond, tally, agree, match, accord, harmonize

coincidence NOUN

The resemblance was just coincidence.
▶ accident, chance, fluke, luck, providence

coincidental ADJECTIVE

Any resemblance is purely coincidental.
▶ accidental, fortuitous, by chance, unintentional

cold ADJECTIVE

1 *a cold day   cold weather*
▶ chilly, cool, fresh, freezing, icy, raw, bitter, biting, perishing, wintry, (*more informal*) nippy, (*more informal*) parky
AN OPPOSITE IS hot

2 *I was feeling cold.*
▶ chilly, chilled, shivery, freezing, frozen
AN OPPOSITE IS hot

3 *a cold reception*
▶ unfriendly, unsympathetic, unwelcoming, cool, frosty, lukewarm, forbidding, indifferent, unenthusiastic
OPPOSITES ARE warm, friendly

cold NOUN

We all feel the cold in winter.
▶ coldness, chill, chilliness

cold-blooded ADJECTIVE

cold-blooded murder
▶ cruel, brutal, savage, barbaric, callous, inhuman, pitiless, merciless, sadistic
AN OPPOSITE IS humane

collaborate VERB

1 *Several companies have collaborated to develop a new vaccine.*
▶ cooperate, combine, unite, work together, join forces, team up

2 *Several villagers were accused of collaborating with the enemy.*
▶ conspire, fraternize, collude, consort, cooperate

collaboration NOUN

1 *The work was done in collaboration with a British firm.*
▶ association, cooperation, partnership, combination, alliance, tandem

2 *collaboration with the enemy*
▶ collusion, connivance, conspiring

collaborator NOUN

1 *She wrote the book with the help of a collaborator*
▶ associate, colleague, partner, co-worker, co-author

2 *After the war he was accused of being a collaborator*
▶ traitor, fraternizer, colluder, defector, fifth-columnist, quisling

collapse VERB

1 *Part of the floor collapsed.*
▶ fall in, cave in, fall down, give way, crumble, crumple, tumble down, buckle, disintegrate

2 *People were collapsing in the heat.*
▶ faint, pass out, lose consciousness, black out, keel over, (*more informal*) flake out

3 *Harriet collapsed exhausted in her chair.*
▶ fall, sink, slump

4 *The banking system was about to collapse.*
▶ fail, break down, founder, come to grief

collapse NOUN

1 *the collapse of part of the floor*
▶ cave-in, disintegration, subsidence

2 *the collapse of peace talks*
▶ breakdown, failure, foundering

colleague NOUN

It is important to get on with your colleagues.
▶ workmate, fellow worker, co-worker, teammate, associate

collect VERB

1 *He collected data from over fifty countries.*
▶ accumulate, gather, assemble, amass, accrue, bring together

2 *The squirrels scurried round collecting nuts.*
▶ gather, heap, hoard, lay up, pile up, put by, reserve, save, scrape together, stockpile, store
AN OPPOSITE IS scatter

3 *People collected to watch the fireworks.*
▶ assemble, gather, come together, congregate, crowd round, convene, converge, flock, group, muster
AN OPPOSITE IS disperse

4 *We are collecting money for charity.*
▶ raise, appeal for, ask for, seek, solicit

5 *I must collect the children from school.*
▶ fetch, get, meet, go and get, bring, call for
OPPOSITES ARE take, drop off

collection NOUN

1 *a collection of strange objects*
▶ assortment, accumulation, hoard, array, cluster, conglomeration, heap, mass, pile, supply, stock, set, stack

2 *a collection of people outside the ground*
▶ group, crowd, gathering, band, accumulation

3 *a collection of poems*
▶ anthology, selection, compilation, treasury, miscellany

collective ADJECTIVE

collective action to bring about change
▶ combined, concerted, united, unified, joint, corporate, common, group, shared, composite, cooperative, democratic
AN OPPOSITE IS individual

---

collective nouns PLURAL NOUN

COLLECTIVE NAMES FOR GROUPS OF BIRDS AND ANIMALS

general words: brood or clutch (of chickens), flock (of birds and sheep), flight (of birds flying), drove (of cattle), herd (of cows and other cattle, and large animals such as elephants and giraffes), gaggle (of geese on the ground), litter (of young born in large numbers, such as puppies, kittens, fox cubs, and pigs), pack (animals that hunt in a group, such as hounds and wolves), pride (of lions), school (of sea mammals such as dolphins and whales), shoal (of fish), swarm (of densely flying insects, e.g. bees and locusts), team (of horses and other draught animals), troop (of monkeys).
USAGE There are many other names that come from collections made by antiquarian writers in the 18th and 19th centuries, for example an *exaltation of larks* and a *bloat of hippopotamuses*. These are all fanciful names that are not used in normal writing. Some names have special meanings, e.g. a swarm of bees is not just a group of bees but a dense mass of bees flying to make a new colony.

---

college NOUN

a college of art
▶ school, academy, institute, conservatory

collide VERB

1 collide with *A van collided head on with the stolen vehicle.*
▶ crash into, smash into, hit, strike

2 *The two vehicles collided head on.*
▶ crash, hit each other, run into each other, meet

collision NOUN

a collision on the motorway
▶ crash, accident, smash, pile-up

colloquial ADJECTIVE

colloquial language
▶ informal, conversational, everyday, casual, vernacular
AN OPPOSITE IS formal

collude VERB

Officials colluded with the smugglers at the border.
▶ conspire, connive, collaborate, plot, scheme, intrigue

collusion NOUN

collusion between officials and the smugglers
▶ conspiracy, connivance, collaboration, complicity, intrigue, scheming

colonist NOUN

the first European colonists in North America
▶ settler, colonizer, pioneer, immigrant, newcomer

colonize VERB

Settlers colonized the southern part of the country.
▶ settle in, found a colony in, move into, occupy, people, populate

colony NOUN

1 *Britain's former colonies in the region*
▶ territory, possession, dependency, dominion, protectorate, province, settlement, outpost

2 *the British colony in New York*
▶ population, community

colossal ADJECTIVE

A colossal building
▶ huge, massive, enormous, gigantic, immense, vast, giant, towering, mammoth, monumental, elephantine
AN OPPOSITE IS tiny

---

colour NOUN

1 *You can choose from over thirty beautiful colours.*
▶ hue, shade, tint, tone, tinge, pigment, tincture, colouring

2 *The exercise put some colour back in her cheeks.*
▶ bloom, redness, pinkness, glow, rosiness, ruddiness

3 colours *the team's new colours*
▶ strip, kit, uniform, livery, outfit

4 colours *the regimental colours*
▶ banner, ensign, flag, standard

NAMES OF COLOURS

The colours are listed in an order that goes from pale (or bright) to dark (or deep). Many colours are named after things of the same colour, including flowers and fruits (eg *cherry* and *rose*), gems and precious stones (eg *emerald* and *ruby*), minerals (eg *coral*), and wines (eg *burgundy* and *claret*).

reds: cerise, pink, magnolia (creamy-pink), vermilion, scarlet, cherry, orange (yellowish-red), pink rose (warm pink), peach (pinkish-orange), flame (bright orange-red), plum (purplish-red), fuchsia (purplish-red), crimson, cardinal (deep scarlet), claret (deep purplish-red), ruby, burgundy, copper (brownish-red), auburn (brownish-red), rust (brownish-red), sepia (brownish-red), maroon (brownish-red), magenta (reddish-mauve), puce (purplish-brown), purple (bluish-red).

yellows: cream (whitish-yellow), primrose, lemon, canary, straw, saffron, amber (honey-yellow), gold, topaz, sand (pale brownish-yellow), cinnamon (brownish-yellow), ochre (brownish-yellow), bronze (brownish-yellow), mustard (brownish-yellow).

▶▶

blues: azure, sky blue, aquamarine (greenish-blue), jade (greenish-blue), turquoise (greenish-blue), cyan (greenish-blue), sapphire, lavender (pale bluish-mauve), lilac (pale pinkish-violet), slate (greyish-blue), cerulean, cobalt, royal blue, Oxford blue, Prussian blue, navy, indigo, violet (bluish-purple), gentian (bluish-purple).

greens: emerald, chartreuse, pea green, viridian (bluish-green), sea green (bluish-green), sap green (yellowish-green), bottle green, sage (greyish-green), olive (greyish-green).

browns: biscuit, fawn, sable, taupe (brownish-grey), sludge, burnt ochre (yellowish-brown), sienna (yellowish-brown), tawny (yellowish-brown), umber (yellowish-brown), chocolate.

greys and blacks: silver, charcoal, ebony, pitch, jet.

whites: ivory, off-white (greyish-white), pearl (greyish-white).

colour VERB
1 *Why not colour it blue?*
▶ paint, tint, tinge, dye, stain, shade, colourwash
2 *Her face began to colour.*
▶ blush, flush, redden, go red
OPPOSITES ARE fade, go pale
3 *The experience had coloured his judgement.*
▶ influence, affect, prejudice, sway, impinge on, slant, bias, distort, pervert

colourful ADJECTIVE
1 *a colourful bunch of flowers*
▶ brilliant, bright, showy, radiant, vibrant, gaudy, iridescent, multicoloured, psychedelic
OPPOSITES ARE colourless, dull
2 *a colourful account of the incident*
▶ graphic, vivid, dramatic, picturesque, animated, exciting, stimulating, striking, florid, picturesque, rich
OPPOSITES ARE dull, plain
3 *music and colourful dancing*
▶ lively, flamboyant, glamorous, energetic, dashing, vigorous, flashy
AN OPPOSITE IS restrained

colourless ADJECTIVE
1 *a bottle of colourless liquid*
▶ transparent, uncoloured, neutral, watery
2 *a colourless complexion*
▶ pale, pallid, wan, anaemic, sickly
3 *a colourless personality*
▶ dull, uninteresting, unexciting, boring, tedious, insipid, dismal, drab, characterless, dreary, vapid, lacklustre, monotonous
AN OPPOSITE IS colourful

column NOUN
1 *The temple stood on massive columns.*
▶ pillar, support, pilaster, post, upright

2 *His sister writes a column in the local newspaper.*
▶ article, report, feature, review, editorial
3 *a column of figures*
▶ list, line, string
4 *The troops advanced in three columns.*
▶ line, row, rank

comb VERB
1 *He looked for a mirror to comb his hair.*
▶ groom, tidy, neaten, arrange, smarten up, smooth out, untangle
2 *Police combed the house and garden for signs of a struggle.*
▶ search, scour, explore, rake, ransack, hunt, sweep

combat NOUN
Many men were killed in the combat that followed.
▶ action, battle, fight, fighting, hostilities, warfare, engagement, encounter, armed conflict, contest, clash

combat VERB
new measures to combat crime
▶ fight, battle against, tackle, contest, counter, contend against, stand up to, strive against, struggle against, withstand, face up to, grapple with, oppose, resist

combination NOUN
1 *a combination of luck and good judgement*
▶ blend, mixture, amalgamation, fusion, synthesis
2 *The evidence was considered in combination with other factors.*
▶ conjunction, association

combine VERB
1 *His father combines a social visit with a trip to the laundry.*
▶ merge, amalgamate, join (to)
2 *Several drivers combined to get everyone home.*
▶ cooperate, collaborate, join forces, pool resources, come together, get together, link up, unite

come VERB
1 *Our friends came last night.*
▶ arrive, appear, visit, (*more informal*) turn up
2 *Spring came early this year.*
▶ occur, happen
3 **come to** *Eventually they came to a river.*
▶ reach, arrive at, get to, come across, happen on, approach, near
4 **come to** *The shirt came to his knees.*
▶ reach, extend to
come about
▶ happen, occur, (*more formal*) come to pass
come across *I came across an old friend.*
▶ find, encounter, discover, chance upon, meet, (*more informal*) bump into
come apart *One of my shoes came apart.*
▶ disintegrate, fall to pieces, break up
come clean *You'd better come clean before they find out.*
▶ confess, own up
come out with *Goodness knows what he'll come out with next.*

▶ say, let out, utter, disclose

come round *It took nearly an hour for her to come round after the operation.*
▶ recover, wake, awake

to come up *Something has come up and she has had to leave.*
▶ arise, occur, happen, crop up

to come upon *He came upon a little hut in the wood.*
▶ find, discover, (*more informal*) bump into

comeback NOUN
The band has achieved an amazing comeback.
▶ recovery, revival, resurgence, rally, upturn

comedian NOUN
a well-known television comedian
▶ comic, entertainer, humorist, wit, jester, buffoon, clown, fool, joker, wag

comedown NOUN
His new job was a bit of a comedown.
▶ anticlimax, humiliation, let-down, disappointment

comedy NOUN
The show contained a great deal of comedy.
▶ humour, farce, wit, jesting, facetiousness, clowning, satire, slapstick, fun, joking, buffoonery, hilarity

comfort NOUN
1 *They like to live in comfort.*
▶ ease, tranquillity, luxury, opulence, prosperity, relaxation, well-being
OPPOSITES ARE discomfort, hardship
2 *We tried to offer the unfortunate woman some words of comfort.*
▶ consolation, sympathy, condolence, commiseration, encouragement, moral support, reassurance, solace, succour, support, aid, help
OPPOSITES ARE misery, grief

comfort VERB
Her sister tried to comfort her.
▶ console, soothe, cheer, assuage, hearten, encourage, reassure, solace, sympathize with

comfortable ADJECTIVE
1 *a comfortable chair   a comfortable house*
▶ snug, cosy, relaxing, convenient, pleasant, easy, enjoyable, roomy, plush, soft, well furnished, warm, (*more informal*) comfy
AN OPPOSITE IS uncomfortable
2 *comfortable shoes*
▶ well-fitting, well-made, snug
3 *a comfortable lifestyle*
▶ prosperous, affluent, pleasant, well-off, luxurious, agreeable

comic ADJECTIVE
The effect of the speech was almost comic.
▶ comical, humorous, funny, amusing, entertaining, diverting, laughable, facetious, hilarious, absurd, ridiculous, ludicrous

comic NOUN
1 *The show included a rather feeble comic.*
▶ comedian, entertainer, jester, clown, humorist
2 *A girl was buying a comic to read on the train.*
▶ magazine, cartoon paper

command NOUN
1 *Officers shouted commands.*
▶ order, instruction, directive, direction, requirement
2 *He has twenty men under his command.*
▶ authority, control, direction, charge, leadership, supervision, jurisdiction
3 *She has a good command of French and German.*
▶ knowledge, mastery, grasp, understanding, comprehension, grip, fluency (in)

command VERB
1 *He commanded his men to advance.*
▶ order, instruct, direct, tell, call on, require, bid
2 *Meredith commands a squadron.*
▶ be in charge of, be in command of, have charge of, lead, head, manage, supervise, rule, control, govern

commandeer VERB
The army commandeered all vehicles in the area.
▶ seize, appropriate, requisition, impound, sequester, take over, take possession of, confiscate

commander NOUN
Army commanders were discouraged from getting involved in politics.
▶ chief, leader, officer, general, head, captain, commanding officer

commemorate VERB
The ceremony commemorated those who died in war.
▶ celebrate, honour, salute, remember, be a memorial to, be a reminder of, pay respects to, pay tribute to

commence VERB
1 *Work will commence in the spring.*
▶ begin, start, get under way
2 *He has now commenced his contract with an Italian club.*
▶ begin, start, inaugurate, launch, open, get under way

commend VERB
1 *The committee commended her for a thorough and useful report.*
▶ praise, compliment, congratulate, applaud, salute, acclaim
AN OPPOSITE IS criticize
2 *They have done well and I commend them unreservedly.*
▶ recommend, endorse, support, vouch for

comment NOUN
1 *I have had some very positive comments about it.*
▶ remark, opinion, criticism, observation, reference, statement, mention
2 *He added a few comments at the end of the paper.*
▶ note, annotation, footnote, gloss
3 *The news caused a lot of comment in the press.*
▶ discussion, debate, interest, consideration

comment VERB

comment on *The article commented on the problems of travel in the area.*
▶ mention, discuss, refer to, allude to, remark on, touch on, speak about

commentary NOUN

1 *a commentary on the test match*
▶ description, report, narration, account
2 *The second part contains a commentary on the text.*
▶ analysis, criticism, critique, explanation, review, interpretation, treatise, discourse, elucidation, notes

commentator NOUN

a radio commentator
▶ announcer, reporter, narrator, broadcaster, journalist

commerce NOUN

Settlers came to Gaul for the sake of commerce.
▶ trade, trading, buying and selling, business, dealing, traffic, (*old-fashioned*) merchandising

commercial ADJECTIVE

1 *The ships were built for commercial use*
▶ trading, trade, business, economic, financial, mercantile
2 *She turned to writing as a commercial venture.*
▶ business, monetary, financial, profitable, profit-making, viable, lucrative

commercial NOUN

The drama was ruined by so many breaks for commercials.
▶ advertisement, promotion, (*more informal*) ad, (*more informal*) advert

commercialized ADJECTIVE

Christmas has become so commercialized.
▶ commercial, mercenary, profit-orientated, materialistic

commiserate VERB

commiserate with *We commiserated with the victims.*
▶ sympathize with, express sympathy for, console, feel for, comfort

commission NOUN

a commission to paint the family's portraits
▶ assignment, appointment, contract, order, mandate, charge, instruction, project, undertaking, task

commission VERB

They went on to commission him to build a palace for the queen.
▶ appoint, engage, contract, recruit, employ, hire, retain, delegate, select, nominate

commit VERB

1 *He swore he had not committed any crime.*
▶ carry out, be guilty of, be responsible for, perform, perpetrate, do, effect, enact, execute, (*more informal*) pull off

2 *The child was committed to her care.*
▶ entrust, consign, hand over, give over, turn over, deliver, deposit

commit yourself to *Students often have to commit themselves to long leases on lodgings.*
▶ undertake, pledge, guarantee, promise, contract

commitment NOUN

1 *The contract included a commitment to complete the work by the end of the year.*
▶ promise, pledge, undertaking, guarantee, assurance, liability, duty
2 *The team felt a commitment to continue the search.*
▶ determination, resolution, obligation, responsibility, dedication, devotion
3 *There are only a few commitments this week.*
▶ engagement, duty, appointment

committed ADJECTIVE

a committed member of the group
▶ dedicated, active, devoted, keen, staunch, loyal, faithful, devout, enthusiastic, diligent, resolute, ardent, earnest, fervent
AN OPPOSITE IS apathetic

committee NOUN

A committee will be set up to supervise the project.
▶ board, panel, council, supervisory body, advisory group, task force

common ADJECTIVE

1 *This is a common question. Accidents are quite common on this stretch of road.*
▶ frequent, regular, usual, normal, habitual, customary, familiar, standard, typical, routine, everyday
2 *Her parents had thought some of her friends were too common for her.*
▶ inferior, low-class, ill-bred, vulgar, coarse, crude
3 *There is a common belief in these superstitions.*
▶ widespread, general, popular, universal, prevalent, conventional, established, accepted
4 *working for the common good*
▶ collective, communal, public, shared, joint

common NOUN

Local children play ball games on the common.
▶ heath, park

commonplace ADJECTIVE

1 *a commonplace occurrence*
▶ common, regular, normal, typical, familiar, routine, standard, everyday, unremarkable
AN OPPOSITE IS unusual
2 *a commonplace style of writing*
▶ ordinary, plain, simple, unremarkable, undistinguished, average, indifferent, humdrum, pedestrian, prosaic
OPPOSITES ARE remarkable, original

commonsense ADJECTIVE

a commonsense approach to life
▶ sensible, practical, level-headed, down-to-earth, pragmatic, no-nonsense, realistic, sane, sound
OPPOSITES ARE unreasonable, unrealistic

ommotion NOUN

She was distracted by the commotion across the street.
▶ disturbance, uproar, racket, tumult, hullabaloo, hubbub, rumpus, fracas, furore, upheaval, agitation, excitement

ommunal ADJECTIVE

communal washing facilities
▶ collective, shared, joint, common, public, general, mutual, open
AN OPPOSITE IS private

ommune NOUN

She lived for several years in a commune in Chicago.
▶ community, collective, settlement, colony, fellowship, kibbutz

ommunicate VERB

1 *Somebody has to communicate the bad news to her.*
convey, announce, report, reveal, declare, disclose, impart, pass on, relate

USAGE You can also say *Somebody has to tell her the bad news,* or *Somebody has to inform her of the bad news,* or *Somebody has to acquaint her with the bad news.*

2 communicate with *Parents and teachers need to communicate with one another regularly.*
speak to, talk to, make contact with, liaise with

3 communicate with *Each bedroom communicates with its own bathroom.*
▶ connect with, adjoin, lead to

4 *It is possible to communicate the disease through ordinary contact.*
▶ transmit, pass on, infect someone with, spread, transfer, give

communication NOUN

1 *She received an official communication from the tax office.*
▶ message, letter, correspondence, advice
2 *There has been little communication between them for several years.*
▶ contact, dealings, association, relations, correspondence, intercourse
3 *The newsletters are used for the communication of information.*
▶ transmission, imparting, disclosure, dissemination, reporting, passing on

NAMES FOR TYPES OF COMMUNICATION

spoken communication: conversation, dialogue, message, rumour, gossip, phone conversation; broadcasting, radio, television; advertising.

written communication: letter, correspondence, postcard, note, memo (in offices), cable.

official communication: announcement, statement, notice, bulletin, dispatch, memorandum, proclamation; newsflash. ▶▶

electronic communication: email, network, Internet, fax, text messages.

the mass media: newspapers, journalism, the press, magazine, television, films.

communicative ADJECTIVE

They are always friendly and communicative.
▶ forthcoming, outgoing, informative, candid, uninhibited, frank, open, sociable, talkative
OPPOSITES ARE uncommunicative, secretive

community NOUN

1 *He had the interests of the community in mind.*
▶ population, populace, society, people, residents, inhabitants, local people, general public
2 *a small farming community in the Borders*
▶ district, region, locality, neighbourhood
3 *a community of gay men*
▶ group, colony, commune, coterie, band, society

commute VERB

1 *The death sentence will be commuted to life imprisonment.*
▶ reduce, lessen, cut, lighten, remit, moderate, adjust
2 *Her husband commutes to the city every day.*
▶ travel, journey, shuttle

compact ADJECTIVE

1 *a compact machine that will fit in a small suitcase*
▶ small, little, petite, portable
2 *a compact encyclopedia*
▶ concise, succinct, condensed, brief

compact NOUN

the government's compact with the unions
▶ agreement, pact, accord, deal, bargain, arrangement, understanding

companion NOUN

He turned to speak to his companions.
▶ friend, associate, comrade, colleague, partner, mate, escort

company NOUN

1 *I miss her company.*
▶ companionship, fellowship, society, presence, friendship
2 *We are expecting company tomorrow evening.*
▶ visitors, guests, callers
3 *He works for an insurance company.*
▶ firm, business, corporation, establishment, concern, enterprise, office, bureau
4 *a performance by the local theatre company*
▶ group, troupe, society, ensemble, association
5 *a company of friends*
▶ group, circle, community, band, gang, gathering

comparable ADJECTIVE

Customers will look elsewhere for better service at comparable prices. Interest rates are not comparable to those in the rest of Europe.
▶ similar, equivalent, corresponding, proportionate, commensurate (with), analogous, parallel, compatible (with), equal, related
AN OPPOSITE IS dissimilar

comparative ADJECTIVE

He would have to leave the comparative comfort he had enjoyed up to now.
▶ relative

compare VERB

1 *We have to compare this year's results with last year's.*
▶ check (against), contrast, correlate, juxtapose, set side by side, weigh, draw parallels between, make connections between, match, relate
2 *You can't compare the book to the video.*
▶ liken, equate, draw a parallel between (*the book and the video*), regard (*the book*) as the same as (*the video*)
compare with *Our achievements hardly compare with yours.*
▶ match, equal, compete with, emulate, rival, vie with

comparison NOUN

1 *There is no comparison between the two versions of the story.*
▶ resemblance, likeness, similarity, correspondence, parallel, correlation, equivalence, analogy
2 *The conclusions are based on a comparison of Hackney and Westminster.*
▶ analysis, collation, correlation, juxtaposition, contrast

compartment NOUN

1 *He then discovered that the case had a secret compartment.*
▶ section, space, pocket, cavity, recess
2 *The shed has a small compartment at the back for tools.*
▶ alcove, space, niche, cubby-hole, chamber, division

compassion NOUN

She felt for him the compassion of an elder sister.
▶ sympathy, pity, concern, understanding, commiseration, tenderness, warmth, fellow feeling, mercy
OPPOSITES ARE indifference, heartlessness

compatible ADJECTIVE

1 *The couple were never compatible.*
▶ well suited, well matched, harmonious, like-minded, suitable
2 *The injuries are not compatible with its having been an accident.*
▶ consistent, reconcilable, consonant, accordant, congruent, matching
AN OPPOSITE IS incompatible

compel VERB

1 *The court could compel him to give evidence.*
▶ force, oblige, coerce, constrain, order, pressure, pressurize
2 **be compelled to** *In the end Jem was compelled to admit the truth.*
▶ have to, be obliged to, be bound to, have no choice but to

compelling ADJECTIVE

a compelling argument
▶ forceful, convincing, cogent, persuasive, powerful, irresistible

compensate VERB

1 *If you have lost money you will be compensated for i*
▶ recompense, repay, reimburse, pay back, remunerate
2 **compensate for** *Nothing can compensate for such dreadful loss.*
▶ make up for, make amends for, balance, offset, counteract, cancel out, neutralize, redress, atone f

compensation NOUN

1 *You will receive compensation for any loss.*
▶ reparation, recompense, reimbursement, repayment, restitution, amends
2 *The balmy evenings were some compensation for th unpleasantness of the day.*
▶ consolation, recompense, comfort

compère NOUN

the compere of a TV programme
▶ host, presenter, anchorman, anchorwoman, anchorperson, announcer, Master of Ceremonies, MC

compete VERB

1 *The boys were competing in a five-a-side tournamen*
▶ take part, participate, perform, enter, go in for
2 *You will have to compete with children over twice yo age.*
▶ contend, vie
3 **compete with** *No one can compete with him whe he's on good form.*
▶ match, rival, compare with, equal, challenge, emulate, keep up with

competent ADJECTIVE

1 *a competent builder*
▶ capable, proficient, accomplished, qualified, abl skilful, efficient, adept
AN OPPOSITE IS incompetent
2 *a competent performance*
▶ adequate, satisfactory, acceptable, decent, reasonable

competition NOUN

1 *We face some fierce competition this year.*
▶ opposition, rivalry, contention, struggle, contest
2 *Lisa came third in the competition.*
▶ contest, match, tournament, game, championship, race

ompetitive ADJECTIVE

1 *a competitive sport*
▶ combative, contentious, aggressive, antagonistic

2 *a competitive player*
▶ ambitious, aggressive, combative

3 *Banking is a highly competitive business.*
▶ ruthless, aggressive, contentious, fierce, cut-throat

4 *top quality at competitive prices*
▶ reasonable, moderate, affordable, keen, economical
OPPOSITES ARE exorbitant, uncompetitive

ompetitor NOUN

1 *Every competitor has to take a blood test.*
▶ candidate, contestant, entrant, participant, contender

2 *We have to improve on our business competitors*
▶ rival, challenger, adversary, opponent

ompile VERB

An editor is needed to compile a new encyclopedia.
▶ assemble, put together, edit, organize, compose, gather together, collect together

omplacent ADJECTIVE

We are doing a good job but we must not be complacent.
▶ smug, self-satisfied, overconfident, oversatisfied, pleased with yourself, self-congratulatory, self-righteous, unconcerned, contented, untroubled
AN OPPOSITE IS dissatisfied

omplain VERB

1 *We'll wait till we get home before complaining.*
▶ protest, make a complaint, grumble

2 complain about *The neighbours complained about the noise.*
▶ protest about, grumble about, make a fuss about, object to, carp about, find fault with, criticize, condemn, (*more informal*) whinge about, (*more informal*) go on about

omplaint NOUN

1 *After a series of complaints about his behaviour he was sent back to England.*
▶ protest, objection (to), criticism (of), accusation, grumble, censure, fault-finding, (*more informal*) gripe

2 *Supporters have little cause for complaint.*
▶ grievance, dissatisfaction, disapproval, criticism, grumbling, fuss

3 *Her breathing difficulty was due to a lung complaint.*
▶ disorder, disease, illness, infection, sickness, upset, affliction, ailment, indisposition, malady, malaise

complement NOUN

The ship was carrying its full complement of passengers.
▶ capacity, quota, amount, total, allowance, aggregate

USAGE Do not confuse *complement* with *compliment.*

complement VERB

The restaurant's wine list complements its good food perfectly.
▶ accompany, complete, go with, round off, enhance, make complete, make perfect

USAGE Do not confuse *complement* with *compliment.*

complete ADJECTIVE

1 *The complete report will be published tomorrow.*
▶ whole, full, entire, unabridged, unedited, unexpurgated, total, unabbreviated
AN OPPOSITE IS incomplete

2 *The exercise is now complete.*
▶ completed, finished, concluded, ended, accomplished, achieved
AN OPPOSITE IS incomplete

3 *He was acting like a complete fool.*
▶ absolute, utter, out-and-out, thorough, thoroughgoing, outright
OPPOSITES ARE qualified, partial

4 *The story was complete rubbish.*
▶ utter, absolute, downright, sheer, pure, total, unqualified, unmitigated

complete VERB

1 *She will complete her training in two years.*
▶ finish, end, conclude, terminate, finalize, fulfil, round off, accomplish, achieve, carry out, clinch, close, do, perfect, perform, (*informal*) wind up

2 *Please complete the application form attached.*
▶ fill in, fill out, fill up, answer

completely ADVERB

He was completely honest about what had happened.
▶ totally, absolutely, utterly, entirely, perfectly, quite

completion NOUN

the completion of the project
▶ finish, conclusion, realization, achievement, fulfilment

complex ADJECTIVE

a complex subject
▶ complicated, intricate, involved, elaborate, convoluted, tortuous, tangled, diverse, manifold
OPPOSITES ARE simple, straightforward

complexion NOUN

1 *a young girl with a pale complexion*
▶ colouring, colour, appearance, skin, skin colour

2 *The latest revelation put a new complexion on things.*
▶ perspective, angle, slant

3 *political views of different complexions*
▶ type, kind, sort, nature, character

complicate VERB

His odd attitude complicated his relationships.
▶ make more difficult, confuse, muddle, tangle, mix up
AN OPPOSITE IS simplify

complicated ADJECTIVE
a complicated story   a complicated set of rules
▶ complex, intricate, involved, elaborate, convoluted, tortuous, tangled, diverse, manifold
OPPOSITES ARE simple, straightforward

complication NOUN
1 *Patients can leave hospital after three days if no complications occur.*
▶ problem, setback, repercussion, difficulty, drawback, snag, complexity, ramification
2 *the complication of modern city life*
▶ intricacy, complexity, confusion

complicity NOUN
their complicity in the crime
▶ collusion, collaboration, connivance, involvement

compliment NOUN
She blushed at the unexpected compliment.
▶ praise, flattery, tribute, accolade, approval, eulogy, (*more informal*) pat on the back
AN OPPOSITE IS insult
USAGE Do not confuse *compliment* with *complement. Flattery* usually means insincere praise.

compliment VERB
He complimented her on the performance.
▶ praise, applaud, commend, congratulate, flatter
OPPOSITES ARE criticize, insult
USAGE See the note at the previous entry.

complimentary ADJECTIVE
1 *The comments were all complimentary.*
▶ appreciative, approving, favourable, congratulatory, laudatory, admiring, commendatory, eulogistic, flattering, fulsome, generous, rapturous, supportive
OPPOSITES ARE critical, insulting
2 *You get a complimentary lunch on the day of arrival.*
▶ free, gratis, courtesy

comply VERB
comply with *He was anxious to comply with their wishes.*
▶ abide by, accede to, observe, obey, follow, fulfil, acquiesce in, submit to, yield to, agree to, assent to, conform to, consent to, defer to, fall in with, perform, satisfy
OPPOSITES ARE ignore, defy

component NOUN
a store full of components for computers
▶ part, piece, bit, constituent part, spare part, unit, element, ingredient, item, (*more informal*) spare

compose VERB
1 *The village was composed of small huts*
▶ build, compile, constitute, construct, fashion, form, frame, make, put together
2 *That year he composed mainly film music.   She sat down to compose a letter.*
▶ write, create, arrange, devise, imagine, make up, produce

compose yourself *He began to tremble and tried t compose himself.*
▶ calm down, control yourself, settle down, pull yourself together
be composed of *The government was composed of individuals rather than parties.*
▶ consist of, comprise, contain, embody, incorporate, involve, comprehend, embrace, include

composed ADJECTIVE
She looked stunning that day and very composed.
▶ calm, confident, self-controlled, placid, relaxed, a ease, unruffled

composition NOUN
1 *the composition of the new team*
▶ structure, make-up, formation, constitution, content, establishment, formulation
2 *the composition of a group of poems*
▶ writing, creation, devising, production
3 *a musical composition*
▶ piece, work, (*technical*) opus

composure NOUN
She acted with great composure.
▶ self-control, dignity, calmness, coolness, tranquillity, (*more informal*) cool

compound NOUN
1 *a chemical compound*
▶ amalgam, synthesis, alloy, blend, mixture, composite, composition, fusion
2 *a compound of energy and enthusiasm*
▶ combination, blend, mixture, synthesis
3 *a compound for animals*
▶ enclosure, pen, run

compound VERB
The bad weather compounded our difficulties.
▶ aggravate, exacerbate, intensify, increase, worsen, complicate

comprehend VERB
I tried to comprehend what he was saying.
▶ understand, grasp, conceive, fathom, make sense of, appreciate, conceive, discern, fathom, follow, perceive

comprehensible ADJECTIVE
The explanation was thorough and comprehensible.
▶ understandable, intelligible, clear, straightforward, lucid, meaningful
AN OPPOSITE IS incomprehensible

comprehension NOUN
She spoke in a dialect that was beyond my comprehension.
▶ understanding, grasp, knowledge, perception

comprehensive ADJECTIVE
a comprehensive account of the topic
▶ inclusive, complete, full, broad, exhaustive, compendious, wide-ranging, detailed, extensive, all-embracing, thorough, total, universal, encyclopedic
OPPOSITES ARE selective, partial

ompress VERB

1 *The activities can be compressed into an eight-hour day.*
▶ squeeze, press, squash, jam

2 *The text has been compressed into a mere ten pages.*
▶ condense, abridge, shorten, cut, summarize

omprise VERB

The building comprises several apartments.
▶ consist of, contain, be composed of, include, incorporate, embody, embrace, involve

ompromise NOUN

Eventually the two sides reached a compromise.
▶ understanding, accommodation, settlement, agreement, middle course, middle way

ompromise VERB

1 *In the end we had to compromise.*
▶ make concessions, meet halfway, strike a balance, concede a point, negotiate, settle

2 *The scandal has severely compromised his reputation.*
▶ undermine, discredit, jeopardize, weaken, prejudice, risk, dishonour, imperil

ompromising ADJECTIVE

Before he left he tore up the compromising letter.
▶ embarrassing, damaging, scandalous, discreditable, dishonourable, improper

ompulsion NOUN

1 *There is no compulsion to go.*
▶ obligation, necessity, constraint, pressure

2 *She felt a strong compulsion to tell the whole story.*
▶ urge, impulse, desire, longing, obsession

ompulsive ADJECTIVE

1 *He felt a compulsive urge to jump out.*
▶ irresistible, uncontrollable, overpowering, overwhelming, besetting, compelling, driving, involuntary, powerful

2 *Not all fat people are compulsive over-eaters.*
▶ habitual, obsessive, addicted, persistent, incorrigible, incurable

ompulsory ADJECTIVE

Each exam paper has one compulsory question. Carrying an identity card is now compulsory.
▶ obligatory, mandatory, binding, required, stipulated, unavoidable, de rigueur, imperative, imposed, incumbent, inescapable, official
AN OPPOSITE IS optional

ompunction NOUN

He had no compunction about lying.
▶ scruples, misgivings, qualms, guilt feelings, conscience

ompute VERB

Interest is computed daily.
▶ calculate, reckon, work out, assess, add up, total, count, estimate, evaluate, measure

computer NOUN

WORDS ASSOCIATED WITH COMPUTERS

types of computer: mainframe, personal computer (PC), laptop, notebook, palmtop, workstation, word processor.

parts of a computer: hardware, system, network, server, terminal; disk drive or hard disk, central processing unit (CPU), motherboard, memory, buffer (temporary memory), cache (extra memory for high-speed retrieval), clipboard (temporary storage area for copied or cut data), floppy disk, CD-ROM, CD-ROM drive, sound card, graphics card; monitor or visual display unit (VDU), desktop, speaker; keyboard, mouse, cursor, icon; modem; bus (set of conductors), parallel port, USB (universal serial bus) port, gateway.

peripherals: printer, scanner.

software and documents: program, BIOS (Basic Input-Ouput System), firmware (software permanently installed), code (program instructions), application (piece of software for a particular purpose), applet (small application within a larger program), file, directory (group of files), data, database, spreadsheet, record, batch (group of records processed together), bit (unit of information), byte (group of units), hyperlink, hypertext; screen saver.

processes: boot (starting up), data processing, saving, autosave, back-up, bookmark, Boolean operator; click, double-click, drag, cut-and-paste, download (file from system or network), import, export, exit (leave a program or system); zip (compressing files), unzip.

Internet and emailing: service provider (ISP), browser (for displaying Internet websites), website, cookie (data sent by an Internet server to a browser); email, attachment; online, offline.

problems: crash (complete failure of system), freeze (sudden locking of computer screen), bug (error in a program), virus (harmful code).

comrade NOUN

The officers went back up the slope to their comrades.
▶ companion, associate, colleague, friend, partner, mate, escort

con NOUN

The offer proved to be just a con.
▶ trick, cheat, swindle, deception, fraud

con VERB

They conned the couple out of their life savings.
▶ trick, cheat, swindle, dupe, deceive, inveigle, hoodwink, (*more informal*) bamboozle

conceal VERB

1 *She concealed the device in her camera A mass of cloud concealed the sun.*
▶ hide, cover up, disguise, secrete, blot out, mask,

obscure, screen, veil, bury, cloak, envelop, camouflage
OPPOSITES ARE reveal, expose, uncover
2 *He could barely conceal his frustration.*
▶ hide, suppress, keep secret, hush up, keep dark, keep quiet
AN OPPOSITE IS reveal

concealed ADJECTIVE
The house stood behind a concealed entrance.
▶ hidden, invisible, camouflaged, disguised, secret, cloaked, furtive, unobtrusive
OPPOSITES ARE obvious, visible

concede VERB
1 *I conceded that I might have been wrong.*
▶ admit, acknowledge, accept, grant, agree, recognize, allow, confess
AN OPPOSITE IS deny
2 *The country conceded some of the territory to its neighbour.*
▶ surrender, yield, give up, relinquish, cede, hand over, submit

conceit NOUN
She said it without conceit, simply as a fact.
▶ vanity, arrogance, pride, boastfulness

conceited ADJECTIVE
Without sounding conceited, I think we offer the best service.
▶ vain, boastful, immodest, arrogant, haughty, self-satisfied, proud, complacent, (*more informal*) cocky
AN OPPOSITE IS modest

conceivable ADJECTIVE
There is no conceivable reason for agreeing.
▶ imaginable, credible, believable, possible

conceive VERB
1 *She was unable to conceive.*
▶ get pregnant, become pregnant, have a baby
2 *The plan was conceived after the war.*
▶ think up, devise, originate, create, form, formulate, invent, design
3 *It is hard to conceive what it must have been like for them.*
▶ imagine, envisage, visualize, picture, appreciate, comprehend, apprehend, grasp

concentrate VERB
1 **concentrate on** *Sharon was concentrating on the video.*
▶ pay attention to, keep your mind on, put your mind to, apply yourself to, focus on, be engrossed in, be absorbed in, attend to, think about
2 *Troops concentrated on the border.*
▶ gather, mass, collect, congregate, converge, crowd, accumulate
AN OPPOSITE IS disperse
3 *We need to concentrate our efforts on improving public services.*
▶ focus, direct (to), aim (at), intensify
OPPOSITES ARE reduce, dilute

concentrated ADJECTIVE
1 *concentrated fruit juice*
▶ condensed, undiluted, reduced, rich, dense, strong, evaporated
AN OPPOSITE IS diluted
2 *making concentrated efforts*
▶ intense, strenuous, intensive, concerted, vigorous, committed, thorough, hard, (*more informal*) all-out
AN OPPOSITE IS half-hearted

concentration NOUN
1 *The work calls for long periods of concentration.*
▶ attention, application
AN OPPOSITE IS inattention
2 *the concentration of power in the hands of a few companies*
▶ accumulation, consolidation, centralization, collection, compression, focusing

concept NOUN
It's not an easy concept to grasp.
▶ idea, notion, principle, theory, thought, hypothesis, image, conception

conception NOUN
1 *They have no conception of how difficult life can be in the country.*
▶ understanding, knowledge, comprehension, appreciation, perception, inkling, grasp, idea
2 *The proposal took three months from conception to implementation.*
▶ creation, origination, inception, genesis, formulation

concern NOUN
1 *concern for others*
▶ regard, consideration, thought, care, attention (to), interest (in)
2 *It's no concern of ours.*
▶ affair, business, matter, responsibility, problem
3 *a cause for great concern*
▶ anxiety, worry, disquiet, unease, distress, apprehension
4 *a publishing concern*
▶ company, firm, business, enterprise, establishment, organization, corporation

concern VERB
1 *What I have to say concerns everyone.*
▶ affect, involve, apply to, refer to, relate to, be relevant to, be important to, interest, matter to, (*more formal*) pertain to
2 *The book concerns various aspects of the subject.*
▶ deal with, be about, treat, describe, review, relate to
3 *Her news concerned us deeply.*
▶ worry, disturb, upset, trouble, distress, bother

concerned ADJECTIVE
1 *His parents looked concerned.*
▶ worried, anxious, troubled, bothered, disturbed, distressed, fearful, upset
AN OPPOSITE IS unconcerned

2 *If you want more information, talk to the people concerned.*
▶ connected, interested, involved, relevant

concerning PREPOSITION
the part of the treaty concerning boundaries
▶ about, relating to, regarding, relevant to, dealing with, germane to, involving, with reference to, with regard to

concert NOUN
a concert at the town hall
▶ recital, musical performance, show, production, session

concerted ADJECTIVE
1 *a concerted effort to deal with the financial crisis*
▶ intense, strenuous, intensive, concentrated, vigorous, committed, thorough, hard, (*more informal*) all-out
2 *We have to take concerted action.*
▶ joint, collective, cooperative, collaborative, united, combined, mutual, shared

concession NOUN
You get a concession if you are a student or pensioner.
▶ reduction, discount, adjustment, allowance
make a concession *The management refuses to make any concessions over pay.*
▶ compromise, give way, concede a point

concise ADJECTIVE
a concise account of events in the war
▶ brief, succinct, compact, short, condensed, concentrated, compressed, abridged, abbreviated, pithy, terse
OPPOSITES ARE lengthy, diffuse

conclude VERB
1 *Hostilities concluded at midnight.*
▶ finish, end, stop, cease, terminate, be over, come to a close, be brought to an end
OPPOSITES ARE start, commence
2 *The jury concluded that the witness had been lying.*
▶ infer, deduce, decide, gather, judge, suppose, think, reckon, surmise, assume
3 *an attempt to conclude a treaty*
▶ negotiate, agree, come to terms on, arrange, effect, bring about, broker

conclusion NOUN
1 *A few gentle jokes formed the conclusion of her speech.*
▶ end, finish, close, completion, termination, culmination, finale, rounding-off, peroration
2 *The court's original conclusion in the case has been proved correct.*
▶ deduction, decision, judgement, verdict, opinion, interpretation, inference, resolution, belief, conjecture, assumption, presumption, surmise

conclusive ADJECTIVE
It will be difficult to provide conclusive proof.
▶ decisive, definitive, definite, indisputable, incontrovertible, irrefutable, unequivocal, unambiguous, unarguable, convincing, persuasive, unanswerable
AN OPPOSITE IS inconclusive

concoct VERB
She didn't have much time to concoct her story.
▶ make up, think up, invent, fabricate, contrive, formulate, prepare, devise, create, develop, (*more informal*) cook up

concrete ADJECTIVE
1 *concrete objects*
▶ solid, physical, material, palpable, substantial, tactile, touchable, visible
2 *The case lacks concrete evidence. The proposals are not yet concrete.*
▶ firm, solid, objective, tangible, material, physical, factual, real, actual, definite, existing
OPPOSITES ARE abstract, theoretical

condemn VERB
1 *He condemned all forms of violence.*
▶ deplore, denounce, castigate, criticize, censure
OPPOSITES ARE commend, approve of
2 *The committee condemned them for their behaviour.*
▶ criticize, censure, denounce, reprehend, deprecate, disparage, berate, revile
3 *After a lengthy trial the court finally condemned them.*
▶ convict, find guilty, sentence, pass judgement, prove guilty, punish, judge
AN OPPOSITE IS acquit

condensation NOUN
The windows were misty with condensation.
▶ moisture, steam, water-drops

condense VERB
1 *She condensed the ten episodes into a single hour-long drama.*
▶ shorten, reduce, abridge, compress, cut, contract, telescope, summarize
AN OPPOSITE IS expand
2 *The liquid is slowly condensed.*
▶ distil, reduce, concentrate, solidify, thicken
AN OPPOSITE IS dilute

condescend VERB
Eventually an official condescended to see us.
▶ deign, consent, see fit, vouchsafe, stoop, lower yourself

condescending ADJECTIVE
She narrowed her eyes at us in a condescending manner.
▶ superior, supercilious, disdainful, patronizing, haughty, imperious, lofty, (*more informal*) snooty

condition NOUN
1 *Check that your vehicle is in good condition.*
▶ order, state, shape, (*more informal*) trim, (*more informal*) nick
USAGE If you use *state* you have to say *in a good state.*
2 *She was told she had a medical condition.*
▶ disorder, illness, disease, complaint, ailment, infirmity
3 *There are some conditions attached to membership.*
▶ requirement, proviso, terms, qualification, restriction, stipulation, limitation, obligation

conditional ADJECTIVE

The offer of a place was a conditional one.
▶ provisional, qualified, dependent, limited, restricted
AN OPPOSITE IS unconditional

condom NOUN

Stay with one partner, or use a condom every time.
▶ sheath, contraceptive, (*more informal*) French letter, (*more informal*) johnny

condone VERB

We cannot condone this sort of behaviour.
▶ tolerate, endorse, disregard, overlook, pardon, forgive, ignore, allow, connive at, excuse, let someone off
OPPOSITES ARE condemn, punish

conducive ADJECTIVE

The noise in the room was not conducive to concentration.
▶ advantageous, beneficial, encouraging, favourable, helpful, supportive (of)

conduct NOUN

1 *good conduct*
▶ behaviour, demeanour, attitude, bearing, manner, ways, actions
2 *the conduct of the nation's affairs*
▶ management, direction, handling, organization, running, supervision, administration, control, discharge

conduct VERB

1 *Visitors are conducted round the building in small groups.*
▶ escort, guide, accompany, take, usher, lead, convey, shepherd
2 *The group conducted a survey into children's eating habits.*
▶ organize, administer, coordinate, carry out, manage, direct, run, handle, preside over
conduct yourself *He conducted himself in a typically high-handed manner.*
▶ behave, act, carry on, acquit yourself

confer VERB

1 *The King conferred a knighthood on him.*
▶ bestow, award, accord, give, grant, honour with, invest
USAGE Note that with all the alternatives apart from *bestow*, you say (for example) *The King awarded him a knighthood*. If you use *bestow* you follow the same pattern as for *confer*.
2 *He asked for a pause to confer with his colleagues.*
▶ consult, discuss things, have a discussion, speak, communicate, deliberate

conference NOUN

1 *an international conference on the environment.*
▶ congress, convention, meeting, symposium, summit
2 *They gathered round the table for a conference.*
▶ discussion, consultation, deliberation, exchange of views, talks

confess VERB

1 *Several of the suspects later confessed.*
▶ admit guilt, plead guilty, own up, accept blame, (*more informal*) come clean
2 *She confessed that she had broken the man's window*
▶ own up, admit, acknowledge, concede
3 *I confess I agree with all they have said.*
▶ admit, concede, grant, allow

confession NOUN

The interrogators failed to get a confession out of him
▶ admission of guilt, acknowledgement of guilt, declaration, disclosure, profession, revelation

confide VERB

1 *He confided his fears to his wife.*
▶ reveal, disclose, divulge, admit, declare
2 **confide in** *He is not easy to confide in.*
▶ unburden yourself to, tell all to, trust in

confidence NOUN

1 *We can face the future with confidence. She shows lot of confidence.*
▶ optimism, assurance, positiveness, conviction, certainty, credence, faith, hope, reliance, trust
OPPOSITES ARE doubt, scepticism, diffidence
have confidence in *They have confidence in your abilities.*
▶ trust , believe, be sure of

confident ADJECTIVE

1 *We are confident that the money can be found.*
▶ optimistic, hopeful, sure, certain, convinced, sanguine, positive, trusting
AN OPPOSITE IS doubtful
2 *She lifted her head in a confident gesture.*
▶ self-assured, self-confident, assertive, assured, self-possessed, self-reliant, positive, bold, composed, definite, fearless, secure, unafraid
AN OPPOSITE IS diffident

confidential ADJECTIVE

1 *All conversations are strictly confidential.*
▶ secret, top secret, private, personal, classified, restricted, suppressed, intimate, (*more informal*) hush-hush, (*more informal*) off the record
2 *a confidential secretary*
▶ personal, private, trusted

confine VERB

1 *She confined her writing to poems and short stories.*
▶ restrict, limit, keep
2 *During the winter months the animals are confined in a small field near the buildings. He was confined in the Tower to await his trial.*
▶ enclose, imprison, keep, shut, close, fence, box, cage, incarcerate, intern, isolate

confinement NOUN

1 *a period of confinement*
▶ imprisonment, incarceration, detention, internment, custody, captivity, restraint
OPPOSITES ARE freedom, liberty
2 *She was admitted to hospital for her confinement.*
▶ labour, delivery, childbirth

confines PLURAL NOUN
the confines of the park
▶ limits, boundaries, bounds, perimeter, edge, extremities

confirm VERB
1 *What happened next day confirmed her suspicions about the place.*
▶ support, corroborate, bear out, back up, upheld, validate, approve, give credence to, substantiate
OPPOSITES ARE contradict, disprove
2 *The hotel will need a deposit to confirm the booking (informal).*
▶ verify, guarantee, clinch, endorse, validate, ratify, formalize, make legal, make official
AN OPPOSITE IS cancel
3 *I confirm that I will be arriving on Saturday.*
▶ affirm, assert, assure you, give an assurance

confirmation NOUN
1 *The DNA evidence provided confirmation of his guilt.*
▶ proof, corroboration, verification, testimony, substantiation
2 *Confirmation of the appointment will follow shortly.*
▶ ratification, endorsement, approval, validation, formalization

confiscate VERB
The police confiscated his passport.
▶ seize, take possession of, impound, appropriate, remove, sequester, take away
OPPOSITES ARE return, restore

conflict NOUN
1 *conflict between management and workers*
▶ dispute, disagreement, discord, contention, confrontation, dissension, antagonism, hostility, friction, strife, clash
AN OPPOSITE IS harmony
2 *a military conflict*
▶ war, struggle, confrontation, contest, clash, campaign, encounter, engagement, action, battle, combat, feud, fight, quarrel, skirmish, warfare

conflict VERB
This fact conflicts with statements made back in September.
▶ clash, disagree, differ (from), be incompatible, be inconsistent, be at variance, be at odds
OPPOSITES ARE support, agree with

conform VERB
1 *I conform because I think it gives a good impression.*
▶ comply, acquiesce, follow convention, fit in, obey the rules, play by the rules, keep in step
OPPOSITES ARE rebel, disobey, differ
2 **conform to** *You have to conform to strict rules of etiquette.*
▶ comply with, follow, obey, abide by, accept, accede to, fit in with, uphold, fulfil
3 **conform to** *Our experiences do not always conform to our beliefs.*
▶ match, fit, suit, correspond to, agree with, tally with, harmonize with, accord with, compare with, square with

conformity NOUN
There is a lot of conformity among young people.
▶ conventionality, orthodoxy, uniformity, compliance, obedience, submission
OPPOSITES ARE eccentricity, rebellion

confound VERB
Their successes confounded all the critics.
▶ astonish, astound, amaze, surprise, stagger, startle, disconcert, dumbfound, shock, flabbergast, perplex, stun, stupefy, bewilder

confront VERB
1 *He confronted an intruder in the hallway.*
▶ challenge, accost, approach, stand up to, take on, tackle, defy, face, meet, oppose, withstand, argue with, brave
AN OPPOSITE IS avoid
2 *He realized he had to confront his problems and sort himself out.*
▶ tackle, face up to, address, deal with, cope with

confrontation NOUN
a serious confrontation with the authorities
▶ conflict, dispute, disagreement, discord, contention, dissension, antagonism, hostility, friction, strife, clash

confuse VERB
1 *All these comments only confuse the issue.*
▶ complicate, muddle, obscure, cloud, obfuscate
2 *Too much detail will confuse us.*
▶ bewilder, perplex, baffle, puzzle, mystify, bemuse, disconcert, confound, (*more informal*) flummox, (*more informal*) floor

confused ADJECTIVE
1 *The children were very confused about what was happening.*
▶ bewildered, perplexed, baffled, puzzled, mystified, bemused, disconcerted, confounded, (*more informal*) flummoxed
AN OPPOSITE IS clear
2 *Her clothes lay in a confused pile on the floor.*
▶ untidy, disorderly, disorganized, muddled, jumbled
OPPOSITES ARE tidy, organized
3 *confused accounts of the incident*
▶ vague, muddled, unclear, indistinct
AN OPPOSITE IS clear

confusion NOUN
1 *a lot of confusion about which system to buy*
▶ uncertainty, indecision, misunderstanding, hesitation, doubt, ignorance
2 *People were wandering about in confusion.*
▶ bewilderment, perplexity, bafflement, mystification, shock
3 *The kitchen was in a terrible state of confusion.*
▶ disorder, disorganization, untidiness, clutter, chaos, mayhem, disarray, muddle, jumble, mess, shambles

congeal VERB
Blood had congealed around the wound.
▶ clot, coagulate, thicken, harden, set, solidify

congested ADJECTIVE

More traffic will be forced on to already congested roads.
▶ crowded, overcrowded, clogged, packed, full, teeming, swarming, stuffed
AN OPPOSITE IS clear

congratulate VERB

I must congratulate Freda on her success.
▶ praise, compliment, commend, applaud, acclaim

congratulations PLURAL NOUN

1 *We sent our congratulations on their wedding.*
▶ compliments, good wishes, greetings, felicitations
2 *You all deserve warm congratulations on the success of the enterprise.*
▶ praise, commendation, applause

congregate VERB

A large crowd had congregated in the town square.
▶ gather, assemble, come together, collect, converge, convene, crowd together, rally, rally round, meet, flock together, join up, swarm, muster, throng round, accumulate

conjure VERB

The magician seemed to conjure eggs from behind people's ears.
▶ magic, charm, rouse, summon, raise
conjure up *Her words conjured up a vision of a beautiful landscape.*
▶ produce, evoke, recall, bring to mind, call to mind, summon up, stir up

connect VERB

1 *The speakers are connected to a powerful amplifier.*
▶ link, attach, couple, join, fasten
AN OPPOSITE IS disconnect.
2 *Police believe the two crimes could be connected.*
▶ associate, link, relate, couple, compare, tie up, bracket together, put together
AN OPPOSITE IS dissociate

connection NOUN

There is a connection between money and power.
▶ relationship, link, association, correlation, correspondence, bond, affinity, coherence, contact, interrelationship, join, unity, (*more informal*) tie-up
AN OPPOSITE IS distinction

connoisseur NOUN

a connoisseur of good food
▶ expert (on), good judge, authority (on), specialist (in), epicure, gourmet, pundit

conquer VERB

1 *Napoleon's attempt to conquer Europe.*
▶ seize, capture, overrun, occupy, invade, take possession of, subjugate, take, win, annex, subject
2 *William of Normandy conquered the English at the Battle of Hastings.*
▶ defeat, beat, overcome, conquer, vanquish, subdue, crush, overpower, rout
3 *With a great effort she conquered her fears.*
▶ overcome, suppress, master, control, curb, surmount, prevail over

conqueror NOUN

He entered the capital of Bengal as a conqueror.
▶ victor, subjugator, defeater, winner, champion, master

conquest NOUN

Alexander's conquest of the Persian Empire
▶ defeat, subjection, subjugation, capture, invasion, occupation, annexation, appropriation, overthrow, triumph (over), victory (over), (*more informal*) takeover

conscience NOUN

1 *His conscience forced him to admit the truth in the end.*
▶ moral sense, principles, morals, ethics, standards
2 *Large organizations have no conscience about getting rid of people.*
▶ scruples, compunction, misgivings, qualms, reservations

conscientious ADJECTIVE

a conscientious worker
▶ hard-working, diligent, industrious, painstaking, thorough, meticulous, punctilious, accurate, attentive, dedicated, rigorous, careful, dutiful, unflagging, assiduous, scrupulous
OPPOSITES ARE careless, irresponsible, lazy

conscious ADJECTIVE

1 *Despite the blow to his head, he remained conscious.*
▶ awake, aware, alert, compos mentis, sensible
AN OPPOSITE IS unconscious
2 *It was a conscious attempt to deceive us.*
▶ deliberate, intended, intentional, calculated, knowing, planned, premeditated, studied, wilful
AN OPPOSITE IS accidental

consecrate VERB

The Bishop had come to consecrate the new cathedral.
▶ sanctify, dedicate, bless, devote, beatify, make sacred

consecrated ADJECTIVE

A churchyard is consecrated ground.
▶ holy, sacred, sanctified, blessed, hallowed

consecutive ADJECTIVE

Interest rates have remained unchanged for six consecutive months.
▶ continuous, successive, uninterrupted, running (*six months running*), in succession (*six months in succession*), in a row (*six months in a row*)

consent VERB

1 *In the end she consented to do something about it.*
▶ agree, be willing, undertake
OPPOSITES ARE refuse, decline
2 **consent to** *He said the girl had consented to his advances.*
▶ agree to, allow, approve, concede, grant, authorize, permit, comply with
OPPOSITES ARE refuse, forbid

consent NOUN
The authorities refused their consent.
▶ agreement, assent, permission, authorization, approval, backing, endorsement, (*more informal*) go-ahead

consequence NOUN
1 *Cooling of the stratosphere was seen as a consequence of the greenhouse effect.*
▶ result, effect, outcome, aftermath, by-product, corollary, repercussion, sequel, side-effect, upshot
2 *These small losses are of little consequence*
▶ importance, significance, account, concern, moment, note, value, weight

consequent ADJECTIVE
We hope the consequent effects are not too serious.
▶ resulting, resultant, ensuing, consequential, subsequent, following

conservation NOUN
the conservation of energy and resources
▶ preservation, protection, safeguarding, saving, careful management, economy, maintenance, upkeep
AN OPPOSITE IS destruction

conservative ADJECTIVE
1 *conservative ideas his conservative father*
▶ traditional, conventional, orthodox, reactionary, old-fashioned, die-hard, hidebound, moderate, narrow-minded, sober, unadventurous
OPPOSITES ARE progressive, radical
2 *the conservative section of the party*
▶ right-wing, right-of-centre, reactionary, traditionalist, Tory
OPPOSITES ARE radical, socialist
3 *Fifty pounds is a conservative estimate.*
▶ cautious, moderate, reasonable, understated, unexaggerated
AN OPPOSITE IS extreme

conservative NOUN
a political conservative
▶ conformist, reactionary, right-winger, Tory, traditionalist, diehard

conservatory NOUN
The family were sitting in the conservatory.
▶ summer house, glasshouse, greenhouse, hothouse

conserve VERB
It is important to conserve energy.
▶ save, preserve, protect, sustain, maintain, safeguard, be economical with, use sparingly, keep, look after, store up
OPPOSITES ARE waste, squander

consider VERB
1 *Donna paused to consider the possibilities.*
▶ think about, contemplate, ponder, reflect on, weigh up, mull over, cogitate, deliberate, muse, meditate on, discuss, ruminate, study, (*informal*) turn over

2 *I consider it a privilege.*
▶ regard (as), deem, count, think, judge, reckon, believe (to be)

considerable ADJECTIVE
There was a considerable amount of traffic on the road.
He had inherited a considerable sum from his grandparents.
▶ substantial, sizeable, appreciable, significant, reasonable, respectable, tolerable, worthwhile, large, comfortable, noteworthy, noticeable, perceptible
AN OPPOSITE IS negligible

considerate ADJECTIVE
We are encouraged to be polite, modest, and considerate to others.
▶ kind, thoughtful, attentive, helpful, caring, obliging, generous, sensitive, accommodating
OPPOSITES ARE inconsiderate, selfish

consideration NOUN
The matter needs careful consideration.
▶ thought, attention, deliberation, reflection, examination, contemplation, meditation, scrutiny, review

consign VERB
1 *May we consign this to your care?*
▶ commit, assign, entrust, hand over, deliver, devote, give, pass on
2 *The packet was consigned by an international carrier.*
▶ send, dispatch, transmit, convey, ship, transfer

consignment NOUN
another consignment of goods
▶ shipment, delivery, load, batch, cargo, shipload, lorryload

consist VERB
consist of *Audiences consist of very different types of people.*
▶ be composed of, comprise, be made of, include, contain, incorporate, involve

consistency NOUN
1 *The pudding had an odd consistency.*
▶ thickness, density, firmness, viscosity
2 *The figures show a remarkable consistency.*
▶ uniformity, regularity, stability, steadiness, constancy, evenness

consistent ADJECTIVE
1 *a consistent pattern of behaviour*
▶ steady, uniform, stable, regular, even, constant, unchanging, unvarying, dependable, reliable, predictable, unfailing
2 *The theory is consistent with recent research.*
▶ compatible, in accordance, in agreement, in harmony
AN OPPOSITE IS inconsistent

consolation NOUN
I tried to offer her some consolation for her loss.
▶ comfort, solace, sympathy, commiseration, compassion, reassurance, support, succour, encouragement, cheer, ease, help, relief

console VERB

His friends tried to console him.
▶ comfort, solace, hearten, encourage, relieve, soothe, sympathize with, calm, cheer

consolidate VERB

1 *attempts to consolidate their reputation in Europe*
▶ strengthen, reinforce, fortify, enhance, stabilize, make secure, make strong
AN OPPOSITE IS weaken

2 *All the resources need to be consolidated.*
▶ amalgamate, combine, integrate, merge, unify, bring together, fuse

consort VERB

consort with *consorting with the opposition*
▶ associate with, socialize with, have dealings with, befriend, fraternize with, keep company with, mix with, be friends with, be seen with

conspicuous ADJECTIVE

1 *Her bright clothes made her conspicuous.*
▶ prominent, distinct, clearly visible, easily seen, noticeable, apparent, perceptible
AN OPPOSITE IS inconspicuous

2 *The infantry showed conspicuous bravery that day.*
▶ obvious, manifest, evident, outstanding, exceptional, marked, pronounced, unmistakable

conspiracy NOUN

They were involved in a conspiracy to kill the king.
▶ plot, scheme, intrigue, machination, plan, stratagem

conspirator NOUN

Three of the conspirators were executed.
▶ plotter, schemer, intriguer, traitor

conspire VERB

They twice conspired to overthrow the dictatorship.
▶ plot, scheme, intrigue, plan, hatch a plot, collude, connive, collaborate, consort, be in league

constant ADJECTIVE

1 *the constant hum of traffic on the bypass*
▶ continuous, continual, persistent, ceaseless, incessant, endless, unending
OPPOSITES ARE changeable, irregular

2 *The wheel should turn at a constant speed.*
▶ steady, regular, stable, uniform, even, invariable, fixed

3 *She proved to be a constant friend.*
▶ faithful, loyal, devoted, staunch, true, firm, dependable, reliable, dedicated
OPPOSITES ARE fickle, unreliable

constantly ADVERB

The train times are constantly changing.
▶ always, continually, repeatedly, all the time, forever

constitute VERB

1 *Their attitude constitutes a form of discrimination.*
▶ amount to, be equivalent to, be tantamount to, compose, comprise, form, make up

2 *A Scottish Parliament was constituted in 1999.*
▶ establish, set up, inaugurate, create, found, appoint

constrain VERB

1 *He felt constrained to write an account of the whole affair.*
▶ compel, force, oblige, coerce, order, pressure, pressurize

2 *Financial dependence constrained women's freedom.*
▶ restrict, limit, restrain, impede, frustrate, curtail, hinder, hamper

constraint NOUN

Political constraints prevented him from speaking his mind.
▶ restriction, restraint, limitation, inhibition, control, hindrance, check

constrict VERB

Excessive fat constricts the arteries.
▶ narrow, tighten, compress, contract, shrink, squeeze

constriction NOUN

He felt a constriction in his throat.
▶ tightening, tightness, narrowing, pressure, stricture

construct VERB

1 *The local council wants to construct a new bridge over the railway line.*
▶ build, erect, put up, set up, assemble

2 *We must construct a new form of society.*
▶ create, devise, develop, formulate, fashion, design, invent

construction NOUN

1 *In 1858 the construction of the present chapel was put in hand.*
▶ building, erection, assembly, creation, establishment, putting-up, setting-up, erecting

2 *The new building was a mainly timber construction.*
▶ building, edifice, erection, structure, framework

constructive ADJECTIVE

The talks proved to be helpful and constructive.
▶ positive, useful, worthwhile, beneficial, advantageous, creative, helpful, practical, valuable
AN OPPOSITE IS destructive

consult VERB

1 *He wanted to consult the workforce before introducing any changes.*
▶ speak to, confer with, refer to, seek advice from, debate with, discuss matters with, exchange views with

2 *Consult your doctor before attempting these exercises.*
▶ see, ask, get advice from, refer to

3 *He consulted a list pinned to the wall.*
▶ refer to, turn to, look something up in

consume VERB

1 *A lot of food and drink was consumed that day.*
▶ eat, drink, devour, digest, swallow, feast on, (more informal) gobble up

2 *The factory consumes thousands of tons of fuel each year.*
▶ use, use up, utilize, expend, absorb, swallow up, deplete, drain, eat into, employ, exhaust

3 *Fire consumed a row of buildings.*
▶ destroy, demolish, devastate, wipe out, annihilate, wreck, ravage, ruin

4 *George was consumed by guilt.*
▶ overcome, overwhelm, preoccupy, obsess, absorb

consumer NOUN
Consumers want good value above all.
▶ customer, purchaser, shopper, buyer, user, end-user, client

contact NOUN
1 *He had been avoiding physical contact with her all day.*
▶ touch, touching, proximity

2 *Contact between Europe and Africa can be traced back hundreds of years.*
▶ communication, connection, association

3 *Make sure all electrical contacts are secure.*
▶ connection, join

4 *I will ask one of my contacts in Italy.*
▶ associate, connection, acquaintance, liaison

contact VERB
I'll contact them when I have more information.
▶ notify, communicate with, get in touch with, get hold of, approach, correspond with, call, call on, phone, ring, speak to, talk to, (*more informal*) drop a line to

contagious ADJECTIVE
a contagious disease
▶ infectious, communicable, catching, spreading, transmittable, transmissible
AN OPPOSITE IS non- infectious

contain VERB
1 *The box contained bottles of red wine.*
▶ hold, accommodate

2 *The atlas contains photographs taken from space.*
▶ include, incorporate, comprise, consist of, be composed of

3 *You will have to contain your impatience.*
▶ restrain, curb, suppress, control, hold back, keep back, repress, check, stifle, limit

container NOUN
a watertight container
▶ receptacle, vessel, holder, repository, canister, case

contaminate VERB
Farming contaminates watercourses every day.
▶ pollute, adulterate, defile, infect, poison, foul, soil, taint
AN OPPOSITE IS purify

contemplate VERB
1 *He contemplated her over his glasses.*
▶ look at, view, observe, regard, survey, watch, eye, gaze at, stare at, (*in literature*) behold

2 *She could not even contemplate what might happen.*
▶ think about, consider, cogitate, deliberate, examine, mull over, plan, reflect on, study, work out

3 *He contemplated leaving.*
▶ consider, think about, envisage, have in mind, intend (to), propose

4 *She sat quietly and contemplated* (*informal*).
▶ ponder, reflect, ruminate, think, meditate, muse

contemporary ADJECTIVE
1 *The historical information comes from contemporary accounts.*
▶ contemporaneous, concurrent, synchronous, coinciding, simultaneous, coexistent, of the time

2 *a concert of contemporary music*
▶ modern, current, present-day, recent, fashionable, the latest, newest

contempt NOUN
She had nothing but contempt for them.
▶ disgust, scorn, disdain, loathing, abhorrence, derision, disparagement, detestation, dislike, disrespect, hatred, ridicule
AN OPPOSITE IS admiration

feel or **show contempt for** *He showed contempt for their extreme views.*
▶ despise, spurn, revile, detest

contemptible ADJECTIVE
a contemptible insult
▶ despicable, shameful, disgraceful, detestable, hateful, deplorable, ignominious, loathsome, odious, mean, vile, low, cheap
AN OPPOSITE IS admirable

contemptuous ADJECTIVE
a contemptuous tone of voice
▶ scornful, disdainful, scathing, disrespectful, insulting, derisive, dismissive, supercilious, condescending, insolent, haughty, mocking, withering, arrogant
AN OPPOSITE IS admiring

be contemptuous of
▶ denigrate, disparage, revile, malign, belittle, decry, impugn, abuse

contend VERB
1 *political parties contending for power*
▶ compete, struggle, vie, strive, fight , grapple, oppose one another, rival one another, contest, dispute .

2 *She contended that she had been given bad advice.*
▶ claim, declare, maintain, aver, hold, assert, allege, argue, affirm, plead

3 **contend with** *They have a lot to contend with.*
▶ cope with, deal with, put up with, sort out, manage, organize

content ADJECTIVE
He seems content now that he's got his way.
▶ happy, contented, satisfied, pleased, gratified, glad, cheerful, smug

content NOUN

1 *The article is admired more for its content than its style*
▶ subject matter, subject, theme, substance, argument, message

2 *Butter has a high fat content.*
▶ element, ingredient, substance

3 *She smiled with content.*
▶ happiness, contentment, satisfaction, pleasure

content VERB

The answer seemed to content him.
▶ satisfy, please, placate, appease, pacify, soothe

contented ADJECTIVE

a contented feeling
▶ happy, content, satisfied, pleased, gratified, glad, cheerful, smug
OPPOSITES ARE discontented, dissatisfied

contention NOUN

Her contention is that the action would be illegal.
▶ argument, claim, opinion, view, assertion, submission, belief, position

contentious ADJECTIVE

1 *a contentious issue*
▶ controversial, debatable, disputed, disputable, vexed

2 *a contentious group of people*
▶ quarrelsome, argumentative, disputatious, difficult

contentment NOUN

They achieved contentment in the country.
▶ happiness, well-being, comfort, pleasure, content, contentedness, gratification, satisfaction, peace of mind, tranquillity, ease, fulfilment, relaxation, serenity
OPPOSITES ARE dissatisfaction, unhappiness

contest NOUN

1 *a song contest   a boxing contest*
▶ competition, tournament, match, bout, encounter, fight, battle, dispute

2 *a contest for the leadership*
▶ struggle, challenge, confrontation, duel

contest VERB

1 *Seven candidates will contest the election.*
▶ enter, compete in, take part in, participate in, contend in, fight in, (*informal*) make a bid for, strive for, struggle for, take up the challenge of, vie for

2 *They decided to contest the decision.*
▶ oppose, challenge, dispute, object to, argue against, take issue with, query, refute, resist, debate, doubt, question

contestant NOUN

The winner beat fifteen other contestants.
▶ competitor, candidate, contender, participant, entrant, player

context NOUN

The events have to be put in their historical context.
▶ background, circumstances, surroundings, framework, situation, ambience, frame of reference, milieu, position

contingency NOUN

The arrangement needs to provide for all contingencies
▶ eventuality, circumstance, event, incident, occurrence, accident

continual ADJECTIVE

She needed continual reassurance.   The service is affected by continual breakdowns.
▶ constant, repeated, frequent, regular, perpetual, ceaseless, incessant, persistent
OPPOSITES ARE occasional, sporadic

continuation NOUN

1 *He returned to the clinic for the continuation of his treatment.*
▶ resumption, maintenance, continuing, continuance, carrying on, extension, prolongation

2 *the continuation of a story*
▶ sequel, supplement, addition, appendix, postscript

continue VERB

1 *Police continued the search until dark.*
▶ carry on, maintain, keep up, keep going, persevere with, proceed with, prolong, pursue, (*more informal*) stick at

2 *Shall we continue after lunch?*
▶ resume, restart, begin again, recommence

3 *Talks continued all week.*
▶ last, carry on, go on, endure, persist, keep on, linger, live on, remain, stay, survive

continuous ADJECTIVE

three days of continuous rain
▶ uninterrupted, unbroken, constant, steady, ceaseless, endless, incessant, persistent, non-stop
OPPOSITES ARE intermittent, sporadic

contorted ADJECTIVE

lengths of contorted metal
▶ twisted, misshapen, buckled, deformed, distorted, screwed up

contour NOUN

the contours of the distant hills
▶ outline, form, profile, shape, line, silhouette, curve, relief

contract NOUN

A contract is legally binding.
▶ agreement, settlement, covenant, compact, commitment, deal, bond, pact, concordat, bargain, indenture, lease, treaty, understanding, undertaking

contract VERB

1 *The glass contracts as it cools.   Labour markets contracted in this area.*
▶ shrink, lessen, diminish, reduce, become smaller, condense, shrivel, decrease, dwindle, wither, close

up, draw together, fall away, narrow, slim down, thin out
OPPOSITES ARE expand, enlarge

2 *The company contracted to build an extension to the house.*
▶ sign an agreement, undertake, covenant, make a deal, promise, agree, arrange

3 *The woman might have contracted smallpox.*
▶ develop, catch, get, become infected by, be taken ill with

contraction NOUN

1 *a contraction of overseas markets*
▶ shrinking, shrivelling, diminution, decline, decrease

2 *"Goodbye" is a contraction of "God be with you".*
▶ abbreviation, diminutive, short form, shortened form

contradict VERB

1 *I didn't like to contradict him but I really didn't agree.*
▶ disagree with, challenge, oppose, speak against, impugn

2 *The new evidence contradicts earlier conclusions.*
▶ conflict with, be at odds with, be inconsistent with, run counter to, challenge, disprove

3 *The statement was later contradicted by the Prime Minister*
▶ deny, repudiate, rebut, dispute, counter
AN OPPOSITE IS confirm

contradictory ADJECTIVE

The two points of view are completely contradictory.
▶ opposite, opposed, conflicting, contrary, incompatible, inconsistent, irreconcilable, different, discrepant, antithetical
OPPOSITES ARE consistent, compatible

contraption NOUN

Above his head was a contraption consisting of springs and wires.
▶ device, contrivance, gadget, apparatus, mechanism, invention, machine

contrary ADJECTIVE

1 (with the stress on *con-*) *Others may take the contrary view.*
▶ opposite, opposing, opposed, contradictory, conflicting, contrasting, reverse, converse, different, other
AN OPPOSITE IS similar

2 (with the stress on *-trary*, pronounced like *Mary*) *a contrary child*
▶ perverse, awkward, difficult, uncooperative, obstinate, unhelpful, tiresome, disobedient, vexatious, (*more informal*) bolshie, (*more informal*) stroppy
AN OPPOSITE IS cooperative

3 **contrary to** *The result was contrary to all expectations.*
▶ in conflict with, at odds with, at variance with, counter to

contrast NOUN

a noticeable contrast between what they say and what they do
▶ difference, dissimilarity, disparity, variance, divergence, contradiction, opposition
AN OPPOSITE IS similarity

contrast VERB

1 *People contrast the two brothers.*
▶ differentiate, distinguish, make distinctions between, discriminate between, compare

2 **contrast with** *Her fair hair contrasted with her dark dress.*
▶ set off, complement, clash with

contrasting ADJECTIVE

contrasting colours   contrasting opinions
▶ complementary, conflicting, different, opposing, opposite
AN OPPOSITE IS similar

contribute VERB

1 *Employers have to contribute a set amount to the fund.*
▶ give, subscribe, donate, provide, put up, supply, add, grant, bestow

2 **contribute to** *The weather contributed to the success of the occasion.*
▶ play a part in, add to, be a factor in, have a hand in, make for, enhance, help, reinforce, support, encourage

contribution NOUN

All income comes from charitable contributions.
▶ donation, benefaction, payment, gift, subscription, allowance, endowment, grant, offering, sponsorship, (*more informal*) handout

contributor NOUN

1 *The charity has acquired several new contributors.*
▶ donor, benefactor, subscriber, supporter, patron, sponsor, giver, backer, helper

2 *a regular contributor to the magazine*
▶ writer, columnist, correspondent, freelance, journalist, reporter

contrivance NOUN

The blinds were opened by a strange contrivance at the side.
▶ device, contraption, gadget, apparatus, mechanism, invention, machine

contrived ADJECTIVE

He looked at her with a contrived smile.
▶ affected, artificial, studied, unnatural, strained, forced

control NOUN

1 *this theme of giving back control over civic affairs to the local people*
▶ jurisdiction, administration, management, regulation, authority, charge, power, government, supervision, command, direction, oversight, organization, guidance, influence

2 *He needs to exercise a little more control and not lose his temper so much.*
▶ restraint, self-control, self-command, self-possession, composure
3 *Some of the controls were difficult to reach.*
▶ switch, knob, button, lever, handle, dial
gain control of *The Portuguese had gained control of the Indian Ocean a century earlier.*
▶ take over, dominate, usurp, win, annex, seize, steal

control VERB
1 *You have to be able to control all the resources.*
▶ be in charge of, manage, administer, have authority over, supervise, govern, oversee, run, operate, look after
2 *He found it hard to control his temper.*
▶ restrain, check, contain, curb, confine, keep in check, master, repress, subdue, suppress

controversial ADJECTIVE
He wrote a controversial article on the death penalty.
▶ contentious, controvertible, debatable, disputable, questionable, doubtful, polemical, problematical, arguable
OPPOSITES ARE uncontroversial, straightforward

controversy NOUN
There is controversy over new road-building plans.
▶ disagreement, dispute, contention, altercation, dissension, debate, argument, issue, polemic, quarrel, war of words, wrangle

convalesce VERB
She needed several weeks to convalesce after her illness.
▶ recuperate, recover, get better, get well, regain strength, improve, make progress, mend

convene VERB
1 *The chairman convened a meeting*
▶ call, summon, assemble, bring together, (more formal) convoke
2 *The committee convened at two o'clock.*
▶ assemble, meet, gather, come together

convenient ADJECTIVE
1 *He asked when it would be convenient to interview her.*
▶ suitable, appropriate, opportune, fitting, agreeable, neat, timely, usable
OPPOSITES ARE inconvenient, awkward
2 *Fast foods are often the most convenient option.*
▶ practical, handy, useful, helpful, labour-saving
3 *There is a regular bus service and convenient shops.*
▶ nearby, accessible, handy, at hand, available
4 convenient for *The house was so convenient for London.*
▶ accessible to, within easy reach of, well situated for, handy for
AN OPPOSITE IS inconvenient

convention NOUN
1 *All these social conventions can become tedious.*
▶ custom, practice, tradition, rule, protocol, canon, formality, matter of form, matter of etiquette

2 *American-style political conventions*
▶ conference, meeting, congress, assembly, symposium
3 *a convention signed by all the countries of the area*
▶ agreement, treaty, accord, compact, understanding

conventional ADJECTIVE
1 *He was willing to follow conventional ideas.*
▶ orthodox, established, traditional, customary, prevalent, mainstream, commonplace, routine, unoriginal, hackneyed
OPPOSITES ARE unconventional, unorthodox
2 *Kevin was a conventional man.*
▶ conservative, hidebound, traditional, traditionalist, conformist, formal, correct, proper, bourgeois, stereotyped, unadventurous, unimaginative, unoriginal, (more informal) stuffy, (more informal) fuddy-duddy
OPPOSITES ARE unconventional, radical
3 *A conventional telephone can be a lot less fiddly than many mobiles.*
▶ standard, normal, regular, traditional, ordinary

converge VERB
The light rays converge to form a sharp image.
▶ merge, combine, meet, join, come together, coincide
OPPOSITES ARE separate, diverge

conversation NOUN
The rest of the conversation was in French.
▶ discussion, talk, discourse, dialogue, exchange, consultation, (more informal) chat

converse NOUN (with the stress on *con-*)
The converse is true.
▶ opposite, reverse, contrary, antithesis, obverse

converse VERB (with the stress on *-verse*)
They conversed for hours about the old days.
▶ talk, speak, chat, discourse, chatter, gossip

conversion NOUN
1 *the conversion of waste into forms of energy*
▶ change, changing, turning, transformation
2 *The house has had a loft conversion.*
▶ adaptation, alteration, renovation, reconstruction, rebuilding, modification
3 *a religious conversion*
▶ rebirth, regeneration, reformation, change of heart

convert VERB
1 *We plan to convert the loft into a workroom. Most of her novels have now been converted into films.*
▶ adapt, change, turn, rebuild, reconstruct, renovate, modify, reorganize
2 *a device for converting digital data into audio signals*
▶ turn, change, transform, translate

convey VERB
1 *A shuttle service conveys passengers form the city to the suburbs.*
▶ transport, carry, take, transfer, deliver, bring, fetch, move

2 *The dancer's movements can convey a variety of meanings.*
► communicate, signify, indicate, impart, disclose, relate, imply, mean, reveal, put across, get across

convict NOUN (with the stress on *con-*)
He looked like a convict in his striped pyjamas.
► prisoner, criminal, condemned person

convict VERB (with the stress on *-vict*)
A jury had earlier convicted Duncan of assault.
► condemn, declare guilty, find guilty
OPPOSITES ARE acquit, clear

conviction NOUN
1 *He spoke with complete conviction.*
► confidence, assurance, certainty, sureness, positiveness, firmness
AN OPPOSITE IS uncertainty
2 *She has keenly felt political convictions.*
► belief, opinion, view, principle, persuasion, creed, faith, tenet

convince VERB
It will be difficult to convince them. She tried to convince herself that nobody would have heard her.
► persuade, assure, prove to, reassure, satisfy, sway, win over, bring round

convincing ADJECTIVE
1 *a convincing argument*
► strong, powerful, conclusive, cogent, decisive, compelling, definite, persuasive, unambiguous, unarguable, unequivocal
AN OPPOSITE IS inconclusive
2 *a convincing victory*
► decisive, conclusive, resounding, emphatic, impressive

convoy NOUN
a convoy of ships
► group, fleet, armada, procession

convulsion NOUN
1 *The convulsions stopped and Charles lay back exhausted.*
► fit, seizure, spasm, attack, paroxysm
2 *seismic convulsions   a political convulsion*
► upheaval, disturbance, tremor, turbulence, eruption, outburst

convulsive ADJECTIVE
convulsive movements
► spasmodic, jerky, shaking, uncontrolled, uncoordinated, violent, (*more informal*) twitchy

cook NOUN
the hotel's new cook
► chef

cook VERB
She cooked them both a romantic dinner.
► prepare, make, get, put together, (*more informal*) fix
RELATED ADJECTIVE culinary
cook something up *He cooked up an idea for getting her to go with him.*
► concoct, devise, contrive, plot, scheme

cool ADJECTIVE
1 *the cool air of early morning*
► fresh, bracing, crisp, brisk, chilly, chilled, (*more informal*) nippy
OPPOSITES ARE warm, balmy
2 *We got a cool response.*
► unfriendly, chilly, lukewarm, unwelcoming, frigid, hostile, unsympathetic, reserved, aloof, (*informal*) standoffish
OPPOSITES ARE warm, friendly, enthusiastic
3 *He was determined to keep cool in the crisis.*
► calm, composed, collected, clear-headed, self-controlled, self-possessed, unflustered, unruffled
4 (*informal*) *She seems to think she's so cool.*
► fashionable, trendy, stylish, sophisticated, chic
5 (*informal*) *It's a cool song.*
► good, excellent, super, superb

cool NOUN
He finally lost his cool and started shouting.
► composure, self-control, self-possession, calm, calmness

cool VERB
1 *He threw open the shutters to cool the room.*
► chill, make cooler, lower the temperature of
2 *Cool the mixture in the fridge for about an hour.*
► chill, refrigerate, make cold
3 *Their enthusiasm had begun to cool. Recent events had cooled their enthusiasm.*
► lessen, reduce, moderate, dampen, diminish, abate, take the edge off or lose its edge

cooped up ADJECTIVE
She doesn't like being cooped up at home all day.
► confined, shut in, shut up, caged, trapped, locked up, imprisoned, incarcerated

cooperate VERB
1 *Several police forces cooperated in the operation.*
► collaborate, combine, unite, work together, join forces, team up
2 **cooperate with** *He absolutely refused to cooperate with them.*
► assist, help, support, work with

cooperation NOUN
1 *wise cooperation between management and workers*
► collaboration, coordination, joint action, teamwork, unity, mutual support
OPPOSITES ARE conflict, rivalry
2 *She thanked them all for their cooperation.*
► assistance, help, helpfulness, support, backing

cooperative ADJECTIVE
1 *The staff were pleasant and cooperative.*
► helpful, obliging, accommodating, supportive, constructive, willing, keen
AN OPPOSITE IS uncooperative
2 *The project was achieved by a cooperative effort*
► joint, combined, collective, concerted, coordinated, corporate, shared, communal
AN OPPOSITE IS individual

coordinate VERB
A committee will coordinate all the sporting activities.
▶ harmonize, organize, bring together, synchronize, systematize

cope VERB
1 *She is too old now to cope by herself.*
▶ manage, survive, carry on, get by, fend for yourself, make do
2 **cope with** *We found so many problems at once difficult to cope with.*
▶ deal with, handle, manage, contend with, endure, tolerate

copious ADJECTIVE
They sat listening and writing copious notes. a long breakfast of croissants and copious coffee
▶ plenty of, abundant, plentiful, extensive, substantial, profuse, lavish, generous, ample, numerous, full
OPPOSITES ARE sparse, meagre

copy NOUN
1 *Keep a copy of your letter.*
▶ duplicate, photocopy, Xerox, facsimile, transcript, clone, double, pattern, print, representation, tracing
2 *The painting is only a copy.*
▶ reproduction, replica, imitation, likeness, model, fake, forgery, twin
AN OPPOSITE IS original
USAGE You use *fake* or *forgery* when you mean a copy that is intended to deceive people.

copy VERB
1 *Copy the passage from the book.*
▶ write out, reproduce, make a copy of, duplicate, repeat
2 *He copied several drawings by Hogarth.*
▶ reproduce, make a copy of, forge, fake, plagiarize, counterfeit, crib, follow
USAGE You use *fake* or *forge* or *counterfeit* when you mean make a copy that is intended to deceive people.
3 *A lot of musicians have tried to copy their sound.*
▶ imitate, mimic, reproduce, emulate, ape, impersonate, parrot, poach

cord NOUN
I tightened the cord on the hood of my jacket.
▶ string, thread, strap, tape, rope, strand, cable

cordial ADJECTIVE
a cordial greeting
▶ friendly, warm, genial, amiable, affectionate, fond, good-natured, heartfelt, enthusiastic

core NOUN
1 *the earth's core*
▶ centre, nucleus, heart, middle, inside
2 *the core of the problem*
▶ heart, essence, crux, nub, central issue, kernel, (*more informal*) nitty-gritty

core ADJECTIVE
the core issue
▶ central, key, chief, basic, fundamental, principal, crucial, vital

cork NOUN
Ken pulled the corks from all the bottles.
▶ stopper, plug, bung

corn NOUN
a field of corn
▶ grain, cereal, cereal crop, wheat, barley

corner NOUN
1 *Turn left at the corner.*
▶ bend, curve, turning
2 *Three women sat in a corner of the room.*
▶ nook, niche, recess, alcove
3 *Stuart felt he was in a bit of a corner.*
▶ predicament, plight, quandary, dilemma, awkward situation, mess, (*more informal*) spot, (*more informal*) scrape, (*more informal*) stew
round the corner *The shops are round the corner.*
▶ nearby, close at hand, not far away, within reach

corner VERB
The animal had cornered its prey.
▶ trap, shut in, bring to bay, run to ground, capture, catch

corny ADJECTIVE
corny jokes
▶ hackneyed, banal, stereotyped, stale, feeble, tired

corporation NOUN
1 *a business corporation*
▶ company, firm, organization, concern, enterprise
2 *a city corporation*
▶ council, town council, local authority

corpse NOUN
Police found the corpse under the floorboards.
▶ body, dead body, remains, cadaver, carcass, skeleton

correct ADJECTIVE
1 *What is the correct time? Not all the information proved correct.*
▶ right, accurate, exact, true, precise, genuine, authentic, reliable, factual, faithful, faultless, flawless, strict
OPPOSITES ARE inaccurate, wrong
2 *She wanted to know the correct course of action.*
▶ right, proper, appropriate, fitting, suitable, acceptable, just
OPPOSITES ARE inappropriate, wrong
3 *correct behaviour*
▶ proper, decent, well-mannered, tactful, unexceptionable

correct VERB
1 *Please correct your mistakes.*
▶ rectify, put right, make good, amend, remedy, cure, redress, adjust, alter, repair, right
2 *Your work will be corrected within two days.*
▶ mark, assess, evaluate, appraise
3 *She corrected him for his rudeness.*
▶ scold, admonish, rebuke, chastise, punish

correction NOUN

the correction of errors
▶ rectification, righting, putting right, resolution, adjustment, amendment

correspond VERB

1 **correspond to** *The translator must choose words that correspond to the sense of the original.*
▶ match, fit, conform to, accord with, agree with, be consistent with, parallel, concur with, harmonize with, square with, tally with, convey

2 *Emma and I corresponded for many years.*
▶ communicate, exchange letters, write to each other

correspondence NOUN

1 *a collection of the composer's published correspondence*
▶ letters, communications, memoranda, notes

2 *There is some correspondence between the two ideas.*
▶ correlation, similarity, resemblance, comparability, agreement

corresponding ADJECTIVE

Climate change brings a corresponding change in average temperature.
▶ matching, equivalent, commensurate, related, analogous, appropriate, complementary, parallel

corroborate VERB

The witness corroborated his story.
▶ confirm, support, endorse, verify, back up, reinforce

corrode VERB

1 *Damp conditions will corrode the metal.*
▶ rust, tarnish, erode, consume, wear away, eat away, oxidize, rot

2 *Iron corrodes rapidly in damp conditions.*
▶ rust, tarnish, deteriorate, perish, disintegrate, crumble

corrugated ADJECTIVE

a corrugated surface
▶ ridged, ribbed, fluted, grooved, furrowed, wrinkled, crinkled, (*more informal*) crinkly

corrupt ADJECTIVE

1 *The government is accused of being corrupt and incompetent.*
▶ dishonest, dishonourable, unprincipled, unscrupulous, untrustworthy, underhand, disreputable, discreditable, bribable, unsound, false, (*more informal*) bent
OPPOSITES ARE honest, reputable

2 *They were involved in some form of corrupt practice.*
▶ dishonest, crooked, criminal, fraudulent, unethical

3 *Some people say society is getting more corrupt.*
▶ sinful, immoral, decadent, degenerate, depraved, dissolute, debauched, rotten, wicked, evil, iniquitous, low, perverted, profligate, venal
AN OPPOSITE IS moral

corrupt VERB

1 *Some firms even try to corrupt local officials.*
▶ bribe, suborn, buy off, pay off, influence, (*more informal*) fix

2 *Pornography corrupts the innocent.*
▶ pervert, deprave, debauch, lead astray, make corrupt, contaminate, degrade, tempt, seduce

corruption NOUN

1 *He was found guilty of treason, espionage, and corruption.*
▶ dishonesty, deception, misconduct, bribery, fraud
AN OPPOSITE IS honesty

2 *all kinds of moral corruption*
▶ sin, immorality, degradation, depravity, degeneracy, impurity
OPPOSITES ARE morality, purity

cosmetic ADJECTIVE

The improvements were largely cosmetic
▶ superficial, surface, external, decorative, insubstantial
OPPOSITES ARE fundamental, substantial

cosmetics NOUN

I had all the cosmetics a woman could want, and I liked to dress up.
▶ make-up, beauty products, face paint, toiletries

cosmic ADJECTIVE

a musical work of cosmic proportions
▶ vast, huge, immense, boundless, endless, infinite, limitless, universal

cosmopolitan ADJECTIVE

1 *a large city with a cosmopolitan atmosphere*
▶ international, multicultural, sophisticated
AN OPPOSITE IS provincial

2 *cosmopolitan attitudes*
▶ worldly, well-travelled, sophisticated, urbane, liberal

cost NOUN

1 *The cost of a ticket has increased.*
▶ price, charge (for), expense, amount, payment (for), levy (on), tariff (on), outlay (on), expenditure (on), rate (for), value, fare, figure

2 *The cost in human lives is too great.*
▶ sacrifice, loss, penalty, price, suffering

cost VERB

1 *Each item on this shelf costs a pound.*
▶ be priced at, sell for, go for, come to, fetch, realize, (*more informal*) set you back

2 *We must cost your proposals before we take them any further.*
▶ price, put a price on, value, estimate the cost of

costly ADJECTIVE

The five-star service is very costly.
▶ expensive, dear, overpriced, exorbitant, (*more informal*) pricey

costume NOUN

a prize for the best costume
▶ outfit, dress, ensemble, clothing, suit, attire, (*informal*) get-up

cosy ADJECTIVE

They lived in a cosy little house.
▶ snug, comfortable, warm, homely, restful, secure, intimate, reassuring, relaxing, soft, (*more informal*) comfy
AN OPPOSITE IS uncomfortable

cottage NOUN

a cottage in the country
▶ little house, bungalow, cabin, chalet, (*mainly Scottish*) bothy

couch NOUN

a cat sat next to her on the couch.
▶ sofa, settee, chesterfield, ottoman, divan

council NOUN

1 *The council is responsible for maintaining the roads.*
▶ local authority, legislature, corporation, assembly
2 *a meeting of the society's administrative council*
▶ board, committee, commission, panel

counsel NOUN

We look to her for wise counsel.
▶ advice, guidance, direction, instruction, suggestions

counsel VERB

She is good at counselling her staff.
▶ advise, guide, give help to, discuss matters with

counsellor NOUN

A trained counseller will help you.
▶ adviser, consultant, therapist

count VERB

1 *He was counting the number of cars parked along the street.*
▶ add up, total, calculate, work out, reckon, check, (*more informal*) tot up
2 *It's important for people to feel that they count.*
▶ matter, be important, have significance, signify
3 **count on** *You can count on my support*
▶ rely on, depend on, bank on, be sure of, trust, believe in, expect, have faith in

count NOUN

1 *There were over a hundred members at the last count.*
▶ calculation, reckoning, counting, tally, poll, census
2 *a high calorie count*
▶ total, sum, amount, tally, number

counter NOUN

1 *He had left his glasses on the counter.*
▶ worktop, work surface, work table
2 *You play the game with counters.*
▶ token, disc, piece

counteract VERB

new laws to counteract terrorism
▶ prevent, resist, oppose, curb, forestall, fight against, act against, work against, thwart, frustrate, foil, reduce, neutralize, withstand

counterbalance VERB

High interest rates counterbalance the high level of risk.
▶ compensate for, make up for, offset, balance, equalize, even out, counteract

counterfeit ADJECTIVE

a counterfeit £20 note
▶ forged, fake, imitation, bogus, sham, copied, (*more informal*) phoney
AN OPPOSITE IS genuine

counterfeit VERB

1 *The notes had been counterfeited.*
▶ copy, fake, forge
2 *His brother managed to counterfeit his signature.*
▶ forge, fake, copy, reproduce, falsify, imitate, simulate

counterpart NOUN

Heads of department were to meet their counterparts from neighbouring schools.
▶ equivalent, opposite number, peer, equal

countless ADJECTIVE

They have to make countless decisions every day.
▶ innumerable, untold, myriad, numerous, numberless, unnumbered, endless, immeasurable, incalculable, infinite, many, measureless, limitless
AN OPPOSITE IS few

country NOUN

1 *a country of warlike people*
▶ nation, land, state, territory, realm
2 *They could return to their own country at last.*
▶ homeland, home, native land, native soil, mother country, country of origin, birthplace
3 *The prime minister would appeal to the country in an election.*
▶ people, nation, public, populace, population, community
4 *You drive through lovely open country.*
▶ terrain, landscape, countryside, scenery, surroundings, environment
RELATED ADJECTIVE rural

couple NOUN

1 *A couple were dancing on the balcony.*
▶ pair, twosome, partners, duo, husband and wife
2 *Let me know if you see him in the next couple of days.*
▶ few, two or three
USAGE You can also say *in the next day or so.*

couple VERB

A second locomotive is coupled to the train at Crewe.
▶ connect, attach, join, link, fasten, hitch, yoke, unite (with), combine (with), pair

coupon NOUN

1 *The offer includes money-saving coupons.*
▶ voucher, token, ticket, certificate
2 *For more information fill in the coupon below.*
▶ form, tear-off slip, slip

courage NOUN

It needs courage to argue with them.
▶ bravery, audacity, boldness, daring, nerve, pluck, gallantry, determination, fearlessness, fortitude, heroism, (*more informal*) bottle, (*more informal*) grit, (*more informal*) guts, (*much more informal*) spunk
AN OPPOSITE IS cowardice

courageous ADJECTIVE

It was a courageous attempt against all the odds.
▶ brave, valiant, daring, audacious, spirited, intrepid, plucky, adventurous, fearless
AN OPPOSITE IS cowardly

courier NOUN

1 *A courier brought a package.*
▶ messenger, carrier, dispatch rider, runner
2 *She worked as a courier for a travel firm.*
▶ representative, guide, tour guide

course NOUN

1 *a beginner's course in German*
▶ programme of study, course of study, educational programme, classes, lessons, studies
2 *The aircraft had changed its course again.*
▶ direction, route, way, tack, path, flight path, bearing, itinerary
3 *an event that changed the course of history*
▶ progress, progression, development, advance, evolution, flow, unfolding, future
4 *the best course to adopt*
▶ plan, plan of action, procedure, approach, method, programme, policy
5 *They had only just started the main course.*
▶ dish, part of a meal, menu item
6 *six laps of the course*
▶ track, circuit, ground, stadium

court NOUN

1 *The court acquitted them all.*
▶ lawcourt, court of law, bench, tribunal
2 *entertainment for the Queen's court*
▶ entourage, followers, royal household, establishment
3 *a court for ball games*
▶ enclosure, playing area, ground, field

courteous ADJECTIVE

The staff are always helpful and courteous.
▶ polite, civil, obliging, considerate, respectful, well-mannered, affable, civilized, refined

courtesy NOUN

Everyone is entitled to the same level of courtesy.
▶ politeness, consideration, civility, respect, attention

courtyard NOUN

People gathered in a courtyard behind the house.
▶ yard, quadrangle, (*more informal*) quad, court, enclosure, forecourt, patio

cover NOUN

1 *The computer screen has its own plastic cover.*
▶ covering, envelope, wrapper, case
2 *Lift the cover and look inside.*
▶ lid, top, cap
3 *The book has a blue cover.*
▶ jacket, dust jacket, dust cover, wrapper
4 *a thick cover of snow*
▶ covering, layer, coat, coating, blanket, carpet, cloak, overlay
5 *The trees provide some sort of cover.*
▶ shelter, protection, refuge, shield, haven, defence

6 *The business is a cover for spying activities.*
▶ front, facade, pretext, disguise, screen

cover VERB

1 *She covered her knees with a blanket.*
▶ envelop, enclose, protect, overlay
USAGE You can also say *She put* (or *placed*) *a blanket over her knees.*.
2 *The car was covered in mud.*
▶ coat, cake, encrust, plaster, smother, spread
3 *The book covers most of the main topics.*
▶ deal with, treat, consider, include, contain, comprise, encompass, embrace, provide for, incorporate
4 *The money should cover most of our needs.*
▶ cater for, be enough for, meet, suffice for, pay for

covering NOUN

a light covering of snow
▶ cover, layer, coat, coating, blanket, carpet, cloak, overlay

cover-up NOUN

The fraud had taken years to be discovered because of a massive cover-up at high level.
▶ concealment, deception, suppression, disguise, pretence

covet VERB

Claudia looked longingly at the smoky-blue suit she coveted.
▶ desire, long for, crave, yearn for, hanker after, dream of, (*more informal*) fancy

coward NOUN

(*informal*) *He accused them of being cheats and cowards.*
▶ weakling, faint-heart, (*more informal*) chicken, (*more informal*) wimp
AN OPPOSITE IS hero

cowardice NOUN

Her husband had been executed for cowardice.
▶ cowardliness, faint-heartedness, spinelessness, timorousness, timidity
OPPOSITES ARE bravery, courage

cowardly ADJECTIVE

The thieves ran off, showing how cowardly they are.
The decision was feeble and cowardly.
▶ faint-hearted, lily-livered, spineless, craven, weak, timid, pusillanimous, (*more informal*) gutless, (*more informal*) yellow
OPPOSITES ARE brave, courageous

cowed ADJECTIVE

The regime ruled over a cowed people.
▶ frightened, scared, subdued, overawed, browbeaten, disheartened, daunted, unnerved

cower VERB

The children cowered in fear.
▶ cringe, shrink, crouch, recoil, flinch, quail, pull back, back away, grovel, hide, shiver, skulk

coy ADJECTIVE

Don't be coy: come and be introduced
► shy, bashful, reserved, diffident, embarrassed, inhibited, self-conscious, hesitant, timid, reserved, retiring
OPPOSITES ARE assertive, forward, bold

crack NOUN

1 *a plate with a crack in it*
► break, chip, chink, split, fracture, fissure, gap
2 *a crack on the head*
► blow, bang, knock, smack, hit, punch, (*more informal*) bash
3 *the crack of a rifle   a crack of thunder*
► bang, report, crash, explosion, burst, snap, pop
4 *a cheap crack*
► joke, jest, quip, wisecrack, gibe, dig, (*more informal*) gag
5 *have a crack at it*
► try, attempt, (*more informal*) go, (*more informal*) shot, (*more informal*) stab

crack VERB

1 *She dropped a cup and cracked it.*
► break, split, shatter, splinter, chip, fracture
2 *Guns cracked in the distance.*
► burst, bang, go bang, explode, thump, boom, pop, crackle, crash
3 *She cracked him round the head.*
► strike, smack, thump, slap, hit, (*more informal*) bash, (*more informal*) whack
4 *The problem proved hard to crack.*
► solve, resolve, work out, puzzle out, fathom, decipher, break
5 *A suspect finally cracked and confessed.*
► break down, give in, give way, collapse, yield
crack down on *a drive to crack down on street crime*
► reduce, suppress, end, stop, eradicate, get tough on, clamp down on
crack up
1 *I'm so anxious I could be cracking up (informal).*
► break down, have a breakdown, lose control, go to pieces, go mad, go crazy
2 *The remark made everyone want to crack up.*
► burst out laughing, roar with laughter, laugh uncontrollably

crackle VERB

The fire began to crackle.
► sizzle, fizzle, crack, fizz, hiss, sputter

cradle NOUN

a baby's cradle
► cot, crib, bed

cradle VERB

She cradled a mug of tea in her hands.
► hold, support, nurse, tend, protect

craft NOUN

1 *the traditional craft of hand weaving*
► handicraft, trade, business, pursuit, activity, occupation, profession, work, job
2 *Pete demonstrated the blacksmith's craft*
► skill, art, technique, expertise, mastery, talent, ability

3 *The harbour was teeming with river craft.*
► vessels, ships, boats

craftsman NOUN

Passers-by could watch the craftsmen at work.
► artisan, artist, craftsperson, master

craftsmanship NOUN

an age when craftsmanship in building reached a peak
► skill, technique, expertise, workmanship, artistry, ability, dexterity, handiwork, (*more informal*) know-how

crafty ADJECTIVE

That's a crafty way of avoiding the problem.
► cunning, clever, shrewd, ingenious, wily, artful, canny

crag NOUN

a high crag overlooking the bay
► cliff, bluff, ridge, rock, precipice

craggy ADJECTIVE

a craggy cliff
► rocky, rough, rugged, jagged, steep

cram VERB

1 *They were busy cramming burgers into their mouths. The shelves were crammed with books.*
► stuff, force, press, squeeze, jam, pack, overfill
2 *I'll never know how we managed to cram into such a tiny car.*
► crowd, crush, squeeze, pack
3 *Many of the students are still cramming for tomorrow's exam.*
► study hard, (*more informal*) swot, (*more informal*) mug up

cramped ADJECTIVE

It was hard to sleep in the cramped quarters of the submarine.
► restricted, confined, poky, constricted, narrow, tight, uncomfortable
AN OPPOSITE IS roomy

crash NOUN

1 *There was a loud crash in the kitchen.*
► bang, smash, clash, clatter, clang, racket, thump, thud, boom
2 *She had been injured in a car crash.*
► accident, collision, smash, bump, pile-up, derailment, disaster, impact, knock, wreck
3 *a stock-market crash*
► collapse, failure, depression, fall, ruin

crash VERB

1 **crash into** *The car crashed into a tree.*
► hit, strike, smash into, collide with, bump into, knock into, lurch into, pitch into
2 *The company had crashed in the recession.*
► fail, collapse, fold up, go under, founder, become bankrupt
3 *Parts of the roof crashed to the ground.*
► collapse, fall, plunge, topple, hurtle

crass ADJECTIVE
It had been a crass thing to do, and he apologized for it.
▶ stupid, foolish, blundering, insensitive, mindless, witless

crate NOUN
Three crates of books stood by the door.
▶ case, packing case, box, carton, tea chest

crater NOUN
Volcanic peaks tower above deep craters.
▶ pit, hole, chasm, hollow, cavity, opening, abyss

crave VERB
The chapel might provide the privacy she craved.
▶ long for, yearn for, hunger for, dream of, hanker after, desire, seek

craving NOUN
the body's natural craving for food
▶ longing, desire, hankering, hunger, thirst, appetite

crawl VERB
1 *He escaped by crawling out of the back of the house.*
▶ creep, edge, inch, slither, clamber
2 *(informal) You can get their support without having to crawl to them all the time.*
▶ grovel, pander, kowtow, fawn (over), be obsequious, (more informal) suck up
be crawling with *The place is crawling with visitors in the summer months.*
▶ be full of, be overrun by, be teeming with, be packed with, be crowded with

craze NOUN
the latest craze to sweep the country
▶ fad, trend, vogue, fashion, rage, mania, diversion, enthusiasm, infatuation, novelty, obsession, passion, pastime

crazy ADJECTIVE
1 *It was crazy to expect them to agree.*
▶ absurd, ridiculous, ludicrous, preposterous, foolish, idiotic, stupid, foolhardy, unwise, (more informal) barmy
2 *She was going crazy with all the work.*
▶ mad, insane, out of your mind, off your head, unbalanced, demented, deranged
3 *The whole family are crazy about golf.*
▶ mad, passionate, keen (on), devoted (to), smitten (with), taken (with), (more informal) potty

creak VERB
The door began to creak.
▶ squeak, grate, groan, scrape, grind, rasp

cream NOUN
1 *Rub in some skin cream.*
▶ lotion, ointment, rub, salve, moisturizer
2 *the cream of the country's jockeys*
▶ pick, elite, choice, finest, best
AN OPPOSITE IS dregs

creamy ADJECTIVE
The powder makes a creamy paste when mixed with water.
▶ smooth, thick, rich, velvety, milky, oily

crease NOUN
The cloth was full of creases and would have to be ironed.
▶ wrinkle, crinkle, pucker, fold, furrow, groove, line, pleat, ridge, ruck, tuck, corrugation

crease VERB
I tried not to crease my clothes.
▶ crumple, crinkle, wrinkle, pucker, crush, crimp, rumple, ruck, fold, furrow, pleat, ridge

create VERB
1 *A new work had to be created from scratch.*
▶ produce, make, generate, develop, compose, devise, design
2 *His father had created the business fifty years before.*
▶ set up, start, begin, found, establish, institute, initiate
3 *The appointment created a lot of resentment.*
▶ cause, bring about, lead to, engender, prompt, produce, result in, give rise to

creation NOUN
1 *the creation of a modern industrial society*
▶ making, formation, foundation, fashioning, establishment, institution, conception, birth, development, origination, production
OPPOSITES ARE disintegration, destruction
2 *The decor was entirely her creation.*
▶ work, effort, conception, invention, design, devising, achievement, handiwork, brainchild, product, work of art

creative ADJECTIVE
Students need to be creative in their thinking.
▶ imaginative, inventive, expressive, resourceful, original, productive, fertile, artistic, positive, ingenious, clever, inspired, talented, visionary
AN OPPOSITE IS destructive

creator NOUN
1 *the creator of many good novels*
▶ writer, author, producer, composer, designer, deviser, initiator, inventor, maker, manufacturer, parent
2 *the creators of the Assyrian Empire*
▶ architect, builder, originator, begetter

creature NOUN
1 *Whales are the largest living creatures.*
▶ animal, living thing, beast, being, brute
2 *The poor creature had been out in the rain all night.*
▶ fellow, individual, person, wretch, beggar, chap

credentials NOUN
1 *A police officer checked the driver's credentials.*
▶ documents, papers, identity papers, authorization, permit, licence, proof of identity, passport, warrant
2 *Her credentials for the job were impeccable.*
▶ qualifications, references, accreditation

credibility NOUN
The details give credibility to the story.
▶ plausibility, conviction, integrity, believability, reliability, probability, trustworthiness

credible ADJECTIVE

The man was unable to give any credible explanation for his presence there.
▶ believable, plausible, reasonable, tenable, conceivable, possible, convincing, imaginable, likely, persuasive
AN OPPOSITE IS incredible

credit NOUN

1 *Gary helped him with his chemistry and deserves a lot of the credit for the good grades he got.*
▶ praise, acclaim, approval, recognition, acknowledgement, commendation, distinction, prestige, merit, esteem, fame, glory, honour, (*more informal*) kudos, reputation, status
AN OPPOSITE IS dishonour
2 *Kate had better taste than she'd been given credit for.*
▶ recognition, acknowledgement, approval

credit VERB

1 *It is difficult to credit such an unlikely story*
▶ accept, believe, subscribe to, trust, have confidence in, have faith in, rely on, depend on, count on, endorse, reckon on, (*more informal*) swallow, (*informal*) buy
AN OPPOSITE IS disbelieve
2 *The idea is credited to Aristotle.*
▶ attribute to, ascribe to, assign to, attach to, associate (with)

creditable ADJECTIVE

The team were on good form and put on a creditable performance.
▶ commendable, laudable, respectable, estimable, admirable, praiseworthy, worthy, excellent, good, honourable, meritorious, well thought of
AN OPPOSITE IS unworthy

creed NOUN

1 *All are welcome regardless of race or creed.*
▶ faith, religion, beliefs, persuasion, convictions
2 *a belief in the religion's creed*
▶ doctrine, dogma, principles, tenets, system of belief

creek NOUN

There used to be a toll bridge crossing the creek.
▶ inlet, estuary, arm of the sea, bay

creep VERB

1 *She watched him creep under the table.*
▶ crawl, slither, slink, wriggle, worm your way, writhe, edge, inch, move slowly
2 *Gilly packed a suitcase and crept down the stairs.*
▶ slip, sneak, steal, move quietly, tiptoe

creepy ADJECTIVE

The place gave her creepy feelings.
▶ frightening, eerie, spooky, scary, weird, sinister, uncanny, unearthly, macabre, ominous
AN OPPOSITE IS pleasant

crest NOUN

1 *a bird with a bright crest*
▶ plume, tuft, comb
2 *We reached the crest of the hill.*
▶ peak, crown, brow, ridge, summit, top, apex

3 *the royal crest*
▶ insignia, regalia, emblem, badge, seal, sign, symbol

crew NOUN

1 *a ship's crew*
▶ company, complement, sailors, seamen
2 *a road-mending crew*
▶ team, gang, unit, party, squad

---

crime NOUN

1 *The report shows a decrease in street crime.*
▶ lawbreaking, lawlessness, delinquency, wrongdoing, transgression, misconduct, dishonesty, illegality
2 *Blackmail is a serious crime.*
▶ offence, misdeed, misdemeanour, transgression, illegal act, unlawful act, (*more informal*) racket, (*old use*) felony

NAMES FOR TYPES OF CRIME
These are names in general use, and not all of them are legal terms.

crimes involving killing: homicide, murder (intentional killing), manslaughter (unintentional killing), assassination (killing of a prominent figure).

crimes involving stealing: theft, robbery, burglary, mugging, pilfering; handling stolen goods.

other violent crimes against people: assault, rape (sexual assault), grievous bodily harm ((*informal*) GBH), actual bodily harm (less serious than grievous), battery; kidnapping, abduction, hijacking, piracy, terrorism.

violent crimes against property: sabotage, vandalism, arson (setting fire to property), criminal damage; drink-driving, joy-riding, being drunk and disorderly.

other, usually non-violent, crimes against the state or against individuals: treason; fraud, forgery, counterfeiting, corruption, embezzlement, extortion, blackmail, bribery, smuggling, drug-peddling; perjury (lying on oath).

---

criminal NOUN

His friends were criminals, working with the smugglers.
▶ lawbreaker, offender, villain, wrongdoer, delinquent, miscreant, convict, culprit, (*more informal*) crook

criminal ADJECTIVE

Hardship can never justify criminal behaviour.
▶ illegal, unlawful, illicit, dishonest, corrupt, nefarious, (*more informal*) crooked, (*more informal*) bent
OPPOSITES ARE legal, honest

cringe VERB

1 *The old man cringed, his hands shaking.*
▶ cower, shrink back, draw back, recoil, flinch, shy away, quail, tremble, crouch, quiver, dodge, duck, grovel

2 *I cringe when I hear those songs these days.*
► wince, blench, squirm, blush

ripple VERB
1 *The car hit her, crippling her for life.*
► disable, incapacitate, maim, injure, lame, damage, paralyse
2 *Industry was crippled by a series of strikes.*
► ruin, destroy, crush, paralyse, scupper, bring to a standstill, put out of action, spoil

rippled ADJECTIVE
1 *His crippled right leg is bent back at the knee.*
► disabled, deformed, lame, incapacitated, physically impaired, injured, maimed, paralysed, handicapped, hurt, invalid, mutilated
2 *Witnesses watched the crippled car being winched on to the Relay tender.*
► immobilized, damaged, incapacitated, out of action, sabotaged, useless

risis NOUN
1 *Events in Europe were reaching a crisis.*
► climax, critical point, turning point, moment of truth
2 *The following year there was another economic crisis.*
► emergency, predicament, problem, danger, difficulty

risp ADJECTIVE
1 *crisp biscuits*
► crunchy, crispy, brittle, crackly, fragile, crumbly
AN OPPOSITE IS soft
2 *a crisp morning in November*
► fresh, brisk, bracing, exhilarating, refreshing
3 *a crisp style of writing*
► terse, incisive, pithy, succinct, sparing, laconic

riterion NOUN
The main criterion of good training is to reach the government's official standard.
► basis, yardstick, measure, benchmark, point of reference, justification, principle, gauge

ritic NOUN
1 *the most famous music critic of the time*
► commentator, reviewer, authority, expert, pundit, judge, analyst
2 *a major critic of government policy*
► detractor, attacker

ritical ADJECTIVE
1 *a critical assessment of the available literature*
► analytical, objective, evaluative, discerning, perceptive
2 *He is highly critical of American foreign policy.*
► disapproving, censorious, derogatory (about), disparaging (about), scathing (about), uncomplimentary (about)
OPPOSITES ARE appreciative, complimentary (about)
3 *He only escaped death by moving his head at the critical moment.*
► crucial, vital, decisive, essential, all-important

4 *She was taken to hospital where her condition is described as critical.*
► serious, grave, dangerous, precarious
AN OPPOSITE IS safe

criticism NOUN
1 *The management have come in for a lot of criticism.*
► disapproval, blame, censure, disparagement, fault-finding, reproach, stricture, tirade, verbal attack, (*more informal*) flak
2 *Their work will be submitted for criticism.*
► evaluation, assessment, appraisal, analysis, judgement, appreciation

criticize VERB
1 *Police criticized motorists for using mobile phones while driving.*
► condemn, censure, find fault with, denounce, blame, castigate, disparage, denigrate, deprecate, (*more informal*) knock, (*more informal*) slam, (*more informal*) pan
AN OPPOSITE IS praise
2 *a review criticizing the work of four modern poets*
► appraise, assess, evaluate, analyse, judge, review

crockery NOUN
The table had been laid and the crockery brought out.
► dishes, plates, tableware, china, crocks, earthenware, porcelain, pottery, ceramics

TYPES OF CROCKERY
things for eating off: dinner service, tea set; plate, side plate, dinner plate, dessert plate.
things for eating out of: bowl, cereal bowl, soup bowl, salad bowl, sugar bowl.
things for drinking from: cup (and saucer), teacup, coffee cup, mug, beaker.
containers: jug, milk jug, pot, teapot, coffee pot, percolator, cafetière; dish, butter dish, tureen, gravy boat, cruet.

crook NOUN
1 *His head was lying in the crook of her arm.*
► bend, curve, angle
2 *She accused them of being crooks.*
► criminal, lawbreaker, villain, wrongdoer

crooked ADJECTIVE
1 *The picture looks slightly crooked.*
► askew, awry, lopsided, offcentre, slanting, angled, (*more informal*) skew-whiff
2 *The garden was a maze of crooked paths.*
► winding, twisting, tortuous, twisty, zigzag
3 *She put a crooked finger to her lips*
► bent, misshapen, deformed, bowed, curved, curving
4 *Several officials were probably crooked.*
► criminal, dishonest, corrupt, nefarious, (*more informal*) bent

crop NOUN
My crop of Brussels sprouts are ready to eat.
► harvest, yield, produce, gathering

crop VERB

1 *Sheep cropped grass in the fields.*
▶ graze on, browse on, eat, nibble, bite off
2 *She had to crop her long blonde hair.*
▶ cut short, cut, clip, trim, snip, shear
crop up *The same names keep cropping up over the years.*
▶ occur, arise, appear, come up, turn up, emerge, spring up, happen

cross ADJECTIVE

Dad got cross and said I was setting a bad example.
▶ angry, annoyed, testy, tetchy, upset, vexed, irate, bad-tempered, cantankerous, crotchety, ill-tempered, irascible, irritable, peevish, short-tempered, (*more informal*) grumpy
AN OPPOSITE IS good- humoured

cross NOUN

1 *a difficult cross to bear*
▶ burden, problem, difficulty, misfortune, trial, tribulation, trouble, worry, grief, sorrow, affliction
2 *a cross between a yak and a cow*
▶ hybrid, cross-breed, amalgam (of), blend (of), combination (of), half-way house, mixture (of)

cross VERB

1 *The roads cross north of the town.*
▶ intersect, intertwine, meet
2 *There is only one place you can cross the river.*
▶ go across, pass over, ford, traverse
3 *It's better not to cross the common in the dark.*
▶ go across, walk across, traverse
4 *A stone bridge crossed the stream.*
▶ span, bridge, arch, go across, extend across, pass across
5 *He blew up if anyone crossed him.*
▶ oppose, annoy, defy, argue with, obstruct, thwart
cross out *He crossed out part of the sentence and rewrote it.*
▶ delete, strike out, erase, cancel

crossroads NOUN

A large van was waiting at the crossroads.
▶ junction, intersection, interchange

crouch VERB

The boys crouched behind a large tree.
▶ squat, kneel, stoop, bend, bob down, bow down, cower, cringe, duck, hunch, huddle

crowd NOUN

1 *The crowd dispersed quickly.*
▶ throng, multitude, mob, masses, horde, gathering, company, rabble, crush
2 *a large crowd at the ground*
▶ gate, attendance, audience, spectators

crowd VERB

1 *Some of them had crowded round a drinks machine.*
▶ gather, collect, cluster, congregate, huddle, muster, mass, swarm, surge
2 *The guests were crowding into the dining room.*
▶ stream, push, pile, pack, squeeze, swarm, flock, surge, jostle

crowded ADJECTIVE

It was hard to find a space on the crowded beach.
▶ packed, congested, overcrowded, swarming, teeming, thronging, cramped, full, busy, jammed, jostling, overflowing
OPPOSITES ARE empty, deserted

crown NOUN

1 *The Queen was wearing her crown.*
▶ coronet, diadem, tiara
2 *He paused at the crown of the hill*
▶ brow, crest, top, summit, peak, ridge, head, ape

crown VERB

1 *William was crowned in Westminster Abbey on Christmas Day.*
▶ install, enthrone, anoint
2 *He crowned his career with a diplomatic post in America.*
▶ cap, round off, top off, complete, conclude, consummate, fulfil, finish off, perfect

crucial ADJECTIVE

1 *Police investigation plays a crucial role in the crimina process.*
▶ major, central, pivotal, decisive, critical, important, momentous, serious
OPPOSITES ARE minor, unimportant
2 *Secrecy is crucial in this matter.*
▶ paramount, essential, vital, critical, indispensabl

crude ADJECTIVE

1 *increased production of crude oil*
▶ unrefined, unpurified, unprocessed, natural, raw
AN OPPOSITE IS refined
2 *a crude method of counting votes*
▶ primitive, simple, basic, rudimentary, rough, makeshift, improvised, homespun, clumsy, unrefined, amateurish, awkward, inelegant, inept
OPPOSITES ARE sophisticated, advanced
3 *He went in for a very crude type of humour.*
▶ coarse, indecent, vulgar, bawdy, lewd, offensive, obscene
USAGE *Obscene* is a very strong word and often implies an intention to offend or corrupt people.

cruel ADJECTIVE

1 *Their opponents were huge cruel men. Hunting is widely regarded as a cruel sport.*
▶ brutal, savage, vicious, fierce, ferocious, barbaric callous, heartless, cold-blooded, pitiless, ruthless, merciless, vile, sadistic, brutish
OPPOSITES ARE gentle, humane, kind, compassionate
2 *Her father's sudden death was a cruel blow.*
▶ severe, harsh, bitter, grim, painful
OPPOSITES ARE mild, gentle

cruelty NOUN

The rebellion was put down with great cruelty.
▶ brutality, savagery, viciousness, ferocity, barbarity, callousness, heartlessness, cold-bloodedness, ruthlessness

ruise NOUN

a sea cruise
▶ voyage, journey, trip, sail

ruise VERB

The family decided to cruise in the Mediterranean.
▶ sail, voyage, travel, journey, take a cruise

rumb NOUN

crumbs of bread   a small crumb of comfort
▶ fragment, grain, morsel, scrap, bit, speck, particle, shred

rumble VERB

1 *The damaged buildings were beginning to crumble.*
▶ disintegrate, break up, collapse, fall apart, fall down, decay, decompose, deteriorate

2 *He crumbled the soil into a fine powder.*
▶ crush, grind, pound, powder, pulverize, break into pieces, fragment

rumbly ADJECTIVE

crumbly cake
▶ powdery, friable, granular
AN OPPOSITE IS solid

rumple VERB

It's hard not to crumple your clothes in such a tiny car.
▶ crease, crush, crinkle, wrinkle, squash

runch VERB

1 *She sat there crunching biscuits.*
▶ munch, chomp, champ, masticate, devour

2 *He was fed up with getting his head crunched in rugger matches.*
▶ crush, pound, pulverize, grind, smash

runch NOUN

(informal) The crunch came when all the men returned from the war.
▶ critical time, moment of truth, crisis, crux, decision time

rusade NOUN

a crusade against street crime
▶ campaign, movement, drive, effort, struggle, fight, push

rush VERB

1 *He nearly crushed his arm in the lift doors.*
▶ squash, squeeze, mangle, crunch, scrunch, compress, mash, break, bruise, grind

2 *She was afraid she would crush her dress.*
▶ crease, crumple, crinkle, wrinkle, squash

3 *The army crushed the rebellion in a short time.*
▶ suppress, subdue, quell, quash, put down, defeat, vanquish, overcome

rush NOUN

There was quite a crush by the doors.
▶ crowd, throng, congestion, jam, press, multitude, mob

rust NOUN

The paint left in the pot had formed a hard crust.
▶ covering, skin, surface, shell, exterior, outside

crusty ADJECTIVE

1 *a meal of dry crusty bread and cheese*
▶ crisp, crispy, brittle, crunchy

2 *He seems so crusty these days.*
▶ irritable, grumpy, gruff, grouchy, tetchy, testy, bad-tempered, irascible, fractious

crux NOUN

Here lay the crux of the matter.
▶ essence, nub, heart, core, kernel, central point, crucial issue, main issue

cry VERB This word is often overused. Here are some alternatives:

1 *Debbie looked upset and about to cry.*
▶ weep, shed tears, sob, howl, whimper, snivel, blubber, bawl, wail
USAGE The last six synonyms are unfriendly or disapproving, and *sob* means to cry uncontrollably and unattractively. *Weep* and *shed tears* are more neutral in tone, although *weep* is more literary.

2 *'Come on!' cried Sam.*
▶ call, yell, exclaim, shout, shriek, scream, bawl
cry off *The game was cancelled when three players cried off.*
▶ withdraw, back out, cancel, excuse yourself
cry out *Somebody was crying out in the darkness.*
▶ call out, yell, scream, screech, shout, shriek

cry NOUN

1 *a cry of pain*
▶ call, shout, yell, shriek, scream, screech, roar, bellow

2 *a cry for help*
▶ appeal, plea, entreaty

cryptic ADJECTIVE

a cryptic note about a ransom
▶ mysterious, obscure, puzzling, enigmatic, unclear, perplexing, unintelligible, coded, veiled, secret
OPPOSITES ARE clear, straightforward

cuddle VERB

So far he had only kissed and cuddled her.
▶ hug, caress, embrace, hold, clasp, pet, fondle, huddle against, snuggle against

cue NOUN

A quick glance was her cue to speak.
▶ signal, sign, prompt, hint, reminder

cuff VERB

She cuffed him round the head.
▶ hit, box, smack, thump, biff, clout, strike

culminate VERB

culminate in *The campaign culminated in a massive demonstration in central London.*
▶ build up to, lead up to, come to a climax with, rise to a peak with, reach a finale with, conclude with, end with, finish with, terminate with, close with

culmination NOUN

These events marked the culmination of a two-month festival.
▶ climax, pinnacle, high point, peak, height, conclusion, crowning moment

culprit NOUN

New evidence showed that he was not the culprit after all.
▶ guilty party, person responsible, offender, criminal, wrongdoer, miscreant, transgressor

cult NOUN

1 *a cult that worshipped the moon*
▶ sect, religious group, denomination
2 *The sport had become a cult in parts of the country.*
▶ craze, fashion, trend, vogue, enthusiasm

cultivate VERB

1 *Peasants cultivated the land.*
▶ farm, till, dig, work, plough
2 *They were helped with cultivating food crops.*
▶ grow, raise, rear, sow, plant, tend, produce
3 *We need to cultivate a better attitude to work.*
▶ develop, foster, nurture, encourage, promote, pursue, try to achieve, cherish, further, improve

cultural ADJECTIVE

a country's cultural heritage
▶ artistic, intellectual, aesthetic, educational, elevating, enlightening, improving

culture NOUN

1 *modern popular culture*
▶ civilization, society, intellectual activity, arts, traditions, customs, education, learning
2 *a person of culture*
▶ intellectual awareness, achievement, enlightenment, education, discernment, good taste

cultured ADJECTIVE

a pleasant, cultured man
▶ cultivated, educated, well-educated, well-read, enlightened, civilized, erudite, artistic, refined, urbane, highbrow, knowledgeable, scholarly
AN OPPOSITE IS ignorant

cumbersome ADJECTIVE

The suitcases were cumbersome rather than heavy.
▶ unwieldy, awkward, bulky, clumsy, hefty, burdensome

cunning ADJECTIVE

1 *a cunning plan*
▶ crafty, wily, artful, sly, devious, knowing, guileful, disingenuous, machiavellian
OPPOSITES ARE ingenuous, guileless
2 *The crime was solved by cunning detective work.*
▶ skilful, clever, shrewd, astute, adroit, subtle, ingenious

cunning NOUN

The defence counsel will need quite a bit of cunning.
▶ guile, craftiness, artfulness, shrewdness, astuteness, adroitness, deviousness

cup NOUN

1 *They were drinking tea from pretty cups.*
▶ teacup, coffee cup, mug, tankard
2 *a silver cup for the winner*
▶ trophy, award, prize

cupboard NOUN

The tools and nails were kept in a cupboard.
▶ cabinet, closet, locker, dresser, (for clothes) wardrobe, (for food) larder

curb VERB

He tried to curb his temper.
▶ restrain, suppress, control, contain, check, hold back, stifle
AN OPPOSITE IS release

curdle VERB

The milk began to curdle.
▶ coagulate, congeal, clot, thicken, turn, turn sour, go lumpy, go sour

cure VERB

1 *A long period of rest will cure his ailment.*
▶ heal, remedy, treat, alleviate, counteract, ease, help, palliate, relieve
OPPOSITES ARE aggravate, worsen
2 *The fault may be difficult to cure.*
▶ correct, rectify, mend, repair, put right, solve, (more informal) fix

cure NOUN

1 *a cure for cancer*
▶ remedy, treatment, antidote, medicine, prescription, restorative, panacea, palliative, therapy
2 *Her unexpected cure amazed the doctors*
▶ recovery, healing, restoration to health

curiosity NOUN

1 *I found it hard to contain my curiosity.*
▶ inquisitiveness, interest, nosiness, prying, meddling, snooping
USAGE The last four synonyms are unfavourable in tone, whereas the first two are neutral.
2 *He had an elephant's head displayed as a curiosity in his house.*
▶ novelty, oddity, curio, rarity, collector's item

curious ADJECTIVE

1 *I was curious about the reason for this unexpected visit.*
▶ inquisitive, intrigued, interested, puzzled, eager to know, agog
OPPOSITES ARE incurious, unconcerned, indifferent
2 *He walked off with a curious jerking motion.*
▶ strange, odd, peculiar, queer, funny, bizarre, unusual, extraordinary, eccentric
AN OPPOSITE IS normal

curl NOUN

1 *Her hair was a mass of curls.*
▶ ringlet, wave, coil, loop, kink
2 *a pattern with repeated curls*
▶ loop, spiral, swirl, twist, bend, circle, curve, scroll, turn

3 *There was a curl of smoke in the distance.*
▶ spiral, coil, swirl, twirl, whorl, corkscrew

url VERB
1 *Smoke curled from the tall chimney.*
▶ coil, spiral, twirl, swirl, furl
2 *The path curls round old tree trunks.*
▶ wind, twist, curve, meander, snake, writhe, zigzag
3 *Sarah curled an arm round his waist.*
▶ wind, twine, entwine, wrap, twist
4 *a treatment to curl the hair*
▶ crimp, wave, frizz, perm

urly ADJECTIVE
thick curly hair
▶ wavy, curled, curling, crinkly, kinky, frizzy, fuzzy, crimped, permed
AN OPPOSITE IS straight

urrency NOUN
1 *The euro simplifies the business of getting foreign currency.*
▶ money, legal tender, coinage, cash, coins, banknotes
2 *This view of the matter has gained currency in the last few years.*
▶ acceptance, popularity, circulation, prevalence
USAGE You can also say ... *has become more widespread* or ... *has become more prevalent*.

urrent ADJECTIVE
1 *keeping abreast of current events*
▶ modern, contemporary, present-day, topical
AN OPPOSITE IS past
2 *The opinion is still current.*
▶ common, prevalent, prevailing, widespread, popular, accepted
AN OPPOSITE IS obsolete
3 *a current driving licence*
▶ valid, usable, up to date
OPPOSITES ARE out of date, expired
4 *the current administration in the White House*
▶ present, incumbent, existing, extant, reigning
OPPOSITES ARE past, former

urrent NOUN
1 *a current of air*
▶ stream, flow, draught, jet, course
2 *The girls were in danger from the strong currents.*
▶ tide, undertow, drift

urriculum NOUN
the school curriculum
▶ syllabus, programme of study, course

urse NOUN
1 *John caught his finger in the door and let out a curse.*
▶ swear word, oath, expletive, profanity, obscenity, blasphemy, exclamation
2 *The witch had put a curse on them.*
▶ malediction, imprecation, jinx
3 *the curse of unemployment*
▶ affliction, blight, scourge, plague, bane, misfortune, torment, evil

curse VERB
I listened to him cursing and shouting.
▶ swear, utter profanities, blaspheme, damn, fulminate
be cursed with *The family was cursed for years with sickness and poverty.*
▶ be afflicted with, be blighted with, be plagued with, be troubled by, be burdened with

cursory ADJECTIVE
a cursory read of the newspaper
▶ brief, perfunctory, superficial, desultory, hasty, hurried, quick, fleeting, casual
OPPOSITES ARE thorough, intensive

curt ADJECTIVE
Carl dismissed the idea with a curt grunt.
▶ abrupt, blunt, harsh, terse, gruff, rude, offhand, brusque, insensitive, outspoken, plain-spoken
OPPOSITES ARE polite, courteous

curtail VERB
1 *Bad weather forced them to curtail their holiday.*
▶ shorten, break off, truncate, cut
AN OPPOSITE IS extend
2 *economic measures needed to curtail public spending*
▶ reduce, decrease, limit, cut back, restrict, restrain, control

curtain NOUN
Clive closed the curtains.
▶ drape, drapery, hanging, blind, screen

curve NOUN
1 *a series of curves in the road*
▶ bend, turn, twist, loop
2 *a tall window with a curve at the top*
▶ arch, arc, bow, crescent

curve VERB
The river curved to the west.
▶ bend, twist, wind, loop, snake, turn, swerve

curved ADJECTIVE
1 *a tall building with a curved roof*
▶ arched, bowed, rounded, humped, crescent, vaulted, convex, bent
OPPOSITES ARE flat, straight
2 *The road was narrow and curved.*
▶ twisty, twisted, sinuous, meandering, serpentine, sweeping
AN OPPOSITE IS straight

cushion NOUN
1 *She put a cushion behind her and leaned back.*
▶ pillow, bolster, headrest, hassock, pad, beanbag
2 *a cushion against inflation*
▶ protection, buffer, shield, defence

cushion VERB
Buffers would cushion the impact of a collision.
▶ absorb, soften, deaden, lessen, reduce, mitigate, muffle

cushy ADJECTIVE
(informal) a cushy job
▶ easy, undemanding, comfortable, secure, *(informal)* jammy

custody NOUN

1 *Sean had given custody of the baby to her brother.*
▶ care, guardianship, charge, protection, safe-keeping, keeping, possession

2 *He had died when still in police custody.*
▶ detention, captivity, confinement, imprisonment, incarceration, (on) remand

custom NOUN

1 *local customs dating back to the thirteenth century*
▶ tradition, practice, usage, institution, convention, procedure, observance, form, habit, way, etiquette, manner, formality, routine

2 *It is our custom to visit relatives at the weekends.*
▶ practice, habit, routine, way, rule, policy, wont

3 *The shop offers discounts to attract custom*
▶ business, trade, customers, buyers, patronage, support

customary ADJECTIVE

1 *It is customary to stand during the playing of the anthem. the customary rules of behaviour*
▶ traditional, normal, usual, common, conventional, established, expected, general, ordinary, popular, prevailing, routine, fashionable
AN OPPOSITE IS unusual

2 *Dr Ali fell once again into his customary silence.*
▶ usual, accustomed, regular, wonted, habitual, typical

customer NOUN

The business is trying to attract younger customers.
▶ shopper, buyer, purchaser, client, consumer, patron
AN OPPOSITE IS seller

cut NOUN

1 *He had a cut on his hand.*
▶ gash, wound, injury, nick, incision, scratch, graze
USAGE *Scratch* and *graze* do not normally involve breaking of the skin and escape of blood.

2 *She had to accept a small cut in pay.*
▶ reduction, decrease, lowering (of), lessening (of)

3 *The leader of the gang demanded a higher cut.*
▶ share, portion, slice, (*more informal*) whack

cut VERB

1 *He had cut his finger with a kitchen knife.*
▶ gash, pierce, wound, injure, slash, nick, incise, scratch, graze
USAGE *Scratch* and *graze* do not normally involve breaking of the skin and escape of blood.

2 *Cut the vegetables into small pieces.*
▶ slice, chop, dice, cube, divide, pare

3 *She was going to have her hair cut. It will soon be time to start cutting the grass again.*
▶ trim, clip, crop, mow

4 *The supermarkets have cut prices on a wide range of goods.*
▶ reduce, lower, lessen, (*more informal*) slash

5 *Parts of the story were cut to make the film version.*
▶ omit, remove, delete, excise, take out, edit out

6 *You will have to cut your essay by about a third.*
▶ shorten, abridge, condense, reduce, precis, truncate

7 *The remarks were spiteful and cut her deeply.*
▶ hurt, offend, upset, wound

cut down
1 *Men are cutting the trees down.*
▶ fell, hew, lop

2 *I'm trying to cut down some of these expenses.*
▶ reduce, decrease, lower, lessen

cut in *Tessa cut in with a remark that made everyone laugh.*
▶ interrupt, butt in, break in, interject, intervene, intrude

cut off
1 *The blade nearly cut off her finger.*
▶ sever, chop off, amputate, hack off, remove

2 *The Gas Board threatened to cut off the supply.*
▶ disconnect, discontinue, interrupt, suspend
OPPOSITES ARE restore, reconnect

3 *Storms cut off the village for several days.*
▶ isolate, separate, seclude

4 *Her family had cut her off without a penny.*
▶ disinherit, disown, reject, repudiate, cast aside

cut out *The report mentioned several ways in which we could cut out inefficiencies.*
▶ remove, eliminate, excise, get rid of

cut up *Cut up the meat into small cubes.*
▶ chop, slice, dice, carve

cutback NOUN

cutbacks in spending
▶ reduction, cut, decrease, saving, economy, limit (to)

cute ADJECTIVE

When I was young I had a cute little collie dog.
▶ appealing, lovely, delightful, attractive, pretty, endearing, adorable, engaging

cutting ADJECTIVE

They had to endure some cutting remarks about their lifestyle.
▶ hurtful, scathing, caustic, sharp, sarcastic, acid, acerbic, bitter, spiteful, vicious, abrasive

cutting NOUN

a newspaper cutting
▶ clipping, snippet, extract, excerpt

cycle NOUN

a cycle of growth and decline lasting 75 years
▶ pattern, sequence, round, circle, series, era, period, revolution, rotation

cyclical ADJECTIVE

cyclical changes in the climate
▶ recurring, recurrent, periodic, repeated, seasonal

cylinder NOUN

The paper is rolled up to form a cylinder.
▶ column, tube, drum, reel, spool

cynic NOUN

Only a cynic would think her dishonest.
▶ sceptic, doubter, pessimist, doom merchant
OPPOSITES ARE optimist, idealist

cynical ADJECTIVE

I may be unduly cynical in thinking they are only in it for the money.
▶ sceptical, distrustful, suspicious, disbelieving, pessimistic, negative, doubting, questioning
AN OPPOSITE IS optimistic

cynicism NOUN

The touch of cynicism in his voice struck a sour note.
▶ scepticism, doubt, disbelief, suspicion, incredulity, pessimism

cyst NOUN

If a cyst forms in the eye, it will need to be removed.
▶ growth, abscess, blister, (*technical*) vesicle

Dd

dab VERB

He dabbed paint on the scratch.
▶ pat, daub, touch, apply (to)

dabble VERB

1 *The children dabbled their feet in the water.*
▶ dip, paddle, splash, wet

2 **dabble in** *She began to dabble in astrology.*
▶ toy with, dip into, tinker with, trifle with

daft ADJECTIVE

a daft idea
▶ silly, stupid, absurd, foolish, crazy, unwise, idiotic

daily ADJECTIVE

a daily occurrence
▶ everyday, day-to-day, regular

dainty ADJECTIVE

1 *a dainty lace handkerchief*
▶ delicate, elegant, exquisite, neat, charming, fine, graceful, pretty
OPPOSITES ARE clumsy, crude

2 *a dainty eater*
▶ fastidious, choosy, fussy, finicky, discriminating, careful
AN OPPOSITE IS gross

dally VERB

There's not enough time to dally.
▶ dawdle, delay, linger, loiter, waste time, idle, loaf, play about, procrastinate, (*more informal*) hang about, (*informal*) dilly-dally, (*literary*) tarry

dam NOUN

The dam could burst after such heavy rain.
▶ barrier, barrage, embankment, bank, dike, wall, weir

dam VERB

The river has been dammed to form a lake.
▶ block, obstruct, barricade, check, hold back, restrict, stem, stop

damage NOUN

Fortunately the thieves caused little damage.
▶ harm, injury, destruction, devastation, havoc, hurt, mutilation

damage VERB

High winds damaged properties along the sea front.
▶ harm hurt, injure, spoil, wreck, blemish, disfigure, deface, mutilate

damn VERB

1 *The voices damned him to hell.*
▶ curse, put a curse on, (*more formal*) execrate

2 *They had been damned for something that was not their fault.*
▶ condemn, censure, blame, abuse, revile, criticize, denounce, castigate, reprove

damnation NOUN

condemned to eternal damnation
▶ doom, perdition, condemnation, hell, ruin
AN OPPOSITE IS salvation

damp ADJECTIVE

1 *Someone had applied a damp cloth to her head.*
▶ moist, dampened, moistened, wet, wetted, soggy

2 *The air was damp and cold.*
▶ wet, drizzly, muggy, humid

dampen VERB

1 *Dampen a soft cloth.*
▶ moisten, wet, damp

2 *Nothing could dampen their enthusiasm now.*
▶ lessen, diminish, deaden, dull, stifle, muffle, restrain, smother, discourage, dishearten

---

dance NOUN

My grandparents first met at a dance.
▶ ball, disco, (*more informal*) hop
RELATED ADJECTIVE choreographic
RELATED NOUN choreography

NAMES FOR TYPES OF DANCE

main styles of dance: ballet, ballroom dancing, country dancing, barn dancing, folk dance, formation dancing, line dancing, lap dance, old-time dancing, rock and roll, tap dance.

some dances from around the world: waltz, veleta, quickstep, foxtrot, two-step, beguine, tango, rumba, mambo, samba, bossa nova, paso doble, fandango, flamenco, bolero, charleston, cha-cha, tarantella, black bottom, cakewalk, can-can, clog dance, tap dance, jig, morris dance, rigadoon, turkey trot, Highland fling, bhangra, lambada, belly dance, Bharata Natyan, Kathak, Capoeira, Noh dance-drama, Mapouka, kabuki, skank, meringue, hula.

group dances: ecossaise, eightsome reel, strathspey, hokey-cokey, Paul Jones, line dancing, quadrille, reel, roundelay, conga, roundelay, square dance, strip the willow. ▶▶

A
B
C
D
E
F
G
H
I
J
K
L
M
N
O
P
Q
R
S
T
U
V
W
X
Y
Z

old dances (often also a piece of music in the same time): waltz, minuet, polonaise, gavotte, allemande, bourrée, galop, chaconne, courante, galliard, gigue, hornpipe, mazurka, passepied, pavane, polka, sarabande, siciliano.

modern dances: bop, body-popping, boogaloo, boogie, break-dancing, disco, jive, salsa, shake, shimmy, shuffle, skank, stomp, twist.

dance VERB
Children danced around playfully.
▶ caper, cavort, frisk, frolic, skip, prance, leap, gambol, hop, jig, jump

danger NOUN
1 *There is a danger of flooding on low ground.*
▶ risk, threat, chance, probability, possibility, likelihood, prospect, liability

2 *The contamination could become a danger to public health.*
▶ threat, hazard, menace, risk

3 *There was a real sense of danger about the place.*
▶ insecurity, vulnerability, uncertainty, precariousness

4 *Their very lives were in danger.*
▶ peril, jeopardy, (at) risk
AN OPPOSITE IS safety

dangerous ADJECTIVE
1 *Building at such a height can be dangerous work.*
▶ hazardous, perilous, risky, unsafe, precarious, insecure, tricky

2 *He was charged with dangerous driving.*
▶ reckless, careless

3 *a dangerous criminal*
▶ ruthless, violent, vicious, desperate

dangle VERB
1 *There were curtains dangling above my head.*
▶ hang, droop, swing, flap, sway, trail, be suspended, wave about

2 *She dangled the keys in his face.*
▶ wave, swing, brandish, flourish, hold

dank ADJECTIVE
the dank basement
▶ damp, musty, chilly, clammy, moist, unaired

dare VERB
1 *No one dared to say anything.*
▶ have the courage, be brave enough, take the risk (of), take a chance, venture

2 *She dared him to jump.*
▶ challenge, defy, provoke, goad, taunt

daring ADJECTIVE
a daring attack
▶ bold, brave, courageous, adventurous, audacious, intrepid, gallant, confident, dauntless, enterprising, heroic, valiant, (*more informal*) plucky
AN OPPOSITE IS timid

daring NOUN
a feat of great daring
▶ audacity, boldness, bravery, courage, enterprise

dark ADJECTIVE
1 *a dark room*
▶ dim, dingy, dull, gloomy, unlit, unilluminated, shadowy
OPPOSITES ARE light, bright

2 *a dark night*
▶ black, pitch-black, starless, moonless, unlit, unilluminated
OPPOSITES ARE light, bright

3 *a dark colour*
▶ deep, strong, heavy
OPPOSITES ARE pale, light

4 *a dark secret*
▶ mysterious, enigmatic, hidden, obscure, impenetrable, cryptic

5 *dark thoughts*
▶ pessimistic, gloomy, sinister, sombre, grim, dismal, bleak, cheerless, fatalistic
AN OPPOSITE IS optimistic

dark NOUN
afraid of the dark
▶ darkness, blackness, gloom, night, night-time
AN OPPOSITE IS light

darken VERB
1 *The sky darkened.*
▶ become dark, become overcast, cloud over
OPPOSITES ARE lighten, brighten

2 *These fears darkened his life for many years.*
▶ overshadow, shadow, blacken, threaten, dim, make gloomy
OPPOSITES ARE lighten, brighten

darling ADJECTIVE
his darling wife
▶ dear, dearest, beloved, adored, cherished, treasured

darling ADJECTIVE
his darling wife
▶ dear, dearest, beloved, adored, cherished, treasured

darling NOUN
1 *Jane had always been his darling.*
▶ beloved, loved one, love, sweetheart, dear, dearest

2 *the darling of the gods*
▶ favourite, pet, idol

dart VERB
Children were darting about everywhere.
▶ dash, rush, hurtle, leap, shoot, spring, bound, flit, fly, move suddenly, (*more informal*) whiz, (*more informal*) zip

dart NOUN
a poisoned dart
▶ bolt, arrow, shaft, missile

dash NOUN
They made a dash for the door.
▶ rush, bolt, leap, sprint, spurt, race, run, chase

dash VERB
1 *We dashed home as soon as we could.*
▶ rush, race, bolt, tear, hasten, hurry, speed, shoot, run, sprint, chase, dart, fly, hasten, (*informal*) zoom
2 *He dashed the plate against the wall.*
▶ smash, crash, hurl, strike, throw, knock

dashing ADJECTIVE
a dashing captain in the Scots Guards
▶ handsome, debonair, stylish, elegant, flamboyant, lively

data NOUN
a group collecting data on teenage pregnancies
▶ information, details, particulars, facts and figures, statistics, evidence, material

date NOUN
1 *coins and pottery from a very early date*
▶ time, age, era, period
2 *She was in danger of missing her date with Paul.*
▶ meeting, appointment, rendezvous, engagement, assignation, fixture
3 *Mary was his date for the evening.*
▶ partner, escort, girlfriend (or boyfriend)

dated ADJECTIVE
The design looks rather dated.
▶ old-fashioned, outdated, archaic, obsolete, antiquated, (*more informal*) out of the ark

daub VERB
The walls of the house were daubed with graffiti.
▶ smear, plaster, cover, bedaub, spatter, smother

daunt VERB
It's a situation that would daunt much tougher people than me.
▶ intimidate, alarm, deter, discourage, unnerve, frighten, overawe, put off, dismay, dishearten, dispirit, depress
AN OPPOSITE IS encourage

daunting ADJECTIVE
They had set themselves the daunting task of writing two thousand words a day.
▶ arduous, difficult, onerous, tough

dauntless ADJECTIVE
a spirited and dauntless young woman
▶ fearless, resolute, determined, courageous, brave, intrepid, plucky, gritty

dawdle VERB
Ruth dawdled back through the wood, reluctant to return.
▶ linger, dally, take your time, delay, idle, (*more informal*) dilly-dally
AN OPPOSITE IS hurry

dawn NOUN
1 *We got up at dawn.*
▶ daybreak, sunrise, break of day, first light, (*more informal*) first thing
AN OPPOSITE IS dusk

2 *the dawn of modern civilization*
▶ beginning, start, birth, origin, genesis, advent, emergence

day NOUN
1 *He looked after Lucy during the day while I was at work.*
▶ daytime, daylight
AN OPPOSITE IS night
2 *The girls are required to plan their own day.*
▶ working day, working time, work time, period of work
3 *He was the leading musician of the day.*
▶ age, period, time, era, epoch

daydream NOUN
She tried to shake off her daydreams.
▶ reverie, fantasy, trance, fancy, dream, vision, imagining, absent-mindedness, meditation, musing, illusion, pipe dream

daydream VERB
He went out, leaving me to dress and daydream.
▶ fantasize, dream, muse, meditate, be lost in thought, imagine

daylight NOUN
Until eight o'clock there is no daylight in our room.
▶ sunlight, light of day, natural light

daze VERB
1 *The fall dazed him for a few minutes.*
▶ stun, stupefy, shock
2 *She was dazed by the news.*
▶ astound, amaze, astonish, startle, dumbfound, bewilder, stagger

dazzle VERB
1 *The sunlight burst through the window and dazzled him.*
▶ daze, blind
2 *The beauty of the place dazzled her.*
▶ overpower, overwhelm, overawe, impress, amaze, astonish

dead ADJECTIVE
1 *Both her parents were dead.*
▶ deceased, departed, passed on, gone
OPPOSITES ARE alive, living
2 *There was a dead animal on the road.*
▶ lifeless, killed, inanimate
3 *Latin is a dead language.*
▶ extinct, obsolete, defunct, disused, died out
AN OPPOSITE IS existing
4 *My feet were dead with cold.*
▶ numb, deadened, insensitive, paralysed, without feeling
AN OPPOSITE IS sensitive
5 *The battery was dead.*
▶ flat, unresponsive, defunct, inoperative, not working, burnt out, used up, useless, worn out
AN OPPOSITE IS operational
6 *When Sheila picked up the phone again the line was dead.*
▶ not working, inoperative, out of order, unresponsive

7 *The place is dead on a Friday night.*
▶ lifeless, dreary, uninteresting, boring, dull, moribund, slow
OPPOSITES ARE lively, exciting
8 (*informal*) *He felt dead by the time he got home.*
▶ exhausted, worn out, drained, tired
9 *He is the dead image of his brother.*
▶ exact, absolute, perfect, complete, utter, downright

dead ADVERB
The road ahead was dead straight.
▶ completely, absolutely, perfectly, utterly

deaden VERB
1 *Mufflers deaden the noise.*
▶ muffle, soften, mute, damp, reduce, quieten, smother, stifle, suppress, weaken, cushion, lessen, check, hush
OPPOSITES ARE amplify, sharpen
2 *A local anaesthetic will deaden the pain.*
▶ numb, stifle, dull, blunt, suppress, alleviate, soothe, desensitize, anaesthetize
OPPOSITES ARE intensify, aggravate

deadline NOUN
a new deadline for withdrawing troops
▶ time limit, target date, latest time

deadlock NOUN
The talks had reached deadlock
▶ stalemate, impasse, standstill, stand-off
AN OPPOSITE IS breakthrough

deadly ADJECTIVE
1 *a deadly poison*
▶ lethal, noxious, harmful, mortal, dangerous
AN OPPOSITE IS harmless
2 *a deadly disease*
▶ terminal, fatal, life-threatening, destructive
AN OPPOSITE IS mild
3 (*informal*) *The party turned out to be deadly.*
▶ dull, boring, dreary, tedious, unexciting, uninteresting
OPPOSITES ARE lively, exciting
4 *He fired an arrow with a deadly aim.*
▶ unerring, unfailing, true, perfect

deaf ADJECTIVE
1 *By this time he was deaf and nearly blind.*
▶ hard of hearing
2 **deaf to** *They were deaf to all our pleas.*
▶ indifferent to, unmoved by, heedless of, oblivious to, unconcerned with

deafening ADJECTIVE
a deafening roar
▶ loud, noisy, piercing, ear-splitting, booming, thunderous, overpowering

deal NOUN
1 *He was good at business deals and not much more.*
▶ agreement, arrangement, negotiation, transaction, settlement, contract, bargain, understanding

2 *Shoppers should look around for the best deal.*
▶ buy, bargain, transaction
a good deal or **a great deal** *We have already achieved a great deal.*
▶ a lot, much, plenty, a large amount, a large quantity

deal VERB
1 *She dealt the cards for another round.*
▶ give out, distribute, share out, dispense, apportion, allot, assign, divide, (*informal*) dole out
2 *The man dealt him a blow on the head*
▶ deliver, inflict, give, administer, apply, mete out
3 *He deals in stocks and shares.*
▶ trade, do business, buy and sell, traffic
4 **deal with** *a difficult issue to deal with*
▶ handle, manage, tackle, cope with, attend to, come to grips with, resolve, control, consider, grapple with, look after, see to, sort out, take action on
5 **deal with** *The book deals with several important topics.*
▶ be concerned with, treat, cover, tackle, explain

dealer NOUN
an antique dealer   a dealer in second-hand cars
▶ trader, supplier, merchant, wholesaler, retailer, merchandiser, shopkeeper, stockist, tradesman

dear ADJECTIVE
1 *They soon became dear friends.*
▶ beloved, close, intimate, lovable, loved, valued, darling
AN OPPOSITE IS hated
2 *Fruit is dear at this time of year.*
▶ expensive, costly, high-priced, overpriced, exorbitant, (*more informal*) pricey
AN OPPOSITE IS cheap

dear NOUN
Everyone agrees he's a dear.
▶ darling, lovable person, treasure, pet

dearly ADVERB
She loved Simon dearly.
▶ deeply, intensely, profoundly, fondly, tenderly, very much, a great deal

death NOUN
1 *Charles phoned to tell her of her uncle's death.*
▶ dying, passing, passing away, end
RELATED ADJECTIVE mortal
2 *The disaster caused many deaths*
▶ casualty, fatality
RELATED ADJECTIVE fatal
3 *The news meant the death of all their dreams.*
▶ end, ending, finish, collapse, ruin, destruction, termination, cessation
put to death *The king put all the conspirators to death.*
▶ execute, kill, have killed

debase VERB
We debase art by praising such trashy work.
▶ degrade, demean, devalue, cheapen, sully, discredit, defile, dishonour, vulgarize, lower the tone of, pollute

debatable ADJECTIVE
It is debatable whether the public wants this sort of sensationalism.
▶ arguable, questionable, disputable, doubtful, dubious, a moot point, open to doubt, open to question, contentious, controversial, controvertible, problematical, uncertain
AN OPPOSITE IS indisputable

debate NOUN
a debate about personal freedom
▶ discussion, argument, exchange of views, controversy, deliberation, contention, dialogue, dispute, (*more formal*) dialectic, (*more formal*) disputation

debate VERB
1 *Parliament will debate schemes for reducing traffic in cities.*
▶ discuss, consider, deliberate, confer about, exchange views on, dispute, argue, weigh up
2 *I am debating whether to get in touch with them.*
▶ consider, think over, ponder, deliberate, contemplate, reflect, (*more informal*) mull over

debris NOUN
1 *There was debris all around from the collapsed buildings.*
▶ rubbish, rubble, ruins, remains, wreckage
2 *Use rubber gloves to clean out debris from the gutters.*
▶ waste, remains, detritus, refuse, litter, bits, dregs, scraps

debt NOUN
1 *The state is encouraging students to build up large debts.*
▶ money owed, arrears, financial obligation, financial commitment, bill
2 *I owe you a great debt for your kindness*
▶ duty, indebtedness, obligation
in debt *By the end of the year he was heavily in debt.*
▶ owing money, in arrears, insolvent
in someone's debt *I shall be forever in your debt.*
▶ grateful to, indebted to, obliged to, beholden to

debtor NOUN
Debtors who fail to pay their hotel bill are not usually sent to prison any more.
▶ bankrupt, defaulter

debut NOUN
The new car has made its debut in Birmingham.
▶ first appearance, launch, entrance, inauguration, initiation, introduction

decadent ADJECTIVE
a decadent society
▶ immoral, dissolute, degenerate, dissipated, corrupt, depraved, declining
AN OPPOSITE IS moral

decay VERB
1 *The skulls were in good condition but the bones had decayed.*
▶ decompose, rot, putrefy, go bad, waste away, perish, deteriorate, degrade, disintegrate
2 *Inner cities had been allowed to decay.*
▶ decline, deteriorate, degenerate, crumble, corrode, disintegrate, wither, fall apart, go downhill

decay NOUN
1 *Today I found a dead blackbird in an advanced state of decay.*
▶ decomposition, rotting, festering, putrefaction
2 *Television is often blamed for the so-called decay in social values.*
▶ deterioration, decline, degradation, collapse, fall, disintegration

deceit NOUN
They achieved much by lies and deceit.
▶ deception, duplicity, trickery, pretence, cheating, misrepresentation, fraud, guile, subterfuge, artifice, ruse
OPPOSITES ARE honesty, openness

deceitful ADJECTIVE
George got used to the fact that I was deceitful and irresponsible.
▶ dishonest, untruthful, insincere, untrustworthy, deceptive, duplicitous, underhand, false, fraudulent, (*more informal*) two-faced

deceive VERB
It had not been too difficult to deceive him.
▶ trick, fool, mislead, hoodwink, delude, dupe, cheat, swindle, (*more informal*) take in

decelerate VERB
I get a whine from the gearbox every time I decelerate in fourth gear.
▶ slow down, go slower, reduce speed, lose speed, decrease speed, brake
AN OPPOSITE IS accelerate

decency NOUN
She said she had been brought up to respect honesty and decency.
▶ good behaviour, propriety, respectability, courtesy, correctness, morality

decent ADJECTIVE
1 *Mum always said it wasn't decent to watch people undress.*
▶ proper, respectable, appropriate, suitable, fitting, seemly, becoming, nice, modest, decorous, tasteful
AN OPPOSITE IS indecent
2 *Apart from that, he seemed a decent enough bloke.*
▶ obliging, courteous, honest, trustworthy, reliable, dependable, upright, polite, honourable
3 *It was her first decent meal of the day.*
▶ good, satisfactory, nice, pleasant, agreeable
AN OPPOSITE IS unsatisfactory

deception NOUN

For a spy, I'm not very good at deception.
▶ deceit, duplicity, trickery, pretence, cheating, misrepresentation, fraud, guile, subterfuge, artifice, ruse
OPPOSITES ARE honesty, openness

deceptive ADJECTIVE

1 *Similarities can be deceptive.*
▶ misleading, illusory, false, unreliable, delusive, fallacious, fraudulent, insincere, specious, spurious, treacherous
AN OPPOSITE IS genuine

2 *deceptive practices*
▶ dishonest, deceitful, fraudulent, underhand, duplicitous, sham, bogus
AN OPPOSITE IS honest

decide VERB

1 *He decided to become a journalist.*
▶ resolve, determine, make up your mind, choose, reach a decision, opt, plan, aim

2 *We don't have enough evidence to decide the issue.*
▶ determine, judge, adjudicate on, make a judgement on, pronounce on

decipher VERB

It was hard to decipher the writing.
▶ decode, unscramble, interpret, make sense of, read, understand, construe, (*more informal*) crack, (*more informal*) make out

decision NOUN

1 *the jury's decision on damages*
▶ verdict, finding, ruling, conclusion, judgement, pronouncement, adjudication

2 *The King agreed with this decision.*
▶ resolution, conclusion, outcome, result, recommendation, resolve, determination

decisive ADJECTIVE

1 *The car's faster speed proved to be a decisive advantage.*
▶ conclusive, definite, significant, crucial, critical, positive, deciding, determining, convincing, final, influential
OPPOSITES ARE inconclusive, insignificant

2 *His decisive no-nonsense manner had given him quite a reputation. They showed themselves capable of decisive action.*
▶ resolute, determined, firm, strong-willed, strong-minded, forceful, forthright, unhesitating, incisive, decided, definite
OPPOSITES ARE indecisive, hesitant

declaration NOUN

1 *a joint declaration by the four heads of state*
▶ announcement, proclamation, notification, promulgation, edict, manifesto

2 *a declaration of trust in the government*
▶ affirmation, assertion, acknowledgement, profession, confirmation, pledge, avowal

declare VERB

1 *Both sides declared their intentions.*
▶ announce, proclaim, express, voice, affirm, revea divulge

2 *He declared that he was ready to do a deal.*
▶ assert, insist, maintain, announce, aver, state, claim, certify, vow, avow

decline NOUN

1 *a decline in profits*
▶ reduction, decrease, drop, fall, downturn, falling off, recession, slump, diminution (of), loss (of), failing (of)

2 *a decline in their fortunes*
▶ deterioration, degeneration, worsening (of)

decline VERB

1 *He declined all our invitations.*
▶ refuse, reject, dismiss, turn down, pass up, forgo
AN OPPOSITE IS accept

2 *After the accident her health declined.*
▶ worsen, deteriorate, weaken, degenerate, flag, die away, fail, fall off, sink, wane, wilt
AN OPPOSITE IS improve

3 *Profits have declined for the third year in succession.*
▶ decrease, diminish, be reduced, lessen, go down, drop away, dwindle, ebb

decode VERB

(informal) The messages were quickly decoded.
▶ decipher, unscramble, interpret, make sense of, understand, construe, solve, read, (*more informal*) crack, (*more informal*) make out, (*more informal*) figure out
OPPOSITES ARE code, encode

decompose VERB

The severed hand was already decomposing.
▶ decay, rot, putrefy, go bad, waste away, perish, deteriorate, degrade, disintegrate

decor NOUN

The decor is tasteful and includes many fine paintings.
▶ decoration, design, interior design, style, colour scheme, furnishing

decorate VERB

1 *a nursery chair decorated with little rabbits*
▶ adorn, ornament, embellish, trim, beautify, enhance

2 *We will decorate the house before moving in.*
▶ paint, renovate, smarten up, refurbish, redecorate, paper, wallpaper, (*more informal*) do up

3 *He was decorated for bravery at the end of the war.*
▶ honour, reward, give a medal to, mention in dispatches

decoration NOUN

1 *a tall ceiling with elaborate decoration*
▶ ornamentation, adornment, embellishment, trimmings, filigree, tracery, frill, scroll

2 *a decoration for bravery*
▶ award, badge, medal, ribbon, star, (*more informal*) gong

decorative ADJECTIVE
a decorative mirror in a frame
▶ ornamental, ornate, fancy, adorning, embellishing, enhancing, elaborate, non-functional
AN OPPOSITE IS functional

decorous ADJECTIVE
decorous behaviour
▶ proper, seemly, decent, becoming, correct, suitable, tasteful, respectable
AN OPPOSITE IS unbecoming

decorum NOUN
He treated the occasion with respect and decorum.
▶ propriety, decency, dignity, seemliness, politeness, respectability, good taste, good manners, gravity, modesty

decoy NOUN
They set up a decoy to distract our attention.
▶ lure, bait, trap, enticement

decoy VERB
His enemies had decoyed him to another part of the country.
▶ lure, entice, induce, inveigle, ensnare, seduce, tempt, bait, draw, lead

decrease NOUN
a decrease in crime levels
▶ reduction, decline, lessening (of), falling off, drop, downturn
AN OPPOSITE IS increase

decrease VERB
1 *We need to decrease our costs.*
▶ reduce, lessen, lower, cut, cut down, curtail
AN OPPOSITE IS increase
2 *The aircraft's speed was rapidly decreasing.*
▶ diminish, lessen, reduce, fall off, dwindle
AN OPPOSITE IS increase

decree NOUN
a presidential decree banning all protest meetings
▶ order, edict, command, mandate, proclamation, dictum, enactment

decree VERB
The law decreed that Sunday should be a day of rest.
▶ order, command, declare, prescribe, ordain, proclaim, pronounce, direct, rule, decide, determine, dictate

decrepit ADJECTIVE
1 *He lived in a decrepit old cottage.*
▶ dilapidated, battered, ramshackle, tumbledown, worn out, broken down, derelict
2 *a decrepit old woman*
▶ feeble, frail, weak, infirm

decry VERB
She decried the quality of commercial broadcasting.
▶ denounce, condemn, criticize, censure, deplore, damn, rail against

dedicate VERB
1 *The church is dedicated to St Peter.*
▶ consecrate, sanctify, hallow, set apart

2 *He dedicated the book to his father's memory*
▶ inscribe, address
3 *We need to dedicate a whole week to the task.*
▶ devote, commit, assign, allot, allocate

dedicated ADJECTIVE
1 *a dedicated musician*
▶ devoted, committed, keen, staunch, steadfast, fervent, loyal, enthusiastic, zealous, wholehearted, single-minded, faithful
2 *a dedicated computer terminal*
▶ customized, specific, exclusive

dedication NOUN
1 *She appreciated all his hard work and dedication.*
▶ devotion, commitment, allegiance, faithfulness, loyalty, adherence, single-mindedness
2 *The book bore a dedication to his wife.*
▶ inscription

deduce VERB
He deduced that she must be a good cook.
▶ conclude, come to the conclusion, reason, work out, gather, infer, surmise, glean

deduct VERB
(informal) The cost of the breakage will be deducted from his allowance.
▶ subtract, knock off, take away, debit (to)
OPPOSITES ARE add (to), credit (to)

deduction NOUN
USAGE from the verb *deduct.*
1 *Income is subject to the deduction of tax.*
▶ subtraction, taking away, taking off, removal, stoppage
USAGE from the verb *deduce.*
2 *Her deduction was quite correct.*
▶ conclusion, inference, reasoning

deed NOUN
1 *a heroic deed*
▶ act, action, feat, exploit, endeavour, enterprise, achievement, adventure, effort, performance, undertaking
2 *The Bank will keep the deeds of the property.*
▶ title (to), papers, records, contract, documents

deem VERB
the changes they deem desirable
▶ regard as, consider, judge, view as, believe to be, reckon as

deep ADJECTIVE
1 *The well is deep.*
▶ bottomless, fathomless, cavernous, yawning
AN OPPOSITE IS shallow
2 *a deep disappointment*
▶ intense, profound, extreme, serious
3 *a deep mystery*
▶ obscure, secret, mysterious, unfathomable, fathomless, arcane
4 *deep affection*
▶ intense, heartfelt, fervent, ardent, deep-seated
5 *a deep thinker*
▶ wise, intelligent, profound, perceptive, learned, discerning

6 *They were deep in conversation.*
▶ rapt, absorbed, engrossed, immersed, preoccupied, riveted
7 *a deep sound*
▶ low, low-pitched, bass, resonant, booming
8 *a deep colour*
▶ dark, rich, vivid, strong, intense

deepen VERB
1 *Their love had deepened over the years.*
▶ increase, intensify, grow, grow stronger
2 *The hole had been deepened.*
▶ dig out, make deeper, hollow, scoop out

deep-seated ADJECTIVE
He had a deep-seated fear of flying.
▶ profound, intense, fundamental, ingrained, deep, deep-rooted
OPPOSITES ARE superficial, temporary

deface VERB
Graffiti had defaced the monument.
▶ disfigure, spoil, mar, injure, mutilate, vandalize, damage

defamatory ADJECTIVE
The remarks are defamatory.
▶ insulting, abusive, slanderous, libellous, disparaging, derogatory, malicious

default NOUN
a large number of defaults on loans
▶ non-payment, failure to pay, neglect, deficiency, lapse, (*more informal*) welshing

defeat NOUN
1 *the defeat of Napoleon at Waterloo*
▶ conquest, subjugation, overthrow, beating, victory (over)
2 *The home side faced defeat.*
▶ failure, loss, setback, humiliation, disappointment, reverse, trouncing
AN OPPOSITE IS victory

defeat VERB
1 *The French army defeated the enemy in a long engagement.*
▶ overcome, beat, conquer, overpower, subdue, vanquish, subjugate, quell, rout
2 *The complexity of the task defeated them.*
▶ confound, baffle, frustrate, fox, (*more informal*) flummox

defect NOUN (with the stress on *de-*)
The machinery showed several defects.
▶ fault, flaw, imperfection, deficiency, weakness, failing, inadequacy, blemish, error, (*more informal*) bug

defect VERB (with the stress on *-fect*)
MPs might defect to other parties.
▶ desert, go over, change sides, revolt

defective ADJECTIVE
The car's brakes were defective.
▶ faulty, out of order, deficient, broken, malfunctioning, inoperative

defence NOUN
1 *Several friends spoke in defence of his actions.*
▶ support, vindication, justification, endorsement
2 *a defence against attack*
▶ protection, resistance (to), shield, deterrent, barricade, bulwark

defenceless ADJECTIVE
defenceless victims
▶ helpless, vulnerable, powerless, impotent, unprotected, exposed
AN OPPOSITE IS protected

defend VERB
1 *An air squadron helped to defend the country against enemy attack.*
▶ protect, guard, safeguard, secure, shield, shelter, screen, cover
2 *He found it hard to defend his actions.*
▶ justify, vindicate, make a case for

defendant NOUN
The defendant stood in the dock.
▶ accused, prisoner, appellant, offender

defensive ADJECTIVE
1 *The aircraft formed a defensive circle.*
▶ defending, protective, protecting, guarding
AN OPPOSITE IS aggressive
2 *Her attitude seemed nervous and defensive.*
▶ wary, watchful, cautious, apologetic, self-justifying
AN OPPOSITE IS assertive

defer VERB
1 *She had decided to defer unpacking to the following day.*
▶ postpone, put off, delay, adjourn, hold over, suspend, (*more informal*) shelve
2 **defer to** *He agreed to defer to his parents' wishes.*
▶ yield to, submit to, respect, accede to, give way to, agree to, surrender to

defiance NOUN
Her dark eyes were ablaze with defiance.
▶ opposition, confrontation, resistance, challenge, audacity, bravado, contempt

defiant ADJECTIVE
He remained defiant in spite of the threats.
▶ obstinate, determined, intransigent, resistant, confrontational, recalcitrant, unyielding
OPPOSITES ARE cooperative, apologetic

deficiency NOUN
a vitamin deficiency
▶ insufficiency, shortage, inadequacy, lack, deficit, shortfall

deficient ADJECTIVE
1 *a diet deficient in vitamins*
▶ lacking, wanting, defective, inadequate, insufficient
OPPOSITES ARE adequate, excessive

2 *deficient leadership*
▶ defective, flawed, faulty, unsound, imperfect, inadequate, (*more informal*) duff
AN OPPOSITE IS perfect

deficit NOUN
a deficit in the budget
▶ loss, shortfall, deficiency, lack
AN OPPOSITE IS surplus

define VERB
1 *We can define evidence as information about whether a particular thing is true or not.*
▶ explain, interpret, clarify, formulate, give the meaning of
2 *The fence defines the boundary of the estate.*
▶ mark, mark out, indicate, set, determine, demarcate, outline

definite ADJECTIVE
1 *She came to some definite conclusions.*
▶ clear, clear-cut, explicit, express, precise, established, fixed, concrete, plain, hard
AN OPPOSITE IS indefinite
2 *There are definite signs of improvement.*
▶ distinct, clear, plain, discernible, obvious, perceptible, noticeable, positive, unmistakable, marked, pronounced, apparent
AN OPPOSITE IS imperceptible

definitely ADVERB
She definitely hadn't been there before.
▶ certainly, positively, surely, unquestionably, beyond doubt, assuredly, for certain, indubitably, doubtless, without doubt, without fail

definition NOUN
1 *It is hard to write a good definition of 'left' and 'right'.*
▶ explanation, description, elucidation, interpretation, meaning
2 *The photograph lacked definition.*
▶ clarity, clearness, sharpness, precision, focus

definitive ADJECTIVE
1 *the definitive film guide*
▶ authoritative, standard, classic, recognized, accepted, official, ultimate, complete, reliable
2 *a definitive reply*
▶ decisive, conclusive, categorical, final
AN OPPOSITE IS provisional

deflate VERB
1 *Someone had deflated two of the tyres.*
▶ let down, let the air out of, flatten
AN OPPOSITE IS inflate.
2 *The news deflated him.*
▶ subdue, humble, humiliate, dishearten, dispirit, dismay, chasten, mortify
OPPOSITES ARE encourage, boost

deflect VERB
He managed to deflect the blow.
▶ divert, turn aside, parry, fend off, intercept, avert, head off, prevent, ward off

deformed ADJECTIVE
He was so deformed the gods took pity on him.
▶ misshapen, contorted, crippled, crooked, distorted, disfigured, twisted, malformed, maimed, bent, warped, mutilated, buckled, mangled, defaced, gnarled, grotesque, ugly

deformity NOUN
His strange position gave the impression of a deformity.
▶ malformation, misshapenness, disfigurement, defect, abnormality, irregularity

defraud VERB
He was defrauding the state by making false tax claims.
▶ swindle, cheat, dupe, (*more informal*) con, (*more informal*) diddle, (*more informal*) fleece, (*more informal*) rip off

deft ADJECTIVE
He tipped back his glass with a deft movement of his arm.
▶ adroit, skilful, adept, neat, agile, expert, delicate, dexterous, nimble, (*more informal*) nifty
OPPOSITES ARE clumsy, awkward

defunct ADJECTIVE
a defunct coal mine
▶ disused, obsolete, unused, inoperative, extinct, discontinued

defy VERB
1 *He was arrested for defying a court order to hand over the property.*
▶ disobey, refuse to obey, flout, disregard, violate, contravene, infringe, breach, resist
AN OPPOSITE IS obey
2 *She defied Robin to admit the truth.*
▶ challenge, dare
3 *The situation defied all attempts at rational explanation.*
▶ elude, escape, defeat, frustrate, thwart, resist

degenerate ADJECTIVE
degenerate behaviour
▶ immoral, corrupt, decadent, depraved, dissolute, debauched

degrading ADJECTIVE
Asking for money can be a degrading experience.
▶ humiliating, demeaning, shaming, mortifying, embarrassing, ignominious, undignified
OPPOSITES ARE uplifting, ennobling

degree NOUN
The work involves a high degree of trust.
▶ level, order, measure, extent, range, stage, intensity, standard
to some degree *The risk will still be present to some degree.*
▶ partly, to some extent, up to a point

deify VERB
The emperor was deified on his death.
▶ treat as a god, make a god, idolize, venerate, worship

deign VERB

She practised all the things she would say to him when he deigned to contact her.
▶ condescend, see fit, consent, descend, stoop

deity NOUN

statues of deities
▶ god, goddess, divinity, demigod, idol, immortal

dejected ADJECTIVE

Lisa was looking dejected.
▶ downcast, depressed, despondent, dispirited, disheartened, downhearted, unhappy, fed up, sad, down, glum, melancholy, miserable, cast down
OPPOSITES ARE cheerful, happy

delay NOUN

1 *Traffic is subject to long delays.*
▶ hold-up, wait, waiting period, stoppage, obstruction
2 *A delay in the proceedings followed.*
▶ deferment, postponement, suspension

delay VERB

1 *Heavy traffic delayed many of the guests.*
▶ detain, hold up, make late, hamper, impede
2 *We might have to delay the start of the game.*
▶ postpone, put off, defer, suspend, adjourn, hold over
OPPOSITES ARE advance, bring forward
3 *There is no time to delay.*
▶ linger, dally, take your time, (*more formal*) procrastinate, (*more informal*) drag your feet, (*more informal*) hang about

delegate NOUN

trade-union delegates
▶ representative, agent, envoy, legate, messenger, spokesperson, ambassador

delegate VERB

1 *The council delegated a member to speak to the press.*
▶ appoint, authorize, commission, nominate, designate, empower, mandate
2 *She delegates routine tasks to an assistant.*
▶ assign, entrust, pass on, hand over, devolve, consign

delegation NOUN

There was a delegation from Nigeria.
▶ deputation, commission, legation, delegacy, mission, representative group, contingent

delete VERB

One paragraph was deleted from the article.
▶ remove, cut out, take out, erase, expunge, cross out

deliberate ADJECTIVE

1 *The disaster may have been an accident rather than deliberate sabotage.*
▶ intentional, calculated, conscious, planned, culpable, premeditated, wilful
OPPOSITES ARE unplanned, accidental, fortuitous
2 *She could hear the slow deliberate footsteps.*
▶ careful, measured, steady, cautious, unhurried, considered, methodical
AN OPPOSITE IS hasty

deliberate VERB

They deliberated for a long time about what to do.
▶ reflect, consider, think, debate, ponder, cogitate, meditate

deliberation NOUN

1 *After some deliberation, he agreed.*
▶ consideration, thought, reflection, contemplation, discussion, consultation
2 *She went to the door with deliberation.*
▶ care, caution, circumspection
AN OPPOSITE IS haste

delicacy NOUN

1 *lacework of great delicacy*
▶ fineness, exquisiteness, daintiness, fragility, intricacy, precision, accuracy, care
2 *It was an unpleasant matter that called for some delicacy.*
▶ sensitivity, subtlety, tact, discrimination, finesse
3 *Several plates of delicacies were brought in.*
▶ titbit, rarity, speciality, treat

delicate ADJECTIVE

1 *The tablecloths were made of beautiful, delicate fabrics.*
▶ fine, exquisite, elegant, intricate, graceful, flimsy, fragile
OPPOSITES ARE coarse, crude
2 *He awoke feeling somewhat delicate, after his night on the town.*
▶ unwell, sickly, ill, unfit, poorly, frail, weak
OPPOSITES ARE healthy, fit, robust
3 *The old clock had a delicate mechanism.*
▶ precise, intricate, accurate, exact
4 *a delicate shade of blue*
▶ subtle, muted, soft, pale, gentle, pastel, subdued
5 *Angie made a tiny, delicate gesture with her hand.*
▶ gentle, deft, adroit, neat, skilful
6 *The next issue to come up was delicate, to put it mildly.*
▶ difficult, tricky, sensitive, awkward, embarrassing, problematical
7 *The matter called for delicate handling.*
▶ sensitive, careful, discriminating
8 *It would not be easy to cater for their delicate taste in food.*
▶ fastidious, discriminating, fussy, (*more informal*) choosy, (*more informal*) pernickety, (*more informal*) faddy, (*more informal*) picky

delicious ADJECTIVE

1 *You can have a delicious meal at the local pub.*
▶ tasty, appetizing, palatable, delectable, enjoyable, luscious, succulent, choice, savoury, (*more informal*) mouth-watering, (*more informal*) scrumptious, (*more informal*) yummy
OPPOSITES ARE unpleasant, uneatable

2 *a delicious feeling of contentment*
▶ delightful, exquisite, lovely, pleasurable, heavenly, glorious

delight NOUN
Florence laughed with delight.
▶ pleasure, happiness, joy, enjoyment, bliss, rapture, ecstasy

delight VERB
1 *She delighted her father by singing for him.*
▶ please, charm, thrill, gratify, enchant, captivate, enthral, entrance, amuse, (*more informal*) bowl over
OPPOSITES ARE displease, disgust
2 **delight in** *Fran delighted in the flowers he gave her.*
▶ relish, enjoy, love, savour, revel in
OPPOSITES ARE hate, dislike, loathe

delighted VERB
He was delighted to see that Jenny had arrived.
▶ pleased, happy, glad, thrilled, overjoyed, gratified, excited, ecstatic
OPPOSITES ARE dismayed, disappointed

delightful ADJECTIVE
He told Julie how delightful it had been to meet her.
▶ pleasant, lovely, enjoyable, pleasing, pleasurable, gratifying, satisfying, marvellous, wonderful

delinquency NOUN
attacking the root causes of delinquency
▶ crime, wrongdoing, criminality, lawbreaking, misconduct, misbehaviour

delinquent ADJECTIVE
She was quite good with delinquent adolescents.
▶ lawless, lawbreaking, errant, unruly, offending, criminal, unmanageable, uncontrollable

delinquent NOUN
It was not fair to label them delinquents.
▶ offender, lawbreaker, wrongdoer, young offender, criminal, hooligan, hoodlum, miscreant, (*informal*) tearaway

delirious ADJECTIVE
1 *The illness made Luke delirious for days on end.*
▶ demented, raving, incoherent, hysterical, irrational, feverish, frenzied
2 *She was delirious with joy.*
▶ ecstatic, elated, thrilled, beside yourself, exultant, wild

deliver VERB
1 *The books will be delivered to your address within the next week.*
▶ send, convey, transport, bring, supply, take, dispatch
2 *The court delivered its verdict.*
▶ utter, give, make, read, announce, declare, pronounce, speak
3 *He delivered a powerful blow to the back of the head.*
▶ administer, deal, launch, aim, strike, hit
4 *The hostages were all delivered from their captors.*
▶ rescue, save, set free, liberate, release, redeem, ransom

delivery NOUN
1 *There is a daily delivery of fresh vegetables.*
▶ consignment, batch, shipment, distribution
2 *The delivery of the message was timed at 3.30.*
▶ dispatch, transmission, conveyance

delude VERB
You are deluding yourself if you think that.
▶ deceive, mislead, fool, take in, hoodwink, beguile, bamboozle, trick

deluge NOUN
The deluge left many homes under water.
▶ downpour, rainstorm, inundation, flood, rainfall, spate

deluge VERB
Callers deluged the help lines all day.
▶ overwhelm, swamp, engulf, flood, inundate, drown, submerge

delusion NOUN
The idea that he might win was a delusion.
▶ fantasy, misconception, misapprehension, deception, dream, hallucination, illusion, mirage, mistake

delve VERB
He delved in his coat pocket.
▶ burrow, rummage, probe, search, explore, dig, investigate

demand NOUN
1 *She refused to give way to their demands.*
▶ request, requirement, claim, ultimatum, stipulation, insistence
2 *There is much less demand for hardback books.*
▶ call, market, need, necessity

demand VERB
1 *The workers demanded a 10% pay rise.*
▶ call for, ask for, claim, want, insist on, require, request, expect
2 *'Where are they?' he demanded*
▶ ask, enquire, challenge, question

demanding ADJECTIVE
1 *a demanding child*
▶ insistent, trying, tiresome, importunate, nagging
2 *a demanding task*
▶ difficult, challenging, testing, exacting, taxing, hard, tough, onerous, arduous, formidable

demeaning ADJECTIVE
He found the job unpleasant and demeaning.
▶ degrading, humiliating, shaming, mortifying, embarrassing, ignominious, undignified
OPPOSITES ARE uplifting, ennobling

demeanour NOUN
an anxious and nervous demeanour
▶ attitude, bearing, manner, disposition

demented ADJECTIVE
A severely demented person might not be able to respond at all.
▶ mad, deranged, delirious, insane, crazy

demise NOUN
the demise of the Assyrian Empire
▶ downfall, collapse, end, disappearance, failure

democratic ADJECTIVE
a democratic government
▶ elected, elective, popular, representative, chosen, popular, egalitarian
AN OPPOSITE IS undemocratic

demolish VERB
The explosion demolished a row of houses.
▶ destroy, wreck, flatten, level, knock down, tear down, break down, obliterate, reduce to ruins
OPPOSITES ARE construct, assemble

demolition NOUN
The houses face demolition.
▶ destruction, dismantling, levelling, pulling down, flattening, clearance

demon NOUN
demons from hell
▶ devil, fiend, spirit, goblin, imp

demonstrable ADJECTIVE
a demonstrable connection between the two crimes
▶ verifiable, provable, incontrovertible, irrefutable, clear, evident, palpable, certain, positive, undeniable

demonstrate VERB
1 *The evidence demonstrates a major change in the role of women.*
▶ show, indicate, establish, display, exhibit, point to, prove, substantiate, verify, exemplify, illustrate, manifest, represent
2 *People demonstrated in the streets.*
▶ protest, rally, hold a rally, lobby, march, parade, picket

demonstration NOUN
1 *a demonstration of skill and creativity*
▶ display, exhibition, manifestation, indication, revelation, expression, presentation, embodiment
2 *(informal) a demonstration against the war.*
▶ protest, demo, rally, march, parade, sit-in, vigil

demonstrative ADJECTIVE
a demonstrative person
▶ affectionate, expressive, emotional, effusive, open, uninhibited, unreserved, unrestrained, fulsome, loving
OPPOSITES ARE reserved, inhibited

demoralize VERB
Poor pay demoralized the staff.
▶ discourage, dishearten, depress, deject, dispirit, disconcert

demote VERB
Some of the less successful managers were demoted.
▶ downgrade, reduce, put down, lower in rank
AN OPPOSITE IS promote

demur VERB
Her husband demurred, despite wanting to support her.
▶ object, raise objections, disagree, dissent, protest

demure ADJECTIVE
She was sitting demure, her hands in her lap.
▶ modest, reserved, bashful, unassuming, diffident, reticent, prim, shy, sober, strait-laced
OPPOSITES ARE brazen, forward

den NOUN
He worked all evening in his den upstairs.
▶ study, retreat, sanctum, hideaway, hideout, lair, sanctuary, private place, secret place

denial NOUN
1 *Reports of a threatened strike met with a firm denial.*
▶ contradiction, renunciation, repudiation, disavowal, dismissal, abnegation, disclaimer, negation, rejection
AN OPPOSITE IS admission
2 *the denial of rights to certain minorities*
▶ refusal, withholding, withdrawal, veto

denigrate VERB
Do not denigrate our city so quickly.
▶ belittle, disparage, revile, malign, vilify, deprecate, defame, (more informal) run down
AN OPPOSITE IS praise

denomination NOUN
1 *a Christian denomination*
▶ religion, religious group, church, sect, communion, persuasion, creed, cult
2 *coins of several denominations*
▶ unit, value, category, designation, class, size, type

denote VERB
A snort from the corner denoted disagreement.
▶ indicate, mean , express, signify, stand for, represent, symbolize, be the sign for

denounce VERB
He denounced them for their dishonesty.
▶ condemn, censure, find fault with, criticize, blame, castigate, disparage, denigrate, deprecate, (more informal) knock, (more informal) slam, (more informal) pan

dense ADJECTIVE
1 *a dense crowd   dense undergrowth*
▶ thick, closely packed, tightly packed, impenetrable, massed
AN OPPOSITE IS sparse
2 *dense smoke*
▶ thick, heavy, concentrated
OPPOSITES ARE thin, light
3 *too dense to understand the point*
▶ stupid, foolish, crass, dull, slow, slow-witted, unintelligent
OPPOSITES ARE clever, intelligent

dent NOUN
There were several small dents in the side of the vehicle.
▶ indentation, dint, dimple, dip, concavity, depression, hollow, pit

dent VERB
1 *He dropped the saucepan and dented it.*
▶ make a dent in, push in, knock in, buckle, depress

2 *Nothing much could dent her confidence.*
▶ diminish, reduce, impair, damage, harm, affect

deny VERB

1 *The story was denied by the Prime Minister's office. The accused denied all the charges.*
▶ contradict, repudiate, rebut, reject, dismiss, contest, oppose, refute
USAGE Note that *refute* means 'to disprove by using arguments'.
2 *The authorities have denied them their basic rights.*
▶ refuse, forbid, withhold

depart VERB

1 *The officials departed after lunch.*
▶ leave, go, go away, go off, withdraw, make off, retire, quit, (*old-fashioned*) take your leave, (*old-fashioned*) decamp
AN OPPOSITE IS arrive
2 *At this point the speaker departed from his notes.*
▶ deviate, digress, differ, diverge, drift
AN OPPOSITE IS stick to

department NOUN

1 *He works in a government department.*
▶ division, section, sector, unit, branch, subdivision, office, bureau, agency, ministry
2 (*informal*) *I'm afraid travel arrangements are not my department.*
▶ domain, responsibility, business, affair, concern, field, area, sphere, line, province, function, job, specialism, (*more informal*) pigeon, (*more informal*) baby

departure NOUN

1 *Our departure has been delayed by half an hour.*
▶ leaving, setting off, going, exit, withdrawal, disappearance, embarkation, escape, exodus, retirement, retreat
AN OPPOSITE IS arrival
2 *The book represents a departure from the author's familiar style.*
▶ change, change of direction, deviation, digression, shift, variation, innovation, branching out

depend VERB

1 **depend on** *Choice of university can depend a lot on expected exam grades.*
▶ be dependent on, hinge on, hang on, rest on, revolve around
2 **depend on** *I shall depend on you to help me.*
▶ rely on, count on, need, bank on, trust

dependable ADJECTIVE

She looked at Roland: so strong and dependable.
▶ reliable, trustworthy, faithful, true, loyal, constant, unswerving, sensible, responsible, conscientious, sound, steady, unfailing
AN OPPOSITE IS unreliable

dependence NOUN

1 *Trevor was determined to reduce his dependence on his family.*
▶ reliance, need (for), trust (in), confidence (in)

2 *a rise in drug dependence*
▶ addiction, dependency, reliance, craving, abuse

dependent ADJECTIVE

1 **dependent on** *A lot is dependent on their decision.*
▶ conditional on, contingent on, connected with, controlled by, determined by, liable to, relative to, subject to, vulnerable to
AN OPPOSITE IS independent
2 **dependent on** *Prisoners remain dependent on what visitors bring for them.*
▶ reliant on, supported by, sustained by, needful of
3 **dependent on** *Some of these people are dependent on drugs.*
▶ addicted to, reliant on, enslaved by, (*more informal*) hooked on

depict VERB

1 *The painting depicts a village in winter.*
▶ show, portray, represent, picture, illustrate, reproduce, delineate, describe, draw, narrate, outline, paint, sketch
2 *The author depicts his own childhood in the story.*
▶ describe, relate, narrate, recount, present, record, outline, delineate, portray, characterize

deplete VERB

Local wars have depleted the food supply.
▶ exhaust, use up, consume, expend, reduce, decrease, lessen, drain, cut
OPPOSITES ARE increase, augment, boost

deplorable ADJECTIVE

1 *Their behaviour had been deplorable.*
▶ disgraceful, shameful, inexcusable, unforgivable, disreputable, lamentable, shocking, blameworthy, discreditable, reprehensible, scandalous, unfortunate, unworthy
OPPOSITES ARE admirable, praiseworthy
2 *The troops lived in deplorable conditions.*
▶ lamentable, regrettable, awful, wretched, terrible, miserable, atrocious

deplore VERB

1 *We deplore all forms of violence.*
▶ condemn, disapprove of, denounce, abhor, decry, deprecate
2 *He deplored the past difficulties and promised a brighter future.*
▶ regret, lament, bemoan, express regret for

deploy VERB

1 *The government deployed troops to prevent demonstrations.*
▶ position, station, post, install, establish, bring into action
2 *You will need to deploy all your personal and social skills.*
▶ use, make use of, utilize, employ, exploit, take advantage of

deport VERB

Illegal immigrants were deported.
▶ expel, banish, exile, expatriate, transport, extradite

depose VERB

A military coup deposed the government.
▶ overthrow, overturn, bring down, oust, get rid of, remove, displace, (*more informal*) topple
AN OPPOSITE IS enthrone

deposit NOUN

1 *You will need to pay a deposit to clinch the booking.*
▶ down payment, advance payment, part payment, security, retainer, first payment
2 *a thick deposit of mud*
▶ layer, covering, coating, accumulation, sediment, silt, sludge, dregs, lees, precipitate
3 *a deposit at the bottom of the bottle*
▶ sediment, accumulation, dregs, silt

deposit VERB

1 (*informal*) *She deposited a pile of papers on the desk.*
▶ put down, set down, lay down, place, leave, (*more informal*) dump, (*more informal*) stick, (*more informal*) plonk, (*more informal*) park
2 *The money is deposited each Friday.*
▶ pay in, bank, lodge, save
3 *The flood water deposited layers of mud.*
▶ precipitate, wash up

depot NOUN

1 *a military depot*
▶ store, storehouse, base, cache, depository, arsenal, dump, hoard
2 *a bus depot*
▶ garage, station, terminus, headquarters

depraved ADJECTIVE

a depraved person   depraved behaviour
▶ corrupt, decadent, degenerate, dissolute, sinful, immoral, debauched, rotten, wicked, evil, iniquitous, low, perverted, profligate, venal
AN OPPOSITE IS moral

deprecate VERB

I had always rather deprecated such flashy good looks.
▶ disapprove of, deplore, frown on, condemn, censure, abhor, dislike

depreciate VERB

The value of property is not likely to depreciate.
▶ drop, fall, become less, lessen, lower, reduce, decrease, go down, deflate, slump, weaken
AN OPPOSITE IS appreciate

depress VERB

1 *The latest news depressed everyone.*
▶ sadden, deject, dishearten, dispirit, upset, discourage, grieve, lower the spirits of, oppress, make sad
AN OPPOSITE IS cheer
2 *Aid tends to depress local markets.*
▶ undermine, weaken, impair, inhibit, check, make less active, slow down, bring down, push down, deflate
AN OPPOSITE IS boost

depressed ADJECTIVE

Sam looked tired and depressed.
▶ dejected, downcast, despondent, dispirited, disheartened, downhearted, disconsolate, unhappy, sad, down, glum, melancholy, miserable, cast down
OPPOSITES ARE cheerful, happy

depressing ADJECTIVE

1 *Tuesday was a cold, depressing day.*
▶ gloomy, bleak, dreary, dismal, grim, drab, sombre, dingy, cheerless
2 *He tried to get rid of all such depressing thoughts.*
▶ dispiriting, disheartening, upsetting, distressing, melancholy, painful, morbid

depression NOUN

1 *A sudden feeling of depression took hold of him.*
▶ sadness, dejection, melancholy, sorrow, despondency, unhappiness, low spirits, glumness, desolation, despair, pessimism, (*more informal*) blues, (*more informal*) dumps
AN OPPOSITE IS cheerfulness
2 *an economic depression*
▶ recession, slump, decline, downturn, slowdown, stagnation, hard times
AN OPPOSITE IS boom
3 *a meteorological depression*
▶ area of low pressure, cyclone, low
AN OPPOSITE IS anticyclone
4 *The wheel hit a depression in the ground.*
▶ hollow, indentation, dent, cavity, hole, pothole, dip, dimple, concavity
OPPOSITES ARE bump, protuberance

deprive VERB

deprive of *The war deprived her of her income.*
▶ deny, dispossess of, rob of, divest of, strip of, take away, starve of, refuse, prevent from having

deprived ADJECTIVE

deprived sections of society
▶ disadvantaged, underprivileged, needy, poor, badly off, destitute

depth NOUN

1 *They tried to measure the depth of the water.*
▶ deepness, distance to the bottom, vertical extent, drop
2 *The orchestra's playing showed a great depth of feeling.*
▶ extent, degree, range, breadth, scope

deputation NOUN

A deputation arrived from the King of Spain.
▶ delegation, commission, legation, mission, delegacy, group of envoys, embassy

depute VERB

He was deputed to continue the negotiations.
▶ appoint, designate, nominate, assign, commission, authorize, empower

deputize VERB

deputize for *His job is to deputize for the manager.*
▶ stand in for, act as deputy for, cover for, represent, substitute for, take over from, take the place of, do the job of, replace, understudy

A B C D E F G H I J K L M N O P Q R S T U V W X Y Z

USAGE Note that *understudy* is normally used about an actor who takes the place of the main actor when they are ill or indisposed.

deputy NOUN

During her absence her duties are done by a deputy.
▶ second in command, number two, substitute, assistant, stand-in, representative, understudy
USAGE Note that *understudy* normally means an actor who takes the place of the main actor when they are ill or indisposed.

deranged ADJECTIVE

The jury found that he had been in a deranged state of mind.
▶ insane, mad, disordered, demented, unbalanced, unstable, disturbed, crazed, confused, distraught

derelict ADJECTIVE

The car passed a row of derelict buildings
▶ dilapidated, ramshackle, run down, tumbledown, ruined, deserted, abandoned, neglected, broken down, decrepit

deride VERB

Critics derided the film when it originally appeared.
▶ ridicule, mock, jeer at, scoff at, poke fun at, laugh at, pillory, denigrate, dismiss, (*more informal*) pooh-pooh

derision NOUN

Their excuses were met with derision.
▶ scorn, ridicule, disdain, mockery, contempt, vilification, disparagement, denigration, dismissal

derisive ADJECTIVE

Robyn gave a short, derisive laugh.
▶ mocking, scornful, ridiculing, disdainful, dismissive, contemptuous

derisory ADJECTIVE

The house was sold for a derisory sum.
▶ laughable, ridiculous, inadequate, trifling, paltry, pitiful

derivation NOUN

1 *the derivation of the word 'posh'*
▶ origin, etymology, root, provenance, source
2 *a family of noble derivation*
▶ ancestry, origin, genealogy, descent, provenance

derivative ADJECTIVE

The theme of the story is very derivative.
▶ unoriginal, imitative, uninspired, plagiaristic, second-hand

derive VERB

1 *She derived some comfort from the fact that she knew the truth.*
▶ gain, receive, obtain, draw, acquire, get
2 *The family's wealth derives from oil.*
▶ originate (in), stem, arise, spring, flow, emanate
3 **be derived from** *The word 'yacht' is derived from Dutch.*
▶ come from, originate in, stem from, descend from

derogatory ADJECTIVE

derogatory remarks
▶ uncomplimentary, disparaging, depreciatory, insulting, offensive, defamatory

descend VERB

1 *The little plane descended towards the runway.*
▶ come down, go down, drop, subside, fall, move down, sink, dive, plummet
OPPOSITES ARE ascend, climb
2 *The road descends to a small village.*
▶ slope, dip, drop, fall, incline, slant
AN OPPOSITE IS ascend
3 **be descended from** *We are descended from an Italian family.*
▶ come from, originate in, spring from, stem from
4 **descend from** *He watched her descend from the train.*
▶ get off, alight from, disembark from, dismount from
5 **descend on** *A coach party descended on the local pub.*
▶ engulf, overwhelm, invade
6 **descend to** *In the end they descended to trickery.*
▶ condescend to, stoop to, lower yourself to, resort to, be reduced to, go as far as

descendants PLURAL NOUN

descendants of J S Bach
▶ line, lineage, heirs, family, successors, offspring, progeny, children, issue, posterity
AN OPPOSITE IS ancestors

descent NOUN

1 *the descent into Dentdale from Newby Head*
▶ way down, drop, incline, dip, declivity, slant, slope, fall
AN OPPOSITE IS ascent
2 *a person of British descent*
▶ ancestry, parentage, origin, lineage, extraction, heredity, blood, pedigree, genealogy, background, derivation, family, stock, strain

describe VERB

1 *A witness described the incident in detail.*
▶ report, narrate, relate, set out, explain, recount
2 **describe as** *I would never describe him as 'charming'*
▶ call, speak of, refer to, classify, categorize, characterize as, portray, present, represent
3 *The pencil described a circle.*
▶ draw, mark out, trace

description NOUN

1 *She launched into a detailed description of her day.*
▶ account, explanation, report, narration, commentary (on)
2 *The room was crammed with furniture of every description.*
▶ sort, kind, variety, type, category, class, order

descriptive ADJECTIVE

an exercise using descriptive language
▶ expressive, graphic, colourful, detailed, pictorial, vivid, striking, explanatory, illustrative

desert NOUN (with the stress on *des-*)
lost in the desert
▶ wasteland, wilderness, waste, wilds

desert ADJECTIVE (with the stress on *des-*)
1 *desert conditions*
▶ arid, dry, waterless, parched, barren, infertile, sterile, uncultivated, wild
AN OPPOSITE IS fertile
2 *a desert island*
▶ uninhabited, solitary, lonely, desolate, isolated, lonely, unfrequented
AN OPPOSITE IS inhabited

desert VERB (with the stress on *-sert*)
1 *Her husband had deserted her.*
▶ abandon, leave, strand, forsake, give up, jilt, renounce, betray, (*more informal*) dump, (*more informal*) walk out on, (*more informal*) leave in the lurch
2 *He had decided to desert the party and join the opposition.*
▶ renounce, abandon, leave, quit, disavow, forsake, (*more informal*) have done with
3 *Soldiers were deserting in large numbers.*
▶ abscond, defect, decamp, make off, go absent, turn tail, run away

deserted ADJECTIVE
1 *a deserted village*
▶ uninhabited, empty, unoccupied, evacuated, neglected, desolate, vacant
2 *a deserted wife*
▶ abandoned, stranded, forsaken, jilted, cast off, betrayed

deserter NOUN
a deserter from the army
▶ absconder, runaway, turncoat, absentee, fugitive, renegade, traitor, defector

deserve VERB
1 *You deserve a holiday.*
▶ be entitled to, be worthy of, have earned, have a right to, be good enough for
2 *The work deserves the highest praise.*
▶ merit, justify, warrant, rate

deserving ADJECTIVE
hardworking and deserving people
▶ worthy, laudable, admirable, praiseworthy, meritorious, commendable, creditable, good, worth supporting
AN OPPOSITE IS unworthy

design NOUN
1 *a design for the new building*
▶ plan, blueprint, drawing, outline, pattern, prototype, sketch, draft, model
2 *furniture of a fresh bright design*
▶ pattern, style, form, composition, arrangement, configuration
3 *His design was to travel and enjoy life.*
▶ intention, ambition, aim, aspiration, goal, object, objective, purpose, end, scheme

design VERB
1 *Wren designed several London churches.*
▶ plan, draw plans of, map out, outline, draw, sketch
2 *an engineer who designed a new kind of aero engine*
▶ create, invent, develop, devise, originate, conceive, think up

designate VERB
He has designated me his representative.
▶ appoint, nominate, delegate (to be), name, identify

designation NOUN
1 *She has the designation 'matron'.*
▶ title, name, label, description, epithet
2 *the designation of this land as an area of outstanding natural beauty*
▶ classification, specification, selection, choice

designer NOUN
a designer of women's fashions
▶ creator, deviser, inventor, originator

desirable ADJECTIVE
1 *a very desirable woman*
▶ attractive, beautiful, alluring, appealing, (*more informal*) sexy
2 *It would be desirable for them to express their support.*
▶ advantageous, advisable, helpful, beneficial, worthwhile, preferable, sensible, prudent

desire NOUN
1 *Ed has always had a desire to travel.*
▶ wish, longing, yearning, craving, inclination, eagerness, enthusiasm, impulse, appetite (for), (*more informal*) yen
2 *Her eyes glowed with desire.*
▶ lust, passion, ardour, lasciviousness, libido, love

desire VERB
1 *We all desire peace.*
▶ want, wish for, yearn for, long for, covet, crave, need, hanker after, hunger for, thirst for, pine for, ache for, fancy, like, prefer, (*informal*) set your heart on, (*informal*) itch for, (*informal*) have a yen for
2 *Paris desired Helen of Troy.*
▶ be attracted to, be captivated by, be infatuated by, (*more informal*) have a crush on

desolate ADJECTIVE
1 *They reached a desolate spot near the coast.*
▶ deserted, uninhabited, abandoned, barren, bare, bleak, gloomy, dismal, dreary, godforsaken
2 *Feeling desolate, she asked him to forgive her.*
▶ miserable, sad, unhappy, forlorn, depressed, dejected, downcast, despondent, disconsolate
AN OPPOSITE IS cheerful

despair NOUN
Stephen was in a state of despair.
▶ hopelessness, desperation, despondency, anguish, pessimism, melancholy, gloom, misery, wretchedness, dejection, depression
AN OPPOSITE IS hope

despair VERB
At times like this you can easily despair.
▶ lose hope, give up hope, lose heart, be demoralized
AN OPPOSITE IS hope

desperate ADJECTIVE
1 *He tried not to listen to the desperate cries outside.*
▶ despairing, hopeless, anguished, inconsolable, distraught, distressed, miserable, wretched
2 *There was a desperate shortage of food.*
▶ acute, critical, severe, serious, grave, dire, urgent
3 *a band of desperate criminals*
▶ violent, wild, dangerous, reckless, impetuous

desperation NOUN
1 *In desperation, she decided to go back to London to find him.*
▶ despair, hopelessness, anguish, despondency, distress
2 *The robbery seemed like an act of desperation.*
▶ recklessness, rashness, impetuosity, foolhardiness, frenzy

despicable ADJECTIVE
guilty of despicable crimes
▶ contemptible, loathsome, hateful, vile, shameful, detestable, abhorrent

despise VERB
She despised the methods he used in business.
▶ scorn, disdain, look down on, deride, condemn, deplore, revile, detest, loathe, feel contempt for
AN OPPOSITE IS admire

despondent ADJECTIVE
Perhaps he was feeling despondent about his exam results.
▶ disheartened, dejected, depressed, downhearted, downcast, gloomy, upset, down, miserable, sad

despot NOUN
the brutal methods used by despots to keep power
▶ tyrant, dictator, autocrat, oppressor, (*more informal*) Big Brother

despotic ADJECTIVE
They disliked any form of despotic rule.
▶ dictatorial, autocratic, authoritarian, oppressive, brutal, cruel, harsh, repressive, tyrannical

despotism NOUN
the despotism of some ancient rulers
▶ tyranny, dictatorship, authoritarianism, oppression, repression, brutality

destination NOUN
At last their destination was in sight.
▶ journey's end, stopping place, objective, goal, purpose, target, terminus

destined ADJECTIVE
1 *The universe might be destined to go on expanding for ever.*
▶ fated, doomed, bound, certain

2 *the destined outcome*
▶ predetermined, preordained, predestined, unavoidable, inescapable, inevitable, intended, ordained
3 *a cargo of cement destined for a factory at Tima*
▶ heading, headed, bound, en route, scheduled, consigned (to)

destiny NOUN
1 *Destiny had intervened to help them.*
▶ fate, fortune, chance, luck, providence, karma
2 *He seemed once more in control of his destiny.*
▶ future, fortune, fate, lot

destitute ADJECTIVE
He had left her destitute with two children to care for.
▶ penniless, impoverished, poverty-stricken, impecunious, homeless, indigent, deprived, down and out, insolvent, needy, poor, (*informal*) skint
AN OPPOSITE IS wealthy

destroy VERB
1 *A bomb had destroyed the building.*
▶ demolish, ruin, wreck, obliterate, devastate, shatter, blow up
2 *Disease destroyed all hopes of an economic recovery.*
▶ wreck, ruin, spoil, obliterate, disrupt, upset, put an end to, frustrate, thwart, undermine
OPPOSITES ARE raise, revive
3 *Their intention was to destroy the enemy.*
▶ kill, slaughter, annihilate, slay, eradicate

destruction NOUN
1 *Fires caused widespread destruction.*
▶ devastation, damage, demolition, ruination, havoc
2 *Much wildlife faces destruction. the destruction of all their hopes*
▶ annihilation, obliteration, elimination, extinction, extermination

destructive ADJECTIVE
1 *a destructive storm*
▶ devastating, damaging, ruinous, catastrophic, violent, ravaging
2 *destructive criticism*
▶ hostile, antagonistic, vicious, negative, fierce, disparaging
AN OPPOSITE IS constructive

detach VERB
You can detach the printing head for cleaning.
▶ remove, unfasten, disconnect, take off, separate, disengage, unfix, free
AN OPPOSITE IS attach

detached ADJECTIVE
1 *detached houses set back from the road*
▶ free-standing, separate, unconnected
2 *Her face expressed detached amusement.*
▶ dispassionate, disinterested, impartial, aloof, distant, objective
AN OPPOSITE IS committed

a b c **d** e f g h i j k l m n o p q r s t u v w x y z

detachment NOUN

1 *He regarded the matter with detachment.*
▶ dispassion, objectivity, disinterest, impartiality, neutrality, unconcern, aloofness, remoteness
2 *a detachment of soldiers*
▶ unit, squad, force, troop, corps, brigade, task force

detail NOUN

1 *The copy of the painting was accurate in every detail.*
▶ feature, particular, aspect, characteristic, circumstance, respect, item, point, factor, specific, fact, ingredient
USAGE You can also use *minutiae*, which is a Latin plural word meaning 'details'.
2 *She has an eye for detail.*
▶ precision, exactness, accuracy, rigour, thoroughness
in detail *They commented on the proposals in detail.*
▶ in depth, thoroughly, closely, methodically, minutely, meticulously, point by point, item by item

detail VERB

1 *An appendix details the sources used in the book.*
▶ describe, list, present, explain, recount, spell out
2 *The head boy was detailed to look after the visitors.*
▶ appoint, assign, delegate, commission, nominate, chosen

detailed ADJECTIVE

a detailed description of the scene
▶ precise, exact, comprehensive, complete, elaborate, exhaustive, minute, intricate, specific
OPPOSITES ARE general, summary

detain VERB

1 *The authorities wanted to detain them for questioning.*
▶ hold, arrest, apprehend, hold in custody, confine, restrain, intern, imprison, gaol, capture
AN OPPOSITE IS release
2 *Something must have detained them.*
▶ delay, hold up, impede, hinder, keep, check, prevent, keep waiting, retard, slow, stop, waylay

detect VERB

1 *We detected slight patches of rust.*
▶ notice, become aware of, perceive, discern, make out, recognize, identify, spot
2 *The crime was detected with the help of DNA evidence.*
▶ discover, uncover, expose, reveal, unearth, find out, root out, unmask, track down

detective NOUN

Detectives were quickly on the scene.
▶ investigator, police officer, CID officer, (*more informal*) sleuth, (*more informal*) private eye

detention NOUN

She had spent two months in police detention.
▶ custody, imprisonment, confinement, internment, (under) arrest

deter VERB

1 *It was mainly the expense that deterred them.*
▶ discourage, put off, inhibit, dissuade, intimidate, prevent, exclude
AN OPPOSITE IS encourage
2 *measures to deter crime*
▶ prevent, stop, check, put a stop to, reduce, discourage, counteract

deteriorate VERB

1 *His health deteriorated rapidly after his wife's death.*
▶ worsen, weaken, decline, lapse, fail, fade, fall off, get worse, relapse, slip, collapse, depreciate, (*more informal*) go downhill
AN OPPOSITE IS improve
2 *These materials deteriorate if they are not stored correctly.*
▶ decay, degenerate, disintegrate, decompose, crumble

determination NOUN

1 (*informal*) *His determination to win grew daily stronger.*
▶ resolution, resolve, will, strength of will, intentness
2 *You will need a lot of determination.*
▶ resolve, firmness of purpose, tenacity, persistence, dedication, drive

determine VERB

1 *It can be difficult to determine the sex of pandas.*
▶ find out, discover, ascertain, decide, establish, identify, verify
2 *Certain chromosomes determine the sex of an embryo.*
▶ control, regulate, decide, direct, dictate, govern, influence, affect

determined ADJECTIVE

1 *He is determined he will have his way.*
▶ adamant, resolute, insistent, convinced, bent (on having), resolved (to have), intent (on having)
AN OPPOSITE IS doubtful
2 *a determined young woman*
▶ resolute, purposeful, strong-willed, single-minded, strong-minded, steadfast, tenacious, dogged
AN OPPOSITE IS irresolute

deterrent NOUN

Penalties need to serve as a deterrent to those tempted to offend.
▶ discouragement, disincentive, impediment, warning, caution, brake, check, curb, obstacle, restraint, threat, (*more informal*) turn-off
AN OPPOSITE IS encouragement

detest VERB

I detest that kind of talk.
▶ hate, abhor, loathe, despise, dislike, deplore, recoil from

detestable ADJECTIVE

She needed to get away from that detestable man.
▶ hateful, loathsome, horrible, abhorrent, repellent

detour NOUN
a detour of five miles
▶ deviation, diversion, roundabout route, indirect route

detract VERB
detract from *These criticisms do not detract from the overall quality of the performance.*
▶ reduce, diminish, take away from, minimize, affect

devastate VERB
1 *Storms have devastated the region.*
▶ destroy, damage severely, ravage, demolish, flatten, ruin, wreck, lay waste, level, overwhelm, raze
2 *He was clearly devastated by the news.*
▶ shatter, shock, dismay, stun, distress, overwhelm, upset

develop VERB
1 *Our plans have developed rapidly in the last few weeks.*
▶ progress, advance, evolve, grow, flourish, get better, improve, mature, thrive, move on
AN OPPOSITE IS regress
2 *An argument developed.*
▶ arise, ensue, result, emerge, start, begin, erupt, come about, (*informal*) blow up
3 *The company wants to develop its overseas business.*
▶ expand, extend, diversify, build up, enlarge, increase, swell
4 *Children develop their reading skills at this age.*
▶ evolve, expand, advance, cultivate, acquire
5 *Let's see if we can develop these ideas.*
▶ amplify, augment, elaborate, enlarge on
6 *People were developing the disease at an early age.*
▶ contract, catch, get, succumb to, be infected with, come down with

development NOUN
1 *the development of a national road network*
▶ evolution, growth, advance, furtherance, expansion, spread, enlargement, promotion, improvement
2 *The Cabinet met to discuss recent developments in the Middle East.*
▶ event, happening, occurrence, outcome, result, change, incident
3 *The land has been set aside for industrial development*
▶ exploitation, building, conversion, use

deviate VERB
politicians who deviate from the party policy
▶ diverge, depart, digress, drift, stray, wander, turn aside, differ, part, veer, vary, err

deviation NOUN
Any deviation from the normal routine caused chaos.
▶ departure, divergence, digression, variation, variance, deflection, alteration, fluctuation, change, shift, disparity

device NOUN
1 *a device for converting digital data into audio signals*
▶ implement, apparatus, appliance, contraption, contrivance, tool, utensil, gadget, instrument, invention, machine
2 *a device to avoid prosecution*
▶ ploy, tactic, plan, ruse, scheme, stratagem, manoeuvre, contrivance, trick, stunt, expedient, wile, gambit, gimmick, (*more informal*) dodge
3 *a shield with a device showing the family arms*
▶ emblem, symbol, motif, badge, crest, insignia, seal, figure, logo

devil NOUN
1 *a sermon on the Devil and his works*
▶ Satan, Lucifer, the Evil One, the Prince of Darkness, the Adversary
2 *a painting with green-skinned devils holding tridents*
▶ demon, fiend, imp, spirit
3 *The poor devil looked frozen and soaked through.*
▶ wretch, fellow, soul
4 *cheeky young devils*
▶ rascal, rogue, monkey, scamp

devilish ADJECTIVE
a devilish laugh
▶ diabolical, diabolic, fiendish, wicked, hellish, infernal, satanic, demoniac, demoniacal, evil
AN OPPOSITE IS angelic

devious ADJECTIVE
1 *a devious route round the hills*
▶ circuitous, indirect, winding, rambling, meandering, tortuous, roundabout, erratic, deviating, wandering, crooked
AN OPPOSITE IS direct
2 *devious methods   a devious person*
▶ underhand, deceitful, dishonest, scheming, calculating, cunning, treacherous, evasive, insincere, misleading, sly, sneaky, wily
AN OPPOSITE IS straightforward

devise VERB
Devise a history project that includes role play.
▶ conceive, think up, think out, work out, invent, make up, plan, form, prepare, design, concoct, contrive, scheme, formulate, imagine, plot

devote VERB
He claimed he wanted to devote more time to his family.
▶ set aside, dedicate, assign, allot, commit, give yourself

devoted ADJECTIVE
a devoted wife and mother
▶ loyal, faithful, dedicated, staunch, fond, loving, caring, committed, devout, steadfast, true

devotee NOUN
devotees of rock music
▶ enthusiast, fan, addict, aficionado, admirer, (*more informal*) buff, (*more informal*) freak

devotion NOUN
1 *her devotion to her family*
▶ loyalty, dedication, commitment, faithfulness, staunchness, steadfastness, fondness (for)

2 *a life of religious devotion*
▶ piety, spirituality, devoutness, holiness, sanctity

devour VERB
1 *She watched him as he devoured his meal.*
▶ eat, consume, guzzle, gobble, wolf down, bolt down, (*more informal*) scoff, (*more informal*) demolish
2 *Flames devoured the barn.*
▶ destroy, consume, engulf, envelop, demolish, ravage, wreck, dispatch

devout ADJECTIVE
a devout Muslim
▶ pious, devoted, dedicated, reverent, faithful, dutiful, true

dexterity NOUN
The job needs patience and dexterity.
▶ skill, deftness, adroitness, expertise, proficiency

dexterous ADJECTIVE
a dexterous flick of the wrist
▶ adroit, deft, skilful, adept, neat, agile, expert, delicate, nimble, (*more informal*) nifty
OPPOSITES ARE clumsy, awkward

diabolical ADJECTIVE
1 *The soldiers showed diabolical cruelty.*
▶ outrageous, appalling, atrocious, wicked, vile, shocking, fiendish, devilish
2 (*informal*) *The standard of driving was diabolical.*
▶ dreadful, awful, frightful, terrible, poor, bad

diagnose VERB
The consultant diagnosed a tumour.
▶ identify, detect, recognize, spot, determine, isolate, distinguish, find, pinpoint

diagnosis NOUN
The original diagnosis proved to be incorrect.
▶ identification, explanation, pronouncement, opinion, verdict, analysis, conclusion, interpretation

diagonal ADJECTIVE
She drew a diagonal line across the page.
▶ oblique, slanting, crosswise, angled

diagram NOUN
a diagram showing the workings of the digestive system
▶ chart, plan, drawing, outline, representation, sketch, schematic representation, figure, table, flowchart, graph, illustration, picture

dial NOUN
the control panel was a mass of dials
▶ pointer, instrument, clock, display

dial VERB
He seized the phone and dialled the police.
▶ phone, telephone, call, ring

dialect NOUN
The local dialect was hard to understand.
▶ vernacular, language, speech, patois, accent, brogue, idiom

dialogue NOUN
A concentrated dialogue is needed to resolve the dispute.
▶ conversation, discussion, exchange, series of talks, communication, discourse, conference

diary NOUN
1 *She kept a diary from the age of ten.*
▶ journal, chronicle, daily record, log
2 *Put the date in your diary.*
▶ appointment book, engagement book, organizer, personal organizer

dicey ADJECTIVE
(*informal*) *Crossing the bridge can be dicey in high winds.*
▶ risky, chancy, dangerous, hazardous, unsafe, precarious, insecure, tricky, uncertain, unpredictable
AN OPPOSITE IS safe

dictate VERB
1 *He dictated a letter to his secretary.*
▶ read out, say aloud, recite, utter
2 *She wasn't going to let him dictate how she wore her hair.*
▶ prescribe, lay down, direct, order, ordain, impose, command, decree, enforce, give orders about, make the rules about, (*informal*) lay down the law about
dictate to *He does rather tend to dictate to his friends.*
▶ order about, boss, tyrannize, bully, domineer, lord it over, (*more informal*) push around, (*more informal*) walk all over

dictator NOUN
what I would do if I were dictator for a day
▶ tyrant, despot, autocrat, oppressor, (*more informal*) Big Brother

dictatorial ADJECTIVE
a dictatorial regime
▶ autocratic, authoritarian, (*informal*) bossy, despotic, totalitarian, tyrannical, domineering, oppressive, absolute, intolerant, overbearing, repressive, undemocratic
AN OPPOSITE IS democratic

dictatorship NOUN
The army imposed a dictatorship in the 1960s.
▶ autocracy, totalitarian state, despotism, tyranny

diction NOUN
1 *unlcear diction*
▶ enunciation, articulation, speech, elocution, intonation
2 *poetic diction*
▶ phraseology, choice of words, phrasing, expression, vocabulary

dictionary NOUN
a word that was not in their dictionary
▶ lexicon, glossary, vocabulary, wordbook, wordfinder, thesaurus

dictum NOUN
1 *Kipling's dictum that 'never the twain shall meet'*
▶ saying, maxim, proverb, epigram, precept
2 *an official dictum*
▶ pronouncement, proclamation, ruling, direction, decree, edict, fiat

die VERB

1 *He was sixteen when his father died.*
► pass away, pass on, lose your life, meet your end, breathe your last, expire, (*more formal*) decease, (*more informal*) snuff it, (*more informal*) bite the dust, (*more informal*) kick the bucket

2 *Hopes are dying of a peaceful settlement*
► fade, dwindle, sink, disappear, vanish, wither, melt away, dissolve

3 *The engine spluttered and died.*
► fail, cut out, stall

diehard ADJECTIVE

a group of diehard socialists
► reactionary, intransigent, hardline, fanatical

diet NOUN

1 *You need a healthy diet.*
► nutrition, nourishment, nutriment, food, fare

2 *His doctor put him on a diet.*
► dietary regime, regimen, abstinence, fast

diet VERB

She had been dieting for several months.
► follow a diet, slim, watch your weight, reduce weight, fast

differ VERB

1 *Opinions on the matter differed.*
► vary, diverge, be different

2 *Our beliefs differ from those of other religious groups.*
► diverge, vary, deviate, be different, contrast (with)
AN OPPOSITE IS conform (to)

3 *The ministers differed about what to do next.*
► disagree, argue, dispute, dissent, clash, conflict, be at odds, oppose each other, contradict each other, fall out, quarrel
AN OPPOSITE IS agree

difference NOUN

There is a big difference in their ages.
► dissimilarity, divergence, contrast, disparity, discrepancy, distinction, diversity, gap, variety, inconsistency, incompatibility, differential, differentiation, incongruity
AN OPPOSITE IS similarity

difference of opinion *The brothers were trying to resolve their difference of opinion.*
► disagreement, misunderstanding, dispute, argument, clash, conflict, controversy, debate, disharmony, dissent, quarrel, strife, tiff, wrangle

different ADJECTIVE

1 *There were many different answers to the question.*
► dissimilar, unlike, unalike, diverging, divergent, varying, deviating, opposed, inconsistent, incompatible, contradictory, contrary, clashing
OPPOSITES ARE identical, similar

2 *Everything about the house looked different.*
► changed, altered, transformed, strange, unfamiliar
AN OPPOSITE IS unchanging

3 *We want to try something different.*
► unusual, unorthodox, uncommon, new, fresh, original, unconventional, unique, abnormal, extraordinary, irregular
AN OPPOSITE IS conventional

4 *Every person's fingerprint is different.*
► distinct, unique, distinctive, individual, special, peculiar, personal, particular, specific
OPPOSITES ARE identical, indistinguishable

differentiate VERB

It was hard to differentiate fact from fiction.
► distinguish, tell apart, tell the difference between, discriminate between

difficult ADJECTIVE

1 *a difficult problem*
► complicated, complex, hard, intricate, involved, intractable, abstruse, obscure, advanced, perplexing, problematical, baffling, deep, enigmatic, (*more informal*) thorny, (*more informal*) tricky
OPPOSITES ARE easy, straightforward

2 *a difficult climb   a difficult task*
► hard, arduous, laborious, demanding, strenuous, tough, formidable, wearisome, burdensome, exacting, challenging
OPPOSITES ARE easy, light

3 *difficult neighbours   a difficult child*
► unmanageable, troublesome, trying, tiresome, uncooperative, intractable, unruly, unhelpful, perverse
OPPOSITES ARE manageable, tractable, accommodating

difficulty NOUN

1 *They found themselves in some difficulty.*
► trouble, distress, hardship, adversity, need, predicament, embarrassment, (*more informal*) fix, (*more informal*) mess

2 *The cost of the holiday might be a difficulty.*
► problem, complication, snag, obstacle, hindrance, stumbling block, hurdle, pitfall, (*more informal*) headache, (*more informal*) hiccup

diffidence NOUN

She replied with some diffidence.
► reserve, shyness, bashfulness, timidity, modesty, humility, hesitancy, uncertainty, unassertiveness, self-consciousness

diffident ADJECTIVE

a diffident smile
► shy, coy, reserved, bashful, sheepish, inhibited, embarrassed, modest, self-conscious, hesitant, timid, reserved, retiring
OPPOSITES ARE assertive, forward, bold, confident

a b c **d** e f g h i j k l m n o p q r s t u v w x y z

diffuse VERB

The sound was diffused by specially designed reflectors.
▶ spread, disperse, scatter, distribute, disseminate, dissipate
OPPOSITES ARE concentrate, collect

dig VERB

1 *The little dog was digging a hole in the garden.*
▶ burrow, excavate, scoop, tunnel, gouge out, hollow out, mine, quarry, delve
2 *Dinah dug him in the ribs.*
▶ poke, prod, jab, nudge, shove

dig up
1 *The police dug up the remains.*
▶ disinter, extricate, exhume
2 *Can you dig up some more information?*
▶ uncover, find out, discover

digest VERB

1 *The food is stodgy and difficult to digest.*
▶ absorb, assimilate, process, dissolve, break down
2 *There is a lot of information to digest.*
▶ take in, consider, absorb, ponder, study, understand

digest NOUN

a digest of the latest research
▶ summary, synopsis, outline, precis

digit NOUN

1 *Add up the digits*
▶ numeral, figure, number, integer
2 *We tried to bring the blood back to our frozen digits.*
▶ finger, toe, extremity

dignified ADJECTIVE

Dr McNab combined an air of authority with a calm and dignified manner.
▶ stately, solemn, noble, majestic, imposing, distinguished, honourable, becoming, august, proper, grand, grave, decorous, sedate
AN OPPOSITE IS undignified

dignify VERB

Customs that are dignified with the name of laws.
▶ honour, distinguish, exalt, graced, adorn

dignitary NOUN

The occasion was attended by numerous foreign dignitaries.
▶ VIP, grandee, worthy, important person, (*more informal*) bigwig, (*more informal*) big shot

dignity NOUN

1 *They accepted their misfortune with great dignity.*
▶ calmness, decorum, gravity, propriety, self-respect, eminence
2 *the dignity of a state occasion*
▶ majesty, grandeur, formality, solemnity, stateliness, magnificence, glory, greatness, honour, importance, nobility, pride, respectability, seriousness

digress VERB

We have digressed from our main theme.
▶ diverge, deviate, stray, wander, depart, go off at a tangent, ramble, veer

digs NOUN

My father paid for my digs in Paddington.
▶ lodgings, room(s), accommodation, living quarters, bedsit, flat, (*more informal*) place, (*more informal*) pad

dilapidated ADJECTIVE

a row of dilapidated Victorian houses
▶ run-down, ramshackle, decrepit, tumbledown, rickety, derelict, broken down, crumbling, neglected, ruined, decayed, tottering, uncared for
OPPOSITES ARE smart, well-maintained

dilemma NOUN

(*informal*) *The need to earn money while still studying placed him in a dilemma.*
▶ quandary, difficulty, predicament, awkward situation, (*more informal*) catch-22

diligent ADJECTIVE

She had been diligent about her piano lessons.
▶ conscientious, industrious, hard-working, painstaking, thorough, meticulous, punctilious, accurate, attentive, dedicated, rigorous, careful, dutiful, unflagging, assiduous, scrupulous
OPPOSITES ARE careless, irresponsible, lazy

dilute VERB

a glass of wine diluted with water
▶ weaken, thin, water down, mix, adulterate, make less concentrated, reduce the strength of
AN OPPOSITE IS concentrate

dim ADJECTIVE

1 *dim shapes in the distance   dim memories of their childhood*
▶ vague, indistinct, shadowy, unclear, fuzzy, blurred
OPPOSITES ARE distinct, clear
2 *a dim room*
▶ dark, sombre, dingy, gloomy, murky, dismal
AN OPPOSITE IS bright
3 (*informal*) *You probably think I'm awfully dim.*
▶ stupid, dense, obtuse, (*more informal*) thick

dim VERB

1 *The sky slowly dimmed*
▶ grow dark, darken, blacken, dull, cloud over
2 *He insisted on dimming the lights.*
▶ turn down, fade, lower, dip, shade, obscure
OPPOSITES ARE turn up, brighten

dimension NOUN

dimensions *a palace of huge dimensions*
▶ proportions, magnitude, size, scale, capacity, extent, scope

diminish VERB

1 *His angry feelings diminished in time.*
▶ decrease, reduce, lessen, decline, subside, wane, become less, depreciate, dwindle, peter out, shrink, shrivel, contract
AN OPPOSITE IS increase
2 *We must not diminish their achievement.*
▶ belittle, disparage, demean, minimize, undervalue, devalue
OPPOSITES ARE exaggerate, magnify

diminutive ADJECTIVE

a woman leading a diminutive poodle
▶ tiny, miniature, minuscule, minute, midget, undersized, dwarf, pygmy, small

dimple NOUN

Her smile produced an instant dimple in each cheek.
▶ hollow, dip, depression, dint, cleft

din NOUN

It was hard to hear anything above the din.
▶ uproar, racket, rumpus, commotion, hubbub, clamour, tumult, hullabaloo, noise, outcry, pandemonium, row, shouting

dine VERB

We will be dining at eight o'clock.
▶ have dinner, eat, feed, feast

dingy ADJECTIVE

The front door opened on to a dingy hallway.
▶ gloomy, dismal, dim, dreary, sombre, dark, drab, dull, murky
OPPOSITES ARE bright, cheerful

---

dinosaur NOUN

WORDS FOR TYPES OF DINOSAUR

large dinosaurs: Allosaurus, Ankylosaurus, Brachiosaurus, Brontosaurus, Diplodocus, Iguanodon, Ornithomimus, Parasaurolophus, Spinosaurus, Stegosaurus, Styracosaurus, Trachodon, Triceratops, Tyrannosaurus.

smaller dinosaurs: Archaeopteryx, Coleophysis, Dimetrodon, Dromaeosaurus, Elasmosaurus, Proceratops, Saltopus.

sea-dwelling dinosaurs: Elasmosaurus, Ichthyosaurus.

flying dinosaurs: Archaeopteryx, Pteranadon, Rhamphorhynchus.

---

dip NOUN

1 *We reached a dip in the ground.*
▶ slope, incline, depression, declivity, dent, hollow, fall, hole, concavity
2 *There will be a dip in sales after Christmas.*
▶ decrease, fall, decline, downturn, falling off
3 *He likes a quick dip in the river.*
▶ bathe, swim, dive, plunge, splash, paddle .

dip VERB

1 *She dipped her hand in the water.*
▶ immerse, lower, plunge, submerge, douse, dunk, drop, duck
2 *The path dips towards the village.*
▶ descend, slope down, go down, subside, dive, slump
3 *He would just smile and dip his head a little.*
▶ lower, drop

diplomacy NOUN

1 *They gave up the war and tried diplomacy.*
▶ negotiation, discussion, consultation, dialogue, statesmanship, statecraft
2 *Her answer combined honesty and diplomacy.*
▶ tact, tactfulness, sensitivity, politeness, discretion, delicacy

diplomat NOUN

1 *An Iranian diplomat has been ordered to leave London.*
▶ envoy, official, ambassador, consul
2 *Ever the diplomat, he offered them his help.*
▶ mediator, conciliator, peacemaker, tactful person

diplomatic ADJECTIVE

He tried to be diplomatic but the news was not good.
▶ tactful, sensitive, considerate, discreet, subtle, polite, understanding, politic, careful, delicate, judicious, prudent, thoughtful
OPPOSITES ARE tactless, outspoken

dire ADJECTIVE

1 *The economy was in a dire state.*
▶ terrible, dreadful, awful, appalling, disastrous, catastrophic
2 *a dire warning*
▶ ominous, portentous, dreadful, gloomy, grim
3 *in dire need of help*
▶ urgent, desperate, pressing, sore, serious, grave

direct ADJECTIVE

1 *Travel by the direct route.*
▶ straight, undeviating, shortest, quickest, nonstop, unswerving
AN OPPOSITE IS indirect
2 *We want a direct answer.*
▶ straightforward, honest, frank, candid, unequivocal, sincere, blunt
AN OPPOSITE IS evasive
3 *The sisters are direct opposites in character.*
▶ absolute, exact, complete, diametrical, downright, thorough, utter, head-on, (*informal*) out-and-out

direct VERB

1 *Earlier in her career she directed a child-growth project.*
▶ manage, run, administer, be in charge of, be responsible for, control, preside over, lead, organize
2 *An official directed them to the meeting room.*
▶ show the way, tell the way, indicate the way, give directions to, guide, point, route
3 *The books are mainly directed at teenagers.*
▶ target, aim, point, design (for), orient (towards)

4 *The judge directed the jury to return a verdict of not guilty.*
▶ instruct, order, tell, command, require, advise, charge, bid, enjoin

direction NOUN

1 *She left an hour later and went off in another direction.*
▶ route, way, course, line, bearing, orientation
2 directions *The nursing staff receive regular directions on new medicines.*
▶ instructions, guidelines, guidance, indications, briefing, plans, orders

directive NOUN

an EU directive on pollution
▶ ruling, instruction, order, regulation, direction, law

directly ADVERB

1 *She will join us directly.*
▶ immediately, at once, instantly, right away, straight away, in a moment, forthwith, presently
2 *You can fly directly from here to Montreal.*
▶ straight, immediately, by a direct route

director NOUN

the directors of the main London museums
▶ head, chief, manager, administrator, principal, (*more informal*) boss

directory NOUN

a business directory
▶ register, index, list, listing, catalogue

dirt NOUN

1 *The area in front of the house was covered in dirt.*
▶ grime, filth, muck, refuse, rubbish, garbage, dust, slime, sludge, mess, mire, pollution
2 *Chickens were scratching about in the dirt*
▶ earth, soil, mud, loam, clay

dirty ADJECTIVE

1 *a dirty room   dirty clothes*
▶ filthy, grimy, grubby, soiled, stained, mucky, dingy, unwashed, squalid
AN OPPOSITE IS clean
2 *dirty water*
▶ impure, muddy, murky, polluted, untreated, cloudy
AN OPPOSITE IS pure
3 *dirty tricks*
▶ corrupt, dishonest, illegal, mean, treacherous, unfair, ungentlemanly, unsporting, (*more informal*) low-down
OPPOSITES ARE honest, sporting
4 *a dirty joke*
▶ rude, indecent, obscene, coarse, crude, smutty, suggestive, improper, risqué, offensive, vulgar
AN OPPOSITE IS clean
5 *a dirty look*
▶ angry, hostile, resentful, peeved, black

dirty VERB

Try not to dirty the towels.
▶ soil, stain, mess up, spoil, taint, tarnish
AN OPPOSITE IS clean

disability NOUN

A disability can make the most routine tasks extremely difficult.
▶ handicap, incapacity, infirmity, disablement, impairment, affliction, complaint, abnormality, weakness

disable VERB

1 *The injury disabled her for several months.*
▶ incapacitate, injure, immobilize, cripple, debilitate, enfeeble, handicap, impair, lame, maim, paralyse, weaken, (*informal*) hamstring
2 *The army succeeded in disabling the device.*
▶ incapacitate, put out of action, deactivate, disarm, make useless, stop working
OPPOSITES ARE restore, repair

disabled ADJECTIVE

The house caters well for disabled visitors.
▶ handicapped, physically handicapped, physically impaired, incapacitated, immobilized, bedridden, crippled, deformed, lame, paralysed
AN OPPOSITE IS able-bodied

disadvantage NOUN

Heavy traffic is a major disadvantage of road travel.
▶ drawback, snag, downside, inconvenience, weakness, nuisance, handicap, hardship, liability, privation, trouble, hindrance, impediment, (*more informal*) minus

disadvantaged ADJECTIVE

schools in disadvantaged areas
▶ deprived, underprivileged, depressed, impoverished, needy

disadvantageous ADJECTIVE

in a disadvantageous position
▶ unfavourable, inauspicious, unfortunate, unlucky, bad

disagree VERB

1 *We constantly disagree.*
▶ dissent, differ, argue, conflict, clash, fall out, quarrel, squabble, wrangle, bicker
AN OPPOSITE IS agree
2 disagree with *She disagrees with everything he says.*
▶ oppose, contradict, counter, argue with, dissent from, object to, take issue with, be at variance with, deviate from
3 disagree with *Onions disagree with me*
▶ make ill, make unwell, upset

disagreeable ADJECTIVE

a disagreeable taste a disagreeable person
▶ unpleasant, nasty, horrible, horrid, offensive, repugnant, revolting, repellent

disagreement NOUN

1 *The two brothers had a disagreement.*
▶ argument, altercation, clash, quarrel, dispute, contretemps, misunderstanding, squabble, wrangle, (*more informal*) tiff, (*more informal*) barney
AN OPPOSITE IS agreement

2 *There is some disagreement between the two versions of the story.*
▶ difference, disparity, variance, dissimilarity, discrepancy, incompatibility, divergence

disappear VERB

1 *The crowd rapidly disappeared.*
▶ vanish, disperse, recede, clear, evaporate, fade, melt away, wane, dissolve, dwindle, cease to exist, ebb

2 *She disappeared round a corner.*
▶ go, pass, withdraw, run away, walk away, depart, retire, escape, flee, fly
AN OPPOSITE IS appear

3 *a way of life that has almost disappeared*
▶ die out, become extinct, vanish, perish
OPPOSITES ARE emerge, appear

disappoint VERB

1 *We will try not to disappoint you.*
▶ let down, fail, dissatisfy, disillusion, disenchant, dishearten
AN OPPOSITE IS satisfy

2 *In the end their hopes were disappointed.*
▶ thwart, frustrate, dash, defeat, foil

disappointed ADJECTIVE

I was disappointed when you didn't come.
▶ saddened, unhappy, upset, let down, dissatisfied, dejected, despondent, downcast, downhearted, crestfallen, discontented, disenchanted, disgruntled, disillusioned, frustrated
OPPOSITES ARE dissatisfied, contented

disappointment NOUN

1 *She could not hide her feeling of disappointment.*
▶ regret, sorrow, sadness, displeasure, dissatisfaction, disapproval, dismay, disillusionment, discontent

2 *The exam result had been a disappointment*
▶ let-down, setback, misfortune, blow, anticlimax

disapproval NOUN

Her face clearly showed her disapproval.
▶ dislike, displeasure, dissatisfaction, criticism, anger, disapprobation, disfavour, dissent, reproach, hostility, censure, condemnation, reprimand
AN OPPOSITE IS approval

disapprove VERB

disapprove of *They disapprove of gambling*
▶ dislike, condemn, deplore, deprecate, object to, frown on, look askance at, be displeased by, take exception to, reject, criticize, denounce, censure, disparage, make unwelcome, regret, (*more informal*) take a dim view of
AN OPPOSITE IS approve of

disapproving ADJECTIVE

(*informal*) *a disapproving glance*
▶ reproachful, critical, censorious, deprecatory, disparaging, slighting, unfavourable, unfriendly
AN OPPOSITE IS approving

disarray NOUN

The room was by now in some disarray. The opposition parties were in disarray.
▶ disorder, confusion, chaos, mess, muddle

disaster NOUN

1 *the world's worst air disaster*
▶ catastrophe, calamity, tragedy, misfortune, mishap, affliction, cataclysm, blow
2 (*informal*) *It would be a complete disaster for him if she came back.*
▶ failure, fiasco, catastrophe, setback, reversal
AN OPPOSITE IS success

SOME TYPES OF NATURAL DISASTER
earthquake, volcanic eruption, avalanche, hurricane, tornado, landslide, mudslide, flood; tidal wave, tsunami, seaquake; famine.

disastrous ADJECTIVE

a disastrous fire a disastrous choice
▶ catastrophic, calamitous, cataclysmic, devastating, ruinous, terrible, tragic, crippling, destructive, dire, dreadful, fatal, bad
OPPOSITES ARE fortunate, successful

disband VERB

The team disbanded once the work was done.
▶ break up, disperse, scatter, separate, part company, go your own way

disbelief NOUN

He looked at her in disbelief
▶ incredulity, distrust, scepticism, doubt, mistrust, suspicion
OPPOSITES ARE belief, credence

disbelieve VERB

He disbelieved everything we said.
▶ doubt, mistrust, reject, suspect, discount, discredit, have no faith in, be sceptical of
AN OPPOSITE IS believe

disbelieving ADJECTIVE

Her manner was disbelieving.
▶ incredulous, mistrustful, distrustful, sceptical

disc NOUN

1 *the disc of the sun*
▶ circle, round, ring
2 *a new disc from the same band*
▶ CD, compact disc, record, album, single

discard VERB

I decided to discard some old clothes.
▶ get rid of, dispose of, dispense with, throw away, cast off, reject, eliminate, jettison, scrap, shed, dump, (*more informal*) chuck away, (*more informal*) ditch

discern VERB

We discerned a tower in the distance.
▶ perceive, spot, make out, pick out, detect, recognize, distinguish, become aware of

discernible ADJECTIVE

His face was clearly discernible to her all the time.
▶ visible, perceptible, observable, noticeable, distinct, manifest, conspicuous

discerning ADJECTIVE

a discerning critic
▶ discriminating, perceptive, refined, judicious, cultivated, enlightened, perspicacious

discharge VERB

1 *Factories along the river were discharging thick smoke.*
▶ emit, give out, pour out, give off, exude, belch, release, secrete, produce, send out, eject, expel
2 *He discharged the gun by accident.*
▶ fire, shoot, detonate, let off, explode
3 *Three employees were discharged on the same day.*
▶ dismiss, fire, make redundant, remove, sack, throw out
4 *The authorities discharged him from prison on a Sunday.*
▶ release, liberate, free, allow to leave, dismiss, excuse

discharge NOUN

1 *discharge from prison*
▶ release, liberation
2 *the discharge of a duty*
▶ accomplishment, execution, completion, fulfilment, achievement

disciple NOUN

a disciple of Aristotle
▶ follower, pupil, adherent, devotee, student, supporter, acolyte, admirer, apostle

disciplinarian NOUN

a strict disciplinarian
▶ taskmaster, authoritarian, autocrat, martinet, despot
AN OPPOSITE IS libertarian

discipline NOUN

1 *Good financial discipline is important.*
▶ control, regulation, order, authority, orderliness, management, self-control, strictness, system, training, obedience
2 *Their mother had been responsible for administering discipline.*
▶ punishment, chastisement, correction
3 *Sociology is a fairly new discipline.*
▶ field of study, field, branch of knowledge speciality

discipline VERB

1 *Families have different ways of disciplining their children.*
▶ train, control, instruct, educate, restrain, break in drill
2 *Several staff have been disciplined.*
▶ punish, reprimand, reprove, penalize, chasten, chastise

disciplined ADJECTIVE

a disciplined workforce
▶ orderly, well-trained, well-behaved
AN OPPOSITE IS undisciplined

disclaim VERB

The company disclaimed all responsibility for the pollution.
▶ deny, reject, renounce, repudiate, disown, forswear
OPPOSITES ARE acknowledge, accept, admit

disclose VERB

This information should not be disclosed to anyone outside this room.
▶ divulge, reveal, communicate, make known, pass on

discolour VERB

Spilt liquid had discoloured the paintwork.
▶ stain, mark, tarnish, tinge, fade, bleach

discomfort NOUN

Her arm felt numb but she managed to hide the discomfort.
▶ pain, soreness, ache, irritation, distress, hardship
AN OPPOSITE IS comfort

disconcerting ADJECTIVE

He answered all the questions with disconcerting honesty.
▶ unsettling, unnerving, offputting, confusing, disturbing, perplexing, upsetting, worrying
AN OPPOSITE IS reassuring

disconnect VERB

1 *The power company had disconnected the supply.*
▶ cut off, break off, stop
OPPOSITES ARE reconnect, restore
2 *The engine was disconnected at Crewe.*
▶ uncouple, detach, disengage, decouple, separate
OPPOSITES ARE attach, connect
3 *Televisions should be disconnected at night.*
▶ unplug, deactivate
OPPOSITES ARE connect, plug in

disconnected ADJECTIVE
a disconnected argument
▶ incoherent, disjointed, garbled, confused, disorganized, rambling, uncoordinated
OPPOSITES ARE coherent, logical

discontent NOUN
Soon their grumblings became open discontent.
▶ dissatisfaction, unease, disquiet, disgruntlement, unhappiness

discontented ADJECTIVE
He felt discontented with his lot in life.
▶ dissatisfied, unhappy, aggrieved, resentful, disgruntled, disaffected, (*more informal*) fed up, (*more informal*) browned off

discontinue VERB
The ferry to the island will be discontinued next year.
▶ stop, end, finish, cease, break off, terminate, suspend, abandon, cancel, bring to an end

discord NOUN
Families can so often become a source of discord.
▶ strife, conflict, friction, disagreement, dissension, disunity, argument, hostility
AN OPPOSITE IS agreement

discordant ADJECTIVE
discordant sounds
▶ unharmonious, dissonant, jarring, cacophonous
AN OPPOSITE IS harmonious

discount NOUN
a £5 discount on the sticker price
▶ reduction, deduction, concession, cut, allowance, rebate, (*more informal*) markdown

discount VERB
We discounted all these rumours.
▶ disregard, reject, disbelieve, overlook, ignore

discourage VERB
1 *The audience was discouraged from asking questions.*
▶ deter, dissuade, restrain, prevent, hinder, put off, warn off
2 *Her cool response discouraged them.*
▶ dishearten, dispirit, demoralize, disappoint, dismay, depress, unnerve, intimidate

discouragement NOUN
Strong police presence is a discouragement to crime.
▶ deterrent, disincentive, constraint, hindrance, impediment, restraint, obstacle, setback, (*informal*) damper (on)
AN OPPOSITE IS encouragement

discouraging ADJECTIVE
The latest news is discouraging.
▶ depressing, dispiriting, disheartening, demoralizing, disappointing, daunting

discourse NOUN (with the stress on *dis-*)
1 *They continued their discourse well into the night.*
▶ conversation, disquisition, literature, speech
2 *a discourse on semantics*
▶ dissertation, essay, treatise, monograph, thesis, paper

discourse VERB (with the stress on -*course*)
He likes to discourse on his favourite topics.
▶ speak, hold forth, expatiate, pontificate

discourteous ADJECTIVE
It would be discourteous to refuse.
▶ rude, impolite, bad-mannered, ill-mannered, disrespectful, uncivil, churlish, ungracious, boorish

discourtesy NOUN
He had committed the grave discourtesy of not turning up for the speech.
▶ rudeness, bad manners, ill manners, disrespect, incivility, churlishness

discover VERB
1 *The children had discovered a secret door at the bottom of the garden.*
▶ find, locate, come across, uncover, chance on, stumble on
2 *We discovered that he had been lying.*
▶ find out, learn, realize, come to know, come to realize, work out, perceive
3 *Faraday discovered electricity.*
▶ originate, develop, pioneer, invent
USAGE Note that *discover* and *invent* do not mean quite the same: you discover something natural that was always there (e.g. electricity), and you invent something new that did not exist before (e.g. television).

discovery NOUN
1 *a major new discovery*
▶ invention, innovation, revelation, breakthrough, disclosure, exploration, (*more informal*) find
2 *the discovery of the body*
▶ finding, location, locating, detection, uncovering, unearthing

discredit VERB
1 *His enemies are looking for information that might discredit him.*
▶ disparage, defame, disgrace, smear, slander, dishonour, ruin the reputation of, slur, vilify
2 *The new evidence discredits the witness's story.*
▶ disprove, prove false, invalidate, challenge, refute, raise doubts about, (*more informal*) explode, (*more informal*) show up

discredit NOUN
The arms sales brought discredit on the government.
▶ disgrace, dishonour, disrepute, shame, ignominy, censure, blame

discreet ADJECTIVE
USAGE Do not confuse this word with *discrete*, which means 'distinct' or 'separate'.
I made a few discreet enquiries.
▶ careful, circumspect, cautious, guarded, wary, tactful, judicious, prudent, considerate, delicate, diplomatic, sensitive, thoughtful, polite, politic
OPPOSITES ARE indiscreet, rash

discrepancy NOUN
There is a discrepancy between the two versions of the story.
▶ inconsistency, difference, disparity, variance,

conflict, dissimilarity, divergence, incompatibility, incongruity
AN OPPOSITE IS similarity

discrete ADJECTIVE

USAGE Do not confuse this word with *discreet*, which means 'careful' or 'cautious'.
teaching the course in discrete units
▶ distinct, separate, individual, detached

discretion NOUN

1 *The police conducted their enquiries with discretion.*
▶ diplomacy, tact, sensitivity, good sense, judgement, maturity, prudence, responsibility, wisdom
AN OPPOSITE IS indiscretion

2 *Payment of interest is at the Bank's discretion.*
▶ choice, option, judgement, will, wish, preference

discriminate VERB

1 *It is hard to discriminate between the two theories.*
▶ differentiate, distinguish, make a distinction, tell the difference

2 *Some employment practices still discriminate against women.*
▶ be biased, be prejudiced, show discrimination, be intolerant (towards)

discriminating ADJECTIVE

a discriminating art collector
▶ discerning, perceptive, astute, judicious, fastidious, critical, particular, selective, (*more informal*) choosy
AN OPPOSITE IS undiscriminating

discrimination NOUN

1 *She shows discrimination in her choice of music*
▶ discernment, good taste, insight, judgement, perceptiveness, refinement, selectivity, subtlety, taste

2 *victims of discrimination*
▶ prejudice, bias, bigotry, intolerance, chauvinism, favouritism, male chauvinism, racism, sexism, unfairness
AN OPPOSITE IS impartiality

discuss VERB

It was good to discuss other people's problems.
▶ debate, consider, talk about, confer about, consult about, deliberate, examine, deal with

discussion NOUN

a lively discussion about funding universities
▶ debate, deliberation, conference, dialogue, consultation, conversation, argument, discourse, consideration, examination, exchange of views, symposium, talk

disease NOUN

suffering from a disease   *a country afflicted by disease*
▶ illness, sickness, bad health, ailment, malady, disorder, infirmity
RELATED ADJECTIVE morbid

diseased ADJECTIVE

poor and diseased villagers
▶ ill, sick, unhealthy, unwell, ailing, infected
AN OPPOSITE IS healthy

disentangle VERB

1 *The cord had a knot that was difficult to disentangle*
▶ untangle, undo, untie, untwist, sort out, straighten, unknot, unravel
AN OPPOSITE IS entangle

2 *She disentangled his hand from her twisted clothing*
▶ free, release, extricate, extract, remove, disengage, liberate, separate
AN OPPOSITE IS enmesh

disfigure VERB

A new motorway will disfigure the landscape.
▶ mar, scar, deface, deform, mutilate, spoil, damage
OPPOSITES ARE enhance, beautify

disgrace NOUN

1 *the public disgrace of being prosecuted for shoplifting*
▶ dishonour, shame, humiliation, ignominy, degradation, slur, stain, stigma, discredit, embarrassment, opprobrium, scandal
AN OPPOSITE IS honour

2 (*informal*) *The local facilities for children were a disgrace.*
▶ outrage, scandal, affront, insult
OPPOSITES ARE credit, asset

disgrace VERB

He very nearly disgraced his friends by reciting an improper poem.
▶ shame, bring shame on, defame, humiliate, scandalize

disgraceful ADJECTIVE

Their behaviour had been disgraceful.
▶ shameful, deplorable, shocking, dreadful, despicable, dishonourable, reprehensible, appalling, bad

disgruntled ADJECTIVE

complaints from disgruntled customers
▶ dissatisfied, discontented, aggrieved, resentful, disappointed, unhappy, indignant, angry

disguise NOUN

She looked quite convincing in her nun's disguise.
▶ costume, outfit, impersonation, camouflage, concealment, pretence, cloak, cover, fancy dress, make-up, front, mask, (*more informal*) get-up

disguise VERB

1 *Her long sleeves disguised her burns.*
▶ hide, conceal, cover, mask, screen, shroud, veil, camouflage, dress up, make inconspicuous

2 *He made no attempt to disguise his anger.*
▶ hide, conceal, cover up, gloss over, misrepresent

3 **disguise yourself as** *I changed my identity and disguised myself as one of the locals.*
▶ dress up as, impersonate, pretend to be, pose as, counterfeit, imitate, mimic, (*more informal*) take off

disgust NOUN

She turned and looked in disgust at the body on the back seat.
▶ revulsion, repugnance, repulsion, abhorrence, distaste, aversion, antipathy, contempt, loathing, detestation, nausea, dislike, hatred
OPPOSITES ARE liking, relish

disgust VERB

The hospital food disgusted me.
▶ revolt, nauseate, offend, appal, repel, sicken, be distasteful to, displease, horrify, outrage, put off, shock, (*more informal*) turn your stomach
OPPOSITES ARE please, appeal to

disgusting ADJECTIVE

The smell was disgusting. They showed disgusting bigotry.
▶ revolting, nauseating, offensive, sickening, loathsome, repugnant, repulsive, unpleasant
OPPOSITES ARE pleasant, appealing, attractive

dish NOUN

1 *He tipped the pasta into a dish.*
▶ plate, bowl, platter
2 *a nutritious vegetarian dish*
▶ food, recipe

dish VERB

dish out *The children helped by dishing out piles of books.*
▶ distribute, give out, hand round, deal out, issue
dish up *Shirley was busy dishing up burgers and hot dogs.*
▶ serve, serve up, provide, dispense

dishearten VERB

The result disheartened them so much they almost gave up.
▶ discourage, dispirit, dismay, depress, disappoint, deter, put off, sadden
OPPOSITES ARE hearten, encourage

dishevelled ADJECTIVE

She ran a hand through her dishevelled hair
▶ untidy, bedraggled, disordered, unkempt, scruffy, disarranged, tangled, ruffled, rumpled, slovenly, tousled, uncombed, messy
OPPOSITES ARE neat, tidy

dishonest ADJECTIVE

Their solicitor proved to be dishonest. a dishonest statement
▶ deceitful, untruthful, lying, fraudulent, false, double-dealing, cheating, swindling, corrupt, underhand, untrustworthy, (*more informal*) crooked
OPPOSITES ARE honest, truthful

dishonesty NOUN

a charge of dishonesty against former colleagues
▶ corruption, fraud, fraudulence, cheating, deceit, deception, deviousness, lying, falsity, falsehood, (*more informal*) crookedness, (*more informal*) shadiness
AN OPPOSITE IS honesty

dishonour NOUN

I have no wish to bring dishonour on you or your family.
▶ disgrace, shame, discredit, degradation, humiliation, ignominy, stigma, opprobrium, indignity
OPPOSITES ARE honour, credit

dishonourable ADJECTIVE

It would be dishonourable to refuse to pay.
▶ disgraceful, shameful, discreditable, ignominious, contemptible, reprehensible

dishy ADJECTIVE

Judging by the photograph, the author's dishy, too.
▶ attractive, good-looking, charming, sexy, appealing

disillusioned ADJECTIVE

They soon became disillusioned by the reality of wedded bliss.
▶ disappointed, disenchanted, disabused, let down, discouraged
AN OPPOSITE IS enthusiastic

disinclined ADJECTIVE

He held Madeleine's hand, which she seemed disinclined to remove.
▶ reluctant, unwilling, loath, hesitant, resistant (to moving), averse (to moving)

disinfect VERB

An aromatic plant is used to disinfect houses where malaria is present.
▶ sterilize, sanitize, clean, cleanse, purify, fumigate
OPPOSITES ARE infect, contaminate

disinfectant NOUN

She wiped the surface down with disinfectant.
▶ antiseptic, sterilizer, germicide, carbolic, cleaner

disintegrate VERB

The aircraft caught fire and disintegrated in the air.
▶ break up, fall apart, fall to pieces, explode, come apart, decompose

disinterested ADJECTIVE

Her advice would always be disinterested.
▶ impartial, neutral, unbiased, unprejudiced, dispassionate, open-minded, even-handed
AN OPPOSITE IS biased
USAGE Note that *disinterested* means 'impartial' and does not mean the same as *uninterested*.

disjointed ADJECTIVE

She turned her disjointed thoughts over in her mind.
▶ disconnected, incoherent, confused, disordered, unconnected, disorganized, jumbled, rambling, fitful, erratic
AN OPPOSITE IS coherent

dislike VERB

She dislikes me because I won't do what she says.
▶ not like, detest, hate, object to, abhor, disapprove of, despise
AN OPPOSITE IS like

dislike NOUN

He had a fear and dislike of big cities.
▶ aversion (to), distaste (for), antagonism (to), antipathy (to), contempt (for), disgust (for), revulsion (from), detestation, disapproval, hatred, loathing
AN OPPOSITE IS liking

dislocate VERB

He had dislocated his left shoulder in a Rugby game.
▶ put out of joint, disjoint, displace, disengage, (*more informal*) put out

dislodge VERB

Several stones had been dislodged, causing a hazard to passers-by.
▶ displace, disarrange, dislocate, disturb, misplace, move, shift, remove, knock out of place, knock out of position

disloyal ADJECTIVE

His colleagues criticized him for being disloyal in his comments.
▶ unfaithful, faithless, treacherous, subversive, seditious, dissident, false, traitorous
OPPOSITES ARE loyal, faithful

disloyalty NOUN

She felt a sense of guilt, of disloyalty.
▶ unfaithfulness, infidelity, betrayal, duplicity, faithlessness, falseness, inconstancy, perfidy, treachery, treason, double-dealing
AN OPPOSITE IS loyalty

dismal ADJECTIVE

1 *She led them into a dismal little room.*
▶ gloomy, dingy, dim, dreary, sombre, dark, drab, dull, murky
OPPOSITES ARE bright, cheerful
2 (*informal*) *a row of dismal performances*
▶ dreadful, awful, terrible, feeble, disgraceful
3 *We looked at the dismal faces around us.*
▶ glum, gloomy, sad, miserable, melancholy, sombre, forlorn, despondent, downcast, sorrowful, mournful, woeful

dismantle VERB

Before they left, the soldiers dismantled the row of huts.
▶ take apart, take to pieces, take down, knock down, break up, demolish, strip down
OPPOSITES ARE assemble, build

dismay NOUN

Laura gave a yelp of dismay as she caught sight of the time on her watch.
▶ alarm, shock, surprise, consternation, concern, distress, apprehension, agitation, trepidation, fright, horror

dismay VERB

You should not be dismayed by these comments.
▶ alarm, daunt, horrify, shock, appal, discourage, dishearten, dispirit, distress, deject, depress, devastate, disappoint, unnerve, frighten, scare
AN OPPOSITE IS encourage

dismember VERB

Thugs slaughtered and dismembered a pet goat.
▶ cut up, disjoint, divide, remove the limbs of

dismiss VERB

1 *Elaine dismissed her husband with a wave of her hand.*
▶ send away, discharge, free, let go, release
2 (*informal*) *Three employees were dismissed on the spot*
▶ give someone notice, discharge, lay off, (*more informal*) sack, (*more informal*) fire
3 *She had dismissed Nina's allegations as rubbish.*
▶ reject, discount, disregard, set aside, repudiate, discard, spurn, drop, get rid of, give up, shelve, wave aside, (*more informal*) pooh-pooh
4 *He tried to dismiss these thoughts from his mind.*
▶ banish, dispel, remove, reject, shrug off

disobedience NOUN

They were punished for their disobedience.
▶ insubordination, naughtiness, misbehaviour, bad behaviour, misconduct, unruliness, rebelliousness, wilfulness

disobedient ADJECTIVE

The children had been disobedient and demanding.
▶ naughty, badly behaved, insubordinate, troublesome, disorderly, disruptive, fractious, rebellious, unruly, wayward, intractable, obstreperous, wilful, contrary
AN OPPOSITE IS obedient

disobey VERB

1 *The Queen was angry that so many people had disobeyed her orders.*
▶ defy, flout, rebel against, contravene, disregard, ignore, infringe, break, resist, transgress, violate
2 *Remember never to disobey.*
▶ be disobedient, rebel, revolt
AN OPPOSITE IS obey

disorder NOUN

1 *They were arrested for acts of public disorder.*
▶ disturbance, unrest, agitation, disruption, upheaval, tumult, insurrection, rebellion
OPPOSITES ARE order, peace
2 *The house is in total disorder.*
▶ untidiness, disarray, disorganization, confusion, chaos, a jumble, a mess, a muddle, a shambles
OPPOSITES ARE order, tidiness

disorderly ADJECTIVE

1 *behaving in a disorderly manner*
▶ unruly, rowdy, rebellious, disruptive, undisciplined, disobedient, boisterous, rough, wild
OPPOSITES ARE orderly, disciplined
2 *a disorderly arrangement*
▶ untidy, disorganized, messy, muddled, confused, chaotic
OPPOSITES ARE orderly, tidy

disorganized ADJECTIVE

1 *The room looked completely disorganized.*
▶ untidy, disorderly, messy, muddled, confused, chaotic
OPPOSITES ARE neat, systematic

2 *I was accused of being careless and disorganized.*
▶ unmethodical, slapdash, slovenly, absent-minded, scatterbrained, inefficient

isown VERB
Her family disowned her when she married Jem.
▶ reject, renounce, repudiate, cast off, abandon, end relations with

isparaging ADJECTIVE
make disparaging remarks
▶ derogatory, depreciatory, insulting, abusive, uncomplimentary

ispassionate ADJECTIVE
a dispassionate assessment of the situation
▶ objective, impartial, detached, neutral, unemotional, calm, cool, impersonal, level-headed
OPPOSITES ARE emotional, biased

ispatch NOUN
A messenger brought dispatches.
▶ bulletin, communiqué, letter, message, report

ispatch VERB
1 *Reminders will be dispatched next week.*
▶ send, post, transmit, consign, convey, forward
2 *In the film the good guy has to dispatch a host of vicious villains.*
▶ kill, put an end to, put to death, dispose of, finish off

ispel VERB
It was a feeling that he found difficult to dispel.
▶ banish, eliminate, dismiss, get rid of, drive away

ispense VERB
1 *Waiters were there to dispense drinks.*
▶ distribute, give out, pass round, mete out, provide, allocate, allot, apportion, deal out, dole out, share
2 *The local chemist dispenses medicines.*
▶ supply, prepare, make up
3 **dispense with** *We can dispense with the formalities.*
▶ waive, disregard, ignore, forgo, do without, pass over, drop, omit, cancel, dispose of, get rid of

isperse VERB
1 *Troops arrived to disperse the demonstrators.*
▶ break up, split up, separate, scatter, drive away, send away, disband, dispel, dismiss
OPPOSITES ARE assemble, collect
2 *The crowd dispersed quickly.*
▶ break up, split up, disband, separate, scatter, dissolve, disappear, vanish, melt away
OPPOSITES ARE collect, gather, assemble
3 *Birds disperse the seed.*
▶ scatter, spread, disseminate, distribute, strew
AN OPPOSITE IS centralize

ispirited ADJECTIVE
He felt tired and dispirited.
▶ disheartened, depressed, dejected, downcast, despondent, downhearted, disconsolate, unhappy, sad, down, glum, melancholy, miserable, cast down
OPPOSITES ARE cheerful, happy

displace VERB
1 *The gales have displaced many roof tiles.*
▶ dislodge, disarrange, dislocate, disturb, misplace, move, shift, remove, knock out of place, knock out of position
2 *The recent land reforms have displaced thousands of people.*
▶ force out, drive out, eject, expel, oust, remove, supplant

display NOUN
an air display   a display of horsemanship
▶ exhibition, demonstration, show, spectacle, pageant, presentation, parade

display VERB
1 *A room will be built to display the marbles.*
▶ exhibit, show, put on show, present
2 *He displayed a good knowledge of the subject.*
▶ show, reveal, demonstrate, manifest, flaunt, produce, betray, air, evince

displease VERB
The decision clearly displeased him.
▶ annoy, irritate, infuriate, incense, anger, enrage, vex, exasperate, madden, aggravate, antagonize, inflame, make angry, (*more informal*) needle, (*more informal*) rile, (*more informal*) bug, (*more informal*) rub up the wrong way

disposable ADJECTIVE
1 *a large disposable income*
▶ available, usable, accessible, spendable
2 *disposable plates*
▶ expendable, replaceable, single-use, (*more informal*) throwaway

disposal NOUN
1 *the disposal of troops for battle*
▶ arrangement, disposition, order, grouping, mustering
2 *the disposal of radioactive waste*
▶ removal, elimination, discarding, destruction, riddance

dispose VERB
1 *A general disposes his troops for battle*
▶ arrange, array, group, place, position, set out
2 **dispose of** *Equipment was needed to dispose of soiled nappies.*
▶ deal with, get rid of, destroy, discard, jettison, scrap, sell, throw away, (*more informal*) dump
be disposed to *Brian was not disposed to question this idea.*
▶ be inclined to, be ready to, be willing to, be liable to, be likely to

disposition NOUN
1 *the disposition of the armed forces*
▶ arrangement, disposal, order, grouping, mustering
2 *a nervous disposition*
▶ temperament, character, nature, humour, inclination, tendency, leaning, make-up, constitution

disproportionate ADJECTIVE

Small tasks can take up a disproportionate amount of time.
▶ undue, uneven, unequal, unreasonable, inordinate, excessive, unbalanced
OPPOSITES ARE proportional, reasonable

disprove VERB

New evidence has disproved the original verdicts.
▶ invalidate, refute, overturn, confute, contradict, controvert, discredit, negate, rebut, expose, (*more informal*) explode
OPPOSITES ARE prove, confirm

dispute NOUN

a matter of great dispute
▶ debate, discussion, controversy, contention, argument, disagreement, conflict, dissension

dispute VERB

1 *We disputed with them deep into the night.*
▶ debate, argue, contend, exchange views, quarrel
2 *No one can dispute their claim.*
▶ challenge, contest, question, oppose, deny, doubt, contradict, controvert, impugn, argue against, quarrel with
AN OPPOSITE IS accept

disqualify VERB

He was disqualified from driving for a year.
▶ ban, bar, debar, prohibit, forbid (to drive), preclude

disquiet NOUN

The decision caused a lot of public disquiet.
▶ unease, concern, worry, distress, anxiety, alarm, anguish

disregard VERB

Anne tried to disregard the noise.
▶ ignore, take no notice of, pay no attention to, discount, overlook, pass over, make light of, brush aside
AN OPPOSITE IS heed

disrepair NOUN

The house is in a serious state of disrepair.
▶ dilapidation, deterioration, decay, neglect, collapse, bad condition, ruin, shabbiness
AN OPPOSITE IS good repair

disreputable ADJECTIVE

1 *disreputable minicab drivers without proper licences*
▶ dishonest, suspect, dubious, discreditable, dishonourable, notorious, corrupt, (*more informal*) sleazy, (*more informal*) shady
AN OPPOSITE IS reputable
2 *His bare feet and stubbly chin gave him a disreputable appearance.*
▶ scruffy, shabby, unkempt, dishevelled, bedraggled, raffish, unconventional
AN OPPOSITE IS respectable

disrespectful ADJECTIVE

He was often disrespectful towards his elders.
▶ rude, discourteous, impertinent, impolite, insolent, impudent, cheeky
OPPOSITES ARE respectful, polite

disrupt VERB

A strike of air-traffic controllers has disrupted holiday travel.
▶ interrupt, break up, dislocate, disturb, upset, interfere with, throw into disorder, break the routine of

disruptive ADJECTIVE

Disruptive behaviour often leads to considerable stress.
▶ unruly, troublesome, rowdy, undisciplined, disorderly, rebellious, misbehaving, errant

dissatisfaction NOUN

There is widespread dissatisfaction with the quality of service.
▶ discontent, discontentment, disappointment, disquiet, disgruntlement, frustration, annoyance, irritation, unhappiness, displeasure, anger, exasperation, chagrin, dismay, regret
AN OPPOSITE IS satisfaction

dissatisfied ADJECTIVE

They were clearly dissatisfied with our answer.
▶ discontented, disappointed, unsatisfied, unhappy, disgruntled, displeased, aggrieved (by), disaffected (by), frustrated (by), (*more informal*) fed up, unfulfilled
OPPOSITES ARE satisfied, contented

dissect VERB

1 *He had to dissect his dumpling with the edge of his fork.*
▶ cut up, take apart, dismember
2 *The argument was dissected and the various aspects considered.*
▶ analyse, split up, examine, inspect, investigate, study, scrutinize, sift, probe

dissension NOUN

The tax cuts were an attempt to head off possible dissension.
▶ disagreement, dissent, discord, dispute, conflict, contention, strife, friction, argument

dissent NOUN

The military government would not tolerate dissent or criticism.
▶ disagreement, objection, protest, insubordination, argument, disapproval

dissent VERB

dissent from *I do not dissent from the ideas you propose.*
▶ disagree with, differ from, demur from, diverge from, dispute, object to, take issue with, quibble with

disservice NOUN
You have done a disservice to the African people.
▶ unkindness, wrong, injustice, disfavour, bad turn, mischief, harm, injury, damage, offence
AN OPPOSITE IS favour

dissident NOUN
dissidents who had been imprisoned by the regime
▶ protester, dissenter, agitator, rebel, nonconformist, (*more informal*) refusenik
AN OPPOSITE IS conformist

dissimilar ADJECTIVE
1 *a wide range of dissimilar tasks*
▶ different, differing, diverse, distinct, unrelated, varying, unlike, disparate, heterogeneous
2 **dissimilar to** *This catfish shows a parental care not dissimilar to that of the cuckoo.*
▶ unlike, different from or to, unrelated to
AN OPPOSITE IS similar

dissipate VERB
1 *Her good humour soon dissipated.*
▶ disappear, vanish, evaporate, dissolve, subside, disperse
OPPOSITES ARE grow, develop
2 *He went on to dissipate his entire fortune.*
▶ waste, squander, fritter, fritter away, misspend, consume, burn up, drain, exhaust
OPPOSITES ARE save, preserve

dissociate VERB
We decided to dissociate ourselves from the more extravagant claims being made.
▶ break away, back away, detach, distance, separate, cut off, divorce, isolate
AN OPPOSITE IS associate

dissolve VERB
1 *The acids dissolve in water.*
▶ liquefy, become liquid, diffuse, disperse, melt, deliquesce, disappear, disintegrate
2 *Dissolve salts in the water to keep it pure.*
▶ liquefy, melt, disintegrate, disperse
3 *His anger began to dissolve.*
▶ disappear, vanish, evaporate, dissipate, subside, disperse
OPPOSITES ARE grow, develop
4 *The Assembly was dissolved after the revolution.*
▶ disband, terminate, abolish, close down, suspend, break up, dismiss, end, bring to an end, cancel, (*more informal*) wind up

dissuade VERB
dissuade from *He dissuaded his colleagues from taking strike action.*
▶ discourage from, prevent from, deter from, divert from, disincline (to take), talk out of, urge against, advise against, persuade not (to take)
AN OPPOSITE IS persuade (to)

distance NOUN
1 *the distance between the two vehicles*
▶ space, interval, gap, extent, length, range, reach, separation

2 *She keeps her distance.*
▶ aloofness, reserve, detachment, reticence, coolness, remoteness, coldness
AN OPPOSITE IS closeness

in the distance *a church spire visible in the distance*
▶ far away, far off, in the background, on the horizon, yonder

distance VERB
distance yourself *The President had to distance himself from these men.*
▶ withdraw, detach yourself, dissociate yourself, separate yourself, remove yourself, keep your distance, keep at arm's length, set yourself apart, keep away, stay away
OPPOSITES ARE involve yourself (with), become close (to)

distant ADJECTIVE
1 *distant countries*
▶ far-off, faraway, remote, outlying, isolated
AN OPPOSITE IS close
2 *a distant memory*
▶ vague, dim, faint, indistinct, obscure, indefinite
3 *a distant manner*
▶ aloof, detached, impersonal, reserved, reticent, unfriendly, withdrawn, cool
OPPOSITES ARE friendly, warm

distaste NOUN
1 *George looked with distaste at the man sitting opposite.*
▶ disgust, revulsion, abhorrence, repugnance, disdain, disfavour, dislike
2 *a distaste for politics*
▶ dislike (of), aversion (to), repugnance (for), disapproval (of)

distasteful ADJECTIVE
The day was hot and their work distasteful.
▶ unpleasant, disagreeable, offensive, repulsive, objectionable, unappealing, unpalatable, repugnant, abhorrent, unsavoury

distinct ADJECTIVE
1 *four distinct categories*
▶ discrete, separate, individual, detached
OPPOSITES ARE indistinct, fuzzy
2 *a distinct improvement*
▶ clear, definite, marked, sharp, decided, unmistakable, obvious, plain

distinction NOUN
1 *There is a clear distinction between politicians and the rest of us.*
▶ difference, contrast, dissimilarity, divergence, variance, variation, differentiation, discrimination, distinctiveness
AN OPPOSITE IS similarity
2 *a writer of distinction*
▶ importance, significance, note, consequence, account, greatness, renown, celebrity, eminence, fame, reputation, repute, prestige, honour
AN OPPOSITE IS mediocrity

3 *treating people without distinction of race, age, creed, or sex*
▶ differentiation, discrimination (between)

4 *He served with distinction in the war.*
▶ honour, credit, merit, courage, valour

distinctive ADJECTIVE
This duck has a distinctive white neck.
▶ distinguishing, characteristic, typical, individual, peculiar, unique, special, singular, different, original, idiosyncratic, unusual

distinguish VERB
1 *the capacity to distinguish between good and bad in literature*
▶ differentiate, discriminate, decide, tell the difference, pick out (good and bad), determine (what is good and bad)

2 *We could distinguish a line of trees in the darkness.*
▶ make out, identify, discern, perceive, recognize, observe, notice, glimpse

distinguished ADJECTIVE
a distinguished statesman
▶ eminent, famous, prominent, well known, celebrated, acclaimed, renowned, illustrious, famed, notable, noteworthy, esteemed, respected, honoured, outstanding

distort VERB
1 *His face was distorted with pain.*
▶ twist, contort, warp, deform, misshape, bend, wrench

2 *That explanation distorts the truth.*
▶ twist, misrepresent, pervert, slant, falsify, misstate, garble, put a slant on, (*more informal*) put a spin on

distorted ADJECTIVE
a distorted version of the events
▶ twisted, slanted, misrepresented, perverted, coloured, false, biased, one-sided, prejudiced, inaccurate

distract VERB
1 *A noise across the street distracted him.*
▶ divert, sidetrack, disturb

2 *Helen appeared to be distracted by the back of the cereal packet.*
▶ puzzle, bewilder, disconcert, confuse, perplex, trouble, worry

distraction NOUN
1 *the distractions of life in a big city*
▶ amusement, entertainment, diversion, pleasure, recreation, enjoyment, fun, interest, pastime

2 *The baby's crying drove her to distraction.*
▶ frenzy, distress, insanity, madness, delirium

distraught ADJECTIVE
The poor woman looked distraught.
▶ upset, overwrought, distressed, distracted, agitated, frantic, (*more informal*) beside yourself

distress NOUN
1 *She put her hand over her mouth to hide her distress*
▶ anguish, suffering, misery, torment, discomfort, wretchedness, unhappiness, disquiet, despair, desolation, agony, grief
OPPOSITES ARE happiness, comfort

2 *the distress of extreme poverty*
▶ hardship, adversity, tribulation, destitution, privation, trial
AN OPPOSITE IS prosperity

distress VERB
I was distressed by the fact that everyone seemed to turn against him.
▶ upset, perturb, disturb, trouble, bother, worry, sadden, afflict, torment
OPPOSITES ARE comfort, soothe

distribute VERB
1 *They spent the day distributing pamphlets.*
▶ circulate, issue, spread, disperse, hand out, make available

2 *The house was sold and the money distributed among his heirs.*
▶ share out, divide up, apportion, allocate

3 *The seed should be distributed evenly.*
▶ scatter, spread, disperse, strew, disseminate, arrange

district NOUN
the shopping district of the town
▶ area, region, quarter, locality, zone, neighbourhood, sector, vicinity, part

distrust VERB
On the whole the public distrusts politicians.
▶ mistrust, suspect, be suspicious of, be sceptical about, have misgivings about, have qualms about, be wary of, disbelieve, doubt, question
AN OPPOSITE IS trust

distrustful ADJECTIVE
He was distrustful of the people who were most trying to help him.
▶ suspicious, mistrustful, unsure, sceptical (about), doubtful (about), cautious (about)

disturb VERB
1 *He crept into the house quietly so as not to disturb his sleeping parents.*
▶ bother, annoy, interrupt, intrude on, disrupt, upset, alarm, wake

2 *Try not to disturb the books and papers.*
▶ muddle, mix up, disarrange, disorganize, confuse

disturbance NOUN
People were injured in violent disturbances in the capital.
▶ commotion, uproar, racket, tumult, hullabaloo, hubbub, rumpus, fracas, furore, upheaval, agitation, excitement

disused ADJECTIVE
An unexploded bomb was found in a disused cellar.
▶ abandoned, neglected, obsolete, unused, unoccupied, discontinued, idle, discarded
AN OPPOSITE IS operational

ditch NOUN

Some sheep had fallen into a ditch and had to be rescued.

▶ trench, channel, gully, watercourse, conduit, dike, drain, gutter, moat

ditch VERB

(informal) We will have to ditch that idea.

▶ abandon, drop, scrap, jettison, throw out, shelve, discard, forget, (*more informal*) dump, (*more informal*) pull the plug on

dither VERB

He dithered over which suit to wear that day.

▶ hesitate, waver, be in two minds, vacillate, (*more informal*) shilly-shally

dive VERB

1 *A young girl dived into the water.*

▶ plunge, leap, jump, drop

2 *The hawk dived rapidly towards its prey.*

▶ swoop, plunge, plummet, descend, nose-dive, drop, pitch

diverge VERB

1 *The roads diverged at this point.*

▶ separate, divide, part, split, branch, deviate, fork

OPPOSITES ARE converge, come together, join

2 *Clearly our opinions diverge.*

▶ differ, disagree, clash, be different

OPPOSITES ARE agree, coincide

diverse ADJECTIVE

information from diverse sources

▶ various, varying, different, sundry, assorted, miscellaneous, mixed, distinct, (*more formal*) manifold

diversify VERB

The company wishes to diversify into producing hang gliders.

▶ expand, branch out, spread out

diversion NOUN

1 *a traffic diversion*

▶ detour, deviation, alternative route

2 *a large city with plenty of diversions*

▶ entertainment, amusement, recreation, relaxation, distraction, pastime, game, hobby, play, sport

diversity NOUN

a great diversity of fruit and vegetables

▶ variety, assortment, miscellany, mixture, range, array, multiplicity

OPPOSITES ARE uniformity, similarity

divert VERB

1 *The plane was diverted to another airport.*

▶ redirect, reroute, deflect, turn aside, switch

2 *We tried to divert them with funny stories.*

▶ amuse, entertain, distract, occupy, interest, cheer up, delight, keep happy, recreate, regale

divide VERB

1 *The river divides north of the city. We divided into two groups*

▶ separate, diverge, split, split in two, fork, branch

AN OPPOSITE IS converge

2 *We divided the food between us*

▶ share out, allocate, allot, apportion, distribute, pass round

3 *We divide the eggs according to size.*

▶ sort, classify, grade, group, arrange, organize, categorize, sort out, separate, subdivide

AN OPPOSITE IS combine

divine ADJECTIVE

1 *divine worship*

▶ holy, sacred, religious

2 *a divine being*

▶ supernatural, godlike, superhuman, heavenly, spiritual, immortal, deific

divinity NOUN

1 *a statue of the divinity*

▶ deity, god, goddess, divine being

2 *arguments about Christ's divinity*

▶ godhead, divine nature

3 *She wanted to study divinity.*

▶ theology, religion, religious studies

division NOUN

1 *divisions in modern society*

▶ split, disunity, rupture, breach, disunion, schism, disagreement, conflict

2 *the division of Germany after the war*

▶ dividing, splitting, partitioning, separation

3 *the overseas division of the company*

▶ department, branch, arm, sector, office, bureau, subsidiary

4 *the division of the spoils*

▶ distribution, dividing up, sharing out, allocation, apportionment, allotment

divorce NOUN

One in three marriages ends in divorce.

▶ separation, annulment, (*more informal*) break-up, (*more informal*) split-up

divorce VERB

Her parents divorced last year.

▶ separate, end a marriage, (*more informal*) split up

divulge VERB

The article did not divulge the whereabouts of the individuals.

▶ disclose, reveal, communicate, make known, pass on

dizzy ADJECTIVE

All that leaping about made her feel dizzy.

▶ giddy, faint, shaky, wobbly, light-headed, (*more informal*) woozy

do VERB

1 *I have a lot of work to do.*

▶ carry out, undertake, perform, achieve, fulfil, complete, discharge

2 *You can do as you please.*
► behave, act, conduct yourself

3 *If there's no tea, a glass of water will do.*
► suffice, satisfy, serve, be enough, be adequate

4 *Shall I do the lunch now?*
► prepare, make, get ready, fix, organize, provide

5 *She went upstairs to do her hair.*
► arrange, groom, style, brush, comb, wash, fix

6 *He will be doing languages at university.*
► study, read, learn, take a course in

7 *She has been doing very well in the new job.*
► get on, progress, succeed

do away with

1 *We want to do away with outdated practices.*
► abolish, get rid of, discontinue, put an end to, dispense with, terminate, suppress

2 *I was afraid his enemies might want to do away with him.*
► kill, murder, put to death, assassinate, eliminate, exterminate

do up

1 *He stopped to do up his laces.*
► tie, fasten, secure

2 *They have bought an old farmhouse to do up.*
► renovate, restore, refurbish, decorate, revamp, (*more informal*) make over

do without

I cannot do without my eight hours' sleep.
► forgo, dispense with, give up, renounce, abstain from

docile ADJECTIVE
Hannah has a docile nature.
► gentle, compliant, meek, mild, obedient, amenable, cooperative, submissive, deferential

dock NOUN
The boat was moored at the end of the dock.
► harbour, quay, wharf, jetty, landing stage, marina, dockyard, boatyard, waterfront

dock VERB

1 *The ship docked the next morning.*
► moor, berth, tie up, put in, anchor, drop anchor

2 *The dog's tail had been docked.*
► cut short, cut off, crop, shorten

3 *The company will dock your wages for any misdemeanour.*
► reduce, cut, lessen, decrease

doctor NOUN
Jane is unwell and should see a doctor.
► GP, physician, medical officer, consultant, (*more informal*) medic
RELATED ADJECTIVE medical

TYPES OF DOCTOR

doctors who treat types of patient: general practitioner (GP: local doctor consulted first), geriatrician (for treatment of old people), gynaecologist (for treatment of women and girls), obstetrician (for treatment of diseases to do with childbirth), paediatrician (for treatment of children). ▶▶

doctors who treat parts of the body: brain surgeon, cardiologist (for heart diseases), chiropractor (for treatment of the joints), chiropodist (for treatment of the feet), dentist (for treatment of the teeth), dermatologist (for skin diseases), gastroenterologist (for stomach and intestine diseases), haematologist (for blood disorders), heart surgeon, immunologist (studies immunity), laryngologist (for treatment of the air passage to the lungs), nephrologist (for treatment of the kidneys), neurologist (for treatment of the nervous system), oculist (for treatment of the eyes), oncologist (for the treatment of tumours), ophthalmologist (for disorders of the eyes), orthodontist (for disorders of the teeth and jaws), orthopaedist (for disorders of the bones and muscles), periodontist (for treatment of the gums and other parts supporting the teeth), plastic surgeon (repairs and rebuilds body tissue), podiatrist (for treatment of the feet), rheumatologist (for treatment of the joints and ligaments), trichologist (for treatment of the hair and scalp), urologist (for treatment of the bladder and urinary system).

other names: anaesthetist (gives anaesthetics), clinician (any doctor who treats patients as distinct from doing research), consultant (senior specialist in a hospital), embryologist (studies embryos), epidemiologist (studies spread of diseases), pathologist (studies the causes and effects of diseases), radiologist (gives X-rays), radiotherapist (treats diseases by using radiation), registrar (hospital doctor of middle rank), surgeon (performs operations).

doctrine NOUN
Christian doctrine
► belief, creed, dogma, teaching, tenet, principle, conviction, orthodoxy, set of beliefs

document NOUN
a legal document
► paper, certificate, contract, deed, record, charter, (*technical*) instrument

dodge NOUN
a clever dodge
► ruse, ploy, trick, device, scheme, tactic, manoeuvre, stratagem, (*informal*) wheeze

dodge VERB

1 *He flicked his head to one side as if dodging a blow.*
► avoid, duck, fend off, evade, move out of the way of, swerve away from, turn away from, veer away from

2 *The Minister may try to dodge the issue.*
► avoid, evade, shun, equivocate over, get out of, fudge, sidestep, (*more informal*) duck

3 *He managed to dodge between parked cars.*
► dart, dive, duck, leap, swerve, jump

dodgy ADJECTIVE
1 (informal) Avoid dodgy travel agents at all costs.
▶ dishonest, suspect, unreliable, underhand
2 (informal) He took out a dodgy-looking sausage sandwich.
▶ suspicious, suspect, dubious, unappealing, inferior, nasty

dog NOUN
She was walking her dog along the beach.
▶ hound, mongrel, pedigree, pup, puppy, whelp, bitch, dingo

dogged ADJECTIVE
She was found again by the dogged efforts of her father.
▶ determined, persistent, resolute, persevering, tenacious, steadfast, single-minded, unflagging, relentless

dogma NOUN
religious dogma
▶ belief, creed, doctrine, teaching, tenet, principle, conviction, orthodoxy, set of beliefs

dogmatic ADJECTIVE
He was far too dogmatic to argue with.
▶ opinionated, doctrinaire, assertive, peremptory, insistent, arrogant, categorical, overbearing
AN OPPOSITE IS open-minded

dole NOUN
(informal) He lived on the dole for three years.
▶ unemployment benefit, state benefit, benefit, social security, income support

dole VERB
dole out Mum started doling out cornflakes.
▶ distribute, give out, share out, hand round, dish up, issue

domain NOUN
1 the king's domain
▶ realm, kingdom, empire, dominion, territory, country
2 the domain of science education
▶ field, sphere, area, concern, speciality, department

domestic ADJECTIVE
1 fuel for domestic use
▶ household, home, family, private
AN OPPOSITE IS public
2 goods for the domestic market
▶ national, inland, internal, local, state
AN OPPOSITE IS foreign
3 a domestic type of person
▶ home-loving, homely, domesticated

domesticated ADJECTIVE
domesticated animals
▶ tame, tamed, domestic, house-trained, trained
AN OPPOSITE IS wild

dominant ADJECTIVE
1 She was the dominant member of the partnership.
▶ leading, primary, prime, main, principal, foremost, uppermost, prominent, pre-eminent
2 The leader plays a dominant role.
▶ controlling, leading, authoritative, powerful, influential, assertive
3 the dominant feature of the landscape
▶ conspicuous, prominent, imposing

dominate VERB
London no longer dominates the British arts scene.
▶ control, monopolize, govern, rule, direct, overshadow, predominate in

domineering ADJECTIVE
He had a domineering mother.
▶ overbearing, authoritarian, autocratic, tyrannical, dictatorial, despotic, oppressive, harsh, strict

dominion NOUN
1 a British dominion
▶ dependency, territory, colony, protectorate
2 The Persians wished to extend their dominion to the Greek mainland.
▶ power, authority, control, mastery, hegemony, overlordship, sovereignty, suzerainty, supremacy, ascendancy

donate VERB
He agreed to donate his fee to charity.
▶ give, present, contribute, subscribe

donation NOUN
The organization depends on voluntary donations.
▶ gift, contribution, subscription, benefaction

donor NOUN
a large gift from an anonymous donor
▶ benefactor, contributor, philanthropist, provider, sponsor, giver
AN OPPOSITE IS recipient

doom NOUN
There was a feeling of doom about the place.
▶ ruin, downfall, catastrophe, destruction, disaster

doomed ADJECTIVE
The project seemed doomed from the start.
▶ ill-fated, ill-omened, condemned, damned, fated, cursed, jinxed, hopeless, hapless

doomsday NOUN
He kept bomb-making equipment for a doomsday scenario.
▶ apocalypse, end of the world, judgement day

door NOUN
She walked out through the door.
▶ doorway, entrance, exit

dope NOUN
1 (informal) smuggling dope
▶ drugs, narcotics, cannabis, heroin
2 (informal) He must have looked a real dope.
▶ fool, idiot, dolt, dimwit, nincompoop

dopey ADJECTIVE
He grew dopey and fell asleep.
▶ dazed, groggy, befuddled, drowsy

dormant ADJECTIVE

1 *The animals remain dominant until the next rainy season.*
▶ asleep, sleeping, hibernating, comatose, resting
AN OPPOSITE IS awake

2 *The volcano has been dormant for centuries.*
▶ inactive, passive, inert, latent, quiescent, quiet
AN OPPOSITE IS active

dose NOUN

a dose of cough mixture
▶ measure, prescribed amount, dosage, portion, quantity

dot NOUN

The picture consists of tiny dots.
▶ spot, speck, point, mark, particle

dot VERB

Small houses dot the landscape.
▶ sprinkle, scatter, fleck, punctuate, pepper

dote VERB

dote on *She doted on the boy for years.*
▶ adore, love, be fond of, idolize, worship, cherish

double ADJECTIVE

double yellow lines on the road
▶ dual, twin, duplicate, matched, matching, twofold, duple
AN OPPOSITE IS single

double NOUN

It was either you or your double.
▶ lookalike, clone, replica, spitting image

double VERB

We must double our efforts.
▶ increase, multiply, magnify, enlarge, repeat
double back *He doubled back, crossed the bridge, and reached home.*
▶ turn back, backtrack, retrace your steps, return
double up *She doubled up with pain.*
▶ collapse, crumple up, fold over, fold up, bend over

double-cross VERB

He was double-crossing his friends.
▶ cheat, betray, deceive, defraud, (*more informal*) two-time

doubt NOUN

1 *There was some doubt about the identity of the father.*
▶ uncertainty, hesitation, confusion, difficulty
2 *I was plagued by doubt.*
▶ indecision, uncertainty, misgiving, lack of confidence, distrust, mistrust, suspicion, reservation, qualm

doubt VERB

1 *I doubt whether they will be there.*
▶ question, think it unlikely
2 *I do not doubt their motives.*
▶ disbelieve, distrust, question, query, suspect

doubtful ADJECTIVE

1 *At first I was doubtful about taking him with me. The woman sounded doubtful.*
▶ hesitant, uncertain, unsure, undecided, dubious,

irresolute, ambivalent, wavering, tentative, sceptical, in two minds
OPPOSITES ARE confident, assured

2 *It was doubtful whether the witness would back him up.*
▶ dubious, uncertain, questionable, debatable, in doubt, open to question
AN OPPOSITE IS certain

3 *We are very doubtful of the conclusions they reached*
▶ suspicious, distrustful, mistrustful, cautious, wary, uneasy (about), sceptical, unsure
OPPOSITES ARE confident, trusting

4 *The chances of success are fairly doubtful.*
▶ unlikely, improbable, uncertain, dubious, remote
OPPOSITES ARE probable, likely

doubtless ADVERB

They will doubtless forget all about it.
▶ undoubtedly, without doubt, indubitably, certainly, surely, probably, presumably, of course, most likely

dowdy ADJECTIVE

a woman in a dowdy black dress
▶ drab, shabby, unattractive, dull, dingy, dreary, old-fashioned, inelegant, frumpy, (*more informal*) tatty
OPPOSITES ARE smart, colourful, fashionable

down ADJECTIVE

He felt down all day.
▶ depressed, dejected, sad, unhappy, miserable, downcast, despondent, dispirited, disheartened, disconsolate, glum, melancholy, cast down
OPPOSITES ARE cheerful, happy

down and out ADJECTIVE

down and out in the streets of a big city
▶ destitute, homeless, penniless, vagrant, living rough
OPPOSITES ARE prosperous, affluent, well-off

downcast ADJECTIVE

Their mother often looked downcast.
▶ dejected, depressed, despondent, dispirited, disheartened, downhearted, unhappy, sad, down, glum, melancholy, miserable, cast down
OPPOSITES ARE cheerful, happy

downfall NOUN

the downfall of the military regime
▶ ruin, undoing, fall, overthrow, collapse, failure, debacle

downgrade VERB

The consulate in Moscow has been downgraded.
▶ demote, lower in status, reduce in importance
OPPOSITES ARE upgrade, promote

downhearted ADJECTIVE

Steve tried not to look too downhearted.
▶ dejected, depressed, despondent, dispirited, disheartened, downcast, unhappy, sad, down, glum, melancholy, miserable, cast down
OPPOSITES ARE cheerful, happy

downpour NOUN
On the way home we were caught in a downpour.
► rainstorm, cloudburst, deluge

downright ADJECTIVE
They were telling half-truths and downright lies.
► utter, absolute, total, complete, out-and-out, outright, positive, categorical, sheer, unmitigated

downtrodden ADJECTIVE
a country downtrodden during years of dictatorship
► oppressed, subjugated, repressed, tyrannized, subdued, crushed, ground down, abused

downturn NOUN
a downturn in the family's fortunes
► decline, reversal (of), failure (of), collapse (of), foundering (of)

downward ADJECTIVE
Take the downward path. a downward trend in prices
► descending, downhill, falling, sloping, going down
AN OPPOSITE IS upward

doze VERB
He began to doze by the fire.
► sleep lightly, nap, catnap, drowse, (more informal) snooze, (more informal) have a snooze, (more informal) have forty winks

doze NOUN
She needed a short doze before her guests arrived.
► nap, catnap, light sleep, siesta, (more informal) snooze, (more informal) forty winks

drab ADJECTIVE
The room had a few pieces of drab furniture.
► dowdy, shabby, dreary, dingy, dull, shabby, sombre, lacklustre, unattractive, uninteresting, (more informal) tatty
OPPOSITES ARE bright, colourful

draconian ADJECTIVE
the country's draconian security measures
► harsh, severe, strict, stringent, drastic, swingeing, punitive, authoritarian

draft NOUN
USAGE Do not confuse this word with *draught*.
1 *a draft of a speech*
► outline, sketch, abstract, first version, rough version, plan
2 *a bank draft*
► cheque, order, banker's order, money order

draft VERB
USAGE Do not confuse this word with *draught*.
1 *He went off to draft his letter.*
► plan, prepare, sketch out, outline, compose, work out, write a draft of
2 *Lawrence had been drafted into the army.*
► conscript

drag VERB
1 *She dragged another chair over to the table.*
► pull, draw, haul, heave, (more informal) yank
AN OPPOSITE IS push

2 *Time began to drag.*
► become tedious, crawl, go slowly, move slowly, pass slowly
OPPOSITES ARE fly, pass quickly

drag NOUN
(informal) Working six days a week can become a drag.
► bore, nuisance, bother, pest, annoyance, trial, (informal) pain in the neck

drain NOUN
The drain had become clogged with leaves.
► channel, conduit, culvert, pipe, drainpipe, outlet, duct, gutter, sewer, watercourse

drain VERB
1 *There is a tap to drain water from the tank.*
► draw off, empty, remove, bleed, clear, take off
2 *Lisa drained the cocoa from her mug.*
► empty, drink up, quaff, gulp, swallow, finish off, polish off
3 *The water drains through into the river.*
► seep, leak out, ooze, strain, trickle
4 *The colour had drained from her face.*
► fade, vanish, disappear, wane, evaporate
5 *The expense drained all my funds.*
► exhaust, consume, deplete, use up, sap, spend

drama NOUN
1 *Ruth is studying drama.*
► acting, dramatics, dramatic art, the theatre, the stage, stagecraft
2 *Hardly a day goes by without some family drama or other.*
► scene, incident, excitement, spectacle, crisis, commotion, disturbance, fracas

dramatic ADJECTIVE
1 *a dramatic production*
► theatrical, stage
2 *a dramatic rescue at sea*
► exciting, striking, thrilling, stirring
OPPOSITES ARE unexciting, routine
3 *a dramatic change in the weather*
► substantial, significant, marked, pronounced
AN OPPOSITE IS insignificant

dramatize VERB
1 *The novel has been dramatized for television.*
► adapt, make into a play, rewrite
2 *He tends to dramatize small difficulties.*
► exaggerate, overplay, overstate, overdo, make too much of

drape VERB
She draped a cloth over the table.
► wrap, hang, drop, fold, arrange, swathe

drastic ADJECTIVE
drastic measures to reduce pollution
► extreme, harsh, severe, radical, rigorous, draconian, desperate, dire

draught NOUN
USAGE Do not confuse this word with *draft*.
1 *The draught made her shiver.*
► current of air, puff, wind, breeze

d

2 *He took another draught of his beer.*
▶ drink, gulp, swallow, mouthful, (*more informal*) swig

draw NOUN
She won a prize in the office draw.
▶ raffle, lottery

draw VERB
1 *Neil drew a shape on his beer mat.*
▶ sketch, depict, trace, outline, mark out, pencil, map out, (*more formal*) delineate
2 *The secretary drew another chair up to the desk.*
▶ pull, drag, haul, heave, (*more informal*) yank
3 *His aunt went over to draw the curtains.*
▶ close, shut, pull together, open, part
USAGE Note that *draw* can mean either 'close' or 'open' when referring to curtains.
4 *By Saturday the show was drawing huge audiences.*
▶ attract, bring in, win, entice, allure, persuade
5 *That is the conclusion I drew.*
▶ reach, arrive at, deduce, infer
6 *The teams drew after extra time.*
▶ tie, be even, be equal
draw out *We could draw out the conversation for hours.*
▶ prolong, extend, protract, stretch, lengthen
draw up
1 *The lawyers will draw up a contract.*
▶ formulate, compose, prepare, write, draft
2 *A car drew up outside the house.*
▶ stop, pull up, come to a halt, come to a standstill

drawback NOUN
The weather was rather a drawback.
▶ disadvantage, snag, hitch, nuisance, weakness, (*more informal*) fly in the ointment
OPPOSITES ARE advantage, benefit

drawing NOUN
She made drawings of the children.
▶ sketch, picture , illustration, study, portrayal, design, outline

dread VERB
He dreaded the telephone call that might take her away from him.
▶ fear, be afraid of, shrink from, be anxious about, worry about

dread NOUN
With a mounting feeling of dread I went to answer the door.
▶ fear, trepidation, apprehension, foreboding, anxiety

dreadful ADJECTIVE
1 *a dreadful accident a dreadful mistake*
▶ terrible, frightful, horrible, awful, fearful, ghastly, hideous, shocking, frightening, terrifying
2 *a dreadful person*
▶ unpleasant, disagreeable, nasty, awful, deplorable

dream NOUN
1 *I had a dream about lizards.*
▶ fantasy, nightmare, delusion, vision, hallucination, illusion, reverie, trance

2 *She was walking around in a dream.*
▶ daydream, reverie, trance, daze
3 *It had always been his dream to run a country pub.*
▶ ambition, wish, desire, yearning, aspiration, pipedream, daydream, ideal

dream VERB
1 *She dreamed she was on a journey.*
▶ have a dream, imagine, fantasize, fancy
2 *I have always dreamt of playing for England.*
▶ long (to play), yearn (to play), hanker (after), fantasize (about)
dream up *There's not much time to dream up an excuse.*
▶ invent, devise, think up, concoct, contrive, work out

dreary ADJECTIVE
1 *a dreary story*
▶ dull, uninteresting, drab, tedious, boring, monotonous, unexciting
OPPOSITES ARE exciting, interesting
2 *dreary countryside*
▶ gloomy, dismal, bleak, drab, sombre, murky

dregs NOUN
1 *dregs at the bottom of a bottle*
▶ sediment, deposit, grounds, lees, remains
2 *the dregs of society*
▶ rabble, riff-raff, outcasts, scum

drench VERB
Rain drenched the countryside.
▶ soak, saturate, douse, inundate, flood, swamp, submerge

dress NOUN
1 *Guests must wear formal dress.*
▶ clothes, clothing, costume, attire, apparel, garb, garments, ensemble, outfit, (*more informal*) gear
RELATED ADJECTIVE sartorial
2 *She wore a beautiful red dress.*
▶ frock, gown, robe, shift
USAGE A *robe* is usually a long dress, and a *shift* is usually a short one.

dress VERB
1 *She had to dress her disabled husband.*
▶ clothe, provide clothes for, put clothes on
AN OPPOSITE IS undress
2 *He dressed quickly and left the house.*
▶ put on clothes, get dressed
3 *A nurse dressed the wound.*
▶ bandage, put a dressing on, bind up, tend, treat, attend to

dribble VERB
1 *A dog lay in the hearth dribbling.*
▶ drool, slaver, slobber, salivate
2 *Water dribbled from the end of the hose.*
▶ trickle, seep, drip, ooze, flow, leak, run

drift NOUN
1 *a drift of deep snow*
▶ pile, heap, bank, mass, mound, ridge, accumulation

2 *the drift of the story*
▶ gist, essence, core, substance, thrust, import, tenor, purport

drift VERB
1 *The boat began to drift downstream*
▶ be carried, be borne, float, stray, coast, move slowly
2 *People drifted out into the gardens.*
▶ wander, ramble, stray, meander, move casually, dawdle, potter
3 *The snow had drifted across the road.*
▶ pile up, bank up, heap up, accumulate, gather, form drifts

drill NOUN
1 *three months of military drill*
▶ training, instruction, discipline, exercise, practice
2 *Everyone knows the drill.*
▶ routine, procedure, system

drill VERB
1 *He filed the edges and drilled a series of holes.*
▶ bore, make a hole, pierce, penetrate
2 *A sergeant was drilling the new recruits.*
▶ train, instruct, coach, teach, exercise

drink NOUN
1 *She had another drink of her coffee.*
▶ sip, swallow, gulp, swill, (*more informal*) swig
2 *In the end he turned to drink.*
▶ alcohol, liquor, alcoholic drink, strong drink, (*more informal*) booze

drink VERB
1 *She drank her tea.*
▶ swallow, sip, gulp down, quaff, swill
2 *an upright citizen who never drank.*
▶ take alcohol, indulge, (*more informal*) tipple, (*more informal*) booze

drip NOUN
1 *You could hear the drips from the blocked gutters.*
▶ drop, dribble, splash, plop, trickle
2 (*informal*) *He thought he must have seemed a complete drip.*
▶ weakling, idiot, (*informal*) ninny, (*informal*) wimp, (*informal*) weed, (*informal*) wally

drip VERB
Water was dripping on the floor.
▶ drop, plop, splash, dribble, leak, drizzle, fall in drips, sprinkle, trickle

drive NOUN
1 *a short drive into town*
▶ trip, run, ride, excursion, journey, outing, jaunt
2 *a young woman with plenty of drive*
▶ motivation, ambition, initiative, enterprise, determination, enthusiasm, energy, keenness, persistence, zeal, (*more informal*) push
3 *a drive to recruit blood donors*
▶ campaign, crusade, effort, appeal

drive VERB
1 *I'll drive them to the station.*
▶ take, transport, ferry, carry

2 *Can you drive a tractor?*
▶ operate, control, manage, handle
3 *She drives everywhere.*
▶ go by car, travel by car, (*old-fashioned*) motor
4 *Most teachers drove their students very hard.*
▶ work, push, urge, direct
5 *Poverty drove them to crime.*
▶ force, compel, urge, push
6 *He drove a nail into the wall.*
▶ hammer, bang, ram
7 **drive at** *What was he driving at?*
▶ imply, suggest, intimate, insinuate, allude to, refer to, hint at, (*more informal*) get at

droop VERB
The flowers began to droop.
▶ wither, wilt, flop, sag, slump, go limp, hang, bend, dangle, fall

drop NOUN
1 *a drop of water*
▶ droplet, drip, globule, bead, bubble
2 *It needs a drop of glue.*
▶ dash, spot, dab, trace, pinch, small amount
3 *a drop of 100 metres*
▶ descent, fall, dive, plunge
4 *She walked to the edge of the cliff and peered at the drop below her.*
▶ precipice, chasm, gorge, abyss, slope
5 *a drop in prices*
▶ reduction, decrease, cut, falling off, downturn, slump
AN OPPOSITE IS rise

drop VERB
1 *A maid had dropped a tray in the hallway.*
▶ let fall, let go of
2 *They all dropped to their knees.*
▶ sink, fall, go down
3 *The union decided to drop some of its claims.*
▶ abandon, give up, relinquish, discontinue
4 *She dropped many of her friends after leaving university.*
▶ desert, abandon, renounce, give up, disown, reject, discard
5 *Many outlets have dropped their prices.*
▶ reduce, lower, cut
6 *He was dropped from the team.*
▶ exclude, leave out (of), discard, expel
7 *The aeroplane dropped a thousand feet.*
▶ descend, fall, plunge, plummet, dive, nosedive, sink

drown VERB
1 *He fell into the water and nearly drowned.*
▶ submerge, sink, go under
2 *Noises from the street drowned our conversation.*
▶ overwhelm, overpower, drown out, engulf, make inaudible, silence

drowsy ADJECTIVE
We became drowsy in the heat.
▶ sleepy, dozy, lethargic, somnolent, (*more informal*) snoozy

drudge NOUN

Sometimes he felt he was no more than a drudge.
▶ menial, servant, hack, (*more informal*) dogsbody, (*more informal*) lackey

drudgery NOUN

She disliked drudgery and tried to make the work interesting.
▶ hard work, hard labour, tedium, (*more informal*) donkey work

drug NOUN

1 *Her doctor prescribed a new drug.*
▶ medicine, medication, medicament, remedy, potion
2 *under the influence of drugs*
▶ narcotic, hallucinogen, stimulant, (*more informal*) dope, (*more informal*) junk

drug VERB

The victim seems to have been drugged before being driven off.
▶ anaesthetize, knock out, stupefy, (*more informal*) dope

drum NOUN

a drum of oil
▶ barrel, canister, cask, butt, keg, tub, tun

drunk ADJECTIVE

The men got drunk and waved bottles around.
▶ intoxicated, inebriated, tipsy, drunken, under the influence, (*more informal*) plastered, (*more informal*) tight, (*more informal*) sloshed

dry ADJECTIVE

1 *Ahead lay miles of dry desert.*
▶ arid, parched, barren, waterless, desiccated, scorched, torrid
2 *a dry story*
▶ dull, tedious, boring, dreary, monotonous
3 *dry humour*
▶ droll, ironic, wry, sardonic, subtle

dry VERB

It wasn't easy drying clothes in such a wet climate.
▶ get dry, make dry

dual ADJECTIVE

The tool has a dual purpose.
▶ double, twofold, twin, combined

dubious ADJECTIVE

1 *I was dubious about the idea.*
▶ doubtful, hesitant, uncertain, unsure, undecided, irresolute, ambivalent, wavering, tentative, sceptical, in two minds
OPPOSITES ARE confident, assured
2 *a dubious excuse*
▶ suspect, suspicious, untrustworthy, unreliable, (*more informal*) fishy, (*more informal*) shady

duck VERB

1 *The boys ducked behind a bush.*
▶ crouch, stoop, bob down
2 *I ducked to avoid an overhanging branch*
▶ dodge, sidestep, bend, swerve, bob down

3 *They ducked him in the river.*
▶ dip, immerse, plunge, submerge, lower

dud ADJECTIVE

The light bulb was dud.
▶ faulty, defective, useless

dud NOUN

Some of the fireworks were duds.
▶ failure, flop, disappointment

due ADJECTIVE

1 *Your subscription is due this week.*
▶ owing, owed, payable, outstanding
2 *She drove with due care.*
▶ proper, rightful, fitting, appropriate, necessary, suitable, adequate
3 *the respect due to an eminent statesman*
▶ deserved (by), merited (by), earned (by), fitting, appropriate, suitable (for)

due to

1 *Death was due to a heart attack.*
▶ caused by, the result of, attributable to
2 *The game was cancelled due to bad weather.*
▶ owing to, because of, on account of, as a consequence of, as a result of, in view of, thanks to

due NOUN

We must give them their due.
▶ deserts, entitlement, rightful treatment, rights, merits, reward

duel NOUN

The Count was killed in a duel.
▶ single combat, fight, encounter, affair of honour

dull ADJECTIVE

1 *dull colours*
▶ drab, dreary, sombre, dark, lacklustre
AN OPPOSITE IS bright
2 *a dull winter morning*
▶ gloomy, overcast, dark, dim, dismal, bleak, murky, sunless
OPPOSITES ARE sunny, bright
3 *The report makes dull reading.*
▶ boring, tedious, uninteresting, unexciting, monotonous, tiresome, insipid
OPPOSITES ARE interesting, exciting
4 *a dull pupil*
▶ stupid, slow, unintelligent, dim, slow-witted, dense
OPPOSITES ARE clever, bright

dumb ADJECTIVE

1 *He kept dumb while the others argued.*
▶ mute, silent, speechless, tongue-tied, unable to speak
2 *He's not as dumb as he makes out.*
▶ stupid, unintelligent, foolish, slow-witted, dull, dim

dumbfounded ADJECTIVE

I gazed back at him, dumbfounded.
▶ astonished, astounded, amazed, surprised, staggered, startled, nonplussed, disconcerted,

speechless, shocked, flabbergasted, perplexed, stunned, stupefied, bewildered, (*more informal*) thunderstruck

dummy NOUN
1 *The gun was only a dummy.*
▶ imitation, fake, sham, substitute, toy, copy, model, counterfeit
2 *a ventriloquist's dummy*
▶ doll, puppet, manikin, figure

dummy ADJECTIVE
a dummy attack
▶ simulated, pretended, trial, mock, practice, bogus, (*more informal*) pretend

dump NOUN
1 *We've a lot to take to the dump.*
▶ tip, refuse dump, rubbish heap, junk yard
2 *an ammunition dump*
▶ cache, depot, hoard, store

dump VERB
1 *Worn-out cars had been dumped at the side of the road.*
▶ dispose of, discard, get rid of, jettison, reject, scrap, (*more informal*) ditch
2 (*informal*) *She dumped her shopping by the door.*
▶ put down, set down, throw down, deposit, drop, tip, place, unload, (*more informal*) park

duplicate ADJECTIVE
The manager opened his room with a duplicate key.
▶ matching, identical, twin, second, alternative, copied, corresponding

duplicate NOUN
The document in the file is a duplicate.
▶ copy, facsimile, photocopy, carbon copy, reproduction, replica

duplicate VERB
The documents have been duplicated.
▶ copy, photocopy, print, reproduce

durable ADJECTIVE
1 *a coat made of durable material*
▶ hard-wearing, tough, strong, sturdy, stout, substantial
2 *a durable peace settlement*
▶ lasting, enduring, abiding, stable, secure

duress NOUN
The statement was obtained by duress.
▶ force, coercion, intimidation, constraint, pressure, threats

dusk NOUN
It was only four o'clock and already dusk.
▶ twilight, evening, sundown, sunset, gloaming, gloom
AN OPPOSITE IS dawn

dust NOUN
The surfaces were covered in dust.
▶ dirt, grime, grit, filth, smut, particles, powder

dusty ADJECTIVE
1 *The tables were dusty.*
▶ dirty, filthy, grubby
2 *a light dusty substance*
▶ powdery, chalky, crumbly, granular, sandy

dutiful ADJECTIVE
His dutiful parents were there waiting for him.
▶ devoted, conscientious, responsible, dedicated, faithful, attentive, scrupulous, obedient
OPPOSITES ARE irresponsible, remiss

duty NOUN
1 *He felt a strong sense of duty.*
▶ responsibility, loyalty, obligation, allegiance, faithfulness, obedience, service
2 *One of his duties was to make the afternoon tea.*
▶ job, role, task, assignment, function, (*more informal*) chore
3 *an increased duty on cigarettes*
▶ tax, levy, tariff, excise, toll, dues

dwarf ADJECTIVE
a dwarf cactus
▶ miniature, small, little, undersized, diminutive

dwarf NOUN
The little dwarf sat on the floor, directing operations.
▶ person of restricted growth, midget, pygmy
USAGE *Person of restricted growth* is the least offensive of these terms.

dwarf VERB
The tower blocks dwarf the old cathedral.
▶ dominate, tower over, overshadow

dwell VERB
dwell in *Hermits used to dwell in these caves.*
▶ inhabit, live in, populate, lodge in, (*more formal*) reside in

---

dwelling NOUN
Several dwellings have disappeared from the village.
▶ house, residence, home

TYPES OF DWELLING

town and city houses: house, bungalow (on one floor), mansion (large and grand), town house (usually in a terrace), detached house (completely separate), semi-detached house (or semi, joined to another house on one side), terraced house (joined to other houses on both sides).

houses in the country: country house (large), grange (large country house with farm buildings), manor (large house with a lot of land), villa (usually in the country with its own grounds), farmhouse, cottage (small), dacha (Russian-style house in the country).

special houses: palace (for royalty and heads of state), parsonage (for clergy), rectory (for clergy), vicarage (for clergy). ▶▶

a b c **d** e f g h i j k l m n o p q r s t u v w x y z

small houses: hut, cabin, chalet, hovel (small and unpleasant), lodge (small house on a country estate, often at the entrance), mud hut, prefab (small temporary house), shack, igloo, caravan, tent, tepee.

homes in parts of buildings: flat, apartment, flatlet (small flat), penthouse (large apartment at the top of a building), maisonette (second floor flat with front door on ground level), studio flat (having one large main room), bed-sitting room (or bedsit, in one room).

buildings for a short stay: hotel, guest house, hostel, motel; gîte (holiday house in France).

dwindle VERB
After the war the population dwindled.
▶ decrease, decline, diminish, shrink, contract, peter out, wane, fall off, die out

dye NOUN
a yellow dye
▶ colouring, colourant, pigment, stain, tint, tinge

dye VERB
She dyed the curtains to match the new paint.
▶ colour, tint, stain, pigment, colour-wash

dynamic ADJECTIVE
The country needs dynamic leadership.
▶ energetic, vigorous, forceful, spirited, positive, effective, bold, vital, active

dynasty NOUN
The ruling dynasty went back to medieval times.
▶ family, house, line, bloodline, succession, regime

Ee

eager ADJECTIVE
1 *It was good to see smiling, eager faces.*
▶ keen, enthusiastic, avid, fervent, zealous
OPPOSITES ARE apathetic, unenthusiastic
2 *They were eager to find a seat near the front.*
▶ keen, anxious, determined
3 *The young ones are eager for more adventure.*
▶ longing, yearning, intent (on)

eagerness NOUN
Her eyes shone with eagerness.
▶ enthusiasm, keenness, fervour, ardour, earnestness, excitement, intentness, longing, passion
OPPOSITES ARE apathy, indifference

ear NOUN
He had the ear of the President.
▶ attention, heed, notice, consideration, regard
RELATED ADJECTIVE aural

early ADJECTIVE
1 *early symptoms of the disease*
▶ initial, first, advance, preliminary, forward
AN OPPOSITE IS late
2 *early civilizations*
▶ ancient, primitive, prehistoric
USAGE Note that *prehistoric* means 'before the time of written records'. *Primitive* means 'early in history', but can also mean 'not advanced, simple', and so it is not always a good choice for the meaning shown here. .

earn VERB
1 *She earns a six-figure salary.*
▶ receive, be paid, make, (*more informal*) bring in, (*more informal*) take home
2 *They have all earned our gratitude.*
▶ deserve, merit, warrant, justify, be worthy of, gain, secure, obtain
OPPOSITES ARE lose, forfeit

earnest ADJECTIVE
1 *an earnest attempt to help*
▶ committed, determined, resolute, conscientious, devoted, diligent, purposeful, eager, industrious, involved
OPPOSITES ARE casual, flippant
2 *He was an earnest, church-going man.*
▶ serious, serious-minded, thoughtful, solemn, grave, sober, staid, humourless
OPPOSITES ARE casual, half-hearted

earnings NOUN
He looked for ways to supplement his earnings.
▶ income, pay, salary, wages, remuneration

earth NOUN
1 *life on earth*
▶ this world, the planet, the globe
RELATED ADJECTIVE terrestrial
2 *The fork turned the soft earth.*
▶ soil, topsoil, loam, clay, sod, ground, humus, land

earthly ADJECTIVE
USAGE Do not confuse this word with *earthy*.
our earthly environment
▶ terrestrial, material, physical, mundane, human, materialistic, secular, temporal
AN OPPOSITE IS spiritual

earthquake NOUN
The town had been damaged by earthquakes.
▶ tremor, convulsion, shock, (*more informal*) quake, upheaval
RELATED ADJECTIVE seismic

earthy ADJECTIVE
USAGE Do not confuse this word with *earthly*.
an earthy sense of humour
▶ rude, crude, coarse, vulgar, bawdy, indelicate, racy, smutty

ease NOUN
1 *Most people can recognize road symbols with ease.*
▶ effortlessness, straightforwardness, no trouble, no problem, facility, simplicity
AN OPPOSITE IS difficulty

2 *Notice the ease with which he completed the task.*
▶ skill, dexterity, facility, naturalness, deftness, mastery, cleverness

3 *a life of ease*
▶ affluence, comfort, contentment, enjoyment, relaxation, luxury, leisure, wealth, prosperity
AN OPPOSITE IS stress

ease VERB

1 *The medicine will ease the pain.*
▶ relieve, alleviate, mitigate, soothe, assuage, allay, lessen, deaden, dull, calm, lighten, moderate, quell, comfort
OPPOSITES ARE aggravate, worsen

2 *measures taken to ease the tension*
▶ reduce, relax, decrease, slacken, take off
AN OPPOSITE IS increase

3 *He eased the stopper out of the bottle.*
▶ guide, slide, slip, edge, inch, manœuvre, move gradually

ease off *The rain eased off*
▶ abate, subside, let up, slacken off, die out, lessen

easily ADVERB

1 *She is easily the brightest student of her year.*
▶ by far, without doubt, undoubtedly, indubitably, indisputably, undeniably, definitely, certainly, patently

2 *In the end I managed the work easily.*
▶ effortlessly, comfortably, with ease, simply, straightforwardly, with no difficulty

easy ADJECTIVE

1 *an easy task*
▶ straightforward, undemanding, effortless, light, pleasant, painless, (*more informal*) cushy
OPPOSITES ARE difficult, heavy

2 *easy instructions to follow*
▶ simple, straightforward, elementary, clear, uncomplicated, understandable, plain, user-friendly, foolproof, manageable
OPPOSITES ARE complicated, difficult

3 *an easy manner*
▶ relaxed, easy-going, affable, natural, friendly, tolerant, informal, open, docile, amenable, accommodating, undemanding, (*more informal*) laid-back
OPPOSITES ARE difficult, intolerant

4 *I long for an easy life.*
▶ comfortable, carefree, untroubled, leisurely, peaceful, restful, serene, relaxed, contented, cosy, tranquil
AN OPPOSITE IS stressful

easy-going ADJECTIVE

Despite his easy-going nature he was extraordinarily energetic.
▶ relaxed, easy, affable, natural, friendly, tolerant, informal, open, docile, amenable, accommodating, undemanding, (*more informal*) laid-back

eat VERB This word is often overused. Here are some alternatives:
1 *The condemned man ate a hearty breakfast.*
▶ consume, devour, swallow, (*more informal*) put away, (*more informal*) tuck into, (*more informal*) scoff, (*more informal*) polish off, (*more informal*) get stuck into
RELATED ADJECTIVE edible
2 *Where shall we eat tonight?*
▶ have a meal, have dinner, dine, (*more informal*) feed
3 eat into *Rust was eating into the bodywork.*
▶ corrode, erode, wear away, wear through, rot, decay

eatable ADJECTIVE

The food is a little overcooked, but still eatable.
▶ palatable, wholesome, edible, fit to eat, safe to eat, digestible
OPPOSITES ARE uneatable, inedible
USAGE Note that *edible* does not mean quite the same as *eatable*. You say that something is *edible* when you mean it is suitable as food and is not (for example) poisonous, whereas you use *eatable* about food that is good enough to eat and not (for example) burnt or undercooked.

eavesdrop VERB

eavesdrop on *He tried as hard as he could to eavesdrop on the conversation in the next room.*
▶ listen in on, overhear, monitor, spy on, snoop on, intrude on

ebb VERB

1 *The tide ebbed late in the morning.*
▶ go out, recede, fall back, flow back, retreat
AN OPPOSITE IS come in
2 *Her strength was beginning to ebb.*
▶ dwindle, decline, fade, wane, diminish, disappear, vanish, weaken
OPPOSITES ARE increase, revive

eccentric ADJECTIVE

His eccentric behaviour was worrying.
▶ unconventional, abnormal, irregular, odd, strange, peculiar, weird, bizarre, extraordinary, idiosyncratic, capricious, quirky, erratic
OPPOSITES ARE ordinary, conventional

eccentric NOUN

She too had a reputation as an eccentric.
▶ individualist, nonconformist, oddity, (*more informal*) oddball, (*more informal*) weirdo, (*more informal*) crackpot

echo NOUN

The mountains are full of strange echoes.
▶ reverberation, reiteration, reflection of sound

echo VERB

1 *The slightest sound echoes across the hall. The words echoed in Isabel's head.*
▶ reverberate, resound, ring, resonate

2 *These thoughts were echoed by another speaker.*
▶ repeat, reiterate, reproduce, say again, ape, copy, imitate, mimic

eclipse VERB

1 *The sun is eclipsed by the moon.*
▶ blot out, block out, obscure, veil, cloud, cover, shade, darken, extinguish

2 *This achievement eclipsed all previous attempts.*
▶ overshadow, outshine, surpass, excel, outdo, put into the shade, dim

eclipse NOUN

1 *a lunar eclipse on 6 August*
▶ darkening, obscuration, blotting out, shading

2 *the eclipse of the ancient empires*
▶ decline, fall, deterioration, degeneration, sinking

economic ADJECTIVE

USAGE The main meanings of *economic* are 'to do with economics or use of money' (the first meaning below) and 'providing good value or profit' (the second meaning below). If you mean 'careful in using money' you should use *economical* or its synonyms.

1 *an outline of the government's economic policies*
▶ financial, monetary, commercial, fiscal, budgetary, business, money-making, trading

2 *The railway line was closed because it was no longer economic.*
▶ profitable, lucrative, fruitful, productive

economical ADJECTIVE

USAGE See the note at the entry for *economic*.

1 *It may be more economical to use an alternative form of fuel.*
▶ inexpensive, cost-effective, reasonable
OPPOSITES ARE wasteful, extravagant

2 *She is very economical with what money she has.*
▶ thrifty, careful, prudent, provident, sensible, canny
AN OPPOSITE IS expensive

economize VERB

One way of economizing is to grow your own vegetables.
▶ save, save money, cut back, cut costs, cut expenditure, spend less, (*more informal*) tighten your belt
AN OPPOSITE IS be extravagant

economy NOUN

1 *You can enjoy life and still exercise economy.*
▶ thrift, frugality, prudence, parsimony, providence
AN OPPOSITE IS wastefulness

2 *To avoid debt we had to make some economies.*
▶ saving, cut

3 *the country's economy*
▶ financial system, wealth, budget

ecstasy NOUN

He ran out in ecstasy, doing cartwheels across the grass.
▶ rapture, bliss, joy, delight , elation, euphoria, exultation

ecstatic ADJECTIVE

They were ecstatic as they returned with the good news.
▶ elated, rapturous, exultant, delighted, euphoric, enraptured, joyful, overjoyed, blissful, delirious, gleeful, happy, (*more informal*) over the moon, (*more informal*) on top of the world

eddy NOUN

There were small eddies near the river bank.
▶ swirl, whirl, whirlpool, vortex

eddy VERB

The water eddied around the rocks.
▶ swirl, whirl, seethe

edge NOUN

1 *We sat by the edge of the lake.*
▶ border, bank, fringe, extremity, verge, perimeter

2 *They now have the edge over their competitors.*
▶ advantage, upper hand, superiority

3 *Her excitement gave an edge to her voice.*
▶ sharpness, pointedness, pungency, asperity, bite

edge VERB

1 *a dress edged with lace*
▶ trim, decorate, finish, fringe, border

2 *She edged closer to the table.*
▶ creep, inch, slink, steal, sidle, move stealthily

edgy ADJECTIVE

The thought of what was coming made her edgy.
▶ tense, nervous, anxious, on edge, apprehensive, uneasy, ill at ease, twitchy, nervy

edible ADJECTIVE

USAGE See the note at the entry for *eatable*.
The decorations on the tree were all edible.
▶ fit to eat, safe to eat, eatable, wholesome
AN OPPOSITE IS inedible

edict NOUN

a royal edict
▶ decree, order, command, mandate, proclamation, dictum, enactment

edifice NOUN

a huge edifice outlined against the sky
▶ building, structure, construction, erection, development, property

edit VERB

1 *She mentioned that she had edited the school magazine.*
▶ direct, manage, be the editor of, be in charge of, supervise

2 *You need to edit the text to make it clearer.*
▶ revise, improve, adapt, modify, rework

edition NOUN

1 *the Christmas edition of the magazine*
▶ issue, number

2 *a first edition of a book*
▶ printing, publication, impression, version

educate VERB

They hired a tutor to educate the children at home.
▶ teach, tutor, instruct, coach, train, drill, cultivate, school

educated ADJECTIVE

an educated woman named Fiona
▶ learned, knowledgeable, cultivated, cultured, well-read, informed, refined, enlightened, civilized, erudite, literate, numerate, sophisticated
AN OPPOSITE IS uneducated

education NOUN

He had received a first-class education.
▶ schooling, training, teaching, instruction, tuition, coaching, curriculum, enlightenment, guidance

eerie ADJECTIVE

an eerie silence
▶ weird, strange, uncanny, sinister, frightening, (*more informal*) spooky, (*more informal*) creepy, (*more informal*) scary

effect NOUN

1 *The effect of all these announcements was to confuse everyone.*
▶ result, consequence, upshot, outcome, conclusion
2 *Sandy and I were feeling the effect of our long day.*
▶ consequence, repercussion, result, influence, aftermath
3 *The violence of those years had a profound effect on people.*
▶ impression, impact
4 *The drug was losing its effect.*
▶ effectiveness, efficacy, power, potency
in effect *He was now in effect a figurehead with little real power.*
▶ in fact, effectively, really, actually, in truth, to all intents and purposes
take effect *The change takes effect next April.*
▶ come into force, be effective, become operative, become valid, be implemented
AN OPPOSITE IS lapse

effect VERB

USAGE Do not confuse this word, which means 'to achieve or bring about', with *affect*, which means 'to cause a change in'.
We need to effect a compromise.
▶ achieve, accomplish, bring about, carry out, initiate, make, put into effect, cause, create, execute, implement

effective ADJECTIVE

1 *There is no effective alternative.*
▶ useful, workable, successful, fruitful, productive, worthwhile, potent, powerful, effectual, efficient, real, strong, (*more formal*) efficacious
AN OPPOSITE IS ineffective
2 *The government still lacks an effective opposition.*
▶ capable, competent, able, proficient, useful
3 *He produced several effective arguments.*
▶ convincing, cogent, persuasive, compelling, telling, striking, meaningful
OPPOSITES ARE weak, unconvincing
4 *The changes will be effective from midnight.*
▶ operative, in force, valid
OPPOSITES ARE inoperative, invalid

effeminate ADJECTIVE

His speech and manner were somewhat effeminate.
▶ womanish, girlish, effete, unmanly, camp, (*more informal, disapproving*) pansy, (*more informal, disapproving*) sissy
AN OPPOSITE IS manly

effervescent ADJECTIVE

effervescent drinks
▶ sparkling, carbonated, fizzy, bubbling, bubbly, foaming

efficiency NOUN

1 *These measures can increase the efficiency of the business.*
▶ productivity, cost-effectiveness
2 *She was praised for her efficiency.*
▶ competence, proficiency, ability, capability, good organization, expertise

efficient ADJECTIVE

1 *The housekeeping was extremely efficient.*
▶ methodical, systematic, well-organized, cost-effective
AN OPPOSITE IS inefficient
2 *She was lucky to have found such an efficient young assistant.*
▶ capable, competent, proficient, able, well-organized, businesslike

effort NOUN

1 *We will make an effort to complete the task in time.*
▶ attempt, endeavour, try, (*more informal*) shot, (*more informal*) stab
2 *It took considerable effort to get the boiler working again.*
▶ exertion, energy, trouble, force, application, pains
3 *It was a tremendous team effort.*
▶ achievement, accomplishment, performance, feat, undertaking, success

effortless ADJECTIVE

She showed the effortless fluency of an experienced speaker.
▶ easy, simple, undemanding, painless, trouble-free, smooth

effrontery NOUN

(*usually disapproving*) *He had the effrontery to offer his story to the papers.*
▶ cheek, audacity, nerve, boldness, temerity, impudence, impertinence, insolence, presumptuousness, shamelessness, (*more informal*) sauce

effusive ADJECTIVE

He spoke with effusive politeness.
▶ unrestrained, extravagant, fulsome, lavish, demonstrative

egg VERB

egg on *One of the group was egging the others on.*
▶ urge, goad, drive, provoke, incite, encourage

egotistic, egotistical ADJECTIVE

an egotistic attitude to life
▶ self-centred, egocentric, egomaniacal, conceited, self-interested, self-absorbed

ejaculate VERB

'No!' he ejaculated, startled.
▶ exclaim, shout, yell, cry out, call out, scream

eject VERB

1 *Two heavy bouncers arrived to eject him from the club.*
▶ expel, throw out, evict, remove, dismiss, (*more informal*) kick out

2 *A tall chimney was ejecting black smoke.*
▶ emit, discharge, send out, pour out, spew out, give off, belch, disgorge

elaborate ADJECTIVE

1 *elaborate schemes to raise money*
▶ complicated, complex, intricate, detailed, extensive, well worked out, involved
AN OPPOSITE IS simple

2 *elaborate wood carvings*
▶ ornate, decorative, ornamental, intricate, fancy, baroque, rococo, showy
OPPOSITES ARE simple, plain

elaborate VERB

elaborate on *He would not elaborate on his news until he had washed.*
▶ expand on, enlarge on, add to, give details of, amplify, develop, supplement, expatiate on, fill out
AN OPPOSITE IS simplify

elapse VERB

Several years elapsed before we returned to the house in Corfu.
▶ pass, go by, slip by, lapse

elastic ADJECTIVE

1 *An elastic cord is tied to an ankle.*
▶ flexible, plastic, pliable, pliant, rubbery, bendy, ductile, yielding, (*more informal*) bouncy, (*more informal*) springy, (*more informal*) stretchy
AN OPPOSITE IS rigid

2 *The arrangements can be made more elastic if you wish.*
▶ flexible, adaptable, adjustable, variable, accommodating
OPPOSITES ARE rigid, fixed

elated ADJECTIVE

Her huge win left her feeling elated.
▶ thrilled, exhilarated, ecstatic, exultant, delighted, euphoric, overjoyed, (*more informal*) over the moon, (*more informal*) on top of the world

elbow VERB

She tried to elbow him out of her way.
▶ push, force, shoulder, muscle

elderly ADJECTIVE

the increase in the number of elderly people
▶ aged, ageing, old, senile

elect VERB

The Party elects a leader every four years.
▶ choose, select, vote for, pick, adopt, appoint, decide on, name, nominate

election NOUN

1 *the election of a president*
▶ selection, choosing, ballot (for), poll (for), vote (for)

2 *She became an MP in the 1997 election.*
▶ poll, vote, ballot
RELATED NOUN psephology

electric ADJECTIVE

The atmosphere in the room was electric.
▶ electrifying, exciting, dramatic, thrilling, tense, charged

electrifying ADJECTIVE

an electrifying performance
▶ thrilling, exciting, astounding, hair-raising, stimulating, amazing, astonishing, electric

elegant ADJECTIVE

1 *Fire destroyed an elegant building in the Old Town.*
▶ handsome, stylish, graceful, gracious, smart, tasteful
AN OPPOSITE IS inelegant

2 *A tall elegant woman walked in.*
▶ graceful, fashionable, beautiful, chic, smart

3 *an elegant solution to an awkward problem*
▶ neat, ingenious, clever, deft, effective

element NOUN

1 *That is only one element of the situation.*
▶ component, factor, part, ingredient, constituent, piece, strand, aspect

2 *There is an element of truth in the story.*
▶ trace, hint, touch, suspicion, smattering, soupçon

3 *James was in his element messing about with old cars.*
▶ environment, domain, habitat, sphere

the elements *We could brave the elements in our cagoules.*
▶ the weather, the wind and rain

elementary ADJECTIVE

1 *an elementary maths course*
▶ basic, rudimentary, fundamental, introductory, primary
AN OPPOSITE IS advanced

2 *The answer to the question is elementary.*
▶ simple, easy, straightforward, uncomplicated

elevated ADJECTIVE

1 *an elevated roadway*
▶ raised, overhead, high

2 *elevated discussions*
▶ grand, dignified, noble, superior, exalted, lofty

elicit VERB

The police were unable to elicit any more information.
▶ obtain, extract, bring out, draw out, derive, evoke

eligible ADJECTIVE
be eligible for *You would be eligible for tax relief on donations.*
▶ be entitled to, qualify for, be allowed, be permitted
AN OPPOSITE IS ineligible

eliminate VERB
1 *We can eliminate sabotage as a cause of the accident.*
▶ exclude, discount, disregard, remove
2 *The junta went on to eliminate many of their opponents.*
▶ get rid of, do away with, eradicate, exterminate, kill, murder, stamp out

elite NOUN
1 *Higher wages are earned by an elite of urban craftsmen.*
▶ the best, the cream, the flower
2 *the social elite*
▶ aristocracy, nobility, gentry, establishment

elocution NOUN
lessons in elocution
▶ diction, pronunciation, articulation, delivery

eloquence NOUN
She spoke with great eloquence.
▶ expressiveness, fluency, articulacy, sensitivity

eloquent ADJECTIVE
After dinner he made an eloquent speech.
▶ expressive, articulate, fluent, moving, stirring, forceful, potent, persuasive, powerful, unfaltering
AN OPPOSITE IS inarticulate

elude VERB
For many years they managed to elude justice.
▶ escape, avoid, evade, circumvent, dodge, shake off, foil, get away from

elusive ADJECTIVE
1 *Despite his phone calls she continued to be elusive for several days.*
▶ evasive, hard to find, difficult to track down, shifty
2 *The play's meaning is elusive*
▶ obscure, subtle, indefinable, intangible, ambiguous, difficult

emaciated ADJECTIVE
Her hair had turned grey and she grew pale and emaciated.
▶ thin, skeletal, bony, haggard, wasted, attenuated

emanate VERB
The leak emanated from a government department.
▶ originate, stem, arise, proceed, spring, derive, emerge, issue

embargo NOUN
There is an embargo on weapon supplies to the area.
▶ ban, bar, prohibition, moratorium, proscription, restriction

embark VERB
1 *Passengers may embark from eight o'clock this evening.*
▶ board, go aboard, go on board
OPPOSITES ARE disembark, land

2 **embark on** *He was ready to embark on a career in medicine.*
▶ begin, start, enter on, commence, undertake, take up, set about

embarrass VERB
He gazed at her until he realized he was embarrassing her.
▶ make (someone) uncomfortable, make (someone) feel embarrassed, disconcert, distress, upset, shame, mortify, fluster, nonplus, humiliate

embarrassed ADJECTIVE
Geoff's outspoken remarks left him feeling embarrassed.
▶ awkward, self-conscious, disconcerted, uncomfortable, abashed, mortified, ashamed, confused, distressed, flustered, nonplussed, humiliated, shamed, upset, (*more informal*) red in the face

embarrassing ADJECTIVE
She was afraid of making an embarrassing mistake.
▶ awkward, humiliating, shaming, shameful, disconcerting, distressing, mortifying, upsetting

embarrassment NOUN
Jane tried to hide her embarrassment.
▶ awkwardness, self-consciousness, discomfort, unease, mortification, humiliation, distress

embassy NOUN
the American embassy
▶ consulate, legation, mission

embezzle VERB
He admitted embezzling thousands of pounds from the company.
▶ steal, misappropriate, pilfer, take fraudulently, appropriate

embezzlement NOUN
They were found guilty of embezzlement.
▶ fraud, theft, stealing, misappropriation, appropriation

embittered ADJECTIVE
He was left tired and embittered by the experience.
▶ bitter, disillusioned, disaffected, resentful, envious, sour

emblem NOUN
America's national emblem, the bald eagle
▶ symbol, sign, token, mark, insignia, badge, crest, device, image, regalia, seal

embody VERB
1 *a spiritual fellowship embodying everything that is true and good*
▶ embrace, include, incorporate, contain, assimilate, take in
2 *They embody everything associated with the culture of the sixties.*
▶ personify, represent, exemplify, symbolize, epitomize, encapsulate, stand for

embrace VERB
1 *The old man got up and embraced his son.*
▶ hug, clasp, hold, cuddle, grasp, squeeze

2 *Imelda could not embrace the idea of life without a husband.*
▶ accept, espouse, welcome, take on, receive
3 *The county embraces the best part of two national parks.*
▶ comprise, embody, include, incorporate, bring together, contain, assimilate, take in

embryonic ADJECTIVE
An urban community existed there in embryonic form.
▶ rudimentary, undeveloped, unformed, early, immature, incipient, incomplete

emend VERB
The text was published in an emended version.
▶ alter, edit, modify, correct, revise, rewrite

emerge VERB
1 *A cyclist emerged from the entrance.*
▶ come out, appear, come into view, issue, emanate
AN OPPOSITE IS disappear
2 *Another version of the story later emerged.*
▶ become known, become evident, be revealed, come to light, surface, unfold, (*more informal*) crop up

emergency NOUN
She offered a helping hand in an emergency.
▶ crisis, danger, difficulty, predicament, urgent situation, extremity, (*more informal*) tight spot

eminent ADJECTIVE
an eminent scientist and scholar
▶ distinguished, famous, prominent, well known, celebrated, acclaimed, renowned, illustrious, famed, notable, noteworthy, esteemed, respected, honoured, outstanding

emission NOUN
carbon dioxide emissions
▶ discharge, release, issue, outpouring, emanation

emit VERB
Vehicle exhausts emit hydrocarbons.
▶ discharge, release, give off, give out, pour out, radiate

emotion NOUN
He spoke with a voice full of emotion.
▶ feeling, passion, sentiment, intensity, warmth, agitation, excitement, fervour
AN OPPOSITE IS indifference

emotional ADJECTIVE
1 *an emotional tribute*
▶ poignant, passionate, impassioned, intense, moving, touching, warm-hearted
2 *an emotional woman*
▶ passionate, demonstrative, fervent, sensitive, temperamental, excitable, romantic

emotive ADJECTIVE
Hunting is an emotive issue.
▶ sensitive, inflammatory, controversial, contentious, delicate

emphasis NOUN
This year there is a special emphasis given to creative writing.
▶ importance, significance, prominence, priority, urgency, weight, stress, attention

emphasize VERB
The spokesman emphasized the need to remain calm.
▶ stress, underline, focus on, highlight, point up, draw attention to, play up, make a point of
OPPOSITES ARE understate, play down

emphatic ADJECTIVE
an emphatic refusal
▶ absolute, firm, forceful, vehement, vigorous, definite, unequivocal, direct, positive, energetic, out-and-out

empire NOUN
the Babylonian Empire
▶ kingdom, realm, domain, dominion, territory
RELATED ADJECTIVE imperial

employ VERB
1 *The business employs over a hundred people.*
▶ engage, hire, pay, take on, retain, use the services of, give work to, have on the payroll
2 *This medical practice employs the most modern techniques.*
▶ use, utilize, apply

employee NOUN
He was an employee of his own brother's bank.
▶ worker, member of staff, member of the workforce
employees *measures to improve working conditions for the employees*
▶ staff, workforce

employer NOUN
1 *His employer was younger than he was.*
▶ boss, manager, manageress, proprietor, chief executive, head
2 *The Health Service is the country's largest employer.*
▶ business, management, company, organization

employment NOUN
She found employment as a bank clerk.
▶ work, a job, a post, a position, a situation, a livelihood

empower VERB
The edict empowered local governors to arrest suspects.
▶ authorize, entitle, permit, allow, enable, sanction, warrant

empty ADJECTIVE
1 *The house had been empty for years.*
▶ vacant, unoccupied, uninhabited, abandoned, deserted
2 *Without him her life felt empty.*
▶ aimless, futile, worthless, purposeless, unimportant, hollow
3 *These warnings were not just empty threats.*
▶ vain, idle, meaningless, ineffectual

empty VERB

1 *No one had troubled to empty the washing machine.*
► unload, unpack, clear
OPPOSITES ARE fill, load

2 *He emptied the glass for a second time.*
► drain, exhaust, drink up
AN OPPOSITE IS fill

enable VERB

1 *The new law will enable individuals to own shares in these companies.*
► authorize, permit, allow, qualify, empower, equip, aid, assist

2 *Wells took time off work to enable him to train twice a day.*
► allow, permit, let, help, make it possible for, provide the means for
AN OPPOSITE IS prevent

enamoured ADJECTIVE

enamoured of *She was jealous because the prince was clearly enamoured of her sister and not her.*
► in love with, infatuated with, fond of, keen on, taken with, smitten with, captivated by, (*more informal*) crazy about, (*more informal*) nuts about

enchant VERB

The scenery never ceased to enchant me.
► delight, please, captivate, bewitch, charm, entrance, enthral, mesmerize
OPPOSITES ARE repel, disgust

enclose VERB

1 *A tall fence enclosed the garden.*
► surround, circle, encircle, bound, border, skirt, encompass, shut in, fence in, confine, contain

2 *Please enclose payment with your order.*
► include, insert, put in

enclosed ADJECTIVE

an enclosed area
► confined, fenced, walled, shut in, contained, surrounded, encircled, limited, restricted
AN OPPOSITE IS open

enclosure NOUN

1 *Dogs drove the animals into the enclosure.*
► pen, compound, fold, paddock, stockade, corral

2 *an enclosure in an envelope*
► contents, inclusion, insertion

encompass VERB

The talks encompass a wide range of subjects.
► include, embrace, cover, incorporate, comprise, deal with

encounter VERB

1 *One day, they encountered a beautiful blonde on the beach.*
► meet, run into, come across, chance on, (*more informal*) bump into

2 *You may encounter a few problems.*
► experience, be faced with, come up against, suffer, undergo

encounter NOUN

1 *an encounter with a wizard*
► meeting, rendezvous

2 *an encounter with the enemy*
► battle, clash, fight , conflict, confrontation, struggle, collision

encourage VERB

1 *The cries of support encouraged the players.*
► hearten, cheer, inspire, buoy up, uplift, motivate, stimulate, animate, invigorate, spur, rally, reassure

2 *The government is keen to encourage small businesses.*
► support, promote, endorse, stimulate, aid, advance, assist, aid, foster, strengthen

3 *Clever marketing encourages sales.*
► promote, increase, boost, generate, foster, further, be conducive to, be an incentive to, engender, help, induce

4 *Her mother encouraged her to take up medicine.*
► persuade, prompt, urge, invite
AN OPPOSITE IS discourage

encouragement NOUN

All they need is a little encouragement.
► reassurance, support, inspiration, stimulation, cheering up

encouraging ADJECTIVE

The first results were very encouraging.
► reassuring, heartening, promising, favourable, gratifying, hopeful, auspicious, cheering, comforting, optimistic

encroach VERB

encroach on *I did not want to encroach on their privacy.*
► intrude on, trespass on, impinge on, invade, violate, enter on

---

end VERB This word is often overused. Here are some alternatives:
1 *The programme ends at midnight. The bus route ends at this point.*
► finish, conclude, terminate, come to an end, close
OPPOSITES ARE start, begin
2 *He wanted to end his relationship with Greta.*
► break off, stop, halt, discontinue, wind up
OPPOSITES ARE maintain, continue
3 *The government plans to end the benefit next year.*
► abolish, terminate, finish, extinguish, put an end to

---

endanger VERB

She could not be moved any distance without endangering her life.
► risk, jeopardize, imperil, threaten, put at risk, expose to risk
AN OPPOSITE IS protect

endearing ADJECTIVE

She has the endearing habit of kissing you on both cheeks.
▶ charming, appealing, attractive, enchanting, engaging, lovable, winning, disarming
AN OPPOSITE IS unappealing

endeavour VERB

We will endeavour to answer these questions later.
▶ attempt, try, venture, undertake, strive, set out

endeavour NOUN

The company will support them in their endeavour.
▶ attempt, venture, effort, striving

ending NOUN

The story has an exciting ending.
▶ end, conclusion, finish, close, resolution, completion, climax, denouement

endless ADJECTIVE

1 *an endless source of good ideas*
▶ boundless, infinite, unlimited, unbounded
2 *He sipped endless cups of strong coffee.*
▶ ceaseless, countless, innumerable, constant, perpetual, interminable, eternal

endorse VERB

We entirely endorse the conclusions reached.
▶ approve, support, back, uphold, confirm, subscribe to, agree with, condone

endurance NOUN

1 *The race is a test of endurance*
▶ stamina, staying power, fortitude, perseverance, determination, tenacity, resoluteness, resolution, strength, (*more informal*) grit, (*more informal*) bottle
2 *Such suffering is beyond anyone's endurance.*
▶ toleration, tolerance, bearing, sufferance, forbearance

endure VERB

1 *The pain is greater than anyone could endure.*
▶ tolerate, bear, withstand, suffer, cope with, undergo, submit to
2 *Their love will endure for ever.*
▶ last, survive, abide, persist, prevail, continue, remain, stay

enduring ADJECTIVE

an enduring friendship
▶ lasting, persisting, abiding, continuing, durable, steadfast, constant

enemy NOUN

The country faces a new and more dangerous enemy.
▶ foe, adversary, opponent, antagonist, opposition
OPPOSITES ARE friend, ally

energetic ADJECTIVE

1 *an energetic young person*
▶ dynamic, active, lively, spirited, animated, enthusiastic, indefatigable, tireless, unflagging
OPPOSITES ARE inactive, lethargic, lazy
2 *energetic exercises*
▶ strenuous, vigorous, rigorous, arduous, brisk

3 *an energetic sales promotion*
▶ forceful, vigorous, aggressive, determined, powerful
OPPOSITES ARE feeble, half-hearted

energy NOUN

1 *She felt full of energy.*
▶ vitality, vigour, drive, liveliness, spirit, verve, zest, zeal, exuberance, strength, (*more informal*) zip
AN OPPOSITE IS lethargy
2 *new and cleaner sources of energy*
▶ power, fuel

enforce VERB

There was no one left to enforce the laws.
▶ apply, impose, administer, implement, execute, carry out, put into effect

engage VERB

1 **engage in** *She is always eager to engage in conversation.*
▶ participate in, take part in, become involved in, go in for, enter into, share in
2 *They decided to engage a nanny for the younger children.*
▶ employ, hire, recruit, take on, appoint, retain
3 *These activities do not always engage the imagination very well.*
▶ occupy, absorb, engross, attract, interest, capture, captivate, grip
4 *The infantry engaged the enemy early the next day.*
▶ fight, do battle, clash with, encounter, enter into battle with
5 *The lowest gear did not engage properly.*
▶ connect, mesh, interlock

engaged ADJECTIVE

1 *an engaged couple*
▶ betrothed, affianced, attached
2 *He was engaged in his work.*
▶ occupied, busy, engrossed, absorbed, immersed, preoccupied

engagement NOUN

1 *They have broken off their engagement.*
▶ betrothal, promise to marry
2 *He had a business engagement that afternoon.*
▶ appointment, arrangement, commitment, obligation, meeting, date
3 *A series of military engagements followed.*
▶ battle, conflict, encounter, fight, clash, skirmish, offensive

engaging ADJECTIVE

an engaging little girl
▶ charming, attractive, appealing, delightful, lovely, pleasing, likeable, lovable

engender VERB

Modern art engenders a lot of argument.
▶ generate, cause, produce, rouse, provoke, give rise to, be the cause of, result in

engine NOUN

1 *a car engine*
▶ motor, power unit, mechanism

2 *a railway engine*
▶ locomotive

engineer NOUN
the engineer's drawings
▶ designer, planner, inventor, architect

engineer VERB
Near the election the government will engineer an economic boom.
▶ devise, create, bring about, produce, contrive, plan, construct, manage

engineering NOUN
BRANCHES OF ENGINEERING
aerodynamics, aeronautical engineering, agricultural engineering, astronautics, automotive engineering, chemical engineering, civil engineering, electrical engineering, environmental engineering, fluid dynamics, geotechnics, hydraulics, mechanical engineering, mining engineering, naval engineering, nuclear engineering, production engineering, structural engineering.

engrave VERB
The watch is engraved with a dedication on the back.
▶ inscribe, etch, print, mark, cut

engraving NOUN
an engraving of the two younger children
▶ etching, print, impression, woodcut, carving

engrossed ADJECTIVE
Fran was engrossed in her book.
▶ absorbed, immersed, involved, interested, engaged, preoccupied (by), gripped (by), captivated (by), occupied (by), enthralled (by), fascinated (by), riveted (by)

enhance VERB
These successes enhanced his reputation.
▶ improve, further, increase, heighten, reinforce, boost, intensify, strengthen, build up

enigma NOUN
We never did solve the enigma of the missing passenger.
▶ puzzle, mystery, riddle, problem, conundrum, paradox

enigmatic ADJECTIVE
an enigmatic smile
▶ mysterious, puzzling, perplexing, strange, obscure, impenetrable
AN OPPOSITE IS straightforward

enjoy VERB
1 *We all enjoy our outings. She enjoyed playing the piano.*
▶ like, love, appreciate, be fond of, be keen on, be pleased by, take pleasure from or in, delight in, indulge in, rejoice in, relish, revel in, savour
OPPOSITES ARE dislike, hate
2 *Visitors enjoy many privileges.*
▶ benefit from, have the benefit of, have the advantage of, experience, use

3 *enjoy yourself*
▶ have fun, have a good time, celebrate, (*informal*) have a ball, (*informal*) let your hair down

enjoyable ADJECTIVE
You can have a good meal in enjoyable surroundings.
▶ agreeable, pleasant, delightful, gratifying, likeable, satisfying, delicious, pleasurable, rewarding, entertaining, amusing
OPPOSITES ARE unpleasant, disagreeable

enlarge VERB
1 *The new emperor sought to enlarge his territory to the east.*
▶ increase, expand, augment, develop, add to, stretch
2 enlarge on *He didn't want to enlarge on his remarks.*
▶ elaborate on, expand on, amplify, develop, broaden, supplement, flesh out

enlighten VERB
If you really don't know perhaps we should enlighten you.
▶ inform, illuminate, advise, explain to, update, notify

enlightened ADJECTIVE
an enlightened attitude to funding the arts
▶ informed, educated, liberal, sophisticated, knowledgeable, civilized, cultivated, refined, open-minded

enlist VERB
1 *Arafat enlisted thousands of young people in his army.*
▶ recruit, enrol, conscript, engage, muster
2 enlist in *The brothers enlisted in the Royal Engineers.*
▶ enrol in, sign up for, join, enter, join up for, volunteer (for)
3 *In Paris, he enlisted the aid of an influential American physician.*
▶ obtain, secure, procure, engage, win

enliven VERB
A little humour often helps to enliven a dull subject.
▶ liven up, brighten up, make more interesting, animate, enhance, improve

enmity NOUN
people who live in a state of enmity with one another
▶ hostility, antagonism, animosity, strife, opposition (towards), antipathy (towards), acrimony (towards)
AN OPPOSITE IS friendship

enormity NOUN
1 *the enormities of the Nazi years*
▶ atrocity, outrage, horror, crime, abomination, wickedness
2 *the enormity of the task*
▶ immensity, hugeness, magnitude, vastness, seriousness, enormousness

E

USAGE Note that *enormity* is not correct when the reference is simply to physical size, e.g. *the enormity of the building*. It's better to say *the huge size of the building* or use one of the synonyms given above. .

enormous ADJECTIVE

An enormous insect crept across the floor.
▸ huge, gigantic, immense, massive, colossal, (*more informal*) whopping, (*more informal*) ginormous

enough ADJECTIVE

Do you have enough food? £10 will not be enough.
▸ sufficient, adequate, ample, as much (food) as you need

enquire VERB

She enquired about times of the trains home.
▸ ask, make enquiries, seek information, want to know

USAGE Note that *inquire* is normally used in the meaning 'to make an official investigation', as in *a committee appointed to inquire into the incident.*

enquiry NOUN

routine telephone enquiries
▸ query, question

USAGE Note that *inquiry* is normally used in the meaning 'official investigation', as in *The opposition called for a public inquiry into the incident.*

enrage VERB

Such a casual attitude enraged her.
▸ anger, annoy, irritate, infuriate, exasperate, incense, vex, madden, aggravate, antagonize, displease, incite, inflame, make angry, (*more informal*) needle, (*more informal*) rile, (*more informal*) bug, (*more informal*) rub up the wrong way
OPPOSITES ARE pacify, placate

enrol VERB

enrol in *You can enrol in your course any evening this week.*
▸ register for, sign up for, join

enslave VERB

The invading armies enslaved the population.
▸ make slaves of, subjugate, suppress, disenfranchise, dominate, subject, take away the rights of
OPPOSITES ARE liberate, emancipate

ensue VERB

A fierce argument ensued.
▸ follow, result, develop, arise, occur, come about

ensure VERB

USAGE Note that *ensure* means 'to make sure' whereas *insure* means 'to take out insurance'.
A mild sedative ensured a good night's sleep.
▸ guarantee, make sure, secure, confirm, make certain

entail VERB

Travel home entailed a five-hour drive.
▸ involve, necessitate, require, call for, demand, occasion

entangle VERB

By switching hands she entangled the dog's lead in her shopping bags.
▸ tangle, twist, catch, intertwine, mix up, knot

enter VERB

1 *Soldiers entered the building.*
▸ go in or into, come in or into, gain access to, set foot in, pass into
AN OPPOSITE IS leave

2 *While the sign is up please do not enter.*
▸ go in, come in
AN OPPOSITE IS leave

3 *A bullet had entered his chest.*
▸ penetrate, pierce, puncture, perforate, make a hole in

4 *That year the Americans entered the war.*
▸ join, take part in, participate in

5 *I'm going to enter a competition.*
▸ go in for, become a contestant in, enrol for

6 *Please enter your details on the form.*
▸ record, register, note, write down

enterprise NOUN

1 *a dangerous enterprise*
▸ undertaking, endeavour, venture, pursuit, operation, project, adventure, business, effort

2 *a charitable enterprise*
▸ organization, business, establishment, company, firm

3 *Success in the job calls for considerable enterprise.*
▸ initiative, resourcefulness, resource, adventurousness, spirit, drive, determination, imagination

enterprising ADJECTIVE

An enterprising buyer can get quite a bargain at this time of year.
▸ adventurous, resourceful, daring, bold, enthusiastic, energetic, imaginative, inventive, creative
AN OPPOSITE IS unadventurous

entertain VERB

1 *He told stories to entertain his children.*
▸ amuse, divert, delight, gladden, cheer up, make laugh, raise a smile, (*more informal*) tickle

2 *We will be entertaining friends this Christmas.*
▸ receive, play host to, cater for, welcome

3 *She refused to entertain the idea.*
▸ consider, contemplate, countenance, accept, agree to

entertainer NOUN

a television entertainer
▸ performer, artiste, artist

entertaining ADJECTIVE

an entertaining story
▸ amusing, enjoyable, witty, funny, diverting, pleasing

entertainment NOUN
The holiday includes free evening entertainment.
▶ amusement, diversion, enjoyment, recreation, pastime, play, fun, pleasure, sport, distraction

TYPES OF ENTERTAINMENT

home entertainment: television, video, home cinema, CD, minidisc, DVD, radio, hi-fi, computer games, board games.

public entertainment: theatre, cinema or film, concert hall, opera, pantomime, musical, variety show, music hall, revue, cabaret, nightclub, casino, circus, waxworks, puppet show; dance, disco, ceilidh, karaoke, magic show, ice-skating show, street entertainment.

outdoor entertainment: firework show, air show, fair, funfair, gymkhana, rodeo, zoo; son et lumière (at a historic building), tattoo, laser-light show, carnival, pageant, fete, barbecue, festival.

enthralling ADJECTIVE
They watched an enthralling series of singles matches.
▶ exciting, fascinating, engrossing, captivating, dazzling

enthusiasm NOUN
1 *They will take on their new role with enthusiasm. He has a new-found enthusiasm for the game.*
▶ eagerness, excitement, keenness, ardour, relish, commitment, zeal, zest, fervour, ambition, drive, panache, spirit, verve
AN OPPOSITE IS apathy
2 *Their latest enthusiasm is swimming.*
▶ interest, pursuit, pastime, diversion, hobby, passion, craze, (informal) fad

enthusiast NOUN
an amateur radio enthusiast
▶ devotee, fan, fanatic, aficionado, follower, lover, (more informal) buff

enthusiastic ADJECTIVE
The visitors got an enthusiastic reception a group of enthusiastic supporters
▶ eager, keen, ardent, fervent, devoted, passionate, wholehearted
OPPOSITES ARE unenthusiastic, apathetic

entice VERB
A friend of mine enticed me to go to a club with him.
▶ persuade, tempt, lure (into going), induce, coax

entire ADJECTIVE
1 *He spent his entire life on the island.*
▶ whole, complete, total, full
2 *The arch of one of the gates is entire.*
▶ intact, complete, undamaged

entirely ADVERB
I entirely agree with you.
▶ completely, absolutely, fully, totally, utterly, thoroughly

entitle VERB
1 **entitle to** *The voucher entitles you to free entrance to the gallery.*
▶ qualify for, authorize to, allow, permit, warrant
2 *The story is entitled 'A Day in the Life of My Dog'*
▶ call, name, title, designate

entitlement NOUN
their entitlement to the money
▶ right, title, claim, ownership (of)

entity NOUN
a separate entity
▶ being, thing, body, organism

entrance NOUN
1 *The main entrance to the building is round the corner.*
▶ entry, way in, access, door, doorway, gateway, approach
2 *At the entrance of the hosts a silence fell on the room.*
▶ entry, appearance, arrival, approach, coming in, going in, (more formal) ingress
3 *Several people were refused entrance.*
▶ admission, admittance, entry, access

entrant NOUN
There are over a hundred entrants in the competition.
▶ candidate, competitor, contender, contestant, entry, participant, player

entreaty NOUN
She ignored their entreaties.
▶ plea, appeal, pleading, exhortation

entrust VERB
1 *She entrusted her brother with the task.*
▶ charge, give responsibility for, put in charge of, trust, (more informal) saddle
2 *She entrusted the task to her brother.*
▶ assign, allocate, commit, delegate, confer (on), turn over

entry NOUN
1 *The entry to the grounds was closed.*
▶ entrance, way in, access, door, doorway, gateway, approach
2 *They were allowed entry on production of a passport.*
▶ admission, admittance, entrance, access
3 *the entry in the diary*
▶ item, record, statement, note, insertion
4 *an entry in a competition*
▶ candidate, competitor, contender, contestant, entrant, participant, player

envelop VERB
A poison gas enveloped the place.
▶ cover, surround, enfold, blanket, enwrap, engulf, cloak, cocoon

envelope NOUN
He put the money in an envelope
▶ wrapper, wrapping, cover, sleeve

enviable ADJECTIVE
She has the enviable job of entertaining celebrities.
▶ attractive, desirable, favourable

envious ADJECTIVE
He was envious of his brother's success.
▶ jealous, resentful, grudging, begrudging, bitter (about), covetous, dissatisfied, *(more informal)* green with envy (about or over)

environment NOUN
1 *a natural environment for wild birds*
▶ habitat, location, setting, surroundings, conditions, situation, milieu, territory
2 **the environment** *industrial activities that threaten the environment*
▶ the natural world, the earth, the planet, the world we live in

envisage NOUN
1 *It is hard to envisage what might happen.*
▶ imagine, visualize, picture, contemplate
2 *We envisage many changes.*
▶ foresee, predict, expect, intend, propose

envoy NOUN
an envoy from Spain
▶ ambassador, representative, delegate, agent, intermediary

envy NOUN
He could not help feeling envy at her good luck.
▶ jealousy, bitterness, resentment, covetousness, cupidity, dissatisfaction, ill-will

envy VERB
He envied her success.
▶ be jealous of, be envious of, begrudge, grudge, resent

epidemic NOUN
a measles epidemic
▶ outbreak, plague, upsurge

episode NOUN
1 *a happy episode in my life*
▶ incident, event, occurrence, happening, occasion, circumstance
2 *the final episode of the series*
▶ instalment, part, section, programme

epitome NOUN
He was the epitome of an English gentleman.
▶ personification, embodiment, essence, quintessence, representation, model, type

equal ADJECTIVE
1 *a row of houses of equal size*
▶ identical, similar, uniform, the same, like, corresponding, comparable, commensurate
OPPOSITES ARE unequal, different, varying
2 *an equal contest*
▶ even, balanced, level, evenly matched
OPPOSITES ARE unequal, uneven
3 **equal to** *We thought he was equal to the task.*
▶ capable of, fit for, adequate for, good enough for, suitable for, suited for
AN OPPOSITE IS incapable of

equal NOUN
They treated him as their equal.
▶ peer, equivalent, counterpart, fellow

equal VERB
1 *Her performance almost equalled the world record.*
▶ match, reach, be as good as, compete with, rival
2 *Three and ten equals thirteen.*
▶ total, amount to

equality NOUN
1 *an equality of supply and demand*
▶ evenness, similarity, balance (between), parity, uniformity, correspondence, identity
2 *equality before the law*
▶ fairness, justice, equal rights, impartiality

equalize VERB
1 *The law equalizes pay for men and women.*
▶ balance, make equal, level, match, even up, *(more informal)* square
2 *Celtic equalized after ten minutes.*
▶ level the score, draw level

equate VERB
She would not equate good looks with lack of brains.
▶ identify, compare, juxtapose, liken, match, parallel

equip VERB
1 *Each seat is equipped with a set of headphones.*
▶ provide, supply, furnish, fit, fit up
2 *qualifications that will equip you for your careers*
▶ qualify, prepare

equipment NOUN
equipment needed to record the concert
▶ apparatus, appliances, tools, gear

equivalent ADJECTIVE
a degree or an equivalent qualification
▶ comparable, similar, identical, corresponding

era NOUN
a new era of peace
▶ age, period, epoch

eradicate VERBS
progress in eradicating malnutrition among the aged
▶ eliminate, suppress, weed out, remove, abolish

erase VERB
They erased a sentence that might cause offence.
▶ delete, remove, rub out

erect ADJECTIVE
an erect posture
▶ upright, rigid, stiff

erect VERB
They will erect a walkway to join the two buildings
▶ build, construct, assemble, put up

erection NOUN
the erection of houses
▶ construction, building, assembly

erode VERB
Rainwater has eroded the soil.
▶ wear away, wear down, eat away, corrode

erotic ADJECTIVE
erotic art
▶ sensual, sexual, amatory, carnal, titillating, (*disapproving*) pornographic, (*disapproving*) salacious, (*disapproving*) lewd, (*disapproving*) suggestive

err VERB
1 *The authorities had erred in not making the information known.*
▶ be wrong, make a mistake, misjudge, miscalculate, blunder, slip up
2 *They were punished if they erred.*
▶ misbehave, do wrong, be bad, be naughty, disobey, transgress

errand NOUN
They did errands for their parents.
▶ task, job, duty, assignment, commission, mission

erratic ADJECTIVE
It is hard to explain such erratic behaviour.
▶ changeable, unpredictable, inconstant, irregular, unstable, variable
OPPOSITES ARE consistent, stable

erroneous ADJECTIVE
The argument was based on an erroneous conclusion.
▶ incorrect, inaccurate, mistaken, false, wrong, invalid, unsound, untrue, faulty, flawed

error NOUN
The report contained many factual errors.
▶ mistake, inaccuracy, slip, blunder, fault, flaw, miscalculation

erupt VERB
1 *Lava continued to erupt from the volcano.*
▶ spew, spout, spurt, gush, issue, pour out, shoot out, belch, be discharged, be emitted, be expelled
2 *Violence erupted on the streets of the city.*
▶ break out, flare up

eruption NOUN
1 *an eruption of Vesuvius   an eruption of violence*
▶ outbreak, outburst, discharge, burst, explosion
2 *a skin eruption*
▶ rash, inflammation

escalate VERB
The dispute might escalate into an all-out war.
▶ grow, develop, build up, heighten, intensify, accelerate

escalation NOUN
an escalation of the conflict
▶ intensification, heightening, aggravation, worsening, enlargement, deterioration

escapade NOUN
a dangerous escapade
▶ adventure, exploit, prank, caper, mischief, romp, antic, spree, fling, scrape, stunt, (*more informal*) lark

escape NOUN
1 *an escape from prison*
▶ breakout, getaway, absconding, bolt, flight, flit, retreat, running away
2 *an escape of gas*
▶ leak, leakage, emission, seepage, discharge

3 *an escape from life's troubles*
▶ distraction, diversion, relief, avoidance, relaxation

escape VERB
1 *They must have had help to escape.*
▶ get away, break free, break out, break loose, run away, abscond, make a break for it
2 *Oil was escaping from a crack in the hull.*
▶ leak, seep, ooze, discharge, drain, pour out, run out
3 *The passengers all escaped serious injury.   We managed to escape a lot of the work.*
▶ avoid, evade, elude, dodge, miss

escapism NOUN
People need escapism in these difficult times.
▶ fantasy, pretence, unreality, wishful thinking, romance, reverie

escort NOUN
1 *The police provided an escort.*
▶ guard, guide, bodyguard, convoy
2 *a royal escort*
▶ attendant, entourage, train, retinue

escort VERB
A representative will escort you to your seat.
▶ accompany, conduct, guide, lead, take, show, usher

especially ADVERB
1 *Property is especially expensive in the central area of the city.*
▶ particularly, exceptionally, extremely, peculiarly, extraordinarily, remarkably, uncommonly
2 *Patients, especially those with head injuries, become disoriented.*
▶ chiefly, mainly, principally, particularly, in particular, above all, primarily

essay NOUN
I have to write an essay by the end of the week.
▶ article, piece of writing, composition, assignment, study

essence NOUN
1 *The essence of good detective work is patience.*
▶ nature, substance, quintessence, core, kernel, basis, crux, essential part
2 *Add a little vanilla essence.*
▶ extract, concentrate

essential ADJECTIVE
The leaflet provides essential travel information.
▶ necessary, basic, vital, important, indispensable, crucial, fundamental, principal, key, primary, requisite, indispensable, main
AN OPPOSITE IS inessential

establish VERB
1 *The new evidence established their guilt.*
▶ prove, demonstrate, substantiate, confirm, indicate, affirm, verify, certify, authenticate
2 *The Bank aims to establish branches throughout the world.*
▶ set up, install, found, initiate, institute, organize, inaugurate, create, base

established ADJECTIVE

an established practice
▶ accepted, confirmed, orthodox, traditional, customary, prevailing, well-known, well-tried, familiar, entrenched, long-standing, routine

establishment NOUN

1 *the establishment of a new republic*
▶ creation, institution, introduction, constitution, formation, foundation, inauguration, inception, composition
2 *an old publishing establishment*
▶ business, concern, enterprise, venture, undertaking, company

estate NOUN

1 *The family lived in a housing estate*
▶ development, area, land
2 *Her grandfather had left an estate worth several millions.*
▶ assets, possessions, wealth, property, belongings, holdings

esteem NOUN

She was held in high esteem by all her friends.
▶ respect, admiration, favour, honour, regard, opinion, acclaim, estimation, credit, reverence, veneration

estimate NOUN

1 *Our estimate of the situation is fairly dire.*
▶ assessment, appraisal, evaluation, estimation, judgement, opinion, view
2 *The painter will let us have an estimate.*
▶ price, quotation, reckoning, specification, valuation, calculation

estimate VERB

The agents estimated the selling price of the house at over a million pounds.
▶ reckon, consider, assess, evaluate, calculate, gauge, work out

estimation NOUN

The builders had done a good job in my estimation.
▶ judgement, opinion, view, assessment, consideration, reckoning, estimate, evaluation, appraisal, appreciation, calculation

estranged VERB

the rift between her and her estranged husband
▶ separated, alienated, disaffected, divided, antagonized, divorced
AN OPPOSITE IS reconciled

estuary NOUN

a river estuary
▶ mouth, delta, creek, fjord, inlet, (*Scottish*) firth

eternal ADJECTIVE

1 *eternal happiness*
▶ everlasting, never-ending, unending, undying, enduring, abiding, timeless, infinite
OPPOSITES ARE transient, ephemeral

2 *I'm tired of your eternal complaining.*
▶ constant, continual, interminable, ceaseless, unceasing, incessant, everlasting, never-ending, perpetual, persistent, unremitting
OPPOSITES ARE occasional, intermittent

eternity NOUN

1 *the eternity after death*
▶ afterlife, eternal life, infinity, perpetuity, immortality
2 **an eternity** (*informal*) *We waited an eternity for a train.*
▶ ages, hours, a long time, for ever

ethical ADJECTIVE

It would not be ethical to increase the cost of health care
▶ morally correct, proper, just, right, principled, fitting, appropriate

ethics NOUN

the ethics of medical research
▶ morality, moral code, morals, principles, propriety, standards, values, ideals, rights and wrongs

ethnic ADJECTIVE

1 *people with different ethnic backgrounds*
▶ cultural, national, indigenous, genetic, tribal, racial
2 *men and women in ethnic dress*
▶ local, traditional, national, folk

ethos NOUN

The head teacher helps determine the ethos of a school.
▶ spirit, character, atmosphere, climate, mood

etiquette NOUN

He showed an easy charm that made up for any lack of etiquette.
▶ protocol, manners, courtesy, civility, politeness, decorum, ceremony, good manners, correct behaviour

euphoria NOUN

It was hard not to get caught up in the euphoria of victory.
▶ elation, joy, happiness, exhilaration, jubilation, ecstasy, thrill

evacuate VERB

1 *It is essential to evacuate everybody from the building.*
▶ remove, clear, move out, send away
2 *Police decided to evacuate the area.*
▶ vacate, leave, quit, relinquish, withdraw from, abandon, decamp from, desert, empty

evacuation NOUN

1 *the evacuation of buildings*
▶ clearance, vacation, abandonment
2 *the evacuation of civilians*
▶ removal, clearance, eviction

evade VERB

1 *Charlie was clearly guilty of evading his responsibilities.*
▶ avoid, shirk, shun, dodge, duck, sidestep, steer clear of, turn your back on
AN OPPOSITE IS accept

2 *They did all they could to evade capture.*
▶ avoid, elude, escape, escape from, fend off, circumvent

evaluate VERB
A panel of doctors will evaluate the treatment.
▶ assess, value, gauge, appraise, rate, calculate

evaluation NOUN
The results need proper evaluation.
▶ assessment, appraisal, valuation, analysis, estimation, reckoning

evaporate VERB
1 *The water quickly evaporates.*
▶ disperse, dry up, vaporize
AN OPPOSITE IS condense
2 *With this news all their hopes evaporated.*
▶ disappear, fade, vanish, melt away, come to an end, dissolve, dissipate
AN OPPOSITE IS materialize

evasive ADJECTIVE
Lydia was evasive, not having a good answer ready.
▶ prevaricating, elusive, equivocal, equivocating, ambiguous, devious, misleading, unforthcoming, disingenuous, non-committal, uninformative
AN OPPOSITE IS straightforward

even ADJECTIVE
1 *an even surface*
▶ flat, smooth, level, flush, true, unbroken
AN OPPOSITE IS rough
2 *an even temperament*
▶ calm, stable, equable, even-tempered, placid, composed, serene, steady
OPPOSITES ARE moody, excitable
3 *the even ticking of the clock*
▶ steady, regular, constant, uniform, unvarying
AN OPPOSITE IS irregular
4 *The scores were even.*
▶ level, equal, identical, balanced, the same
AN OPPOSITE IS unequal

even VERB
even out *I tried to even out the wrinkled carpet.*
▶ smooth, straighten, flatten, level
even up *Another point will even up the scores*
▶ level, balance, equalize, (*more informal*) square

evening NOUN
It was evening when we reached home.
▶ dusk, sunset, sundown, nightfall, twilight, (*poetic*) eventide, (*poetic*) gloaming

event NOUN
1 *an annual event*
▶ occurrence, happening, occasion, affair, episode, experience, activity, function, business, circumstance, contingency, eventuality, incident, chance
2 *a sporting event*
▶ game, match, competition, tournament
in the event *In the event, the plan was abandoned.*
▶ as it turned out, as it happened, in the end, in actual fact, as a result, as a consequence

even-tempered ADJECTIVE
Sam was an even-tempered chap and took it well.
▶ calm, stable, equable, placid, composed, serene
OPPOSITES ARE excitable, moody

eventful ADJECTIVE
It had been a long and eventful week.
▶ busy, lively, active, full, action-packed, remarkable, noteworthy, momentous
OPPOSITES ARE routine, uneventful, dull

eventual ADJECTIVE
We will have to wait for the eventual verdict.
▶ final, ultimate, ensuing, resulting, prospective, future

eventually ADVERB
Eventually they agreed.
▶ in the end, by and by, finally, at length

everlasting ADJECTIVE
The gift would be an everlasting reminder of her evening.
▶ eternal, never-ending, unending, undying, enduring, abiding, timeless, infinite
OPPOSITES ARE transient, ephemeral

everyday ADJECTIVE
Road accidents were an everyday occurrence.
▶ commonplace, common, frequent, ordinary, regular, familiar

everyone NOUN
She was afraid everyone would know by now.
▶ everybody, the whole world, every person, one and all, (*more informal*) every Tom, Dick, and Harry

everywhere ADVERB
He looked everywhere for his keys.
▶ all over, in every place, far and wide, high and low

evict VERB
If they didn't pay their rent that week they would be evicted.
▶ expel, eject, throw out, remove, (*more informal*) kick out, (*more informal*) give (someone) the boot

evidence NOUN
1 *evidence of life on other planets*
▶ confirmation, verification, proof, corroboration, substantiation, authentication
2 *Her evidence helped convict all four of them.*
▶ testimony, statement, information

evident ADJECTIVE
It was evident that he didn't like her.
▶ obvious, apparent, clear, plain, noticeable, observable, transparent, discernible
AN OPPOSITE IS unclear

evil ADJECTIVE
1 *an evil act   the most evil person he had met*
▶ wicked, bad, wrong, sinful, vile, immoral, depraved
OPPOSITES ARE good, virtuous

2 *An evil smell came from the drains.*
▶ nasty, foul, noxious, unpleasant, offensive, unspeakable, vile, pestilential, poisonous, troublesome
AN OPPOSITE IS pleasant
3 *an evil influence*
▶ harmful, hurtful, pernicious, destructive, deadly, poisonous

evil NOUN
1 *a crime of the utmost evil*
▶ wickedness, wrong, sinfulness, depravity, immorality, vileness, vice, iniquity
2 *a great social evil*
▶ catastrophe, affliction, disaster, enormity, calamity, curse, misfortune

evoke VERB
The scene evoked memories of her childhood.
▶ arouse, stir up, summon up, bring to mind, call to mind, call up, raise, stimulate, inspire, awaken, conjure up, elicit, excite, kindle, produce, provoke, suggest

evolution NOUN
the evolution of scientific methods
▶ development, emergence, growth, improvement, maturing, progress, unfolding

evolve VERB
The plan evolved from quite a simple idea.
▶ develop, grow, derive, progress, mature, emerge, expand

exact ADJECTIVE
1 *Stacey likes to be exact in her work.*
▶ careful, precise, accurate, meticulous, methodical, painstaking, rigorous
2 *These are the exact measurements of the room.*
▶ precise, accurate, correct, definite
3 *Is this an exact copy?*
▶ identical, faithful, close

exacting ADJECTIVE
an exacting task
▶ demanding, taxing, tough, difficult, laborious, strenuous

exactly ADVERB
1 *She looks exactly like her mother at that age.*
▶ precisely, entirely, absolutely, completely, totally, utterly, every inch
2 *Describe the scene exactly.*
▶ accurately, precisely, faithfully, in detail

exaggerate VERB
The press reports exaggerated the scale of the fire.
▶ overstate, over-emphasize, overestimate, overstress, overdo, inflate, magnify, make too much of, amplify, enlarge, maximize, (*more informal*) play up
OPPOSITES ARE understate, underestimate

examination NOUN
1 *the annual examination of the accounts*
▶ inspection, scrutiny, study, scanning, analysis, appraisal

2 *a written examination in history*
▶ exam, test, paper
3 *a medical examination*
▶ check-up, check, inspection, review

examine VERB
1 *The Fraud Squad will examine the company account for the last ten years.*
▶ inspect, scrutinize, study, investigate, check, analyse, review, scan, probe
2 *Students are examined at the end of each year.*
▶ test, assess, appraise
3 *The defence counsel will examine the witness tomorrow.*
▶ cross-examine, interrogate, cross-question

example NOUN
1 *a fine example of a Tudor building*
▶ specimen, sample, case, exemplar, illustration, instance, occurrence
2 *We ought to follow their example.*
▶ precedent, model, pattern, ideal, standard
3 *They were convicted as an example to others.*
▶ warning, lesson, deterrent, caution

exasperate VERB
This stupid behaviour exasperated us.
▶ infuriate, incense, anger, annoy, irritate, enrage, vex, (*more informal*) rile

excavate VERB
1 *Moles had excavated tunnels under the grass.*
▶ dig, bore, burrow, hollow out
2 *A coin hoard was excavated from the ancient site.*
▶ unearth, dig up, uncover, discover, reveal

exceed VERB
1 *Total luggage weight must not exceed 300 kilos.*
▶ be more than, be greater than, go over
2 *Police stopped her for exceeding the speed limit.*
▶ break, go beyond, go faster than
3 *The amount exceeded all our expectations.*
▶ surpass, beat, outstrip, better, outdo, excel, pass, top

exceedingly ADVERB
an exceedingly good meal
▶ extremely, exceptionally, especially, supremely, outstandingly, immensely, amazingly, unusually, extraordinarily, tremendously, really, very

excel VERB
1 *One choir excelled all the others and was invited back for next year.*
▶ surpass, outdo, outclass, outstrip, do better than, beat, exceed
2 *He excels at most things he turns his hand to.*
▶ shine, do well, be good, stand out, be outstanding

excellent ADJECTIVE
an excellent idea   The book is excellent.
▶ outstanding, very good, first-class, first-rate, superlative, superb, remarkable, exceptional, splendid, wonderful, marvellous, tremendous

xcept PREPOSITION

The restaurant is open every evening except Monday.
▶ excluding, except for, apart from, other than, besides

xception NOUN

Most countries are represented, although there are a few exceptions.
▶ abnormality, irregularity, oddity, peculiarity, deviation, anomaly, departure, eccentricity, special case, freak, quirk, rarity
take exception to *She takes exception to people smoking in the house.*
▶ object to, disapprove of, complain about, demur at, resent, be offended by

xceptional ADJECTIVE

1 *a woman of exceptional ability*
▶ outstanding, excellent, very good, first-class, first-rate, superlative, superb, remarkable
2 *exceptional weather patterns*
▶ unusual, abnormal, untypical, extraordinary, strange, irregular, peculiar, freakish

xcerpt NOUN

(formal) We read excerpts from his new book.
▶ extract, passage, selection, section, portion, quotation, snippet

xcess NOUN

1 *an excess of vitamin E*
▶ surplus, surfeit, superfluity, oversufficiency, superabundance, abundance, glut
OPPOSITES ARE scarcity, deficit
2 *a lifestyle characterized by excess*
▶ extravagance, overindulgence, intemperance, lavishness, prodigality

xcessive ADJECTIVE

1 *excessive drinking*
▶ immoderate, inordinate, extreme, extravagant, disproportionate, superfluous
2 *The cost proved excessive.*
▶ unreasonable, exorbitant, inordinate, (more informal) steep

xchange NOUN

1 *The two sides agreed to an exchange of prisoners.*
▶ switch, interchange, replacement, substitution, (informal) swap
2 *This misunderstanding led to a series of bitter exchanges.*
▶ argument, altercation, recrimination, war of words
3 *Archaeological evidence points to an exchange of goods between the two areas.*
▶ trade, traffic, barter, dealing

xchange VERB

1 *The players exchanged shirts at the end of the game.*
▶ swap, change, switch, interchange
2 *I exchanged my old bike for a smart new one.*
▶ swap, barter, trade, substitute

excitable ADJECTIVE

She was afraid to tell him everything as he could be so excitable.
▶ emotional, volatile, temperamental, sensitive, highly strung, nervous, irascible, jumpy

excite VERB

The prospect of a day out excited them.
▶ thrill, exhilarate, elate, enliven, stimulate
AN OPPOSITE IS bore

excited ADJECTIVE

The children were becoming excited.
▶ animated, stimulated, worked up, boisterous, lively, elated, restless, overwrought, vivacious

excitement NOUN

1 *They could hardly conceal their excitement.*
▶ enthusiasm, exhilaration, agitation, elation, eagerness, stimulation
2 *There will be a lot of excitement at the party this afternoon.*
▶ commotion, activity, adventure

exciting ADJECTIVE

an exciting story
▶ thrilling, stirring, exhilarating, rousing, stimulating, invigorating, enthralling, gripping, dramatic, sensational
OPPOSITES ARE dull, unexciting

exclaim VERB

He exclaimed that he had never been there.
▶ cry, cry out, call, yell, shout, shriek, scream

exclamation NOUN

With an exclamation of horror she rushed upstairs.
▶ cry, yell, call, shout, shriek, interjection, (old-fashioned) ejaculation

exclude VERB

1 *They were anxious to exclude the inevitable gatecrashers from the house.*
▶ keep out, deny access to, ban, disallow, prevent, prohibit, deter, debar, reject
2 *He excluded his own name from the list.*
▶ omit, leave out, miss out, fail to include, rule out
3 *These figures exclude any allowance for inflation.*
▶ omit, be exclusive of, not include

exclusive ADJECTIVE

1 *The room is for your exclusive use.*
▶ sole, unique, private, unshared, undivided, unrestricted
2 *one of London's most exclusive clubs*
▶ select, elite, fashionable, restrictive, private, premier, (more informal) classy, (more informal) posh

excursion NOUN

an excursion to Brighton
▶ trip, outing, jaunt, journey, expedition, day out, drive, run

excuse NOUN

1 *He trotted out the usual feeble excuses.*
▶ defence, pretext, explanation, alibi, plea, reason

2 *There is no excuse for what you did.*
▶ justification, vindication

excuse VERB
1 *We cannot excuse bad behaviour.*
▶ justify, defend, condone, tolerate, overlook, ignore, sanction, mitigate
2 *She found it hard to excuse them this time.*
▶ forgive, pardon, absolve

execute VERB
1 *The manoeuvre is particularly hard to execute in heavy traffic.*
▶ carry out, implement, perform, complete, accomplish, achieve, do, effect
2 *The State no longer executes convicted murderers.*
▶ put to death, apply the death penalty to, hang, behead, electrocute

execution NOUN
1 *the execution of the plan*
▶ implementation, carrying out, performance, accomplishment, achievement, prosecution
2 *a sentence of execution*
▶ capital punishment, the death penalty, hanging, beheading, electrocution

executive NOUN
a meeting of company executives
▶ manager, director, chief, principal

executive ADJECTIVE
executive powers
▶ administrative, decision-making, managerial, supervisory

exemplary ADJECTIVE
Their exemplary behaviour impressed everyone.
▶ ideal, perfect, impeccable, exceptional, model, admirable, faultless, flawless

exemplify VERB
The case exemplifies many of today's problems.
▶ typify, epitomize, symbolize, demonstrate

exempt ADJECTIVE
Students should be exempt from health charges
▶ excused, excepted, absolved, immune, excluded, released, free, let off, spared
AN OPPOSITE IS liable (to)

exempt VERB
We hope they will exempt him from jury service.
▶ excuse, release, free, let (someone) off

exercise NOUN
1 *Regular exercise will keep you fit.*
▶ physical activity, working out, exertion, training
2 *the exercise of authority*
▶ use, application, practice
3 **exercises** *army exercises*
▶ operations, manoeuvres

exercise VERB
1 *She exercises every day.*
▶ work out, do exercises, keep fit
2 *Please exercise a little patience.*
▶ use, have, employ, apply

3 *The problem continues to exercise us.*
▶ trouble, worry, bother, make anxious

exert VERB
1 *She exerts a considerable influence on the children.*
▶ exercise, wield, bring to bear, apply
2 **exert yourself** *He exerted himself to get the job don on time.*
▶ strive, endeavour, try hard, make an effort, go to some trouble

exertion NOUN
They were all panting from the exertion.
▶ effort, strain, toil

exhale VERB
He exhaled a misty cold breath.
▶ breathe out, puff out, blow out

exhaust VERB
1 *We exhausted the fuel supply after only a week.*
▶ use up, consume, drain, empty, deplete, dry up, finish off, go through, spend, sap, void
2 *Her day out had exhausted her.*
▶ tire out, wear out, fatigue, weary, tax, strain

exhaust NOUN
a vehicle exhaust
▶ emission, discharge, fumes, gases, smoke

exhausted ADJECTIVE
1 *They went to bed exhausted that night.*
▶ tired out, worn out, weary, fatigued, shattered, (*more informal*) dead tired, (*more informal*) played out (*more informal*) washed out
2 *exhausted money reserves*
▶ depleted, used up, spent

exhausting ADJECTIVE
an exhausting journey
▶ tiring, wearying, fatiguing, wearing, arduous, strenuous, taxing, gruelling, demanding, laborious, punishing, sapping, difficult, hard, severe
AN OPPOSITE IS refreshing

exhaustion NOUN
He had to stop from sheer exhaustion.
▶ fatigue, weariness, tiredness, debility, weakness
AN OPPOSITE IS vigour

exhaustive ADJECTIVE
An exhaustive search failed to produce the missing ring.
▶ comprehensive, thorough, intensive, meticulous extensive, far-reaching, full-scale, all-out, careful

exhibit VERB
1 *The gallery will exhibit a collection of new paintings.*
▶ show, display, put on display, present, set up
2 *He exhibited great pride in his family.*
▶ show, reveal, display, demonstrate, manifest, disclose, express
OPPOSITES ARE hide, conceal

exhibition NOUN
an exhibition of Greek sculpture
▶ display, presentation, show, showing, demonstration

exhilarated ADJECTIVE

The day's events left them feeling exhilarated.
► excited, elated, thrilled, animated, stimulated, worked up
AN OPPOSITE IS dejected

exhilarating ADJECTIVE

The ride was an exhilarating experience.
► exciting, thrilling, stirring, rousing, stimulating, invigorating, enthralling, gripping, dramatic, sensational
OPPOSITES ARE dull, unexciting

exhilaration NOUN

a feeling of exhilaration
► excitement, enthusiasm, elation, eagerness, stimulation

exile NOUN

1 *The poet was punished with exile.*
► banishment, expulsion, deportation, expatriation, extradition
2 *a group of political exiles*
► émigré, exiled person, displaced person, deportee, expatriate, outcast, refugee

exile VERB

The new regime immediately exiled the dictators.
► expel, banish, deport, drive out, eject, expatriate, send away

exist VERB

1 *animals that no longer exist*
► live, occur, be alive, be in existence
2 *They had to exist for years on a meagre income.*
► survive, subsist, live, hold out, keep going, continue, endure, last

existence NOUN

1 *The new law threatens the very existence of these old institutions.*
► survival, continuance, continuation, being, actuality, life, living, reality
AN OPPOSITE IS non-existence
2 *a dreary existence in a remote part of the country*
► way of life, livelihood, lifestyle

existing ADJECTIVE

The existing arrangements were proving inadequate.
► current, present, available, prevailing, actual, existent, extant
USAGE You can also say *the arrangements already in place* or *the arrangements already in force.*

exit NOUN

1 *A passage on the right leads to the exit.*
► way out, door, doorway, egress, gate, gateway
AN OPPOSITE IS entrance
2 *They made a quick exit.*
► departure, withdrawal, retreat, leaving, exodus
OPPOSITES ARE entrance, arrival
3 *Take the exit marked Leeds.*
► turning, turn-off, turn, road

exit VERB

A regal-looking woman then exited.
► leave, depart, go out
OPPOSITES ARE enter, arrive

exonerate VERB

The letter exonerated him.
► clear, absolve, vindicate, acquit

exorbitant ADJECTIVE

The cost of rail travel can be exorbitant.
► extortionate, excessive, unreasonable, prohibitive, inordinate, unrealistic, outrageous, expensive, extravagant, high, overpriced
OPPOSITES ARE reasonable, competitive

exotic ADJECTIVE

1 *exotic places in the Far East*
► faraway, distant, remote, foreign, romantic, unfamiliar, alien
AN OPPOSITE IS familiar
2 *an exhibition of exotic birds*
► foreign, non-native, tropical, alien, unnaturalized, imported
AN OPPOSITE IS native
3 *exotic dress*
► colourful, striking, unusual, unfamiliar, unconventional, outlandish
AN OPPOSITE IS conventional

expand VERB

1 *a good opportunity to expand the business*
► develop, enlarge, extend, broaden, build up, diversify, increase, amplify, augment, elaborate, fill out, make bigger
OPPOSITES ARE contract, reduce
2 *Metal expands when heated.*
► increase in size, become larger, swell, dilate, grow, stretch, thicken, widen
AN OPPOSITE IS contract

expanse NOUN

a vast expanse of water
► extent, area, stretch, surface, sweep, range, breadth, sheet, tract

expansive ADJECTIVE

After a few drinks he became quite expansive.
► talkative, communicative, forthcoming, outgoing, sociable, unreserved, uninhibited, voluble, conversational, open
OPPOSITES ARE curt, unfriendly

expect VERB

1 *We expect a large number of visitors this year.*
► hope for, look for, look forward to, envisage, predict, anticipate, await, bank on
2 *We expect complete discretion.*
► demand, insist on, require, call for, count on, rely on, want
3 *I expect they missed the train.*
► suppose, assume, presume, imagine, believe, guess, judge, think, (*more informal*) reckon

e

expectant ADJECTIVE
1 *Hundreds of expectant fans waited outside the theatre.*
▶ eager, excited, hopeful, watchful, anxious
2 *an expectant mother*
▶ pregnant, expecting

expedient ADJECTIVE
It seemed expedient to leave.
▶ advantageous, convenient, suitable, useful, beneficial, prudent, in your own interests

expedition NOUN
a major scientific expedition
▶ journey , voyage, mission, quest, exploration, mission, safari

expel VERB
1 *He was expelled from the country.*
▶ banish, exile, deport, drive out, throw out, cast out, evict, expatriate
2 *The machinery was expelling thick smoke.*
▶ discharge, emit, let out, release, disgorge, spew out

expend VERB
It may not be worth expending a lot of effort on this task.
▶ use up, consume, spend, drain, devote (to)

expendable ADJECTIVE
the theory that males are expendable
▶ dispensable, replaceable, superfluous, non-essential, unnecessary, unimportant
OPPOSITES ARE indispensable, essential

expenditure NOUN
the need to cut back on local expenditure
▶ spending, outlay, expense, outgoings, payment

expense NOUN
1 *the increasing expense of running a car*
▶ cost, price, spending
2 *unexpected expenses*
▶ expenditure, outlay, charges, outgoings, overheads, payment

expensive ADJECTIVE
an expensive holiday
▶ costly, dear, high-priced, extravagant, lavish, exorbitant, (*more informal*) pricey
OPPOSITES ARE cheap, inexpensive

experience NOUN
1 (*informal*) *You learn by experience.*
▶ practice, involvement, participation, familiarity, observation, taking part
2 (*informal*) *Salary will depend partly on experience.*
▶ skill, knowledge, background, understanding, (*more informal*) know-how
3 *a terrifying experience*
▶ incident, event, episode, affair, happening, occurrence, ordeal, adventure

experience VERB
She experienced some harassment at work.
▶ meet, encounter, undergo, face, run into, suffer

experienced ADJECTIVE
1 *an experienced actor*
▶ expert, skilled, skilful, qualified, trained, practised, knowledgeable, professional, specialized, well-versed
AN OPPOSITE IS inexperienced
2 *an experienced man of the world*
▶ mature, seasoned, sophisticated, worldly-wise, knowing, wise
OPPOSITES ARE innocent, naive

experiment NOUN
1 *She conducted experiments using laser technology.*
▶ test, investigation, trial, enquiry, demonstration, observation, analysis, piece of research
2 *The new library hours are an experiment.*
▶ trial, trial run, try-out

experiment VERB
experiment with *You need to experiment with the camera's different settings.*
▶ test, try out, investigate, explore, do tests on, conduct an experiment on, do research on

experimental ADJECTIVE
1 *The new designs are still at an experimental stage.*
▶ exploratory, investigatory, provisional, tentative, preliminary, speculative, trial, test
2 *experimental forms of music*
▶ innovative, innovatory, radical, avant-garde, original

expert ADJECTIVE
1 *You can get independent expert advice quite cheaply.*
▶ skilled, professional, qualified, specialist
2 *I am an expert swimmer.*
▶ skilful, skilled, accomplished, proficient, competent, talented, outstanding, exceptional, formidable

expert NOUN
1 *You need to get advice from an expert.*
▶ specialist, professional, authority, (*more informal*) pro
2 (*informal*) *He is an expert at board games.*
▶ authority, master, past master, connoisseur, genius, virtuoso, (*more informal*) ace, (*more informal*) whizz, (*more informal*) wizard, (*more informal*) dab hand, (*disapproving*) know-all
AN OPPOSITE IS novice

expertise NOUN
A high level of expertise is required.
▶ skill, competence, proficiency, ability, knowledge, capability, professionalism

expire VERB
1 *The animals were expiring in the heat.*
▶ die, perish, pass away
2 *Our television licence has expired.*
▶ run out, become invalid, lapse, finish

explain VERB

1 *I will try to explain the problem.*
▶ describe, clarify, make clear, spell out, elucidate, interpret, demonstrate, express, put into words
2 *It is hard to explain such stupidity.*
▶ account for, justify, excuse, defend, vindicate, give reasons for, make excuses for, rationalize

explanation NOUN

1 *I owe you an explanation for what happened.*
▶ justification, reason, account, excuse, defence, rationale
2 *What on earth can the explanation be?*
▶ cause, motive, reason
3 *The summary at the end gives a brief explanation of the ideas discussed.*
▶ account, clarification, elucidation, interpretation, demonstration

explanatory ADJECTIVE

a few explanatory comments
▶ descriptive, explaining, illustrative, interpretive, revelatory, helpful, illuminating, (*more formal*) expository

explicit ADJECTIVE

1 *The advance party had received explicit instructions to turn back.*
▶ clear, plain, direct, definite, express, precise, distinct, exact, emphatic, specific, positive, categorical, unambiguous, unmistakable, unequivocal
AN OPPOSITE IS vague
2 *The film contains a number of sexually explicit scenes.*
▶ candid, open, direct, frank, unreserved, undisguised, plain
OPPOSITES ARE implicit, suggestive

explode VERB

1 *A bomb exploded in the centre of the city.*
▶ go off, blow up, detonate
2 *The findings explode a number of myths about cancer treatment.*
▶ disprove, rebut, refute, expose, debunk, discredit, destroy, put an end to

exploit NOUN (with the stress on *ex-*)

Their exploits gave them a fearsome reputation.
▶ feat, deed, adventure, accomplishment, achievement

exploit VERB (with the stress on -*ploit*)

1 *The newcomers exploited the land's mineral resources.*
▶ make use of, utilize, use, take advantage of, draw on, benefit from, capitalize on
2 (*informal*) *They are accused of exploiting an impoverished workforce.*
▶ take advantage of, mistreat, ill-treat, abuse, oppress, manipulate, cheat, swindle, (*more informal*) fleece

explore VERB

1 *an outing to explore the neighbourhood*
▶ tour, travel through, reconnoitre, survey, inspect, take a look at
2 *We'd like to explore the possibility of working together.*
▶ investigate, examine, look into, consider, study, review, probe, analyse

explorer NOUN

Roberts was a keen explorer as well as an artist.
▶ traveller, discoverer, voyager, rover, globetrotter

explosion NOUN

A loud explosion shook the building.
▶ blast, bang, boom, burst, crash, report, detonation, discharge

explosive ADJECTIVE

1 *explosive substances*
▶ volatile, inflammable, combustible, unstable
2 *an explosive situation*
▶ tense, highly charged, critical, fraught, hazardous, dangerous, perilous, sensitive
AN OPPOSITE IS stable

explosive NOUN

a large supply of explosives
▶ bomb, device, incendiary device

export VERB

Most of the country's produce is exported.
▶ sell abroad, trade abroad, send abroad
USAGE You can use *overseas* instead of *abroad* in all these synonyms.

expose VERB

1 *The investigation exposed many faults.*
▶ reveal, uncover, bring to light, disclose, unveil, unmask
2 **expose someone to** *They were exposed to serious danger.*
▶ put at risk of, subject to, lay open to

exposure NOUN

1 *He feared exposure of the scandal in the tabloid press.*
▶ revelation, disclosure, uncovering, unmasking, divulgence
2 **exposure to** *exposure to criticism*
▶ experience of, contact with, introduction to, acquaintance with

express VERB

They expressed their wishes clearly.
▶ communicate, articulate, utter, convey, voice, vent, give vent to, release, air, phrase, put into words, ventilate

express ADJECTIVE

1 *It was his express wish.*
▶ explicit, clear, plain, direct, definite, precise, distinct, exact, emphatic, specific, positive, categorical, unambiguous, unmistakable, unequivocal
2 *an express train*
▶ fast, rapid, high-speed, non-stop

e

expression NOUN

1 *He liked to use old-fashioned expressions.*
▶ phrase, idiom, statement, saying, turn of phrase, phraseology, wording, cliché, formula, remark, term
2 *She bore a puzzled expression.*
▶ look, countenance, aspect, air, face, appearance, mien
3 *She read out the letter with expression.*
▶ emotion, feeling, passion, intensity, poignancy, sensibility, sensitivity, sympathy, understanding
4 *The regime forbids the expression of opposing ideas.*
▶ utterance, uttering, voicing, assertion

expressive ADJECTIVE

1 *He raised his hand in an expressive gesture.*
▶ meaningful, telling, revealing, informative, emphatic, communicative, demonstrative, significant
2 *an expressive voice*
▶ eloquent, articulate, lively, modulated, varied
AN OPPOSITE IS expressionless
3 *an expressive piece of music*
▶ emotional, passionate, intense, poignant, evocative, powerful
AN OPPOSITE IS unemotional

expulsion NOUN

The culprits faced expulsion.
▶ dismissal, removal, exclusion, banishment, eviction

exquisite ADJECTIVE

1 *a ring with exquisite little jewels*
▶ beautiful, lovely, delicate, dainty
2 *She always showed exquisite taste.*
▶ refined, discriminating, discerning, sensitive, impeccable

extend VERB

1 *The emperor sought to extend his power.*
▶ expand, enlarge, develop, build up, broaden, spread
AN OPPOSITE IS reduce
2 *The meeting was extended to allow for questions.*
▶ prolong, lengthen, continue, protract, draw out, make longer
3 *We extend our thanks to all contributors.*
▶ offer, proffer, advance, bestow, confer, hold out, present, accord
4 *The fields extend as far as the river.*
▶ reach, go, continue, carry on, spread

extension NOUN

1 *The new owners built a huge extension to the house.*
▶ addition, annexe, wing
2 *We needed an extension of the deadline.*
▶ postponement, deferral, delay
3 *the extension of the royal territories the extension of knowledge*
▶ enlargement, increase, expansion, broadening, development, growth

extensive ADJECTIVE

1 *a country house with extensive gardens*
▶ large, large-scale, substantial, considerable, spacious, expansive
2 *an extensive knowledge of Indian languages*
▶ comprehensive, thorough, complete, exhaustive, wide-ranging, broad, vast, wide

extent NOUN

1 *The estate is about three acres in extent*
▶ area, size, expanse, scope, dimensions, spread, distance
2 *It was only later that we saw the extent of the damage.*
▶ degree, scale, scope, size, magnitude, amount, measure, quantity, range

exterior NOUN

the exterior of the building
▶ outside, outside surface, outward aspect, facade, shell
AN OPPOSITE IS interior

exterior ADJECTIVE

the exterior walls
▶ outer, outside, external, outermost
AN OPPOSITE IS interior

exterminate VERB

They came with orders to exterminate all alien life.
▶ eradicate, annihilate, eliminate, wipe out, do away with, massacre, kill

external ADJECTIVE

an external surface
▶ outer, outside, exterior, outermost

extinct ADJECTIVE

1 *an extinct volcano*
▶ inactive, extinguished
OPPOSITES ARE active, dormant
2 *an extinct species*
▶ lost, vanished, defunct, died out, dead, destroyed, obsolete, exterminated
OPPOSITES ARE extant, living, surviving

extinction NOUN

Some breeds face extinction.
▶ disappearance, extermination, eradication, annihilation, death, obliteration

extinguish VERB

Extinguish all fires before leaving the site.
▶ put out, douse, quench, smother, damp down, snuff out
AN OPPOSITE IS light

extort VERB

He went around extorting money from local residents.
▶ force, exact, extract, wrest, coerce, bully, (*more informal*) screw

extortionate ADJECTIVE

Rents have become extortionate in this area.
▶ exorbitant, excessive, unreasonable, prohibitive, inordinate, unrealistic, outrageous, expensive, extravagant, high, overpriced
OPPOSITES ARE reasonable, competitive

extra ADJECTIVE
1 *She had a second job to bring in extra money.*
▶ additional, more, further, added, increased, supplementary, fresh
2 *There was a lot of extra food in the house.*
▶ spare, excess, surplus, superfluous, unused, leftover
3 *The large stores take on extra staff before Christmas.*
▶ temporary, ancillary, auxiliary, supernumerary

extra ADVERB
He worked extra hard just before the exams.
▶ especially, exceptionally, particularly, extremely, unusually

extra NOUN
The Monday holiday was a welcome extra.
▶ addition, supplement, bonus, extension

extract VERB
1 *The dentist extracted her tooth.*
▶ pull out, take out, draw out, remove, withdraw
AN OPPOSITE IS insert
2 *It was difficult to extract any information from them.*
▶ obtain, wrest, draw, glean, elicit, derive, gather, get

extract NOUN
1 *a drink of beef extract*
▶ essence, concentrate, distillation, decoction
2 *He was copying out extracts from a newspaper.*
▶ excerpt, passage, selection, clipping, cutting, piece, citation, quotation, clip

extraordinary ADJECTIVE
What an extraordinary story! Their behaviour was quite extraordinary.
▶ remarkable, exceptional, amazing, astonishing, astounding, wonderful, startling, staggering, stunning, breathtaking, fantastic, phenomenal, incredible
AN OPPOSITE IS ordinary

extravagance NOUN
The new outfit was bought in a fit of extravagance.
▶ indulgence, lavishness, prodigality, profligacy, excess, squandering, improvidence, wastefulness
AN OPPOSITE IS thrift

extravagant ADJECTIVE
an extravagant lifestyle
▶ indulgent, lavish, spendthrift, improvident, squandering, wasteful
AN OPPOSITE IS thrifty

extreme ADJECTIVE
1 *a sure sign of extreme tiredness*
▶ great, intense, exceptional, extraordinary, utter, acute, downright
AN OPPOSITE IS slight
2 *The situation called for extreme measures.*
▶ drastic, serious, radical, dire, desperate, severe, tough, harsh, strict
AN OPPOSITE IS mild
3 *in the extreme north of the country*
▶ farthest, furthest, far-off, distant, remotest, faraway

4 *a person of extreme political opinions*
▶ radical, extremist, fanatical, diehard, zealous
AN OPPOSITE IS moderate

extreme NOUN
These theories go from one extreme to the other.   an attitude pushed to its extreme
▶ limit, extremity, height, end

extremity NOUN
at the southern extremity of the island
▶ limit, edge, end, tip, boundary, margin

extrovert NOUN
Most of the volunteers are extroverts by nature.
▶ socializer, outgoing person, mixer
AN OPPOSITE IS introvert

extrovert ADJECTIVE
an extrovert personality
▶ outgoing, extroverted, sociable, gregarious, positive, active, confident
AN OPPOSITE IS introvert

exuberant ADJECTIVE
a witty and exuberant style of humour
▶ lively, ebullient, high-spirited, sparkling, effusive, enthusiastic, exhilarated, cheerful, outgoing

exult VERB
The staff exulted at the good news about the business.
▶ rejoice, delight, celebrate, be joyful, be glad, be delighted

exultant ADJECTIVE
The exultant winners waved to the crowd.
▶ jubilant, joyful, triumphant, exhilarated, joyous, ecstatic

eye NOUN
1 *He has a sharp eye.*
▶ eyesight, vision, power of sight, visual perception
RELATED ADJECTIVES ocular, ophthalmic
2 *Not much escaped her attentive eye.*
▶ watch, observation, vigilance, notice
3 **eyes** *It was a dreadful mistake in our eyes.*
▶ opinion, view, judgement, way of thinking, viewpoint, (to our) mind
an eye for *an eye for detail*
▶ an appreciation of, an awareness of, an understanding of, a perception of, a sensitivity for, an instinct for

eye VERB
He eyed the visitors carefully.
▶ look at, watch, observe, view, gaze at, glance at, scrutinize, examine

eye-witness NOUN
The police case depends on the evidence of an eye-witness.
▶ bystander, looker-on, onlooker, witness, observer, spectator, watcher

a
b
c
d
e
f
g
h
i
j
k
l
m
n
o
p
q
r
s
t
u
v
w
x
y
z

Ff

fable NOUN
the fable of the fox and the crow
▶ story, tale, parable, moral tale

fabric NOUN
1 *Special fabrics are often used for the seats.*
▶ cloth, material, stuff, textile
2 *The bomb did some damage to the fabric of the building.*
▶ structure, framework, frame, construction, make-up

fabricate VERB
The witness had fabricated his evidence.
▶ invent, falsify, make up, concoct, trump up

fabulous ADJECTIVE
1 *They had a fabulous time in Morocco.*
▶ wonderful, marvellous, fantastic, splendid, magnificent
2 *fabulous places you read about in stories*
▶ legendary, mythical, imaginary, fictitious, fantastic

façade NOUN
1 *the façade of the house*
▶ front, frontage, exterior, aspect
2 *their constant joking was just a façade*
▶ show, front, display, pretence, affectation, posture, act, pose, sham

face NOUN
1 *She has a lovely face.*
▶ features, countenance, visage, profile, physiognomy
2 *His face became angry.*
▶ expression, look, appearance, manner, bearing, countenance
3 *A cube has six faces.*
▶ side, surface, plane, aspect
4 *the north face of the house*
▶ aspect, façade
5 *He put on a brave face for the sake of his visitors.*
▶ front, show, display, act

face VERB
1 *The hotel faces the lake.*
▶ overlook, be opposite (to), front, give on to
2 *You will face a lot of criticism.*
▶ meet, encounter, experience, confront
face up to *She faced up to all her obligations.*
▶ accept, come to terms with, recognize, acknowledge, deal with, cope with

facet NOUN
every facet of the situation
▶ aspect, feature, characteristic, detail, particular

facetious ADJECTIVE
That's enough of the facetious remarks, thank you.
▶ flippant, frivolous, jocular, humorous, funny, witty, amusing, comical, glib
AN OPPOSITE IS serious

facile ADJECTIVE
a facile explanation
▶ simplistic, superficial, over-simple, shallow, glib, pat
AN OPPOSITE IS profound

facilitate VERB
Use of video and other classroom aids will facilitate rapid learning.
▶ assist, support, enable, allow, promote, encourage, further, make way for

facility NOUN
1 *She has a great facility for singing.*
▶ aptitude, talent, flair, faculty, adeptness, skill (in) expertise (in)
2 *This facility is used for copying music to a CD.*
▶ function, device, provision
3 **facilities** *the use of a sauna and sports facilities*
▶ amenities, resources, services, equipment, provisions

fact NOUN
It is a fact that car use has risen steeply in the last decade.
▶ reality, truth, actuality, certainty, fait accompli
AN OPPOSITE IS fiction
the facts *The jury has to take all the facts into account*
▶ evidence, information, details, data, circumstances, particulars, aspects

faction NOUN
Fighting between the two rival factions began almost immediately.
▶ group, side, party, section, contingent, camp, clique, cabal

factor NOUN
Cost was a key factor in the decision.
▶ circumstance, element, feature, component, ingredient, influence, aspect, determinant

factory NOUN
I worked in a factory that made parts for tractors.
▶ manufacturing plant, workshop, works, assembly line

factual ADJECTIVE
a factual description of the events
▶ truthful, accurate, historical, authentic, genuine, realistic, faithful, objective

faculty NOUN
1 *the faculty of speech*
▶ power, capability, capacity, facility
2 *a faculty for settling disputes*
▶ aptitude, talent, facility, flair, adeptness, skill (in), expertise (in)
3 **faculties**
▶ senses, wits, intelligence, reason, powers

fad NOUN
Rap music was not just a passing fad.
► craze, fashion, trend, vogue, whim, passion, enthusiasm, obsession, compulsion, (*more informal*) rage, (*more informal*) thing

faddy ADJECTIVE
(*informal*) *Luke was such a faddy eater.*
► fussy, finicky, (*informal*) picky, (*informal*) choosy

fade VERB
1 *The light has faded the colours.*
► blanch, bleach, discolour, whiten
AN OPPOSITE IS brighten
2 *The music began to fade.*
► weaken, decline, decrease, diminish, dwindle, dim, wane, disappear, evanesce, fail, melt away, pale, vanish
AN OPPOSITE IS intensify
3 *The flowers had faded by now.*
► wither, wilt, droop, flag, perish, shrivel
AN OPPOSITE IS bloom
4 *Their enthusiasm was fading.*
► decline, diminish, dwindle, fail, flag, sink, disappear

fail VERB
1 *In the end all attempts failed.*
► be unsuccessful, go wrong, miscarry, fall through, come to grief, collapse
AN OPPOSITE IS succeed
2 *The business had failed and the family faced ruin.*
► collapse, founder, go under, go bankrupt, (*more informal*) fold
AN OPPOSITE IS prosper
3 *She was angry with her daughter who had failed to contact her.*
► neglect, forget, omit
4 *Her health was failing.*
► deteriorate, decline, weaken, sink, collapse
AN OPPOSITE IS improve
5 *They believe we have failed them.*
► let down, disappoint, betray, desert
AN OPPOSITE IS support
6 *He failed one of his exams.*
► be unsuccessful in, not pass
AN OPPOSITE IS pass

failing NOUN
She loved him despite his failings.
► fault, weakness, shortcoming, flaw, defect
OPPOSITES ARE strength, strong point

failure NOUN
1 *The negotiations ended in failure.*
► disappointment, lack of success, defeat, disaster
2 *The plan proved to be a failure.*
► disaster, catastrophe, fiasco, debacle, blunder, mistake, (*more informal*) flop, (*more informal*) damp squib
3 *a failure in the power supply*
► breakdown, fault, malfunction
4 *To do nothing might be regarded as a failure of duty.*
► dereliction, neglect, omission, deficiency

faint ADJECTIVE
1 *There was a faint smell of gas.*
► slight, indistinct, vague, weak
AN OPPOSITE IS strong
2 *The sky had a faint pink colour.*
► pale, light, hazy, weak
AN OPPOSITE IS bright
3 *We heard a faint cry from the next room.*
► quiet, muted, muffled, feeble, weak
AN OPPOSITE IS loud
4 *There is a faint possibility of an improvement in the weather.*
► slight, slim, slender, remote, small, vague, doubtful
AN OPPOSITE IS strong
5 *She was feeling faint and had to lie down.*
► dizzy, giddy, light-headed, weak, (*more informal*) woozy

faint VERB
He grew pale and seemed about to faint.
► pass out, lose consciousness, black out, collapse, (*more informal*) flake out, (*literary*) swoon

fair ADJECTIVE
1 *It doesn't seem fair to blame the children.*
► just, equitable, reasonable, honourable
AN OPPOSITE IS unfair
2 *They gave a fair assessment of the situation.*
► honest, impartial, reasonable, objective, dispassionate, neutral, even-handed
OPPOSITES ARE unreasonable, biassed
3 *She believes she has a fair chance of success. He had achieved a fair result in his exams.*
► moderate, reasonable, average, satisfactory, adequate, acceptable, tolerable, respectable, decent
OPPOSITES ARE excellent, outstanding
4 *There was a fair amount of traffic going past.*
► considerable, moderate, average
5 *She had blue eyes and fair hair.*
► blond(e), light, pale, yellow
6 *It was a good match played in fair weather.*
► fine, dry, bright, clear, sunny, warm
OPPOSITES ARE bad, wet, inclement

fair NOUN
1 *a country fair*
► fete, gala, carnival, funfair, festival
2 *an antiques fair*
► market, sale, mart, bazaar
3 *a book fair*
► exhibition, display, show, presentation

fairly ADVERB
The news is fairly good.
► reasonably, moderately, tolerably, quite, rather, somewhat, (*more informal*) pretty
AN OPPOSITE IS extremely

fairy tale, **fairy story** NOUN
fairy tales about witches and dragons
► folk tale, legend, myth, story

faith NOUN

1 *His employers had complete faith in him.*
► trust, confidence, hope, belief, reliance
2 *Her faith is very precious to her.*
► religion, belief, religious conviction

faithful ADJECTIVE

1 *He wondered if Clara had a faithful partner waiting for her at home.*
► loyal, devoted, constant, dependable, dutiful, reliable, staunch, steadfast, trusty, trustworthy, close, consistent, unswerving
OPPOSITES ARE unfaithful, disloyal
2 *He kept a faithful record of the events of that day.*
► accurate, true, truthful, precise, exact, authentic
AN OPPOSITE IS inaccurate

fake ADJECTIVE

1 *You could tell the diamonds were fake.*
► imitation, artificial, simulated, synthetic, unreal, false, bogus, sham, (*more informal*) phoney
2 *He brought out a wad of fake banknotes.*
► counterfeit, forged, false, sham, bogus, fraudulent, (*more informal*) phoney
AN OPPOSITE IS genuine

fake NOUN

1 *One of the paintings was a fake.*
► forgery, copy, imitation, reproduction, replica, duplicate, hoax, sham, simulation, (*more informal*) phoney
2 *The man who claimed to be a surgeon is a fake.*
► fraud, charlatan, impostor, cheat, (*more informal*) quack, (*more informal*) phoney

fake VERB

They would have to fake a death certificate.
► forge, fabricate, counterfeit, falsify, (*more informal*) fiddle

fall VERB

1 *He stumbled and fell.*
► tumble, fall over, topple, trip over, keel over, collapse
AN OPPOSITE IS get up
2 *Flood levels began to fall at last.*
► drop, go down, subside, recede
AN OPPOSITE IS rise
3 *Bombs continued to fall all night.*
► drop, descend, plummet, rain down
4 *Prices are expected to fall soon.*
► go down, decrease, decline, diminish
OPPOSITES ARE rise, increase
5 *The Empire in the East did not fall for several more centuries.*
► decline, collapse, disintegrate, deteriorate
AN OPPOSITE IS flourish
6 *Thousands fell in the war.*
► die, be killed, be lost, lose your life, perish, (*literary*) be slain
7 *Her birthday falls on a Saturday this year.*
► occur, come, happen, take place
fall apart *The sheds fell apart in the high winds.*
► collapse, disintegrate, break up, fragment, crumble, fall to pieces, shatter

fall asleep *She couldn't help falling asleep.*
► doze off, drop off, go to sleep, (*more informal*) nod off
fall in *The roof has fallen in.*
► collapse, come down, cave in
fall off *Demand for these products has fallen off lately.*
► decline, slacken, decrease, lessen, drop off
fall out *They fell out over money.*
► quarrel, argue, disagree, fight, squabble, bicker, clash
fall through *In the end the plan fell through.*
► come to nothing, fail, miscarry, founder, collapse
OPPOSITES ARE go ahead, succeed

fall NOUN

1 *He was hurt in a fall.*
► tumble, spill, topple, stumble
2 *Economists expect a fall in house prices.*
► drop, decline, fall-off, decrease, dip, lessening, reduction, slump
OPPOSITES ARE rise, increase
3 *an epic poem on the fall of Troy*
► surrender, capitulation, submission, defeat
4 *the fall of the Roman Empire*
► downfall, collapse, ruin, failure, demise, destruction

fallacy NOUN

It is a fallacy to think we can change our character.
► misconception, delusion, mistake, falsehood, error, myth

fallible ADJECTIVE

Humans are fallible beings.
► imperfect, erring, error-prone, weak
AN OPPOSITE IS infallible

false ADJECTIVE

1 *a false alibi*
► untrue, fictitious, invented, concocted, fabricated, invalid, spurious
AN OPPOSITE IS genuine
2 *a false friend*
► unfaithful, disloyal, unreliable, dishonourable, untrustworthy
AN OPPOSITE IS faithful
3 *false hair*
► artificial, unreal, imitation, synthetic, simulated, fake, sham
AN OPPOSITE IS real
4 *a false belief*
► incorrect, erroneous, mistaken, fallacious, wrong
AN OPPOSITE IS correct

falsify VERB

The date of the entry had been falsified.
► tamper with, fake, fabricate, alter, pervert

falter VERB

1 *The country must not falter in the face of such danger.*
► hesitate, waver, delay, vacillate, flinch, hold back, lose confidence, be indecisive, get cold feet
AN OPPOSITE IS persevere
2 *He faltered for a moment over an awkward name.*
► stammer, stumble, stutter

fame NOUN

Their fame spread all over the world.
► renown, celebrity, stardom, popularity, notability, prestige, reputation, glory, name, stature, standing, prominence

familiar ADJECTIVE

1 *The room was full of familiar faces.*
► well-known, recognizable, accustomed, everyday, commonplace
2 *a familiar friend*
► close, intimate, dear
3 *The atmosphere in the house was friendly and familiar.*
► informal, casual, relaxed, natural, open, unreserved, free and easy, unceremonious

familiarity NOUN

1 *A familiarity with at least one European language is needed.*
► acquaintance, knowledge (of), understanding (of)
2 *They spoke to one another with a great deal of familiarity.*
► informality, intimacy, closeness, friendliness, naturalness, casualness

familiarize VERB

familiarize with *Our aim is to familiarize the public with basic word-processing programs.*
► introduce (to), accustom (to), acclimatize (to), make familiar (with), teach

---

family NOUN

1 *a large house divided to accommodate two families*
► household
2 *She sends a yearly newsletter to family and friends.*
► relatives, relations, kin, kinsmen, clan
USAGE Kin and kinsmen are words you normally find only in stories and literature.
3 *parents clearly devoted to their family*
► children, offspring, daughters and sons
RELATED ADJECTIVE domestic

same generation: sister, brother, sibling (= brother or sister), twin, triplet; half-sister, half-brother (= a sister or brother having one parent the same); stepbrother, stepsister (= a child of a step-parent from a previous marriage); cousin; fiancé (= the man a woman is going to marry), fiancée (= the woman a man is going to marry), husband, wife, spouse (= a husband or wife), partner; widow (= a woman whose husband has died), widower (= a man whose wife has died).

older generation: ancestor, forebear, forefather; grandparent, grandmother, grandfather; parent, mother, father; step-parent, stepmother, stepfather; guardian, godparent, godmother, godfather; aunt, uncle.   ►►

---

younger generations: descendant, offspring, heir; child, daughter, son; stepchild, stepdaughter, stepson; ward (= a child looked after by a guardian); godchild, goddaughter, godson; niece, nephew; grandchild, granddaughter, grandson.

---

famine NOUN

a country constantly threatened by famine
► hunger, malnutrition, scarcity, shortage, starvation, dearth, want
AN OPPOSITE IS plenty

famous ADJECTIVE

a famous singer
► well-known, celebrated, renowned, acclaimed, admired, prominent, revered, distinguished, honoured, eminent, exalted, illustrious, great, notable, noted
OPPOSITES ARE unknown, obscure

fan NOUN

1 *a fan of rock music*
► devotee, enthusiast, admirer, lover, fanatic, addict, aficionado, (*more informal*) freak
2 *A ceiling fan cooled the room.*
► ventilator, blower, extractor, air-conditioner

fanatic NOUN

1 *a religious fanatic*
► extremist, zealot, militant, activist, diehard
2 *a fitness fanatic*
► enthusiast, devotee, admirer, lover, fan, addict, aficionado, (*more informal*) freak

fanatical ADJECTIVE

His ancestors had been fanatical royalists.
► extreme, fervent, passionate, zealous, militant, single-minded, rabid, frenzied, immoderate, irrational, obsessive, bigoted
AN OPPOSITE IS moderate

fanciful ADJECTIVE

full of fanciful ideas
► unrealistic, far-fetched, fantastic, imaginary, whimsical, illusory, visionary, romantic

fancy ADJECTIVE

1 *The belts are decorated with fancy patterns.*
► elaborate, decorative, ornamental, ornate
2 *They don't like wearing fancy clothes.*
► showy, ostentatious, gaudy

fancy NOUN

1 *The little cottage caught our fancy.*
► imagination, ingenuity, whim
2 *I had a fancy they might be there.*
► notion, idea, belief, impression, suspicion, hunch

fancy VERB

1 *I fancied I could see a light in the sky.*
► imagine, think, suppose, believe, suspect
2 *I fancy a doughnut.*
► feel like, wish for, want, desire

3 *This was the boy she had fancied for so long.*
► be attracted to, find attractive, have a crush on, desire, want

fantastic ADJECTIVE
1 *We had a fantastic time.*
► wonderful, marvellous, fabulous, splendid, magnificent
2 *It's a fantastic idea.*
► fanciful, extraordinary, incredible, unbelievable

fantasy NOUN
a fantasy about living on a desert island
► dream, daydream, pipe dream, delusion, fancy

far ADJECTIVE
He'd been to many far places.
► distant, faraway, far off, remote, our of the way, outlying

farce NOUN
1 *They went to see a farce at the local theatre.*
► comedy, slapstick
2 *The trial had been a farce.*
► travesty, absurdity, sham, mockery, charade

fare NOUN
a standard-class rail fare
► price, charge, cost, payment, fee

far-fetched ADJECTIVE
The storyline was too far-fetched and the acting was poor.
► improbable, unlikely, implausible, incredible, dubious, doubtful, unconvincing

farm NOUN
a farm of 200 acres
► smallholding, farmstead, estate, grange

farm VERB
The same family had farmed the land for centuries.
► cultivate, work, till, plough

farming NOUN
Farming makes an important contribution to the country's economy.
► agriculture, cultivation, husbandry, land management, tillage, crofting, agronomy
RELATED ADJECTIVES agricultural, pastoral

fascinate VERB
Most people are fascinated by the way words change their meaning.
► interest (in), engross, captivate, enthrall, absorb, beguile, entrance, attract, charm

fascinating ADJECTIVE
a fascinating book about the invention of the camera
► interesting, engrossing, intriguing, captivating, enthralling, absorbing, beguiling, entrancing, attractive, charming

fashion NOUN
1 *the fashion for long dresses*
► trend, vogue, craze
2 *She was behaving in a very odd fashion.*
► way, manner, mode, method

fashionable ADJECTIVE
a fashionable hotel in central London
► stylish, popular, chic, elegant, modish, (*more informal*) trendy
AN OPPOSITE IS unfashionable

fast ADJECTIVE
1 *She drives a fast car   The race was run at a fast pace   Delivery is always fast.*
► quick, rapid, speedy, swift, brisk, lively, sprightly, flying, high-speed, (*more informal*) nippy
AN OPPOSITE IS slow

fast ADVERB
1 *The train was travelling fast towards the tunnel.*
► quickly, rapidly, swiftly, speedily, at full speed, at full tilt, briskly
AN OPPOSITE IS slowly
2 *The wheels were stuck fast in the mud.*
► tightly, securely, immovably
3 *By now she was fast asleep.*
► deeply, sound, completely

fast VERB
a month in which many people are fasting
► go without food, abstain, deny yourself
AN OPPOSITE IS overeat

fasten VERB
1 *a sleeveless jacket that you fasten at the back*
► do up, tie, close, button up
OPPOSITES ARE unfasten, undo
2 *We were told to fasten all windows.*
► close, secure, lock, bolt
AN OPPOSITE IS unfasten
3 *Brackets are fastened to the wall.*
► fix, attach, secure, bolt
AN OPPOSITE IS remove

fastidious ADJECTIVE
Louise had always been fastidious about her appearance.
► particular, punctilious, discriminating, scrupulous, fussy, choosy, finicky, (*more informal*) pernickety

---

fat ADJECTIVE This word is often overused. Here are some alternatives:
1 *A fat woman came into the room.*
► plump, stout, large, overweight, corpulent, rotund, podgy, obese, tubby, portly
OPPOSITES ARE thin, slim
2 *He was reading a fat book.*
► thick, bulky, chunky, substantial
3 (*informal*) *A fat cheque arrived just before Christmas.*
► large, substantial, sizeable, generous

---

fat NOUN
He has a lot of fat to get rid of.
► fatness, obesity, blubber, (*technical*) adipose tissue, (*more informal*) flab

fatal ADJECTIVE
1 *He delivered a fatal blow with the axe.*
► deadly, mortal, lethal

2 *She contracted a fatal illness in the Far East.*
▶ deadly, terminal, mortal, incurable, malignant

3 *That decision proved to be a fatal mistake.*
▶ disastrous, catastrophic, calamitous, destructive

fatality NOUN
There were several fatalities from the blast.
▶ casualty, death, loss

fate NOUN
1 *I am ready for whatever fate has to offer.*
▶ destiny, chance, providence, fortune, the future, luck, the stars, karma, kismet

2 *He was to meet a terrible fate.*
▶ death, demise, end, ruin, doom

fated ADJECTIVE
They were fated not to meet again.
▶ destined, doomed, predestined, preordained, predetermined, meant, bound, certain, intended

fateful ADJECTIVE
The fateful meeting took place that week.
▶ momentous, decisive, crucial, critical, historic
OPPOSITES ARE trivial, unimportant

father NOUN
His father was now living in Bristol.
▶ male parent, (*more informal*) dad, (*more informal*) daddy, (*more informal*) pop, (*old-fashioned*) pater
RELATED ADJECTIVE paternal

fathom VERB
There was a look on his face that she couldn't quite fathom.
▶ understand, comprehend, work out, make out, get to the bottom of

fatigue NOUN
Fatigue got the better of them.
▶ tiredness, weariness, exhaustion, lethargy, debility, feebleness, weakness
OPPOSITES ARE vitality, energy

fatten VERB
Farmers fatten their livestock.
▶ feed up, build up, make fat

fatty ADJECTIVE
fatty food
▶ greasy, oily, fat, (*technical*) oleaginous

fault NOUN
1 *a fault in the manufacturing process*
▶ defect, deficiency, failure, failing, flaw, weakness, imperfection, shortcoming, blemish, malfunction, snag

2 *There is a fault in their argument.*
▶ flaw, error, fallacy, inaccuracy, miscalculation, mistake

3 *He had his faults, but carelessness was not one of them.*
▶ failing, weakness, shortcoming, flaw, defect
OPPOSITES ARE strength, strong point

4 *The problem was my fault.*
▶ responsibility, liability, mistake, error

fault VERB
I cannot fault your reasoning.
▶ criticize, find fault with, censure, impugn, (*more informal*) pick holes in

faultless ADJECTIVE
Her French is faultless.
▶ perfect, flawless, impeccable, exemplary, fluent

faulty ADJECTIVE
The light bulb was faulty.
▶ broken, defective, not working, malfunctioning, inoperative, out of order, deficient

favour NOUN
1 *She regards us with great favour.*
▶ approval, approbation, commendation, goodwill, kindness, friendliness, benevolence, esteem
OPPOSITES ARE disfavour, disapproval

2 *Could you do me a favour?*
▶ good turn, benefit, kindness, kind act, courtesy, indulgence, good deed

favour VERB
1 *I favour casual clothes.*
▶ prefer, choose, opt for, approve of, like

2 *The government favours a policy of peace.*
▶ recommend, support, back, subscribe to, promote, advocate, espouse, endorse, champion

favourable ADJECTIVE
1 *CDs at favourable prices*
▶ advantageous, beneficial, competitive, convenient

2 *a favourable assessment of their ability*
▶ positive, encouraging, enthusiastic, complimentary, sympathetic, approving, agreeable

favourite ADJECTIVE
John was her favourite nephew.
▶ best-loved, most-liked, preferred, favoured, treasured, dearest, special, chosen, pet

favourite NOUN
(*informal*) *Sarah had always been one of his favourites.*
▶ first choice, preference, darling, pet, idol, apple of your eye

favouritism NOUN
We want to be fair and avoid favouritism.
▶ preferential treatment, partiality, one-sidedness, partisanship, bias, prejudice

fear NOUN
1 *I remember the shock of fear when I heard her scream.*
▶ terror, fright, horror, alarm, panic, dread, trepidation

2 *He found it hard to overcome his fears.*
▶ anxiety, concern, foreboding, unease, misgiving

fear VERB
1 *They all feared Ted and kept away from him.*
▶ be afraid of, be scared of, dread, be terrified of, tremble at, worry about

2 *We fear a bad outcome. I fear you may be right.*
▶ suspect, expect, foresee, anticipate

fearful ADJECTIVE

1 *The generals were fearful of enemy reprisals.*
▶ afraid, frightened, scared, nervous, apprehensive (about), anxious (about), uneasy (about), (*more informal*) jittery (about)

2 *She felt a fearful pain in her leg.*
▶ terrible, dreadful, frightful, horrible, awful

3 (*informal*) *There would be a fearful row if anyone found out.*
▶ major, very great, dreadful, terrible, awful

feasible ADJECTIVE

With luck the plan might be feasible.
▶ practicable, practical, workable, achievable, realizable, attainable, possible, viable
OPPOSITES ARE impractical, impossible

feast NOUN

a feast fit for a king
▶ banquet, meal, dinner, (*more formal*) repast, (*more informal*) spread, (*more informal*) binge

feast VERB

They feasted for three whole days.
▶ eat your fill, wine and dine, gorge yourself

feat NOUN

a feat of great daring
▶ deed, exploit, act, accomplishment, achievement, undertaking, action, attainment, performance

feature NOUN

1 *This latest incident has some notable features.*
▶ characteristic, circumstance, aspect, point, facet, detail, peculiarity, quality, trait

2 *a magazine feature*
▶ article, report, story, item, piece, column

3 **features** *Her coiled hair accentuated her fine features.*
▶ face, countenance, expression, lineaments, look, (*more formal*) physiognomy

feature VERB

1 *This year's concerts will feature new young performers.*
▶ present, promote, highlight, focus on, give prominence to, spotlight

2 *The players will feature in a charity promotion.*
▶ appear, participate, take part, play a role, star

fed up ADJECTIVE

1 *You look tired and fed up.*
▶ depressed, dejected, dispirited, despondent, disheartened, miserable, cast down, sad, down, glum

2 **be fed up with** *I was totally fed up with all their whinging.*
▶ be sick of, be tired of, be weary of, have had enough of

fee NOUN

1 *You can have your order delivered for a small fee.*
▶ charge, payment, cost, sum, price

2 *The membership fee is due in April.*
▶ subscription, charge, dues

feeble ADJECTIVE

1 *My feeble attempts to protest were ignored.*
▶ weak, ineffective, inadequate, tame, poor, flimsy, shallow

2 *The illness left him too feeble to stand.*
▶ weak, weakened, frail, delicate, sickly, poorly, infirm, incapacitated, helpless

3 *Her brother was a feeble character.*
▶ spineless, timid, weak, ineffective, ineffectual

feed VERB

1 *She has a large family to feed.*
▶ nourish, sustain, provide for, cater for

2 *He was feeding information to the enemy.*
▶ supply, provide, deliver, present

3 *They spend all their time feeding and sleeping.*
▶ eat, take food, have a meal, dine

4 **feed on** *The local wildlife feeds on these plants.*
▶ eat, live on, exist on, consume, devour

feel VERB

1 *He felt the back of his head with his hand.*
▶ touch, stroke, finger, handle, caress, fondle

2 *She felt the muzzle of a gun in her side.*
▶ sense, perceive, detect, be aware of, be conscious of, discern

3 *Did you feel any pain?*
▶ experience, suffer, undergo, endure, go through

4 *We feel you should apologize to her.*
▶ believe, think, consider, consider it right, reckon, judge

5 *The fabric feels soft.*
▶ seem, appear, strike you as

feel for *She had had a bad time and I felt for her.*
▶ feel sorry for, sympathize with, pity, commiserate with

feel like *Do you feel like a drink?*
▶ fancy, wish for, want, desire

feel NOUN

1 *The wood had a warm feel.*
▶ texture, quality, surface, touch, impression

2 *She has a good feel for the music.*
▶ aptitude, flair, talent, gift, knack

feeling NOUN

1 *They enjoyed the feeling of power and superiority*
▶ sensation, sense, awareness, consciousness, perception

2 *I had a feeling she wouldn't be coming.*
▶ suspicion, inkling, notion, idea, hunch, fancy, premonition

3 *There was a friendly feeling about the place.*
▶ atmosphere, aura, air, ambience, climate, quality, mood

4 *She spoke with great feeling.*
▶ emotion, passion, intensity, concern, tenderness, warmth, ardour

5 *He had lost all feeling in his arm.*
▶ sensation, perception, sense of touch

fell VERB

1 *A guard felled him with a single blow.*
▶ knock down, knock over, bring down, flatten, prostrate, (*more informal*) floor

2 *Dead trees have to be felled fairly quickly.*
▶ chop down, cut down

fellow NOUN
He's a decent fellow, always ready to help out.
▶ chap, man, boy, individual, (*more informal*) bloke, (*more informal*) guy

female ADJECTIVE
female characteristics
▶ feminine, womanly

feminine ADJECTIVE
a feminine young woman who revels in her freedom
▶ womanly, ladylike, girlish, female

fence NOUN
The area was surrounded by a tall fence.
▶ railing, enclosure, barrier, wall, paling, hedge

fence VERB
fence in *You will need to fence in the hens.*
▶ confine, pen in, coop up, shut in, close in, hedge in
fence off *More land would be fenced off.*
▶ enclose, surround, encircle, separate off, section off, partition off, cut off

fend VERB
fend for yourself *They can fend for themselves for a few days.*
▶ look after yourself, care for yourself, take care of yourself, manage, cope, (*more informal*) get by
fend off *A small force might not be enough to fend off an attack.*
▶ repel, repulse, resist, ward off, beat off, fight off, hold back, thwart

ferment NOUN (with the stress on *fer-*)
Constant change leaves the organization in a state of ferment.
▶ turmoil, upheaval, agitation, unrest, commotion, excitement, disruption, confusion, disorder

ferment VERB (with the stress on *-ment*)
Low pay ferments resentment.
▶ cause, bring about, rouse, stir up, foment, engender, provoke, incite, stimulate

ferocious ADJECTIVE
He was the victim of a ferocious attack.
▶ fierce, brutal, violent, savage, cruel, vicious, barbaric, callous, heartless, cold-blooded, pitiless, ruthless, merciless, vile, sadistic, brutish
OPPOSITES ARE gentle, humane

ferocity NOUN
The police were surprised by the ferocity of the attack.
▶ savagery, brutality, cruelty, viciousness, fierceness, barbarity, callousness, heartlessness, cold-bloodedness, ruthlessness
AN OPPOSITE IS gentleness

fertile ADJECTIVE
1 *fertile soil*
▶ fruitful, productive, prolific, rich, fecund
AN OPPOSITE IS infertile
2 *a fertile mind*
▶ imaginative, inventive, creative, resourceful, ingenious

fertilize VERB
1 *The sperm has a tail that allows it to swim before fertilizing the egg.*
▶ impregnate, inseminate
2 *Insects fertilize the plants.*
▶ pollinate
3 *After ploughing the land is fertilized.*
▶ enrich, feed, dress, compost, manure

fertilizer NOUN
Farmers depend on good fertilizer.
▶ manure, dung, compost, dressing

fervent ADJECTIVE
1 *a fervent hope that we can be friends*
▶ heartfelt, earnest, eager, intense, keen, strong
2 *a fervent cricket supporter*
▶ eager, ardent, passionate, impassioned, avid, zealous, keen, enthusiastic

fester VERB
1 *The wound in his side had festered.*
▶ become infected, turn septic, suppurate, ulcerate, putrefy, discharge, gather, go bad, decay
2 *He did not want to spend years festering in jail.*
▶ languish, waste away, wither, rot, moulder

---

festival NOUN
The city has a music festival in the spring.
▶ jubilee, pageant, carnival, gala, fête, jamboree, celebration, festivities, anniversary
NAMES FOR RELIGIOUS FESTIVALS
Buddhist festivals: Buddha Day, Nirvana Day.
Christian festivals: Lent, Easter, Christmas Day.
Hindu festivals: Holi, Diwali.
Muslim festivals: Ramadan, Eid.
Jewish festivals: Passover, Rosh Hashanah, Yom Kippur, Hanukkah.
Sikh festivals: Baisakhi, Birth of Guru Nanak.

---

festive ADJECTIVE
A festive atmosphere encourages the children to have a good time.
▶ jolly, joyous, joyful, happy, merry, cheerful, cheery, jubilant, convivial, celebratory, gay, gleeful, jovial, light-hearted
OPPOSITES ARE gloomy, sombre

festivities PLURAL NOUN
The family returned home in time for the New Year festivities.
▶ celebrations, revels, revelry, festival, party, entertainments, amusements, fun, jollification

fetch VERB
1 *She went to fetch a bucket from the cupboard.*
▶ get, bring, collect, pick up, retrieve, obtain, bear, call for, carry, convey, import, transfer, transport
2 *Will you fetch your brother from the station?*
▶ collect, pick up, transport, bring, get, convey, conduct
3 *We had better fetch the doctor.*
▶ send for, call for, summon, go for, get, bring

4 *By this time he reckoned the house might fetch a cool million.*
▶ sell for, be sold for, be bought for, raise, realize, bring in, earn, go for, make, produce

fetching ADJECTIVE
The children wore fetching little outfits.
▶ pretty, attractive, appealing, delightful, charming
AN OPPOSITE IS unattractive

fete NOUN
a village fete
▶ gala, fair, festival, pageant, bazaar, garden party, jubilee, carnival

feud NOUN
The family feud came to a head this week.
▶ vendetta, dispute, conflict, rivalry, strife, quarrel , antagonism, hostility, enmity, animosity

fever NOUN
1 *He caught some sort of fever and never got over it.*
▶ feverishness, high temperature, delirium
2 *We were in a fever of impatience waiting for them to return.*
▶ frenzy, ferment
3 *World Cup football fever*
▶ excitement, agitation, passion, frenzy

feverish ADJECTIVE
1 *She looked flushed and feverish.*
▶ fevered, burning, hot, febrile, inflamed, delirious
2 *The house was a scene of feverish activity.*
▶ frenzied, frantic, frenetic, excited, hectic, agitated, hurried, hasty, impatient, restless
OPPOSITES ARE calm, gentle

few ADJECTIVE
1 *Few details are available about the crash* (*informal*) *A few people had gathered at the gates.*
▶ not many, hardly any, a small number of, a handful of
AN OPPOSITE IS many
2 *Buses are few at this time of night.*
▶ scarce, scant, meagre, in short supply, thin on the ground, few and far between

few PRONOUN
I only have a few left.
▶ small number, handful, sprinkling, couple, one or two
AN OPPOSITE IS lot

fiasco NOUN
The invasion attempt ended up as a fiasco.
▶ failure, debacle, catastrophe, disaster, shambles, farce, (*more informal*) washout, (*more informal*) cock-up

fib NOUN
It was obvious that he was telling fibs.
▶ lie, untruth, story, falsehood

fibre NOUN
1 *The fibres are then spun, either by hand or by machine.*
▶ thread, strand, hair, filament

2 *clothes in natural fibres*
▶ cloth, fabric, stuff, material, substance
3 *a diet low in fat and high in fibre*
▶ roughage, bulk, fibrous material
4 *a person of great moral fibre*
▶ character, backbone, toughness, courage, determination, spirit, tenacity

fickle ADJECTIVE
His fickle supporters soon deserted him.
▶ changeable, disloyal, unfaithful, inconstant, changing, erratic, faithless, variable, unreliable, unstable, vacillating, volatile, unpredictable
OPPOSITES ARE loyal, faithful, constant

---

fiction NOUN
1 *a course in twentieth-century fiction*
▶ novels, stories, creative writing
AN OPPOSITE IS non-fiction
2 *The allegations were a total fiction.*
▶ invention, fabrication, concoction, deception, fantasy, figment, flight of fancy, pack of lies, (*more informal*) tall story
OPPOSITES ARE fact, truth

NAMES FOR TYPES OF FICTION

novel, short story; drama, play, poetry; gothic novel (19th-century horror and mystery), ghost story, adventure story, picaresque (adventures of a hero), romantic novel, epistolary novel (story told through exchanges of letters), historical novel (set in a historical period), detective story, science fiction (or sci fi), spy fiction, fantasy, myth, fairy story.

---

fictional ADJECTIVE
a fictional character
▶ imaginary, invented, fabulous, fanciful, legendary, made-up, make-believe, mythical
AN OPPOSITE IS factual

fictitious ADJECTIVE
He used a fictitious name.
▶ invented, false, fake, assumed, spurious, fabricated, fraudulent, unreal, untrue, apocryphal
OPPOSITES ARE genuine, true

fiddle NOUN
1 *a group of fiddle players*
▶ violin
2 (*informal*) *He was involved in a huge tax fiddle.*
▶ fraud, swindle, cheat, trick

fiddle VERB
1 fiddle with *Stephen was fiddling with the CD player.*
▶ tinker with, play about with, tamper with, meddle with, twiddle, finger
2 (*informal*) *The auditors will find out if anyone has fiddled the accounts.*
▶ falsify, misrepresent, rig, alter, interfere with, tamper with, (*more informal*) doctor, (*more informal*) cook

fiddling ADJECTIVE
I get fed up with the fiddling little details
▶ trivial, petty, trifling, paltry, unimportant

fiddly ADJECTIVE
(*informal*) *a row of fiddly buttons and switches*
► intricate, complicated, inaccessible

fidelity NOUN
The nobles were expected to show fidelity to the king.
► loyalty, allegiance, obedience, fealty

fidget VERB
The heat in the room made me fidget.
► wriggle, twitch, jiggle, shuffle about, be jittery

fidgety ADJECTIVE
The audience became bored and fidgety.
► restless, twitchy, jittery, impatient, restive, uneasy, agitated, nervous, on edge
OPPOSITES ARE controlled, still

field NOUN
1 *There was a bull in the next field.*
► enclosure, paddock, pasture
2 *The field was too wet to play on.*
► pitch, ground, sports field, playing field, (*more informal*) park
3 *great names in the field of medicine*
► sphere, domain, area, speciality, subject, discipline
4 *The house lay outside our field of vision.*
► range, scope, extent

fiend NOUN
1 *It was as if he had been possessed by some fiend.*
► demon, devil, evil spirit, imp, bogie
2 *the fiend who had attacked her*
► brute, beast, monster, villain
3 *She was a bit of a fitness fiend.*
► fanatic, enthusiast, addict, devotee, (*more informal*) freak, (*more informal*) nut

fiendish ADJECTIVE
1 *All sorts of fiendish tortures might be awaiting them.*
► wicked, cruel, diabolical, brutal, barbaric, vicious, unspeakable
2 *a fiendish plot to kill the king*
► cunning, clever, ingenious, canny, devious, wily

fierce ADJECTIVE
1 *a fierce dog*
► ferocious, vicious, savage, wild, brutal
OPPOSITES ARE gentle, tame
2 *fierce competition*
► strong, intense, powerful, keen, aggressive, cutthroat
AN OPPOSITE IS mild
3 *fierce resentment*
► passionate, ardent, intense, strong, powerful
4 *a fierce pain*
► acute, severe, strong, powerful, intense

fiery ADJECTIVE
1 *a fiery furnace*
► burning, blazing, flaming, raging, glowing, scorching, red-hot
2 *She remained calm, despite her fiery temperament.*
► passionate, ardent, fervent, excitable, spirited, lively, volatile, explosive, violent, hot-headed
3 *The sky was a fiery red.*
► bright, vivid, brilliant, intense, vibrant, rich, strong

fight NOUN
1 *He had got into a fight on the way home.*
► brawl, fracas, tussle, struggle
2 *She hated having fights with her boyfriend.*
► quarrel, argument, row, squabble, wrangle, contretemps, altercation, difference of opinion, (*more informal*) bust-up, (*more informal*) slanging match
3 *the fight for women's rights*
► struggle, battle, campaign, effort
4 *a championship fight*
► contest, match, bout, meeting, fixture

fight VERB
1 *Some men were fighting in the street.*
► brawl, tussle, struggle, grapple, wrestle, have a fight, exchange blows
2 *Her sons all fought in the war.*
► serve, be a soldier, join up, take up arms
3 *She and her boyfriend are always fighting.*
► quarrel, argue, row, squabble, wrangle
4 *The unions will fight any proposals to cut jobs.*
► oppose, resist, contest, challenge, defy, object to, combat, withstand
5 *women who fought for their basic freedoms*
► campaign, battle, strive, crusade

fighter NOUN
an enemy fighter
► soldier, combatant, fighting man, fighting woman, warrior

figurative ADJECTIVE
a figurative expression
► metaphorical, symbolic, allegorical, fanciful, non-literal
AN OPPOSITE IS literal

figure NOUN
1 *The final figure was higher than last year.*
► total, sum, amount, number
2 *The third figure is an eight.*
► digit, numeral, character, number
3 *It's hard to put an exact figure on it.*
► amount, price, cost, sum
4 *Jane has a lovely figure.*
► shape, physique, build, proportions, body, frame
5 *By now she had become a public figure.*
► personality, character, celebrity, dignitary, person, individual, personage
6 *He did not want to be seen as a figure of fun.*
► symbol, personification, embodiment, epitome

figure VERB
an animal that figures in many ancient myths
► feature, appear, play a role, has a place

file NOUN
1 *He keeps his business letters in A4 files.*
► folder, binder, portfolio, wallet, sleeve
2 *There is a file on these people at headquarters.*
► dossier, record, set of notes

3 *A file of soldiers was walking up the road.*
▶ line, column, string, train, procession, convoy, stream

file VERB
1 *Completed forms are filed by year in the top drawer.*
▶ classify, arrange, organize, put in order, enter, store, keep, archive
2 *She was sitting filing her nails.*
▶ smooth, shape, rub, polish
3 *The children filed through the door into the sunshine.*
▶ stream, troop, march, parade, walk in a line, proceed in a line

fill VERB
1 *She soon filled a suitcase with the things she needed.*
▶ pack, load
2 *Fill the holes and gaps before you start papering.*
▶ plug, stop, stop up, bung up, block up, seal
3 *With thirty guests we will fill the house.*
▶ crowd, throng, pack, pack into, congest
4 *A smell of coffee filled the room.*
▶ spread through, pervade, permeate, penetrate
5 *Recruits will fill the new posts by the end of the year.*
▶ occupy, take up, be appointed to, move into
6 *A bank loan will fill their needs for now.*
▶ fulfil, satisfy, meet, supply, furnish

fill in
1 *You have to fill in this form.*
▶ complete, fill out, answer
2 *I am filling in for Shirley while she is away.*
▶ deputize, cover, stand in, substitute
3 *Ken will fill us in on the details.*
▶ brief, inform (of), advise (of), apprise (of)

filling NOUN
The cushion was losing its filling.
▶ stuffing, padding, wadding, insides, contents

filling ADJECTIVE
a filling meal
▶ satisfying, nourishing, nutritious, ample, square, solid, substantial

---

film NOUN
1 *There was a film of dust on the table.*
▶ layer, covering, coat, coating, dusting, patina, sheet, veil, skin, screen
2 *The boys are going to see a film this evening.*
▶ movie, picture, feature, (*old-fashioned*) motion picture

NAMES FOR TYPES OF CINEMA FILM

feature film, documentary, cartoon, war film, western, romance, (*informal*) weepie, love story, (*informal*) biopic, science fiction film, horror film, comedy film.

---

filter NOUN
Pass the liquid through a filter.
▶ sieve, strainer, gauze, membrane, mesh, screen

filter VERB
You have to filter the rainwater.
▶ sieve, strain, sift, filtrate, purify, clarify, percolate

filth NOUN
1 *I needed a hose to get the filth off my boots.*
▶ dirt, muck, grime, mud, slime, sludge, garbage, excrement
2 *The newspaper had several pages of filth.*
▶ pornography, smut, indecency, obscenity, (*more informal*) porn

filthy ADJECTIVE
1 *The house was filthy.*
▶ dirty, grubby, mucky, squalid, uncleaned, unwashed
AN OPPOSITE IS clean
2 *Everyone agreed it was a filthy trick.*
▶ nasty, mean, vile, despicable, contemptible, disgusting, shabby
3 *They were accused of using filthy language.*
▶ rude, indecent, coarse, vulgar, lewd, improper, obscene
OPPOSITES ARE clean, polite
4 *He was in a filthy mood.*
▶ bad, foul, bad-tempered, irritable

final ADJECTIVE
1 *the final month of their course*
▶ last, closing, concluding, finishing, end
OPPOSITES ARE first, initial
2 *the final minutes of the match*
▶ last, closing, dying
3 *The judges' decision is final.*
▶ irrevocable, definitive, absolute, indisputable, unalterable, decisive, incontrovertible

finalize VERB
We can now finalize the arrangements for the trip.
▶ complete, conclude, settle, clinch, resolve, decide, confirm, (*more informal*) wrap up

finally ADVERB
The bank finally agreed to loan the money.
▶ eventually, ultimately, in the end, at length, at last

finance NOUN
1 *He needs to learn more about finance.*
▶ economics, money management, accounting, banking, fiscal matters
2 *The company is seeking longer-term finance.*
▶ funding, funds, capital, assets, revenue, income, financial backing
3 *His finances are in a fairly good state.*
▶ resources, assets, financial affairs, money affairs

finance VERB
Private sponsors will finance the venture.
▶ fund, back, subsidize, support, provide money for, invest in, underwrite, pay for, sponsor

financial ADJECTIVE
financial affairs
▶ monetary, fiscal, pecuniary, economic

find VERB
1 *I found some old coins in the cupboard.*
▶ discover, locate, retrieve, track down, come across, chance on, unearth, uncover

2 *We found it odd that there were so many complaints.*
▶ consider, think, believe, reckon, see as, regard as, look on as, view as

3 *You will find that it's helpful to number each paragraph.*
▶ realize, discover, learn, perceive, notice, become aware

4 *I hope you find the success you deserve.*
▶ achieve, attain, win, obtain, acquire, reach, secure, get

find out

1 *At last we will find out what happened.*
▶ learn, ascertain, discover, perceive

2 *The culprits were soon found out.*
▶ reveal, expose, unmask, uncover, (*more informal*) rumble

find NOUN
An ancient ship burial was among the exciting finds.
▶ discovery, acquisition

findings NOUN
The inquiry will announce its findings tomorrow.
▶ judgement, conclusion, recommendation, verdict, decision

fine ADJECTIVE

1 *It was a fine achievement.*
▶ excellent, outstanding, admirable, remarkable, exceptional, commendable, first-class, good

2 *The next day was fine.*
▶ bright, fair, dry, clear, sunny, warm, cloudless
OPPOSITES ARE bad, wet, inclement

3 *He brought out the fine china.*
▶ delicate, fragile

4 *A pen with a fine tip.*
▶ thin, narrow, slender, slim

5 *a beach of fine warm sand*
▶ powdery, minute

6 *He likes fine clothes*
▶ elegant, stylish, smart, chic, fashionable

7 *The mechanism needs a fine adjustment.*
▶ small, minor, subtle

8 *It's fine to write to me here.*
▶ all right, acceptable, suitable, agreeable

fine NOUN
He got a parking fine
▶ penalty, charge

finger VERB
He fingered the ring on his finger.
▶ touch, feel, handle, stroke, rub, fondle, caress, twiddle

finicky ADJECTIVE
a finicky eater
▶ fussy, fastidious, particular, choosy, (*more informal*) picky

finish NOUN

1 *The race had an exciting finish.*
▶ ending, end, close, last stage, conclusion, result

2 *They went out to celebrate the finish of the work.*
▶ completion, conclusion, end, cessation, termination

3 *Mix the paint well for an even finish.*
▶ appearance, surface, texture, lustre, polish, shine, gloss, smoothness

finish VERB

1 *We have to finish the work today.*
▶ complete, conclude, end, finalize

2 *They never seem to finish complaining.*
▶ stop, cease, end

3 *We've finished the biscuits.*
▶ use up, eat, consume, devour, exhaust, (*more informal*) polish off

4 *The film finishes at ten.*
▶ end, conclude, terminate

5 *Another year of losses will finish the company.*
▶ destroy, ruin, overwhelm, overpower

finite ADJECTIVE
We have a finite amount of land to build on.
▶ limited, restricted, fixed, definable, defined, known, measurable, numbered, calculable
OPPOSITES ARE infinite, limitless

fire NOUN

1 *The building was destroyed in a fire.*
▶ blaze, conflagration, inferno, flames, burning, combustion, holocaust, pyre

2 *She spoke with fire in her eyes.*
▶ passion, feeling, enthusiasm, intensity, vigour, fervour, ardour, dynamism, exuberance

fire VERB

1 *The engine began to fire.*
▶ ignite, start, catch, (*more informal*) get going

2 *The guerrillas fired a rocket.*
▶ launch, discharge, shoot, detonate, set off, let off, let fly with

3 *The idea fired their imagination.*
▶ excite, stimulate, arouse, inspire, enliven, stir up

4 *(informal) They fired him for misconduct.*
▶ dismiss, discharge, sack, give someone notice, lay off

firm ADJECTIVE

1 *The ground is fairly firm at this point.*
▶ hard, solid, unyielding, hardened, compact, compressed, resistant, stable
AN OPPOSITE IS soft

2 *The house lacked firm foundations.*
▶ secure, steady, strong, sturdy, fast, fixed, stable, tight, anchored

3 *Firm action is essential.*
▶ resolute, determined, decided, steadfast, adamant, dogged, obstinate, persistent, unshakeable, unwavering, unflinching

4 *We need a firm commitment*
▶ definite, agreed, settled, unchangeable

5 *Sally was a firm friend of hers.*
▶ devoted, constant, faithful, loyal, reliable, dependable

firm NOUN
Dave joined an accountancy firm.
▶ company, establishment, organization, business, concern, corporation

first ADJECTIVE

1 *Our first attempts didn't work.*
► initial, opening, preliminary
2 *The first inhabitants were hunters.*
► original, earliest, oldest, primeval, primitive
3 *The first consideration is the welfare of the children.*
► principal, prime, paramount, primary, main, chief, key, foremost, supreme, overriding

first-class ADJECTIVE

a first-class meal
► excellent, first-rate, top-quality, outstanding, superb, superlative, top-flight

first-hand ADJECTIVE

She has first-hand knowledge of the city.
► direct, personal

firstly ADVERB

Firstly, we must learn each other's names.
► first, to begin with, to start with, at the outset, as a start

first-rate ADJECTIVE

a first-rate piece of work
► excellent, outstanding, first-class, top-quality, superb, superlative, top-flight

---

fish NOUN

SOME COMMON TYPES OF FISH

flatfish: brill, dab, Dover sole, flounder, fluke, halibut, lemon sole, megrim, plaice, scaldfish, sole, turbot.

freshwater fish: barb, barbel, barramundi, bass, bream, carp, catfish, chub, dace, grayling, gudgeon, guppy, loach, lungfish, minnow, perch, pike, piranha, roach, rudd, salmon (partly freshwater), stickleback, sucker, tench, trout.

sea fish: angler fish, barracuda, brisling, catfish, cod, coelacanth, conger (eel), dory, eel, garfish, goby, goldfish (kind of carp), gunnel, haddock, hake, herring, jellyfish, ling (type of cod), mackerel, monkfish, moonfish, mullet, pilchard, rockfish, salmon (partly sea fish), sardine, shad, shark, skate, snapper, sprat, starfish, surgeon, swordfish, tuna, whitebait, whiting, wrasse.

crustaceans and molluscs: barnacle, crab, crayfish, cuttlefish, lobster, prawn, shellfish, shrimp; clam, cockle, conch, cowrie, cuttlefish, limpet, mussel, nautilus, octopus, oyster, scallop, sea slug, sea snail, shellfish, squid, triton, whelk, winkle.
RELATED ADJECTIVE piscine

---

fish VERB

fish for *He seemed to be fishing for compliments.*
► invite, seek, solicit

fishy ADJECTIVE

(informal) The price was so low it all seemed a bit fishy.
► suspicious, dubious, doubtful, suspect, peculiar, strange, odd, queer, funny

fit ADJECTIVE

1 *She looked remarkably fit for a fifty-two-year-old.*
► healthy, well, able-bodied, robust, hale and hearty, in good form
OPPOSITES ARE unfit, unhealthy
2 *The vehicles are all fit for commercial use.*
► suitable, appropriate, prepared, equipped, ready, proper, right, correct
OPPOSITES ARE unfit, unsuitable
3 *Do you think he is fit to be a parent?*
► competent, able, capable (of being), qualified, worthy
OPPOSITES ARE unfit, incapable

fit NOUN

1 *He might have an epileptic fit at any time.*
► seizure, convulsion, paroxysm, spasm, attack
2 *She was having a fit of hysterics.*
► outbreak, outburst, spell, bout, attack, explosion

fit VERB

1 *It takes a long time to fit all the pieces together.*
► arrange, assemble, build, construct, dovetail, install, interlock, join, match, position, put in place, put together
2 *Make the punishment fit the crime.*
► suit, match, accord with, be appropriate to, correspond with or to, be fitting for, conform with

fitful ADJECTIVE

There was time for a few hours' fitful sleep.
► spasmodic, intermittent, disturbed, uneven, broken, patchy, irregular
OPPOSITES ARE constant, regular

fitted ADJECTIVE

1 *He clearly isn't fitted for the job.*
► suited, suitable, right, equipped, appropriate
2 *It was a modern house with fitted cupboards everywhere you looked.*
► built-in, integral, incorporated, customized

fitting ADJECTIVE

The concert was a fitting tribute to a fine singer.
► suitable, apt, appropriate, apposite, proper, timely, felicitous
OPPOSITES ARE inappropriate, unsuitable

fittings PLURAL NOUN

The bathroom fittings were cheap and flimsy.
► fixtures, fitments, equipment, accessories, furnishings

fix VERB

1 *You can fix the notice to a lamppost.*
► fasten, tie, pin, attach, affix, secure
2 *The farmer had fixed posts into the ground.*
► set, embed, cement, place, position
3 *I can fix it for you to get an invitation.*
► arrange, organize, manage
4 *Let's fix a date to meet.*
► set, decide on, agree on, arrange, settle, determine
5 *The television needs to be fixed.*
► mend, repair, put right

fix NOUN
(*informal*) *I'm in a bit of a fix.*
▶ difficulty, predicament, mess, plight, dilemma, (*informal*) hole, (*informal*) jam, quandary, corner

fixed NOUN
The licence is for a fixed period.
▶ set, definite, decided, established, settled, predetermined, firm

fizz VERB
She dropped in a tablet and the water fizzed.
▶ bubble, effervesce, foam, froth, fizzle, sizzle, hiss

fizzy ADJECTIVE
There are fizzy drinks in the garden.
▶ sparkling, effervescent, bubbly, carbonated, foaming
AN OPPOSITE IS still

flabbergasted ADJECTIVE
He just stood there, flabbergasted.
▶ astonished, amazed, astounded, surprised, staggered, startled, disconcerted, dumbfounded, speechless, shocked, perplexed, stunned, stupefied, bewildered, (*more informal*) thunderstruck

flabby ADJECTIVE
(*informal*) *When he took her hand in his, it was soft and flabby.*
▶ slack, limp, loose, floppy, flaccid, weak, feeble
OPPOSITES ARE firm, stiff

flag NOUN
The route was decorated with flags.
▶ banner, standard, ensign, pennant, pennon, streamer, bunting, colours

flag VERB
Our energy was beginning to flag.
▶ fade, fail, decline, diminish, dwindle, sink, disappear

flair NOUN
1 *He has a flair for games.*
▶ talent, aptitude, gift, ability, genius, faculty, capacity, adeptness
2 *She dresses with great flair.*
▶ style, elegance, taste, discernment, panache, finesse

flake NOUN
First remove any loose flakes of old paint.
▶ scale, sliver, chip, splinter, shaving, bit, leaf, slice, wafer

flamboyant ADJECTIVE
He was well known for his flamboyant appearance.
▶ ostentatious, showy, colourful, gaudy, brilliant, resplendent, extravagant

flaming ADJECTIVE
a flaming torch
▶ burning, blazing, fiery, glowing, brilliant

flap VERB
1 *The washing was flapping in the wind*
▶ flutter, sway, swing, quiver, wave about

2 *The swan flapped its wings angrily.*
▶ beat, flutter, shake, agitate, quiver, thrash
3 *He tried hard to avoid flapping.*
▶ panic, fuss, become agitated, become flustered

flare VERB
The match flared in his cupped hands.
▶ blaze, flame, flash, burn, erupt, sparkle
flare up
1 *This border war could flare up at any time.*
▶ break out, burst out, erupt, blow up, recur
2 *They annoyed her and she flared up at them.*
▶ lose your temper, lose control, fly into a rage, become angry

flash VERB
Lights flashed in the distance.
▶ shine, blaze, flare, gleam, beam, glint, sparkle, spark

flash NOUN
1 *a flash of light*
▶ blaze, burst, flare, glare, gleam, glint, sparkle, flicker, twinkle, ray
2 *a flash of inspiration*
▶ burst, wave, surge, rush

flashy ADJECTIVE
Lily held out her hand with a flashy ring on one finger.
▶ showy, gaudy, ostentatious, vulgar, (*more informal*) tacky

flat ADJECTIVE
1 *a flat surface*
▶ level, smooth, even, horizontal, plane
OPPOSITES ARE bumpy, uneven
2 *She lay flat on the bed.*
▶ outstretched, prostrate, spread out, recumbent
3 *a flat sea*
▶ calm, still, smooth, waveless, tranquil
OPPOSITES ARE rough, choppy
4 *His voice was flat and lifeless.*
▶ dull, monotonous, uninteresting, unexciting, tedious, boring, bland, dreary, insipid, colourless, featureless, unexpressive, weak
AN OPPOSITE IS emotional
5 *The request met with a flat refusal.*
▶ outright, direct, straight, plain, absolute, positive

flat NOUN
They lived in a small flat for several years.
▶ apartment, maisonette, set of rooms, flatlet, penthouse

flatten VERB
1 *Tom flattened the crumpled paper against his knee.*
▶ smooth, press, even out, iron out, level out, roll
OPPOSITES ARE roughen, crumple
2 *People had walked over the beds and flattened the plants.*
▶ squash, trample, crush, compress, run over
3 *The hurricane had flattened hundreds of buildings.*
▶ demolish, destroy, devastate, knock down, level, raze

4 (*informal*) *He's quite capable of flattening you with a single blow.*
▶ knock down, knock over, fell, prostrate, (*informal*) floor, (*informal*) lay out

flatter VERB
1 *He enjoyed teasing and flattering her.*
▶ praise, compliment, humour, fawn on, play up to, (*more informal*) sweet-talk, (*more informal*) butter up
USAGE Note that to *flatter* is to compliment someone in an insincere way, whereas to *praise* is to pay genuine compliments.
2 *She wore a dress that flattered her small figure.*
▶ suit, enhance, set off, look good on, show to advantage

flattering ADJECTIVE
1 *flattering remarks*
▶ complimentary, favourable, appreciative, adulatory, effusive, obsequious, fawning, fulsome, ingratiating
OPPOSITES ARE insulting, sincere
2 *a flattering outfit*
▶ becoming, fetching, enhancing

flattery NOUN
We succumb to flattery because it makes us feel good.
▶ praise, compliments, adulation, blandishments, admiration, fawning, obsequiousness, servility
USAGE Note that *flattery* is always insincere, whereas *praise* is usually genuine.

flaunt VERB
He loved flaunting his knowledge about cars.
▶ show off, display, parade, exhibit, flourish, vaunt, make a show of

flavour NOUN
1 *The food had a spicy flavour.*
▶ taste, tang, savour
2 *a story with an oriental flavour*
▶ character, quality, atmosphere, aura, ambience, mood, feel, style, feeling, aspect

flavour VERB
You can flavour the stew with mixed herbs.
▶ season, spice, enliven, liven up, enrich

flavouring NOUN
Add some gentle flavouring.
▶ seasoning, additive, spice, essence, extract

flaw NOUN
There is a flaw in this reasoning. a glass with a tiny flaw you can hardly see
▶ defect, blemish, fault, imperfection, deficiency, weakness, failing, shortcoming

flawed ADJECTIVE
The argument was obviously flawed.
▶ defective, unsound, faulty, imperfect, weak, deficient

flawless ADJECTIVE
Her skin was flawless.
▶ perfect, faultless, immaculate, unblemished, unmarked, spotless

fleck NOUN
white with flecks of blue
▶ speck, patch, dot, point, streak, dab, splash

flee VERB
She left the others and fled to her room.
▶ run off, bolt, fly, take off, clear off, hurry off, escape, disappear

fleet NOUN
A large fleet of ships sailed out.
▶ flotilla, armada, naval force, convoy, navy, squadron, task force

fleeting ADJECTIVE
We had a fleeting glimpse of the queen.
▶ brief, momentary, transient, cursory, passing, short
AN OPPOSITE IS lasting

flesh NOUN
an animal's flesh
▶ meat, muscle, tissue, carrion, fat
USAGE Note that *carrion* is the decaying flesh of a dead animal.

flex NOUN
a flex for an electric iron
▶ cable, lead, wire

flex VERB
She flexed her arms and swept back her hair.
▶ bend, bow, curve, double up, hook, cock, angle

flexible ADJECTIVE
1 *flexible working practices*
▶ adaptable, adjustable, variable, fluid, open
OPPOSITES ARE inflexible, rigid
2 *a flexible rod used as an aerial*
▶ bendable, pliable, pliant, malleable, stretchable
OPPOSITES ARE rigid, fixed

flick VERB
He flicked a finger lightly against her cheek.
▶ stroke, wag, brush, wave, sweep, flip, jerk

flick NOUN
1 *The king dismissed his page with a flick of his head.*
▶ jerk, toss, flip, sweep
2 *He gave the table a few flicks with a duster.*
▶ dab, touch, brush, swipe, stroke

flicker VERB
1 *The candle flickered in the breeze.*
▶ glimmer, twinkle, sparkle, shimmer, blink
2 *The eyelids can flicker when you dream.*
▶ tremble, quiver, waver, flutter

flight NOUN
1 *a short history of flight*
▶ flying, aviation, aeronautics, air travel
2 *the flight of a missile*
▶ path, trajectory, track
3 *the king's flight to safety*
▶ escape , getaway, retreat, fleeing

flimsy ADJECTIVE
1 *He moved the flimsy barrier and walked past.*
▶ fragile, rickety, shaky, makeshift, insubstantial, frail, weak
AN OPPOSITE IS substantial
2 *She wore a flimsy nightdress.*
▶ light, lightweight, thin, fine, diaphanous, silky, filmy
3 *We heard the usual flimsy excuses.*
▶ feeble, weak, poor, thin, unconvincing, implausible

flinch VERB
She flinched as he put out his hand.
▶ wince, recoil, start, shrink, pull back, draw back, shy away, shrink back
flinch from *He never flinches from his duty.*
▶ shrink from, shirk, avoid, evade, balk at

fling VERB
He flung the gun over the bridge.
▶ throw, hurl, toss, sling, cast, pitch, heave

flip VERB
1 *He flipped a coin in the air.*
▶ toss, flick, spin, threw
2 *The beetle flipped on to its back.*
▶ turn, spin, tip, topple
flip through *She was flipping through the pages of a magazine.*
▶ flick through, thumb through, skim through, scan, peruse

flippant ADJECTIVE
a flippant remark
▶ facetious, frivolous, jocular, humorous, funny, witty, amusing, comical, glib
AN OPPOSITE IS serious

flirt VERB
flirt with
1 *He loves flirting with the girls.*
▶ tease, trifle with, lead on, make up to, (*more informal*) chat up
2 *an idea I had been flirting with for some time*
▶ consider, entertain, toy with, trifle with, dabble in

flit VERB
insects flitting from plant to plant
▶ dart, flip, fly, flutter, whisk, skim, dance

float VERB
1 *little boats floating on the water*
▶ sail, bob, drift
2 *A cloud floated across the sun.*
▶ drift, glide, hover, slip, slide, waft
3 *We want to float a few ideas.*
▶ suggest, propose, put forward, submit, raise, present, come up with, moot
4 *The company was floated on the Stock Market.*
▶ launch, set up, promote, initiate, offer

flock NOUN
1 *a flock of sheep*
▶ herd, drove, group
2 *a flock of birds*
▶ flight, group
3 *a flock of anxious relatives*
▶ crowd, throng, horde, gathering, bunch, huddle, mob, mass

flock VERB
People flocked from all quarters.
▶ gather, collect, assemble, come together, congregate, crowd, convene, converge, muster

flog VERB
The executioner flogged the woman on her back.
▶ whip, beat, flay, lash, scourge, thrash, flagellate, birch, cane

flood NOUN
1 *The flood cut off several villages.*
▶ inundation, deluge, torrent, downpour
2 *a flood of protests*
▶ succession, torrent, barrage, spate, storm, volley, excess, abundance, profusion, plethora
AN OPPOSITE IS trickle

flood VERB
1 *The dam burst, flooding the town.*
▶ inundate, swamp, submerge, engulf, overwhelm, drown, deluge, immerse
2 *Light flooded the room.*
▶ fill, swamp, saturate
3 *The loo flooded yesterday.*
▶ overflow, run over, brim over
4 *The press flooded back into the courtroom.*
▶ pour, stream, surge, swarm, flock, crowd, throng

floor NOUN
1 *The floor was sopping wet.*
▶ ground, flooring, base
2 *Take the lift to the third floor.*
▶ level, storey, stage, landing

flop VERB
1 *His white hair flopped over his eyes.*
▶ dangle, droop, hang down, slump, flag, sag, wilt
2 *All she wanted was to flop into a chair.*
▶ drop, fall, sink, slump, collapse, tumble
3 *The idea flopped spectacularly.*
▶ fail, founder, misfire, be unsuccessful, fold

flop NOUN
The show was a flop.
▶ failure, disaster, debacle, fiasco, (*more informal*) washout

floppy ADJECTIVE
a girl in pigtails, wearing a large floppy woollen hat
▶ limp, droopy, drooping, dangling, loose, saggy, sagging, hanging
AN OPPOSITE IS stiff

flounder VERB
The infantry floundered in the swampy ground. He was floundering in a situation of his own making.
▶ struggle, falter, grope, wallow, stumble, fumble, stagger

flourish VERB

1 *Plants flourish in this good soil. The farmers flourished, aided by good weather.*
▶ thrive, prosper, bloom, blossom, succeed, boom, be strong, be vigorous, progress
2 *She went out, flourishing an umbrella.*
▶ brandish, wave, wield, swirl, swing, flaunt

flourish NOUN

With a flourish he produced a small bag of sweets.
▶ gesture, wave, sweep, show, fanfare

flourishing ADJECTIVE

a flourishing chain of supermarkets
▶ thriving, successful, prosperous, booming, vigorous, buoyant, productive, lucrative

flout VERB

He had no intention of flouting a court order.
▶ disobey, defy, violate, contravene, infringe, break, spurn, scorn
OPPOSITES ARE respect, observe

flow VERB

1 *Water was flowing through the pipes.*
▶ run, stream, spurt, trickle, ooze, squirt, gush, flood, cascade
2 *Several issues flow from these proposals.*
▶ result, proceed, follow, arise, spring, proceed, emerge, emanate

flow NOUN

1 *Alcohol increases the flow of blood to the brain.*
▶ movement, circulation, stream, motion, course, current, passage, surge
2 *a steady flow of correspondence*
▶ stream, current, deluge, cascade, flood, gush, spate

flower NOUN

1 *Mandy picked flowers from the garden*
▶ bloom, blossom, floret, bud
2 *the flower of a nation's youth*
▶ finest, best, pick, cream, choice, elite

flowery ADJECTIVE

flowery language
▶ fancy, elaborate, florid, ornate, flamboyant, overblown

fluctuate VERB

Their income fluctuates from year to year.
▶ vary, change, alter, shift, differ, rise and fall

fluent ADJECTIVE

1 *She is fluent in five European languages.*
▶ articulate, able to speak
2 *It is important to speak in a fluent and interesting manner.*
▶ articulate, natural, expressive, eloquent, effortless, flowing, polished, ready, smooth, unhesitating, (*disapproving*) glib, (*disapproving*) facile
AN OPPOSITE IS inarticulate

fluff NOUN

The sofa is covered in fluff.
▶ fuzz, dust, nap, down, floss, thistledown

fluffy ADJECTIVE

She padded into the bedroom wrapped in a big fluffy towel.
▶ furry, woolly, fleecy, fuzzy, downy, velvety, soft

fluid ADJECTIVE

1 *fluid substances*
▶ liquid, aqueous, flowing, watery, running, gaseous, liquefied, melted, molten, (*more informal*) runny
AN OPPOSITE IS solid
2 *fluid movements*
▶ graceful, flowing, smooth
3 *My plans are still fairly fluid.*
▶ flexible, adaptable, adjustable, variable, open, changeable, unstable, indefinite, unsettled
OPPOSITES ARE firm, fixed, definite
USAGE Be careful when you use *changeable* or *indefinite*, because they have other meanings.

fluid NOUN

Drink lots of fluids and eat fibre-rich foods.
▶ liquid, juice

fluke NOUN

By a lucky fluke she came along at that moment.
▶ chance, accident, piece of luck, stroke of luck

flurry NOUN

1 *a snow flurry*
▶ swirl, whirl, gust
2 *a flurry of activity*
▶ spate, wave, burst, spell, stir, spurt, outbreak, commotion

flush ADJECTIVE

1 *He had just been paid and was feeling flush.*
▶ rich, wealthy, well off, prosperous
2 *The opening needs to be flush with the wall.*
▶ level, flat, even, square, true

flush VERB

1 *Nancy flushed with embarrassment.*
▶ blush, go red, redden, colour, glow
2 *Fruit helps flush toxins from the body.*
▶ cleanse, rinse out, wash out, swill
3 *The police tried to flush the suspects out.*
▶ chase out, drive out, expel, send up

flustered ADJECTIVE

She looked shocked and flustered.
▶ confused, bewildered, bemused, perplexed, baffled, puzzled, mystified, disconcerted, confounded

flutter VERB

1 *Butterflies fluttered around the garden.*
▶ flit, flitter, dance
2 *The bird fluttered its wings.*
▶ flap, beat, shake, agitate, quiver, thrash

fly VERB

1 *A flock of birds flew past.*
▶ glide, flit, flutter, hover, soar, wing
2 *A gull flew into the air.*
▶ rise, soar, ascend, mount

3 *He refused to fly the aircraft until it had been checked.*
▶ pilot, operate, take off in, travel in
4 *A flag was flying at half mast.*
▶ flutter, flap, wave
5 *The ship was flying a neutral flag.*
▶ display, show, exhibit
6 fly at *Charley flew at him, shaking his fist.*
▶ attack, assault, go for, set upon, weigh into, let fly at, hit out at, lash out at

foam NOUN
1 *The sea looked like white crests of foam.*
▶ froth, spume, surf, spray, lather, scum, suds
2 *There was at least an inch of foam on his beer.*
▶ head, bubbles, effervescence

foam VERB
The water heaved and foamed.
▶ froth, fizz, seethe, ferment, bubble, effervesce, lather, boil

fob VERB
fob off
1 *It's no good fobbing us off with promises.*
▶ stall, put off, palm off, deceive, saddle
2 *He fobbed off the most difficult job on Trevor.*
▶ inflict, impose, dump, unload

focus NOUN
1 *Get the camera into focus*
▶ clarity, correct adjustment, sharpness
2 *The television has become a main focus of the living room.*
▶ centre, focal point, heart, hub, core, pivot

focus VERB
focus on *We need to focus on the events of this coming week.*
▶ concentrate on, direct attention to, fix attention on, home in on, zero in on, spotlight, think about, aim at, centre on, look mainly at

fog NOUN
Don't go out if there's fog.
▶ mist, smog, bad visibility, haze

foggy ADJECTIVE
Outside it was dull and foggy.
▶ misty, smoggy, hazy, murky, gloomy, dingy, dim
AN OPPOSITE IS clear

foil VERB
She foiled their efforts by walking in at the wrong moment.
▶ thwart, frustrate, obstruct, impede, hamper, hinder, baffle, scotch, check, prevent, stop

foist VERB
She doesn't want to foist her opinions on her kids.
▶ impose, force, thrust, offload, palm off, saddle someone with

fold VERB
1 *Fold the sheets and put them in a drawer.*
▶ double, double over, turn over, bend, tuck, overlap, crease, pleat

2 *She stood there, folding her arms.*
▶ clasp, wrap, cradle, enfold, enclose, embrace, entwine, envelop, hug
3 *I'll fold the chair and put it away.*
▶ close, collapse, let down, put down
4 *The business folded during the recession.*
▶ fail, collapse, crash, founder, close down

fold NOUN
1 *Neatly arrange the folds in the curtains.*
▶ pleat, crease, tuck, furrow, bend
2 *a fold for sheep*
▶ enclosure, pen, paddock, compound

folder NOUN
I need a folder for these papers.
▶ file, binder, portfolio, wallet, sleeve

folk, folks PLURAL NOUN
1 *It was good news for the folk back home.*
▶ people, individuals, citizens, inhabitants
2 *She would visit her folks at the weekend.*
▶ family, parents, relatives, people, kinsfolk

follow VERB
1 *He followed them as far as the corner.*
▶ go after, come after, walk behind, tread on the heels of, trace the footsteps of
2 *She hoped to follow her father as chief executive of the company.*
▶ succeed, replace, take the place of, take over from, supplant, supersede, step into someone's shoes
3 *An undercover police officer followed him everywhere.*
▶ pursue, stalk, track, shadow, trail, go after, (more informal) tail
4 *Make sure you follow the instructions on the packet.*
▶ observe, comply with, adhere to, carry out, obey, note, heed, conform to, keep to
5 *Many benefits followed from their membership of the community.*
▶ result, ensue, emanate, arise, develop
6 *I found it hard to follow his meaning.*
▶ understand, comprehend, grasp, fathom, take in, catch
7 *Which team do you follow?*
▶ support, be a fan of

follower NOUN
the leader's closest followers
▶ supporter, adherent, devotee, backer, disciple, companion

following ADJECTIVE
She went home on the following day
▶ next, ensuing, subsequent, succeeding
OPPOSITES ARE preceding, previous

following NOUN
These successes brought him a strong following.
▶ support, backing, retinue, patronage, body of adherents

folly NOUN

It would be an act of folly to start a war.
▶ foolishness, stupidity, senselessness, recklessness, silliness, madness, lunacy, idiocy

fond ADJECTIVE

1 *her fond father*
▶ loving, adoring, devoted, doting, caring, attentive, kind

2 *a fond hope*
▶ foolish, unrealistic, naive, vain, empty

3 **be fond of** *She's fond of dancing I'm very fond of Jo.*
▶ be keen on, be partial to, be attached to, like, love, (*more informal*) be hooked on, (*more informal*) be wild about, (*more informal*) be crazy about

fondle VERB

He stooped down to fondle the cat.
▶ stroke, caress, pat, pet, cuddle, play with

---

food NOUN

1 *He had gone a week without food.*
▶ nourishment, sustenance, nutriment, subsistence
RELATED ADJECTIVE alimentary

2 *Have you brought any food?*
▶ provisions, refreshments, eatables, something to eat, (*old use*) victuals, (*more informal*) grub

WORDS FOR BASIC TYPES OF FOOD

cereals and cereal products: barley, maize, oats, rice, rye, sweetcorn, wheat; bread, chapatti, chollah, ciabatta, naan, roll, pitta, matzo, croissant, baguette, bagel, pumpernickel, tortilla, flour; branflakes, cornflakes; semolina; pasta, lasagne, macaroni, noodles, spaghetti; dumplings; porridge.

dairy products: butter, cheese, cream, curds, eggs, milk, yoghurt.

fish: carp, cod, brill, flounder, haddock, halibut, kipper, mackerel, plaice, salmon, sardine, sole, trout, turbot, whitebait.

fruit: ackee, apple, apricot, banana, berry, cherry, citrus fruits, coconut, currant, date, fig, grape, grapefruit, kiwi, lemon, lime, lychee, mango, melon, olive, orange, papaya, paw-paw, peach, pear, pineapple, plantain, plum, prune, raisin, raspberry, rhubarb, strawberry, sultana, tangerine, tomato.

meat: bacon, beef, chicken, corned beef, game, gammon, ham, lamb, mutton, pork, poultry, tripe, turkey, veal, venison.

puddings and other sweet foods: biscuit, cake, chocolate, cookie, custard, fruit salad, ice-cream, jelly, mousse, pie, tart.

savoury foods: broth, chop suey, crisps, curry, fritter, goulash, lasagne, moussaka, nuts, pastry, pie, pizza, quiche, pudding, risotto, seafood, soup. ▶▶

---

vegetables: asparagus, aubergine, brinjal, sweet potato, courgette, yam, zuchinni, mealy, okra, beans, beetroot, Brussels sprouts, cabbage, carrot, cauliflower, celery, greens, kale, leek, marrow, onion, parsnip, pea, potato, pumpkin, runner bean, spinach, swede, tomato, turnip.

---

fool NOUN

1 *He was acting like a fool.*
▶ idiot, ass, halfwit, dimwit, blockhead, dunderhead, nincompoop, imbecile, moron, clown, buffoon, clot, chump, (*more informal*) dope, (*more informal*) prat, (*more informal*) ninny, (*more informal*) twit, (*more informal*) twerp

2 (*old-fashioned*) *a fool at the court of the king*
▶ jester, clown, buffoon, comic, stooge

fool VERB

1 *We easily fooled him.*
▶ deceive, trick, hoodwink, hoax, dupe

2 *I thought you were just fooling.*
▶ pretend, joke, jest, tease, make believe, put on an act

fool about *Some children were fooling about.*
▶ play about, lark about, misbehave

USAGE You can use *around* instead of *about* in all these synonyms.

foolhardy ADJECTIVE

a foolhardy venture
▶ reckless, rash, impetuous, imprudent, ill-advised, unwise, irresponsible

foolish ADJECTIVE

a foolish remark She had been extremely foolish.
▶ stupid, silly, ill-advised, unwise, crazy, mad, insane, (*more informal*) daft
OPPOSITES ARE wise, sensible

foolishness NOUN

They shook their heads at her foolishness in going back to France.
▶ stupidity, folly, senselessness, recklessness, silliness, madness, lunacy, idiocy

foolproof ADJECTIVE

The system is foolproof if you follow the instructions carefully.
▶ infallible, unfailing, dependable, straightforward, simple, (*more informal*) idiot-proof

foot NOUN

1 *The animal had hurt its foot.*
▶ paw, hoof, trotter, claw

2 *The house was at the foot of the hill.*
▶ bottom, base

footing NOUN

1 *He tried not to lose his footing on the narrow stairs.*
▶ foothold, hold, grip, balance

2 *They would put the club on a sound financial footing.*
▶ basis, base, foundation, standing, support, terms

footprint NOUN
There were huge footprints in the snow.
▶ footmark, footstep, track, print, trace, spoor
USAGE You use *spoor* only when referring to an animal.

footstep NOUN
She heard footsteps in the hall.
▶ step, footfall, tread

forbid VERB
She forbids the use of calculators in this exercise.
▶ ban, prohibit, bar, disallow, rule out, exclude, proscribe, veto, outlaw, refuse, preclude
OPPOSITES ARE permit, allow

forbidden ADJECTIVE
1 *Ball games are forbidden on the grass outside the building.*
▶ banned, prohibited, barred, disallowed, proscribed, illegal, against the law, outlawed, unauthorized, unlawful
AN OPPOSITE IS permissible
2 *This part of the house is forbidden to them.*
▶ out of bounds, restricted, closed

forbidding ADJECTIVE
The house has a dark, forbidding appearance.
▶ grim, ominous, menacing, threatening, gloomy, stern, unfriendly, uninviting, unwelcoming
AN OPPOSITE IS friendly

force NOUN
1 *It needed some force to get the door open.*
▶ strength, might, vigour, effort, energy, muscle, power, drive, pressure, weight
2 *The force of the explosion was felt for miles.*
▶ intensity, impact, effect, shock, momentum
3 *They used force to get their way.*
▶ violence, coercion, compulsion, aggression, constraint, duress
4 *I could see the force of the argument.*
▶ strength, cogency, effectiveness, validity, persuasiveness, weight, rightness
5 *a peace-keeping force*
▶ body, group, corps, unit, team, detachment, troops, army

force VERB
1 *If necessary we will force them to do it.*
▶ compel, make, oblige, coerce, constrain, pressure, pressurize, order, impel, bulldoze, drive, press-gang
2 *The intruders had to force a door.*
▶ break open, burst open, prise open, smash, use force on, wrench
3 *They tried to force their opinions on us*
▶ impose, inflict, thrust

forceful ADJECTIVE
1 *a forceful personality*
▶ strong, dynamic, powerful, assertive, commanding, self-assured, energetic
2 *forceful arguments*
▶ strong, cogent, compelling, convincing, potent, plausible, effective

foreboding NOUN
1 *Lucy was full of foreboding about the day ahead.*
▶ anxiety, fear, apprehension, misgiving, trepidation, dread, worry
2 *Their forebodings proved right.*
▶ premonition, presentiment, suspicion, intuition, inkling, hunch, portent, bad omen

forecast NOUN
The figures were based on an inaccurate forecast and had to be revised.
▶ prediction, prophecy, projection, prognosis, calculation, outlook, expectation, prognostication

forecast VERB
We forecast increased rain levels over the coming months.
▶ predict, foretell, foresee, prophesy, expect, anticipate, reckon on

foreign ADJECTIVE
1 *I like travelling to foreign countries.*
▶ overseas, distant, remote, exotic, faraway, far-flung
2 *the Company's foreign branches*
▶ overseas, international, external
AN OPPOSITE IS domestic
3 *Jealousy is foreign to her nature.*
▶ unknown, familiar, alien, strange
AN OPPOSITE IS natural

foreigner NOUN
Many foreigners come to live in this city.
▶ overseas visitor, visitor, immigrant, alien, outsider, newcomer, stranger
AN OPPOSITE IS native

foreman NOUN
He asked the foreman what to do next.
▶ supervisor, manager, overseer, superintendent, team leader

foremost ADJECTIVE
the foremost musicians of the day
▶ leading, principal, chief, main, greatest, supreme, primary

foresee VERB
We could never have foreseen what would happen.
▶ forecast, anticipate, predict, foretell, expect, envisage, prophesy

foresight NOUN
She had the foresight to write a will.
▶ forethought, prudence, perspicacity, farsightedness, prescience, vision, circumspection, preparedness
AN OPPOSITE IS improvidence

forestall VERB
The Government will try to forestall criticism by conceding some of the objections.
▶ prevent, pre-empt, anticipate, stave off, fend off, thwart, frustrate

f

foretell VERB

We could not foretell what might happen.
▶ predict, forecast, foresee, anticipate, prophesy, forewarn

forever ADVERB

They are forever complaining.
▶ constantly, continually, always, perpetually, incessantly, endlessly, ceaselessly

forfeit NOUN

You are liable to a forfeit if you disobey.
▶ penalty, fine, charge, damages

forfeit VERB

The original owner can forfeit his right to claim back his property.
▶ lose, relinquish, surrender, sacrifice, forgo, renounce, give up

forge NOUN

a blacksmith's forge
▶ smithy, workshop, furnace

forge VERB

1 *The smithy forged swords and knives for the army.*
▶ work, cast, make, mould, shape, hammer out, beat into shape
2 *He would have a go at forging the signature.*
▶ fake, falsify, counterfeit, imitate, copy, reproduce
3 *He had been highly successful in forging a strong team.*
▶ build, create, develop, establish, set up
forge ahead *The Persians forged ahead through Thrace.*
▶ advance, make progress

forgery NOUN

He thinks they sold him a forgery.
▶ fake, copy, imitation, reproduction, replica, duplicate, hoax, sham, simulation, (*more informal*) phoney

forget VERB

1 *I forgot my passport.*
▶ leave behind, overlook, mislay
AN OPPOSITE IS remember
2 *She forgot to lock the door.*
▶ omit, neglect, fail
AN OPPOSITE IS remember
3 *This is not something we can easily forget.*
▶ ignore, disregard, overlook, dismiss, think no more of, stop thinking about

forgetful ADJECTIVE

As he grew older he became more forgetful.
▶ absent-minded, inattentive, neglectful, abstracted, oblivious, vague, dreamy, lax, heedless

forgive VERB

1 *He found it hard to forgive them.*
▶ excuse, pardon, exonerate, absolve, let off, spare, (*more formal*) exculpate
2 *We cannot forgive such rudeness.*
▶ excuse, condone, overlook, ignore, disregard

forgiveness NOUN

He begged their forgiveness.
▶ pardon, absolution, exoneration, understanding, tolerance, mercy

forgiving ADJECTIVE

He seemed kind and forgiving.
▶ merciful, lenient, tolerant, compassionate, understanding, clement, humane
AN OPPOSITE IS vindictive

forgo VERB

They would have to forgo their morning swim.
▶ do without, go without, miss, give up, sacrifice, eschew, abandon, renounce

fork VERB

1 *The road forks at the bottom of the hill.*
▶ branch, split, separate
fork out (*informal*) *If necessary they would just have to fork out the money.*
▶ pay, produce, (*informal*) cough up

forked ADJECTIVE

a bird with a forked tail
▶ split, branched, divided, pronged, V-shaped, (*technical*) bifurcate

forlorn ADJECTIVE

She looked so forlorn.
▶ sad, unhappy, miserable, sorrowful, dejected, wretched, disconsolate, downcast, crestfallen, pitiful

form NOUN

1 *a form of blackmail*
▶ kind, type, sort, class, order, variety
2 *the human form*
▶ body, frame, shape, figure, build
3 *They wanted to know the correct form for these occasions.*
▶ etiquette, custom, protocol, usage, procedure, convention
4 *There is a form to fill in.*
▶ document, questionnaire, sheet
5 *Her son moved into a new form at school.*
▶ class, year, grade, set, group, stream
6 *The form of the landscape has hardly changed for centuries.*
▶ appearance, shape, formation, configuration, structure, outline, silhouette
7 *He exercised hard to get into good form.*
▶ condition, shape, health, fettle, fitness

form VERB

1 *We must form a plan.*
▶ devise, formulate, develop, prepare, draw up, put together, work out, conceive
2 *The pots were formed from clay.*
▶ make, fashion, shape, model
3 *They decided to form a club.*
▶ set up, establish, found, launch, institute, begin
4 *Ice was forming on the windows.*
▶ materialize, appear, take shape, develop, emerge, grow

5 *Six players form a team.*
▶ make up, constitute, compose, comprise

formal ADJECTIVE
1 *a formal manner*
▶ aloof, prim, staid, stiff, starchy, punctilious
2 *a formal occasion*
▶ solemn, official, ceremonious, conventional, dignified
3 *a formal education*
▶ prescribed, conventional, institutional

formality NOUN
1 *He behaved towards her with greater formality.*
▶ aloofness, remoteness, staidness, correctness, decorum, ceremony
2 **formalities** *Certain formalities have to be observed.*
▶ procedures, conventions, rules, customs, protocol

formation NOUN
the formation of a joint company
▶ establishment, setting up, institution, inauguration, creation, inception

former ADJECTIVE
1 *She met her former husband in town.*
▶ ex-, past, one-time, previous, late
2 *The fields were a lake in former times.*
▶ earlier, past, bygone, ancient

formerly ADVERB
The work had formerly been done by volunteers.
▶ previously, in the past, at one time, once, earlier, hitherto

formidable ADJECTIVE
We face a formidable task.
▶ difficult, daunting, demanding, challenging, onerous, strenuous, awesome, overwhelming

formula NOUN
1 *a legal formula*
▶ form of words, phrase, rubric
2 *a formula for success*
▶ recipe, prescription, blueprint, procedure, method, rule, way

formulate VERB
The party formulated a ten-point programme.
▶ form, devise, develop, prepare, draw up, put together, work out, conceive

forsake VERB
1 *He found it hard to forsake his old ways.*
▶ give up, renounce, abandon, relinquish, discard, set aside
2 *He would not forsake his wife and family.*
▶ abandon, desert, disown, leave behind, turn your back on

fort NOUN
A small garrison was left to defend the fort.
▶ fortress, fortification, stronghold, castle, citadel, tower

forthcoming ADJECTIVE
1 *He would be a candidate in the forthcoming election.*
▶ imminent, impending, approaching, coming, future, next
2 *She is not always particularly forthcoming.*
▶ communicative, talkative, expansive, informative, voluble, chatty, sociable
AN OPPOSITE IS uncommunicative
3 *No reply was forthcoming.*
▶ available, ready, on offer, at hand
AN OPPOSITE IS unavailable

forthright ADJECTIVE
She was forthright in her reply.
▶ frank, candid, direct, blunt, outspoken, plain-speaking, straightforward, unequivocal
AN OPPOSITE IS cautious

fortify VERB
1 *The knights fortified the citadel.*
▶ strengthen, reinforce, secure, defend, protect, garrison
2 *She fortified herself with a strong drink.*
▶ strengthen, support, sustain, invigorate, hearten, reassure, encourage, boost, cheer
OPPOSITES ARE weaken, subdue

fortitude NOUN
He accepted his fate with great fortitude.
▶ courage, bravery, resolution, determination, valour, firmness, hardihood, willpower, strong-mindedness

fortuitous ADJECTIVE
It was fortuitous that they arrived on the same day.
▶ accidental, coincidental, unintentional, chance

fortunate ADJECTIVE
1 *He was fortunate not to be shown a red card.*
▶ lucky, favoured
2 *These events provided them with a fortunate opportunity.*
▶ favourable, advantageous, auspicious, providential, welcome, happy, lucky

fortune NOUN
1 *a major change of fortune*
▶ fate, destiny, luck
2 *By good fortune he was able to take up the offer.*
▶ chance, luck, accident, providence
3 *She decided she would leave her fortune to charity.*
▶ wealth, riches, property, possessions, (more informal) pile

fortune-teller NOUN
He had the solemn voice of a fortune-teller.
▶ clairvoyant, crystal-gazer, soothsayer, palmist, prophet

forward ADJECTIVE
1 *The animal's long rear legs enable a fast forward movement.*
▶ onward, advancing, frontal, front, leading, progressive
AN OPPOSITE IS backward

a b c d e f g h i j k l m n o p q r s t u v w x y z

2 *forward planning*
▶ advance, future, early, prospective, forward-looking
AN OPPOSITE IS retrospective.
3 *His manner on the phone had been a little too forward.*
▶ bold, brazen, barefaced, brash, audacious, daring, presumptuous, familiar, uninhibited, precocious, assertive, over-confident, cheeky, (*more informal*) fresh, (*more informal*) pushy
OPPOSITES ARE shy, diffident

forward VERB
1 *Will you forward my letter?*
▶ send on, redirect
2 *The goods are forwarded by air.*
▶ dispatch, send, transport, transmit, convey, carry
3 *I will try to forward my plans during my visit.*
▶ advance, progress, develop, expedite, promote

forwards, forward ADVERB
The car shot forwards.
▶ ahead, in front, onwards

foster VERB
1 *activities that foster good health*
▶ encourage, promote, cultivate, stimulate, nurture, advance, further
2 *The couple had fostered several children.*
▶ bring up, rear, raise, care for, take care of, look after, nurture, parent, mother
USAGE You can also use *adopt*, but it has a special legal meaning.

foul ADJECTIVE
1 *You can recognize the animal from its foul smell.*
▶ nasty, horrible, unpleasant, disgusting, revolting, repulsive, repellent, dreadful, terrible, vile
AN OPPOSITE IS pleasant
2 *There was a foul mess on the floor.*
▶ dirty, filthy, unclean, nasty, mucky
AN OPPOSITE IS clean
3 *He had committed a foul crime.*
▶ wicked, evil, vile, contemptible, despicable, obnoxious, shameful, abhorrent, repellent, loathsome
AN OPPOSITE IS pleasant
4 *She had been subjected to taunts and foul language.*
▶ obscene, indecent, coarse, vulgar, offensive, crude, lewd
AN OPPOSITE IS mild
5 *The game was spoilt by a series of foul tackles.*
▶ illegal, unfair, prohibited
OPPOSITES ARE legal, fair
6 *The weather was foul all day.*
▶ unpleasant, bad, vile, disagreeable, inclement
AN OPPOSITE IS fine
7 *He apologized for having been so foul to her.*
▶ unkind, unfriendly, unpleasant, disagreeable, bad-tempered
OPPOSITES ARE kind, friendly

foul VERB
1 *Chemical waste was fouling the water.*
▶ pollute, contaminate, dirty, soil, sully, stain

2 *Silt was fouling the river mouth.*
▶ clog, choke, block, obstruct, stop up
3 *The ship had fouled its own nets.*
▶ entangle, snarl, catch, ensnare, twist

found VERB
1 *He founded the business in the 1880s.*
▶ establish, set up, start, create, begin, institute, inaugurate, initiate, organize, endow, fund
2 *Democracy is founded on the principle of free speech.*
▶ base, build, ground, construct, erect

foundation NOUN
1 *the foundation of the company in the eighteenth century*
▶ founding, establishment, institution, inauguration, initiation, setting up, starting, beginning
2 *There was no foundation for the claim.*
▶ basis, ground, reason, justification, rationale
3 **foundations** *The building had weak foundations*
▶ base, substructure, footing, underpinning, basis, bottom, cornerstone, bedrock
4 **foundations** *the foundations of the subject*
▶ fundamentals, rudiments, basic principles, elements, essentials, origins

founder NOUN
His grandfather had been the founder of the college.
▶ originator, creator, initiator, benefactor

founder VERB
The scheme foundered for lack of money.
▶ fail, collapse, miscarry, come to grief, come to nothing, (*more informal*) fold

fountain NOUN
The fountains are switched off in the cold months.
▶ jet, spout, spray, spring, fount

fox VERB
The question completely foxed them.
▶ baffle, confuse, perplex, bemuse, disconcert, confound, (*more informal*) flummox, (*more informal*) floor

fraction NOUN
They could only raise a fraction of the amount needed.
▶ part, division, portion, percentage, section, subdivision
USAGE You can use *small* or *tiny* with any of these words to help with the meaning.

fractious ADJECTIVE
He was feeling tired and fractious.
▶ irritable, bad-tempered, peevish, disagreeable, tetchy

fracture NOUN
She suffered a fracture in her leg.
▶ break, crack, breakage, fissure, split, chip, cleft, gap, opening, rent, rift

fracture VERB
He had fallen and fractured his skull.
▶ break, crack, split, cause a fracture in, suffer a fracture in

ragile ADJECTIVE

1 *She put away her fragile china.*
▶ breakable, brittle, delicate, weak, easily damaged
AN OPPOSITE IS strong

2 *The fragile ceasefire was barely holding.*
▶ precarious, tenuous, insecure, flimsy, vulnerable,
(*more informal*) dodgy

ragment NOUN (with the stress on *frag-*)

Fragments of broken pottery lay around.
▶ piece, bit, particle, chip, sliver, scrap, shiver,
shred, remnant, snippet, speck, atom, crumb, part

ragment VERB (with the stress on *-ment*)

The impact made the glass fragment.
▶ break, shatter, splinter, split, disintegrate, shiver,
crumble, come to pieces

ragmentary ADJECTIVE

*They couldn't tell much from the fragmentary
information available.*
▶ scrappy, incomplete, piecemeal, partial,
disconnected, disjointed, bitty
USAGE Be careful when you use *partial*,
because it has other meanings.

ragrance NOUN

The herbs gave off a gentle aromatic fragrance.
▶ scent, smell, perfume, bouquet, aroma, balm

ragrant ADJECTIVE

She went back to her own pretty and fragrant bedroom.
▶ sweet-scented, sweet-smelling, scented,
perfumed, aromatic

rail ADJECTIVE

1 *The old lady was very frail since breaking her hip.*
▶ weak, infirm, feeble, puny
OPPOSITES ARE strong, robust

2 *houses made of frail materials*
▶ flimsy, fragile, insubstantial, delicate, brittle,
breakable

3 *She clung to her frail memories.*
▶ weak, faint, dim

frailty NOUN

1 *the frailty of the very old*
▶ weakness, infirmity, debility, incapacity

2 *human frailties*
▶ weakness, failing, foible, deficiency, imperfection,
susceptibility

frame NOUN

1 *The vehicle has a strong lightweight frame.*
▶ framework, shell, skeleton, chassis, structure,
construction, bodywork

2 *a portrait in a gilt frame*
▶ surround, mount, mounting, border, setting,
edging

frame VERB

1 *The artists frame their own pictures.*
▶ mount, surround, encase, set

2 *The lawyers will frame the proposals.*
▶ compose, formulate, draw up, plan

framework NOUN

1 *The models are built round a wooden framework.*
▶ frame, shell, skeleton, structure, construction,
armature

2 *the changing framework of human life*
▶ structure, fabric, scheme, organization

frank ADJECTIVE

At least he is frank about his opinions.
▶ honest, candid, sincere, genuine, direct, open,
forthright, ingenuous, straightforward, straight,
truthful, unequivocal
OPPOSITES ARE insincere, disingenuous

frantic ADJECTIVE

1 *Her parents were frantic about her safety.*
▶ anxious, agitated, worried, distraught, fraught,
overwrought, (*more informal*) beside yourself
OPPOSITES ARE calm, composed

2 *There are frantic attempts to locate the luggage.*
▶ hectic, feverish, frenzied, wild
AN OPPOSITE IS calm

fraud NOUN

1 *He was accused of fraud.*
▶ fraudulence, swindling, cheating, sharp practice,
deceit, deception

2 *The offer turned out to be a fraud.*
▶ swindle, deception, trick, hoax, sham

3 *They exposed him as a fraud.*
▶ impostor, charlatan, cheat, trickster, (*more
informal*) phoney

fraudulent ADJECTIVE

fraudulent dealings on the stock exchange
▶ dishonest, illegal, unlawful, illicit, corrupt,
criminal, bogus, (*more informal*) crooked
AN OPPOSITE IS honest

fraught ADJECTIVE

By the end of the day she looked tired and fraught.
▶ anxious, apprehensive, agitated, tense, worried,
concerned, nervous, fearful, uneasy, troubled,
distressed
AN OPPOSITE IS calm

frayed ADJECTIVE

He wore a shirt with a frayed collar
▶ worn, tattered, ragged, threadbare, shabby,
untidy

freak ADJECTIVE

The south of the country was battered by freak storms.
▶ unusual, exceptional, abnormal, untypical,
anomalous, unpredictable, extraordinary
AN OPPOSITE IS normal

freak NOUN

1 *The animal is a genetically engineered freak.*
▶ oddity, aberration, abnormality, irregularity,
anomaly, quirk, monster, monstrosity, mutant,
malformation

2 (*informal*) *a weight-training freak*
▶ fanatic, devotee, enthusiast, admirer, lover, fan,
addict, aficionado

free ADJECTIVE

1 *Tickets to the concert are free.*
▶ without charge, free of charge, gratis, complimentary, gratuitous, on the house
AN OPPOSITE IS to be paid for

2 *The people longed to be free.*
▶ independent, self-governing, autonomous, emancipated
OPPOSITES ARE subjugated, dependent

3 *The wanted man is still free.*
▶ at liberty, on the loose, at large, unrestrained
AN OPPOSITE IS captive

4 *We don't have much free time.*
▶ spare, available, idle, unused

5 *The bathroom is free now.*
▶ vacant, unoccupied, empty, available, not in use
OPPOSITES ARE occupied, engaged

6 *She is very free with her money.*
▶ generous, lavish, liberal, unstinting, bounteous
OPPOSITES ARE mean, tight

7 *Are you free on Friday?*
▶ available, unoccupied, able to come
AN OPPOSITE IS occupied

8 *They are free to choose.*
▶ able, allowed, permitted, in a position, at leisure
AN OPPOSITE IS unable

9 **free of** *We are free of any commitments now.*
▶ relieved of, unaffected by, unencumbered by, unhindered by, lacking, without
AN OPPOSITE IS encumbered by

10 *the free movement of people and goods*
▶ unrestricted, unimpeded, unobstructed, unhindered, unlimited, clear, open
AN OPPOSITE IS obstructed

free VERB

1 *The new government freed all political prisoners.*
▶ release, liberate, set free, set at liberty, let loose, set loose, turn loose, deliver
OPPOSITES ARE confine, lock up

2 *The jury freed all three accused.*
▶ acquit, clear, exonerate, absolve, discharge, pardon
AN OPPOSITE IS condemn

3 *Firefighters managed to free the trapped victims.*
▶ rescue, release, extricate, remove, pull out, pull free

4 *She struggled hard to free her hand.*
▶ clear, loose, extricate, disentangle, disengage, untie, untangle
AN OPPOSITE IS tangle

freedom NOUN

1 *The prisoners longed for their freedom.*
▶ liberty, liberation, release, deliverance
OPPOSITES ARE captivity, confinement

2 *Only a revolution would give the country its freedom.*
▶ independence, self-government, self-determination
AN OPPOSITE IS dependence

3 *Parents should have the freedom to choose the education for their children.*
▶ ability, opportunity, chance, facility, power, licence, scope, leeway
AN OPPOSITE IS restriction

freely ADVERB

He found it hard to talk freely.
▶ openly, candidly, frankly, plainly, honestly

freeze VERB

1 *In winter the river freezes.*
▶ ice over, become ice, become solid, solidify, harden

2 *We had no fire and were beginning to freeze.*
▶ feel cold, go numb with cold

3 *If you have too much fruit you can freeze it.*
▶ deep-freeze, dry-freeze, refrigerate, chill, preserve

4 *a government plan to freeze prices*
▶ fix, peg, hold, curb, limit, keep as they are

freezing ADJECTIVE

It was a freezing morning.
▶ bitterly cold, frosty, raw, biting, piercing

freight NOUN

1 *a mixture of passenger and freight services*
▶ cargo, goods, merchandise

2 *Air freight charges are extremely high.*
▶ transportation, shipment, carriage, conveyance

frenzy NOUN

1 *The audience was in a state of frenzy.*
▶ hysteria, fever, delirium, turmoil, agitation, mania, derangement

2 *a frenzy of anger*
▶ fit, spasm, outburst, paroxysm, ferment

frequent ADJECTIVE (with the stress on *fre-*, pronounced like *free*)

1 *An airport bus leaves at frequent intervals.*
▶ regular, numerous, repeated, constant, recurring, continual

2 *Claire is a frequent visitor here.*
▶ habitual, constant, regular, common

frequent VERB (with the stress on *-quent*)

He frequents wine bars in the town.
▶ visit, patronize, haunt, attend

fresh ADJECTIVE

1 *Good eating habits include fresh fruit and vegetable.*
▶ natural, raw

2 *The party needs new members and fresh ideas*
▶ new, original, innovative, novel, recent, up-to-date

3 *The army has a batch of fresh recruits*
▶ young, youthful, inexperienced, callow

4 *Next day was fresh and bright.*
▶ cool, crisp, refreshing, clear

5 *She was feeling fresh after her shower.*
▶ refreshed, rested, restored, revived, invigorated

6 *They walked out to a fresh wind.*
▶ cold, brisk, bracing, invigorating

7 She told him not to get fresh.
▶ impudent, impertinent, insolent, cheeky, saucy, familiar, disrespectful, forward

eshen VERB
The cool water freshened him.
▶ refresh, invigorate, restore, revive, stimulate, fortify

et VERB
He stopped fretting about his life and the future.
▶ worry, be anxious, agonize, concern yourself, brood, mope, be upset

iction NOUN
1 The rope is restrained by friction.
▶ rubbing, abrasion, grip, chafing, resistance, scraping
2 There was some friction between the different ethnic groups.
▶ conflict, disagreement, antagonism, discord, strife, dissension, contention, clashing, quarrelling, fighting, rivalry

iend NOUN
He can stay with a friend while his parents are away.
▶ acquaintance, companion, associate, (*more informal*) mate, (*more informal*) pal, (*more informal*) buddy, (*more informal*) chum

iendliness NOUN
They liked him for his friendliness and humour.
▶ kindness, sociability, goodwill, hospitality, warmth

iendly ADJECTIVE
1 The staff are very friendly and helpful.
▶ pleasant, agreeable, kind, amiable, kindly, kind-hearted, well-disposed, likeable, genial, congenial, sympathetic, approachable, receptive, sociable, outgoing
2 Volunteers are on hand to give friendly advice. The hotel is small with a friendly atmosphere.
▶ cordial, good-natured, sympathetic, amicable, warm, welcoming
3 The girls had been friendly since their childhood.
▶ close, affectionate, intimate, familiar, (*more informal*) chummy, (*more informal*) pally, (*more informal*) matey

iendship NOUN
1 He thanked his colleagues for their friendship and support.
▶ friendliness, affection, goodwill, comradeship, cordiality
OPPOSITES ARE hostility, enmity
2 Their friendship grew over the coming months.
▶ relationship, affection, intimacy, closeness, love, attachment

ight NOUN
1 The blast gave everyone a fright.
▶ scare, shock, surprise, start, turn, jolt
2 Amy was overcome by fright.
▶ fear, alarm, terror, trepidation, consternation, horror, dismay, dread, panic

frighten VERB
The noises outside began to frighten them.
▶ scare, startle, alarm, terrify, shock, agitate, disturb, fluster, panic, intimidate, disconcert
AN OPPOSITE IS reassure

frightened ADJECTIVE
The children were tired and frightened.
▶ scared, afraid, alarmed, terrified, petrified, fearful, shaken, shocked, panicky

frightening ADJECTIVE
a frightening experience
▶ terrifying, alarming, fearsome, daunting, (*more informal*) scary

frightful ADJECTIVE
1 We had to eat frightful food.
▶ awful, terrible, dreadful, ghastly, appalling, horrible
2 a scene of frightful devastation
▶ shocking, horrible, terrible, gruesome, harrowing, hideous, grisly, horrid, macabre

frigid ADJECTIVE
1 the frigid northern climate
▶ bitter, bitterly cold, freezing, frozen, icy, arctic
2 Leo glared back in frigid indignation.
▶ stiff, stony, formal, unfeeling, austere, distant, aloof

frill NOUN
1 a skirt with deep frills
▶ fringe, ruff, ruffle, flounce
2 a small hotel with no frills
▶ extra, luxury, embellishment, extravagance

fringe NOUN
1 a fringe round the edge of a curtain
▶ border, edging, flounce, frill, gathering, trimming, valance
2 on the fringe of the town
▶ edge, outskirts, limits, periphery, perimeter, borders, margin
AN OPPOSITE IS centre

frisk VERB
1 The dogs frisked about on the grass.
▶ leap, cavort, frolic, caper, bound, jump, play, sport, spring, bounce, gambol, skip
2 She was frisked by a police officer.
▶ search, body-search, examine, inspect

frisky ADJECTIVE
a frisky young calf
▶ lively, playful, skittish, high-spirited, spirited, frolicsome, jaunty, sprightly

fritter VERB
He frittered away all the money he had been given.
▶ squander, waste, misspend, dissipate, get through

frivolous ADJECTIVE

They often made frivolous comments.
▶ flippant, facetious, trivial, trifling, silly, shallow, stupid, foolish, jocular, flighty, ridiculous, superficial, unimportant, vacuous
AN OPPOSITE IS serious

frock NOUN

a red cotton frock
▶ dress, gown, shift, robe

frolic VERB

Lambs frolicked in the fields.
▶ play, cavort, frisk, caper, leap, jump, sport, spring, bounce, gambol, skip, bound

front NOUN

1 *the front of the house*
▶ facade, facing, exterior
AN OPPOSITE IS back

2 *the front of a boat*
▶ prow, bow, forepart
OPPOSITES ARE back, stern

3 *the front of a car*
▶ nose, forepart
AN OPPOSITE IS rear

4 *the front of the queue*
▶ head, start, beginning, lead
OPPOSITES ARE back, end

5 *Young recruits were sent to the front.*
▶ front line, battle line, combat zone

6 *He managed to keep up a brave front.*
▶ appearance, manner, show, pose, bearing

front ADJECTIVE

The front runners came into view.
▶ first, leading, foremost, most advanced
AN OPPOSITE IS back

frontier NOUN

the French-German frontier
▶ border, boundary, borderline, dividing line, limit

frosty ADJECTIVE

1 *a frosty autumn morning*
▶ freezing, bitter, ice-cold, crisp
2 *I'm afraid we'll get a frosty reception.*
▶ unfriendly, unwelcoming, unsympathetic, cool, stony

froth NOUN

1 *Claude wiped the champagne froth from his moustache.*
▶ foam, bubbles, effervescence, head
2 *He shook his hand in the water to make a froth.*
▶ lather, suds, foam

frown VERB

The woman frowned at them.
▶ scowl, glower, glare, lour, grimace, knit your brow, look sullen, (*more informal*) give a dirty look
frown on *They frown on bad language.*
▶ disapprove of, view with disfavour, look askance at, object to, disfavour, dislike, discourage

frown NOUN

He had a frown on his face.
▶ scowl, glare, grimace, black look,
(*more informal*) dirty look

frozen ADJECTIVE

1 *The lake is frozen.*
▶ iced over, ice-covered, icebound, solidified
2 *She felt frozen in the keen wind.*
▶ freezing, very cold, numbed

frugal ADJECTIVE

1 *a frugal meal*
▶ meagre, paltry, plain, simple
2 *They lead a frugal life.*
▶ economical, thrifty, sparing, parsimonious, abstemious

fruit NOUN

SOME COMMON TYPES OF FRUIT

apples: Blenheim orange, Bramley, Cox (Cox's orange pippin), crab apple (small and sour), Golden Delicious, Granny Smith, Gravenstein, Pearmain, pippin, Red Delicious, russet ; eating apple, cooking apple; crab apple.

pears: Bartlett, Comice, Conference, Jargonelle, Williams.

citrus fruits: clementine (tangerine), grapefruit, Jaffa (orange), kumquat, lemon, lime, mandarin (orange), navel orange (seedless), orange, ortanique (cross between orange and tangerine), pomelo, satsuma (tangerine), Seville orange (bitter, used for marmalade), tangerine, Ugli fruit.

stone fruits: apricot, avocado, cherry, damson, date, greengage, lychee, nectarine, olive, peach, plum.

fleshy fruits: banana, cantaloupe (small melon), cucumber, fig, guava, honeydew (melon), kiwi fruit, mango, mangosteen, melon, persimmon, pineapple, pomegranate, pumpkin, tomato.

berries: bilberry, blackcurrant, blueberry, cranberry, elderberry, gooseberry, grape, jujube, loganberry, raspberry, redcurrant, strawberry.

fruitful ADJECTIVE

1 *a fruitful crop*
▶ abundant, copious, productive, rich, prolific, fertile, plenteous, profuse
AN OPPOSITE IS unproductive
2 *Talks have proved fruitful.*
▶ successful, productive, beneficial, profitable, useful, effective, worthwhile, gainful, rewarding
AN OPPOSITE IS fruitless

fruitless ADJECTIVE
three days of fruitless negotiations
► futile, vain, abortive, unsuccessful, unfruitful, unproductive, profitless, unavailing, pointless, useless, disappointing, unprofitable, unrewarding
AN OPPOSITE IS fruitful

frustrate VERB
1 *The lack of progress was clearly frustrating them.*
► exasperate, discourage, dispirit, irritate
OPPOSITES ARE satisfy, please
2 *Bad weather frustrated all attempts at a rescue.*
► thwart, foil, defeat, forestall, inhibit, prevent

frustrated ADJECTIVE
He felt let down and frustrated.
► disappointed, thwarted, inhibited

frustration NOUN
He shook his head in frustration.
► exasperation, annoyance, anger, irritation, disappointment, dissatisfaction

fudge VERB
1 *The Government were accused of trying to fudge the issue.*
► evade, dodge, skirt, gloss over
2 *The accountants won't let you fudge the figures.*
► falsify, fake, distort, misrepresent

fudge NOUN
The proposals are regarded as a bit of a fudge.
► compromise, evasion, equivocation, (*more informal*) cop-out

fuel NOUN
1 *Vehicles were running out of fuel on the motorway jams.*
► petrol, propellant, diesel oil
2 *The inspectors' report added fuel to the war cause.*
► encouragement, provocation, incentive

fuel VERB
The pictures fuelled rumours of an affair.
► encourage, stimulate, intensify, sustain, stoke up, feed, nurture

fugitive NOUN
He spent three months as a fugitive and was finally captured.
► escapee, runaway, escaper, deserter, renegade, refugee

fulfil VERB
1 *She was fulfilling her life's ambition of seeing the world.*
► achieve, realize, carry out, accomplish, succeed in, attain, effect, perform
2 *They have to work twelve hours a day to fulfil their obligations.*
► meet, complete, implement, execute, comply with, satisfy, respond to, answer, conform to
OPPOSITES ARE fail in, neglect

fulfilment NOUN
The fulfilment of these plans would take time.
► achievement, completion, accomplishment, execution, performance, discharge

full ADJECTIVE
1 *His glass was still full.*
► filled, loaded, topped up
AN OPPOSITE IS empty
2 *The trains would be full on a Friday afternoon.*
► crowded, packed, crammed, congested, thronged, teeming, swarming, stuffed, mobbed, (*more informal*) jam-packed
AN OPPOSITE IS empty
3 *By the end of the meal they were too full to talk.*
► well fed, satisfied, satiated, replete, sated, (*more informal*) bursting
4 *The bureau can give you a full list of local hotels and guest houses.*
► complete, comprehensive, exhaustive, thorough, copious
5 *The article did not tell the full story.*
► entire, complete, total, unabridged, unexpurgated
6 *She had led a full life and was looking forward to a period of quiet.*
► exciting, eventful, interesting, busy, lively, hectic
7 *The new piano had a full sound.*
► rich, resonant, sonorous, full-bodied, deep

fully ADVERB
We fully accept that there must be changes. I don't think you fully understand.
► completely, entirely, wholly, totally, thoroughly, quite, altogether, positively, without reserve
AN OPPOSITE IS partially

fumble VERB
1 *He fumbled for his wallet.*
► grope, feel about, fish, delve
2 *Without any light she could only fumble about.*
► stumble, blunder, flounder, lurch, stagger, totter
3 *Then, unfortunately, the keeper fumbled the ball.*
► mishandle, miss, drop, fail to catch, fail to keep

fumes PLURAL NOUN
fumes from an old tractor
► exhaust, smoke, gases, vapour, fog, pollution, smog

fuming ADJECTIVE
Dad was pacing back and forth, fuming.
► angry, furious, enraged, seething, raging, incensed

fun NOUN
After their exams they just wanted some fun.
► enjoyment, entertainment, amusement, recreation, diversion, distraction, relaxation, jollity, play

function NOUN
1 *The organization has several functions.*
► role, responsibility, obligation, purpose, concern, use, job, task
2 *I had seen him at an official function*
► event, occasion, party, gathering, reception, dinner, (*more informal*) do

function VERB

1 *To stop the machine functioning, switch it off.*
▶ work, operate, run, perform
2 **function as** *The office also functions as an advice centre.*
▶ act as, serve as, operate as, constitute, form, have the role of

functional ADJECTIVE

1 *an ugly functional building*
▶ practical, utilitarian, serviceable, useful
OPPOSITES ARE impractical, decorative
2 *The drinks machine is not yet functional.*
▶ working, operational, operative, in working order
OPPOSITES ARE inoperative, out of order

fund NOUN

1 *an emergency fund for refugees*
▶ pool, kitty, store, reserve, cache, source, supply
2 **funds** *Funds are running low.*
▶ money, cash, capital, finances, assets, reserves, savings

fund VERB

Private capital will help fund the railways.
▶ pay for, finance, capitalize, sponsor, subsidize, back, endow, maintain

fundamental ADJECTIVE

fundamental political principles
▶ basic, elementary, essential, primary, underlying, axiomatic, key, prime, principal, important, main, necessary
OPPOSITES ARE secondary, inessential

funeral NOUN

I attended his funeral last week.
▶ burial, interment, cremation, committal, laying to rest, obsequies, wake

funnel NOUN

Smoke poured from the funnel.
▶ chimney, flue, vent, shaft

funny ADJECTIVE

1 *a funny story*
▶ amusing, humorous, comic, comical, witty, hilarious, facetious, droll, entertaining, silly, absurd, ridiculous
AN OPPOSITE IS serious
2 *a funny coincidence*
▶ peculiar, strange, odd, curious, puzzling, queer, weird, bizarre

furious ADJECTIVE

She was furious when she found out.
▶ angry, enraged, infuriated, incensed, fuming, annoyed, cross, displeased, irritated, irate, indignant, outraged
OPPOSITES ARE pleased, calm

furnish VERB

They have furnished the rooms tastefully.
▶ decorate, appoint, fit out, fit up, equip

furniture NOUN

After the fire they had to buy new furniture.
▶ furnishings, fitments, fittings, effects, household goods, equipment, movables, possessions

furrow NOUN

a potato field with deep furrows
▶ channel, trench, groove, rut, ditch

furrow VERB

He furrowed his brow.
▶ crease, wrinkle, crinkle, pucker, knit, screw up

furry ADJECTIVE

All her furry little pets had died.
▶ fleecy, woolly, fuzzy, hairy, downy, feathery

further ADJECTIVE

We need further information
▶ more, additional, extra, fresh, new, supplementary

further VERB

She wants to further her career in business.
▶ advance, promote, foster, forward, develop, boost, assist, expedite, accelerate

furtive ADJECTIVE

They cast furtive glances round the room.
▶ secret, secretive, surreptitious, covert, stealthy, shifty, sly, concealed, disguised, hidden, conspiratorial, underhand, (*more informal*) sneaky
AN OPPOSITE IS open

fury NOUN

1 *She could not hide her fury.*
▶ anger, rage, wrath, passion
2 *The storm hit the town with immense fury.*
▶ force, ferocity, fierceness, violence, turbulence, severity, savagery

fuse VERB

The programme fuses news information with comment.
▶ blend, combine, merge, join, amalgamate, compound, unite, meld, weld

fuss NOUN

1 *There was a lot of fuss about the missing money.*
▶ commotion, agitation, excitement, confusion, upset, worry
2 *He wanted to get the job done with as little fuss as possible.*
▶ bother, trouble, difficulty, inconvenience, effort, (*more informal*) hassle

fuss VERB

He begged her not to fuss.
▶ fret, worry, get worked up, agitate, bother, complain, (*more informal*) flap, (*more informal*) create

fussy ADJECTIVE

1 *They are both fussy about their food.*
▶ finicky, fastidious, particular, choosy, (*more informal*) picky
2 *The menu is a little fussy and over-rich.*
▶ fancy, elaborate, ornate, florid, detailed

futile ADJECTIVE
In the end the rebels abandoned the futile struggle.
▶ fruitless, pointless, vain, ineffectual, unsuccessful, useless, abortive, unavailing, unproductive, barren
AN OPPOSITE IS fruitful

futility NOUN
She shook her head, aware of the futility of trying to explain herself.
▶ pointlessness, uselessness, ineffectiveness, unproductiveness, absurdity, aimlessness, emptiness, hollowness, vanity, wasted effort
OPPOSITES ARE usefulness, effectiveness

future NOUN
1 *There is a bright future for them.*
▶ outlook, prospects, expectations, destiny
2 *our plans for the future*
▶ time to come, time ahead
AN OPPOSITE IS past

future ADJECTIVE
Future generations may find themselves living on a warmer planet.
▶ later, following, coming, succeeding, subsequent, prospective, approaching, forthcoming, impending
AN OPPOSITE IS past

fuzzy ADJECTIVE
1 *The baby had a large fuzzy head.*
▶ downy, frizzy, fluffy, woolly, fleecy, velvety, feathery
2 *good sound but a fuzzy picture*
▶ blurred, bleary, unfocused, ill-defined, indistinct, vague, hazy, shadowy, unclear, cloudy, dim, faint, misty
OPPOSITES ARE clear, sharp

Gg

gadget NOUN
a kitchen full of gadgets
▶ tool, utensil, appliance, contraption, contrivance, device, implement, machine, invention, instrument

gaffe NOUN
Anne was taking a day off trying to forget her gaffe.
▶ mistake, blunder, error, slip, indiscretion

gag NOUN
His latest gag was quite funny for a change.
▶ joke, jest, quip, funny remark, witticism, wisecrack

gag VERB
1 *The food had a strange taste that made her gag.*
▶ retch, choke, heave
2 *The regime found effective ways of gagging the press.*
▶ silence, muzzle, stifle, keep quiet, suppress, smother, restrain, prevent from speaking

gaiety NOUN
1 *There was gaiety in her voice.*
▶ cheerfulness, cheer, joy, happiness, merriment, jollity, delight
2 *They headed for the gaiety of a London bar.*
▶ festivity, fun, celebration, revelry, jollification

gaily ADVERB
1 *She waved gaily back.*
▶ merrily, cheerfully, cheerily, happily, joyfully, blithely
OPPOSITES ARE sadly, drearily
2 *She wore a gaily coloured sari.*
▶ brightly, brilliantly, flamboyantly
AN OPPOSITE IS drably
3 *There was Ben, gaily waving the traffic past.*
▶ casually, nonchalantly, heedlessly, airily, breezily, lightly, unthinkingly, uncaringly
AN OPPOSITE IS anxiously

gain NOUN
1 *We are all motivated by the prospect of financial gain. There was no personal gain in it for me.*
▶ profit, earnings, income, advantage, benefit, return, reward, proceeds, yield, acquisition, asset, attainment, dividend, increase, winnings
AN OPPOSITE IS loss
2 **gain** or **gains** *Labour made modest gains in the local elections in the spring.*
▶ advances, progress, advancement, headway

gain VERB
1 *She gained a huge income from her investments.*
▶ earn, gross, clear, bring in, obtain, acquire, procure
2 *They gained a wide reputation from the publicity.*
▶ earn, achieve, acquire, win, secure
3 *Trevor raised his head to gain a better view.*
▶ get, achieve, attain
4 *The car began to gain speed.*
▶ increase, gather, pick up
USAGE You can also say *the car began to accelerate.*
5 **gain on** *We were gaining on the vehicle in front.*
▶ catch up with, draw nearer to, narrow the gap between, creep up on, approach

gala NOUN
the annual summer gala
▶ festival, carnival, jamboree, fete, fair, fiesta, celebration, revelry, party

gale NOUN
1 *Rain and gales are frequent.*
▶ storm, squall, high wind, hurricane
2 *She collapsed in gales of laughter.*
▶ outburst, burst, eruption, paroxysm, fit, peal, howl, hoot, roar

gallant ADJECTIVE
1 *a gallant band of soldiers*
▶ brave, courageous, valiant, daring, fearless, intrepid, heroic, doughty, noble, manly
AN OPPOSITE IS cowardly

G

2 *A gallant gentleman at the next table came over to help her.*
► courteous, chivalrous, respectful, considerate, obliging, gracious
OPPOSITES ARE discourteous, rude

gallery NOUN
1 *She walked to the end of the gallery and through a door at the end.*
► passage, passageway, corridor
2 *They had seats up in the gallery.*
► balcony, circle, upper circle, (*more informal*) gods

gallop VERB
A horse galloped past.
► race, run, canter, rush, dash, speed, sprint

galvanize VERB
Seeing her in this state galvanized him into action.
► jolt, shock, spur, prod, urge, stimulate

gambit NOUN
It was a daring gambit and might just work.
► plan, stratagem, tactic, ruse, move, manoeuvre, trick

gamble VERB
1 *He drinks and gambles and chases women.*
► bet, game, risk money, wager, (*more informal*) have a flutter
2 *We gambled and were lucky.*
► take a risk, take a chance, try your luck, speculate, venture

---

game NOUN
1 *The children were playing a new game.*
► pastime, diversion, amusement, entertainment, sport, activity
2 *I know how to deal with his little game.*
► scheme, trick, plot, plan, dodge
3 *It was the big game on Saturday.*
► match, contest, tournament, competition, event, meeting
4 *They were just playing a game on us.*
► joke, trick, prank, hoax

NAMES FOR TYPES OF GAME

board games: chess, draughts, ludo, Monopoly, Scrabble; backgammon.

card games: beggar-my-neighbour, blackjack or pontoon or vingt-et-un, bridge, bezique, canasta, cribbage, faro, old maid, patience (for one player), piquet, poker, rummy, snap, whist.

other indoor games: billiards, snooker, pool; cards, solitaire; darts; dominoes; dice; lotto, bingo; marbles, tiddlywinks; table tennis, (*informal*) ping-pong); bagatelle; charades, eye spy, consequences, hide-and-seek, pass the parcel; computer games.

outdoor games: roller skating, rollerblading, skateboarding; skating, sledging; hopscotch, leapfrog; conkers.

---

game ADJECTIVE
1 *She was always game for anything.*
► willing, ready, eager, keen, prepared, in the mood
2 *You will need to be game to take on this job.*
► brave, daring, bold, courageous, plucky, intrepid

gang NOUN
1 *a gang of teenagers*
► band, group, crowd, pack, mob
2 *a gang working on the road*
► team, squad, troop, shift, detachment, working party
3 *I was never a part of his gang.*
► circle, set, group, ring, clan, clique

gang VERB
gang together or **up** *They always gang up to get their way.*
► combine, conspire, cooperate, work together, team up

gangster NOUN
a mob of armed gangsters
► hoodlum, bandit, robber, mobster, brigand, criminal, crook, desperado, gunman, thug

gaol NOUN, VERB, SEE **jail**

gap NOUN
1 *a gap in a wall*
► opening, breach, break, chink, space, hole, cleft, crack, cranny, crevice, rift, void
2 *a gap in the fighting*
► pause, break, interruption, lull, intermission, interval
3 *the gap between rich and poor*
► divide, gulf, rift, chasm, disparity, imbalance

gape VERB
He gaped at her in surprise.
► stare, gaze, goggle, (*more informal*) gawk, (*more informal*) gawp

garage NOUN
1 *The house had a large garage, which the new owner turned into a study.*
► car-port
2 *She had stopped to fill up the tank at a local garage.*
► filling-station, petrol station, service station

garbled ADJECTIVE
The story seems garbled and may be nonsense.
► confused, muddled, mixed up, twisted, jumbled, scrambled
AN OPPOSITE IS clear

garden NOUN
1 *a house with a garden*
► plot, allotment, patch, yard
2 **gardens** *a walk through the gardens*
► grounds, park
RELATED ADJECTIVE horticultural
RELATED NOUN horticulture

garland

garland NOUN

a garland of flowers

▶ wreath, chain, festoon, circle, loop, ring

garment NOUN

These fabrics are ideal for children's garments.

▶ piece of clothing, item of clothing, costume, outfit, habit, robe

garnish VERB

Garnish the fish with cucumber.

▶ decorate, adorn, trim, embellish, enhance

garrison NOUN

1 *A small garrison defended the town.*

▶ force, unit, platoon, contingent, detachment

2 *An enemy force surrounded the garrison.*

▶ stronghold, fortress, fort, fortification, barracks, post, camp, citadel

gash NOUN

Blood was pouring from a gash on his head.

▶ cut, slash, wound, injury, slit, laceration, abrasion

gash VERB

Frank gashed his hand on a broken glass.

▶ cut, slash, lacerate, wound, injure, gouge

gasp VERB

She gasped and sat back, her face pale.

▶ catch your breath, pant, choke, gulp, blow

gasp NOUN

The boy fell back with a gasp.

▶ pant, heave, wheeze, puff, blow

gasping ADJECTIVE

The effort left them gasping.

▶ breathless, exhausted, tired out, puffed

gate NOUN

Some children came through the gate.

▶ gateway, doorway, door, entrance, entry, exit, (*poetic*) portal

gather VERB

1 *A crowd gathered near the entrance.*

▶ assemble, collect, come together, congregate, crowd round, convene, converge, flock, group, muster

AN OPPOSITE IS disperse

2 *She spent some time gathering her books.*

▶ collect, assemble, accumulate, bring together, heap up

3 *They went into the garden to gather flowers and berries.*

▶ pick, pluck, garner, harvest

4 *I gather you have been unwell.*

▶ understand, believe, be told, be given to understand, learn, hear, be informed, deduce, infer, surmise

5 *You can gather the dress at the waist.*

▶ pleat, fold, crimp, ruffle, pucker

gathering NOUN

a gathering of families

▶ assembly, meeting, company, group , mass, party, function, social, (*informal*) get-together

gauche ADJECTIVE

a gauche young man with a slight stammer

▶ awkward, ungainly, gawky, inelegant, graceless

OPPOSITES ARE elegant, sophisticated

gaudy ADJECTIVE

She wore dull clothes, nothing gaudy.

▶ garish, lurid, flashy, loud, glaring, vulgar

OPPOSITES ARE sober, dull

gauge NOUN

1 *He checked the pressure gauge.*

▶ meter, instrument, dial, reading

2 *The track was the wrong gauge for the new rolling stock.*

▶ size, width, measure, standard

3 *The local elections will be seen as a gauge of public opinion.*

▶ measure, indicator, test, guide (to), touchstone, benchmark

gauge VERB

1 *A special scoring table will gauge which competitor does best.*

▶ assess, evaluate, appraise, calculate, reckon

2 *Instruments can gauge the distance precisely.*

▶ measure, calculate, compute, quantify, determine

gaunt ADJECTIVE

His arms were wrapped round his gaunt body.

▶ haggard, drawn, lank, emaciated, wasted, skinny, scrawny, shrivelled, skeletal, cadaverous

gawky ADJECTIVE

She had been a thin, gawky adolescent

▶ awkward, ungainly, inelegant, ungraceful, graceless, gangling, gauche, inept, lumbering, bumbling, maladroit, uncoordinated

AN OPPOSITE IS graceful

gay ADJECTIVE

1 *a club for gay people*

▶ homosexual, (*female*) lesbian, (*more informal*) queer

2 *He was so gay and lively.*

▶ cheerful, happy, carefree, lively, merry, jolly, jovial, glad

gaze VERB

He continued to gaze out of the window.

▶ stare, look, gape

gear NOUN

(*informal*) *You can put your gear in here.*

▶ equipment, paraphernalia, belongings, possessions, stuff, things, tackle

gem NOUN
1 *a tiara made of gems and pearls*
▶ jewel, precious stone, gemstone
2 *The anthology contains some real gems.*
▶ pearl, wonder, treasure, masterpiece, outstanding example

SOME COMMON TYPES OF GEM AND GEMSTONES

agate, alexandrine, almandine, amber, amethyst, aquamarine, beryl, bloodstone, cairngorm, carbuncle, carnelian, cat's-eye, chalcedony, chrysolite, chrysoprase, corundum, diamond, emerald, garnet, girasol, greenstone, jacinth, jade, jasper, lapis lazuli, marcasite, moonstone, morganite, moss agate, onyx, opal, rhodolite, rose quartz, ruby, sapphire, sardonyx, sunstone, tanzanite, topaz, tourmaline, turquoise, zircon.

general ADJECTIVE
1 *The idea is sound in general terms*
▶ broad, rough, sweeping, vague, loose, indefinite
AN OPPOSITE IS specific
2 *This model is more suitable for general use.*
▶ widespread, universal, popular, regular, typical, normal, ordinary, everyday, conventional
OPPOSITES ARE specialist, restricted
3 *a general pay increase*
▶ comprehensive, inclusive, overall, universal

generally ADVERB
It is generally a mistake to ignore these factors.
▶ normally, as a rule, by and large, on the whole, broadly, mainly, mostly, in the main, predominantly, usually

generate VERB
a move to generate more business
▶ create, produce, bring about, make, cause, give rise to, propagate, engender, beget, breed, (*more informal*) whip up

generation NOUN
1 *people of an earlier generation*
▶ age, age group
2 *the generation of new jobs*
▶ creation, production, origination, initiation, genesis

generosity NOUN
Thanks to the generosity of sponsors the games can continue.
▶ kindness, munificence, liberality, philanthropy, benevolence, bounty, charity, largess

generous ADJECTIVE
1 *a person of a good and generous nature*
▶ kind, kind-hearted, magnanimous, benevolent, unselfish, charitable, big-hearted, beneficent, philanthropic

2 *She was always generous on the children's birthdays.*
▶ bountiful, liberal, lavish, munificent, indulgent, bounteous
3 *a generous helping of pudding*
▶ large, lavish, ample, copious, plentiful, abundant

genial ADJECTIVE
The guests were welcomed by their genial host.
▶ friendly, affable, cordial, congenial, kindly, pleasant, cheerful, good-natured, companionable, hospitable, jolly, warm-hearted, easygoing
AN OPPOSITE IS unfriendly

genius NOUN
1 *They have a genius for getting attention.*
▶ talent, gift, flair, aptitude, bent, intellect, knack
2 *It doesn't take a genius to work out his little game.*
▶ mastermind, great thinker, great brain, prodigy, past master, expert, intellectual

gentle ADJECTIVE
1 *The mild, gentle face looked back at him.*
▶ kind, kindly, tender, sympathetic, compassionate, warm-hearted, soft-hearted, placid, calm
OPPOSITES ARE unkind, harsh
2 *A gentle breeze was blowing.*
▶ light, faint, soft
OPPOSITES ARE strong, fierce
3 *There was a gentle slope up to the house.*
▶ gradual, slight, easy
AN OPPOSITE IS steep

genuine ADJECTIVE
1 *A genuine Picasso hung on the wall.*
▶ authentic, original, bona fide, actual, real, true, authenticated
AN OPPOSITE IS fake
2 *She's a very genuine person.*
▶ sincere, honest, unaffected, frank, truthful, devout, candid, earnest, true
AN OPPOSITE IS insincere

germ NOUN
1 *the germ of a great idea*
▶ beginning, nucleus, seed, start, genesis, embryo, cause, origin
2 *a cleaner that also kills germs*
▶ microbe, micro-organism, bacterium, (*more informal*) bug, virus

gesture NOUN
1 *She sent them away with an irritable gesture of her hand.*
▶ signal, sign, motion, movement, flourish, gesticulation
2 *a gesture of goodwill*
▶ act, action, indication, deed

gesture VERB
He gestured for them to leave.
▶ signal, motion, gesticulate, make a gesture, sign

get VERB This word is often overused. Here are some alternatives:

1 *She got her degree at St Andrews.*
▶ obtain, receive, acquire, come by, achieve, procure

2 *It's getting cold.*
▶ become, turn, grow

3 *We'll get there soon.*
▶ arrive, reach, come to

4 *Will you get my book?*
▶ fetch, bring, collect, pick up

5 *I got a cold.*
▶ catch, come down with, develop

6 *I'll get her to come tomorrow.*
▶ persuade, urge, induce, make

get across *It's hard to get the idea across.*
▶ communicate, convey, impart, transmit

get ahead *people who want to get ahead*
▶ succeed, prosper, flourish, get on well

get along
1 *They do seem to get along with each other.*
▶ agree, see eye to eye, be friendly, be compatible

2 *We are getting along quite well now.*
▶ manage, cope, get on, make out, progress, advance

get at *What are you getting at?*
▶ suggest, imply, intend, insinuate, mean

get away *Tom and Fiona wanted to get away for the weekend*
▶ escape, leave, (*more informal*) make off

get back *We won't get our money back.*
▶ recover, recoup, regain, retrieve

get by *We have enough money to get by.*
▶ survive, manage, cope, make do, muddle along, muddle through

get down *All the talk of war got them down.*
▶ depress, deject, dishearten, dispirit, sadden

get in *The train gets in at 7 o'clock.*
▶ arrive, come

get on
1 *We'd better get on the bus.*
▶ board, embark, mount, ascend

2 *How did they get on during their holiday?*
▶ cope, manage, fare, get along, make out

get out *Some of the prisoners had got out.*
▶ escape, break out, break free, get away, flee

get over
1 *She's just got over flu.*
▶ recover from, shake off, survive

2 *difficulties that we can never get over*
▶ overcome, surmount, deal with

get round
1 *a problem they tried to get round*
▶ avoid, evade, overcome, get the better of

2 *He always got round his mother when he needed something.*
▶ persuade, cajole, prevail on, win over, beguile

get together *Let's get together next week.*
▶ meet, meet up, see one another   ▶▶

get up
1 *She got up from her chair.*
▶ rise, stand, stand up

2 *They would have to get up early to leave for the airport.*
▶ rise, get out of bed

getaway NOUN
a quick getaway
▶ escape, breakout, breakaway

ghastly ADJECTIVE
1 *a ghastly murder*
▶ terrible, frightful, horrible, horrific, horrifying, gruesome

2 *a ghastly time*
▶ unpleasant, disagreeable, nasty, horrid, revolting
AN OPPOSITE IS lovely

ghost NOUN
1 *They say there's a ghost in the house.*
▶ phantom, spectre, spirit, wraith, vision

2 *a ghost of a smile*
▶ trace, hint, suggestion, glimmer, semblance, shadow

ghostly ADJECTIVE
The ghostly figure seemed to belong to a dream.
▶ unearthly, spectral, eerie, phantom, uncanny, weird, supernatural, (*informal*) spooky, (*informal*) creepy, (*informal*) scary

giant NOUN
A giant of a man stood in the doorway.
▶ monster, colossus, titan, Goliath, ogre
AN OPPOSITE IS dwarf

giant ADJECTIVE
The thrust from the four giant engines pushed him back in his seat.
▶ huge, enormous, gigantic, colossal, immense, massive, mighty, vast, large, elephantine, gargantuan, mammoth, monstrous, prodigious, titanic, (*more informal*) whopping, (*more informal*) jumbo, (*more informal*) king-size
OPPOSITES ARE tiny, miniature

gibberish NOUN
He kept up a stream of gibberish.
▶ nonsense, rubbish, balderdash, (*more informal*) drivel, (*more informal*) gobbledegook, (*more informal*) hogwash

gibe VERB, SEE **jibe**

giddy ADJECTIVE
The heat of the sun made her giddy.
▶ dizzy, faint, weak, light-headed, unsteady, wobbly, (*more informal*) woozy

gift NOUN
1 *He made the library a generous gift.*
▶ present, donation, benefaction, contribution, largesse, handout, offering, grant, gratuity, bequest, endowment

2 *a gift for languages*
▶ talent, flair, aptitude, capacity, genius, knack, ability, bent, capability

gifted ADJECTIVE

a gifted young musician
▶ talented, able, accomplished, capable, skilful, skilled

gigantic ADJECTIVE

a gigantic old building
▶ huge, enormous, colossal, immense, massive, mighty, vast, large, giant, (*more informal*) whopping, (*more informal*) jumbo, (*more informal*) king-size

giggle VERB

The silly hat made them giggle.
▶ snigger, titter, chuckle, laugh

gimmick NOUN

the latest publicity gimmicks
▶ stunt, trick, device, ploy, stratagem

gingerly ADVERB

They stepped gingerly into the road.
▶ cautiously, carefully, warily, charily, hesitantly, nervously, timidly, tentatively, guardedly

girdle NOUN

They wore girdles round their waists.
▶ belt, sash, band, waistband, corset

girl NOUN

a pretty little girl
▶ lass, daughter, female child

gist NOUN

The gist of the story is clear.
▶ main idea, drift, point, meaning, essence, substance, significance, general sense, quintessence, nub, direction

give VERB

1 *He would give them another hundred pounds.*
▶ provide with, present with, supply with, allow, award, bestow on, donate, make over

2 *Will you give her a message?*
▶ pass on, convey, communicate, transmit, send, deliver

3 *three brothers who had given their lives in the Great War*
▶ sacrifice, lose, relinquish, devote

4 *a note giving details of Christmas opening times*
▶ show, list, provide, display

5 *The boys gave no trouble.*
▶ cause, make, create, start

6 *The right herbs will give your food a better flavour.*
▶ afford, produce, yield, lend

7 *We are going to give a party*
▶ hold, lay on, organize, arrange

8 *He saw her and gave a shout.*
▶ utter, emit, let out

9 *The roof was giving under the weight.*
▶ collapse, yield, break, fall in

10 *She would give them a warning.*
▶ issue, deliver, administer, impose on

give away *She tried not to give away their secret.*
▶ reveal, disclose, divulge, betray

give in *They had to give in after a while.*
▶ submit, surrender, capitulate, yield, succumb, comply

give off *The fire gave off grey fumes.*
▶ produce, emit, send out, discharge, exude, release

give out

1 *Please give out the books.*
▶ hand out, hand round, distribute, dole out, deal out

2 *The money gave out after four days.*
▶ run out, be used up, be exhausted, dry up

give up *Don't give up now.*
▶ quit, stop, concede defeat, admit defeat, resign, despair

glad ADJECTIVE

1 *I am glad you came.*
▶ pleased, happy, delighted, thrilled, overjoyed

2 *They were glad to help*
▶ pleased, willing, eager, keen

glamorous ADJECTIVE

1 *a glamorous woman*
▶ beautiful, elegant, captivating, alluring, gorgeous, smart, lovely, entrancing, stylish, fashionable

USAGE Be careful when you use *smart*, because it has another important meaning.

2 *a glamorous lifestyle*
▶ exciting, colourful, dazzling, glittering, alluring, smart

glamour NOUN

1 *She offered that extra bit of glamour.*
▶ beauty, attractiveness, elegance, style, charm, seductiveness

2 *the glamour of living in a big city*
▶ appeal, excitement, attraction, allure, glitter, lustre, magic

glance VERB

1 *She glanced at her watch.*
▶ look, peek, peep, take a look at

2 **glance at** or **through** *I only had time to glance at the article.*
▶ scan, skim, read quickly, run your eye over

glance NOUN

He gave us a quick glance.
▶ look, peek, peep, glimpse

glare VERB

1 *She glared at him.*
▶ stare angrily, glower, scowl, frown

2 *The lights of oncoming cars glared in the darkness.*
▶ dazzle, blaze, be blinding, flare, beam

glare NOUN

1 *an angry glare*
▶ stare, scowl, glower, frown, black look

2 *the glare of the lights*
▶ dazzle, shine, blaze, brilliance, beam, flare

glaring ADJECTIVE
a glaring error
▶ obvious, conspicuous, blatant, flagrant, patent, plain, overt, inescapable

glaze NOUN
pots with a bright glaze
▶ varnish, coating, lustre, gloss, shine

gleam VERB
The brass door knob gleamed in the moonlight.
▶ glimmer, glint, glow, shine, flash, glisten, glitter, sparkle, shimmer

gleam NOUN
the gleam of lights in the distance
▶ glimmer, glint, glow, glitter, sparkle, shimmer

glib ADJECTIVE
a glib talker   an answer that was merely glib
▶ slick, pat, smooth, facile, superficial, insincere, articulate, fluent, plausible, quick, ready
OPPOSITES ARE sincere, thoughtful

glide VERB
1 *A boat glided past.*
▶ slide, move smoothly, slip, sail, coast, skim
2 *The gulls were gliding overhead.*
▶ drift, soar, wheel, hover, sail, float, fly

glimmer VERB
The moonlight glimmered on the great sweep of lawn.
▶ gleam, glint, glow, shine, flash, glisten, glitter, sparkle, shimmer, twinkle

glimmer NOUN
There was a faint glimmer in his eyes.
▶ gleam, glint, glow, glitter, sparkle, shimmer, twinkle

glimpse VERB
I glimpsed Auntie sitting on the bottom stair.
▶ spot, spy, catch sight of, make out

glimpse NOUN
I caught a quick glimpse of the house.
▶ glance, peep, look, sight, sighting, view, (*more informal*) squint

glint VERB
Her blue eyes glinted like ice.
▶ gleam, glow, shine, flash, glisten, glitter, sparkle, shimmer

glint NOUN
a glint in the mirror
▶ gleam, glimmer, glow, glitter, sparkle, shimmer

gloat VERB
A group of lads was gloating over a rugby victory.
▶ boast, brag, crow, triumph, exult, rejoice, show off

global ADJECTIVE
1 *global communications*
▶ worldwide, international, world, intercontinental, universal

2 *a global solution to the problem*
▶ total, comprehensive, general, all-inclusive, wide-ranging

globe NOUN
1 *people from all over the globe*
▶ world, earth, planet
2 *the shape of a globe*
▶ ball, orb, sphere, round

gloom NOUN
1 *They peered out into the gloom*
▶ darkness, dimness, semi-darkness, murk, murkiness, shade, shadow, twilight, cloudiness, dullness, dusk, obscurity
2 *Her feeling of gloom lifted.*
▶ depression, dejection, despondency, low spirits, melancholy

gloomy ADJECTIVE
1 *They walked through the front door into a gloomy hall.*
▶ dark, dingy, dim, dismal, dreary, dull, shadowy, sombre, cheerless
AN OPPOSITE IS bright
2 *a gloomy expression*
▶ miserable, downcast, downhearted, dejected, dispirited, glum, unhappy
OPPOSITES ARE cheerful, happy
3 *a gloomy outlook for the economy*
▶ pessimistic, unfavourable, unpromising, depressing, bleak, downbeat
OPPOSITES ARE optimistic, upbeat

glorious ADJECTIVE
1 *a glorious victory*
▶ magnificent, splendid, illustrious, celebrated, acclaimed, distinguished, renowned, great
2 *a glorious view across the hills*
▶ wonderful, spectacular, magnificent, superb, beautiful, stunning

glory NOUN
1 *the glory of competing for your country   successes that bring much glory*
▶ distinction, honour, renown, prestige, kudos, fame, credit, triumph, success
2 *glory to God*
▶ adoration, homage, praise, thanksgiving, veneration, worship
3 *the glories of New England in the autumn*
▶ beauty, magnificence, grandeur, majesty, radiance, splendour

gloss NOUN
The new paint has a fine gloss.
▶ shine, sheen, brightness, brilliance, lustre, burnish, polish

gloss VERB
gloss over *He tended to gloss over arguments that didn't fit his theories.*
▶ conceal, cover up, disguise, evade, explain away
OPPOSITES ARE highlight, emphasize

glossy ADJECTIVE

a glossy tile floor

▶ bright, burnished, glassy, glazed, gleaming, lustrous, polished, reflective, shiny, silky, sleek, smooth

AN OPPOSITE IS dull

glow VERB

1 *Lights glowed from the windows.*

▶ shine, gleam, glimmer, flicker, flare

2 *She glowed with pleasure at having said the right thing.*

▶ shine, flush, blush, colour, redden

glow NOUN

1 *the glow of the street lights*

▶ shine, gleam, glimmer, radiance, luminosity, brilliance

2 *There was a distinct glow in her cheeks.*

▶ flush, blush, rosiness, pinkness, warmth

3 *We felt a glow of excitement.*

▶ ardour, fervour, enthusiasm, feeling, intensity, passion

glower VERB

Harry glowered at him from the table.

▶ scowl, glare, stare angrily, frown, lour

glowing ADJECTIVE

1 *glowing street lights*

▶ bright, shining, luminous, radiant

2 *glowing cheeks*

▶ bright, rosy, red, pink, blushing, flushed

3 *a glowing report*

▶ complimentary, enthusiastic, highly favourable, fervent, admiring, eulogistic, ecstatic

glue NOUN

a tube of glue

▶ adhesive, paste, gum, fixative, sealant, cement

glue VERB

Glue the pieces together.

▶ fix, stick, fasten, affix, paste, cement, bond, gum, seal

glum ADJECTIVE

Tony looked glum.

▶ miserable, downcast, downhearted, dejected, dispirited, gloomy, unhappy

OPPOSITES ARE cheerful, happy

glut NOUN

a glut of fresh fruit

▶ surplus, surfeit, excess, superfluity, plenty, abundance

AN OPPOSITE IS scarcity

gnaw VERB

1 *The dog was gnawing a bone.*

▶ chew, bite, nibble, munch, eat

2 **gnaw at** *Doubts continued to gnaw at her.*

▶ worry, torment, plague, niggle, distress

---

go VERB This word is often overused. Here are some alternatives:

1 *She started to go towards the entrance.*

▶ move, advance, proceed, walk, make your way, progress

2 *We are going to London on Friday.*

▶ travel, journey, make a trip

3 *Several of the guests had already gone.*

▶ leave, depart, go away, withdraw, make off, (*more informal*) clear off

4 *My purse had gone.*

▶ disappear, vanish, be taken, be stolen

5 *The path goes to the village.*

▶ lead, take you, continue, extend, stretch

6 *All the money goes to charity.*

▶ be given, be donated, be granted, be presented

7 *All our money has gone.*

▶ be used up, be spent, be exhausted

8 *His hair had gone grey.*

▶ turn, become, grow

9 *I hope things go well for them.*

▶ work out, turn out, develop

10 *The coat and hat don't go.*

▶ match, harmonize, blend, suit one another

11 *The car won't go.*

▶ start, work, function, operate, run

12 *Where do these books go?*

▶ belong, be placed, be kept, have a place

13 *Has the bell gone?*

▶ sound, ring, chime, peal

14 *The time will go quickly.*

▶ pass, go by, elapse, lapse

go ahead *The plan will go ahead*

▶ begin, proceed, continue, take place

go away *She wanted them all to go away.*

▶ leave, depart, (*more informal*) clear off

go back *I'll have to go back and look for it.*

▶ return, turn round

go down *Prices are expected to go down.*

▶ fall, drop, decrease, get lower

go for

1 *Which one will you go for?*

▶ choose, take, favour, prefer

2 *He went for her with a hammer.*

▶ attack, assault, set at, lunge at

go in for *We are going in for a competition.*

▶ enter, take part in, participate in

go into *The lawyers will go into it in detail.*

▶ discuss, consider, think about, investigate, probe, delve into, review

go off

1 *A bomb went off.*

▶ explode, detonate, blow up

2 *The milk's gone off.*

▶ go bad, go sour, turn

▶▶

go on
1 *The programme went on for over two hours.*
▶ continue, extend, carry on, run
2 *She went on about how lucky we were.*
▶ chatter, witter, ramble, (*more informal*) rabbit
go over *Shall we go over the figures?*
▶ study, check, review, examine, analyse, scrutinize, investigate
go through *It's hard to comprehend what they must have gone through.*
▶ suffer, experience, undergo, endure, withstand
go with
1 *Will you go with them?*
▶ accompany, escort
2 *I'm not sure this tie goes with my shirt.*
▶ match, suit, harmonize with, blend with

goad VERB
The latest unemployment figures might goad the minister to take action.
▶ provoke, stimulate, spur, move, rouse, urge, motivate, encourage

go-ahead NOUN
The plan will be given the go-ahead next week.
▶ approval, permission, authorization, clearance, consent, assent, agreement

goal NOUN
The overall goal is to promote the use of good English.
▶ aim, objective, object, ambition, intention, purpose, target, aspiration, design, end

gobble VERB
He stopped talking to gobble his food.
▶ guzzle, devour, bolt, gulp, eat

god, goddess NOUN
the gods and goddesses of ancient Olympus
▶ deity, divinity, divine being, immortal
RELATED ADJECTIVE divine

godsend NOUN
A cut in interest rates would be a godsend to homeowners.
▶ blessing, boon, miracle, stroke of good luck, windfall

golden ADJECTIVE
1 *a golden carriage*
▶ gilt, gilded
2 *golden hair*
▶ blond, blonde, yellow
3 *a golden opportunity*
▶ excellent, unique, special, promising, auspicious, propitious

good ADJECTIVE This word is often overused. Here are some alternatives:
1 *She is basically a good person.*
▶ virtuous, exemplary, righteous, moral, honest, upright, worthy, trustworthy
OPPOSITES ARE bad, wicked, immoral
2 *Can you recommend a good hotel?*
▶ fine, high-quality, satisfactory, acceptable, excellent, superb, outstanding
AN OPPOSITE IS poor
3 *The children were exceptionally good all evening.*
▶ well-behaved, obedient, well-mannered
AN OPPOSITE IS naughty
4 *That would be a good thing to do.*
▶ proper, right, correct, appropriate, auspicious
AN OPPOSITE IS inappropriate
5 *He is not a good swimmer. She has always been good at music.*
▶ capable, able, proficient, accomplished, talented, skilled
OPPOSITES ARE poor, inept
6 *She was a good friend.*
▶ true, loyal, close, dear, trusty, reliable, trustworthy, dependable
AN OPPOSITE IS distant
7 *It was a good party.*
▶ enjoyable, pleasant, agreeable, pleasing
8 *Tom gave the car a good clean*
▶ thorough, complete
9 *a good number of people*
▶ considerable, substantial, appreciable, sizeable, fair, ample
10 *It is good of you to come.*
▶ kind, generous, considerate, obliging
AN OPPOSITE IS unkind
11 *When is a good time to call?*
▶ convenient, suitable, appropriate, opportune, fitting
OPPOSITES ARE bad, unsuitable
12 *food that is good for you*
▶ healthy, wholesome, nutritious, nourishing
OPPOSITES ARE bad, unhealthy
13 *a pub that serves good food*
▶ delicious, appetizing, tasty
14 *There are several good reasons for going.*
▶ valid, genuine, cogent, real, convincing
AN OPPOSITE IS poor

goodbye NOUN
Roddy said goodbye and left us
▶ farewell, (*more informal*) cheerio, (*French*) adieu, (*French*) au revoir

good-for-nothing ADJECTIVE
a good-for-nothing layabout
▶ worthless, useless, inept, lazy, idle, (*more informal*) no-good

good-humoured ADJECTIVE
He was patient and good-humoured.
▶ genial, affable, cordial, congenial, amiable, easygoing
AN OPPOSITE IS ill-humoured

good-looking ADJECTIVE
a good-looking woman
▶ attractive, handsome, nice-looking, presentable, beautiful, pretty, lovely
AN OPPOSITE IS ugly

good-natured ADJECTIVE
He had a blunt good-natured face.
▶ kind, kindly, gentle, warm-hearted, amiable, friendly, neighbourly, benevolent
AN OPPOSITE IS ill-natured

goodness NOUN
There is a lot of goodness in these people, criminals though they are.
▶ virtue, good, uprightness, generosity, goodwill, honesty
AN OPPOSITE IS wickedness

goods PLURAL NOUN
1 *the supply of goods and services*
▶ merchandise, produce, products, articles, stock
2 *The dead man's goods did not amount to much.*
▶ property, possessions, effects, chattels

good-tempered ADJECTIVE
He remained patient and good-tempered despite the difficulties.
▶ calm, placid, equable, unflustered, composed, self-possessed, tranquil
AN OPPOSITE IS bad-tempered

goodwill NOUN
People come here full of goodwill and good intentions.
▶ kindness, benevolence, generosity, friendliness, consideration
OPPOSITES ARE hostility, ill-will

gorge NOUN
The drive is spectacular: gorges and tropical rain forests.
▶ ravine, gully, canyon, defile, chasm, pass, fissure

gorge VERB
gorge on We gorged on fresh sardines and salads from the local market.
▶ gobble, guzzle, wolf, devour, cram down, (*more informal*) tuck into, (*more informal*) stuff yourself with

gorgeous ADJECTIVE
1 *a gorgeous young woman*
▶ beautiful, lovely, glamorous, dazzling, pretty, stunning, striking
2 *a gorgeous view*
▶ magnificent, spectacular, splendid, superb, glorious

gory ADJECTIVE
an account of the battle with all the gory details
▶ grisly, gruesome, ghastly, violent, bloody, brutal, horrific, repulsive

gossip NOUN
1 *He liked gossip and knew something about everybody.*
▶ idle talk, tittle-tattle, tattle, prattle, rumour, hearsay, chatter, scandal
2 *The sisters were both dreadful gossips.*
▶ scandalmonger, gossipmonger, talebearer, busybody, tattler

gossip VERB
The landlord was busy gossiping to the other customers.
▶ chat, chatter, prattle, spread stories, (*informal*) natter, (*informal*) tattle

gouge VERB
Engineers had gouged a tunnel out of the rock.
▶ dig, hollow, scoop, chisel, excavate, cut

govern VERB
1 *A coalition was formed to govern the country.*
▶ run, rule, administer, be in charge of, conduct the affairs of, direct, manage, preside over
2 *the rules that govern the way we treat each other*
▶ regulate, determine, control, direct, affect, influence, shape
3 *She tried to govern her feelings.*
▶ control, master, restrain, curb, check, bridle, discipline, regulate, tame, keep in check, keep under control

government NOUN
1 *The new government takes office next week.*
▶ administration, executive, regime, ministry
2 *a country that badly needs a period of stable government*
▶ rule, direction, leadership, management, guidance, regulation

NAMES FOR TYPES OF GOVERNMENT
terms ending in -cracy (from a Greek word kratia meaning 'power or rule'): autocracy (by one ruler), bureaucracy (by state officials), democracy (by representatives elected by the people), meritocracy (by able or qualified people), plutocracy (by the rich), theocracy (by a god through priests).
terms ending in -archy (from a Greek word arkhein meaning 'to rule'): monarchy (by a king or queen), oligarchy (by a few powerful people).
terms ending in -ism: communism (with public ownership of wealth and resources), constitutionalism (according to a constitution), despotism (by a despot), fascism (by an extreme right-wing group), federalism (by a union of states running their own internal affairs), imperialism (by an empire or emperor), totalitarianism (by an oppressive ruler or rulers).
other terms: dictatorship (by a dictator), tyranny (by a tyrant).

governor NOUN
1 *a prison governor*
▶ administrator, director, principal, superintendent

2 *the governor of a province*
▶ ruler, overseer, viceroy, commissioner, administrator

gown NOUN
a beautiful silk gown
▶ dress, robe, costume, frock

grab VERB
1 *She grabbed him by his arm.*
▶ seize, grasp, catch, grip, take hold of, clutch at
2 *Someone grabbed her credit card while she wasn't looking.*
▶ snatch, steal, take, (*more informal*) nab, (*more informal*) pinch

grace NOUN
1 *The dancers moved with considerable grace.*
▶ elegance, poise, gracefulness, refinement
2 *He conceded the point with good grace.*
▶ courtesy, civility, decorum, decency, charm, generosity
3 *They did not want to see another president fall from grace.*
▶ favour, approval, esteem, regard, support
4 *by the grace of the monarch*
▶ generosity, favour, benevolence, indulgence, goodwill

graceful ADJECTIVE
Mary's clothes were light and graceful.
▶ elegant, flowing, stylish, tasteful, smooth, beautiful

gracious ADJECTIVE
1 *a kind and gracious man*
▶ courteous, polite, civil, refined, considerate, compassionate, benevolent, generous, magnanimous, decorous
2 *a gracious building*
▶ elegant, handsome, graceful, opulent, grand

grade NOUN
1 *She is trying for a higher grade in the exam.*
▶ mark, score, level, grading, assessment, standard
2 *a hotel in the top grade*
▶ class, category, classification
3 *officers in the lower grades*
▶ rank, level, status, echelon, step

grade VERB
1 *Eggs are graded according to size.*
▶ sort, classify, categorize, differentiate, group, range, arrange, rank
2 *An external examiner will grade the coursework.*
▶ mark, assess, evaluate, rank, rate

gradient NOUN
The road is on a steep gradient
▶ slope, incline, rise, ascent, bank, declivity, hill

gradual ADJECTIVE
1 *a gradual change in the weather*
▶ steady, slow, moderate, progressive, continuous, regular, step-by-step
AN OPPOSITE IS sudden
2 *a gradual slope*
▶ gentle, moderate, slight, easy
AN OPPOSITE IS steep

gradually ADVERB
The colours fade gradually in the sunlight.   *Gradually she eased the drawer back in its place.*
▶ slowly, little by little, steadily, gently, cautiously, progressively, imperceptibly

grain NOUN
1 *a good grain harvest*
▶ corn, cereal, seed
2 *grains of sand*
▶ granule, particle, speck, crumb, fragment
3 *not a grain of truth in the story*
▶ trace, hint, ounce, scrap
4 *wood with a strong grain*
▶ texture, marking, surface, pattern

grand ADJECTIVE
1 *a grand palace*
▶ magnificent, splendid, majestic, glorious, stately, imposing
2 *a grand old lady*
▶ distinguished, illustrious, august, eminent, prominent, celebrated
3 (*informal*) *They are doing a grand job.*
▶ excellent, very good, fine, splendid, first-class, first-rate

grandeur NOUN
the grandeur of the royal ceremonies
▶ splendour, magnificence, glory, resplendence, stateliness

grandiose ADJECTIVE
a grandiose scheme
▶ ambitious, bold, daring, grand, ostentatious, pretentious, showy, extravagant, flamboyant, (*more informal*) over the top
AN OPPOSITE IS modest

grant VERB
1 *The award body can grant you a scholarship.*
▶ give, award, allow, confer on you, pay, provide you with
2 *The court granted her request.*
▶ allow, consent to, accede to, permit
3 *We grant that the difference is small.*
▶ admit, concede, acknowledge, agree, accept, confess

grant NOUN
1 *They were given a local authority grant to repair their roof.*
▶ award, allowance, subsidy, subvention, endowment, contribution, donation, allocation
2 *a student grant*
▶ bursary, scholarship, sponsorship, loan

graph NOUN
a graph showing the rise in house prices
▶ table, chart, diagram, grid, pie chart, column-graph

graphic ADJECTIVE
a graphic description of the accident
▶ vivid, explicit, striking, forceful, dramatic, lurid, detailed, colourful
AN OPPOSITE IS vague

g

grapple VERB
1 *They grappled for the gun on the wet grass.*
▶ struggle, wrestle , tussle, scuffle, brawl, fight
2 **grapple with** *The Prime Minister has a major problem to grapple with.*
▶ contend with, tackle, attend to, cope with, deal with, manage, handle, come to grips with, engage with, get involved with, try to solve, (*more informal*) have a go at
AN OPPOSITE IS avoid

grasp VERB
1 *He got up and grasped her hand.*
▶ grip, clasp, clutch, grab, seize, catch, snatch, hold, get hold of, hang on to
2 *He got impatient if they failed to grasp a point.*
▶ understand, comprehend, follow, take in, apprehend, perceive, master, learn, realize, (*more informal*) cotton on to

grasp NOUN
1 *She managed to escape his grasp.*
▶ grip, hold, clutch, embrace, control
2 *His ultimate goal was within his grasp.*
▶ reach, power, command
3 *They now have a good grasp of the subject.*
▶ understanding, comprehension, perception, mastery, familiarity (with)

grass NOUN
A notice told them to keep off the grass.
▶ lawn, turf, green

grate VERB
1 *She started to grate some cheese.*
▶ shred, grind, cut up, mince
2 *His whining voice began to grate.*
▶ irritate, jar, rankle, be irksome

grateful ADJECTIVE
The families are grateful for all the support they have received.
▶ thankful, appreciative (of), indebted, obliged
AN OPPOSITE IS ungrateful

gratitude NOUN
His letter expressed gratitude for the help he had been given.
▶ thanks, appreciation (of), acknowledgement (of), indebtedness

gratuitous ADJECTIVE
This is no time for gratuitous insults.
▶ unjustified, unwarranted, uncalled for, undeserved, needless, unmerited, superfluous, inappropriate
OPPOSITES ARE justifiable, unnecessary

grave ADJECTIVE
1 *a grave error   grave matters*
▶ serious, important, significant, crucial, critical, momentous, vital, acute, weighty
AN OPPOSITE IS unimportant
2 *a grave offence*
▶ criminal, indictable, punishable
AN OPPOSITE IS minor

3 *a grave expression*
▶ serious, solemn, sombre, earnest, severe, subdued, dignified, gloomy, thoughtful, unsmiling, grim, long-faced
AN OPPOSITE IS happy

grave NOUN
He visited the graves of his ancestors.
▶ burial place, tomb, vault, mausoleum, sepulchre

gravity NOUN
1 *the gravity of the situation*
▶ seriousness, severity, acuteness, magnitude, momentousness, danger, importance
2 *the gravity of his manner*
▶ solemnity, dignity, sobriety, earnestness, ceremony, pomp, sedateness
3 *the force of gravity*
▶ gravitation, pull, weight, heaviness, downward force

graze VERB
1 *She fell and grazed her knee.*
▶ scrape, cut, scratch, scuff, abrade
2 *Cattle grazed in the fields.*
▶ feed, browse, crop, ruminate, pasture

graze NOUN
a graze on his elbow
▶ cut, abrasion, laceration, raw spot

greasy ADJECTIVE
1 *She had greasy hair and worried about her weight.*
▶ oily, shiny, waxy
AN OPPOSITE IS dry
2 *His hand left greasy fingerprints on the glass.*
▶ fatty, oily, smeary, slimy, buttery
3 *He sidled up in his usual greasy manner.*
▶ obsequious, ingratiating, unctuous, sycophantic, fawning, grovelling, flattering, fulsome, (*more informal*) smarmy

---

great ADJECTIVE This word is often overused. Here are some alternatives:
1 *A great hill rose before them.*
▶ large, huge, big, enormous, gigantic, massive, colossal
AN OPPOSITE IS small
2 *Speaking a foreign language is a great advantage. She is a person of great courage.*
▶ considerable, special, much, extreme
OPPOSITES ARE small, little
3 *He read through the list of great statesmen.*
▶ famous, eminent, celebrated, distinguished, honoured, renowned, acclaimed, prominent, revered, exalted, illustrious
OPPOSITES ARE unknown, obscure
4 *The invasion proved a great mistake.   a talk on the great advances in medicine*
▶ important, significant, crucial, critical, big, vital
OPPOSITES ARE insignificant, unimportant
5 *We went to a great party.*
▶ excellent, enjoyable, marvellous, wonderful, fantastic, first-rate
AN OPPOSITE IS poor

G

greed NOUN

1 *I ate my supper with undisguised greed.*
▶ hunger, gluttony, ravenousness, overeating, over-indulgence
2 *Material greed is not one of their faults.*
▶ avarice, acquisitiveness, covetousness, rapacity, cupidity, craving, desire, selfishness
3 *He was clearly motivated by a greed for power.*
▶ appetite, desire, urge, need, lust, longing, craving

greedy ADJECTIVE

1 *a greedy eater*
▶ gluttonous, ravenous, voracious, insatiable
2 *greedy for money*
▶ avaricious, covetous, acquisitive, mercenary, grasping
3 *greedy for power*
▶ eager, avid, longing, craving, (*more informal*) itching

green ADJECTIVE

1 *a green garden*
▶ leafy, grassy, verdant
OPPOSITES ARE barren, bare
2 *green with envy*
▶ envious, covetous, jealous, resentful
3 *a green recruit*
▶ inexperienced, raw, naive, innocent, immature, untried, credulous, gullible
OPPOSITES ARE experienced, worldly wise
4 *green issues*
▶ environmental, ecological, conservationist

greenery NOUN

vases stuffed with flowers and greenery
▶ foliage, leaves, leafage, plants, vegetation

greet VERB

She greeted her visitors one by one.
▶ welcome, say hello to, acknowledge, receive, give a greeting to, hail, salute

greeting NOUN

1 *She called out a greeting.*
▶ hello, salutation, welcome
2 **greetings** *birthday greetings*
▶ good wishes, best wishes, congratulations, compliments

gregarious ADJECTIVE

He is cheerful, hard-working, and gregarious.
▶ sociable, outgoing, extrovert, friendly, convivial, companionable, affable

grey ADJECTIVE

1 *His grey beard had grown very long.*
▶ silver, silvery, slate-grey, whitish, greying, grizzled, grizzly, hoary
2 *Her face was grey with worry.*
▶ pale, ashen, leaden, wan, sallow, pasty, drawn
3 *The day began grey and dull.*
▶ cloudy, overcast, gloomy, dismal, dreary, bleak

grid NOUN

1 *He had broken the stone to which the iron grid was fixed.*
▶ grating, grille, lattice, mesh, framework
2 *The information is shown in the form of a grid.*
▶ graph, matrix, network

grief NOUN

His letters made her grief for her mother more bearable.
▶ sadness, sorrow, mourning, bereavement, unhappiness, distress, misery, affliction, desolation
AN OPPOSITE IS joy

come to grief *The scheme came to grief from lack of financial support.*
▶ fail, go wrong, miscarry, be unsuccessful, fall through, collapse

grievance NOUN

The public can call in with any grievances about local services.
▶ complaint, protest, criticism, objection, grudge, (*more informal*) moan, (*more informal*) grouse

grieve VERB

1 *She grieved for her mother constantly.*
▶ mourn, sorrow, lament, weep, cry
2 *They were deeply grieved by the unkind newspaper reports.*
▶ hurt, wound, upset, sadden, distress

grim ADJECTIVE

1 *His face bore a grim expression.*
▶ stern, severe, harsh, dour, forbidding, sullen, morose, gloomy
OPPOSITES ARE cheerful, pleasant
2 *the grim knowledge that she might die*
▶ unpleasant, dreadful, terrible, grisly, gruesome, macabre, distressing, fearsome, horrid, shocking
AN OPPOSITE IS pleasant
3 *a grim little mining town*
▶ dreary, bleak, dismal, gloomy, dingy

grime NOUN

The shelves were covered in grime.
▶ dirt, filth, muck, dust, soot

grimy ADJECTIVE

The other office was dark and grimy.
▶ dirty, grubby, filthy, messy, smutty, soiled

grin VERB

She grinned at us and left the room.
▶ smile, beam, smirk

grin NOUN

He had a silly grin on his face.
▶ smile, smirk

grind VERB

1 *He ground the coffee into a fine powder.*
▶ crush, pound, grate
2 *The kitchen had a wheel for grinding knives.*
▶ sharpen, whet, hone, file
3 *The old car grinds slowly up the hill.*
▶ struggle, crawl, strain, chug

grip VERB

1 *He gripped Helen's hand.*
▶ grasp, clasp, clutch, grab, seize, catch, snatch, hold, get hold of, hang on to
2 *The story gripped everyone.*
▶ engross, enthral, absorb, captivate, fascinate, rivet, mesmerize

grip NOUN

She kept a firm grip on the back of the chair.
▶ hold, grasp, clasp, clutch
get to grips with *a book that gets to grips with the main issues*
▶ deal with, cope with, grasp, tackle
AN OPPOSITE IS avoid

gripe VERB

(*informal*) *I was griping to her about the people at work.*
▶ complain, grumble, protest, whine, grouch, (*informal*) moan, (*informal*) whinge, (*more informal*) bellyache

grisly ADJECTIVE

a grisly little story about a serial murderer
▶ gruesome, gory, ghastly, violent, bloody, brutal, horrific, repulsive, frightful, hideous, macabre, revolting, repellent

grit NOUN

1 *The problem was caused by pieces of grit in the carburettor.*
▶ gravel, dust, sand
2 (*informal*) *Ambition and sheer grit got them where they are today.*
▶ determination, toughness, stamina, tenacity, perseverance, courage, bravery, pluck, spirit, (*informal*) guts

grit VERB

1 *Sara gritted her teeth and said nothing.*
▶ clench, gnash, grind, grate
2 *Lorries have gone out to grit the roads.*
▶ treat, salt, sand

grizzle VERB

(*informal*) *a grumpy child who was always grizzling*
▶ cry, whimper, snivel, whine, (*informal*) whinge

groan VERB

She heard him groaning in his sleep.
▶ moan, cry out, sigh, wail

groan NOUN

He let out a weary groan.
▶ moan, sigh, cry, wail

groom VERB

Martha was grooming her hair.
▶ brush, comb, smooth, dress, arrange, tidy

groove NOUN

The water had worn a groove in the rock.
▶ channel, furrow, hollow, rut, indentation, slot, track

grope VERB

She groped around for her clothes.
▶ fumble, cast about, feel about, flounder, search blindly

gross ADJECTIVE

1 *a gross exaggeration*
▶ extreme, blatant, flagrant, glaring, obvious, conspicuous, sheer, outright
2 *gross indecency*
▶ coarse, vulgar, crude, obscene, lewd, improper
3 *He looked gross and he knew it.*
▶ obese, fat, corpulent, overweight, big
4 *gross income*
▶ total, inclusive, overall, aggregate, whole, full
5 *gross misshapen versions of the human form*
▶ disgusting, repellent, abhorrent, loathsome, sickening

grotesque ADJECTIVE

a grotesque creature with a flattened body and a squashed-looking head
▶ deformed, malformed, misshapen, distorted, weird, freakish, bizarre, hideous, mangled

ground NOUN

1 *The ground was wet and spongy.*
▶ earth, terrain, soil, turf, loam
2 *The little plane slowly rose from the ground.*
▶ land, surface
3 **grounds** *a large house in its own grounds*
▶ land, estate, gardens, surroundings

groundless ADJECTIVE

Their fears proved to be groundless.
▶ baseless, needless, unfounded, unjustified, unwarranted, unsubstantiated, uncalled for, false, gratuitous, imaginary, irrational
AN OPPOSITE IS justifiable

group NOUN

1 *Divide the children into groups for a game.*
▶ set, circle, section
2 *The reading group meets once a month.*
▶ club, circle, society, association
3 *a small group of islands off the north-east coast*
▶ cluster, collection, formation, bunch, mass, clump
4 *A group of fans waited at the stage door.*
▶ crowd, band, body, gathering, flock, assembly, gang, pack
5 *They sorted the books into different groups.*
▶ category, class, type, sort, kind, set

group VERB

group together
1 *Farmers began to group together to form cooperatives.*
▶ unite, join together, join forces, team up, come together
2 *Comfortable chairs are grouped around coffee tables.*
▶ arrange, organize, dispose, assemble, collect, cluster
3 *We group the books according to their size.*
▶ classify, categorize, sort, range, band

grovel VERB

1 *grovelling on the floor*
► crawl, creep, crouch
2 *I don't like to see them grovelling to him.*
► kowtow, crawl, behave obsequiously, demean yourself, (*more informal*) suck up

grow VERB

1 *The baby grew fast.*
► get bigger, get larger, increase in size, fill out, put on growth
2 *Their debts are growing.*
► increase, mount up, multiply
AN OPPOSITE IS decrease
3 *She grows roses in her garden.*
► cultivate, produce, propagate, farm
4 *At about 4 o'clock it grows dark.*
► become, turn, come to be
5 *The business was growing.*
► expand, develop, flourish, thrive, prosper, succeed, boom
OPPOSITES ARE decline, fail

growl VERB

The dog growled at him.
► snarl, snap, yap

grown-up ADJECTIVE

Chris has a grown-up sister.
► adult, fully grown, mature

growth NOUN

1 *a steady growth in population*
► increase, expansion, development
OPPOSITES ARE decline, decrease
2 *hormones that aid growth*
► growing, development, maturing
3 *measures to increase economic growth*
► expansion, development, progress, advance
AN OPPOSITE IS decline
4 *She has to have a growth removed.*
► tumour, lump, swelling, cyst

grub NOUN

The fruit was riddled with grubs.
► larva, maggot, caterpillar

grub VERB

grub about or **around** *He began grubbing around under the table.*
► rummage, delve, scrabble, ferret, poke

grubby ADJECTIVE

He had not yet changed out of his grubby overalls.
► dirty, filthy, grimy, soiled, messy

grudge NOUN

The letter was written by someone with a grudge.
► grievance, resentment, umbrage, pique, bitterness, rancour, bad feelings

grudge VERB

He grudged the money he would have to pay out.
► resent, begrudge, object to, be angry about

grudging ADJECTIVE

She was pleased by this approval, grudging though it was.
► reluctant, unwilling, unenthusiastic, half-hearted, resentful, hesitant, guarded, cautious, ungracious
AN OPPOSITE IS enthusiastic

gruelling ADJECTIVE

a gruelling journey back from the Himalayas
► exhausting, arduous, tiring, wearying, exacting, demanding, punishing, hard, taxing, strenuous, laborious, (*more informal*) killing
AN OPPOSITE IS easy

gruesome ADJECTIVE

The gruesome remains had to be analysed.
► grisly, gory, ghastly, bloody, horrific, repulsive, frightful, hideous, macabre, revolting, repellent

gruff ADJECTIVE

1 *His voice was gruff in the darkness.*
► harsh, rough, hoarse, husky, throaty
2 *his unique gruff manner*
► abrupt, brusque, curt, blunt, bad-tempered, churlish

grumble VERB

Everyone was grumbling about the heat.
► complain, carp, protest, whine, grouch, (*informal*) moan, (*informal*) whinge, (*more informal*) bellyache, (*more informal*) gripe

grumble NOUN

constant grumbles about the weather
► complaint, moan, groan, protest, objection

grumpy ADJECTIVE

I'm always grumpy early in the morning.
► bad-tempered, irritable, irascible, testy, grouchy, touchy, crotchety, cantankerous, peevish, fractious, cross, (*more informal*) stroppy, (*more informal*) shirty
OPPOSITES ARE good-humoured, good-tempered

guarantee NOUN

1 *Used cars come with a six-month guarantee.*
► warranty, warrant, covenant
2 *We cannot give a guarantee that these measures will succeed.*
► assurance, pledge, promise, commitment, surety, oath

guarantee VERB

1 *He could not guarantee that they would keep their jobs.*
► promise, swear, pledge, assure, certify, give a guarantee, give your word, vouch, vow
2 *You need a reservation to guarantee a seat.*
► secure, ensure, make sure of

guard VERB

1 *Troops guarded the house.*
► protect, stand guard over, watch over, shield, safeguard, defend, cover
2 *An escort guarded the prisoners.*
► supervise, watch over, control

3 guard against *Take care to guard against over-tiredness in the first few weeks.*
▶ beware of, be alert to, try to prevent

guard NOUN

1 *We were turned back by the guards at the border.*
▶ sentry, sentinel, custodian, lookout, patrol, watchman

2 *He felt the guard's hand on his shoulder.*
▶ jailer, prison officer, warder, warden

off your guard or **off guard** *He was caught off guard for a moment and the water surged over him.*
▶ unprepared, unready, unsuspecting

on your guard *Thieves are operating in this area, so be on your guard.*
▶ alert, watchful, vigilant, heedful, circumspect, chary

guarded ADJECTIVE

Their reaction was guarded and unfriendly.
▶ cautious, wary, chary, unenthusiastic, non-committal, discreet

guardian NOUN

1 *the child's guardian*
▶ adoptive parent, foster parent

2 *the guardian of international peace*
▶ protector, defender, preserver, custodian, keeper, minder, steward

guess VERB

1 *You have to guess the weight of a large cake.*
▶ estimate, reckon, judge, predict, gauge, determine

2 *I guess I should say sorry.*
▶ suppose, believe, think, imagine, expect, assume, consider, reckon

guess NOUN

My guess was he would head for the motorway.
▶ theory, hypothesis, prediction, feeling, belief, opinion, conjecture, supposition, notion, idea, intuition

guest NOUN

1 *They joined their guests for dinner.*
▶ visitor, company, caller

2 *The hotel could take up to thirty guests.*
▶ resident, patron, client, lodger, boarder, customer, tenant

guidance NOUN

His supervisor offered him guidance.
▶ advice, direction, instruction, help, counsel, teaching, support, pointers, guidelines

guide VERB

1 *I asked her to guide me back to the town.*
▶ lead, direct, show, show the way, take, accompany, escort, conduct

2 *The students have to be guided carefully through this stage of their work.*
▶ advise, counsel, direct, supervise, instruct, teach

guide NOUN

1 *Your guide will show you the way.*
▶ escort, leader, courier, navigator, pilot, attendant

2 *The sample is only meant to be a guide.*
▶ model, indication, example, gauge, guideline, pointer

3 *We explored the city with the help of a pocket guide.*
▶ guidebook, tourist guide, handbook, manual

guilt NOUN

1 *The jury was quite sure of his guilt.*
▶ guiltiness, culpability, liability, responsibility, blame, blameworthiness, wrongfulness, criminality
AN OPPOSITE IS innocence

2 *There is no need to feel guilt about it.*
▶ shame, remorse, self-reproach, self-accusation, bad conscience, penitence, contrition, dishonour, guilty feelings, regret
AN OPPOSITE IS virtue

guilty ADJECTIVE

1 *Brown was found guilty of assault.*
▶ culpable, blameworthy, at fault, liable, responsible, blameable, in the wrong, reprehensible
AN OPPOSITE IS innocent

2 *She felt guilty about deceiving her friends.*
▶ ashamed, remorseful, sorry, repentant, regretful, contrite, penitent, conscience-stricken, shamefaced, sheepish
AN OPPOSITE IS unrepentant

gulf NOUN

1 *Here ships turn into the gulf.*
▶ bay, inlet, creek, estuary, sound

2 *the gulf between rich and poor*
▶ gap, contrast, chasm, divergence, divide, rift, split, division

gullible ADJECTIVE

Wayne is very gullible when he's had too much to drink.
▶ credulous, over-trusting, trustful, suggestible, easily taken in
OPPOSITES ARE suspicious, astute

gulp VERB

Brian gulped his beer and stood to leave.
▶ swallow, swill down, (*more informal*) swig, (*more informal*) knock back
AN OPPOSITE IS sip

gulp NOUN

She finished her juice in one gulp.
▶ swallow, mouthful, (*more informal*) swig

gum NOUN

You can stick the pictures in with gum.
▶ glue, adhesive, paste

gum VERB

The photos were gummed to the page.
▶ stick, glue, paste, fix

gun NOUN
He threatened her with a gun.
▶ firearm, weapon, pistol, revolver, rifle, shotgun, (*more informal*) shooter

gurgle VERB
1 *The baby gurgled in a corner.*
▶ burble, babble, chuckle
2 *The stream gurgled beside the path.*
▶ babble, burble, trickle, murmur

gurgle NOUN
The water rushed out with a loud gurgle.
▶ burble, babble, trickle, ripple

gush VERB
1 *Blood gushed from the wound in his head.*
▶ pour, spurt, squirt, stream, flow, rush, cascade, spout, surge
OPPOSITES ARE trickle, ooze
2 *They gushed all afternoon about their holiday plans.*
▶ enthuse, rave, effuse, chatter, jabber, (*more informal*) go on

gush NOUN
Turning the tap slightly produced a gush of scalding water.
▶ rush, spurt, surge, stream, torrent, cascade, flood, flow, jet, spout, squirt, burst

gust NOUN
They felt a sudden gust of wind.
▶ blast, flurry, rush, puff, squall

gusto NOUN
He ate his dinner with gusto.
▶ enthusiasm, vigour, relish, enjoyment, satisfaction, liveliness, spirit, verve, zest

gut NOUN
1 **gut** or **guts** (*informal*) *He felt a sharp pain in his gut.*
▶ stomach, belly, bowels, intestines, innards, insides
RELATED ADJECTIVE visceral
2 **guts** (*informal*) *It takes guts to say what you think.*
▶ courage, nerve, bravery, audacity, boldness, daring, (*informal*) bottle

gut ADJECTIVE
I had a gut feeling Eric was the right man for us.
▶ instinctive, intuitive, deep-seated, spontaneous, innate, reflex

gutter NOUN
The recent rains had filled the gutters.
▶ guttering, channel, conduit, drain, duct, sluice

guy NOUN
He's a clever guy.
▶ bloke, chap, fellow, man, boy, individual

guzzle VERB
They came in and guzzled all the food.
▶ gobble, gobble up, wolf, wolf down, devour, (*more informal*) scoff, (*more informal*) tuck into, (*more informal*) polish off

gyrate VERB
Couples were gyrating to loud music.
▶ turn, twirl, rotate, wheel, revolve, spin, swirl, circle, spiral, pirouette

Hh

habit NOUN
1 *healthy eating habits*
▶ practice, custom, pattern, routine, tendency, way, rule
2 *her habit of twirling her hair as she spoke*
▶ mannerism, quirk, trick, gesture, custom, practice
3 *They stole money to fund their drug habit*
▶ addiction, dependence, craving, fixation, compulsion, obsession, weakness
4 *a nun's habit*
▶ costume, robe, garment, outfit, attire, garb
in the habit of *He was in the habit of practising on his flute when he went to bed.*
▶ used to, accustomed to, given to, inclined to

habitat NOUN
the panda's natural habitat
▶ environment, surroundings, element, territory, terrain, haunt, domain, ecosystem

WORDS FOR ANIMAL HABITATS
terrestrial habitats (land): burrow, copse, desert, ditch, field, forest, garden, grassland, heathland, meadow, moorland, mountain, pasture, rainforest, scrub, soil, tree, towns and cities, tundra, walls, woodland.
aquatic and semi-aquatic habitats (water): bog, coral reef, ditch, fen, lake, mangrove swamp, marsh, ocean, pond, river, rock pool, sea, seashore, stream, swamp.

habitual ADJECTIVE
1 *She expected his habitual response to such suggestions.*
▶ usual, customary, normal, regular, characteristic, typical, fixed, routine, accustomed, established
AN OPPOSITE IS unaccustomed
2 *their habitual criticism of everything we did*
▶ constant, persistent, continual, recurrent, incessant, interminable, unremitting, endless, relentless
AN OPPOSITE IS infrequent
3 *habitual smokers*
▶ confirmed, regular, addicted, persistent, inveterate, hardened, compulsive, chronic
AN OPPOSITE IS occasional

hack VERB
The victim's head had been hacked off.
▶ cut, chop, lop, slash, saw

hackneyed ADJECTIVE
hackneyed expressions
▶ overused, clichéd, banal, commonplace, stale, tired, worn, trite, (*more informal*) corny
OPPOSITES ARE original, fresh

hag NOUN
an old hag
▶ crone, witch, gorgon, termagant, woman

haggard ADJECTIVE
He saw tears on her white, haggard cheeks.
▶ drawn, careworn, shrunken, pinched, gaunt, wan, withered, wasted
OPPOSITES ARE fresh, healthy

haggle VERB
He could spend all afternoon haggling over a few dollars.
▶ barter, bargain, negotiate, argue, quibble, discuss terms, wrangle

hail VERB
A friend hailed him from a top window.
▶ greet, call out to, shout to, wave to, salute

hail NOUN
a hail of bullets
▶ barrage, volley, shower, deluge, torrent, stream, flood, burst

hair NOUN
1 *She ran her hand through her hair.*
▶ locks, tresses, curls, (*more informal*) mop
2 *a dog with short hair*
▶ coat, fur, hide

hairdresser NOUN
an appointment with the hairdresser
▶ hair stylist, stylist, coiffeur, (*for men*) barber

hair-raising ADJECTIVE
the hair-raising events of the days leading up to war
▶ terrifying, frightening, horrifying, shocking, alarming, chilling, petrifying

hairstyle NOUN
A new hairstyle will give you a new lease of life.
▶ haircut, cut, coiffure, style, (*more informal*) hairdo

hairy ADJECTIVE
His shirt was open, revealing a hairy chest.
▶ shaggy, fuzzy, bristly, downy, hirsute, fleecy, furry, long-haired, stubbly, woolly
OPPOSITES ARE hairless, smooth-skinned

half-hearted ADJECTIVE
She made a half-hearted attempt to brush away his hand.
▶ unenthusiastic, weak, feeble, apathetic, indifferent
AN OPPOSITE IS committed

halfway ADJECTIVE
the halfway point in the journey
▶ midway, central, part-way

halfway ADVERB
He stopped halfway along the path.
▶ midway, part-way, in the middle

hall NOUN
1 *The meeting will be in the village hall.*
▶ assembly hall, meeting room, auditorium, concert hall, theatre
2 *You can leave your coat in the hall.*
▶ hallway, entrance hall, lobby, foyer, corridor, passage, vestibule

hallucination NOUN
He suffered from hallucinations for weeks after the accident.
▶ delusion, illusion, apparition, fantasy, figment of the imagination, mirage, vision, daydream, dream

halo NOUN
Her hair sparkled like a halo round her head.
▶ ring of light, aureole, aureola, corona, nimbus

halt VERB
1 *A series of strikes halted production for several weeks.*
▶ stop, terminate, obstruct, arrest, impede, block, check, curb
OPPOSITES ARE start, continue
2 *Traffic halted on the bridge.*
▶ stop, wait, come to a halt, come to rest, draw up, pull up
OPPOSITES ARE start, continue
3 *Work on the building halted during the holiday period.*
▶ cease, stop, break off, end, terminate
OPPOSITES ARE start, resume

halt NOUN
1 *The train came to a halt.*
▶ stop, standstill, break, interruption, pause, stoppage
2 *a halt in the output of spare parts*
▶ stoppage, cessation, break, interruption, pause

halting ADJECTIVE
She spoke at best a halting English.
▶ hesitant, faltering, stumbling, uncertain, underconfident, unsure, erratic, irregular, stammering, stuttering
AN OPPOSITE IS fluent

halve VERB
1 *Halve the pears and remove the cores.*
▶ cut in half, split in two, divide in two, bisect
2 *Their income halved over the next year.*
▶ lessen by half or by fifty percent, decrease by half or by fifty percent

hammer NOUN
He hit the nail with a hammer.
▶ mallet, gavel

hammer VERB
The soldiers hammered on the door.
▶ beat, batter, bash, pummel, pound, strike, knock

hamper VERB
1 *Bad weather hampered the rescue operation.*
▶ obstruct, hinder, hold up, interfere with, restrict, thwart, prevent, curb, curtail, foil
AN OPPOSITE IS facilitate
2 *Her bandaged hand hampered her.*
▶ hinder, encumber, impede, restrain, entangle, handicap, hold back
AN OPPOSITE IS aid

hand NOUN
1 *a person's hand*
▶ fist, palm
RELATED ADJECTIVE manual

2 *the hand of a gauge*
► pointer, indicator
3 *The factory took on more hands.*
► worker, employee, labourer
4 hands *The property came into his sister's hands.*
► possession, control, charge, custody, power, responsibility
at or **on** or **to hand**
► close by, handy, accessible, available, present, waiting, within reach
give somebody a hand *Let me give you a hand with the dinner.*
► help, assist

hand VERB
He handed her a letter.
► give, offer, pass, present (her with a letter), submit (a letter to her), convey, deliver
hand down *The family property is handed down from one generation to the next.*
► pass down, pass on, bequeath, leave as a legacy, will
hand out or **round** *A flight attendant handed out forms.*
► distribute, circulate, give out, deal out, share out
hand over
1 *She handed over a large sum.*
► pay, donate, tender, surrender
2 *The prisoners were handed over to the local police.*
► deliver up, entrust, turn over

handbook NOUN
a UCAS handbook and application form
► guide, instruction book, manual, reference manual

handful NOUN
a handful of complaining letters
► small number, smattering, sprinkling, trickle

handicap NOUN
1 *Their poor French was a handicap when travelling.*
► disadvantage, difficulty, drawback, shortcoming, hindrance, inconvenience, limitation, encumbrance, stumbling block, restriction, obstacle, problem, nuisance
OPPOSITES ARE advantage, benefit
2 *He was born with a severe physical handicap.*
► disability, defect, abnormality, impairment, impediment
USAGE Note that *handicap* is often regarded as offensive in this meaning.

handicap VERB
They were handicapped by the fact that they had not been taught science.
► hamper, impede, limit, disadvantage, restrict, hinder, hold back
AN OPPOSITE IS help

handicapped ADJECTIVE
learning methods for handicapped pupils
► disabled, disadvantaged, incapacitated
USAGE Note that *handicapped* is often regarded as offensive in this meaning.

handiwork NOUN
I stood back to admire my handiwork.
► creation, work, product, handicraft, craftwork, achievement, invention

handle NOUN
The head flew off the handle and cracked our only mirror.
► haft, shank, stock, shaft, grip

handle VERB
1 *A notice asked visitors not to handle the exhibits.*
► touch, feel, hold, finger, fondle, pick up, grip, grasp
2 *It would not be easy to handle such a tense meeting. He was used to handling temperamental singers.*
► manage, deal with, cope with, control, tackle, contend with
3 *The firm handles a lot of overseas business.*
► deal in, trade in, market
4 *He needed a smaller car that he could handle more easily.*
► control, drive, manoeuvre, operate, steer

handout NOUN
1 handouts *They lived on benefits and handouts for several months.*
► donations, charity, aid
2 *There are handouts for each talk at the back of the room.*
► leaflet, circular, pamphlet, notice, brochure

handsome ADJECTIVE
1 *a handsome man*
► good-looking, nice-looking, attractive, comely, personable, (*more informal*) dishy
OPPOSITES ARE ugly, unattractive
2 *a handsome building*
► elegant, striking, imposing, stately, well-proportioned, attractive
OPPOSITES ARE ugly, hideous
3 *a handsome profit*
► large, big, sizeable, substantial, considerable, ample
AN OPPOSITE IS meagre
4 *a handsome offer*
► generous, gracious, liberal, magnanimous, munificent
AN OPPOSITE IS mean

handwriting NOUN
large clear handwriting
► writing, script, hand, calligraphy, penmanship

handy ADJECTIVE
1 *The brush is handy for cleaning up stubborn dust.*
► useful, convenient, practical, helpful, effective
2 *He's handy with a screwdriver.*
► skilful, adept, dexterous, proficient, practical, able, deft
3 *Keep your timer handy.*
► accessible, available, ready, at or to hand, close by, nearby

h

hang VERB

1 *Baskets of flowers hung from the lampposts.*
► be suspended, dangle, swing, sway
2 *Rich exotic curtains hang from every window.*
► drape, drop, droop, cascade, trail
3 *Make sure you hang the pictures at eye level.*
► fix, attach, fasten, display, suspend, stick
4 *A damp mist hung in the air.*
► float, hover, drift, linger, cling, remain

hang about (*informal*) *Don't hang about if you want to take advantage of this offer.*
► delay, wait, procrastinate

hang around (*informal*) *small groups hanging around coffee bars*
► linger in, loiter in, frequent, haunt

hang back *He hung back, afraid to go in.*
► hesitate, demur, hold back, recoil, shy away

hang on *If they can hang on a few more days it will help us.*
► stay, persevere, remain, continue, carry on, persist

hang on to *If you have cash, hang on to it.*
► keep, hold on to, retain, preserve

hang out (*informal*) *She enjoyed hanging out with members of the band.*
► associate, mix, spend time, keep company, fraternize, socialize

hang-up NOUN

(*informal*) *Wally has a hang-up about his appearance.*
► fixation, obsession, neurosis, inhibition, anxiety, (*more informal*) thing

hanker VERB

1 *He could see that she hankered to go back.*
► long, yearn, be aching, crave, want, wish
2 **hanker after** or **for** *They hankered after the bright city lights.*
► long for, crave, miss, be pining for

haphazard ADJECTIVE

the haphazard spray of machine-gun fire   things strewn about in a haphazard fashion
► random, indiscriminate, arbitrary, chaotic, disorderly, disorganized, casual, irregular, unmethodical
AN OPPOSITE IS orderly

happen VERB

1 *The collision happened as the pursuing boat tried to turn.   Something strange was happening that day.*
► occur, take place, come about, arise, result, ensue, transpire
2 **happen to** *We never knew what happened to her.*
► become of, befall

happening NOUN

There is a record of all the happenings of that week.
► event, incident, occurrence, circumstance, episode, affair

happiness NOUN

A feeling of great happiness filled her.
► contentment, joy, joyfulness, gladness, pleasure, bliss, elation, ecstasy
OPPOSITES ARE unhappiness, sorrow

happy ADJECTIVE This word is often overused. Here are some alternatives:
1 *a room full of happy faces*
► contented, cheerful, joyful, jolly, delighted, merry, smiling
2 *I will be happy to help.*
► pleased, glad, willing, disposed, delighted
3 *By a happy chance a film crew was there to record the scene.*
► fortunate, lucky, felicitous, favourable, fitting

harass VERB

The men continued to harass her.
► pester, torment, badger, hound, persecute, trouble, harry, hassle, annoy, vex

harassed ADJECTIVE

good news for harassed mums and dads
► stressed, harried, worn, troubled, (*informal*) exhausted
AN OPPOSITE IS carefree

harbour NOUN

Boats bobbed up and down in the harbour.
► port, dock, marina, mooring, quay, waterfront

harbour VERB

1 *He was arrested for harbouring a criminal.*
► hide, protect, shelter, conceal, shield, give refuge to, give asylum to, give sanctuary to
2 *Better not to harbour a grudge.*
► bear, hold, nurse, nurture, entertain, foster, cling to

hard ADJECTIVE This word is often overused. Here are some alternatives:
1 *The ground is too hard to play on.*
► solid, firm, unyielding, hardened, tough, compact
AN OPPOSITE IS soft
2 *three weeks of hard work*
► strenuous, arduous, exhausting, fatiguing, demanding
AN OPPOSITE IS easy
3 *a hard problem to solve*
► difficult, complicated, complex, involved, knotty, baffling, puzzling
AN OPPOSITE IS simple
4 *a hard taskmaster*
► strict, harsh, firm, stern, demanding, severe
OPPOSITES ARE mild, easy-going
5 *a hard blow*
► heavy, forceful, strong, powerful, violent
AN OPPOSITE IS light

hard up *We were too hard up to buy fancy clothes.*
► poor, impoverished, poverty stricken, badly off, impecunious

hard ADVERB

1 *She works hard at school.*
▶ diligently, industriously, steadily, earnestly, energetically
2 *It has been raining hard.*
▶ heavily, steadily, (*more informal*) cats and dogs
3 *She looked hard at them.*
▶ intently, intensely, closely, attentively, keenly

harden VERB

1 *The cement hardens after two hours.*
▶ set, solidify, become hard, stiffen
2 *These experiences hardened their determination to continue.*
▶ strengthen, reinforce, increase, intensify, fortify, toughen

hard-hearted ADJECTIVE

No one could be so hard-hearted as to ignore such desperate appeals for help.
▶ unfeeling, heartless, unsympathetic, callous, uncaring, unconcerned

hardly ADVERB

1 *It is hardly surprising that so many people have considered leaving.*
▶ not at all, by no means, barely, scarcely
2 *John said he hardly knew her.*
▶ scarcely, barely, only just, only slightly, only faintly

hardship NOUN

Drought caused the population much hardship.
▶ suffering, privation, misery, misfortune, adversity, affliction, austerity, destitution, difficulty, need, trouble, unhappiness, want

hardware NOUN

tanks and other military hardware   computer hardware
▶ equipment, machinery, implements, tools, instruments

hard-wearing ADJECTIVE

outdoor clothes that are hard-wearing
▶ durable, strong, tough, resilient, lasting, sturdy, well-made, stout
OPPOSITES ARE flimsy, delicate

hardy ADJECTIVE

a good expedition for hardy walkers
▶ fit, robust, sturdy, hearty, healthy, tough, vigorous, strong, resilient, rugged
OPPOSITES ARE tender, delicate

harm NOUN

1 *a way of dealing with waste without causing any harm to the public*
▶ injury, damage, suffering, hurt, detriment, inconvenience
AN OPPOSITE IS benefit
2 *We can't see any harm in their idea.*
▶ wrong, disadvantage, snag

harm VERB

1 *If they harmed any of the hostages the police would have to go in.*
▶ hurt, injure, maltreat, mistreat, ill-treat, wound, molest, abuse, (*more informal*) lay a finger on
2 *effluence that harms the environment*
▶ damage, spoil, ruin, hurt, do damage to, do harm to

harmful ADJECTIVE

the harmful effects of smoking
▶ damaging, detrimental, injurious, dangerous, noxious, destructive, unhealthy
OPPOSITES ARE harmless, beneficial

harmless ADJECTIVE

1 *a harmless substance*
▶ safe, innocuous, non-toxic, non-poisonous, benign
AN OPPOSITE IS harmful
2 *It was just a bit of harmless fun. He looked as harmless as a tired sparrow.*
▶ safe, inoffensive, innocuous, unobjectionable, gentle
AN OPPOSITE IS objectionable

harmonious ADJECTIVE

1 *harmonious sounds*
▶ tuneful, melodious, melodic, euphonious, sweet-sounding, mellifluous
AN OPPOSITE IS discordant
2 *a harmonious relationship*
▶ friendly, cordial, amicable, congenial
OPPOSITES ARE unfriendly, hostile
3 *a harmonious balance of colour and tone*
▶ matching, coordinated, proportional, balanced, pleasing, congruous
OPPOSITES ARE unbalanced, incongruous

harmonize VERB

1 *The colours harmonize well.*
▶ match, blend, tone in, go together, coordinate, balance, fit together
2 *There is an argument for harmonizing taxes across Europe.*
▶ coordinate, correlate, reconcile, bring together, make uniform, make consistent

harmony NOUN

1 *different ethnic groups living in harmony*
▶ friendship, agreement, concord, peace, amity, fellowship, goodwill, unity
OPPOSITES ARE disagreement, enmity
2 *musical harmony*
▶ tunefulness, euphony, concord, melody
AN OPPOSITE IS discord

harness VERB

attempts to harness the forces of nature
▶ use, control, utilize, make use of, exploit, tame, keep under control, mobilize

harrowing ADJECTIVE

a harrowing tale of betrayal and murder
▶ distressing, traumatic, disturbing, upsetting, shocking, frightening

harry VERB

1 *They were harried all morning by news reporters.*
▶ harass, pester, torment, persecute, badger, trouble, annoy, vex

2 *The fleet was given a free hand to harry the enemy's supply lines.*
▶ attack, ravage, ransack, plunder, devastate

harsh ADJECTIVE

1 *He spoke in a high, harsh voice.*
▶ shrill, grating, strident, rasping

2 *harsh measures to combat street crime*
▶ severe, punitive, strict, draconian

3 *They exchanged harsh words.*
▶ sharp, bitter, unfriendly, unkind

4 *the harsh rule of a tyrant*
▶ cruel, savage, brutal, despotic, hard, strict, intolerant

harvest NOUN

a bumper harvest
▶ crop, yield, produce, return

harvest VERB

crops that have to be harvested by hand
▶ gather, reap, take in, bring in, collect, garner, mow, pick

hash NOUN

make a hash of
▶ bungle, botch, mismanage, mishandle, muff, make a mess of

hassle NOUN

1 *It's always such a hassle trying to park.*
▶ bother, nuisance, inconvenience, struggle, difficulty

2 *She started getting hassle from the kids coming to her.*
▶ harassment, trouble, annoyance, argument, (*more informal*) aggravation

hassle VERB

Some of the passengers were hassling the driver.
▶ harass, pester, badger, trouble, harry, annoy

haste NOUN

He was working with great haste.
▶ speed, hurry, urgency, swiftness, rapidity, promptness, impetuosity

hasten VERB

1 *The king hastened back from Berwick.*
▶ hurry, rush, speed, make haste

2 *A rise in interest rates will hasten the ruin of many small businesses.*
▶ quicken, accelerate, speed up, bring nearer, precipitate

hasty ADJECTIVE

1 *They made a hasty retreat back to the house.*
▶ hurried, swift, rapid, brisk, quick, headlong

2 *The decision seemed hasty.*
▶ rash, precipitate, impulsive, imprudent, impetuous, reckless

hat NOUN

SOME COMMON TYPES OF HAT

men's hats: bowler, trilby, top hat, Homburg, porkpie, deerstalker, stetson, boater, sun-hat, sombrero, panama, straw hat.

women's hats: bonnet, Juliet cap, cloche, toque.

soft informal hats: cap, beret, baseball cap, balaclava, skull cap, beanie.

ceremonial and official hats: busby, helmet, mortar board, biretta, mitre.

some other hats: bobble hatglengarry, yarmulke, taj, tam-o'shanter, turban.

hatch VERB

A plan was hatching in her mind.
▶ develop, form, grow

hatch up *The little scheme they hatched up.*
▶ devise, concoct, conceive, contrive, formulate, think up, brew up, dream up, cook up

hate VERB

1 *The brothers hated each other.*
▶ loathe, detest, abhor, dislike, abominate, (*more informal*) can't bear, (*more informal*) can't stand

2 *I hate to bother them.*
▶ be sorry, hesitate, regret, be reluctant

hate NOUN

1 *feelings of hate*
▶ hatred, loathing, detestation, dislike, distaste, revulsion, abhorrence

2 *They made a list of their pet hates.*
▶ dislike, bugbear, bane, bête noire

hateful ADJECTIVE

I'll never come back to this hateful country.
▶ detestable, loathsome, horrible, horrid, awful, nasty
AN OPPOSITE IS lovable

hatred NOUN

The war left a legacy of fear and hatred.
▶ hate, loathing, detestation, revulsion, repugnance, hostility, enmity, bad feeling
OPPOSITES ARE love, liking

haughty ADJECTIVE

He walked out with a haughty toss of his head.
▶ proud, arrogant, self-important, supercilious, disdainful, contemptuous, scornful, superior, lofty, overbearing
AN OPPOSITE IS modest

haul VERB

A special locomotive is needed to haul these trains. She hauled him up from the floor.
▶ pull, drag, heave, tug, tow
AN OPPOSITE IS push

haunt VERB

1 *He likes to haunt old junk shops.*
▶ frequent, spend time in, keep returning to, visit frequently, (*more informal*) hang around in

2 *Her words came back to haunt her.*
▶ obsess, torment, trouble, worry, prey on

haunt NOUN
one of their favourite haunts in town
▶ meeting place, retreat, rendezvous, spot

haunting ADJECTIVE
haunting and lyrical poetry
▶ evocative, touching, emotive, memorable, poignant, nostalgic, wistful, plaintive
AN OPPOSITE IS unmemorable

have VERB
1 *They have a house in France.*
▶ own, possess, be the owner of, boast, keep, enjoy
AN OPPOSITE IS lack
2 *We have coffee at eleven.*
▶ drink, take
3 *What did you have for lunch?*
▶ eat, consume
4 *She had a letter from her boyfriend.*
▶ receive, get, be sent, obtain, acquire
OPPOSITES ARE send, reject
5 *They are having a party next door.*
▶ hold, give, organize, arrange, throw, provide, lay on
6 *The apartment has five rooms.*
▶ contain, comprise, consist of, include, incorporate, be made up of
7 *We had trouble parking.*
▶ experience, encounter, undergo, meet with, run into, suffer, face
8 *I have a bad cold.*
▶ be suffering from, be afflicted by, be affected by, be troubled by
9 *The boys had a lot of fun.*
▶ enjoy, experience, go through
10 *Mike had guests at the weekend.*
▶ entertain, receive, be host to, cater for, invite
11 *Julia has had her baby.*
▶ give birth to, bear, produce, be delivered of, bring into the world

haven NOUN
1 *a haven for ships on the north coast*
▶ harbour, port, anchorage, mooring
2 *a safe haven in time of trouble*
▶ refuge, retreat, shelter, sanctuary, asylum

havoc NOUN
Frost and snow caused havoc in the area.
▶ chaos, confusion, disruption, mayhem, disorder, devastation, destruction

haywire ADJECTIVE
A virus can make your PC go haywire.
▶ out of control, erratic, faulty, chaotic, disorganized, topsy-turvy

hazard NOUN
a serious health hazard
▶ risk, threat, danger, menace

hazard VERB
1 *a business that is too risky to hazard money on*
▶ risk, chance, jeopardize
2 *I wouldn't want to hazard a guess about that.*
▶ offer, put forward, venture, advance

hazardous ADJECTIVE
He knew how hazardous the road could be in the dark.
▶ dangerous, risky, perilous, precarious, uncertain, unpredictable, unsafe, chancy, (*more informal*) dicey
OPPOSITES ARE safe, secure

haze NOUN
The clear sky suddenly filled with haze.
▶ mist, fog, cloud, vapour, film, obscurity

hazy ADJECTIVE
1 *The weather was good, if a little hazy.*
▶ misty, cloudy, foggy, smoky
2 *hazy memories of childhood*
▶ vague, indistinct, blurred, fuzzy, unclear, faint, dim

head NOUN
1 *He hit his head on a beam.*
▶ skull, crown, cranium, (*more informal*) nut, (*more informal*) bonce
RELATED ADJECTIVE cephalic
2 *the head of a publishing firm*
▶ chief, chairman, chief executive, president, principal
3 *You need a good head for this work.*
▶ brain, intellect, intelligence, wit
4 *She has quite a head for figures.*
▶ aptitude, gift, talent, bent, knack
lose your head *Connie lost her head and ran off.*
▶ panic, lose control, go to pieces, (*more informal*) lose your cool
off your head *He was quite off his head, spouting complete nonsense.*
▶ mad, crazy, insane, out of your mind, unbalanced, demented, deranged

head ADJECTIVE
the head chef
▶ chief, senior, principal, leading

head VERB
1 *She headed a team of researchers.*
▶ lead, be in charge of, be at the head of, manage, direct, oversee, supervise
2 **head for** *They were heading for the station.*
▶ go or move towards, make for, aim for, point to

heading NOUN
1 *He turned the page and read the chapter heading.*
▶ title, headline, caption, rubric
2 *The subject is discussed under several headings.*
▶ category, division, section, class, group

headland NOUN
You can gaze out over the headland to the sea.
▶ promontory, cape, head, point, foreland

headline NOUN
a newspaper headline
▶ heading, title, caption

headlong ADJECTIVE
a headlong dash to the river
▶ hasty, breakneck, precipitate, impetuous, reckless

headstrong ADJECTIVE
Imaginative and headstrong, he became an art student.
▶ stubborn, wilful, obstinate, intractable, perverse, contrary

headway NOUN
make headway *The sales team has begun to make good headway.*
▶ make progress, progress, advance, gain ground, move forward

heady ADJECTIVE
a mood of heady excitement
▶ exhilarating, intoxicating, thrilling, euphoric, ecstatic, elated

heal VERB
1 *Madra's wounds began to heal.*
▶ get better, recover, knit, mend, unite
2 *an ointment to heal her injured finger*
▶ make better, cure, treat, remedy, restore
3 *The rift between father and son was never completely healed.*
▶ mend, repair, put right, settle, remedy, reconcile, patch up

health NOUN
1 *He is now in excellent health and back at work.*
▶ condition, shape, form, fettle, constitution
2 *Hormone levels are important to health.*
▶ fitness, wellbeing, healthiness, good health
RELATED ADJECTIVE sanitary

healthy ADJECTIVE
1 *We try to promote a healthy lifestyle.*
▶ health-giving, wholesome, beneficial, bracing, invigorating
2 *I think I am fit, healthy, and looking good again.*
▶ well, in good health, in good condition, in good shape, in good trim
3 *a healthy respect for the opposite sex*
▶ sound, strong, rigorous

heap NOUN
1 *a heap of old newspapers*
▶ pile, stack, mass, mound, mountain, collection, hoard
2 **heaps** *We've got heaps of time.*
▶ plenty, a lot, a great deal, (*more informal*) lots, (*more informal*) masses, (*more informal*) piles

heap VERB
1 *She heaped more cakes on their plates.*
▶ pile, stack, mass, bank, collect
2 *The praise heaped on them was well deserved.*
▶ lavish, shower, bestow, confer

hear VERB
1 *You can hear the traffic in the distance.*
▶ make out, catch, listen to, perceive, discern, detect.
RELATED ADJECTIVE audible
USAGE Note that all these words, except for *listen to*, can also be used about seeing, and so you might need to make the meaning clear by saying, for example, *You can make out the sound of traffic in the distance.* Note also that *listen to* implies something you try to do, whereas *hear* can refer to sounds that you might be aware of by chance.
2 *I heard that you were leaving.*
▶ be told, be informed, learn, gather, find out, discover
3 *A female judge heard the case.*
▶ try, judge, sit in judgement on

hearing NOUN
1 *He made the comment out of our hearing.*
▶ earshot, range, reach.
RELATED ADJECTIVE acoustic
2 *a judicial hearing*
▶ trial, court case, inquiry, investigation, tribunal, review, proceedings

hearsay NOUN
evidence based on hearsay
▶ rumour, gossip, talk, word of mouth, tittle-tattle

heart NOUN
1 *His heart had stopped beating.*
▶ organ of circulation, (*more informal*) ticker
RELATED ADJECTIVE cardiac
2 *an air link into the heart of the city*
▶ centre, middle, nucleus, core, hub, inside, kernel
3 *the heart of the problem*
▶ essence, nub, crux, root, focus
4 *He won't allow his heart to rule his head.*
▶ feelings, emotion, sentiment
5 *The lack of support made them lose heart.*
▶ enthusiasm, eagerness, courage, bravery, resolution, determination
6 *She may be stern but she has a lot of heart.*
▶ compassion, feeling, sympathy, tenderness, understanding, affection, humanity, kindness, love

heartbreaking ADJECTIVE
heartbreaking sobs from the bedroom
▶ distressing, harrowing, pitiful, saddening, tragic, grievous, heart-rending

heartbroken ADJECTIVE
He was heartbroken at having to sell his home.
▶ broken-hearted, inconsolable, devastated, grief-stricken, desolate, despairing
AN OPPOSITE IS happy

hearten VERB
It had heartened her that she could still win against Ivor.
▶ encourage, comfort, reassure, console, cheer, cheer up, (*more informal*) buck up
AN OPPOSITE IS dishearten

heartfelt ADJECTIVE
a heartfelt message of good luck
▶ sincere, genuine, deeply felt, profound, wholehearted, enthusiastic, earnest, ardent, fervent

heartless ADJECTIVE
heartless thieves who stole a boy's bicycle
▶ callous, hard-hearted, mean-spirited, insensitive, cruel

hearty ADJECTIVE
1 *The remark brought a loud hearty laugh.*
▶ enthusiastic, sincere, warm, jovial, cordial, exuberant, cheerful, uninhibited
2 *Beth always had a hearty appetite*
▶ big, healthy, strong, robust, vigorous
3 *They looked forward to a hearty meal and a good night's sleep.*
▶ substantial, generous, sizeable, solid, large, ample, wholesome

heat NOUN
1 *The fire gave out a lot of heat.*
▶ warmth, hotness, glow
RELATED ADJECTIVES thermal, calorific
2 *The summer heat was exhausting.*
▶ hot weather, warmth, humidity, sultriness, swelter
3 *There is too much heat in these arguments.*
▶ passion, intensity, ardour, warmth, vehemence, anger, fury

heat VERB
1 *You can heat the food under the grill, if you prefer.*
▶ cook, heat up, reheat
2 *The room has two external walls and is difficult to heat.*
▶ keep warm, warm up

heated ADJECTIVE
1 *The discussion soon became heated.*
▶ passionate, vehement, animated, impassioned, bitter, tempestuous
OPPOSITES ARE dispassionate, calm
2 *Rachael grew heated as she talked about her ordeal.*
▶ excited, roused, worked up, keyed up, animated, impassioned
AN OPPOSITE IS calm

heave VERB
Two men heaved back the great iron gates.
▶ haul, drag, pull, throw, draw, tow, tug, hoist, lift, lug, raise

heaven NOUN
1 *You might get your reward in heaven, if you are lucky.*
▶ paradise, the next world, the hereafter, the afterlife
2 *In that heat a cool drink was absolute heaven.*
▶ ecstasy, bliss, joy, rapture, delight
AN OPPOSITE IS hell
3 **the heavens** *The moon caused a glow in the heavens.*
▶ the sky, the skies, the firmament, the blue
RELATED ADJECTIVE celestial

heavenly ADJECTIVE
1 *the sound of joyful, heavenly music*
▶ beautiful, celestial, divine, angelic, blissful, exquisite
OPPOSITES ARE devilish, infernal
2 *They had a heavenly time.*
▶ delightful, marvellous, wonderful, lovely, pleasant

heavy ADJECTIVE
1 *too heavy to lift*
▶ weighty, massive, bulky, hefty
2 *a heavy man*
▶ large, fat, corpulent, overweight
3 *heavy smoking*
▶ excessive, immoderate, intensive, uncontrolled
4 *a heavy meal*
▶ substantial, hearty, filling, sizeable, solid, stodgy
5 *a heavy blow*
▶ hard, forceful, violent, powerful, hefty
6 *heavy losses a heavy fine*
▶ large, substantial, considerable
7 *a heavy burden of responsibility*
▶ onerous, demanding, formidable, challenging, severe
8 *heavy work*
▶ arduous, strenuous, taxing
9 *heavy reading*
▶ serious, tedious, dull
10 *heavy rain*
▶ strong, intense, teeming, torrential

heckle VERB
Some of the speakers came close to being heckled.
▶ barrack, jeer, shout down, interrupt, harass, disrupt

hectic ADJECTIVE
We spent three hectic days getting the house in order.
▶ busy, frantic, feverish, frenzied, manic, chaotic
OPPOSITES ARE leisurely, quiet

hector VERB
An official hectored them into leaving.
▶ bully, browbeat, intimidate, chivvy, harass

hedge NOUN
1 *The garden was enclosed by a hedge.*
▶ fence, hedgerow, barrier, screen
2 *Savings form a hedge against loss of income.*
▶ safeguard, protection, shield, buffer, cushion

hedge VERB
The next question made him hedge.
▶ prevaricate, equivocate, vacillate, stall, be evasive, quibble, hesitate, temporize, (*more informal*) beat about the bush
hedge in *They were hedged in by their lack of information.*
▶ confine, hinder, obstruct, impede, restrict, limit

heed VERB
She refused to heed him.
▶ listen to, pay attention to, take notice of, regard, obey, follow
AN OPPOSITE IS disregard

heedless ADJECTIVE

heedless of *They were heedless of the suffering around them.*
▶ inattentive to, unconcerned about, unmindful of, neglectful of, uncaring of, careless about, unsympathetic towards
AN OPPOSITE IS heedful

hefty ADJECTIVE

A hefty young man stood in their way.
▶ burly, beefy, sturdy, well-built, strapping, brawny, hulking, muscular, powerful, stocky, stout, athletic, big, heavy
OPPOSITES ARE slight, thin

height NOUN

1 *We wanted to know the height of the tower.*
▶ tallness, highness, vertical measurement, elevation, altitude
2 **heights** *reaching the mountain heights*
▶ summit, top, peak, crest, crown, tip
3 *They were at the height of their fame.*
▶ peak, high point, acme, climax, zenith
OPPOSITES ARE nadir, low point

heighten VERB

1 *The architects proposed heightening the roof levels.*
▶ raise, make higher, lift up, elevate, build up
AN OPPOSITE IS lower
2 *The presence of police heightened their sense of alarm.*
▶ increase, magnify, intensify, add to, sharpen, strengthen, augment, boost, enhance
AN OPPOSITE IS lessen

hell NOUN

1 *religions that believe in a hell*
▶ netherworld, eternal punishment, infernal regions, lower regions
AN OPPOSITE IS heaven
RELATED ADJECTIVE infernal
2 *Living with Patrick must be hell.*
▶ agony, torture, a misery, a nightmare, an ordeal, a torment

hellish ADJECTIVE

It was a hellish experience they wanted never to repeat.
▶ dreadful, ghastly, horrible, terrible, frightful

help VERB

1 *Will you help me move this bed?*
▶ assist, aid, lend a hand
2 *I couldn't help laughing.*
▶ prevent yourself, restrain yourself from, refrain from, resist
3 *A small donation will help those in need.*
▶ support, contribute to, encourage, promote
4 *Foreign visits will help your languages.*
▶ improve, enhance, bolster
5 *She took aspirin to help her headache.*
▶ relieve, reduce, ease, soothe, alleviate, remedy, lessen

help NOUN

1 *We could do with some help.*
▶ assistance, support, aid, guidance, cooperation, advice
AN OPPOSITE IS hindrance
2 *Would a screwdriver be of help?*
▶ use, service, benefit, utility

helper NOUN

1 *A chain of helpers passed buckets of water along.*
▶ supporter, volunteer, worker
2 *All her helpers were away that day.*
▶ assistant, colleague, collaborator, subordinate, associate, co-worker

helpful ADJECTIVE

1 *The shop assistant was friendly and helpful.*
▶ obliging, willing, cooperative, thoughtful, considerate, sympathetic, eager to please, friendly
2 *A hammer might be helpful. A sceptical attitude won't be helpful.*
▶ useful, of use, beneficial, worthwhile, profitable, productive, constructive, valuable

helping NOUN

a good helping of pudding
▶ portion, serving, plateful, bowlful, share, amount, ration, (*more informal*) dollop

helpless ADJECTIVE

She felt helpless and frustrated.
▶ powerless, impotent, incapable, dependent, weak, forlorn, vulnerable, defenceless, destitute

hem NOUN

She lowered the hem of her skirt.
▶ hemline, edge, border, fringe

hem VERB

hem in *We were hemmed in by a group of tourist buses.*
▶ shut in, close in, box in, enclose, surround, confine, restrict

herald NOUN

1 *A herald announced the end of hostilities.*
▶ courier, messenger, town crier, crier
2 *The buds in the park are a herald of spring.*
▶ harbinger, sign, indicator, indication, prelude, forerunner, precursor

---

herb NOUN

SOME COMMON HERBS

angelica, anise, balm, balsam, basil, bay leaf, bergamot, borage, camomile, caraway, chervil, chicory, chive, coriander, cumin, dill, fennel, fenugreek, hyssop, lavender, lemon balm, lovage, marjoram, mint, oregano, parsley, peppermint, rosemary, rue, saffron, sage, savory, sorrel, spearmint, tansy, tarragon, thyme, wintergreen.

herd NOUN
1 *herds of farm animals*
▶ drove, pack, flock, fold
2 *She cut her way through the herd of lunchtime drinkers.*
▶ crowd, mass, throng, horde, crush

herd VERB
1 *They herded the sheep into the pens.*
▶ drive, lead, guide, round, gather, collect
2 *We all herded into a meeting room.*
▶ crowd, pack, throng, flock, huddle, squash

hereditary ADJECTIVE
1 *the hereditary right to place the crown on the king's head*
▶ ancestral, inherited, bequeathed, handed down, transmitted, family
2 *a hereditary disease   hereditary characteristics*
▶ genetic, congenital, inherent, transmissible, transmittable, inborn, inbred, innate
AN OPPOSITE IS acquired

heritage NOUN
part of our national heritage
▶ tradition, culture, history, inheritance, legacy

hermit NOUN
caves occupied by hermits
▶ recluse, solitary, ascetic, anchorite

hero NOUN
1 *His father had been decorated as a war hero.*
▶ champion, brave man
2 *James had always been her hero.*
▶ idol, star, ideal, paragon, favourite, darling
3 *The story had no real hero.*
▶ principal character, lead character, protagonist

heroic ADJECTIVE
All his heroic efforts might come to nothing.
▶ brave, courageous, noble, valiant, bold, daring, gallant, intrepid
AN OPPOSITE IS cowardly

heroine NOUN
the heroine of the film
▶ leading or principal female character, female lead, female star, leading lady

hesitant ADJECTIVE
They were hesitant about what to do next.   He took a hesitant step back.
▶ uncertain, tentative, cautious, faltering, doubtful, half-hearted, irresolute, indecisive, undecided, dithering
OPPOSITES ARE decisive, resolute

hesitate VERB
She hesitated before searching in her bag for her keys.
▶ pause, delay, falter, dither, hold back, vacillate, waver, wait, have second thoughts

hesitation NOUN
He answered without any hesitation.
▶ pause, delay, equivocation, reluctance, vacillation, misgivings, second thoughts, qualms, reservation, doubt, uncertainty

hidden ADJECTIVE
1 *a hidden entrance   a hidden camera*
▶ concealed, secret, unseen, invisible, disguised, camouflaged, covered
2 *The message may have a hidden meaning.*
▶ unknown, obscure, cryptic, secret, abstruse, mysterious, ulterior

hide VERB
1 *Sam hid in a cupboard.*
▶ conceal yourself, take cover, keep hidden, lie low, keep out of sight
2 *Where did they hide the jewels?*
▶ conceal, secrete, store away, bury, (more informal) stash
AN OPPOSITE IS expose
3 *Richard tried to hide his disapproval.*
▶ disguise, conceal, keep hidden, suppress, repress, mask
OPPOSITES ARE disclose, flaunt
4 *Passing clouds hid the moon.*
▶ obscure, shadow, block out, conceal, obstruct
AN OPPOSITE IS reveal

hide NOUN
an animal's hide
▶ skin, pelt, coat, fur, leather

hideous ADJECTIVE
1 *His mouth was twisted in a hideous grin.*
▶ ugly, unsightly, repulsive, repellent, revolting, gruesome, disgusting, macabre
AN OPPOSITE IS beautiful
2 *It is one of the most hideous experiences we have had in our lives.*
▶ horrible, ghastly, horrific, terrible, appalling, shocking, sickening, dreadful, frightful, grim, grisly, odious

hide-out NOUN
Police stormed his hideout in the suburbs.
▶ hiding place, hideaway, retreat, refuge, lair, den, shelter, sanctuary, bolt-hole

hiding NOUN
I was given a good hiding.
▶ beating, thrashing, caning, spanking, belting, whacking

high ADJECTIVE
1 *a high mountain   a high building*
▶ tall, lofty, elevated, towering
OPPOSITES ARE low, short
2 *a high position in the government*
▶ senior, prominent, high-ranking, top-ranking, leading, distinguished, important, influential, powerful
OPPOSITES ARE junior, low- ranking
3 *high moral principles*
▶ noble, lofty, honourable, high-minded
AN OPPOSITE IS base
4 *high prices*
▶ inflated, excessive, exorbitant, top, costly
AN OPPOSITE IS low

5 *the high notes*
► high-pitched, soprano, treble, shrill, sharp, piercing
OPPOSITES ARE low, bass
6 *the highest standards*
► excellent, outstanding, exceptional, exemplary
OPPOSITES ARE low, poor
7 *high winds*
► strong, powerful, violent, stiff, blustery
AN OPPOSITE IS gentle
8 *I have a high opinion of them.*
► favourable, positive, good, approving
OPPOSITES ARE low, unfavourable

highbrow ADJECTIVE
highbrow tastes in music
► intellectual, sophisticated, cultivated, cultured, serious

high-class ADJECTIVE
The restaurant is high-class and in a good location.
► superior, high-quality, high-grade, exclusive, excellent

highlight NOUN
one of the highlights of a long career
► high point, high spot, climax, peak, best moment

highlight VERB
The news reports tend to highlight party disagreements.
► emphasize, accentuate, spotlight, focus on, play up, show up

highly ADVERB
a form of waste that is highly toxic
► very, extremely, considerably, exceedingly, distinctly, decidedly, immensely

highly-strung ADJECTIVE
a young highly-strung performer
► nervous, nervy, sensitive, excitable, jumpy, temperamental, tense

hijack VERB
A man was charged with hijacking a Russian plane to Stockholm.
► seize, commandeer, take over, skyjack, expropriate

hike VERB
They hiked across the moors for several miles.
► trek, go on foot, walk , ramble, tramp, trudge, traipse, slog

hike NOUN
a twenty-mile hike
► trek, walk , ramble, tramp, trudge, slog

hilarious ADJECTIVE
A group clustered round a hilarious puppet show.
► comical, funny, amusing, entertaining, uproarious, riotous, (*more informal*) hysterical, (*more informal*) side-splitting

hill NOUN
1 *the house at the top of the hill*
► high ground, elevation, hillock, ridge, peak, mount

2 *The car stalled on a steep hill.*
► slope, rise, gradient, incline, ascent

hinder VERB
Power failures have hindered production.
► hamper, hold up, interfere with, obstruct, restrict, thwart, prevent, curb, curtail, foil
AN OPPOSITE IS facilitate

hindrance NOUN
Our presence might be as much a hindrance to you as a help.
► impediment, obstacle, obstruction, encumbrance, handicap, restriction, limitation, restraint, inconvenience, complication, disadvantage, drawback
AN OPPOSITE IS help

hinge VERB
Everything hinges on next month's elections.
► depend, rest, hang, revolve, turn

hint NOUN
1 *She would drop a few casual hints about leaving. I can take a hint that I'm not wanted.*
► clue, sign, signal, indication, reminder, inkling, intimation
2 *His father kept turning up to offer handy hints.*
► tip, piece of advice, pointer
3 *There was a hint of sadness in her voice.*
► trace, tinge, touch, suggestion

hint VERB
1 *He hinted that a new project was being considered.*
► suggest, imply, indicate, intimate
2 **hint at** *I'm not sure what she was hinting at.*
► allude to, refer to, imply, suggest

hire VERB
1 *We could hire a car and drive to London.*
► rent, lease, book, charter
2 *The new bosses want to hire more freelance workers.*
► employ, engage, recruit, appoint

hiss VERB
1 *She turned the tap until she heard the gas hiss.*
► fizz, fizzle, whistle
2 *The audience hissed him and threw things on the stage.*
► jeer, boo, catcall

historic ADJECTIVE
a historic meeting of the heads of state
► famous, notable, epoch-making, celebrated, momentous, significant, important
AN OPPOSITE IS unimportant

historical ADJECTIVE
a story based on historical events
► real, real-life, true, actual, authentic, documented, attested, verifiable
OPPOSITES ARE fictitious, fictional

history NOUN
1 *their interest in history*
► the past, former times, days of old, antiquity
2 *a history of the civil wars*
► chronicle, record, narrative

hit VERB This word is often overused. Here are some alternatives:
1 *He hit the tree with his fist.*
▶ strike, smack, slap, thump, whack, (*more informal*) slug
2 *Several lorries hit the central barrier.*
▶ crash into, run into, collide with, smash into
3 *The industry has been hit by lightning strikes.*
▶ affect, hurt, harm, damage
4 *It suddenly hit me that I should have confirmed the booking.*
▶ strike, occur to, dawn on, come to, cross your mind
5 *Contributions should hit the million mark.*
▶ reach, achieve

hit NOUN
1 *He got a hit on the head.*
▶ blow, punch, thump, knock, smack, slap, whack
2 *The party had been a huge hit.*
▶ success, triumph, winner, best-seller, (*more informal*) knockout

hitch NOUN
The moves all went without any hitch.
▶ problem, difficulty, snag, setback, hindrance

hitch VERB
1 *The farmer hitched a tractor to the cart.*
▶ fasten, attach, hook, couple, connect
2 *Diana hitched up her skirts and entered the water.*
▶ pull, lift, raise, hoist, jerk, (*more informal*) hike

hoard NOUN
The tomb contained a huge hoard of jewellery.
▶ cache, store, stock, pile, stockpile, heap, supply, treasure-trove

hoard VERB
The refugees had hoarded their supplies.
▶ store, amass, accumulate, mass, put by, save, stockpile, pile up, collect, gather, keep, lay up, treasure, (*more informal*) stash away
AN OPPOSITE IS squander

hoarse ADJECTIVE
a voice that was hoarse from shouting
▶ rough, harsh, gruff, husky, throaty, rasping, croaking, grating, gravelly, growling, raucous

hoax NOUN
The virus warning was a hoax
▶ joke, practical joke, prank, trick, spoof, deception, fake, fraud, imposture, cheat, swindle, (*more informal*) leg-pull, (*more informal*) con

hoax VERB
It's not a good time to hoax people.
▶ trick, fool, dupe, deceive, take in, hoodwink, cheat, (*more informal*) con, (*more informal*) pull someone's leg

hobble VERB
The old man hobbled down the road.
▶ limp, shuffle, shamble, totter, falter, stagger

hobby NOUN
Kevin took up fishing as a hobby.
▶ pastime, leisure activity, leisure pursuit, recreation, diversion, interest, relaxation

hoist VERB
The crew hoisted more cargo on deck.
▶ raise, lift, pull up, heave, winch up

hoist NOUN
a hand-operated pneumatic hoist
▶ crane, jack, pulley, winch, lift, lifting gear, block and tackle, davit, windlass, derrick

hold VERB
1 *He was holding a black briefcase.*
▶ clasp, clutch, grip, cling to, cling on to
2 *I wanted to hold her in my arms.*
▶ hug, embrace, clasp, fold, cradle
3 *Visitors must hold a valid passport.*
▶ possess, bear, have, own
4 *The society holds a general meeting in March.*
▶ call, convene, summon, conduct, assemble
5 *Police are holding him pending further investigation.*
▶ detain, keep in custody, imprison, lock up, arrest
6 *She held a senior position in a bank.*
▶ occupy, fill, (*more informal*) hold down
7 *The house holds six to eight people.*
▶ take, accommodate, have room for, have space for, contain
8 *The sect holds that killing animals is a sin.*
▶ believe, consider, maintain, contend, think, take the view
9 *I hope the good weather will hold.*
▶ continue, last, carry on, persist, endure

hold back
1 *Joe held back his anger.*
▶ suppress, control, restrain, curb, check, keep back, hold in
AN OPPOSITE IS release
2 *The lack of information held us back.*
▶ hinder, hamper, inhibit, impede, thwart, restrain
AN OPPOSITE IS help
3 *There is no need to hold back if you have things to say.*
▶ hesitate, pause, desist, shrink
AN OPPOSITE IS proceed

hold forth *Ivor was holding forth about his adventures.*
▶ discourse, declaim, speak at length, spout, rant

hold off
1 *The rain held off until lunch time.*
▶ stay away, desist
2 *He held the attackers off as long as he could.*
▶ resist, fend off, ward off, stave off, repel, rebuff

hold out
1 *Supplies will not hold out much longer.*
▶ last, remain, continue
AN OPPOSITE IS run out
2 *The garrison held out for a whole month.*
▶ resist, persevere, stand fast, hang on
OPPOSITES ARE give in, yield

hold up
1 *The bridge is held up by concrete columns.*
▶ support, bear, shore up, carry, raise

h

2 *Work on the roof was held up by bad weather.*
▶ delay, detain, hinder, impede
AN OPPOSITE IS facilitate

hold with *We do not hold with violence.*
▶ approve of, agree with, support, condone, countenance, subscribe to
AN OPPOSITE IS disapprove of

hold NOUN

1 *She released her hold on the handle.*
▶ grip, grasp, clutch
2 *Tim had some kind of hold over them.*
▶ influence, power, control, sway, (*more informal*) clout

holder NOUN

1 *She put the knife back in its holder.*
▶ case, container, receptacle, casing, cover, sheath, stand, rest
2 *holders of EU passports*
▶ bearer, possessor, owner

hold-up NOUN

1 *There was a hold-up at the bank.*
▶ robbery, raid, burglary
2 *We faced several hold-ups on the motorway.*
▶ delay, wait, hitch, setback, stoppage

hole NOUN

1 *The work gang dug a large hole in the road.*
▶ opening, orifice, trench, ditch
2 *There were holes in the plaster caused by damp.*
▶ gap, split, cavity, crack, fissure, pit, puncture, hollow, depression, tear
3 *The animal crawled out of its hole.*
▶ burrow, lair, retreat
4 *We were out of money and in a bit of a hole.*
▶ predicament, mess, difficulty, tight corner, quandary, plight, crisis, emergency

holiday NOUN

1 *Her doctor told her she needed a holiday.*
▶ vacation, break, rest, time off, leave
2 *Monday is a public holiday.*
▶ bank holiday, festival, feast day

holiness NOUN

Her holiness affected everyone who saw her.
▶ sanctity, devoutness, spirituality, piety, saintliness, godliness, righteousness

hollow ADJECTIVE

1 *a hollow space*
▶ empty, concave, sunken, deep, depressed
AN OPPOSITE IS solid
2 *a hollow laugh*
▶ dull, low, flat, muffled, muted
3 *a hollow promise*
▶ insincere, artificial, false, empty, deceptive
AN OPPOSITE IS sincere
4 *a hollow victory*
▶ worthless, futile, vain, meaningless, pointless, pyrrhic
AN OPPOSITE IS worthwhile

hollow NOUN

an ancient theatre built in the hollow of a hillside
▶ depression, cavity, dimple, dip, crater, hole, indentation, bowl, concavity, dent, dint, dish

hollow VERB

hollow out *Engineers hollowed out a tunnel.*
▶ dig out, excavate, gouge out, burrow, scoop

holy ADJECTIVE

1 *holy men and women*
▶ saintly, godly, pious, devout, religious, spiritual, virtuous, pure
2 *a holy place*
▶ sacred, hallowed, consecrated, sanctified, revered, venerated

homage NOUN

an act of homage to the king
▶ respect, recognition, acknowledgement, devotion, tribute, honour, admiration, esteem, deference, veneration

pay homage to *He paid homage to all who had sacrificed their lives in the war.*
▶ honour, praise, salute, acclaim, applaud

home NOUN

1 *People were forced to leave their homes.*
▶ house, dwelling, place of residence, address, accommodation
RELATED ADJECTIVE domestic
2 *They had travelled thousands of miles from home.*
▶ native land, homeland, birthplace, motherland, fatherland
3 *He refused to go into a home.*
▶ institution, nursing home, residential home, hospice, shelter

homeless ADJECTIVE

increasing numbers of homeless people
▶ destitute, vagrant, down-and-out, outcast, unhoused, wandering, evicted, forsaken, abandoned, itinerant, nomadic

homely ADJECTIVE

The hotel offers a warm welcome and a homely atmosphere.
▶ friendly, informal, relaxed, easygoing, familiar, intimate, congenial, comfortable, cosy, natural, simple, unaffected, unpretentious
AN OPPOSITE IS formal

homosexual ADJECTIVE

homosexual couples
▶ gay, queer, (*female*) lesbian
AN OPPOSITE IS heterosexual

honest ADJECTIVE

1 *He's a fair and honest man.*
▶ upright, honourable, virtuous, law-abiding, high-minded, scrupulous, moral, decent, principled, upstanding
AN OPPOSITE IS dishonest
2 *business practices that are barely honest*
▶ legal, lawful, ethical, legitimate, above-board, (*more informal*) on the level
AN OPPOSITE IS dishonest

3 *It was an honest mistake.*
▶ genuine, real, authentic, legitimate
AN OPPOSITE IS deliberate

4 *Let us have your honest opinion. I've tried to be perfectly honest with you.*
▶ sincere, objective, candid, direct, open, frank, truthful, impartial, unbiased, unprejudiced, balanced
OPPOSITES ARE insincere, untruthful, biased

honestly ADVERB
1 *He said he had come by the money honestly.*
▶ fairly, legally, lawfully, legitimately, honourably
2 *She could honestly say she had had nothing to do with the incident.*
▶ frankly, sincerely, truthfully, genuinely

honesty NOUN
1 *She demanded complete honesty from her staff.*
▶ truthfulness, trustworthiness, integrity, goodness, morality, honour, uprightness, veracity, fairness, probity, rectitude, reliability, scrupulousness
AN OPPOSITE IS dishonesty

2 *They were encouraged to speak with complete honesty.*
▶ sincerity, candour, directness, frankness, straightforwardness, bluntness, outspokenness, plainness
AN OPPOSITE IS insincerity

honour NOUN
1 *He defended the President, calling him a man of honour.*
▶ honesty, integrity, morality, principle, distinction, decency, probity
2 *She received many honours from the film industry.*
▶ award, accolade, tribute, distinction, commendation, acknowledgement, recognition
3 *I appreciate the honour of speaking at this assembly.*
▶ privilege, distinction, cachet, kudos
4 *They were received with honour by the king.*
▶ praise, acclaim, homage, admiration, adulation

honour VERB
1 *a grand parade to honour the distinguished visitors*
▶ praise, applaud, acclaim, salute, celebrate, commend, pay homage to
2 *They intend to honour their commitment to the peace process.*
▶ fulfil, respect, observe, carry out, keep, discharge

honourable ADJECTIVE
1 *No one doubted that her motives were entirely honourable. honourable people who were fighting for the common good*
▶ honest, sincere, reputable, noble, worthy, just, straight, trustworthy, principled, virtuous, upright, proper
2 *a respected politician who has done honourable service in the Treasury*
▶ distinguished, illustrious, eminent, great

hoodwink VERB
The man had hoodwinked him into parting with a large sum of money.
▶ deceive, trick, dupe, cheat, swindle, fool, mislead, delude, (*more informal*) take in

hook NOUN
1 *He hung his coat on one of the hooks.*
▶ peg, nail
2 *a dress fastened at the back with a hook and eye*
▶ fastener, fastening, clasp, clip, hasp
3 *a fishing hook*
▶ barb, snare

hook VERB
1 *David hooked a 64 pound carp.*
▶ catch, take, land, net, bag
2 *He hooked a trailer to the car.*
▶ hitch, fasten, attach, couple, connect

hooligan NOUN
hooligans messing around in the dodgems
▶ troublemaker, hoodlum, lout, ruffian, vandal, thug, bully, delinquent, tough, rough, tearaway, (*more informal*) yob

hoop NOUN
a hoop of metal
▶ band, loop, ring, round, circle, circlet, girdle

hoot VERB
1 *An owl hooted.*
▶ screech, call, tu-whit tu-whoo
2 *The driver became impatient and hooted.*
▶ beep, toot, honk, sound the horn
3 *The audience hooted in derision.*
▶ shout, shriek, yell, jeer, call out

hoot NOUN
1 *the hoot of an owl*
▶ screech, call, tu-whit tu-whoo
2 *hoots of laughter*
▶ shriek, shout, scream, yell, jeer

hop VERB
He hopped along beside her. She hopped on a bus and went home.
▶ jump, leap, skip, spring, trip, bound, dance, flit, limp, prance, caper

hop NOUN
1 *With one hop he was free.*
▶ jump, leap, skip, spring, bound
2 *a short hop across the Channel*
▶ trip, journey, jaunt, ride, distance

hope VERB
1 *I hope to answer all your questions.*
▶ aim, intend, plan, have it in mind, aspire
2 **hope for** *We are hoping for a quick response.*
▶ expect, look for, wish for, want
USAGE It is better to avoid *anticipate* in this sense, because it has other meanings.

hope NOUN
1 *She has the hope of being in the national team.*
▶ ambition, aspiration, expectation, dream, desire, wish

a b c d e f g h i j k l m n o p q r s t u v w x y z

2 *There's some hope of a better future.*
▶ prospect, expectation, likelihood, optimism, assumption

hopeful ADJECTIVE

1 *We are still hopeful about avoiding a conflict.*
▶ optimistic, confident, positive, expectant, sanguine
AN OPPOSITE IS pessimistic

2 *hopeful signs of an economic recovery*
▶ promising, encouraging, favourable, heartening, reassuring, propitious, auspicious, cheering
AN OPPOSITE IS discouraging

hopefully ADVERB

1 *'Are we going back?' she asked hopefully.*
▶ expectantly, optimistically, confidently, with hope
AN OPPOSITE IS pessimistically

2 *Hopefully the work will be completed next week.*
▶ all being well, most likely, with luck, conceivably, probably

hopeless ADJECTIVE

1 *He looked at her in hopeless bewilderment.*
▶ despairing, desperate, dejected, downhearted, downcast, wretched, pessimistic

2 *The doctors regarded his case as hopeless.*
▶ impossible, incurable, irremediable, beyond hope, beyond recovery, lost, unattainable

3 *The situation seemed hopeless, now that the food had run out.*
▶ desperate, critical, serious, dire, impossible, beyond hope, useless, futile

4 *He is hopeless at board games.*
▶ incompetent, ineffective, ineffectual, poor, inept, (*more informal*) pathetic, (*more informal*) useless, (*more informal*) rubbish

horde NOUN

A horde of journalists waited outside the house.
▶ crowd, throng, pack, mob, swarm, band, gang, group

horizon NOUN

A ship was visible on the horizon
▶ skyline, vista, range of view

horrible, horrid ADJECTIVE

1 *a horrible accident on the bypass*
▶ dreadful, horrific, horrifying, horrendous, frightful, fearful, terrible, ghastly, hideous, sickening

2 *Saturday was a wet, horrible day. The smell was horrid.*
▶ unpleasant, nasty, disagreeable, awful, beastly, dreadful, ghastly, revolting, terrible
OPPOSITES ARE pleasant, agreeable

3 *Nora was a horrible person. The teachers were horrid to him.*
▶ nasty, disagreeable, odious, objectionable, loathsome, hateful, offensive
OPPOSITES ARE nice, kind

horrific ADJECTIVE

He died from horrific head injuries.
▶ dreadful, appalling, horrific, horrifying, horrendous, frightful, fearful, terrible, hideous, ghastly, sickening

horrified ADJECTIVE

Horrified residents escaped the flames over garden fences.
▶ frightened, horror-stricken, horror-struck, shocked, appalled, disgusted, sickened, stunned

horrify VERB

1 *He wrote stories that horrified his readers.*
▶ terrify, frighten, scare, alarm, petrify, terrorize

2 *The news would have horrified her.*
▶ shock, appal, outrage, scandalize, offend, sicken, disgust, revolt, nauseate, unnerve, alarm
OPPOSITES ARE please, delight

horror NOUN

1 *People screamed in horror.*
▶ terror, fear, fright, alarm

2 *Public opinion reacted with horror.*
▶ shock, outrage, disgust, revulsion, repugnance, consternation
AN OPPOSITE IS delight

3 *Newspaper reports described the full horror of the attack.*
▶ ghastliness, awfulness, frightfulness, hideousness, savagery, barbarity

horse NOUN

a woman on a horse
▶ (*for riding*) mount, (*small breed*) pony, (*adult male*) stallion, (*young male*) colt, (*large and strong*) cob, (*adult female*) mare, (*young female*) filly, (*new-born horse*) foal
RELATED ADJECTIVES equestrian, equine

hospitable ADJECTIVE

a kind, hospitable family
▶ friendly, sociable, welcoming, congenial, cordial, convivial, amicable, generous, gracious, receptive
OPPOSITES ARE inhospitable, unfriendly

hospital NOUN

Joe was lying in a bed in the hospital.
▶ infirmary, clinic, nursing home, sanatorium, medical institution, convalescent home, hospice

hospitality NOUN

1 *We needed hospitality for the night.*
▶ accommodation, catering, entertainment

2 *Thank you for your hospitality.*
▶ kindness, friendliness, sociability, welcome, conviviality, warm reception

host NOUN

1 *A host of people headed for the town.*
▶ crowd, throng, band, horde, swarm, group

2 *The host of the restaurant welcomed his guests.*
▶ proprietor, landlord

3 *the host of a television programme*
▶ presenter, compère, anchorman, anchorwoman, announcer, link person

hostage NOUN

The hijackers released some of the hostages.
► captive, prisoner, detainee

hostel NOUN

We could stay at a hostel near the city.
► boarding house, guest house

hostile ADJECTIVE

1 *a hostile crowd   a hostile attack*
► aggressive, antagonistic, belligerent, confrontational, bellicose, pugnacious, angry, militant, unfriendly, malevolent, ill-disposed, warlike
AN OPPOSITE IS friendly

2 *a hostile climate*
► harsh, unfavourable, adverse, inhospitable, bad, contrary, unpropitious
AN OPPOSITE IS favourable

3 hostile to *They are hostile to the idea.*
► opposed to, averse to, unsympathetic to, antagonistic to, against

hostility NOUN

1 *They reacted with hostility.*
► antagonism, enmity, animosity, opposition, malice, hatred, ill-will
AN OPPOSITE IS friendship

2 *their hostility to our suggestion*
► opposition, antipathy, disapproval (of), aversion, antagonism

hot ADJECTIVE

1 *hot weather*
► warm, balmy, summery, boiling, blazing, roasting, scorching, sweltering, sultry
OPPOSITES ARE cold, chilly

2 *What we need is a hot meal.*
► cooked, heated, piping, sizzling

3 *a hot dish with peppers*
► spicy, peppery, piquant, sharp, pungent
AN OPPOSITE IS mild

4 *a hot temper*
► fierce, angry, raging, intense, violent, passionate

hotchpotch NOUN

a hotchpotch of different plants and shrubs.
► mixture, assortment, jumble, miscellany, ragbag, mishmash, confusion, mess

hotel NOUN

We stayed in a hotel by the river.
► guest house, boarding house, inn, pension, motel

hound VERB

The reporters went on hounding her.
► harass, pursue, harry, hassle, pester, persecute, trouble

house NOUN

1 *a row of terraced houses*
► home, dwelling, abode, residence

2 *the house of Stuart*
► dynasty, clan, family, tribe

house VERB

The cabins housed twenty people.
► accommodate, provide room for, lodge, quarter, shelter, take in, billet, board, (*more informal*) put up

household NOUN

a large household with lots of children
► family, home, ménage, establishment, (*more informal*) set-up

housing NOUN

an acute need for better housing
► accommodation, houses, homes, habitation, shelter

hovel NOUN

The little cottage was not much better than a hovel.
► shack, shanty, shed, slum, hut

hover VERB

1 *A police helicopter hovered above the crowd.*
► float, hang, flutter, drift, fly

2 *He hovered outside the room waiting to be called in.*
► linger, dally, pause, wait about, waver, loiter, hesitate, (*informal*) hang about

howl VERB

A dog howled in the distance.
► yowl, bay, cry

howl NOUN

howls of laughter
► shriek, hoot, roar, gale, scream, yell

hub NOUN

1 *He gripped the hub of the rear wheel.*
► centre, middle, pivot, axis

2 *The foyer will be the hub of activity in this part of the building.*
► focus, focal point, heart, pivot, nucleus

hubbub NOUN

Seb listened to the growing hubbub.
► commotion, noise, din, disturbance, uproar, racket, tumult, hullabaloo, rumpus

huddle VERB

1 *They huddled together in twos and threes.*
► crowd, gather, cluster, squeeze, pack, throng, flock, herd, pile, press
AN OPPOSITE IS scatter

2 *He huddled under the duvet.*
► cuddle, curl up, nestle, snuggle

huddle NOUN

There was a huddle of people round the enquiry desk.
► crowd, throng, crush, knot, flock, cluster

hue NOUN

1 *gloss paint in a range of hues*
► colour, shade, tone, tint, tinge

2 *people of all political hues*
► complexion, kind, type, nature, character

huff NOUN

He went off in a huff.
► sulk, fit of pique, rage, bad mood

h

huffy ADJECTIVE

They didn't have an answer and became huffy when we asked.
▶ irritable, irritated, annoyed, unfriendly, grumpy, prickly, piqued, testy, petulant
AN OPPOSITE IS friendly

hug VERB

Mary was kissed and hugged by her workmates.
▶ embrace, clasp, cuddle, squeeze, cling to, enfold, fold in your arms, hold close, nurse, snuggle against

hug NOUN

They met with tears and hugs.
▶ embrace, clasp, cuddle, squeeze

huge ADJECTIVE

a huge building   a huge tax increase
▶ enormous, gigantic, immense, massive, colossal, vast, large, big, great, giant, (*more informal*) whopping, (*more informal*) ginormous
AN OPPOSITE IS tiny

hulk NOUN

the hulk of an old ship
▶ wreck, shell, ruin, body, carcass, frame, hull

hulking ADJECTIVE

A hulking figure came through the door.
▶ huge, large, bulky, clumsy, cumbersome, awkward, heavy, ungainly, unwieldy
OPPOSITES ARE small, delicate

hum VERB

The engine was still humming.
▶ purr, whirr, drone, murmur, throb, vibrate

human ADJECTIVE

1 *the human race*
▶ anthropoid
2 *They are only human and make mistakes.*
▶ mortal, fallible, imperfect, weak
3 *a very human reaction to the problem*
▶ compassionate, humane, kind, considerate, understanding, sympathetic, merciful, philanthropic
AN OPPOSITE IS inhuman

human beings
▶ men and women, humankind, humanity, mortals, people, folk

humane ADJECTIVE

a humane way to control the fox population
▶ kind, compassionate, considerate, understanding, sympathetic, merciful

humanity NOUN

1 *If they have a shred of humanity in them they will hand over the suspects.*
▶ compassion, understanding, sensitivity, fellow feeling, sympathy, tolerance
2 *a decision that could affect the whole of humanity*
▶ humankind, the human race, mankind, mortals, people

humble ADJECTIVE

1 *He acted in a humble and contrite manner.*
▶ meek, self-effacing, unassuming, deferential, respectful, submissive
AN OPPOSITE IS proud
2 *I live in a humble house in the suburbs.*
▶ modest, simple, plain, ordinary, unpretentious, unostentatious
OPPOSITES ARE grand, pretentious
3 *She comes from a humble background.*
▶ lowly, undistinguished, poor, common, ordinary
OPPOSITES ARE distinguished, noble

humdrum ADJECTIVE

Most of the work is repetitive and humdrum.
▶ tedious, dull, mundane, dreary, boring, routine, monotonous, ordinary, banal

humid ADJECTIVE

a hot and humid day
▶ muggy, clammy, sultry, sticky, damp, dank, moist, steamy, sweaty
AN OPPOSITE IS fresh

humiliate VERB

He liked to humiliate them with constant reminders of their mistakes.
▶ embarrass, humble, mortify, demean, shame, put to shame

humiliating ADJECTIVE

Rome inflicted a humiliating defeat on its neighbour.
▶ embarrassing, mortifying, ignominious, degrading, demeaning, humbling, chastening, crushing, inglorious, discreditable, dishonourable, shaming, undignified
AN OPPOSITE IS glorious

humiliation NOUN

At immigration he suffered the humiliation of a body search.
▶ embarrassment, indignity, ignominy, mortification, shame, disgrace, degradation, dishonour

humility NOUN

I'm not sure I have the humility to admit my mistakes.
▶ modesty, deference, humbleness, meekness, self-effacement, unpretentiousness, lowliness
AN OPPOSITE IS pride

humorous ADJECTIVE

a love story with humorous episodes
▶ amusing, funny, comic, comical, jocular, hilarious, entertaining

humour NOUN

1 *a conversation spiced with humour*
▶ wit, jocularity, badinage, repartee, jokes, jesting, hilarity, comedy, drollery
2 *in a bad humour*
▶ mood, temper, frame of mind, state of mind, disposition, spirits

humour VERB
She humoured him to keep him happy.
▶ indulge, pander to, gratify, pamper, mollify, cater to, give way to, go along with

hump NOUN
a hump in the road
▶ bump, protuberance, bulge, mound, rise, curve, knob, lump, swelling

hunch NOUN
The theory was no more than a hunch.
▶ feeling, intuition, inkling, guess, impression, suspicion, idea

hunch VERB
He sat in a corner and hunched his shoulders.
▶ arch, curve, bend, hump, shrug, huddle, curl up

hunger NOUN
1 *She had no hunger that day.*
▶ appetite, desire for food
2 *He grew faint with hunger.*
▶ lack of food, malnutrition, starvation, deprivation, famine
3 *a hunger for knowledge*
▶ desire, yearning, longing, craving, appetite, thirst

hungry ADJECTIVE
I was hungry again by 3 o'clock.
▶ in need of food, ravenous, famished, starving, (*more informal*) peckish

hunk NOUN
a hunk of bread
▶ lump, chunk, block, wedge, piece, portion, slab

hunt NOUN
the hunt for clues
▶ search, quest, pursuit (of), chase

hunt VERB
1 *They hunt foxes and deer.*
▶ chase, give chase to, stalk, track, trail, course, pursue
2 *She spent ages hunting for her keys.*
▶ search, look, rummage, scour, root around

hurdle NOUN
1 *He hit the last hurdle and fell.*
▶ fence, jump, barrier, obstacle
2 *There was one more hurdle to overcome before they could claim success.*
▶ obstacle, difficulty, handicap, problem, snag, stumbling block

hurl VERB
She hurled a book at Roger.
▶ throw, fling, toss, cast, pitch, heave

hurly-burly NOUN
the hurly-burly of city life
▶ bustle, hustle, commotion, hubbub, turmoil

hurricane NOUN
a region hit by floods and hurricanes
▶ gale, tornado, storm, typhoon, whirlwind, cyclone

hurried ADJECTIVE
1 *hurried attempts to change the venue.*
▶ hasty, hectic, rushed, speedy, precipitate, swift, rapid
2 *He gave the paper a hurried read.*
▶ brief, cursory, superficial, swift, rapid

hurry VERB
1 *If I don't hurry I'll be late.*
▶ be quick, hurry up, hasten, make speed, move faster, (*more informal*) buck up, (*more informal*) shift, (*more informal*) step on it
AN OPPOSITE IS dawdle
2 *Sarah hurried to the library.*
▶ rush, hasten, dash, speed, chase, hurtle, hustle, move quickly, (*more informal*) belt
OPPOSITES ARE go slowly, amble
3 *She hurried the children into the bathroom.*
▶ hustle, hasten, push on, urge on, drive
AN OPPOSITE IS delay

hurry NOUN
In our hurry we forgot the food.
▶ haste, bustle, confusion, urgency, agitation

hurt VERB
1 *My arm hurts.*
▶ be sore, be painful, ache, throb, sting
2 *Derek hurt his leg.*
▶ injure, wound, maim, bruise, damage, disable
3 *The criticism hurt her deeply.*
▶ upset, distress, offend, grieve

hurt NOUN
1 *She rubbed the hurt on her leg.*
▶ injury, wound, soreness, pain, aching
2 *She loved him in spite of the hurt he had caused her.*
▶ distress, suffering, pain, wrong, sadness, anguish, torment

hurt ADJECTIVE
1 *A hurt animal lay in the road.*
▶ injured, wounded, maimed, bruised, scarred
2 *He felt hurt by the words she had used.*
▶ upset, pained, distressed, wounded

hurtful ADJECTIVE
She forgot all the hurtful remarks and remembered the good times.
▶ upsetting, distressing, unkind, spiteful, mean, cruel, malicious, wounding, painful
OPPOSITES ARE kind, comforting

hurtle VERB
1 *A train was hurtling towards them.*
▶ speed, rush, race, career, charge, dash, fly, tear, chase, shoot
2 *The plane hurtled to the ground.*
▶ plunge, plummet, nosedive, drop

husband NOUN
Their husbands had taken their cars to the rally.
▶ spouse, partner, (*more formal*) consort, (*more informal*) man, (*more informal*) mate, (*more informal*) better half

a b c d e f g h i j k l m n o p q r s t u v w x y z

hush NOUN
A hush fell on the room.
▶ silence, quiet, quietness, calm, stillness, tranquillity
OPPOSITES ARE noise, clamour

hush VERB
She wanted to hush their fears.
▶ calm, soothe, allay, ease, assuage, quieten
hush up *The government is accused of hushing up the dangers.*
▶ conceal, cover up, keep secret, keep quiet, hide, stifle, suppress

hush-hush ADJECTIVE
The news is still rather hush-hush.
▶ secret, confidential, restricted, classified, (*more informal*) under wraps

husk NOUN
There were seed husks scattered over the floor.
▶ shell, case, pod, covering

husky ADJECTIVE
1 *He gave a low husky laugh.*
▶ gruff, throaty, hoarse, croaky
2 *Eyes turned to the big husky guy who came.*
▶ hefty, beefy, burly, brawny, strong, muscular

hustle VERB
The MPs were hustled out of the building.
▶ rush, hasten, bustle, jostle, bundle, force, shove

hut NOUN
a hut in the woods
▶ cabin, shack, shed, shelter, shanty, den, hovel

hybrid NOUN
a hybrid of two species
▶ cross, cross-breed, mixed breed, blend, amalgam, combination, composite, compound, mixture, fusion

hybrid ADJECTIVE
hybrid roses
▶ cross-bred, composite, mixed, compound, mongrel
AN OPPOSITE IS pure-bred

hygiene NOUN
acceptable standards of hygiene
▶ cleanliness, sanitariness, sanitation, health, wholesomeness
RELATED ADJECTIVE sanitary

hygienic ADJECTIVE
Hygienic conditions are essential.
▶ sanitary, clean, germ-free, sterilized, sterile, aseptic, disinfected, healthy, pure, salubrious, unpolluted, wholesome
OPPOSITES ARE unhygienic, insanitary, dirty

hypnotic ADJECTIVE
The music has a hypnotic beat.
▶ mesmeric, mesmerizing, soporific, sleep-inducing, spellbinding, compelling, fascinating, irresistible, magnetic, soothing

hypnotism NOUN
She returned under hypnotism to an earlier part of her life.
▶ hypnosis, (*old use*) mesmerism

hypnotize VERB
She was hypnotized by the sight of the body on the floor.
▶ mesmerize, bewitch, entrance, captivate, enthral, transfix, fascinate, dominate, magnetize, stupefy

hypocrisy NOUN
He wanted to be completely honest and avoid accusations of hypocrisy.
▶ insincerity, double-talk, duplicity, sanctimoniousness, sanctimony, pretence, deceit, deception, cant, falsity, inconsistency, (*more informal*) humbug

hypocritical ADJECTIVE
It would be hypocritical to condemn them for something I'd like to do myself.
▶ insincere, false, inconsistent, sanctimonious, deceptive, (*more informal*) phoney, (*more informal*) two-faced

hypothesis NOUN
a hypothesis about the origin of the universe
▶ theory, thesis, premise, conjecture, proposition, supposition, guess

hypothetical ADJECTIVE
There is a hypothetical risk of damage.
▶ theoretical, speculative, conjectural, notional, putative, imaginary, assumed, supposed, suppositional, unreal

hysteria NOUN
He was overexcited, on the verge of hysteria.
▶ frenzy, hysterics, panic, mania, madness
OPPOSITES ARE composure, calmness

hysterical ADJECTIVE
1 *The fans were screaming and hysterical.*
▶ overwrought, frenzied, uncontrollable, uncontrolled, crazed, berserk, delirious, demented, frantic, wild, raving, distraught
2 (*informal*) *A dog set off the security alarm with hysterical results.*
▶ hilarious, crazy, comical, funny, amusing, uproarious, (*informal*) killing, (*informal*) side-splitting

Ii

icy ADJECTIVE
1 *An icy blast of air hit Dad full in the face.*
▶ freezing, biting, bitter, frosty, arctic, cold
2 *Few people had braved the icy streets.*
▶ frozen, frozen over, ice-covered, glacial, glassy, slippery, (*more informal*) slippy
3 *She looked at him with an icy stare.*
▶ unfriendly, hostile, cold, frosty, stony

idea NOUN
1 *The idea of an afterlife appeals to him.*
► concept, notion, conception, image, perception, hypothesis
2 *Our idea is to go abroad this year.*
► plan, intention, scheme, object, objective, aim, goal, proposal, project
3 *I have other ideas on that subject.*
► view, thought, opinion, viewpoint, theory, feeling
4 *Did you have an idea this might happen?*
► suspicion, feeling, fancy, inkling, impression, notion
5 *We need some idea of the cost.*
► estimate, estimation, approximation, guess, (*more informal*) guesstimate

ideal ADJECTIVE
1 *The conditions for skiing were ideal.*
► perfect, excellent, optimum, exemplary, suitable, best, classic, faultless, model
2 *Such things are only possible in an ideal world.*
► Utopian, visionary, unattainable, hypothetical, imaginary, unreal, impractical

ideal NOUN
1 *an ideal to aim at*
► model, example, pattern, standard, yardstick, epitome, paradigm, archetype
2 *a person of high ideals*
► principle, standard, value, belief, conviction

idealistic ADJECTIVE
an idealistic picture of family life
► unrealistic, perfectionist, utopian, visionary, over-optimistic, romantic, quixotic, starry-eyed
AN OPPOSITE IS realistic

identical ADJECTIVE
1 *The two houses looked identical.*
► alike, similar, the same, indistinguishable
2 *Successive tests produced identical results.*
► the same, corresponding, matching, equal, equivalent

identification NOUN
1 *The Bank will need to see your identification.*
► ID, proof of identity, identity card, papers, credentials, documents
2 *An early identification of problems is important.*
► recognition, detection, diagnosis, discovery, classification, establishment
3 *their identification with independence struggles in Africa*
► association, sympathy, empathy, involvement, rapport, fellow feeling

identify VERB
1 *The suspect was identified by three witnesses.*
► recognize, pick out, single out, name
2 *The report identifies three areas for action.*
► establish, determine, recognize, diagnose, detect, discover, distinguish, pinpoint, spot
3 **identify with** *Readers can easily identify with the chief character in the story.*
► empathize with, relate to, feel for, sympathize with, (*informal*) put yourself in the shoes of

identity NOUN
1 (*informal*) *There was nothing to show the owner's identity.*
► name, ID
2 *a case of mistaken identity*
► identification, recognition, picking out
3 *She might lose her identity if she married him.*
► individuality, character, personality, selfhood, uniqueness, distinctiveness, singularity

idiom NOUN
1 *He uses 'spiffing' and other outdated idioms.*
► expression, phrase, turn of phrase, choice of words, manner of speaking, colloquialism, usage
2 *the poet's idiom*
► language, mode of expression, style, usage, phraseology

idiomatic ADJECTIVE
idiomatic expressions
► colloquial, natural, well-phrased

idiosyncrasy NOUN
One of his idiosyncrasies is sleeping in his clothes.
► oddity, peculiarity, eccentricity, quirk, whim, trait, habit, mannerism

idiosyncratic ADJECTIVE
The grammar was faulty and the spelling idiosyncratic.
► odd, peculiar, eccentric, distinctive, unconventional, quirky, individual, personal, singular
AN OPPOSITE IS common

idiot NOUN
The mistake made him feel an idiot.
► fool, ass, dolt, imbecile, simpleton, blockhead, ignoramus, dunderhead, dunce, halfwit, moron, cretin, (*more informal*) dope, (*more informal*) dimwit, (*more informal*) nitwit, (*more informal*) chump, (*more informal*) ninny

idiotic ADJECTIVE
How idiotic it seemed for a man of his age to fall in love.
► stupid, silly, foolish, absurd, senseless, nonsensical, (*more informal*) daft
AN OPPOSITE IS sensible

idle ADJECTIVE
1 *The chief problem with Jack was that he was idle.*
► lazy, indolent, slothful, work-shy
2 *The computers had been idle all day.*
► out of use, unused, dormant, out of service, inoperative
3 *She refused to indulge in idle speculation*
► futile, pointless, aimless, vain, meaningless, trivial, frivolous, fatuous

idle VERB
1 *Jane idled across the park.*
► saunter, amble, dawdle, wander
2 *Richard had finished his work and idled until it was time to go home.*
► do nothing, laze, take it easy, kill time, loaf, slack

3 *A car was idling in the driveway.*
► tick over

idle away *We idled away an hour or two.*
► fritter away, while away, pass, spend

idol NOUN
1 *a temple in which idols were worshipped*
► image, icon, statue, deity, god
2 *the newest pop idols*
► star, superstar, icon, hero, heroine, favourite

idolize VERB
The man she had once idolized was now a racist.
► hero-worship, worship, revere, admire, look up to, adulate, adore, venerate
AN OPPOSITE IS vilify

idyllic ADJECTIVE
They spent an idyllic week in Paris.
► blissful, delightful, heavenly, perfect, lovely, peaceful, happy, unspoiled
AN OPPOSITE IS desolate

ignite VERB
1 *The fuel will not ignite.*
► fire, burn, catch fire, light
2 *Resentment can ignite disobedience or even rioting.*
► cause, kindle, trigger, spark, set off, whip up

ignoble ADJECTIVE
They were accused of starting a war for ignoble motives.
► dishonourable, unworthy, base, shameful, despicable, disgraceful, vile
AN OPPOSITE IS noble

ignominious ADJECTIVE
an ignominious defeat
► humiliating, undignified, mortifying, degrading, inglorious, shameful, disgraceful

ignorance NOUN
1 *She seemed amused by Rashid's obvious ignorance of the subject.*
► unawareness, unfamiliarity (with), incomprehension, lack of knowledge, inexperience
OPPOSITES ARE knowledge, familiarity (with)
2 *They could not hide their ignorance.*
► foolishness, unintelligence, naivety, stupidity

ignorant ADJECTIVE
1 *He called his wife an ignorant peasant.*
► uneducated, illiterate, unread, unschooled, untaught, untutored, simple, stupid
2 *We are hopelessly ignorant of events in this part of the world.*
► unaware, uninformed (about), unenlightened (about), ill-informed, oblivious, (more informal) clueless (about)

ignore VERB
1 *The complaints are too serious to ignore.*
► disregard, overlook, take no notice of, neglect, pass over, set aside
2 *Helen had ignored him, out of spite.*
► snub, spurn, shun, give the cold shoulder to

ill ADJECTIVE
1 *Jenny began to feel ill in the taxi home.*
► sick, unwell, poorly, out of sorts, off colour, indisposed, ailing, peaky, queasy, nauseous
2 *She suffered no ill effects from her night out.*
► harmful, damaging, adverse

illegal ADJECTIVE
Under-age drinking is illegal.
► unlawful, prohibited, criminal, wrong, forbidden, barred
OPPOSITES ARE legal, lawful, permitted

illegible ADJECTIVE
The signature was illegible.
► unreadable, indecipherable, unintelligible, indistinct, obscure, unclear
OPPOSITES ARE legible, readable

illegitimate ADJECTIVE
1 *There were three illegitimate children from an earlier affair.*
► natural, (old use) bastard
2 *Support from the Church was propping up an illegitimate regime.*
► illegal, unlawful, illicit, spurious

illicit ADJECTIVE
trade in illicit drugs
► illegal, unlawful, prohibited, proscribed, unauthorized

illiterate ADJECTIVE
Though not as good a singer as her sister, she was by no means musically illiterate.
► uneducated, ignorant, backward, untaught, untrained, unlearned, unschooled
AN OPPOSITE IS literate

illness NOUN
The doctors were unsure of the exact nature of the illness.
► disease, disorder, sickness, infirmity, complaint, indisposition, ailment, malady, affliction

illogical ADJECTIVE
The conclusion, however illogical it seems, was correct.
► irrational, unreasonable, fallacious, invalid, unsound, absurd, inconsequential, inconsistent, senseless
AN OPPOSITE IS logical

ill-treat VERB
Their father had ill-treated them.
► maltreat, mistreat, abuse, misuse, harm, injure, (more informal) knock about

illuminate VERB
1 *Blazing torches illuminated the path.*
► light, light up, brighten, floodlight, make brighter, shine on
2 *a series of articles illuminating current events*
► clarify, elucidate, throw or shed light on, illustrate, clear up, enlighten, explain

illumination NOUN
The full moon provided some illumination.
► light, lighting, radiance, brightness

illusion NOUN
1 *an illusion created by mirrors*
▶ hallucination, apparition, mirage, deception, delusion, fantasy, figment of the imagination, trick
2 *We have no illusions about the difficulty of the task.*
▶ delusion, misapprehension, misconception, fantasy

illusory ADJECTIVE
These signs of progress may be illusory.
▶ deceptive, misleading, delusive, deluding, false, illusive, imaginary, unreal, sham
OPPOSITES ARE real, genuine

illustrate VERB
1 *The book is illustrated with photographs and drawings.*
▶ decorate, adorn, embellish
2 *A few examples will illustrate the argument.*
▶ clarify, elucidate, throw or shed light on, illuminate, clear up, enlighten, explain

illustration NOUN
1 *a children's book with beautiful illustrations*
▶ picture, drawing, plate, sketch, photograph, figure, depiction
2 *a good illustration of the difficulties involved*
▶ example, instance, specimen, demonstration, case

illustrious ADJECTIVE
an illustrious naval commander
▶ distinguished, eminent, famous, prominent, well known, celebrated, acclaimed, renowned, famed, notable, noteworthy, esteemed, respected, honoured, outstanding

image NOUN
1 *There were images of the saints along the church walls.*
▶ picture, portrait, representation, likeness, icon, effigy, figure
2 *The image on the screen was a little fuzzy.*
▶ picture, reproduction
3 *The image the company gives is one of ruthless profiteering.*
▶ impression, perception, conception, idea, notion

imaginable ADJECTIVE
It was the worst outcome imaginable.
▶ conceivable, thinkable, possible
OPPOSITES ARE unimaginable, inconceivable

imaginary ADJECTIVE
a story set in an imaginary country
▶ imagined, fictitious, fictional, invented, made-up, make-believe, fanciful, unreal, non-existent, hypothetical, mythical, fabulous
OPPOSITES ARE real, actual

imagination NOUN
The writing shows a great deal of imagination.
▶ creativity, inventiveness, originality, inspiration, vision, ingenuity, insight, sensitivity, resourcefulness, artistry, cleverness, fancy, thought

imaginative ADJECTIVE
an imaginative dramatization for television
▶ creative, inventive, original, inspired, ingenious, resourceful, enterprising, fanciful, clever
AN OPPOSITE IS unimaginative

imagine VERB
1 *Can you imagine life on a desert island?*
▶ visualize, envisage, picture, conceive, conceptualize
2 *I imagine you'd like us to pay you now.*
▶ suppose, assume, presume, expect, take it

imbecile NOUN
I'd have to be an imbecile to do such a thing.
▶ fool, idiot, ass, simpleton, blockhead, dunderhead, halfwit, moron, cretin

imitate VERB
1 *June liked to imitate her mother's social life.*
▶ copy, emulate, follow, model yourself on, echo
2 *He was good at imitating politicians.*
▶ mimic, impersonate, do an impression of, parody, caricature, send up, spoof

imitation NOUN
1 *a good imitation of the human voice*
▶ impersonation, impression, parody, travesty
2 *The stolen jewels turned out to be imitations.*
▶ copy, reproduction, replica, duplicate, fake, counterfeit

imitation ADJECTIVE
The weapon was an imitation firearm.
▶ fake, artificial, simulated, sham, counterfeit, dummy, mock, model
OPPOSITES ARE real, genuine

imitative ADJECTIVE
a painting done in an imitative style
▶ derivative, unoriginal, conventional, copied, plagiarized, unimaginative
AN OPPOSITE IS original

immaculate ADJECTIVE
She wore an immaculate blue suit.
▶ perfect, spotless, pristine, impeccable

immature ADJECTIVE
an immature young man behaving in a silly way
▶ childish, babyish, inexperienced, callow

immediate ADJECTIVE
1 *We need to take immediate action*
▶ instant, instantaneous, prompt, urgent, speedy, swift, quick, rapid, direct, pressing, top-priority
OPPOSITES ARE delayed, low- priority
2 *our immediate neighbours*
▶ nearest, closest, close, near, adjacent, next
AN OPPOSITE IS remote

immediately ADVERB
1 *I went back to London immediately.*
▶ straight away, at once, directly, forthwith, instantly, promptly, right away, unhesitatingly
2 *The wall has a damp patch immediately below the window.*
▶ directly, exactly, precisely, squarely, dead, close

immense ADJECTIVE
a cathedral with two immense towers
▶ huge, great, enormous, gigantic, massive, colossal, vast, giant, (*more informal*) whopping, (*more informal*) ginormous
AN OPPOSITE IS tiny

immerse VERB
You need to immerse your hair in warm water.
▶ plunge, submerge, submerse, bathe, dip, dunk, drench, douse, duck, lower

immersed ADJECTIVE
I was immersed in my work.
▶ absorbed, engrossed, preoccupied (by), occupied (by), busy (with), involved, wrapped up, interested, engaged

immigrant NOUN
a large number of Spanish-speaking immigrants
▶ incomer, settler, newcomer
AN OPPOSITE IS emigrant

imminent ADJECTIVE
An invasion of Crete seemed imminent.
▶ close, near, at hand, in the offing, in the air, impending, threatening, about to happen, approaching, looming, coming, foreseeable

immobilize VERB
The authorities will immobilize illegally parked vehicles.
▶ put out of action, make immobile, make inoperative, deactivate, disable, clamp

immoral ADJECTIVE
immoral behaviour
▶ wrong, unethical, morally wrong, wrongful, disreputable, degenerate, sinful, wicked, unscrupulous, unprincipled, evil, bad
AN OPPOSITE IS moral

immortal ADJECTIVE
She might place her immortal soul in deadly peril.
▶ eternal, undying, everlasting, ageless, timeless, deathless, endless, perpetual, unchanging
AN OPPOSITE IS mortal

immortality NOUN
the gods' immortality
▶ eternal life, endless life, agelessness, permanence, timelessness

immune ADJECTIVE
immune to the disease immune from prosecution
▶ safe (from), free (from), resistant, invulnerable, exempt (from), protected (from), unaffected (by)

immunity NOUN
1 *immunity to malaria*
▶ resistance, resilience, protection (from)
2 *immunity from prosecution*
▶ exemption, freedom, impunity, dispensation, protection

impact NOUN
1 *She suffered a broken ankle in the impact.*
▶ crash, collision, smash, clash, blow, jolt, bump, bang, knock

2 *High street technology is having a huge impact on modern life.*
▶ effect, influence, impression, repercussions, consequences (for)

impair VERB
An illness has impaired his hearing.
▶ damage, injure, weaken, harm, diminish

impartial ADJECTIVE
Counsellors are on hand to give you free and impartial advice.
▶ objective, unbiased, disinterested, dispassionate, balanced, detached, neutral, non-partisan, open-minded, equitable, even-handed, fair, fair-minded, just, unprejudiced
AN OPPOSITE IS biased

impatience NOUN
1 *There was a tremor of impatience in her voice.*
▶ irritability, agitation, shortness, intolerance, brusqueness, frustration, nervousness
2 *his impatience to start work*
▶ eagerness, keenness, haste

impatient ADJECTIVE
1 *As time passed Michael grew impatient.*
▶ restless, agitated, fretful, irritated, tetchy, testy, anxious, ill at ease, keyed up, jumpy
2 *The army was impatient to engage the enemy.*
▶ anxious, eager, keen, avid

impeccable ADJECTIVE
a young person of impeccable character
▶ perfect, exemplary, flawless, spotless, blameless, model, untarnished, irreproachable

impede VERB
Various problems have impeded progress on the project.
▶ obstruct, hinder, hold up, hamper, interfere with, restrict, inhibit, thwart, check, curb, handicap
AN OPPOSITE IS facilitate

impediment NOUN
1 *Her humble origins were not seen as an impediment to the marriage.*
▶ obstacle, obstruction, barrier, bar, hindrance, handicap, block, check, curb
AN OPPOSITE IS aid
2 *a speech impediment*
▶ handicap, defect, stammer, stutter

impel VERB
Her love for Gerry impelled her to stand by him.
▶ force, compel, oblige, constrain, motivate, inspire, urge, instigate, propel

impending ADJECTIVE
There were looks of dismay at her impending departure.
▶ imminent, approaching, coming, forthcoming, looming

imperative ADJECTIVE
It is imperative that we find them.
▶ essential, vital, crucial, necessary, obligatory, compulsory, urgent
OPPOSITES ARE unimportant, optional

imperceptible ADJECTIVE
The movement was slow and imperceptible.
▶ indiscernible, undetectable, indistinguishable, unnoticeable, infinitesimal, insignificant, negligible, slight, small, subtle
AN OPPOSITE IS noticeable
USAGE You can also use *inaudible* when you are referring to sounds, and *invisible* when you are referring to sight.

imperfect ADJECTIVE
The goods were imperfect and had to be sent back.
▶ faulty, defective, deficient, flawed, damaged, broken, incomplete, shop-soiled
AN OPPOSITE IS perfect

imperfection NOUN
She handed over her work, hoping they would not notice its many imperfections.
▶ defect, fault, deficiency, shortcoming, weakness, flaw, failing, blemish, inadequacy
AN OPPOSITE IS perfection

imperial ADJECTIVE
1 *The imperial armies moved east.*
▶ royal, regal, sovereign
2 *her imperial manner*
▶ majestic, grand, dignified, imposing, magnificent

imperil VERB
He did not wish to imperil their chances of success.
▶ endanger, harm, risk, jeopardize, threaten, compromise

impersonal ADJECTIVE
His manner was brusque and impersonal.
▶ detached, aloof, distant, formal, unemotional, unfriendly, unsympathetic, businesslike, remote, cold, cool
AN OPPOSITE IS friendly

impersonate VERB
She tried to impersonate the queen.
▶ imitate, mimic, parody, caricature, mock, pose as

impertinence NOUN
They were unclear whether the remark was a joke or a piece of impertinence.
▶ rudeness, cheek, insolence, impudence, effrontery, audacity, impoliteness, discourtesy, disrespect
AN OPPOSITE IS politeness

impertinent ADJECTIVE
A question like that would seem impertinent from anyone else.
▶ rude, impolite, insolent, impudent, disrespectful, audacious, brazen
OPPOSITES ARE respectful, polite

impetuous ADJECTIVE
With hindsight the decision looked impetuous rather than decisive.
▶ impulsive, rash, hasty, reckless, foolhardy
AN OPPOSITE IS cautious

impetus NOUN
1 *Their enthusiasm began to lose impetus.*
▶ momentum, force, power, drive, motivation, stimulus, energy, impulse, incentive, push, spur
2 *A new product would give the sales campaign an added impetus.*
▶ boost, stimulus, inducement, incentive, push, spur

impinge VERB
impinge on *The noise in the next room was impinging on her concentration.*
▶ encroach on, intrude on, affect, interfere with, influence, invade

implacable ADJECTIVE
They voiced their implacable opposition.
▶ relentless, inexorable, remorseless, adamant, unswerving, unrelenting, inflexible, outright, utter

implausible ADJECTIVE
The suggestion seemed implausible.
▶ unconvincing, improbable, unlikely, questionable, unreasonable, doubtful, dubious, far-fetched, incredible, fanciful, suspect, flimsy, weak, feeble
AN OPPOSITE IS plausible

implement NOUN
garden implements
▶ tool, utensil, appliance, device, gadget, instrument, contraption

implement VERB
The measures would be costly to implement.
▶ put into practice, carry out, execute, bring about, accomplish, effect, realize, enforce, fulfil, perform, try out

implicate VERB
The evidence implicated them in several crimes.
▶ involve, embroil, entangle, incriminate, inculpate, associate (with), connect (with)

implication NOUN
1 *He did not like the implication that he had been dishonest.*
▶ suggestion, insinuation, intimation, imputation, innuendo, inference
USAGE Strictly, *inference* means 'a conclusion you draw' rather than 'a conclusion you suggest', so it is better to use one of the other words given here.
2 *They are suspected of implication in the crime.*
▶ involvement, association, connection, entanglement, incrimination

implicit ADJECTIVE
1 *The article makes a number of implicit assumptions.*
▶ implied, indirect, tacit, hinted at, insinuated, unspoken, unstated
AN OPPOSITE IS explicit
2 *an implicit belief in their ability*
▶ absolute, utter, total, wholehearted, complete, unqualified, unreserved, unquestioning

implore VERB
His family implored him to come home.
▶ beg, entreat, urge, appeal to, call on, exhort, (*literary*) beseech

imply VERB
1 *He seemed to imply that we were wrong.*
▶ suggest, hint, insinuate, intimate, indicate
USAGE You will sometimes see *infer* used as a synonym of *imply*, but *infer* properly means 'to draw a conclusion' rather than 'to suggest a conclusion', so it is better to use one of the other words given here.
2 *The traffic measures imply a need for better public transport.*
▶ entail, involve, point to, indicate, suggest, signify, necessitate

impolite ADJECTIVE
It would have been impolite to leave the party so early.
▶ rude, bad-mannered, discourteous, disrespectful, inconsiderate, ungracious

importance NOUN
1 *an event of the greatest importance*
▶ significance, consequence, seriousness, import, substance, gravity, urgency
2 *a person of importance*
▶ power, influence, authority, prominence, status, distinction, eminence

important ADJECTIVE
1 *an important decision*
▶ significant, momentous, crucial, critical, vital, far-reaching, consequential, historic
2 *It is important to get there early.*
▶ crucial, vital, essential
3 *an important person*
▶ powerful, influential, prominent, distinguished, eminent

impose VERB
1 *The library will impose a fine on the late return of books.*
▶ exact, enforce, introduce, fix, inflict, levy, prescribe, set, place
2 **impose on** *They were afraid they might be imposing on us.*
▶ intrude on, presume on, inconvenience, encroach on, obtrude on, force yourself on, take advantage of

imposing ADJECTIVE
an imposing mock-baronial building
▶ grand, stately, impressive, magnificent, majestic, splendid, distinguished, striking, dignified, grandiose
OPPOSITES ARE unimposing, modest

imposition NOUN
1 *the imposition of a windfall tax*
▶ introduction, levying, charging, exacting, enforcing, fixing, setting
2 *Asking for help might seem an imposition.*
▶ intrusion, encroachment, presumption, liberty, burden, encumbrance

impossibility NOUN
They had to admit to the impossibility of the task.
▶ impracticality, unlikelihood, hopelessness
OPPOSITES ARE possibility, feasibility

impossible ADJECTIVE
1 *The tears made speaking impossible.*
▶ impractical, hopeless, inconceivable, unthinkable, out of the question, unachievable
2 *They had succeeded against impossible odds.*
▶ unrealistic, hopeless, overwhelming, insurmountable, implausible, unbelievable, preposterous, ludicrous, unattainable
AN OPPOSITE IS possible

impostor NOUN
The official turned out to be an impostor.
▶ impersonator, masquerader, charlatan, fraud, cheat, hoaxer, trickster, (*more informal*) phoney

impotent ADJECTIVE
They felt impotent against the power pitted against them.
▶ powerless, helpless, ineffectual, weak, useless, feeble, inadequate, incapable, incompetent, ineffective, unable
OPPOSITES ARE powerful, effective

impoverished ADJECTIVE
an impoverished family
▶ poor, poverty-stricken, penniless, destitute, impecunious, insolvent, ruined

impractical ADJECTIVE
an impractical suggestion
▶ unrealistic, unworkable, impossible, unreasonable
AN OPPOSITE IS practical

imprecise ADJECTIVE
an imprecise description
▶ vague, loose, inexact, inaccurate, hazy, woolly, equivocal
OPPOSITES ARE precise, exact

impregnable ADJECTIVE
The enemy were in an impregnable position.
▶ invulnerable, invincible, unassailable, unconquerable, safe, secure, strong, impenetrable
AN OPPOSITE IS vulnerable

impress VERB
1 *This evidence did not impress the jury.*
▶ move, stir, influence, affect, excite, make an impression on, have an impact on, (*more informal*) grab
2 **impress on** *We must impress on Chris what good work he has done.*
▶ emphasize to, bring home to, instil in, inculcate in

impression NOUN
1 *We got the impression they were hiding something.*
▶ feeling, sense, suspicion, conviction, awareness, notion, idea, hunch, inkling
2 *The experience left a good impression on him.*
▶ effect, impact, influence

3 *He had formed a favourable impression of them.*
▶ opinion, view, perception, assessment, estimation, judgement, verdict
4 *She did a good impression of the Queen Mother.*
▶ imitation, impersonation, parody, caricature, (*more informal*) send-up
5 *The mug had left a circular impression in the cloth.*
▶ indentation, dent, hollow, stamp, mark, print, outline

impressive ADJECTIVE
1 *She has made an impressive concert debut.*
▶ striking, accomplished, masterly, first-class, exciting, stirring
AN OPPOSITE IS insignificant
2 *The conference is held in an impressive building near the university.*
▶ magnificent, imposing, splendid, grand, stately, monumental

imprison VERB
The judge imprisoned him for five years.
▶ jail, incarcerate, send to prison, put in prison, detain, lock up, confine, (*more informal*) put away, (*more informal*) send down

imprisonment NOUN
The penalty is life imprisonment.
▶ incarceration, internment, detention, confinement, custody

improbable ADJECTIVE
The excuse was most improbable.
▶ unlikely, implausible, incredible, doubtful, questionable, far-fetched, unbelievable, unconvincing, preposterous
AN OPPOSITE IS probable

impromptu ADJECTIVE
an impromptu talk on famous battles
▶ unrehearsed, improvised, extempore, unscripted, spontaneous, ad-lib
AN OPPOSITE IS rehearsed

improper ADJECTIVE
1 *It would be improper to accept payment.*
▶ wrong , inappropriate, unsuitable, irregular, out of place, unacceptable, unprofessional, incorrect, inopportune, uncalled for, unwarranted
2 *In those days such behaviour would have been thought improper.*
▶ indecent, unseemly, indecorous, unbecoming, unfitting, shocking, vulgar
AN OPPOSITE IS proper

improve VERB
1 *We are always looking for ways to improve the service.*
▶ make better, better, enhance, reform, upgrade, develop
2 *Relations between the employers and unions have improved markedly.*
▶ get better, progress, advance, develop, make headway, rally, (*more informal*) look up
3 *Reduce the dose as soon as the patient begins to improve.*
▶ recover, get better, recuperate, regain strength

4 *They are hoping to improve their offer shortly.*
▶ increase, raise, supplement, enlarge, augment, top up
5 improve on *It will be hard to improve on work of that quality.*
▶ surpass, outdo, do better than, exceed

improvement NOUN
1 *The weather showed a little improvement. an improvement in East-West relations*
▶ recovery, advance, upturn, progress, enhancement, amelioration, development, rectification, betterment, gain, rally, reformation
2 *We have carried out a lot of improvements to the house.*
▶ renovation, alteration, extension, modernization, modification, (*informal*) face-lift

improvise VERB
1 *The boys improvised a raft.*
▶ devise, contrive, rig, put together, concoct
2 *an entertainer who is good at improvising.*
▶ extemporize, ad-lib

impudence NOUN
They soon forgave him his impudence.
▶ cheek, insolence, impertinence, effrontery, audacity, rudeness, impoliteness, discourtesy, disrespect
AN OPPOSITE IS politeness

impudent ADJECTIVE
She thought him an impudent bully.
▶ rude, insolent, impertinent, impolite, disrespectful, audacious, brazen
OPPOSITES ARE respectful, polite

impulse NOUN
1 *His first impulse was to call the police.*
▶ instinct, urge, inclination, compulsion, whim, caprice, desire
2 *His actions were so often governed by impulse.*
▶ impetuosity, spontaneity, rashness, recklessness
3 *Emotion is one of the main impulses of poetry.*
▶ stimulus, inspiration, motivation

impulsive ADJECTIVE
With an impulsive gesture she flounced out of the room.
▶ impetuous, spontaneous, rash, reckless, hasty, uninhibited, instinctive, passionate
AN OPPOSITE IS deliberate

impure ADJECTIVE
1 *The water was found to be impure.*
▶ contaminated, polluted, tainted, unclean, foul, defiled, dirty, filthy, infected, unhygienic, unwholesome, adulterated
2 *impure thoughts*
▶ immoral, indecent, unclean, corrupt, wicked, degenerate

impurity NOUN
1 *An instrument measured the impurity of the air.*
▶ contamination, pollution, dirtiness, uncleanliness, foulness, filthiness

a
b
c
d
e
f
g
h
i
j
k
l
m
n
o
p
q
r
s
t
u
v
w
x
y
z

2 *water full of impurities*
▶ contaminant, pollutant, adulterant, foreign matter

inability NOUN
their inability to agree on a single point
▶ incapacity, incapability, impotence, powerlessness, lack of ability

inaccessible ADJECTIVE
More of the countryside is becoming inaccessible.
▶ unreachable, cut off, out of reach, isolated, remote, godforsaken, hard to find, out-of-the-way, in the middle of nowhere, in the back of beyond, secluded, unfrequented, (*informal*) unget-at-able
AN OPPOSITE IS accessible

inaccuracy NOUN
The information is marred by inaccuracies
▶ mistake, error, miscalculation, blunder, imprecision, fault, defect, flaw, slip, oversight
OPPOSITES ARE accuracy, precision

inaccurate ADJECTIVE
The road map is very inaccurate.
▶ inexact, imprecise, incorrect, erroneous, faulty, imperfect, defective, unsound

inactive ADJECTIVE
1 *Illness left me inactive for several weeks.*
▶ idle, immobile, inert, lethargic, listless, sluggish
2 *The alarm was inactive at the time of the break-in.*
▶ inoperative, idle, non-functioning, turned off, out of action, out of use

inadequate ADJECTIVE
1 *The army suffered from bad pay and inadequate training.*
▶ insufficient, unsatisfactory, not enough, deficient, scanty, sparse
2 *It's a difficult job and they may prove inadequate.*
▶ incapable, ineffectual, incompetent, not up to scratch

inadvisable ADJECTIVE
It was inadvisable for him to drive or operate machinery.
▶ unwise, ill-advised, imprudent, foolish, misguided, silly
AN OPPOSITE IS advisable

inane ADJECTIVE
a series of inane remarks
▶ silly, foolish, stupid, fatuous, idiotic, absurd, mindless, vacuous, futile, pointless

inanimate ADJECTIVE
an inanimate object
▶ lifeless, insentient, inert, dead, dormant, inactive, unconscious
OPPOSITES ARE animate , living

inappropriate ADJECTIVE
The police decided a prosecution would be inappropriate.
▶ unsuitable, out of place, inapt, ill-suited, unfitting, untimely, ill-timed, improper, incongruous
OPPOSITES ARE appropriate, suitable

inattentive ADJECTIVE
The performance suffered from an inattentive audience.
▶ distracted, preoccupied, heedless, unobservant, dreamy, daydreaming, dreaming, absent-minded, lacking concentration
OPPOSITES ARE attentive, alert

inaudible ADJECTIVE
From that distance the voices were inaudible.
▶ indistinct, hard to hear, unclear, quiet, silent, weak, undetectable, unidentifiable, muted, faint, low, muffled, mumbled
AN OPPOSITE IS audible

incapable ADJECTIVE
Those who feel incapable in their work can get advice.
▶ incompetent, ineffective, ineffectual, inadequate, impotent, inept, unable, useless, weak
AN OPPOSITE IS capable

incentive NOUN
the introduction of more financial incentives
▶ inducement, stimulus, motivation, spur, encouragement, reward, (*more informal*) sweetener, (*more informal*) carrot

incessant ADJECTIVE
incessant noise from the road works outside
▶ continuous, continual, constant, ceaseless, endless, unceasing, interminable, non-stop
OPPOSITES ARE temporary, intermittent

incident NOUN
1 *He recalled an amusing incident from his childhood.*
▶ event, episode, occurrence, happening, occasion, affair, experience, activity, business, circumstance
2 *Police were called to an incident in the centre of town.*
▶ disturbance, commotion, fracas, scene, brawl, rumpus, fight

incidental ADJECTIVE
We can ignore the incidental details.
▶ secondary, subsidiary, ancillary, subordinate, inessential, unimportant, minor, trivial, petty, peripheral
AN OPPOSITE IS essential

incite VERB
1 *She had incited him to commit the crime.*
▶ urge, encourage, provoke, goad, push, impel, egg on
2 *They were accused of inciting racial hatred.*
▶ stir up, instigate, rouse, whip up, foment

inclination NOUN
1 *He showed no inclination to leave.*
▶ readiness, desire, impulse, wish, disposition, predisposition, predilection
AN OPPOSITE IS disinclination
2 *She had no inclination for work that day.*
▶ liking, partiality, appetite, taste, fondness, penchant
AN OPPOSITE IS dislike
3 *an inclination of 45°*
▶ gradient, incline, slope, angle, slant

incline VERB
The uprights incline slightly to the right.
▶ lean, slant, tilt, tip, slope, veer
be inclined *We are inclined to believe him.*
▶ be disposed, be minded, be willing, be ready

include VERB
1 *Sports activities include swimming and aerobics.*
▶ incorporate, involve, comprise, contain, embrace, encompass, consist of, take in, make room for, subsume
2 *The package includes flights, hotels costs, and all outings.*
▶ cover, allow for, take into account, add in
AN OPPOSITE IS exclude

incoherent ADJECTIVE
The letter was long and incoherent.
▶ unclear, confused, muddled, unintelligible, disorganized, incomprehensible, inarticulate, garbled, rambling, hard to follow, disjointed, disordered, illogical
OPPOSITES ARE coherent, intelligible

income NOUN
1 *Her income has gone up significantly in the last year.*
▶ earnings, salary, pay, remuneration, wages, money
2 *taxes on business income*
▶ revenue, receipts, takings, profits, gains, proceeds, takeover
OPPOSITES ARE expenditure, outgoings

incomparable ADJECTIVE
the city's incomparable beauty
▶ unparalleled, unequalled, unrivalled, matchless, peerless, inimitable

incompatible ADJECTIVE
1 *The two versions of the incident are incompatible.*
▶ inconsistent, irreconcilable, conflicting, contradictory, discrepant, incongruous, at variance, clashing, contrasting, different
2 *She and her partner seem totally incompatible.*
▶ unsuited, mismatched, (*more informal*) poles apart
AN OPPOSITE IS compatible

incompetent ADJECTIVE
They were all either too lazy or too incompetent to do an honest day's work.
▶ inept, incapable, unqualified, inefficient, unskilful, unfit, inadequate, unproficient, bungling, blundering, clumsy, ineffectual
AN OPPOSITE IS competent

incomplete ADJECTIVE
They have to move into the house even though it's still incomplete.
▶ unfinished, uncompleted, half-finished, not finished, unready

incomprehensible ADJECTIVE
1 *She made some incomprehensible remark.*
▶ unintelligible, incoherent, unfathomable, baffling, confusing, perplexing, obscure, cryptic, opaque, mysterious, inscrutable, enigmatic
AN OPPOSITE IS comprehensible

2 *The writing was incomprehensible.*
▶ illegible, indecipherable, unintelligible
OPPOSITES ARE intelligible, legible

inconceivable ADJECTIVE
It was inconceivable that the king would agree to these demands.
▶ unimaginable, unthinkable, implausible, incredible, unbelievable, undreamed of, (*more informal*) mind-boggling
OPPOSITES ARE conceivable, credible

inconclusive ADJECTIVE
The opinion polls are inconclusive.
▶ unconvincing, indefinite, undecided, ambiguous, equivocal, indecisive, indeterminate, uncertain, unsettled, open
AN OPPOSITE IS conclusive

incongruous ADJECTIVE
the incongruous sound of an electric doorbell
▶ inappropriate, out of place, discordant, unsuitable, ill-suited, incompatible, inconsistent, conflicting, odd, clashing, contrasting, ill-matched, uncoordinated, irreconcilable
AN OPPOSITE IS appropriate

inconsiderate ADJECTIVE
inconsiderate behaviour It was very inconsiderate of them.
▶ thoughtless, insensitive, unthinking, uncaring, unkind, discourteous, impolite, unconcerned, tactless

inconsistent ADJECTIVE
1 *Their attitudes are inconsistent and hard to understand.*
▶ changeable, unreliable, erratic, capricious, unstable, variable, fickle, inconstant, unpredictable, (*more informal*) up-and-down
2 *There are several inconsistent versions of the legend.*
▶ conflicting, contradictory, incompatible, irreconcilable, discrepant, incongruous, at variance, clashing, contrasting, different
AN OPPOSITE IS consistent

inconsolable ADJECTIVE
Lisa was inconsolable when she arrived back from the accident.
▶ heartbroken, broken-hearted, devastated, grief-stricken, desolate, despairing

inconspicuous ADJECTIVE
1 *The building is small and inconspicuous.*
▶ unobtrusive, undistinguished, unremarkable, unostentatious, camouflaged, hidden, out of sight, insignificant, ordinary, invisible
2 *Jane did her best to remain inconspicuous.*
▶ retiring, self-effacing, unassuming, modest, restrained
OPPOSITES ARE conspicuous, noticeable

incontrovertible ADJECTIVE
These are all incontrovertible facts.
▶ indisputable, incontestable, irrefutable, undeniable, unquestionable, unarguable, self-evident

inconvenience NOUN
The road works have caused a great deal of inconvenience.
▶ trouble, bother, difficulty, disruption, awkwardness, nuisance, hindrance, irritation, fuss, upset, annoyance, disadvantage, drawback, encumbrance
AN OPPOSITE IS convenience

inconvenience VERB
We hope the delay will not inconvenience you too much.
▶ trouble, bother, disturb, put out, incommode, annoy, irritate, disadvantage, embarrass, (*informal*) put you out

inconvenient ADJECTIVE
Shirley arrived at an extremely inconvenient moment.
▶ awkward, difficult, unsuitable, inappropriate, inopportune, untimely, ill-timed, embarrassing, annoying, bothersome, irritating, troublesome
AN OPPOSITE IS convenient

incorporate VERB
1 *The peace treaty incorporated the region into Italy.*
▶ absorb, merge, assimilate, subsume, embody, include (in), contain (in)
2 *The leaflet incorporates a sponsorship form.*
▶ include, contain, embrace

incorrect ADJECTIVE
The next three answers were incorrect.
▶ wrong, erroneous, mistaken, inaccurate, imprecise, inexact, false, untrue

incorrigible ADJECTIVE
an incorrigible flirt
▶ incurable, inveterate, irredeemable, hardened, hopeless

increase NOUN
an increase in size   an increase in demand
▶ growth, rise, development, enlargement, expansion, swelling, intensification, upsurge, upturn
AN OPPOSITE IS decrease

increase VERB
1 *Applications for jobs have increased.*
▶ rise, grow, swell, multiply, expand, spread, proliferate
OPPOSITES ARE decrease, decline
2 *Prosperity increases consumer demand.*
▶ raise, heighten, boost, enhance, add to, strengthen, intensify, develop, expand, escalate, augment
OPPOSITES ARE reduce, lower

incredible ADJECTIVE
1 *an incredible feat of engineering*
▶ magnificent, marvellous, spectacular, remarkable, wonderful, extraordinary, amazing, astounding
2 *Their story is incredible.*
▶ unbelievable, implausible, far-fetched, improbable, unlikely, questionable, unreasonable, doubtful, dubious
AN OPPOSITE IS credible

incredulous ADJECTIVE
She was incredulous when they told her the cost.
▶ disbelieving, unbelieving, doubtful, dubious, sceptical, unconvinced, distrustful, questioning, suspicious, uncertain
AN OPPOSITE IS credulous

incriminate VERB
The evidence incriminated the whole family.
▶ implicate, involve, accuse, blame, embroil, (*more formal*) inculpate, (*more informal*) point the finger at
OPPOSITES ARE exonerate, clear

incur VERB
actions that might incur a penalty
▶ earn, sustain, attract, provoke, run up, suffer, get, expose you to, bring upon yourself

incurable ADJECTIVE
1 *an incurable illness*
▶ untreatable, inoperable, irremediable, irreparable, terminal, fatal, chronic, hopeless
AN OPPOSITE IS curable
2 *Jenny is an incurable romantic.*
▶ inveterate, incorrigible, hardened, dyed-in-the-wool

indecent ADJECTIVE
Customs officers discovered indecent photographs in his luggage.
▶ obscene, pornographic, dirty, filthy, bawdy, lewd, licentious

indecision NOUN
She wanted to act, but indecision prevented her.
▶ hesitation, irresolution, indecisiveness, uncertainty, doubt, ambivalence, vacillation, equivocation
OPPOSITES ARE decisiveness, resolution

indecisive ADJECTIVE
1 *He came across as an indecisive leader.*
▶ hesitant, irresolute, tentative, equivocating, uncertain, weak, dithering
2 *The result of the tests was indecisive.*
▶ uncertain, doubtful, unsure

indefensible ADJECTIVE
That sort of abusive talk is quite indefensible.
▶ inexcusable, unjustifiable, unpardonable, unacceptable, unsupportable, untenable, wrong, misguided

indefinite ADJECTIVE
1 *The inspectors are here for an indefinite period.*
▶ unspecified, unknown, uncertain, unlimited
AN OPPOSITE IS definite
2 *a word like 'get', with an indefinite meaning*
▶ vague, unclear, unspecific, imprecise, hazy

indefinitely ADVERB
The problem could be with us indefinitely.
▶ for ever, continuously, continually, endlessly, for all time

indelible ADJECTIVE
1 *indelible ink*
▶ permanent, ineradicable, fixed, lasting, fast, ingrained
2 *The experience left an indelible impression on her.*
▶ unforgettable, ineradicable, lasting, enduring
AN OPPOSITE IS erasable.

indelicate ADJECTIVE
1 *It seemed a little indelicate to ask.*
▶ insensitive, tactless, indiscreet, undiplomatic, indecent
2 *His sense of humour could be indelicate at times.*
▶ indecent, coarse, vulgar, gross, crude, lewd, bawdy, obscene

independence NOUN
1 *The country gained its independence in the 1950s.*
▶ self-government, autonomy, freedom, individualism, liberty, nonconformity
AN OPPOSITE IS dependence
2 *The judges must be able to act with complete independence.*
▶ impartiality, neutrality, disinterest, detachment, objectivity, freedom

independent ADJECTIVE
1 *an independent country*
▶ autonomous, sovereign, self-governing
2 *an independent person*
▶ free, unconstrained, self-reliant, self-sufficient, free-thinking, liberated
AN OPPOSITE IS dependent
3 *an independent opinion*
▶ impartial, unbiased, disinterested, objective

indicate VERB
1 *A linesman raised his flag to indicate a goal.*
▶ signify, denote, register, record, designate
2 *Good sales indicate the book's popularity.*
▶ show, demonstrate, be a sign of, testify to, suggest, imply, attest
3 *Indicate your choice of prize on the form.*
▶ specify, point out

indication NOUN
1 *His secretary could give no clear indication of when he was expected back.*
▶ clue, hint, inkling, intimation, suggestion, explanation
2 *Pain may be an indication of injury.*
▶ sign, indicator, symptom, mark, evidence, manifestation

indifference NOUN
He reacted with complete indifference to their predicament.
▶ unconcern, apathy, coolness, disregard, nonchalance, inattention

indifferent ADJECTIVE
1 *His voice showed how indifferent he was.*
▶ unconcerned, apathetic, uncaring, nonchalant
2 *After an indifferent meal he went off to bed.*
▶ mediocre, ordinary, inferior, unexceptional, average

indigenous ADJECTIVE
indigenous people from rainforests across the world
▶ native, aboriginal, original, local

indignant ADJECTIVE
The newspaper received indignant letters from outraged readers.
▶ irate, angry, affronted, aggrieved, incensed, outraged, resentful, offended, vexed, piqued, heated, furious, fuming

indignation NOUN
The false accusations filled him with indignation.
▶ anger, fury, resentment, outrage, affront, umbrage, vexation

indignity NOUN
He suffered the indignity of having his application rejected.
▶ humiliation, shame, embarrassment, mortification, disgrace, dishonour, stigma

indirect ADJECTIVE
1 *The convoy took a quieter indirect route.*
▶ roundabout, circuitous, meandering, out-of-the-way
2 *It was an insult, if only an indirect one.*
▶ disguised, ambiguous, equivocal, oblique, implicit, implied, inexplicit
AN OPPOSITE IS direct

indiscreet ADJECTIVE
Her mum would never have done anything so indiscreet.
▶ imprudent, unwise, injudicious, tactless, ill-advised, ill-considered, ill-judged, unthinking, impolite, impolitic, undiplomatic, careless, incautious, unguarded
OPPOSITES ARE discreet, careful

indiscretion NOUN
It is important to be careful and avoid any indiscretion.
▶ imprudence, rashness, recklessness, tactlessness, foolhardiness

indiscriminate ADJECTIVE
Congestion soon occurs if indiscriminate parking is allowed.
▶ haphazard, random, unsystematic, general, wholesale, undiscriminating, aimless, desultory, general
OPPOSITES ARE selective, systematic

indispensable ADJECTIVE
Charles regarded him as an indispensable source of wisdom and experience.
▶ essential, vital, crucial, required, requisite, basic, central, imperative, key, necessary, much-needed
AN OPPOSITE IS unnecessary

indisposed ADJECTIVE
Mark had to stand in for the soloist, who was indisposed.
▶ ill, unwell, sick, infirm, poorly

indisputable ADJECTIVE

Charles returned in triumph, indisputable King of Aquitaine.
▶ incontrovertible, incontestable, acknowledged, undeniable, indubitable, unassailable, unequivocal
OPPOSITES ARE questionable, debatable

indistinct ADJECTIVE

1 *In the photocopies, some of the letters were indistinct.*
▶ blurred, fuzzy, unclear, out of focus, ill-defined, dim, faint, hazy, misty, obscure, vague, shadowy, bleary
2 *She murmured, but her voice was indistinct.*
▶ muffled, muted, faint, weak, inaudible, slurred
AN OPPOSITE IS distinct

indistinguishable ADJECTIVE

The boys are indistinguishable.
▶ identical, interchangeable, alike, the same
AN OPPOSITE IS different

individual ADJECTIVE

1 *music with an individual style*
▶ characteristic, distinctive, distinct, particular, special, specific, unique, peculiar, exclusive, idiosyncratic, private, personal
2 *Individual countries can make their own decisions.*
▶ separate, single, discrete
AN OPPOSITE IS collective

individual NOUN

In the corner sat a strange individual.
▶ person, being, human being, soul, mortal

indoctrinate VERB

With their psychological techniques they were able to indoctrinate large numbers of people.
▶ brainwash, propagandize, re-educate, instruct, train, teach

induce VERB

1 *Their leaders induced them to continue fighting.*
▶ persuade, convince, prevail upon, press, urge, encourage
2 *Conversations like these induce close friendship.*
▶ bring about, cause, create, effect, instigate, engender, develop, produce, lead to, give rise to, arouse, kindle

inducement NOUN

Paying off student loans is an inducement to join the profession.
▶ incentive, encouragement, enticement, stimulus, motivation, spur, lure, bait

indulge VERB

1 *She decided to indulge her passion for music.*
▶ satisfy, gratify, fulfil, pander to, go along with, humour
2 *She could not be accused of indulging her children.*
▶ spoil, pamper, cosset, mollycoddle
3 **indulge in** *Here we stopped and indulged in a cream tea.*
▶ enjoy, revel in

indulgent ADJECTIVE

He could see the looks of indulgent amusement on their faces.
▶ tolerant, compliant, patient, permissive, easygoing, lenient, liberal, overgenerous, fond, genial, kind
AN OPPOSITE IS strict

industrial ADJECTIVE

an industrial area north of the city
▶ industrialized, manufacturing, business

industrious ADJECTIVE

an industrious and studious youth
▶ diligent, hard-working, conscientious, assiduous, enterprising, painstaking, energetic, active, keen, productive, zealous, sedulous, tireless
OPPOSITES ARE lazy, indolent

industry NOUN

1 *the American oil industry*
▶ business, trade, commerce, manufacturing
2 *The garden looked a hive of industry.*
▶ activity, hard work, industriousness, diligence, effort, toil, energy, vigour, application, commitment, determination, keenness, labour, perseverance, persistence, tirelessness, zeal
OPPOSITES ARE laziness, indolence

inedible ADJECTIVE

a joke recipe for baking an inedible cake
▶ uneatable, unpalatable, unwholesome, poisonous, noxious
AN OPPOSITE IS edible

ineffective ADJECTIVE

1 *The protests were quite ineffective.*
▶ unsuccessful, unproductive, useless, futile, vain, fruitless, unavailing, worthless
OPPOSITES ARE effective, fruitful
2 *an ineffective leader*
▶ inadequate, ineffectual, weak, feeble, inept, incompetent
AN OPPOSITE IS effective

inefficient ADJECTIVE

1 *He must be the world's most inefficient gardener.*
▶ ineffective, ineffectual, unproductive, disorganized, incompetent, inept, inexpert
2 *The wood stoves are extremely inefficient for cooking food.*
▶ uneconomical, unproductive, extravagant, wasteful, awkward, clumsy
AN OPPOSITE IS efficient

inelegant ADJECTIVE

'Sunken building' is an inelegant term for these small structures.
▶ unattractive, graceless, awkward, cumbersome, unrefined, ugly, crude

ineligible ADJECTIVE

The club was fined for fielding ineligible players.
▶ disqualified, inappropriate, unacceptable, unfit, unsuitable
AN OPPOSITE IS eligible

inept ADJECTIVE
The Banks have proved inept at merging.
▶ unskilful, incompetent, bungling, clumsy, maladroit

inequality NOUN
a growth in crime, caused by unemployment and social inequality
▶ imbalance, disparity, unfairness, divergence, difference, dissimilarity
AN OPPOSITE IS equality

inert ADJECTIVE
He prodded the inert body on the floor.
▶ motionless, lifeless, immobile, inanimate, dormant, inactive

inertia NOUN
There was a danger of lapsing into inertia.
▶ inactivity, inaction, passivity, lethargy, listlessness, apathy, torpor, immobility, lassitude, indolence, idleness, laziness, numbness, sluggishness
AN OPPOSITE IS liveliness

inescapable ADJECTIVE
For the king, Parliament was an inescapable reality when taxes had to be raised.
▶ unavoidable, inevitable, necessary, obligatory, mandatory
AN OPPOSITE IS avoidable

inevitable ADJECTIVE
There have been the inevitable delays.
▶ unavoidable, inescapable, obligatory, mandatory, ineluctable

inexcusable ADJECTIVE
The insult was inexcusable.
▶ indefensible, unforgivable, intolerable, unpardonable, reprehensible

inexpensive ADJECTIVE
a simple and inexpensive method
▶ cheap, low-priced, low-cost, economical, affordable, modest
AN OPPOSITE IS expensive

inexperienced ADJECTIVE
School-leavers and inexperienced people often get jobs in riding schools.
▶ inexpert, untrained, unskilled, unpractised, unaccustomed, immature, callow, amateur, fresh, green, raw
AN OPPOSITE IS experienced.

inexplicable ADJECTIVE
For some inexplicable reason she felt suddenly afraid.
▶ unexplainable, mysterious, puzzling, strange, unaccountable, incomprehensible, unfathomable, baffling, mystifying, enigmatic
AN OPPOSITE IS understandable

infallible ADJECTIVE
1 *The idea works well, but it is not infallible.*
▶ foolproof, unfailing, guaranteed, perfect, certain
AN OPPOSITE IS fallible

2 *Kate always adopted her infallible routine.*
▶ dependable, reliable, unerring, accurate

infamous ADJECTIVE
a series of infamous murders
▶ notorious, scandalous, shameful, ill-famed, disreputable
AN OPPOSITE IS reputable

infant NOUN
an age at which infants are learning to walk
▶ baby, child, tot, (*informal*) toddler

infatuated ADJECTIVE
He seemed to be infatuated with every girl her met.
▶ besotted, obsessed, taken, (*more informal*) smitten, (*more informal*) head over heels

infatuation NOUN
(*informal*) *Her mother regarded Sarah's feelings for him as a girlish infatuation.*
▶ obsession, fixation, passion, (*more informal*) crush

infect VERB
1 *The organism may infect the eye of the infant with a 'sticky eye'.*
▶ cause an infection in, spread disease to
2 *The water supply had become infected.*
▶ contaminate, pollute, poison, taint, blight
3 *Her cheerful humour infects everyone she meets.*
▶ affect, influence, inspire, animate, touch

infection NOUN
1 *a bladder infection*
▶ disease, virus, disorder, complaint
2 *The dressing will keep the wound free of infection.*
▶ contamination, contagion, bacteria, poisoning

infectious ADJECTIVE
1 *the conquest of infectious diseases*
▶ contagious, communicable, catching, transmissible, transmittable, spreading
2 *infectious laughter*
▶ contagious, irresistible, spreading

infer VERB
What can we infer from the table of results?
▶ conclude, deduce, extrapolate, reason, gather, assume, work out, guess, understand
USAGE See the note at *imply*.

inferior ADJECTIVE
1 *inferior rank*
▶ lesser, lower, subsidiary, subordinate, junior, secondary, second-class, ancillary, low, humble
2 *inferior quality*
▶ poor, mediocre, substandard, shoddy, tawdry, bad, cheap, indifferent

infernal ADJECTIVE
1 *the infernal regions of the underworld*
▶ hellish, nether, lower, diabolical, devilish
2 *Having to leave so early was an infernal nuisance.*
▶ wretched, damned, diabolical, accursed

infinite ADJECTIVE
1 *You will need infinite patience in detailed work like this.*
▶ endless, limitless, boundless, immeasurable, unlimited, incalculable, immense, prodigious
OPPOSITES ARE limited, finite
2 *Along the rooflines were infinite numbers of chimneys.*
▶ countless, innumerable, numberless, incalculable
OPPOSITES ARE limited, finite

inflamed ADJECTIVE
Her skin had become inflamed.
▶ swollen, reddened, raw, smarting, infected, poisoned, septic, festering

inflammable ADJECTIVE
inflammable chemicals
▶ flammable, combustible, volatile, burnable
OPPOSITES ARE non- flammable, incombustible

inflammation NOUN
inflammation of the skin
▶ swelling, redness, soreness, burning, tenderness, infection

inflate VERB
1 *We have ten minutes to inflate fifty balloons.*
▶ pump up, blow up, puff up, dilate, distend, swell
2 *News reports have greatly inflated the number of casualties.*
▶ exaggerate, magnify, overstate, overplay, overdramatize

inflexible ADJECTIVE
1 *The boots felt rather narrow and inflexible.*
▶ rigid, stiff, firm, hard, unbending, unyielding, hardened, immovable, fixed, solid
2 *An inflexible approach to the problem won't work.*
▶ strict, stubborn, obstinate, entrenched, immutable, intractable, intransigent, unaccommodating, unalterable, uncompromising, unhelpful
AN OPPOSITE IS flexible

inflict VERB
1 *He was determined to inflict some sort of penalty on them.*
▶ impose, administer (to), mete out (to), deal out (to), apply (to), perpetrate, wreak, enforce, force
2 *No one really wants an elderly relative inflicted on them for months.*
▶ impose, foist, thrust, saddle someone (with), burden someone (with)

influence NOUN
The local organizations can have a large influence on the party at national level.
▶ effect, impact, control, sway, hold, pressure, pull, power (over), direction (over), authority (over), dominance (over)

influence VERB
1 *Parents influence their children enormously in the first few years.*
▶ affect, have an effect on, guide, exert an influence on, direct, control

2 *There had been several attempts to influence the jury.*
▶ sway, bias, coerce, pressurize, prejudice, suborn, lead astray, bribe, corrupt

influential ADJECTIVE
1 *a respected and influential politician*
▶ important, authoritative, leading, powerful, dominant
OPPOSITES ARE uninfluential, insignificant
2 *a piece of writing that has been highly influential*
▶ significant, persuasive, pivotal, seminal, crucial, effective, far-reaching, telling
OPPOSITES ARE uninfluential, unimportant

influx NOUN
a huge influx of tourists
▶ rush, stream, flood, flow, inflow, inundation, invasion

inform VERB
1 *I'll inform them that we are ready to leave.*
▶ tell, notify, advise, let someone know, send word to, apprise
2 **inform on** *No one wants to inform on a friend.*
▶ denounce, betray, report, incriminate, tell on, (*more informal*) shop

informal ADJECTIVE
1 *We were having an informal conversation*
▶ casual, relaxed, natural, easy-going
2 *The style of the article was very informal.*
▶ colloquial, idiomatic, vernacular, demotic, popular
3 *You can wear informal clothes.*
▶ casual, everyday, comfortable, leisure

information NOUN
You can get more information from the website.
▶ details, particulars, facts, data, guidance, material, documentation, advice, knowledge, (*more informal*) info

informative ADJECTIVE
The two- day course is too short to be informative.
▶ instructive, useful, helpful, communicative, enlightening, revealing, illuminating, factual
OPPOSITES ARE uninformative, uncommunicative

informed ADJECTIVE
She seems highly informed on the subject.
▶ knowledgeable, enlightened, conversant (with), familiar (with), abreast (of), au fait (with)
OPPOSITES ARE ill- informed, ignorant

infringe VERB
1 *behaviour that infringes all the rules*
▶ break, violate, contravene, disobey, breach, flout, transgress
2 *measures that infringe civil liberties*
▶ undermine, encroach on, impair, compromise, damage

infuriate VERB
His stubborn refusal began to infuriate her.
▶ anger, enrage, exasperate, incense, annoy, irritate, vex, madden, aggravate, antagonize,

displease, make angry, (*more informal*) needle, (*more informal*) rile
OPPOSITES ARE placate, appease, please

ingenious ADJECTIVE
an ingenious solution to the difficulty
▶ inventive, imaginative, creative, clever, original, cunning, resourceful, astute, shrewd, inspired, skilful, subtle
AN OPPOSITE IS unimaginative

ingenuity NOUN
You need ingenuity to write computer programs like these.
▶ inventiveness, imagination, creativity, originality

ingenuous ADJECTIVE
The look on his face was ingenuous and sincere.
▶ innocent, naive, frank, guileless, honest, open, artless
OPPOSITES ARE disingenuous, artful

ingredient NOUN
Fruit is the missing ingredient in their diet.
▶ component, constituent, element, part, piece, portion

inhabit VERB
(*old-fashioned*) *a cave complex that hermits used to inhabit*
▶ live in, occupy, dwell in, people, populate, settle in

inhabitant NOUN
the inhabitants of the town
▶ resident, citizen, native, local, occupant, dweller, (*plural*) population, (*plural*) townsfolk

inhabited ADJECTIVE
an inhabited island
▶ populated, settled, occupied, peopled, colonized
AN OPPOSITE IS uninhabited

inherent ADJECTIVE
the inherent goodness of humankind
▶ intrinsic, innate, inborn, inbred, ingrained, congenital, fundamental, essential, hereditary, immanent, native, natural
AN OPPOSITE IS acquired

inherit VERB
His son will inherit the business on his death.
▶ receive, be left, be bequeathed, succeed to

inheritance NOUN
She bought a house with her inheritance.
▶ legacy, bequest, estate, fortune, heritage

inhibit VERB
the problems that inhibit progress
▶ obstruct, hinder, hold up, hamper, impede, interfere with, restrict, thwart, check, curb, handicap

inhibited ADJECTIVE
He felt inhibited about discussing money.
▶ shy, reticent, embarrassed, awkward, self-conscious, reserved, diffident, bashful, (*more informal*) hung up

inhibition NOUN
1 *The state places no inhibition on press freedom.*
▶ restraint, bar, check, barrier, interference, impediment
2 **inhibitions** *Not everyone can overcome their inhibitions so easily.*
▶ shyness, reticence, diffidence, reserve, self-consciousness, insecurity, repression, (*informal*) hang-ups

inhuman ADJECTIVE
the inhuman treatment of political prisoners
▶ inhumane, brutal, cruel, barbaric, barbarous, harsh, callous, bestial, savage, merciless, pitiless, ruthless, unnatural, bloodthirsty, diabolical, fiendish, heartless
OPPOSITES ARE humane, compassionate

inhumane ADJECTIVE
It would be inhumane to take away their freedom.
▶ cruel, inhuman, harsh, callous, sadistic, barbaric, barbarous, uncivilized
AN OPPOSITE IS humane

initial ADJECTIVE
1 *Their initial reaction was one of anger.*
▶ first, original, provisional, earliest
OPPOSITES ARE final, eventual
2 *an initial payment of £100*
▶ opening, preliminary, starting, commencing, inaugural, introductory
OPPOSITES ARE final, closing

initially ADVERB
I had initially intended to send an email.
▶ at first, originally, to begin with, to start with, at the start

initiate VERB
The local authority has initiated a youth enterprise scheme.
▶ institute, inaugurate, instigate, launch, begin

initiative NOUN
1 *Employers are looking for initiative in candidates for jobs.*
▶ enterprise, resourcefulness, drive, inventiveness, innovativeness, energy, dynamism, leadership, originality, ambition
2 *We are in danger of losing the initiative.*
▶ advantage, upper hand, edge, lead
3 *a new initiative for peace*
▶ proposal, plan, scheme, strategy, measure

injure VERB
1 *He was injured in a street fight.*
▶ hurt, harm, wound , maim, cripple, disfigure
2 *She injured her arm.*
▶ hurt, damage, break, crush

injury NOUN
1 *His hand injury had fully recovered.*
▶ wound, cut, damage, fracture, lesion
2 *The suit will protect you from personal injury*
▶ harm, hurt, suffering

a b c d e f g h **i** j k l m n o p q r s t u v w x y z

injustice NOUN

1 *He shook his head at the cruel injustice of the world.*
▶ unfairness, unjustness, inequality, inequity, oppression, discrimination, dishonesty, partiality, wrongness
AN OPPOSITE IS justice

2 *She felt her treatment to be a grave injustice.*
▶ wrong, injury, affront, grievance, offence, crime, iniquity, outrage

inkling NOUN

I got some inkling that this one would be different.
▶ idea, notion, impression, suspicion

innate ADJECTIVE

a decor that shows innate good taste.
▶ inherent, inborn, inbred, intrinsic, natural, ingrained, congenital, fundamental, essential
AN OPPOSITE IS acquired

inner ADJECTIVE

1 *the inner part of the building*
▶ interior, central, innermost, internal, inside
AN OPPOSITE IS outer

2 *She kept her inner feelings to herself.*
▶ private, secret, personal, intimate

innocent ADJECTIVE

1 *He always swore that he was innocent.*
▶ guiltless, blameless, free from blame
AN OPPOSITE IS guilty

2 *At her age she looked so innocent.*
▶ pure, virtuous, chaste, fresh, childlike, trusting, guileless, artless

3 *They claimed it had just been innocent fun.*
▶ harmless, innocuous, inoffensive

innovation NOUN

There will be some innovations when the new management takes over.
▶ change, alteration, reform, departure, new feature, novelty, revolution

innovative ADJECTIVE

innovative ideas
▶ new, fresh, original, inventive, resourceful

innuendo NOUN

language full of double meanings and innuendo
▶ insinuation, intimation, aspersion, slur

innumerable ADJECTIVE

the light from innumerable fires
▶ countless, numerous, very many, untold, numberless, unnumbered, incalculable, infinite

inoffensive ADJECTIVE

a few inoffensive remarks about their local MP
▶ harmless, innocuous, unobjectionable, unexceptionable

input NOUN

They went to the meeting armed with input from their survey.
▶ information, data, facts and figures, statistics

inquire VERB

inquire into *The committee will inquire into all these matters.*
▶ investigate, look into, examine, probe, scrutinize, explore

USAGE Note that *enquire* is normally used in the more general meaning 'to ask about something', as in *'She enquired about his health'*.

inquiry NOUNS

The government has set up a formal inquiry into the incident.
▶ investigation, inquest, scrutiny, inquisition, inspection

inquisitive ADJECTIVE

Gareth possessed a sharp and inquisitive mind.
▶ curious, questioning, inquiring, interested, probing, prying

insane ADJECTIVE

1 *She was declared insane on the recommendation of two doctors.*
▶ mad, deranged, crazy, demented, mentally ill

2 *It would be insane to think they could do the journey in a day.*
▶ crazy, foolish, stupid, senseless, ludicrous, absurd, mad

insanity NOUN

1 *Insanity ran in the family.*
▶ madness, mental disorder, mental illness, derangement, lunacy, dementia

2 *A loan at such a high rate of interest would be insanity.*
▶ folly, foolishness, stupidity, madness, lunacy

insatiable ADJECTIVE

an insatiable appetite for debate
▶ unquenchable, unsatisfiable, voracious, ravenous, immoderate, prodigious

---

insect NOUN

Some insects are disguised as a leaf or a twig.
▶ bug, pest, (*more informal*) creepy-crawly

SOME COMMON INSECTS

flies: fly, blackfly, bluebottle, gadfly, gnat, horsefly, housefly, hoverfly, midge, mosquito, sandfly, tsetse fly.

bees: bee, worker, drone, queen bee; bumblebee, carpenter bee, drone, honeybee, mason bee.

wasps: wasp, hornet, ichneumon (= 'tracker'), sawfly; (*informal*) yellow jacket.

beetles: beetle, black beetle (= cockroach), chafer, click beetle, cockchafer, Colorado beetle, death-watch beetle, dung beetle, firefly (having soft body), glow-worm (having soft body), ladybird, soldier beetle, stag beetle, weevil.

▶▶

other flying insects: ant; aphid (blackfly,
greenfly); crane fly (daddy-long-legs),
damselfly, dragonfly, lacewing; locust; mayfly;
butterfly, moth.
jumping insects: flea, grasshopper, cricket,
cicada.
non-flying insects: ant, cockroach, earwig,
louse, mantis, sawyer, stick insect, termite,
thrip, water boatman.
other creatures loosely called insects:
centipede, worm, earthworm, mite, slug,
woodlouse.
other words: larva (e.g. caterpillar or tadpole),
grub (larva), maggot (larva), leatherjacket
(larva of crane fly), woodworm (larva of a
beetle), nit (egg), pupa (stage between larva
and adult), chrysalis (butterfly or moth pupa),
imago (adult stage).

insecure ADJECTIVE
1 *Police warned that the house was insecure.*
▶ unsafe, unprotected, ill-protected, vulnerable,
exposed, ill-defended, defenceless
2 *All this bold talk made him feel insecure.*
▶ anxious, worried, concerned, unconfident,
diffident

insensible ADJECTIVE
1 *She lay insensible on a couch.*
▶ unconscious, inert, senseless
2 **insensible to** *We are not insensible to the risks
involved.*
▶ unaware of, ignorant of, unconscious of,
unresponsive to
USAGE Note that *insensible* is not the opposite
of *sensible* in its normal meaning 'having good
sense'.

insensitive ADJECTIVE
1 *It was insensitive to criticize them at a time like this.*
▶ unfeeling, uncaring, tactless, thoughtless, callous
2 *a part of the body insensitive to pain*
▶ hardened, resistant, impervious, immune,
unaffected (by)

insert VERB
He inserted a new film in the camera.
▶ put, place, push, slip, install, locate

inside ADJECTIVE
The inside walls of the house were damp.
▶ inner, interior, internal, innermost, indoor
OPPOSITES ARE outside , outer, exterior

inside NOUN
The inside of the box should be lined with silver paper.
▶ interior, inner surface, inner part, core

insides PLURAL NOUN
He felt total panic in his insides.
▶ guts, stomach, intestines, organs, (*more informal*)
tummy

insidious ADJECTIVE
*Mocking little phrases found their insidious way into her
mind.*
▶ stealthy, surreptitious, sneaking, cunning, furtive

insight NOUN
Her experience and insight proved invaluable.
▶ understanding, appreciation, awareness, grasp,
perception, intuition, acumen, discernment

insignificant ADJECTIVE
The differences are mostly insignificant.
▶ unimportant, negligible, trivial, trifling, small,
footling, inconsequential, inconsiderable, irrelevant,
meaningless
AN OPPOSITE IS significant

insincere ADJECTIVE
He flashed a gleaming, insincere smile.
▶ false, deceitful, dishonest, disingenuous,
pretended, feigned, hypocritical, devious
AN OPPOSITE IS sincere

insinuate VERB
He insinuated that they had lied.
▶ imply, suggest, hint, intimate, give to understand

insipid ADJECTIVE
They sipped bowls of pale insipid soup.
▶ bland, tasteless, weak, watery

insist VERB
1 *He insisted he had done everything they had asked.*
▶ maintain, contend, assert, hold, aver, claim,
declare, state, stress
2 **insist on** *parents who insist on an early bedtime*
▶ demand, enforce, require, stipulate

insistence NOUN
1 *her insistence that they should go with her*
▶ demand, requirement, entreaty, urging
2 *Jane's insistence that she loved him*
▶ assertion, declaration, contention, claim, avowal

insistent ADJECTIVE
There were insistent requests for financial support.
▶ persistent, demanding, unrelenting, unremitting,
urgent, emphatic, relentless, repeated, forceful,
assertive

insolence NOUN
She accused him of insolence.
▶ cheek, impertinence, impudence, effrontery,
audacity, rudeness, impoliteness, discourtesy,
disrespect

insolent ADJECTIVE
The boy was constantly insolent.
▶ rude, impolite, impertinent, impudent,
disrespectful, audacious, brazen
OPPOSITES ARE respectful, polite

insoluble ADJECTIVE
one of the world's insoluble problems
▶ unsolvable, unresolvable, inexplicable,
unanswerable, unfathomable, incomprehensible,
mysterious, mystifying, baffling, enigmatic, puzzling
AN OPPOSITE IS soluble

inspect VERB

The houses had been inspected by a surveyor.
▶ check, examine, investigate, scrutinize, supervise, oversee

inspection NOUN

The machinery needs a regular inspection.
▶ examination, check, check-up, investigation, review, scrutiny, survey

inspector NOUN

Inspectors are sent out each week to assess the work done.
▶ examiner, investigator, supervisor, tester, controller, official, superintendent

inspiration NOUN

1 *writing that relies on inspiration*
▶ creativity, imagination, inventiveness, ingenuity, enthusiasm, genius, influence
2 *The success proved an inspiration to everyone involved in the project.*
▶ stimulus, spur, motivation, filip, boost
3 *Emma had a sudden inspiration*
▶ idea, thought, brainwave, revelation

inspire VERB

a simple tune that inspired him to write a musical
▶ stimulate, influence, motivate, prompt, encourage, enthuse, galvanize, reassure, spur, stir, animate, arouse, (*more informal*) egg on

instability NOUN

The world economy is in a state of instability.
▶ unsteadiness, variability, unreliability, changeability, precariousness, fluctuation, unpredictability

install VERB

1 *We want to install central heating on all floors.*
▶ put in, establish, fix, introduce, set up
2 **install yourself** *She installed herself in a sofa by the fire.*
▶ ensconce yourself, settle, place yourself , plant yourself , (*more informal*) park yourself

instalment NOUN

1 *You can pay for your licence in monthly instalments.*
▶ payment, part
2 *a serial in four instalments*
▶ episode, part, section

instance NOUN

We could not find a single instance of discrimination.
▶ example, occurrence, case, illustration, sample

instant ADJECTIVE

The website gives you instant access to the information you need.
▶ immediate, instantaneous, on-the-spot, prompt, fast, quick, rapid, speedy, direct, swift

instant NOUN

The incident was over in an instant.
▶ moment, second, minute, flash, split second, (*more informal*) tick, (*more informal*) twinkling

instantly ADVERB

He fell asleep instantly.
▶ immediately, at once, straight away, right away, there and then, in a trice, directly

instigate VERB

1 *The police will instigate formal inquiries.*
▶ initiate, set in motion, establish, institute
2 *A few troublemakers managed to instigate a disturbance.*
▶ start, spark, incite, generate, encourage, prompt, whip up, kindle

instinct NOUN

Her instinct was to find out more about them.
▶ impulse, inclination, intuition, hunch, feeling, presentiment, sixth-sense, tendency, urge

instinctive ADJECTIVE

Their instinctive reaction is to find someone to blame.
▶ intuitive, natural, innate, automatic, reflex
OPPOSITES ARE deliberate, conscious

institute VERB

The Academy has instituted a new research programme.
▶ establish, inaugurate, initiate, launch, introduce, found, create, originate, set up, begin, start

institution NOUN

1 *the institution of a new language course*
▶ introduction, establishment, setting up, formation, creation, launching, inauguration, inception, initiation, founding, opening
2 *He did not want to spend the rest of his life in an institution.*
▶ home, hospital, asylum
3 *an academic institution*
▶ establishment, school, academy, college
4 *A spring holiday has become a family institution.*
▶ custom, convention, tradition, routine, practice, ritual, habit

instruct VERB

1 *A private tutor instructed the children in French.*
▶ coach, educate, train, drill, ground, teach
2 *The officials instructed us to wait.*
▶ order, direct, command, require, call on, advise

instruction NOUN

1 *It is important to listen out for instructions.*
▶ direction, directive, order, command, guidance
2 *basic instruction in mathematics*
▶ education, tuition, teaching, schooling, coaching, tutoring, grounding

instructive ADJECTIVE

an instructive experience
▶ educational, enlightening, informative, illuminating, revealing, edifying, helpful, improving

instrument NOUN

a sharp instrument
▶ implement, tool, device, utensil, contrivance, contraption, apparatus, appliance, equipment, gadget, machine, mechanism

instrumental ADJECTIVE

He was instrumental in getting the information we needed.
▶ active, influential, involved, contributory (to), helpful, useful

insubordinate ADJECTIVE

His older son had been difficult and insubordinate.
▶ disobedient, unruly, rebellious, badly behaved, wayward, undisciplined, defiant, mutinous
AN OPPOSITE IS obedient

insult NOUN (with the stress on in-)

The two men threw insults at each other.
▶ affront, abuse, indignity, slight, snub
AN OPPOSITE IS compliment

insult VERB (with the stress on -sult)

She put her head out of the window to insult passers-by.
▶ abuse, affront, malign, revile, offend, mock, snub, vilify, sneer at
AN OPPOSITE IS compliment

insulting ADJECTIVE

They directed their insulting remarks at anyone they happened to see.
▶ abusive, rude, offensive, disparaging, contemptuous, deprecatory, scornful, scurrilous, slanderous, insolent, condescending, mocking, patronizing, (more informal) snide
OPPOSITES ARE polite, complimentary

intact ADJECTIVE

Several buildings remained intact despite heavy bombing.
▶ whole, undamaged, untouched, unharmed, complete, entire

intangible ADJECTIVE

Dusk gave the scene an intangible quality
▶ impalpable, untouchable, imperceptible, unreal, ethereal, incorporeal, shadowy, disembodied, elusive, abstract, airy
AN OPPOSITE IS tangible

integral ADJECTIVE

1 Speech is an integral part of human interaction.
▶ essential, constituent, indispensable, intrinsic, irreplaceable, necessary, requisite
AN OPPOSITE IS incidental
2 The equipment is sold as an integral system.
▶ complete, integrated, combined, indivisible, whole

integrate VERB

The army command integrated several units into a single force.
▶ merge, amalgamate, combine, consolidate, unify, unite, fuse, join, blend, bring together
AN OPPOSITE IS separate

integrity NOUN

No one doubts their integrity.
▶ honesty, honour, morality, sincerity, reliability, virtue, fidelity, uprightness, honourableness, righteousness, goodness, incorruptibility, loyalty, principle
AN OPPOSITE IS dishonesty

intellect NOUN

a story that appeals to the intellect rather than the emotions
▶ mind, reason, intelligence, judgement, wits

intellectual ADJECTIVE

1 intellectual powers.
▶ mental, cerebral, rational, cognitive, conceptual
2 an intellectual person
▶ intelligent, academic, cultured, scholarly, studious, thoughtful, highbrow

intellectual NOUN

Opposition to the regime is strongest among intellectuals.
▶ academic, scholar, highbrow, thinker, member of the intelligentsia, intelligent person

intelligence NOUN

1 a person of great intelligence
▶ intellect, brainpower, powers of reasoning, perceptiveness, acumen, wisdom, wits, understanding, comprehension, (more informal) nous
AN OPPOSITE IS stupidity
2 constant intelligence regarding terrorist attacks
▶ information, report, warning, news, notification, data, facts, knowledge, (more informal) tip-off

intelligent ADJECTIVE

She is a highly intelligent writer.
▶ clever, bright, acute, sharp, perceptive, profound, shrewd

intelligible ADJECTIVE

The message was barely intelligible.
▶ understandable, comprehensible, coherent, decipherable, legible, clear, lucid, meaningful
OPPOSITES ARE unintelligible, incomprehensible

intend VERB

1 I intend to apply for a grant.
▶ propose, mean, plan, have it in mind, have a mind, aim, contemplate (applying), determine, purpose
2 The book is intended for learners of English.
▶ design, destine, mean

intense ADJECTIVE

She was suffering from intense pain. The experience rouses intense emotions.
▶ extreme, acute, severe, fierce, sharp, strong, powerful, profound, potent
OPPOSITES ARE moderate, mild

intensify VERB

1 The dizzy feeling in his head intensified.
▶ increase, strengthen, grow, escalate
AN OPPOSITE IS weaken
2 We must intensify our efforts.
▶ increase, escalate, step up, reinforce, sharpen, concentrate
AN OPPOSITE IS reduce

intensive ADJECTIVE
Police have made an intensive search of the area.
▶ thorough, exhaustive, comprehensive, rigorous, detailed, complete, full, all-out, concentrated

intent ADJECTIVE
1 *She was intent on visiting her friends in Spain.*
▶ keen (to), resolved (to), determined (to), bent, fixed
AN OPPOSITE IS reluctant
2 *He had an intent look on his face.*
▶ attentive, engrossed, absorbed, preoccupied, steadfast
OPPOSITES ARE vacant, blank

intention NOUN
Our intention is to accept the offer.
▶ aim, purpose, objective, object, plan, ambition, design, end, goal

intentional ADJECTIVE
The remarks were intentional.
▶ deliberate, premeditated, intended, planned, calculated, conscious, considered, meant, designed, prearranged, wilful
AN OPPOSITE IS unintentional

interaction NOUN
the interaction of two influences
▶ effect on each other, exchange, (*informal*) give and take, interplay, reciprocal effect, (*informal*) to and fro

intercept VERB
He intercepted her at the kitchen door.
▶ stop, catch, check, interrupt, obstruct, cut off, block, deflect, head off, thwart, trap

interest NOUN
1 *a matter of great interest to both of them*
▶ importance, significance, consequence, moment, note, value
2 *Her interests include rock-climbing.*
▶ activity, pursuit, hobby, pastime, diversion, preoccupation
show interest in *John was showing interest in the idea.*
▶ take notice of, pay attention to, be concerned about, be curious about, have regard for, show involvement in, show commitment to

interest VERB
an idea that interests me
▶ appeal to, attract, excite, fascinate, intrigue, engage, engross, concern, stimulate, arouse the curiosity of, capture the imagination of, divert, entertain, involve, (*more informal*) turn on
AN OPPOSITE IS bore

interested ADJECTIVE
1 *None of them appeared to be interested.*
▶ curious, enthusiastic, excited, keen, responsive, fascinated, absorbed, attentive, engrossed, intent
AN OPPOSITE IS uninterested.

2 *At the meeting various problems were explained to the interested parties.*
▶ affected, involved, concerned, connected
AN OPPOSITE IS disinterested
be interested in *The owners were interested in the idea of selling off part of the land.*
▶ like, be attracted by, fancy

interesting ADJECTIVE
an interesting idea
▶ attractive, appealing, engrossing, stimulating, exciting, intriguing, fascinating, thought-provoking

interfere VERB
1 **interfere in** *She did not wish to interfere in her friends' lives.*
▶ intervene, intrude in, meddle in, butt into, pry into, snoop into, encroach on
2 **interfere with** *A headache interfered with his thoughts.*
▶ inhibit, hinder, hamper, impede, get in the way of

interference NOUN
He would not tolerate any interference.
▶ intrusion, intervention, meddling, snooping, involvement

interfering ADJECTIVE
She blamed his interfering brother.
▶ meddlesome, meddling, nosy, prying, snooping, intrusive

interim ADJECTIVE
An interim report is being prepared.
▶ provisional, temporary, stopgap, short-term, acting, halfway

interior NOUN
the interior of the building
▶ inside, inside surface, inward aspect, heart, core
AN OPPOSITE IS exterior

interior ADJECTIVE
the interior walls
▶ inner, inside, internal, innermost
AN OPPOSITE IS exterior

interlude NOUN
a quiet interlude in a hectic day
▶ interval, pause, respite, spell, break, breathing space

intermediary NOUN
They used an intermediary to conclude the agreement.
▶ mediator, go-between, negotiator, conciliator, middleman

intermediate ADJECTIVE
French classes at intermediate level
▶ midway, halfway, transitional

interminable ADJECTIVE
It was a week of interminable meetings and interviews.
▶ endless, never-ending, ceaseless, incessant, constant, continuous, continual, perpetual, everlasting

intermittent ADJECTIVE
A day of intermittent rainstorms followed.
▶ sporadic, periodic, occasional, irregular,
recurrent, spasmodic, fitful, (*informal*) on and off
AN OPPOSITE IS continuous

internal ADJECTIVE
1 *The house was built round an internal courtyard.*
▶ inner, interior, inside, central
AN OPPOSITE IS external
2 *the country's internal affairs*
▶ domestic, home, interior, local, civil

international ADJECTIVE
the growth of fast international travel
▶ global, worldwide, intercontinental, universal

interpret VERB
wise men who interpret the sacred laws
▶ explain, expound, clarify, elucidate, translate

interpretation NOUN
We have a different interpretation of the story.
▶ explanation, understanding, clarification, reading,
analysis, definition, gloss, version

interrogate VERB
The secret police wanted to interrogate them.
▶ question, cross-examine, examine, investigate,
(*more informal*) grill, (*more informal*) quiz

interrogation NOUN
The police interrogation continued all morning.
▶ questioning, cross-examination, investigation,
examination, (*more informal*) grilling

interrupt VERB
1 *He opened his mouth to interrupt.*
▶ butt in, break in, cut in, intervene
2 *People at the back of the hall began to interrupt her.*
▶ heckle, disrupt, butt in on, cut in on
3 *The news from home led them to interrupt their
holiday.*
▶ suspend, break off, discontinue, delay, postpone,
put off, defer
4 *The new building will interrupt the view.*
▶ break, break up, divide, disturb

interruption NOUN
1 *There were several interruptions during the speech.*
▶ intervention, intrusion, disruption, cutting in,
disturbance
2 *A note through the letterbox warned of interruptions
in the water supply.*
▶ break, disruption, suspension, pause, check,
hiatus, stop

interval NOUN
1 *There will be an interval of 20 minutes halfway
through the show.*
▶ intermission, interlude, break, pause
2 *The next class will be in a week's time and you can
revise in the interval.*
▶ interim, meantime, meanwhile, pause, delay

intervene VERB
1 *A week intervened before I saw her again*
▶ come between, happen, intrude, occur

2 *Someone has to intervene to sort out the
disagreement.*
▶ step in, intercede, interrupt, interfere, intrude,
mediate, arbitrate, butt in

intervention NOUN
*Their intervention was resented by both sides in the
dispute.*
▶ intrusion, involvement, intercession, mediation

interview NOUN
Interviews for the job will be held next week.
▶ meeting, discussion, conference, audience,
questioning

interview VERB
A journalist wants to interview her about her new book.
▶ talk to, question, ask questions, have a discussion
with, interrogate, examine

intimate ADJECTIVE
1 *an intimate friendship*
▶ close, loving, affectionate, personal, familiar,
friendly, informal, sexual
2 *an intimate atmosphere*
▶ friendly, welcoming, warm, informal, relaxed,
cosy
3 *intimate thoughts*
▶ personal, private, secret, confidential
4 *an intimate knowledge of the area*
▶ detailed, exhaustive, profound, deep, in-depth

intimidate VERB
*He wanted to get his way without appearing to
intimidate them.*
▶ threaten, bully, frighten, coerce, browbeat,
menace, persecute, scare, terrify, terrorize, cow,
daunt, hector, make afraid

intolerable ADJECTIVE
The noise had become intolerable.
▶ unbearable, unendurable, unacceptable,
insufferable, insupportable, excruciating,
impossible
OPPOSITES ARE tolerable, bearable

intolerant ADJECTIVE
He was extremely intolerant about religion.
▶ bigoted, dogmatic, narrow-minded, opinionated,
prejudiced, chauvinistic, illiberal
AN OPPOSITE IS tolerant

intrepid ADJECTIVE
*The four intrepid climbers had to turn back because of
fierce winds.*
▶ bold, courageous, daring, brave, gallant, fearless,
plucky, valiant

intricate ADJECTIVE
intricate designs   intricate relationships
▶ complex, elaborate, ornate, detailed,
complicated, convoluted, tangled, delicate,
involved, sophisticated, tortuous
AN OPPOSITE IS simple

intrigue NOUN

1 *a leader vulnerable to jealousy and intrigue*
▶ conspiracy, plotting, scheming, machination, trickery, subterfuge

2 *a family abuzz with romantic intrigues*
▶ affair, liaison, amour, flirtation, dalliance, intimacy

intrigue VERB

1 *These stories have always intrigued young children.*
▶ interest, fascinate, engross, captivate, enthrall, absorb, beguile

2 *The men were suspected of intriguing against the king*
▶ plot, conspire, scheme, connive, manoeuvre

intriguing ADJECTIVE

an intriguing account of a trip round the world
▶ interesting, fascinating, engrossing, captivating, enthralling, absorbing, beguiling

intrinsic ADJECTIVE

The jewellery has little intrinsic value.
▶ inherent, innate, fundamental, essential, basic, real

introduce VERB

1 *Jane introduced us to her husband.*
▶ present, make known, acquaint

2 *The new owners have introduced some new features.*
▶ bring in, institute, initiate, establish, set up, start, begin, create, offer, propose, suggest, pioneer

3 *a new star to introduce the show*
▶ present, host, compère, announce

introduction NOUN

1 *the introduction of a democratic government*
▶ institution, establishment, foundation, inauguration, beginning, development

2 *The author thanks his friends in the book's introduction.*
▶ foreword, preface, preamble, front matter, opening

introductory ADJECTIVE

1 *The speaker began with some introductory remarks.*
▶ opening, preliminary, preparatory, initial, prefatory
AN OPPOSITE IS concluding

2 *a short introductory course*
▶ basic, elementary, preliminary, preparatory, primary

introvert NOUN

He enjoyed a social life despite being an introvert.
▶ shy person, reserved person
AN OPPOSITE IS extrovert
USAGE For other synonyms see the words in the next entry.

introverted ADJECTIVE

a quiet and introverted character
▶ shy, reserved, retiring, introvert, introspective, inward-looking, thoughtful, meditative, withdrawn, contemplative, pensive, self-contained, unsociable
AN OPPOSITE IS extrovert

intrude VERB

intrude on *No one has the right to intrude on a person's privacy in this way.*
▶ encroach on, break in on, interrupt, interfere with, butt in on, eavesdrop on, intervene in, gatecrash

intruder NOUN

Intruders had left the house in a mess.
▶ trespasser, interloper, invader, burglar, housebreaker, prowler, robber, thief, raider

intrusion NOUN

Please forgive this intrusion.
▶ interruption, interference, encroachment, intervention, disruption
AN OPPOSITE IS withdrawal

intuition NOUN

1 *He relied on his intuition to get him out of the difficulty.*
▶ instinct, intuitiveness, sixth sense, insight

2 *What you say confirms all my intuitions.*
▶ feeling, gut feeling, hunch, suspicion, premonition

intuitive ADJECTIVE

She has an intuitive understanding of languages.
▶ instinctive, innate, inborn, inherent, natural, unconscious, involuntary

inundate VERB

The waters inundated the city. We were inundated with letters.
▶ flood, deluge, engulf, submerge, overrun, overwhelm

invade VERB

The allies invaded the country from the south.
▶ march into, occupy, enter, penetrate, overrun, raid, subdue, violate, attack, descend on, encroach on

invalid ADJECTIVE (with the stress on -*val*-)

1 *His licence would be invalid in America.*
▶ void, unacceptable, unusable, worthless, null and void
AN OPPOSITE IS valid

2 *It was not difficult to prove the idea invalid.*
▶ false, fallacious, unfounded, unreasonable, unsound, incorrect, untrue, illogical, irrational, unconvincing, unscientific
AN OPPOSITE IS valid

invalid ADJECTIVE (with the stress on *in*-)

Kate has an invalid husband.
▶ sick, ailing, infirm, disabled, incapacitated, bedridden

invaluable ADJECTIVE

James is an invaluable member of the team.
▶ crucial, indispensable, irreplaceable, precious, priceless, useful, valuable, incalculable, inestimable
AN OPPOSITE IS worthless
USAGE Note that *invaluable* is not the opposite of *valuable*: for this you should use *valueless*.

invasion NOUN
1 *an air invasion of the island*
▶ attack (on), occupation, incursion, seizure, annexation, overrunning, onslaught, raid
2 *the annual invasion of tourists*
▶ influx, incursion, inundation, flood, horde, spate, stream, swarm, throng, infestation

invent VERB
1 *He invented a new board game.*
▶ create, devise, conceive, formulate, improvise, originate
2 *They invented any excuse to avoid going near the swimming pool.*
▶ make up, concoct, fabricate, manufacture, (*more informal*) cook up

invention NOUN
1 *the invention of printing*
▶ development, origination, creation, devising, innovation, pioneering
2 *writing that shows a lot of invention*
▶ originality, creativity, imagination, ingenuity, inventiveness, resourcefulness, inspiration
3 *The excuse was pure invention.*
▶ fabrication, fantasy, fiction, deceit, concoction

inventive ADJECTIVE
an inventive artist
▶ creative, original, imaginative, innovative, ingenious, resourceful, enterprising, fertile, inspired
AN OPPOSITE IS imitative

inventor NOUN
the inventor of the telephone
▶ creator, originator, designer, discoverer, architect, author, maker

invert VERB
A storm inverted the little boat.
▶ overturn, reverse, turn upside down, upset, capsize

invest VERB
invest in *She invested in her son's business.*
▶ put money into, buy shares in, fund, back

investigate VERB
Police are investigating the discovery of a body.
▶ inquire into, look into, follow up, probe, examine, explore, consider, study, gather evidence about, scrutinize, (*more informal*) go into

investigation NOUN
The problem needs further investigation. There will have to be an official investigation.
▶ examination, inquiry, research, scrutiny, study, survey, inspection, inquisition, (*informal*) probing

investment NOUN
You need good advice before you make any investments.
▶ venture, expenditure, outlay

invigorating ADJECTIVE
an invigorating early morning walk
▶ stimulating, exhilarating, revitalizing, refreshing, bracing, enlivening, fresh, health-giving, healthy, rejuvenating
AN OPPOSITE IS tiring

invincible ADJECTIVE
the invincible power of the invading armies
▶ unbeatable, unassailable, indestructible, indomitable, unconquerable, invulnerable, mighty

invisible ADJECTIVE
The house was invisible in the dark.
▶ hidden, obscured, concealed, undetectable, unnoticeable, imperceptible, unnoticed, unseen, out of sight, covered, disguised, inconspicuous
AN OPPOSITE IS visible

invitation NOUN
1 *an invitation to attend the conference*
▶ call, summons, request
2 *An open door is an invitation to any passing thief.*
▶ temptation, encouragement, enticement, lure, provocation, inducement

invite VERB
1 *They've invited us to dinner on Saturday.*
▶ ask, request the company of, welcome, summon
2 *Using emotive language might invite trouble.*
▶ provoke, cause, generate, engender, foster, elicit

inviting ADJECTIVE
the inviting sight of a buffet lunch
▶ attractive, appealing, welcome, pleasant, enticing, agreeable, appetizing, seductive

invoke VERB
1 *The prosecutor invoked an old law of the previous century.*
▶ refer to, appeal to, cite
2 *She clasped her hands and invoked her patron saint.*
▶ pray to, appeal to, entreat, supplicate, beseech, implore

involuntary ADJECTIVE
She gave an involuntary shudder.
▶ reflex, automatic, unconscious, spontaneous, unthinking, unintentional, conditioned, impulsive, instinctive
AN OPPOSITE IS deliberate

involve VERB
1 *Her job involves a lot of travel.*
▶ necessitate, entail, require, demand, mean
2 *These are decisions that involve everybody.*
▶ affect, concern, interest, include, embrace, take in, touch
3 *The project involved them in community work.*
▶ occupy, engage, absorb, engross
4 *A drug habit can rapidly involve them in crime.*
▶ implicate, associate, embroil, entangle

involved ADJECTIVE

1 *a long and involved story*
▶ complex, complicated, convoluted, elaborate, intricate, tangled, confusing, difficult, (*more informal*) knotty
AN OPPOSITE IS straightforward

2 *She is totally involved in her work.*
▶ occupied, engrossed, absorbed, engaged, preoccupied, caught up, committed (to), dedicated (to)
AN OPPOSITE IS uninvolved

involvement NOUN

1 *her involvement in charity work.*
▶ interest, participation, activity

2 *There was no doubting their involvement in the plot.*
▶ complicity, connivance, participation, entanglement, association

invulnerable ADJECTIVE

No one is invulnerable to these dangers.
▶ safe (from), secure (from), impervious, immune, insusceptible
AN OPPOSITE IS vulnerable

irate ADJECTIVE

The helpline has to deal with hundreds of irate callers.
▶ angry, enraged, furious, incensed, infuriated, indignant, displeased, outraged

ironic ADJECTIVE

1 *The tone of Sarah's voice was sharply ironic.*
▶ sarcastic, ironical, satirical, wry, derisive, double-edged, mocking

2 *It is ironic that after criticizing London so much he should end up living there.*
▶ paradoxical, strange, peculiar, odd, weird, incongruous

irrational ADJECTIVE

an irrational fear of flying
▶ illogical, baseless, unreasonable, senseless, arbitrary, unsound, absurd
AN OPPOSITE IS rational

irregular ADJECTIVE

1 *an irregular surface*
▶ uneven, rough, coarse, bumpy, pitted

2 *an irregular heartbeat   an irregular pattern*
▶ variable, fluctuating, erratic, fitful, haphazard, unsystematic, intermittent

3 *Her appointment was most irregular.*
▶ improper, abnormal, unorthodox, anomalous, unconventional, against the rules

irrelevant ADJECTIVE

Don't waste time on irrelevant details.
▶ inappropriate, unnecessary, inessential, extraneous, peripheral, immaterial, inapplicable, pointless, unconnected, unrelated
AN OPPOSITE IS relevant

irreparable ADJECTIVE

A power failure can cause irreparable damage.
▶ permanent, irretrievable, irreversible, irremediable, unrectifiable, lasting, irrecoverable, unalterable, incurable
AN OPPOSITE IS reparable

irreplaceable ADJECTIVE

a work of art that is irreplaceable
▶ unique, inimitable, indispensable, matchless, priceless, rare
OPPOSITES ARE replaceable, common

irrepressible ADJECTIVE

He loved her irrepressible high spirits
▶ ebullient, lively, boisterous, uninhibited, unstoppable, sparkling, bubbling, vivacious, vigorous, bouncy, resilient, uncontrollable, ungovernable
AN OPPOSITE IS sluggish

irresistible ADJECTIVE

1 *The temptation to laugh was irresistible.*
▶ overpowering, overwhelming, inescapable, inexorable, powerful, seductive, unavoidable, compelling, persuasive

2 *She has an irresistible laugh.*
▶ attractive, appealing, enticing, alluring, seductive, fetching, captivating, beguiling

irresponsible ADJECTIVE

1 *an irresponsible attitude*
▶ reckless, rash, inconsiderate, thoughtless, careless, immoral, selfish, shiftless
AN OPPOSITE IS responsible

2 *They sometimes behave like irresponsible teenagers.*
▶ immature, unreliable, feckless, unthinking, untrustworthy

irreverent ADJECTIVE

an irreverent approach to authority
▶ disrespectful, discourteous, disdainful, insolent, impertinent, impudent, scornful, flippant, casual, rude
OPPOSITES ARE reverent, respectful

irrevocable ADJECTIVE

an irrevocable decision
▶ unalterable, unchangeable, irreversible, immutable, binding, final, firm, fixed, settled, hard and fast
AN OPPOSITE IS reversible

irritable ADJECTIVE

Harry sat back with an irritable look on his face.
▶ bad-tempered, irascible, grumpy, testy, grouchy, touchy, tetchy, crotchety, cantankerous, peevish, fractious, cross, (*more informal*) stroppy, (*more informal*) shirty
OPPOSITES ARE good-tempered, good-humoured, affable

irritate VERB

I was letting silly things irritate me.
▶ annoy, displease, anger, infuriate, enrage, exasperate, incense, peeve, vex, madden, aggravate, antagonize, inflame, make angry, (*more*

informal) needle, (*more informal*) rile, (*more informal*)
bug, (*more informal*) rub up the wrong way
OPPOSITES ARE please, gratify

rritation NOUN
It was hard to hide our irritation at such rudeness.
▶ annoyance, indignation, displeasure,
exasperation, pique, chagrin, vexation

solate VERB
1 *Their extreme political views tended to isolate them
from their contemporaries.*
▶ separate, set apart, keep apart, cut off, segregate,
detach, insulate, seclude, alienate, exclude, single
out
2 *Sophisticated cameras can easily isolate offending
vehicles.*
▶ identify, recognize, pick out, single out, pinpoint,
distinguish

solated ADJECTIVE
1 *an isolated town in eastern Malaysia*
▶ remote, outlying, secluded, solitary, inaccessible,
out of the way, deserted
AN OPPOSITE IS accessible
2 *an isolated occurrence*
▶ unique, special, exceptional, untypical, abnormal

ssue NOUN
1 *The society debates political issues.*
▶ matter, concern, subject, topic, affair, point,
question, argument, controversy, dispute, problem
2 *a special issue of the magazine*
▶ edition, number, instalment, publication, printing

ssue VERB
1 *Smoke issued from the top of the building.*
▶ emerge, emanate, erupt, flow out, rise, appear,
come out, gush, leak, spring
2 *The ambassador issued a formal statement.*
▶ publish, publicize, release, circulate, distribute,
give out, print, produce, send out

tch NOUN
1 *I have an itch in my back.*
▶ itchiness, tickle, tingling, irritation, need to
scratch
2 *She felt an itch to start painting.*
▶ desire, hankering, longing, yearning, urge, wish,
impulse, lust, need, ache, impatience, restlessness,
(*more informal*) yen

tch VERB
1 *The warmth made my skin itch.*
▶ tickle, tingle, be irritated
2 *They were itching to leave.*
▶ long, hanker, yearn, be eager, be keen

tem NOUN
1 *an item of equipment*
▶ article, bit, object, component, ingredient
2 *a news item*
▶ report, article, account, feature, notice, piece
3 *several items on the agenda*
▶ topic, subject

jab VERB
He laughed and jabbed his friend in the ribs.
▶ poke, prod, dig, nudge, elbow, shove

jack VERB
jack up *He got a passer-by to help him jack up the car
and change the tyre.*
▶ lift, raise, hoist, lever up

jacket NOUN
1 *He wore a blue jacket and cream shirt.*
▶ coat
2 *books with lurid jackets*
▶ cover, wrapper, coat, covering, folder
3 *The boiler needs an insulating jacket.*
▶ casing, sheath, sleeve, envelope, skin, wrapping

jackpot NOUN
Three winners will share the jackpot this week.
▶ top prize, first prize, big prize
hit the jackpot (*informal*)
▶ be successful, win a fortune, strike it lucky, make a
packet

jaded ADJECTIVE
The long day left me feeling jaded.
▶ weary, tired, drained, exhausted, fatigued, listless,
spent, (*more informal*) done in
AN OPPOSITE IS fresh

jagged ADJECTIVE
He gashed his head against a jagged branch.
▶ spiky, uneven, broken, irregular, ragged, rough,
toothed, serrated, zigzag
OPPOSITES ARE even, smooth

jail NOUN
a building that used to be the town jail
▶ prison, jailhouse, guardhouse, (*more informal*) nick,
(*more informal*) clink

jail VERB
If he's found guilty he'll be jailed.
▶ send to prison, put in prison, imprison, give a
custodial sentence to

jailer NOUN
The jailer's wife brought the prisoner some food.
▶ prison guard, prison officer, guard, warder,
warden

jam NOUN
1 *a long jam on the motorway*
▶ tailback, hold-up, obstruction, blockage,
bottleneck
2 *We're in a bit of a jam.*
▶ predicament, quandary, embarrassment,
difficulty, dilemma, tight corner, trouble, plight,
(*more informal*) fix, (*more informal*) hole
3 *Have some home-made jam.*
▶ preserve, conserve, jelly, marmalade

jam VERB

1 *They try to jam too many people in the lifts.*
► cram, pack, squeeze, stuff, crowd, crush, ram, squash

2 *Protesters jammed one side of the motorway.*
► block, clog, obstruct, congest

3 *I'll jam the door open with a newspaper.*
► prop, stick, wedge

4 *The window has jammed.*
► stick, become stuck, become wedged, become lodged, seize

jangle VERB

He jangled his keys as he walked to the door. Bracelets jangled on her wrists.
► jingle, clink, tinkle, clang

janitor NOUN

a school janitor
► caretaker, custodian, watchman, maintenance man

jar NOUN

a jar of honey
► pot, drum, glass, crock, container

jar VERB

1 **jar on** *His whining voice jarred on me.*
► grate on, annoy, irritate, irk, exasperate, set your teeth on edge

2 *The fall jarred her whole body.*
► jolt, jerk, shake, shock, vibrate

jargon NOUN

The instructions are full of difficult jargon.
► technical language, parlance, idiom, (*more informal*) gobbledegook

jarring ADJECTIVE

a sequence of jarring chords
► clashing, discordant, conflicting, harsh, grating, grinding, raucous, jangling, unpleasant, disagreeable

jaundiced ADJECTIVE

a jaundiced view of life
► bitter, pessimistic, resentful, disillusioned, cynical, sceptical

jaunt NOUN

a jaunt round the old city
► trip, outing, excursion, tour, expedition, journey

jaunty ADJECTIVE

His cap was pushed to one side, giving him a jaunty air.
► cheerful, bright, lively, jolly, carefree, spirited, perky, airy, breezy, frisky, sprightly
OPPOSITES ARE dejected, dismal

jazzy ADJECTIVE

1 *jazzy music*
► animated, lively, rhythmic, spirited, syncopated

2 *a jazzy colour scheme*
► bright, bold, colourful, gaudy, showy, loud, flashy
OPPOSITES ARE sober, dull

jealous ADJECTIVE

1 *Jason was jealous of her ability to come up with good ideas.*
► envious, resentful, grudging, covetous, desirous
OPPOSITES ARE proud, admiring

2 *the story of a beautiful woman who is locked away by her jealous lover*
► suspicious, distrustful, possessive, protective, dominating
AN OPPOSITE IS trusting

3 *They are very jealous of their privileges.*
► protective, defensive, watchful, mindful
AN OPPOSITE IS unconcerned (about)

jealousy NOUN

1 *He was overcome by jealousy at their good fortune.*
► envy, resentment, bitterness, discontent, covetousness

2 *She could no longer stand her lover's jealousy.*
► suspicion, distrust, mistrust, possessiveness

jeer VERB

The demonstrators were jeering the police.
► mock, taunt, scoff, deride, sneer at, abuse, insult, barrack, heckle
AN OPPOSITE IS cheer

jeer NOUN

comments that brought jeers from his schoolmates
► taunt, sneer, jibe, insult, boo, hiss, ridicule, disapproval
AN OPPOSITE IS cheer

jeopardize VERB

He wouldn't jeopardize his career by taking risks now.
► threaten, endanger, put at risk, compromise, harm, imperil, expose

jeopardy NOUN

in jeopardy *With the country at war the empire was in jeopardy*
► in danger, in peril, at risk, vulnerable, under threat
AN OPPOSITE IS secure

jerk VERB

1 *She jerked her hand from his and turned away.*
► pull, tug, pluck, wrench, yank, tweak

2 *The car jerked forward.*
► jolt, lurch, bump, bounce

jerk NOUN

1 *He pulled away his hand with a jerk.*
► tug, pull, wrench, yank, twitch

2 *The bus stopped with a jerk.*
► jolt, lurch, start, bump, shock

jerky ADJECTIVE

Her voice had grown jerky and breathless.
► fitful, spasmodic, convulsive, shaky, twitchy, jumpy, uncoordinated, incoherent
OPPOSITES ARE steady, smooth

jest NOUN

The men talked and exchanged jests.
► joke, witticism, quip, banter

jest VERB

He admitted that he had been jesting.
▶ joke, fool, hoax, tease, (*more informal*) kid

jet NOUN

1 *a jet of water*
▶ stream, spurt, squirt, gush, spout, spray, flow, fountain, rush
2 *He pointed the jet at the flames.*
▶ nozzle, sprinkler

jetty NOUN

We landed at a rickety jetty.
▶ pier, quay, wharf, landing stage, breakwater, groyne, mole

jewel NOUN

1 *a tiara encrusted with jewels*
▶ gem, gemstone, precious stone
2 *His girlfriend was a jewel.*
▶ treasure, angel, paragon, pearl, wonder

---

jewellery NOUN

A street fair was selling ethnic jewellery.
▶ gems, jewels, ornaments, (*more informal*) sparklers

ITEMS OF JEWELLERY

worn on the head and neck: diadem, tiara; earring, ear stud; nose ring, nose stud; necklace, beads, chain, pendant; choker.

worn on the arms and hands: armlet, bangle, bracelet, charm bracelet, circlet, wristlet; cuff links; ring, eternity ring, signet ring.

worn on the body: anklet, brooch, clasp, locket, pin, tiepin, stud.

JEWELS AND JEWELLERY STONES

amber, cairngorm, carnelian or cornelian, coral, diamond, emerald, garnet, ivory, jade, jasper, jet, lapis lazuli, moonstone, onyx, opal, pearl, rhinestone, ruby, sapphire, topaz, turquoise.

METALS USED TO MAKE JEWELLERY

gold, platinum, silver.

---

jibe NOUN

He'll have to put up with the jibes of his friends.
▶ taunt, jeer, sneer, snide remark

jiggle VERB

The boy was jiggling in his chair.
▶ fidget, wriggle, squirm

jilt VERB

Perhaps Hugh had done her a favour by jilting her.
▶ reject, desert, discard, abandon, (*more informal*) ditch

jingle NOUN

1 *He could hear the jingle of her bracelet.*
▶ jangle, clink, tinkle
2 *An advertising jingle kept coming into his head.*
▶ slogan, song, catchline, ditty, refrain

jingle VERB

The coins jingled in their pockets.
▶ jangle, clink, tinkle, clang

jingoism NOUN

the jingoism of some war films
▶ chauvinism, nationalism, extreme patriotism, xenophobia

jinx NOUN

They wondered whether the jinx would strike again.
▶ curse, spell, evil eye, bad luck

jinxed ADJECTIVE

It was almost as if the house was jinxed.
▶ cursed, bewitched, bedevilled, under a spell

jitters PLURAL NOUN

a fit of jitters
▶ nervousness, nerves, anxiety, agitation, tension, edginess, restlessness

jittery ADJECTIVE

He felt jittery about meeting her again.
▶ nervous, anxious, agitated, tense, edgy, fretful, restless, ill at ease

job NOUN

1 *The job involves some weekend work.*
▶ occupation, employment, position, situation, post, work, career
2 *Painting the house will be a long job.*
▶ task, piece of work, undertaking, operation, assignment, project, chore
3 *It's my job to lock up in the evenings.*
▶ responsibility, duty, task, concern, role, function
4 (*informal*) *We had a job finding the house.*
▶ problem, difficulty, difficult task, hard time, struggle

jobless ADJECTIVE

Two percent of the population is jobless.
▶ unemployed, out of work, laid off, redundant
OPPOSITES ARE employed, in work

jocular ADJECTIVE

a few jocular remarks
▶ humorous, funny, witty, comical, amusing, droll, joking
AN OPPOSITE IS serious

USAGE Remember that *funny* can mean 'peculiar' as well as 'jocular', and it is sometimes better to use another word.

jog VERB

1 *He jogged her elbow as he walked past.*
▶ nudge, prod, jolt, jar, bump, jostle
2 *I need a clue to jog my memory.*
▶ prompt, stir, arouse, stimulate, remind
3 *They were jogging through the park.*
▶ trot, run, jogtrot

join VERB

1 *Join the two pieces together.*
▶ connect, fasten, attach, couple, merge, stick, tie, glue

2 *Her son wanted to join the army.*
► enlist in, enrol in, sign up in, enter, volunteer for, become a member of
3 *We joined the peace march along the route.*
► follow, go along with, tag along with, accompany
4 *The two roads join here.*
► meet, come together, converge

join NOUN
You have to look hard to see the join.
► joint, connection, seam, knot, link, mend

joint NOUN
the joint between the wall and the flat roof
► join, connection, junction, seam

joint ADJECTIVE
The two artists are holding a joint exhibition.
► combined, shared, common, collaborative, coordinated, cooperative, collective, communal, concerted, united, mutual
OPPOSITES ARE separate, discrete, individual

joke NOUN
(informal) They sat all evening telling each other jokes.
► funny story, jest, witticism, wisecrack, pleasantry, quip, crack, (more informal) gag

joke VERB
1 *He laughed and joked with his friends.*
► tell jokes, crack jokes, jest, clown, have a laugh, be facetious
2 *From the look on her face I'd say she was only joking.*
► fool, tease, hoax, (more informal) kid

joker NOUN
She seems quite a joker, but she has her serious side.
► jester, comedian, comic, humorist, wag, wit, clown

jolly ADJECTIVE
We had a jolly time. He was in a jolly mood when he came back.
► cheerful, merry, cheery, happy, jovial, exuberant, hearty

jolt VERB
1 *The car jolted along the rough roads.*
► bump, bounce, jerk, jog, shake, shudder
2 *The fierceness of his remarks jolted her.*
► startle, surprise, shock, disturb, disconcert, upset, discompose, astonish, nonplus

jostle VERB
1 *She was afraid of being jostled by the crowds.*
► push, shove, hustle, press, crowd in on
2 *People jostled for a good view.*
► struggle, scramble, jockey

jot VERB
jot down *The man jotted down my details.*
► write down, note down, take down, scribble, make a note of

journal NOUN
1 *an academic journal*
► periodical, publication, magazine, gazette, digest
2 *She kept a journal of the voyage.*
► diary, log, record, chronicle, account

journalist NOUN
A journalist wanted to hear his story.
► reporter, correspondent, columnist, feature-writer, contributor, writer

journey NOUN
The journey takes you through three countries.
► trip, route, itinerary, travels, voyage, peregrination
USAGE You normally use *voyage* to mean a long journey by sea.

journey VERB
They journeyed north.
► travel, go, voyage, go on a journey, sail, cruise, trek

jovial ADJECTIVE
A jovial old man greeted them.
► jolly, cheerful, cheery, affable, genial, merry

joy NOUN
There was a look of joy on her face.
► delight, bliss, pleasure, happiness, gladness, ecstasy, elation, joyfulness, exultation, rapture, euphoria, exuberance
OPPOSITES ARE sorrow, misery

joyful ADJECTIVE
Kate set off with joyful enthusiasm.
► cheerful, happy, joyous, jubilant, bright, sunny, lively, elated, animated, contented, buoyant, good-humoured, light-hearted, chirpy
AN OPPOSITE IS sad

jubilant ADJECTIVE
Jubilant fans surged on to the pitch.
► delighted, joyful, overjoyed, exultant, joyous, elated, ecstatic, thrilled

jubilee NOUN
a royal jubilee
► anniversary, celebration, festival, gala, carnival, commemoration

judge NOUN
1 *The judges could not agree on a winner.*
► adjudicator, arbiter, arbitrator, assessor, moderator, referee, umpire
2 *a good judge of art*
► connoisseur, authority (on), expert (on), critic

judge VERB
1 *A magistrate will judge the case.*
► try, hear, sit in judgement on, adjudicate on, decide
2 *A panel of experts will judge the ten best entries.*
► assess, appraise, decide, evaluate, review, examine
3 *We judged that she had been misled.*
► conclude, decide, consider, believe, think, reckon, determine, come to the view, form the opinion

judgement NOUN
1 *the judgement of the court*
► verdict, decision, adjudication, ruling, finding, pronouncement, sentence

2 *He showed a lack of judgement.*
▶ understanding, discernment, perception, wisdom, sense, common sense, acumen, prudence
3 *my judgement of the situation*
▶ assessment, appraisal, evaluation, estimate, analysis, view, opinion, belief

judicial ADJECTIVE
a judicial review
▶ legal, judiciary, official, impartial

judicious ADJECTIVE
a judicious approach to the teaching of English
▶ sensible, prudent, appropriate, shrewd, thoughtful, well judged, wise, astute, expedient

jug NOUN
a jug of water
▶ pitcher, carafe, flagon, ewer, crock, vessel

juggle VERB
She learned to juggle her hours so she could spend more time at home.
▶ manipulate, rearrange, alter, change, move about

juice NOUN
Add the juice of a lemon.
▶ liquid, fluid, extract, essence

juicy ADJECTIVE
1 *a juicy pear*
▶ succulent, tender, moist, soft, ripe
AN OPPOSITE IS dry
2 *a juicy piece of gossip*
▶ interesting, lurid, spicy, colourful, racy

jumble NOUN
Clothes lay on the floor in a jumble.
▶ muddle, hotchpotch, mess, clutter, chaos, confusion, disorder

jumble VERB
I'll try not to jumble the photographs.
▶ muddle, disorganize, mix up, shuffle, confuse, disarrange, (*more informal*) mess up
AN OPPOSITE IS organize

jump VERB
1 *A dog jumped off the chair.*
▶ leap, spring, bound, bounce, hop
2 *All the horses jumped the first fence.*
▶ vault, clear
3 *The children were jumping about in the garden.*
▶ skip, dance, frolic, prance, cavort
4 *A noise made him jump.*
▶ start, jerk, jolt, flinch, recoil
5 *Attendance had jumped by more than 20 percent.*
▶ rise, increase, leap, go up, escalate

jump NOUN
1 *With a jump he reached the other side.*
▶ leap, bound, spring, vault, hop
2 *The horse cleared the last jump comfortably.*
▶ fence, hurdle, ditch, barrier, obstacle, gap, gate
3 *a huge jump in house prices*
▶ rise, increase, escalation, upturn
4 *She woke up with a jump.*
▶ start, jerk, jolt, shock, shudder, lurch

jumpy ADJECTIVE
He was tired and jumpy.
▶ nervous, edgy, jittery, tense, anxious, agitated, apprehensive

junction NOUN
1 *a road junction*
▶ intersection, crossing, interchange, turn-off
2 *the junction of two rivers*
▶ confluence, convergence, meeting

junior ADJECTIVE
a junior official
▶ low-ranking, lower-ranking, subordinate, subsidiary, younger, lesser, minor, secondary
AN OPPOSITE IS senior

junk NOUN
a cupboard full of old junk
▶ rubbish, clutter, oddments, odds and ends, garbage, refuse, scrap, trash, waste

just ADJECTIVE
1 *a just ruler   a just settlement*
▶ fair, equitable, fair-minded, honourable, even-handed, unprejudiced, unbiased, neutral, non-partisan
AN OPPOSITE IS unjust
2 *a just punishment*
▶ fair, fitting, deserved, merited, appropriate, suitable, reasonable, legitimate
OPPOSITES ARE undeserved, unfair

justice NOUN
1 *He appealed to their sense of justice.*
▶ fairness, justness, fair play, integrity, equity, honesty, impartiality, legality, right
AN OPPOSITE IS injustice
2 *the administration of justice*
▶ the law, legal proceedings

justifiable ADJECTIVE
a justifiable reaction
▶ reasonable, justified, valid, legitimate, defensible, excusable, well-founded, understandable, warranted, acceptable
AN OPPOSITE IS unjustifiable

justification NOUN
1 *There is no justification for such callousness.*
▶ excuse, reason, grounds, basis, warrant, foundation
2 *Such extreme measures call for some justification*
▶ explanation, defence, vindication, argument, rationalization

justify VERB
Tiredness cannot justify this kind of reckless behaviour.
▶ excuse, defend, absolve, mitigate, account for, vindicate, exonerate, warrant, validate, uphold, support

jut VERB
jut out *A set of shelves jutted out on one wall.*
▶ project, protrude, stick out, extend, overhang, poke out

juvenile ADJECTIVE
1 *juvenile behaviour*
▶ immature, childish, babyish, infantile, puerile
AN OPPOSITE IS mature
2 *juvenile novels*
▶ adolescent, young, youthful

juvenile NOUN
The people involved were all juveniles.
▶ youth, young person, minor, under-age person

Kk

keen ADJECTIVE
1 *Competition is keen and a good honours degree is essential.*
▶ intense, acute, fierce, extreme, strong
2 *France was keen to attract more foreign investment.*
▶ eager, anxious, determined, impatient, ambitious, intent (on attracting)
3 *William is a keen devotee of science fiction.*
▶ enthusiastic, eager, avid, fervent, impassioned, committed, conscientious
4 *a knife with a keen cutting edge*
▶ sharp, sharp-edged, razor-sharp, honed
5 *Patience, nimble fingers, and keen eyesight are needed to operate the tool.*
▶ sharp, acute, clear, sensitive, strong, powerful
6 *She still displays a keen sense of humour.*
▶ sharp, piercing, incisive, penetrating, pungent, trenchant

keep VERB
1 *an in-flight magazine for you to read and keep*
▶ retain, hold on to, hang on to, possess
2 *They did their best to keep quiet.*
▶ remain, stay, continue to be, carry on being
3 *He keeps twitching his ears.*
▶ persist in, go on, continue, carry on
4 *We'll try not to keep you too long.*
▶ detain, delay, hold up, keep waiting
5 *These problems shouldn't keep you from continuing.*
▶ deter, constrain, hinder, impede, obstruct
6 *You must keep your promise.*
▶ observe, fulfil, comply with, obey, respect, keep faith with
7 *Where do you keep the coats?*
▶ store, put, stow, house
8 *Keeping a family can be expensive.*
▶ support, maintain, provide for, look after, care for, be responsible for

keeper NOUN
1 *the keeper of the museum*
▶ curator, custodian, administrator, superintendent
2 *the prisoners and their keeper*
▶ jailer, warden, guard, custodian
3 *He said he was not his brother's keeper.*
▶ guardian, protector, minder

keepsake NOUN
She gave him a ring as a keepsake.
▶ memento, souvenir, reminder, token

kernel NOUN
the juicy kernel of the nut
▶ core, heart, seed, middle

key NOUN
1 *the key to a problem*
▶ clue, indicator, pointer, lead, secret, solution, answer, interpretation
2 *a key to a map*
▶ guide, legend, index, table, explanation, glossary

key ADJECTIVE
the key question
▶ fundamental, crucial, vital, critical, essential, important

---

keyboard NOUN

THE MAIN KEYBOARD MUSICAL INSTRUMENTS

large standing instruments: piano, pianoforte, grand piano, fortepiano, clavier; harpsichord, clavichord, spinet, virginals, celesta; organ, harmonium.

electronic instruments: electric organ, synthesizer.

other instruments: accordion.

---

kick NOUN
1 *He gave the television a kick.*
▶ hit, boot, blow
2 *(informal) Some people might get a kick out of crossing the Atlantic in an old bath.*
▶ thrill, excitement, (*informal*) buzz

kick VERB
1 *Merv kicked the ball out.*
▶ boot, hit , drive, send, punt, heel
2 *(informal) a habit I have to kick*
▶ give up, quit, break, abandon, cease, desist from

kid VERB
(*informal*)
1 *I think they were only kidding.*
▶ tease, fool, bluff, lie
2 *Are you kidding me?*
▶ hoodwink, pull your leg, have you on, deceive

kidnap VERB
The group was allegedly preparing to kidnap a businessman.
▶ abduct, capture, seize, carry off, run away with, snatch

kill VERB
1 *The gang would not hesitate to kill the prisoners.*
▶ murder, put to death, slay, slaughter, dispatch, eliminate, exterminate, assassinate, (*more informal*) bump off
USAGE You use *assassinate* to refer to an important person, especially a statesman or stateswoman. *Slay* and *dispatch* are literary words.

2 *The war killed all hopes of continuing archaeological investigation at the site.*
▶ end, destroy, put an end to, dash, extinguish, finish
3 *Take aspirin to kill the pain.*
▶ soothe, alleviate, assuage, deaden, suppress, dull, blunt, reduce, stifle, extinguish
4 (*informal*) *She complained that her back was killing her.*
▶ hurt, pain, torment, torture, give discomfort to, give pain to
5 *We arrived early and had an hour to kill.*
▶ occupy, fill up, while away, pass, spend
6 (*informal*) *She nearly killed herself getting the work finished in time.*
▶ exhaust, wear out, tire out, sap, debilitate

killer NOUN
A witness was able to identify the killers.
▶ murderer, assassin, gunman, (*more informal*) hitman

killing NOUN
a brutal killing that shocked the community
▶ murder, assassination, slaughter, massacre, execution
USAGE Note that *slaughter* and *massacre* refer to the killing of a large number of people.

kind ADJECTIVE
A kind friend helped him home. It was kind of her to ring.
▶ caring, good, kind-hearted, kindly, considerate, sympathetic, thoughtful, obliging, tender-hearted, benevolent
OPPOSITES ARE unkind, unfriendly

kind NOUN
a new kind of rock music
▶ sort, type, style, form, variety, category, genre

kindle VERB
1 *Bonfires are kindled on Midwinter's Day.*
▶ light, burn, ignite, fire, set fire to
2 *These events kindled strong feelings.*
▶ stir up, stimulate, arouse, give rise to, evoke, induce, inflame, call forth

kindly ADJECTIVE
a kindly old man
▶ kind, kind-hearted, benevolent, caring, good, considerate, sympathetic, thoughtful, obliging, tender-hearted

kindness NOUN
She had shown them much kindness over many years.
▶ consideration, thoughtfulness, generosity, goodwill, benevolence, favour, understanding

king NOUN
After the war the country expelled its king.
▶ ruler, monarch, sovereign, crowned head
RELATED ADJECTIVES regal, royal

kingdom NOUN
a small kingdom in Asia Minor
▶ monarchy, realm, dominion

kink NOUN
1 *a kink in the road.*
▶ bend, corner, angle
2 *kinks in the line*
▶ twist, curl, loop, knot, tangle

kiss VERB
She stooped to kiss the little boy.
▶ caress, embrace, (*more informal*) peck

kiss NOUN
He gave her a long kiss.
▶ caress, embrace, (*more informal*) peck, (*more informal*) snog

kit NOUN
1 *a tool kit*
▶ equipment, gear, implements, appliances, tackle
2 *They made the furniture from kits.*
▶ outfit, set of parts, self-assembly set, flatpack
3 *a football kit*
▶ outfit, strip, colours, clothes

knack NOUN
He has a knack of hitting the nail on the head.
▶ gift, flair (for), talent (for), instinct (for), ability (to hit), skill (for)

knead VERB
Knead the dough until it is smooth.
▶ work, squeeze, press, pummel, manipulate, pound

kneel VERB
She knelt by the bed to pray.
▶ bend, bow, crouch, stoop, squat, fall to your knees, genuflect

knickers NOUN
She wore bright blue knickers.
▶ panties, pants, underpants, briefs, drawers

knife VERB
The victim had been knifed repeatedly.
▶ stab, gash, slash, pierce, cut, wound

knit VERB
knit together *The new arrangements took a few months to knit together.*
▶ unite, become unified, come together, combine, connect

knob NOUN
1 *He held the door knob as he looked into the room.*
▶ handle
2 *She wore her hair in a knob on top.*
▶ bump, lump, bulge, swelling, boss, projection, protuberance

knock VERB
1 *He swore as he knocked his knee on the edge of the desk.*
▶ bump, hit, strike, bang, crack, rap
2 *The man knocked on the door and waited.*
▶ bang, rap, tap, thump, pound
knock about *He knocks about with some lads from Walsall.*

▶ mix, associate, go around
knock down
1 *They are going to knock down the entire row of houses.*
▶ demolish, level, raze, destroy
2 *He knocked her down with one blow.*
▶ fell, topple, flatten, floor
knock off (*informal*)
1 *We knock off early tonight.*
▶ finish work, go home
2 *Someone had knocked off the vicar's car.*
▶ steal, take, (*informal*) pinch, (*informal*) nick
knock out
1 *I hit him and knocked him out.*
▶ stun, strike unconscious
2 (*informal*) *The long walk knocked us out.*
▶ exhaust, tire out, wear out
3 (*informal*) *music that knocked me out*
▶ overwhelm, amaze, astound

knock NOUN
The car has taken a few knocks.
▶ blow, bump, bang, shock, collision, smash

knockout NOUN
The event was a knockout.
▶ success, sensation, triumph, winner, hit

knot NOUN
1 *a knot in a rope*
▶ tie, twist, splice, hitch
2 *a knot of people*
▶ cluster, bunch, clump, group

knot VERB
She knotted a scarf round her neck.
▶ tie, secure, bind, fasten, do up, entwine
OPPOSITES ARE unknot, untie

know VERB
1 *Does she know we are here?*
▶ realize, be aware, understand, appreciate
2 *I speak French but don't know any German.*
▶ understand, speak, have knowledge of, be familiar with, be conversant with, have a grasp of
3 *Gerry knows me from our student days.*
▶ be acquainted with, have met, be friendly with, have had dealings with
4 *He had known much better times.*
▶ experience, live through, go through, undergo

know-all NOUN
(*informal*) *He's such a know-all he's bound to be able to tell us.*
▶ smart alec, wise guy, show-off, wiseacre, expert, pundit

know-how NOUN
(*informal*) *technical know-how*
▶ expertise, knowledge, skill, proficiency, understanding

knowing ADJECTIVE
1 *She gave a knowing look.*
▶ meaningful, expressive, significant, suggestive, eloquent, shrewd, artful
AN OPPOSITE IS innocent

2 *a knowing young woman*
▶ clever, astute, crafty, cunning

knowledge NOUN
1 *an extensive knowledge of the local history*
▶ understanding, comprehension, mastery, command, grasp
2 *technical knowledge*
▶ expertise, skill, proficiency, understanding, (*more informal*) know-how
3 *I have no knowledge of these people.*
▶ acquaintance (with), familiarity (with)
4 *people with a wide range of knowledge*
▶ learning, education, erudition, scholarship

knowledgeable ADJECTIVE
1 *a knowledgeable man*
▶ educated, erudite, learned, well informed
2 *knowledgeable about modern art*
▶ well informed, versed (in), acquainted (with), conversant (with), familiar (with), au fait (with)
AN OPPOSITE IS ignorant

kowtow VERB
kowtow to *It's good not to have to kowtow to the bosses any more.*
▶ grovel to, defer to, pander to, fawn on, toady, flatter, curry favour with, make up to, (*more informal*) suck up to

Ll

label NOUN
1 *Always read the label on the packet.*
▶ tag, tab, sticker, ticket, docket, marker
2 *a new independent record label*
▶ brand, company, organization

label VERB
The authorities were too ready to label people as troublemakers.
▶ identify, mark, categorize, class, classify, define, describe, regard, name, stamp, brand, call

laborious ADJECTIVE
Restoring your data is a long and laborious process.
▶ arduous, hard, heavy, difficult, stiff, tough, exhausting, fatiguing, gruelling, wearisome, onerous, strenuous, burdensome, back-breaking, tiresome, uphill
OPPOSITES ARE easy, straightforward

labour NOUN
1 (*informal*) *Keeping the place clean involved a lot of labour.*
▶ work, toil, effort, exertion, industry, drudgery, donkey work, (*more informal*) grind, (*more informal*) sweat

2 *The company took on extra labour to cope with the seasonal rush.*
▶ staff, workers, employees, workforce, (*more informal*) hands
3 *Agnes went into labour about lunchtime.*
▶ childbirth, labour pains, contractions, delivery, (*technical*) parturition

labour VERB
1 *Levin laboured day and night on the project.*
▶ work , work hard, toil, drudge, grind, exert yourself, (*more informal*) beaver, (*more informal*) slave, (*more informal*) sweat
2 *As he laboured to get back on course another blast threw the boat lopsided.*
▶ struggle, strive, endeavour, work, do your utmost, go all out
3 *We have made our point and there is no need to labour it.*
▶ overdo, overemphasize, dwell on, elaborate, exaggerate, make heavy weather of

labourer NOUN
labourers working in the fields
▶ worker, workman, workperson, hired hand

labyrinth NOUN
a labyrinth of streets and lanes
▶ maze, warren, network, complex, jungle, tangle

lace NOUN
1 *a cloth trimmed with lace*
▶ lacework, openwork, filigree, net, tatting
2 *One shoe had a lace missing.*
▶ shoelace, bootlace, shoestring, cord, string, thong

lace VERB
1 *He laced his shoes.*
▶ fasten, do up, tie up, secure
2 *She laced her fingers into his.*
▶ twine, entwine, intertwine, interweave

lack NOUN
suffering from a lack of vitamins
▶ deficiency, shortage, want, scarcity, absence, dearth, paucity, deprivation, need, privation, famine
OPPOSITES ARE sufficiency, abundance

lack VERB
The film lacks drama.
▶ be without, be short of, be deficient in, miss, want, need, require

lacking ADJECTIVE
1 **lacking** or **lacking in** *a relationship lacking in affection*
▶ wanting, needing, without, missing, short of, weak in, deficient in, inadequate in, defective in
2 *Convincing arguments are lacking.*
▶ absent, missing, unavailable, non-existent

lad NOUN
a young lad of ten
▶ boy, youth, youngster, schoolboy, fellow, (*more informal*) kid, (*more informal*) guy

laden ADJECTIVE
an old man laden with shopping
▶ loaded, burdened, encumbered, weighed down, hampered, oppressed

lady NOUN
He met the lady again on his way out.
▶ woman, female, (*more informal*) dame

ladylike ADJECTIVE
behaviour that was not especially ladylike
▶ proper, genteel, refined, respectable, polite, dainty, modest, prim and proper, well-bred

lag VERB
1 (*informal*) *Some of the runners were lagging behind.*
▶ straggle, trail, fall behind, drop behind, hang back, linger, dally, dawdle, bring up the rear, come last, idle
OPPOSITES ARE keep up, take the lead
2 *material for lagging water pipes*
▶ insulate, wrap up

laid-back ADJECTIVE
He took a laid-back attitude despite the difficulties.
▶ relaxed, unruffled, nonchalant, philosophical, casual, easygoing, at ease, informal
OPPOSITES ARE tense, uptight

lair NOUN
1 *an animal's lair*
▶ den, burrow, haunt, hole, earth
2 *a criminal's lair*
▶ hideaway, hideout, hiding place, refuge, retreat, shelter, sanctuary

lake NOUN
a house by the lake
▶ lagoon, sea, tarn, lido, pond, pool, reservoir, water, (*Scottish*) loch, (*literary*) mere

lame ADJECTIVE
1 *a young child who was sick and lame*
▶ disabled, handicapped, incapacitated, crippled
2 *As excuses went, this one was pretty lame.*
▶ feeble, weak, flimsy, thin, unconvincing, implausible, hard to believe
OPPOSITES ARE convincing, persuasive

lament NOUN
The villagers sang a lament for their dead.
▶ dirge, elegy, lamentation, requiem, threnody

lament VERB
We sat on the beach, lamenting the loss of our dry clothes.
▶ bemoan, bewail, regret, mourn, grieve over, deplore, complain about, express sorrow about, weep over

lamentable ADJECTIVE
a lamentable failure
▶ regrettable, deplorable, woeful, unfortunate, distressing, pitiful, ignominious

land NOUN
1 *a large house with several acres of land*
▶ grounds, ground, estate, property, farmland, open space
2 *Egypt is a land steeped in history.*
▶ country, nation, state, region
3 *The ship reached land at last.*
▶ dry land, terra firma, shore

land VERB
1 *Allied troops landed in Kuwait.*
▶ disembark, debark, go ashore, alight, arrive, berth, come ashore, dock, end a journey, reach landfall
AN OPPOSITE IS embark
2 *The ship will land at Calais.*
▶ dock, berth, moor, anchor, reach shore
OPPOSITES ARE set sail, put to sea
3 *The plane landed ten minutes ahead of schedule.*
▶ touch down, come in to land
AN OPPOSITE IS take off

landmark NOUN
1 *The church steeple was a landmark visible for miles around.*
▶ feature, sight, spectacle, marker, high point
2 *a landmark in history*
▶ turning point, milestone, watershed, new era

landscape NOUN
1 *the landscape of the Scottish Highlands.*
▶ scenery, countryside, topography, terrain, environment, rural scene, scene
2 *a landscape painting*
▶ panorama, vista, view, outlook, prospect

landslide NOUN
After the flooding came the landslides.
▶ landslip, earthfall, rockfall, avalanche

landslide ADJECTIVE
a landslide election victory
▶ decisive, overwhelming, runaway, emphatic

lane NOUN
a country lane
▶ road, byroad, byway, track, trail, path

language NOUN
1 *the language of the media*
▶ vocabulary, usage, style, speech
2 *The forms are written in plain language.*
▶ wording, phraseology, phrasing
3 *the grammar of language*
▶ speech, writing, communication, utterance, discourse
4 *How many languages do you know?*
▶ tongue
RELATED ADJECTIVE linguistic   ▶▶

Indo-European languages: Abanian, Armenian, Belorussian, Bengali, Breton, Bulgarian, Catalan, Croatian, Czech, Danish, Dutch, English, Flemish, French, Frisian, Gaelic, German, Greek, Gujarati, Hindi, Hindustani, Icelandic, Iranian, Irish, Italian, Kashmiri, Kurdish, Latvian, Lithuanian, Macedonian, Manx, Moldavian, Nepali, Norwegian, Pashto, Polish, Portuguese, Provençal, Punjabi, Romanian, Romany, Russian, Serbian, Sinhalese, Slovak, Slovenian, Spanish, Swedish, Tajik, Ukrainian, Urdu, Welsh, Yiddish.

Finno-Ugric languages: Estonian, Finnish, Hungarian (Magyar), Lappish (Sami).

Turkic languages Azerbaijani, Turkish, Uzbek.

Languages of the Caucasus: Armenian, Azerbaijani, Chechen, Georgian, Ossetian.

Dravidian languages: Malayalam, Tamil.

Sino-Tibetan languages: Burmese, Chinese, Laotian, Thai, Tibetan.

Semitic languages: Arabic, Aramaic, Assyrian, Chaldean, Hebrew, Maltese.

African languages: Congolese, Coptic, Sesotho, Setswana, Kiswahili.

Asian and Polynesian languages: Balinese, Fijian, Hawaiian, Javanese, Khmer, Malagasy, Malay, Maori, Samoan, Sundanese, Tagalog, Tahitian, Tongan, Vietnamese.

Languages of unknown origin: Basque, Korean, Japanese.

Extinct languages: Akkadian, Anglo-Saxon, Avestan, Babylonian, Gaulish, Gothic, Hittite, Latin, Norn, Old Norse, Old Prussian, Phoenician, Phrygian, Pictish, Prakrit, Sanskrit, Sogdian, Sumerian, Syriac, Tocharian, Ugaritic.

Artificial languages: Esperanto, Ido, Volapük.

languish VERB
1 *All the plants languished and died.*
▶ wilt, droop, wither, weaken, waste away
2 *Political prisoners languished for years in the country's jails*
▶ rot, moulder, decline, waste away, be abandoned, be neglected, be forgotten

lanky ADJECTIVE
a lanky young man
▶ tall, gangling, gaunt, gawky, lean, spindly, scraggy

lap NOUN
1 *A cat was sitting on her lap.*
▶ knee or knees, thighs
2 *They managed three laps of the track.*
▶ circuit, round, orbit, circle, loop, stretch, course

lap VERB
1 *Waves lapped against the rocks.*
▶ wash, splash, dash, beat, strike, surge, rush
2 *The dog lapped a bowl of water.*
▶ drink, sip, lick, slurp, gulp

lapse NOUN

1 *a temporary lapse of attention*
▸ failure, error, weakness, relapse, failing, fault, slip, mistake, omission, flaw, shortcoming
2 *a lapse into crime*
▸ decline, descent, fall, falling, deterioration
3 *The family returned after a lapse of ten years.*
▸ interval, gap, pause, break, interruption

lapse VERB

1 *They soon lapsed into their bad old habits.*
▸ slide, slip, drop, fall, decline, deteriorate, degenerate
2 *Membership will lapse at the end of the month.*
▸ expire, run out, finish, stop, terminate, become invalid

large ADJECTIVE

1 *a large house elected with a large majority*
▸ big, great, huge, sizeable, substantial, enormous, gigantic, immense, massive, colossal, vast, giant, (*more informal*) whopping, (*more informal*) ginormous
2 *a large man*
▸ big, burly, hefty, bulky, stocky, hulking, strapping
3 *a large supply of food*
▸ plentiful, abundant, copious, generous, lavish, profuse, ample, liberal
4 *large areas of conifers*
▸ widespread, extensive, wide-ranging, large-scale

largely ADVERB

She was largely responsible for getting us into this mess.
▸ mainly, chiefly, principally, primarily, mostly, to a large extent

lark NOUN

(*informal*) *It all seemed just a lark to them.*
▸ prank, bit of fun, joke, laugh, game, escapade, amusement

lash VERB

1 *Driving rain lashed the windows.*
▸ beat against, dash against, batter, pound
2 *She lashed him with a belt.*
▸ whip, beat, thrash
lash out at *The speaker lashed out at his critics.*
▸ attack, condemn, denounce, lambaste, castigate, censure

last ADJECTIVE

1 *There was none of the violence associated with the last protest.*
▸ previous, preceding, recent, former
2 *She realized she was still the last person in the queue.*
▸ final, rearmost, endmost
OPPOSITES ARE first, leading
3 *She decided to have one last look.*
▸ final, concluding, ultimate
OPPOSITES ARE initial, opening
4 *I am the last person to complain.*
▸ least likely, most unlikely
OPPOSITES ARE first, most likely

last VERB

The storm lasted all night.
▸ continue, carry on, keep on, persist, endure, linger, remain, stay, hold, hold out, live, survive
OPPOSITES ARE stop, cease, fade

lasting ADJECTIVE

The reforms will produce lasting change.
▸ permanent, enduring, continuing, long-lasting, long-standing, unceasing, undying, unending, long-term, long-lived, durable, indestructible, indissoluble, lifelong, stable, abiding
AN OPPOSITE IS temporary

latch NOUN

He lifted the latch and opened the door.
▸ catch, fastening, bolt, clasp, lock

late ADJECTIVE

1 *The train was over an hour late.*
▸ overdue, delayed, slow, behind-hand, belated, dilatory, tardy, unpunctual
AN OPPOSITE IS early
2 *her father, the late king*
▸ deceased, dead, departed, former
3 *He had taken part in the late conflict.*
▸ recent, previous, preceding, former

lately ADVERB

He had been out a lot lately.
▸ recently, latterly, of late

latent ADJECTIVE

the latent power of the media
▸ dormant, potential, hidden, undeveloped, undiscovered, invisible

later ADJECTIVE

The issue would be dealt with at a later meeting.
▸ subsequent, future, following, succeeding

later ADVERB

We will meet you later.
▸ afterwards, in a while, subsequently, eventually, next

lateral ADJECTIVE

1 *lateral movements*
▸ side, sideways, sideward, sidelong, edgeways
2 *lateral thinking*
▸ unorthodox, creative, inventive, original, ingenious

lather NOUN

1 *soapy lather*
▸ foam, froth, suds, bubbles
2 *in a lather*
▸ state of excitement, dither, frenzy, fluster, flutter, flap, fever

latitude NOUN

(*informal*) *The brief gives some latitude for on-the-spot decisions.*
▸ freedom, leeway, liberty, scope, room, elbow room, space

latter ADJECTIVE

There are more games in the latter part of the month.
► later, closing, concluding, last, recent, second
AN OPPOSITE IS former

laudable ADJECTIVE

the laudable objective of controlling pollution
► admirable, praiseworthy, commendable, creditable, worthy
AN OPPOSITE IS shameful

USAGE Do not confuse *laudable* with *laudatory* (see next entry), which has a different meaning.

laudatory ADJECTIVE

a highly laudatory character reference
► complimentary, congratulatory, approving, approbatory, flattering

USAGE Do not confuse *laudatory* with *laudable* (see previous entry), which has a different meaning. Note that *flattering* suggests praise beyond what is really deserved, and you should only use it when you mean this.

laugh VERB This word is often overused. Here are some alternatives:
1 *Joe's antics began to make them laugh.*
► giggle, chuckle, chortle, snigger, titter, guffaw, (*more informal*) scream
2 **laugh at** *I didn't say anything in case the others laughed at me.*
► mock, ridicule, make fun of, scoff at, deride, jeer

laugh NOUN

1 *She gave a loud laugh.*
► chuckle, chortle, snigger, titter, guffaw
2 *Being with Henry was always a laugh.*
► joke, piece of fun, adventure, (*more informal*) scream

laughable ADJECTIVE

1 *The money they were offering was laughable.*
► absurd, ridiculous, ludicrous, preposterous, risible, derisory
2 *laughable attempts to steer the boat*
► funny, comic, comical, amusing, hilarious, farcical

laughter NOUN

sounds of conversation and laughter from the next room
► laughing, mirth, laughs, chuckling, sniggering, hilarity, tittering, giggling, guffaws, merriment, (*more informal*) hysterics

launch VERB

1 *In its heyday the dockyard launched a ship every year.*
► float, set afloat, put in the water
2 *It was decided to launch the shuttle from a different site.*
► fire, propel, send off, blast off, set off
3 *The enemy launched a counter-offensive. A new business will be launched next year.*
► begin, start, initiate, open, set up, embark on, establish, found, inaugurate

lavatory NOUN

There's another lavatory downstairs.
► toilet, cloakroom, convenience, (*more informal*) loo, (*old-fashioned*) WC

lavish ADJECTIVE

After the show there will be a lavish supper.
► sumptuous, elaborate, copious, extravagant, luxurious, generous, liberal, abundant, plentiful, bountiful, exuberant, munificent, opulent, unstinting
AN OPPOSITE IS meagre

law NOUN

1 *a new law closing tax loopholes*
► regulation, statute, act, bill, ruling, rule, enactment, edict
RELATED ADJECTIVE legal, judicial

USAGE Note that a *bill* is a government's proposal for a law, and an *act* is the bill after it has been passed and received the royal assent.

2 *the laws of logic*
► rule, principle, precept, prescription, guideline, tenet, maxim, doctrine
3 (*informal*) *on the run from the law*
► police, authorities

law-abiding ADJECTIVE

law-abiding citizens
► well-behaved, respectable, honest, decent, orderly, peaceable, peaceful, compliant, disciplined, good, obedient
OPPOSITES ARE lawless, criminal

lawful ADJECTIVE

1 *The police were making a lawful arrest.*
► legal, legitimate, permissible, permitted, allowable, allowed, just, right
2 *people going about their lawful business*
► legitimate, rightful, proper, valid, recognized, authorized, regular, legal, documented, prescribed
AN OPPOSITE IS illegal

lawless ADJECTIVE

a lawless rabble
► disorderly, unruly, riotous, mutinous, wild, rowdy, rebellious, disruptive, undisciplined, seditious, reckless, anarchic, anarchical, chaotic
AN OPPOSITE IS law-abiding

lawlessness NOUN

The toppling of the regime was followed by weeks of lawlessness.
► anarchy, disorder, chaos, unruliness, insurrection, mob rule, rebellion, rioting
AN OPPOSITE IS order

lawsuit NOUN

The newspaper did not want to provoke a lawsuit.
► legal action, suit, litigation, proceedings

lawyer NOUN

This is a matter for the lawyers.
► solicitor, legal practitioner, legal adviser, barrister, QC, advocate, attorney

L

USAGE A *barrister* is a lawyer who presents a case in a lawcourt, and an *advocate* is a name for a barrister in Scotland. A *QC* (= Queen's Counsel) is a specially appointed senior barrister. *Attorney* has special meanings in the USA.

lax ADJECTIVE
lax discipline in schools
► slack, slipshod, casual, easygoing, lenient, permissive, careless, loose, neglectful, negligent, remiss, vague
AN OPPOSITE IS strict

lay VERB
1 *He laid the map on the seat beside him.*
► put, place, set, set down, spread, deposit, leave
2 *We began to lay plans for a spring holiday.*
► form, make, devise, prepare, work out, hatch, concoct
3 *Be careful where you lay the blame for this.*
► assign, attach, attribute, ascribe, allot, apportion, fix, impute
4 *The landlady laid a table for breakfast.*
► arrange, set out, organize
lay in *The men laid in a supply of beer.*
► stock up with, put aside, put by, collect, store
lay into (*informal*) *His father laid into him when he got home.*
► scold, rebuke, berate, castigate, criticize, censure
lay off
1 (*informal*) *You really should lay off smoking.*
► give up, stop, cut out
2 *Over a hundred staff were laid off just before Christmas.*
► make redundant, dismiss, discharge, release, (*more informal*) sack
lay on *His mother laid on a marvellous tea.*
► provide, supply, furnish, give
lay out
1 *Richard laid out the plans on the table.*
► arrange, set out, spread, display
2 (*informal*) *The blow laid him out for an hour.*
► knock out, make unconscious, flatten

layabout NOUN
It's odd for such a lively lad to have a layabout for a brother.
► idler, loafer, good-for-nothing, sluggard, (*more informal*) slob, (*more informal*) couch potato
OPPOSITES ARE hard-worker, beaver

layer NOUN
1 *an extra layer of paint*
► coating, coat, covering, surface, film, sheet, skin, thickness
2 *a layer of rock*
► seam, stratum, substratum

layout NOUN
The layout of the house takes some getting used to.
► arrangement, organization, design, plan, disposition, (*more informal*) set-up

laze VERB
Young girls lazed in the sun.
► relax, idle, loaf, lounge, loll
AN OPPOSITE IS work

laziness NOUN
His report mentioned lateness and laziness.
► idleness, indolence, slothfulness, sloth, lethargy, loafing, lounging about, dilatoriness, inactivity, slowness, sluggishness
AN OPPOSITE IS industry

lazy ADJECTIVE
1 *No one can accuse them of being lazy after all they've achieved.*
► idle, indolent, slothful, work-shy, inactive, lethargic, slack
AN OPPOSITE IS industrious
2 *They headed for a lazy weekend in the country.*
► quiet, relaxing, peaceful

lead NOUN
1 *The older students provide a lead for the younger ones.*
► example, guidance, leadership, direction
2 (*informal*) *Detectives are following an important new lead.*
► clue, hint, tip, tip-off, line of inquiry
3 *One of the Ferrari team took the lead.*
► first place, front position, spearhead, vanguard
4 *She will play the lead in his new film.*
► principal role, chief part, starring role, title role
5 *The toaster needs a new lead.*
► cable, flex, wire
6 *He let the dog off the lead.*
► leash, tether, rein, chain, strap, cord

lead VERB
1 *She led her guests out on the terrace.*
► conduct, guide, show, escort, usher, marshal, shepherd, steer, pilot
AN OPPOSITE IS follow
2 *Smith was appointed to lead the delegation.*
► head, be in charge of, be the leader of, preside over, direct, manage, command, govern, supervise, rule
3 *The Oxford boat was leading for most of the distance.*
► be in front, be in the lead, head the field
AN OPPOSITE IS trail
4 *They have led a very happy life.*
► pass, spend, have, experience, undergo
lead to *Asking awkward questions might lead to trouble.*
► cause, bring about, result in, give rise to, produce, generate, create, precipitate, induce, stimulate
lead on *She was accused of leading them on.*
► mislead, deceive, entice, beguile, hoodwink, string along

leader NOUN
1 *the leader of the marketing team*
► head, chief, director, manager, principal, superior, (*more informal*) boss
2 *one of the country's former leaders*
► ruler, chief, governor

leading ADJECTIVE

The book is acknowledged as the leading authority on the subject.
▶ principal, foremost, chief, major, key, main, primary, pre-eminent, outstanding, dominant, important, inspiring, prominent, well-known

leaflet NOUN

Adam grabbed a leaflet from the counter.
▶ handout, flyer, brochure, circular, pamphlet, booklet

league NOUN

1 *The countries came together to form a league.*
▶ association, alliance, federation, confederation, confederacy, syndicate
2 *On Saturday they face the league leaders.*
▶ group, class, championship

leak VERB

1 *Oil was leaking from the tank.*
▶ seep, escape, ooze, spill, trickle, drip, exude
2 *We still haven't discovered who leaked the information.*
▶ reveal, disclose, divulge, pass on, give away, let out, make known

leak NOUN

1 *several leaks in the roof*
▶ hole, opening, crack, drip, perforation, puncture
2 *a gas leak*
▶ escape, seepage, discharge
3 *a leak of information*
▶ disclosure, divulgence, revelation

leaky ADJECTIVE

a leaky roof
▶ leaking, dripping, cracked, holed, perforated, punctured
AN OPPOSITE IS watertight

lean ADJECTIVE

1 *a tall lean figure*
▶ thin, spare, skinny, slender, slim, gaunt, lanky, wiry, bony, emaciated
AN OPPOSITE IS fat
2 *a lean harvest*
▶ meagre, scanty, sparse, poor, mean, barren, inadequate

lean VERB

1 *The trees were leaning in the wind.*
▶ slant, incline, bend, tilt, tip, bank, heel over, list, loll, slope
2 *Mary leaned against the fence.*
▶ rest, support yourself, prop yourself up, recline
3 **lean towards** *We lean towards a peaceful solution.*
▶ favour, prefer, tend towards, incline towards

leaning NOUN

He had a leaning towards socialism.
▶ inclination, tendency, bent, bias, partiality (for), penchant (for), predilection (for), propensity (for), instinct (for), liking (for), preference (for), taste (for)

leap VERB

1 *The dog leapt over the gate.*
▶ jump, spring, vault, bound
2 *Claire leapt to her feet*
▶ spring, jump
3 *Prices have leapt in the last few months.*
▶ soar, rise, rocket, surge, increase
OPPOSITES ARE tumble, plummet, fall
4 **leap at** *He leapt at the opportunity.*
▶ seize, grasp, accept eagerly, (*more informal*) go for
OPPOSITES ARE turn down, reject

learn VERB

1 *It is important to learn the language when living in a foreign country.*
▶ master, acquire a knowledge of, acquire, understand, assimilate, pick up
2 *If I want to learn a poem I stick it on the fridge.*
▶ memorize, learn by heart, know

learned ADJECTIVE

a learned piece of writing
▶ scholarly, erudite, intellectual, academic, cultured, educated, highbrow

learner NOUN

At this stage he is just a learner.
▶ beginner, novice, apprentice, pupil, starter, newcomer, cadet, trainee, tiro

learning NOUN

a person of great learning
▶ scholarship, erudition, knowledge, culture, education, schooling, wisdom, information

least ADJECTIVE

1 *I haven't the least idea what he means.*
▶ slightest, smallest, tiniest
AN OPPOSITE IS greatest
2 *Choose a place that involves the least travel.*
▶ minimum, minimal, smallest amount of
OPPOSITES ARE maximum, most

leave VERB

1 *It is time to leave now.*
▶ depart, set off, go, go away, go out, take your leave, withdraw, retire, say goodbye, (*more informal*) disappear
AN OPPOSITE IS arrive
2 *She left the house that afternoon.*
▶ depart from, quit, vacate
3 *His wife has left him.*
▶ desert, abandon, forsake
4 *He's going to leave his job at the end of the month.*
▶ quit, give up, resign from, relinquish
5 *I've left my case on the train.*
▶ lose, mislay, leave behind
6 *Leave it to me to sort out.*
▶ entrust, refer, hand over, consign
7 *When he died he left them the house.*
▶ bequeath, will, endow

leave NOUN

1 *The judge granted him leave to appeal against the verdict.*
▶ permission, consent, authorization, approval, liberty

2 *Greg was having some leave from the army.*
▶ free time, time off, holiday, absence, sabbatical, vacation

lecture NOUN

1 *a lecture on modern poetry*
▶ talk, discourse, speech, address, lesson

2 *He got a stern lecture about being late.*
▶ reprimand, scolding, rebuke, harangue

lecture VERB

1 *Anna lectures at the university.*
▶ teach, give lectures, give lessons, take students

2 *Professor Jones will lecture on advances in genetics.*
▶ give a lecture, speak, talk, discourse, (*more informal*) hold forth

3 *She lectured us on our bad manners*
▶ reprimand, scold, rebuke, admonish, chide

leg NOUN

1 *the first leg of the journey*
▶ stage, part, phase, stretch, lap, step

2 *a table leg*
▶ support, upright, prop

legal ADJECTIVE

1 *legal advice*
▶ judicial, judiciary

2 *activity that is not legal*
▶ lawful, legitimate, licit, permissible, authorized, permitted, aboveboard, allowable, allowed, rightful, proper, constitutional, valid
AN OPPOSITE IS illegal

legend NOUN

legends from the past
▶ myth, story, folk tale, fable, tradition

legendary ADJECTIVE

legendary beasts and heroes
▶ mythical, fabled, fabulous, fictional, fictitious, story-book, invented, made-up, non-existent
AN OPPOSITE IS real

legible ADJECTIVE

The writing was barely legible.
▶ readable, clear, decipherable, intelligible, distinct, neat, plain
AN OPPOSITE IS illegible

legitimate ADJECTIVE

1 *They have legitimate reasons for the action they took.*
▶ valid, sound, cogent, admissible, well-founded, acceptable, justifiable

2 *The Duke lacked a legitimate heir.*
▶ lawful, legal, rightful, acknowledged, true, proper

leisure NOUN

1 *They lead a life of leisure.*
▶ ease, relaxation, enjoyment, inactivity, pleasure, amusement, recreation, retirement

2 *She never had enough leisure to do the things she wanted.*
▶ free time, spare time, time off, freedom, liberty, rest

leisurely ADJECTIVE

a leisurely stroll through the park
▶ slow, gentle, unhurried, relaxed, relaxing, restful, sedate, comfortable, easy, lingering, peaceful
OPPOSITES ARE brisk, hurried

lend VERB

1 *He asked me to lend him the money.*
▶ loan, advance, let someone have
AN OPPOSITE IS borrow

2 *Her presence lent dignity to the occasion.*
▶ add, give, bring, impart, afford, bestow (on), confer (on)
AN OPPOSITE IS detract (from)

length NOUN

1 *The snakes grew to a length of twenty feet or more.*
▶ extent, measurement, stretch, distance

2 *People began to grumble about the length of the wait.*
▶ duration, extent, protractedness, period, time

lengthen VERB

1 *The days begin to lengthen in March.*
▶ grow longer, get longer, draw out, stretch, enlarge, elongate, expand, extend, get longer, increase, prolong, pull out
AN OPPOSITE IS shorten

2 *You will need to lengthen the cooking time.*
▶ extend, increase, prolong, continue
AN OPPOSITE IS shorten

lengthy ADJECTIVE

The family faced a lengthy journey.
▶ long, protracted, drawn out, tedious, extended
OPPOSITES ARE short, brief

lenient ADJECTIVE

He always said his mother had been too lenient with him.
▶ soft, easygoing, tolerant, soft-hearted, indulgent, merciful, forgiving, mild, kind
OPPOSITES ARE strict, severe

lessen VERB

1 *He took an aspirin to lessen the pain.*
▶ reduce, lower, decrease, deaden, alleviate, assuage, mitigate, make less, minimize, tone down

2 *Her love for him would never lessen.*
▶ diminish, decrease, abate, fade, dwindle, weaken, grow less, recede, shrink
AN OPPOSITE IS increase

lesson NOUN

1 *a French lesson*
▶ class, period, lecture, seminar, tutorial, instruction

2 *The experience might be a lesson to all of them.*
▶ example, warning, deterrent, moral

let VERB

1 *His parents wouldn't let him go on the trip.*
▶ allow, permit, give permission, authorize, consent to, agree to
OPPOSITES ARE prevent, forbid
USAGE If you use *allow, permit,* or *authorize* you have to add *to,* e.g. *His parents wouldn't allow him to go.* If you use *give permission,* you have to say *His parents wouldn't give him permission to go* or *His parents wouldn't give him permission for him to go.* If you use *consent* or *agree* you have to say *His parents wouldn't agree* or *consent to his* or *him going.*
2 *The landlord will let rooms for six months.*
▶ rent out, lease out, hire out
let down *They felt the manager had let them down.*
▶ fail, disappoint, betray, abandon, desert
let off *They decided to let him off with a warning.*
▶ pardon, forgive, excuse, spare, release
let up *The rain let up for a while.*
▶ ease, subside, abate, slacken, diminish
AN OPPOSITE IS intensify

let-down NOUN

After all the excitement, the holiday was a complete let-down.
▶ disappointment, anticlimax, comedown, (*more informal*) washout, (*more informal*) damp squib

lethal ADJECTIVE

execution by lethal injection
▶ deadly, fatal, mortal, poisonous

lethargic ADJECTIVE

I felt tired and lethargic all weekend.
▶ sluggish, inactive, inert, listless, languid, lazy, sleepy, slow, torpid, apathetic
OPPOSITES ARE vigorous, energetic

lethargy NOUN

The best way to shake off winter lethargy is with a good long stretch.
▶ sluggishness, listlessness, inactivity, inertia, apathy, laziness, slowness, torpor

letter NOUN

1 *She wrote a letter to her MP.*
▶ message, note, communication, dispatch, missive, (*more formal*) epistle
RELATED ADJECTIVE epistolary
2 *The wall was daubed with large letters.*
▶ character, figure, sign, symbol, device

level ADJECTIVE

1 *Make sure the surface is level before spreading the paper on it.*
▶ flat, even, smooth, uniform, flush, regular, horizontal, plane
AN OPPOSITE IS uneven
2 *The scores were level at half time.*
▶ equal, even, matching, balanced, the same, (*more informal*) neck-and-neck

level NOUN

1 *Soon she was promoted to a senior level.*
▶ rank, status, position, class, echelon

2 *There is a high level of absenteeism.*
▶ amount, quantity, extent, degree, proportion
3 *The water rose to a dangerous level.*
▶ height, elevation, altitude
4 *There are offices on this level of the building.*
▶ floor, storey, tier

level VERB

1 *He piled on the earth, levelling it with his hands.*
▶ smooth, even out, flatten, rake
2 *A series of violent tremors levelled the area.*
▶ raze, demolish, destroy, devastate, knock down, lay low
3 *His hand was shaking, making it difficult to level the gun.*
▶ aim, point, direct, train

level-headed ADJECTIVE

Belinda was too level-headed to fool herself in this way.
▶ sensible, balanced, practical, prudent, realistic, self-possessed, commonsensical, judicious

lever NOUN

You push the lever down and leave it there.
▶ switch, handle, knob, bar

lever VERB

He picked up a crowbar and levered open the window.
▶ prise, force, wrench, heave

liability NOUN

1 *The driver of the other car admitted liability for the accident.*
▶ responsibility, blame, culpability, accountability
2 *Taking the dog with us could prove a liability.*
▶ nuisance, inconvenience, encumbrance, hindrance, burden, handicap, drawback, (*more informal*) drag

liable ADJECTIVE

1 *The company is not liable for any damage that might be caused.*
▶ responsible, accountable, answerable, to blame
AN OPPOSITE IS exempt (from)
2 *The shaft is liable to break under pressure.*
▶ likely, apt, prone, inclined, given (to falling), disposed, predisposed, ready
AN OPPOSITE IS unlikely

liar NOUN

Parkin was either a coward or a liar, or both.
▶ deceiver, fabricator, falsifier, (*more informal*) storyteller, (*more informal*) fibber

libel NOUN

He said the newspaper article amounted to libel.
▶ defamation of character, misrepresentation, an insult, a slur, a smear
USAGE You can also use *slander* when the insult is spoken rather than printed.

libellous ADJECTIVE

Lawyers check whether there is anything libellous in the writing.
▶ defamatory, derogatory, false, insulting
USAGE You can also use *slanderous* when the insult is spoken rather than printed.

liberal ADJECTIVE

1 *a liberal supply of liquid refreshment*
▶ copious, generous, plentiful, lavish, abundant, ample, bounteous, bountiful, munificent, unstinting
AN OPPOSITE IS mean

2 *liberal social attitudes*
▶ broad-minded, tolerant, enlightened, moderate, easygoing, magnanimous, lenient, unbiased, unprejudiced, permissive, free
AN OPPOSITE IS narrow- minded

3 *liberal political views*
▶ progressive, radical, forward-looking
AN OPPOSITE IS conservative

liberate VERB
the intention to liberate all people from every kind of slavery
▶ free, set free, release, discharge, deliver, rescue, save, emancipate, unfetter, loose, ransom, untie
OPPOSITES ARE enslave, subjugate

liberty NOUN
You can enjoy the liberty to follow your own interests.
▶ freedom, independence, emancipation, liberation, release

at liberty

1 *The escaped prisoners were at liberty for three months.*
▶ free, on the run, on the loose

2 *She is at liberty to use her money as she wishes.*
▶ free, entitled, permitted, allowed, authorized
AN OPPOSITE IS forbidden

licence NOUN

1 *I needed a licence to play music in my shop.*
▶ permit, certificate, document, authorization, warrant

2 *the licence to act as you see fit*
▶ authority, authorization, permission, entitlement, prerogative, privilege

license VERB
The local authority will license the restaurant to serve alcoholic drinks.
▶ authorize, permit, give a licence to, entitle, allow, empower
OPPOSITES ARE prohibit (from serving), ban (from serving)

lick VERB

1 *Tessa was licking a lollipop.*
▶ suck, taste

2 *(more informal) They licked the visiting side 4-0.*
▶ beat, defeat, overcome, trounce, rout, thrash

3 *By now the flames were licking the ceiling.*
▶ touch, reach, brush, flicker round, dance round

lid NOUN
The lid was stuck to the jar.
▶ top, cap, stopper, cover, covering

lie NOUN
He can't help telling lies.
▶ untruth, falsehood, falsification, fabrication, deception, invention, falsity, deceit, fiction, (*more informal*) fib
OPPOSITES ARE truth, fact

lie VERB

1 *He lied about where he'd been.*
▶ tell an untruth, invent a story, dissemble, (*more informal*) fib

2 *She was lying on the bed.*
▶ recline, stretch out, rest, lounge, sprawl

3 *The town lies twenty miles from the coast.*
▶ be situated, be located, be placed, be found, be sited

life NOUN

1 *the joy of giving life*
▶ existence, breath, being

2 *Their dog still looked full of life*
▶ vitality, energy, liveliness, vigour, verve, spirit, vivacity, zest, activity, (*more informal*) go

3 *He's reading a life of John Lennon*
▶ biography, autobiography, life story

4 *The contract covers the life of the project.*
▶ duration, course, span, extent

lifeless ADJECTIVE

1 *The lifeless body fell into the grave.*
▶ dead, deceased, inanimate, defunct, comatose, inert
AN OPPOSITE IS living

2 *a lifeless desert*
▶ barren, arid, bare, sterile
AN OPPOSITE IS fertile

3 *The voice was dull and lifeless.*
▶ lacklustre, lethargic, unexciting, apathetic, tedious, boring, flat, slow
AN OPPOSITE IS animated

lifelike ADJECTIVE
The new portrait was unusually lifelike.
▶ realistic, true to life, authentic, natural, graphic, convincing, photographic
AN OPPOSITE IS unrealistic

lifelong ADJECTIVE
Ramesh had been his lifelong friend.
▶ lasting, constant, long-term

lift VERB

1 *She lifted the twins into their special chairs.*
▶ raise, pick up, hoist, heave
OPPOSITES ARE lower, drop

2 *The plane lifted off the ground*
▶ rise, ascend, go up, soar
OPPOSITES ARE land, touch down

3 *The sight of the sea lifted their spirits.*
▶ raise, boost, buoy up, revive, enliven, perk up
OPPOSITES ARE lower, subdue

4 *The six-month ban has now been lifted.*
▶ cancel, revoke, rescind, remove, withdraw
AN OPPOSITE IS impose

5 *By now the mist had lifted.*
▶ clear, disperse, disappear, vanish, dissolve, rise
OPPOSITES ARE come down, appear

lift NOUN
She took the lift to the top floor.
▶ elevator, escalator, hoist

light ADJECTIVE
1 *a light load*
▶ slight, lightweight, portable, insubstantial, weightless, flimsy, feathery
AN OPPOSITE IS heavy
2 *a light blue*
▶ pale, faint, pastel, fair
AN OPPOSITE IS dark
3 *a light meal*
▶ modest, frugal, simple, skimpy, insubstantial
OPPOSITES ARE heavy, rich
4 *light music   a little light reading*
▶ entertaining, lightweight, diverting, undemanding, easy
5 *She looked light on her feet.*
▶ nimble, deft, agile, graceful

light NOUN
1 *The gas lamp did not give out much light.*
▶ brightness, illumination, radiance, luminescence, glow, lustre
2 *There was a light on in the bedroom.*
▶ lamp, lantern, torch, bulb
3 *She saw the problem in a new light.*
▶ aspect, complexion, angle, standpoint, point of view, slant, approach
USAGE With the last five synonyms you use *from* instead of *in*, e.g. *She saw the problem from a new standpoint.*
4 *In an hour they would be working in the light.*
▶ daylight, light of day, daytime, sunlight

light VERB
1 *The boys wanted to light a fire.*
▶ kindle, ignite, set alight, set burning, put a match to, set fire to, switch on
OPPOSITES ARE put out, extinguish
2 *Hundreds of searchlights lit the sky.*
▶ illuminate, light up, lighten, brighten, irradiate, floodlight, cast light on, shed light on, shine on
AN OPPOSITE IS darken

lighten VERB
1 *Pale streaks lightened the sky.*
▶ light, light up, illuminate, brighten, irradiate
AN OPPOSITE IS darken
2 *The sky lightened in the east.*
▶ brighten, grow lighter
AN OPPOSITE IS darken
3 *The gift lightened their financial burden.*
▶ ease, reduce, relieve, alleviate, mitigate, moderate
OPPOSITES ARE increase, intensify

light-headed ADJECTIVE
She felt nauseous and light-headed from the shock.
▶ dizzy, giddy, faint, shaky, (*more informal*) woozy

light-hearted ADJECTIVE
His light-hearted banter had a serious side.
▶ cheerful, carefree, jolly, playful, jovial, bright

like ADJECTIVE
The cousins are very like each other.
▶ similar to, the same as, identical
AN OPPOSITE IS unlike

like VERB This word is often overused. Here are some alternatives:
1 *I have always liked Rosamund.*
▶ be fond of, be attached to, care for, adore, admire, respect, esteem, (*old-fashioned*) hold dear, (*more informal*) have a soft spot for, (*more informal*) take a shine to, (*more informal*) fancy
2 *Do you like dancing?*
▶ enjoy, care for, appreciate, be keen on, be partial to, (*more informal*) love, (*more informal*) fancy

likeable ADJECTIVE
The person appointed needs to be likeable and a good mixer.
▶ pleasant, personable, nice, friendly, attractive, charming, congenial, pleasing, endearing
AN OPPOSITE IS hateful

likelihood NOUN
Neither side has shown any likelihood of winning.
▶ possibility, probability, prospect, chance, hope

likely ADJECTIVE
1 *It was likely that there would be an inquiry.*
▶ probable, possible, expected, foreseeable, envisaged, (*more informal*) odds-on
2 *Try to think of a more likely explanation.*
▶ credible, believable, plausible, convincing, reasonable
3 *It was a likely place for them to meet.*
▶ suitable, appropriate, proper, apposite, promising, hopeful

liken VERB
He likened a computer to the human brain.
▶ compare, equate, match, parallel, relate, correlate, associate (with)

likeness NOUN
1 *The photograph was a good likeness of their mother.*
▶ representation, image, depiction, portrayal, picture, portrait, copy, replica
2 *His likeness to Alan is remarkable.*
▶ resemblance, similarity, affinity, correspondence
AN OPPOSITE IS dissimilarity

liking NOUN
a liking for rock music
▶ fondness, partiality, taste, desire, attraction, weakness, penchant, predilection, fancy
OPPOSITES ARE dislike (of), aversion (to)

limb NOUN
1 *His limbs ached.*
▶ arm, leg, extremity, appendage
2 *the limbs of a tree*
▶ branch, bough

limber VERB

limber up *She was limbering up for the next race.*
▶ warm up, loosen up, work out, prepare, get ready, exercise

limelight NOUN

Peter was excited about being back in the limelight again.
▶ spotlight, stardom, focus of attention, prominence

limit NOUN

1 *There was a limit to what they could do to help. There is a limit of ten thousand tickets for away supporters.*
▶ restriction, maximum, ceiling, cut-off point, curb, restraint, limitation
2 *They drove out as far as the city limits.*
▶ boundary, border, edge, perimeter, confine

limit VERB

The organizers have to limit numbers in the interests of safety.
▶ restrict, curb, put a limit on, restrain, check, control, circumscribe, demarcate, confine, fix

limitation NOUN

1 *a limitation on numbers*
▶ limit, restriction, ceiling, cut-off point, curb, restraint
2 *I am aware of my limitations.*
▶ weakness, shortcoming, deficiency, imperfection, inadequacy, defect

limited ADJECTIVE

Resources are limited.
▶ restricted, circumscribed, finite, short, controlled, rationed, defined, determinate, fixed, inadequate, insufficient, narrow, reduced, small
OPPOSITES ARE unlimited, limitless

limitless ADJECTIVE

The opportunities are limitless.
▶ endless, unending, never-ending, boundless, unbounded, unlimited, without limit, countless, incalculable, inexhaustible, infinite, vast, unimaginable
AN OPPOSITE IS limited

limp ADJECTIVE

(informal) The man held out a limp hand.
▶ soft, loose, flabby, drooping, slack, weak, sagging, wilting, bendy, flexible, pliable, yielding, *(more informal)* floppy
OPPOSITES ARE firm, rigid

limp VERB

She limped back into the house.
▶ hobble, hop, falter, shuffle, stumble, totter

line NOUN

1 *A line of cars was waiting at the lights.*
▶ queue, row, file, column, procession, chain, string
2 *He drew a line under his signature. From their window they could see lines in the sand.*
▶ stroke, rule, underline, strip, band, bar, streak
3 *As she grew older the lines on her face increased.*
▶ crease, wrinkle, furrow, groove

4 *They walked in a straight line across the field*
▶ direction, path, route, course, track
5 *The courts are taking a tough line with repeat offenders. Cabinet members are obliged to support the government line.*
▶ approach, course, course of action, procedure, policy, position, stance, tactic
6 *There aren't many opportunities in my line.*
▶ field, line of work, occupation, business, calling, speciality, trade, work, province, domain
7 *Mark attached a line to the post.*
▶ cord, rope, string, cable, wire, thread, flex
8 *the handsome lines of a classical building*
▶ shape, contour, profile, figure, features, silhouette
9 *The ball had not crossed the line.*
▶ limit, boundary, border, edge, demarcation
10 *She comes from a noble line related to the royal family.*
▶ ancestry, family, descent, lineage, extraction, pedigree, genealogy, stock, background

line VERB

1 *She lined the cat's box with blankets.*
▶ cover, face, pad, stuff, reinforce
2 *The drive was lined with trees.*
▶ border, edge, fringe, bound, skirt
line up *The children lined up by the door.*
▶ form a line, form a queue, queue, queue up, fall in, form a crocodile

lineage NOUN

a noble lineage
▶ ancestry, line, family, descent, extraction, pedigree, genealogy, stock, background

line-up NOUN

a dazzling line-up of performers
▶ cast, list, bill, programme, array

linger VERB

1 *Most of the crowd leave promptly but some tend to linger.*
▶ wait around, lag behind, loiter, dally, tarry, hang on, stay put, delay
2 *An aroma of coffee lingered all morning.*
▶ persist, last, continue, remain, endure, stay

lining NOUN

a coat with a thick lining
▶ padding, inner layer, interfacing, inlay, liner, interlining

link NOUN

1 *She fostered links between the two families*
▶ bond, tie, relationship, attachment
2 *a rail link between the city centre and the airport*
▶ connection, communication, line
3 *an important link in the organization*
▶ element, component, constituent, piece
4 *a chain of hardened steel links*
▶ loop, ring, connector, connection

link VERB

1 *Police are linking this crime with a series of other robberies.*
▶ connect, associate, relate (to), draw a connection between

2 *The two trains were linked together.*
▶ couple, join, connect, attach, fasten

lip NOUN

Coffee poured over the lip of the jug.
▶ rim, brim, brink, mouth, edge

liquefy VERB

The gas will only liquefy at a low temperature.
▶ become liquid, condense, dissolve, liquidize, melt
AN OPPOSITE IS solidify

liquid NOUN

The doctor says he can only take liquids for a few days.
▶ fluid, liquid substance, juice, drink, solution

liquid ADJECTIVE

The pudding had become liquid in the heat.
▶ runny, fluid, thin, watery, sloppy, sloshy, wet, aqueous, molten, running, flowing
AN OPPOSITE IS solid

liquidate VERB

USAGE Do not confuse this word with *liquidize*, which has a different meaning.

1 *The ruling clan liquidated all its rivals.*
▶ kill, slaughter, annihilate, massacre, eliminate, destroy, purge, (*more informal*) do away with, (*more informal*) get rid of

2 *The company was liquidated at the cost of a hundred jobs.*
▶ close down, wind up, dissolve, put into liquidation

liquidize VERB

USAGE Do not confuse this word with *liquidate*, which has a different meaning.

Liquidize the vegetables to make a smooth paste.
▶ blend, crush, purée, pulp, make into liquid

liquor NOUN

Persons under 18 may not buy liquor.
▶ alcohol, alcoholic drink, spirits, strong drink, intoxicant, (*more informal*) hard stuff

list NOUN

I had a list of over 7,000 names.
▶ register, inventory, catalogue, index, file, roll, roster, schedule

list VERB

1 *We have listed names of contributors in alphabetical order.*
▶ record, register, itemize, enter, index, file, enumerate, catalogue

2 *The ship was listing in the heavy seas.*
▶ tilt, lean, lean over, tip, heel, pitch, keel over

listen VERB

1 *I don't think they were listening.*
▶ pay attention, take notice

2 **listen to** *a doctor who listens to what his patients tell him*
▶ pay attention to, take notice of, hear, heed, attend to, concentrate on, (*old-fashioned*) hark
AN OPPOSITE IS ignore

listless ADJECTIVE

a young woman clutching a pale, listless child
▶ lethargic, sluggish, enervated, lackadaisical, torpid, inert, apathetic, unenthusiastic
AN OPPOSITE IS lively

literal ADJECTIVE

1 *a literal translation*
▶ word-for-word, verbatim, faithful, strict, exact, close, plain, prosaic, unimaginative

2 *the literal truth of the Bible*
▶ strict, plain, bare, exact, precise, straightforward, unvarnished, narrow

literary ADJECTIVE

1 *a collection of literary works*
▶ written, printed, published, dramatic, poetic, imaginative

2 *a literary style of writing*
▶ formal, stylish, ornate, polished, sophisticated, imaginative, recognized as literature

3 *a group of literary friends*
▶ cultured, educated, literate, scholarly, refined, well-read, widely read, erudite, learned

literate ADJECTIVE

1 *At 15 he was barely literate.*
▶ able to read and write, educated

2 *a literate piece of writing*
▶ well-written, readable, lucid, eloquent, stylish

3 *a literate society*
▶ cultured, educated, literary, scholarly, refined, well-read, widely read, erudite, learned

literature NOUN

1 *We can pick up some literature about the place from the tourist office.*
▶ brochures, leaflets, pamphlets, handouts, circulars

2 *a class in English literature*
▶ writings, books

lithe ADJECTIVE

a lithe young gymnast
▶ agile, graceful, pliant, supple, flexible, limber, lissom, loose-jointed

litter NOUN

1 *It took days to clear up all the litter.*
▶ rubbish, refuse, junk, waste, debris, clutter, garbage, mess, scraps, bits and pieces, odds and ends, trash, jumble

2 *a litter of puppies*
▶ brood, family, (*more formal*) progeny

litter VERB

They had littered the room with a half-eaten takeaway.
▶ clutter, mess up, make untidy, scatter, strew

little ADJECTIVE This word is often overused. Here are some alternatives:
1 *a little book*
▶ small, tiny, minute, miniature, mini, petite, (*Scottish*) wee, (*more informal*) teeny
2 *a little person*
▶ small, slight, short, diminutive, (*Scottish*) wee
3 *in a little while*
▶ short, brief, fleeting, (*Scottish*) wee
4 *We have a little problem*
▶ minor, trivial, unimportant, insignificant, inconsequential, negligible
5 a little *Add a little water.*
▶ some, a small amount of, a bit of, a touch of, a spot of, a taste of

little NOUN
You only need a little.
▶ bit, dash, pinch, small amount, touch, modicum

little ADVERB
The singers are little known in this country.
▶ scarcely, barely, hardly, slightly, not much

live VERB
1 *We live in Glasgow.*
▶ reside, have a home, dwell, lodge
2 *He hardly earns enough to live on.*
▶ exist, subsist, survive, endure, stay alive
3 *I'm not sure these plants will live much longer.*
▶ last, survive, stay alive
4 *She has led a happy life.*
▶ pass, spend, experience, undergo

live ADJECTIVE
1 *live animals*
▶ living, alive, breathing, animate
2 *a live show*
▶ real-time, actual, unrecorded
3 *a live rail*
▶ electrified, charged, powered, connected
4 *a live issue*
▶ topical, current, relevant, pertinent, contemporary, vital, controversial

livelihood NOUN
The printing business was his main livelihood.
▶ income, source of income, means of support, living, subsistence, occupation, employment

liveliness NOUN
She has a liveliness which is quite extraordinary for her age.
▶ enthusiasm, exuberance, vitality, vigour, sprightliness, verve, vivacity, energy, dynamism, activity, boisterousness, (*more informal*) go
OPPOSITES ARE tiredness, inactivity

lively ADJECTIVE
1 *The bars are lively late in the evening.*
▶ busy, hectic, bustling, crowded, swarming
OPPOSITES ARE quiet, dead

2 *an attractive and lively young woman*
▶ vivacious, high-spirited, exuberant, animated, alert, active, spirited, exciting, cheerful
OPPOSITES ARE lifeless, dull
3 *a lively colour scheme*
▶ bright, vivid, colourful, striking, bold
OPPOSITES ARE dull, bland

liven VERB
liven up *The room needed a few pictures to liven it up.*
▶ brighten up, animate, cheer up, vitalize, put life into, (*more informal*) perk up, (*more informal*) pep up

livery NOUN
1 *the pageboys in their blue livery*
▶ uniform, costume, outfit, suit, regalia, garb, (*more informal*) get-up
2 *railway coaches repainted in their old maroon livery*
▶ colours, colour scheme, paintwork

livestock NOUN
If you plan to keep livestock, the security of fences and gates is vital.
▶ cattle, farm animals

livid ADJECTIVE
1 *A row of livid bruises began to form on his skin.*
▶ bluish-grey, purplish, dark, discoloured
2 *He was livid with me.*
▶ furious, angry, fuming, seething, raging, enraged, infuriated

living ADJECTIVE
all living creatures
▶ live, alive, breathing, animate, existing, vital, active, sentient, surviving, vigorous
OPPOSITES ARE dead, extinct

living NOUN
He was washing cars for a living.
▶ livelihood, income, source of income, means of support, subsistence, occupation, employment

living room NOUN
Music was playing in the living room.
▶ sitting room, drawing room, lounge, reception room

load NOUN
1 *a load of goods*
▶ cargo, consignment, freight, vanload, lorryload, truckload, shipment, boatload, (*more formal*) lading
2 *a heavy load of work*
▶ burden, commitment, obligation, weight
3 a load of (*informal*) *a load of rubbish*
▶ a lot of, a great deal of, a wealth of

load VERB
1 *We loaded the luggage into the car.*
▶ pack, stow, store, stack, cram, heap, pile
AN OPPOSITE IS unload (from)
2 *They've loaded me with more responsibilities.*
▶ burden, encumber, weigh down, saddle
AN OPPOSITE IS relieve (of)

loaded ADJECTIVE
1 *He had a loaded gun in his hand.*
▶ primed, charged, filled, ready

2 *A loaded trolley trundled up the platform.*
▶ full, filled, laden, burdened, inundated, piled high, weighed down, crammed

3 *a loaded argument*
▶ one-sided, biased, tendentious, prejudiced, unfair, distorted, emotive, partial

4 *(informal) Their parents are loaded and can easily afford the fees.*
▶ wealthy, well-off, rich, affluent, prosperous, moneyed

loaf VERB
He can't go on loafing around any longer.
▶ laze, idle, lounge, waste time, kill time
OPPOSITES ARE work, toil

loafer NOUN
(informal) education that produces a generation of loafers
▶ layabout, idler, lounger, shirker, wastrel, (informal) skiver, (informal) lazybones, (informal) good-for-nothing

loan NOUN
A bank loan would help develop the business.
▶ advance, credit, mortgage

loan VERB
1 *We will loan you the money for a period of 5 years.*
▶ lend, advance, credit

2 *The gallery loans pictures all over the world.*
▶ lend, give on loan, provide on loan

loath ADJECTIVE
They were loath to admit their mistake.
▶ reluctant, unwilling, disinclined, averse (to admitting)

loathe VERB
She loathed living in the suburbs.
▶ hate, detest, abhor, abominate, dislike, despise
OPPOSITES ARE love, like, adore

loathing NOUN
Loathing for the other woman rose in her chest.
▶ hatred, detestation, abhorrence, repugnance (for), revulsion (for)
AN OPPOSITE IS love

loathsome ADJECTIVE
a loathsome crime
▶ detestable, horrible, horrid, awful, nasty
OPPOSITES ARE pleasant, likeable

lob VERB
He lobbed the ball in the air.
▶ throw, toss, hurl, pitch, fling, loft, shy, bowl, cast, chuck, sling

lobby NOUN
1 *We can wait for her in the hotel lobby.*
▶ entrance hall, foyer, vestibule, hallway

2 *the anti-abortion lobby*
▶ pressure group, campaign, ginger group, campaigners, supporters

lobby VERB
1 *The paper urged readers to lobby their MPs.*
▶ petition, pressurize, solicit, persuade, seek to influence, urge

2 **lobby for** *a group lobbying for lower rail fares*
▶ campaign for, crusade for, press for, advocate, champion, demand, promote

local ADJECTIVE
1 *the local library*
▶ nearby, neighbourhood, neighbouring

2 *Try the local cuisine.*
▶ regional, district, provincial, community
OPPOSITES ARE national, global

3 *a local infection*
▶ confined, restricted, limited, localized, circumscribed
AN OPPOSITE IS general

local NOUN
The restaurant is filled with locals.
▶ inhabitant, resident, parishioner, native

locality NOUN
1 *There are several good schools in the locality.*
▶ region, area, neighbourhood, vicinity, location, district, community, parish

2 *new housing in an attractive locality*
▶ position, location, setting, situation, place

locate VERB
1 *He located the skylight window he had noticed from the outside.*
▶ find, discover, identify, pinpoint, track down, detect, light on

2 *The boiler room is located in the basement.*
▶ situate, site, position, place

location NOUN
The firm is moving to a new location.
▶ position, site, locality, locale, place, point, situation, spot, venue, whereabouts

lock NOUN
1 *a lock on a door*
▶ fastening, latch, clasp

2 *a lock of hair*
▶ curl, tress, tuft

lock VERB
We lock the door at night.
▶ fasten, secure, shut, bolt, close, seal
lock up *He was locked up for causing criminal damage.*
▶ jail, imprison, put behind bars

lodge NOUN
a hunting lodge
▶ cabin, cottage, hut, chalet

lodge VERB
1 *The family lodged at a guest house for a few weeks.*
▶ board, stay, live, reside

2 *I will lodge a formal complaint.*
▶ submit, register, enter, place, present

lodger NOUN
Her husband had once been a lodger of hers.
▶ boarder, paying guest, tenant, resident, inmate, guest

lodgings NOUN
She had lodgings in Camden Town.
▶ accommodation, rooms, quarters, apartments, residence, (*more informal*) digs, (*more informal*) pad

log NOUN
a log of telephone calls
▶ record, register, tally, list, account, journal

log VERB
All calls are logged and monitored.
▶ record, register, book, file, note, write down

logic NOUN
We accept the logic of your case.
▶ reasoning, rationale, sense, validity, argumentation, rationality, cogency

logical ADJECTIVE
The conclusions are logical.
▶ rational, reasonable, cogent, coherent, clear, sound, valid, consistent, intelligent, methodical, sensible, systematic
AN OPPOSITE IS illogical

loiter VERB
With so much to do there was no time to loiter in the shopping malls.
▶ linger, dally, potter, dawdle, tarry, (*more informal*) loaf about, (*more informal*) mooch about

lone ADJECTIVE
a lone cyclist   a lone tree
▶ solitary, single, solo, isolated, individual, unaccompanied, separate

loneliness NOUN
The feeling of loneliness drove him to move on.
▶ isolation, solitude, solitariness, friendlessness, seclusion, rejection, unpopularity

lonely ADJECTIVE
1 *I walked through the garden feeling very lonely.*
▶ alone, solitary, friendless, abandoned, lonesome, neglected, forlorn
AN OPPOSITE IS popular
2 *The cart drove along the lonely road*
▶ deserted, unfrequented, remote, secluded, isolated, abandoned, desolate, forsaken, out of the way, uninhabited, (*informal*) off the beaten track
AN OPPOSITE IS crowded

loner NOUN
Although most of the group are sociable, Tony is a loner.
▶ recluse, introvert, lone wolf, hermit, outsider

long ADJECTIVE
1 *long blonde hair*
▶ lengthy
AN OPPOSITE IS short
2 *a long wait*
▶ lengthy, prolonged, extended, extensive, long-lasting
OPPOSITES ARE short, brief

long VERB
long for *We longed for the holidays.*
▶ yearn for, crave, dream of, hanker after, hunger for, pine for

longing NOUN
He felt a longing for his home
▶ yearning, hankering (after), craving, desire, hunger, need, thirst, urge, wish, (*informal*) yen

long-lasting ADJECTIVE
We need long-lasting solutions to these problems.
▶ enduring, abiding, long-running, durable, permanent, prolonged

long-standing ADJECTIVE
a long-standing arrangement
▶ well-established, long-established, time-honoured, firm

long-suffering ADJECTIVE
He went home to his long-suffering mother.
▶ patient, forbearing, tolerant, uncomplaining

long-winded ADJECTIVE
a long-winded speech
▶ lengthy, long, rambling, diffuse, verbose, wordy, tedious, boring

---

look VERB This word is often overused. Here are some alternatives:
1 *Everywhere you look there are trees.*
▶ see, observe, regard, survey, glance, scrutinize, scan
2 *Things looked difficult that day.*
▶ seem, appear
look after *Jane had to look after her father during his last illness.*
▶ take care of, care for, tend, attend to, provide for, mind, nurse, supervise, watch over, (*more informal*) keep an eye on
look at *I knew if I looked at her we'd both start laughing.*
▶ glance at, watch, observe
look down on *The family looked down on all their neighbours.*
▶ despise, disdain, scorn, hold in contempt, sneer at, (*more informal*) look down one's nose at
look for
1 *I was still looking for my wallet.*
▶ search for, hunt for, seek, try to find
2 *Behaviour like that is looking for trouble.*
▶ ask for, provoke, invite, attract, court, incite, tempt, cause, encourage, generate, (*more informal*) stir up
look into *The official said he would look into the complaint.*
▶ investigate, find out about, inquire into, study, explore, examine
look out *A ball can easily hit you if you don't look out.*
▶ beware, watch out, be careful, be vigilant, pay attention, keep your eyes open ▶▶

a b c d e f g h i j k l m n o p q r s t u v w x y z

---

look up

1 *You can look up the answer in an encyclopedia.*
▶ find, search for, research, track down
2 (*informal*) *We can look up some friends on our way home.*
▶ visit, call on, stop by, (*informal*) drop in on, (*informal*) look in on
3 *Things were beginning to look up.*
▶ improve, progress, show an improvement, revive
look up to *Susan looked up to her father.*
▶ admire, respect, esteem, revere, have a high regard for, have a high opinion of, think highly of

---

look NOUN
1 *We had a look at the house.*
▶ glance, glimpse, peek, peep, sight (of), observation (of), view (of), (*informal*) squint
2 *You could see he was angry from the look on his face.*
▶ expression, mien
3 *a house with a Tudor look*
▶ appearance, aspect, facade, guise, quality, atmosphere, semblance
4 *this year's new look*
▶ fashion, vogue, style, trend, craze, rage
5 looks *All the sisters enjoyed stunning good looks.*
▶ appearance, features

lookalike NOUN
a Madonna lookalike
▶ double, twin, exact likeness, spitting image, replica, clone, (*more informal*) spit

lookout NOUN
1 *a lookout on the bridge*
▶ sentry, guard, sentinel, scout, watchman
2 *It might not work but that's their lookout.*
▶ concern, responsibility, business, affair, problem

loom VERB
1 *The cathedral loomed above them.*
▶ soar, tower, rise, appear, rear up
2 *Blurred shapes loomed out of the mist.*
▶ appear, emerge, come into view, reveal itself
3 *Without action, big problems loom.*
▶ threaten, impend, be imminent, menace, overshadow

loop NOUN
He slipped a loop of wire over the handle and pulled it tight.
▶ coil, noose, ring, twist, curl, hoop, turn, bend, circle, kink

loop VERB
Loop a rope round the animal's neck.
▶ coil, wind, twist, bend, curl, entwine, turn

loophole NOUN
a loophole in the regulations
▶ means of escape, ambiguity, flaw, (*more informal*) get-out, (*more informal*) let-out

loose ADJECTIVE
1 *a loose screw*
▶ insecure, unfastened, untied, unfixed, wobbly
OPPOSITES ARE tight, secure
2 *a wild animal loose in the grounds*
▶ free, at large, unconfined, on the loose, at liberty
AN OPPOSITE IS confined
3 *loose trousers*
▶ baggy, slack, loose-fitting, roomy
OPPOSITES ARE tight, close-fitting
4 *a loose translation*
▶ free, imprecise, vague, inexact
OPPOSITES ARE literal, exact

loosen VERB
1 *He tried to loosen the knots.*
▶ ease, free, slacken, undo, untie, unfasten, release
2 *She loosened her grip.*
▶ weaken, relax, lessen
AN OPPOSITE IS tighten

loot NOUN
a bag full of the thieves' loot
▶ booty, spoils, plunder, haul, (*more informal*) swag

loot VERB
Soldiers looted the deserted buildings.
▶ raid, plunder, pillage, ransack, rifle, rob, steal from

lop VERB
With a single blow he lopped off the mighty branch.
▶ cut, chop, hack, slice, pare

lopsided ADJECTIVE
a tractor pulling a lopsided load
▶ uneven, unbalanced, tilting, askew, asymmetrical, crooked, (*more informal*) cock-eyed

lord NOUN
1 *the lord of the manor*
▶ master, overlord, leader, chief, prince
2 *He has been made a lord.*
▶ peer, noble, baron, earl, duke

lordly ADJECTIVE
1 *lordly titles*
▶ noble, aristocratic, princely, courtly
2 *He spoke in a lordly manner.*
▶ haughty, imperious, disdainful, condescending, domineering, overbearing, high-handed

lose VERB
1 *I've lost my passport.*
▶ mislay, misplace, lose track of, forget
AN OPPOSITE IS find
2 *We've already lost a lot of time. They lost money on the deal.*
▶ waste, use up, squander, dissipate, forfeit, exhaust
OPPOSITES ARE gain, make
3 *The home side lost 3-0.*
▶ be beaten, be defeated, fail, suffer defeat
AN OPPOSITE IS win

loser NOUN
1 *There are many losers and few winners in this game.*
▶ runner-up
AN OPPOSITE IS winner
2 *(informal) He's a complete loser.*
▶ failure, non-achiever, nobody, *(informal)* no-hoper

loss NOUN
1 *The loss of all his money ruined the holiday.*
▶ losing, theft, deprivation, disappearance
2 *The loss of her husband devastated her.*
▶ death, demise, passing, decease
3 *The company faced a huge loss.*
▶ deficit, debit, debt, lack of profit
4 *Loss of the game was a major blow.*
▶ defeat (in), failure (in), forfeiture
5 *The army suffered heavy losses.*
▶ casualty, fatality, mortality, victim

lost ADJECTIVE
1 *The lost keys never turned up.*
▶ missing, mislaid, misplaced, vanished
2 *I became lost in the complications of the plot.*
▶ confused, baffled, bewildered, perplexed
3 *many lost opportunities*
▶ missed, neglected, wasted, squandered
4 *She appeared to be lost in thought.*
▶ absorbed, engrossed, preoccupied

lot NOUN
1 **a lot of** or **lots of** *She has a lot of friends. We need lots of money.*
▶ many, plenty of, a large amount or number of, a great deal of
2 *On Monday a new lot of tourists arrives.*
▶ set, collection, group, batch, crowd
3 *He was not at all happy with his lot.*
▶ fate, destiny, fortune, future
4 *The money was divided into three lots.*
▶ share, portion, allocation, quota

lottery NOUN
She won a thousand pounds in a lottery.
▶ draw, raffle, sweepstake, sweep, gamble

loud ADJECTIVE
1 *loud music*
▶ noisy, blaring, deafening, booming, thunderous
AN OPPOSITE IS quiet
2 *loud colours*
▶ gaudy, garish, bold, lurid, flashy, showy
AN OPPOSITE IS subdued

lounge VERB
Miranda lounged on the sofa all morning.
▶ laze, loll, recline, relax, sprawl, slump, slouch, luxuriate, idle, waste time

lounge NOUN
We will have our drinks in the lounge.
▶ living room, sitting room, drawing room, day room

lousy ADJECTIVE
(informal) He had been a lousy father.
▶ awful, terrible, dreadful, atrocious, appalling, frightful, poor, bad
OPPOSITES ARE wonderful, lovely

lout NOUN
a group of drunken louts
▶ hooligan, hoodlum, ruffian, *(more informal)* yob

loutish ADJECTIVE
loutish behaviour
▶ uncouth, rude, ill-mannered, coarse, crude, vulgar, *(more informal)* yobbish

lovable ADJECTIVE
a lovable little kitten
▶ adorable, dear, sweet, charming, appealing, likeable, attractive, cuddly, enchanting, endearing, engaging, lovely, pleasing, taking, winning
AN OPPOSITE IS hateful

love VERB
1 *She told him she loved him.*
▶ care for, feel deeply for, adore, cherish, hold dear, treasure
OPPOSITES ARE hate, loathe, detest
2 *We all love the holidays.*
▶ like, like very much, enjoy, take pleasure in, appreciate, desire, look forward to, *(more informal)* fancy
AN OPPOSITE IS dislike

love NOUN
1 *He gave her flowers to show his love.*
▶ fondness, affection, adoration, devotion, admiration, ardour, desire, friendship, infatuation, liking, passion
2 *Emma was his true love.*
▶ beloved, loved one, darling, dear, dearest, lover
in love with *He had been in love with her all his life.*
▶ devoted to, enamoured with, fond of, infatuated with
RELATED ADJECTIVES amatory, erotic

love affair NOUN
a passionate love affair
▶ relationship, romance, affair, liaison, intrigue, courtship

loveless ADJECTIVE
a loveless marriage
▶ passionless, unloving, unfeeling, heartless, unresponsive, cold, frigid, undemonstrative
AN OPPOSITE IS loving

lovely ADJECTIVE This word is often overused. Here are some alternatives:
1 *a lovely young woman* *You look lovely.*
▶ beautiful, attractive, good-looking, exquisite, pretty, enchanting, charming, delightful, appealing
OPPOSITES ARE unattractive, hideous, ugly
2 *a lovely spring morning*
▶ pleasant, delightful, glorious, wonderful, fine
OPPOSITES ARE horrible, unpleasant

lover NOUN
There is a rumour that she has a secret lover.
▶ admirer, sweetheart, boyfriend, girlfriend, man friend, lady friend

loving ADJECTIVE
He adored her loving nature
▶ affectionate, tender, fond, friendly, kind, warm, amorous, ardent, demonstrative, devoted, doting, passionate
AN OPPOSITE IS loveless

low ADJECTIVE
1 *a low wall*
▶ short, small, squat, shallow
AN OPPOSITE IS high
2 *Prices are now low.*
▶ reasonable, cheap, inexpensive
OPPOSITES ARE high, exorbitant
3 *Supplies were getting low.*
▶ sparse, scarce, meagre, inadequate, depleted, paltry
OPPOSITES ARE plentiful, abundant
4 *He was feeling low that day.*
▶ depressed, dispirited, downcast, unhappy
AN OPPOSITE IS happy
5 *a low trick*
▶ mean, base, despicable, shameful, contemptible
AN OPPOSITE IS admirable
6 *a low rumbling sound*
▶ muted, soft, deep
AN OPPOSITE IS loud

lower VERB
1 *The soldier lowered the flag.*
▶ bring down, drop, let down, take down
OPPOSITES ARE raise, hoist
2 *a need to lower interest rates*
▶ reduce, decrease, bring down, lessen
OPPOSITES ARE raise, increase
3 *Did he have to lower himself in this way?*
▶ demean, degrade, humiliate, shame, discredit

lowly ADJECTIVE
He is just a lowly administrator.
▶ modest, simple, humble, obscure, insignificant, meek, low

loyal ADJECTIVE
a loyal friend
▶ faithful, true, devoted, steadfast, staunch, constant, dependable, reliable, sincere
AN OPPOSITE IS disloyal

loyalty NOUN
His first loyalty was to his family.
▶ allegiance, faithfulness, fidelity, devotion, constancy, dependability, fealty, honesty, patriotism, reliability, staunchness, steadfastness, trustworthiness
AN OPPOSITE IS disloyalty

lubricate VERB
She went out to lubricate her cycle.
▶ grease, oil

lucid ADJECTIVE
a lucid explanation of the problem
▶ clear, intelligible, coherent, cogent, plain, simple

luck NOUN
1 *They could not believe their luck.*
▶ good fortune, good luck, success
2 *She hopes her luck will change.*
▶ fate, fortune, lot, destiny
3 *It was luck that brought them here.*
▶ chance, accident, serendipity

lucky ADJECTIVE
1 *a lucky chance a lucky guess*
▶ fortunate, auspicious, providential, opportune, expedient, timely
2 *He is lucky to have such a good friend as you.*
▶ fortunate, blessed, favoured, advantaged

lucrative ADJECTIVE
a lucrative business
▶ profitable, profit-making, productive, rewarding, gainful

ludicrous ADJECTIVE
a ludicrous suggestion
▶ absurd, ridiculous, laughable, incredible, farcical, preposterous, risible, foolish, idiotic, (*more informal*) crazy, (*more informal*) daft, (*more informal*) barmy, (*more informal*) zany
OPPOSITES ARE reasonable, sensible

lug VERB
He lugged his old suitcase up the hill.
▶ drag, pull, haul, carry, heave, hump

luggage NOUN
Trevor put his luggage on the rack.
▶ bags, cases, baggage, things, paraphernalia, belongings

lukewarm ADJECTIVE
1 *She pulled a face over her lukewarm tea.*
▶ tepid, warm
2 *a lukewarm response*
▶ unenthusiastic, indifferent, half-hearted, offhand, cool, apathetic

lull NOUN
a lull in the fighting
▶ pause, respite, break, calm, gap, interval, rest, (*more informal*) let-up

lull VERB
The singing lulled her to sleep.
▶ soothe, calm, subdue, hush, pacify, quell, quieten, tranquillize
AN OPPOSITE IS agitate

lumber VERB
1 (*informal*) *We were lumbered with paying the bill.*
▶ saddle, burden, encumber, load
2 *Henry lumbered down the stairs.*
▶ shamble, trudge, tramp, plod, shuffle, blunder, move clumsily

lumber NOUN
1 *cutting lumber in the forest*
▶ timber, wood

2 *a loft full of lumber*
► jumble, clutter, junk, odds and ends, bits and pieces, rummage, rubbish, trash

luminous ADJECTIVE
a luminous dial
► glowing, luminescent, lustrous, radiant, bright, phosphorescent, shining

lump NOUN
1 *a lump of bread*
► chunk, hunk, block, wedge, piece, portion, slab, wad
2 *The blow left a lump on his head*
► swelling, bump, growth, protuberance

lump VERB
lump together *The newspaper reports lumped together several stories.*
► combine, amalgamate, merge, bunch
lump it *(informal) We're not going and we'll just have to lump it.*
► accept it, put up with it, tolerate it, endure it

lunacy NOUN
1 *a scene of despair and lunacy*
► insanity, madness, mental disorder, mental illness, derangement, dementia
2 *It would be lunacy to try a rescue in this weather.*
► folly, foolishness, stupidity, madness, insanity

lunatic NOUN
a dangerous lunatic
► maniac, madman, madwoman, (*more informal*) loony

lunatic ADJECTIVE
a lunatic scheme
► crazy, foolish, stupid, senseless, ludicrous, absurd, mad

lunge VERB
The man lunged at him.
► thrust, charge, pounce, rush, throw yourself, dash, dive, lurch

lurch VERB
James lurched into the bathroom.
► stagger, stumble, totter, reel, roll, list, lunge, sway, pitch, heave, lean, plunge, wallow

lurch NOUN
leave in the lurch *They felt they had been left completely in the lurch.*
► let down, desert, abandon, forsake

lure VERB
Advertising can lure people into debt.
► tempt, entice, allure, attract, induce, coax, seduce, draw, inveigle, invite, lead on, persuade

lurid ADJECTIVE
1 *window blinds of lurid colours*
► garish, gaudy, flashy, loud, glaring, vulgar
OPPOSITES ARE sober, dull
2 *The report included all the lurid details.*
► sensational, melodramatic, graphic, salacious, gruesome, macabre

lurk VERB
men lurking in doorways
► skulk, loiter, lie in wait, lie low, crouch, hide

luscious ADJECTIVE
luscious fruit hanging from the trees
► delicious, juicy, succulent, mouth-watering, appetizing

lush ADJECTIVE
1 *lush vegetation*
► rich, luxuriant, abundant, profuse, exuberant, prolific, flourishing
2 *a lush penthouse*
► luxurious, sumptuous, grand, opulent, lavish

lust NOUN
1 *He watched her with obvious lust.*
► sexual desire, sexual longing, ardour, passion, lechery, licentiousness
2 *a lust for power*
► greed, desire, craving, longing, hunger, appetite, itch

luxurious ADJECTIVE
luxurious surroundings
► sumptuous, grand, opulent, lavish, comfortable, lush, magnificent, plush, splendid
OPPOSITES ARE austere, simple, spartan

luxury NOUN
They led a life of luxury.
► opulence, sumptuousness, splendour, affluence, extravagance, comfort, ease, enjoyment, indulgence, pleasure, relaxation, self-indulgence, voluptuousness

lying ADJECTIVE
He was just a lying schemer.
► deceitful, dishonest, double-dealing, two-faced, false, untrustworthy, untruthful
AN OPPOSITE IS truthful

lying NOUN
She was no good at lying, even to save her own skin.
► falsehood, untruthfulness, deceit, dishonesty, mendacity, (*more formal*) perjury

lyrical ADJECTIVE
a lyrical poem a lyrical description
► expressive, poetic, emotional, inspired, songlike, rhapsodic

Mm

macabre ADJECTIVE
the macabre business of the switched bodies
► gruesome, grisly, grim, gory, morbid, eerie, weird, lurid, dreadful, horrible, ghoulish

machine NOUN
The machine started to make a noise.
▶ apparatus, appliance, contrivance, device, contraption, instrument, tool, gadget, mechanism
RELATED ADJECTIVE mechanical

machinery NOUN
1 *a factory equipped with modern machinery*
▶ equipment, machines, plant, instruments, hardware, gear
2 *the agreed machinery for resolving disputes*
▶ procedure, organization, structure, system, constitution, method

macho NOUN
macho jobs like bricklaying
▶ manly, male, masculine, virile, (*more informal*) butch, (*more informal*) laddish

mad ADJECTIVE
1 *He thought he was going mad.*
▶ insane, mentally ill, deranged, demented, crazy, (*more informal*) out of your mind, (*more informal*) off your head, (*more informal*) potty, (*more informal*) nutty, (*more informal*) nuts
2 *It was a mad idea but they liked it.*
▶ foolish, crazy, insane, absurd, senseless, wild, preposterous
3 (*informal*) *Is she still mad with you for ditching her?*
▶ angry, cross, furious, enraged, infuriated, irate
4 **mad about** (*informal*) *Jenny is mad about jazz.*
▶ keen on, crazy about, enthusiastic about, eager for, devoted to, addicted to

madden VERB
It's their pretence that maddens me most.
▶ infuriate, exasperate, anger, enrage, incense, annoying, craze, irritate, vex, provoke

maddening ADJECTIVE
The traffic moved with maddening slowness.
▶ infuriating, exasperating, irritating, annoying, vexing, irksome

madness NOUN
1 *There was a gleam of madness in his eyes.*
▶ insanity, dementia, lunacy, delirium, frenzy, hysteria, derangement, eccentricity, mania, mental illness, psychosis
2 *It is madness to let children roam about after dark.*
▶ foolishness, folly, stupidity, insanity, lunacy

magazine NOUN
1 *a pile of magazines on the dining-room table*
▶ journal, periodical, colour supplement, weekly, monthly, comic
2 *a magazine of weapons*
▶ arsenal, ammunition dump, storehouse, depot

magic NOUN
1 *It was so real it had to be magic.*
▶ sorcery, wizardry, witchcraft, devilry, the black arts, the supernatural
2 *No children's party is complete without the magic.*
▶ conjuring, conjuring tricks, illusion, sleight of hand, (*technical*) prestidigitation
3 *The place had lost none of its magic.*
▶ charm, fascination, appeal, allure, glamour

magic ADJECTIVE
a magic spell
▶ supernatural, magical, miraculous

magical ADJECTIVE
They would remember this magical day for the rest of their lives.
▶ wonderful, marvellous, extraordinary, delightful, enchanting

magician NOUN
A magician would finish off the day's entertainment.
▶ conjuror, entertainer, illusionist, wizard, sorcerer

magnanimous ADJECTIVE
With luck on her side Dora could afford to be magnanimous.
▶ generous, bountiful, beneficent, liberal, unstinting

magnate NOUN
an oil magnate
▶ industrialist, tycoon, mogul, baron, businessman, captain of industry

magnetic ADJECTIVE
her magnetic personality
▶ attractive, fascinating, captivating, alluring, charming, appealing, charismatic, seductive, compelling, hypnotic, irresistible
AN OPPOSITE IS repulsive

magnetism NOUN
the sheer magnetism of her personality
▶ attraction, charm, appeal, fascination, allure, charisma, seductiveness, lure, power

magnificent ADJECTIVE
1 *a magnificent view*
▶ spectacular, splendid, impressive, imposing, noble, glorious, gorgeous, sumptuous
2 *a magnificent achievement*
▶ brilliant, masterly, superb, marvellous, wonderful, very fine

magnify VERB
1 *The device magnifies the image.*
▶ enlarge, maximize, amplify, make larger, augment, expand, increase, intensify, (*more informal*) blow up
AN OPPOSITE IS reduce
2 (*informal*) *It is easy to magnify the difficulties involved.*
▶ exaggerate, inflate, maximize, overdo, overestimate, overstate, make too much of, blow up out of all proportion, dramatize
AN OPPOSITE IS minimize.

magnitude NOUN
1 *They realized the magnitude of the task*
▶ size, immensity, vastness, hugeness, extent, enormousness
2 *events of tragic magnitude*
▶ importance, significance, consequence, import, moment

maid NOUN
A maid cleared the room.
▶ servant, serving girl, maidservant, domestic

maiden NOUN
a young maiden
▶ girl, lass, (*literary*) damsel

mail NOUN
The letter came with the morning mail.
▶ post, letters, delivery, packages, packets, parcels, correspondence

mail VERB
I'll mail you the package tomorrow.
▶ post, send, dispatch, forward

maim VERB
Many people were killed or maimed in the attack.
▶ injure, disable, mutilate, wound , disfigure, cripple, handicap

main ADJECTIVE
These are the main issues.
▶ chief, principal, primary, prime, most important, overriding, foremost, fundamental, key, crucial, central, paramount, predominant, basic, essential

mainly ADVERB
The staff are mainly trainees.
▶ chiefly, primarily, principally, mostly, predominantly, especially, essentially

maintain VERB
1 *The villagers pay to maintain the private road.*
▶ keep up, preserve, service, look after, take care of
2 *We need to maintain our links with industry.*
▶ sustain, continue, keep up, conserve, retain, preserve, prolong
3 *They maintain that they were never there.*
▶ assert, claim, affirm, insist, make out, declare, contend, argue

maintenance NOUN
1 *The buildings need a good deal of regular maintenance.*
▶ upkeep, repairs, preservation, care, servicing, conservation, looking after
2 *Absent fathers have to pay maintenance.*
▶ financial support, subsistence, alimony, allowance

majestic ADJECTIVE
a majestic range of mountains
▶ magnificent, grand, spectacular, splendid, impressive, imposing, noble, glorious, gorgeous, sumptuous

majesty NOUN
1 *The procession continued with great majesty.*
▶ dignity, stateliness, solemnity, glory, splendour, grandeur, nobility
2 *the Queen's majesty*
▶ sovereignty, royalty, dominion, authority

major ADJECTIVE
a major achievement
▶ important, considerable, significant, noteworthy, substantial, sizeable, appreciable

majority NOUN
1 *The majority of older people are poor.*
▶ greater number, preponderance, bulk
2 *the age of majority*
▶ adulthood, coming of age, manhood, maturity, womanhood
AN OPPOSITE IS minority
be in the majority
▶ predominate, preponderate, be greater, dominate, outnumber, prevail

make VERB
1 *He makes reproduction furniture.*
▶ build, construct, assemble, put together, manufacture, produce
2 *She made me tell her the whole story.*
▶ force, coerce, oblige, compel, prevail on, pressure, urge
USAGE You need to use the word *to* after all these synonyms, e.g. *She forced me to tell her the whole story.* If you use *prevail* you have to say *She prevailed on me to tell her the whole story.*
3 *The animals make such a noise.*
▶ cause, create, generate, engender, give rise to
4 *She made a little bow.*
▶ perform, execute, give, do, effect, carry out
5 *The town made him their mayor.*
▶ appoint, name, designate, nominate, elect, vote
6 *We seem to have made some mistakes.*
▶ commit, perpetrate, be responsible for, be guilty of
7 *The scheme is bound to make money.*
▶ earn, bring in, gain, acquire
AN OPPOSITE IS lose
8 *James's mother went out to make the lunch.*
▶ prepare, get ready, cook, put together, concoct
9 *I make the total over £500.*
▶ estimate, calculate, work out
USAGE You need to use the word *at* after all these synonyms, e.g. *I estimate the total at over £500.*
10 *We must make a decision.*
▶ reach, come to, arrive at, settle on
11 *I think she'll make a good leader.*
▶ be, constitute, act as, serve as

make off *The thieves made off with the money.*
▶ escape, run off, get away, leave, bolt, (*more informal*) clear off

make out
1 *We could make out a tower in the distance.*
▶ see, discern, distinguish, perceive, detect, recognize, catch sight of, glimpse
2 *They made out we owed them money.*
▶ maintain, assert, claim, affirm, insist, declare, contend, argue
3 *How did you make out at the interview?*
▶ manage, get on, get along, do, cope, (*more formal*) fare

4 *The old man had made out a will.*
▶ draw up, write, complete

make up

1 *Such a story is not something anyone could make up.*
▶ invent, fabricate, contrive, concoct, think up, devise, create, (*more informal*) cook up

2 *They decided to kiss and make up.*
▶ be friends again, make peace, settle your differences, bury the hatchet, mend fences
AN OPPOSITE IS quarrel

make up for *The fine acting made up for all the problems with the production.*
▶ compensate for, offset, counterbalance, counteract, make amends for, redress

make NOUN
a new make of car
▶ brand, marque, model, sort, kind, type, variety

make-believe NOUN
The secret garden was only make-believe.
▶ fantasy, pretence, fiction, fancy, illusion, invention, imagination
AN OPPOSITE IS reality

make-believe ADJECTIVE
a make-believe world of elves and fairies
▶ imaginary, fanciful, pretended, sham, simulated, unreal, feigned, made-up, mock, (*more informal*) pretend
AN OPPOSITE IS real

maker NOUN
a maker of toy cars
▶ manufacturer, producer, creator, designer, originator, constructor, builder

makeshift ADJECTIVE
He arranged a row of chairs to form a makeshift bed.
▶ temporary, standby, rough-and-ready, improvised, stopgap, pernicious, hurtful

make-up NOUN
1 *Ambition is an important part of his make-up.*
▶ character, nature, temperament, constitution, disposition

1 *Her make-up started to run.*
▶ cosmetics, powder, paint

male ADJECTIVE
male characteristics
▶ masculine, manly, virile

malevolent ADJECTIVE
the malevolent gaze of his eyes
▶ malicious, hostile, spiteful, baleful, malign, vindictive, malignant, pernicious, hurtful, offensive, venomous

malice NOUN
actions prompted by malice
▶ malevolence, ill will, spite, spitefulness, animosity

malicious ADJECTIVE
malicious remarks
▶ malevolent, hostile, spiteful, baleful, malign, vindictive, malignant, mischievous, pernicious, offensive, hurtful, venomous
OPPOSITES ARE benevolent, kind

malign ADJECTIVE
a malign influence
▶ harmful, malevolent, hostile, spiteful, baleful, vindictive, malignant, pernicious, offensive, hurtful, venomous
OPPOSITES ARE benevolent, kind

malign VERB
She accused them of maligning her.
▶ defame, vilify, disparage, smear, slander, libel

malignant ADJECTIVE
1 *a malignant disease*
▶ fatal, incurable, terminal, virulent, destructive
2 *a malignant growth*
▶ cancerous, poisonous, non-benign, spreading
AN OPPOSITE IS benign
3 *a malignant stare*
▶ malevolent, hostile, spiteful, baleful, malign, pernicious, offensive, hurtful, venomous
OPPOSITES ARE benevolent, kind

malinger VERB
We do all the work while Charlie goes on malingering.
▶ shirk, sham, (*more informal*) skive, (*more informal*) swing the lead

malleable ADJECTIVE
a malleable substance
▶ soft, pliable, tractable, workable, ductile, plastic
AN OPPOSITE IS brittle

malnutrition NOUN
a country blighted by poverty and malnutrition
▶ hunger, starvation, under-nourishment, famine

malpractice NOUN
a lawyer accused of malpractice
▶ misconduct, wrongdoing, impropriety, dereliction of duty, negligence

maltreat VERB
He was a bully and often maltreated his wife.
▶ ill-treat, mistreat, abuse, misuse, harm, injure, molest, (*more informal*) knock about

mammoth ADJECTIVE
It would be a mammoth task getting the house to rights again.
▶ huge, enormous, gigantic, immense, massive, colossal, vast, large, big, giant, (*more informal*) whopping, (*more informal*) ginormous
AN OPPOSITE IS tiny

man NOUN
1 *a man in a smart suit*
▶ male, gentleman, fellow, (*more informal*) chap, (*more informal*) bloke
2 *All men are fallible.*
▶ person, individual, human being

3 *the evolution of modern man*
► humanity, humankind, mankind, the human race, humans, Homo sapiens
4 *The men have gone on strike.*
► worker, employee
RELATED ADJECTIVES male, masculine

man VERB
We need to man the reception desk from 8 till 5.
► staff, provide personnel for, provide staff for, occupy

manage VERB
1 *She manages a team of 20.*
► be in charge of, run, head, lead, supervise, oversee, control
2 *a course in managing money*
► organize, administer, deal with, regulate
3 *I could only just manage the extra work I had to do.*
► undertake, accomplish, achieve, finish, complete, carry out
4 *I don't know how we'll manage without her.*
► cope, get along, survive, fare, make do
5 *a horse that's difficult to manage*
► control, handle, master, cope with, deal with

manageable ADJECTIVE
1 *a manageable task*
► achievable, doable, practicable, feasible, reasonable, attainable, viable
AN OPPOSITE IS awkward
2 *a manageable horse*
► controllable, obedient, tractable, compliant, amenable, disciplined, docile
OPPOSITES ARE unmanageable, disobedient

management NOUN
1 *The local cinema is under new management.*
► administration, control, direction, supervision, charge, care
2 *The union is in dispute with the management.*
► managers, employers, directors, proprietors, executives

manager NOUN
a meeting of departmental managers
► director, administrator, head, executive, supervisor, principal, controller, boss, chief

mandate NOUN
The government claims it has an election mandate for these measures.
► authority, authorization, approval, endorsement, sanction

mandatory ADJECTIVE
a mandatory UN resolution
► compulsory, obligatory, binding, required

mangle VERB
Henry was staring at the man's mangled hand.
► maul, mutilate, maim, crush, damage, disfigure, injure, wound , lacerate, squash, tear

mangy ADJECTIVE
1 *a mangy dog*
► dirty, unkempt, scabby

2 *a mangy old sofa*
► scruffy, shabby, worn, moth-eaten, shoddy, (*more informal*) tatty

manhandle VERB
1 *The gun crews manhandled the weapons into position.*
► heave, haul, shove, push, manoeuvre
2 *We were spat on, sworn at, and manhandled.*
► maltreat, mistreat, maul, abuse, (*more informal*) knock about

mania NOUN
a mania for old cars
► obsession, passion, enthusiasm, fad, craze, infatuation (with), preoccupation (with)

maniac NOUN
a homicidal maniac
► lunatic, madman or madwoman, psychopath, (*more informal*) loony

manifest ADJECTIVE
a manifest error
► clear, obvious, plain, apparent, patent, unmistakable

manifesto NOUN
a political manifesto
► statement, programme, declaration, policy

manipulate VERB
1 *You need to know how to manipulate all the machine's knobs and levers.*
► operate, work, wield, control, negotiate, twiddle
2 *Governments try to manipulate the economy before elections.*
► influence, control, exploit
3 *It is not difficult to manipulate the data to get the result you want.*
► alter, distort, falsify, doctor, massage, tinker with, fiddle with, fudge, rig, (*more informal*) cook

mankind NOUN
They want to save nature from mankind.
► humanity, humankind, the human race, humans, man, Homo sapiens

manly ADJECTIVE
1 *a manly physique*
► virile, masculine, muscular, sturdy, robust, well-built
2 *manly deeds*
► brave, courageous, bold, heroic, valiant, gallant, chivalrous

man-made ADJECTIVE
a man-made fibre
► synthetic, artificial, manufactured, simulated, imitation
AN OPPOSITE IS natural

manner NOUN
1 *They dealt with the problem in a very efficient manner.*
► way, fashion, style, method, means, procedure, process, mode

2 *I don't much like his unfriendly manner.*
▶ attitude, demeanour, disposition, air, look, bearing, behaviour, character, conduct, mien
3 *We've seen all manner of things there.*
▶ kind, sort, type, variety, category, class
4 **manners** *He needs to learn some manners.*
▶ politeness, refinement, civility, courtesy, etiquette, good behaviour, good conduct, breeding, gentility

mannerism NOUN
He has the annoying mannerism of impatiently snapping his fingers.
▶ peculiarity, idiosyncrasy, quirk, trait, oddity, habit, characteristic

manoeuvre NOUN
1 *She parked the car with a deft manoeuvre.*
▶ movement, move, action, operation
2 *a diplomatic manoeuvre*
▶ stratagem, strategy, tactic, move, plan, plot, ploy, ruse, dodge, gambit, trick
3 *military manoeuvres*
▶ exercise, movement, operation, training

manoeuvre VERB
He manoeuvred the trunk down the stairs.
▶ manipulate, negotiate, move, engineer, guide, navigate, pilot, steer

manual ADJECTIVE
manual work
▶ labouring, physical, by hand

manual NOUN
a training manual
▶ handbook, guide, guidebook, reference book

manufacture VERB
The country could manufacture a nuclear weapon within five years.
▶ make, construct, create, build, prefabricate, assemble, fabricate, mass-produce, process, (*informal*) turn out

manufacturer NOUN
a manufacturer of cosmetics
▶ maker, producer, creator

many ADJECTIVE
There are many reasons.
▶ a lot of, plenty of, numerous, countless, various, copious, profuse, innumerable, umpteen, (*more informal*) lots of
AN OPPOSITE IS few

map NOUN
a map of Europe
▶ chart, diagram, plan
RELATED ADJECTIVE cartographic
RELATED NOUN cartography

map VERB
Aircraft were used to map the region.
▶ chart, survey
map out *We mapped out a plan.*
▶ outline, set out, formulate, detail

mar VERB
His good looks were marred by stubble and red eyes.
▶ spoil, impair, disfigure, ruin, deface, detract from, tarnish

marauder NOUN
An array of jagged glass kept out marauders.
▶ bandit, brigand, raider, robber, buccaneer, pirate, plunderer, invader

march VERB
A company of soldiers marched past.
▶ file, troop, parade, stride, pace, walk

march NOUN
1 *a three-day march*
▶ trek, hike, tramp, slog
2 *a protest march*
▶ procession, rally, demonstration, parade, (*more informal*) demo
3 *the march of time*
▶ advance, progress, progression, passage, evolution

margin NOUN
1 *the margin of the lake*
▶ edge , border, boundary, verge, perimeter, side
2 *They won by a narrow margin.*
▶ difference, gap, surplus

marginal ADJECTIVE
The extra cost is marginal.
▶ negligible, minimal, insignificant, unimportant, minimal, borderline
OPPOSITES ARE significant, important

mark NOUN
1 *a dirty mark*
▶ spot, stain, blot, blotch, smudge, blemish
2 *a mark of respect*
▶ sign, token, symbol, indication, proof, evidence, gesture
3 *Donations have passed the million mark.*
▶ stage, point, level
4 *a comment that hit the mark*
▶ target, objective, purpose, aim
5 *He got a better mark for French than for German.*
▶ grade, grading, score, assessment, evaluation

mark VERB
1 *She took great care not to mark her white dress.*
▶ stain, blemish, smudge, dirty, discolour, blot
2 *All possessions should be clearly marked.*
▶ label, tag
3 *The capture of the rebel stronghold marked a new stage in the war.*
▶ represent, signify, herald, denote, identify, characterize
4 *a festival to mark the Golden Jubilee*
▶ celebrate, recognize, observe, commemorate, remember
5 *Mark my words carefully.*
▶ heed, note, mind, take notice of, listen to, regard
6 *She had exam papers to mark that evening.*
▶ assess, grade, correct, evaluate, appraise

marked ADJECTIVE
a marked improvement in health
▶ distinct, noticeable, decided, pronounced, plain, clear, emphatic, palpable
AN OPPOSITE IS slight

market NOUN
1 *The local market is every Saturday.*
▶ bazaar, fair, sale, marketplace
2 *The market for second-hand cars is thriving.*
▶ demand, call, need, requirement

market VERB
The firm markets reproduction furniture
▶ sell, trade in, merchandise, retail

maroon VERB
a story about a group of boys marooned on a desert island
▶ strand, cast away, abandon, isolate, leave, desert, forsake

marriage NOUN
1 *The couple will celebrate their 50 years of marriage.*
▶ matrimony, wedlock, partnership, union
2 *The marriage took place in the local register office.*
▶ wedding, wedding ceremony, match, nuptials
RELATED ADJECTIVES conjugal, marital, matrimonial, nuptial

marry VERB
1 *They never married.*
▶ get married, wed, (*more informal*) tie the knot
OPPOSITES ARE separate, divorce
2 *He married Jessica in Italy.*
▶ wed, (*more informal*) get hitched to
OPPOSITES ARE separate from, divorce
3 *The exhibition marries information with entertainment.*
▶ combine, unite, link, merge, connect, join, ally

marsh NOUN
The car had plunged into a marsh.
▶ swamp, bog, marshland, wetland, mire, morass, quagmire, quicksands, fen, slough, mudflats, saltmarsh, saltings

marshal VERB
The king marshalled a huge army. The police marshalled their evidence with great care.
▶ gather, assemble, collect, organize, muster, set out, deploy, draw up, group, line up, arrange
OPPOSITES ARE disperse, scatter

martial ADJECTIVE
1 *martial law*
▶ military
AN OPPOSITE IS civil
2 *a martial nation*
▶ warlike, bellicose, militant, aggressive, belligerent, pugnacious
AN OPPOSITE IS peaceable
3 *martial exploits*
▶ military, soldierly, valiant, brave, courageous

marvel VERB
marvel at *Everyone marvelled at their courage.*
▶ admire, be amazed by, wonder at, applaud, praise, appreciate, respect, be astonished by, be surprised by

marvel NOUN
a marvel of precision engineering
▶ miracle, wonder, sensation, phenomenon

marvellous ADJECTIVE
1 *a marvellous achievement*
▶ remarkable, amazing, extraordinary, wonderful, magnificent, astonishing, astounding
AN OPPOSITE IS ordinary
2 *We had a marvellous time*
▶ excellent, wonderful, fantastic, splendid, lovely, delightful, smashing, (*more informal*) terrific
OPPOSITES ARE awful, dreadful

masculine ADJECTIVE
1 *She wore a masculine shirt with rolled-up sleeves.*
▶ male, man's or men's, manlike
AN OPPOSITE IS feminine
2 *a powerfully masculine man*
▶ manly, virile, muscular, well-built, strapping, vigorous
OPPOSITES ARE weak, timid

mash VERB
Mash the potatoes and put them on top.
▶ crush, pulp, cream, purée, pulverize, pound, smash, squash, grind, mangle, beat

mask NOUN
They wore masks to hide their faces.
▶ disguise, veil, camouflage, cover, screen, shield, façade

mask VERB
A row of trees masked the view.
▶ conceal, cover, obscure, screen, shield, hide, shroud, veil, blot out, camouflage, cloak, disguise

mass NOUN
1 *a mass of wet leaves*
▶ pile, heap, load, accumulation, collection, conglomeration
2 *a mass of cars heading for the coast*
▶ multitude, throng, crowd, troop, mob, quantity, large number
3 *The mass of people declined to vote at all.*
▶ majority, greater part, bulk, body
4 *an object having a large mass*
▶ weight, size, magnitude, bulk

mass ADJECTIVE
a mass protest
▶ wholesale, universal, large-scale, widespread, comprehensive, general, popular
AN OPPOSITE IS small-scale

mass VERB
Spectators massed under the trees during the downpour.
▶ gather, assemble, collect, flock

massacre NOUN
the massacre of innocent civilians
▶ slaughter, killing, mass murder, extermination, butchery, carnage, annihilation

massacre VERB
The army massacred most of the population.
▶ slaughter, butcher, exterminate, annihilate, murder, liquidate, eliminate

massive ADJECTIVE
a massive building   massive debts
▶ huge, enormous, gigantic, immense, colossal, vast, large, big, giant, (*more informal*) whopping, (*more informal*) ginormous
AN OPPOSITE IS tiny

mast NOUN
1 *a tall mast*
▶ flagpole, maypole, aerial, pylon, transmitter
2 *a ship's mast*
▶ spar, boom, yard

master NOUN
1 *He became master of the country after a bloody coup.*
▶ ruler, chief, head, lord, overlord, governor
2 *a dog's master*
▶ owner, keeper
3 *a master of disguises*
▶ expert (at), genius, past master, maestro, virtuoso

master VERB
1 *He managed to master his feelings.*
▶ control, restrain, check, contain, curb, confine, keep in check, repress, subdue, suppress
2 *She mastered the language after a few months.*
▶ learn, grasp, acquire, be expert in, (*more informal*) get the hang of

masterful ADJECTIVE
USAGE Do not confuse this word with *masterly*, which has a different meaning.
the most masterful sovereign in English history
▶ authoritative, commanding, powerful, domineering, overbearing, arrogant, dictatorial, tyrannical, bossy

masterly ADJECTIVE
USAGE Do not confuse this word with *masterful*, which has a different meaning.
a masterly survey of the subject
▶ expert, skilful, adept, adroit, accomplished, consummate, intelligent, fine

mastermind NOUN
the mastermind behind the robbery
▶ originator, planner, creator, engineer, prime mover, architect, inventor, manager, (*more informal*) brain, (*more informal*) brains

mastermind VERB
They brought him back to mastermind the new operation.
▶ control, direct, plan, organize, coordinate, conduct, supervise, carry through

masterpiece NOUN
The portrait is the artist's masterpiece.
▶ masterwork, finest work, (*Latin*) magnum opus, (*French*) chef-d'oeuvre

mastery NOUN
1 *a mastery of languages*
▶ command, knowledge, grasp, comprehension, understanding, proficiency (in)
2 *work done with great mastery*
▶ proficiency, capability, expertness, skill, adroitness, dexterity

match NOUN
1 *a cricket match*
▶ game, contest, competition, fixture, test match, tie, tournament
2 *The dress and shoes are a good match.*
▶ combination, pair
3 *She found a match for the tall vase.*
▶ copy, replica, complement, counterpart, duplicate, twin
4 *The enemy tanks were no match for ours in speed and range.*
▶ equal, rival, equivalent, counterpart
5 *a love match*
▶ marriage, union, friendship, partnership, relationship, alliance

match VERB
1 *The hat matches her dress.*
▶ go with, suit, harmonize with, tone with, blend with, complement
AN OPPOSITE IS clash with
2 *The two versions of the story don't match.*
▶ agree, correspond, tally
3 *No one can match him at Scrabble.*
▶ equal, rival, compete with

matching ADJECTIVE
The curtains have a matching duvet cover.
▶ corresponding, coordinating, equivalent, harmonizing, toning, complementing
AN OPPOSITE IS incongruous

matchless ADJECTIVE
her matchless beauty
▶ incomparable, unequalled, inimitable, unmatched, unrivalled, peerless, unique

mate NOUN
1 *a plumber's mate*
▶ assistant, helper, apprentice, colleague
2 *He went to see a film with his mates.*
▶ friend, pal, chum, companion
3 *He's still looking for his ideal mate.*
▶ partner, wife or husband, spouse, lover, consort

mate VERB
The zoo is trying to get the pandas to mate.
▶ breed, copulate, couple

material NOUN
1 *material for making curtains*
▶ fabric, cloth, textile, stuff

2 *organic material*
► matter, substance, stuff
3 *We are collecting material for an article on surfing.*
► data, information, facts, statistics, evidence, particulars

material ADJECTIVE
1 *the material world as distinct from the spiritual world*
► physical, corporeal, tangible, earthly, concrete
OPPOSITES ARE spiritual, abstract
2 *information that is material to our enquiries*
► relevant, pertinent, applicable, germane
OPPOSITES ARE irrelevant, immaterial

materialize VERB
1 *A vague form materialized at the end of the path.*
► appear, take shape, form, loom, arise
AN OPPOSITE IS disappear
2 *The expected deliveries had not in fact materialized.*
► happen, occur, come about, take place

matter NOUN
1 *Excess vegetable matter can be kept in a separate waste bin.*
► material, substance, stuff
2 *The last sentence of his statement goes to the heart of the matter.*
► affair, business, subject, topic, issue, concern
3 *It's of little matter now.*
► importance, consequence, significance, moment

matter VERB
Does it matter what I wear?
► make a difference, be important, count, signify

matter-of-fact ADJECTIVE
(*informal*) *He described the place in a very matter-of-fact way.*
► deadpan, down-to-earth, factual, mechanical, prosaic, unemotional, unimaginative, to the point, unadorned
OPPOSITES ARE emotional, imaginative

mature ADJECTIVE
1 *a mature woman*
► adult, grown-up, grown, full-grown, advanced, well-developed
OPPOSITES ARE immature, adolescent
2 *He seems very mature for his age.*
► responsible, sensible, dependable, reliable
OPPOSITES ARE immature, childish
3 *mature cheese   mature fruit*
► mellow, ready, ripened, seasoned
AN OPPOSITE IS unripe

mature VERB
1 *Bella had matured into a beautiful young woman.*
► grow, grow up, develop, blossom
2 *Their friendship matured rapidly.*
► develop, grow, blossom, bloom, flourish, thrive

maul VERB
1 *He pulled me to the ground and started mauling on my back and neck.*
► savage, attack, claw, manhandle, molest, maltreat, ill-treat, mutilate, lacerate

2 *The new production was mauled by the critics.*
► criticize, attack, savage, pillory, lambaste, (*more informal*) hammer, (*more informal*) slam

maximum ADJECTIVE
a maximum speed of 80 kph
► greatest, highest, top, full, utmost, extreme, fullest, largest, most, biggest, supreme
AN OPPOSITE IS minimum

maximum NOUN
Production has reached its maximum.
► upper limit, limit, peak, ceiling, highest point, pinnacle, top level
AN OPPOSITE IS minimum

mayhem NOUN
I decided I'd caused enough mayhem for one day.
► confusion, chaos, disorder, muddle, bedlam, pandemonium, anarchy, disorganization, lawlessness, shambles, tumult
AN OPPOSITE IS order

maze NOUN
a maze of rooms and corridors
► labyrinth, warren, network, web, tangle, confusion

meadow NOUN
sheep grazing in a meadow
► field, paddock, pasture, (*poetic*) mead, (*poetic*) lea

meagre ADJECTIVE
1 *He had a few coins in his pocket, his meagre earnings for the day.*
► paltry, scanty, scant, sparse, negligible, pitiful, miserable, modest, (*more informal*) mingy, (*more informal*) measly
OPPOSITES ARE plentiful, abundant
2 *a tall, meagre youth*
► thin, lean, skinny, scrawny, scraggy, lanky

---

meal NOUN
A meal would be waiting for them when they got home.
► bite to eat, (*literary*) repast, (*more informal*) spread, (*more informal*) feed
RELATED ADJECTIVE prandial

SOME WORDS FOR MEALS

main meals: breakfast, continental breakfast, lunch ((*more formal*) luncheon), tea, high tea, dinner.

large or grand meals: banquet, dinner party, feast; (*more informal*) blowout, beanfeast.

outdoor meals picnic, barbecue.

light or informal meals: snack, elevenses, brunch (combined breakfast and lunch), buffet, supper, fork supper, takeaway, TV dinner.

---

mean ADJECTIVE
1 *He was too mean to leave a tip.*
► miserly, niggardly, stingy, parsimonious, (*more informal*) mingy, (*more informal*) tight-fisted, (*more informal*) penny-pinching

2 *It was mean of them to leave her like that.*
▶ unkind, nasty, shameful, unpleasant, callous, cruel, spiteful

3 *His room was a cold mean affair.*
▶ squalid, shabby, wretched, dismal, humble, lowly

mean VERB

1 *The sign means you have to stop.*
▶ indicate, signify, denote, convey, show

2 *What do you think they mean by these remarks?*
▶ intend, suggest, imply

3 *I mean to find him come what may.*
▶ intend, plan, aim, want, wish, propose, purpose, aspire

4 *Her promotion meant a lot more travel.*
▶ involve, entail, necessitate, lead to, result in

5 *Your help means a lot to me.*
▶ matter, be important, have importance

meander VERB

A group of tourists meandered across the square.
▶ wander, stroll, ramble, amble, roam, saunter

meaning NOUN

1 *I didn't understand the meaning of her remarks.*
▶ significance, sense, import, implication, force, thrust, connotation

2 *Some words have several meanings.*
▶ sense, definition, denotation, explanation

3 *Life has little meaning for them now.*
▶ value, worth, point, purpose, significance

meaningful ADJECTIVE

meaningful remarks
▶ expressive, significant, relevant, consequential, pointed, suggestive, meaning
AN OPPOSITE IS meaningless

meaningless ADJECTIVE

1 *a meaningless compliment*
▶ empty, worthless, insincere, hollow, fatuous, nonsensical
AN OPPOSITE IS meaningful

2 *Life seemed meaningless.*
▶ pointless, senseless, worthless, inconsequential, insignificant

means NOUN

1 *modern means of communication*
▶ method, mode, way, medium, channel, vehicle, instrument, course

2 *I don't have the means for such a lifestyle.*
▶ resources, funds, money, wherewithal, income, finance

3 *a person of means*
▶ wealth, riches, substance, property

measly ADJECTIVE

(informal) All he could find was a measly ten-pence piece.
▶ meagre, paltry, scanty, scant, sparse, negligible, pitiful, miserable, modest, (more informal) mingy
AN OPPOSITE IS generous

measure NOUN

1 *These successes earned them a measure of glory. Add three measures of liquid.*
▶ share, portion, amount, allocation, quota, ration

2 *personal income as a measure of success*
▶ gauge, criterion, yardstick, standard, touchstone, meter, test

3 *special measures to monitor noise levels*
▶ step, action, procedure, process, means, control, operation

measure VERB

1 *It's not easy to measure the effects of such a disaster.*
▶ evaluate, assess, gauge, appraise, determine, fathom

2 **measure up to** *attempts to measure up to the expected standards.*
▶ achieve, meet, satisfy, match, comply with

measured ADJECTIVE

He was walking at a measured pace.
▶ steady, regular, even, rhythmic, constant, sustained, sedate, slow, firm, resolute

---

measurement NOUN

1 *Measurements are given in metric units.*
▶ dimension, size, extent, proportions

2 *an instrument used in the measurement of air speed*
▶ calculation, computation, mensuration, evaluation, assessment

SOME METRIC MEASUREMENTS WITH UNITS (* = SI UNITS)

length: kilometre (km, = 1,000 metres), metre (m) centimetre (cm), milimetre (mm).

mass: *kilogram (kg, = 1,000 grams), gram (g).

time: milennium (1,000 years), century (100 years), year, month, week, minute, second.

temperature: *kelvin (K), degree Celsius, Centigrade.

strength of light: *candela (cd).

amount of substance: *mole (mol).

force: *newton (N).

work, nergy, heat: *joule (j).

power: watt (W).

electric current: *ampere (A).

electric charge: coulomb (C).

electrical resistance: *ohm (Ω).

electric voltage: *volt.

frequency: *hertz.

pressure: *pascal (Pa).

radioactivity: *becquerel (Bq).

---

mechanic NOUN

a motor mechanic
▶ engineer, technician

mechanical ADJECTIVE

1 *a mechanical doll*
▶ mechanized, automated, machine-driven, motor-driven, automatic
AN OPPOSITE IS manual

2 *The voice sounded detached and mechanical.*
► unemotional, unfeeling, matter-of-fact, perfunctory, unthinking, cold, inhuman, lifeless, routine, soulless
AN OPPOSITE IS thoughtful

mechanism NOUN
1 *A trigger mechanism activates the bolt.*
► apparatus, machine, device, appliance, system, tool
2 *Mechanisms are in place for correcting mistakes.*
► procedure, process, system, means, channel, structure

medal NOUN
Their son had won a medal for bravery.
► medallion, honour, decoration, award, reward, trophy, prize

meddle VERB
We don't want them meddling in our affairs.
► interfere, pry, intrude, poke, nose, snoop, (more informal) stick your nose in

meddlesome ADJECTIVE
We can do without meddlesome relatives.
► interfering, meddling, prying, intrusive, officious, intruding

mediate VERB
He tried to mediate between Franklin and the British government.
► negotiate, arbitrate, intercede, act as mediator, liaise

mediator NOUN
last-minute pressure from diplomat and UN mediators
► arbitrator, negotiator, intermediary, broker, go-between, peacemaker

medicinal ADJECTIVE
They collected berries, nuts, and medicinal plants.
► healing, curative, remedial, restorative, therapeutic, medical

medicine NOUN
1 *examples of how modern medicine has helped to prolong life*
► medical science, healing, surgery, therapeutics, treatment of diseases
2 *He poured a dose of the medicine into the glass.*
► medication, medicament, remedy, cure, drug, prescription, treatment
RELATED ADJECTIVES clinical, pharmaceutical

mediocre ADJECTIVE
Fred turned a mediocre business into one that was thriving.
► ordinary, commonplace, indifferent, average, undistinguished, middle-of-the-road, run-of-the-mill, unexceptional, middling, passable, tolerable, second-rate
OPPOSITES ARE exceptional, outstanding

meditation NOUN
He fell silent for a while, as if in meditation.
► contemplation, prayer, reflection, yoga

meditate VERB
meditate on *They were meditating on the meaning of life.*
► consider, contemplate, ponder, cogitate, reflect on, brood on, mull over, speculate on

medium ADJECTIVE
She is of medium height.
► average, middling, middle, normal, ordinary, standard, usual, intermediate, midway, moderate

medium NOUN
1 *Television is a powerful medium of communication.*
► method, means, channel, mode, way, vehicle, instrument, course
2 *a happy medium between quality and quantity*
► average, midpoint, middle way, middle ground, compromise
3 *I went to see a medium and she told me I would be rich one day.*
► clairvoyant, spiritualist, psychic

medley NOUN
a medley of popular tunes
► mixture, assortment, miscellany, variety, selection, collection, hotchpotch, assembly

meek ADJECTIVE
She seemed meek but could be fiercely passionate.
► gentle, mild, demure, submissive, compliant, modest, docile, unassuming, self-effacing, unassertive, forbearing
AN OPPOSITE IS assertive

meet VERB
1 *She met an old friend in town.*
► encounter, come across, run across, run into, chance on, stumble on
2 *I'll meet you at the airport.*
► collect
3 *They met the challenge bravely.*
► face, undergo, encounter, experience, endure, suffer
4 *The equipment does not meet our requirements.*
► satisfy, fulfil, answer, measure up to, match up to, conform to
5 *The board meets every month.*
► gather, assemble, come together, convene, hold a meeting
6 *The two roads meet north of the city.*
► join, converge, merge, come together, connect, intersect

meeting NOUN
1 *He rushed back to be in time for the meeting.*
► gathering, assembly, conference, forum, convention
2 *He adored her from their very first meeting.*
► encounter, rendezvous, contact, assignation, get-together, date
3 *The town stands at the meeting of three mighty rivers.*
► convergence, coming together, junction, confluence, union, concourse

melancholy ADJECTIVE

1 *melancholy music*
▶ sad, sorrowful, mournful, reflective
2 *a melancholy mood*
▶ unhappy, downhearted, despondent, gloomy, dispirited, depressed, dejected, downcast
OPPOSITES ARE joyful, happy, elated

melancholy NOUN

a feeling of melancholy
▶ sadness, sorrow, dejection, unhappiness, depression, dejection, despondency, gloom
OPPOSITES ARE joy, happiness, elation

mellow ADJECTIVE

1 *a mellow voice*
▶ smooth, melodious, dulcet, tuneful, sweet
2 *a mellow temperament*
▶ easy-going, tolerant, amiable, good-natured, affable, kind-hearted
3 *mellow fruit*
▶ ripe, mature, juicy, tender, sweet

melodious ADJECTIVE

melodious sounds
▶ tuneful, musical, melodic, harmonious, euphonious, lyrical, sweet-toned

melody NOUN

a beautiful melody
▶ tune, air, strain, theme, song

melt VERB

The sun soon melted the snow, The ice was beginning to melt.
▶ thaw, unfreeze, defrost, liquefy, soften, dissolve
melt away *The crowds rapidly melted away.*
▶ disperse, dissolve, dwindle, vanish, evaporate, disappear, fade

member NOUN

new members of the sports club
▶ associate, subscriber, fellow, adherent

memento NOUN

a memento of the occasion
▶ souvenir, keepsake, token, reminder, memorial

memoirs PLURAL NOUN

He published his memoirs in 1990.
▶ reminiscences, recollections, autobiography, life story

memorable ADJECTIVE

1 *a memorable event*
▶ unforgettable, notable, remarkable, outstanding, extraordinary
OPPOSITES ARE commonplace, forgettable
2 (*informal*) *a memorable tune*
▶ catchy, haunting

memorial NOUN

a memorial to victims of the war
▶ monument, remembrance, shrine, cenotaph, plaque, tablet

memorize NOUN

Long numbers are hard to memorize.
▶ remember, commit to memory, learn by heart, retain
AN OPPOSITE IS forget

memory NOUN

1 *My mother always had a good memory.*
▶ recall, retention, ability to remember, recollection
2 *happy memories of a lovely occasion*
▶ reminiscence, recollection, remembrance, reminder, souvenir, impression
3 *a plaque in memory of local writers*
▶ commemoration, remembrance, tribute, honour, recognition

menace NOUN

1 *a menace to society*
▶ danger, threat, hazard, risk
2 *That child is a menace.*
▶ nuisance, pest, annoyance
3 *a situation full of menace*
▶ threat, ominousness, intimidation

menace VERB

The state should not menace its own citizens.
▶ threaten, intimidate, frighten, bully

mend VERB

1 *An electrician was mending faulty wiring.*
▶ repair, fix, restore, renovate
AN OPPOSITE IS break
2 *a pile of socks to mend*
▶ patch, repair, darn
3 *a quarrel that a few kind words can mend*
▶ put right, resolve, sort out, straighten out, remedy, rectify, redress
AN OPPOSITE IS make worse

menial ADJECTIVE

Someone has to do the menial tasks.
▶ humble, lowly, routine, unskilled, low-grade, humdrum, inferior, degrading, demeaning
OPPOSITES ARE skilled, important

menial NOUN

They are treated like menials.
▶ servant, drudge, minion, domestic, (*more informal*) skivvy

mental ADJECTIVE

1 *The work calls for considerable mental concentration.*
▶ intellectual, cerebral, abstract, rational, cognitive, theoretical
2 *Your mental attitude affects your behaviour.*
▶ psychological, temperamental, emotional, subjective

mentality NOUN

They seem to have an ostrich-like mentality.
▶ attitude, way of thinking, outlook, predisposition, disposition, frame of mind, character, temperament, personality, (*more informal*) make-up

mention VERB

1 *Nick mentioned that he would be here next week.*
▶ state, say, remark, observe, reveal, indicate, disclose, divulge
2 *Better not to mention the score.*
▶ refer to, allude to, touch on, speak about, comment on, disclose, hint at, let out, reveal, (*more informal*) let drop

merciful ADJECTIVE

They believe in a merciful God.
▶ compassionate, forgiving, humane, gracious, understanding, sympathetic, generous, beneficent
OPPOSITES ARE merciless, cruel

merciless ADJECTIVE

a leader who was merciless to his enemies
▶ cruel, pitiless, ruthless, heartless, unsparing, unforgiving, unrelenting, harsh, severe
AN OPPOSITE IS merciful

mercy NOUN

1 *The prisoners begged for mercy.*
▶ clemency, compassion, leniency, pity, sympathy, forbearance, forgiveness, understanding
AN OPPOSITE IS cruelty
2 *It is a mercy that more people weren't killed.*
▶ blessing, godsend, boon, favour, piece of good fortune

merge VERB

1 *It seems a good idea to merge the two organizations.*
▶ combine, amalgamate, integrate, unite, join together, consolidate, coalesce, blend, fuse, link up, put together
2 *The two parties have agreed to merge.*
▶ unite, join together, come together, amalgamate, unify, combine
3 *The motorways merge ahead.*
▶ join, meet, converge
OPPOSITES ARE split, separate

merit NOUN

writers of merit
▶ excellence, goodness, value, virtue, worth, importance, quality, credit, eminence

merit VERB

The idea certainly merits consideration.
▶ deserve, warrant, be worth, be worthy of, be entitled to, justify, rate, earn, incur

merriment NOUN

They could hear bursts of laughter and ripples of merriment.
▶ jollity, enjoyment, cheerfulness, mirth, festivity, conviviality, amusement, revelry, high spirits
OPPOSITES ARE misery, gloom

merry ADJECTIVE

merry crowds of holiday-makers   a merry ringing of bells
▶ jolly, cheerful, light-hearted, carefree, joyful, joyous, festive, happy, gleeful

mesh NOUN

1 *A wire mesh covered the hutch.*
▶ netting, lattice, net, network, web
2 *a mesh of political intrigue*
▶ tangle, entanglement, snare, trap

mesmerize VERB

His hand gripped hers across the table and his voice mesmerized her.
▶ hypnotize, bewitch, entrance, captivate, enthral, transfix, fascinate, dominate, magnetize

mess NOUN

1 *There's quite a mess in the kitchen.*
▶ muddle, untidiness, disarray, jumble, confusion, clutter, shambles
2 *It was a mess of his own making and he would have to find a way out.*
▶ predicament, quandary, difficulty, trouble, (*more informal*) fix

make a mess of *I'm afraid I've made a mess of the assignment.*
▶ ruin, spoil, botch, bungle, mishandle, mismanage, fluff, muff, mess up, (*more informal*) make a hash of, (*much more informal*) cock up, (*much more informal*) screw up
OPPOSITES ARE succeed in, bring off

mess VERB

mess about or **around** *They need to stop messing around and get on with something.*
▶ fool about or around, play about or around, (*more informal*) muck about or around
mess up
1 *They had messed up the garden in less than ten minutes.*
▶ jumble, muddle, make a mess of, dirty, dishevel, disrupt, disarrange
2 *A new assignment: try not to mess this one up.*
▶ ruin, spoil, botch, bungle, mishandle, mismanage, fluff, muff, make a mess of, (*more informal*) make a hash of, (*much more informal*) cock up, (*much more informal*) screw up

message NOUN

Sarah sent a message with her brother.
▶ communication, note, letter, word, memo, dispatch, missive

messenger NOUN

A messenger brought the news.
▶ courier, emissary, go-between, envoy, runner, dispatch-rider

messy ADJECTIVE

1 *All these jobs can be messy and produce a lot of debris.*
▶ dirty, filthy, mucky, grubby, grimy
2 *The bathroom had become very messy. Her hair was tangled and messy.*
▶ untidy, dishevelled, unkempt, disorganized, chaotic, sloppy
OPPOSITES ARE tidy, neat, organized

m

metal NOUN
a lump of metal
▶ ingot, nugget

WORDS FOR TYPES OF METAL

metals: lithium, beryllium, sodium, magnesium, aluminium, potassium, calcium, scandium, titanium, vanadium, chromium, manganese, iron, cobalt, nickel, copper, zinc, gallium, strontium, zirconium, molybdenum, silver, cadmium, tin, barium, tungsten, platinum, gold, mercury, lead, bismuth, uranium.

metal alloys: brass (copper and zinc), bronze (copper and tin), cast iron (iron and carbon), electrum (gold and silver), pewter (tin and lead, or tin, copper and antimony), solder (lead and tin), steel (iron, carbon and other elements).

method NOUN
a new method of gathering vital data
▶ way, approach (to), procedure (for), manner, mode, technique (for), style, plan (for)

methodical ADJECTIVE
a methodical approach to working
▶ organized, orderly, systematic, meticulous, painstaking, efficient, businesslike, meticulous, logical, tidy, precise, neat
OPPOSITES ARE disorganized, inefficient

meticulous ADJECTIVE
He continued his meticulous inspection of the machine.
▶ careful, methodical, scrupulous, diligent, painstaking, systematic, thorough, rigorous

middle ADJECTIVE
Remove the middle pin.
▶ central, midway, mean, medial, median, half-way, inner, inside

middle NOUN
1 *There was a large table in the middle of the room.*
▶ centre, midpoint
OPPOSITES ARE edge, border
2 *a journey to the middle of the earth*
▶ centre, core, heart, kernel
OPPOSITES ARE surface, circumference

middling ADJECTIVE
She speaks middling to good Japanese.
▶ average, medium, fair, ordinary, moderate, everyday, modest, passable

midget NOUN
houses so small they must have been occupied by midgets
▶ person of restricted growth, small person, dwarf, pygmy

USAGE *Person of restricted growth* is the term you should use to avoid causing offence, as all the other words have derogatory overtones.

midget ADJECTIVE
a midget car
▶ miniature, baby, dwarf, small

miffed ADJECTIVE
(informal) She felt miffed at being ignored.
▶ annoyed, irritated, angry, cross, displeased, vexed, infuriated, incensed, enraged, (*more informal*) put out

might NOUN
I hit it with all my might.
▶ strength, force, power, energy, vigour

mighty ADJECTIVE
a mighty blow to the head
▶ powerful, forceful, violent, vigorous, ferocious, hefty, savage
AN OPPOSITE IS weak

mild ADJECTIVE
1 *She spoke in a mild voice.*
▶ gentle, soft, tender, calm, tender-hearted, easygoing, sympathetic
AN OPPOSITE IS harsh
2 *The weather turned mild.*
▶ warm, calm, fair, temperate
OPPOSITES ARE severe, cold

militant ADJECTIVE
militant opponents of the regime
▶ belligerent, active, aggressive, combatant, assertive, positive
OPPOSITES ARE restrained, peaceful

military ADJECTIVE
a military command   military units
▶ fighting, service, armed, martial, belligerent, enlisted, uniformed
AN OPPOSITE IS civilian

military NOUN
The town came under the control of the military.
▶ army, armed forces, services, militia, soldiers, soldiery
AN OPPOSITE IS civilian

milk VERB
Unscrupulous moneylenders can milk unwary clients.
▶ exploit, take advantage of, cash in on, squeeze, bleed

milky ADJECTIVE
1 *her beautiful milky skin*
▶ pale, white, cream, creamy
2 *a milky liquid*
▶ cloudy, chalky, misty, opaque, whitish
AN OPPOSITE IS clear
RELATED ADJECTIVE lactic

mill NOUN
1 *a paper mill*
▶ factory, plant, processing plant, works, workshop
2 *a pepper mill*
▶ grinder, crusher, roller

mill VERB

The wheat is milled into flour.
▶ grind, crush, roll, pulverize, powder

mill about or **around** *Outside, people were still milling about.*
▶ throng, swarm, stream, surge, wander about, move aimlessly

mime VERB

She mimed a telephone conversation.
▶ act out, mimic, simulate, gesture, impersonate

mimic NOUN

He was entertaining and a good mimic.
▶ impersonator, impressionist, imitator

mimic VERB

She could mimic anyone after a few minutes listening to them.
▶ imitate, impersonate, copy, ape, caricature, do an impression of, parody, parrot, pretend to be, simulate, (*more informal*) take off

mince VERB

1 *He took the meat and minced it.*
▶ grind, chop, dice, crumble, cube

2 not mince words *She doesn't mince her words when she's angry.*
▶ speak plainly, speak straight, get to the point, not pull your punches

mind NOUN

1 *people with brilliant minds*
▶ brain, intellect, intelligence, sense, wits, understanding, mentality, power of reasoning, (*more informal*) grey matter
RELATED ADJECTIVE mental

2 *It's hard to keep my mind on my work.*
▶ attention, concentration, thinking

3 *I couldn't get her words out of my mind.*
▶ memory, recollection, remembrance

4 *I've a mind to go and complain.*
▶ inclination, wish, desire, fancy, intention, disposition, tendency

mind VERB

1 *I'll mind your bags while you're gone.*
▶ look after, watch, guard, take care of, attend to, (*more informal*) keep an eye on

2 *You'd better mind what they say.*
▶ be careful of, beware of, heed, pay attention to, look out for, watch out for, take notice of, note, remember

3 *Will you mind if I eat my lunch?*
▶ care, object, bother, disapprove, grumble, take offence, worry, be resentful, complain

mindful ADJECTIVE

mindful of *Rob flew with care, mindful of the lives of his crew.*
▶ aware of, conscious of, heedful of, alive to, attentive to, careful of
OPPOSITES ARE heedless of, oblivious to

mindless ADJECTIVE

1 *The occasion was spoilt by incidents of mindless violence.*
▶ senseless, wanton, gratuitous, thoughtless

2 *People are reduced to mindless automatons, unable to think for themselves.*
▶ stupid, idiotic, brainless, witless, foolish

mine NOUN

1 *a coal mine*
▶ pit, colliery, coalfield, deposit, mineshaft

2 *He was killed by a mine.*
▶ landmine, explosive

3 *The book is a mine of information.*
▶ store, wealth, fund, treasury, repository, hoard, rich supply

mine VERB

Gold is mined in these hills.
▶ excavate, extract, quarry, dig for, remove

---

mineral NOUN

SOME COMMON MINERALS

alabaster, albite, anhydrite, asbestos, aventurine, azurite, bentonite, bloodstone, Blue John, borax, cairngorm, calamine, calcite, cassiterite, chalcedony, chlorite, chrysoberyl, cinnabar, corundum, dolomite, emery, feldspar, fluorite or fluorspar, fool's gold, galena, graphite, gypsum, haematite, halite, hornblende, idocrase, jacinth, jargoon, kaolinite, lapis lazuli, lazurite, magnetite, malachite, mica, microcline, montmorillonite, orthoclase, pitchblende, pyrites, quartz, realgar, rock salt, rutile, sanidine, siderite, smithsonite, sodalite, spar, sphalerite, spinel, talc, uraninite, vesuvianite, wurzite, zircon.

---

mingle VERB

1 *Guests mingled in the gardens.*
▶ socialize, circulate, get together, merge, mix, fraternize, associate, move about, rub shoulders, intermingle

2 *Open air smells mingled with the aroma of food cooking.*
▶ combine, merge, fuse, unite, join, coalesce

mingy ADJECTIVE

(*informal*) *All I got was a mingy five pounds.*
▶ meagre, measly, paltry, miserable, scanty, scant, sparse, negligible, pitiful, modest, (*informal*) mouldy
AN OPPOSITE IS generous

miniature ADJECTIVE

a miniature village
▶ tiny, small-scale, scaled-down, diminutive, minute, baby, model

minimal ADJECTIVE

Increases in rent this year have been minimal.
▶ very little, negligible, slight, least, smallest, minimum, token, nominal

minimize VERB

1 *They banned smoking to minimize the danger of fire*
▶ reduce, keep down, cut down, lessen, curtail, diminish
OPPOSITES ARE maximize, increase

2 *He should not minimizes the value of their contribution.*
▶ underestimate, gloss over, make light of, play down
OPPOSITES ARE maximize, exaggerate

minimum ADJECTIVE

The pay is well above the minimum wage.
▶ lowest, least, smallest, minimal, bottom

minimum NOUN

Costs are kept to a minimum
▶ lower limit, limit, base, lowest point, bottom level
AN OPPOSITE IS maximum

minion NOUN

He gives the worst jobs to his minions.
▶ assistant, underling, lackey, hireling, stooge, hanger-on, attendant

minister NOUN

1 *a minister of the church*
▶ clergyman, clergywoman, cleric, parson, priest, vicar, preacher

2 *a government minister*
▶ official, office-holder, executive, secretary of state

USAGE A *secretary of state* is a head of a government department (such as transport) and a member of the cabinet; not all ministers are secretaries of state.

minister VERB

minister to *Paramedics were ministering to the injured.*
▶ tend, attend to, care for, look after, nurse, treat, assist, help

minor ADJECTIVE

minor alterations to the treaty
▶ small, trivial, unimportant, insignificant, inconsequential, negligible, secondary, lesser, trifling, petty
AN OPPOSITE IS major

minority NOUN

A minority voted for a return to work.
▶ small number, lesser number, smaller number
be in a minority
▶ be outnumbered, be less, be the smaller number

mint ADJECTIVE

in mint condition
▶ brand new, pristine, immaculate, perfect, new, unblemished, unmarked, unused, fresh

mint NOUN

(informal) They made a mint from the deal.
▶ fortune, heap, (*informal*) packet, (*informal*) pile, (*informal*) stack

mint VERB

Special coins were minted to celebrate the jubilee.
▶ strike, cast, manufacture, stamp out, coin, forge, make

minuscule ADJECTIVE

a minuscule room
▶ tiny, minute, infinitesimal, microscopic

minute ADJECTIVE

a minute insect
▶ tiny, minuscule, infinitesimal, diminutive, miniature

minute NOUN

I'll only be a minute.
▶ moment, short while, second, (*more informal*) tick

miracle NOUN

a miracle of modern technology
▶ marvel, wonder, sensation, phenomenon, feat

miraculous ADJECTIVE

a miraculous escape
▶ amazing, astounding, astonishing, extraordinary, unbelievable, incredible, inexplicable, marvellous, wonderful, mysterious

mirage NOUN

The lake turned out to be a mirage.
▶ illusion, optical illusion, hallucination, vision, delusion

mirror NOUN

1 *She took a quick look in the mirror on her way out.*
▶ looking glass, glass, reflector

2 *art as a mirror of life*
▶ reflection, image, likeness, copy, double

mirror VERB

Jody's views mirrored her own.
▶ reflect, correspond to, match, imitate, copy, echo

mirth NOUN

sounds of mirth from the terrace
▶ merriment, amusement, revelry, jollity, enjoyment, cheerfulness, festivity, conviviality, high spirits
OPPOSITES ARE misery, gloom

misbehave VERB

Little Mary was misbehaving again.
▶ behave badly, be naughty, be disobedient, (*more informal*) play up, (*more informal*) fool about

misbehaviour NOUN

In those days any form of misbehaviour was punished.
▶ bad behaviour, misconduct, naughtiness, disobedience, indiscipline, insubordination, mischief, mischief-making, wrongdoing

miscalculate VERB

We miscalculated the amount of fuel we would need.
▶ misjudge, make a mistake over, get wrong, underestimate or overestimate, blunder over

miscalculation NOUN

The problem arises from miscalculations by officials.
▶ mistake, error, error of judgement, blunder

miscellaneous ADJECTIVE
He made money from gardening and miscellaneous jobs.
▶ various, varied, different, assorted, mixed, sundry, multifarious

mischief NOUN
1 *He was always plotting some mischief with his brother.*
▶ misbehaviour, naughtiness, bad behaviour, mischievousness, misconduct, disobedience, pranks
2 *A faulty fuel pipe can cause much mischief.*
▶ trouble, difficulty, harm, damage, injury, bother, nuisance

mischievous ADJECTIVE
1 *mischievous children*
▶ naughty, badly behaved, misbehaving, disobedient, insubordinate, troublesome, vexatious
2 *There was a mischievous grin on his face.*
▶ playful, impish, roguish, teasing
3 *The house was full of mischievous rumours.*
▶ malicious, malevolent, hostile, unfriendly, spiteful, vicious, pernicious

misconception NOUN
a popular misconception about volcanoes
▶ misunderstanding, misapprehension, misbelief, delusion, fallacy

misconduct NOUN
1 *They were accused of professional misconduct.*
▶ wrongdoing, malpractice, impropriety, misbehaviour, negligence
2 *Any misconduct will be reported.*
▶ misbehaviour, bad behaviour, naughtiness, misdemeanour

miser NOUN
an old miser who kept his money hidden under the floorboards
▶ scrooge, penny-pincher, hoarder, niggard, (*informal*) skinflint
AN OPPOSITE IS spendthrift

miserable ADJECTIVE
1 *She was too miserable to eat.*
▶ unhappy, sad, dejected, despondent, downcast, downhearted, down, disheartened, disconsolate, glum, melancholy, cast down
2 *The house was cramped and miserable.*
▶ dreary, dismal, gloomy, cheerless, joyless, squalid
3 *It was a miserable way to treat people.*
▶ contemptible, despicable, disgraceful, deplorable, shameful
4 *They kept us waiting for hours and all we got was a miserable cup of tea.*
▶ measly, paltry, meagre, wretched, niggardly, pitiful, (*more informal*) mingy, (*more informal*) mouldy

miserly ADJECTIVE
He was miserly for all his life and died rich as a result.
▶ mean, niggardly, penny-pinching, parsimonious, tight, stingy
AN OPPOSITE IS generous

misery NOUN
1 *the misery of unemployment*
▶ hardship, suffering, privation, affliction, distress, misfortune, tribulation, anguish
2 *She put her hands to her face in silent misery.*
▶ unhappiness, distress, wretchedness, despair, grief, suffering
3 (*more informal*) *He can be fun but a lot of the time he's a real misery.*
▶ spoilsport, killjoy, pessimist, (*more informal*) wet blanket

misfire VERB
The plan had misfired.
▶ fail, fall through, founder, miscarry, go wrong, (*more informal*) flop
AN OPPOSITE IS succeed

misfit NOUN
a bunch of misfits and weirdos
▶ eccentric, nonconformist, maverick, dropout, individualist, (*more informal*) oddball

misfortune NOUN
Bruce had the misfortune to break a bone in his wrist. The family had suffered several generations of misfortune
▶ bad luck, mischance, mishap, trouble, setback, tribulation, hardship
AN OPPOSITE IS good luck

misgiving NOUN
We agreed to the proposal with several misgivings.
▶ doubt, reservation, qualm, scruple, diffidence
AN OPPOSITE IS confidence

misguided ADJECTIVE
a misguided policy on immigration
▶ mistaken, misconceived, erroneous, fallacious, unsound, unfounded, ill-judged, ill-considered

mishap NOUN
an unfortunate mishap in the kitchen
▶ accident, misfortune, misadventure, setback, problem, difficulty

misjudge VERB
He misjudged the distance and hit a parked car.
▶ miscalculate, overestimate, underestimate, get wrong, guess wrongly, make a mistake about, misinterpret, misunderstand

mislay VERB
I seem to have mislaid my passport.
▶ lose, misplace, lose track of, forget

mislead VERB
Colin had evidently tried to mislead her.
▶ deceive, delude, fool, hoodwink, take in, misguide, misinform, lead astray

misleading ADJECTIVE
a misleading answer
▶ confusing, deceptive, equivocal, ambiguous, evasive, dishonest, unreliable

a b c d e f g h i j k l **m** n o p q r s t u v w x y z

mismanage VERB
The redundancies had been badly mismanaged..
▶ mishandle, bungle, botch, ruin, spoil, fluff, muff, mess up, make a mess of, (*more informal*) make a hash of, (*much more informal*) cock up, (*much more informal*) screw up

misrepresent VERB
The statement misrepresented the views of the government.
▶ misreport, misstate, falsify, distort, pervert, misconstrue

miss VERB
1 *The bullet missed him by inches.*
▶ fail to hit, fall short of
2 *It was an easy catch but he still missed it.*
▶ drop, fumble, fail to catch, let slip, mishandle
3 *If we're not careful we'll miss the last train.*
▶ be too late for, fail to catch
4 *He was ill and had to miss the party.*
▶ be absent from, skip
5 *I will miss Debbie terribly.*
▶ pine for, long for, yearn for, feel the loss of
6 *He swerved and managed to miss an oncoming car.*
▶ avoid, dodge, evade, escape, circumvent
7 *Don't miss your chance.*
▶ let slip, let go, forfeit, pass by, pass up, disregard

missing ADJECTIVE
A few books are still missing.
▶ lost, mislaid, misplaced, gone astray, straying, unaccounted for, absent, disappeared

mission NOUN
1 *a mission to Africa*
▶ expedition, assignment, operation, exploration, journey, sortie, voyage
2 *his mission in life*
▶ calling, vocation, goal, aim, purpose, function

mist NOUN
1 *The sun was breaking through the early morning mist.*
▶ haze, fog, vapour, cloud, mistiness
2 *She wiped a hole to peep through the mist on the windows*
▶ condensation, film, steam

mistake NOUN
It's easy to make mistakes when you are tired.
▶ error, slip, blunder, lapse, misjudgement, miscalculation, oversight, (*more informal*) gaffe

mistake VERB
I mistook the meaning of the instruction.
▶ misunderstand, misinterpret, confuse, get wrong, misjudge, misread, misconstrue, (*informal*) get the wrong end of the stick about, mix up

mistaken ADJECTIVE
These conclusions are mistaken, in our view.
▶ wrong, incorrect, erroneous, misguided, unfounded, unsound, ill-judged, inappropriate

mistreat VERB
Some of the prisoners had been mistreated.
▶ ill-treat, maltreat, abuse, misuse, harm, injure, molest, (*more informal*) knock about

mistress NOUN
His wife never knew he had a mistress.
▶ lover, girlfriend, (*more informal*) bit on the side, (*more informal*) fancy woman

mistrust VERB
I mistrust their intentions.
▶ distrust, suspect, be suspicious of, be sceptical about, have misgivings about, have qualms about, be wary of, disbelieve, doubt, question
AN OPPOSITE IS trust

misty ADJECTIVE
1 *misty weather*
▶ hazy, foggy, murky, cloudy
AN OPPOSITE IS clear
2 *a misty window*
▶ misted, clouded
3 *misty memories*
▶ indistinct, vague, hazy, unclear, obscure, nebulous
OPPOSITES ARE sharp, distinct

misunderstand VERB
I must have misunderstood - I thought you were coming with us.
▶ make a mistake, misapprehend, misinterpret, mishear, get it wrong, (*more informal*) get hold of the wrong end of the stick

misunderstanding NOUN
1 *The suggestion was based on a misunderstanding of the issues.*
▶ misapprehension, misconception, misinterpretation, misjudgement, false impression, delusion (about), (*informal*) mix-up
2 *It wasn't a row, just a slight misunderstanding.*
▶ difference of opinion, disagreement, dispute, quarrel, squabble, argument, contretemps

misuse NOUN
1 *the misuse of confidential information*
▶ wrong use, misappropriation, misapplication, exploitation
2 *the misuse of innocent people*
▶ ill-treatment, maltreatment, mistreatment
3 *the misuse of drugs*
▶ abuse, careless use, ill-use, mishandling

misuse VERB
1 *He was accused of misusing public money.*
▶ misapply, misemploy, embezzle, put to wrong use
2 *She had been misused by successive partners.*
▶ ill-treat, maltreat, mistreat, abuse, harm, injure, molest, (*more informal*) knock about

mitigate VERB
The treatment mitigated the worst effects of the injury.
▶ alleviate, lessen, reduce, diminish, allay, deaden, temper, soften

mitigating ADJECTIVE
The defence lawyers pointed to mitigating circumstances.
▶ extenuating, moderating, vindicating, justifying, qualifying

mix VERB
1 *Mix the ingredients together.   Oil and water don't mix.*
▶ blend, mingle, combine, merge, fuse, unite, coalesce, amalgamate
2 *He mixes with all sorts of people.*
▶ associate, consort, fraternize, socialize, mingle, (*more informal*) hang about with
mix up *I've mixed up the two dates.*
▶ confuse, muddle, muddle up, jumble up, mistake

mix NOUN
The work calls for a good mix of basic skills.
▶ mixture, combination, blend, assortment, fusion, set

mixed ADJECTIVE
1 *a mixed collection*
▶ assorted, varied, diverse, miscellaneous, heterogeneous, different
2 *mixed ingredients*
▶ combined, integrated, amalgamated, united, composite, hybrid, joint
3 *Their reactions were mixed.*
▶ ambivalent, equivocal, uncertain, unsure, confused, muddled, ambiguous

mixture NOUN
a strange mixture of people
▶ assortment, variety, medley, combination, blend, miscellany, jumble, hotchpotch, assemblage, gathering

moan VERB
1 *The injured man was moaning with pain.*
▶ groan, cry, howl, whimper
2 *Everyone moaned about the food.*
▶ complain, grumble, grouse, grouch, carp, whine, (*more informal*) whinge

moan NOUN
1 *moans of pain*
▶ groan, cry, howl, whimper
2 *moans about the awful food*
▶ complaint, grumble, grouse, grouch, carping, whining, (*more informal*) whinging

mob NOUN
(*informal*) *An angry mob gathered at the gate.*
▶ crowd, throng, mass, horde, rabble, swarm, bunch, gang, group, herd, pack, riot

mob VERB
Her fans mobbed her all the way to her car.
▶ crowd round, swarm round, throng round, jostle, surround, besiege, hem in, harass, hassle

mobile ADJECTIVE
1 *She was soon mobile again after her operation.*
▶ moving, walking, able to move

2 *The village is visited by a mobile library once a week.*
▶ travelling, itinerant, peripatetic, roving, wandering
3 *It helps to be mobile in furthering a career.*
▶ adaptable, flexible, versatile, adjustable
4 *Her mobile features showed anger and regret.*
▶ expressive, suggestive, changing, changeable

mobilize VERB
1 *The army was mobilized to fight the rebels.*
▶ summon, assemble, call up, enlist, levy, marshal, muster
2 *The spin doctors mobilize support for government policy.*
▶ rally, generate, activate, stir up, stimulate, promote, galvanize, organize

mock VERB
Her brother had grinned and mocked her behind her back.
▶ ridicule, jeer, make fun of, laugh at, taunt, scorn, sneer at, deride, disparage, tease

mock ADJECTIVE
He shook his head in mock disbelief.
▶ pretend, imitation, simulated, false, fake, sham, feigned

mockery NOUN
1 *There was a note of mockery in her voice.*
▶ ridicule, derision, contempt, scorn, sarcasm, disdain
2 *The trial was a mockery of justice.*
▶ travesty, parody, caricature, sham

mocking ADJECTIVE
His smile was coldly mocking.
▶ derisive, contemptuous, scornful, sarcastic, disdainful
AN OPPOSITE IS friendly

mode NOUN
The normal mode of transport is by road.
▶ method, means, manner, system

model ADJECTIVE
1 *a model railway*
▶ miniature, toy, replica
2 *a model pupil*
▶ ideal, perfect, exemplary, impeccable, faultless

model NOUN
1 *a working model of a high-speed train*
▶ replica, copy, representation, facsimile, imitation
2 *a model of good behaviour*
▶ ideal, paragon, epitome, personification
3 *laws based on the American model*
▶ pattern, example, type, standard, paradigm, prototype, version, mould

model VERB
1 *The artist modelled the figure in bronze.*
▶ form, make, fashion, mould, sculpt, design
2 *Characters who are modelled on real life.*
▶ base, draw (from), derive (from)

moderate ADJECTIVE
1 *a moderate success*
▶ average, modest, mediocre, tolerable, passable
2 *a moderate drinker*   *Prices are moderate this year.*
▶ reasonable, sensible, restrained, controlled, modest, fair

moderate VERB
1 *The wind has moderated.*
▶ abate, die down, ease off, subside, decrease, become less extreme
2 *Can we do something to moderate the noise?*
▶ control, curb, check, reduce, lessen, mitigate, alleviate, allay, subdue

moderately ADVERB
a moderately successful attempt
▶ fairly, reasonably, somewhat, passably, quite, rather, slightly, (*more informal*) pretty

moderation NOUN
He always showed moderation in exercising authority.
▶ restraint, caution, fairness, reasonableness, sobriety, temperance

modern ADJECTIVE
1 *modern art*
▶ contemporary, present-day, current
2 *She wears very modern clothes.*
▶ fashionable, stylish, modish, voguish, advanced

modernize VERB
(*informal*) *The factory needs to modernize its production methods.*
▶ update, renovate, refurbish, renovate, regenerate, improve, rebuild

modest ADJECTIVE
1 *a modest increase in income*
▶ moderate, reasonable, limited, slight, small
AN OPPOSITE IS large
2 *He is always modest about his achievements.*
▶ unassuming, unpretentious, humble, reserved, discreet, retiring, bashful
AN OPPOSITE IS boastful

modesty NOUN
She shows admirable modesty about her abilities.
▶ humility, reserve, reticence, discretion, self-effacement, shyness, lack of pretension

modify VERB
These events have led us to modify our views.
▶ change, alter, amend, adapt, revise, adjust, reform

moist ADJECTIVE
He dug into the dark moist earth.
▶ damp, soggy, clammy, wet, watery

moisten VERB
Moisten the compost if it becomes dry.
▶ dampen, wet, damp, soak, moisturize, make moist, humidify
AN OPPOSITE IS dry

moisture NOUN
The windows were covered in moisture.
▶ dampness, condensation, damp, humidity, liquid, steam, vapour, wetness, wet

molest VERB
The woman had been molested by a group of men.
▶ harass, pester, beset, torment, persecute, harry

moment NOUN
1 *She waited for a moment before going in.*
▶ minute, second, little while, short time
2 *We can leave the moment the rain stops.*
▶ instant, minute, second, point
3 *These matters are of little moment to most people.*
▶ importance, import, significance, consequence, interest, weight, value

momentary ADJECTIVE
He had a momentary glimpse of her face.
▶ brief, fleeting, passing, quick, temporary, transient, transitory
AN OPPOSITE IS permanent

momentous ADJECTIVE
a momentous decision
▶ important, significant, fateful, epoch-making, historic, critical, crucial, decisive
AN OPPOSITE IS unimportant

momentum NOUN
The car began to gain momentum.   *a momentum for change*
▶ impetus, force, velocity, power, impulse, incentive, thrust

monarch NOUN
They swore loyalty to the monarch.
▶ sovereign, ruler, king, queen
RELATED ADJECTIVES regal, royal

monarchy NOUN
the abolition of the monarchy
▶ royalty, kingship, kingdom, realm

money NOUN
1 *I don't have enough money to buy it.*
▶ cash, means, funds, capital, finance, change, (*more informal*) dosh
2 *How much money shall we take on holiday?*
▶ currency, cash
RELATED ADJECTIVES financial, monetary, pecuniary

monitor NOUN
1 *Watch the monitor.*
▶ screen, set, television, VDU = *visual display unit*
2 *a heart monitor*
▶ scanner, detector

monitor VERB
Special equipment will monitor noise levels.
▶ check, watch, keep track of, observe, record, scan

monopolize VERB
He tends to monopolize the conversation.
▶ dominate, control, corner, take over, shut others out of, (*more informal*) hog
AN OPPOSITE IS share

monotonous ADJECTIVE
a monotonous piece of work
▶ boring, tedious, dull, dreary, uninteresting, tiresome, wearisome, repetitive, repetitious
OPPOSITES ARE interesting, varied

monotony NOUN
the monotony of their working lives
▶ dullness, boredom, tedium, sameness, repetitiveness, repetitiousness, weariness, dreariness, routine, uniformity

monster NOUN
1 *a huge monster of a man*
▶ giant, colossus, mammoth, leviathan
2 *He was behaving like a monster.*
▶ beast, brute, fiend, savage, ogre

monster ADJECTIVE
She came in eating a monster ice cream. The film was a monster hit.
▶ huge, enormous, massive, colossal, gigantic, immense, (*informal*) ginormous

monstrous ADJECTIVE
1 *A monstrous wave loomed over the ship.*
▶ huge, enormous, massive, colossal, gigantic, immense, (*informal*) ginormous
2 *a monstrous winged creature*
▶ grotesque, hideous, gruesome, horrible, grisly, repulsive
3 *a monstrous injustice*
▶ appalling, dreadful, shocking, outrageous, abominable, disgraceful, scandalous, hideous, wicked, vile, foul, evil

monument NOUN
1 *a monument to local heroes*
▶ memorial, obelisk, statue, shrine, mausoleum
2 *a monument over his grave*
▶ gravestone, headstone, tombstone
3 *The book is a monument to years of research.*
▶ testament, record, token, evidence

monumental ADJECTIVE
1 *a monumental plaque*
▶ commemorative, memorial
2 *a monumental task*
▶ huge, great, enormous, immense, awesome, grand, impressive

mood NOUN
1 *He was in a bad mood for most of the day.*
▶ temper, humour, disposition, spirit, frame of mind, state of mind, vein
2 *The music sets the right mood for the story.*
▶ atmosphere, feeling, tone, spirit, ambience

moody ADJECTIVE
Charles was quiet and moody, and this worried her.
▶ changeable, temperamental, volatile, unpredictable, sulky, sullen, gloomy, morose

moon NOUN
by the light of a full moon
RELATED ADJECTIVE lunar

moon VERB
There was not much to do and the young ones were mooning about.
▶ mope, loaf, idle, waste time, (*more informal*) mooch

moor NOUN
a windswept moor
▶ heath, moorland, upland, fell

moor VERB
The boat was moored by a jetty.
▶ tie up, secure, fasten, anchor, berth, dock

mop VERB
A man was mopping the floor.
▶ wash, clean, sponge, wipe

mope VERB
She realized it was no use moping.
▶ brood, fret, sulk, pine, be miserable, grieve

moral ADJECTIVE
1 *moral issues*
▶ ethical, social, behavioural
2 *a very moral person*
▶ good, honest, virtuous, upright, principled, honourable, decent, proper, pure, blameless, upstanding, responsible, trustworthy
AN OPPOSITE IS immoral
3 *moral support*
▶ emotional, psychological

moral NOUN
There's a clear moral to this story.
▶ lesson, message, meaning, point, significance, import, principle

morale NOUN
A series of wins boosted the team's morale.
▶ confidence, self-confidence, self-esteem, state of mind, spirit, mood, (*informal*) heart

morality NOUN
standards of morality
▶ ethics, morals, ideals, principles, integrity, honesty, goodness, propriety, conduct, behaviour, manners
AN OPPOSITE IS immorality

morbid ADJECTIVE
1 *a morbid obsession with death*
▶ macabre, ghoulish, unhealthy, gruesome, grisly, unwholesome
2 *The thought of old age made her morbid.*
▶ gloomy, depressed, dejected, melancholy, downhearted, pessimistic
AN OPPOSITE IS cheerful

more ADJECTIVE
They want more money.
▶ additional, extra, further, added, increased, fresh, supplementary, other
AN OPPOSITE IS less

morning NOUN
It was nearly morning when they finally reached home.
▶ daybreak, dawn, daylight, sunrise, first light

m

morose ADJECTIVE
Back home dad was looking very morose.
▶ sullen, gloomy, bad-tempered, ill-tempered, glum, sour, surly, moody, tetchy, crabby
AN OPPOSITE IS cheerful

morsel NOUN
a few morsels of food
▶ bite, mouthful, nibble, taste, fragment, piece, scrap, crumb, titbit

mortal ADJECTIVE
1 *The coffins contained the mortal remains of the victims.*
▶ physical, bodily, corporeal, earthly, worldly, perishable
2 *She struck him a mortal blow.*
▶ deadly, fatal, lethal
3 *mortal enemies*
▶ deadly, bitter, irreconcilable
4 *living in mortal fear*
▶ extreme, intense, grave, dire

mortal NOUN
a tale of mortals battling with divine forces.
▶ human being, human, mortal creature, individual, person, man or woman, earthling

mortified ADJECTIVE
He would be mortified if his friends knew.
▶ humiliated, embarrassed, shamed, ashamed, crushed

mostly ADVERB
She reads books all day, mostly novels.
▶ mainly, chiefly, predominantly, primarily, principally, normally, typically, usually, generally, largely
OPPOSITES ARE rarely, hardly

mother NOUN
Her mother picked her up every day from school.
▶ female parent, (*more informal*) mum, (*more informal*) mummy, (*more informal*) ma, (*old-fashioned*) mater
RELATED ADJECTIVE maternal

mother VERB
She was fond of mothering the residents when they were sick.
▶ look after, care for, nurse, comfort, pamper, protect, cherish, fuss over

motherly ADJECTIVE
a motherly woman
▶ maternal, protective, caring, kind, loving

motif NOUN
wallpaper with a repeated floral motif
▶ design, device, pattern, symbol, ornament, figure, emblem

motion NOUN
The motion of the bus made her queasy.
▶ movement, moving, action, shifting, progress
RELATED ADJECTIVES dynamic, kinetic

motion VERB
He motioned to them to go in.
▶ gesture, signal, beckon, direct

motionless ADJECTIVE
1 *The traffic ahead was motionless.*
▶ static, stationary, immobile, still, at a standstill, at rest
AN OPPOSITE IS moving
2 *They stood motionless for several minutes, neither wanting to speak first.*
▶ still, stock-still, immobile, unmoving, paralysed, rooted to the spot, frozen, inert
OPPOSITES ARE moving, active

motivate VERB
Money is what motivated them most.
▶ prompt, drive, urge, stimulate, provoke, influence, activate, incite, persuade, impel

motivation NOUN
the motivation to learn
▶ incentive, stimulus, impulse, drive, inspiration, inducement, encouragement, spur

motive NOUN
The police could not establish any motive for the attacks.
▶ reason, grounds, rationale, motivation, object, intention, purpose, thinking, aim, cause

motto NOUN
Their guiding motto was 'You scratch my back, and I'll scratch yours'.
▶ saying, maxim, watchword, dictum, proverb, adage, precept, slogan, axiom

mould NOUN
1 *The cheese had mould on it.*
▶ mildew, fungus, must, growth
2 *The molten metal is poured into a mould.*
▶ cast, die, form, matrix, template

mould VERB
1 *The figures are moulded in bronze.*
▶ shape, form, fashion, forge, model, create, sculpt
2 *Education helps to mould your character.*
▶ form, shape, influence, determine, direct

mouldy ADJECTIVE
1 *a hunk of mouldy bread*
▶ mildewed, mildewy, mouldering, decaying, musty, rotten, stale
2 (*informal*) *The prize was just a mouldy book token.*
▶ measly, paltry, miserable, meagre, wretched, niggardly, pitiful, (*informal*) mingy

mound NOUN
1 *a mound of dirty socks*
▶ pile, heap, stack
2 *The common had several mounds to climb.*
▶ hill, hillock, hummock, rise, ridge, embankment

mount VERB

1 *The gallery mounts a special exhibition every year.*
▶ put on, organize, present, display, show, exhibit
2 *June mounted her pony. The guest of honour mounted the platform.*
▶ climb on to, jump on to, get on, get up on, get astride
OPPOSITES ARE get off, climb down from
3 *Our savings were mounting at last.*
▶ grow, increase, accumulate, pile up
OPPOSITES ARE dwindle, decrease

mountain NOUN

1 *several mountains to climb in the area*
▶ peak, summit, height
RELATED ADJECTIVE alpine
2 *a mountain of work to get through*
▶ heap, pile, load, mound, stack, mass, great deal, backlog

mountainous ADJECTIVE

1 *mountainous country*
▶ hilly, craggy, rocky, alpine, highland, precipitous
2 *mountainous waves*
▶ huge, enormous, gigantic, colossal, immense, towering, (*more informal*) ginormous

mourn VERB

1 *He hid himself away, mourning his dead wife.*
▶ grieve for, sorrow over, lament for, weep for, pine for
2 *We all mourn the loss of so many precious artefacts.*
▶ regret, deplore, bewail
AN OPPOSITE IS rejoice over

mournful ADJECTIVE

mournful music a mournful cry
▶ sad, sorrowful, melancholy, unhappy, doleful, desolate, heartbroken, tragic, sombre

mouth NOUN

1 *He opened his mouth.*
▶ jaws, lips, (*more informal*) gob
RELATED ADJECTIVE oral
2 *the mouth of the cave*
▶ entrance, opening, entry, aperture
3 *the mouth of a river*
▶ outfall, outlet, estuary, firth

mouth VERB

Thank you, I answered, mouthing the words carefully.
▶ utter, enunciate, pronounce, articulate, form, say

mouthful NOUN

1 *a mouthful of food*
▶ bite, taste, morsel, nibble, gobbet, spoonful, swallow
2 *a mouthful of water*
▶ gulp, draught, sip, swallow, (*more informal*) swig

movable ADJECTIVE

They took all the movable furniture when they left.
▶ portable, transportable, transferable, mobile, detachable
AN OPPOSITE IS immobile

move VERB This word is often overused. Here are some alternatives:

1 *He got up and moved to the bench under the tree.*
▶ go, walk, march, proceed, advance, stroll, amble
2 *The traffic moved slowly forward.*
▶ edge, creep, crawl, slide
3 *I'll move the chair closer to the table.*
▶ carry, take, shift, transport
4 *We need to move quickly to secure a place.*
▶ act, take action, take steps, make a move, take the initiative
5 *At long last things are starting to move.*
▶ progress, make progress, make headway, develop, (*more informal*) get somewhere
6 *She moved from London to the country last year.*
▶ relocate, move house, move home, migrate, decamp, depart
7 *The beautiful performance moved them deeply.*
▶ touch, affect, impress, disturb, agitate
8 *The language course moved her to find out about living abroad.*
▶ prompt, stimulate, motivate, persuade, rouse, impel, induce, inspire

move NOUN

1 *The group got together to talk over their next move.*
▶ step, action, initiative, tactic, ploy, ruse
2 *It's your move.*
▶ turn, go, opportunity, chance

movement NOUN

1 *the movement of goods and animals*
▶ transportation, carrying, relocation, conveyance, transferral, repositioning
2 *She joined a left-wing political movement in her student days.*
▶ party, organization, faction, group, grouping, campaign
3 *A movement in the bushes caught his eye.*
▶ motion, move, activity, action
4 *There has been little movement on our grant application.*
▶ progress, change, advance
5 *a movement towards equal pay for men and women*
▶ trend, tendency, swing, current

movie NOUN

1 *a horror movie*
▶ film, picture, feature, motion picture
2 *Let's go to the movies.*
▶ cinema, films

moving ADJECTIVE

1 *a moving train*
▶ travelling, mobile, active, on the move, under way
OPPOSITES ARE stationary, motionless
2 *a moving story*
▶ touching, affecting, poignant, emotive, stirring, emotional, heart-warming, inspiring, exciting, stimulating
AN OPPOSITE IS unemotional

mow VERB
Someone should mow the grass.
▶ cut , trim, clip, crop

much NOUN
We don't have much to do.
▶ a lot, a great deal, plenty

much ADJECTIVE
Do you need much help?
▶ a lot of, a great deal of, plenty of, considerable, substantial

muck NOUN
1 *He went out to clean the muck off the windows.*
▶ dirt, grime, filth, slime, sludge, mess, mud, (*more informal*) gunge
2 *spreading muck in the fields*
▶ manure, dung

muck VERB
muck about or **around** (*informal*) *John was mucking about with an old engine.*
▶ fool about or around, play about or around, tinker, (*informal*) mess about or around

mucky ADJECTIVE
She took off her mucky shoes.
▶ dirty, messy, muddy, filthy, grubby, soiled, foul, grimy
AN OPPOSITE IS clean

mud NOUN
He slipped and fell in the mud.
▶ sludge, slime, slurry, clay, soil, dirt, mire, muck, ooze, silt

muddle NOUN
1 *a muddle over the time of the train*
▶ confusion, misunderstanding, mistake, mix-up
2 *Look at the muddle in the kitchen.*
▶ mess, shambles, jumble, clutter, chaos, untidiness, disorder, tangle

muddle VERB
1 *Her explanation merely muddled him.*
▶ confuse, bewilder, mix up, perplex, puzzle, disorientate, mislead
AN OPPOSITE IS enlighten
2 *Don't muddle the papers on the desk.*
▶ disorganize, disarrange, mix up, mess up, jumble up, make a mess of, disorder
OPPOSITES ARE tidy, clear up

muddled ADJECTIVE
He felt muddled and couldn't think what to do.
▶ confused, disorganized, bewildered, mixed up, perplexed, puzzled, disorientated

muddy ADJECTIVE
1 *They came in to change their muddy boots.*
▶ dirty, messy, mucky, filthy, grubby, soiled, foul, grimy
AN OPPOSITE IS clean
2 *The ground was wet and muddy.*
▶ waterlogged, boggy, marshy, sodden, soft, spongy, sloppy

3 *The water looked muddy.*
▶ cloudy, misty, opaque, messy
AN OPPOSITE IS clear

muffle VERB
He muffled the sound of the gun with cushions.
▶ deaden, dull, dampen, smother, soften, suppress, muzzle
muffle up *She went out, muffling herself up against the cold.*
▶ wrap up, cover up, envelop, swathe, enclose

muffled ADJECTIVE
a muffled cry
▶ faint, indistinct, muted, deadened, dull, unclear
OPPOSITES ARE distinct, loud

mug NOUN
1 *We drank tea from mugs.*
▶ beaker, cup
2 *He was rather a mug to drive so fast.*
▶ fool, simpleton, idiot, clot

mug VERB
They were mugged on their way home.
▶ attack, assault, molest, rob, steal from, set on, jump on
mug up *He's mugging up for his driving test.*
▶ study, learn, read up, cram

muggy ADJECTIVE
muggy weather
▶ humid, close, clammy, sultry, oppressive, sticky, stuffy, airless

mull VERB
mull over *a few suggestions to mull over*
▶ consider, ponder, think about, contemplate, reflect on, weigh up, turn over in your mind

multiply VERB
1 *The problems began to multiply.*
▶ increase, proliferate, grow, mount up, spread, become numerous
OPPOSITES ARE decrease, diminish
2 *The hedgehogs multiplied rapidly.*
▶ breed, propagate, reproduce, procreate

multitude NOUN
a multitude of people a multitude of questions to answer
▶ mass, host, myriad, swarm, throng, lots, large number, legion

mumble VERB
She walked off, mumbling quietly.
▶ mutter, murmur, whisper, burble

mumbo-jumbo NOUN
The form was covered in mumbo-jumbo.
▶ jargon, gobbledegook, gibberish, nonsense

munch VERB
The children waited, munching their rolls.
▶ chomp, crunch, eat, bite, chew, gnaw

mundane ADJECTIVE
She hoped such mundane matters would keep him occupied for a while.
▶ everyday, routine, commonplace, day-to-day, humdrum, tedious, dull, boring, unexceptional
OPPOSITES ARE extraordinary, exceptional

murder NOUN
Reports are coming in of a brutal murder.
▶ killing , homicide, slaughter (= killing of many people), assassination (= killing of an important person), fratricide (= killing of a brother), infanticide (= killing of a child), matricide (= killing of a mother), parricide (= killing of a parent or close relative), patricide (= killing of a father), regicide (= killing of a king or queen)

murder VERB
A gang had tried to murder him.
▶ kill, put to death, assassinate

murderer NOUN
The murderer was never caught.
▶ killer, assassin

murderous ADJECTIVE
a murderous assault
▶ homicidal, deadly, lethal, brutal, bloodthirsty, barbarous, savage, ferocious, vicious

murky ADJECTIVE
The sky was murky and drizzle was falling.
▶ gloomy, grey, dark, overcast, leaden, misty, dim, dull, cloudy, foggy, sombre
AN OPPOSITE IS clear

murmur VERB
He murmured an apology and left.
▶ mutter, mumble, whisper, burble

muscular ADJECTIVE
He's tall and muscular.
▶ brawny, muscly, athletic, strong, well built, beefy, strapping, sinewy

mushy ADJECTIVE
1 *The fruit was mushy and overripe.*
▶ soft, pulpy, pappy, slushy, sloppy, squidgy
2 *They read a mushy article about being good neighbours.*
▶ sentimental, mawkish, emotional, slushy

---

music NOUN

NAMES FOR TYPES OF MUSIC
traditional music: classical music, chamber music, instrumental music, orchestral music, choral music, opera; ballet music; folk music.
rock and popular music: pop music, rock, rock and roll, reggae, soul, jive, swing; acid house, funk, rap, hip-hop, garage, goth, grunge, heavy metal, punk, new wave, techno.
jazz music: jazz, traditional jazz (or trad), blues, ragtime, salsa, bebop, skiffle; .
religious music: church music, gospel music; hymn, anthem, cantata, spiritual, qawwali; bhjan.

NAMES FOR MUSICAL INSTRUMENTS
keyboard instruments: piano, pianoforte, grand piano, fortepiano, clavier; harpsichord, clavichord, spinet, virginals, celesta; organ, harmonium; electric organ, synthesizer; accordion.
wind instruments: bassoon, clarinet; oboe, cor anglais; flute, piccolo; recorder; saxophone; harmonica, mouth organ; bagpipes; ocarina (bird-shaped).
brass instruments: trumpet, bugle, cornet; trombone; horn, tuba, sousaphone, euphonium.
stringed instruments: violin, viola, cello, double bass; guitar, banjo, mandolin, lute, lyre, ukulele; balalaika (Russian guitar with triangular body), bouzouki (Greek mandolin), harp; sitar (Indian lute with a long neck), sarod (classical Indian lute), tamboura (large four-stringed Indian lute).
percussion instruments: drum, timpani (plural), kettledrum, snare drum, side drum, bongo, tom-tom, tam-tam, cymbal, triangle; tambourine, xylophone, glockenspiel, gongs, chimes; castanets, maracas, marimba; gamelan (band in Java and Bali), tabla (small hand drums used in Indian music), goombay (West Indian goatskin drum).

---

musical ADJECTIVE
musical sounds
▶ tuneful, melodic, melodious, euphonious, harmonious, lyrical, pleasant, sweet-sounding
AN OPPOSITE IS discordant

musician NOUN
A small group of musicians were playing on the terrace.
▶ performer, player, instrumentalist

muster VERB
The king mustered a large army.
▶ assemble, marshal, mobilize, gather, call together, summon, rally, convene, collect, get together

musty ADJECTIVE
There is a musty smell in the room.
▶ mouldy, stale, stuffy, airless, damp, dank, fusty, mildewy

mute ADJECTIVE
Yvonne remained mute.
▶ silent, speechless, unspeaking, dumb, tongue-tied, voiceless

mutilate VERB
Some of the bodies had been mutilated.
▶ mangle, disfigure, cripple, dismember, cut up, lacerate, maim, disable, injure, lame, wound

mutinous ADJECTIVE
mutinous soldiers
▶ rebellious, insubordinate, seditious, insurgent, rebel

mutiny NOUN
a mutiny on board ship   a mutiny by government MPs
▶ rebellion, revolt, protest, uprising, insurrection

mutiny VERB
The troops mutinied over pay.
▶ rebel, revolt, rise up, protest, go on strike

mutter VERB
Her husband mutters in his sleep.
▶ mumble, murmur, whisper, burble

mutual ADJECTIVE
an agreement based on mutual trust
▶ joint, shared, reciprocal, reciprocated, common, complementary

muzzle NOUN
the dog's muzzle
▶ snout, nose, mouth, jaws

muzzle VERB
crude attempts to muzzle the press
▶ silence, restrain, stifle, suppress, censor, gag

muzzy ADJECTIVE
a muzzy feeling in the head
▶ dazed, hazy, blurred, confused, muddled

mysterious ADJECTIVE
His friends had disappeared in mysterious circumstances.
▶ strange, puzzling, odd, peculiar, curious, weird, obscure, baffling, unexplained, unknown
AN OPPOSITE IS straightforward

mystery NOUN
1 *Their disappearance remains a mystery.*
▶ puzzle, enigma, riddle, conundrum
2 *events surrounded in mystery*
▶ secrecy, obscurity, uncertainty, ambiguity

mystical ADJECTIVE
a mystical experience
▶ spiritual, religious, supernatural, metaphysical, transcendental, mysterious, abnormal, occult

mystify VERB
The work he did mystified his contemporaries.
▶ puzzle, perplex, baffle, bewilder, bamboozle, confuse

mythical ADJECTIVE
a story based on mythical events
▶ legendary, mythological, imaginary, fabled, fabulous, fictional, invented, fanciful, make-believe
AN OPPOSITE IS real

mythological ADJECTIVE
mythological gods and heroes
▶ mythical, fabled, legendary, traditional

mythology NOUN
creatures in mythology
▶ legend, myth, tradition, folklore

Nn

nab VERB
(informal) A police car nabbed him on his way home.
▶ catch, arrest, apprehend, take into custody

nag VERB
He's been nagging me about it for weeks.
▶ harass, badger, pester, chivvy, hound, (*more informal*) keep on at, (*more informal*) go on at, (*more informal*) moan at

nail NOUN
1 *The nail's fallen out so I'll have to use a screw.*
▶ tack, pin, stud
2 *He broke his nail opening a carton.*
RELATED ADJECTIVE ungual

nail VERB
Nail it to the wall.
▶ hammer, pin, tack, fasten, attach, secure, fix

naive ADJECTIVE
I was very naive in those days but I've learned a lot since then.
▶ innocent, ingenuous, unsophisticated, inexperienced, credulous, artless, raw, green
OPPOSITES ARE sophisticated, experienced, knowing

naked ADJECTIVE
1 *a naked statue*
▶ nude, bare, unclothed, uncovered, undressed, unclad
AN OPPOSITE IS clothed
2 *the naked truth*
▶ plain, undisguised, unadorned, unvarnished, simple, bald, unmitigated

name NOUN
His name is Carl.
▶ first name, forename, (*more formal*) denomination, (*more formal*) appellation
RELATED ADJECTIVES nominal, onomastic

name VERB
1 *Her father had wanted to name her Clio.*
▶ call, dub, style, christen, baptize
2 *The victim will not be named until relatives have been notified.*
▶ identify, specify
3 *The king has to name a successor.*
▶ choose, designate, nominate, decide on, specify, appoint

nameless ADJECTIVE
pictures by a nameless artist
▶ unnamed, unidentified, anonymous, unheard of

nap NOUN
He was on the sofa, having a nap.
▶ snooze, doze, sleep, rest, lie-down, (*more informal*) forty winks

narrate VERB
The story is narrated by the governess.
▶ tell, relate, recount, report, describe, unfold, detail, relay, chronicle

narrative NOUN
a chronological narrative of the events of the last five years
▶ account, summary, narration, commentary, description, sketch

narrow ADJECTIVE
1 *a narrow path* *She was elected by a narrow majority.*
▶ slim, thin, slender, fine
2 *a narrow space*
▶ tight, close, confined, cramped, enclosed, limited, constricting
AN OPPOSITE IS wide
3 *a narrow point of view*
▶ narrow-minded, intolerant, conservative, illiberal, insular, parochial, small-minded, bigoted, hidebound
OPPOSITES ARE broad- minded, open- minded, tolerant

narrow-minded ADJECTIVE
a narrow-minded outlook
▶ small-minded, intolerant, narrow, bigoted, conservative, illiberal, insular, parochial, short-sighted, hidebound
OPPOSITES ARE broad- minded, open- minded, tolerant

nasty ADJECTIVE
1 *The pudding had a nasty taste*
▶ unpleasant, disagreeable, disgusting, horrible, disgusting, repellent
OPPOSITES ARE pleasant, nice, lovely
2 *He can be very nasty at times.*
▶ unkind, unfriendly, unpleasant, disagreeable, malicious, mean, spiteful, vindictive
3 *The weather turned nasty.*
▶ unpleasant, rough, squally
OPPOSITES ARE fine, pleasant

nation NOUN
1 *The president will broadcast to the nation.*
▶ people, population, country, community, society
2 *the nations of the world*
▶ country, people, civilization, land, power, race, state
RELATED ADJECTIVE ethnic

national ADJECTIVE
1 *a national strike*
▶ nationwide, countrywide, general, widespread
2 *national costume*
▶ ethnic, popular, domestic

national NOUN
an Italian national
▶ citizen, subject, native, resident, inhabitant

nationalism NOUN
the surge of nationalism in Europe
▶ patriotism, (*disapproving*) chauvinism, (*disapproving*) jingoism, (*disapproving*) xenophobia

native ADJECTIVE
1 *native inhabitants*
▶ original, aboriginal, indigenous
2 *a native instinct for politics*
▶ innate, inherent, inborn, inbred, natural, congenital, hereditary, inherited

native NOUN
a native of New York
▶ inhabitant, resident, citizen, national

natter VERB
They nattered on for hours.
▶ chatter, chat, prattle, blather, burble, talk

natural ADJECTIVE
1 *a natural tendency to self-preservation*
▶ innate, inborn, instinctive, intuitive, inherent
2 *Her manner is fresh and natural.*
▶ genuine, sincere, unaffected, uninhibited, ingenuous, open
3 *It was natural for them to want more information.*
▶ understandable, reasonable, logical, unsurprising, predictable
4 *Kim proved to be a natural leader.*
▶ born, spontaneous, untaught
5 *The bay forms a natural port on this side of the island.*
▶ ready-made

nature NOUN
1 *the beauties of nature*
▶ the natural world, the living world, the environment, the countryside, the landscape
2 *It's not in his nature to make complaints.*
▶ character, personality, temperament, disposition, constitution, make-up
3 *decisions that by their nature cause resentment*
▶ essence, characteristics
4 *coins, medals, and things of that nature*
▶ kind, type, sort, category, description

naughty ADJECTIVE
1 *a naughty child*
▶ badly behaved, mischievous, misbehaving, disobedient, insubordinate, troublesome, vexatious
2 *a naughty film*
▶ indecent, suggestive, obscene, pornographic

nausea NOUN
He had a bad headache and a feeling of nausea.
▶ sickness, queasiness, biliousness, retching, vomiting

nauseating ADJECTIVES
She disliked his nauseating self-importance.
▶ sickening, disgusting, revolting, repulsive, repellent, loathsome, offensive

nauseous ADJECTIVE
The stench made him feel nauseous.
▶ sick, disgusted, queasy, bilious

nautical ADJECTIVE
eating seafood in a nautical atmosphere
▶ maritime, naval, marine, seafaring, seagoing

naval ADJECTIVE
Mediterranean naval bases
▶ nautical, maritime, marine

navel NOUN
She wore a bright stud in her navel.
▶ (*more informal*) belly button, (*more informal*) tummy button, (*technical*) umbilicus
RELATED ADJECTIVE umbilical

navigate VERB
1 *She navigated the yacht round the world.*
▶ steer, pilot, direct, handle, manoeuvre, (*more informal*) skipper
2 *Parts of the river are hard to navigate.*
▶ negotiate, cross, traverse, sail over

navy NOUN
an officer in the navy
▶ fleet, armada, convoy, flotilla, naval force

near ADJECTIVE
1 *She is a near neighbour of ours.*
▶ nearby, close, adjacent, adjoining, next-door, bordering, connected, neighbouring
OPPOSITES ARE distant, faraway
2 *A decision is near.*
▶ close, approaching, imminent, coming, forthcoming, impending, (*more informal*) round the corner
3 *near relatives*
▶ close, dear, familiar, intimate
AN OPPOSITE IS distant

nearby ADVERB
Her children all live nearby.
▶ close by, not far away, at hand, within reach, in the vicinity

nearly ADVERB
The work is nearly finished.
▶ almost, practically, virtually, about, more or less, as good as, just about, around

neat ADJECTIVE
1 *The room was neat and newly decorated.*
▶ tidy, orderly, trim, spick-and-span, spruce, immaculate
OPPOSITES ARE untidy, messy
2 *hair tied in a neat bun at the back*
▶ compact, elegant, trim, well formed, simple
OPPOSITES ARE clumsy, awkward
3 *neat writing*
▶ regular, precise, well formed, elegant
4 *a neat solution to the problem*
▶ clever, ingenious, adroit, deft, inventive, resourceful, slick
AN OPPOSITE IS inept
5 *a glass of neat whisky*
▶ undiluted, straight, pure, unmixed, unadulterated
AN OPPOSITE IS diluted

nebulous ADJECTIVE
We need more than a few nebulous ideas.
▶ vague, hazy, uncertain, muddled, confused, half-formed, (*more informal*) half-baked

necessary ADJECTIVE
necessary repairs to the bridge
▶ essential, indispensable, vital, unavoidable, requisite, needed, needful, obligatory, imperative, compulsory, mandatory
AN OPPOSITE IS unnecessary

necessitate VERB
Measures as drastic as these would necessitate legislation.
▶ require, involve, entail, demand, call for, mean, compel

necessity NOUN
1 *A mobile phone is now regarded as a necessity by most people.*
▶ essential, requirement, prerequisite
2 *Necessity compelled thousands to emigrate.*
▶ need, poverty, hardship, destitution, penury, deprivation
3 *the necessity for caution*
▶ need, demand, indispensability (of)

need VERB
1 *The room needs redecorating.*
▶ require, want, be in need of, demand, call for
2 *We need more milk.*
▶ require, want, be short of, lack
3 *He needed her so much now.*
▶ yearn for, long for, pine for, crave, depend on, rely on
4 **need to** *Do we need to come?*
▶ have to, be obliged to, be required to, be compelled to, be under an obligation to

need NOUN
1 *There is no need to say anything.*
▶ necessity, obligation, call, requirement
2 *basic human needs like food and water*
▶ requirement, essential, necessity, want, prerequisite

needle VERB
You shouldn't let them needle you like that.
▶ annoy, irritate, goad, hassle, rile, niggle

needless ADJECTIVE
a lot of needless expense
▶ unnecessary, unwanted, inessential, unneeded, gratuitous, superfluous, pointless

needy ADJECTIVE
day centres for the frail and needy
▶ poor, deprived, destitute, impoverished, underprivileged, penniless

negate VERB
The decision negates years of hard work.
▶ nullify, invalidate, undo, reverse, cancel, neutralize, abrogate, countermand

negative ADJECTIVE
1 *a negative response*
▶ dissenting, saying 'no', rejecting, refusing
OPPOSITES ARE affirmative, positive

2 *They have been criticized for their negative attitudes.*
▶ pessimistic, unenthusiastic, uncooperative, defeatist, dismissive, antipathetic
AN OPPOSITE IS positive

neglect VERB
1 *He'd been neglecting his work for the past week.*
▶ pay no attention to, ignore, let slide, shirk, skip, disregard, overlook, forget, leave alone
AN OPPOSITE IS concentrate on
2 *She neglected her son and had a succession of boyfriends.*
▶ fail to take care of, fail to look after, abandon, spurn, forsake
AN OPPOSITE IS look after
3 *He was being neglected by all his friends.*
▶ ignore, disregard, abandon, rebuff, disdain, slight
AN OPPOSITE IS appreciate

neglect NOUN
The building had suffered from years of neglect.
▶ negligence, carelessness, dereliction of duty, inattention, indifference, slackness
OPPOSITES ARE attention, care

neglected ADJECTIVE
The back of the house overlooked a neglected garden.
▶ untended, uncared for, derelict, dilapidated, run-down, ramshackle, overgrown

negligence NOUN
The company was accused of negligence.
▶ dereliction of duty, remissness, irresponsibility, carelessness, failure to take proper care
AN OPPOSITE IS conscientiousness

negligent ADJECTIVE
He claimed that the doctors had been negligent.
▶ neglectful, careless, irresponsible, inattentive
OPPOSITES ARE conscientious, careful

negligible ADJECTIVE
The difference in price is negligible.
▶ tiny, trifling, trivial, insignificant, unimportant, inconsequential, imperceptible, inconsiderable, minor, slight, small
OPPOSITES ARE considerable, significant

negotiate VERB
1 *We would like to negotiate a better deal.*
▶ work out, hammer out, agree on, reach agreement on, settle, transact
2 *The other side refused to negotiate.*
▶ consult, confer, discuss terms, deal, talk, parley
3 *The road has several sharp bends to negotiate.*
▶ get round, clear, pass round, deal with, overcome

negotiation NOUN
The negotiations will begin in Rome next week.
▶ discussion, consultation, bargaining, arbitration, mediation, conciliation, transaction, debate, diplomacy

neighbourhood NOUN
a quiet neighbourhood
▶ district, area, locality, vicinity, region, place, community, environs, surroundings, zone

neighbouring ADJECTIVE
The neighbouring buildings have parking facilities.
▶ nearby, adjacent, adjoining, nearest, closest, next-door, bordering, close
OPPOSITES ARE distant, remote

neighbourly ADJECTIVE
a neighbourly offer of help
▶ friendly, amiable, obliging, considerate, kind, helpful, genial, sociable, companionable

nerve NOUN
1 *The manoeuvre takes some nerve and a good sense of timing. He lost his nerve at the last moment and couldn't go through with it.*
▶ courage, bravery, boldness, daring, gallantry, determination, fearlessness, fortitude, heroism, (*more informal*) bottle, (*more informal*) grit, (*more informal*) guts, (*more informal*) pluck, (*much more informal*) spunk
2 *They had the nerve to ask for more money.*
▶ cheek, audacity, effrontery, temerity, impertinence, impudence, insolence, presumptuousness, shamelessness, (*more informal*) sauce
3 *the nerves in your body*
RELATED ADJECTIVE neural

nervous ADJECTIVE
1 *a nervous girl who always wore black*
▶ highly-strung, nervy, anxious, excitable
2 *He was getting a little nervous out there, all by himself.*
▶ anxious, worried, apprehensive, agitated, concerned, (*more informal*) jumpy, (*more informal*) jittery

nestle VERB
The children nestled together in the back of the car.
▶ huddle, cuddle, nuzzle, snuggle, curl up, lie comfortably

net NOUN
The gardener put nets on the trees to catch falling fruit.
▶ mesh, netting, webbing, lattice

net VERB
1 *He managed to net the fish at last.*
▶ catch, land
2 *Top executives can net enormous bonuses as well as their massive salaries.*
▶ earn, get, make, receive, bring in, clear, accumulate

nettle VERB
remarks that began to nettle him
▶ annoy, irritate, displease, anger, infuriate, enrage, exasperate, incense, vex, madden, aggravate, antagonize, inflame, make angry, (*more informal*) needle, (*more informal*) rile, (*more informal*) bug, (*more informal*) rub up the wrong way

a
b
c
d
e
f
g
h
i
j
k
l
m
n
o
p
q
r
s
t
u
v
w
x
y
z

network NOUN
1 *a network of tiny tubes*
▶ web, grid, mesh, net, netting, crisscross pattern, labyrinth, lattice, maze, tracery
2 *a computer network the rail network*
▶ system, complex, organization

neurotic ADJECTIVE
He always tries to depict me as incompetent and neurotic.
▶ unstable, mentally unbalanced, disturbed, maladjusted, nervous, obsessive, overwrought

neutral ADJECTIVE
1 *He would be the perfect neutral umpire.*
▶ impartial, unbiased, objective, disinterested, unprejudiced, even-handed
OPPOSITES ARE biased, prejudiced
2 *neutral colours*
▶ dull, indefinite, indeterminate, intermediate, characterless, colourless, middle
AN OPPOSITE IS distinctive

neutralize VERB
Alkalis neutralize acids.
▶ counteract, counterbalance, cancel out, invalidate, make ineffective, negate, nullify, offset

never-ending ADJECTIVE
They were having never-ending rows.
▶ constant, continual, endless, incessant, persistent, interminable

new ADJECTIVE This word is often overused. Here are some alternatives:
1 *new ways of beating crime*
▶ modern, recent, up-to-date, advanced
2 *We need some new ideas.*
▶ fresh, original, innovative, novel, creative, different
3 *The school has had some new labs built.*
▶ additional, extra, more, further, supplementary, fresh
4 *After the operation I felt a new person.*
▶ changed, improved, restored, revived, invigorated

newcomer NOUN
She watched the newcomers suspiciously from her open door.
▶ new arrival, outsider, settler, stranger, immigrant, novice, beginner

news NOUN
The news of his death stunned his colleagues.
▶ report, announcement, story, account, tidings, information (about), disclosure (about), statement, revelation

next ADJECTIVE
1 *Her friend lived in the next street*
▶ adjacent, neighbouring, adjoining, connecting, closest, nearest
AN OPPOSITE IS distant
2 *The next train is not for another hour.*
▶ following, soonest, succeeding, subsequent
AN OPPOSITE IS previous

nibble VERB
She nibbled her sandwich while she waited.
▶ munch, pick at, gnaw, eat

nice ADJECTIVE This word is often overused. Here are some alternatives:
1 *We had a nice time in Greece.*
▶ pleasant, agreeable, enjoyable, marvellous, wonderful, delightful, splendid
2 *They are such nice people.*
▶ pleasant, likeable, agreeable, personable, friendly, congenial, genial
3 *That's rather a nice distinction.*
▶ fine, subtle, delicate, fastidious

niche NOUN
1 *A little statue stood in a niche in the wall.*
▶ recess, alcove, nook, cavity
2 *She felt she had found her niche in life.*
▶ place, slot, position, calling, vocation

nick VERB
1 *He had nicked his skin while shaving.*
▶ cut
2 *(informal) Someone nicked my pen.*
▶ steal, take, (informal) pinch

nick NOUN
1 *a nick in the wood*
▶ cut, notch, chip, groove, scar
2 *(informal) The car is in good nick.*
▶ condition, shape, repair, order, trim, fettle

nickname NOUN
Her nickname is 'Posh'.
▶ pet name, sobriquet, tag, alias

night NOUN
It had rained in the night.
▶ night-time, dark
RELATED ADJECTIVE nocturnal

nightmare NOUN
1 *After the accident he had a series of nightmares.*
▶ bad dream
2 *Getting the tyre fixed had been a nightmare.*
▶ ordeal, trial, torment

nimble ADJECTIVE
He was surprisingly light and nimble on his feet.
▶ agile, lithe, lively, sprightly, deft, quick, graceful, (informal) nippy

nip VERB
1 *The dog nipped her leg.*
▶ bite, peck, snap at, pinch, tweak
2 *(informal) I'll nip round and see how he's getting on.*
▶ go, dash, drop, (informal) pop

nippy ADJECTIVE
1 *(informal) She drives a nippy two-seater.*
▶ speedy, fast, nimble, quick, rapid
2 *(informal) The weather's quite nippy for June.*
▶ chilly, cold, raw

nitty-gritty NOUN
(*informal*) *Her job involves getting stuck into the nitty-gritty.*
▶ basics, essentials, hard work, (*informal*) slog

nobility NOUN
1 *actions that showed true nobility*
▶ honour, dignity, nobleness, uprightness, virtue, worthiness, greatness, integrity, magnanimity, morality
2 *The king had the support of the nobility.*
▶ aristocracy, gentry, nobles, lords, peerage

noble ADJECTIVE
1 *He came from a noble family.*
▶ aristocratic, high-born, patrician, princely, (*informal*) blue-blooded
AN OPPOSITE IS humble
2 *a noble deed*
▶ honourable, virtuous, worthy, brave, chivalrous, courageous, gallant, glorious, heroic, magnanimous
AN OPPOSITE IS ignoble
3 *a noble building*
▶ imposing, impressive, magnificent, elegant, grand, majestic, splendid, stately, dignified, distinguished, great
AN OPPOSITE IS unimpressive

noble NOUN
War was the principal activity of many of the nobles in Edward's reign.
▶ aristocrat, nobleman, noblewoman, lord, peer, grandee, lady, peers

nod VERB
1 *She nodded to him to go in.*
▶ signal, gesture, indicate, sign
2 *He nodded his head in agreement.*
▶ incline, bob, dip, lower
nod off *She nodded off and started to snore.*
▶ fall asleep, go to sleep, doze off, drop off

nod NOUN
He gave us a discreet nod.
▶ signal, gesture, cue

noise NOUN
The noise from below battered her eardrums.
▶ sound, din, clamour, racket, uproar, tumult, commotion, crash, clatter, clash, (*more informal*) hullabaloo
AN OPPOSITE IS silence

noisy ADJECTIVE
1 *He loved this noisy, busy city.*
▶ loud, clamorous, rackety, tumultuous, turbulent, deafening
2 *The plane completed its noisy take-off.*
▶ loud, deafening, ear-splitting, thunderous
3 *They were disturbed by the noisy argument going on in the next room.*
▶ loud, vociferous, raucous, rowdy, strident, shouting, shrieking

nomad NOUN
a group of nomads driving cattle
▶ traveller, wanderer, itinerant, migrant, rover

nomadic ADJECTIVE
nomadic peoples
▶ travelling, wandering, itinerant, roving

nominal ADJECTIVE
1 *The president is nominal head of the organization but has few real powers.*
▶ formal, official, ostensible, supposed, theoretical, in name only
2 *The family continued to live in the house for a nominal rent.*
▶ token, symbolic, minimal, small, peppercorn

nominate VERB
It is a good idea to nominate an adult to supervise the children's activities.
▶ choose, appoint, designate, name, select, elect

nonchalant ADJECTIVE
Kate leant back, trying to look nonchalant.
▶ unconcerned, detached, relaxed, indifferent, dispassionate, unemotional, unruffled, blasé, calm, casual, cool, (*more informal*) laid-back
AN OPPOSITE IS anxious

non-committal ADJECTIVE
He held up a hand in a non-committal gesture.
▶ guarded, cautious, wary, discreet, (*more informal*) cagey

nondescript ADJECTIVE
The town was a nondescript, cheerless place.
▶ ordinary, undistinguished, commonplace, average, dull, uninspiring
OPPOSITES ARE distinctive, remarkable

nonentity NOUN
a nonentity incapable of making decisions
▶ nobody, nothing, cipher, person of straw, person of no importance

non-existent ADJECTIVE
The cupboard had a row of hangars for my non-existent dozen suits.
▶ imaginary, fictitious, mythical, supposed, unreal, hypothetical, imagined, legendary, made-up
AN OPPOSITE IS existing

---

non-fiction NOUN

TYPES OF NON-FICTION WRITING
anthology (collection of short items), article (short essay in a magazine or newspaper), journalism; autobiography, biography, memoir, essay; travel writing, monograph (short book on a specific subject), reference, encyclopedias, dictionaries, thesauruses, gazetteers, atlases; sacred writing, holy books.

OTHER TYPES OF NON-FICTION
report, recount, advice text, persuasive text, revue, instruction, explanation text.

---

nonplussed ADJECTIVE
The confusion left us feeling nonplussed.
▶ surprised, disconcerted, astonished, astounded, bewildered, stunned, flummoxed, stupefied, perplexed, (*more informal*) thunderstruck

nonsense NOUN

1 *They're talking nonsense.*
▶ rubbish, balderdash, gibberish, claptrap, drivel, gobbledegook, (*more informal*) rot, (*more informal*) twaddle

2 *The idea was a complete nonsense.*
▶ absurdity, folly, mistake, inanity

nonsensical ADJECTIVE

The suggestion was nonsensical and shouldn't be taken seriously.
▶ absurd, ludicrous, meaningless, ridiculous, senseless, unreasonable, incomprehensible, foolish, crazy, laughable, silly, stupid, fatuous, inane, illogical, irrational
AN OPPOSITE IS sensible

non-stop ADJECTIVE

non-stop fun and laughter
▶ continuous, constant, endless, uninterrupted, unending, never-ending, ceaseless

non-stop ADVERB

We worked non-stop to get the job finished.
▶ continuously, all the time, unceasingly, incessantly, steadily, round the clock

nook NOUN

a nook in the corner with magazines to read
▶ recess, alcove, niche, hollow, cubbyhole

norm NOUN

Society imposes its own norms of behaviour.
▶ standard, principle, yardstick, benchmark, pattern, basis, guide (to)

normal ADJECTIVE

1 *They seem like a perfectly normal couple.*
▶ ordinary, average, typical, run-of-the-mill, standard, conventional, everyday

2 *During the holidays you can borrow books in the normal way.*
▶ usual, customary, standard, regular, routine, habitual, established

normality NOUN

The household returned to something like normality.
▶ routine, regularity, typicality, usualness

normally ADVERB

1 *Reminders are normally sent out at the beginning of the month.*
▶ usually, ordinarily, customarily, typically
AN OPPOSITE IS exceptionally

2 *They just wanted to be able to live normally again.*
▶ as normal, in the normal way

nose NOUN

1 *He stood scratching the side of his nose.*
▶ nostrils, (*technical*) proboscis, snout
RELATED ADJECTIVE nasal

2 *The nose of a boat appeared at the harbour entrance.*
▶ prow, bow, front

nose VERB

He nosed the car into a gap in the traffic.
▶ ease, inch, edge, move, manoeuvre
nose about *Her friend was nosing about downstairs.*
▶ explore, ferret, search, snoop, prowl
nose into *I wish they would stop nosing into our business.*
▶ interfere in, meddle in, pry into, snoop in

nostalgic ADJECTIVE

The smell of the place aroused nostalgic feelings.
▶ evocative, wistful, emotional, yearning, regretful, sentimental, romantic, maudlin

nosy ADJECTIVE

He always wanted to help, but sometimes he seemed too nosy for his own good.
▶ inquisitive, prying, intrusive, curious, (*more informal*) snoopy

notable ADJECTIVE

1 *Musicians (with some notable exceptions) are highly practical people.*
▶ significant, noteworthy, remarkable, important, memorable
AN OPPOSITE IS insignificant

2 *a notable American statesman*
▶ prominent, famous, distinguished, noted, eminent, illustrious
OPPOSITES ARE obscure, unknown

notch NOUN

1 *The bow string fits into a notch in the arrow.*
▶ nick, groove, incision, cut

2 *His spirits lifted a notch.*
▶ degree, step, point, level

notch VERB

notch up *He hoped to notch up another good mark with Harriet.*
▶ earn, score, gain, achieve, acquire

note NOUN

1 *Leave me a note before you go.*
▶ message, communication, letter, memo, line

2 *I'll make a note of her new address.*
▶ record, entry, reminder

3 *Someone had written notes in the margin.*
▶ comment, annotation, gloss, remark

4 *a writer of some note*
▶ importance, distinction, renown, eminence, acclaim

note VERB

1 *Note the new cafeteria built since our last visit.*
▶ observe, notice, see, remark

2 *I'll be happy to note your suggestion.*
▶ consider, heed, bear in mind, make a note of, take into account

3 *Note the dates in your diary.*
▶ write down, jot down, enter, record, scribble

notebook NOUN

She wrote the details in a notebook.
▶ exercise book, jotter, writing book, diary

noted ADJECTIVE
a noted local celebrity
▶ famous, well-known, renowned, notable
OPPOSITES ARE obscure, unknown

noteworthy ADJECTIVE
a noteworthy addition to his collection
▶ important, significant, notable, remarkable,
striking
OPPOSITES ARE insignificant, unimportant

notice NOUN
1 *There was a notice pinned on the classroom door.*
▶ announcement, message, note, information
sheet, poster, sticker, sign, placard, warning
2 *Nothing escaped her notice that day.*
▶ attention, observation, awareness, perception,
heed
take no notice of *Take no notice of the shouting.*
▶ ignore, disregard, pay no attention to, pass over

notice VERB
1 *Did you notice the window was open?*
▶ observe, perceive, see, spot
2 *I noticed a smell of gas in the kitchen.*
▶ detect, perceive, note

noticeable ADJECTIVE
a noticeable reduction in the cost
▶ perceptible, appreciable, observable,
conspicuous, recognizable, distinct, marked,
significant, unmistakable
AN OPPOSITE IS imperceptible

notify VERB
Parents will be notified of any changes.
▶ inform, advise, tell, apprise, let somebody know

notion NOUN
1 *Paul was a dreamer, his head full of wild notions.*
▶ idea, belief, concept, thought, image, perception,
opinion
2 *He had no notion of what her words meant.*
▶ understanding, idea, knowledge, clue

notional ADJECTIVE
the notional line along the horizon
▶ theoretical, hypothetical, conjectural, putative,
imaginary

notoriety NOUN
*He was fast achieving notoriety as a writer of racy
stories.*
▶ infamy, ill repute, dishonour, discredit, scandal

notorious ADJECTIVE
one of the most notorious villains in London
▶ infamous, disreputable, dishonourable,
ignominious, ill-famed

nought NOUN
1 *Her card number has a lot of noughts in it.*
▶ zero, nil, O
2 *One of the contestants scored a resounding nought.*
▶ nil, zero, nothing, (more informal) zilch

nourish VERB
They had just enough money to nourish their children.
▶ feed, provide for, support, sustain, maintain

nourishing ADJECTIVE
a nourishing diet
▶ nutritious, wholesome, sustaining, healthy,
nutritive, beneficial, health-giving

nourishment NOUN
the nourishment that elderly people require
▶ sustenance, nutriment, nutrition, diet, food,
subsistence, goodness

novel ADJECTIVE
a novel idea for its time
▶ new, original, innovative, unconventional,
unfamiliar, unusual, fresh, imaginative, different,
singular, surprising, uncommon
OPPOSITES ARE familiar, common, hackneyed

novelty NOUN
1 *the beauty and novelty of the poetry*
▶ freshness, originality, unfamiliarity,
unconventionality, imaginativeness, newness
2 *a little shop selling sweets and novelties*
▶ knick-knack, trinket, souvenir, bauble, curiosity,
gimmick

novice NOUN
He admitted he was only a novice at sailing.
▶ beginner, learner, newcomer, new recruit,
neophyte

now ADVERB
1 *You need to decide now.*
▶ immediately, straight away, here and now, on the
spot, without delay
2 *The box office is closed now.*
▶ at present, at the moment, at the minute,
currently

noxious ADJECTIVE
noxious substances
▶ poisonous, harmful, toxic, foul, unwholesome,
destructive, corrosive, noisome
OPPOSITES ARE innocuous, harmless

nub NOUN
Money is the nub of the problem.
▶ crux, essence, central point, core, gist

nucleus NOUN
These three chapters form the nucleus of the description.
▶ heart, core, centre, kernel

nude ADJECTIVE
Nude bathing is forbidden.
▶ naked, unclothed, undressed, uncovered, bare

nudge VERB
Every time he laughed she nudged him in his side.
▶ poke, prod, shove, jog, jolt, bump, hit , touch

nuisance NOUN
1 *What a nuisance for you, having to go back into
hospital.*
▶ inconvenience, annoyance, bother, bore, trial,
irritant, irritation, worry, pest, vexation, trouble,
(more informal) pain
2 *I'm sorry if I'm being a nuisance.*
▶ pest, bother, trial, burden

nullify VERB

The opposition has promised to nullify the current legislation.
▶ cancel, repeal, rescind, revoke, abolish, annul, do away with, invalidate, negate, neutralize

numb ADJECTIVE

My hands were numb with cold.
▶ dead, frozen, numbed, benumbed, insensitive, unfeeling
AN OPPOSITE IS sensitive

numb VERB

Sheer terror had numbed her senses.
▶ deaden, paralyse, desensitize, freeze, immobilize, make numb, anaesthetize

number NOUN

1 *The paper had a line of numbers written on it.*
▶ figure, numeral, integer, digit, unit
RELATED ADJECTIVE numerical
2 *a large number of children*
▶ quantity, amount, collection, sum, total, crowd, multitude, aggregate
3 *The film included a few musical numbers.*
▶ item, piece, song
4 *the spring number of the magazine*
▶ issue, edition, publication, impression, printing

number VERB

Visitors to the city this year numbered over ten million.
▶ total, add up to, amount to, come to

numeral NOUN

Items over a hundred are written in numerals.
▶ figure, digit, integer, number

numerous ADJECTIVE

Numerous reasons have been given to justify the invasion.
▶ many, several, a lot of, plenty of, copious, abundant, profuse, multitudinous, diverse, sundry
AN OPPOSITE IS few

nurse VERB

1 *She nursed her old father for years.*
▶ look after, care for, take care of, tend, treat
2 *A woman was nursing a baby.*
▶ breastfeed, feed, suckle
3 *hopes that have to be nursed until they become reality*
▶ preserve, sustain, support, cherish, maintain, encourage
4 *They went on nursing their grievance all their lives.*
▶ harbour, foster, bear

nursery NOUN

The youngest children were at the nursery.
▶ nursery school, playgroup, kindergarten, crèche

nurture VERB

1 *nurturing young children*
▶ bring up, look after, care for, provide for, nourish, educate, rear
2 *She nurtured a deep interest in the classical world.*
▶ foster, cultivate, encourage, promote, stimulate

nut NOUN

KINDS OF NUT INCLUDE
almond, areca, beechnut, brazil, cashew, chestnut, cob-nut, coconut, filbert, hazel, monkey nut, peanut, pecan, pistachio, walnut.

nutritious ADJECTIVE

nutritious food
▶ nourishing, wholesome, sustaining, healthy, nutritive, beneficial, health-giving

Oo

oaf NOUN

She called him a loud-mouthed oaf.
▶ lout, fool, dolt, ass, idiot, clod, clot

oath NOUN

1 *The nobles refused to take the oath of allegiance to the king.*
▶ vow, pledge, promise, affirmation, avowal
2 *He uttered a terrible oath.*
▶ swear word, profanity, expletive, imprecation, curse, obscenity

obedient ADJECTIVE

She was described as a good girl, always obedient.
▶ dutiful, compliant, deferential, respectful, well-behaved, subservient, submissive, acquiescent, amenable, biddable, tractable
AN OPPOSITE IS disobedient

obese ADJECTIVE

The proportion of obese men has risen to 8 percent.
▶ fat, overweight, outsize, corpulent, rotund

obey VERB

1 *I obeyed him without question.*
▶ do what someone says, take orders from, submit to, defer to
2 *He was not too good at obeying orders.*
▶ follow, carry out, perform, discharge, execute
3 *Her legs wouldn't obey her brain's command to move.*
▶ respond to, respect, abide by

object NOUN

1 *It's an object I found on the beach.*
▶ article, body, item, thing
2 *Research is published regularly with the object of providing the most up-to-date findings.*
▶ objective, purpose, intention, aim, point, target, end, goal, intent

object VERB

1 *I'll open a window if you don't object.*
▶ mind, protest, demur
2 **object to** *I hope they don't object to us coming.*
▶ oppose, protest against, be against, disapprove of, take exception to

objection NOUN
The scheme went ahead despite many objections.
▶ protest, protestation, challenge, complaint, exception, dissent, disapproval, opposition, remonstration

objectionable ADJECTIVE
He can be objectionable when he wants to be. There was an objectionable smell in the room.
▶ unpleasant, offensive, disagreeable, obnoxious, intolerable, unacceptable, nasty, repellent, distasteful

objective ADJECTIVE
1 *The case lacks objective evidence.*
▶ impartial, unbiased, disinterested, neutral, detached, dispassionate
AN OPPOSITE IS subjective
2 *a research programme based on objective investigation*
▶ factual, scientific, rational

objective NOUN
The main objective is to build a strong business.
▶ object, purpose, intention, aim, point, target, end, goal, intent

obligation NOUN
She believed she had an obligation to help.
▶ responsibility, duty, liability, commitment, requirement, need

obligatory ADJECTIVE
Use of seat-belts in the back seats is now obligatory.
▶ compulsory, mandatory, binding, required, stipulated, unavoidable, de rigueur, imperative, imposed, incumbent, inescapable, official
AN OPPOSITE IS optional

oblige VERB
We cannot oblige them to agree, but we can persuade them.
▶ force, compel, require, constrain, make

obliged ADJECTIVE
We'd be obliged if you would let us know when you arrive.
▶ grateful, indebted, gratified, appreciative, thankful

obliging ADJECTIVE
Richard is an obliging sort of chap.
▶ helpful, accommodating, considerate, cooperative, thoughtful, willing, agreeable, civil, courteous, friendly, kind, neighbourly, polite
OPPOSITES ARE disobliging, unhelpful

oblique ADJECTIVE
an oblique line
▶ slanting, angled, diagonal, inclined, sloping, tilted, aslant

obliterate VERB
The explosion might obliterate the entire building.
▶ destroy, demolish, wipe out, ruin, wreck, devastate, shatter, blow up

oblivion NOUN
1 *She sank further into oblivion.*
▶ unconsciousness, insensibility, stupor, senselessness, blackness, unawareness
OPPOSITES ARE consciousness, awareness
2 *achievements that history has consigned to oblivion*
▶ obscurity, nothingness, non-existence
AN OPPOSITE IS prominence

oblivious ADJECTIVE
oblivious of what is going on
▶ unaware, unconscious, heedless, unmindful, insensible (to), insensitive (to), disregardful, blind (to), deaf (to), ignorant, unconcerned (with), unresponsive (to)
OPPOSITES ARE conscious, aware

obnoxious ADJECTIVE
a thoroughly obnoxious individual
▶ unpleasant, objectionable, disagreeable, disgusting, loathsome, odious, repulsive, repellent

obscene ADJECTIVE
obscene literature
▶ pornographic, indecent, improper, immodest, immoral, depraved, salacious, shocking, suggestive

obscenity NOUN
1 *laws against obscenity*
▶ indecency, immodesty, impurity, impropriety, pornography, licentiousness, grossness, indelicacy
2 *The crime was an obscenity.*
▶ atrocity, abomination, outrage, enormity, evil
3 *louts uttering obscenities*
▶ swear word, profanity, curse, expletive

obscure ADJECTIVE
He was suffering from an obscure disease that made his hand shaky.
▶ unknown, little-known, unheard-of, mysterious, dubious

obscure VERB
1 *Clouds obscured the sun.*
▶ hide, conceal, cover, veil, shroud, mask, envelop
2 *Their evidence has merely obscured the issues.*
▶ confuse, complicate, muddle, obfuscate

obsequious ADJECTIVE
the mafia leader and his obsequious followers
▶ servile, grovelling, unctuous, sycophantic, ingratiating, fawning, toadying, subservient, smarmy

observant ADJECTIVE
Her observant eye took in every detail.
▶ alert, attentive, vigilant, watchful, perceptive, percipient, eagle-eyed, sharp-eyed, heedful, quick
AN OPPOSITE IS inattentive

observation NOUN
1 *He was sent to hospital for observation.*
▶ monitoring, scrutiny, examination, inspection, surveillance, attention
2 *Put any further observations on a separate sheet of paper.*
▶ remark, comment, statement, opinion

observe VERB

1 *She observed her friends over by the bar.*
▶ notice, see, perceive, discern, spot, descry, behold
2 *James observed that Rachel looked unhappy.*
▶ remark, comment, mention, note, declare, announce, state
3 *From her window she could observe what was going on in the street.*
▶ watch, view, survey, regard, monitor, witness, scrutinize

observer NOUN

Brian was merely an observer and took no part in the action.
▶ spectator, onlooker, looker-on, bystander, viewer, watcher, commentator, eye-witness, witness

obsess VERB

1 *Thoughts of death obsessed him.*
▶ preoccupy, dominate, haunt, prey on, engross, possess, take a hold on
2 **be obsessed with** or **by** *I was totally obsessed with food and controlling my weight.*
▶ be fixated with or by, be preoccupied with or by, (*more informal*) be hung up on

obsession NOUN

These memories rapidly became an obsession.
▶ fixation, preoccupation, mania, passion, infatuation, compulsion, addiction

obsessive ADJECTIVE

His jealousy was becoming obsessive.
▶ compulsive, consuming, all-consuming, dominating, controlling, fanatical, addictive

obsolescent ADJECTIVE

obsolescent forms of recording
▶ declining, waning, disappearing, ageing, dying out, moribund, (*informal*) on the way out
USAGE Note that something is *obsolescent* when it is dying out, i.e. will soon be obsolete, and is *obsolete* when it has died out.

obsolete ADJECTIVE

The machinery installed in the 1990s had become obsolete.
▶ out of date, outdated, outmoded, anachronistic, antiquated, extinct, superseded, old-fashioned, passé, disused, dated, primitive
OPPOSITES ARE current, up to date

obstacle NOUN

a major obstacle in the peace process
▶ barrier, hurdle, hindrance, stumbling block, obstruction, drawback, difficulty, impediment, problem, snag, bar, interference

obstinate ADJECTIVE

They were too obstinate to see the advantages of the scheme.
▶ stubborn, inflexible, intractable, immovable, intransigent, unbending, unyielding, dogged, headstrong
OPPOSITES ARE amenable, open-minded

obstreperous ADJECTIVE

The shop was full of obstreperous customers.
▶ unruly, awkward, unmanageable, disorderly, disruptive, rowdy, rough, (*more informal*) stroppy
OPPOSITES ARE well-behaved, restrained

obstruct VERB

1 *The opposite side of the road was obstructed by cars.*
▶ block, jam, clog up, choke up
2 *He was charged with obstructing the course of justice.*
▶ impede, hinder, hamper, frustrate, thwart, hold up, inhibit, retard, interfere with
OPPOSITES ARE assist, further

obstruction NOUN

an obstruction to learning
▶ barrier, hurdle, hindrance, stumbling block, drawback, difficulty, impediment, problem, snag, bar, interference

obstructive ADJECTIVE

He accused her of being deliberately obstructive.
▶ uncooperative, unhelpful, awkward, difficult, disobliging, stalling
OPPOSITES ARE helpful, cooperative

obtain VERB

You will need to obtain the necessary permission.
I obtained the books at half price.
▶ get, acquire, secure, procure, come by, achieve

obtrusive ADJECTIVE

A motorway through the valley would be very obtrusive.
▶ conspicuous, prominent, noticeable, obvious, out of place, intrusive, protuberant, ugly
OPPOSITES ARE unobtrusive, inconspicuous

obtuse ADJECTIVE

He seemed too obtuse to understand what I was saying.
▶ stupid, slow, dense, crass, unintelligent, dull-witted, slow-witted, (*more informal*) thick

obvious ADJECTIVE

It's obvious that she's keen on Bill. He spoke with an obvious French accent.
▶ clear, plain, evident, self-evident, patent, apparent, glaring, perceptible
AN OPPOSITE IS imperceptible

obviously ADVERB

She was obviously very upset.
▶ clearly, plainly, patently, evidently, discernibly, indubitably, manifestly, unmistakably, without doubt

occasion NOUN

1 *She had spoken to him on several occasions.*
▶ instance, point, time, moment
2 *His eighteenth birthday would be a special occasion.*
▶ event, affair, celebration
3 *I'll mention it if the occasion arises.*
▶ opportunity, chance, opening, right moment

4 *I've never had any occasion to complain.*
▶ reason, cause, grounds, excuse, need, justification, pretext

occasional ADJECTIVE
There were still occasional air raids.
▶ intermittent, periodic, sporadic, infrequent, irregular, isolated, odd, rare, random

occasionally ADVERB
Tess turned her head occasionally to look at him.
▶ sometimes, from time to time, now and then, every so often, intermittently, periodically, sporadically, infrequently, irregularly

occult ADJECTIVE
the occult power of the priests
▶ supernatural, mystical, magic, magical, transcendental, paranormal, secret, esoteric, arcane, obscure

occult NOUN
the occult *Mary had a strong interest in the occult.*
▶ the supernatural, the paranormal, supernaturalism, black magic, diabolism, witchcraft, sorcery

occupant NOUN
The apartment had two occupants at the time.
▶ resident, inhabitant, tenant, occupier, lodger, householder

occupation NOUN
1 *Passports no longer specify your occupation.*
▶ job, profession, work, line of work, walk of life, employment, business
2 *The occupation of the country continued for much longer than predicted.*
▶ invasion, annexation, seizure, takeover, occupancy, possession
3 *a house built for multiple occupation*
▶ occupancy, residence, habitation, tenancy, possession, use
4 *Board games are one of their favourite leisure occupations.*
▶ pastime, hobby, interest, activity, diversion

occupy VERB
1 *Colin occupies the top floor.*
▶ live in, inhabit, be the tenant of, reside in, lodge in, possess, have possession of, own
2 *These problems occupied her mind for several days.*
▶ absorb, engage, hold, preoccupy, engross, divert
3 *The army occupied the country in the spring.*
▶ capture, seize, invade, take over, take possession of, overrun, annex, conquer, garrison

occur VERB
1 *We need to know everything that occurred that morning.*
▶ happen, take place, come about
2 *The disease occurs only in tropical climates.*
▶ be found, exist, be prevalent, appear, show itself, manifest itself

3 occur to *It occurred to him that she might still be waiting there. It never occurred to us that we'd have to pay extra.*
▶ cross your mind, enter your head

occurrence NOUN
Bicycle theft has become a common occurrence.
▶ event, happening, incident, experience, circumstance, affair, occasion, phenomenon

odd ADJECTIVE
1 *It was an odd thing to do.*
▶ strange, peculiar, weird, unusual, bizarre, curious, eccentric
2 *His friends thought him quite odd.*
▶ eccentric, strange, peculiar, abnormal, weird
3 *the odd numbers*
▶ uneven
4 *Do you have any odd change you could give him?*
▶ spare, leftover, miscellaneous, sundry, available
5 *She noticed he was wearing odd socks.*
▶ unmatched, different, unpaired, clashing

oddity NOUN
1 *people remembered chiefly for their oddity*
▶ strangeness, abnormality, peculiarity, idiosyncrasy, quirkiness
2 *He is regarded as a bit of an oddity.*
▶ eccentric, crank, misfit, maverick, curiosity, character

oddments PLURAL NOUN
oddments left over from a jumble sale
▶ bits and pieces, odds and ends, scraps, fragments, remnants, leftovers, offcuts

odds PLURAL NOUN
The odds are that they have left the country.
▶ likelihood, probability, chances
USAGE If you use *likelihood* or *probability* you should use a singular verb, e.g. *The likelihood is that they have left the country.*

odious ADJECTIVE
odious methods of dealing with their political opponents
▶ hateful, offensive, repulsive, repellent, obnoxious, unpleasant, abhorrent, detestable, abominable

odorous ADJECTIVE
odorous fumes from parked lorries
▶ foul-smelling, evil-smelling, smelly, stinking, reeking

odour NOUN
1 *an odour of urine*
▶ smell, stink, stench
2 *a delicious odour of hot bread*
▶ aroma, smell, savour

off ADJECTIVE
1 *The milk is off.*
▶ bad, rotten, putrid

a b c d e f g h i j k l m n o p q r s t u v w x y z

2 *The game is now off.*
▶ postponed, cancelled
3 *I think their remarks were a bit off, to put it mildly.*
▶ unacceptable, objectionable, unsatisfactory, disappointing

offbeat ADJECTIVE
an offbeat humour
▶ unconventional, unorthodox, idiosyncratic, strange, weird, bizarre, quirky

off colour ADJECTIVE
He was feeling a bit off colour and decided to stay at home.
▶ unwell, poorly, ill, queasy, peaky, nauseous

offence NOUN
1 *The company might even be guilty of a criminal offence.*
▶ crime, misdemeanour, wrong, wrongdoing, misdeed, fault, transgression
2 *We don't want to cause any offence.*
▶ annoyance, anger, resentment, hard feelings, indignation, irritation, upset, displeasure, disgust
take offence *She made it clear she had taken offence.*
▶ be or feel offended, be upset, be or feel aggrieved, be or feel affronted, take umbrage

offend VERB
1 *I didn't mean to offend you.*
▶ give or cause offence to, upset, hurt, displease, annoy, affront, insult, anger, irritate, disgust, make angry, outrage, provoke, rile, vex
2 *A large percentage of prisoners released early went on to offend again.*
▶ break the law, commit a crime, do wrong, transgress
be or **feel offended**
▶ take offence, be upset, be or feel aggrieved, be or feel affronted, take umbrage

offender NOUN
A higher proportion of offenders were sentenced to three months or less.
▶ wrongdoer, lawbreaker, criminal, malefactor, miscreant, delinquent, culprit, transgressor

offensive ADJECTIVE
The remarks were clearly offensive.
▶ insulting, derogatory, depreciatory, disrespectful, abusive, objectionable, provocative, discourteous, insolent, uncivil, rude
OPPOSITES ARE complimentary, courteous

offer VERB
1 *Counsellors are on hand to offer advice and support.*
▶ provide, give, extend, make available, put forward, hold out, suggest
2 *Many local people offered to help in the search.*
▶ volunteer, come forward, present yourself, show willing
3 *The job offers good career prospects.*
▶ provide, afford, present, hold out, involve, entail

offer NOUN
1 *a business offer*
▶ bid, proposal, tender, proposition, submission

2 *kind offers of help*
▶ proposal, proposition, overture

offering NOUN
an offering of a few silver coins
▶ contribution, donation, gift, benefaction, present

offhand ADJECTIVE
His manner was most offhand.
▶ casual, indifferent, cool, cavalier, brusque, abrupt, aloof, curt, uncooperative, perfunctory
OPPOSITES ARE polite, courteous

offhand ADVERB
I can't think of a better way offhand.
▶ on the spur of the moment, at the drop of a hat, right now, without consideration, impromptu

office NOUN
1 *Her office was just a few blocks away.*
▶ workplace, place of work, place of business, bureau
2 *The new Prime Minister took up his office immediately.*
▶ post, position, appointment, function, task, duty, responsibility, situation

officer NOUN
The trade union had few full-time officers.
▶ official, functionary, office-holder, representative, executive, administrator

official ADJECTIVE
1 *There were calls for an official inquiry into the matter. a member of an official organization*
▶ authorized, accredited, approved, proper, authentic, authenticated, certified, formal
2 *They were dressed for an official function.*
▶ formal, ceremonial

official NOUN
An official came down to escort us to the president's office.
▶ officer, functionary, office-holder, representative, executive, administrator

officiate VERB
officiate at *The Vice-President officiates at the annual ceremony.*
▶ be in charge of, preside over, conduct, direct, oversee, supervise, manage, be responsible for, have official authority over

officious ADJECTIVE
An officious waiter led us to a table in a poky corner.
▶ self-important, bumptious, bossy, over-zealous, dictatorial, interfering, meddling, (more informal) pushy

off-putting ADJECTIVE
She tried to think of some off-putting remark to make them go away.
▶ discouraging, unpleasant, intimidating, unnerving, unsettling, disconcerting, unappealing, unattractive, disagreeable, distasteful

offset VERB
Charges are offset by interest earned on deposit accounts.
▶ counterbalance, balance, cancel, neutralize, compensate for, counteract

offshoot NOUN
The business has offshoots all over Europe.
▶ branch, subsidiary, (*more informal*) spin-off

offspring NOUN
1 *the core of the family: parents and their offspring*
▶ children, sons and daughters, progeny, family

2 *Their latest offspring was playing in the garden.*
▶ child, baby, infant, little one, son, daughter, youngster

often ADVERB
She often asks about you.
▶ frequently, regularly, repeatedly, constantly, again and again, many times, time after time

ogre NOUN
1 *an ogre who ate children*
▶ giant, monster, bogey

2 *He was not such an ogre as he seemed.*
▶ fiend, brute, monster, devil

oil VERB
She went to the shed to oil her bike.
▶ lubricate, grease

oily ADJECTIVE
1 *oily skin an oily substance*
▶ greasy, oleaginous, slimy

2 *an oily manner*
▶ smooth, unctuous, fawning, ingratiating, obsequious, (*more informal*) smarmy

ointment NOUN
She rubbed ointment on her skin.
▶ lotion, cream, salve, liniment, embrocation, balm, unguent

OK, okay ADJECTIVE This word is often overused.
Here are some alternatives:
(*informal*) *Is everything OK now? The film is OK.*
▶ all right, satisfactory, fine, in order, acceptable, adequate, reasonable

OK, okay INTERJECTION
(*informal*) *OK, I'll go with you.*
▶ all right, very well, very good, right you are, right, fine

OK, okay NOUN
(*informal*) *The manager gave his OK.*
▶ permission, approval, consent, authorization, agreement, assent

OK, okay VERB
(*informal*) *Get a parent to okay your proposal.*
▶ agree to, approve, authorize, consent to, endorse, ratify

old ADJECTIVE This word is often overused. Here are some alternatives:
1 *an old man*
▶ elderly, aged, advanced in years, senile
2 *old buildings*
▶ antiquated, dilapidated, ramshackle, ruined, historic
3 *old clothes*
▶ worn, shabby, threadbare, frayed, moth-eaten
4 *in the old days*
▶ past, former, bygone, early, ancient, olden
5 *an old practice*
▶ long-standing, time-honoured, traditional, established, familiar
6 *an old joke*
▶ hackneyed, stale, tired, overworked

old-fashioned ADJECTIVE
a big old-fashioned bathroom with noisy pipes
▶ outdated, out of date, outmoded, antiquated, obsolescent
OPPOSITES ARE up to date, modern, fashionable

omen NOUN
an omen of things to come
▶ sign, portent, signal, token, foreboding, indication, premonition, augury, auspice, presage, warning

ominous ADJECTIVE
an ominous dark sky an ominous warning
▶ threatening, menacing, portentous, sinister, inauspicious, unpropitious, baleful, forbidding, grim
OPPOSITES ARE auspicious, propitious

omission NOUN
There are some unfortunate omissions from the list.
▶ exclusion, gap, oversight, deletion, blank

omit VERB
1 *Someone had omitted her name from the list.*
▶ leave out, miss out, exclude, ignore, cut, drop, overlook, edit out, eliminate
OPPOSITES ARE include, add, insert
2 *I omitted to tell you.*
▶ forget, neglect, fail
AN OPPOSITE IS remember

once ADVERB
We were good friends once.
▶ at one time, in the past, formerly, previously

onerous ADJECTIVE
an onerous task
▶ difficult, burdensome, troublesome, arduous, strenuous

one-sided ADJECTIVE
1 *a one-sided account of the conflict*
▶ biased, prejudiced, partisan, partial, preferential, slanted, unfair
OPPOSITES ARE impartial, fair
2 *a one-sided argument*
▶ unequal, uneven, unbalanced
AN OPPOSITE IS even

o

ongoing ADJECTIVE

1 *an ongoing problem with noisy neighbours*
▶ continuous, continuing, persistent, constant, ceaseless
2 *A road improvement programme is ongoing.*
▶ under way, in progress, developing, progressing, evolving, continuing, current, extant, existing

onlooker NOUN

An onlooker had videoed the entire incident.
▶ observer, bystander, eyewitness, witness, spectator

only ADJECTIVE

She is their only child
▶ sole, single, solitary, lone, unique

onset NOUN

With the onset of winter came the snow.
▶ beginning, start, arrival, opening, inception

onslaught NOUN

The onslaught on the city lasted for several days.
▶ attack, assault, offensive, bombardment

onus NOUN

The onus is on Scott to raise the issue.
▶ responsibility, obligation, liability, burden, duty

ooze VERB

Blood oozed from a wound on his arm.
▶ seep, leak, issue, exude, escape, flow, dribble

opaque ADJECTIVE

The glass of the bottle was opaque so the contents could not be seen.
▶ cloudy, non-transparent, obscure, blurred, misty, dark, hazy, unclear
OPPOSITES ARE clear, transparent

open ADJECTIVE

1 *an open door*
▶ unclosed, ajar, unlocked
AN OPPOSITE IS closed
2 *an open box*
▶ uncovered, unfastened, unsealed, lidless
OPPOSITES ARE closed, fastened
3 *open access*
▶ free, unrestricted, clear, unobstructed, wide, available
AN OPPOSITE IS restricted
4 *open country*
▶ sweeping, rolling, broad, extensive, unenclosed
5 *an open secret*
▶ plain, evident, overt, obvious, conspicuous, noticeable
AN OPPOSITE IS closed
6 *an open question*
▶ unresolved, unsettled, undecided, debatable, moot
AN OPPOSITE IS closed
7 *open about his feelings*
▶ frank, honest, candid, unreserved, natural
OPPOSITES ARE reserved, guarded
8 *a procedure open to abuse*
▶ vulnerable, subject, susceptible, liable

open VERB

1 *A young woman opened the door.*
▶ unfasten, unlock, unbolt
2 *He started to open the packet.*
▶ unwrap, undo, untie, unseal
3 *A new superstore will open next month.*
▶ start trading
4 *The story opens with a train journey.*
▶ begin, start, (*more formal*) commence
5 *The chairman then opened the meeting.*
▶ begin, start, inaugurate, set in motion

open-air ADJECTIVE

an open-air swimming pool
▶ outdoor, out-of-doors, alfresco
AN OPPOSITE IS indoor

opening NOUN

1 *an opening in the wall*
▶ doorway, gateway, entry, aperture, breach, chink, crack, cleft, hole, fissure
2 *looking for openings in accountancy*
▶ opportunity, chance, (*more informal*) break

opening ADJECTIVE

the opening line of the poem
▶ first, initial, beginning, introductory, inaugural
AN OPPOSITE IS final

operate VERB

1 *The alarms had been switched off and were not operating.*
▶ work, function, run, act, perform, be operative, go
2 *a machine that's difficult to operate*
▶ work, use, utilize, handle, manage, deal with, drive
3 *X-rays will show whether doctors will need to operate on him.*
▶ perform surgery, carry out an operation

operation NOUN

1 *There are few other business operations the size of ours.*
▶ enterprise, undertaking, procedure, proceeding, process, transaction
2 *Military operations have been delayed by the weather.*
▶ campaign, exercise, action, activity, manuvre, movement, effort
3 *a committee to ensure the smooth operation of the system*
▶ running, functioning, working, direction, control, management
4 *a surgical operation*
▶ biopsy, surgery, transplant

operational ADJECTIVE

Two new reactors were operational the following year.
▶ functioning, operating, working, up and running, going, usable

operative ADJECTIVE

Perhaps you're right: the operative word is 'perhaps'.
▶ key, significant, important, principal, relevant, crucial, effective

opinion NOUN

You can have an opinion but you must back it up with facts or reasons.
▶ belief, judgement, view, point of view, viewpoint, thought, attitude, standpoint, stance, idea, notion, feeling

opinionated ADJECTIVE

He always seemed patronizing and opinionated.
▶ dogmatic, doctrinaire, inflexible, pompous, cocksure, self-important, arrogant, stubborn, uncompromising

opponent NOUN

1 *He threw the ball at an opponent's head.*
▶ adversary, opposer, rival, antagonist, competitor, contestant, enemy, foe, opposition
OPPOSITES ARE ally, partner
2 *an opponent of reform*
▶ objector (to), opposer, dissident, dissenter

opportune ADJECTIVE

It was an opportune moment to speak out.
▶ appropriate, suitable, timely, auspicious, convenient, favourable, propitious, advantageous, lucky, right
OPPOSITES ARE unsuitable, inconvenient

opportunity NOUN

(informal) This was a good opportunity to make some money.
▶ chance, occasion, possibility, moment, opening, time, (more informal) break

oppose VERB

1 *There was a large group of protesters who opposed the plans for a new runway.*
▶ object to, be against, protest against, disapprove of, take exception to
OPPOSITES ARE support, defend
2 *If you want to go I shan't oppose you*
▶ resist, counter, withstand, take issue with, defy, confront

opposed ADJECTIVE

opposed to *The village was opposed to the scheme for a new hostel.*
▶ against, hostile to, antagonistic to, antipathetic to, unsympathetic to

opposite ADJECTIVE

1 *She lived in a house opposite the church.*
▶ facing, across from
2 *There is a long mirror on the opposite wall.*
▶ opposing, facing
3 *They were brothers who had fought on opposite sides in the civil war.*
▶ rival, opposing, conflicting, contrary, enemy
AN OPPOSITE IS allied

opposite NOUN

He always says one thing and does the opposite.
▶ contrary, reverse, other extreme, antithesis, converse
AN OPPOSITE IS same

opposition NOUN

1 *The suggestion met with fierce opposition.*
▶ resistance, hostility, antagonism, disapproval, scepticism, unfriendliness, competition
AN OPPOSITE IS support
2 *In the argument she quickly won over the opposition.*
▶ opponents, opposing side, other side

oppress VERB

1 *He could not get rid of the gloomy feelings that oppressed him.*
▶ depress, cast down, weigh down, burden, hang over, dispirit
2 *a people that had been oppressed by successive invaders*
▶ persecute, abuse, maltreat, tyrannize, repress, suppress, subjugate, subdue, keep down

oppressed ADJECTIVE

oppressed minorities in the community
▶ persecuted, downtrodden, repressed, abused, maltreated, tyrannized, suppressed
AN OPPOSITE IS privileged

oppressive ADJECTIVE

1 *an oppressive dictatorship*
▶ dictatorial, autocratic, authoritarian, despotic, brutal, cruel, harsh, repressive, tyrannical
2 *oppressive weather*
▶ humid, muggy, sultry, stuffy, airless, close, hot, stifling, heavy

oppressor NOUN

The angry mob thirsted for the blood of its oppressors.
▶ persecutor, intimidator, tormentor, despot, tyrant, autocrat

opt VERB

opt for *They opted for a hotel near the beach.*
▶ choose, pick, pick out, select, settle on, fix on

optimism NOUN

Despite the difficulties he tried to keep up a note of optimism.
▶ confidence, hopefulness, hope, positiveness, cheerfulness, good cheer
AN OPPOSITE IS pessimism

optimistic ADJECTIVE

1 *Women are less optimistic about their health prospects than men.*
▶ cheerful, confident, positive, hopeful, upbeat, sanguine, cheerful, buoyant
AN OPPOSITE IS pessimistic
2 *The accounts included an optimistic assessment of the financial outlook.*
▶ favourable, encouraging, hopeful, upbeat, bright, rosy
AN OPPOSITE IS pessimistic

optimum ADJECTIVE

The announcement is timed to have the optimum effect.
▶ best, maximum, most favourable, most advantageous, highest, ideal, perfect
AN OPPOSITE IS worst

a
b
c
d
e
f
g
h
i
j
k
l
m
n
o
p
q
r
s
t
u
v
w
x
y
z

option NOUN
We had little option but to agree.
▶ choice, alternative, possibility

optional ADJECTIVE
The exam consists of two compulsory questions and an optional essay.
▶ voluntary, discretionary, non-compulsory, elective
OPPOSITES ARE compulsory, obligatory

opulent ADJECTIVE
a house with an air of opulent grandeur
▶ luxurious, sumptuous, lavish, splendid, magnificent, wealthy, rich
OPPOSITES ARE stark, restrained

oral ADJECTIVE
Witnesses give oral evidence to the inquiry.
▶ spoken, unwritten, verbal, by mouth, said
AN OPPOSITE IS written

orbit NOUN
1 *the earth's orbit round the sun*
▶ course, path, circuit, track, trajectory, rotation, revolution
2 *This question is outside the orbit of the ordinary officials.*
▶ domain, sphere, range, scope, ambit

orbit VERB
other planets that orbit the sun
▶ circle, go round, travel round

ordeal NOUN
She helped nurse him back to health after his four-year ordeal as a captive.
▶ trial, tribulation, suffering, difficulty, test, torture, unpleasant experience, nightmare

order NOUN
1 *He gave the order to charge.*
▶ command, directive, instruction, direction, decree, edict
2 *It would not be easy to restore order.*
▶ peace, control, calm, quiet, law and order, discipline, harmony
3 *The plants were put in in a set order.*
▶ sequence, arrangement, disposition
4 *I've put in an order for a hundred storage boxes.*
▶ request, requisition, booking, demand, application
5 *the lowest orders in society*
▶ class, rank, hierarchy
6 *an ancient order of craftsmen*
▶ association, society, guild, company, lodge, brotherhood, sisterhood
7 *skills of a very high order*
▶ type, kind, sort, nature, variety, category

out of order
1 *The ticket machine was, as usual, out of order.*
▶ broken, not working, inoperative
2 *Remarks like that would be ruled out of order.*
▶ improper, uncalled-for, unacceptable, irregular, unwarranted

order VERB
1 *She ordered them to leave the room.*
▶ instruct, command, direct, charge, enjoin
2 *I ordered the tickets on the Internet.*
▶ book, reserve, apply for, requisition
3 *He tried hard to order his thoughts.*
▶ arrange, organize, sort out, set in order, regulate

orderly ADJECTIVE
1 *The army began an orderly withdrawal.*
▶ methodical, systematic, ordered, regular, well organized, well regulated
AN OPPOSITE IS disorganized
2 *The children were told to form an orderly queue.*
▶ neat, tidy, controlled, well behaved
AN OPPOSITE IS disorderly

ordinary ADJECTIVE
1 *just an ordinary day's work*
▶ usual, normal, typical, habitual, customary
OPPOSITES ARE unusual, abnormal
2 *Susan is not like ordinary women.*
▶ average, normal, typical, conventional
OPPOSITES ARE abnormal, unconventional
3 *My life seemed so ordinary; I needed a change.*
▶ routine, humdrum, run-of-the-mill, dull, routine, unremarkable, uninteresting, unexceptional, unexciting, commonplace
OPPOSITES ARE exceptional, unique

organic ADJECTIVE
1 *an organic substance*
▶ natural, animate, live, living, biological
AN OPPOSITE IS inorganic
2 *organic foods*
▶ natural, additive-free, pesticide-free, non-chemical
3 *society as an organic whole*
▶ integrated, organized, structured, coherent, systematic, harmonious
AN OPPOSITE IS disparate

organism NOUN
a living organism
▶ living thing, being, creature, animal, plant

organization NOUN
1 *Sara is responsible for the organization of trips and visits.*
▶ planning, administration, coordination, running
2 *Organization is an important aspect of essay writing.*
▶ structure, planning, arrangement, composition
3 *an international organization with branches throughout the world*
▶ institution, enterprise, operation, company, (more informal) outfit, (more informal) set-up

organize VERB
1 *The protesters used mobile phones and the Internet to organize a demonstration.*
▶ arrange, coordinate, plan, make arrangements for, assemble, bring together, run
2 *Try to organize your ideas on paper.*
▶ order, marshal, structure, assemble, develop, coordinate, establish, systematize, put in order, form, shape

organized ADJECTIVE
a well organized sales promotion
► systematic, coordinated, efficient, well ordered, well planned, well run, meticulous, methodical, orderly, scientific, structured
OPPOSITES ARE disorganized, inefficient

orient, orientate VERB
1 *After her husband's death she had to orientate herself to a new way of life.*
► adapt, adjust, accommodate, familiarize, acclimatize, accustom
2 **orient** or **orientate yourself** *They looked out for landmarks to orient themselves.*
► get your bearings, get the lie of the land

oriental ADJECTIVE
oriental countries
► eastern, Far Eastern, Asian, Asiatic

origin NOUN
1 *a discussion of the origin of the universe*
► beginning, start, birth, genesis, dawning, emergence, inception, source
OPPOSITES ARE end, conclusion
2 *a man of Irish origins*
► descent, ancestry, parentage, extraction, family, pedigree, background, stock

original ADJECTIVE
1 *the original inhabitants of North America*
► earliest, first, indigenous, native, aboriginal, initial
AN OPPOSITE IS recent
2 *an original idea for a story*
► new, creative, innovative, novel, fresh, unfamiliar, unique, unusual, first-hand, imaginative, inventive, unconventional
OPPOSITES ARE unoriginal, commonplace
3 *an original painting by Picasso*
► authentic, genuine, real

originate VERB
1 *Where did the rumour originate?*
► arise, start, begin, emerge, emanate, evolve, be born, crop up
2 *It is not clear who originated the idea.*
► conceive, invent, create, initiate, introduce, inaugurate, discover, inspire, pioneer, be the inventor of, give birth to, institute, launch

ornament NOUN
1 *a plain style of clothing without ornament*
► decoration, adornment, embellishment, trimming, accessory, filigree, frill, frippery, finery, garnish, jewel, tracery
2 *a shelf covered with ornaments*
► trinket, knick-knack, bauble, gewgaw

ornamental ADJECTIVE
an ornamental ceiling
► decorative, fancy, attractive, ornate, ornamented, showy

ornate ADJECTIVE
1 *an ornate mirror over the fireplace*
► ornamented, decorated, elaborate, showy
AN OPPOSITE IS plain

2 *ornate language*
► elaborate, florid, fancy, grandiose, affected, pretentious

orthodox ADJECTIVE
He has orthodox views on most things.
► conventional, mainstream, established, conservative, standard, traditional, conformist
OPPOSITES ARE unorthodox, unconventional

ostentatious ADJECTIVE
Their ostentatious attempts to look busy fools nobody.
► showy, pretentious, conspicuous, flamboyant, obtrusive, vulgar, theatrical, overdone
AN OPPOSITE IS modest

oust VERB
The president knew that his opponent would never unite to oust him.
► depose, overthrow, remove, drive out, expel, unseat, defeat

out-and-out ADJECTIVE
an out-and-out success
► complete, utter, outright, thoroughgoing, downright, absolute, thorough, unmitigated

outbreak NOUN
1 *an outbreak of SARS new outbreaks of violence*
► eruption, upsurge, outburst, epidemic, rash, spate
2 *the outbreak of war*
► start, beginning, onset

outburst NOUN
At this there was a loud outburst of laughter.
► eruption, burst, explosion, outbreak, surge, spasm

outcast NOUN
a social outcast
► reject, pariah, leper, outsider, exile, outlaw, castaway

outclass VERB
She won every game, outclassing every rival.
► surpass, outdo, outstrip, outshine, beat, exceed, eclipse, excel, be better than

outcome NOUN
speculation about the outcome of the next election
► result, consequence, conclusion, upshot, issue, conclusion

outcry NOUN
an outcry about the state of the railways
► protest, complaint, furore, clamour, tumult

outdated ADJECTIVE
an outdated road network
► out-of-date, obsolete, old-fashioned, dated, decrepit, antiquated, ancient

outdo VERB
Everyone tried to outdo each other with stories of how exciting their holidays had been.
► surpass, outstrip, outshine, exceed, eclipse, excel, be better than, outclass, beat

outdoor ADJECTIVE
an outdoor sport such as archery
► open-air, outside, alfresco

outer ADJECTIVE
1 *It was so hot they began to shed their outer clothing.*
► outermost, exterior, external, outside, outward, surface, superficial
2 *superstores built in the outer areas of cities*
► outlying, distant, remote, peripheral, further, suburban
AN OPPOSITE IS inner

outfit NOUN
1 *a complete photography outfit*
► equipment, kit, apparatus, (*more informal*) gear, (*more informal*) set-up
2 *The weather was still too cold for summer outfits.*
► costume, ensemble, suit, dress, clothing, (*informal*) get-up, (*informal*) turn-out, (*more informal*) gear, (*more informal*) togs

outgoing ADJECTIVE
1 *She was in a bright, outgoing mood that day.*
► sociable, friendly, amiable, genial, congenial, demonstrative, pleasant, agreeable, kind, kindly, kind-hearted, well-disposed, sympathetic, likeable, approachable, receptive
2 *the outgoing president*
► departing, leaving, retiring, former, ex-
AN OPPOSITE IS incoming

outgoings PLURAL NOUN
His monthly outgoings had risen alarmingly.
► expenses, expenditure, spending, disbursements, overheads

outing NOUN
family outings to the coast
► trip, excursion, jaunt, expedition, drive, run, ride, joyride

outlandish ADJECTIVE
We could dream up all sorts of outlandish ideas.
► weird, strange, extraordinary, odd, queer, eccentric, bizarre, quirky

outlast VERB
Don't forget that leather outlasts denim.
► outwear, last longer than, survive

outlaw NOUN
those notorious outlaws Jesse and Frank James
► bandit, brigand, fugitive, desperado, renegade, robber, marauder, criminal, outcast

outlaw VERB
The state in effect outlawed political opposition.
► ban, prohibit, bar, forbid, disallow, banish, embargo, condemn, veto

outlay NOUN
The trip involves a small outlay.
► expense, expenditure, cost, price, (*more formal*) disbursement

outlet NOUN
1 *The boiler has an outlet for fumes.*
► vent, duct, channel, opening, orifice, exit, mouth, way out
2 *We need a better outlet for complaints.*
► channel, process, means
3 *High Street outlets for these goods*
► shop, store, retailer, market

outline NOUN
1 *the outline of a low building*
► profile, silhouette, shape, form, contour, shadow, figure
2 (*informal*) *He sat down and wrote an outline of his essay.*
► summary, sketch, framework, skeleton, plan, draft, rough idea, bare bones

outline VERB
In this chapter we will outline ways of acting out your chosen scenario.
► sketch out, summarize, indicate, rough out

outlive VERB
She outlived her husband by more than twenty years.
► survive, live longer than, outlast

outlook NOUN
1 *The house has a glorious outlook over the downs.*
► view, vista, prospect, panorama, aspect, vantage point
2 *The sisters were totally different in character and outlook.*
► attitude, way of thinking, standpoint, viewpoint, frame of mind, point of view
3 *Lower interest rates will improve the economic outlook.*
► prospects, expectations, forecast, hopes, future, prognosis, prediction, (*more informal*) lookout

outlying ADJECTIVE
Take a boat trip to one of the outlying islands.
► outer, distant, remote, outermost, far-flung, far-off, faraway
AN OPPOSITE IS central

outmoded ADJECTIVE
outmoded ways of storing information
► old-fashioned, outdated, out-of-date, obsolete, dated, obsolescent

outnumber VERB
On these occasions males usually outnumber females.
► exceed, be more than, outstrip

out-of-date ADJECTIVE
1 *He handed over an out-of-date passport.*
► expired, lapsed, invalid, void
2 *She was using a machine that was totally out of date.*
► old-fashioned, outdated, obsolete, dated, obsolescent

out-of-the-way ADJECTIVE
out-of-the-way places
► distant, outlying, faraway, remote, isolated, far-flung, far-off

output NOUN
a marked increase in industrial output
▶ production, productivity, product, yield, manufacture

outrage NOUN
1 *I can remember the sense of outrage when I first saw those blancmange-coloured walls.*
▶ anger, indignation, fury, disgust, affront, horror
2 *The country's suffering is an outrage.*
▶ scandal, disgrace, atrocity, enormity, barbarity, infamy

outrageous ADJECTIVE
1 *an outrageous slur on his character*
▶ disgraceful, shocking, scandalous, appalling, monstrous, shameful, dreadful, intolerable, wicked, heinous
AN OPPOSITE IS mild
2 *We were invited to tell outrageous stories about people we knew.*
▶ far-fetched, extravagant, preposterous, unlikely, questionable, dubious
AN OPPOSITE IS reasonable
3 *If you're not careful about the extras the cost can become outrageous.*
▶ excessive, exorbitant, extortionate

outright ADJECTIVE
By now it was clear the whole story was an outright fabrication.
▶ complete, utter, out-and-out, thoroughgoing, downright, absolute, thorough, unmitigated
AN OPPOSITE IS indefinite

outright ADVERB
I decided I would have to tell her outright.
▶ directly, explicitly, candidly, plainly, bluntly, openly, honestly

outset NOUN
The answer was clear from the outset.
▶ start, beginning, opening, inception
OPPOSITES ARE conclusion, end

outside ADJECTIVE
1 *An outside light will improve security.*
▶ exterior, external, outer, outdoor, outward
AN OPPOSITE IS inside
2 *We must resist all outside interference*
▶ external, extraneous, foreign, alien
AN OPPOSITE IS inside
3 *There is an outside chance of thunder.*
▶ slight, remote, slender, slim, faint, negligible

outside NOUN
The outside of the building is covered in ivy.
▶ exterior, facade, surface, outer surface, shell, skin
AN OPPOSITE IS inside

outsider NOUN
I still felt an outsider after years of living in the village.
▶ stranger, visitor, foreigner, alien, newcomer, incomer, interloper, intruder, immigrant, non-resident, outcast
AN OPPOSITE IS insider

outskirts PLURAL NOUN
a group of buildings on the outskirts of the city
▶ outer areas, outlying districts, edge, fringe, suburbs, margin, periphery, purlieus
OPPOSITES ARE centre, heart

outspoken ADJECTIVE
some outspoken remarks
▶ frank, forthright, candid, direct, blunt, plain-speaking, straightforward, unequivocal
OPPOSITES ARE guarded, diplomatic

outstanding ADJECTIVE
1 *She is an outstanding musician.*
▶ excellent, exceptional, superb, superlative, fine, extraordinary, distinguished, celebrated
OPPOSITES ARE mediocre, unexceptional
2 *All outstanding questions will be answered.*
▶ unresolved, unsettled, remaining, pending

outstrip VERB
Demand for fuel was outstripping supply.
▶ exceed, surpass, outdo, overtake, outdistance, eclipse

outward ADJECTIVE
His outward manner was bright and cheerful.
▶ external, outer, outside, surface, apparent, ostensible, superficial, visible
OPPOSITES ARE inward, inner

outweigh VERB
The benefits of the scheme have to outweigh the costs.
▶ exceed, be better than, be greater than, prevail over, override, have the edge on

outwit VERB
The besieged garrison managed to outwit the enemy.
▶ outsmart, dupe, fool, hoodwink, hoax, cheat, deceive, trick, (*more informal*) take in, (*more informal*) outfox

oval ADJECTIVE
an oval lawn
▶ egg-shaped, elliptical, ovoid

overall ADJECTIVE
It was a good overall result.
▶ general, all-inclusive, all-embracing, comprehensive, inclusive
AN OPPOSITE IS specific

overall ADVERB
Things have improved overall.
▶ generally, in general, generally speaking, altogether, all in all, for the most part, on the whole, in the main, on balance, on average

overbearing ADJECTIVE
Don't be intimidated by his overbearing attitude.
▶ arrogant, haughty, conceited, self-important, high-handed, lordly, superior, condescending, supercilious, disdainful, cavalier, imperious
AN OPPOSITE IS meek

o

overcast ADJECTIVE
The sky was dull and overcast.
▶ cloudy, grey, dull, dark, sombre, sunless, gloomy, stormy
OPPOSITES ARE clear, bright

overcome VERB
1 *Neither army was strong enough to overcome the other.*
▶ defeat, beat, conquer, overpower, vanquish, overwhelm, trounce
2 *It would be be easy to overcome his fear of flying.*
▶ control, master, get the better of, repress, subdue

overcrowded ADJECTIVE
an overcrowded beach
▶ packed, overfull, congested, bursting, jam-packed, chock-full, crammed, overpopulated, swarming, filled to capacity, jammed

overdo VERB
She spoilt her case by overdoing the emotion.
▶ exaggerate, overstate, overplay, overemphasize, overdramatize
OPPOSITES ARE underplay, play down

overdue ADJECTIVE
1 *The train is overdue.*
▶ late, delayed, behind time, tardy, unpunctual, slow
AN OPPOSITE IS early
2 *Our phone bill is overdue.*
▶ unpaid, unsettled, outstanding, owing, in arrears

overeat VERB
The food was so dreadful at least there was no danger of them overeating.
▶ overindulge, eat too much, be greedy, gorge, guzzle, binge, (more informal) stuff yourself, (more informal) make a pig of yourself
OPPOSITES ARE diet, fast, undereat

overflow VERB
The water tank overflowed, causing damage to the roof.
▶ spill over, flow over, pour over, run over, brim over, flood

overgrown ADJECTIVE
The garden was overgrown from years of neglect.
▶ unkempt, untidy, wild, tangled, untrimmed, unweeded, weedy

overhaul VERB
Cars used for hire are overhauled regularly.
▶ service, maintain, check over, examine, inspect, repair, refurbish

overhead ADJECTIVE
an overhead power line
▶ aerial, elevated, raised, high, suspended, projecting, overhanging
AN OPPOSITE IS underground

overhead ADVERB
A flock of birds passed overhead.
▶ above, up above, on high, high up, (more literary) aloft

overjoyed ADJECTIVE
Brian was overjoyed at the birth of his daughter.
▶ thrilled, delighted, ecstatic, pleased, excited, happy, glad
OPPOSITES ARE dejected, disappointed

overload VERB
At peak times the staff were constantly overloaded with work.
▶ overburden, weigh down, strain, encumber

overlook VERB
1 *a mistake we are willing to overlook*
▶ ignore, disregard, take no notice of, pay no attention to, discount, overlook, pass over, let pass, excuse, forget, make light of, brush aside, (more informal) turn a blind eye to
AN OPPOSITE IS penalize
2 *The house overlooks a car park.*
▶ look out on, have a view of, look on to, look over, face, front

overpower VERB
The prisoners could easily have overpowered their guards.
▶ overwhelm, subdue, prevail over, get the better of, gain mastery over, get control over, master, overturn

overpowering ADJECTIVE
1 *an overpowering feeling of sorrow*
▶ overwhelming, irrepressible, irresistible, uncontrollable, oppressive, intense
OPPOSITES ARE slight, weak
2 *The smell was overpowering.*
▶ stifling, suffocating, nauseating, sickening, pungent
AN OPPOSITE IS mild
3 *overpowering evidence of their guilt*
▶ compelling, irrefutable, undeniable, incontrovertible, conclusive, forceful, powerful, strong
OPPOSITES ARE unconvincing, inconclusive

overrated ADJECTIVE
His achievements are often overrated.
▶ exaggerated, overvalued, magnified, glorified, rated too highly
AN OPPOSITE IS underrated

overrule VERB
A higher court overruled the decision.
▶ overturn, override, revoke, reverse, cancel, rescind, quash, set aside, countermand
OPPOSITES ARE confirm, endorse, allow

overrun VERB
The country was overrun by its neighbours.
▶ invade, occupy, subdue, violate, attack, enter, penetrate, raid

overshadow VERB
Both countries were overshadowed by the superior power of Russia.
▶ dominate, eclipse, dwarf, overpower, put in the shade, outshine, outclass

oversight NOUN
The delay was caused by oversight.
▶ omission, lapse, carelessness, neglect, error

overt ADJECTIVE
signs of overt racism
▶ open, obvious, manifest, plain, blatant, unconcealed, undisguised
OPPOSITES ARE disguised, hidden, covert

overtake VERB
1 *Huge lorries were overtaking one another.*
▶ pass, pull ahead of, go past, overhaul, catch up with
2 *Fruit had overtaken oil as the country's main export.*
▶ outstrip, exceed, surpass, outdo
3 *Another disaster overtook the family.*
▶ befall, overwhelm, overpower, strike, hit, afflict, engulf

overthrow VERB
The emperor was finally overthrown by his own guard.
▶ depose, oust, remove, drive out, expel, unseat, defeat

overthrow NOUN
the overthrow of the tyrant
▶ downfall, defeat, removal, fall, collapse, deposing, ousting, expulsion, unseating

overtone NOUN
The word 'compulsory' has threatening overtones
▶ connotation, association, implication, undertone, undercurrent, reverberation, suggestion

overturn VERB
1 *The boat overturned in a squall.*
▶ capsize, turn over, tip over, keel over, turn turtle, overbalance
2 *Someone had overturned a box of tools over the garage floor.*
▶ upset, spill, knock over, tip over, topple
3 *The decision was overturned in the House of Lords.*
▶ overrule, override, revoke, reverse, cancel, rescind, quash, set aside, countermand

overweight ADJECTIVE
I had put on two stone and was noticeably overweight.
▶ fat, obese, corpulent, gross
OPPOSITES ARE underweight, undernourished

overwhelm VERB
1 *The home side overwhelmed the visitors in the league game.*
▶ defeat, overcome, crush, overpower, rout, trounce, win against, conquer, vanquish, subdue, get the better of, (*more informal*) thrash
2 *Monsoons would soon overwhelm the region.*
▶ overrun, inundate, submerge, engulf, flood, deluge, bury
3 *She bent her head, overwhelmed by grief.*
▶ overcome, overpower, strike, crush

overwhelming ADJECTIVE
1 *The campaign received overwhelming support.*
▶ strong, massive, formidable, sweeping, forceful, powerful
2 *The army suffered another overwhelming defeat.*
▶ crushing, devastating, great, overpowering

overwrought ADJECTIVE
They were overwrought and needed sleep.
▶ tense, agitated, keyed up, worked up, nervous, upset, excited
OPPOSITES ARE calm, unexcited

owing ADJECTIVE
There is a small amount of money still owing.
▶ due, outstanding, unpaid, payable, owed, unsettled, overdue
owing to *He would not use the lifts, owing to his claustrophobia.*
▶ because of, as a result of, on account of, as a consequence of, by reason of, thanks to

own VERB
Many more people own their own house.
▶ possess, be the owner of, have, hold
own up to *He was waiting for a good moment to own up to the mistake.*
▶ confess, admit, acknowledge, tell the truth about, (*more informal*) come clean about, (*more informal*) make a clean breast of

owner NOUN
1 *Maintenance of the service road is the responsibility of the properties' owners.*
▶ possessor, proprietor, freeholder, landlord, landlady
2 *Dog owners should not let their pets foul the pavements.*
▶ keeper, master, mistress

Pp

pace NOUN
1 *She moved back a few paces.*
▶ step, stride
2 *The traffic was moving at a slow pace.*
▶ speed, rate, velocity, movement, quickness, gait, (*informal*) lick
3 *They quickened their pace to a run.*
▶ stride, gait, tread, walk, march, speed, progress

pace VERB
Richard paced up and down for ages before going in.
▶ walk, stride, tread, march

pacifism NOUN
a supporter of pacifism and tolerance
▶ non-violence, peaceful solutions
AN OPPOSITE IS militarism

pacifist NOUN
Her parents had been strong pacifists during the cold war.
▶ peace-lover, peacemaker
AN OPPOSITE IS militarist

pacify VERB
It was too late to pacify her now, and she stormed off.
▶ appease, placate, calm, conciliate, mollify, soothe, assuage, propitiate, quieten
AN OPPOSITE IS anger

pack NOUN
1 *The bookshelves come in a self-assembly pack. A pack of cigarettes lay on the table.*
▶ package, packet, container, carton, box, parcel, bundle
2 *a group of walkers with packs on their backs*
▶ backpack, rucksack, knapsack, kitbag
3 *a pack of wolves*
▶ group, herd, troop
4 *a pack of youths*
▶ group, crowd, band, gang, set, throng, horde, mob

pack VERB
1 *The children helped to pack the hamper.*
▶ fill, load, stuff, put things in
2 *She decided to pack her belongings and leave.*
▶ bundle, parcel, wrap, stow, store
3 *On rainy days visitors pack the local museums.*
▶ throng, crowd into, cram into, squash into, squeeze into, fill, jam
pack in (*informal*) *James has decided to pack in his job.*
▶ give up, leave, resign from, (*informal*) quit, (*informal*) chuck in
pack up
1 (*informal*) *The microwave chose that very moment to pack up.*
▶ break down, stop working, go wrong, fail, develop a fault, (*more formal*) malfunction, (*informal*) play up, (*informal*) act up
2 (*informal*) *If you're not having a good time perhaps it's time to pack up.*
▶ stop, break off, call it a day

package NOUN
A strange package arrived by special delivery.
▶ parcel, packet, container, consignment

packed ADJECTIVE
a packed room
▶ crowded, full, crammed, jam-packed, chock-a-block

packet NOUN
1 *a packet of sugar*
▶ pack, carton, bag, box, container
2 **a packet** (*informal*) *new shoes that cost a packet*
▶ a fortune, a small fortune, a huge amount, a king's ransom, (*informal*) an arm and a leg

pact NOUN
The two countries signed a non-aggression pact.
▶ treaty, alliance, agreement, settlement, truce, protocol, understanding

pad NOUN
1 *Take a pad to sit on as the seats are hard.*
▶ cushion, pillow, padding, squab, bolster, wad
2 *She made notes on a small pad.*
▶ notebook, notepad, jotter, sketchbook

pad VERB
1 *You can pad the cushion with plastic foam.*
▶ stuff, pack, fill, line, upholster
2 *He padded along to the bathroom.*
▶ walk, creep, tiptoe
pad out *Try not to pad out your letter with irrelevant detail.*
▶ expand, inflate, fill out, elaborate, lengthen, spin out, stretch out

padding NOUN
1 *The sofa burst open and masses of grey padding fell out.*
▶ stuffing, wadding, filling, cushioning
2 *The story could be much shorter but for all the tedious padding.*
▶ verbiage, verbosity, wordiness, (*informal*) waffle

paddle NOUN
You'll need to use the paddle to reach the shore.
▶ oar, scull

paddle VERB
1 *We paddled furiously to get to safety.*
▶ row, scull, pull
2 *You can paddle a long way out at low tide.*
▶ dabble, wade, splash about

paddock NOUN
horses in a paddock
▶ field, meadow, pasture, enclosure

pagan NOUN
pagans who worshipped nature
▶ heathen, infidel, non-believer, unbeliever
USAGE You should only use *pagan* with reference to people in the past. It is an unfavourable term used by Christians and other believers in God to refer to non-believers. It is not an ordinary equivalent to words such as *atheist*, which is a more neutral term for someone who believes there is no God.

pagan ADJECTIVE
pagan festivals
▶ heathen, infidel, ungodly, atheistic, godless, idolatrous, irreligious, unchristian
USAGE See the note at the previous entry.

page NOUN
1 *He had written a whole page by the time she returned.*
▶ side, sheet, folio, leaf
2 *Clare's little brother had been a page at her friend's wedding.*
▶ pageboy, attendant, train-bearer

pageant NOUN
the annual pageant in the city centre
▶ parade, procession, spectacle, extravaganza, display, tableau

A
B
C
D
E
F
G
H
I
J
K
L
M
N
O
P
Q
R
S
T
U
V
W
X
Y
Z

pageantry NOUN

Visitors love all the pageantry associated with royalty.
▶ pomp, ceremony, ritual, show, spectacle, splendour, grandeur, glamour, magnificence, display, formality

pain NOUN

1 *The pain in his tooth was fading.*
▶ ache, soreness, hurt, tenderness, throb, discomfort
2 *How could anyone be expected to put up with so much pain?*
▶ suffering, discomfort, agony, affliction
3 *the pain of losing a child*
▶ grief, sorrow, distress, torment, anguish, misery, trauma
4 (*informal*) *Younger brothers could be a pain at times like this.*
▶ nuisance, pest, bother, bore, trial, tribulation, inconvenience

pain VERB

It pained him to think of all the trouble they had been through.
▶ hurt, sadden, grieve, distress, mortify

pained ADJECTIVE

He wore a pained expression as he told them the news.
▶ hurt, upset, injured, distressed, aggrieved, offended

painful ADJECTIVE

1 *The knight had a painful wound in his side.*
▶ sore, hurting, tender, agonizing, excruciating
2 *The journey had been a painful experience.*
▶ unpleasant, traumatic, disagreeable, bitter, wretched
OPPOSITES ARE pleasant, agreeable

painless ADJECTIVE

There is no completely painless way to travel
▶ comfortable, easy, effortless, pain-free, simple, trouble-free, undemanding
AN OPPOSITE IS painful

painstaking ADJECTIVE

She showed a painstaking attention to detail.
▶ meticulous, careful, thorough, assiduous, punctilious, scrupulous
OPPOSITES ARE careless, slapdash

paint NOUN

They chose a bright paint for the walls.
▶ colour, pigment, tint, colouring, stain

paint VERB

1 *Kim couldn't make up her mind whether to paint the room or paper it.*
▶ colour, tint, use paint on, coat with paint, apply paint to, decorate
2 *The article paints a vivid picture of life in rural Wales.*
▶ describe, depict, portray, present, sketch, outline, delineate

painting NOUN

She was eager to buy one of his larger paintings.
▶ picture, oil painting, watercolour

KINDS OF PAINTING INCLUDE

cave painting, fresco (painted on wet plaster), icon (religious portrait), landscape, miniature, mural (painted on dry wall), nude, oil, panorama, portrait, seascape, still life, wall painting, watercolour.

pair NOUN

1 *a pair of earrings*
▶ set, set of two
2 *The guests drank to the happy pair.*
▶ couple, partners, husband and wife, man and wife
3 *The pair sang, one standing and the other at the piano.*
▶ couple, duo, two, twosome

pair VERB

She couldn't find a jersey to pair with her skirt.
▶ match, couple, twin, partner, put together

pal NOUN

(*informal*) *The boys had been pals since primary school.*
▶ friend, companion, (*informal*) mate, (*informal*) buddy, (*informal*) chum

palace NOUN

a royal palace open to the public
▶ official residence, château, mansion, stately home, castle
RELATED ADJECTIVE palatial

palatable ADJECTIVE

1 *The little hotel serves meals that are more than palatable.*
▶ tasty, pleasant, appetizing, eatable, edible, nice to eat, enjoyable
AN OPPOSITE IS unpalatable
2 *Some of the news is not very palatable.*
▶ acceptable, agreeable, easy to take
AN OPPOSITE IS unpalatable

palatial ADJECTIVE

a palatial residence in the heart of the old city
▶ grand, magnificent, splendid, impressive, imposing, noble, luxurious, sumptuous
OPPOSITES ARE modest, humble

pale ADJECTIVE

1 *He frowned and turned pale.*
▶ white, pallid, wan, ashen, anaemic, sallow
AN OPPOSITE IS flushed
2 *a pale shade of pink*
▶ light, soft, muted, pastel, faint, weak
OPPOSITES ARE dark, strong
3 *a pale light*
▶ dim, weak, watery, feeble
OPPOSITES ARE bright, strong

pale VERB

She paled suddenly and clenched her hands.
▶ turn white or go white, become pale, lose colour, whiten, blanch, lighten

pall NOUN
a thick pall of carbon monoxide
▶ cloud, cloak, mantle, blanket, covering

pall VERB
The constant business travel soon began to pall
▶ become tedious, become boring, weary, cloy, irk, lose its attraction, become uninteresting

pallid ADJECTIVE
His face was pallid with fear.
▶ pale, white, wan, ashen, anaemic, sallow
AN OPPOSITE IS flushed

pally ADJECTIVE
The two men had become quite pally over the years.
▶ friendly, close, on good terms, intimate, (*informal*) matey, (*informal*) chummy

palm VERB
palm off *They palmed off the worst wines on their visitors.*
▶ foist, fob off, get rid of, dispose of, offload, (*more informal*) unload

palpable ADJECTIVE
The tension in the room was palpable.
▶ perceptible, noticeable, discernible, recognizable, unmistakable, obvious, plain, clear

paltry ADJECTIVE
All he gave was a paltry five pounds.
▶ meagre, negligible, pitiful, miserable, modest, scanty, scant, sparse, (*more informal*) mingy, (*more informal*) measly
OPPOSITES ARE generous, extravagant

pamper VERB
His mother tended to pamper him.
▶ spoil, indulge, overindulge, cosset, mollycoddle, coddle, humour, pander to

pamphlet NOUN
a pamphlet on bee-keeping
▶ leaflet, brochure, booklet, handout, folder, notice

pan NOUN
Fry the mushrooms and onions in a large pan.
▶ frying-pan, saucepan, container, vessel, pot

pan VERB
(*informal*) *The reviews all panned the film mercilessly.*
▶ criticize, attack, lambaste, censure, (*informal*) hammer, (*informal*) take apart, (*informal*) knock
OPPOSITES ARE praise, commend, recommend

panacea NOUN
a panacea for our troubles
▶ cure, remedy, perfect solution, magic formula

panache NOUN
Julian produced the flowers with all the panache of a successful conjuror.
▶ confidence, enthusiasm, flourish, spirit, style, verve, zest

pandemonium NOUN
The meeting ended in pandemonium.
▶ chaos, uproar, bedlam, mayhem, confusion, disorder, muddle

pander VERB
pander to *Susan was prepared to pander to some of their foibles, but there were limits.*
▶ gratify, indulge, satisfy, cater to

pane NOUN
She went to the window and pressed her face against the pane.
▶ glass, sheet of glass, windowpane

panel NOUN
1 *He stared at the control panel, looking for the right switch.*
▶ console, fascia, board
2 *The case will be decided by a panel of judges.*
▶ group, team, body, board, council, commission

pang NOUN
1 *Pangs of hunger came over them.*
▶ spasm, twinge, stab
2 *She felt a slight pang of regret*
▶ qualm, misgiving, scruple, twinge, prick

panic NOUN
They rushed out in panic.
▶ alarm, fright, fear, trepidation, consternation, horror, terror, frenzy

panic VERB
There is no need to panic yet.
▶ be alarmed, take fright, lose your head, lose your nerve, overreact, (*more informal*) flap

panicky ADJECTIVE
Her voice became breathless and panicky.
▶ panic-stricken, alarmed, frantic, hysterical, frightened, overexcited, terror-stricken, unnerved
AN OPPOSITE IS calm

panorama NOUN
There is a lovely panorama across the city from the top of the tower.
▶ view, vista, prospect, outlook, landscape, perspective, scene

panoramic ADJECTIVE
a panoramic view of the hills
▶ wide, sweeping, broad, extensive, comprehensive

pant VERB
He lay there panting from the exertion.
▶ gasp, puff, heave, wheeze, breathe quickly

pants NOUN
a pair of pants
▶ underpants, briefs, trunks, shorts, (*for men*) boxer shorts, (*for men*) Y-fronts, (*for women*) panties, (*for women*) knickers

paper NOUN
1 *They had to show their papers at the border.*
▶ document, credentials, identification, authorization, certificate
2 *I'll go and buy a paper.*
▶ newspaper, daily, broadsheet (= large newspaper), tabloid (= small newspaper), magazine
3 *Her father was writing a paper for a medical journal.*
▶ article, essay, study, lecture, dissertation, thesis

parade NOUN
a military parade
▶ procession, march, cavalcade, spectacle, display, pageant, review, show

parade VERB
1 *The teams will parade through the city.*
▶ process, troop, march past
2 *He paraded up and down in the corridor.*
▶ stride, strut, walk
3 *She was eager to parade her knowledge.*
▶ show off, display, demonstrate, exhibit, make a show of

paradise NOUN
1 *non-Christian theories about Paradise*
▶ heaven, Utopia, Eden, Elysium, nirvana
2 *Their holiday had been absolute paradise.*
▶ bliss, heaven, joy, delight, ecstasy

paradox NOUN
the paradox of high prices at a time of low demand
▶ anomaly, contradiction, self-contradiction, incongruity, oddity

paradoxical ADJECTIVE
It seems paradoxical to reduce taxes when more money is needed for public services.
▶ absurd, anomalous, conflicting, contradictory, illogical, incongruous, self-contradictory

parallel ADJECTIVE
1 *a pair of parallel lines*
▶ equidistant
2 *parallel methods of achieving the same objective*
▶ similar, analogous, corresponding, matching

parallel NOUN
1 *There is a parallel between her experience and ours.*
▶ similarity, resemblance, analogy, correspondence, comparison, likeness, match
2 *It would be hard to find an exact parallel to this problem.*
▶ counterpart, equivalent, analogue, likeness, duplicate

parallel VERB
Their lives parallel each other in many respects.
▶ resemble, match, be similar to, compare with, correspond to

paralyse VERB
1 *The injury paralysed his right leg for a time.*
▶ disable, immobilize, cripple, incapacitate, deaden
2 *The country was paralysed by a wave of strikes.*
▶ bring to a standstill, immobilize, bring to a halt, cripple, halt, freeze

paralysed ADJECTIVE
I had a paralysed right arm.
▶ disabled, handicapped, incapacitated, immobilized, crippled, lame, unusable

paralysis NOUN
1 *a disease that can cause paralysis*
▶ immobility, incapacity, paraplegia
2 *paralysis of the country's transport system*
▶ shutdown, immobilization, stopping, standstill

parameter NOUN
It is important to define the parameters for this research.
▶ criterion, guideline, framework, limit, boundary

paramount ADJECTIVE
an issue of paramount importance
▶ supreme, prime, primary, central, pre-eminent, highest, cardinal, foremost, utmost

paraphernalia NOUN
all the paraphernalia needed to build our own greenhouse
▶ equipment, apparatus, tackle, stuff, things, (*more informal*) odds and ends

parcel NOUN
a parcel of food
▶ package, packet, pack, consignment, bale, bundle, carton

parcel VERB
parcel out *Land was parcelled out in small plots.*
▶ divide up, distribute, share out, apportion, portion out, split up

parched ADJECTIVE
1 *The back lawn is so parched it hardly needs cutting.*
▶ scorched, dry, arid, baked, barren, waterless, dehydrated, lifeless, sterile
2 *We felt parched in the hot afternoon sun.*
▶ thirsty, dehydrated, dry, (*more informal*) gasping

pardon VERB
1 *The king would pardon them if they admitted their guilt.*
▶ forgive, excuse, absolve, grant a pardon to, reprieve, amnesty, acquit
AN OPPOSITE IS punish
2 *These are faults we can pardon and even admire.*
▶ forgive, excuse, condone

pardon NOUN
A pardon was offered to the rebels.
▶ amnesty, reprieve, release, discharge

pare VERB
pare down *The business has been pared down and several branches closed.*
▶ reduce, diminish, decrease, cut , prune, slim down, curtail, trim

parent NOUN
She had an elderly parent to look after.
▶ mother or father, guardian

parentage NOUN
a young man of Indian parentage
▶ origin, ancestry, lineage, pedigree, extraction, descent, heredity, pedigree, roots, stock, derivation, blood, ancestors, forebears

parish NOUN
1 *a large London parish*
▶ district, community
2 *The vicar had a large parish to look after.*
▶ congregation, flock, fold

a
b
c
d
e
f
g
h
i
j
k
l
m
n
o
p
q
r
s
t
u
v
w
x
y
z

park NOUN
The children went off to play in the park.
▶ recreation ground, public gardens, playground, parkland

park VERB
She parked the car outside her friend's house.
▶ leave, position, station, stop, place

parliament NOUN
The country's parliament dates back to the Middle Ages.
▶ legislature, congress, assembly, council, government, senate, conclave, convocation

parody NOUN
1 He swivelled his hips in a parody of the belly dance.
▶ caricature, lampoon, comic imitation, mimicry, mockery, skit, (more informal) take-off, (more informal) spoof, (more informal) send-up
2 The article was no more than a parody of the truth.
▶ travesty, distortion, mockery, caricature

parody VERB
Jane Austen parodied the gothic novel. Alice bit back her tears and parodied a smile.
▶ caricature, satirize, mimic, lampoon, travesty, ape, imitate, (more informal) send up, (more informal) take off

parry VERB
Stephen managed to parry the blow.
▶ fend off, ward off, avert, deflect, block, dodge, stave off, avoid, evade, sidestep, repel, repulse, push away

parson NOUN
The parson shook hands outside the church.
▶ clergyman, clergywoman, cleric, minister, priest, vicar, preacher

part NOUN
1 This is only one part of the story.
▶ bit, piece, portion, segment, section, episode, chapter, constituent
OPPOSITES ARE whole, entirety
2 A part of the house had been closed off.
▶ section, portion
3 The washing machine has broken and needs a new part.
▶ component, element, unit
4 Deborah would take the lead part in the school play.
▶ role, character
5 Her parents lived in another part of town.
▶ region, district, neighbourhood, quarter, section, sector
6 Their part in the affair had not been very distinguished.
▶ involvement, role, function, concern, responsibility, contribution (to)

part VERB
1 They did not want to part on such bad terms.
▶ separate, leave, say goodbye, say farewell, break up, go away
OPPOSITES ARE meet, reunite
2 The authorities are anxious not to part the children.
▶ separate, divide, split

3 **part with** advertising designed to persuade shoppers to part with their money.
▶ give up, relinquish, hand over, let go of, give up, forgo, surrender, discard

partial ADJECTIVE
1 The economic collapse was followed by a partial recovery.
▶ limited, incomplete, qualified, restricted, imperfect, unfinished
AN OPPOSITE IS complete
2 **be partial to** She had always been partial to a cream tea.
▶ like, love, enjoy, be fond of, have a fondness for, be keen on, appreciate, (more informal) go for

participant NOUN
There were over a hundred participants in the race.
▶ participator, entrant, competitor

participate VERB
A million people participated in the vote by using their mobiles.
▶ take part, join in, be involved, cooperate, engage, share, assist, help

participation NOUN
They sought an active participation in the political life of the country
▶ involvement, cooperation, sharing, contribution (to), partnership, sharing

particle NOUN
There was not a single particle of food left.
▶ bit, piece, morsel, scrap, shred, crumb, drop, fragment, grain, iota, jot, sliver, speck

particular ADJECTIVE
1 The article criticized a particular group of companies.
▶ specific, certain, distinct, definite, discrete
2 This is a matter of particular interest to us.
▶ special, exceptional, marked, unusual, uncommon, noteworthy, remarkable
3 He was not too particular about the methods they used.
▶ fussy, discriminating, finicky, fastidious, (more informal) choosy

particulars PLURAL NOUN
A police officer will call to take your particulars.
▶ details, facts, information, circumstances

particularly ADVERB
The river trip is particularly enjoyable.
▶ especially, exceptionally, remarkably, unusually, distinctly, notably

parting NOUN
1 It will be an emotional parting.
▶ farewell, goodbye, departure, leaving
OPPOSITES ARE meeting, reunion
2 They would tell their son and daughter that evening about their intended parting.
▶ separation, breakup, split-up, divorce
AN OPPOSITE IS reconciliation

partisan NOUN
The country was swarming with Tito's partisans.
► supporter, follower, adherent, devotee, champion, guerrilla, fighter

partisan ADJECTIVE
the bitterly partisan nature of the debate
► biased, one-sided, prejudiced, coloured, partial, slanted, factional

partition NOUN
1 *the partition of the country after the war*
► division, dividing, splitting, breaking-up
2 *A partition separated the two parts of the room.*
► screen, panel, divider, barrier, dividing wall

partition VERB
A UN resolution partitioned the country into two states.
► divide, split, subdivide, separate

partly ADVERB
The work was now partly finished
► partially, in part, to some extent, up to a point

partner NOUN
1 *Jack had been his business partner for many years.*
► colleague, associate, collaborator, ally, confederate, comrade, companion
2 *Staff were encouraged to bring their partners to the party.*
► girlfriend or boyfriend, husband or wife, spouse, mate

partnership NOUN
1 *a business partnership*
► company, firm, corporation, organization, syndicate, alliance, combination, cooperative, affiliation
2 *a partnership between nations*
► cooperation, association, coalition, collaboration

party NOUN
1 *a flat-warming party*
► celebration, gathering, festivity, function, merrymaking, (*humorous*) jollification, (*more informal*) get-together, (*more informal*) do
2 *a political party*
► group, faction, grouping, league, alliance, association, cabal, coalition
3 *a search party*
► team, crew, squad, company, group

pass VERB
1 *Lots of heavy traffic passed through the village.*
► drive, go, move, stream, progress
2 *She went to pass him the sugar and spilled it.*
► hand, give, deliver
3 *Eventually the storm passed.*
► blow over, go away, fade, fade away, disappear, come to an end
4 *As time passed he gradually forgot her.*
► elapse, go by, advance, progress, tick by
pass away *He passed away in his sleep.*
► die, pass on, lose your life, meet your end, breathe your last, expire
pass off *The meeting passed off without any trouble.*
► happen, take place, go off, occur, turn out

pass out *She must have passed out.*
► faint, lose consciousness, black out, (*more informal*) flake out
pass over *Perhaps we can pass over these mistakes.*
► disregard, overlook, ignore, forget, take no notice of, pay no attention to, discount
pass up *He was not one to pass up a chance of a free holiday.*
► turn down, forgo, reject, refuse, miss out on

pass NOUN
1 *a pass through the mountains*
► route, way, defile, gap, gorge, ravine, canyon
2 *Your pass will get you into all the city's museums.*
► permit, ticket, warrant, authority, authorization, licence

passable ADJECTIVE
1 *The food was no more than passable.*
► adequate, acceptable, satisfactory, tolerable, moderate, ordinary, sufficient, all right, fair, mediocre, middling, (*more informal*) so-so
AN OPPOSITE IS unacceptable
2 *The road is passable again after being closed because of floods.*
► open, traversable, navigable, usable, unblocked, clear
AN OPPOSITE IS impassable

passage NOUN
1 *the passage of time*
► passing, advance, course, march, progress, progression, moving on
2 *a sea passage*
► crossing, journey , voyage, trip, cruise, sail
3 *a narrow passage leading to the garden*
► corridor, passageway, walkway, thoroughfare, hallway, way through
4 *a passage between the two houses*
► alley, alleyway, path, pathway, way, lane, track
5 *a passage from The Amber Spyglass*
► excerpt, extract, section, episode, scene, paragraph, piece, quotation

passenger NOUN
Passengers were told to get out at the next station.
► traveller, commuter, voyager, rider

passer-by NOUN
Passers-by stopped and looked.
► bystander, onlooker, observer, spectator, watcher, witness, eyewitness

passing ADJECTIVE
a passing feeling of regret
► brief, temporary, short-lived, transient, momentary, cursory, short

passion NOUN
1 *You could talk about your passion for hang-gliding.*
► enthusiasm, fondness, eagerness, keenness (on), mania, appetite, interest (in), fanaticism, zeal, craving, commitment (to)
OPPOSITES ARE indifference (to), apathy

2 *He recalled the passion with which she had kissed him.*
▶ feeling, ardour, intensity, emotion, fervour, love, longing, craving, desire, excitement, fire, heat
AN OPPOSITE IS detachment
3 *He spoke with a fierce passion.*
▶ emotion, feeling, vehemence, anger, rage, fury, frenzy, paroxysm
OPPOSITES ARE coolness, indifference

passionate ADJECTIVE
1 *a passionate appeal for help*
▶ impassioned, emotional, heartfelt, intense, ardent, fervent, impulsive
OPPOSITES ARE half- hearted, cool
2 *a passionate embrace*
▶ loving, amorous, sensual, lustful, erotic, (*more informal*) steamy
AN OPPOSITE IS cold
3 *His passionate temperament got the better of him.*
▶ excitable, hot-blooded, intense, fiery, wild, violent
OPPOSITES ARE placid, phlegmatic

passive ADJECTIVE
1 *a passive acceptance of hardship*
▶ submissive, resigned, compliant, impassive, docile, long-suffering, non-violent, indifferent, patient, unresisting
OPPOSITES ARE active, lively
2 *Tim had played a passive role in the affair.*
▶ inactive, uninvolved, non-participating
OPPOSITES ARE active, assertive

past ADJECTIVE
memories of past happiness
▶ former, bygone, previous, earlier, ended, finished, gone, (*more informal*) over and done with
OPPOSITES ARE present, future

past NOUN
She was trying hard to forget the past.
▶ antiquity, days gone by, history, old days, olden days, past times
OPPOSITES ARE present, future

---

pasta NOUN
How revolting to want chips with pasta.
SOME COMMON KINDS OF PASTA
cannelloni, fusilli, lasagne, macaroni, noodles, penne, ravioli, rigatoni, spaghetti, tagliatelle, tortellini, vermicelli.

---

paste NOUN
1 *He used paste to fix his photos in an album.*
▶ glue, gum, adhesive, fixative
2 *Mix the ingredients into a smooth paste.*
▶ purée, spread, mixture, pulp

paste VERB
She was busy pasting wallpaper.
▶ fix, fasten, glue, gum, hang

pastime NOUN
a time when art was a rich man's pastime
▶ hobby, activity, recreation, diversion, amusement, entertainment, occupation, game, sport, relaxation

pastoral ADJECTIVE
1 *a pastoral scene of trees and cows*
▶ rural, rustic, country, outdoor, agrarian, bucolic, farming, idyllic
AN OPPOSITE IS urban
2 *the pastoral duties of a vicar's wife*
▶ ecclesiastical, priestly, parochial, ministerial, caring

pasture NOUN
a farm with a hundred acres of pasture
▶ grass, grassland, meadow, field, paddock, pasturage, grazing

pasty ADJECTIVE
a row of people with pasty faces
▶ pale, pallid, white, wan, sickly, anaemic, unhealthy
OPPOSITES ARE healthy, ruddy

pat VERB
Les leaned forward to pat her hand.
▶ tap, touch, dab, stroke, rub, fondle

pat ADJECTIVE
His answers sounded pat, as if he'd rehearsed them.
▶ glib, slick, facile, simplistic, smooth, unconvincing, perfunctory, superficial

pat ADVERB
off pat *They have the right language off pat.*
▶ by heart, by rote, word for word, parrot-fashion

patch NOUN
1 *old jeans covered in patches*
▶ mend, repair
2 *The family was going through a difficult patch.*
▶ period, time, spell, phase, stretch
3 *Harry had a vegetable patch up the road.*
▶ plot, piece of ground, strip, row, area

patch VERB
He had got someone to patch his jacket at the elbow.
▶ mend, repair, reinforce, put a patch on, cover, darn, fix, sew up, stitch up

patchy ADJECTIVE
1 *They drove through stretches of patchy fog.*
▶ irregular, uneven, sporadic, intermittent, variable, erratic, inconsistent, unpredictable, bitty, changeable
AN OPPOSITE IS constant
2 *a piece of patchy grass*
▶ uneven, speckled, mottled, dappled, multicoloured
3 *Their story was patchy and confusing.*
▶ fragmentary, deficient, variable, limited, inadequate
OPPOSITES ARE comprehensive, complete

patent ADJECTIVE
The action was a patent violation of the agreement.
▶ obvious, clear, plain, evident, blatant, manifest, apparent, palpable, undisguised
OPPOSITES ARE hidden, unclear

path NOUN
1 *a path by the railway line*
▶ footpath, pathway, track, alley, lane
2 *His path was blocked by the barricades.*
▶ way, route, course, passage, progress

pathetic ADJECTIVE
1 *a pathetic wave of the hand*
▶ pitiful, pitiable, poignant, plaintive, sad, touching, moving, affecting, distressing, heartrending, lamentable, wretched
2 (*informal*) *He added up his pathetic savings.*
▶ inadequate, paltry, meagre, feeble, derisory, miserable, wretched, worthless

pathos NOUN
her speech of pathos and wifely love
▶ sadness, poignancy, emotion, feeling, pity, tragedy

patience NOUN
1 *Great care and patience is needed to avoid damaging the plants.*
▶ diligence, perseverance, persistence, self-control, stoicism, endurance, fortitude
2 *Will's behaviour was stretching their patience to the limit.*
▶ toleration, forbearance, composure, calmness, restraint, equanimity, resignation

patient ADJECTIVE
1 *She tried to be patient while her husband hunted for the key.*
▶ calm, self-controlled, composed, restrained, forbearing, indulgent, tolerant, lenient, understanding, philosophical
OPPOSITES ARE impatient, intolerant
2 *The task called for a great deal of patient work.*
▶ diligent, persistent, persevering, tenacious, determined, dogged, resolved, purposeful

patient NOUN
the relation between doctor and patient
▶ invalid, sick person, sufferer, case

patio NOUN
In summer they would sit on the patio.
▶ terrace, courtyard, paved area

patriotic ADJECTIVE
Many of his patriotic songs have a stirring lilt.
▶ nationalistic, loyal, flag-waving, (*disapproving*) jingoistic, (*disapproving*) chauvinistic

patrol NOUN
1 *Security guards remain on patrol all night.*
▶ surveillance, watch, guard, duty
2 *A four-man patrol set off through the jungle.*
▶ guard, lookout, party, task force, convoy, detail

patrol VERB
Guards with dogs patrol the estate.
▶ police, tour, inspect, keep watch on, be on patrol on, go the rounds of

patron NOUN
1 (*informal*) *a patron of the arts*
▶ sponsor, supporter, benefactor, champion, backer, defender
2 *Parking outside the shops is for patrons only.*
▶ client, customer, (*more informal*) regular

patronage NOUN
1 *State patronage of the arts is a thing of the past.*
▶ sponsorship, backing, support
2 *The management thanked customers for their patronage over the years.*
▶ custom, business, trade

patronize VERB
1 *The parents of girls like Sally patronized the little shop.*
▶ do business with, be a customer of, frequent, shop at, buy from, deal with
2 *The nobility patronized music and the arts.*
▶ sponsor, support, finance, back, foster, encourage
3 *She accused them of patronizing her.*
▶ talk down to, condescend to, look down on, put down

patronizing ADJECTIVE
The British should learn to adopt a less patronizing tone.
▶ condescending, supercilious, superior, disdainful, haughty, lofty, paternalistic, snobbish
OPPOSITES ARE humble, modest

patter VERB
1 *Rain pattered against the window.*
▶ beat, tap, rattle, clatter, pitter-patter
2 *The children pattered up to their rooms.*
▶ scurry, scamper, scuttle

patter NOUN
1 *the patter of feet*
▶ pattering, pitter-patter, scurrying, scuttling
2 *a salesman's patter*
▶ chatter, babble, line, (*more informal*) spiel

pattern NOUN
1 *patterns drawn in the sand*
▶ design, device, figure, motif, shape, figuration, arrangement, decoration, ornamentation
2 *Their actions might set a pattern*
▶ example, model, standard, guide, norm, original, precedent, archetype, criterion, prototype, sample, specimen
3 *The insects have a special behaviour pattern.*
▶ system, order, method, scheme

paunch NOUN
He leaned back in his chair and spread his finger over his paunch.
▶ belly, pot belly, gut, pot

pauper NOUN
The revolution left the family almost paupers.
▶ beggar, bankrupt, insolvent, down and out

pause VERB
She paused for a moment before going in.
▶ wait, hesitate, stop, delay, halt, waver, hang back, break off, rest, have a pause

pause NOUN
There was a short pause while the band regrouped.
▶ break, interruption, interval, delay, rest, wait, interlude, intermission, lull, stoppage, respite, stop, suspension, (*more informal*) breather

pave VERB
1 *She decided to pave part of the garden to put a table on.*
▶ cover, concrete, flag, tile, asphalt
2 **pave the way for** *Tax cuts paved the way for an economic recovery.*
▶ prepare for, lay the foundations for, clear the way for, herald, precede

pavement NOUN
A parked car was blocking the pavement.
▶ footpath, path, walkway, (*American*) sidewalk

paw NOUN
She stroked the cat's paw.
▶ foot, pad

paw VERB
The young animals were pawing one another.
▶ touch, poke, maul

pawn NOUN
The nobles used the young prince as a pawn in their power struggle.
▶ puppet, dupe, tool, stooge, hostage

pay NOUN
Her pay would go up in April.
▶ income, earnings, salary, wages, payment, (*more formal*) remuneration, (*more formal*) emolument

pay VERB
1 *I'd rather pay more and get a better machine.*
▶ spend, expend, pay out, part with, (*more informal*) shell out, (*more informal*) dish out
2 *He said he'd pay me for the broken window.*
▶ reimburse, recompense, refund, repay, pay back
3 *Stella is trying to pay her debts.*
▶ settle, discharge, pay off, meet, clear, honour
4 *I'll make them pay for this.*
▶ suffer, make amends, atone, answer
5 *It would pay us to wait until the new model comes out.*
▶ benefit, profit, be an advantage to

payment NOUN
1 *You can settle in six or twelve monthly payments.*
▶ instalment, contribution, remittance
2 *There is a discount for prompt payment.*
▶ settlement, remittance
3 *You get extra payment for working late.*
▶ pay, wages, income, remuneration

peace NOUN
1 *It's not easy to get any peace in this house.*
▶ calm, quiet, silence, tranquillity, relaxation, hush
OPPOSITES ARE disturbance, noise

2 *The country longed for peace after years of civil unrest.*
▶ order, harmony, harmoniousness, non-violence
AN OPPOSITE IS disorder
3 *A peace will be signed and the war ended.*
▶ armistice, truce, ceasefire, treaty, agreement, concord

peaceable ADJECTIVE
a peaceable nation
▶ peace-loving, unwarlike, non-violent, pacific, peaceful, placid, conciliatory, cooperative, friendly, harmonious
OPPOSITES ARE aggressive, warlike, belligerent

peaceful ADJECTIVE
1 *a peaceful part of the country*
▶ quiet, restful, serene, tranquil, secluded, undisturbed, unruffled, untroubled, calm, still, pleasant, relaxing, balmy
OPPOSITES ARE noisy, troubled
2 *The country wants to resolve the dispute in a peaceful manner.*
▶ non-violent, calm, cordial, amicable, friendly, orderly
3 *Tanya had a peaceful temperament.*
▶ calm, placid, serene, amicable, friendly, unruffled, pacific, gentle
OPPOSITES ARE turbulent, agitated

peak NOUN
1 *the peaks of the mountains*
▶ summit, tip, top, crest, pinnacle, crown, point
2 *Ruth had reached the peak of her career.*
▶ height, highest point, zenith, acme, climax, culmination
OPPOSITES ARE nadir, trough

peaky ADJECTIVE
Josh had been looking peaky all morning, and stayed at home.
▶ pale, pallid, pasty, unwell, sickly, poorly, queasy, out of sorts

peal NOUN
a peal of bells
▶ chime, carillon, ringing, clang

peal VERB
The bells pealed
▶ chime, ring, toll, resound, resonate

peasant NOUN
1 *There were rows of peasants picking tomatoes in the fields.*
▶ countryman, rustic, farmhand, yokel
2 (*informal*) *He became angry and called them a bunch of peasants.*
▶ lout, oaf, bumpkin

peculiar ADJECTIVE
1 *Something peculiar was happening to her computer.*
▶ strange, odd, unusual, weird, curious, funny, extraordinary, bizarre, abnormal
OPPOSITES ARE normal, ordinary
2 *By that stage of the journey we were all feeling a bit peculiar.*
▶ unwell, ill, sick, poorly, queasy, out of sorts

3 *Norman had his own peculiar way of doing things.*
▶ special, characteristic, distinctive, individual, particular, singular, unique, idiosyncratic, (*more informal*) wacky, (*more informal*) screwy

peculiarity NOUN
1 *Find out about the peculiarities of the local weather when you go abroad. He had a strange physical peculiarity.*
▶ oddity, peculiar or special feature, abnormality, foible, idiosyncrasy, quirk, trait, characteristic, eccentricity
2 *We will have to accept the peculiarity of this arrangement.*
▶ strangeness, abnormality, oddness, oddity, eccentricity, bizarreness

pedantic ADJECTIVE
1 *He has a pedantic style of writing.*
▶ academic, bookish, formal, humourless, learned, old-fashioned, pompous, scholarly, schoolmasterly, stilted
AN OPPOSITE IS informal
2 *a pedantic application of the rules*
▶ strict, inflexible, precise, over-scrupulous, unimaginative, (*more informal*) nit-picking
AN OPPOSITE IS flexible

peddle VERB
a company peddling cheap software in the third world
▶ sell, trade in, traffic in, market, vend, tout, (*more informal*) flog

pedestal NOUN
a statue on a tall pedestal
▶ base, plinth, stand, support, mounting, column, pillar

pedestrian ADJECTIVE
1 *a pedestrian walkway*
▶ pedestrianized, traffic-free
2 *a pedestrian performance*
▶ dull, tedious, ordinary, mediocre, run-of-the-mill, monotonous, boring

pedestrian NOUN
Pedestrians should use the footbridge.
▶ walker, person on foot

pedigree ADJECTIVE
a pedigree dog
▶ pure-bred, thoroughbred

pedigree NOUN
cattle with a pedigree that goes back to Roman Britain
▶ ancestry, descent, lineage, line, stock, descent, parentage

pedlar NOUN
a pedlar of cheap watches and electronic games
▶ seller, hawker, travelling salesman, street-trader, vendor

peek VERB
A face peeked round the doorway.
▶ peep, peer, glance, look

peek NOUN
He took a quick peek at the recipe.
▶ peep, glance, glimpse, look

peel NOUN
Orange peel lay in a spiral on the table.
▶ rind, skin, covering, zest

peel VERB
Jeff peeled an apple.
▶ pare, skin, strip

peep VERB
Jane peeped through the keyhole.
▶ peek, peer, glance, look

peep NOUN
Have a peep at the baby.
▶ peek, glance, glimpse, look

peer VERB
A woman peered at us from a corner of the room.
▶ gaze, look, glance, squint, peep, peek

peeved ADJECTIVE
Paula still felt peeved about it.
▶ annoyed, irritated, angry, cross, displeased, vexed, infuriated, incensed, enraged, (*more informal*) miffed, (*more informal*) put out
AN OPPOSITE IS pleased

peevish ADJECTIVE
Ellen replied in a slightly peevish tone.
▶ irritable, petulant, fractious, irascible, fretful, touchy, sullen, snappy, crotchety
OPPOSITES ARE good-humoured, agreeable

peg NOUN
She put her coat on a peg.
▶ hook, pin, spike, knob

peg VERB
1 *Make sure you peg the tent to the ground.*
▶ fasten, fix, secure, attach
2 *Prices will be pegged for six months.*
▶ fix, hold, hold down, keep down, freeze, control

pelt VERB
1 *The men were pelting each other with snowballs.*
▶ bombard, shower, attack, assail, batter
2 *It was pelting down outside.*
▶ pour, teem, rain cats and dogs
3 *The players pelted back to the dressing room.*
▶ rush, dash, run, hurry, sprint, charge, streak

pen NOUN
1 *sheep in a pen*
▶ enclosure, compound, paddock, stockade
2 *He wrote it down with a pen.*
▶ ballpoint, biro, felt-tipped pen, fountain pen

penalize VERB
The authorities can penalize parents of children who miss school.
▶ punish, impose a penalty on, fine, discipline
AN OPPOSITE IS reward

penalty NOUN
a fixed penalty for illegal parking
▶ punishment, fine, forfeit
AN OPPOSITE IS reward

pending ADJECTIVE
A decision is pending.
▶ imminent, impending, forthcoming, in the offing, about to happen

penetrate VERB
1 *Make sure the screws do not penetrate the top surface of the shelf.*
▶ pierce, puncture, perforate, bore through, make a hole in
2 *An advance force penetrated the city's outer defences.*
▶ infiltrate, enter, get through, slip through, probe
3 *Damp had penetrated the stone-work.*
▶ impregnate, permeate, pervade, seep into

penetrating ADJECTIVE
1 *She looked away from his penetrating dark eyes.*
▶ piercing, probing, staring, sharp, keen
2 *The students asked some penetrating questions.*
▶ perceptive, sharp, acute, intelligent, incisive, profound, searching
3 *The silence was interrupted by a penetrating scream.*
▶ shrill, piercing, strident, ear-splitting, deafening

penniless ADJECTIVE
Epstein was a penniless student in Paris.
▶ poor, impoverished, destitute, poverty-stricken, moneyless, (more informal) skint

pensive ADJECTIVE
He sipped his coffee with a pensive expression on his face.
▶ thoughtful, reflective, contemplative, absorbed, meditative, ruminative, preoccupied, wistful, serious

people NOUN
1 *By mid-afternoon many people were hungry People like to read books like these.*
▶ persons, individuals, human beings, humans, folk, mortals, humanity, humankind, mankind
USAGE Note that *humanity, humankind*, and *mankind* are all singular nouns and you use a singular verb with them, e.g. *Humankind likes to read books like these.*
2 *The government will appeal to the people in a general election.*
▶ nation, electorate, voters, electors, community
3 *a shopping centre that serves the people of the area a proud and brave people*
▶ populace, population, citizens, inhabitants, public, society, common people, community, electorate, nation
RELATED ADJECTIVES ethnic, national
4 *Her people live in Ireland.*
▶ family, relatives, relations, parents, clan, kith and kin
USAGE Note that *family* and *clan* are singular nouns but you can use a singular or plural

verb with them, e.g. *Her family lives in Scotland* or *Her family live in Scotland.*

people VERB
the inhabitants who once peopled this fine island
▶ populate, inhabit, occupy, live in, settle, colonize

pep NOUN
(informal) The project needed a lot more pep.
▶ energy, vigour, vitality, spirit, verve, exuberance, fizz

pep VERB
pep up *He added some herbs to pep up the flavour.*
▶ liven up, vitalize, enhance, intensify

peppery ADJECTIVE
Dried chillies add a peppery touch.
▶ hot, spicy, pungent, peppered, sharp

perceive VERB
1 *Those in the room perceived voices outside.*
▶ hear, discern, distinguish, make out, notice, recognize, become aware of
2 *Some animals cannot perceive colour.*
▶ see, discern, distinguish, recognize, observe, identify
3 *I began to perceive her meaning.*
▶ understand, comprehend, apprehend, grasp, realize, sense, deduce, gather, know
4 *We all perceive the world in different ways.   an enemy perceived as a major threat*
▶ regard, consider, view, judge, deem, think of, look on

perceptible ADJECTIVE
1 *There followed a perceptible pause in the conversation.*
▶ noticeable, perceivable, distinct, evident, marked, palpable, detectable, appreciable, obvious, audible
AN OPPOSITE IS imperceptible
2 *The coast was perceptible from the aircraft windows.*
▶ visible, discernible, observable, recognizable

perception NOUN
1 *The public's perception of the government's honesty has changed.*
▶ impression, consciousness, apprehension, sense, view, awareness, cognition, comprehension, understanding, recognition, sensation
2 *She speaks with great perception on these problems.*
▶ insight, perceptiveness, discernment, understanding, perspicacity, astuteness, shrewdness, intelligence, observation

perceptive ADJECTIVE
A few perceptive questions can liven up the interview.
▶ discerning, astute, shrewd, intelligent, insightful, perspicacious
OPPOSITES ARE obtuse, inept

perch VERB
A monkey came in and perched on a table.
▶ sit, settle, rest, balance, alight

perfect ADJECTIVE (with the stress on *per-*)
1 *It was the start to a perfect day.*
▶ superb, excellent, superlative, wonderful, marvellous, idyllic, blissful
2 *a second-hand book in perfect condition*
▶ impeccable, flawless, immaculate, spotless, pristine
OPPOSITES ARE imperfect, flawed
3 *a copy so perfect you can't tell it from the original*
▶ exact, precise, faithful, accurate, true, close
AN OPPOSITE IS inaccurate
4 *A digital radio will make a perfect birthday present.*
▶ ideal, suitable, fitting, apt, appropriate
OPPOSITES ARE unsuitable, inappropriate
5 *He felt a perfect fool. They had never met; they were perfect strangers.*
▶ complete, absolute, utter, total, entire, thoroughgoing

perfect VERB (with the stress on *-fect*)
He is spending some time perfecting his speech.
▶ improve, make perfect, refine, complete, finish, fulfil, realize

perfection NOUN
1 *the perfection of her complexion*
▶ faultlessness, flawlessness, excellence, beauty, completeness, ideal, wholeness
AN OPPOSITE IS imperfection
2 *the perfection of their plans*
▶ completion, consummation, fulfilment, realization, accomplishment, fruition, achievement

perfectionist NOUN
He was such a perfectionist he wouldn't allow any mistakes.
▶ idealist, purist, precisionist, (*more informal*) stickler

perfectly ADVERB
1 *He brought in a perfectly baked cake.*
▶ superbly, impeccably, faultlessly, flawlessly, beautifully, excellently
2 *I'm perfectly happy to let them use the house. He can be perfectly horrid at times.*
▶ absolutely, completely, entirely, totally, utterly
3 *You know perfectly well what I mean.*
▶ very, quite, full, (*more informal*) jolly

perforate VERB
a teabag perforated with tiny holes
▶ pierce, prick, puncture, penetrate, bore through, drill

perform VERB
1 *The two devices perform the same function. She has her duties to perform.*
▶ fulfil, exercise, carry out, execute, discharge, accomplish, achieve
2 *The company performed the new play in London.*
▶ present, stage, put on, produce, mount
3 *The speakers perform best at a fairly high volume.*
▶ work, function, operate, behave

performance NOUN
1 *the performance of their duties*
▶ carrying out, execution, discharge, accomplishment, fulfilment, completion, implementation
2 *The music received a fine performance.*
▶ rendition, interpretation, rendering, account
3 *The review praised the new range of cars for their performance*
▶ operation, running, functioning, behaviour
4 *He made a huge performance of thanking them.*
▶ fuss, exhibition, act, scene, parade

performer NOUN
The song was sung by the original performers.
▶ singer, entertainer, artist, artiste, musician, player, star, actor, actress

perfume NOUN
1 *With a final spray of exotic perfume she left the room.*
▶ scent, toilet water, eau de cologne
2 *the fresh, sweet perfume of roses*
▶ smell , scent, fragrance, aroma, odour, whiff

perfunctory ADJECTIVE
They greeted each other with perfunctory grunts.
▶ cursory, desultory, fleeting, casual, hurried, offhand, half-hearted, unthinking, mechanical, automatic
OPPOSITES ARE enthusiastic, careful

perhaps ADVERB
Perhaps they took the train to Glasgow.
▶ maybe, possibly, conceivably, feasibly

peril NOUN
1 *the perils of the sea*
▶ danger, hazard, risk, menace, uncertainty
OPPOSITES ARE security, safety
in peril *The climbers found themselves in great peril.*
▶ in danger, at risk, in jeopardy

perilous ADJECTIVE
a perilous journey through tropical swamps
▶ dangerous, hazardous, fraught, unsafe, risky
AN OPPOSITE IS safe

perimeter NOUN
1 *The airport perimeter is closely guarded.*
▶ boundary, periphery, confines, edge, fringe, border, margin, borderline, bounds, circumference
2 *The perimeter is about twelve miles.*
▶ circumference, outer edge

period NOUN
1 *They suffered from several long periods of separation.*
▶ spell, interval, stretch, term, bout, run, span, phase, session
2 *the Hanoverian period of English history*
▶ age, era, years, epoch, time
3 *There was a double period of maths on Monday.*
▶ lesson, class, session

periodic ADJECTIVE
He suffered periodic lapses of memory.
▶ occasional, regular, intermittent, recurrent, repeated, spasmodic

periodical NOUN

The library has a special catalogue of periodicals.
► journal, magazine, review, monthly, quarterly, weekly

peripheral ADJECTIVE

1 *migrants travelling from peripheral parts of Europe*
► distant, outermost, outlying, outer
AN OPPOSITE IS central

2 *These issues are peripheral to the main question.*
► secondary, subsidiary, inessential, non-essential, incidental, marginal, borderline, minor, irrelevant, unimportant
OPPOSITES ARE essential, crucial

perish VERB

1 *Many people perished in the floods.*
► die, be killed, lose your life, pass away

2 *The tyres had started to perish.*
► decay, decompose, disintegrate, crumble away, rot

perk NOUN

(informal) company cars and other perks
► benefit, extra, bonus, *(more formal)* perquisite, *(more informal)* plus

perk up VERB

He perked up when he saw Susan coming.
► cheer up, liven up, brighten, take heart, pick up, bounce back

perky ADJECTIVE

Margaret was in one of her perky moods.
► lively, cheerful, vivacious, animated, bubbly, bouncy, buoyant, sparkly

permanent ADJECTIVE

1 *We are looking for a permanent solution to the problem.*
► lasting, continuing, durable, fixed, long-term, unchangeable, irreversible, everlasting, perpetual, eternal

2 *Leslie has got his first permanent job.*
► stable, fixed, established, secure, firm

permeate VERB

A delicious smell permeated the whole house.
► pervade, pass through, spread through, filter through, flow through, penetrate, percolate through, saturate

permissible ADJECTIVE

Pollution exceeds permissible levels.
► permitted, allowable, allowed, legal, lawful, legitimate, acceptable, admissible, authorized
OPPOSITES ARE forbidden, unacceptable

permission NOUN

We will need permission to miss the afternoon classes.
► authorization, authority, leave, consent, approval, agreement, licence, assent, clearance, dispensation, *(more informal)* the go-ahead, *(informal)* the green light

permissive ADJECTIVE

the permissive society of the sixties and seventies
► liberal, broad-minded, open-minded, tolerant, free-and-easy, indulgent, lenient

permit VERB

1 *The authorities would not permit release of the documents.*
► allow, authorize, endorse, agree to, consent to, approve of, give permission for, sanction, license, tolerate
OPPOSITES ARE prohibit, prevent, ban

2 *His club will permit him to play in the national side.*
► allow, authorize, give an opportunity, make it possible
OPPOSITES ARE forbid, prohibit (from)

permit NOUN

The warden asked to see his permit.
► authorization, licence, pass, warrant, certification, passport, visa, charter

perpetual ADJECTIVE

1 *The Arctic is in almost perpetual daylight.*
► continuous, constant, uninterrupted, permanent, ceaseless, everlasting, eternal, non-stop
AN OPPOSITE IS temporary

2 *Their perpetual rows upset the children.*
► continual, interminable, incessant, constant, eternal, endless, ceaseless
OPPOSITES ARE occasional, intermittent

perplex VERB

a helpline that answers any questions that perplex you
► baffle, bewilder, puzzle, mystify, confuse, bemuse, disconcert, confound, fox, *(more informal)* flummox, *(more informal)* floor

persecute VERB

1 *In Rome, Christians were being persecuted by the Emperor Nero.*
► oppress, victimize, martyr, discriminate against, maltreat, ill-treat, tyrannize

2 *He thought everyone was persecuting him.*
► harass, hound, pester, pursue, bother, plague, torment, intimidate, bully, terrorize

persecution NOUN

victims of political persecution
► oppression, victimization, discrimination, harassment, maltreatment, martyrdom, tyranny, abuse

perseverance NOUN

The job required perseverance and patience.
► persistence, tenacity, determination, resolve, doggedness, diligence, dedication, application, commitment, endurance, stamina

persevere VERB

He decided to persevere, in spite of some early failures.
► continue, persist, keep going, carry on, press on, endure, *(more informal)* soldier on, *(more informal)* hang on, *(more informal)* keep at it, *(informal)* stick at it, *(more informal)* plug away
OPPOSITES ARE give up, stop

persist VERB

1 *The officer persisted with his questions.*
▶ continue, persevere, keep going, carry on, press on, endure, (*more informal*) soldier on, (*more informal*) hang on, (*more informal*) keep at it, (*informal*) stick at it, (*more informal*) plug away
OPPOSITES ARE desist, give up, stop

2 *If the pain persists, you should see a doctor.*
▶ continue, carry on, keep on, go on, linger, last, remain
AN OPPOSITE IS cease

3 **persist in** *He would persist in interrupting her*
▶ keep on, insist on

persistent ADJECTIVE

1 *The company should respond to its more persistent critics.*
▶ determined, tenacious, persevering, resolute, single-minded

2 *They were interrupted by a persistent knocking at the door.*
▶ continuing, constant, steady, incessant, endless, non-stop

person NOUN

We must find the person responsible. She was the first person to arrive. There was not a person to be seen.
▶ individual, man or woman, being, human being, soul, body

personal ADJECTIVE

1 *a story based on the author's personal experiences*
▶ own, individual, particular, special, exclusive
OPPOSITES ARE general, public

2 *The letter was marked 'personal'.*
▶ private, confidential, secret

personality NOUN

1 *He has a warmth of personality and a generous nature.*
▶ character, nature, disposition, temperament, identity, individuality, (*more informal*) make-up

2 *a television personality*
▶ celebrity, star, superstar, name

personify VERB

The dancers are meant to personify Spring.
▶ represent, symbolize, personalize, epitomize, allegorize, embody, give a human shape to, incarnate

personnel NOUN

An alert has been sent out to security personnel.
▶ staff, workers, employees, manpower, workforce, force, crew, people

perspective NOUN

Since the war we see history from a different perspective.
▶ outlook, viewpoint, point of view, slant, view, angle

in perspective *To put this in perspective, ten percent of buyers admitted to being dissatisfied with what they had bought.*
▶ in context, in proportion

perspire VERB

Women glow and men perspire.
▶ sweat, break out in a sweat, exude, drip

persuade VERB

Will you be able to persuade Susie to go back to England?
▶ convince, tempt, prevail on or upon, induce, coax, talk into, make, entice, influence, pressure, pressurize, urge, bring round, cajole, inveigle
AN OPPOSITE IS dissuade

persuasion NOUN

1 *I shall need a lot of persuasion to change my mind.*
▶ persuading, coaxing, coercion, convincing, inducement, exhortation, cajolery, enticement, argument

2 *people with a wide range of political persuasions*
▶ belief, conviction, view, opinion, faith

persuasive ADJECTIVE

There's a lot of persuasive talk but not much action.
▶ convincing, compelling, cogent, sound, valid, plausible, reasonable, forceful, strong, telling, credible, effective, eloquent, influential, logical, watertight
OPPOSITES ARE unconvincing, unpersuasive

pert ADJECTIVE

The barmaid was a pert, slightly plump girl called Rose.
▶ cheeky, impudent, impertinent, insolent, impolite, disrespectful, brazen, audacious, forward

pertinent ADJECTIVE

The questions he asked me were very pertinent.
▶ relevant, apposite, suitable, fitting, apt, material, to the point

perturb VERB

Her arrival did not perturb him in the slightest.
▶ alarm, disturb, upset, dismay, distress, unnerve, agitate, shock, fluster, daunt, (*more informal*) put the wind up
AN OPPOSITE IS reassure

peruse VERB

Visitors can relax in the reading room, perusing books or using the online facilities.
▶ read, study, browse through, inspect, glance at, look through, skim through, thumb through, scrutinize

pervade VERB

A pleasant smell of cooking pervaded the room.
▶ permeate, pass through, spread through, filter through, flow through, penetrate, affect, imbue, percolate through, saturate

pervasive ADJECTIVE

Their jaunty behaviour masked a pervasive sense of anxiety.
▶ prevalent, pervading, widespread, inescapable, insidious, permeating, general, ubiquitous, universal, rife
USAGE Note that *rife* is only used after a verb, e.g. *A sense of anxiety was rife.*

perverse ADJECTIVE

He has the perverse habit of calling all young girls 'madam' and all older women girls.
► contrary, wayward, awkward, unreasonable, tiresome, capricious, wilful, obstinate, stubborn, unhelpful, rebellious
OPPOSITES ARE reasonable, obliging

perversion NOUN

1 *The evidence was a perversion of the truth.*
► distortion, misrepresentation, falsification, travesty, debasement, corruption, aberration, twisting
2 *new attitudes to sexual perversion*
► deviation, abnormality, deviance, unnaturalness, (*more informal*) kinkiness

pervert NOUN (with the stress on *per-*)

They called him a sexual pervert.
► deviant, degenerate, (*more informal*) perv, (*more informal*) weirdo, (*more informal*) sicko

pervert VERB (with the stress on *-vert*)

1 *He was charged with perverting the course of justice.*
► distort, subvert, twist, bend, abuse, falsify, undermine
2 *a dictator perverted by years of power*
► corrupt, deprave, lead astray, debase, degrade

perverted ADJECTIVE

Just put it down to my perverted sense of humour.
► unnatural, deviant, twisted, warped, distorted, depraved, debased, abnormal, degenerate, (*more informal*) sick, (*more informal*) kinky
OPPOSITES ARE natural, normal

pessimism NOUN

His pessimism prevented him from taking any risks.
► despondency, fatalism, negativeness, hopelessness, gloom, despair, resignation, unhappiness, cynicism
AN OPPOSITE IS optimism

pessimistic ADJECTIVE

Manufacturers are pessimistic about the economic future.
► negative, fatalistic, gloomy, downbeat, downhearted, unhopeful, defeatist, despairing, despondent, resigned, unhappy, cynical
AN OPPOSITE IS optimistic

pest NOUN

1 *Vincent's demands for attention were becoming a pest.*
► nuisance, bother, annoyance, irritation, curse, trial, bore, bane, vexation, (*more informal*) pain, (*more informal*) pain in the neck
2 *the rise in crop pests*
► insect, bug, parasite, (*more informal*) creepy-crawly

pester NOUN

Claire was nice and didn't pester him with silly questions.
► annoy, bother, irritate, badger, harass, nag, harry,

chivvy, hound, trouble, besiege, (*more informal*) hassle, (*more informal*) bug, (*more informal*) keep on at, (*more informal*) go on at

pet NOUN

(*informal*) *They teased him and called him teacher's pet.*
► favourite, darling, treasure, blue-eyed boy or girl

pet ADJECTIVE

1 *Whoever heard of a pet rattlesnake?*
► tame, domestic
2 *The shop was very much his own pet scheme.*
► favourite, cherished, prized, precious, special, personal

pet VERB

Kim sat holding the kitten and petting it.
► pat, stroke, pamper, caress, cuddle, fondle, kiss, touch

peter out VERB

The traffic began to peter out.
► dwindle, diminish, decrease, subside, disappear, fall off, die out, wane, shrink

petite ADJECTIVE

She had a slender petite figure and a lovely complexion.
► small, slight, delicate, elfin, gamine

petition NOUN

a petition protesting at the new building plans
► appeal, list of signatures, application, supplication, entreaty, plea

petition VERB

After his death his widow petitioned the governor for justice.
► appeal to, call upon, make a plea to, plead with, supplicate, beseech, apply to, solicit

petrified ADJECTIVE

The child stood petrified with fright.
► terrified, paralysed, terror-struck, horrified, frozen

petty ADJECTIVE

1 *The meeting was called for petty reasons.*
► trivial, minor, trifling, unimportant, insignificant, slight, secondary, paltry
2 *The criticisms were unfair and petty.*
► spiteful, small-minded, vindictive, mean, ungenerous, grudging

petulant ADJECTIVE

He sounded as petulant as an obstinate child.
► bad-tempered, peevish, irritable, fractious, irascible, fretful, touchy, sullen, snappy, crotchety
OPPOSITES ARE good-humoured, agreeable

phantom NOUN

1 *a phantom that appeared at night*
► ghost, spectre, spirit, apparition, wraith, (*more informal*) spook
2 *He realized that what he had seen had been a phantom of his own mind.*
► hallucination, figment, illusion, delusion, vision
3 *a phantom pregnancy*
► imaginary, imagined, false, unreal

phase NOUN
1 *the final phase of the war*
► stage, part, period, step, chapter
2 *The marriage was going through a difficult phase.*
► period, stage, spell, time, state

phase out VERB
The old version of the software has been phased out.
► withdraw, remove, close, eliminate, terminate

phenomenal ADJECTIVE
Lutyens had a phenomenal memory for detail.
► remarkable, extraordinary, outstanding, amazing, astonishing, astounding, staggering, sensational, breathtaking
OPPOSITES ARE ordinary, run-of-the-mill

phenomenon NOUN
1 *Retirement was a largely twentieth-century phenomenon*
► occurrence, circumstance, feature, experience, event, situation, thing
2 *The band became a cult phenomenon.*
► sensation, wonder, marvel, spectacle, prodigy

philanthropic ADJECTIVE
He donated the money for genuinely philanthropic motives.
► charitable, altruistic, beneficent, benevolent, humanitarian, public-spirited, generous, bountiful, munificent, caring, humane, kind
AN OPPOSITE IS misanthropic

philanthropist NOUN
a cricket-loving Edwardian philanthropist
► benefactor, patron, donor, contributor, sponsor, backer

philanthropy NOUN
Nineteenth-century philanthropy seeking to protect the elderly
► benevolence, generosity, beneficence, humanitarianism, public-spiritedness, patronage, liberality, altruism, munificence

philosopher NOUN
Thales, the first Greek philosopher
► thinker, sage, student of philosophy, theorizer

philosophical ADJECTIVE
1 *a new approach to old philosophical ideas*
► theoretical, analytical, rational, reasoned, abstract, academic, metaphysical, ideological, intellectual, learned, logical, wise, erudite
2 *He felt in a philosophical mood.*
► thoughtful, reflective, contemplative, meditative, introspective, studious, ruminative
3 *Jane was philosophical about life's problems.*
► calm, composed, collected, resigned, unemotional, unruffled, stoical, self-possessed, patient
AN OPPOSITE IS emotional

philosophy NOUN
1 *a student of philosophy*
► thinking, reasoning, metaphysics, wisdom, knowledge, logic

2 *Taylor spent his life promoting his philosophy.*
► convictions, beliefs, ideology, principles, theories, credo, attitudes, viewpoint

phlegmatic ADJECTIVE
Ronnie, in his own phlegmatic way, could live with the problem better than most.
► calm, cool, composed, placid, impassive, unemotional, unexcitable, cool-headed, serene
OPPOSITES ARE excitable, passionate

---

phobia NOUN
He has a phobia about noise.
► aversion (to), dread (of), fear (of), anxiety, obsession, neurosis, revulsion, dislike (of), hatred (of), horror, *(more informal)* hang-up, *(more informal)* thing

TYPES OF PHOBIA
The three most common **phobia** words are
agoraphobia: fear of open spaces.
claustrophobia: fear of enclosed spaces.
xenophobia: hostility to foreigners.

OTHER TYPES OF FEAR ARE:
aerophobia: aeroplanes.
zoophobia: animals.
homophobia: homosexuals.
haemophobia: blood.
ailurophobia: cats.
cryophobia: cold.
cyberphobia: computers.
ochlophobia: crowds.
scotophobia: darkness.
thanatophobia: death.
cynophobia: dogs.
panphobia: everything.
phasmophobia: ghosts.
acrophobia: heights.
photophobia: light.
androphobia: men.
hypnophobia: sleep.
triskaidekaphobia: the number thirteen.
brontophobia: thunder.
hydrophobia: water.
gynophobia: women.
ergophobia: work.

---

phone VERB
She tried to phone home on her mobile.
► call, ring, telephone, reach, dial

phoney ADJECTIVE
He gave a phoney name.
► false, bogus, sham, fake, made-up, invented, fictitious, assumed, spurious
OPPOSITES ARE genuine, authentic

phoney NOUN
The lawyer was a phoney.
▶ impostor, sham, fraud, fake, charlatan, swindler

photograph NOUN
She published her best photographs in a magazine.
▶ photo, picture, snapshot, snap, image, print, slide, transparency

photograph VERB
I photographed them as people first and models second.
▶ shoot, snap, take a picture of

phrase NOUN
He searched in his mind for the right phrase to describe his feelings.
▶ expression, wording, group of words, form of words, construction, idiom

phrase VERB
She thought about how to phrase the question.
▶ express, word, put in words, formulate, couch, frame, present

physical ADJECTIVE
1 *It is hard to describe his physical appearance*
▶ bodily, corporal, corporeal, carnal
AN OPPOSITE IS mental
2 *our physical existence*
▶ earthly, material, mortal, terrestrial, tangible, fleshly, substantial
AN OPPOSITE IS spiritual

physique NOUN
He had the physique of a rugby forward.
▶ body, build, figure, frame, physical condition, proportions, form, muscles, shape

pick VERB
1 *We spent the afternoon picking fruit.*
▶ gather, collect, pluck, harvest, garner
2 *He picked a card and held it to his chest. Pick a time and place that suit you.*
▶ choose, select, take, decide on, opt for, settle on, fix on, single out
pick on *They are always picking on Freddie.*
▶ victimize, bully, persecute, tease, (*more informal*) get at
pick out *It was difficult to pick anything out in the fog.*
▶ see, discern, spot, distinguish, make out, recognize, identify
pick up
1 *It was too heavy to pick up.*
▶ lift, raise, take up, hoist
2 *You can pick up a bargain at the car-boot sales.*
▶ find, discover, obtain, acquire, get hold of, buy, purchase
3 *Lisa picked up some Spanish during her stay abroad.*
▶ learn, acquire, absorb, get to know, master
4 *He offered to pick up the children from school.*
▶ collect, fetch, go to get, call for
5 *The weather began to pick up.*
▶ improve, recover, get better, brighten
6 *Be careful you don't pick up an infection.*
▶ catch, contract, get, come down with

pick NOUN
1 *Take your pick.*
▶ choice, preference, selection, option
2 *the pick of the bunch*
▶ best, finest, prime, top, cream, choicest, élite

picket VERB
Over a hundred workers picketed the depot.
▶ blockade, cordon off, surround, enclose, demonstrate at, protest at

pickle VERB
Mary likes to pickle most of her fruit.
▶ preserve, conserve, bottle, marinade, souse

pictorial ADJECTIVE
a mosaic with pictorial designs
▶ illustrated, graphic, diagrammatic, representational, illustrative

picture NOUN
1 *the famous picture of Bubbles*
▶ painting, portrait, likeness, portrayal, representation, depiction, profile, image
2 *Kevin wanted to take a picture of them.*
▶ photograph, snapshot, snap, shot
NAMES FOR TYPES OF PICTURE
paintings: oil painting, watercolour, pastel; landscape, portrait, still-life, abstract; frieze (along the top of a wall), mural (large painting on a wall), fresco (watercolour painted on plaster when still wet), impasto (using thick layers of paint); transfer; reproduction (copy of a painting); collage (made from small pieces of paper and fabric).
drawings: drawing, sketch, doodle, engraving, etching, print, tracing; silhouette (outline of subject coloured in black).
photographs: photogrpah ((*informal*)photo, pic), snapshot, portrait, enlargement ((*informal*) blow-up), vignette (subject fading into background); print, positive, negative, transparency or slide; Polaroid; still (taken from a cinema film); digital.

picturesque ADJECTIVE
1 *He had spent the morning painting picturesque views of his master.*
▶ attractive, pretty, beautiful, charming, pleasant, scenic
AN OPPOSITE IS ugly
2 *She was trying to find a more picturesque way to describe it.*
▶ colourful, graphic, descriptive, expressive, vivid, imaginative, poetic
AN OPPOSITE IS prosaic

piece NOUN
1 *a piece of cheese a piece of stone*
▶ bit, chunk, lump, hunk, portion, fragment, morsel, particle
2 *a piece of furniture*
▶ item, article

piece

3 *She wrote a piece for the local newspaper.*
▶ article, story, feature, essay, account

piece VERB
piece together *It is difficult to piece the evidence together into a convincing case.*
▶ assemble, compose, fit together, join together

piecemeal ADJECTIVE
a few piecemeal changes
▶ intermittent, gradual, disjointed

pied ADJECTIVE
a breed of pied cattle
▶ dappled, flecked, mottled, particoloured, piebald, spotted, variegated

pier NOUN
1 *Boats were tied up at the pier.*
▶ jetty, quay, wharf, dock , landing stage, breakwater
2 *Immense piers supported a high vault.*
▶ column, pillar, support, buttress, upright, pile

pierce VERB
a spear that could pierce the thickest armour
▶ penetrate, puncture, perforate, make a hole in, probe, enter, transfix, impale

piercing ADJECTIVE
1 *From the wood comes a piercing screech.*
▶ shrill, sharp, penetrating, shattering, ear-splitting, high-pitched, strident, deafening, loud
2 *a piercing wind*
▶ freezing, bitter, biting, wintry, stinging
3 *a piercing pain*
▶ stabbing, intense, excruciating, agonizing, stinging

piety NOUN
a priest respected for his piety
▶ devoutness, devotion, piousness, holiness, godliness, saintliness, sanctity, religion, faith
AN OPPOSITE IS impiety

pig NOUN
1 *(informal) He was always a bit of a pig when it came to food.*
▶ glutton, guzzler, gourmand, (*informal*) greedy guts
2 *Her husband can be a real pig at times.*
▶ brute, monster, beast, fiend, animal, demon

pile NOUN
1 *a pile of stones*
▶ heap, stack, mass, mound, mountain, collection, hoard
2 *We have piles of work to do.*
▶ plenty, a lot, a great deal, (*more informal*) lots, (*more informal*) masses, (*more informal*) heaps

pile VERB
They piled everything into a corner.
▶ heap, stack, pack, jam, accumulate, amass, load, mass, store, collect, gather, hoard
pile up *Problems were beginning to pile up*
▶ build up, mount up, increase, grow, accumulate

pilfer VERB
People were pilfering bricks from building sites.
▶ steal, take, snatch, pinch, filch, (*more informal*) swipe, (*more informal*) nick, (*more informal*) knock off

pillar NOUN
A row of pillars supports the roof.
▶ column, pier, support, buttress, upright, pile

pillow NOUN
She rested her head on a pillow.
▶ cushion, bolster, headrest, pad

pilot NOUN
1 *the pilot of an aircraft*
▶ airman or airwoman, (*old-fashioned*) aviator
2 *a harbour pilot*
▶ navigator, helmsman, steersman, coxswain, guide

pilot ADJECTIVE
a pilot scheme
▶ experimental, trial, test, sample, model

pilot VERB
He piloted the little plane to the island.
▶ fly, guide, lead, navigate, steer, direct, drive

pimple NOUN
a face covered in pimples
▶ spot, blackhead, swelling, (*more informal*) zit

pin NOUN
The notice was attached by a pin.
▶ tack, nail, spike, brad, skewer

pin VERB
She pinned a badge on him
▶ fasten, attach, fix, stick

pinch VERB
1 *She pinched his arm.*
▶ nip, squeeze, crush, tweak
2 *Someone has pinched my pen.*
▶ steal, take, pilfer, snatch, filch, (*more informal*) swipe, (*more informal*) nick, (*more informal*) knock off

pine VERB
He thinks you were pining from love.
▶ languish, wither, fade, droop, sicken
pine for *The Smiths were pining for their home.*
▶ long for, yearn for, hanker after, miss, crave

pinnacle NOUN
1 *This win marked the pinnacle of her career in athletics.*
▶ peak, climax, height, highest point, summit, zenith, acme, apex, top
OPPOSITES ARE nadir, trough
2 *tall pinnacles of rock*
▶ peak, spire, steeple, turret, crest

a b c d e f g h i j k l m n o p q r s t u v w x y z

pinpoint VERB
Black boxes in trains can pinpoint the cause of accidents.
▶ identify, determine, discover, distinguish, locate, detect, track down

pioneer NOUN
1 *pioneers of the American West*
▶ settler, colonist, colonizer, discoverer, explorer
2 *a pioneer of birth control*
▶ developer, innovator, originator, pathfinder, groundbreaker

pioneer VERB
a scientist who pioneered genetic fingerprinting
▶ develop, introduce, evolve, create, discover, invent, originate, initiate, spearhead

pious ADJECTIVE
1 *His second wife was a remarkably pious woman.*
▶ religious, devout, devoted, spiritual, dutiful
OPPOSITES ARE impious, irreligious
2 *The remark was no more than a pious platitude.*
▶ sanctimonious, insincere, self-righteous
AN OPPOSITE IS sincere

pipe NOUN
a water pipe
▶ duct, channel, tube, conduit, hose, pipeline

pipe VERB
The liquid is piped into containers.
▶ channel, funnel, siphon, carry, run

pipe down (*informal*) *He got annoyed and told them to pipe down.*
▶ be quiet, be silent, quieten down, stop talking, hush

pique NOUN
He walked out in a fit of pique
▶ irritation, annoyance, anger, displeasure, petulance, exasperation

pirate NOUN
Pirates attacked the ship.
▶ marauder, privateer, (*historical*) buccaneer, (*old-fashioned*) corsair

pirate VERB
A large number of CDs are pirated.
▶ plagiarize, copy illegally, poach

pit NOUN
1 *A deep pit had been dug in the ground.*
▶ hole, ditch, trench, shaft, hollow, depression, trough, cavity, chasm, abyss
2 *increasing pit closures*
▶ mine, coal mine, colliery, quarry, shaft, working

pitch NOUN
1 *Their voices rose in pitch with the excitement.*
▶ tone, timbre, key, modulation
2 *His anger reached such a pitch that he became almost violent.*
▶ level, point, height, degree, intensity

3 *the pitch of the roof*
▶ steepness, angle, gradient, incline, slope, slant, tilt
4 *The referee ordered the players off the pitch.*
▶ playing field, field, park, ground

pitch VERB
1 *This is where we pitch our tents for the night.*
▶ put up, raise, fix, erect, set up
2 *She picked up the ball and pitched it into the neighbouring garden.*
▶ throw, fling, toss, hurl, lob, sling, bowl, heave, cast, (*more informal*) bung, (*more informal*) chuck
3 *Several lads pitched into the water.*
▶ plunge, dive, plummet, drop, topple
4 *The boat was pitching in the storm.*
▶ lurch, toss, wallow, rock, roll, reel, flounder, dip up and down

pitch in *Everyone needs to pitch in to get the work done.*
▶ help out, lend a hand, do your bit

piteous ADJECTIVE
She gave a long piteous cry.
▶ plaintive, mournful, pathetic, pitiful, pitiable, sad, sorrowful, wretched, touching, affecting, distressing, heartbreaking, heartrending

pitfall NOUN
Drama producers no longer need to fear the pitfalls of live television.
▶ hazard, snag, trap, danger, peril, snare, difficulty, drawback, catch

pitiful ADJECTIVE
1 *She was a pitiful sight, still lying where she had fallen.*
▶ sad, pathetic, pitiable, sorrowful, wretched, touching, affecting, distressing, heartbreaking, heartrending
2 *He trudged off with the pitiful few pounds he had made that day.*
▶ meagre, negligible, paltry, miserable, modest, scanty, scant, sparse, (*more informal*) mingy, (*more informal*) measly
OPPOSITES ARE generous, extravagant

pitiless ADJECTIVE
Dinah did not break under the pitiless criticism.
▶ merciless, relentless, ruthless, unrelenting, callous, cruel, hard, heartless, inexorable, unfeeling
OPPOSITES ARE merciful, compassionate

pittance NOUN
She cleaned people's houses for a pittance.
▶ crumb, tiny sum, (*more informal*) peanuts

pitted ADJECTIVE
a pitted surface
▶ scarred, uneven, marked, pockmarked, blemished, rough
AN OPPOSITE IS smooth

pity NOUN
1 *He had never felt pity for anyone in his life.*
▶ compassion, sympathy, commiseration, tenderness, understanding, feeling, forbearance, mercy, forgiveness, humanity, kindness
OPPOSITES ARE indifference, animosity
2 **a pity** *It's a pity it was dark and we couldn't see the garden.*
▶ a shame, unfortunate, a piece of bad luck, a cause for regret

pity VERB
He always pitied people who had to ask for money.
▶ feel sorry for, feel pity for, feel for, sympathize with, commiserate with, take pity on

pivot NOUN
The weight turns on a pivot.
▶ axis, axle, fulcrum, spindle, linchpin, centre, swivel, hub

pivot VERB
She watched as Leo pivoted on one foot.
▶ swivel, rotate, turn, swing, spin, twirl, whirl, revolve

placate VERB
He was placated by a glass of beer that was put before him.
▶ pacify, calm, appease, mollify, soothe, win over, conciliate, assuage

place NOUN
1 *She rose quietly from her place at the table.*
▶ seat, chair, position, space
2 *They would choose a foreign place for their next holiday.*
▶ locality, region, resort, city, town, village
3 *'Seaview' is the ideal place to write and work quietly.*
▶ spot, locale, location, venue, point
4 *They badly wanted a place of their own.*
▶ home, house, residence, dwelling, property, flat, apartments, establishment, accommodation
5 *She was offered a place on the company's board.*
▶ position, post, appointment, situation
6 *I know my place and won't interfere.*
▶ status, position, station, standing, rank
in place of *The bed was supported by a pile of books in place of a missing leg.*
▶ instead of, in lieu of, as a replacement for, as a substitute for
out of place *a remark that seemed out of place*
▶ inappropriate, unsuitable, improper, unseemly, unbecoming
take place *The competition will take place next month.*
▶ happen, occur, be held, come about

place VERB
1 *He placed the shopping on the table.*
▶ put, set, lay, deposit, leave, (*more informal*) stick, (*more informal*) dump, (*more informal*) plonk
2 *The judges placed her second overall.*
▶ rank, grade, position
3 *The face was familiar but I couldn't quite place it.*
▶ recognize, identify, remember

placid ADJECTIVE
1 *My normally placid father became a raging bull.*
▶ even-tempered, calm, equable, tranquil, collected, composed, level-headed, self-possessed, imperturbable, unruffled, gentle, mild, cool, unexcitable, phlegmatic
AN OPPOSITE IS excitable
2 *a four-mile stretch of placid water*
▶ calm, quiet, tranquil, peaceful, unruffled, undisturbed, motionless
OPPOSITES ARE stormy, rough

plagiarize VERB
She accused him of plagiarizing the results of her research.
▶ copy, pirate, steal, poach, reproduce, (*more informal*) lift, (*more informal*) crib

plague NOUN
1 *a study of the effects of the plague on two major cities*
▶ pestilence, blight, epidemic, contagion, infestation, outbreak
2 *a plague of flies*
▶ infestation, invasion, nuisance, scourge, swarm
3 *the plague of street crime in the area*
▶ curse, blight, bane, scourge, affliction, cancer

plague VERB
1 *The fears which had menaced her before returned to plague her.*
▶ afflict, bedevil, beset, torment, hound, torture, persecute
2 *He was being plagued with questions.*
▶ pester, badger, harass, trouble, annoy, bother, disturb, irritate, molest, vex, worry, (*more informal*) nag

plain ADJECTIVE
1 *The forms are written in plain English.*
▶ clear, simple, straightforward, understandable, intelligible, direct
OPPOSITES ARE obscure, unclear
2 *It was plain that someone had been in the house before them.*
▶ obvious, clear, evident, apparent, manifest
3 *They thought some plain speaking was needed.*
▶ frank, candid, outspoken, blunt, direct, explicit, unequivocal
4 *The house had a rather plain appearance.*
▶ unattractive, ordinary, unprepossessing, ugly
AN OPPOSITE IS attractive
5 *The room was decorated in a plain style.*
▶ simple, basic, restrained, unadorned, unembellished, unelaborate, unpretentious
OPPOSITES ARE elaborate, fancy

plain NOUN
the movement of wildebeest across the plains of Africa
▶ grassland, flatland, prairie, savannah, steppe, prairie

plain ADVERB

Many people are just plain scared of making the change.
▶ downright, completely, totally, utterly, really, thoroughly, absolutely, simply

plaintive ADJECTIVE

the faint, plaintive wail of her two-month-old baby
▶ sad, mournful, sorrowful, piteous, pitiful, doleful, melancholy, wistful

plan NOUN

1 *(informal) a plan of the building*
▶ chart, diagram, map, layout, blueprint, representation
2 *a clever plan for raising money*
▶ scheme, idea, proposal, project, programme, strategy, suggestion, proposition

plan VERB

1 *She began planning tomorrow's journey.*
▶ organize, arrange, work out, think out, prepare
2 *some tips for anyone planning a new garden*
▶ design, devise, contrive, sketch out
3 *We plan to go abroad this year.*
▶ intend, propose, aim, mean, envisage, contemplate, be thinking of

USAGE If you use any of the last three synonyms, you need to say *going* instead of *to go*, e.g. *We envisage going abroad this year.*

plane NOUN

1 *The plane rose gently in the air.*
▶ aeroplane, aircraft, jet, airliner, craft
2 *The thought that came to her now was on a more creative plane.*
▶ level, stage, degree, position

planet NOUN

the population of the planet
▶ globe, world, orb

PLANETS OF THE SOLAR SYSTEM (SHOWN WITH INCREASING DISTANCE FROM THE SUN)

Mercury, Venus, Earth, Mars, Jupiter, Saturn, Uranus, Neptune.

plank NOUN

a plank of wood
▶ board, floorboard, beam, timber

plant NOUN

1 **plants**
▶ greenery, growth, flora, undergrowth, vegetation
2 *industrial plant*
▶ machinery, machines, equipment, apparatus
3 *a plant of British intelligence*
▶ informer, informant, spy, agent, infiltrator, mole   ▶▶

USAGE Many plants produce flowers or cones in which seeds form. Some of the simpler ones do not have seeds; instead they reproduce with tiny objects called spores. There are several large groups of plants, examples of which are given below.

NAMES FOR TYPES OF PLANTS

flowering plants (having flowers and seeds; fruit and vegetables come from these): apple, ash, bluebell, buttercup, carnation, chrysanthemum, cornflower, cowslip, crocus, daffodil, daisy, dandelion, forget-me-not, foxglove, geranium, hollyhock, hyacinth, iris, lilac, lupin, marigold, oak, orchid, pansy, pear, peony, plum, poppy, primrose, rose, strawberry, sunflower, tulip, vegetables, violet, wallflower, water-lily.

coniferous (cone-bearing) plants: fir, juniper, larch, monkey puzzle, pine, redwood, spruce, yew.

flowerless plants (reproducing with spores) : algae (seaweeds and other simple water plants); mosses, liverworts; ferns, horsetails.

plant VERB

1 *Plant the seeds in September.*
▶ sow, bury, set out, put in the ground
2 *Someone had planted the idea in her mind.*
▶ put, establish, introduce, fix, lodge, impress, instil, imprint

plaster NOUN

1 *He stripped the wall down to the plaster.*
▶ plasterwork, mortar, stucco
2 *A nurse put a plaster on the cut.*
▶ dressing, sticking plaster, bandage

plaster VERB

The floor was plastered with mud.
▶ cover, daub, coat, smother, smear, spread

plastic ADJECTIVE

They were drinking warm beer from plastic tumblers.
▶ PVC, polystyrene, polyurethane, celluloids

plate NOUN

1 *She helped herself to a plate of food.*
▶ dish, platter, dinner plate, plateful, helping, serving, portion, bowl
2 *Someone had removed the plates from the end of the book.*
▶ illustration, picture, print, photograph, lithograph
3 *There was a brass plate by the front door.*
▶ plaque, nameplate, sign

platform NOUN

1 *A speaker addressed the audience from the platform.*
▶ dais, rostrum, podium, stand, stage
2 *the Liberal Democrats' election platform*
▶ policy, programme, manifesto, plan, party line

platitude NOUN

She ignored the somewhat patronizing platitude.
▶ commonplace, banality, truism, cliché, chestnut

plausible ADJECTIVE
1 *He knew he had presented a plausible explanation.*
▶ credible, reasonable, believable, convincing, persuasive, tenable, likely, feasible, probable, possible, acceptable, conceivable
AN OPPOSITE IS implausible
2 *He had the sort of plausible charm that Georgina was wary of.*
▶ smooth, smooth-talking, glib, specious

play NOUN
1 *a balance between work and play*
▶ amusement, entertainment, relaxation, recreation, enjoyment, leisure, pleasure, diversion, fun
2 *a play by Shakespeare*
▶ drama, theatrical work, stage play, tragedy, comedy, production, performance, show
3 *There was some play in the mechanism.*
▶ movement, freedom of movement, looseness, flexibility, latitude, leeway

play VERB
1 *The children were playing in the garden.*
▶ amuse yourself, have fun, enjoy yourself, play games, romp, frolic, caper
2 *I enjoy playing indoor sports.*
▶ take part in, engage in, participate in, join in, compete in
3 *The two sides play each other next week.*
▶ compete against, take on, challenge, oppose, vie with
4 *We need someone to play Hamlet.*
▶ act, perform, portray, act the part of, play the part of, take the role of
5 *He regretted not being able to play a musical instrument.*
▶ perform on, make music on
play down *The Government played down the effect of the tax increases.*
▶ minimize, make light of, gloss over, underplay
OPPOSITES ARE exaggerate, play up
play on *advertising that plays on people's anxieties*
▶ exploit, take advantage of, make use of, capitalize on, trade on
play up *Some of the children began to play up.*
▶ misbehave, behave badly, be naughty, cause trouble

playboy NOUN
Maria realized that she had married an unreliable playboy.
▶ womanizer, philanderer, ladies' man, libertine, rake

player NOUN
1 *The team has bought some new players.*
▶ team member, sportsman or sportswoman, competitor, contestant
2 *players on stage*
▶ actor or actress, performer, artist, entertainer
3 *players in an orchestra*
▶ musician, performer, instrumentalist, soloist, artist

playful ADJECTIVE
1 *She came back from the party in a playful mood.*
▶ frisky, lively, jolly, spirited
2 *a few playful remarks*
▶ light-hearted, joking, teasing, jocular, frivolous

playground NOUN
a playground behind the school
▶ play area, recreation ground, amusement park

playing field NOUN
The train passed a playing field where a game was going on.
▶ sports ground, ground, pitch, recreation ground

playwright NOUN
an Elizabethan playwright
▶ dramatist, writer, tragedian

plea NOUN
1 *a plea for mercy*
▶ appeal, petition, request, entreaty, supplication, invocation, prayer
2 *His plea was that he had been ill.*
▶ claim, excuse, defence, justification, pretext

plead VERB
The prisoners pleaded for their lives.
▶ beg, implore, entreat, petition, request, solicit, appeal, ask, importune

pleasant ADJECTIVE
1 *It was a pleasant afternoon.*
▶ enjoyable, pleasing, agreeable, satisfying, delightful, lovely, nice
AN OPPOSITE IS unpleasant
2 *The assistants are all very pleasant.*
▶ friendly, agreeable, congenial, likeable, personable, good-humoured, nice
OPPOSITES ARE unpleasant, disagreeable

please VERB
1 *She did her best to please them.*
▶ make happy, satisfy, give pleasure to, gladden, gratify, amuse, content, delight, entertain
2 *Do what you please*
▶ want, like, wish, desire, feel like

pleased ADJECTIVE
We were so pleased to see you.
▶ happy, glad, delighted, satisfied, overjoyed, thrilled
OPPOSITES ARE displeased, annoyed

pleasing ADJECTIVES
a very pleasing result
▶ pleasant, agreeable, gratifying, satisfying, welcome, acceptable

pleasure NOUN
1 *She found great pleasure in fashionable clothes.*
▶ enjoyment, gratification, happiness, satisfaction, amusement, contentment, fulfilment, delight, comfort, entertainment, gladness, joy, solace
2 *the pleasures that children bring*
▶ joy, delight, enjoyment

a
b
c
d
e
f
g
h
i
j
k
l
m
n
o
p
q
r
s
t
u
v
w
x
y
z

pledge NOUN
1 *Labour's pledge to spend billions on education*
▶ promise, undertaking, assurance, commitment, guarantee
2 *She gave her rings as a pledge.*
▶ surety, security, bond, deposit, bail

pledge VERB
They all pledged their loyalty to the Queen.
▶ promise, swear, vow, guarantee, undertake

plentiful ADJECTIVE
a plentiful supply of fruit
▶ abundant, copious, ample, liberal, profuse, generous, lavish, rich, bountiful, prolific, inexhaustible
OPPOSITES ARE sparse, scarce

plenty NOUN
1 *a time of plenty*
▶ prosperity, wealth, affluence, opulence, luxury, well-being, comfort
2 **plenty of** *There is plenty of time before they arrive.*
▶ a lot of, a great deal of, much, enough, (*more informal*) lots of, (*more informal*) heaps of, (*more informal*) loads of, (*more informal*) masses of

pliable ADJECTIVE
1 *a pliable material*
▶ flexible, bendable, pliant, supple, plastic, springy, (*more informal*) bendy
AN OPPOSITE IS stiff
2 *a pliable mind*
▶ adaptable, impressionable, responsive, suggestible, compliant, flexible, tractable, biddable, accommodating
AN OPPOSITE IS rigid

plight NOUN
the plight of the homeless
▶ difficulty, predicament, danger, trouble, extremity, quandary, straits

plod VERB
1 *Mary plodded up the path.*
▶ trudge, tramp, lumber, stomp
2 *It will take hours to plod through the whole book.*
▶ plough, wade, trawl, labour, persevere, grind on

plot NOUN
1 *He grew vegetables in a plot behind the house.*
▶ piece of ground, patch, allotment, smallholding, lot
2 *The novel has a complicated plot.*
▶ storyline, story, outline, action, thread, scenario, narrative
3 *A plot was revealed against the government.*
▶ conspiracy, intrigue, plan, scheme, cabal, machination

plot VERB
1 *The president's brother was plotting his downfall.*
▶ plan, scheme, concoct, devise, hatch
2 *He was accused of plotting against the government.*
▶ conspire, scheme, intrigue
3 *They plotted their course on the map.*
▶ chart, mark, map

plough VERB
1 *Farmers ploughed the fields.*
▶ cultivate, till, work, turn over
2 *A van had ploughed into a shop window.*
▶ plunge, crash, career, smash, bulldoze

ploy NOUN
It was just a ploy to get rid of Doreen.
▶ trick, ruse, move, device, stratagem, manoeuvre

pluck NOUN
It must have taken a lot of pluck to walk along a path marked 'danger'.
▶ courage, daring, nerve, audacity, boldness, heroism, (*more informal*) bottle, (*more informal*) grit, (*more informal*) guts

pluck VERB
1 *She began to pluck hairs off her skirt.*
▶ pick, pull, take off, snatch
2 *He sang and plucked a guitar.*
▶ pick, twang, strum, finger
3 *The girls stood plucking fruit from the trees.*
▶ pick, gather, collect, harvest, garner

plucky ADJECTIVE
a plucky young woman's tale of escape
▶ brave, courageous, bold, daring, intrepid, valiant, resolute
OPPOSITES ARE timid, cowardly

plug NOUN
1 *He put a plug in the top of the bottle.*
▶ stopper, cork, bung
2 (*informal*) *They put in a plug for their new song.*
▶ advertisement, piece of publicity, mention, (*informal*) puff, (*informal*) boost

plumb ADVERB
The arrow hit the target plumb in the middle.
▶ exactly, precisely, dead, (*more informal*) slap

plumb VERB
They seem to have plumbed the depths of despair.
▶ penetrate, probe, sound, explore, measure

plummet VERB
A stone came loose and plummeted to the ground.
▶ plunge, fall, hurtle, drop, crash, dive

plump ADJECTIVE
a plump little boy
▶ chubby, podgy, tubby, fat, dumpy, rotund, round, overweight, stout, portly, pudgy
OPPOSITES ARE thin, slim, skinny

plump VERB
Jill plumped down on the sofa and fell asleep.
▶ sink, drop, flop, fall, collapse
plump for *I'm going to plump for the vegetarian meal.*
▶ choose, opt for, go for, pick, decide on

plunder VERB
Pirates plundered towns and villages near the coast.
▶ loot, pillage, raid, ransack, ravage, despoil, rifle, rob, sack, steal from

plunder NOUN
The army was bent on plunder and murder.
▶ looting, robbery, pillage, pillaging, marauding

plunge VERB
1 *The plane plunged to the ground.*
▶ dive, plummet, fall, hurtle, drop, crash, swoop, nosedive
2 *I plunged into the lake.*
▶ dive, leap, jump, throw yourself, hurl yourself
3 *He plunged the knife into the man's back.*
▶ thrust, force, stab, shove, stick, push
4 *She plunged a hand in the water.*
▶ dip, immerse, submerge, sink

poach VERB
The new company was poaching staff from its rivals.
▶ steal, purloin, filch, (*more informal*) pinch, (*more informal*) nick

pocket NOUN
There were some pockets of resistance to the new regime.
▶ area, patch, centre, cluster

pocket VERB
The management was accused of pocketing all the profits.
▶ take, steal, appropriate, help yourself to, take for yourself

podgy ADJECTIVE
She looked a bit podgy.
▶ plump, chubby, tubby, fat , dumpy, rotund, round, overweight, pudgy
OPPOSITES ARE thin, slim, skinny

---

poem NOUN
He read her some of his poems.
▶ verse, rhyme, poetry
NAMES FOR TYPES OF POEM
longer narrative poems: epic, ballad, lay, chanson.
poems for singing: chanson, madrigal, lay, dithyramb (ancient choral hymn), ballad.
laments: elegy.
short pastoral and romantic poems: eclogue, pastoral, georgic, idyll.
short poems and rhymes: lyric, ode, sonnet (of fourteen lines), nursery rhyme, epigram, limerick, clerihew, nonsense verse, lay.
Japanese poems: haiku, tanka.
NAMES FOR POETIC FEATURES
verse, stanza; rhyme, enjambement, free verse, rhythm, couplet, imagery, metre, alliteration (use of similar sounds at the beginning of a sequence of words), assonance (similarity of syllables in words, e.g. *stone* and *cold*), simile, metaphor; blank verse (without end-of-line rhymes), concrete poetry (with the meaning echoed by visual patterns in the words).

---

poet NOUN
She wrote stories and was a poet.
▶ writer of verse, rhymester, rhymer, lyricist, versifier, bard

poetic ADJECTIVE
poetic language
▶ expressive, lyrical, poetical, emotive, metrical, imaginative
AN OPPOSITE IS prosaic

poetry NOUN
a book of poetry
▶ poems, verses, rhymes

poignant ADJECTIVE
a poignant moment of farewell
▶ touching, moving, affecting, sad, tender, emotional, pitiful, pathetic, sorrowful

point NOUN
1 *the point of the needle*
▶ tip, end, sharp end, spike, extremity
2 *points of light*
▶ spot, speck, dot, fleck
3 *At this point, the door opened.*
▶ moment, instant, time, stage
4 *I wish they would get to the point.*
▶ essence, crux, meaning, thrust
5 *a few points of detail*
▶ detail, item, issue, factor, consideration, particular, facet, feature
6 *She admitted he had some good points*
▶ characteristic, feature, attribute, aspect, peculiarity, side
7 *There didn't seem much point in staying.*
▶ purpose, reason, object, aim, goal, advantage, benefit
8 *They could get on the train at a point further up the line.*
▶ place, position, location, spot, site, locality

point VERB
1 **point** or **point to** *An official pointed the way. He pointed to a picture on the stairs.*
▶ indicate, point out, draw attention to, show, signal
2 *She saw the man was pointing a gun at her.*
▶ aim, direct, level, train
3 *I'll point you in the right direction.*
▶ direct, guide, lead, steer

point-blank ADJECTIVE
1 *The gun was fired at point-blank range.*
▶ close
2 *Their request met with a point-blank refusal.*
▶ blunt, direct, straight, plain, frank, open, explicit, forthright

point-blank ADVERB
She told him point-blank that it was over.
▶ bluntly, directly, straight, straight out, frankly, openly, plainly, clearly, forthrightly

pointed ADJECTIVE
1 *He used the pointed end of a stick.*
▶ sharp, tapered, spiky

2 *Kathleen greeted this pointed remark with a smile.*
► cutting, biting, trenchant, caustic, acerbic, scathing, barbed, sharp, insinuating, hurtful
AN OPPOSITE IS bland

pointer NOUN
The pointer moved into 'danger'.
► needle, indicator, hand, arrow

pointless ADJECTIVE
The country was being dragged into a pointless military conflict. It was pointless to try to catch them now.
► futile, senseless, fruitless, useless, needless, vain, aimless, meaningless, unprofitable
OPPOSITES ARE useful, valuable

poise NOUN
Claudia admired her poise.
► calmness, composure, equanimity, aplomb, assurance, self-confidence, self-control, coolness, dignity, elegance, equilibrium

poised ADJECTIVE
1 *Both forces were poised to take the city.*
► prepared, ready, set, waiting, keyed up
2 *She gave a poised performance.*
► assured, self-assured, self-confident, dignified, composed, graceful, elegant

poison NOUN
1 *A gram of the poison is enough to kill a man.*
► toxin, venom
2 *a poison in society*
► blight, contamination, contagion, cancer

poison VERB
1 *The murderer had poisoned his victim.*
► kill
2 *Chemicals are poisoning the country's rivers.*
► pollute, contaminate, infect, foul, taint
3 *The media were accused of trying to poison people's minds.*
► prejudice, subvert, corrupt, embitter, colour, warp, affect, pervert

poisonous ADJECTIVE
1 *a poisonous insect*
► venomous, deadly, virulent
2 *a cloud of poisonous gases*
► toxic, lethal, noxious, fatal, mortal
3 *a poisonous remark*
► malicious, malevolent, hostile, vicious, spiteful, vitriolic

poke VERB
They poked burning sticks at him. He poked her with his elbow.
► prod, dig, jab, nudge, thrust, stab, shove, stick
poke about or **around** *Someone was poking about in the cupboard.*
► search, rummage, root around
poke fun at *They laughed and poked fun at him.*
► ridicule, mock, make fun of, jeer at
poke out *A hand was poking out of the back window.*
► protrude, stick out, jut out, peek, project

poke NOUN
Amy gave him a poke.
► prod, dig, jab, nudge, shove

poky ADJECTIVE
a poky room with one chair
► tiny, small, confined, cramped, uncomfortable, restrictive
AN OPPOSITE IS spacious

pole NOUN
1 *The fence was held up by a series of poles.*
► post, pillar, stake, stick, upright, support, shaft, spar
2 *Their opinions are at opposite poles.*
► extreme, extremity, limit
poles apart *Our political views are poles apart.*
► completely different, worlds apart, like chalk and cheese, irreconcilable, incompatible

police NOUN
The police soon arrived at the scene.
► police force, constabulary, (*more informal*) the Law, (*more informal*) the Fuzz, (*more informal*) the Bill

police VERB
It would be difficult to police such a large area
► control, supervise, watch over, monitor, patrol, keep in order, keep the peace at, provide a police presence at

policeman, policewoman NOUN
A policeman stood at the gate.
► police officer, officer, constable, (*more informal*) bobby, (*more informal*) cop, (*more informal*) copper

policy NOUN
1 *the school's policy on truancy*
► strategy, code of practice, code of conduct, approach (to), procedure
2 *It's always a good policy to read the instructions carefully.*
► practice, habit, custom, rule

polish VERB
I must polish my shoes.
► shine, brush up, clean, buff up, burnish, brighten, rub down, rub up, wax
polish off *The boys polished off a plate of burgers.*
► finish, eat up
polish up *She sat down to polish up her essay.*
► improve, refine, enhance, brush up

polish NOUN
1 *The table had a lovely bright polish.*
► shine, sheen, gloss, lustre, patina, finish
2 *His years abroad had given him polish.*
► refinement, sophistication, suavity, urbanity, class, finesse, grace, style, elegance

polished ADJECTIVE
1 *a polished table*
► shiny, shining, bright, glossy, gleaming, lustrous, burnished, glassy
OPPOSITES ARE dull, tarnished

2 *polished manners*
▶ refined, sophisticated, suave, urbane, polite, cultured, elegant, gracious, perfected, (*more informal*) posh
OPPOSITES ARE rough, crude
3 *a polished performance*
▶ accomplished, skilful, masterly, expert, flawless, faultless

polite ADJECTIVE
They were too polite to complain.
▶ well-mannered, courteous, respectful, civil, well behaved, considerate, cultivated
AN OPPOSITE IS rude

politics NOUN
Fiona took an interest in local politics.
▶ political affairs, government, political science, public affairs

poll NOUN
1 *There would have to be a second poll to decide the winner.*
▶ ballot, vote, election
2 *The store organized a poll to determine views on smoking.*
▶ survey, opinion poll, sampling, census, plebiscite, referendum

pollute VERB
Industrial waste has polluted the lake.
▶ contaminate, poison, taint, foul, defile, infect

pollution NOUN
pollution caused by city traffic
▶ contamination, impurity, poisoning, defilement, dirtiness, adulteration

pomp NOUN
He gave up the pomp of courtly life.
▶ splendour, magnificence, grandeur, ostentation, pageantry, ritual, solemnity, spectacle, ceremonial, ceremony, display, formality, show

pompous ADJECTIVE
He sounded so pompous I couldn't help giggling.
▶ self-important, grandiose, overbearing, haughty, arrogant, conceited, pretentious, puffed up, condescending, domineering
AN OPPOSITE IS modest

ponder VERB
ponder or **ponder about** *It was a good time to ponder the events of the last week.*
▶ consider, think about, contemplate, reflect on, meditate on, review, mull over

ponderous ADJECTIVE
He spoke in a slow ponderous way.
▶ clumsy, awkward, lumbering, cumbersome, ungainly
OPPOSITES ARE elegant, graceful

pool NOUN
1 *a pool of water*
▶ pond, puddle, lake, mere, tarn
2 *a pool of hire cars*
▶ supply, stock, reserve

pool VERB
They could buy more if they pooled their money.
▶ combine, amalgamate, put together, merge, share

poor ADJECTIVE
1 *The scheme was intended to rehouse poor families.*
▶ impoverished, poverty-stricken, badly off, impecunious, hard-up, destitute, penniless
OPPOSITES ARE rich, wealthy
2 *The workmanship was of poor quality.*
▶ inferior, substandard, deficient, defective, unsatisfactory, mediocre, second-rate, shoddy
OPPOSITES ARE superior, fine
3 *The poor man had to wait ten hours for a train.*
▶ unfortunate, unlucky, luckless, wretched, pitiful, unhappy
OPPOSITES ARE fortunate, lucky

poorly ADJECTIVE
She began to feel poorly in the taxi home.
▶ ill, unwell, sick, out of sorts, off colour, indisposed, ailing, peaky, queasy, nauseous

pop VERB
Corks were popping everywhere.
▶ crack, go bang, explode, go off, burst, snap

pop NOUN
the pop of an air rifle
▶ crack, bang, explosion, burst, snap

popular ADJECTIVE
1 *a popular student*
▶ well-liked, favoured, favourite, liked, admired, accepted
2 *a popular line in women's clothing*
▶ fashionable, modish, sought-after, well-known, current, (*more informal*) trendy

popularize VERB
1 *a campaign to popularize their new products*
▶ make popular, bring into vogue or fashion, promote, spread
2 *There are several good books that popularize the subject.*
▶ simplify, make accessible, make easy, present in a popular way, universalize

populate VERB
The island is populated mainly by visitors.
▶ inhabit, occupy, people, live in

population NOUN
the population of the country
▶ inhabitants, people, populace, residents, citizens, occupants, community

populous ADJECTIVE
the most populous city in the north
▶ densely or heavily populated, heavily settled, crowded, congested, populated

porch NOUN
He sat all day in a rocking chair in the porch.
▶ vestibule, entrance, entrance hall, lobby, portico, doorway

pore VERB
pore over *She was poring over a map of Greece.*
▶ study, peruse, scan, scrutinize, be absorbed in, be engrossed in

pornographic ADJECTIVE
a pornographic film
▶ obscene, indecent, lewd, erotic, titillating

porous ADJECTIVE
a porous substance
▶ permeable, pervious, absorbent, spongy, cellular, holey
AN OPPOSITE IS impermeable

port NOUN
A large liner had entered the port.
▶ harbour, seaport, marina, anchorage, dock, dockyard, haven

portable ADJECTIVE
a portable computer
▶ transportable, mobile, movable, lightweight, compact, easy to carry, handy, light, manageable, small

porter NOUN
1 *The apartment block had its own porter.*
▶ caretaker, doorkeeper, doorman, janitor, commissionaire, concierge
2 *A porter helped her with her luggage.*
▶ baggage-carrier, baggage-handler, baggage-attendant, bearer, carrier

portion NOUN
1 *a large portion of rice*
▶ helping, serving, plateful, bowlful, share, amount, ration, (*more informal*) dollop
2 *Use the rear portion of the train.*
▶ section, part, segment
3 *Her portion of the inheritance came to several millions.*
▶ share, allocation, quota, division, ration, percentage

portly ADJECTIVE
a portly figure in a dark suit
▶ stout, plump, podgy, tubby, fat, chubby, dumpy, rotund, round, overweight, pudgy
OPPOSITES ARE thin, slim, skinny

portrait NOUN
a portrait of the Prince Regent
▶ painting, picture, drawing, portrayal, depiction, representation, image, likeness

portray VERB
1 *The artist portrayed her in profile.*
▶ paint, draw, sketch, depict, show
2 *The novel portrays London life in Victorian England.*
▶ describe, depict, picture, characterize, represent, illustrate, show, delineate, evoke

pose VERB
1 *River levels pose a threat at this time of year.*
▶ present, constitute, create, produce

2 *The article poses a number of important questions.*
▶ raise, put forward, advance, offer, posit, broach, suggest
3 *She posed for a local artist on Saturday afternoons.*
▶ sit, model, be a model
4 *From his manner it was clear he was only posing.*
▶ pretend, put on an act, strike a pose, put on airs, feign, masquerade
5 **pose as** *He decided to pose as a police officer.*
▶ impersonate, pretend to be, masquerade as, pass yourself off as

pose NOUN
1 *a model in a suggestive pose*
▶ attitude, position
2 *His behaviour was only a pose.*
▶ pretence, act, affectation, façade, show, front, masquerade, posture

poser NOUN
1 (*informal*) *How to get home in time was a bit of a poser.*
▶ problem, difficulty, dilemma, puzzle
2 (*informal*) *The bar was full of posers showing off to the girls.*
▶ exhibitionist, poseur, (*informal*) phoney, (*informal*) pseud, (*informal*) show-off

posh ADJECTIVE
(*informal*) *The car was parked outside a posh hotel.*
▶ smart, stylish, high-class, luxury, luxurious, fashionable, elegant, plush, showy, (*informal*) classy, (*informal*) swanky, (*informal*) snazzy, (*informal*) swish

position NOUN
1 *The map shows the position of the house.*
▶ location, situation, setting, locality, site, point
2 *She rose to a standing position.*
▶ posture, pose, stance, attitude
3 *His lack of money left him in an awkward position.*
▶ situation, circumstances, predicament, plight
4 *They well knew their position in society.*
▶ status, standing, level, role, rank, grade
5 *advertisements for positions in banking*
▶ job, post, situation, appointment, vacancy
6 *the opposition's position on the war*
▶ point of view, viewpoint, attitude, policy, stand, standpoint, stance, outlook

position VERB
Chairs had been positioned along the walls.
▶ put, arrange, deploy, dispose, locate, place, settle, situate, stand, station

positive ADJECTIVE
1 *I was positive they would come back.*
▶ certain, sure, convinced, confident, satisfied, assured
OPPOSITES ARE uncertain, unsure
2 *The case lacked positive proof.*
▶ definite, conclusive, categorical, unequivocal, incontrovertible, irrefutable, indisputable, clear, explicit
OPPOSITES ARE doubtful, unclear

P

3 *The criticism was positive.*
► helpful, constructive, practical, useful
AN OPPOSITE IS negative
4 *a positive advantage*
► definite, conclusive, clear, unmistakable, emphatic, unequivocal, undeniable
AN OPPOSITE IS vague
5 *a positive attitude*
► optimistic, confident, hopeful, assured
AN OPPOSITE IS pessimistic
6 *The journey was a positive nightmare.*
► absolute, utter, complete, sheer, perfect

possess VERB
1 *The family possessed a house in France.*
► own, have, be in possession of
2 *Foreign armies possessed the country*
► seize, occupy, take over, acquire, control, dominate, govern, rule
3 *A strange feeling possessed him.*
► preoccupy, obsess, dominate, haunt, consume

possession NOUN
1 *She came into possession of the fortune.*
► ownership, control, title, tenure, custody
2 **possessions** *She put her few possessions in the van.*
► belongings, things, property, chattels, effects, assets, goods, bits and pieces

possessive ADJECTIVE
He was very possessive and grew angry when she wanted to leave.
► jealous, overprotective, proprietorial, clinging, domineering, selfish

possibility NOUN
1 *There was still a possibility they might come.*
► chance, likelihood, probability, prospect, hope, fear
2 *the possibility of starting their own business*
► feasibility, practicality, capability, potentiality
3 *They even considered the possibility of going to war.*
► option, alternative, choice

possible ADJECTIVE
1 *An improvement next year might be possible.*
► feasible, practicable, achievable, attainable, viable, workable
AN OPPOSITE IS impossible
2 *There is another possible explanation.*
► conceivable, imaginable, plausible, likely, believable, tenable, credible
OPPOSITES ARE unlikely, inconceivable
3 *He is regarded as a possible party leader.*
► potential, prospective, probable, promising, likely
OPPOSITES ARE unlikely, improbable

possibly ADVERB
1 *Possibly Jane will be there too.*
► maybe, perhaps, conceivably
2 *Could you possibly bring some food?*
► by any chance, conceivably, at all

post NOUN
1 *a flat roof supported by wooden posts*
► pole, pillar, stake, stick, upright, support, shaft, spar
2 *The post hasn't come yet.*
► mail, letters, delivery
3 *The post will be advertised in the local newspaper.*
► job, position, situation, appointment, vacancy

post VERB
1 *An announcement had been posted on all notice boards.*
► display, pin up, put up, stick up, advertise, announce
2 *I must go and post a letter.*
► mail, send, dispatch, put in the post, send off, get off

poster NOUN
He collects old film posters.
► notice, placard, display, sign, bill, sticker, advertisement, announcement, playbill

posterity NOUN
Everything that happened has been recorded for posterity.
► future generations, the future, descendants, heirs, offspring, successors

postpone VERB
The game was postponed for a fortnight.
► put off, defer, delay, put back, adjourn, hold over, suspend, put on ice

posture NOUN
He bent his head forward in a posture of respect.
► position, stance, pose, attitude, bearing, deportment

posy NOUN
a posy of violets and freesias
► bouquet, bunch, spray, nosegay, buttonhole, corsage

pot NOUN
a pot of stew
► pan, saucepan, vessel, casserole, cauldron, stewpot, stockpot, crock, urn

potent ADJECTIVE
1 *a potent drug*
► strong, powerful, pungent, intoxicating
2 *a potent influence*
► strong, powerful, vigorous, compelling, impressive, dominant, overpowering, weighty

potential ADJECTIVE
a potential cause of trouble
► probable, likely, imminent, impending, prospective, latent, dormant, possible, promising, budding, embryonic, future

potential NOUN
The area has great potential for industrial expansion.
► possibilities, capacity, capability, scope, prospects, promise

a b c d e f g h i j k l m n o **p** q r s t u v w x y z

potion NOUN
a love potion
▶ mixture, concoction, draught, elixir, brew, dose, drug, philtre, tonic

potter VERB
potter about or **around** *I love pottering around the house.*
▶ mess about or around, amuse yourself, pass time

pottery NOUN
a sale of local pottery
▶ ceramics, earthenware, porcelain, stoneware, china, crockery

potty ADJECTIVE
1 (*informal*) *Maybe I'm going potty.*
▶ mad, insane, crazy, (*informal*) round the bend, (*informal*) bonkers
2 **potty about** *She's potty about her two sons.*
▶ devoted to, infatuated with, smitten with, mad about, crazy about

pounce VERB
pounce on *The animal pounced on its prey.*
▶ jump on, spring on, leap on, swoop on, bound at, lunge at, attack, ambush

pound VERB
1 *Hans pounded his huge fists on the desk and glared.*
▶ beat, strike, thump, thud, batter, bang, bash
2 **pound on** *He pounded on the gates, shouting wildly.*
▶ batter, beat, thump, pummel, bang on, strike, hit
3 *Her heart was pounding.*
▶ throb, pulsate, thump, thud, race
4 *Pound the garlic with a little salt.*
▶ crush, grind, powder, mash, pulverize

pour VERB
1 *Blood poured from his wound.*
▶ spill, issue, stream, run, discharge, flow, gush, spout
2 *She poured milk from the jug.*
▶ serve, tip, decant

pout VERB
Carrie pouted, complaining that she had been left out.
▶ sulk, pull a face, look petulant, scowl, mope

poverty NOUN
The region suffered from years of poverty.
▶ want, penury, privation, destitution, hardship, shortage, need, necessity
AN OPPOSITE IS wealth

powdery ADJECTIVE
a white powdery deposit
▶ dusty, sandy, grainy, chalky, crumbly, fine, granular, loose, pulverized

power NOUN
1 *His father had a stroke and lost the power of speech.*
▶ faculty, property, capability, capacity, ability, competence
2 *Who knows where the real power lies.*
▶ control, authority, influence, dominance, mastery, domination

3 *The governor has the power to impose a curfew.*
▶ right, prerogative, authorization, authority
4 *a speech of great power*
▶ force, strength, potency, vigour, intensity, energy
AN OPPOSITE IS weakness

powerful ADJECTIVE
1 *a powerful blow*
▶ violent, hard, strong, forceful
AN OPPOSITE IS weak
2 *a powerful ruler*
▶ strong, dominant, commanding, forceful, vigorous, effective
OPPOSITES ARE weak, ineffective
3 *a powerful physique*
▶ strong, muscular, sturdy, hefty, mighty, solid, burly
OPPOSITES ARE weak, puny
4 *a powerful argument*
▶ strong, convincing, compelling, cogent, overwhelming
OPPOSITES ARE weak, unconvincing

powerless ADJECTIVE
1 *We felt powerless in the face of such determination.*
▶ helpless, impotent, ineffectual, ineffective, incapable, defenceless, feeble, weak
OPPOSITES ARE powerful, strong
2 *The police were powerless to act.*
▶ unable, incapable (of acting), without power

practicable ADJECTIVE
Such a detailed plan would not be practicable.
▶ realistic, feasible, viable, workable, achievable, attainable, possible, sensible, practical
OPPOSITES ARE impracticable, impractical

practical ADJECTIVE
1 *You need practical experience of the work before you apply for the job.*
▶ real, actual, hands-on, empirical, relevant
AN OPPOSITE IS theoretical
2 *We can't think of any practical alternatives.*
▶ workable, feasible, realistic, viable, reasonable, sensible, possible, achievable
AN OPPOSITE IS impractical
3 *Let's be practical and not try far-fetched ideas.*
▶ sensible, realistic, pragmatic, down-to-earth, commonsensical, hard-headed
AN OPPOSITE IS impractical
4 *a cute little gadget that is also practical*
▶ handy, functional, useful, serviceable, utilitarian
OPPOSITES ARE impractical, useless

practically ADVERB
The place was practically deserted.
▶ almost, nearly, virtually, just about, more or less, close to

practice NOUN
1 *It has become a common practice to use robots to disarm devices.*
▶ custom, procedure, convention, policy, routine, method, system
2 *It takes a lot of practice to play that well.*
▶ training, rehearsal, preparation, exercise, drill

3 *He was better at the theory than the practice of medicine.*
▶ use, application, exercise, execution, implementation
4 in practice *The idea is good but probably won't work in practice.*
▶ in real life, for real, in reality, in actuality, in effect, in operation

practise VERB
1 *They practised these pieces for weeks.*
▶ do exercises, drill, exercise, prepare, rehearse, train, warm up
2 *These customs are still practised in some parts of the world.*
▶ follow, carry out, perform, put into practice, observe, apply, engage in

pragmatic ADJECTIVE
a pragmatic approach to the problem
▶ practical, sensible, realistic, down-to-earth, commonsensical, hard-headed
AN OPPOSITE IS impractical

praise VERB
1 *The judge praised her for her bravery.*
▶ commend, applaud, pay tribute to, express approval of, compliment, congratulate, admire, acclaim, acknowledge, eulogize
2 *They praised God for the good harvest.*
▶ worship, glorify, honour, exalt, adore

praise NOUN
1 *The rescue services deserve all our praise.*
▶ approval, acclaim, admiration, commendation, applause, adulation, recognition, tribute
2 *Give praise to God.*
▶ homage, honour, worship, thanks, thanksgiving, glory, adoration

praiseworthy ADJECTIVE
a praiseworthy attempt to put things right
▶ commendable, laudable, admirable, creditable, worthy, estimable, exemplary, deserving, honourable, meritorious
OPPOSITES ARE deplorable, blameworthy

prance VERB
James was prancing about wrapped in a towel.
▶ dance, cavort, romp, jump, leap, skip, hop, frolic, gambol

prank NOUN
It had been a prank that had gone tragically wrong.
▶ trick, practical joke, escapade, game, hoax, stunt, (*more informal*) lark

pray VERB
pray to *The village prayed to God for a good harvest.*
▶ ask, beg, call upon, entreat, beseech, invoke, supplicate, say prayers to

prayer NOUN
The priest murmured some prayers.
▶ invocation, devotion, supplication, entreaty

preach VERB
1 *The bishop will preach in the cathedral.*
▶ give or deliver a sermon, speak
2 *We try to preach tolerance.*
▶ teach, advocate, urge, recommend, champion
3 preach to *You are in no position to preach to us about honesty.*
▶ moralize to, pontificate to, lecture, harangue

precarious ADJECTIVE
The cliff walk looked more and more precarious.
▶ dangerous, risky, insecure, shaky, unstable, unsteady, vulnerable, wobbly, uncertain, perilous, rocky, unsafe
OPPOSITES ARE secure, safe

precaution NOUN
As an extra precaution, tell a neighbour when you are going to be away.
▶ safeguard, safety measure, insurance, protection, defence, provision

precede VERB
1 *Three months of advertising preceded the launch of the new models.*
▶ come before, go before, lead up to, pave the way for, usher in
2 *He preceded his speech with an announcement.*
▶ preface, introduce, open, prefix, start, lead into
AN OPPOSITE IS follow

precedent NOUN
They were reluctant to give way because it might create a precedent.
▶ pattern, model, standard, example, previous instance

precinct NOUN
These streets now form a pedestrian precinct.
▶ area, zone, sector, quarter, region

precious ADJECTIVE
1 *a collection of precious paintings*
▶ valuable, priceless, choice, costly, inestimable, rare
2 *The ring was her most precious possession.*
▶ treasured, cherished, valued, prized, favourite, dearest, beloved
3 *This action gained them a few precious minutes.*
▶ valuable, priceless, vital

precipitate VERB
The police action precipitated a riot.
▶ cause, spark off, trigger off, induce, occasion, bring on, encourage

précis NOUN
a précis of the story
▶ summary, synopsis, resumé, outline, abstract, abridgement, short version

precise ADJECTIVE
1 *I don't know the precise time. Here are the precise measurements of the room.*
▶ exact, accurate, correct, detailed, definite
OPPOSITES ARE imprecise, approximate, rough

2 *The train stopped at that precise moment.*
▶ exact, particular, specific, actual
3 *The workmanship is very precise.*
▶ careful, meticulous, exact, detailed, finicky, punctilious, scrupulous
AN OPPOSITE IS careless

precisely ADVERB
1 *The plane took off at three o'clock precisely.*
▶ exactly, on the dot, promptly
2 *The house is precisely what we are looking for.*
▶ exactly, absolutely, entirely, altogether, in every way

precocious ADJECTIVE
From an early age he showed a precocious talent for computing.
▶ advanced, clever, gifted, talented, forward, mature, quick
OPPOSITES ARE backward, slow

predecessor NOUN
1 *a programme about our Victorian predecessors*
▶ ancestor, forerunner, forefather, forebear
AN OPPOSITE IS descendant
2 *The Prime Minister learned from his predecessor's mistakes.*
▶ precursor, forerunner, antecedent
AN OPPOSITE IS successor

predicament NOUN
Can't you see the predicament I'm in?
▶ difficulty, dilemma, mess, crisis, plight, quandary, jam, embarrassment, emergency, (*more informal*) pickle, (*more informal*) spot, (*more informal*) hole, (*more informal*) corner

predict VERB
The polls predicted a landslide victory.
▶ forecast, prophesy, foretell, foresee, divine, forewarn, anticipate, envisage

predictable ADJECTIVE
David's reaction was entirely predictable.
▶ foreseeable, to be expected, likely, probable, certain
AN OPPOSITE IS unpredictable

prediction NOUN
A little later, the prediction came true.
▶ prophecy, forecast, conjecture, prognosis

predominant ADJECTIVE
The predominant feeling was one of relief.
▶ chief, main, principal, overriding, primary, prime

predominantly ADVERB
The guests in the hotel were predominantly American.
▶ chiefly, mainly, primarily, principally, mostly, especially, essentially

predominate VERB
Bright colours predominate in these designs.
▶ dominate, prevail, preponderate, be in the majority, be most common, outnumber

pre-eminent ADJECTIVE
Spain was then the pre-eminent power in Europe.
▶ leading, foremost, greatest, chief, principal, major

prefer VERB
1 *I prefer tea thanks.*
▶ like better, would rather have, favour, go for, opt for, plump for
2 prefer to *We'd prefer to travel by car.*
▶ would rather, would sooner, would like better

preferable ADJECTIVE
Many people find self-catering preferable.
▶ better, more suitable, advantageous, more desirable, superior, nicer, advisable, preferred
OPPOSITES ARE disadvantageous, undesirable

preference NOUN
1 *Our preference is for winter holidays.*
▶ liking, choice, inclination, option, partiality, predilection, leaning, wish, fancy
2 *Preference will be given to applicants with a foreign language.*
▶ precedence, priority, favour, advantage

preferential ADJECTIVE
I'm not asking for preferential treatment, only what I deserve.
▶ special, better, favoured, privileged, advantageous

pregnant ADJECTIVE
It is probably best to cut out alcohol altogether when pregnant.
▶ expecting a baby, carrying a child, expectant, (*more informal*) expecting

prehistoric ADJECTIVE
Stonehenge is a unique and powerful prehistoric monument.
▶ ancient, early, primitive
USAGE Note that *prehistoric* strictly refers to ancient times before there were written records. It is best to avoid using *primitive* because it also has an unfavourable meaning.

prejudice NOUN
They were the victims of widespread prejudice.
▶ discrimination, bigotry, bias, partisanship, chauvinism, favouritism, intolerance, racialism, racism, sexism
AN OPPOSITE IS tolerance

prejudice VERB
1 *He feared the accused's attitude might prejudice the jury.*
▶ influence, bias, sway, predispose, colour
2 *The reports might prejudice his election chances.*
▶ damage, harm, injure, be detrimental to, adversely affect, undermine

prejudiced ADJECTIVE
1 *Racially prejudiced attitudes are thought to be widespread.*
▶ biased, discriminatory, chauvinistic, intolerant, partial
2 *The staff seemed prejudiced against the poor.*
▶ biased, intolerant (of), partial, conditioned

prejudicial ADJECTIVE

a procedure that is prejudicial to public health
► harmful, detrimental, injurious, damaging, unfavourable
OPPOSITES ARE beneficial, advantageous

preliminary ADJECTIVE

1 *I should like to make a few preliminary remarks.*
► opening, introductory, initial

2 *A preliminary report will be issued next month.*
► provisional, initial, first, preparatory

prelude NOUN

The trade agreement is seen as a prelude to full membership of the EU.
► introduction, preliminary stage, preparation, precursor, curtain raiser
AN OPPOSITE IS epilogue

premature ADVERB

1 *His career was cut short by his premature death.*
► early, untimely, unseasonable

2 *Congratulations at this stage might be premature.*
► hasty, overhasty, rash, precipitate, too soon

premeditated ADJECTIVE

The attack was clearly premeditated.
► planned, intentional, pre-planned, calculated, deliberate, intended, pre-arranged, predetermined, wilful, conscious, considered
OPPOSITES ARE unpremeditated, spontaneous

premise NOUN

The argument is based on a false premise.
► proposition, assumption, thesis, hypothesis, postulate, presupposition

premises PLURAL NOUN

The premises are locked every evening.
► building or buildings, property, establishment, site, office

premonition NOUN

The situation was like a bad dream, with premonitions of the events to come.
► foreboding, presentiment, intuition, suspicion, inkling, portent, warning, forewarning, misgiving, omen

preoccupied ADJECTIVE

1 *He looked anxious and preoccupied.*
► pensive, thoughtful, lost in thought, absent-minded, rapt

2 **preoccupied with** *Sarah became more and more preoccupied with her child.*
► engrossed in, absorbed in, obsessed with, involved with, taken up with, concerned with, wrapped up in, engaged in, immersed in

preparation NOUN

1 *They devoted the next week to the preparation of plans.*
► devising, drawing up, putting together, development, formulation

2 *More staff were taken on to help with the preparations for the hotel's opening.*
► arrangements, plans, provisions, preliminaries, groundwork

preparatory ADJECTIVE

Preparatory negotiations were going on in the Austrian capital.
► preliminary, provisional, initial, first

prepare VERB

1 *Students have to prepare their presentations well in advance.*
► draw up, write, compose, construct, put together, get ready, make ready

2 *The cooks have to start preparing the food early each morning.*
► make ready, get ready, make, assemble, cook

3 *We should begin to prepare for the future.*
► plan, make arrangements, make provision or provisions, get ready

prepare yourself *We prepared ourselves for the worst.*
► brace yourself, gird yourself, steel yourself, fortify yourself

prepared ADJECTIVE

1 *We are prepared to wait for the right person to be found.*
► willing, ready, disposed, predisposed, inclined, able, set
AN OPPOSITE IS unwilling

2 *His solicitor read out a prepared statement.*
► pre-arranged, arranged, agreed, organized

preposterous ADJECTIVE

Anyone who maintained such a preposterous theory would be considered mad.
► absurd, ridiculous, ludicrous, laughable, incredible, farcical, risible, foolish, idiotic, (*more informal*) crazy, (*more informal*) daft, (*more informal*) barmy, (*more informal*) zany
OPPOSITES ARE reasonable, sensible

prerequisite NOUN

A knowledge of computing would be helpful but is not a prerequisite of the course.
► requirement, precondition, condition, stipulation, essential, qualification

prerogative NOUN

The government has the exclusive prerogative to allow an amnesty.
► right, entitlement, privilege, authority, sanction

prescribe NOUN

1 *The doctor decided to prescribe penicillin.*
► write a prescription for, authorize, advise, recommend

2 *The teachers would prescribe the topics to be dealt with.*
► specify, stipulate, lay down, assign, fix, impose, ordain, dictate

prescription NOUN
1 *Some of these medicines can be bought without a prescription.*
▶ authorization, order, instruction, direction
2 *She ran to the chemist to fetch her prescription before closing time.*
▶ medicine, medication, mixture, pills, tablets, drug

presence NOUN
1 *She could not explain the presence of Richard's car outside her flat.*
▶ existence, being there
2 *He requested the presence of a solicitor.*
▶ attendance, company, appearance, support
3 *She had a strong presence which gave her added authority.*
▶ aura, air, demeanour, bearing, manner, appearance, charisma
4 *the presence of her family in the area*
▶ proximity, nearness, closeness, vicinity
5 *They felt some sort of presence in the room*
▶ spirit, ghost, spectre, phantom

present ADJECTIVE (with the stress on *pres-*)
1 *A police officer should be present whenever possible.*
▶ in attendance, at hand, nearby, attending, available, there or here
AN OPPOSITE IS absent
2 *The shares are not expected to maintain their present high value.*
▶ current, present-day, existing, prevailing, contemporary
at present or **at the present time** *We have no plans to increase taxes at present.*
▶ just now, right now, at the moment, at this time, currently

present NOUN (with the stress on *pres-*)
1 *a history of the family from the sixteenth century to the present*
▶ present day, modern times, today
2 *She let him keep the pen as a present.*
▶ gift, donation, gratuity, contribution, offering

present VERB (with the stress on *-sent*)
1 *She presented a prize to the winners.*
▶ hand out, give out, hand over, award, grant, bestow (on)
2 *The committee has presented its report.*
▶ submit, tender, hand in, offer, proffer, publish
3 *The situation presents some novel features.*
▶ show, demonstrate, display, exhibit
4 *A compère presented each act.*
▶ introduce, announce

presentable ADJECTIVE
He wanted to go and buy some presentable clothes.
▶ respectable, smart, neat, tidy, elegant, decent, suitable, satisfactory
OPPOSITES ARE untidy, shabby

presentation NOUN
1 *They will give a presentation, with slides, on their recent trip to Kenya.*
▶ talk, lecture, address, lecture, display, demonstration

2 *the presentation of the evidence*
▶ submission, advancing, offering, propounding

present-day ADJECTIVE
the archaeology of Persia, present-day Iran
▶ modern, contemporary, present

presently ADVERB
1 *We'll be there presently.*
▶ shortly, soon, directly, in a while, (*more informal*) in a bit
2 *The family is presently abroad.*
▶ currently, at present, at the moment, now

preserve VERB
1 *Local action can also preserve wildlife.*
▶ protect, safeguard, secure, conserve, maintain, sustain, uphold, defend, guard
OPPOSITES ARE endanger, neglect
2 *She wanted to preserve him from harm.*
▶ protect, defend, guard, safeguard, shield
3 *special containers for preserving fruit*
▶ conserve, bottle, store, keep, save

preside VERB
1 *We elect a chairman to preside at the meeting.*
▶ be in charge, take charge, officiate, take the chair
2 **preside over** *The finance director presides over the annual budget review.*
▶ be in charge of, direct, have responsibility for, manage, be in control of

president NOUN
The society has a new president.
▶ head, director, chief, leader

press VERB
1 *She pressed his hand.*
▶ squeeze, grip, clutch, clinch
2 *He pressed some clothes into a suitcase.*
▶ squash, stuff, cram, push, squeeze, force
3 *Donna needed time to press her clothes.*
▶ iron, smooth, smooth out, flatten
4 *The next process is to press the grapes.*
▶ crush, squeeze, compress, mash, pulp
5 *People pressed round to see what was going on.*
▶ gather, cluster, crowd, swarm, throng
6 *You must press them to give you an answer.*
▶ urge, persuade, pressure, compel, plead with, force, insist on
USAGE If you use *insist on* you say *You must insist on them giving* (or *their giving*) *you an answer.*

press NOUN
1 *There was quite a press round the entrance.*
▶ crowd, throng, crush, mob
2 **the press** *The press would pay huge sums for an interview.*
▶ the newspapers, the papers, the media, journalists, reporters

pressing ADJECTIVE
a pressing need for changes
▶ urgent, acute, critical, crucial, vital, essential, serious, drastic
OPPOSITES ARE non-urgent, inessential

pressure NOUN
1 *The pressure on the foundations caused them to crack.*
► force, load, weight, burden, strain, stress
2 *The team is working under severe pressure.*
► stress, strain, difficulty, (*more informal*) hassle
3 *She was under a lot of pressure to accept the offer.*
► constraint, coercion, duress, harassment, compulsion, intimidation

pressurize VERB
He didn't want to pressurize them into agreeing if they were still uncertain.
► force, coerce, pressure, press, influence, goad, harass, badger, pester, bully, browbeat, bulldoze

prestige NOUN
Achieving an agreement would bring the president added prestige.
► status, reputation, standing, credit, kudos, renown, esteem, fame, glory, honour, importance

prestigious ADJECTIVE
She won a prestigious award for her contributions to medical science.
► distinguished, reputable, highly regarded, honourable, esteemed, acclaimed, respected, celebrated, illustrious

presumably ADVERB
Presumably you won't be coming with us.
► I assume, I presume, I suppose, I expect, doubtless, probably

presume VERB
1 *We presume there will be a call-out charge.*
► assume, expect, suppose, imagine, take it, dare say, guess, conjecture, surmise, believe
2 *Don't presume to take charge yourself.*
► dare, venture, have the nerve, have the temerity, have the audacity, be so bold as, go so far as

presumptuous ADJECTIVE
It was presumptuous to make a decision without consulting us.
► arrogant, audacious, forward, bold, impudent, insolent, bumptious, unwarranted, conceited, impertinent, overconfident, shameless, (*more informal*) pushy, (*more informal*) cheeky

pretence NOUN
Their self-confidence turned out to be just a pretence.
► make-believe, act, show, display, front, affectation, deception, posturing, façade, masquerade, charade, subterfuge, falsehood, sham, pose, ruse, bluff, cover, faking, dissembling

pretend VERB
1 *She pretended to understand, but we were all confused*
► affect, profess, claim, purport
2 *Let's pretend we're ghosts.*
► imagine, make believe, suppose, play being

pretend ADJECTIVE
(*informal*) *He made his room into a pretend cave.*
► imaginary, make-believe, fantasy, fanciful, mythical, pretended

pretentious ADJECTIVE
The best food can often be found in smaller, less pretentious restaurants.
► ostentatious, showy, affected, conspicuous, flashy, grandiose, extravagant
OPPOSITES ARE modest, unassuming

pretext NOUN
He called on the pretext of leaving some plants for Diane.
► excuse, grounds, ploy, pretence, ruse, guise

pretty ADJECTIVE
a pretty little garden
► attractive, lovely, good-looking, beautiful, charming, appealing, pleasing, (*more informal*) cute
OPPOSITES ARE plain, ugly, hideous

pretty ADVERB
(*informal*) *It was a pretty daft thing to do.*
► rather, quite, somewhat, fairly, moderately, (*more informal*) kind of

prevail VERB
1 *attitudes that prevailed in the 1960s*
► exist, hold, be prevalent, be current
2 *Common sense prevailed in the end.*
► win, win through, triumph, reign, rule, predominate
3 *The Greek army prevailed against all the odds.*
► be victorious, triumph, win
4 **prevail on** or **upon** *Can you prevail on her to change her mind?*
► persuade, induce, urge, pressure, pressurize, tempt

prevailing ADJECTIVE
The prevailing view was that war could be avoided.
► current, general, established, popular, widespread, prevalent, predominant, dominant, principal, fashionable

prevaricate VERB
He prevaricated when they asked him personal questions.
► equivocate, be evasive, hedge, cavil, beat about the bush, (*more informal*) shilly-shally, (*more informal*) pussy-foot

prevent VERB
1 *It was too late to prevent the accident.*
► stop, avert, avoid, head off, forestall, frustrate, hinder
2 *I'll try to prevent them from coming in before you're ready.*
► stop, restrain, check, inhibit, block, bar

previous ADJECTIVE
a review of the previous three years
► preceding, foregoing, antecedent, last, earlier, former, prior
AN OPPOSITE IS following

previously ADVERB
Previously she had worked in a nightclub.
► earlier, formerly, in the past, at one time, before this or that, hitherto

prey NOUN
Lions are often slower than their prey.
▶ quarry, victim, game, kill

prey VERB
prey on
1 *Wild dogs will also prey on cattle.*
▶ hunt, catch, kill, eat, feed on
2 *The thought kept preying on his mind.*
▶ trouble, oppress, disturb, distress, haunt, beset, burden, weigh down, worry

price NOUN
1 *The price of your holiday is fully guaranteed.*
▶ cost, terms, rate, amount, charge (for), outlay (on)
2 *What price should you charge?*
▶ amount, figure, sum, fee, rate, charge, levy
3 *Isolation was one price of their peaceful existence.*
▶ consequence, result, penalty, sacrifice, downside

priceless ADJECTIVE
1 *a priceless collection of watercolours   a priceless away goal*
▶ precious, valuable, irreplaceable, inestimable, treasured, prized, costly
2 *(informal) a priceless remark that made them all laugh*
▶ hilarious, riotous, uproarious, funny, (*more informal*) hysterical

prick VERB
1 *He pricked the lid and put it in the microwave.*
▶ pierce, puncture, perforate, make a hole in, stab, jab, punch
2 *The smoke made my eyes start to prick.*
▶ sting, smart, prickle, hurt
3 *His conscience was pricking him.*
▶ trouble, worry, disturb, distress, oppress, torment, afflict

prickle NOUN
1 *The bush was covered with prickles.*
▶ thorn, spike, needle, spine, quill, barb
2 *The shuffling sound outside sent a prickle down my spine.*
▶ tingle, tingling, prickling, chill, thrill

prickle VERB
The grass prickled their legs.
▶ sting, prick, tickle

prickly ADJECTIVE
1 *a prickly bush*
▶ spiky, spiny, thorny, bristly, scratchy, sharp
2 *(informal) He's quite a prickly character.*
▶ irritable, irascible, peevish, testy, edgy, touchy, grumpy, short-tempered, fractious

pride NOUN
1 *Pride prevented him from accepting the offer.*
▶ conceit, vanity, arrogance, snobbery
2 *She took great pride in her work.*
▶ satisfaction, pleasure, delight, joy, comfort, sense of achievement
3 *Their victory was a source of great pride to them.*
▶ self-esteem, self-respect, gratification, honour, dignity

priest NOUN
They looked for a priest to marry them.
▶ clergyman or clergywoman, minister, pastor, vicar, padre
RELATED ADJECTIVE sacerdotal

NAMES FOR PRIESTS AND RELIGIOUS OFFICIALS
ancient: (Roman) augur, flamen, haruspex, pontifex; (Celtic) druid, ovate.
Christian: abbess, abbot, archimandrite, archbishop, archdeacon, bishop, brother, canon, chaplain, clergyman, clergywoman, curate, deacon, deaconess, father, friar, mendicant, minister, monk, mother superior, nun, parson, prior, prioress, rector, sister, vicar.
Buddhist: Dalai Lama, lama, Panchen Lama, pongyi, talapoin.
Hindu: Brahman, guru, mahant, panda, pandit, pujari, rishi.
Jewish:cantor, chief rabbi, hazzan, kohen, Levite, rabbi, rebbe, rebbetzin.
Muslim: ayatollah, caliph, fakir, imam, muezzin, mullah, sheikh.
Sikh: guru.

prig NOUN
She regarded him as an arrogant stand-offish prig.
▶ prude, puritan, hypocrite, killjoy

priggish ADJECTIVE
She too was in danger of seeming priggish and opinionated.
▶ self-righteous, smug, sanctimonious, sententious, prudish, prim, strait-laced, stuffy, starchy

prim ADJECTIVE
She sat behind her desk looking prim.
▶ demure, proper, formal, strait-laced, prissy, prudish, starchy, fastidious
AN OPPOSITE IS broad-minded

primarily ADVERB
The work is primarily funded by a grant from the Lottery Fund.
▶ chiefly, principally, mainly, mostly, predominantly, basically, in the main

primary ADJECTIVE
1 *Their primary aim was to make money.*
▶ main, chief, principal, key, prime, paramount, overriding, ultimate, supreme
2 *the primary cause of the infection*
▶ original, initial, first

prime ADJECTIVE
1 *The prime reason for his decision was a wish for change.*
▶ main, chief, principal, key, primary, paramount, overriding, ultimate, supreme
2 *a hundred acres of prime agricultural land*
▶ best, choice, select, superior, first-class, high-grade, top-quality

primitive ADJECTIVE
1 *primitive peoples*
▶ ancient, early, earliest, prehistoric
AN OPPOSITE IS developed
2 *primitive tools*
▶ crude, basic, rudimentary, simple, undeveloped, elementary, rough
OPPOSITES ARE sophisticated, advanced

principal ADJECTIVE
Traffic noise is the principal objection to the new road scheme.
▶ main, chief, primary, prime, most important, overriding, foremost, fundamental, key, crucial, central, paramount, predominant, basic, essential

principally ADVERB
The place was full of foreigners, principally Americans.
▶ mainly, chiefly, primarily, mostly, predominantly, especially, essentially

principle NOUN
1 *a woman of principle*
▶ honour, integrity, morality, ideals, conscience, scruples, decency, virtue
2 *a basic principle of physics*
▶ rule, law, formula, canon, dictum, axiom, tenet
in principle *In principle the idea is a good one.*
▶ in theory, theoretically, in general, in the main, by and large

principles PLURAL NOUN
1 *They were praised for sticking to their principles.*
▶ morals, values, morality, standards, moral standards, code of behaviour
2 *the first principles of a subject*
▶ essentials, fundamentals, basics, elements, laws

print VERB
1 *The company logo is printed at the top of each page.*
▶ mark, stamp, imprint, impress, engrave, reproduce
2 *The books are printed in the Far East.*
▶ set in print, run off, produce, reproduce, manufacture
3 *The publishers plan to print ten thousand copies of the book.*
▶ publish, issue, produce
4 *Print your name at the top of the form.*
▶ write in capital letters or large letters

print NOUN
1 *The print was difficult to read.*
▶ type, typeface, printing, lettering, letters, characters
2 *There were prints of feet in the sand*
▶ mark, impression, imprint, indentation, stamp
3 *A print would be less costly than an original painting.*
▶ reproduction, engraving, lithograph, copy, duplicate, photograph

prior ADJECTIVE
He said he already had a prior engagement that morning.
▶ previous, earlier, existing, advance

priority NOUN
1 *Traffic from the right has priority.*
▶ right of way, precedence
2 *Education will have priority at this year's conference.*
▶ precedence, preference, first place, first importance, primacy, predominance

prise VERB
She carefully prised off the lid.
▶ lever, wrest, twist, force

prison NOUN
They would spend the next three years in prison.
▶ jail, confinement, detention, custody, place of detention, penitentiary

prisoner NOUN
The prisoners staged a demonstration on the prison roof.
▶ detainee, convict, captive, hostage, inmate, internee, (*more informal*) jailbird

prissy ADJECTIVE
Asking him to stop swearing might sound prissy.
▶ prudish, prim, priggish, stuffy

pristine ADJECTIVE
a book in pristine condition
▶ perfect, immaculate, spotless, mint, unspoilt, unblemished, unmarked

privacy NOUN
The little room gave her some privacy.
▶ seclusion, solitude, tranquillity, peace and quiet, quietness, secrecy, isolation

private ADJECTIVE
1 *He had amassed a huge private fortune.*
▶ personal, exclusive, individual, special
2 *Private talks were held at Chequers.*
▶ secret, confidential, covert, clandestine
OPPOSITES ARE public, open
3 *She had her own private thoughts on the matter.*
▶ personal, secret, hidden, intimate
4 *They needed somewhere private to talk.*
▶ quiet, secluded, undisturbed, out of the way, isolated, solitary, peaceful, tranquil
AN OPPOSITE IS busy
5 *John is a very private sort of person.*
▶ reserved, withdrawn, intimate, reticent, unsocial

privilege NOUN
1 *Full members enjoy special privileges.*
▶ benefit, entitlement, advantage, prerogative, concession, right
2 *It had been a privilege to meet them.*
▶ honour, pleasure

privileged ADJECTIVE
He enjoyed a privileged social position.
▶ advantaged, affluent, prosperous, wealthy, favoured, fortunate, special, superior, élite, powerful
OPPOSITES ARE disadvantaged, underprivileged

prize NOUN
Helen won the prize three years in a row.
▶ award, reward, trophy, honour, accolade

prize VERB
They prize their freedom above all else.
▶ value, appreciate, cherish, esteem, treasure, hold dear, regard, rate, approve of, revere, like

probable ADJECTIVE
Engine failure was the most probable cause of the crash. It is probable that this road was heavily guarded.
▶ likely, plausible, credible, feasible, believable, expected, possible, predictable, presumed, (more informal) odds-on, (more informal) on the cards
OPPOSITES ARE improbable, unlikely

probation NOUN
New staff have six months of probation.
▶ apprenticeship, test, trial period, traineeship

probe VERB
1 The inquiry will probe the circumstances of the accident.
▶ investigate, examine, inquire into, look into, scrutinize, analyse, study, go into
2 Unmanned underwater vehicles probed the ocean depths.
▶ sound, plumb, penetrate, explore, feel

probe NOUN
1 a space probe
▶ exploration, expedition
2 a police probe
▶ inquiry, investigation, examination, study, research, scrutiny

problem NOUN
1 He gave them a page of problems to solve.
▶ puzzle, question, riddle, conundrum, enigma, mystery, (more informal) brainteaser, (more informal) poser
2 Money was becoming a big problem for them.
▶ difficulty, complication, worry, burden, trouble, predicament, quandary, dilemma, set-back, snag, (informal) headache

problematic ADJECTIVE
Unravelling this argument can be problematic.
▶ difficult, complicated, complex, problematical, intractable, tricky, thorny, knotty, taxing, involved, enigmatic, controversial
OPPOSITES ARE straightforward, simple, easy

procedure NOUN
There is a special procedure for dealing with complaints.
▶ course of action, process, routine, system, policy, strategy, approach, proceeding

proceed VERB
1 We still don't know how to proceed.
▶ begin, make a start, act, take action, make a move, progress
2 They turned off the main road and proceeded as far as the village.
▶ advance, continue, progress, make your way, carry on, press on
3 proceed with Despite opposition, they decided to proceed with the changes.
▶ go ahead with, carry out, implement, put into effect

proceedings PLURAL NOUN
1 He began proceedings against the newspaper.
▶ legal action, action, lawsuit, litigation
2 (informal) The proceedings of the meeting will be published shortly.
▶ records, report, transactions, minutes
3 They had enjoyed the day's proceedings more than they expected.
▶ events, activities, happenings, affairs, (more informal) goings-on

proceeds PLURAL NOUN
All proceeds from the sale will go to charity.
▶ profits, receipts, takings, returns, revenue, income, earnings, money

process NOUN
1 Sending email attachments is a simple process.
▶ operation, procedure, activity, exercise, affair
2 a new process for producing colour pictures
▶ system, method, technique, procedure
3 The learning process continues for many years.
▶ progression, course, development, experience, evolution

process VERB
1 Officials hope to process asylum claims more quickly.
▶ deal with, attend to, handle, expedite, treat, see to, sort out
2 The crude oil is processed at this refinery.
▶ refine, convert, make usable, prepare, transform, treat

procession NOUN
A procession passed through the town.
▶ parade, march, cavalcade, spectacle, display, pageant, review, show

proclaim VERB
1 She proclaimed her love for him.
▶ declare, announce, profess, make known, affirm, assert, give out, pronounce
2 The president proclaimed the day a public holiday.
▶ declare, decree, pronounce

proclamation NOUN
The Queen issues a proclamation dissolving Parliament.
▶ decree, edict, order, command, ruling, announcement, declaration

procrastinate VERB
Fear of making a mistake caused him to procrastinate.
▶ delay, put things off, be indecisive, temporize, defer a decision, stall, dither, (more informal) dilly-dally, (more informal) shilly-shally, (more informal) drag your feet

procure VERB
He persuaded a friend to procure him a ticket.
▶ get, obtain, acquire, secure, find, pick up, get hold of, buy

prod VERB

1 *The cook grumbled as he prodded the potatoes. He continued to prod her palms with the needle.*
▶ jab, poke, stab, dig, nudge, push
2 *He always needs someone to prod him into action.*
▶ goad, spur, stir, rouse, prompt, urge, stimulate, egg on, incite, provoke

prod NOUN

1 *She gave him a prod that woke him up.*
▶ jab, poke, stab, dig, nudge, shove, push
2 *The phone call was a prod to remind him to put the bins out that night.*
▶ prompt, reminder, stimulus

prodigy NOUN

Mozart met Thomas, another musical prodigy, in Florence.
▶ genius, marvel, phenomenon, sensation, talent, wonder

produce VERB (with the stress on -*duce*)

1 *The remark produced a wave of sniggers through the room.*
▶ cause, give rise to, occasion, provoke, bring about, result in, generate, effect
2 *He had failed to produce an essay for the third week running.*
▶ present, submit, offer, hand in, supply, provide
3 *He put his hand in his pocket and produced his passport.*
▶ show, display, present, bring out, take out
4 *It would be difficult to produce the required output that year.*
▶ supply, yield, deliver, provide
5 *The company produced Hamlet at the Edinburgh Festival.*
▶ stage, mount, present, put on, show

produce NOUN (with the stress on *prod-*)

an increase in organically grown produce
▶ food, crops, harvest, output, products, commodities, yield, fruit, vegetables

product NOUN

1 *The company will announce its new product at the trade fair.*
▶ commodity, output, production, artefact, produce, end-product, goods, merchandise
2 *The story was the product of a vivid imagination.*
▶ result, consequence, outcome, effect, fruit, upshot

productive ADJECTIVE

1 *He still had years of productive work ahead.*
▶ useful, valuable, worthwhile, constructive, creative, effective, gainful, profitable, profitmaking, rewarding, beneficial, busy
OPPOSITES ARE unproductive, fruitless
2 *a productive area of land*
▶ fertile, fruitful, rich, prolific, lush
OPPOSITES ARE unproductive, barren

profane ADJECTIVE

1 *He used coarse, profane language*
▶ indecent, offensive, obscene, crude, coarse, vulgar, blasphemous
AN OPPOSITE IS respectful
2 *the sacred and the profane*
▶ secular, temporal, worldly, irreligious, unholy, sacrilegious
OPPOSITES ARE religious, sacred, holy

profess VERB

1 *They professed their faith in a moving ceremony.*
▶ declare, proclaim, announce, make known, affirm, assert, give out, pronounce
2 *He professed to hate everything about the place.*
▶ claim, pretend, purport, allege, make out

profession NOUN

She was no longer attracted by the teaching profession.
▶ career, occupation, vocation, line of work, business, calling, employment, work

professional ADJECTIVE

1 *the study of modern languages as a preparation for professional life*
▶ working, business, executive
2 *the use of professional judgement*
▶ expert, qualified, skilled, trained, competent, efficient, proficient
3 *The plays were recorded in a studio with professional actors.*
▶ paid, salaried, full-time
OPPOSITES ARE amateur, voluntary
4 *He was a thoroughly professional journalist.*
▶ conscientious, businesslike, proficient, dutiful, responsible
AN OPPOSITE IS unprofessional

proficiency NOUN

Applicants should have some proficiency in Japanese.
▶ skill, ability, competence, expertise, mastery (of), aptitude

proficient ADJECTIVE

She was now a highly proficient pilot.
▶ able, capable, skilled, accomplished, skilful, expert, qualified, competent, experienced

profile NOUN

1 *a beautiful woman with a perfect profile*
▶ shape, side view, contour, figure, outline, silhouette
2 *a profile of John F Kennedy*
▶ biography, sketch, portrait, study, account
3 *The company has raised its profile in Eastern Europe.*
▶ influence, presence, image

profit NOUN

1 *The company made a modest profit in the last financial year.*
▶ return, surplus, yield, excess
2 **profits** *Two percent of profits contribute to the social fund.*
▶ revenue, income, takings, earnings, proceeds

3 *There would be no profit in continuing.*
▶ advantage, benefit, value, use, gain, point, purpose

profit VERB
1 *It would profit us to wait for a while.*
▶ benefit, advantage, be an advantage to, pay, help
2 **profit by** or **from** *No one profited from these changes.*
▶ benefit from, gain advantage from, do well out of

profitable ADJECTIVE
a profitable undertaking
▶ moneymaking, profitmaking, remunerative, lucrative, paying, productive, fruitful, gainful, rewarding, advantageous, beneficial, commercial, useful, valuable, worthwhile
AN OPPOSITE IS unprofitable

profound ADJECTIVE
1 *I offered my profound sympathy.*
▶ sincere, deep, heartfelt, intense
AN OPPOSITE IS insincere.
2 *a profound disagreement*
▶ complete, total, utter, absolute, extreme
3 *a profound argument*
▶ learned, wise, erudite, intelligent, perceptive, penetrating, thoughtful

profuse ADJECTIVE
She left with profuse goodbyes.
▶ copious, effusive, plentiful, abundant, lavish, extravagant, generous

programme NOUN
1 *a varied programme of events*
▶ schedule, agenda, timetable, calendar, listing, plan, order, scheme, (*more informal*) line-up
2 *a television programme*
▶ broadcast, transmission, performance, production, show

progress NOUN (with the stress on *pro-*)
1 *major progress in medical research*
▶ advance, development, headway, improvement, movement, progression, breakthrough, (*more informal*) step forward
2 *The heavy rain made further progress difficult.*
▶ travel, headway, advance, movement

progress VERB (with the stress on *-gress*)
The plans are progressing slowly.
▶ advance, develop, move forward, make progress, make headway, proceed, prosper, mature, improve, (*more informal*) come on
OPPOSITES ARE regress, deteriorate

progression NOUN
a progression of days and nights
▶ sequence, series, string, succession, cycle, chain, row

progressive ADJECTIVE
1 *a progressive improvement in health*
▶ continuous, continuing, steady, increasing, ongoing, accelerating, growing, escalating
OPPOSITES ARE faltering, fluctuating, unsteady

2 *a party leader with progressive ideas*
▶ liberal, advanced, radical, modern, go-ahead, forward-looking, enlightened, avant-garde, contemporary, enterprising, up-to-date
AN OPPOSITE IS conservative

prohibit VERB
1 *a law prohibiting the advertising of tobacco products.*
▶ forbid, ban, disallow, proscribe, outlaw, make illegal
2 *Her commitments prohibited her from attending the funeral.*
▶ prevent, preclude, rule out, restrict, impede, obstruct

prohibited ADJECTIVE
Dumping waste is prohibited.
▶ forbidden, illegal, not allowed, not permitted, banned

project NOUN (with the stress on *proj-*)
1 *a project to create more conservation areas*
▶ scheme, undertaking, plan, proposal, venture, enterprise, idea
2 *They're doing a history project.*
▶ assignment, piece of research, piece of work, activity, task

project VERB (with the stress on *-ject*)
1 *Balconies project from the upstairs windows.*
▶ stick out, extend, protrude, stand out, jut out, overhang, bulge
2 *The torch projected a strong beam.*
▶ cast, throw, throw out, flash, shine
3 *You can project the year's income from these monthly figures.*
▶ estimate, reckon, forecast, predict, extrapolate

proliferate VERB
The problems proliferated.
▶ multiply, increase, escalate, build up, mushroom, intensify, snowball, spread

prolific ADJECTIVE
1 *a prolific crop of vegetables*
▶ plentiful, abundant, copious, profuse, productive, rich, bountiful, fertile, fruitful
AN OPPOSITE IS unproductive
2 *a prolific writer*
▶ productive, creative, inventive

prolong VERB
She didn't want to prolong the argument.
▶ lengthen, protract, extend, continue, perpetuate, spin out, draw out, increase, make longer, stretch out
OPPOSITES ARE shorten, curtail

prolonged ADJECTIVE
a prolonged trip abroad
▶ long, lengthy, extended, protracted
OPPOSITES ARE short, brief

prominence NOUN
The city was captured, but rose again to prominence.
▶ fame, celebrity, eminence, distinction, renown, importance, greatness

prominent ADJECTIVE
a prominent member of the government
▶ important, well-known, leading, eminent, distinguished, notable, noteworthy, celebrated

promiscuous ADJECTIVE
I went through a promiscuous period after I left Sam.
▶ loose, immoral, licentious, dissolute, abandoned, wanton, casual
OPPOSITES ARE moral, chaste

promise VERB
1 *He promised to pay for the damage.*
▶ undertake, guarantee, agree, contract
2 *He promised she'd be there.*
▶ give your word, say, pledge, swear
3 *The bright sky promised a fine day*
▶ indicate, presage, suggest, signify, augur, predict

promise NOUN
1 *You have my promise.*
▶ word, assurance, word of honour, pledge, undertaking, commitment, guarantee, oath, vow
2 *a group of pupils showing outstanding promise*
▶ potential, ability, aptitude, talent, capability

promising ADJECTIVE
1 *There are promising signs of an improvement.*
▶ encouraging, hopeful, favourable, auspicious, propitious, talented
2 *a promising young talent*
▶ budding, gifted, up-and-coming, able

promontory NOUN
The castle stands on a rocky promontory.
▶ headland, projection, prominence, cape, cliff, foreland, ridge, spit, spur

promote VERB
1 *She was promoted in the recent cabinet reshuffle.*
▶ upgrade, move up, give a promotion to, advance, honour
2 *He will promote his new novel at the Book Fair.*
▶ advertise, publicize, push, sponsor, boost, (*more informal*) plug
3 *an organization promoting equal opportunities*
▶ champion, further, advance, sponsor, encourage, stimulate, foster, nurture, boost

promotion NOUN
1 *He is hoping for a promotion next year.*
▶ advancement, upgrading, elevation, preferment, rise
2 *the promotion of her new film*
▶ marketing, publicity, advertising, backing, selling, pushing, (*more informal*) plugging

prompt ADJECTIVE
We hope for a prompt response.
▶ quick, swift, rapid, speedy, early, punctual, immediate, expeditious
OPPOSITES ARE late, slow

prompt VERB
1 *We are not sure what prompted such an angry outburst.*
▶ cause, give rise to, bring about, occasion, lead to, produce, bring on, precipitate, trigger, spark off
OPPOSITES ARE deter, prevent
2 *A noise prompted her to turn round.*
▶ cause, lead, induce, stimulate, prod, provoke
AN OPPOSITE IS discourage (from)
3 *He forgot what to say and his wife had to prompt him.*
▶ remind, cue, prod, jog the memory

prone ADJECTIVE
1 *A man was lying prone on the floor*
▶ face down, on your front, prostrate
AN OPPOSITE IS upright
2 *People here are prone to exaggerate.*
▶ apt, inclined, liable, susceptible, predisposed, disposed, given
OPPOSITES ARE resistant, immune

prong NOUN
the prong of a fork
▶ point, spike, spur, tine

pronounce VERB
1 *The name is difficult to pronounce.*
▶ say, enunciate, articulate, sound, speak, utter, get your tongue round
2 *The doctor pronounced me well.*
▶ declare, proclaim, judge, announce, affirm, assert
USAGE If you use *affirm* or *assert* you say *The doctor affirmed* or *asserted that I was well.*

pronounced ADJECTIVE
He walked with a pronounced limp
▶ distinct, marked, noticeable, clear, definite, decided, conspicuous, obvious, prominent, unmistakable, striking, evident

pronunciation NOUN
The key to pronunciation of long words is often the stress.
▶ enunciation, articulation, intonation, accent, diction, elocution, inflection

proof NOUN
If there is a problem, return the goods with proof of purchase.
▶ evidence, confirmation, verification, authentication, certification, corroboration, demonstration

prop NOUN
1 *The bridge is supported by steel props.*
▶ post, strut, upright, support, buttress, bolster
2 *She had become the family's emotional prop.*
▶ support, mainstay, pillar, anchor, backbone

prop VERB
He propped his bike against the wall.
▶ lean, rest, stand
prop up *The old tree was propped up with posts.*
▶ support, hold up, brace, strengthen, reinforce, shore up, buttress

propaganda NOUN
a master of political propaganda
▶ information, misinformation, advertising, publicity, brainwashing, indoctrination, persuasion

propagate VERB
1 *The plants are propagated in large greenhouses.*
▶ breed, grow , cultivate, generate
2 *Wild flowers thrive and propagate.*
▶ reproduce, multiply, proliferate, procreate
3 *They were accused of propagating false reports.*
▶ spread, transmit, disseminate, pass on, communicate, put about, circulate, proliferate

propel VERB
1 *He propelled the ball high into the air.*
▶ throw, toss, fling, hurl, pitch, launch, shoot, kick, punt
2 *The little craft was propelled by a small outboard motor.*
▶ drive, move, power, impel, set in motion, push

proper ADJECTIVE
1 *It was about time he found a proper job.*
▶ real, genuine, bona fide
2 *She doesn't think it proper to share a room with him.*
▶ right, correct, decent, respectable, decorous
3 *You have to apply through the proper channels.*
▶ correct, right, appropriate, official, established, usual
4 *(informal) He felt a proper fool.*
▶ complete, utter, perfect, absolute, positive

property NOUN
1 *He left all his property to his nephew.*
▶ possessions, belongings, assets, worldly goods, wealth, valuables, chattels, effects, fortune
2 *Brits looking for property to buy abroad.*
▶ buildings, premises, houses, estate
3 *the medicinal properties of garlic*
▶ quality, attribute, characteristic, power, peculiarity, trait, feature

prophecy NOUN
The prophecy is coming true.
▶ prediction, forecast, prognostication, divination, augury, prognosis

prophesy VERB
Some pessimistic types had prophesied a bad outcome.
▶ predict, forecast, foretell, foresee, forewarn of, prognosticate

prophet NOUN
an Old Testament prophet
▶ seer, soothsayer, clairvoyant, oracle, forecaster, fortune teller

prophetic ADJECTIVE
He wrote a story that proved prophetic of his own future life.
▶ predictive, prescient, far-seeing, oracular, prophesying, apocalyptic

proportion NOUN
1 *the proportion of girls to boys in a class*
▶ ratio, balance, relationship, distribution

2 *A large proportion of the country is forested.*
▶ part, portion, amount, quantity, percentage, section, share, piece, quota
3 **proportions** *a building of huge proportions*
▶ dimensions, measurements, size, magnitude

proportionate ADJECTIVE
Air fares are proportionate to the distance travelled.
▶ proportional, in proportion, commensurate, relative, comparable, corresponding
AN OPPOSITE IS disproportionate

USAGE You can also say *Air fares correspond to (or relate to) the distance travelled.*

proposal NOUN
There is a proposal to build a ring road.
▶ plan, scheme, proposition, suggestion, project, bid, motion , offer, recommendation

propose VERB
1 *Charles proposed Greece for their next holiday.*
▶ suggest, put forward, recommend, offer, come up with, submit, ask for, present
AN OPPOSITE IS withdraw
2 *How do you propose to find the money?*
▶ plan, intend, mean, aim, have in mind
3 *Six candidates have been proposed for election.*
▶ nominate, put up

proposition NOUN
1 *They discussed the proposition that war was inevitable.*
▶ theory, hypothesis, premise, notion, idea
2 *a business proposition*
▶ proposal, plan, scheme, suggestion, project

proprietor NOUN
the proprietor of a shop
▶ owner, manager, boss

propriety NOUN
He always behaves with great propriety.
▶ decorum, delicacy, correctness, appropriateness, decency, good manners, sensitivity, etiquette, politeness, seemliness, tact
AN OPPOSITE IS impropriety

prosaic ADJECTIVE
a prosaic name for such a beautiful place
▶ dull, unimaginative, dry, humdrum, pedestrian, lacklustre, insipid
AN OPPOSITE IS poetic

prosecute VERB
The police are going to prosecute him for dangerous driving.
▶ charge, prefer charges against, institute legal proceedings against, bring to trial, take legal proceedings against, indict

prospect NOUN
1 *She went to India with every prospect of a long stay.*
▶ chance, expectation, likelihood, possibility, probability, promise, hope

2 *There is a magnificent prospect from the penthouse apartment.*
▶ view, vista, outlook, panorama, landscape, perspective, scene, sight, spectacle

3 prospects *His job prospects were looking good.*
▶ future, potential, outlook, possibilities, hopes

prospective ADJECTIVE
A survey is commissioned by the prospective purchaser of the property.
▶ potential, possible, probable, likely, future, eventual, intended, would-be, aspiring, -to-be (purchaser-to-be)

prospectus NOUN
The prospectus included information on part-time courses.
▶ brochure, manifesto, programme, syllabus, pamphlet

prosper VERB
The market in mobiles continues to prosper.
▶ thrive, do well, flourish, boom, blossom, expand, succeed, progress, make progress

prosperity NOUN
The future prosperity of inner cities depends on how safe they are to live in.
▶ success, welfare, wealth, affluence, growth, plenty, profitability

prosperous ADJECTIVE
She took out a dress she had been given by a prosperous banker.
▶ well-off, wealthy, affluent, rich, successful, thriving, prospering, flourishing, well-to-do
AN OPPOSITE IS unsuccessful

protect VERB
1 *The men were anxious to protect their women and children. The city fought a war to protect its democracy.*
▶ defend, safeguard, keep safe, preserve, secure, shield, guard, save

2 *An armed guard protected the convoy.*
▶ escort, guard, accompany, defend, cover, shield

protection NOUN
1 *They looked for some form of protection from the wind and rain.*
▶ shelter, refuge, security, shield

2 *Military strength would be no protection against terrorist activities of that sort.*
▶ barrier, buffer, screen, bulwark, security, insurance

protective ADJECTIVE
1 *protective clothing*
▶ protecting, insulating, shielding, sheltering, defensive

2 *Her parents had always been protective towards her.*
▶ caring, solicitous, watchful, vigilant, jealous, defensive, possessive

protest NOUN (with the stress on *pro-*)
1 *The violence shown in the programme caused a wave of protests.*
▶ complaint, objection, outcry, protestation, remonstrance, cry of disapproval

2 *There will be a large protest in the town square.*
▶ demonstration, rally, march, sit-in, (*more informal*) demo

protest VERB (with the stress on -*test*)
1 *People protested against the export of animals.*
▶ demonstrate, object, make a protest, remonstrate, express disapproval (of)

2 *The neighbours protested that the music was too loud.*
▶ complain, object, grumble, expostulate, fulminate, argue, take exception

3 *He continued to protest his innocence.*
▶ maintain, insist on, claim, profess, proclaim, assert, contend

protocol NOUN
They are real sticklers for protocol.
▶ procedure, formalities, etiquette, propriety, rules of conduct, rules of behaviour, manners, good form, custom

protrude VERB
A long snout protrudes at the front of the animal.
▶ stick out, poke out, project, stand out, jut out

proud ADJECTIVE
1 *He's too proud to admit his mistake.*
▶ conceited, arrogant, vain, big-headed, self-important, full of yourself, presumptuous, boastful
OPPOSITES ARE modest, unassuming, humble

2 *They are a proud people.*
▶ noble, dignified, honourable, self-respecting

3 proud of *Anna was so proud of her garden.*
▶ pleased with, delighted with, thrilled with, satisfied with, happy about, glad about, gratified at, fond of
AN OPPOSITE IS ashamed of

prove VERB
1 *The new evidence proves your innocence.*
▶ confirm, corroborate, demonstrate, establish, substantiate, attest, authenticate, bear out, show to be true, verify
AN OPPOSITE IS disprove

2 *The story proved to be true.*
▶ turn out, happen, be found

proven ADJECTIVE
an actor of proven ability
▶ demonstrated, established, tested, tried, certified, confirmed, proved, undoubted, unquestionable
AN OPPOSITE IS doubtful

proverb NOUN
the old proverb about too many cooks
▶ saying, maxim, adage, dictum, byword, catchphrase

a
b
c
d
e
f
g
h
i
j
k
l
m
n
o
p
q
r
s
t
u
v
w
x
y
z

proverbial ADJECTIVE

the proverbial ruthlessness of business executives
▶ well-known, famous, legendary, traditional, conventional, clichéd, customary

provide VERB

1 *The hotel can provide a picnic.*
▶ supply, furnish, serve, produce, present, contribute, lay on, arrange for

2 **provide for** *He now made enough money to provide for his family.*
▶ support, maintain, feed, keep, sustain, provide food for

3 **provide for** *The agreement provides for arbitration in the case of disputes.*
▶ allow for, make provision for, stipulate, specify, require, call for, arrange for

providence NOUN

the workings of providence
▶ fate, destiny, fortune

provident ADJECTIVE

They are always provident in money matters.
▶ prudent, judicious, far-sighted, shrewd, thrifty

province NOUN

1 *a province of the Roman Empire*
▶ territory, region, department, district, dependency

2 *Politics was not my province at that time.*
▶ responsibility, concern, domain, territory, preserve, sphere

provincial ADJECTIVE

1 *the provincial government*
▶ local, regional, district, territorial

2 *the provincial attitudes of the middle classes*
▶ unsophisticated, insular, parochial, suburban, small-town, narrow-minded, dreary, dull

provisional ADJECTIVE

The provisional total is over a million dollars.
▶ interim, temporary, tentative, conditional, stopgap
OPPOSITES ARE definite, permanent

provisions PLURAL NOUN

The army was running out of provisions.
▶ supplies, food and drink, foodstuff, stores, subsistence, rations, groceries, requirements

proviso NOUN

He allowed friends to use his house, with the proviso that they tend to the garden.
▶ condition, stipulation, provision, requirement, qualification, restriction, understanding

provocation NOUN

(informal) He refused to react despite extreme provocation.
▶ annoyance, goading, aggravation, irritation, harassment, taunting, incitement, inducement, grounds, justification, motivation

provoke VERB

1 *Plans for a new ring road have provoked a lot of interest.*
▶ arouse, rouse, prompt, cause, kindle, instigate, spark off, stimulate, stir up, (*more informal*) whip up
AN OPPOSITE IS allay

2 *She was provoked into making comments that she later regretted.*
▶ goad, spur, prick, sting

3 *Better not to provoke him while he's in a good mood.*
▶ annoy, irritate, anger, incense, offend, tease, taunt

prowess NOUN

1 *the knights' prowess in battle*
▶ bravery, courage, valour, gallantry, heroism, daring, spirit

2 *her prowess as a dancer*
▶ ability, skill, talent, expertise, accomplishment, aptitude, competence, excellence

prowl VERB

Dogs prowled about at night.
▶ slink, skulk, sneak, steal, creep, roam, sidle

proximity NOUN

1 *the proximity of the enemy*
▶ closeness, nearness, presence, propinquity

2 *There are good hotels in the proximity*
▶ vicinity, neighbourhood

prudent ADJECTIVE

1 *It's not always prudent to speak to strangers.*
▶ wise, advisable, sensible, shrewd
AN OPPOSITE IS unwise

2 *a prudent attitude to money*
▶ cautious, careful, shrewd, far-sighted, thoughtful, wary

prudish ADJECTIVE

Her aunt was a rather prudish woman.
▶ puritanical, prim, priggish, easily shocked, strait-laced, narrow-minded, old-fashioned, illiberal, intolerant, proper, (*more informal*) prissy
OPPOSITES ARE broad-minded, permissive, liberal

pry VERB

I didn't mean to pry, I was just curious.
▶ interfere, meddle, delve, poke about, nose about, ferret about, be inquisitive, snoop, (*informal*) stick your nose in

pseudonym NOUN

George Orwell is a pseudonym
▶ alias, assumed name, (*French*) nom de plume, pen name, sobriquet, false name

psychic ADJECTIVE

She seemed to have psychic powers and knew exactly what would happen.
▶ clairvoyant, telepathic, extrasensory, supernatural, mystic, occult, psychical

psychological ADJECTIVE
The effects are mostly psychological.
▶ mental, subconscious, emotional, subjective, irrational
AN OPPOSITE IS physical

puberty NOUN
the age of puberty
▶ adolescence, maturity, pubescence, growing up

public ADJECTIVE
1 *public gardens*
▶ communal, open, free, community, unrestricted
AN OPPOSITE IS private
2 *a public figure*
▶ well-known, prominent, celebrated, leading, eminent, important, distinguished, notable, famous
OPPOSITES ARE unknown, obscure
3 *This is all public knowledge by now.*
▶ general, common, recognized, widely known, open

public NOUN
houses open to the public
▶ people, the populace, the community, the country, the nation, citizens

publication NOUN
1 *Publication of the report will be in July.*
▶ issuing, appearance, publishing, printing, production, dissemination
2 *a list of the latest publications*
▶ book, volume, title, work, tome, opus, newspaper, magazine

publicity NOUN
1 *The film was launched in a blaze of publicity.*
▶ attention, media attention, public interest, exposure
2 *Publicity will include television advertising.*
▶ promotion, marketing, advertising, (*more informal*) hype

publicize VERB
The event is being publicized weeks in advance.
▶ advertise, make known, announce, report, (*more informal*) plug
OPPOSITES ARE suppress, conceal

publish VERB
1 *A sequel to the story was published last year.*
▶ issue, bring out, produce, print
2 *The letters should be published as soon as possible.*
▶ make public, make known, publicize, disseminate, put out, make available

pucker VERB
She felt her lips pucker and her eyes grow moist.
▶ wrinkle, screw up, crease, purse, tighten, compress

pudding NOUN
When Steve arrived the others were starting their pudding.
▶ dessert, sweet, (*more informal*) afters

puddle NOUN
He woke up to find a puddle of water on his sleeping bag.
▶ pool, splash, spill

puerile ADJECTIVE
He was making puerile excuses.
▶ childish, infantile, immature, juvenile, silly, inane, fatuous

puff NOUN
1 *a puff of wind*
▶ gust, blast, breath, rush, draught, flurry
2 *a puff of grey smoke*
▶ cloud, whiff

puff VERB
He was puffing when he reached the top of the stairs.
▶ gasp, pant, wheeze, breathe heavily, blow
puff out *The curtains puffed out in the draught.*
▶ swell, distend, become inflated, billow, rise

puke VERB
She had eaten something that upset her and went off to puke.
▶ be sick, vomit, retch, heave, (*informal*) throw up

pull VERB
1 *She pulled another chair to where she was sitting.*
▶ drag, draw, tug, heave, (*more informal*) yank
2 *Cars were pulling trailers and caravans.*
▶ tow, haul, lug, drag, trail
3 *The match will pull huge crowds.*
▶ attract, draw, bring in, entice, allure, tempt
4 *He had pulled a muscle and was forced to withdraw.*
▶ strain, sprain, wrench
5 *A dentist might need to pull the tooth.*
▶ extract, take out, remove, pull out
pull apart *Only pull the machine apart if you know how to put it together again.*
▶ dismantle, take apart, take to pieces, dismember, separate
pull down *A row of houses will be pulled down to make space for the new complex.*
▶ demolish, knock down, tear down, bulldoze, dismantle
pull someone's leg *They stopped pulling his leg when they realized he was upset.*
▶ tease, rag, make fun of, play tricks on
pull off *The gang have pulled off another bank robbery.*
▶ achieve, accomplish, manage, carry out, bring off, succeed in
pull out *The army will pull out by the end of the year.*
▶ withdraw, retreat, leave, depart, quit, move out
pull through *She is likely to pull through despite severe injuries.*
▶ recover, get better, improve, come through, recuperate
pull together *Everyone has to pull together if we are going to succeed.*
▶ cooperate, work together, work as a team, collaborate

pull NOUN
1 *He gave the handle a pull.*
▶ tug, jerk, heave, (*more informal*) yank

2 *The beauty of the place exerted quite a pull.*
▶ attraction, lure, draw, influence, enticement

pulp NOUN
a fruit with a juicy pulp
▶ flesh, mash, mush, paste, pap

pulp VERB
Pulp the damsons through a sieve.
▶ crush, mash, pound, squash, liquidize, pulverize, purée, smash

pulsate VERB
The machine sprang to life and began pulsating.
▶ throb, pulse, beat, oscillate, palpitate, quiver, drum, tick, vibrate

pulse NOUN
The music lacked a regular pulse
▶ beat, rhythm, throb, oscillation, vibration

pulverize VERB
The seeds are pulverized into a powder.
▶ pound, crush, grind, press, powder

pump VERB
The crew rushed to pump the water out of the boat.
▶ drain, draw off, empty, force, drive, raise, siphon
pump up *We'd better pump up the tyres.*
▶ inflate, blow up, fill

pun NOUN
a pun on the words 'entrance' and 'entrancing'
▶ double meaning, wordplay, play on words

punch VERB
1 *Ken punched him in the stomach.*
▶ hit , strike, bash, thump, box, sock, clout, jab, poke, prod, beat, cuff, slog
2 *He punched a hole in the wall.*
▶ pierce, puncture, perforate

punch NOUN
a punch on the nose
▶ blow, bash, thump, box, poke

punctual ADJECTIVE
We're expected to be punctual.
▶ on time, prompt, in good time, (*more informal*) on the dot
OPPOSITES ARE unpunctual, late

puncture NOUN
Her bike had a puncture on the way home.
▶ flat tyre, burst tyre, (*more informal*) flat

puncture VERB
Vandals had punctured her tyres.
▶ make a hole in, pierce, rupture, let down, deflate

punish VERB
The culprits would be punished.
▶ penalize, discipline, correct, chastise, scold, make an example of

punishment NOUN
The punishment has to be reasonable.
▶ penalty, discipline, correction, chastisement
RELATED ADJECTIVE penal

punitive ADJECTIVE
The court can impose a punitive fine.
▶ harsh, severe, drastic, stringent, exemplary

puny ADJECTIVE
He looked small and puny for his age.
▶ weak, feeble, frail, sickly, undersized, undernourished, stunted
OPPOSITES ARE sturdy, strong

pupil NOUN
She is an able pupil.
▶ student, scholar, schoolgirl or schoolboy, learner

purchase VERB
The library has purchased new computer hardware.
▶ buy, acquire, obtain, invest in, pay for, procure, secure, get
OPPOSITES ARE sell, dispose of, market

pure ADJECTIVE
1 *pure gold*
▶ genuine, unalloyed, unmixed, natural
OPPOSITES ARE impure, adulterated
2 *places where the air is pure*
▶ clean, fresh, clear, untainted, unpolluted, uncontaminated
OPPOSITES ARE impure, polluted
3 *a pure mind*
▶ virtuous, moral, chaste, good, innocent, righteous, blameless
OPPOSITES ARE immoral, dirty

purely ADVERB
The lights are purely for show.
▶ simply, only, solely, entirely, totally, completely, exclusively

purify VERB
Trees help to purify the air.
▶ clean, make pure, refine, sterilize, freshen, disinfect, filter
OPPOSITES ARE pollute, contaminate

puritanical ADJECTIVE
a puritanical attitude to pleasure
▶ moralistic, puritan, austere, strict, severe, disapproving, intolerant, narrow-minded, strait-laced
AN OPPOSITE IS permissive

purity NOUN
1 *the purity of the water*
▶ cleanliness, clearness, freshness, naturalness, wholesomeness
2 *the purity of their thoughts*
▶ goodness, virtue, morality, rightness, uprightness, integrity, honesty

purpose NOUN
1 *They made their purpose clear.*
► intention, motive, justification
2 *I can't see any purpose in doing that.*
► point, advantage, benefit, gain
3 *Their actions show a lot of purpose.*
► determination, resolution, resolve,
single-mindedness, tenacity, enthusiasm
on purpose *He says it was an accident but I'm sure he
did it on purpose.*
► deliberately, intentionally, purposely,
consciously, knowingly

purposeful ADJECTIVE
He cleared his throat in a purposeful manner.
► deliberate, determined, resolute, calculated,
decided, decisive, single-minded, firm, positive,
steadfast, unwavering
AN OPPOSITE IS hesitant

purposely ADVERB
Old trees are left purposely to rot.
► on purpose, deliberately, intentionally,
consciously, knowingly

purse NOUN
1 *Keep your foreign money in a separate purse.*
► pouch, wallet, money bag, bag
2 *activities that are paid for out of the public purse*
► fund or funds, resources, money, kitty, finances,
exchequer

purse VERB
He pursed his lips and thought hard.
► tighten, close, compress, pucker, contract, screw
up

pursue VERB
1 *I pursued a fox to the end of the lane.*
► chase, go after, run after, follow, track
2 *It was an ambitious objective to pursue.*
► strive for, work towards, aim at, aspire to
3 *She is determined to pursue a career in politics.*
► follow, undertake, take up, engage in
4 *He pursues a number of interests in his spare time.*
► carry on, maintain, follow, continue, devote
yourself to

pursuit NOUN
1 *Police gave up the pursuit when they lost the trail in
London.*
► chase, hunt, search, tracking
2 *The family enjoy their outdoor pursuits.*
► activity, pastime, diversion, amusement
3 *the pursuit of knowledge*
► search (for), quest (for), striving (for), aim, goal,
objective

push VERB
1 *She pushed a chair against the door.*
► shove, thrust, press, propel, nudge
AN OPPOSITE IS pull
2 *I pushed a few things into a bag.*
► pack, cram, squash, squeeze, jam, ram, crush, put,
insert

3 *He tried to push his way through the crowd.*
► force, thrust, shove, elbow, jostle, shoulder, prod,
press
4 *Better not to push them to come if they don't want to.*
► press, pressure, pressurize, put pressure on, urge,
persuade, cajole, browbeat, coerce, bully, compel,
(*more informal*) lean on
5 *Each software company wants to push its own
product.*
► promote, publicize, advertise, popularize, make
known, market, (*more informal*) plug

push around *He was fed up with being pushed
around.*
► bully, domineer, boss about or around, trample
on, mistreat

push for *Trade unions are pushing for the repeal of
some of these laws.*
► demand, insist on, press for, urge

push off (*informal*) *She was busy and told us to push
off.*
► go away, leave, be off, run along, depart, (*informal*)
beat it, (*informal*) scram

push NOUN
1 *She felt a push in her back.*
► shove, thrust, prod, nudge, jolt, poke, knock
2 *The enemy's push was aimed at reaching the coast.*
► advance, thrust, drive, offensive, onslaught,
assault

pushy ADJECTIVE
*He needed to appear in control without seeming too
pushy.*
► assertive, dominating, dominant, aggressive,
forceful, officious

put VERB This word is often overused. Here are some
alternatives:
1 *He put the case on the table. They put a guard on
the door.*
► place, leave, set, deposit, position, stand, settle,
station, post
2 *I wanted to say something but I wasn't sure how to
put it.*
► express, word, phrase, formulate, couch
3 *The government will put a tax on it.*
► impose, inflict, levy, apply (to), assign (to)
4 *They put the cost at over a million.*
► estimate, reckon, calculate, assess, evaluate,
measure, judge
5 *We have some ideas to put to you.*
► submit, present, propose, advance, offer,
suggest

put across *The government needs to put its message
across clearly.*
► communicate, convey, get across, spell out,
make clear, express

put aside *We have put aside some money.*
► save, set aside, put by, keep, keep in reserve,
reserve ►►

put back
1 *The meeting has been put back for a week.*
▶ postpone, defer, delay, hold over
AN OPPOSITE IS bring forward
put by *She wanted to put something by each week for emergencies.*
▶ save, set aside, keep, earmark
put down
1 *I'd better put down some details.*
▶ write down, record, enter, note down, make a note of
2 *The army quickly put down the rebellion.*
▶ suppress, crush, quell, quash, defeat
3 *He enjoyed putting people down, especially in public.*
▶ criticize, belittle, disparage, humiliate, mortify
4 *You can put it down to laziness.*
▶ attribute, ascribe, blame (on)
put forward *Stella put forward a new suggestion.*
▶ advance, offer, propose, suggest, present, submit
AN OPPOSITE IS withdraw
put in *You have to put in a new ink cartridge*
▶ insert, install, fit
OPPOSITES ARE remove, take out
put off
1 *The noise put her off.*
▶ deter, discourage, disconcert, unnerve, repel, distract, intimidate
AN OPPOSITE IS attract
2 *We'd better put off a decision.*
▶ postpone, defer, delay, hold over, shelve, reschedule
AN OPPOSITE IS bring forward
put on
1 *He put on an air of importance.*
▶ assume, affect, simulate, feign, sham
2 *The gallery is putting on a special exhibition.*
▶ mount, organize, stage, produce, present
put out
1 *Nina was put out by this criticism.*
▶ offend, annoy, anger, irritate, affront, insult
2 *I hope it won't put you out if I stay a few days.*
▶ inconvenience, bother, trouble, impose on
3 *The BBC put out an appeal.*
▶ announce, publish, broadcast, circulate
put up
1 *He put up a shed in the garden*
▶ erect, build, construct, assemble
OPPOSITES ARE take down, demolish
2 *We can put you up for a few days.*
▶ accommodate, house, lodge, take in, give a bed to, shelter
3 *They have put up their prices.*
▶ increase, raise, lift, (*more informal*) bump up
put up with *She is not prepared to put up with such behaviour.*
▶ tolerate, stand for, accept, bear, take, endure, stomach

puzzle NOUN
It is a hard puzzle to solve.
▶ problem, riddle, question, enigma, paradox
puzzle VERB
Mike's angry response puzzled me.
▶ confuse, perplex, baffle, mystify, bewilder, disconcert, confound, fox, (*more informal*) flummox
puzzle out *She was trying to puzzle out who the caller might have been.*
▶ work out, figure out, resolve, decide, get to the bottom of, make sense of

puzzled ADJECTIVE
Freda had a puzzled look on her face.
▶ confused, baffled, perplexed, mystified, bewildered, at a loss, nonplussed, (*more informal*) stumped

puzzling ADJECTIVE
There was something puzzling about the shape of the house.
▶ confusing, baffling, bewildering, perplexing, mystifying, mysterious, inexplicable, extraordinary
OPPOSITES ARE straightforward, comprehensible

Qq

quagmire NOUN
Heavy rain turned the field into a quagmire.
▶ swamp, morass, marsh, mire, bog

quail VERB
The force of her anger made him quail.
▶ tremble, cower, cringe, shrink, shudder, wince, quake, recoil, blench, flinch

quaint ADJECTIVE
a quaint little shop that served teas
▶ charming, picturesque, antiquated, strange, sweet, old-world, (*more informal*) twee

quake VERB
Passing trains make the walls quake.
▶ tremble, quiver, shake, shiver, quaver, vibrate, shudder, wobble

qualification NOUN
1 *You need a professional qualification in social work.*
▶ certificate, diploma, degree, training, skill, competence, eligibility, fitness
2 *He agreed without any qualification.*
▶ reservation, hesitation, restriction, exception, condition, modification

qualified ADJECTIVE

1 *His two sons were both qualified doctors.*
▶ certified, chartered, skilled, trained, professional, graduate, competent
AN OPPOSITE IS unqualified

2 *She could only give the idea qualified approval.*
▶ limited, modified, conditional, cautious, guarded, reserved, restricted, equivocal, half-hearted
OPPOSITES ARE unqualified, unconditional

qualify VERB

1 *The course qualifies you to teach young children.*
▶ authorize, permit, allow, entitle, prepare, equip, fit
AN OPPOSITE IS disqualify (from)

2 *I may qualify for a discount.*
▶ be eligible, be entitled (to), be allowed

3 *He qualified his conclusion with a few reservations.*
▶ moderate, modify, restrict, mitigate, limit

quality NOUN

1 *work of a high quality*
▶ standard, calibre, class, grade, rank, sort, value, condition, excellence

2 *He has many good qualities*
▶ characteristic, feature, attribute, point, aspect, peculiarity, property, trait

qualm NOUN

She had some qualms about leaving the old man alone.
▶ concern, anxiety, misgiving, unease, disquiet, apprehension, doubt, worry, reservation, scruple

quandary NOUN

James was in a quandary about what to do next.
▶ predicament, state of confusion, state of uncertainty, state of perplexity, plight, dilemma

quantify VERB

The cost will be hard to quantify.
▶ measure, put a figure on, determine, gauge, assess

quantity NOUN

A huge quantity of stolen goods was recovered.
▶ amount, number, total, volume, lot, portion, proportion, consignment

quarrel NOUN

A quarrel developed in which Kemp was struck over the head.
▶ argument, row, disagreement, altercation, difference of opinion, dispute, squabble, clash, tiff
OPPOSITES ARE agreement, reconciliation

quarrel VERB

1 *People quarrel in different ways.*
▶ argue, disagree, row, have a row, squabble, bicker, fall out, tiff, fight
AN OPPOSITE IS agree

2 **quarrel with** *I can't quarrel with your version of what happened.*
▶ disagree with, find fault with, criticize, oppose

quarrelsome ADJECTIVE

He didn't want to stay with such a quarrelsome family.
▶ argumentative, contentious, belligerent, disputatious, aggressive, factious, confrontational, ill-tempered
AN OPPOSITE IS peaceable

quarry NOUN

The cat came in with its quarry still hanging from its mouth.
▶ prey, victim, prize, kill

quarter NOUN

1 *a house in the poor quarter of the city*
▶ district, locality, neighbourhood, vicinity, area, region, part, sector

2 *There was help from an unexpected quarter.*
▶ source, direction, point, location

quarter VERB

The troops were quartered in a country house.
▶ accommodate, house, board, lodge, put up, station, billet

quarters PLURAL NOUN

Her bedroom had once been part of the servants' quarters.
▶ accommodation, rooms, lodging, chambers

quash VERB

1 *The Court of Appeal may quash the sentence.*
▶ overrule, revoke, rescind, overturn, set aside, cancel, retract, repeal, nullify

2 *The rebellion was brutally quashed. The statement failed to quash rumours.*
▶ put an end to, stamp out, suppress, crush, quell, subdue, overthrow

quaver VERB

She broke off as her voice began to quaver.
▶ tremble, quiver, waver, shake, flutter, vibrate, pulsate

quay NOUN

Overlooking the quay was a small hotel.
▶ dock, wharf, pier, harbour, jetty, landing-stage, berth

queasy ADJECTIVE

He had been feeling tired and queasy for the past few days.
▶ sick, nauseous, bilious, unwell, poorly, queer, out of sorts

queen NOUN

She knew she would be queen one day.
▶ ruler, monarch, sovereign, crowned head
RELATED ADJECTIVES regal, royal

queer ADJECTIVE

1 *There was something queer going on.*
▶ odd, strange, unusual, weird, peculiar, funny, curious, bizarre, puzzling, mysterious, remarkable
OPPOSITES ARE ordinary, normal

2 *I was feeling a bit queer.*
▶ sick, unwell, poorly, queasy, out of sorts, nauseous, bilious, faint, dizzy

quell VERB
Troops were sent in to quell the rising.
▶ suppress, put an end to, stamp out, crush, quash, subdue, overthrow

quench VERB
1 *The fire brigade was called in to quench the flames.*
▶ extinguish, put out, smother, damp down, douse, snuff out
2 *We stopped at a small village to quench our thirst.*
▶ relieve, satisfy, sate, slake, cool

query NOUN
Please send a stamped addressed envelope with any queries.
▶ question, enquiry, problem, doubt, uncertainty

query VERB
She had to query the wisdom of such a plan.
▶ question, doubt, suspect, have doubts about, have reservations about, feel uneasy about, challenge, dispute
AN OPPOSITE IS accept

quest NOUN
a quest to find iron-age remains
▶ expedition, mission, search, hunt, crusade

question NOUN
1 *You haven't answered the question.*
▶ enquiry, query, problem
AN OPPOSITE IS answer
2 *There is the question of all his debts.*
▶ issue, matter, business, point, subject, problem
3 *There's some question about who will be in charge.*
▶ uncertainty, doubt, misgiving, argument, reservation, debate, dispute, controversy, objection
out of the question *Sending them more money was out of the question.*
▶ impossible, inconceivable, unthinkable, unrealistic, not feasible, impractical, (*more informal*) not on
OPPOSITES ARE possible, feasible

question VERB
1 *A man is being questioned at Gloucester police station.*
▶ interrogate, interview, cross-examine, investigate, (*more informal*) quiz, (*more informal*) grill, (*more informal*) pump
2 *She never questioned his right to be there.*
▶ query, doubt, suspect, have doubts about, have reservations about, feel uneasy about, challenge, dispute

questionable ADJECTIVE
All these arguments are highly questionable.
▶ debatable, doubtful, dubious, suspect, unreliable, disputable, uncertain, unclear, unprovable, (*more informal*) iffy, (*more informal*) shady
OPPOSITES ARE unquestionable, indisputable, acceptable

questionnaire NOUN
The results of the questionnaire showed that children were enthusiastic about learning science.
▶ question sheet, survey, opinion poll, quiz, test

queue NOUN
1 *To my surprise there was no queue at the Post Office.*
▶ line, line of people
2 *There were traffic queues all down the motorway.*
▶ jam, tailback, file, column, procession

queue VERB
They queued for hours to be sure of tickets.
▶ line up, form a queue, wait in a queue

quibble VERB
He accepted the offer without quibbling.
▶ complain, find fault, carp, cavil, object, equivocate, split hairs, nitpick

quibble NOUN
Her only quibble was about the cost.
▶ complaint, objection, reservation, doubt, query, criticism

quick ADJECTIVE
1 *She gave a quick glance at her watch.*
▶ hasty, brief, cursory, furtive, fleeting, rapid
OPPOSITES ARE long, careful
2 *He was always a quick worker.*
▶ fast, swift, rapid, speedy, lively, sprightly, prompt
AN OPPOSITE IS slow
3 *There is no quick solution to the problem.*
▶ instant, instantaneous, ready, sudden
4 *Kevin wasn't as quick as some of the others in the class.*
▶ bright, clever, intelligent, gifted, able, sharp, alert, acute, (*more informal*) on the ball
AN OPPOSITE IS dull

quicken VERB
The pace quickened.
▶ speed up, accelerate, get or go faster, hasten, hurry
OPPOSITES ARE slow, slow down

quickly ADVERB
1 *She began to walk more quickly.*
▶ fast, swiftly, rapidly, speedily
AN OPPOSITE IS slowly
2 *We quickly realized they had gone.*
▶ soon, at once, straight away, right away, rapidly, immediately, instantly, directly, suddenly

quiet ADJECTIVE
1 *The house is in a quiet village near the river.*
▶ peaceful, tranquil, secluded, isolated, calm, restful, pleasant
OPPOSITES ARE noisy, busy
2 *He spoke in a quiet voice.*
▶ soft, low, muted, muffled
OPPOSITES ARE loud, raised
3 *Can we have a quiet word together?*
▶ private, confidential, secret
4 *Fiona's a lovely, quiet person.*
▶ shy, reserved, private, subdued, taciturn, withdrawn, calm, placid, serene, composed, untroubled, unruffled
AN OPPOSITE IS outgoing
5 *It's hard to keep rumours like that quiet.*
▶ secret, silent, private, confidential, undisclosed
AN OPPOSITE IS public

quieten VERB
1 *The audience quietened when the curtain went up.*
▶ go quiet, fall silent, grow silent, hush, shush, (*more informal*) shut up
2 *He was so excited it was impossible to quieten him.*
▶ calm, calm down, pacify, mollify, appease, assuage

quilt NOUN
He put a quilt on the bed.
▶ eiderdown, bedcover, bedspread, counterpane, duvet

quip NOUN
He finished the speech with a quip.
▶ joke, witticism, witty remark, jest, (*more informal*) wisecrack

quirk NOUN
One of his quirks is that he checks things over and over again.
▶ peculiarity, oddity, idiosyncrasy, foible, whim, caprice

quit VERB
1 *She's much too determined to quit now.*
▶ give up, stop, leave, depart, go, cease
2 *It's time you quit smoking.*
▶ give up, stop, cease, discontinue, drop, (*more informal*) pack in
3 *He decided to quit his job and go abroad.*
▶ leave, resign from, retire from, renounce, forsake, abandon

quite ADVERB
1 *The two sisters are quite different in appearance.*
▶ completely, totally, wholly, entirely, utterly
2 *It was quite late by now.*
▶ rather, fairly, a bit, somewhat, comparatively, relatively, (*more informal*) pretty

quits ADJECTIVE
After four games we were quits.
▶ level, even, square, equal

quiver VERB
The trees quivered in the wind. I sat quivering with fright.
▶ shake, tremble, shudder, shiver, quaver, flutter

quiz NOUN
The day ended with a quiz between the two teams.
▶ competition, questionnaire, test, examination, questioning

quiz VERB
(*informal*) *The police are quizzing a suspect.*
▶ question, interrogate, interview, cross-examine, investigate

quizzical ADJECTIVE
She had a quizzical expression.
▶ puzzled, questioning, enquiring, perplexed, baffled, curious

quota NOUN
He wouldn't take his full quota of leave this year.
▶ allocation, allowance, ration, share, portion

quotation NOUN
1 *a quotation from Shakespeare*
▶ citation, quote, reference, excerpt, extract, piece, passage
2 *First we need a quotation for the work.*
▶ estimate, price, quote, figure, tender

quote VERB
1 *She quoted a few lines from a poem.*
▶ cite, recite, recall, repeat, mention, refer to
2 *The figure the builder quoted was too high.*
▶ estimate, offer, tender, bid, specify

Rr

rabble NOUN
He was met by a rabble of angry, noisy youths.
▶ crowd, throng, horde, mob, gang, group, herd, swarm

race NOUN
1 *people of many different races*
▶ ethnic group, nation, people, clan, tribe
RELATED ADJECTIVES ethnic, racial
2 *Donald won the race easily.*
▶ contest, competition, chase, heat, event

race VERB
1 *The children were racing each other in the garden.*
▶ have a race with, run against, compete with, try to beat
2 *Herds of waterbuck raced across the swamps. She raced towards the house.*
▶ dash, rush, shoot, sprint, streak, dart, hare, hasten, hurry, run, tear, zoom, career, fly, gallop, move fast
3 *All kinds of thoughts raced through my mind.*
▶ rush, dart, fly, shoot, zoom

racial ADJECTIVE
laws against racial discrimination
▶ ethnic, national, cultural

racism NOUN
the struggle to end racism in all its forms
▶ discrimination, racialism, racial hatred, intolerance, prejudice, xenophobia, bigotry, chauvinism

racist ADJECTIVE
racist attitudes
▶ discriminatory, racialist, intolerant, prejudiced, xenophobic, biased, bigoted, chauvinist
OPPOSITES ARE tolerant, unbiased

rack NOUN
a vegetable rack   a luggage rack
▶ stand, shelf, support, framework, frame

racket NOUN

1 (*informal*) *The machines make a frightful racket.*
▶ noise, din, commotion, hubbub, clamour, tumult, rumpus, uproar
2 (*informal*) *He was involved in a stolen car racket.*
▶ swindle, fraud, dodge, fiddle, deception, (*more informal*) con, (*informal*) scam

racy ADJECTIVE

a writer of racy novels
▶ bawdy, spicy, indecent, naughty, risqué

radiant ADJECTIVE

1 *a radiant moon*
▶ bright, shining, brilliant
OPPOSITES ARE dark, dull
2 *a radiant smile*
▶ beautiful, glowing, dazzling, sparkling, beaming, joyful, elated, happy
OPPOSITES ARE faint, weak

radiate VERB

1 *Electric bulbs radiate more heat than light.*
▶ emit, send out, give off, spread, transmit, diffuse, shed
2 *a face that radiates confidence*
▶ show, display, exhibit, emanate, breathe, transmit, send out

radical ADJECTIVE

1 *a radical course of action*
▶ fundamental, drastic, thoroughgoing, thorough, comprehensive, sweeping, rigorous, complete, basic
AN OPPOSITE IS superficial
2 *a government committed to radical change*
▶ revolutionary, extreme, extremist, militant
OPPOSITES ARE moderate, conservative

raffle NOUN

She won a prize in a raffle.
▶ draw, lottery, tombola, sweepstake

rage NOUN

1 *He stormed out of the room in a burst of rage.*
▶ anger, fury, temper, outrage, passion, pique, exasperation
2 *the rage for portable DVD players*
▶ craze, vogue, trend, fashion, passion

rage VERB

1 *He was raging about what had happened.*
▶ fume, storm, seethe, rant, fulminate, be angry
2 *A fierce blizzard raged for days.*
▶ blow, storm, thunder, rampage

ragged ADJECTIVE

1 *She spent the morning mending ragged clothes.*
▶ tattered, torn, frayed, threadbare, ripped, shabby, tatty, unkempt, worn out
2 *He drilled his ragged collection of men.*
▶ disorganized, disordered, disorderly, erratic, irregular, uneven

raid NOUN

1 *Sentries watched out for any air raids.*
▶ attack, assault, strike, swoop, blitz, foray, sortie, onslaught, invasion
2 *He had killed a guard during a bank raid.*
▶ robbery, burglary, break-in, hold-up, (*more informal*) heist

raid VERB

1 *The army raided towns on the border.*
▶ attack, pillage, loot, plunder, ransack, maraud, assault, storm, descend on
2 *Burglars raided local jewellers for the second time.*
▶ rob, hold up, burgle, break into
3 *Police raided homes and offices in the area.*
▶ search, swoop on

railing NOUN

A notice had been put on the railing.
▶ fence, paling, barrier

railway NOUN

They were warned not to cross the railway
▶ track, line, rails

rain NOUN

The rain had started again.
▶ rainfall, wet weather, drizzle, shower, downpour, cloudburst, raindrops, rainstorm, squall, deluge, (*more formal*) precipitation

rain VERB

It rained all afternoon.
▶ pour, bucket, teem, pelt, drizzle, spit

rainy ADJECTIVE

a rainy day
▶ wet, showery, drizzly, damp
AN OPPOSITE IS dry

raise VERB

1 *Ben raised his hand.*
▶ put up, lift
2 *A crane will raise the load to the top of the building.*
▶ lift, hoist
3 *The company was forced to raise its prices.*
▶ increase, put up, push up, lift
4 *United will need to raise their game for the away match.*
▶ improve, enhance, strengthen, heighten, boost, step up, put more life into
5 *We need to raise five thousand pounds.*
▶ collect, get, obtain, gather, net, amass, scrape together, yield, assemble
6 *This good news raised their hopes.*
▶ encourage, increase, improve, arouse, rouse, excite
7 *She raised three children on her own.*
▶ bring up, provide for, nurture, look after, educate
8 *Charles raised several objections to the idea.*
▶ bring up, put forward, advance, present, introduce, pose, offer
9 *The incident raises questions about rail safety.*
▶ give rise to, occasion, cause, bring about, produce, engender

rally NOUN
an anti-war rally
▶ demonstration, meeting, protest, march, (*more informal*) demo

rally VERB
1 *The king rallied his troops at the border. They tried to rally support for the election.*
▶ muster, assemble, marshal, amass, gather, round up, organize
2 *Our spirits rallied.*
▶ recover, improve, pick up, get better, look up, perk up

ram VERB
The getaway van rammed a police car.
▶ hit, strike, smash into, be in collision with, slam into, collide with, crash into

ramble VERB
1 *We spent a week rambling in the countryside.*
▶ walk, roam, trek, tramp, hike, rove, stroll
2 *He was rambling on about his schooldays.*
▶ chatter, blather, prattle, drift, run, maunder, (*more informal*) rabbit, (*more informal*) witter

rambling ADJECTIVE
a long rambling speech
▶ long-winded, verbose, diffuse, disjointed, disconnected, incoherent, roundabout, digressive

ramp NOUN
There's a ramp for wheelchairs
▶ slope, incline, gradient, rise, sloping surface

rampage VERB
A mob rampaged through the streets.
▶ run riot, run amok, go on the rampage, riot, go berserk, go wild, race about, rush about, behave violently

rampant ADJECTIVE
years of rampant corruption
▶ unrestrained, unchecked, unbridled, widespread, pervasive, wild

ramshackle ADJECTIVE
a ramshackle old house
▶ dilapidated, tumbledown, derelict, decrepit, rickety, shaky, unsafe, broken down, ruined, tottering, crumbling
AN OPPOSITE IS sturdy

random ADJECTIVE
Her house came up in a random sample of houses in the area.
▶ indiscriminate, arbitrary, chance, haphazard, casual, unplanned, accidental, unconsidered, unpremeditated, fortuitous, irregular
AN OPPOSITE IS systematic

range NOUN
1 *a range of mountains*
▶ chain, row, line, series, string, file
2 *a wide range of food*
▶ variety, assortment, selection, array, scope, choice, spectrum, extent

3 *an age range between 20 and 30*
▶ span, scope, compass, radius

range VERB
1 *Prices range between £100 and £600*
▶ vary, extend, differ, fluctuate, reach
2 *Sheep ranged over the hills.*
▶ roam, rove, wander, stray, travel
3 *Pupils are ranged by ability.*
▶ classify, class, categorize, rank, order, group

rank NOUN
1 *She was promoted to the rank of assistant manager.*
▶ level, grade, position, status, standing, station, title, class, degree
2 *a family of rank*
▶ high standing, distinction, importance, nobility, aristocracy
3 *The front rank began to move forward.*
▶ row, line, file, column

rank VERB
He's ranked number two in the world.
▶ grade, class, categorize, classify, designate, list

rank ADJECTIVE
1 *a ditch full of rank water*
▶ foul-smelling, noxious, fetid, smelly
2 *There was rank disbelief at the numbers.*
▶ utter, sheer, outright, downright, complete, total, wholesale, absolute

rankle VERB
rankle with *The criticism still rankles with him.*
▶ annoy, upset, anger, offend, irritate, nettle, irk

ransack VERB
1 *Thieves had ransacked the buildings.*
▶ plunder, pillage, loot, raid, rob, ravage, wreck
2 *I ransacked the cupboard for a clean shirt.*
▶ rummage through, hunt through, scour, search, comb, (*more informal*) turn upside down

ransom NOUN
The ransom was set at four million dollars.
▶ pay-off, release money, payment, price

ransom VERB
The kidnappers demanded a million pounds to ransom the girl.
▶ obtain the release of, release, redeem, liberate, free

rant VERB
The old man was ranting in German.
▶ hold forth, shout, yell, roar, bellow, declaim

rap VERB
rap on *He rapped on the big oak door.*
▶ knock on, strike, tap, hit

rape NOUN
a charge of rape
▶ sexual assault, sexual attack, sexual abuse

rape VERB
He raped her at gunpoint.
▶ sexually assault, violate, force yourself on, sexually abuse

rapid ADJECTIVE
They made rapid progress.
► fast, quick, swift, speedy, brisk, lively, smooth, sharp, prompt, headlong
OPPOSITES ARE slow, leisurely

rapt ADJECTIVE
a rapt audience
► engrossed, enthralled, absorbed, captivated, enraptured, fascinated, spellbound

rapture NOUN
They gazed at each other in rapture.
► ecstasy, bliss, joy, delight, happiness, euphoria, wonderment, exaltation

rapturous ADJECTIVE
They got a rapturous reception from the teenage audience.
► ecstatic, joyful, joyous, enthusiastic, euphoric, enraptured, delighted

rare ADJECTIVE
1 *a rare moment of peace*
► uncommon, infrequent, scarce, occasional, sporadic, odd, singular
OPPOSITES ARE frequent, common
2 *a person of rare abilities*
► exceptional, remarkable, incomparable, unusual, uncommon, special, abnormal

raring ADJECTIVE
They were raring to begin.
► eager, keen, enthusiastic, longing, impatient, (*more informal*) itching, (*more informal*) dying

rascal NOUN
1 *One of the rascals had stolen money from the till.*
► rogue, scoundrel, ne'er-do-well
2 *Dad asked, 'What's the little rascal been up to?'*
► scamp, scallywag, monkey, mischief-maker, wretch, monster

rash ADJECTIVE
He regretted making such a rash promise.
► reckless, impulsive, impetuous, foolhardy, hasty, precipitate, imprudent, incautious, injudicious, indiscreet, ill-advised, ill-considered, headstrong, unthinking, heedless, hot-headed, hurried
OPPOSITES ARE cautious, considered, prudent

rash NOUN
1 *Her skin broke out in a rash.*
► spots, eruption, hives
2 (*informal*) *a rash of break-ins in the area*
► outbreak, spate, series, succession

rasping ADJECTIVE
the old man's rasping voice
► hoarse, grating, croaking, jarring, raspy, croaky, rough, harsh, husky, gravelly, gruff

rate NOUN
1 *They were pedalling at a furious rate.*
► speed, pace, tempo, velocity, (*more informal*) lick
2 *You can hire a boat for a reasonable daily rate.*
► charge, amount, price, cost, payment, fare, fee, figure

rate VERB
1 *They do not rate our chances very highly.*
► assess, evaluate, appraise, judge, regard, value, count, weigh, estimate, calculate, consider, measure
2 *The suggestion only rated a brief mention.*
► merit, deserve, warrant, be worthy of
3 (*informal*) *I don't rate this stuff like you do.*
► think much of, think highly of, admire, value, enjoy

rather ADVERB
1 *It sounds rather difficult.*
► fairly, somewhat, quite, slightly, moderately, relatively, (*more informal*) pretty
2 *I'd rather leave it until the weekend.*
► sooner, preferably

ratify VERB
All member countries have to ratify the agreement simultaneously.
► confirm, approve, endorse, affirm, sign, authorize, validate

rating NOUN
The restaurant might lose its five-star rating.
► grade, grading, classification, ranking, category, designation, evaluation, placing, mark

ratio NOUN
The ratio of men to women has changed.
► proportion, balance, relationship, correlation, correspondence

ration NOUN
They decided not to increase their daily ration of biscuits.
► allowance, allocation, quota, share, measure, helping, portion
rations *The expedition might soon run out of rations.*
► supplies, provisions, stores, food, necessaries, necessities

ration VERB
Fuel is strictly rationed in wartime.
► control, limit, restrict, conserve, allocate, allot, apportion

rational ADJECTIVE
1 *Feelings are so high it's difficult to have a rational discussion.*
► reasoned, logical, sensible, coherent, cogent, reasonable, balanced, sane, intelligent, judicious, lucid, normal
OPPOSITES ARE irrational, illogical
2 *In the last year of his life he was often barely rational.*
► lucid, coherent, sane, intelligible, in your right mind

rationale NOUN
The government lacks a rationale for reducing taxes.
► reason, reasoning, logical basis, ground or grounds, philosophy, justification

rationalize VERB

1 *Martin tried to rationalize his behaviour of the day before.*
▶ justify, explain, account for, excuse, defend, make allowances for
2 *a proposal to rationalize the postal services*
▶ reorganize, streamline, make more efficient, trim, slim down, modernize

rattle VERB

1 *He rattled the coins in his purse.*
▶ jangle, clink, clunk
2 *A row of trucks rattled along the track.*
▶ clatter, jolt, shake, bounce
3 *The wind rattled at the doors and windows*
▶ shake, batter, beat
4 *This news had rattled her badly.*
▶ disconcert, disturb, unnerve, fluster, shake, discomfit, (*more informal*) throw
rattle off *He rattled off the words he had learned.*
▶ recite, run through, reel off, repeat, list

rattle NOUN

the rattle of crockery in the kitchen
▶ clatter, clattering, clank, clanking

ratty ADJECTIVE

Upset neighbours can get very ratty.
▶ bad-tempered, irritated, irascible, grumpy, testy, grouchy, touchy, crotchety, cantankerous, peevish, fractious, cross, (*more informal*) stroppy, (*more informal*) shirty

raucous ADJECTIVE

the raucous clamour of alarm bells
▶ noisy, harsh, shrill, strident, jarring, grating, loud, rough

ravage VERB

He let his army ravage the Norman countryside.
▶ devastate, lay waste, ruin, destroy, loot, pillage, plunder, raid, damage, despoil, ransack

rave VERB

1 *He was raving and swearing at them.*
▶ rage, rant, shout, roar, bellow, storm
2 **rave about** *Everyone raved about Leeds that day.*
▶ praise, idolize, be ecstatic about, go into raptures over

rave ADJECTIVE

The film got a rave review.
▶ enthusiastic, rapturous, glowing, ecstatic, wonderful

ravenous ADJECTIVE

By evening the walkers were ravenous.
▶ hungry, famished, ravening, insatiable

ravine NOUN

At this point the river flows in a deep ravine
▶ gorge, canyon, defile, gully, chasm, pass

ravishing ADJECTIVE

She looked ravishing in a summer dress.
▶ beautiful, gorgeous, stunning, enchanting, radiant, dazzling

raw ADJECTIVE

1 *She ate a piece of raw onion.*
▶ uncooked, fresh
2 *the high cost of raw materials*
▶ natural, untreated, unprocessed, basic
3 *His skin had become raw.*
▶ sore, inflamed, red, tender
4 *You could sense the raw passion.*
▶ strong, intense, powerful, fervent, unrestrained
5 *They walked against the raw wind.*
▶ cold, bitter, biting, freezing, piercing, chilly

ray NOUN

1 *A ray of light shone through the branches.*
▶ beam, shaft, stream, streak, finger, glint, glimmer
2 *There was one ray of hope left.*
▶ glimmer, flicker, gleam, spark, trace, sign, hint, indication

raze VERB

Enemy troops razed the buildings to the ground.
▶ demolish, tear down, flatten, destroy, bulldoze

reach VERB

1 *After a while the walkers reached a village.*
▶ arrive at, get to, come to, go as far as, (*more informal*) end up at, (*more informal*) make it to
2 *The Government has not reached any of its major targets yet.*
▶ achieve, attain, succeed in, (*more informal*) hit, (*more informal*) make
3 *I can't reach the switch.*
▶ get hold of, grasp, get your hand to, take, touch
4 *You can reach me on my mobile.*
▶ contact, get in touch with, communicate with
reach out *She reached out her hand.*
▶ stretch out, stick out, hold out, put out, extend, raise

reach NOUN

1 *The station is within easy reach*
▶ distance, range, compass, scope
2 *The fugitives were now beyond the reach of the law.*
▶ jurisdiction, authority, control, sway, command
3 *Aim at achievements that are within your reach.*
▶ capabilities, abilities, capacity

react VERB

Zoe wondered how he would react if she told him everything.
▶ respond, reply, answer, behave, take it, act

reaction NOUN

His reaction had puzzled her.
▶ response, manner of response, reply, answer, rejoinder, retort, behaviour

read VERB

1 *He sat in the sofa, reading the papers.*
▶ peruse, study, scan, skim, glance at, pore over, dip into
2 *She promised to read them a story*
▶ read out, tell, say aloud, recite
3 *The writing is not hard to read.*
▶ make out, decipher, make sense of, understand, decode

r

readable ADJECTIVE

1 *a readable book*
▶ enjoyable, entertaining, interesting, well-written, compulsive, gripping
OPPOSITES ARE boring, unreadable
2 *readable handwriting*
▶ legible, clear, decipherable, understandable, neat, plain
AN OPPOSITE IS illegible

readily ADVERB

1 *Janet readily agreed.*
▶ willingly, gladly, happily, unhesitatingly, promptly, eagerly, freely, voluntarily
AN OPPOSITE IS reluctantly
2 *The town is readily reached from the shore.*
▶ easily, quickly, without difficulty

reading NOUN

1 *He gave the letters a hurried reading.*
▶ study, perusal, scrutiny, scan, browse, glance, look through
2 *This is our reading of the evidence.*
▶ interpretation, understanding, construal, reconstruction

ready ADJECTIVE

1 *We are ready to leave. He wasn't ready for the answer he got.*
▶ prepared, set, primed, (more informal) psyched up
2 *They were more than ready to take us to the station.*
▶ willing, prepared, happy, pleased, eager, keen, agreeable, disposed
3 *Everything was ready to start the game.*
▶ prepared, in place
4 **ready to** *By the time she got home she was ready to collapse.*
▶ about to, close to, likely to, on the point of, on the verge of, on the brink of
5 *He has a ready answer to all criticisms.*
▶ prompt, quick, immediate, telling, perceptive, sharp, astute

real ADJECTIVE

1 *Is that real cream?*
▶ genuine, natural, authentic, bona fide, (German) echt
OPPOSITES ARE false, artificial
2 *Some viewers treat characters in soaps as if they were real people.*
▶ actual, physical, existing, unimaginary
OPPOSITES ARE imaginary, made- up
3 *'Carl' is not his real name.*
▶ true, actual, proper
AN OPPOSITE IS assumed
4 *She began to feel real remorse for what had happened.*
▶ sincere, genuine, honest, heartfelt
AN OPPOSITE IS insincere
5 *(informal) I felt a real idiot.*
▶ complete, utter, absolute, total, (informal) right, (informal) proper

realistic ADJECTIVE

1 *The film was meant to be a realistic portrayal of the events.*
▶ authentic, truthful, true to life, faithful, lifelike, natural, genuine, convincing, recognizable, representational, graphic
OPPOSITES ARE fictional, imaginary
2 *To stand any chance the plan has to be realistic.*
▶ practical, sensible, pragmatic, reasonable, common-sensical
OPPOSITES ARE impractical, idealistic
3 *Wage rises have to be realistic.*
▶ reasonable, moderate, acceptable, adequate, fair, justifiable
OPPOSITES ARE unrealistic, excessive

reality NOUN

He sometimes finds it hard to distinguish reality from fantasy.
▶ truth, fact, actuality, certainty, the real world
AN OPPOSITE IS fantasy

realize VERB

1 *I realized it was going to be difficult.*
▶ understand, grasp, register, comprehend, appreciate, recognize, accept, (more informal) twig
2 *They will realize their life's ambition at last.*
▶ achieve, accomplish, fulfil, attain, bring about, bring off, complete
3 *The picture could realize thousands at auction.*
▶ fetch, sell for, be sold for, earn, bring in, produce

realm NOUN

1 *the defence of the realm*
▶ kingdom, monarchy, state, empire, principality
2 *the realm of scientific research*
▶ sphere, domain, field, area, activity, department

rear NOUN

1 *There is a door at the rear of the house.*
▶ back, back part, other end, other side
2 *We went to the rear of the queue.*
▶ end, tail, back
3 *He gave her a slap on the rear.*
▶ bottom, backside, behind, rump, buttocks, (more informal) bum

rear ADJECTIVE

The animal had hurt one of its rear legs.
▶ back, hind, hindmost, rearmost
AN OPPOSITE IS front

rear VERB

I was born and reared in Liverpool.
▶ bring up, raise, educate, care for, nurture

rearrange VERB

1 *Someone had rearranged the furniture.*
▶ reposition, switch round, swap round, reorganize
2 *We'll have to rearrange our plans for the weekend.*
▶ reorganize, alter, adjust, reschedule, rejig

reason NOUN

1 *Money was his main reason for changing jobs.*
▶ cause, ground or grounds, justification, excuse, pretext, case, motive, explanation, apology, argument, incentive, rationale

2 *arguments based on reason rather than emotion*
▶ reasoning, logic, sense, rationality, intellect, judgement, common sense
3 *She was terrified of losing her reason.*
▶ sanity, mind, mental faculties, senses, wits, (*more informal*) marbles
RELATED ADJECTIVE rational

reason VERB
1 *John reasoned that it was too late to reach home in time now.*
▶ calculate, conclude, come to the conclusion, work out, deduce, judge, consider, infer, resolve
2 *Her husband tried to reason with her.*
▶ persuade, talk round, bring round, prevail on, debate with, argue with, remonstrate with, discuss with

reasonable ADJECTIVE
1 *Any reasonable person would have to agree with you.*
▶ sensible, rational, logical, fair-minded
OPPOSITES ARE unreasonable, irrational
2 *It was a reasonable explanation.*
▶ logical, convincing, credible, compelling, cogent, plausible, sound, viable
OPPOSITES ARE unreasonable, illogical
3 *They charge a reasonable fee for this service.*
▶ modest, moderate, acceptable, tolerable
OPPOSITES ARE unreasonable, excessive

reasoning NOUN
I couldn't follow his reasoning.
▶ thinking, logic, train of thought, rationality, rationale, argumentation, arguments, hypothesis, interpretation

reassure VERB
Danny tried hard to reassure us.
▶ comfort, calm, hearten, support, encourage, assure, bolster up, inspirit, give confidence to
OPPOSITES ARE unnerve, disconcert

reassuring ADJECTIVE
He gave her a reassuring smile.
▶ sympathetic, understanding, comforting, encouraging, calming, caring, supportive
AN OPPOSITE IS disconcerting

rebate NOUN
He was delighted to get a tax rebate.
▶ refund, repayment, discount, concession

rebel NOUN (with the stress on *reb-*)
The rebels took control of the region.
▶ revolutionary, insurgent, revolutionist, guerrilla, dissenter, malcontent, mutineer, renegade

rebel ADJECTIVE (with the stress on *reb-*)
Rebel forces captured the town.
▶ insurgent, revolutionary, rebellious, mutinous

rebel VERB (with the stress on -*bel*)
The people of the south rebelled.
▶ revolt, mutiny, riot, rise up, mount a rebellion

rebellion NOUN
Troops were sent in to crush the rebellion.
▶ uprising, revolt, rising, insurrection, insurgency, sedition, mutiny, insubordination, resistance, revolution

rebellious ADJECTIVE
1 *rebellious troops*
▶ mutinous, insurgent, rebel, rebelling, mutinying, subversive
2 *rebellious staff*
▶ defiant, insubordinate, unruly, ungovernable, unmanageable, uncontrollable, recalcitrant, obstreperous

rebound VERB
1 *The ball rebounded off the wall.*
▶ bounce, bounce back, ricochet, recoil, boomerang
2 (*informal*) *His devious tactics rebounded on him.*
▶ backfire, misfire, recoil, boomerang, come back

rebuff VERB
The offer was rebuffed again. She rebuffed him many times before finally accepting.
▶ reject, refuse, turn down, decline, spurn, dismiss, snub
OPPOSITES ARE accept, welcome

rebuff NOUN
He carried on despite this rebuff.
▶ rejection, refusal, snub, repulse, (*more informal*) put-down, (*more informal*) slap in the face
OPPOSITES ARE acceptance, welcome

rebuild VERB
It will cost a fortune to rebuild the theatre.
▶ reconstruct, renovate, restore, reassemble
AN OPPOSITE IS demolish

rebuke VERB
She didn't want to rebuke him in front of his friends.
▶ tell off, reprimand, reprove, reproach, admonish, scold, chide
OPPOSITES ARE praise, commend

rebuke NOUN
He did not know how to answer this stinging rebuke.
▶ reprimand, reproach, admonishment, admonition, scolding, telling-off, censure

rebut VERB
They were determined to rebut all these charges.
▶ deny, counter, repudiate, refute, disprove, dispute, reject, prove false

recall VERB
She could not recall what he had said.
▶ remember, recollect, call to mind, think, cast your mind back to
AN OPPOSITE IS forget

recede VERB
The flood waters slowly receded.
▶ subside, ebb, retreat, regress, go back, abate, shrink back, decline, retire, return, slacken

receipt NOUN

1 *Make sure you keep the receipt.*
▶ sales slip, proof of purchase, bill, ticket, counterfoil, stub
2 *Receipt of your tickets is guaranteed within three working days.*
▶ delivery, arrival, receiving
receipts *receipts from the sale of council houses*
▶ income, proceeds, revenue, earnings, profits, takings, gains

receive VERB

1 *He received an award for gallantry.*
▶ be given, earn, get, accept, collect, obtain, gain, take, acquire, be sent
OPPOSITES ARE give, present
2 *He received some minor injuries in the accident.*
▶ suffer, sustain, experience, undergo, bear
AN OPPOSITE IS inflict
3 *She received the news in complete silence.*
▶ hear, listen to, respond to, react to, take, greet

recent ADJECTIVE

Recent events have caused them to change their minds.
▶ new, current, fresh, latest, present-day, up-to-date, contemporary, modern, novel
OPPOSITES ARE old, earlier

receptacle NOUN

a receptacle for umbrellas
▶ container, holder, vessel, repository, box, canister, pot, basket

reception NOUN

1 *We got a friendly reception.*
▶ greeting, welcome
2 *A reception will be held at the local hotel.*
▶ party, function, gathering, celebration, get-together, social event, (*more informal*) do

receptive ADJECTIVE

We must be receptive to new ideas.
▶ responsive, open, open-minded, susceptible, sympathetic, welcoming, amenable, interested (in), kindly disposed

recess NOUN

1 *The room has two recesses with fitted bookshelves.*
▶ alcove, bay, niche, nook, hollow, cavity, apse, indentation
2 *The chairman announced a twenty-minute recess.*
▶ break, adjournment, respite, rest, interval, intermission, interlude

recession NOUN

an economic recession
▶ decline, downturn, depression, slump, trough

recipe NOUN

1 *She would try out her new soufflé recipe*
▶ method, procedure, directions, instructions
2 *The measures might prove to be a recipe for disaster.*
▶ prescription, formula, procedure, likely cause (of)

recital NOUN

1 *She gave her first piano recital at the age of eight.*
▶ concert, public performance, programme

2 *a recital of poems*
▶ recitation, rendering, saying aloud, delivery, narration

recite VERB

1 *She announced that she would recite a poem.*
▶ say aloud, read out, deliver, perform, declaim
2 *It would take too long to recite all the events of the week.*
▶ list, enumerate, detail, recount, relate, repeat, run through, reel off, specify

reckless ADJECTIVE

For such a mild man he could be amazingly reckless behind the wheel of a car.
▶ rash, careless, heedless, mindless, thoughtless, negligent, foolhardy, daredevil

reckon VERB

1 *They reckoned the cost at about three thousand pounds.*
▶ assess, estimate, calculate, work out, figure out, gauge, evaluate, count, add up, compute, total
2 (*informal*) *I reckon she's keen on him.*
▶ think, believe, suspect, consider, dare say, have an idea, fancy, guess
3 *These animals are reckoned the most dangerous.*
▶ consider, regard as, deem, judge, count
4 **reckon on** *We didn't reckon on such stiff opposition.*
▶ expect, foresee, plan for, bargain for, figure on

reckoning NOUN

By my reckoning we should make a small profit.
▶ calculation, estimation, estimate, judgement, evaluation

reclaim VERB

1 *You can reclaim your travelling expenses.*
▶ get back, claim back, recover, (*more informal*) put in for
2 *an area of land reclaimed from the sea*
▶ recover, restore, save, make usable, regenerate

recline VERB

His aunt was reclining on a sofa.
▶ lie, rest, lie down, lie back, lean back, stretch out, lounge, loll, sprawl

recognize VERB

1 *I didn't recognize him in his smart suit.*
▶ identify, place, know, remember, recall, call to mind, put a name to
2 *They recognize his abilities without liking his work very much.*
▶ acknowledge, admit, accept, concede, grant, allow, appreciate, confess, realize
3 *The qualification is not recognized in Britain.*
▶ accept, approve, acknowledge, accredit, admit, endorse, support

recoil VERB

She recoiled instinctively as he put his hand out.
▶ flinch, draw back, shy away, jerk back, start, wince, shrink back

recollect VERB

I don't recollect any such promise.

▶ remember, recall, call to mind, think, cast your mind back to

AN OPPOSITE IS forget

recollection NOUN

She had no recollection of what happened

▶ memory, remembrance, recall, impression

recommend VERB

1 *His doctor recommended surgery.*

▶ advise, counsel, propose, advocate, suggest, urge, prescribe

2 *This book is recommended by teachers.*

▶ approve of, advocate, endorse, commend, suggest, praise, speak well of, vouch for, (*more informal*) plug

recommendation NOUN

1 *The governors accepted the main recommendation of the committee.*

▶ advice, counsel, guidance, proposal, suggestion

2 *She supported him with her personal recommendation*

▶ commendation, endorsement, advocacy, testimonial, reference, blessing

reconcile VERB

1 *Their shared grief reconciled them after years of being apart.*

▶ reunite, bring together, conciliate, harmonize, placate

2 **reconcile yourself to** *We have reconciled ourselves to a long wait.*

▶ accept, resign yourself to, learn to live with, get used to, submit to, tolerate

reconnoitre VERB

(*informal*) *Helicopters reconnoitred the area ahead of ground troops.*

▶ survey, patrol, scout, spy out, explore, investigate, scan, examine, gather intelligence about, inspect

reconsider VERB

She refused to reconsider her decision.

▶ rethink, review, reassess, reappraise, think over, alter, modify

reconstruct VERB

1 *They will have to reconstruct a large part of the building.*

▶ rebuild, renovate, restore, reassemble

AN OPPOSITE IS demolish

2 *Police will reconstruct the incident using actors.*

▶ recreate, re-enact

record NOUN (with the stress on *rec-*)

1 *You should keep a record of everything they say.*

▶ account, report, note, log

2 **records** *There are more historical records for these years.*

▶ documents, archives, evidence, accounts, documentation, annals

3 *She stayed in listening to records.*

▶ CD, disc, compact disc, album, recording, LP

4 *There is not a single mistake to tarnish his record.*

▶ background, career, CV

5 *The new time was a world record.*

▶ best performance, fastest time

record VERB (with the stress on -*cord*)

1 *He recorded everything he heard in a notebook.*

▶ note, register, enter, put down, set down, write down, transcribe, log, minute

2 *They wanted to record the song and send it in.*

▶ tape, tape-record, make a recording of, video, preserve, keep

recount VERB

Her brother recounted all his adventures.

▶ tell, describe, relate, report, retail, detail, depict, narrate, recite

recover VERB

1 *She was recovering from a mild stroke.*

▶ recuperate, convalesce, get better, improve, heal, mend, rally, revive, pull round or through, (*more informal*) be on the mend

2 *Police say they have recovered some of the stolen property.*

▶ trace, find, get back, track down, retrieve, reclaim, recoup, repossess, salvage

recovery NOUN

1 *Her recovery is proving slow.*

▶ recuperation, convalescence, return to health, improvement, healing, cure

2 *The economy is showing signs of recovery.*

▶ improvement, revival, upturn, picking up

3 *A reward will be paid on recovery of the stolen paintings.*

▶ retrieval, repossession, restoration, recapture, reclamation, salvaging

recreation NOUN

a study of the use of the countryside for recreation

▶ relaxation, amusement, diversion, enjoyment, pleasure, leisure, entertainment, fun, play, games, pastime

recrimination NOUN

If things go wrong there will be questions and recriminations.

▶ accusation, quarrelling, squabbling, bickering

recruit NOUN

1 *The Army is trying to attract more recruits.*

▶ new member, initiate, conscript

2 *Many recruits to the industry turn out to be unsuitable.*

▶ new entrant, trainee, apprentice, novice, new member, newcomer

recruit VERB

1 *The services recruit a high proportion of graduates.*

▶ enlist, enrol, draft, conscript

2 *The Company provides training for the staff it has recruited.*

▶ hire, employ, enrol, engage, take on, advertise for

OPPOSITES ARE dismiss, lay off, make redundant

rectify VERB
The engineers put in extra work to rectify the problem.
▶ correct, put right, resolve, sort out, deal with, fix, remedy, redress

recuperate VERB
She went to Brighton to recuperate from her illness.
▶ recover, get better, get back to normal, regain your health or strength, improve

recur VERB
The problem is certain to recur if we don't do something about it.
▶ return, happen again, reappear, come again, be repeated, persist

recurrent ADJECTIVE
recurrent attacks of fever
▶ repeated, recurring, continual, persistent, regular, chronic, cyclical, frequent, intermittent, periodic

recycle VERB
The department is advising customers on how to recycle their waste.
▶ reuse, reprocess, reclaim, recover, salvage, use again

red ADJECTIVE
1 *She wore a red dress.*
▶ scarlet, vermilion, ruby, crimson, cherry, claret, maroon, flame-coloured
2 *He was red in the face with embarrassment.*
▶ flushed, blushing, flaming, ruddy, florid, glowing, inflamed, rosy, rubicund
3 *The chemicals in the water made his eyes red.*
▶ bloodshot, inflamed, swollen, sore

redden VERB
Her face reddened.
▶ colour, flush, go red, blush, glow

redeem VERB
1 *Freddie had to redeem his oboe from the pawnbroker's.*
▶ reclaim, retrieve, recover, repossess, buy back
2 **redeem yourself** *He failed the first test but redeemed himself in the second.*
▶ vindicate, absolve
3 *You can redeem your voucher at any branch of the store.*
▶ exchange, cash in, exchange for cash, return, trade in

reduce VERB
1 *The goal is to reduce carbon emissions by 20 percent.*
▶ lessen, lower, decrease, bring down, curtail, moderate
OPPOSITES ARE increase, enlarge
2 *The novel has been greatly reduced in the television adaptation.*
▶ shorten, abridge, condense
AN OPPOSITE IS expand
3 *The father's gambling debts reduced the family to poverty.*
▶ drive, force, bring to the point of

reduction NOUN
1 *a reduction in pollution*
▶ decrease, drop, fall, lessening, lowering, diminution
AN OPPOSITE IS increase
2 *a series of price reductions*
▶ cut, discount, (more informal) slash
AN OPPOSITE IS increase

redundant ADJECTIVE
There are three redundant churches in the area.
▶ unnecessary, unwanted, superfluous, surplus, excessive, too many
AN OPPOSITE IS necessary

make someone redundant *They plan to make twenty members of the workforce redundant just before Christmas.*
▶ lay off, dismiss, sack, discharge

reel VERB
1 *A woman reeled towards him clutching a half-eaten burger.*
▶ stagger, stumble, sway, totter, lurch, swerve
2 **reel from** *When the worst happens you reel from it and the shock is enormous.*
▶ be shaken by, be shocked by, be stunned by, be staggered by, be aghast at

reel off *He reeled off one joke after another.*
▶ recite, rattle off, fire off, run off

refer VERB
1 *His GP referred him to a specialist. The manager referred the matter to head office.*
▶ pass, send, transfer, direct, entrust, hand on, send on
2 **refer to** *The police officer referred to her notes.*
▶ consult, look up, turn to, look in, search in
3 **refer to** *The third paragraph of the article refers to new publications.*
▶ mention, detail, list, touch on, describe, allude to, cite

referee NOUN
1 *The referee blew his whistle.*
▶ umpire, judge, adjudicator, arbitrator, (more informal) ref
2 *Your CV must include the names of two referees.*
▶ supporter, character witness, backer, advocate

reference NOUN
1 *The title 'Brave New World' is a reference to a Shakespeare play.*
▶ allusion, quotation (from), citation (from), example (of), illustration (from), instance (of), mention (of)
2 *His teacher had given him a glowing reference.*
▶ testimonial, recommendation, endorsement, backing
with reference to *She spoke to him with reference to his recent conduct.*
▶ about, with regard to, in relation to, a propos of, on the subject of ▶▶

NAMES FOR TYPES OF REFERENCE SOURCES

books: dictionary, thesaurus, encyclopedia, almanac, directory, companion, guidebook; atlas, gazetteer, catalogue; timetable.

electronic: database, website, Internet, World Wide Web.

places of information: library, archive, museum, gallery; local record office.

---

refill VERB
It was time to refill the tank.
► top up, replenish, refuel, renew

refine VERB
1 *By refining cereals we lose valuable fibre.*
► process, purify, clarify, distil, treat
2 *ways of refining your computing skills*
► improve, perfect, sharpen, polish, hone, touch up

refined ADJECTIVE
1 *refined sugar*
► purified, pure, processed, clarified, distilled, concentrated
2 *a refined man*
► cultivated, sophisticated, urbane, well-mannered

refinement NOUN
1 *Computer programs usually need refinement to get rid of the bugs.*
► improvement, modification, alteration, perfection, fine-tuning, change
2 *the poise, refinement, and eloquence of his playing*
► style, elegance, finesse, polish, sophistication, subtlety, discrimination

reflect VERB
1 *The window reflected their faces staring in.*
► mirror, send back, shine back, throw back
2 *The looks on their faces reflected their feelings.*
► show, indicate, reproduce, demonstrate, correspond to, echo, exhibit, match, reveal, bear witness to
3 **reflect on** *She reflected on the promises she had made to her friends.*
► think about, consider, contemplate, meditate on, ponder, brood on, ruminate on, mull over, muse on, reminisce about, (*more informal*) chew over

reflection NOUN
1 *We could see our reflections in the water.*
► image, likeness
2 *The test will provide an accurate reflection of a child's ability.*
► indication, demonstration, manifestation, expression, evidence, echo, result
3 *After some reflection, he decided to accept the offer.*
► thought, deliberation, consideration, contemplation, thinking, meditation, rumination, pondering, musing

reform VERB
1 *He realized he would have to reform.*
► mend your ways, turn over a new leaf, improve, do better
2 *Everyone agrees on the need to reform the prison system.*
► reorganize, reconstitute, regenerate, purge, remodel, revolutionize

reform NOUN
the need for reform
► improvement, betterment, change, adjustment, reorganization, (*more informal*) shake-up

refrain VERB
refrain from *Please refrain from shouting comments during the speeches.*
► desist from, avoid, do without, forgo, abstain from, eschew, forbear, (*more informal*) quit, (*more informal*) leave off, stop

refresh VERB
1 *A bit of air will refresh us.*
► invigorate, cool, freshen, revive, revitalize, restore, enliven, renew
2 *Revisiting the scene might refresh my memory.*
► prompt, jog, stimulate, remind, prod

refreshing ADJECTIVE
1 *a refreshing drink   a refreshing breeze*
► invigorating, revitalizing, reviving, enlivening, stimulating, bracing, exhilarating, cool, restorative, thirst-quenching, tingling
2 *a refreshing change*
► welcome, stimulating, different, interesting, fresh, new, original

refreshment NOUN
You can get some refreshment in the interval.
► food and drink, sustenance, snack, (*more informal*) eats, (*more informal*) nibbles

refuge NOUN
1 *The homeless seek refuge in doorways and under bridges.*
► shelter, protection, safety, sanctuary, security, cover, hideout, hiding-place, retreat
2 *The mountains provide a refuge for the freedom fighters.*
► sanctuary, shelter, haven, retreat, hideaway, hideout, hiding place, (*more informal*) bolt hole

refugee NOUN
He had come to Britain as a refugee.
► displaced person, asylum seeker, stateless person, exile, fugitive, outcast

refund NOUN (with the stress on *re-*)
Refunds will be given only if you produce a receipt.
► repayment, rebate, reimbursement

refund VERB (with the stress on *-fund*)
We will refund travelling expenses.
► repay, reimburse, pay back, recoup, give back

a
b
c
d
e
f
g
h
i
j
k
l
m
n
o
p
q
r
s
t
u
v
w
x
y
z

refusal NOUN
1 (*informal*) *There have been two refusals to the invitation so far.*
▶ rejection, negative reply, non-acceptance, regrets, no
AN OPPOSITE IS acceptance
2 *Her refusal to see him again caused great distress.*
▶ unwillingness, disinclination, reluctance, aversion

refuse VERB (with the stress on -*fuse*)
1 *He refused several invitations that week.*
▶ turn down, decline, reject, say no to, rebuff, spurn, baulk at, give a negative reply to
AN OPPOSITE IS accept
2 *The local council refused permission for the building to go ahead.*
▶ withhold, deny, not grant, deprive of
AN OPPOSITE IS grant

refuse NOUN (with the stress on *ref-*)
Flies buzzed round the pile of refuse.
▶ rubbish, waste, litter, garbage

refute VERB
It is an argument we can refute quite easily.
▶ disprove, rebut, invalidate, prove wrong, counter, discredit, negate

regain VERB
Government forces regained most of the city.
▶ recover, get back, win back, repossess, recapture, reclaim, retake, take back

regal ADJECTIVE
1 *A regal feast was spread out in front of them.*
▶ grand, splendid, magnificent, impressive, superb, majestic, kingly, noble, princely, queenly, royal, stately
2 *the tombs of his regal ancestors*
▶ royal, kingly, sovereign, princely, queenly, noble

regard VERB
1 *She regarded them closely for a while.*
▶ look at, observe, eye, gaze at, stare at, watch, contemplate, scrutinize, view
AN OPPOSITE IS disregard
2 *We regard these paintings as the best from the 11-14 age group.*
▶ consider, look on, view, judge, rate, deem, reckon, account, esteem, value

regard NOUN
1 *Good planning must have due regard for the costs involved.*
▶ attention, care, concern, consideration, deference, heed, notice, respect, thought
2 *They have a high regard for your opinions.*
▶ respect, esteem, appreciation (of), approval (of), estimation (of), admiration, affection
3 *She became nervous of his constant regard.*
▶ gaze, look, stare, scrutiny

regarding PREPOSITION
She got a letter from the bank regarding her overdraft.
▶ concerning, about, with regard to, with reference to, on the subject of, connected with

regardless ADJECTIVE
1 *The cliff walk was dangerous, but we carried on regardless.*
▶ anyway, anyhow, nonetheless, nevertheless, even so, just the same
2 **regardless of** *Dinghy sailing has something to offer everyone, regardless of age or fitness.*
▶ irrespective of, without regard to, disregarding, no matter
OPPOSITES ARE mindful of, taking account of

regime NOUN
1 *members of the former military regime*
▶ government, administration, rule, reign, jurisdiction, command
2 *It is usually a Monday that slimmers pick for a new health regime.*
▶ programme, plan, system, arrangement, scheme, diet

region NOUN
The family came from the coastal region.
▶ district, area, territory, neighbourhood, locality, sector, quarter, zone, terrain, land
in the region of *It will cost in the region of five million dollars.*
▶ about, approximately, roughly, in the neighbourhood of

register NOUN
The local authority keeps a register of disabled people.
▶ list, official list, directory, record, index, file

register VERB
1 *We wish to register a protest. The car is registered in his wife's name.*
▶ record, put on record, file, log, list, enter, submit, report
2 *You can still register for a place on the course.*
▶ enrol, enlist, put your name down, check in, apply, enter
3 *Their faces registered relief.*
▶ show, display, express, indicate, exhibit, betray, manifest

regret VERB
1 *You may come to regret your decision.*
▶ be sorry about, repent, rue, deplore
2 *She said how much she regretted her uncle's death.*
▶ lament, mourn, grieve over, feel sorrow for, be upset about

regret NOUN
1 *Both men expressed regret for their actions.*
▶ remorse, sorrow, shame, contrition, repentance, guilt
2 *We left our old home with a feeling of regret.*
▶ sadness, sorrow, unhappiness, disappointment

regretful ADJECTIVE
She was regretful about what had happened.
▶ sorry, remorseful, apologetic, repentant, contrite, penitent, ashamed, sorrowful, disappointed, sad
OPPOSITES ARE unrepentant, happy

R

regrettable ADJECTIVE

It was a regrettable thing to say but it was too late to change it.
▶ unfortunate, undesirable, unwelcome, ill-advised, inappropriate, unsuitable, distressing, upsetting, lamentable, shameful
OPPOSITES ARE fortunate, suitable

regular ADJECTIVE

1 *She had a regular route to work each morning.*
▶ routine, habitual, customary, typical, usual, normal, established
2 *There were regular complaints about the noise.*
▶ frequent, periodic, constant, continual, persistent
OPPOSITES ARE rare, occasional
3 *a regular procedure for dealing with enquiries*
▶ systematic, methodical, efficient, well organized, established, approved, conventional
AN OPPOSITE IS haphazard

regulate VERB

1 *a body that regulates the railways*
▶ supervise, oversee, monitor, administer, manage, control, (*more informal*) keep an eye on
2 *The clocks need to be regulated every so often.*
▶ control, manage, adjust, alter, change, moderate

regulation NOUN

1 *A copy of the regulations about working hours is pinned on the notice board.*
▶ rule, ruling, law, order, requirement, procedure, ordnance, statute, decree, edict
2 *the regulation of traffic in the city centre*
▶ control, management, supervision, direction, monitoring, overseeing, administration

rehearsal NOUN

a rehearsal for the school concert
▶ practice, trial performance, preparation, exercise, (*more informal*) run-through

rehearse VERB

We need to rehearse the last scene a bit more.
▶ practise, go over or through, run through, try out, prepare, (*informal*) run over

reign VERB

Victoria reigned for sixty-four years.
▶ rule, be queen or king, be on the throne, wear the crown, govern, be in power
RELATED ADJECTIVE regnal

reign NOUN

She had a long and successful reign.
▶ rule, monarchy, sovereignty

reinforce VERB

1 *Two stone supports reinforce the old wall. These events reinforced all our suspicions.*
▶ strengthen, fortify, support, bolster, buttress, underpin, prop up, hold up, stiffen, toughen, back up, give strength to
2 *Two more legions were sent to reinforce the army on the Rhine.*
▶ strengthen, supplement, increase, augment

reinforcements PLURAL NOUN

The police unit badly needed reinforcements.
▶ support, back-up, additional help

reinstate VERB

He was reinstated as president the following year.
▶ restore, re-establish, reinstall, reappoint, take back, recall
AN OPPOSITE IS dismiss

reject VERB

1 *The union rejected the new offer.*
▶ turn down, refuse, decline, say no to, dismiss, veto
AN OPPOSITE IS accept
2 *Although she loved him, in the end she rejected him.*
▶ rebuff, spurn, jilt, repudiate, cast aside, (*more informal*) dump

rejection NOUN

1 *Their leaders urged rejection of the offer.*
▶ refusal, non-acceptance, dismissal, turning down
AN OPPOSITE IS acceptance
2 *Her rejection of Clive hurt him deeply.*
▶ spurning, repudiation, rebuff, shunning, (*more informal*) dumping

rejoice VERB

Scientists rejoiced at the new discovery.
▶ celebrate, delight, exult, revel, be happy
OPPOSITES ARE lament, be sad

rejoicing NOUN

It was a time for rejoicing.
▶ celebration, festivity, jubilation, euphoria, gladness, happiness
AN OPPOSITE IS mourning

relapse NOUN

The nurses watched her closely in case she suffered a relapse.
▶ worsening, deterioration, setback, regression, turn for the worse, complications, recurrence

relapse VERB

1 *A few patients relapse in spite of the treatment.*
▶ get worse, become ill again, deteriorate, regress, fall back, have a relapse, slip back, weaken, degenerate
2 *No one could think of anything to say, and the meeting relapsed into silence.*
▶ sink, lapse, regress

relate VERB

1 *They have many stories to relate about their adventures abroad.*
▶ tell, recount, narrate, report, present, describe, recite
2 *Police are relating the two crimes.*
▶ link, connect, associate, see a connection between
3 **relate to** *The questions relate to an incident that took place the previous week.*
▶ refer to, concern, have to do with, apply to, bear on, pertain to, involve

r

4 relate to *They wanted a worker who could communicate with the young and relate to them.*
▶ identify with, sympathize with, understand, feel for, have a rapport with

related ADJECTIVE
1 *a set of related ideas*
▶ connected, associated, linked, allied, concomitant, analogous
2 *It turned out that the two women were related.*
▶ of the same family, kindred, kin

relations NOUN
1 *His relations were coming to visit that weekend.*
▶ relatives, family, (*more formal*) kinsmen
2 *He wanted to improve his relations with the eastern bloc.*
▶ dealings, associations, communications, connections

relationship NOUN
1 *the relationship between religion and politics*
▶ connection, relation, link, association, correlation, correspondence, affinity
2 *Her relationship with her stepmother had deteriorated.*
▶ friendship, rapport, understanding, attachment, closeness

relative ADJECTIVE
1 *Assess the relative importance of each fact.*
▶ comparative, respective, corresponding, respective
2 **relative to** *evidence relative to the incident*
▶ related to, relevant to, pertinent to, connected with, germane to, associated with

relative NOUN
She's a relative of mine.
▶ relation, member of the same family, (*more formal*) kinsman or kinswoman

relax VERB
1 *Yoga helps you to relax.*
▶ unwind, unbend, ease up, let up, take it easy
2 *She relaxed her grip on the handle.*
▶ loosen, slacken, loose, let go, weaken, reduce
3 *His presence helped to relax her.*
▶ calm, calm down, soothe, pacify

relaxation NOUN
a few hours left for relaxation
▶ recreation, relaxing, rest, unwinding, enjoyment, loosening up

relaxed ADJECTIVE
a relaxed atmosphere
▶ informal, casual, easygoing, pleasant, carefree
OPPOSITES ARE tense, formal

relay NOUN
a live television relay
▶ broadcast, transmission, programme

relay VERB
They did not relay all the information to the passengers.
▶ pass on, hand on, transmit, communicate, broadcast, send out, spread

release VERB
1 *The guerrillas promised to release one hostage.*
▶ free, liberate, let go
OPPOSITES ARE imprison, detain
2 *The names of the victims were released when the families had been informed.*
▶ make public, make known, publish, reveal, divulge, disclose, publicize, circulate, communicate
OPPOSITES ARE withhold, keep secret

release NOUN
1 *the release of the prisoners*
▶ freeing, liberation, deliverance, letting go, ransom
2 *a new release of the software*
▶ issue, version, edition, publication

relent VERB
The woman calmed down and appeared to relent.
▶ give in, give way, relax, soften, weaken, yield, show pity, become more lenient
OPPOSITES ARE harden, stiffen

relentless ADJECTIVE
The home side faced relentless pressure.
▶ constant, continuous, unrelenting, remorseless, persistent, unremitting, unflagging, merciless, ruthless
AN OPPOSITE IS intermittent

relevant ADJECTIVE
Take a note of any relevant information.
▶ pertinent, applicable, significant, apposite, material, suitable
AN OPPOSITE IS irrelevant

reliable ADJECTIVE
1 *The case lacked any reliable evidence.*
▶ dependable, valid, trustworthy, sound, genuine, authentic
AN OPPOSITE IS unreliable
2 *John was his most reliable friend.*
▶ faithful, trustworthy, dependable, devoted, staunch, constant, true, good

reliance NOUN
She had much reliance on her family's support.
▶ dependence, confidence (in), faith (in), trust (in)

relic NOUN
1 *The book was a relic of her schooldays.*
▶ survival (from), souvenir, memento, remnant, reminder, token, vestige
2 **relics** *a saint's relics*
▶ remains, sacred objects

relief NOUN
1 *It was a relief to find the village after miles of empty countryside.*
▶ reassurance, consolation, comfort, solace
2 *The medicine offered some relief from the pain.*
▶ alleviation (of), easing (of), lessening (of), remedy (for), assuagement (of), mitigation (of)
AN OPPOSITE IS intensification
3 *He needed a little light relief from his work.*
▶ respite, diversion, release, recreation, amusement, entertainment

4 *Aircraft brought relief to the beleaguered inhabitants.*
▶ help, aid, assistance, succour, deliverance

relieve VERB
1 *The pills helped to relieve her headache.*
▶ alleviate, ease, lessen, assuage, mitigate, diminish
2 *A video might relieve the boredom of the afternoon.*
▶ reduce, counteract, lighten, dispel
3 *It relieved us to know she was safely home.*
▶ reassure, comfort, console, soothe, please, gladden
4 *The army sent in supplies to relieve the townspeople.*
▶ help, aid, support, assist, sustain
5 *Her spell of duty was nearly over and a colleague would soon relieve her.*
▶ replace, take over from, stand in for

---

religion NOUN
the country's official religion
▶ faith, belief, form of worship
NAMES FOR WORLD RELIGIONS
Baha'ism, Buddhism, Christianity, Hinduism, Islam, Jainism, Judaism, Shinto, Sikhism, Taoism, Zen, Zoroastrianism.

---

religious ADJECTIVE
1 *religious beliefs religious music*
▶ spiritual, sacred, holy, theological
AN OPPOSITE IS secular
2 *a religious person*
▶ devout, pious, reverent, holy, saintly, God-fearing
AN OPPOSITE IS irreligious
3 *a religious attention to duty*
▶ scrupulous, meticulous, punctilious, zealous, strict, close

relinquish VERB
The dictator relinquished many of his powers.
▶ give up, surrender, hand over, let go, cede, yield, resign, renounce, repudiate, discard, drop

relish NOUN
1 *He ate his meal with relish.*
▶ appetite, delight, enjoyment, enthusiasm, gusto, zest
OPPOSITES ARE disgust, dislike
2 *fish with a spicy relish*
▶ seasoning, condiment, flavouring, dressing, sauce
3 *a spice to add special relish*
▶ piquancy, taste, flavour, tang

relish VERB
He was relishing his moment of triumph.
▶ enjoy, delight in, revel in, take pleasure in, savour, appreciate, like, love

reluctant ADJECTIVE
I was reluctant to admit where I had been.
▶ unwilling, disinclined, averse, hesitant (about), resistant, opposed, loath
OPPOSITES ARE willing, ready, eager

rely VERB
We can rely on them to help us.
▶ depend on, count on, trust, have confidence in, (*more informal*) bank on

remain VERB
1 *He remained in hospital for several weeks.*
▶ stay, continue, stop, linger
2 *Even after the revolution the chief of police remained in power.*
▶ continue, survive, persist, prevail, endure
3 *By the end of the evening only a handful of guests remained.*
▶ be left, be present, survive, stay around

remainder NOUN
1 *They were excused duties for the remainder of the day.*
▶ rest, residue, balance
2 *Finish what you can and do the remainder tomorrow.*
▶ rest, extra, difference, remnant, residue, what is left

remaining ADJECTIVE
1 *She wanted to remove any remaining doubts.*
▶ persisting, surviving, lingering, abiding, continuing, residual
2 *Melt the remaining butter and brush it over the pastry.*
▶ left over, unused, surplus, extra

remains NOUN
1 *He ate the remains of his sandwich in one huge mouthful.*
▶ remainder, rest, residue, remnant
2 *The saint's remains are in the crypt.*
▶ body, corpse, ashes, relics

remark NOUN
We had the usual conversational remarks about the weather.
▶ comment, observation, thought, utterance, reflection, statement, word, opinion

remark VERB
1 *He remarked that it was very quiet in the room.*
▶ comment, observe, mention, note, say, state, declare, reflect
2 *We did not remark anything unusual.*
▶ note, mark, notice, observe, heed, see, perceive

remarkable ADJECTIVE
1 *They were bubbling with excitement after their remarkable journey.*
▶ extraordinary, amazing, astonishing, memorable, unforgettable, wonderful, marvellous, breathtaking, fantastic, strange, incredible, astounding, startling, staggering, stunning
AN OPPOSITE IS ordinary
2 *It was certainly a remarkable achievement.*
▶ outstanding, striking, impressive, noteworthy, exceptional, memorable, phenomenal, distinguished

remedy NOUN
1 *a flu remedy*
▶ cure, treatment, medicine, medication, relief, antidote

r

2 *He suggested a day out as a remedy for their boredom.*
▶ answer, solution, cure, relief, corrective, palliative

remedy VERB
The government will pass a bill to remedy the problem.
▶ put right, correct, rectify, solve, resolve, fix, deal with, sort out, redress, counteract

remember VERB
1 *a lot of facts to remember*
▶ memorize, learn, commit to memory
2 *Do you remember my cousin Alice?   I can't remember where I put my keys.*
▶ recall, recollect, recognize
3 *Remember that she won't be here for several days yet.*
▶ bear in mind, keep in mind, take into account, not forget
4 *They sat on the terrace remembering their childhoods.*
▶ reminisce about, recall, recollect, look back on, muse on, be nostalgic about

remind VERB
1 *A note on the fridge reminded me to feed the cat.*
▶ prompt, nudge, hint at, tell
2 **remind you of** *The music reminded me of my holiday.*
▶ make you think of, take you back to

reminder NOUN
1 *She forgot about him and needed a reminder to phone.*
▶ prompt, nudge, cue, hint, suggestion
2 *The photo was a reminder of a happy time.*
▶ souvenir, memento

reminisce VERB
reminisce about *We reminisced about our schooldays.*
▶ recall, remember, hark back to, think back to, review, be nostalgic about

reminiscences PLURAL NOUN
reminiscences of her wartime childhood
▶ memories, recollections, reflections, remembrances

reminiscent ADJECTIVE
reminiscent of *a story reminiscent of Dickens*
▶ similar to, comparable with, suggestive of, recalling, evocative of, redolent of

remnants PLURAL NOUN
Remnants of the meal lay on the floor.
▶ remains, residue, leavings

remonstrate VERB
He had remonstrated furiously with the referee.
▶ protest (to), complain (to), argue, take issue, expostulate

remorse NOUN
He was filled with remorse for the harm he had done.
▶ guilt, shame, sorrow, repentance, contrition, penitence, compunction, regret, bad conscience

remorseful ADJECTIVE
You felt remorseful because if you hadn't been so late none of this would have happened.
▶ sorry, regretful, repentant, contrite, sad, ashamed, self-reproachful

remorseless ADJECTIVE
The remorseless heat was becoming too much for Hugh.
▶ relentless, unrelenting, persistent, unremitting, constant, continuous, unflagging, merciless, ruthless

remote ADJECTIVE
1 *The works would be sited at a remote place for safety.*
▶ isolated, outlying, secluded, out-of-the-way, distant, faraway, inaccessible, cut-off
AN OPPOSITE IS central
2 *There was a remote chance the decision would be overruled.*
▶ slight, small, slim, slender, faint, unlikely, doubtful, improbable, negligible
AN OPPOSITE IS strong
3 *His manner was remote and unfriendly.*
▶ aloof, detached, distant, withdrawn, reserved, stand-offish, uncommunicative
OPPOSITES ARE warm, friendly

removal NOUN
1 *A local company would take care of the removal.*
▶ relocation, transfer, transportation
2 *The nail took some removal*
▶ extraction, withdrawal, taking out, drawing
3 *The king insisted on the Prime Minister's removal from office.*
▶ dismissal, expulsion, displacement, elimination, ejection, ousting
OPPOSITES ARE restoration, appointment

remove VERB
1 *It took two hours to remove the tooth.*
▶ pull out, take out, extract, withdraw
2 *She decided to remove the last sentence from her letter.*
▶ delete, erase, expunge, efface, rub out, strike out
AN OPPOSITE IS restore (to)
3 *He tidied up the garden and removed some dead branches.*
▶ cut off, pull off, detach, strip off
4 *Karen went into the bathroom and removed her clothes.*
▶ take off, peel off, slip out of, shed, cast off
AN OPPOSITE IS put on
5 *The more severe penalties had been removed.*
▶ abolish, get rid of, eliminate, withdraw, do away with, (*more informal*) axe
OPPOSITES ARE impose, restore

render VERB
1 *The blow rendered him unconscious.*
▶ make, leave, cause to be
2 *People were eager to render assistance.*
▶ offer, give, provide, tender, furnish, supply
3 *Scholars rendered the Latin original into modern English.*
▶ translate, transcribe, adapt

R

renew VERB

1 *It was time to renew her interest in the countryside.*
▶ refresh, revive, restore, revitalize, resurrect, awaken

2 *I'll have to renew my passport next month.*
▶ extend, prolong

3 *The interior of the building was completely renewed in the eighteenth century.*
▶ renovate, restore, rebuild, modernize, refurbish, revamp, reconstruct, redecorate, make over, recondition, overhaul, transform

renewal NOUN

1 *the renewal of their friendship*
▶ revival, resumption, resurgence, resurrection, reawakening, rebirth

2 *the renewal of the inner cities*
▶ renovation, restoration, regeneration, modernization, reconditioning

3 *You are allowed one renewal of your passport.*
▶ updating, revalidation, replacement

renounce VERB

1 *They refused to renounce violence.*
▶ reject, abandon, repudiate, abjure, forsake, forswear, forsake, spurn, declare your opposition to, discard

2 *Edward would renounce his claim to the French throne.*
▶ give up, abandon, relinquish, resign, abdicate, surrender

renovation NOUN

the renovation of an old building
▶ improvement, modernization, overhaul, reconditioning, redevelopment, refit, refurbishment, renewal, repair, restoration, transformation, updating

renovate VERB

The hotel will be renovated for the Olympics.
▶ renew, restore, rebuild, modernize, refurbish, revamp, reconstruct, redecorate, make over, recondition, overhaul, transform

renown NOUN

Their renown spread far and wide.
▶ fame, distinction, reputation, celebrity, eminence

renowned ADJECTIVE

His father had been a renowned film actor.
▶ famous, celebrated, distinguished, prominent, acclaimed, esteemed, notable

rent VERB

1 *You can rent a car at the airport.*
▶ hire, lease, charter

2 *They rent out their apartment during the Festival.*
▶ let, lease, sublet

reorganize VERB

He helped to reorganize the local youth club.
▶ restructure, make changes to, change, alter, rearrange, transform, rationalize, (*more informal*) shake up

repair VERB

Public money will be spent to repair the damage.(informal) He longed to get back with Maggie and repair their broken marriage.
▶ mend, fix, put right, rectify, overhaul, patch up, renew, renovate

repair NOUN

1 *The engine is in dire need of repair.*
▶ mending, fixing, overhaul, maintenance, renovation

2 *The building is in good repair.*
▶ condition, state, shape, fettle

repay VERB

1 *The debt has been completely repaid.*
▶ pay off, pay back, settle, expunge, extinguish

2 *We must repay your train fare.*
▶ refund, reimburse, pay back, recompense, compensate, remunerate, settle

3 *He was eager to repay their kindness*
▶ return, reciprocate, recompense, requite

repeal VERB

Most of the legislation had lapsed or been repealed.
▶ revoke, rescind, abolish, cancel, quash, set aside, withdraw, retract

repeat VERB

1 *Neither of them had any wish to repeat their experience.*
▶ have again, do again, redo, re-experience, reproduce, duplicate

2 *The tale became more colourful every time someone repeated it.*
▶ say again, restate, reiterate, reproduce, recite, relate

repeat NOUN

1 *We are hoping for a repeat of last week's successes.*
▶ repetition, repeating, recurrence, reiteration, rerun, return

2 *I watched a repeat of the programme.*
▶ replay, rerun, reshowing, rebroadcast, repetition

repeated ADJECTIVE

The Russians made repeated attempts to break through the enemy lines.
▶ frequent, persistent, continual, constant, ceaseless, unremitting, recurrent

repeatedly ADVERB

She had repeatedly refused all his proposals of marriage.
▶ often, frequently, constantly, time after time, again and again, over and over

repel VERB

1 *The invaders were repelled at the border.*
▶ drive back, beat back, push back, repulse, ward off, parry, put to flight

2 *a device for repelling cats*
▶ deter, keep away, scare off
AN OPPOSITE IS attract

3 *Such selfishness repelled me.*
▶ revolt, disgust, sicken, offend, nauseate
OPPOSITES ARE delight, please

repellent ADJECTIVE

1 *Reviewers found the programme repellent.*
▶ revolting, disgusting, sickening, repulsive, offensive, repugnant, nauseating
2 *The material is repellent to rainwater.*
▶ resistant, impermeable, impervious

repent VERB

This miraculous event caused him to repent his past life and become a monk.
▶ regret, feel remorse for, be sorry for, be ashamed of, lament, rue, atone

repentance NOUN

He was given a long sentence because he refused to show repentance for what he had done.
▶ regret, remorse, sorrow, penitence, contrition

repentant ADJECTIVE

He admitted blame and was repentant for his part in the crime.
▶ sorry, apologetic, regretful, remorseful, ashamed, contrite, penitent
AN OPPOSITE IS unrepentant

repercussion NOUN

Changes in the environment are having considerable repercussions for neighbouring regions.
▶ consequence, implication, effect, result, outcome, backlash

repetition NOUN

The authorities do not want to see any repetition of last week's incident.
▶ repeat, repeating, recurrence, reiteration, rerun, return, reappearance, duplication

repetitive ADJECTIVE

To him fixing tiles was repetitive and boring.
▶ monotonous, tedious, boring, humdrum, mechanical, repetitious, unchanging, unvaried, (*more informal*) samey
AN OPPOSITE IS varied

replace VERB

1 *She replaced the book on the shelf.*
▶ put back, return, reinstate, restore
2 *He did not need to look far for someone to replace him when he left.*
▶ succeed, follow, take over from, take the place of, supersede, supplant, be a substitute for, come after
3 *a scheme to replace dying trees*
▶ renew, change, provide a substitute for

replacement NOUN

Thomas had lost his mobile and bought a replacement.
▶ substitute, alternative, successor, surrogate, stand-in

replenish VERB

The maid had gone to replenish the jug of milk.
▶ refill, top up, fill up, recharge

replica NOUN

Katie wore a replica of her sister's dress.
▶ copy, duplicate, imitation, reproduction, likeness, double, clone, facsimile, model, reconstruction

reply VERB

1 *She replied that they would just have to wait.*
▶ answer, respond, retort, counter
2 **reply to** *He never replies to letters.*
▶ answer, acknowledge, give a reply to, respond to, react to

reply NOUN

My letter called for a reply.
▶ answer, response, acknowledgement, reaction, rejoinder, retort

report VERB

1 *She threatened to report him to the police.*
▶ inform on, make a complaint against
2 *You must report for duty at 9 o'clock.*
▶ present yourself, arrive, appear, turn up, check in, clock in
3 *The government has reported an increase in exports.*
▶ announce, proclaim, declare, communicate, notify, relate, recount, note

report NOUN

1 *There is a full report of the incident in today's newspaper.*
▶ account, description, review, article, announcement, record, statement, story, (*more informal*) write-up
2 *We heard the report of a gun.*
▶ bang, blast, crack, noise, explosion, detonation, pop

reporter NOUN

A group of reporters waited outside the house.
▶ journalist, correspondent, newspaperman or newspaperwoman

reprehensible ADJECTIVE

Their conduct was reprehensible.
▶ deplorable, disgraceful, shameful, despicable, dishonourable, blameworthy, regrettable, culpable, objectionable, remiss, unworthy, bad, wicked

represent VERB

1 *The picture represents a winter scene.*
▶ show, depict, describe, portray, illustrate, delineate, draw, paint, picture, exhibit, enact
2 *Each character in the play represents a particular human quality.*
▶ stand for, embody, symbolize, typify, personify, epitomize, exemplify
3 *They chose a spokesperson to represent their views.*
▶ speak for, express, present, be an example of

representation NOUN

The bust is a representation of a young woman.
▶ portrayal, depiction, likeness, image, picture, portrait, resemblance, delineation

representative ADJECTIVE

1 *a representative sample of British society*
▶ typical, characteristic, average, archetypal, illustrative, normal
AN OPPOSITE IS abnormal
2 *The Greeks devised forms of representative government.*
▶ democratic, elected, elective, popular, chosen

representative NOUN
1 *the queen's representative abroad*
► ambassador, delegate, deputy, consul, diplomat, spokesperson, spokesman or spokeswoman, proxy, stand-in
2 *a sales representative*
► agent, salesperson, salesman or saleswoman, (*informal*) rep

repress VERB
(*informal*) *It was hard to repress our feelings.*
► control, restrain, suppress, curb, stifle, bottle up, keep down, crush, inhibit, quell
OPPOSITES ARE express, release

repression NOUN
1 *an era of political repression*
► oppression, subjugation, suppression, domination, despotism, dictatorship, totalitarianism, tyranny, authoritarianism
AN OPPOSITE IS freedom
2 (*informal*) *the repression of feelings*
► suppression, restraint, stifling, bottling up, inhibition, suffocation

repressive ADJECTIVE
a repressive military regime
► authoritarian, autocratic, coercive, cruel, despotic, dictatorial, harsh, illiberal, oppressive, restricting, severe, totalitarian, tyrannical, undemocratic, unenlightened
OPPOSITES ARE liberal, democratic

reprieve VERB
He was sentenced to death but later reprieved.
► pardon, spare, set free, let off, forgive

reprimand VERB
They were reprimanded for their bad behaviour.
► rebuke, admonish, reprove, reproach, upbraid, censure, scold, chide, criticize, reprehend, (*more informal*) tell off, (*more informal*) tick off
OPPOSITES ARE praise, commend

reprimand NOUN
The police gave them a formal reprimand.
► telling-off, talking-to, rebuke, admonishment, admonition, reproof, scolding, (*more informal*) ticking-off

reprisal NOUN
He was afraid of reprisals if he owned up.
► retaliation, retribution, revenge, counter-attack, vengeance

reproach VERB
Mr Smith reproached her for being late.
► reprimand , rebuke, admonish, reprove, upbraid, censure, scold, chide, criticize, reprehend, (*more informal*) tell off, (*more informal*) tick off
AN OPPOSITE IS praise

reproach NOUN
a look of reproach
► disapproval, reprimand, scorn, rebuke, admonishment, reproof
AN OPPOSITE IS approval

reproachful ADJECTIVE
She gave him a reproachful frown.
► disapproving, reproving, scornful, accusatory, censorious, critical, withering
AN OPPOSITE IS approving

reproduce VERB
1 *The drawings are reproduced in beautiful colour illustrations.*
► copy, reprint, duplicate, transcribe, print, simulate, reissue, repeat, photocopy
2 *These animals reproduce in large numbers.*
► breed, bear young, produce offspring, multiply, propagate, procreate, spawn, increase

reproduction NOUN
1 *methods of reproduction in fish*
► breeding, propagation, procreation, multiplying
2 *The portrait is only a reproduction.*
► copy, replica, duplicate, facsimile, imitation, fake, forgery, likeness, print
AN OPPOSITE IS original

reproof NOUN
He tutted at her in mild reproof.
► reprimand, rebuke, admonishment, admonition, censure
AN OPPOSITE IS approval

---

reptile NOUN
KINDS OF REPTILE INCLUDE
snakes: snake, serpent, adder, anaconda, asp, boa constrictor, cobra, grass snake, king cobra, mamba, pit viper, puff adder, python, rattlesnake, sidewinder, viper.
alligators and lizards: alligator, basilisk (mythical), blindworm (legless), caiman, chameleon, crocodile, gecko, goanna, gharial, iguana, lizard, monitor lizard, salamander (mythical), skink, slow-worm (legless), tuatara.
other reptiles: loggerhead, terrapin, tortoise, turtle.

---

repudiate VERB
1 *He repudiated all the charges made against him.*
► dispute, rebuff, reject, deny, disagree with, renounce, refute
OPPOSITES ARE accept, acknowledge
2 *She did not want to repudiate their agreement.*
► disown, go back on, recant, rescind, retract, reverse, revoke

repugnant ADJECTIVE
Polygamy may seem repugnant to us.
► abhorrent, repulsive, revolting, repellent, offensive, disgusting, loathsome

repulse VERB
1 *The rebels attacked and were repulsed.*
► drive back, beat back, push back, repel, ward off, parry, put to flight
2 *He showed her affection but was repulsed.*
► reject, rebuff, spurn, snub, jilt

repulsive ADJECTIVE
His appearance was repulsive.
▶ revolting, disgusting, repugnant, repellent, loathsome, obnoxious, hideous
AN OPPOSITE IS attractive

reputable ADJECTIVE
Make sure you get a reputable builder to do the work.
▶ reliable, dependable, highly regarded, well thought of, tried and trusted, respectable, respected, trustworthy, creditable
AN OPPOSITE IS disreputable

reputation NOUN
His reputation had been damaged by the affair.
▶ good name, name, standing, stature, character, esteem, honour, repute, image, prestige

reputed ADJECTIVE
They are reputed to be descended from the French nobility.
▶ thought, believed, rumoured, said, held, considered, supposed, alleged, reckoned

request NOUN
Our request for assistance has been accepted.
▶ appeal, plea, petition, entreaty, application, call, supplication

request VERB
1 *We requested immediate help.*
▶ ask for, appeal for, call for, seek, plead for, require, solicit
2 *They requested us to stop.*
▶ ask, call on, require, implore, beseech

require VERB
1 *One of the victims required immediate surgery.*
▶ need, have to have
2 *The situation required extreme care.*
▶ call for, need, necessitate, involve, entail
3 *An official required me to show my passport.*
▶ order, instruct, direct, command, oblige, request

required ADJECTIVE
This book is required reading for this age group.
▶ essential, indispensable, vital, obligatory, necessary, prescribed, requisite, compulsory, mandatory
AN OPPOSITE IS optional

requirement NOUN
One of the requirements for this work is a quiet place to go and do it.
▶ need, necessity, essential, requisite, prerequisite, stipulation, condition, proviso

requisite ADJECTIVE
She wasn't sure she had the requisite qualifications for the job.
▶ required, necessary, prescribed, obligatory, indispensable, vital

requisition VERB
The army requisitioned the house for the duration of the war.
▶ commandeer, appropriate, seize, take possession of, take over, occupy

rescue VERB
1 *In a few hours someone would come and rescue them.*
▶ set free, free, release, save, liberate, deliver, extricate, ransom
2 *I went back to the house to rescue some of my belongings.*
▶ recover, retrieve, salvage, get back, bring away

rescue NOUN
The news was all about a dramatic sea rescue.
▶ saving, rescuing, recovery, release, deliverance, liberation

research NOUN
More research is needed into the causes of violent crime.
▶ investigation, experimentation, testing, exploration, inquiry, analysis, searching, study

research VERB
The disease has been widely researched.
▶ investigate, study, inquire into, explore, probe, look into

resemblance NOUN
There is a close resemblance between the two accounts.
▶ similarity, correspondence, conformity, agreement, comparison, equivalence, likeness
OPPOSITES ARE difference, dissimilarity

resemble VERB
The garden resembled a wilderness.
▶ look like, be like, remind you of, be similar to, mirror
AN OPPOSITE IS differ from

resent VERB
Jack resented his mother's interference.
▶ begrudge, take exception to, take umbrage at, object to, be annoyed about, be resentful of, dislike

resentful ADJECTIVE
Her parents' constant complaining left her feeling resentful.
▶ aggrieved, indignant, disgruntled, discontented, offended, bitter, hurt, irritated, antagonistic, sour, jealous, (more informal) put out, (more informal) peeved, (more informal) miffed

resentment NOUN
The appointment of an outsider caused intense resentment among the workforce.
▶ indignation, discontent, bad feelings, disgruntlement, rancour, antagonism, irritation

reservation NOUN
1 *You will need to make a reservation if you come on a Friday.*
▶ booking, advance booking, prior arrangement
2 *Some members of the group had reservations about the plan.*
▶ misgiving, doubt, scepticism, unease, scruple, qualification, hesitation, qualm

reserve VERB
1 *Demand will be high so make sure your newsagent reserves you a copy.*
▶ keep, put aside, set aside, hold, retain, earmark

R

2 (*informal*) *Chuck reserved a room at the local hotel.*
▶ book, secure, arrange for, order

reserve NOUN
1 *Her reserve of money was running out.*
▶ supply, fund, stock, store, reservoir, hoard, accumulation
2 *a wildlife reserve*
▶ preserve, reservation, sanctuary, park
3 *His reserve prevented him from joining in the fun.*
▶ shyness, reticence, diffidence, timidity, restraint, modesty, aloofness
AN OPPOSITE IS openness

reserved ADJECTIVE
As a young man he had been rather reserved.
▶ shy, reticent, diffident, retiring, unforthcoming, quiet, timid, restrained, distant, aloof
OPPOSITES ARE forthcoming, outgoing

reside VERB
reside in *Most students reside in halls during their first year.*
▶ live in, stay in, have a room in, dwell in, lodge in, settle in, occupy, have as a home, inhabit

residence NOUN
They spent the summer in their country residence.
▶ home, house , dwelling, domicile, abode, address, mansion, quarters, habitation

resident NOUN
1 *the residents of Boston*
▶ inhabitant, citizen, townsman or townswoman, denizen, native
2 *The hotel's first duty is to ensure the safety of its residents.*
▶ guest, boarder, lodger, client, occupant
AN OPPOSITE IS non- resident

resident ADJECTIVE
1 *People resident in the EU do not need to complete the form.*
▶ living, residing, dwelling
AN OPPOSITE IS non- resident
2 *The family once had a resident butler.*
▶ live-in, living-in, permanent

resign VERB
1 *The manager resigned at the end of the season.*
▶ leave, stand down, step down, give in your notice, quit, (*more informal*) call it a day, give up
2 *She resigned all her rights in the matter.*
▶ renounce, relinquish, abandon, surrender, cede, give up, forsake
AN OPPOSITE IS take up
3 **resign yourself to** *We had resigned ourselves to a long wait.*
▶ reconcile yourself to, become resigned to, accept, come to terms with

resignation NOUN
1 *They faced an uncertain future with resignation.*
▶ patience, forbearance, tolerance, stoicism, endurance, fortitude, sufferance, acceptance, fatalism

2 *There would be many resignations from the right wing of the party.*
▶ departure, notice, standing down, retirement, relinquishment

resilient ADJECTIVE
1 *Use a resilient material for harder wear.*
▶ flexible, supple, pliable, pliant, durable, tough, elastic, springy
AN OPPOSITE IS inflexible
2 *She was still young and resilient.*
▶ adaptable, buoyant, irrepressible, tough, hardy, strong
OPPOSITES ARE vulnerable, sensitive

resist VERB
1 *He resisted all our attempts to persuade him.*
▶ oppose, withstand, stand up to, defy, balk at, fend off, confront, fight
OPPOSITES ARE yield to, submit to
2 *a hard varnish that resists wear for years*
▶ withstand, be proof against, combat, weather, endure, keep out
AN OPPOSITE IS be susceptible to
3 *The temptation was so strong he was unable to resist any longer.*
▶ hold out, desist, restrain yourself, forbear
OPPOSITES ARE yield, give in

resistant ADJECTIVE
1 **resistant to** *a material that is resistant to heat*
▶ impervious to, proof against, repellent to, immune to, unaffected by
AN OPPOSITE IS susceptible
2 **resistant to** *He was always resistant to change.*
▶ opposed to, averse to, hostile to, suspicious of
OPPOSITES ARE receptive to, attracted to

resolute ADJECTIVE
The local people put up a resolute resistance.
▶ determined, purposeful, resolved, firm, steadfast, staunch, tenacious, unflinching, undaunted
OPPOSITES ARE irresolute, half- hearted, feeble

resolution NOUN
1 *They showed great resolution in the face of danger.*
▶ determination, resolve, spirit, boldness, courage, firmness, fortitude, commitment, perseverance, doggedness, staunchness, steadfastness, tenacity, will power
2 *The committee passed the resolution by a large majority.*
▶ motion, proposal, proposition, declaration, decision, judgement
3 *Let's hope financial aid can be a resolution of the country's difficulties.*
▶ settlement, solution, answer (to)

resolve VERB
1 *It will take months to resolve the matter completely.*
▶ settle, sort out, work out, solve, put right, straighten out, rectify, deal with
2 *The boys resolved to keep going until dark.*
▶ determine, decide, make up your mind, take a decision

resolve NOUN
Opposition to his ideas only strengthened his resolve.
▶ determination, resolution, firmness of purpose, steadfastness, tenacity
OPPOSITES ARE indecision, hesitancy

resort NOUN
1 *Going on strike would be a last resort.*
▶ option, choice, alternative, course of action, expedient, recourse, refuge
2 *a seaside resort on the south coast*
▶ holiday town, tourist spot, retreat, spa

resort VERB
resort to *I don't want to have to resort to threats.*
▶ make use of, have recourse to, fall back on, turn to, adopt, utilize, use, sink to, stoop to

resound VERB
Thunder resounded in the hills.
▶ resonate, reverberate, ring, echo, boom, vibrate

resounding ADJECTIVE
1 *His fist hit the table with a resounding thump.*
▶ loud, echoing, booming, resonant, vibrant, reverberating, clear, ringing
2 *The show had been a resounding success.*
▶ decided, emphatic, decisive, thorough, complete, outstanding, tremendous, great

resourceful ADJECTIVE
They were resourceful in using the few materials available.
▶ imaginative, enterprising, inventive, creative, ingenious, innovative, original, talented, clever
AN OPPOSITE IS unimaginative

resources PLURAL NOUN
The business had to survive on limited resources.
▶ assets, funds, wealth, money, riches, capital, reserves

respect NOUN
1 *He showed the respect due to such a great writer.*
▶ esteem, regard, honour, deference, homage, admiration, awe, reverence, veneration, consideration
2 *The conclusions were correct in every respect.*
▶ aspect, regard, particular, point, characteristic, detail, facet, feature, way

respect VERB
1 *We respected them for their honesty.*
▶ admire, esteem, think well of, appreciate, regard, commend
AN OPPOSITE IS despise
2 *She promised to respect her father's wishes.*
▶ comply with, abide by, observe, honour, obey, follow, conform to, adhere to

respectable ADJECTIVE
1 *He came from a respectable family in New England.*
▶ decent, reputable, honourable, respected, upright, worthy
AN OPPOSITE IS disreputable

2 *She found a job and now earns a respectable income*
▶ decent, reasonable, substantial, considerable, sizeable

respectful ADJECTIVE
Two chambermaids were standing at a respectful distance.
▶ polite, deferential, courteous, dutiful, reverential, gracious, civil
OPPOSITES ARE disrespectful, rude

respective ADJECTIVE
We handed the horses back to their respective lads.
▶ separate, individual, own, various, particular, several

respite NOUN
It was good to get a few moments' respite from the noise.
▶ rest, break, breathing space, pause, (more informal) let-up

respond VERB
respond to *He responded to each question with a shrug.*
▶ answer, react to, reply to, acknowledge, greet, counter

response NOUN
The comment brought an angry response.
▶ answer, reply, retort, reaction, rejoinder, riposte, acknowledgement, counter, (more informal) comeback

responsible ADJECTIVE
1 *Mr Jones was one of her most responsible tenants.*
▶ trustworthy, reliable, dependable, conscientious, honest, sensible
AN OPPOSITE IS irresponsible
2 *She has a responsible position in a city bank.*
▶ important, powerful, influential, authoritative, executive
3 **responsible for** *He is responsible for the day-to-day running of the computer system.*
▶ in charge of, accountable for, answerable for
4 **responsible for** *Kim was responsible for the damage*
▶ guilty of, culpable of, liable for

responsive ADJECTIVE
Educational institutions must become more responsive to the needs of students.
▶ alert, alive, aware, impressionable, interested, open, perceptive, receptive, sympathetic, warm-hearted, willing
OPPOSITES ARE insensitive, apathetic

rest NOUN
1 *The rest of the group went to visit a gallery.*
▶ remainder, balance, remains, others
2 *You need a rest, Fran, you look tired.*
▶ break, breathing space, time off, lie-down, nap, snooze, respite, pause, (more informal) breather
3 *alternating periods of rest and exercise*
▶ relaxation, leisure, respite, inactivity, ease, calm, tranquillity

rest VERB

1 *She went to rest in her room*
▶ relax, take a rest, lie down, ease up, have a sleep, have a nap, have a snooze
2 *Her hand rested on his shoulder.*
▶ lie, be laid
3 *She rested her bike against the wall.*
▶ prop, lean, stand, support, place, put
4 *The success of the idea rests on the financial support they can bring in.*
▶ depend, rely, hang, hinge

---

restaurant NOUN
She wondered if the restaurant had a sushi bar.
▶ eating place, eating house

KINDS OF RESTAURANT INCLUDE
bistro (small), brasserie (French), cafe, cafeteria, canteen (in a school, office, etc.), carvery (serving meat joints), chophouse, coffee shop, crêperie (serving pancakes), diner, drive-in, grill, milk bar, pizzeria (serving pizzas), roadhouse (in the country), rotisserie (serving roast meat), snack bar, steakhouse, sushi bar (Japanese), takeaway, tapas bar (Spanish), taqueria (Mexican), taverna (Greek), tea room, transport cafe, trattoria (Italian), wine bar.

---

restful ADJECTIVE
He enjoyed the most restful night he could remember.
▶ relaxing, soothing, calm, peaceful, placid, quiet, tranquil, leisurely, untroubled
OPPOSITES ARE restless, disturbed

restless ADJECTIVE
1 *My mother was restless, waiting for the family to return.*
▶ agitated, anxious, edgy, nervous, restive, fidgety, impatient, jittery, jumpy, worried
AN OPPOSITE IS relaxed.
2 *a restless night of tossing and turning*
▶ sleepless, disturbed, troubled, uncomfortable, unsettled, interrupted
AN OPPOSITE IS restful

restore VERB
1 *The interim government wished to restore democracy as soon as possible.*
▶ bring back, reinstate, reinstitute, reinstall, give back, put back, replace, return
AN OPPOSITE IS abolish
2 *We must restore the property to its rightful owners.*
▶ return, give back, hand back, take back, replace
AN OPPOSITE IS retain
3 *The building has been beautifully restored.*
▶ renovate, repair, rebuild, recondition, reconstruct, refurbish, clean, (*more informal*) do up, renew
AN OPPOSITE IS neglect
4 *An operation was needed to restore the girl's sight.*
▶ bring back, re-establish, rehabilitate, reinstate, reintroduce, revive

restrain VERB
1 *The dogs were restrained by leads.*
▶ bind, fetter, confine, restrict, tie, shackle

2 *She found it hard to restrain her laughter.*
▶ control, hold back, suppress, check, curb, prevent
OPPOSITES ARE encourage, stimulate
3 *He had to restrain himself from jumping up and looking out of the window..*
▶ stop, keep, prevent, hold back
AN OPPOSITE IS force

restrained ADJECTIVE
He was unusually restrained and conventional.
▶ self-controlled, muted, unemotional, undemonstrative, inhibited, quiet, discreet, reserved, reticent, repressed, subdued
AN OPPOSITE IS uninhibited

restrict VERB
1 *A busy working life restricted her opportunities to get away.*
▶ limit, constrain, impede, hinder, hamper, restrain, curtail
AN OPPOSITE IS increase
2 *The prisoners were restricted to their cells*
▶ confine, restrain, enclose, imprison, keep, shut
AN OPPOSITE IS free

restriction NOUN
1 *There is a restriction on the number of places available.*
▶ limit, limitation, constraint, control, curb, restraint, check
2 *a society that imposes restrictions on personal freedom.*
▶ limitation, reduction, diminution, curtailment, cutback

result NOUN
1 *The water shortage is a result of the hot weather*
▶ consequence, effect, outcome, sequel, repercussion, upshot, fruit, issue, product, end-product
2 *the result of a trial*
▶ verdict, decision, judgement
3 *the result of an exam*
▶ mark, grade, score, assessment, ranking
4 *the result of a calculation*
▶ answer, solution

result VERB
1 *What resulted from your interview?*
▶ arise, come about, culminate, develop, emanate, emerge, ensue, eventuate, follow, happen, issue, occur, proceed, spring, stem, take place, turn out
2 **result in** *The accident resulted in serious injuries.*
▶ end in, cause, involve, bring about, lead to, give rise to, achieve, provoke

resume VERB
It is essential to resume talks to reach an agreement.
▶ restart, reopen, recommence, continue, begin again, start again, carry on, proceed with, reconvene

resumption NOUN
Failure of the ceasefire led to a resumption of hostilities.
▶ continuation, renewal, reopening, restarting, recommencement, resurgence

a
b
c
d
e
f
g
h
i
j
k
l
m
n
o
p
q
r
s
t
u
v
w
x
y
z

résumé NOUN
a brief résumé of the facts
▶ summary, outline, overview, precis, abstract

resurgence NOUN
a resurgence of interest in archaeology
▶ renewal, revival, recovery, reawakening, re-emergence

resurrect VERB
It's just an old idea that someone has resurrected.
▶ revive, renew, restore, resuscitate, bring back, revitalize

retain VERB
1 *When he retired he retained his shares in the company.*
▶ keep, hold on to, hang on to, preserve
AN OPPOSITE IS surrender
2 *She retained her composure despite much provocation.*
▶ keep control of, maintain, preserve
AN OPPOSITE IS lose
3 *Some students are good at retaining facts from their reading.*
▶ remember, memorize, keep in mind, learn, recall, recollect
AN OPPOSITE IS forget

retaliate VERB
(informal) After the attack the Egyptians were powerless to retaliate.
▶ fight back, strike back, hit back, respond, reciprocate, take revenge, get even

retaliation NOUN
The best safeguard is the power to threaten retaliation.
▶ reprisal, retribution, revenge, counter-attack, vengeance

reticent ADJECTIVE
She remained reticent about the whole episode.
▶ guarded, reserved, inhibited, unforthcoming, uncommunicative, unresponsive

R

retire VERB
1 *She retired two years ago after a long career in teaching.*
▶ stop working, give up work
2 *Jane retired to her room for the evening.*
▶ withdraw, adjourn, retreat, decamp
3 **retire from** *He intended to retire from Parliament at the next election.*
▶ resign from, withdraw from, give up, leave, quit

retiring ADJECTIVE
He has a quiet, retiring nature
▶ shy, reserved, unassuming, diffident

retort NOUN
She intended to make a sharp retort.
▶ response, answer, reply, riposte, rejoinder, comeback, counter

retort VERB
'It's worth a try, surely,' Jenkins retorted.
▶ reply, answer, respond, counter, react, snap back

retract VERB
1 *The landing gear is retracted on takeoff.*
▶ pull in, draw in, pull back
2 *She apologized and retracted the accusations.*
▶ withdraw, take back, abandon, rescind, reverse, revoke, recant

retreat NOUN
1 *Before he could say anything I made a hasty retreat.*
▶ departure, withdrawal, escape, exit, flight
2 *The family had a holiday retreat in the hills.*
▶ refuge, resort, haven, hideaway, hideout, sanctuary, shelter

retreat VERB
1 *The army retreated in disarray.*
▶ withdraw, retire, draw back, fall back, move back, back away, depart, go away, leave, (*more informal*) run away, (*more informal*) turn tail
AN OPPOSITE IS advance
2 *The tide retreated rapidly.*
▶ go out, recede, shrink back, ebb, flow back
AN OPPOSITE IS come in
3 *The management had to retreat over their modernization plan.*
▶ back down, climb down, change your mind, backtrack, do a U-turn, withdraw
AN OPPOSITE IS persevere

retribution NOUN
The victims' families demanded retribution.
▶ revenge, vengeance, justice, recompense, redress, reprisal, punishment, retaliation, compensation
AN OPPOSITE IS forgiveness

retrieve VERB
1 *She went next door to retrieve her ball.*
▶ get back, fetch back, bring back, recover, regain, rescue, find, reclaim, repossess, track down, salvage, save, trace
2 *It would not be easy to retrieve such an awkward situation.*
▶ put right, set right, rectify, remedy, sort out, straighten out, put to rights

retrograde ADJECTIVE
Pulling out of overseas markets is seen as a retrograde step.
▶ backward, negative, regressive, deteriorating
AN OPPOSITE IS progressive

retrospect NOUN
in retrospect *In retrospect, they could have made a better job of it.*
▶ with hindsight, looking back, on reflection

return VERB
1 *They returned to Paris the next day.*
▶ go back, come back, get back, depart (for), set off (for), set out (for)
2 *I'll see you when I return.*
▶ come back, get back, arrive back, come home, get home, reappear

3 *She had found a stray cat and wanted to return it to its owner.*
▶ give back, send back, take back, restore, deliver, reunite (with)
4 *Things will soon return to their normal state*
▶ go back, be back, revert
5 *After a while the headaches returned.*
▶ happen again, recur, reappear
6 *Neil came to return the money I had lent him.*
▶ give back, repay, refund, reimburse
7 *Jenny was eager to return the favour.*
▶ reciprocate, repay, requite, recompense

return NOUN
1 *Their return was delayed by bad weather.*
▶ setting off back, departure
2 *We look forward to your return*
▶ arrival, homecoming, reappearance
3 *the country's return to normality after the war*
▶ reversion, restoration (of), re-establishment (of)
4 *There is every danger of a return of the problem.*
▶ recurrence, reappearance, repetition
5 *We all want a good return on our investments.*
▶ income, profit, gain, interest
6 *There was a notice requesting the return of all library books.*
▶ replacement, bringing back, giving back, restitution

reveal VERB
1 *Kenny revealed the truth at last.*
▶ admit, confess, impart, divulge, tell, disclose, communicate, expose
OPPOSITES ARE hide, conceal
2 *The police were unwilling to reveal the man's whereabouts.*
▶ disclose, divulge, publicize, broadcast, publish, betray
OPPOSITES ARE conceal, keep secret
3 *He removed the cloth to reveal a beautiful bronze statuette.*
▶ expose, display, exhibit, show, uncover, unveil
AN OPPOSITE IS cover

revel VERB
1 *When the exams were over we revelled all night.*
▶ celebrate, have fun, make merry, enjoy yourself, carouse, roister
2 **revel in** *She always revelled in the limelight.*
▶ delight in, enjoy, love, adore, lap up, wallow in, relish, take pleasure in, rejoice in

revelation NOUN
Further revelations appeared in the next day's tabloids.
▶ disclosure, exposé, discovery, exposure, bringing to light, announcement, admission, confession, unmasking, news

revelry NOUN
a night of wild revelry
▶ celebration or celebrations, festivity, carousing, carousal, partying, enjoyment, conviviality, merrymaking, revelling, revels, roistering, jollity, fun, frolics

revenge NOUN
1 *The family is seeking revenge for Nino's killing.*
▶ vengeance, retribution, retaliation, reprisal, satisfaction
2 *They shot Maria's brother out of revenge.*
▶ vengefulness, vindictiveness, spite, malice, maliciousness, hatred

revenge VERB
He was determined to revenge his brother's ill-treatment.
▶ avenge, take revenge for, retaliate for, have satisfaction for, repay, (*more informal*) get your own back for
be revenged *He would be revenged on them before the year was out.*
▶ take revenge on, have revenge on, retaliate against, get even with

revenue NOUN
The government is looking to increase its revenue from taxes on tobacco.
▶ income, proceeds, receipts, return, yield, gain, profits, takings, money

reverberate VERB
His voice reverberated round the room.
▶ echo, resound, resonate, re-echo, ring, boom, vibrate

revere VERB
They still revere him as a national hero.
▶ respect, honour, esteem, admire, venerate, pay homage to, idolize, exalt, feel reverence for
AN OPPOSITE IS despise

reverence NOUN
a deep reverence for their country's heroic past
▶ respect, esteem, veneration, awe, homage, admiration, adoration (of), devotion (to), deference (to)
OPPOSITES ARE disrespect, contempt

reverent ADJECTIVE
A reverent silence fell on the room.
▶ respectful, reverential, deferential, awe-struck, awed, solemn, devout, dutiful, pious
OPPOSITES ARE irreverent, disrespectful

reversal NOUN
1 *There would soon be a reversal of their fortunes.*
▶ turnround, turnaround, change (in), shift
2 *The two principal actors suggested a reversal of their roles.*
▶ exchange, swap, interchange, change, transposition, inversion

reverse NOUN
The story turned out to be the reverse of the truth
▶ opposite, contrary, converse, inverse, antithesis

reverse VERB
1 *We can reverse the order of events if you like.*
▶ turn round, swap round, change round, transpose, invert, alter

2 *He reversed the car into a tree. The lorry reversed into the opening.*
▶ back, go or drive backwards
3 *The referee refused to reverse his decision.*
▶ change, rescind, retract, revoke, undo, countermand, negate, overturn, repeal

review NOUN
1 *a review of the year's achievements*
▶ survey, report, reappraisal, study, analysis, reassessment, look back (at)
2 *On Saturday the paper has book reviews.*
▶ criticism, critique, notice, appreciation, (*informal*) write-up
3 *The research is described in a scientific review.*
▶ journal, periodical, magazine, publication
4 *a military review*
▶ inspection, parade, display, demonstration

review VERB
1 *Let's review the situation and decide what to do.*
▶ consider, survey, assess, evaluate, appraise, weigh up, go over, study, reconsider, re-examine, scrutinize
2 *She reviewed the book on a television arts programme.*
▶ criticize, discuss, assess, evaluate

revile VERB
The people reviled him as a traitor.
▶ denounce, condemn, abuse, lambaste, rail against

revise VERB
1 *I am not about to revise my opinion.*
▶ reconsider, reassess, rethink, change, alter
2 *She spent the weekend revising for her exam.*
▶ study, read up, cram, (*more informal*) swot, (*more informal*) bone up
3 *The text was revised in the second edition.*
▶ amend, correct, edit, adapt

revival NOUN
a revival of interest in politics
▶ resurgence, reawakening, renewal, recovery, restoration, resurrection, upsurge, rebirth, renaissance, return, revitalization
AN OPPOSITE IS decline

revive VERB
1 *The man was unconscious but soon revived.*
▶ regain consciousness, recover, come round, come to, awake
2 *Hot drinks soon revived us.*
▶ reinvigorate, revitalize, resuscitate, refresh, freshen up, renew, restore, bring back to life

revoke VERB
The new regime revoked his passport.
▶ cancel, withdraw, rescind, abrogate, invalidate, retract, nullify

revolt VERB
1 *The island revolted against Athenian rule.*
▶ rebel, rise up, defect, mutiny
2 *Their cruelty revolted us.*
▶ disgust, sicken, shock, outrage, offend, repel, nauseate

revolt NOUN
a revolt in the Netherlands
▶ rebellion, uprising, revolution, defection, mutiny

revolting ADJECTIVE
There was a revolting mess on the floor.
▶ disgusting, repulsive, nauseating, offensive, sickening, loathsome, repugnant, unpleasant

revolution NOUN
1 *A revolution brought the democrats to power again.*
▶ rebellion, revolt, rising, uprising, coup, coup d'état, mutiny, civil war
2 *a revolution of the earth*
▶ rotation, circuit, cycle, orbit, turn
3 *a revolution in information technology*
▶ transformation, dramatic change, sea change, shift

revolutionary ADJECTIVE
1 *Revolutionary forces attacked the city.*
▶ rebel, rebellious, renegade, seditious, subversive, extremist
2 *a revolutionary idea for traffic control*
▶ original, innovative, innovatory, radical, novel, new, unconventional, progressive, inventive, advanced, experimental, avant-garde, challenging
AN OPPOSITE IS conservative

revolutionize VERB
a technique that will revolutionize heart surgery
▶ transform, change for ever, transfigure, reshape, remould

revolve VERB
1 *The ceiling fan began to revolve.*
▶ turn, go round, rotate, spin, whirl
2 *The moon revolves round the earth.*
▶ circle, orbit, gyrate
3 **revolve around** *Their lives revolved around their dogs.*
▶ concentrate on, centre on, focus on or be focused on, be absorbed in, be preoccupied with

revulsion NOUN
a feeling of revulsion against the savagery of these acts
▶ disgust, repulsion, abhorrence, repugnance, horror, loathing, nausea, contempt (for)

reward NOUN
1 *a reward for years of loyal service*
▶ honour, award, remuneration, prize, bonus, return, decoration, medal
2 *The dog's owners have offered a reward for its safe return.*
▶ payment, recompense, compensation, inducement, present, bounty
AN OPPOSITE IS punishment

reward VERB
1 *All three soldiers were rewarded for their bravery.*
▶ decorate, honour, recognize
AN OPPOSITE IS punish
2 *You will be well rewarded for your work.*
▶ pay, recompense, remunerate, repay, compensate, give a reward to
AN OPPOSITE IS punish

R

rewarding ADJECTIVE
The trip proved to be a rewarding experience.
▶ satisfying, worthwhile, pleasing, gratifying, fulfilling, fruitful, valuable
OPPOSITES ARE unrewarding, thankless

reword VERB
Do you think you should reword the last sentence?
▶ rephrase, recast, rewrite, put another way, express differently, revise, redraft, edit

rhetoric NOUN
1 *a statesman renowned for his rhetoric*
▶ oratory, eloquence, power of speech
2 *Ignore the rhetoric and there are some interesting things in these speeches.*
▶ pomposity, bombast, extravagant language, grandiloquence, verbosity, wordiness, exaggeration, hyperbole

rhyme NOUN
She tried to remember the words of the rhyme.
▶ poem, verse, ditty, ode, song, jingle

rhythm NOUN
1 *the rhythm of the poem*
▶ metre, measure, accent, flow
2 *the heavy rhythm of the rock music upstairs*
▶ beat, throb, pulse
3 *It was all part of the rhythm of their daily lives.*
▶ pattern, flow, pace, tempo

rhythmic ADJECTIVE
the rhythmic beat of the music
▶ pulsing, rhythmical, metrical, throbbing, steady, regular, lilting
AN OPPOSITE IS irregular

rich ADJECTIVE
1 *Rich people pay higher rates of tax.*
▶ wealthy, affluent, moneyed, well-off, well-to-do, prosperous, opulent, (*more informal*) flush, (*more informal*) loaded
OPPOSITES ARE poor, impoverished
2 *a room of rich furnishings*
▶ luxurious, sumptuous, opulent, ornate, lavish, costly, fine, gorgeous, elaborate, splendid
3 *acres of rich agricultural land*
▶ fertile, productive, fruitful, lush
OPPOSITES ARE infertile, unproductive
4 *a rich output of music dramas*
▶ plentiful, abundant, copious, prolific, profuse, plenteous, ample, teeming
5 *the rich colours of autumn*
▶ deep, full, strong, intense, vibrant, vivid, warm
AN OPPOSITE IS pale

riches NOUN
He spoke dreamily of the riches of America.
▶ wealth, money, affluence, fortune, treasure, assets, means, property

rickety ADJECTIVE
a small wild garden with a rickety greenhouse
▶ shaky, unsteady, unstable, wobbly, flimsy, decrepit, ramshackle, dilapidated, broken-down

rid VERB
The builders should rid the house of asbestos and all dangerous substances.
▶ clear, free, strip, purge, cleanse
get rid of *Scotland had got rid of its usurper.*
▶ dispose of, expel, remove, eject, evict, throw out, dispense with, (*more informal*) dump

riddle NOUN
The authorities want to solve the riddle of the man's identity.
▶ enigma, mystery, puzzle, question, problem, conundrum, (*more informal*) poser

riddle VERB
1 *The gunman riddled the door with holes.*
▶ puncture, perforate, pepper, pierce
2 *Her body was riddled with arthritis.*
▶ overrun, infest, permeate, pervade, cripple

ride VERB
1 *I'm learning to ride a horse.*
▶ control, handle, manage, sit on
2 *She rode through the town on a bicycle.*
▶ travel, pedal, drive, steer, progress

ride NOUN
The house is a short ride from the city centre.
▶ journey, trip, drive, run, jaunt, outing, (*more informal*) spin

ridicule NOUN
We will be open to ridicule if we get things wrong.
▶ mockery, derision, scorn, contempt, taunting, jeering, banter, teasing

ridicule VERB
I did not ridicule him as the others did.
▶ mock, make fun of, deride, laugh at, jeer at, sneer at, scoff at, humiliate, taunt

ridiculous ADJECTIVE
It was ridiculous to feel so worried.
▶ absurd, preposterous, ludicrous, senseless, silly, stupid, unreasonable, nonsensical, incredible, irrational, insane, mad

rife ADJECTIVE
Terror and torture were rife then.
▶ widespread, common, prevalent, general, universal, endemic, abundant

rift NOUN
1 *a rift in the ice*
▶ crack, fault, flaw, fracture, split, break, fissure
2 *a rift between the two leaders*
▶ breach, division, disagreement, difference of opinion, falling-out, estrangement, schism, alienation

rig NOUN
1 *He was wearing the rig of an army captain.*
▶ uniform, dress, outfit, livery
2 *She was busy setting up the recording rig for the afternoon.*
▶ equipment, apparatus, machinery, gear, system, kit, tackle

a
b
c
d
e
f
g
h
i
j
k
l
m
n
o
p
q
r
s
t
u
v
w
x
y
z

rig VERB

They were accused of rigging the election.
▶ manipulate, falsify, tamper with, interfere with, gerrymander, influence

right ADJECTIVE

1 *What is the right thing to do? Are you sure he's the right person for the job?*
▶ proper, appropriate, suitable, fitting, ideal
OPPOSITES ARE wrong, unsuitable

2 *She gave the right answer.*
▶ correct, accurate, exact, precise, true, actual, real, apposite, appropriate, apt, factual, genuine, proper
OPPOSITES ARE wrong, incorrect

3 *It's not right for them to be treated in this way.*
▶ fair, just, equitable, lawful, ethical, honourable, moral
AN OPPOSITE IS unjust

right NOUN

1 *Everyone should have the right to say what they believe.*
▶ entitlement, prerogative, freedom, liberty, privilege (of saying), facility

2 *We believe we have right on our side.*
▶ justice, virtue, fairness, goodness, legality, integrity, morality, honesty

right VERB

We will do our best to right the situation.
▶ remedy, rectify, put right, set right, redress, repair, resolve, correct, sort out, make amends for

rightful ADJECTIVE

1 *The car was returned to its rightful owner.*
▶ lawful, legal, legitimate, genuine, approved, authorized, proper, real, true, valid
AN OPPOSITE IS wrongful

2 *He felt he had been denied his rightful place in the company.*
▶ deserved, due, merited, earned, proper, fitting, just, right

rigid ADJECTIVE

1 *It's best to keep your lunch in a rigid container.*
▶ stiff, hard, firm, inflexible

2 *He had not yet established a rigid routine for his work.*
▶ fixed, set, firm, definite, unvarying, hard-and-fast

3 *She had a reputation as a rigid disciplinarian.*
▶ strict, stern, severe, harsh, uncompromising, unyielding
AN OPPOSITE IS flexible

rigorous ADJECTIVE

a rigorous attention to detail
▶ meticulous, thorough, careful, scrupulous, painstaking, conscientious, diligent, fastidious, stringent
OPPOSITES ARE lax, careless

rile VERB

(informal) His companions seemed determined to rile him.
▶ irritate, annoy, anger, enrage, exasperate,

incense, upset, peeve, vex, (*more informal*) needle, (*more informal*) bug, (*more informal*) rub up the wrong way

rim NOUN

They stared over the rim of the crater.
▶ brim, edge, lip, border, brink, verge, circumference

rind NOUN

the rind of a lemon
▶ peel, skin, husk, crust, outer layer

ring NOUN

1 *A ring of fire would protect her.*
▶ circle, loop, round, circuit, halo

2 *a spy ring*
▶ network, organization, syndicate, association, gang, group, cell, cartel

3 *a ring of spectators*
▶ circle, band, group, crowd, throng

4 *a circus ring*
▶ arena, enclosure
RELATED ADJECTIVE annular

ring VERB

1 *Riot police ringed the area.*
▶ surround, circle, encircle, confine, enclose, encompass, form a ring round

2 *Church bells rang all morning.*
▶ peal, chime, toll, clang, resound, jangle, reverberate

3 *I'll ring you tomorrow evening.*
▶ phone, call, telephone, ring up, (*informal*) give a buzz

rinse VERB

Campers were rinsing their plates in the stream.
▶ wash, wash out, swill, bathe, clean, sluice

riot NOUN

The authorities were reluctant to make arrests for fear of sparking a riot.
▶ uproar, insurrection, uprising, rising, tumult, commotion, brawl, street fight, fracas

riot VERB

The crowd rioted and pulled down the gates.
▶ rampage, run riot, create a riot, run amok, go berserk, revolt, rise up, mutiny, rebel

riotous ADJECTIVE

a riotous party
▶ wild, lively, boisterous, roisterous, loud, noisy, uproarious, rollicking
OPPOSITES ARE orderly, restrained

rip VERB

She read the note and ripped it into little pieces. The travellers ripped a way through the foliage.
▶ tear, slash, cut, rend, gash
rip off (*informal*) *The shop had ripped them off.*
▶ overcharge, swindle, cheat, defraud, (*informal*) rob

ripe ADJECTIVE

1 *a ripe melon*
▶ mature, ripened, tender, juicy
OPPOSITES ARE unripe, green

2 *an area ripe for development*
▶ ready, suitable, fit
AN OPPOSITE IS unsuitable

ripen VERB
The apples need time to ripen.
▶ become ripe, mature, develop, mellow

rip-off NOUN
(informal) At that price it was a rip-off.
▶ fraud, cheat, overcharge

rise VERB
1 *The little plane rose into the air.*
▶ ascend, go up, fly up, climb
OPPOSITES ARE fall, descend
2 *The castle walls rose above us.*
▶ tower, soar, loom, reach up
3 *Incomes have risen by an average 3 percent.*
▶ increase, grow, go up, get higher, escalate
OPPOSITES ARE fall, decrease
4 *She rose from her chair.*
▶ stand up, get up, jump up, leap up

rise NOUN
1 *We walked up the rise to the castle.*
▶ slope, incline, elevation, ascent, hill, ramp, bank
2 *another rise in interest rates*
▶ increase, jump, leap, upturn
OPPOSITES ARE fall, drop, decrease

risk NOUN
1 *She faced the risk of being stopped by the police.*
▶ chance, likelihood, possibility, danger
2 *Travelling at such a high speed involved risk.*
▶ hazard, peril, danger, speculation, uncertainty, gamble

risk VERB
1 *He didn't want to risk leaving her alone.*
▶ chance, dare, venture
2 *She risked everything to meet him again.*
▶ endanger, jeopardize, put at risk, put at peril, chance, imperil, hazard

risky ADJECTIVE
1 *Any project involving rockets is always risky.*
▶ dangerous, hazardous, unsafe, perilous, (more informal) dodgy
AN OPPOSITE IS safe
2 *Farming is a risky business.*
▶ uncertain, chancy, precarious, touch-and-go
AN OPPOSITE IS secure

ritual NOUN
1 *a religious ritual*
▶ ceremony, rite, ceremonial, observance, service, liturgy
2 *The Sunday outing had become something of a ritual.*
▶ custom, tradition, habit, formality

rival NOUN
Leo was his main rival for the job.
▶ competitor, adversary, challenger, opponent, contender, contestant

rival ADJECTIVE
A rival supermarket has opened.
▶ competing, competitive, opposing

rival VERB
Few countries rival Greece for its beauty.
▶ compete with, contend with, compare with, equal, match, be as good as, emulate, vie with

rivalry NOUN
There was growing rivalry between the two teams.
▶ competitiveness, competition, contention, opposition, conflict, antagonism
AN OPPOSITE IS cooperation

river NOUN
a trip down the river
▶ stream, waterway, watercourse, brook, rivulet, creek

---

road NOUN
a busy road
▶ roadway, route, way, highway, motorway, street, avenue, boulevard

KINDS OF ROADS AND PATHWAYS

main roads: thoroughfare, trunk road (or arterial road, linking towns and cities), motorway (or (American) freeway), clearway (no stopping), dual carriageway (or (American) highway), bypass (avoiding a town or city), ring road (round a town or city), slip road (leading to and from a main road).

roads in towns and cities: street, avenue (or boulevard, broad with trees) drive, driveway, crescent, cul-de-sac (closed at one end), one-way street, service road (giving access to houses), side road, side street.

minor and country roads: byroad, byway, lane, track, trail, cart track, causeway (across wet ground), bridleway (or bridle path, for horse riding).

paths for walking: alley, path, pathway, footpath, pavement (or (American) sidewalk), beside a road), esplanade (broad open space for walking), walk, walkway, towpath (beside a river or canal, originally for pulling barges).

---

roadworthy ADJECTIVE
a roadworthy vehicle
▶ safe, usable

roam VERB
People like to roam over the hills.
▶ wander, rove, ramble, stroll, amble, walk, meander, travel, stray, range

roar VERB
1 *Bill roared at them to stop.*
▶ shout, bellow, yell, bawl, clamour, shriek
2 *A motorbike roared past.*
▶ speed, zoom, whizz, flash
3 *He had the audience roaring.*
▶ guffaw, howl, hoot, (more informal) split your sides, (more informal) kill yourself laughing

roar NOUN
the roars of the crowd
▶ shout, yell, clamour, bellow, howl

rob VERB
1 *The gang had robbed banks all over the south-east.*
▶ burgle, hold up, steal from, break into, raid, loot, rifle
2 *She was attacked and robbed on her way home that evening.*
▶ mug, steal from, hold up
3 *They thought they had been robbed of their victory.*
▶ cheat, deprive, defraud, swindle

robber NOUN
Robbers attacked the travellers on the road north.
▶ thief, brigand, bandit, raider, highwayman, marauder
USAGE You can also use *burglar* and *housebreaker* for robbers who steal from buildings, and *mugger* for robbers who attack people in the street.

robbery NOUN
a wave of robberies and other crimes
▶ burglary, theft, thieving, stealing, housebreaking, shoplifting, pilfering, hold-up, mugging, (*more informal*) stick-up

robot NOUN
In a future world robots do much of the work.
▶ automaton, computerized machine, automated machine, android

robust ADJECTIVE
1 *a man with a robust physique*
▶ strong, vigorous, hardy, muscular, powerful, rugged, athletic, brawny, healthy, sound
2 *The tools will need to be very robust*
▶ sturdy, durable, strong, tough, serviceable
AN OPPOSITE IS fragile

rock NOUN
1 *a castle high up on a rock*
▶ cliff, crag, outcrop
2 *Rocks were strewn across the road*
▶ boulder, stone
WORDS FOR TYPES OF ROCK
igneous rocks: andesite, basalt, diorite, granite, kimberlite. obsidian, peridotite, rhyolite.
sedimentary rocks: chalk, chert, clay, conglomerate, dolomite, limestone, sandstone.
metamorphic rocks: gneiss, hornfels, marble, quartzite, schist, slate.
minerals: argentite, barite, beryl, cassiterite, cinnabar, diamond, galena, gold, gypsum, magnetite, mica, topaz, tourmaline.

rock VERB
1 *The woman rocked gently in her chair.*
▶ sway, swing, move gently
2 *The ship rocked in the storm*
▶ toss, lurch, sway, pitch, plunge, roll
3 *News of the disaster rocked the nation.*
▶ stun, shake, stagger, astound, astonish, startle, dumbfound

rocket VERB
Prices have rocketed under this government.
▶ shoot up, soar, escalate, spiral, increase rapidly, (*more informal*) go through the roof

rocky ADJECTIVE
1 *a rocky hillside*
▶ stony, rock-strewn, craggy, shingly, pebbly, rugged
2 *The table is rocky.*
▶ unsteady, shaky, wobbly, rickety, tottery
3 *The marriage had become decidedly rocky.*
▶ difficult, precarious, problematic, unstable

rod NOUN
1 *an iron rod*
▶ bar, pole, baton, staff, shaft, sceptre
2 *He was beaten with a rod.*
▶ cane, switch

rodent NOUN
SOME NAMES OF RODENTS
agouti, beaver, capybara (largest), cavy, chinchilla, coypu, degu, dormouse, field mouse, gerbil, gopher, guinea pig, hamster, harvest mouse, jerboa, lemming, marmot, mouse, muskrat, paca, porcupine, rat, squirrel, vole, water rat.

rogue NOUN
In the story, everyone is either a fool or a rogue.
▶ villain, scoundrel, rascal, good-for-nothing, reprobate, crook

role NOUN
1 *The director took a small role in the film.*
▶ part, character, portrayal
2 *He spoke in his role of government adviser.*
▶ capacity, function, position, office, post, job

roll NOUN
1 *a roll of film*
▶ reel, spool, cylinder, drum, scroll
2 *an electoral roll*
▶ register, list, record, index, catalogue, schedule, inventory

roll VERB
1 *The can rolled into the gutter The huge wheels began to roll.*
▶ spin, rotate, revolve, turn, whirl, gyrate
2 *She rolled the paper into a ball.*
▶ wind, fold, coil, twist, curl, screw
3 *The ship began to roll.*
▶ rock, sway, lurch, pitch, toss, reel
4 *He was in the kitchen, rolling pastry.*
▶ smooth, flatten, level, even out
5 *Thunder rolled in the distance.*
▶ rumble, boom, resound, reverberate, thunder
roll up (*informal*) *He rolled up with some friends just as we were leaving.*

▶ arrive, appear, come, show your face, (*informal*) turn up, (*informal*) show up

romance NOUN

1 *a historical romance*
▶ love story, romantic novel, fantasy
2 *the romance of travel*
▶ glamour, excitement, adventure, fascination, mystique
3 *Romance was in the air.*
▶ love, passion, ardour
4 *They were having a wild romance.*
▶ love affair, relationship, attachment

romantic ADJECTIVE

1 *He was handsome and romantic.*
▶ amorous, passionate, loving, tender-hearted, affectionate
2 *romantic stories set in the Far East*
▶ imaginary, fanciful, sentimental, (*more informal*) soppy
3 *a pretty village in a romantic landscape*
▶ idyllic, picturesque, fairy-tale
4 *Their notions about life were highly romantic.*
▶ idealistic, idealized, starry-eyed, unrealistic, visionary, utopian, fanciful, dreamy

romp VERB

The children romped in the garden.
▶ leap about, cavort, caper, run about, skip about, bound about, frisk, frolic, gambol

room NOUN

1 *There wasn't enough room for a bed.*
▶ space, capacity, volume
2 (*informal*) *We need more room to live our own lives.*
▶ freedom, latitude, leeway, allowance, elbow room
3 *There's always room for improvement.*
▶ scope, capacity, margin, opportunity

THE MAIN KINDS OF ROOM ARE

rooms in a house or flat: hall, cloakroom, living room (or drawing room or sitting room or lounge), front room, dining room, study, den, studio (large living room in a flat), breakfast room, conservatory; kitchen, pantry, scullery, utility room; landing, bedroom, boudoir, dressing room, guest room (or spare room), nursery, boxroom, lumber room, playroom (or rumpus room), bathroom, lavatory (or toilet or (*informal*) loo); attic, loft; basement, cellar .

rooms in a school: foyer, lobby, hall, assembly room, cloakroom, office, common room, classroom, library, laboratory (or (*informal*) lab), workshop, music room, gymnasium (or gym), locker room, changing room, lavatories (or toilets), boiler room, storeroom; sickroom, dormitory (in a boarding school).

rooms in an office: foyer, lobby, office, working area (open plan), meeting room, boardroom, lavatories (or toilets), boiler room.

roomy ADJECTIVE

The apartment was bright and roomy.
▶ spacious, capacious, large, sizeable, extensive, commodious, voluminous
OPPOSITES ARE cramped, poky

root NOUN

1 *The plant had long stringy roots.*
▶ tuber, rhizome, rootlet, radicle
2 *Money is the root of the problem.*
▶ source, origin, cause, basis, starting point, seed, germ

root VERB

root out *The magistrates were determined to root out corruption.*
▶ discover, unearth, dig out, ferret out, remove, eliminate, extirpate

rope NOUN

A rope attached the boat to the quayside.
▶ cable, cord, line, halyard, hawser, lanyard

rope VERB

rope in *They roped us in to help too.*
▶ enlist, persuade, talk (into helping), inveigle (into helping), drag

rot NOUN

1 *The surveyor found traces of rot in the roof timbers.*
▶ decay, decomposition, mould, mildew, dry rot, wet rot
2 (*informal*) *You're talking rot*
▶ nonsense, rubbish, gibberish, drivel, codswallop, claptrap

rot VERB

The floorboards had begun to rot.
▶ decay, decompose, perish, become rotten, degenerate, deteriorate, crumble, disintegrate

rota NOUN

a washing-up rota for the week
▶ roster, schedule, list, timetable

rotary ADJECTIVE

rotary motion
▶ rotating, rotatory, revolving, gyrating, twirling, twisting, spinning, turning, whirling

rotate VERB

1 *The arms of the windmill were rotating.*
▶ revolve, turn round, go round, move round, spin, gyrate, twirl, swivel, roll
2 *The role of chairman rotates every year.*
▶ alternate, take turns, change, switch, swap, move round

rotation NOUN

1 *the rotation of the earth*
▶ revolution, turn, orbit, spinning
2 *the rotation of a wheel*
▶ turning, revolving, spinning, gyration

rotten ADJECTIVE

1 *Some of the wood looked rotten.*
▶ decayed, decaying, decomposed, crumbling, disintegrating

2 *the stench of rotten meat*
▶ mouldy, mouldering, putrid, decayed, decaying, foul, tainted
AN OPPOSITE IS fresh

3 (*informal*) *They had a rotten time.*
▶ unpleasant, disagreeable, terrible, bad
OPPOSITES ARE pleasant, good

4 (*informal*) *The builders had done a rotten job. He would make a rotten teacher.*
▶ poor, inferior, inadequate, bad, low-grade, (*informal*) crummy, (*informal*) ropy, (*informal*) lousy
OPPOSITES ARE fine, good

rough ADJECTIVE

1 *She picked her way over the rough ground*
▶ bumpy, rugged, uneven, broken, irregular, rocky, stony, coarse, craggy
AN OPPOSITE IS even

2 *rough skin*
▶ dry, chapped, coarse, hairy, bristly, shaggy, unshaven
AN OPPOSITE IS smooth

3 *rough treatment It was pretty rough on your mother.*
▶ harsh, severe, hard, tough, stern

4 *a rough sea the ability to withstand rough weather*
▶ choppy, turbulent, agitated, stormy, tempestuous, violent, wild
AN OPPOSITE IS calm

5 *a rough voice*
▶ harsh, grating, gruff, rasping, hoarse, husky
AN OPPOSITE IS soft

6 *She doesn't like rough kids.*
▶ rowdy, boisterous, disorderly, unrestrained
AN OPPOSITE IS polite

7 *The tower is of rough workmanship.*
▶ amateurish, careless, clumsy, crude, hasty, imperfect, inept, (*informal*) rough and ready, unfinished, unpolished, unskilful
AN OPPOSITE IS skilful

8 *This gives you a rough idea of what we mean.*
▶ vague, approximate, imprecise, inexact, estimated, hazy, crude
AN OPPOSITE IS exact

9 *To begin with I made a rough drawing.*
▶ quick, sketchy, crude, hasty, preliminary, basic, outline

10 *He went home. He was feeling rough.*
▶ ill, unwell, sick, poorly, out of sorts, queasy, off colour, (*more informal*) lousy, (*more informal*) grotty
OPPOSITES ARE well, fit

roughly ADVERB

1 *There were roughly equal numbers of men and women.*
▶ about, around, approximately, nearly, close to

2 *Geoffrey pulled his arm roughly away.*
▶ violently, forcefully, forcibly, abruptly

round ADJECTIVE

1 *a round window*
▶ spherical, circular, bulbous, curved, cylindrical, globular

2 *a man with a short round figure*
▶ rounded, plump, chubby, rotund, ample, full, fat

round NOUN

1 *the most exciting tie of the second round*
▶ stage, game, series, sequence, contest

2 *an endless round of radio and television interviews*
▶ cycle, series, succession, sequence

round VERB

A large van rounded the corner.
▶ travel round, skirt, turn

round off *We rounded the evening off with some drinks.*
▶ end, finish, complete, conclude, cap, top

round on *Jo rounded on her. 'You're supposed to be looking after this place.'*
▶ turn on, snap at, attack, weigh into, let fly at

round up *His dog, Nell, rounded up 300 sheep.*
▶ herd, drive together, muster, marshal, assemble

roundabout ADJECTIVE

He reached the town square by a roundabout route
▶ indirect, circuitous, devious, winding, rambling, meandering, tortuous, twisting, long
AN OPPOSITE IS direct

roundabout NOUN

1 *Let's play on the roundabout.*
▶ merry-go-round, carousel

2 *Turn right at the next roundabout.*
▶ traffic circle, rotary

rouse VERB

1 *Next morning he was roused by the clanging of church bells.*
▶ arouse, awaken, wake up

2 *His words roused feelings of sympathy in her.*
▶ aroused, provoke, stir up, trigger, spark off, kindle, cause

3 *He can be violent when he's roused.*
▶ anger, annoy, provoke, incite, inflame, incense, work up

rousing ADJECTIVE

a rousing speech
▶ stirring, inspiring, moving, stimulating, exciting

rout VERB

They went on to rout the Royalist forces.
▶ crush, defeat, overwhelm, trounce, thrash, put to flight, drive off, (*more informal*) hammer

A B C D E F G H I J K L M N O P Q R S T U V W X Y Z

rout NOUN
The defence prevented the game from turning into a rout.
► crushing defeat, trouncing, thrashing, debacle

route NOUN
This route is direct but gets tedious in the later stages.
► way, road, course, direction, path, passage, itinerary, journey

routine NOUN
1 *Their evening routine never varied.*
► procedure, pattern, way, method, course of action, practice, system, custom, drill, habit
2 *I've been practising a new dance routine.*
► act, performance, programme, number, turn

routine ADJECTIVE
It is now a fairly routine operation done under local anaesthetic.
► standard, normal, ordinary, everyday, run-of-the-mill

row NOUN (rhymes with *crow*)
a row of small plants
► line, string, chain, series, sequence, cordon, file

row NOUN (rhymes with *cow*)
1 *She and Paul had had a row.*
► quarrel, argument, squabble, fight, scrap, altercation, disagreement, dispute, (*more informal*) slanging match
AN OPPOSITE IS reconciliation
2 (*informal*) *The crowd was making a dreadful row.*
► noise, racket, rumpus, tumult, din, disturbance, uproar, commotion

row VERB (rhymes with *cow*)
They had been shouting and rowing all evening.
► quarrel, argue, wrangle, bicker, squabble, fight, scrap

rowdy ADJECTIVE
a bunch of rowdy men
► unruly, disorderly, riotous, noisy, badly behaved, rough, wild, disruptive, boisterous
OPPOSITES ARE quiet, peaceful

royal ADJECTIVE
1 *the royal family*
► regal, imperial, kingly, princely, queenly, majestic, stately
2 *We received a royal welcome*
► magnificent, splendid, excellent, fine

rub VERB
1 *John rubbed the back of his leg.*
► stroke, knead, massage, caress, smooth
2 *She rubbed lotion on the children's backs.*
► apply (to), smear, smooth, spread, put on
3 *His new shoes were rubbing dreadfully.*
► pinch, chafe, abrade, graze, scrape, hurt
4 *Stella rubbed the table with polish.*
► polish, buff, shine, wipe
rub out *Someone had rubbed out his name.*
► remove, erase, delete, efface, expunge, blot out

rubbish NOUN
1 *Household rubbish is collected on Wednesdays.*
► refuse, waste, garbage, debris, junk, leavings, litter, trash
2 *They are talking rubbish.*
► nonsense, balderdash, gibberish, claptrap, drivel, gobbledegook, (*more informal*) rot, (*more informal*) twaddle

rubble NOUN
Often he had to clear away piles of rubble before he could continue.
► debris, ruins, remains, wreckage, fragments

ruddy ADJECTIVE
a cheerful pipe-smoking man with a ruddy complexion
► reddish, rubicund, flushed, glowing, healthy

rude NOUN
1 *He was sometimes rude, but always honest.*
► impolite, discourteous, disrespectful, impertinent, impudent, insolent, ill-mannered, ill-bred, uncivil, offensive, abusive
OPPOSITES ARE polite, civil
2 *a rude joke*
► vulgar, coarse, dirty, smutty, filthy
AN OPPOSITE IS clean

rudeness NOUN
'You,' she called, with uncharacteristic rudeness.
► impoliteness, bad manners, discourtesy, disrespect, incivility, impertinence, impudence, insolence, churlishness, cheek

rudimentary ADJECTIVE
1 *You'll need a rudimentary knowledge of first aid.*
► simple, basic, elementary, primitive, fundamental, crude
AN OPPOSITE IS advanced
2 *The pelycosaurs tended to develop rudimentary teeth.*
► incomplete, embryonic, vestigial, primitive
3 *a rudimentary language course*
► introductory, basic, elementary, preliminary, initial

ruffian NOUN
A group of ruffians assaulted a university student on his way home.
► thug, hoodlum, hooligan, lout, rogue, scoundrel, brute, bully, villain, mugger, (*more informal*) tough, (*more informal*) yob

ruffle VERB
1 *A light wind ruffled the leaves of the trees.*
► stir, agitate, ripple, disturb
2 *Isobel took off her scarf and ruffled her hair.*
► rumple, tousle, run your fingers through, dishevel, mess up
AN OPPOSITE IS smooth
3 *Don't let their stupid remarks ruffle you.*
► annoy, upset, unsettle, disconcert, fluster, irritate, vex, worry, (*more informal*) nettle, (*more informal*) rattle
AN OPPOSITE IS calm

rug NOUN

1 *The children sat on a rug on the floor.*
▶ mat, runner, matting

2 *She was wrapped in a rug to keep out the cold.*
▶ blanket, coverlet, throw

rugged ADJECTIVE

1 *a Spanish village nestling in rugged hills*
▶ rough, uneven, rocky, craggy, stark, bumpy, jagged, irregular
OPPOSITES ARE smooth, gentle

2 *The only softness about his rugged face was in his lips.*
▶ strong, sturdy, rough, tough, robust, hardy, burly, husky, muscular, weather-beaten

ruin NOUN

1 *They now face financial ruin.*
▶ bankruptcy, insolvency, failure, breakdown, collapse, downfall, ruination, undoing

2 *It was the ruin of all their hopes.*
▶ destruction, disintegration, devastation, overthrow, failure, undoing, ruination

3 *Crackpot Hall is a sad ruin in a beautiful location.*
▶ remnant, shell, group of remains

4 **ruins** *Villagers had discovered three unidentifiable bodies among the ruins of the house.*
▶ remains, rubble, debris, wreckage

ruin VERB

1 *Once again the rain has ruined what promised to be a good contest.*
▶ spoil, wreck, destroy, shatter, blight, wreak havoc on, torpedo, (*more informal*) mess up
OPPOSITES ARE save, rescue

2 *He would be ruined if he had to pay.*
▶ bankrupt, impoverish, financially cripple

ruined ADJECTIVE

the gateway to a ruined fortress
▶ derelict, dilapidated, ramshackle, tumbledown, crumbling

ruinous ADJECTIVE

1 *activity that has a ruinous effect on the environment*
▶ disastrous, catastrophic, devastating, calamitous, destructive, cataclysmic, dire, fatal

2 *They found the building in a ruinous condition*
▶ ruined, dilapidated, derelict

rule NOUN

1 *the rules governing procedures in case of fire*
▶ regulation, law, code, convention, precept, principle, routine, practice, custom

2 *British rule had ended in 1947.*
▶ control, jurisdiction, administration, sovereignty, mastery, command, domination, dominion, authority, government, supremacy, sway

3 *The normal rule is to apply for tickets by letter.*
▶ procedure, practice, protocol, form, custom, convention

rule VERB

1 *How could a city-state like Rome rule an empire?*
▶ govern, administer, manage, run, control, direct, command, dominate, lead, reign over

2 *The king's successor ruled for less than a year.*
▶ reign, be ruler, be in power, be monarch

3 *The judge ruled that the defendant should be awarded the costs of the case.*
▶ decree, order, direct, pronounce, resolve, decide, determine, adjudicate, find, judge

rule out *We cannot rule out suicide as a cause of death.*
▶ exclude, discount, reject, eliminate, dismiss, preclude, disregard

---

ruler NOUN

a much-respected ruler
▶ leader, sovereign, overlord, governor, dynast, monarch, president (of a republic), head of state

NAMES FOR TYPES OF RULER

general words in addition to the ones above: emperor, empress, king, queen, prince, princess, lord, regent (ruling on behalf of someone unable to rule, e.g. a minor), viceroy (representing a monarch in a colony), dictator, tyrant.

historical and regional rulers: aga (Turkish), caesar (Roman), caliph (Muslim), emir (Muslim), Führer (German, title of Hitler), kaiser (German or Austrian), khan (Muslim), Khedive (Turkish viceroy in Egypt), maharajah (Indian prince), maharani (wife or widow of a maharajah), mikado (Japanese), nawab (Mogul governor), pharaoh (ancient Egypt), raja (Indian king or prince), rani (Hindu queen), satrap (ancient Persia), shah (Iranian king), sheikh (Arab leader), shogun (Japan), sultan (Muslim), sultana (wife of a sultan), tsar (Russian emperor before 1917), tsarina (Russian empress before 1917).

---

ruling NOUN

A ruling came from the president himself.
▶ decision, pronouncement, resolution, decree, judgement, adjudication, order, command, instruction

rumble VERB

Thunder rumbled in the distance.
▶ boom, reverberate, resound, echo

rummage VERB

She started to rummage in her handbag for her keys.
▶ search, hunt, scrabble, burrow, root

rumour NOUN

1 *A rumour had started that the company would close.*
► report, story, piece of gossip, whisper
2 *The suggestion was only rumour.*
► gossip, hearsay, talk, tittle-tattle

rumpus NOUN

A terrible rumpus was going on outside.
► commotion, uproar, racket, tumult, hullabaloo, hubbub, fracas, furore, upheaval, agitation, excitement

---

run VERB This word is often overused. Here are some alternatives:
1 *We ran across the field.*
► sprint, race, jog, tear, dash, rush, hasten, speed, streak, bolt, scamper, scoot
2 *The buses don't run on Sundays.*
► operate, function, go, provide a service
3 *The car has been running erratically.*
► function, perform, work, behave
4 *His car was stolen because he had left the engine running.*
► operate, tick over, go
5 *Water ran down the wall.*
► stream, trickle, flow, flood, pour, spill, gush, cascade, dribble, leak
6 *She was running a small business in Leeds.*
► manage, be in charge of, direct, control, administer, conduct, supervise, govern, look after, maintain, rule
7 *He could no longer afford to run a car.*
► maintain, keep, own, use, drive
8 *She ran me back to my house.*
► drive, take, bring, ferry, give a lift to
9 *It is important to run exhaustive tests.*
► carry out, perform, complete, do, fulfil
10 *A sharp pain ran up her arm.*
► pass, move, shoot, travel, go
11 *The road runs north.*
► extend, reach, stretch, go, continue
run across *I ran across your sister in Paris.*
► meet, encounter, come across, run into, chance on
run after *Jill ran after him with his keys.*
► chase, pursue, follow
run away *He threw down his shield and ran away.*
► escape, flee, bolt, abscond, (more informal) make off
run down
1 *A dog ran into the road and he ran it down.*
► run over, knock over, hit, struck
2 *She didn't want to run him down in public.*
► criticize, denigrate, disparage, belittle, find fault with
run into *Did you run into any of your friends?*
► meet, encounter, come across, run across, chance on
run out *My subscription runs out in December.*
► expire, terminate, end, come to an end, cease, dry up

---

run NOUN

1 *a run across the park*
► jog, dash, sprint, spurt, trot, gallop, canter, race
2 *a run in the car*
► drive, ride, trip, excursion, journey, (more informal) spin
3 *a run of bad luck*
► sequence, stretch, series, chain, course
4 *a chicken run*
► enclosure, compound, coop, pen

runaway NOUN

a safe house for young runaways
► fugitive, escapee, refugee, absconder

runner NOUN

1 *There are seven runners in the next race.*
► competitor, entrant, participant, athlete
2 *The commanding officer sent a runner to headquarters*
► courier, messenger

running NOUN

1 *A private company has taken over the running of the school.*
► administration, management, direction, controlling, supervision
2 *These measures will ensure the smooth running of the organization.*
► operation, working, functioning

runny ADJECTIVE

a runny mixture of egg and milk
► watery, thin, fluid, liquid, free-flowing
OPPOSITES ARE solid, viscous

run-of-the-mill ADJECTIVE

The songs are all run-of-the-mill efforts.
► ordinary, routine, average, mediocre, unremarkable, unexceptional, unimpressive

rupture NOUN

The rupture in the blood vessel was not caused by the operation.
► split, crack, tear, puncture, fracture, burst

rupture VERB

The impact ruptured both fuel tanks.
► split, puncture, fracture, crack, tear, burst, sever

rural ADJECTIVE

The majority lived in rural communities outside London.
► country, rustic, pastoral, agricultural, agrarian, countrified
AN OPPOSITE IS urban

rush VERB

She rushed into the garden.
► hurry, hasten, dash, run, sprint, race, tear, dash, hasten, streak, bolt
OPPOSITES ARE dawdle, saunter

rush NOUN

1 *a frantic rush to put out the flames*
► hurry, haste, dash, race, scramble
2 *It stopped the rush of water for a time.*
► flood, gush, spate, cataract

r

3 *There was a sudden rush for the doors*
▶ charge, stampede, surge (towards)

rust VERB
a special coating to prevent the iron from rusting
▶ corrode, become rusty, oxidize, crumble away, decay, rot

rustic ADJECTIVE
1 *a house in rustic surroundings*
▶ rural, country, pastoral, agricultural, agrarian, countrified
AN OPPOSITE IS urban
2 *She sat down on a rustic wooden seat.*
▶ plain, simple, crude, rough, artless, unsophisticated

rustle VERB
The rain rustled in the grass.
▶ crackle, swish, whisper, whoosh

rusty ADJECTIVE
1 *Nothing causes more blisters than using a rusty trowel.*
▶ corroded, rusted, oxidized, rotten, tarnished, discoloured
2 *My French is a little rusty.*
▶ unpractised, neglected, below par, deficient, weak, unused, (*more informal*) creaky

rut NOUN
1 *There were deep ruts in the track.*
▶ furrow, groove, trough, channel, indentation
2 *He was in a rut; comfortable, but in a rut all the same.*
▶ groove, grind, dull routine, treadmill

ruthless ADJECTIVE
1 *a ruthless dictator*
▶ merciless, pitiless, brutal, cruel, callous, unfeeling, heartless, vicious, violent, ferocious, fierce
AN OPPOSITE IS compassionate
2 *He carried out his instructions with ruthless efficiency.*
▶ relentless, unrelenting, inexorable, unremitting, intense, implacable

Ss

sabotage NOUN
The crash was probably caused by engine failure and not sabotage.
▶ wilful damage, deliberate destruction, vandalism, wrecking, disruption, treachery

sabotage VERB
1 *A gang had sabotaged the cash machines in the shopping mall.*
▶ wreck, deliberately damage, destroy, disable, put out of action, cripple, vandalize

2 *Are you telling me he deliberately set out to sabotage your work?*
▶ wreck, ruin, spoil, thwart, undermine, disrupt

sack NOUN
1 *The flour was in an open sack on the floor.*
▶ bag, pack, pouch
2 *When she complained she promptly got the sack.*
▶ notice, dismissal, discharge, your cards, (*more informal*) the boot

sack VERB
1 *Unbelievably, he sacked his son-in-law and replaced him with Trevor.*
▶ dismiss, give notice to, get rid of, lay someone off, let someone go, (*more informal*) fire, (*more informal*) kick out
2 *Edward I had sacked the town in 1296.*
▶ destroy, raid, loot, plunder, pillage, ravage

sacred ADJECTIVE
1 *The new pope was enthroned in the most sacred place in the basilica.*
▶ holy, blessed, consecrated, sanctified, hallowed, dedicated, venerated
OPPOSITES ARE unconsecrated
2 *The recital mixed operatic arias with traditional sacred melodies.*
▶ religious, spiritual, devotional, ecclesiastical
OPPOSITES ARE secular

NAMES FOR SACRED TEXTS AND HOLY BOOKS
Buddhism: Tripitaka.
Christianity: Bible, Old Testament, New Testament, Gospel, Epistle.
Confucianism: I Ching.
Hinduism: Bhagavadgita, Mahabharata, Ramayana, Veda.
Islam: Koran.
Judaism: Talmud, Torah.
Sikhism: Adi Granth.
Zoroastrianism: Zend-Avesta.

sacrifice NOUN
1 *The festival involved a sacrifice of a ram and seven lambs.*
▶ offering, ritual slaughter, votive offering, oblation
2 *The building was rebuilt with some sacrifice of its earlier features.*
▶ loss, abandonment, discarding, rejection, surrender, giving up, yielding, renunciation, renouncing

sacrifice VERB
1 *They have sacrificed their principles and lost their good name. a memorial to the bomber crews who sacrificed their lives in the war*
▶ give up, forfeit, relinquish, surrender, forgo, go without
2 *The goat had been sacrificed at the shrine.*
▶ offer up, kill, slaughter, immolate

sacrilege NOUN
Wearing armour in a holy place was sacrilege.
► blasphemy, desecration, impiety, profanity, irreverence, disrespect, ungodliness
OPPOSITES ARE piety, respect

---

sad ADJECTIVE This word is often overused. Here are some alternatives:
1 *Everyone was sad to be leaving. He looked at her sad face.*
► unhappy, sorrowful, dejected, downcast, despondent, downhearted, depressed, miserable, glum, in low spirits
2 *I told my brother and sister the sad news. The story is sadder than we realized.*
► distressing, upsetting, depressing, grave, tragic, unfortunate, regrettable, serious, heart-rending
3 *This sad state of affairs does not have to continue.*
► sorry, wretched, unfortunate, regrettable, shameful, disgraceful
4 *(informal) They live in a sad little house.*
► pathetic, pitiful, inadequate

---

sadden VERB
That brief reminder of her husband saddened her.
► upset, distress, dispirit, grieve, dishearten
AN OPPOSITE IS cheer up

saddle VERB
It seemed a pity to saddle them with so much work.
► burden, encumber, lumber, load, impose
USAGE If you use *impose* you have to say *It seemed a pity to impose so much work on them.*

sadistic ADJECTIVE
a sadistic killer
► callous, cruel, brutal, brutish, pitiless, cold-blooded, ruthless, merciless, vile

sadness NOUN
She could not hide her sadness.
► unhappiness, sorrow, dejection, misery, melancholy, low spirits, depression, regret

safe ADJECTIVE
1 *The building was safe from attack.*
► secure, protected, guarded, invulnerable, impregnable
2 *The missing children were all safe.*
► unharmed, unhurt, uninjured, out of danger
3 *She is a safe driver. Better safe than sorry.*
► cautious, prudent, circumspect, attentive
4 *He's a safe person to be with.*
► reliable, trustworthy, responsible, sensible, level-headed, upright
5 *a medicine that is safe for young children*
► harmless, innocuous, proven

safeguard NOUN
Burglar alarms are an additional safeguard.
► protection, defence, guard, shield, precaution, security, assurance

safeguard VERB
The charter safeguards your human rights.
► protect, preserve, defend, secure, look after, shield, guard

safety NOUN
1 *The safety of passengers is paramount.*
► security, protection, welfare, well-being
AN OPPOSITE IS danger
2 *The refugees looked for a place of safety.*
► refuge, shelter, sanctuary, protection

safety belt NOUN
The bus was fitted with safety belts.
► seat belt, safety harness

sag VERB
The ceiling sags in the middle.
► hang down, sink, slump, dip, droop, fall

saga NOUN
They longed to tell the saga of their day's adventures.
► tale, story, catalogue, rigmarole

---

sail VERB
1 *John loves sailing his boat.*
► pilot, navigate, skipper, steer, captain
2 *We had a holiday sailing in the Mediterranean.*
► cruise, voyage, boat, yacht, go sailing, navigate
3 *The ferry sails at midday.*
► put to sea, set sail, leave harbour, weigh anchor
SOME TYPES OF SAILING SHIP
barque, brigantine, caique, caravel, catamaran, clipper, cutter, dhow, felucca, frigate, galleon, junk, ketch, longship, lugger, man-of-war, merchantman, merchant ship, monohull, schooner, skiff, sloop, smack, trimaran, xebec, yacht, yawl.

---

sailor NOUN
He did not make a very good sailor.
► seaman, seafarer, mariner, boatman, yachtsman or yachtswoman

saintly ADJECTIVE
a saintly priest
► holy, godly, pious, devout, spiritual, God-fearing, blessed, virtuous
AN OPPOSITE IS unholy

sake NOUN
for the sake of *He did it for the sake of his family.*
► for the good of, in the interests of, for the benefit of, for the advantage of, on behalf of

salary NOUN
She is paid an annual salary of £45,000.
► income, earnings, pay, wages, remuneration, emolument, payment

sale NOUN
laws to control the sale of drugs
► selling, marketing, trading (in), dealing (in), traffic (in), disposal
AN OPPOSITE IS purchase

S

salesperson NOUN
A salesperson must know their products' benefits.
▶ salesman or saleswoman, sales assistant, shop assistant, shopkeeper

sallow ADJECTIVE
a sallow complexion
▶ pale, pallid, wan, sickly, yellowish, anaemic, colourless

salty ADJECTIVE
a thick salty paste used for flavouring
▶ salt, salted, piquant, saline, briny, tangy, spicy
OPPOSITES ARE fresh, bland

salubrious ADJECTIVE
We reached the more salubrious outskirts of the city.
▶ healthy, health-giving, beneficial, wholesome, sanitary, hygienic, invigorating, refreshing, pleasant
OPPOSITES ARE unhealthy, unpleasant

salutary ADJECTIVE
Their experiences offer some salutary warnings.
▶ beneficial, helpful, useful, valuable, advantageous, productive, profitable

salute VERB
1 *You call me 'sir' but you don't salute me, OK?*
▶ greet, acknowledge, hail, address, welcome
2 *I salute them for having the courage to admit their mistakes.*
▶ pay tribute to, acknowledge, celebrate, recognize, honour

salute NOUN
He gave a quick salute.
▶ greeting, acknowledgement, salutation, wave

salvage NOUN
the search and salvage of aircraft wreckage
▶ recovery, rescue, retrieval, saving, reclamation

salvage VERB
1 *We might be able to salvage the car before it goes right under.*
▶ recover, rescue, reclaim, retrieve, save
2 *She strives to salvage her family's battered reputation.*
▶ save, preserve, rescue, recover, regain

salvation NOUN
1 *Faith alone might not be enough to secure salvation.*
▶ redemption, deliverance, saving
AN OPPOSITE IS damnation
2 *The growing mail-order business proved to be the company's salvation.*
▶ deliverance, lifeline, help, rescue, way out

salve NOUN
a lip salve
▶ ointment, cream, lotion, balm

same ADJECTIVE
1 *Is that the same person?*
▶ actual, identical, selfsame
2 **the same** *The witnesses' versions were all essentially the same.*
▶ similar, identical, alike, comparable, equivalent, matching, indistinguishable
OPPOSITES ARE different, unalike

3 **the same** *The timetable tends to remain the same from year to year.*
▶ unchanged, constant, unvarying, identical
4 *Let's celebrate again on the same day next year.*
▶ corresponding

sample NOUN
1 *Finalists will submit samples of their photographic work.*
▶ specimen, example, representative piece, selection, demonstration, illustration, indication, instance, model, pattern
2 *The survey was based on a sample of a thousand voters.*
▶ cross section, sampling

sample VERB
Guests will sample some of the great wines of the world with their dinner.
▶ try out, try, test, check out, inspect, taste

sanctimonious ADJECTIVE
What happened to all the sanctimonious talk about putting his family first?
▶ self-righteous, holier-than-thou, smug, superior, moralizing, priggish, mealy-mouthed, pious, unctuous
AN OPPOSITE IS modest

sanction NOUN
The scheme has official sanction.
▶ permission, consent, authority, approval

sanction VERB
He decided to sanction the work on his own initiative.
▶ authorize, allow, permit, approve, consent to, give permission for, endorse

sanctions PLURAL NOUN
The UN will vote on whether to lift the sanctions.
▶ restrictions, penalties, embargo, boycott, prohibition

sanctity ADJECTIVE
1 *the sanctity of St Francis*
▶ holiness, sacredness, godliness, piety, spirituality, goodness
2 *It is an issue for anyone who cares about the sanctity of human life*
▶ importance, inviolability

sanctuary NOUN
1 *a sanctuary dedicated to Apollo*
▶ holy place, temple, shrine
2 *The place was a quiet sanctuary where they could do their work.*
▶ refuge, haven, retreat, shelter

sand NOUN
The children played on the sand for hours.
▶ beach, sands, shore, seaside, strand

sane ADJECTIVE
Humour was what helped keep them sane.
▶ rational, lucid, normal, balanced, reasonable, sensible, (*informal*) compos mentis, level-headed, sound, stable
AN OPPOSITE IS mad

sanitary ADJECTIVE
The area has cleaner air and more sanitary conditions.
▶ hygienic, clean, aseptic, antiseptic, sterile, healthy, salubrious, germ-free, pure, uncontaminated
AN OPPOSITE IS insanitary

sanity NOUN
He was not sure enough of his own sanity to take these risks.
▶ reason, senses, rationality, balance of mind, mental health, lucidity

sap VERB
a fever that sapped his strength and depressed his mind
▶ drain, exhaust, deplete, erode, bleed, wear away

sarcasm NOUN
She spoke with more than a hint of sarcasm in her voice.
▶ ridicule, derision, mockery, irony, scorn, scoffing

sarcastic ADJECTIVE
If bosses are sarcastic, try not to react.
▶ mocking, contemptuous, sardonic, ironic, derisive, ironic, scornful, scathing, scoffing, sneering, withering

sash NOUN
She wore a girlish blue sash round her waist.
▶ girdle, belt, band, waistband, cummerbund

satire NOUN
a smutty satire about marriage
▶ parody, lampoon, burlesque, caricature, invective, irony, mockery, (*more informal*) spoof, (*more informal*) send-up, (*more informal*) take-off

satirical ADJECTIVE
a satirical cartoon series
▶ ironical, irreverent, mocking, critical, disparaging, disrespectful, sarcastic

satirize VERB
an attempt to satirize films and film-makers
▶ mock, parody, ridicule, caricature, burlesque, criticize, deride, lampoon, travesty, make fun of, (*more informal*) send up, (*more informal*) take off

satisfaction NOUN
1 *This year, she thought with satisfaction, she was well-prepared. Job satisfaction tends to be high.*
▶ contentment, comfort, happiness, pleasure, pride, self-satisfaction, sense of achievement, enjoyment, fulfilment, gratification
AN OPPOSITE IS dissatisfaction
2 *They may have to turn to the courts for satisfaction.*
▶ settlement, reparation, compensation, recompense, reparation, amends, justice, redress

satisfactory ADJECTIVE
There was no satisfactory method of dealing with trivial complaints.
▶ adequate, acceptable, satisfying, suitable, reasonable, tolerable, fair, passable, sufficient, (*more informal*) all right, (*informal*) up to scratch
AN OPPOSITE IS unsatisfactory

satisfy VERB
1 *There are not enough terminals to satisfy demand.*
▶ fulfil, gratify, answer, meet, fill, service, provide for
AN OPPOSITE IS frustrate
2 *Neither place had fully satisfied him.*
▶ content, make happy
AN OPPOSITE IS dissatisfy

saturate VERB
Heavy rainfall had saturated the ground. The Colombian cartel saturated the market with cocaine.
▶ soak, drench, impregnate, permeate, suffuse, steep, wet

saturated ADJECTIVE
1 *Saturated soil lacks air.*
▶ soaked, sodden, waterlogged, steeped (in)
2 *Her clothes had become saturated in the downpour.*
▶ soaked, soaking wet, sopping, drenched, wringing

saucy ADJECTIVE
1 *a saucy child*
▶ cheeky, rude, impudent, insolent, impertinent, disrespectful, pert, brazen, cocky, presumptuous
OPPOSITES ARE polite, respectful
2 *saucy postcards*
▶ rude, suggestive, titillating, lewd

saunter VERB
She sauntered over to the pool.
▶ stroll, amble, wander, drift, dawdle

savage ADJECTIVE
1 *Savage dogs roamed the streets.*
▶ fierce, wild, ferocious, vicious, untamed
AN OPPOSITE IS tame
2 *a savage assault*
▶ fierce, ferocious, brutal, cruel, sadistic
AN OPPOSITE IS humane
3 *The speech was a savage attack on cronyism.*
▶ fierce, scathing, vitriolic, harsh, blistering, searing

save VERB
1 *They wanted to save money for a holiday.*
▶ put by, set aside, store up, conserve, reserve, retain, scrape together, (*more informal*) stash away
OPPOSITES ARE waste, squander
2 *Try to save petrol during the fuel crisis.*
▶ economize on, cut back on, be sparing with, use wisely
AN OPPOSITE IS waste
3 *The crew managed to save all the passengers after an emergency landing.*
▶ rescue, free, release, liberate, recover, retrieve, salvage, set free
4 *A bit of help would have saved me from exhausting myself.*
▶ prevent, preserve, protect, safeguard, defend, guard, shield

saving NOUN
1 *a saving of 20% on the regular price*
▶ reduction, cut, discount

2 savings *With all his savings gone he needed to find work again.*
▸ funds, reserves, nest egg, resources

saviour NOUN
Gorbachev presented himself as the saviour of socialism.
▸ rescuer, liberator, champion, protector, defender, redeemer, guardian

savour VERB
It was his first curry for three months and he was going to savour it.
▸ enjoy, relish, appreciate, delight in, take pleasure in

savoury ADJECTIVE
Sun-dried tomatoes give a pizza a savoury taste.
▸ spicy, piquant, appetizing, mouth-watering, delectable, delicious, luscious

---

say VERB This word is often overused. Here are some alternatives:
1 *She could not say his name.*
▸ speak, utter, voice, articulate, enunciate
2 *'It's snowing,' he said.*
▸ observe, remark, declare, state, announce, answer, reply, respond
3 *Hugh says he didn't do it.*
▸ maintain, claim, assert, insist, contend
4 *He lit a candle and said a prayer.*
▸ recite, utter, speak
5 *What are you trying to say?*
▸ express, put into words, communicate, make known
6 *We cannot say what might happen.*
▸ guess, foretell, imagine, judge, estimate

---

saying NOUN
You know the saying about too many cooks?
▸ proverb, adage, maxim, dictum, aphorism

scale NOUN
1 *people at different ends of the social scale*
▸ hierarchy, ladder, spectrum, ranking, sequence, progression
2 *the scale of a map*
▸ proportion, ratio, measure, relative size
3 *the scale of the tragedy*
▸ size, extent, scope, magnitude, degree, range

scale VERB
The intruders had to scale a 10-foot fence.
▸ climb, ascend, clamber up, scramble up, shin up, go up, go over, mount

scamp NOUN
He was an idle young scamp in those days.
▸ rascal, scallywag, devil, monkey, imp

scamper VERB
Sam scampered off and waited at the gate.
▸ scurry, scuttle, dash, dart, scoot, run, rush, hasten, hurry
scamper about *Dogs scampered about the churchyard.*
▸ run about, gambol, frisk, frolic, romp

scan VERB
1 *We scanned the trees and caught sight of a magpie.*
▸ study, examine, regard, view, watch, gaze at, look at, scrutinize, survey, search, stare at
2 *Mungo scanned the books to see what Vic might like.*
▸ skim, glance through, flick through, have a look at

scandal NOUN
1 *The tabloids loved reporting scandal.*
▸ gossip, rumour, aspersions, notoriety, sensation, slander, calumny, (*more informal*) tittle-tattle
2 *The college had been involved in a drugs scandal.*
▸ wrongdoing, affair, business
3 *It's a scandal that the hospital has to close.*
▸ disgrace, outrage, injustice, affront, insult, shame

scandalize VERB
behaviour that scandalized polite society
▸ shock, outrage, horrify, disgust, appal, sicken, insult

scandalous ADJECTIVE
1 *This is a scandalous way to treat people who have risked their lives for the sake of their country.*
▸ shameful, disgraceful, shocking, outrageous, monstrous, appalling, wicked
2 *This was scandalous behaviour and the Palace gave her a firm warning.*
▸ improper, shameful, discreditable, disreputable
3 *The scandalous rumours had been quickly forgotten.*
▸ shocking, scurrilous, malicious, libellous, slanderous, defamatory

scanty ADJECTIVE
1 *a conclusion based on scanty evidence*
▸ meagre, sparse, scant, paltry, minimal, negligible, pitiful, miserable, modest, (*more informal*) mingy, (*more informal*) measly
AN OPPOSITE IS plentiful
2 *They looked bored and cold in their scanty dresses.*
▸ skimpy, revealing, insubstantial, short, thin

scar NOUN
a scar on his left cheek
▸ mark, injury, wound , disfigurement, blemish, cicatrix

scar VERB
1 *The wound scarred his face.*
▸ disfigure, mark, leave a scar on, deface, brand, damage, spoil
2 *He was scarred for life by his mother's early death.*
▸ traumatize, disturb, distress, upset, damage

scarce ADJECTIVE
(*informal*) *When money became scarce, he tried to go on welfare.*
▸ sparse, meagre, in short supply, hard to find, hard to come by, scanty, at a premium, rare, lacking, deficient
AN OPPOSITE IS plentiful

scarcely ADVERB
There was scarcely enough to go round.
▸ barely, hardly, only just

scarcity NOUN
a scarcity of good job opportunities
▶ shortage, dearth, deficiency, want, paucity, inadequacy, insufficiency, lack
OPPOSITES ARE abundance, surplus

scare VERB
1 *I didn't mean to scare you. I just wanted to talk.*
▶ alarm, startle, shake, unnerve, dismay, shock
AN OPPOSITE IS calm
2 *The bogeyman could not scare him any more.*
▶ frighten, intimidate, terrorize, threaten, make afraid, menace, panic, bully, cow
AN OPPOSITE IS reassure

scare NOUN
Finding the door unlocked gave her a scare.
▶ fright, shock, start, turn, jolt, alarm

scared ADJECTIVE
Many of us are too scared to go out alone.
▶ frightened, afraid, fearful, anxious, alarmed, terrified, panic-stricken

scary ADJECTIVE
It's not so scary now with all these people around.
▶ frightening, scaring, alarming, eerie, spooky, creepy, terrifying, chilling, spine-chilling, intimidating

scathing ADJECTIVE
There followed a scathing attack on the government for its lack of action.
▶ critical, scornful, cutting, withering, caustic, vitriolic, devastating, harsh
AN OPPOSITE IS complimentary

scatter VERB
1 *The crowd quickly scattered.*
▶ disperse, break up, disband, separate, disintegrate, dissolve, go off in all directions
2 *She scattered breadcrumbs across the path.*
▶ strew, sprinkle, spread, throw, fling, toss, shower
AN OPPOSITE IS gather

scatterbrained ADJECTIVE
She was scatterbrained about such things and left everything to Tod.
▶ absent-minded, disorganized, forgetful, dreamy, feather-brained, muddled, empty-headed, unsystematic, vague, (*more informal*) scatty

scavenge VERB
Hens scavenged for bits of food.
▶ search, rummage, forage, look, root about

scene NOUN
1 *Police were called to the scene of the accident.*
▶ location, site, place, position, point, spot, setting, locale, locality, whereabouts
2 *a beautiful scene by the lake*
▶ view, vista, outlook, prospect, panorama, landscape, picture, tableau, sight, spectacle
3 *A large picture of the setting sun formed the scene for the farewell.*
▶ backdrop, scenery, set, stage

4 *The last scene of the novel is set in France.*
▶ part, section, episode, sequence
5 *He lost his money and there was a scene at the checkout.*
▶ fuss, commotion, disturbance, outburst, row, contretemps, exhibition, argument, quarrel, drama, (*more informal*) to-do, (*more informal*) carry-on

scenery NOUN
They stopped to admire the scenery.
▶ landscape, terrain, panorama, scene, vista, outlook, surroundings

scenic ADJECTIVE
There is a scenic route through the mountains.
▶ picturesque, panoramic, pretty, pleasing, attractive, beautiful, lovely, spectacular, striking

scent NOUN
1 *The scent of rose water hung in the air.*
▶ smell , odour, perfume, fragrance, aroma, redolence
2 *a bottle of scent*
▶ perfume, toilet water, lavender water, cologne
3 *The dogs picked up the scent.*
▶ trail, track

scented ADJECTIVE
a smell of scented soap
▶ perfumed, fragrant, aromatic

sceptic NOUN
He is a sceptic about the dangers of global warming.
▶ doubter, unbeliever, sceptical person, cynic, agnostic
AN OPPOSITE IS believer

sceptical ADJECTIVE
He was initially sceptical about her abilities but soon changed his mind.
▶ dubious, doubtful, distrustful, mistrustful, disbelieving, incredulous, suspicious, uncertain, unconvinced, unsure, cynical
AN OPPOSITE IS confident

scepticism NOUN
Others expressed scepticism about using this method.
▶ distrust, mistrust, disbelief, suspicion, doubt, incredulity, lack of confidence, cynicism
AN OPPOSITE IS confidence

schedule NOUN
There was hardly any spare time in her busy schedule. I will organize a schedule of visits.
▶ timetable, agenda, programme, scheme, calendar, diary, list, plan

scheme NOUN
1 *Pitt proposed a national scheme of cash allowances for children.*
▶ plan, project, proposal, programme, venture, enterprise, strategy, system, blueprint, idea, method, procedure
2 *a scheme to steal the jewels*
▶ plot, conspiracy, intrigue, secret plan, ruse, ploy, (*more informal*) racket, (*more informal*) scam

3 *a bright colour scheme*
▶ design, arrangement, pattern, layout

scheme VERB
The emperor's wife schemed to exercise power through her son.
▶ plot, intrigue, connive, conspire, collude, plan

schism NOUN
the widening schism between the king and the church
▶ division, split, rift, breach, break, quarrel, disagreement

scholar NOUN
a leading classical scholar
▶ academic, authority, expert, savant, intellectual, intellect, man or woman of letters

scholarly ADJECTIVE
a serious, scholarly woman
▶ intellectual, learned, erudite, academic, lettered, knowledgeable

scholarship NOUN
1 *a music scholarship worth £2,000 a year*
▶ award, grant, bursary, exhibition
2 *a person of great scholarship*
▶ learning, erudition, knowledge, wisdom, academic achievement, intellectual attainment

school NOUN
Have you asked them what makes a good school?
▶ college, academy, educational institution, centre of learning, institute

schooling NOUN
the last two years of schooling.
▶ education, instruction, tuition, teaching, training, coaching

---

science NOUN
the science of forensic medicine
▶ technology, discipline, field, technique, art

BRANCHES OF SCIENCE AND TECHNOLOGY
acoustics, aeronautics, agricultural science, anatomy, anthropology, artificial intelligence, astronomy, astrophysics, behavioural science, biochemistry, biology, biophysics, botany, chemistry, climatology, computer science, cybernetics, dietetics, domestic science, dynamics, earth science, ecology, economics, electronics, engineering, entomology, environmental science, food science, genetics, geographical science, geology, geophysics, hydraulics, information technology, life science, linguistics, materials science, mathematics, mechanics, medicine (medical science), metallurgy, meteorology, microbiology, mineralogy, ornithology, pathology, pharmacology, physics, physiology, political science, psychology, robotics, sociology, space technology, sports science, telecommunications, thermodynamics, toxicology, veterinary science, zoology.

---

scientific ADJECTIVE
1 *scientific research*
▶ science-based, technical, technological
2 *Our methods are not scientific enough.*
▶ systematic, methodical, analytical, organized, precise, rigorous, thorough, regulated

scientist NOUN
the accusation that scientists are 'playing God'
▶ researcher, scientific expert, technologist, (*more informal*) boffin

scintillating ADJECTIVE
1 *The bright lights looked scintillating reflected in the surface of the water.*
▶ sparkling, glittering, dazzling, shining, bright
2 *The team gave a scintillating display of skill and stamina.*
▶ brilliant, exciting, dazzling, exhilarating, stimulating

scoff VERB
1 **scoff at** *Experts are inclined to scoff at such theories.*
▶ mock, ridicule, sneer at, jeer at, scorn, deride, make fun of, poke fun at
2 (*informal*) *You feel guilty when you scoff a sherry trifle.*
▶ eat up, guzzle, gobble up, wolf, wolf down, devour, (*more informal*) tuck into, (*more informal*) polish off

scold VERB
Busy young mothers scolded their children.
▶ tell off, reprimand, rebuke, admonish, reprove, reproach, upbraid, censure, chide, criticize, reprehend, (*more informal*) tick off
OPPOSITES ARE praise, commend

scoop VERB
scoop out
1 *They would scoop out holes in the sand.*
▶ dig, gouge, scrape, excavate, hollow, cut
2 *Scoop out the flesh of the pineapple halves.*
▶ remove, take out, scrape out, spoon out, extract
scoop up *She scooped up her things and left hurriedly.*
▶ pick up, gather up, grab, collect

scope NOUN
1 *issues that are beyond the scope of the inquiry*
▶ extent, limit, range, competence, terms of reference, remit, ambit, capacity, compass, sphere, reach
2 *There is plenty of scope for new ideas.*
▶ opportunity, chance, latitude, leeway, freedom, room, space

scorch VERB
Some of the walls had been scorched by fire.
▶ burn, singe, char, blacken

scorching ADJECTIVE
The desert is a place of scorching heat by day and bitter cold by night.
▶ blazing, boiling, flaming, baking, roasting, sweltering, burning
OPPOSITES ARE freezing, bitter

score NOUN

1 *The final score did not reflect the balance of the game.*
▶ result, tally, total, mark, number of points
2 *They had a score to settle*
▶ debt, grievance

score VERB

1 *a move that scored double points*
▶ earn, win, gain, achieve, make, (*more informal*) chalk up
2 *A pattern had been scored in the surface.*
▶ cut, engrave, incise, mark, gouge, scratch, scrape, slash

scorn NOUN

She treated that remark with the scorn it deserved.
▶ contempt, disdain, derision, disparagement, ridicule, mockery
AN OPPOSITE IS admiration

scorn VERB

Their haircuts are severe and they scorn make-up.
▶ despise, deride, scoff at, ridicule, mock, spurn, look down on, dismiss
AN OPPOSITE IS admire

scornful ADJECTIVE

Richard was prepared to put up with the scornful disapproval of Eve and Ted.
▶ contemptuous, derisive, disdainful, supercilious, scathing, disparaging, mocking, scoffing, sneering, withering
OPPOSITES ARE admiring, respectful

scotch VERB

Hopes of trying a first kiss were scotched when she fell asleep the moment she got into the car.
▶ end, bring to an end, put paid to, frustrate, shatter, wreck, destroy, scupper

scot-free ADJECTIVE

You wouldn't want to see the real villains getting off scot-free.
▶ unpunished, unscathed, unharmed, unhurt, safe

scoundrel NOUN

It wasn't her fault she had a scoundrel for a grandson.
▶ rascal, rogue, ruffian, ne'er-do-well, good-for-nothing, villain, knave, scallywag, scamp

scour VERB

1 *They were made to scrub kitchen floors and scour out pans.*
▶ scrub, clean, scrape, wash, buff up, burnish, polish, rub
2 *Rita scoured the junk shops for second-hand pieces to fill the rooms.*
▶ search, comb, ransack, rummage through, forage through, hunt through

scourge NOUN

There is hardly an area where the scourge of unemployment is not biting hard.
▶ affliction, bane, curse, misfortune, torment

scout NOUN

Scouts came back with information about the enemy positions.
▶ lookout, outrider, advance guard, spy

scout VERB

scout about or **around** *I asked Claire to scout around to find him a place to stay.*
▶ look about, reconnoitre, search, explore, hunt, investigate, cast about, get information

scowl VERB

She scowled at him and told him to go away.
▶ glower, frown, glare, grimace

scowl NOUN

There was an unmistakable scowl on his face.
▶ frown, glower, grimace

scrabble VERB

She scrabbled about in her pockets until she found her glasses.
▶ rummage, grope, root, fumble, claw, dig

scraggy ADJECTIVE

She kept out of the way of her sister's scraggy old cat.
▶ scrawny, skinny, thin, lanky, gaunt, lean, bony, emaciated, underfed
OPPOSITES ARE plump, fat

scram VERB

(*informal*) *Scram or I'll call the police.*
▶ go away, leave, get going, get moving, (*informal*) beat it, (*informal*) shove off, (*informal*) clear off

scramble NOUN

Getting there in time proved quite a scramble.
▶ struggle, rush, hustle, dash

scramble VERB

1 *I scrambled down the slope towards the car. Daniel scrambled to his feet and left the room.*
▶ clamber, climb, crawl, scrabble, move awkwardly
2 *She saw the two men scramble for the fallen gun.*
▶ scuffle, struggle, tussle, fight, jostle
3 *They quickly scrambled into the plane.*
▶ dash, hasten, hurry, run, rush

scrap NOUN

1 *There were a few scraps of food on the table.*
▶ bit, piece, morsel, particle, crumb, speck, fragment, mouthful
2 *Not a scrap of evidence could be found.*
▶ shred, speck, iota, jot, ounce, trace
3 *a lorry loaded with scrap*
▶ junk, refuse, rubbish, salvage, waste, litter, odds and ends
4 *He wanted to avoid a scrap with Kevin.*
▶ fight, quarrel, disagreement, tussle, brawl

scrap VERB

1 *Local residents want the road plan to be scrapped.*
▶ abandon, cancel, discard, (*informal*) ditch, drop, give up, jettison, throw away, write off
2 *The younger children are always scrapping.*
▶ fight, quarrel, argue, brawl

scrape VERB
1 *Elaine had scraped her skin against the wall.*
▶ graze, scratch, scuff, abrade, bark, lacerate
2 *He scraped his boots before going inside.*
▶ scrub, scour, rub, clean
scrape together *We scraped enough money together to get home*
▶ collect, amass, rake together, dredge up

scrape NOUN
Try not to get into any scrapes
▶ difficulty, predicament, tight spot, mischief, trouble

scrappy ADJECTIVE
The game turned out to be a scrappy affair.
▶ disorganized, disjointed, uneven, slipshod, unsatisfactory
AN OPPOSITE IS well-organized

scratch VERB
1 *Be careful not to scratch the table top.*
▶ scrape, mark, score, gash, cut, damage the surface of, gouge
2 *The thorns were scratching his legs.*
▶ graze, chafe, prick, cut, lacerate

scratch NOUN
1 *There were scratches in the paintwork.*
▶ gash, groove, line, mark, scoring, scrape
2 *He had a long scratch down one side of his face.*
▶ graze, laceration, wound, cut
up to scratch *The work was not up to scratch.*
▶ satisfactory, adequate, acceptable, good enough, passable, all right

scrawl VERB
He scrawled a quick note to his mother.
▶ scribble, dash off, jot down, write

scrawny ADJECTIVE
A bald scrawny man came in.
▶ skinny, scraggy, thin, gawky

scream VERB
She screamed at them to stop.
▶ yell, shriek, shout, bawl, screech, roar, howl, wail

scream NOUN
He let out a scream of pain.
▶ yell, shriek, shout, screech, roar, howl, wail

screen NOUN
1 *a computer with a 17-inch screen*
▶ monitor, display, VDU or visual display unit
2 *A screen divided the room in two.*
▶ partition, divider, curtain, blind

screen VERB
1 *A low hedge screened the dustbins.*
▶ hide, conceal, mask, shield, shelter
2 *Staff are regularly screened in the interests of security.*
▶ vet, scrutinize, examine, investigate

screw VERB
1 *She screwed the lid on the jar.*
▶ fasten, tighten, twist, turn
2 *James screwed the piece of paper into a tight ball.*
▶ twist, wind, wring

3 *The last thing to do was screw the boards back down.*
▶ fix, fasten, secure
4 *(informal) He was not going to let them screw him for money like that again.*
▶ cheat, swindle, defraud, pressurize, extort, squeeze
USAGE If you use *extort* or *squeeze* you have to say (for example) *He was not going to let them extort money from him like that again.*

scribble VERB
He quickly scribbled a shopping list.
▶ scrawl, dash off, jot down, write

scribe NOUN
He would need to get a scribe to write his letter for him.
▶ copyist, clerk, transcriber, amanuensis, scrivener, secretary

script NOUN
1 *The note had been written in an elegant script.*
▶ handwriting, hand, autograph
2 *The film was spoilt by a poor script.*
▶ screenplay, text, dialogue

scrounge VERB
Street urchins scrounged money from the tourists.
▶ beg, cadge, sponge

scrounger NOUN
He was neither a scrounger nor a misfit.
▶ cadger, sponger, parasite

scrub VERB
1 *She decided to scrub the bathroom floor.*
▶ wash, clean, rub, brush, scour
2 *(informal) If interest rates went up again they would have to scrub their holiday.*
▶ cancel, scrap, go without, do without, call off, drop, abandon, (*informal*) ditch

scruffy ADJECTIVE
1 *He had worn scruffy jeans and a T-shirt to his Downing Street breakfast.*
▶ shabby, worn, ragged, worn-out, dirty
AN OPPOSITE IS smart
2 *He was standing in a bar, scruffy and long-haired.*
▶ unkempt, untidy, dishevelled, ungroomed, messy, bedraggled
AN OPPOSITE IS tidy

scruples NOUN
He has no scruples about bending the rules.
▶ qualms, compunction, conscience, misgivings, hesitation, doubts

scrupulous ADJECTIVE
1 *The story had been written with a scrupulous attention to historical accuracy.*
▶ conscientious, diligent, fastidious, meticulous, minute, painstaking, precise, punctilious, rigorous, strict, systematic, thorough
2 *The accounts will be reviewed by the most scrupulous auditor.*
▶ honest, honourable, upright, upstanding, principled, right-minded, fair-minded, ethical
AN OPPOSITE IS unscrupulous

scrutinize VERB
Bernard scrutinized the poster.
▶ examine, inspect, survey, study, peruse, scan, investigate

scrutiny NOUN
She continued her scrutiny of the house.
▶ examination, inspection, investigation, survey, perusal, study, search

scuff VERB
The toe was scuffed and the shoes would need mending.
▶ scrape, scratch, rub, graze, brush

scuffle NOUN
There was a scuffle and the sound of people running.
▶ fight, fracas, brawl, struggle, tussle, scrap, rumpus, commotion, argument

scuffle VERB
Three teenage boys were scuffling and messing around.
▶ fight, brawl, struggle, tussle, scrap, come to blows

sculpture NOUN
a marble sculpture of Venus
▶ carving, figure, statue, effigy, image
USAGE A small sculpture is called a *statuette*. A *bust* is a sculpture of the top part of a person.

scum NOUN
The water had a thick scum on it.
▶ froth, foam, film, impurities

scupper VERB
1 *The captain decided to scupper the ship.*
▶ scuttle, sink, submerge
2 *Lack of funds might scupper the project.*
▶ ruin, wreck, destroy, put paid to, frustrate, shatter, scotch, end, bring to an end

scurrilous ADJECTIVE
a scurrilous attack on their integrity
▶ offensive, abusive, insulting, defamatory, scandalous, slanderous, libellous, unfounded, unwarranted

scurry VERB
Officials scurried about.
▶ scamper, scuttle, dash, dart, rush, hurry

scuttle VERB
1 *The fleet was scuttled next day.*
▶ scupper, sink, submerge
2 *A waitress scuttled past carrying a cake.*
▶ scurry, scamper, dash, dart, scoot, run, rush, hasten, hurry

sea NOUN
1 *They caught sight of the sea in the distance.*
▶ water, ocean, waves
RELATED ADJECTIVES marine, maritime, nautical, naval
2 *sea creatures*
▶ aquatic, marine, seafaring, ocean, salt
3 *a sea voyage*
▶ ocean-going, oceanic, seagoing
4 *a sea of friendly faces*
▶ mass, host, multitude, profusion

seal NOUN
the queen's seal
▶ emblem, crest, insignia, symbol, stamp
seal of approval *The senior partner gave his seal of approval to the scheme.*
▶ endorsement, blessing, ratification, assent, consent

seal VERB
1 *She folded the letter and sealed the envelope.*
▶ stick down, close, fasten, secure
2 *He filled the jar and sealed it.*
▶ stop up, close, plug, stopper
3 *He held out a hand to seal the agreement.*
▶ confirm, clinch, complete, secure, (more informal) sew up
seal off *Police sealed off the city centre.*
▶ close off, shut off, cordon off, fence off, isolate

seam NOUN
1 *Small stitches will ensure a neat seam.*
▶ join, stitching
2 *a seam of coal*
▶ layer, stratum, vein

seamy ADJECTIVE
He had discovered the seamy side of life.
▶ sordid, seedy, sleazy, squalid, disreputable, unpleasant

search VERB
1 *We searched for clues.*
▶ look, hunt, explore, ferret about, nose about, poke about, prospect, pry, seek
2 *Security staff will search passengers and their luggage.*
▶ check, examine, investigate, scrutinize, inspect, (more informal) frisk
3 *I searched the house for my keys.*
▶ hunt through, scour, comb, ransack, rummage through, forage through

search NOUN
We began our search for a place to eat.
▶ hunt, quest, exploration, investigation, look, check

searching ADJECTIVE
1 *You have to ask yourself some searching questions.*
▶ penetrating, probing, incisive, sharp, shrewd, deep
AN OPPOSITE IS superficial
2 *He gave her a searching look.*
▶ observant, perceptive, discerning

seaside NOUN
a trip to the seaside
▶ coast, beach, seashore, shore
RELATED ADJECTIVE littoral

season NOUN
The holiday season lasts until October these days.
▶ period, time of year, time, phase

season VERB
1 *herbs for seasoning fish*
▶ flavour, spice, salt, add seasoning to
2 *The wood should be well seasoned.*
▶ mature, age, temper, condition

seasonable ADJECTIVE
seasonable weather
▶ usual, normal, appropriate, expected, predictable, suitable

seasoned ADJECTIVE
a seasoned traveller
▶ experienced, practised, veteran, well versed

seasoning NOUN
Add the garlic and a little seasoning.
▶ flavouring, salt and pepper, spices, herbs

seat NOUN
1 *There were not enough seats for everyone to sit on.*
▶ chair, bench, stool, pew, place
2 *The capital city is not always the seat of government.*
▶ centre, headquarters, location, site, base, nucleus, heart, hub
3 *a country seat in Scotland*
▶ residence, ancestral, mansion, abode, stately home

seat VERB
1 *She seated her guests round a large oval table.*
▶ place, position, put, settle
2 *The smaller cinema seats thirty.*
▶ accommodate, holds, takes, have seats for, sit

secede VERB
secede from *The southern states seceded from the Union.*
▶ withdraw from, separate from, break away from, leave, quit, split with

secluded ADJECTIVE
The path leads down to a secluded beach.
▶ sheltered, private, concealed, hidden, undisturbed, unfrequented, isolated, remote
OPPOSITES ARE busy, public

seclusion NOUN
a millionaire living in seclusion in Surrey
▶ isolation, solitude, privacy, retreat, retirement, solitariness, concealment, secrecy

second ADJECTIVE
1 *There won't be a second chance.*
▶ another, further, additional, repeated, alternative, extra
2 *We keep a second set of data in another building.*
▶ spare, extra, alternative, backup

second NOUN (with the stress on *sec-*)
1 *They were only gone for a second.*
▶ moment, instant, bit, flash, (*more informal*) jiffy, (*more informal*) tick
2 *Chris was acting as his second.*
▶ assistant, attendant, supporter, right-hand man or woman, helper

second VERB (with the stress on -*cond*)
She was seconded to another branch of the company for a year.
▶ transfer, assign temporarily, move, relocate

secondary ADJECTIVE
1 *issues that are regarded as secondary*
▶ subsidiary, subordinate, minor, lesser, lower, inferior, second-rate
2 *A secondary action was started in support of the main attack.*
▶ extra, ancillary, auxiliary, supplementary, supportive, reinforcing, second, reserve

second-class ADJECTIVE
They felt as though they were second-class citizens.
▶ second-best, second-rate, inferior, lesser, unimportant

second-hand ADJECTIVE
1 *a second-hand car*
▶ used, pre-owned, old
AN OPPOSITE IS new
2 *She was relying on second-hand information.*
▶ indirect, secondary, derivative
AN OPPOSITE IS personal.

second-rate ADJECTIVE
a second-rate holiday camp entertainer
▶ second-class, second-best, substandard, mediocre, middling, ordinary, below par, commonplace, indifferent, inferior, low-grade

secret ADJECTIVE
1 *secret information*
▶ confidential, classified, restricted, (*more informal*) hush-hush
AN OPPOSITE IS public
2 *They met at a secret location.*
▶ private, secluded, hidden, isolated, remote, unknown, undisclosed
OPPOSITES ARE public, well-known
3 *a secret operation*
▶ undercover, clandestine, covert, surreptitious
AN OPPOSITE IS overt

secretary NOUN
She called in her secretary to take notes of the meeting.
▶ assistant, personal assistant or PA, clerk, typist

secrete VERB
1 *He secreted the money in a drawer.*
▶ hide, conceal, stow away, bury
2 *The bladder is a store for urine secreted by the kidneys.*
▶ discharge, emit, exude, produce, ooze, leak

secretion NOUN
the secretion of hormones
▶ discharge, production, emission, exudation

secretive ADJECTIVE
He was being very secretive about his intentions.
▶ uncommunicative, unforthcoming, reticent, tight-lipped, cagey, close, withdrawn
AN OPPOSITE IS communicative

sect NOUN
a religious sect
▶ cult, denomination, faction, group, order

sectarian ADJECTIVE
sectarian politics
▶ factional, schismatic, partisan, parochial, doctrinaire

section NOUN
1 *You must complete every section of the application form*
▶ part, division, portion, paragraph
2 *the reference section of your local library*
▶ department, part, division

sector NOUN
1 *the northern sector of the city*
▶ district, region, section, area, part, quarter, zone
2 *the private sector of industry*
▶ branch, arm, division

secular ADJECTIVE
secular music   a secular ceremony
▶ non-religious, temporal, worldly, earthly, civil, lay
OPPOSITES ARE sacred, religious

secure ADJECTIVE
1 *Check that all doors and windows are secure.*
▶ locked, sealed, closed tight, impregnable, invulnerable
OPPOSITES ARE insecure, vulnerable
2 *We felt secure indoors during the storm.*
▶ safe, protected, unharmed, unhurt, unscathed
OPPOSITES ARE exposed, in danger
3 *The ladder needs to be made secure.*
▶ stable, steady, firm, fast, fixed, immovable
OPPOSITES ARE insecure, unsteady

secure VERB
1 *Secure the front door when you leave.*
▶ fasten, close, lock, shut, seal, bolt
2 *a charter that secures the rights of the individual*
▶ ensure, assure, guarantee, protect, confirm
3 *Jenny secured a senior post in the company.*
▶ obtain, acquire, gain, get, be given

security NOUN
1 *The first priority is the security of passengers.*
▶ safety, protection, care, guarding, freedom from harm
AN OPPOSITE IS vulnerability
2 *The president's visit called for unprecedented levels of security.*
▶ safety measures, safeguards, protection, surveillance

sedate ADJECTIVE
1 *The procession moved forward at a sedate pace.*
▶ steady, unhurried, deliberate, gentle, easy-going, comfortable, slow
OPPOSITES ARE brisk, lively
2 *They enjoyed their sedate suburban life and didn't hanker after the bright lights.*
▶ calm, staid, prim, sober, seemly, demure, dignified, serene

sedate VERB
The patient had to be sedated.
▶ tranquillize, treat with sedatives, pacify, drug

sedative NOUN
The doctor prescribed him a sedative.
▶ tranquillizer, sleeping pill, barbiturate, narcotic

sedentary ADJECTIVE
People with sedentary lifestyles need to take exercise.
▶ seated, sitting, desk-bound, immobile, inactive
AN OPPOSITE IS active

sediment NOUN
There was a thick layer of sediment at the bottom of the bottle.
▶ deposit, dregs, lees, residue, sludge

seduce VERB
They were seduced into buying by the clever sales talk.
▶ entice, allure, lure, attract, beguile, mislead, ensnare, entrap, tempt, inveigle

seduction NOUN
the seductions of city life
▶ attraction, temptation, allure, appeal, enticement

seductive ADJECTIVE
1 *Lori gave him one of her most seductive smiles.*
▶ sexy, alluring, captivating, ravishing, bewitching, appealing, attractive, enticing, irresistible, provocative, tempting
OPPOSITES ARE repulsive, repellent
2 *the seductive warmth of a coal fire*
▶ attractive, appealing, enticing, comforting

see VERB
1 *She saw Eve waiting for her.   Did you see who got into the car with him?*
▶ perceive, glimpse, discern, make out, pick out, recognize, identify, distinguish
RELATED ADJECTIVE visible
2 *She could see how difficult it might be..*
▶ understand, follow, know, comprehend, realize, recognize, take in, grasp, appreciate, fathom
3 *I can see trouble ahead.*
▶ foresee, envisage, picture, visualize, predict, imagine, anticipate, conceive
4 *We'll see what we can do.*
▶ consider, think about, reflect on, weigh up, decide, investigate
5 *They are going to see the game on Saturday.*
▶ watch, attend, be a spectator at
6 *Is she still seeing Stephen?*
▶ go out with, be dating, meet, visit
7 *Keith offered to see her home.*
▶ take, escort, accompany, conduct
8 *Stuart went to see the doctor about his leg.*
▶ visit, consult, confer with, talk to, speak to
9 *I saw an old friend in town.*
▶ meet, encounter, run into, run across, chance on, (more informal) bump into
10 *I must go and see what the dog is up to.*
▶ find out, discover, ascertain, establish

11 see to *Will you see to the repairs?*
▶ attend to, deal with, take care of, look after, sort out, organize, manage

seed NOUN
1 *The male provides the seed to fertilize the female egg.*
▶ sperm, semen, seminal fluid
2 *The birds feed on insects, seed, and shoots.*
▶ grains
3 *The fruit was full of seeds.*
▶ pip, stone
4 *The conflict was the seed for all future troubles.*
▶ source, origin, cause, basis
RELATED ADJECTIVE seminal

seedy ADJECTIVE
a seedy hotel on the seafront
▶ sleazy, squalid, shabby, run-down, sordid, seamy, rough

seek VERB
1 *The fleet sailed south to seek the enemy.*
▶ look for, search for, pursue, follow, try to find, hunt
2 *They will need to seek advice from a lawyer.*
▶ ask for, call on, get
3 *Spain is seeking the extradition of the suspects.*
▶ request, solicit, try to obtain
4 *We seek to please our customers.*
▶ try, attempt, endeavour, strive, aspire

seem VERB
The woman seemed too afraid to speak.
▶ appear, look, sound, give the impression of being

seemly ADJECTIVE
It was not seemly to look too closely.
▶ proper, decent, fitting, suitable

seep VERB
Smoke seeped into the auditorium.
▶ leak, ooze, escape, exude, flow, trickle, dribble

seething ADJECTIVE
1 *Rose was seething about what had happened.*
▶ fuming, furious, angry, livid, infuriated, incensed, outraged
2 *The water in the pan was seething.*
▶ boil, bubble, foam, froth up

segment NOUN
Segments of orange decorated the top of the cake.
▶ section, piece, slice, wedge, chunk

segregate VERB
The school agreed to segregate them for swimming lessons.
▶ separate, isolate, keep apart, set apart, put apart, exclude, cut off

segregation NOUN
1 *Racial segregation has been outlawed.*
▶ apartheid, discrimination, separation
2 *the segregation of smokers and non-smokers in public places*
▶ isolation, separation, keeping apart

seize VERB
1 *He seized the remote and turned up the volume.*
▶ grab, snatch, take hold of
OPPOSITES ARE release, let go of
2 *Rebels have seized an outpost in the jungle.*
▶ capture, take, take possession of, take over, overrun
OPPOSITES ARE abandon, relinquish
3 *Customs officers seized a large cache of drugs.*
▶ confiscate, appropriate, impound
OPPOSITES ARE return, give back
4 *Bandits seized his wife and children.*
▶ kidnap, abduct, take prisoner, capture, (*more informal*) snatch
OPPOSITES ARE release, let go

seizure NOUN
1 *Alexander's seizure of the city.*
▶ capture, occupation, subjugation, annexation
2 *He suffered a seizure on the journey home.*
▶ convulsion, attack, fit, stroke, spasm, paroxysm, apoplexy
3 *the unlawful seizure of goods*
▶ confiscation, impounding, appropriation, sequestration

seldom ADVERB
She was seldom away from home for long.
▶ rarely, not often, hardly ever, infrequently
AN OPPOSITE IS often

select VERB
The committee met to select a chairperson.
▶ choose, pick, appoint, name, elect, vote for, nominate, decide on

select ADJECTIVE
a select group of former pupils
▶ exclusive, élite, privileged, choice, chosen, hand-picked, preferred, special
AN OPPOSITE IS ordinary

selection NOUN
1 *There's a wide selection of food to choose from.*
▶ range, variety, assortment
2 *Mike put a coin in the machine and made his selection.*
▶ choice, pick, option

selective ADJECTIVE
She's very selective in her reading.
▶ discerning, discriminating, particular, careful, (*more informal*) choosy
AN OPPOSITE IS indiscriminate

self-centred ADJECTIVE
Old people tend to become more self-centred as the years go by.
▶ selfish, egocentric, self-absorbed, self-obsessed, inconsiderate

self-confident ADJECTIVE
In self-confident mood, Franco pressed ahead with his plans.
▶ self-assured, self-possessed, sure of yourself, confident, positive, assertive, assured, poised
AN OPPOSITE IS diffident

self-conscious ADJECTIVE
He felt self-conscious about having to borrow money from his father.
► embarrassed, bashful, diffident, uneasy, awkward, uncomfortable, unnatural, coy, shy, ill at ease, nervous
OPPOSITES ARE natural, confident

self-contained ADJECTIVE
1 *The house was converted into four self-contained apartments.*
► complete, separate
2 *This self-contained person was not going to admit anything.*
► independent, self-reliant, self-sufficient, aloof, unemotional
AN OPPOSITE IS sociable

self-control NOUN
He lost self-control and killed her.
► composure, restraint, self-discipline, calmness, coolness, self-command

self-denial NOUN
a life of self-denial and humility
► self-sacrifice, abstemiousness, selflessness, moderation, austerity
AN OPPOSITE IS self-indulgence

self-employed ADJECTIVE
If you are self-employed you need to protect your livelihood.
► freelance, independent, casual

self-evident ADJECTIVES
The reasons are pretty self-evident.
► obvious, plain, clear, apparent, transparent, evident

self-important ADJECTIVE
A self-important figure in uniform was strutting about.
► conceited, pompous, arrogant, bumptious, overbearing

self-indulgent ADJECTIVE
For many, a second home seems a self-indulgent luxury.
► extravagant, pleasure-seeking, hedonistic, intemperate
OPPOSITES ARE restrained, abstemious

selfish ADJECTIVE
People are seen as being more selfish and less tolerant.
► self-centred, egocentric, inconsiderate, self-absorbed, self-obsessed
OPPOSITES ARE unselfish, considerate, generous, selfless

selfishness NOUN
They were motivated by greed and selfishness.
► egotism, self-obsession, self-interest, thoughtlessness, meanness
OPPOSITES ARE unselfishness, generosity

selfless ADJECTIVE
He made a selfless sacrifice for his country.
► unselfish, generous, magnanimous

self-respect NOUN
Under the new president, the country prospered and recovered its self-respect.
► pride, dignity, self-confidence, self-esteem

self-righteous ADJECTIVE
He called her a stuck-up, self-righteous Miss Perfect.
► sanctimonious, holier-than-thou, priggish, smug, self-satisfied, moralizing, unctuous

self-sacrifice NOUN
Day-to-day living was based on constant toil and self-sacrifice.
► self-denial, selflessness, unselfishness

self-satisfied ADJECTIVE
Hilary relaxed and gave a little self-satisfied smile.
► smug, complacent, self-congratulatory

self-supporting ADJECTIVE
measures that would make more colleges self-supporting
► independent, self-sufficient, self-reliant, self-contained

sell VERB
1 *The corner shop sells basic provisions.*
► stock, trade in, deal in, retail, handle, peddle
2 *They are having problems selling their house.*
► put on the market, dispose of, (more formal) vend

seller NOUN
sellers of household goods
► supplier, trader (in), dealer (in), vendor, retailer, stockist, purveyor

semblance NOUN
A semblance of order was restored.
► appearance, show, pretence, air, facade, front

send VERB
1 *I'll send you a letter.*
► post, mail, dispatch, convey, forward
2 *She sent John a message.*
► fax, email, wire, transmit
3 *The space programme will be sending a satellite into orbit.*
► launch, propel, shoot, direct, fire
4 *It's the sort of remark that sends you mad.*
► make, drive, cause to be
send for *They decided to send for the police.*
► call, fetch, summon, ask to come
send out *The chimneys send out grey fumes.*
► discharge, emit, give off, belch
send round *The manager sent round a questionnaire.*
► circulate, distribute, publish, issue
send up *The sketch sent up story-book heroes.*
► satirize, ridicule, parody, make fun of, caricature, lampoon

send-off NOUN
They gave Anthony a magnificent send-off.
► farewell, goodbye, leave-taking

send-up NOUN
a hilarious send-up of a spy movie
► satire, parody, caricature, lampoon, (more informal) spoof

senile ADJECTIVE

Her husband was becoming senile and difficult to cope with.
▶ old, aged, doddering, infirm, feeble, decrepit, (*more informal*) past it
AN OPPOSITE IS in his or her prime

senior ADJECTIVE

1 *a senior pupil*
▶ older, elder
2 *a senior official*
▶ high-ranking, superior, chief
OPPOSITES ARE junior, subordinate

seniority NOUN

The Chief Clerk was next in seniority.
▶ rank, standing, precedence, superiority

sensation NOUN

1 *She felt a sensation of floating.*
▶ feeling, sense, awareness, impression
2 *The affair caused a sensation.*
▶ commotion, excitement, stir, furore, outrage, scandal, surprise, thrill

sensational ADJECTIVE

1 *a sensational murder trial*
▶ shocking, horrifying, lurid, scandalous, thrilling, blood-curdling, breathtaking, exciting, hair-raising
2 *Her singing was sensational.*
▶ amazing, extraordinary, remarkable, wonderful, fabulous, fantastic, magnificent, great, marvellous, spectacular, superb

sense NOUN

1 *She has a strong sense of rhythm.*
▶ feeling, sensation, perception
2 *He felt a sense of guilt.*
▶ feeling, awareness, sensation, perception
3 *They had the sense to get out in time.*
▶ wisdom, common sense, intelligence, wit, shrewdness
4 *I couldn't see the sense of leaving then.*
▶ point, purpose, advantage, benefit
5 *I didn't grasp the sense of their message.*
▶ meaning, significance, substance, implication, import, drift, gist, point
make sense of *It's hard to make sense of these remarks.*
▶ understand, grasp, comprehend

sense VERB

We sensed that they didn't trust us.
▶ feel, suspect, discern, perceive, realize, get the impression, appreciate, guess, notice, be aware, detect

senseless ADJECTIVE

1 *It was a senseless crime.*
▶ pointless, futile, needless, aimless, absurd, nonsensical, foolish, stupid
2 *They found him in the morning, senseless but alive.*
▶ unconscious, comatose, stunned, out cold

sensible ADJECTIVE

1 *Joanna was sensible enough to listen. Everyone agreed that this was a sensible decision.*
▶ wise, prudent, thoughtful, far-sighted, shrewd, judicious, intelligent, pragmatic, responsible, realistic, rational, level-headed
OPPOSITES ARE foolish, unwise
2 *She liked to wear sensible clothes.*
▶ practical, functional, comfortable, useful, (*informal*) no-nonsense
OPPOSITES ARE impractical, fashionable

sensitive ADJECTIVE

1 *The human eye is very sensitive to green.*
▶ responsive, reactive, susceptible, affected (by), conscious (of)
AN OPPOSITE IS insensitive
2 *The problem needs sensitive handling.*
▶ tactful, thoughtful, considerate, sympathetic, understanding, perceptive
OPPOSITES ARE insensitive, tactless
3 *She's a very sensitive girl, so take care what you say.*
▶ emotional, easily offended, easily upset, volatile, thin-skinned, touchy
AN OPPOSITE IS thick- skinned
4 *Take care in the sun if you have a fair sensitive skin.*
▶ delicate, soft, tender, fragile, fine
OPPOSITES ARE tough, resilient
5 *The court ruling comes at a sensitive time for the government.*
▶ awkward, tricky, controversial, delicate
AN OPPOSITE IS uncontroversial

sensual ADJECTIVE

1 *sensual pleasures*
▶ physical, sexual, erotic, carnal, bodily
2 *a beautiful sensual woman*
▶ sexually attractive, sexy, voluptuous, seductive, passionate
USAGE *Sensual* and *sensuous* are often used in the same way, although there is a formal distinction in that *sensual* has stronger sexual connotations whereas *sensuous* is more neutral.

sensuous ADJECTIVE

sensuous music
▶ emotional, lush, rich, affecting, appealing, beautiful, richly embellished
AN OPPOSITE IS simple

sentence NOUN

1 *The judge will decide on a sentence next week.*
▶ judgement, ruling, decision, verdict
2 *Her husband is serving a three-year sentence for robbery.*
▶ prison term, (*more informal*) stretch

sentence VERB

The men will be sentenced at a later date.
▶ pass judgement on, pronounce sentence on, punish

sentiment NOUN

1 *I agree with the sentiments expressed in your letter.*
▶ view, opinion, belief, thought, attitude, idea, judgement
2 *There's not much room for sentiment in this kind of business.*
▶ sentimentality, emotionalism, finer feelings, sensibility, soft-heartedness, mawkishness

sentimental ADJECTIVE

1 *The family held a sentimental attachment to their old home.*
▶ emotional, nostalgic, affectionate, tender, romantic, soft-hearted
2 *a sentimental story about separated twins*
▶ maudlin, mawkish, over-emotional, sickly, saccharine, syrupy, indulgent, gushing, corny, (*more informal*) soppy, (*more informal*) mushy, (*more informal*) treacly
OPPOSITES ARE unsentimental, realistic

sentry NOUN

A sentry was on duty at the gate.
▶ guard, sentinel, lookout, watchman, patrol, picket

separable ADJECTIVE

The components are separable and can be replaced individually. Teaching and research are not completely separable activities.
▶ separate, distinct, detachable, divisible, removable, distinguishable

separate ADJECTIVE

1 *The guards took care to keep the two groups separate.*
▶ apart, segregated, cut off, divided, divorced, fenced off, isolated
OPPOSITES ARE together, united
2 *You may prefer to have the kitchen separate from the dining area. The reports may have been referring to two separate events.*
▶ distinct, detached, different, discrete, unattached (to), unconnected (to)
AN OPPOSITE IS joined

separate VERB

1 *They were arguing so fiercely it was difficult to separate them. The war separated us for many years.*
▶ divide, part, break up, split up, segregate
AN OPPOSITE IS unite
2 *Only a short distance separated them.*
▶ divide, come between
AN OPPOSITE IS unite
3 *We separated at the station and I went home.*
▶ part company, go different ways, split up
AN OPPOSITE IS meet
4 *The path separated and went up the hill.*
▶ diverge, fork, branch off
AN OPPOSITE IS merge
5 *Separate the yolks of the eggs from the whites.*
▶ remove, extract, isolate, abstract, filter out
AN OPPOSITE IS mix
6 *When his parents separated he lived with his mother.*
▶ split up, break up, divorce, part, become estranged, part company

7 **separate from** *She separated herself from the company and formed her own business.*
▶ withdraw from, break away from, leave, quit, dissociate yourself from
AN OPPOSITE IS join

separation NOUN

1 *the separation of church and state*
▶ division, splitting, dissociation, severance, detachment, disconnection, parting, isolation, removal, segregation, cutting off
OPPOSITES ARE merging, unification
2 (*informal*) *The separation of the prince and princess has been formally announced.*
▶ break-up, split, parting, rift, estrangement
AN OPPOSITE IS marriage

septic ADJECTIVE

One of her toes looked septic.
▶ infected, poisoned, putrefying, festering, putrid, inflamed, purulent, suppurating

sequel NOUN

1 *The immediate sequel was a riot in the capital.*
▶ consequence, result, outcome, upshot
2 *a sequel to Daphne du Maurier's 'Rebecca'.*
▶ continuation, (*more informal*) follow-up

sequence NOUN

1 *A similar sequence of events occurred in the Baltic States.*
▶ succession, order, course, progression, series, chain, cycle
2 *Here is a short sequence from her new film.*
▶ excerpt, scene, clip, extract, section, episode

serene ADJECTIVE

Her eyes lit up, and a serene smile spread across her face.
▶ calm, composed, contented, untroubled, unruffled, placid, tranquil, peaceful, imperturbable, quiet
AN OPPOSITE IS agitated

series NOUN

1 *Guerrillas carried out a series of kidnappings.*
▶ succession, sequence, string, chain, wave, spate, rash, outbreak, run
2 *Filming has started on a six-part drama series.*
▶ serial, run of programmes

serious ADJECTIVE

1 *She wore a serious expression.*
▶ solemn, grave, earnest, thoughtful, pensive, sombre, unsmiling, grim, dour
OPPOSITES ARE jovial, cheerful
2 *A serious disagreement arose between them.*
▶ important, significant, momentous, critical, urgent, weighty, crucial, grave
OPPOSITES ARE unimportant, frivolous
3 *She suffered serious injuries when she fell from her horse. robbery, assault, theft, and other serious crimes*
▶ severe, critical, bad, acute, shocking, terrible, appalling, dreadful, grave, grievous
AN OPPOSITE IS trivial

4 *He said he was only interested in serious literature*
► intellectual, scholarly, learned, highbrow, profound, (*more informal*) heavy
5 *Are you serious about leaving?*
► sincere, in earnest, genuine, committed, wholehearted
AN OPPOSITE IS uncommitted

seriously ADVERB
1 *He looked at her seriously, frowning deeply.*
► solemnly, earnestly, thoughtfully, sternly, dourly
2 *The baby was seriously ill in hospital.*
► severely, critically, badly, acutely, gravely
3 *Do you seriously expect me to believe you?*
► really, actually, honestly

sermon NOUN
His sermon on patriotism fell completely flat.
► homily, address, lesson, talk

servant NOUN
A servant appeared, carrying a tray.
► attendant, retainer, domestic, valet, butler, maid, menial, helper, (*more informal*) skivvy, (*more informal*) flunkey

serve VERB
1 *They served their masters well.*
► attend, assist, look after, minister to, work for
2 *He claimed to use his business skills to serve the public interest.*
► further, advance, benefit, advantage, support
3 *The book served as a useful guide to the city's attractions. a slogan that would serve for the whole range of products*
► function, be adequate, be useful
4 *a tool that serves a special purpose*
► fulfil, answer, perform, satisfy, complete, discharge
5 *At that point he went in to serve the food.*
► give out, dish up, distribute, provide
6 *Molly spent the summer serving in a local shop.*
► assist, be an assistant, sell
7 **serve on** *He had served on the committee for ten years.*
► work on, be a member of, sit on, contribute to

service NOUN
1 *The contract lists the terms of service.*
► employment, work, business, labour, duty
2 *They have done us quite a service.*
► favour, benefit, assistance, kindness, good turn
3 *products that will give years of service*
► use, usage, utility
4 *She took the car in for a service.*
► overhaul, maintenance check
5 *a church service*
► ceremony, worship, ritual, rite, observance

service VERB
A local garage services their car.
► maintain, repair, check, mend, overhaul

serviceable ADJECTIVE
1 *He was conscious of his own serviceable but dowdy clothes.*
► functional, practical, dependable, hard-wearing, durable, tough, robust, lasting, strong, sensible
AN OPPOSITE IS impractical
2 *The door of the cottage had stout and serviceable bolts.*
► working, usable, functioning, operational, workable

servile ADJECTIVE
Parents have no right to expect servile obedience from their children.
► obsequious, subservient, submissive, unctuous, abject, craven, cringing, fawning, sycophantic, grovelling, menial, slavish, humble, ingratiating, (*more informal*) bootlicking
AN OPPOSITE IS domineering

serving NOUN
a large serving of pasta
► portion, helping, plateful, plate, share, amount, ration, (*more informal*) dollop

session NOUN
1 *The council held its first session in October.*
► meeting, sitting, assembly, conference, discussion, hearing
2 *More practice sessions were needed.*
► period, time, spell, bout

set NOUN
1 *There was a set of keys on the table. The government will announce a set of new proposals on human rights.*
► collection, group, series, batch, bunch, assortment, array
2 *She belonged to a fashionable London set.*
► circle, clique, group, crowd, coterie, company
3 *a television set*
► apparatus, receiver
4 *a chemistry set*
► kit, outfit, apparatus
5 *The production boasted a spectacular set and lavish costumes.*
► staging, setting, scenery, stage furniture

set VERB
1 *She set the bags on a bench in the porch.*
► put, place, deposit, position, stand, leave, settle, station, post
2 *We should set a date for the next meeting.*
► fix, decide on, agree on, establish, choose, select, name, arrange, schedule
3 *She set the alarm for five the next morning.*
► adjust, regulate, programme, synchronize
4 *The sun was setting.*
► go down, sink, subside, vanish, disappear

5 *Leave the jelly in the fridge to set.*
▶ harden, solidify, thicken, stiffen, gel
set about
1 *He set about the task with gusto.*
▶ begin, start, make a start on, get down to, embark on, tackle
2 *A gang set about them in a dark alley.*
▶ attack, assault, assail, fall on, lay into
set aside
1 *Daphne set aside money each month towards her holiday.*
▶ save, put by, keep, earmark
2 *The decision was set aside in the Appeal Court.*
▶ overrule, overturn, reverse, revoke, quash, annul
set off or **out** *We set off early for the airport.*
▶ start out, leave, depart
set out *He set out his collection of coins.*
▶ lay out, arrange, display, exhibit, present
set up
1 *A statue will be set up in the main square.*
▶ erect, put up, raise, construct
2 *The company plans to set up a branch in New York.*
▶ open, establish, found, start, institute
3 *Her secretary set up a meeting for the following week.*
▶ organize, arrange, fix, schedule

setback NOUN
He had survived a whole series of setbacks.
▶ difficulty, problem, hitch, delay, hold-up, obstacle, reverse, snag, blow, upset, disappointment, complication, misfortune, (*more informal*) glitch, (*more informal*) hiccup
OPPOSITES ARE advance, breakthrough

setting NOUN
1 *a relaxing holiday in a quiet setting*
▶ surroundings, location, position, site, background, environment, locale
2 *diamonds in a silver setting*
▶ mounting, mount, fixture, surround
3 *a drama in a historical setting*
▶ backdrop, context, (*French*) mise en scène, scene, set

settle VERB
1 *Further talks will be held today in an attempt to settle the dispute.*
▶ resolve, conclude, clear up, put an end to, find a solution to, reach an agreement about
2 *The solicitors will settle their affairs.*
▶ arrange, organize, sort out, put in order, order, complete
3 *After the war the family settled in Liverpool.*
▶ move (to), set up home, make your home, establish yourself
4 *We can settle the bill in the morning.*
▶ pay, square, clear
5 *Jack settled into an armchair by the fire.*
▶ sink, fall, drop, subside
6 *A bird settled on a branch.*
▶ land, alight, descend

7 *He needed something to settle his nerves.*
▶ calm, soothe, compose, pacify, quell
AN OPPOSITE IS agitate
settle down *Why can't you settle down?*
▶ calm down, quieten down, be quiet, be still, relax
settle down to *Rachel wanted her to settle down to something.*
▶ get down to, apply yourself to, concentrate on, focus on
settle for *Shelby wasn't a man to settle for a dull life.*
▶ agree to, accept, acquiesce in, compromise on
settle on *It was high time they settled on a date for the wedding.*
▶ decide, choose, fix, agree on, name, arrange, organize, schedule

settlement NOUN
1 *a legal settlement*
▶ agreement, deal, arrangement, treaty, contract
2 *The dispute is no nearer settlement.*
▶ resolution, solution, sorting out, settling
3 *an Iron-Age settlement near the modern trunk road*
▶ community, colony, encampment, commune, town, village

settler NOUN
Settlers had established a town there.
▶ colonist, immigrant, pioneer, newcomer

set-up NOUN
a modern communications set-up   a new constitutional set-up for the EU
▶ system, arrangement, framework, organization, business, operation

sever VERB
1 *The arm had been severed at the shoulder.*
▶ cut off, cut, chop off, hack off, shear off, slice off, separate, amputate, disconnect, remove
2 *Henry VIII severed his relationship with the Church of Rome.*
▶ break off, cut off, terminate, disconnect, cease

several ADJECTIVE
1 *The cable is split into several strands.   He had admitted the murder several times.*
▶ a number of, many, some, a few
2 *There are several ways of looking at the problem.*
▶ various, miscellaneous, a number of, sundry, assorted

severe ADJECTIVE
1 *The region faced a severe threat of mass starvation. Wreckage covered the road, causing severe traffic disruption.*
▶ serious, acute, grave, extreme, critical, dire, grievous
AN OPPOSITE IS minor
2 *Many birds were found injured or dead after the severe weather.*
▶ harsh, hard, extreme, turbulent, stormy
AN OPPOSITE IS mild
3 *Oliver developed a severe stomach ulcer.   The pains could be severe and disruptive.*
▶ acute, intense, painful, excruciating
AN OPPOSITE IS slight

4 *The expedition will be a severe test of their stamina.*
▶ demanding, hard, formidable, difficult, onerous, burdensome
OPPOSITES ARE simple, easy
5 *She did not expect the criticism to be so severe.*
▶ fierce, harsh, sharp, scathing, caustic
AN OPPOSITE IS mild
6 *More severe penalties were needed for hit-and-run drivers. They deplored the imposition of such severe censorship.*
▶ strict, harsh, draconian, ruthless
AN OPPOSITE IS mild
7 *It was described as neoclassical architecture in a severe style.*
▶ plain, simple, spare, stark, unadorned
OPPOSITES ARE ornate, elaborate

sew VERB
His aunt sewed the badge on his sleeve.
▶ stitch, tack, attach, fasten
OPPOSITES ARE unpick, remove
sew up *You need to sew up the hole in your sleeve.*
▶ darn, stitch, mend, patch, repair

sewing NOUN
She always had a piece of sewing tucked in her belt.
▶ embroidery, mending, needlepoint, needlework

sex NOUN
1 *The disease affects children of both sexes.*
▶ gender
2 *There is nothing wrong in asking questions about sex.*
▶ the facts of life, sexual activity, reproduction, sexual reproduction
3 *Unsafe sex in this age group was increasing.*
▶ sexual intercourse, intercourse, making love, lovemaking, sexual relations
have sex *Derek said they'd been having sex.*
▶ have sexual intercourse, make love, go to bed together, (more informal) go all the way

sexual ADJECTIVE
1 *A bit of petting had been the only sexual activity.*
▶ erotic, physical, sensual, carnal, sexy
2 *A diagram of the sexual organs might help.*
▶ reproductive, procreative, genital

sexy ADJECTIVE
1 *'You're young,' he said coolly, 'beautiful, sexy, and intelligent.'*
▶ sexually attractive, desirable, seductive, sensual
2 *Louise stripped to her sexy lace underwear.*
▶ titillating, erotic, suggestive, salacious, lewd, racy, sexually explicit, pornographic, (more informal) steamy

shabby ADJECTIVE
1 *Florrie straightened the lapel of her shabby coat.*
▶ worn, scruffy, ragged, tattered
2 *She went into a shabby coffee bar in the centre of town.*
▶ run-down, scruffy, dilapidated, seedy, dingy, dirty, poky, tatty
3 *He hated resorting to such shabby lying.*
▶ shameful, mean, cheap, contemptible, despicable, rotten

shack NOUN
a shack in the woods
▶ hut, cabin, shanty, shed, hovel

shade NOUN
1 *They spend most of the day lying in the shade.*
▶ shadow, shelter, cover
2 *The shades of evening drew on.*
▶ darkness, twilight, gloominess, dimness, obscurity, shadow
3 *She pulled the shade down over the window.*
▶ blind, screen, curtain, awning, canopy
4 *a mass-produced shirt in a harsh shade of blue*
▶ hue, tinge, tint, tone, colour
5 *All shades of opinion were represented.*
▶ variety, variation, form, nuance, subtlety
6 a shade *Silvio laughed a shade too heartily.*
▶ a little, a bit, a touch, rather, (more informal) a tad

shade VERB
1 *A tall fence shaded most of the garden.*
▶ overshadow, cast a shadow over, screen, shield, shroud, veil, conceal, obscure, mask, protect
2 *You can shade the background with a dark pencil.*
▶ colour in, darken, block in

shadow NOUN
1 *He lingered in the shadow of the corridor outside the room.*
▶ shade, darkness, dimness, semi-darkness, gloom
2 *She saw a shadow on the wall.*
▶ silhouette, outline, shape, profile, contour
3 *There's not a shadow of doubt that they were there at the time of the crime.*
▶ trace, slightest bit, scrap, shred, crumb, ounce, particle, iota, jot
4 *There was a shadow of a smile across her face.*
▶ hint, flicker, suspicion, trace, suggestion, sign

shadow VERB
He continued to shadow the van until forced to return.
▶ follow, trail, track, stalk, pursue

shadowy ADJECTIVE
1 *They made out a shadowy form in front of them.*
▶ indistinct, hazy, vague, blurred, blurry, nebulous, unsubstantial, indeterminate, indistinguishable, unrecognizable
2 *She let herself out into the shadowy hall.*
▶ dark, shady, shaded

shady ADJECTIVE
1 *Mrs Halliday took Dot down a shady footpath.*
▶ shaded, shadowy, sheltered, dark, shrouded, sunless
OPPOSITES ARE sunny, bright
2 *Blake had been authorized to do shady deals with Russian intelligence.*
▶ dubious, suspect, suspicious, disreputable, unethical, dishonest, untrustworthy, (more informal) fishy, (more informal) dodgy, (more informal) shifty
AN OPPOSITE IS honest

shaft NOUN

1 *a wooden shaft*
▶ pole, rod, stick, staff, shank, post
2 *The shaft of a pickaxe lay on the ground.*
▶ handle, stem, stock
3 *The first shaft of light broke through the window.*
▶ ray, beam, gleam, bar, finger
4 *a shaft in a mine*
▶ passage, mineshaft, tunnel, duct

shaggy ADJECTIVE

He had a shaggy coat you could lose a hairdryer in. The big shaggy head turned to look at me.
▶ hairy, bushy, thick, woolly, fleecy, unkempt, dishevelled, unshorn, hirsute
OPPOSITES ARE smooth, sleek

shake VERB

1 *The whole building seemed to shake. We were shaking with fear.*
▶ tremble, quiver, shudder, shiver, convulse, judder, heave, wobble
2 *The wind shook the window frame.*
▶ rattle, vibrate
3 *She shook her umbrella at an approaching taxi.*
▶ wave, waggle, wag, brandish, flourish, jiggle, joggle
4 *The news shook them.*
▶ shock, startle, unnerve, unsettle, upset, alarm, distress, disturb, frighten, perturb

shake something off *Bobby finally shook off his flu and was able to play again.*
▶ get over, recover from, get rid of, (*more informal*) see the back of
shake someone off *He looked round to see if he had shaken off his pursuer.*
▶ escape, elude, get away from, leave behind, give someone the slip

shaky ADJECTIVE

1 *They sat at a shaky table.*
▶ unsteady, flimsy, wobbly, rickety, rocky, weak, frail, ramshackle
2 *She let out a deep, shaky breath.*
▶ trembling, shaking, faltering, quivering
3 *His voice was shaky with emotion.*
▶ quavering, unsteady, faltering, nervous, tremulous
AN OPPOSITE IS steady
4 *He had to admit it was a shaky alibi, but he got away with it.*
▶ precarious, uncertain, unpromising, doubtful, unsound

shallow ADJECTIVE

I do not agree with that shallow view of the situation.
▶ superficial, facile, oversimplified, simplistic, narrow, flimsy, lightweight, surface
OPPOSITES ARE profound, deep

sham NOUN

The lad's appearance and manner could be a sham.
▶ pretence, act, fake, fraud, fiction, lie
AN OPPOSITE IS real thing

sham ADJECTIVE

She felt trapped in a sham marriage.
▶ false, fake, bogus, pretended, simulated, imitation
AN OPPOSITE IS genuine

sham VERB

He wasn't shamming, he was obviously injured.
▶ pretend, fake, dissemble

shambles NOUN

(*informal*) *The room was a shambles. The loans scheme had degenerated into a shambles.*
▶ mess, muddle, chaos, confusion, disorder

shame NOUN

1 *He couldn't face the shame of being found out.*
▶ humiliation, opprobrium, dishonour, disgrace, stigma, remorse, guilt, embarrassment, ignominy, mortification, degradation, discredit
OPPOSITES ARE honour, pride
2 **a shame** *It's a shame he didn't stick to chess instead of cards.*
▶ a pity, unfortunate, a piece of bad luck, a cause for regret
OPPOSITES ARE fortunate, lucky

shame VERB

1 *He had been shamed in public.*
▶ humiliate, mortify, humble, chasten, embarrass, (*more informal*) show up
2 *You have shamed your family name. He would have shamed an angel with his table manners.*
▶ disgrace, dishonour, discredit, degrade, taint, tarnish
OPPOSITES ARE honour, do credit to

shamefaced ADJECTIVE

'I'm sorry,' said Anthony, looking shamefaced.
▶ ashamed, embarrassed, abashed, penitent, repentant, self-conscious, sheepish, hangdog, mortified, sorry
OPPOSITES ARE proud, unrepentant

shameful ADJECTIVE

The scheme had been a shameful waste of money.
▶ disgraceful, deplorable, contemptible, outrageous, reprehensible, scandalous, unworthy, wicked, vile
AN OPPOSITE IS honourable

shameless ADJECTIVE

1 *People said he was a shameless sponger.*
▶ brazen, bold, audacious, forward, incorrigible, abandoned
OPPOSITES ARE reticent, bashful
2 *They knew it was a shameless lie.*
▶ blatant, flagrant, barefaced, unashamed, overt

shape NOUN
1 *The shape of their bodies changes with astonishing speed.*
▶ form, figure, configuration, physique, outline, profile, silhouette, pattern
2 *For his age he was in pretty good shape.*
▶ condition, health, state, trim, fettle, (*more informal*) nick

TWO-DIMENSIONAL GEOMETRICAL SHAPES

shapes with straight sides: decagon (10 sides), diamond, dodecagon (12 sides), hendecagon (11 sides), heptagon (7 sides), hexagon (6 sides), lozenge (diamond shape), nonagon (9 sides), oblong (4 sides with right angles and opposite sides equal in length), octagon (8 sides), parallelogram (4 sides with opposite sides parallel), pentagon (5 sides), polygon (5 or more sides), quadrangle (4 sides), quadrilateral (4 sides), rectangle (4 sides with right angles and opposite sides equal in length), rhombus (4 equal sides), square (4 equal sides with right angles), trapezium (4 sides with 2 opposite sides parallel), triangle (3 sides: an isosceles triangle has two sides equal in length and an equilateral triangle has three sides equal in length).

shapes with curved sides: circle, ellipse, ovoid, semicircle.

THREE-DIMENSIONAL SHAPES

cone, cube, cuboid, cylinder, prism, pyramid, sphere.

shape VERB
She shaped the clay into a tall pot.   A number of factors have shaped their ideas.
▶ form, fashion, mould, cast, make, sculpt

shapeless ADJECTIVE
1 *This shapeless mass was my dinner.*
▶ formless, amorphous, indeterminate, irregular, nebulous, undefined, unformed, vague
AN OPPOSITE IS defined.
2 *Gladys removed a shapeless cardigan and hung it over the chair.*
▶ baggy, saggy, sagging, unshapely, formless, dumpy
AN OPPOSITE IS shapely

shapely ADJECTIVE
advertisements full of shapely hips and pretty faces
▶ well-proportioned, elegant, graceful, attractive, trim
AN OPPOSITE IS shapeless

share NOUN
We will get a share of the profits.
▶ portion, part, division, quota, allocation, allowance

share VERB
1 *Member countries will have to share the costs.*
▶ divide, split, deal out, distribute, ration out, share out, apportion, allocate, allot, go halves with

2 *She had to share a room with two other people.*
▶ use jointly, live in
3 **share in** *It is important for everyone to share in the decision-making process.*
▶ be involved in, take part in, participate in, join in, cooperate in

sharp ADJECTIVE
1 *A sharp knife is essential.*
▶ keen-edged, keen, pointed, spiky
AN OPPOSITE IS blunt
2 *Kittens can strike out with their sharp claws.*
▶ pointed, jagged, cutting
3 *She felt a sharp pain in her arm.*
▶ acute, piercing, intense, fierce, stabbing, severe
OPPOSITES ARE gentle, mild
4 *a cheese with a sharp flavour*
▶ strong, piquant, pungent, bitter
OPPOSITES ARE mild, mellow
5 *There was a sharp cry from outside.   There was a series of sharp raps on the door.*
▶ loud, piercing, shrill, high-pitched
AN OPPOSITE IS soft
6 *A sharp wind blew outside.*
▶ cold, chilly, bitter, keen, brisk, biting, cutting
OPPOSITES ARE gentle, warm
7 *If he disapproves there will be frowns and sharp words.*
▶ harsh, bitter, cutting, scathing, caustic, acerbic, tart
8 *She adjusted the focus to make the image sharper.*
▶ distinct, clear, crisp
OPPOSITES ARE blurred, indistinct
9 *There could be a sharp drop in prices.*
▶ rapid, steep, sudden, abrupt
AN OPPOSITE IS gradual
10 *His sharp eyes spotted something moving.*
▶ keen, perceptive, observant, keen-sighted, acute
AN OPPOSITE IS weak
11 *He had a quick wit and a sharp mind.*
▶ perceptive, incisive, discerning, percipient
OPPOSITES ARE dull, slow

sharpen VERB
You will need to sharpen the knife.
▶ make sharp, whet, hone, grind, strop, file
AN OPPOSITE IS blunt

shatter VERB
1 *The blast was loud enough to shatter windows. The glass shattered like an eggshell.*
▶ break, smash, blow out, splinter, crack
2 *The silence was shattered by a warning shout from the alley.*
▶ destroy, wreck, ruin, dash, overturn, upset

shattered ADJECTIVE
1 *She seemed shattered by the refusal.*
▶ upset, devastated, stunned, shocked, staggered, distraught

shave

2 *By the time he reached home he felt shattered.*
▶ exhausted, tired out, worn out, weary, fatigued, (*more informal*) dead tired, (*more informal*) played out, (*more informal*) washed out

shave VERB
His shot shaved the near post.
▶ brush, graze, touch, glance off
shave off *Michael shaved off his moustache.*
▶ cut off, snip off, crop

sheath NOUN
He had the knife half out of its sheath.
▶ case, casing, covering, sleeve, scabbard

shed NOUN
Marion kept her rabbits in a garden shed.
▶ hut, shack, shelter, storehouse, lean-to, outhouse, potting shed

shed VERB
A lorry had shed its load on the inside lane.
▶ spill, throw off, drop, scatter, cast off, discard, let fall, shower

sheen NOUN
Using the right polish will give the surface a delicate sheen.
▶ shine, gloss, lustre, brightness, gleam, patina, burnish, polish

sheepish ADJECTIVE
His smile turned into a sheepish grin..
▶ embarrassed, shamefaced, abashed, ashamed, bashful, coy, guilty, mortified, self-conscious, shy, timid
AN OPPOSITE IS unabashed

sheer ADJECTIVE
1 *It was sheer chance that Beverley had been to the same hotel. The offence was an act of sheer desperation.*
▶ utter, complete, absolute, total, pure, unmitigated, unqualified, out-and-out
2 *A few yards ahead was a sheer drop.*
▶ vertical, abrupt, precipitous, perpendicular
3 *Sheer fabrics look great in a bathroom setting.*
▶ fine, gauzy, flimsy, see-through, diaphanous, transparent, thin

sheet NOUN
1 *a sheet of paper*
▶ piece, leaf, page, folio
2 *a sheet of ice*
▶ layer, film, covering, strip, expanse, surface
3 *a sheet of glass*
▶ pane, panel, plate

shelf NOUN
She put the vase back on the shelf.
▶ ledge, mantelpiece, sill, rack

shell NOUN
1 *an insect that has no hard shell to protect it*
▶ case, casing, crust, husk, hull, pod
2 *All that was left of the building was its shell.*
▶ frame, framework, skeleton, hull

shelter NOUN
1 *Their house provided shelter for countless escapees.*
▶ protection, refuge, sanctuary, safety, cover, haven, lee, asylum
2 *We set up a shelter against the wind.*
▶ shield, screen, barrier, cover
3 *She ran a shelter for the homeless*
▶ sanctuary, refuge, haven, safe haven, retreat

shelter VERB
1 *The hut sheltered us from the storm.*
▶ protect, keep safe, shield, cover, safeguard, screen, guard
2 *The walkers sheltered in doorways.*
▶ take shelter, take refuge, seek protection, take cover
3 *His family took it in turns to shelter him.*
▶ harbour, accommodate, give shelter to, hide

sheltered ADJECTIVE
1 *a sheltered spot behind the sand dunes*
▶ protected, enclosed, screened, shielded, covered, calm, quiet, windless
AN OPPOSITE IS exposed.
2 *She had led a sheltered life.*
▶ secluded, withdrawn, cloistered, reclusive, isolated, unadventurous, unexciting
AN OPPOSITE IS adventurous

shelve VERB
The plans had to be shelved for the time being.
▶ postpone, defer, put off, put to one side, suspend, abandon, mothball, (*more informal*) put on ice, (*more informal*) put on the back burner
OPPOSITES ARE implement, revive

shield NOUN
One coating will afford the metal a shield against corrosion.
▶ protection, safeguard, guard, screen, shelter, barrier, defence, bulwark

shield VERB
She tried to shield her eyes from the glare of the sun.
▶ protect, shade, screen, cover, defend, guard, keep safe, safeguard, shelter

shift VERB
1 *Les shifted the furniture to make more space.*
▶ move, rearrange, reposition, relocate, adjust, transfer, switch round, haul, lug
2 *It wouldn't be easy to shift all that dirt.*
▶ remove, dislodge, budge
3 *Their opinions had shifted somewhat.*
▶ change, alter, modify, vary, fluctuate

shift NOUN
1 *constant shifts in public opinion*
▶ change, alteration, variation, fluctuation
2 *His mum was working on the night shift.*
▶ period, stint, stretch

shifty ADJECTIVE
She had seen that shifty look before.
▶ dishonest, untrustworthy, deceitful, furtive, underhand, shady, wily, scheming, dubious
AN OPPOSITE IS straightforward

a b c d e f g h i j k l m n o p q r **s** t u v w x y z

shimmer VERB

The lights shimmered on the surface of the water.
▶ glimmer, glint, gleam, glow, glisten, glitter, sparkle, shine, flash

shine VERB

1 *The sun shone through the windows.*
▶ beam, gleam, glow, glisten, glint, sparkle, flash
2 *He had forgotten to shine his shoes.*
▶ polish, brush, buff, brighten
3 *There was one thing they all shone at.*
▶ excel, stand out, be outstanding

shine NOUN

a shine on the furniture
▶ polish, sheen, lustre, patina, burnish, gleam

shining ADJECTIVE

1 *a knight in shining armour*
▶ gleaming, brilliant, radiant, glittering, glowing, luminous, shiny, sparkling
2 *a shining example*
▶ outstanding, conspicuous, splendid, eminent, glorious, praiseworthy, resplendent

shiny ADJECTIVE

He liked her shiny black boots.
▶ bright, glossy, gleaming, shining, glistening, polished, burnished, lustrous
OPPOSITES ARE dull, matt

ship NOUN

Another very big wave hit the ship.
▶ vessel, craft, boat, liner, steamer

ship VERB

Twenty flamingoes were shipped from Tanzania to London.
▶ send, consign, transport, post, mail

shipment NOUN

There's a grain shipment due out tomorrow.
▶ load, cargo, consignment, freight, vanload, lorryload, truckload, boatload, (*more formal*) lading

shirk VERB

We've got responsibilities, and we can't shirk them.
▶ dodge, duck, evade, avoid, shun, get out of, shrink from, neglect

shiver VERB

Maria stood at the door shivering.
▶ tremble, quiver, shake, shudder, palpitate, flutter

shock NOUN

1 *the shock of an explosion*
▶ impact, blow, vibration, collision, concussion, jolt
2 *The news came as a shock.*
▶ blow, upset, surprise, bombshell, bolt from the blue
3 *The state of the room always gave her a shock.*
▶ surprise, fright, scare, jolt, start, (*more informal*) turn
4 *She was in a state of shock for several days.*
▶ trauma, distress

shock VERB

The brutal attack shocked the whole community.
▶ horrify, appal, stun, stagger, alarm, outrage, dismay, scandalize, repel, offend, disgust, sicken, revolt

shocking ADJECTIVE

1 *Next day they heard the whole shocking story.*
▶ horrifying, horrific, appalling, alarming, distressing, terrible, dreadful, awful, frightening, upsetting
2 *Their language was quite shocking.*
▶ offensive, disgusting, outrageous

shoddy ADJECTIVE

1 *the shoddy state of our national services*
▶ inferior, poor-quality, second-rate, cheap, trashy, rubbishy, (*more informal*) tacky
AN OPPOSITE IS well- made
2 *The workmanship was noticeably shoddy.*
▶ careless, slapdash, slipshod, sloppy
OPPOSITES ARE painstaking, careful

shoot VERB

1 *The gunman had been daring the police to shoot him.*
▶ hit, kill, gun down, snipe at, pick off
2 *A motor cycle shot past.*
▶ race, dash, zoom, career, fly, rush, streak, hare
3 *They plan to shoot the outdoor scenes on location in Africa.*
▶ film, make, capture

---

shop NOUN

His father opened a shop in the town.
▶ store, retail store, outlet, emporium
TYPES OF SHOP

large general shops: department store, multiple; hypermarket, supermarket, megastore.

small general shops: convenience store, corner shop; confectioner, grocery, newsagent, tobacconist, paper shop.

shops selling food and drink: bakery (bread and cakes), butcher (meat), charcuterie (cold cooked meats), confectioner (sweets), creamery (dairy products), dairy, delicatessen (special meats, cheeses, spices, etc), fish and chip shop, fishmonger, florist (flowers), greengrocer or greengrocery (fruit and vegetables), grocer or grocery, patisserie (cakes and pastries), takeaway (cooked food to take away), tuck shop (sweets); off licence (alcoholic drinks), vintner (wine), winery.

shops selling clothes: boutique, clothes shop, clothier (old-fashioned), couturier (smart fashionable clothes), dressmaker, haberdasher or haberdashery (dressmaking materials), menswear shop, outfitter (men's clothes), shoe shop or shoemaker, tailor (men's clothes).

shops selling medicines and drugs: chemist, drugstore, pharmacy.   ▶▶

other shops: antique shop, barber, bookshop, bookstall (kiosk), chandler (old-fashioned: general supplies), cleaner (for cleaning clothes), DIY shop, draper (old-fashioned: fabrics), electrician, furniture store, garden centre, hairdresser, hardware store, health-food shop, heel bar (for repairing shoes), herbalist (herbs and medicinal plants), ironmonger, jeweller, launderette, perfumery, post office, stationer (paper and writing materials), toyshop, video shop, watchmaker (selling and repairing clocks and watches).

shopping NOUN
She put her shopping in the back of the car.
▶ goods, purchases

shore NOUN
They stopped for a picnic near the shore.
▶ seashore, beach, sands, coast, foreshore, seaboard, shingle, bank, strand
RELATED ADJECTIVE littoral

short ADJECTIVE This word is often overused. Here are some alternatives:
1 *a short piece of string*
▶ small, little
AN OPPOSITE IS long
2 *a short person*
▶ small, little, petite, squat, stocky, diminutive
AN OPPOSITE IS tall
3 *a short account of the voyage*
▶ brief, concise, succinct, pithy
OPPOSITES ARE long, elaborate, lengthy
4 *Take a short look at this.*
▶ brief, cursory, fleeting, momentary
OPPOSITES ARE prolonged, lengthy
5 *Supplies were short.*
▶ low, meagre, scant, deficient, inadequate, insufficient
OPPOSITES ARE plentiful, abundant
6 *She was rather short with me.*
▶ curt, abrupt, sharp, blunt, brusque, snappy, impatient
OPPOSITES ARE courteous, patient

shortage NOUN
a shortage of water
▶ scarcity, sparseness, dearth, deficiency, insufficiency, lack, want, paucity, shortfall
AN OPPOSITE IS abundance

shortcoming NOUN
He was well aware of his own shortcomings.
▶ defect, failing, fault, imperfection, weakness, drawback, foible, vice
AN OPPOSITE IS strength

shorten VERB
The composer shortened the work for concert performance.
▶ cut down, reduce, condense, compress, cut, trim, abridge
OPPOSITES ARE lengthen, expand

shortly ADVERB
A note arrived shortly afterwards.
▶ soon, presently, directly, before long, by and by

short-sighted ADJECTIVE
The media tend to be short-sighted when dealing with the arts.
▶ narrow-minded, narrow, improvident, intolerant, conservative, illiberal, insular, parochial, small-minded

shot NOUN
1 *A shot rang out.*
▶ bang, blast, report, explosion
2 *This is a shot of us on the beach.*
▶ photo, photograph, snap, snapshot
3 *He managed a winning shot.*
▶ stroke, hit, strike, throw
4 *(informal) He wanted a shot at driving the car.*
▶ attempt, try, go, (informal) bash

shoulder VERB
1 *The Minister shouldered the main responsibility for the new policy.*
▶ bear, carry, accept, sustain, take on, undertake
2 *He shouldered his way through the crowd.*
▶ shove, push, thrust, elbow, force

shout VERB
'Come on,' she shouted.
▶ cry, call, yell, exclaim, shriek, scream, bawl

shove VERB
1 *She shoved the boy into the back of the van.*
▶ push, thrust, drive, propel, force
2 *Several large men shoved past them.*
▶ push, barge, elbow, jostle, hustle, shoulder, crowd

shovel VERB
Supporters helped to shovel snow off the pitch.
▶ dig, scoop, shift, clear, move

show NOUN
1 *Thousands came to watch the show.*
▶ entertainment, performance, production, presentation, spectacle, pageant
2 *They had to put on a show of strength.*
▶ display, exhibition, demonstration, appearance, impression, facade, pretence, illusion, affectation

show VERB
1 *Shall I show you how to do it?*
▶ demonstrate, explain, point out, clarify
2 *There's a hole in the sleeve but it won't show.*
▶ be visible, be seen, be obvious, appear
3 *This shows you what you can achieve with limited resources.*
▶ demonstrate, reveal, illustrate, prove, exemplify
4 *They are showing his watercolours at the local gallery.*
▶ exhibit, display
5 *Finn began to show her impatience.*
▶ reveal, manifest, convey, indicate, communicate, expose
6 *A girl showed them to their seats.*
▶ take, escort, accompany, conduct, walk

a b c d e f g h i j k l m n o p q r **s** t u v w x y z

showdown NOUN

The government expected a showdown with the unions over pay.
▶ confrontation, crisis, clash

shower NOUN

1 *a shower of rain*
▶ fall, drizzle, downpour
2 *a shower of compliments*
▶ spate, wave, flood, rush, volley, barrage, torrent, flurry

shower VERB

1 *A passing lorry showered mud over the pavement.*
▶ spray, spatter, splash, sprinkle, rain
2 *The awards committee showered praise on the winners.*
▶ lavish, pour, heap, load

show-off NOUN

a show-off with a big flashy car
▶ exhibitionist, boaster, poser, bragger, egotist

showy ADJECTIVE

showy fake jewellery
▶ gaudy, flashy, ostentatious, pretentious, flamboyant, conspicuous, garish, tawdry, (*more informal*) tacky
OPPOSITES ARE sober, restrained

shred NOUN

1 *Not a shred of evidence could be found.*
▶ scrap, speck, iota, jot, ounce, trace
2 shreds *The dress had been torn to shreds.*
▶ tatters, ribbons, rags, strips

shred VERB

Shred the vegetables and add them to the blender.
▶ grate, chop finely, tear, mince

shrewd ADJECTIVE

a shrewd politician   a shrewd sense of timing
▶ clever, astute, sharp, acute, canny, prudent, intelligent, quick-witted, perceptive, discerning, crafty, wily
AN OPPOSITE IS stupid

shriek VERB

The audience shrieked with laughter.   'Come and see, quick!' Mary shrieked.
▶ scream, screech, squeal, roar, howl, bellow, yell

shrill ADJECTIVE

'That's not true!' she protested in a shrill voice.
▶ piercing, penetrating, high-pitched, screaming, sharp, strident, screechy
OPPOSITES ARE soft, gentle

shrink VERB

1 *Your sweater has shrunk in the wash.*
▶ become smaller, contract, dwindle, shrivel, wither
AN OPPOSITE IS expand
2 *The woman shrank in alarm.*
▶ draw back, cower, cringe, flinch, hang back, back off, recoil

shrivel VERB

The plants were shrivelling in the heat.
▶ wilt, wither, droop, become parched, dehydrate, dry up, wrinkle, shrink

shroud NOUN

a shroud of mist over the sea   The outfit operates behind a shroud of secrecy.
▶ covering, blanket, mantle, pall, veil

shroud VERB

A mist shrouded the seafront.
▶ cover, envelop, wrap, blanket, cloak, enshroud, hide, mask, conceal, screen, swathe, veil

shrug VERB

shrug off *She shrugged off suggestions that she had been unfair.*
▶ dismiss, disregard, ignore, take no notice of, pay no heed to, set aside

shudder VERB

She still shuddered at the thought of what had happened.
▶ shake, quiver, shiver, tremble, be horrified, convulse, quake, squirm

shudder NOUN

Another mighty shudder passed through the ship.
▶ tremor, spasm, convulsion, trembling, tremble, quiver

shuffle VERB

1 *He shuffled over to the fireplace.*
▶ shamble, hobble, scuffle, stumble, teeter, totter
2 *She shuffled the cards and began dealing.*
▶ mix, mix up, jumble, rearrange, reorganize

shun VERB

The group shunned all forms of publicity.
▶ avoid, shy away from, stay clear of, evade, steer clear of, keep away from

shut VERB

I'll shut the window.
▶ close, fasten, latch, lock, push to, bolt, seal, secure
shut down *They will have to shut down the operation in South Africa.*
▶ close down, discontinue, terminate, cease, suspend
OPPOSITES ARE open up, activate
shut in or **up** *She closed the door to shut the dogs in.*
▶ keep in, confine, detain, enclose, imprison, incarcerate
shut off *They had been shut off without food for two days.*
▶ cut off, isolate, separate, segregate
shut out
1 *He shut them out of the house by mistake.*
▶ lock out, keep out, exclude
AN OPPOSITE IS let in
2 *She tried to shut out those bad memories.*
▶ exclude, keep out, suppress, forget
AN OPPOSITE IS recall
shut up *He told them to say something sensible or shut up.*

► be quiet, be silent, stop talking, say nothing, hold your tongue

shy ADJECTIVE
He was too shy to say his name.
► embarrassed, coy, reserved, diffident, bashful, sheepish, inhibited, modest, self-conscious, hesitant, timid, retiring
OPPOSITES ARE assertive, forward, bold, confident

shy VERB
shy away from *They shied away from any sign of danger.*
► avoid, flinch from, recoil from, hang back from, be chary of

sick ADJECTIVE
1 *He had been sick and had to stay at home.*
► ill, unwell, poorly, out of sorts, off colour, indisposed, ailing, peaky, queasy, nauseous
2 **be sick of** *We are all sick of having to wait so long.*
► be fed up with, be tired of, be weary of, have had enough of

sicken VERB
It sickened us to see so much waste.
► make someone sick, disgust, revolt, nauseate, repel, put off

sickening ADJECTIVE
The stench of burnt fuel oil is sickening. There was a sickening sound of tearing metal.
► revolting, disgusting, nauseating, offensive, repulsive, repellent, appalling

sickly ADJECTIVE
1 *He was a sickly child with a bad chest.*
► unhealthy, poorly, sick, ill, infirm, frail, feeble, weak
2 *She had a sickly complexion.*
► pale, wan, pasty, sallow, pallid, ashen
3 *The walls were painted a sickly green.*
► insipid, pale, wan

sickness NOUN
1 *She was away because of sickness.*
► illness, disease, ailment, disorder
2 *The spells of sickness lasted four or five days.*
► nausea, biliousness, queasiness, vomiting

side NOUN
1 *The box has an address label on one side.*
► surface, face, facet, elevation, flank
2 *A hut stood by the side of the lake.*
► edge, border, verge, boundary, margin, fringe, brink, limit, perimeter, rim
3 *He was driving over the limit on the wrong side of the road.*
► half, part, carriageway
4 *I could see both sides in the argument.*
► point of view, aspect, perspective, standpoint, opinion, stance, angle, view, viewpoint, slant
5 *The family had backed the winning side in the civil war.*
► faction, camp, army, team

6 *The home side was one player short.*
► team, squad, lineup
RELATED ADJECTIVE lateral

side VERB
side with *They didn't know who to side with.*
► support, favour, prefer, take the side of, agree with

side effect NOUN
The drug can have alarming side effects.
► consequence, repercussion, result, by-product

sideline NOUN
He does magic shows as a sideline.
► diversion, second job, secondary activity, additional activity, extra

sidestep VERB
She managed to sidestep the most awkward questions.
► avoid, evade, dodge, circumvent, skirt round, steer clear of, bypass

sidetrack VERB
He was too easily sidetracked by minor difficulties.
► distract, deflect, put off, divert

sideways ADVERB
He fell sideways and hurt his arm.
► to the side, laterally, obliquely

sideways ADJECTIVE
1 *There should be no sideways movement in the shaft.*
► lateral, oblique, indirect
2 *He gave us a sideways glance as he left.*
► oblique, furtive, covert, sidelong, sly

sidle VERB
He sidled into the room hoping not to be seen.
► creep, sneak, slink, slip, steal, slide

siege NOUN
The city was under siege for a year.
► blockade, encirclement, investment

sieve NOUN
Use a sieve to strain the fruit.
► strainer, sifter, colander, filter, riddle, screen

sieve VERB
Sieve the mixture into a bowl.
► strain, sift, filter, riddle, screen

sift VERB
1 *Sift the flour over the eggs and milk.*
► sieve, strain, filter, riddle, screen
2 **sift through** *Police have been sifting through piles of evidence.*
► examine, inspect, sort out, analyse, scrutinize, investigate, review

sigh VERB
1 *She sighed with relief.*
► breathe out, exhale
2 *'Not again,' he sighed.*
► moan, complain, lament, grumble

sight NOUN

1 *His sight was failing.*
▶ eyesight, vision, seeing, visual perception
RELATED ADJECTIVES visual, optic or optical
2 *The enemy was almost in sight.*
▶ range, view, field of vision
3 *In the early afternoon they had their first sight of land.*
▶ view, glimpse, appearance, look (at), glance (at)
4 *Thousands of visitors enjoy the sights every year.*
▶ place of interest, landmark
5 *The fireworks were an impressive sight.*
▶ spectacle, display, show, exhibition, showpiece, scene

sight VERB

A spotter plane sighted the survivors.
▶ spot, discern, make out, glimpse, notice, observe, perceive, distinguish, recognize, see, behold

sign NOUN

1 *There are no signs yet of a change in the weather.*
▶ indication, intimation, hint, warning, forewarning, promise, threat, omen, pointer, portent, presage, augury
2 *He gave the sign to begin.*
▶ signal, cue, gesture , nod
3 *There were signs of a much earlier occupation at the site.*
▶ trace, vestige, clue, proof, reminder
4 *Cards are sent as a sign of affection.*
▶ token, marker, manifestation, symptom
5 *We'll have to put a sign in the window.*
▶ notice, placard, poster, publicity, signboard, advertisement
6 *The walls were daubed with signs and pictures.*
▶ symbol, mark, device, emblem, insignia, badge, logo, cipher, trademark

sign VERB

She signed her name at the bottom of the page.
▶ write, autograph, inscribe, initial, endorse

sign up

1 *The brothers all signed up in the army.*
▶ enlist, enrol, register, join
2 *The company has signed up many more clerical staff.*
▶ enrol, enlist, recruit, engage, take on, hire

signal NOUN

1 *The captain gave the signal to move forward.*
▶ sign, gesture, wave, prompt, cue, nod, (more informal) go-ahead
2 *The city mob took Edward's flight as the signal for an orgy of destruction.*
▶ cue, prompt, occasion, excuse, stimulus

signal VERB

1 *A police officer signalled to him to stop.*
▶ gesture, indicate, motion, sign, wave, beckon, communicate, flag, gesticulate, give a signal
2 *The pointed gun signalled his intentions very clearly.*
▶ indicate, express, reveal, announce, proclaim, declare, show

signature NOUN

He couldn't read his own signature.
▶ autograph, initials, mark, name, endorsement

significance NOUN

He thought hard about the significance of her remarks.
▶ importance, import, force, purport, implication, meaning, relevance, sense, point, signification, message
AN OPPOSITE IS insignificance

significant ADJECTIVE

1 *The tests produced some significant results.*
▶ important, meaningful, revealing, informative, indicative, (more informal) tell-tale
2 *The measures would have a significant effect on prices*
▶ considerable, important, noteworthy, serious, sizeable, remarkable, influential, big
AN OPPOSITE IS insignificant

signify VERB

Red signifies danger.
▶ mean, denote, symbolize, represent, indicate, stand for, imply

silence NOUN

1 *There was silence for a time, while they thought.*
▶ quiet, quietness, stillness, tranquillity, peace, peacefulness, calm, hush
AN OPPOSITE IS noise
2 *The criticism reduced him to silence.*
▶ speechlessness, dumbness, muteness, reticence, taciturnity, uncommunicativeness
OPPOSITES ARE speech, verbosity

silence VERB

1 *The menace in his voice silenced them.*
▶ quieten, keep quiet, make silent, suppress, muzzle, shut up, gag
2 *A special muffler helps to silence exhaust noise*
▶ deaden, muffle, quieten, mute

silent ADJECTIVE

1 *George was silent until they reached the car park.*
▶ quiet, speechless, unspeaking, voiceless, dumb, mute, taciturn, reticent
2 *It was totally silent in the kitchen.*
▶ quiet, hushed, peaceful, tranquil, noiseless, soundless

silhouette NOUN

I made out the long silhouette of a tall man.
▶ outline, profile, contour, shape, figure, form, features

silky ADJECTIVE

She ran her fingers through her dark silky hair.
▶ smooth, soft, sleek, velvety, glossy, fine, satiny

silly ADJECTIVE

People often do silly things. 'I'm not quite as silly as you think,' she said.
▶ foolish, unwise, stupid, imprudent, rash, reckless, foolhardy, senseless, idiotic, crazy, mad, (*more informal*) daft

similar ADJECTIVE

1 *The boys are similar in appearance.*
▶ alike, identical, indistinguishable, close, like, the same
OPPOSITES ARE dissimilar, different

2 *hills and similar features*
▶ comparable, analogous, equivalent

3 **similar to** *Her views are similar to my own.*
▶ like, comparable to, close to
OPPOSITES ARE unlike, dissimilar to, different from

similarity NOUN

There is a startling similarity between them.
▶ resemblance, likeness, affinity, closeness, correspondence, congruity, similitude, sameness, uniformity
AN OPPOSITE IS difference

simmer VERB

1 *Vegetables were simmering on the hob.*
▶ boil gently, bubble, stew

2 *She simmered with suppressed anger.*
▶ fume, seethe, rage, be incensed

simple ADJECTIVE

1 *a simple method of fixing up shelving*
▶ straightforward, easy, uncomplicated, elementary, undemanding
OPPOSITES ARE complicated, difficult

2 *The forms are written in simple language.*
▶ clear, plain, straightforward, unambiguous, direct

3 *They led simple, honest lives. He is a simple sort of guy.*
▶ ordinary, unpretentious, unsophisticated, unassuming, innocent, artless

simplicity NOUN

1 *The solution was amazing for its simplicity.*
▶ straightforwardness, simpleness, ease
AN OPPOSITE IS difficulty

2 *The house appealed because of the simplicity of its style.*
▶ plainness, unpretentiousness, restraint, purity, austerity
AN OPPOSITE IS ornateness

simplify VERB

The rules are difficult to apply and need to be simplified.
▶ make simple, clarify, disentangle, streamline
AN OPPOSITE IS complicate

simplistic ADJECTIVE

The solution is appealing but far too simplistic.
▶ facile, superficial, oversimple, inadequate, naive, pat
AN OPPOSITE IS sophisticated

simply ADVERB

1 *It was simply impossible to tell the difference.*
▶ wholly, absolutely, completely, utterly

2 *She did it simply because we asked her to.*
▶ merely, just, purely, solely, only

3 *It is important to dress simply and avoid flamboyance.*
▶ plainly, soberly, without fuss, without frills, with restraint

4 *He writes simply and effectively.*
▶ clearly, plainly, straightforwardly, intelligibly

5 *They lived simply.*
▶ modestly, unpretentiously, naturally, quietly

simulate VERB

1 *The capsule simulates the actual conditions of space travel.*
▶ imitate, reproduce, replicate, mimic, duplicate, parallel

2 *She did her best to simulate a smile.*
▶ put on, feign, fake, sham, pretend

simultaneous ADJECTIVE

There were three simultaneous bomb attacks in the city.
▶ concurrent, coinciding, synchronized, synchronous, contemporaneous, parallel

sin NOUN

1 *It was a sin against their gods*
▶ offence, wrong, transgression, evil, iniquity

2 *a powerful sermon on the dangers of sin*
▶ wickedness, wrongdoing, sinfulness, immorality, evil
AN OPPOSITE IS virtue

sin VERB

He confessed he had sinned and incurred the wrath of his God.
▶ do wrong, be guilty of sin, transgress, err, go astray, offend

sincere ADJECTIVE

1 *Their praise was completely sincere.*
▶ heartfelt, honest, candid, genuine, truthful, wholehearted, open
AN OPPOSITE IS insincere

2 *Jane is a very sincere person.*
▶ honest, genuine, truthful, straightforward, ingenuous, artless

sincerity NOUN

I trust the sincerity of their intentions.
▶ honesty, genuineness, integrity, openness, straightforwardness, trustworthiness, truthfulness

sinful ADJECTIVE

Such behaviour was sinful.
▶ wicked, wrong, evil, iniquitous, unrighteous, ungodly
AN OPPOSITE IS virtuous

sing VERB

To cheer herself up she began to sing.
▶ chant, croon, hum, intone, trill

a b c d e f g h i j k l m n o p q r **s** t u v w x y z

singer NOUN
an arrangement for a singer with small orchestra
▶ vocalist, soloist, songster

TYPES OF SINGER

general words: chorister, folk singer, opera singer, pop singer or pop star, soloist.

female singers: alto, coloratura soprano (singing high elaborate music), contralto, mezzo-soprano, soprano; choirgirl, diva (famous opera singer), prima donna (chief singer of an opera company).

male singers: baritone, bass, basso profundo (lowest bass), countertenor (higher than tenor), falsetto (singing unusually high notes), tenor, treble; castrato (historical: castrated and higher than tenor), choirboy, crooner, folk singer, minstrel (medieval singer), troubadour (medieval French poet and singer).

single ADJECTIVE
1 *All the chocolates were gone apart from a single orange cream.*
▶ solitary, lone, sole, isolated
2 *He had remained single all his life.*
▶ unattached, unmarried, a bachelor, unwedded
AN OPPOSITE IS married
3 *She listened to every single word.*
▶ individual, particular

single VERB
single out *It would be invidious to single out any individual for praise.*
▶ pick out, choose, select, fix on, separate out

single-handed ADJECTIVE
She ran the guest house single-handed.
▶ alone, by yourself, unaided, without help, independently

single-minded ADJECTIVE
She seemed ambitious and single-minded.
▶ determined, resolute, persevering, unwavering, steadfast, dedicated

singular ADJECTIVE
They acted with singular determination.
▶ extraordinary, remarkable, exceptional, uncommon, unusual, conspicuous, notable

sinister ADJECTIVE
His words had a sinister undertone.
▶ menacing, threatening, ominous, disturbing, alarming, disquieting, malevolent, baleful, (*more informal*) scary, (*more informal*) creepy

sink VERB
1 *The sun sank below the horizon.*
▶ descend, dip, fall, drop, disappear, vanish
AN OPPOSITE IS rise
2 *Their hopes began to sink.*
▶ dwindle, fade, flag, fail, weaken, lessen, subside, collapse
AN OPPOSITE IS revive

3 *The ship sank with the loss of many lives.*
▶ founder, go under, submerge, capsize
OPPOSITES ARE rise, float

sinner NOUN
a sermon about how we are all sinners of one kind or another
▶ wrongdoer, offender, transgressor, reprobate

sip VERB
She sat sipping tea.
▶ drink slowly, taste, sample, (*more informal*) slurp

sip NOUN
He took another sip of his beer.
▶ mouthful, drink, drop, taste, (*more informal*) slurp

sister NOUN
He had a younger sister in Liverpool.
▶ sibling
RELATED ADJECTIVE sororal

sit VERB
1 *Julian sat in an armchair.*
▶ settle, perch, flop, ensconce yourself
2 *The hall sat about a hundred people.*
▶ seat, accommodate, have seats for, holds, takes, has room for
3 *Parliament sits again in a week's time.*
▶ meet, assemble, convene, gather, be in session
4 *She sits her exams this year.*
▶ take, go in for, be a candidate in

site NOUN
the site for the new hospital
▶ location, situation, setting, spot, plot, locality, ground

site VERB
Bus stops are sited at intervals of no more than half a mile.
▶ position, place, situate, locate, erect, station, install

sitting NOUN
a sitting of Parliament
▶ session, assembly, meeting, period

sitting room NOUN
a long sitting room with an open fireplace
▶ living room, drawing room, lounge, front room, reception room

situated ADJECTIVE
a hypermarket situated near the bypass
▶ located, positioned, sited, built, placed, established

situation NOUN
1 *new houses in a pleasant situation*
▶ locality, location, position, setting, site, spot, place
2 *Their financial situation had improved significantly.*
▶ circumstances, position, state, state of affairs, condition, plight, predicament
USAGE You use *plight* and *predicament* about bad situations.
3 *She applied for a situation with an estate agent*
▶ job, position, post, employment

size NOUN
1 *the vast size of the main bedroom*
▶ dimensions, proportions, scale, magnitude, area, volume
2 *the size of the job*
▶ scale, extent, scope, range, immensity

sizeable ADJECTIVE
A sizeable reward is being offered.
▶ large, substantial, considerable, significant, decent, generous, worthwhile, (*more informal*) tidy

sizzle VERB
Food sizzled in the pan.
▶ crackle, frizzle, hiss, sputter

skeleton NOUN
1 *the skeleton of a building*
▶ framework, frame, bones, structure
2 *a skeleton of the plan*
▶ outline, draft, abstract, blueprint, sketch

sketch NOUN
1 *She drew a sketch of the scene.*
▶ drawing, outline, picture, diagram, plan
2 *a biographical sketch*
▶ description, portrait, profile, cameo
3 *a brief sketch of the main events*
▶ outline, summary, synopsis, rundown
4 *a comic sketch from the television series*
▶ scene, skit, turn, routine, number

sketch VERB
He decided to sketch the garden instead of taking a photograph.
▶ draw, make a drawing of, portray, depict, rough out, represent
sketch out *We will sketch out our plan.*
▶ outline, describe, summarize, rough out, draft, give the gist of

sketchy ADJECTIVE
The information was too sketchy to act on.
▶ incomplete, imperfect, perfunctory, bitty, scrappy, skimpy, meagre, rough, vague, imprecise, scanty
OPPOSITES ARE detailed, comprehensive

skilful ADJECTIVE
a skilful negotiator   a skilful use of the materials
▶ expert, skilled, able, capable, accomplished, proficient, adroit, deft, talented, clever, masterly, consummate
AN OPPOSITE IS incompetent

skill NOUN
work that needs a lot of skill
▶ expertise, ability, skillfulness, aptitude, adeptness, dexterity, competence, talent
AN OPPOSITE IS incompetence

skilled ADJECTIVE
a skilled engineer
▶ experienced, trained, qualified, skilful, proficient, accomplished, expert, practised, versed
OPPOSITES ARE unskilled, inexperienced

skim VERB
1 *The boat skimmed across the water.*
▶ glide, skate, plane, slide, float, coast
2 **skim through** *He skimmed through a picture book.*
▶ scan, skip through, flick through, look through, riffle through, read quickly

skimp VERB
Despite the low price you won't skimp on comfort here.
▶ stint on, be frugal with, economize on, cut corners on

skimpy ADJECTIVE
I'd rather have my clothes too long than looking skimpy.
▶ scanty, short, flimsy, low-cut

skin NOUN
1 *The animal has a tough skin.*
▶ hide, pelt
2 *the skin of an apple*
▶ peel, rind, outside

skin VERB
She skinned three tomatoes.
▶ peel, pare, strip

skinflint NOUN
(*informal*) *He's such a skinflint considering how much he must be earning.*
▶ miser, pinchpenny, penny-pincher, niggard, (*informal*) meanie

skinny ADJECTIVE
We have to find skinny people to try our designs on.
▶ thin, scrawny, scraggy, lean, lanky, spindly, emaciated

skip VERB
1 *Cathy skipped along the path.*
▶ dance, prance, trip, frisk
2 *We can skip these details.*
▶ pass over, ignore, omit, leave out, miss out, dispense with, forget
3 *We skipped school to go on the demo.*
▶ miss, be absent from, play truant from, absent yourself from, cut

skirmish NOUN
Other border skirmishes have gone unreported.
▶ encounter, fight, tussle, scrap, conflict, engagement, confrontation, battle

skirt VERB
skirt round
1 *If you stop here we can skirt round the fence.*
▶ go round, pass round, border, encircle, circle, surround
2 **skirt round** *Fran skirted round the answers, aware of who was listening.*
▶ avoid, evade, steer clear of, sidestep, ignore, gloss over

skit NOUN
She plays a pram-pushing mother in a skit on daytime magazine programmes.
▶ parody, satire, caricature, spoof, sketch

a b c d e f g h i j k l m n o p q r s t u v w x y z

skulk VERB

He passed the day skulking around cafés.
▶ loiter, prowl, lurk, slink, sneak

sky NOUN

Suddenly the whole sky around them was filled with birds.
▶ heavens, atmosphere, blue yonder
RELATED ADJECTIVE celestial

slab NOUN

slabs of rock cut from the quarries
▶ block, piece, tablet, chunk, hunk, lump, slice

slack ADJECTIVE

1 *The rope suddenly went slack.*
▶ limp, loose
AN OPPOSITE IS tight

2 *A slack defence let in several goals.*
▶ disorganized, negligent, careless, undisciplined, inattentive, lax, lazy, listless, easygoing
OPPOSITES ARE alert, diligent.

3 *Business tends to be slack just after Christmas.*
▶ sluggish, slow, quiet, inactive, slow-moving, depressed
OPPOSITES ARE brisk, busy

slack VERB

This was no time for slacking.
▶ idle, shirk, be lazy, (*more informal*) skive

slacken VERB

1 *The boat lurched as he slackened his grip on the wheel.*
▶ loosen, relax, release, ease off
AN OPPOSITE IS tighten

2 *The rain might just have slackened by now.*
▶ decrease, ease, lessen, abate, lower, moderate, reduce, slow down

slacker NOUN

There was no room for slackers.
▶ layabout, idler, shirker, loafer, malingerer, sluggard

slam VERB

He stormed out and slammed the door.
▶ bang, shut, fling shut, crash

slander NOUN

He'd sue me for slander if I made the accusations publicly.
▶ defamation, misrepresentation, calumny, libel, slur, aspersion, malicious gossip, scandalmongering
OPPOSITES ARE compliment, praise

slander VERB

She discovered that her friend had been slandering her behind her back.
▶ defame, libel, smear, vilify, besmirch

slanderous ADJECTIVE

The truth can often be slanderous if you put it in a certain way.
▶ defamatory, libellous, disparaging, pejorative, scurrilous, malicious, abusive

slant NOUN

1 *The floor seemed to be on a slant.*
▶ slope, angle, incline, diagonal, gradient, list, rake, ramp, pitch, tilt

2 *The Youth Theatre brings a new slant to Christmas shows.*
▶ point of view, viewpoint, standpoint, angle, perspective, emphasis, bias

slant VERB

1 *The handwriting slants to the right. Joe slanted his gaze towards her.*
▶ tilt, lean, slope, incline, be at an angle, be skewed

2 *He slanted his version of the story to avoid awkward admissions.*
▶ bias, distort, twist, warp, weight, colour, prejudice

slanting ADJECTIVE

The slanting sunlight cast long shadows.
▶ sloping, oblique, angled, inclined, diagonal, listing, raked, askew, skewed, slantwise, tilted
OPPOSITES ARE straight, level

slap VERB

1 *Anne was at the end of her patience and wanted to slap him.*
▶ smack, strike, hit, clout, whack, spank

2 *She had slapped a parking ticket on his Mercedes.*
▶ fling, throw, toss, hurl

3 *Slap some varnish on to seal the surface.*
▶ spread, daub, plaster, apply

slap NOUN

He heard the sound of a slap from the next room.
▶ smack, clout, whack, blow, thump

slapdash ADJECTIVE

The book is full of phoney, slapdash arguments.
▶ careless, slipshod, slovenly, untidy, thoughtless

slash VERB

1 *Someone had slashed the tyres.*
▶ cut, slit, gash, rip, tear, knife

2 *Prices will be slashed out of the high season.*
▶ reduce, cut, drop

slash NOUN

He had a deep slash across his arm.
▶ cut, gash, laceration, wound, injury

slate VERB

(*informal*) *The critics all slated the production, though they like the music.*
▶ criticize, pillory, lambaste, revile, (*informal*) pan

slaughter NOUN

The senseless slaughter of dolphins takes place merely to catch a few extra tuna.
▶ massacre, carnage, killing, butchery, murder, bloodshed

slaughter VERB

A whole legion was ambushed and slaughtered.
▶ massacre, butcher, kill, annihilate, eliminate, murder, slay

slave NOUN
Most of the work was done by slaves at that time.
▶ serf, thrall, vassal, drudge, servant
RELATED ADJECTIVE servile

slave VERB
That's all the thanks you get for slaving over a hot stove all morning.
▶ toil, labour, grind, sweat, work , drudge, exert yourself, work your fingers to the bone, (*more informal*) work your socks off
OPPOSITES ARE relax, skive

slavery NOUN
They were being sent back to torture, slavery, and death.
▶ bondage, enslavement, servitude, captivity, serfdom
AN OPPOSITE IS freedom

slavish ADJECTIVE
1 *He was no slavish follower of a party.*
▶ servile, submissive, abject, cringing, fawning, grovelling, humiliating, menial, obsequious
AN OPPOSITE IS assertive
2 *It was a slavish copying of older ideas.*
▶ unoriginal, unimaginative, close, imitative, literal, uninspired
AN OPPOSITE IS independent

slay VERB
Thousands of men and women were slain in the reprisals.
▶ kill, slaughter, massacre, butcher, murder, put to death, exterminate, annihilate, cut down, (*informal*) finish off

sleazy ADJECTIVE
a sleazy little café on the edge of town
▶ dirty, squalid, shabby, run-down, sordid, seamy, rough

sleek ADJECTIVE
1 *She combed her sleek dark hair.*
▶ silky, glossy, shiny, smooth, brushed, soft, velvety, well-groomed
AN OPPOSITE IS dull
2 *a sleek sports car*
▶ streamlined, graceful, elegant, aerodynamic
3 *a group of sleek young men in smart suits*
▶ stylish, well-groomed, prosperous
·AN OPPOSITE IS unkempt

sleep NOUN
She often had a sleep in the afternoon.
▶ snooze, nap, rest, doze, catnap, siesta, (*more informal*) kip, (*more informal*) forty winks

sleep VERB
He had slept for about an hour.
▶ snooze, doze, rest, slumber, (*more informal*) kip, (*more informal*) drop off, (*more informal*) nod off, (*more informal*) doss down

sleepless ADJECTIVE
The shock caused him sleepless nights for a week.
▶ wakeful, restless, disturbed

sleepy ADJECTIVE
1 *I wasn't sleepy, so I decided to walk round for a bit.*
▶ tired, drowsy, somnolent, lethargic, weary, torpid, sluggish, soporific, heavy-eyed, (*informal*) dopey, ready to sleep
AN OPPOSITE IS awake
2 *a sleepy little town near the border*
▶ quiet, peaceful, tranquil, inactive, dull, unexciting
OPPOSITES ARE lively, busy

slender ADJECTIVE
1 *a slender youth with dark hair*
▶ slim, lean, slight, thin, graceful, svelte
AN OPPOSITE IS fat
2 *a slender thread*
▶ fine, fragile, tenuous, feeble
AN OPPOSITE IS strong
3 *slender hopes*
▶ faint, slim, remote, flimsy
4 *a verdict based on slender evidence*
▶ meagre, scanty, flimsy, tenuous, inadequate
AN OPPOSITE IS adequate

slice NOUN
a slice of bread
▶ piece, sliver (=thin slice), chunk (= thick slice), hunk (= thick slice), tranche, slab

slice VERB
She sliced the cheese into thin pieces.
▶ cut, cut up, chop, carve, divide

slick ADJECTIVE
a slick marketing campaign
▶ smooth, efficient, smart, polished, streamlined, skilful, professional
AN OPPOSITE IS inept

slide VERB
The spoon slid across the table.
▶ glide, slither, skim, skid, slip

slight ADJECTIVE
1 *There was a slight problem with this plan.*
▶ small, modest, tiny, imperceptible, insignificant, negligible, slim, minor, trivial
2 *her slight figure*
▶ slim, slender, delicate, dainty, graceful, petite, svelte
AN OPPOSITE IS big

slight NOUN
He was seething at the slight to his authority.
▶ insult, affront, slur, snub, rebuff

slightly ADVERB
The new models are slightly bigger. He was slightly taken aback by this.
▶ a little, a bit, rather, somewhat, a shade, moderately
AN OPPOSITE IS very

slim ADJECTIVE
1 *She is tall, slim, and dignified.*
▶ slender, lean, slight, thin, graceful, svelte
2 *a slim chance of winning*
▶ faint, slender, remote, flimsy

s

slim VERB
a diet to help you slim
► lose weight, reduce weight, become slimmer, shape up

slime NOUN
The path was covered in a green slime.
► sludge, muck, mucus, mud, ooze

slimy ADJECTIVE
He slid helplessly down the slimy walls.
► slithery, slippery, sticky, oozy, greasy

sling VERB
He slung his coat on a chair.
► throw, hurl, toss, fling, cast, pitch, heave

slink VERB
He slunk round to the back of the house.
► creep, sneak, slip, steal, edge, sidle

slinky ADJECTIVE
(informal) a slinky long dress
► sleek, close-fitting, clinging, tight, sexy

slip VERB
1 *People were slipping on the icy ground.*
► slide, slither, fall, trip, stumble
2 *He got up and slipped quietly out of the door.*
► creep, sneak, slink, steal, edge, sidle
3 *He slipped some money into his pocket.*
► put, tuck, stick, shove, stuff

slip NOUN
1 *a slip of paper*
► piece, scrap, chit, sheet
2 *Did you mean to write 'yes' or was that a slip?*
► mistake, error, gaffe, lapse, blunder

slippery ADJECTIVE
1 *The floor was wet and slippery.*
► slithery, greasy, slimy, slippy
2 *a slippery character*
► devious, unreliable, dishonest, crafty, cunning

slipshod ADJECTIVE
a slipshod performance
► careless, slapdash, slovenly, untidy, thoughtless

slit NOUN
1 *He peeped through a slit in a fence.*
► opening, chink, gap, crack, aperture, slot
2 *She made a slit in the side of the box.*
► cut, incision, gash, tear, slash

slit VERB
Henry looked for a knife to slit open his letter.
► cut, tear, rip, slice

slither VERB
A snake slithered through the grass.
► slide, slink, slip, creep, glide, snake, worm

slobber VERB
The dog slobbered on the carpet.
► drool, dribble, salivate, slaver

slog NOUN
(informal) The work was a year's hard slog.
► toil, labour, struggle, work, (informal) grind

slogan NOUN
a well-known advertising slogan
► jingle, motto, catchphrase, catchword, watchword, saying

slope NOUN
1 *A flat roof must have a slope for drainage.*
► incline, gradient, slant, angle, pitch
2 *They had their picnic on a grassy slope.*
► hillock, hill, bank, rise

slope VERB
The garden slopes gently away from the house.
► slant, fall or rise, fall away, shelve, bank, incline

sloppy ADJECTIVE
1 *The cement mixture was much too sloppy.*
► liquid, runny, slushy, watery, messy, wet
AN OPPOSITE IS solid
2 *sloppy work*
► careless, slovenly, slapdash, slipshod
AN OPPOSITE IS careful

slosh VERB
1 *Water was sloshing about*
► splash, slop, spill, splatter
2 *Michael threatened to slosh anyone else who said anything.*
► hit, thump, bash, clout

slot NOUN
1 *She put another coin in the slot and waited.*
► slit, chink, aperture, opening
2 *a weekly radio slot for listeners' comments*
► spot, time, place, space

slouch VERB
Martin was slouching in a low chair.
► slump, droop, loaf, lounge, flop, hunch, stoop

slovenly ADJECTIVE
1 *He was criticized for his slovenly appearance.*
► untidy, scruffy, messy, dishevelled
AN OPPOSITE IS careful
2 *The work is slovenly and needs to be redone.*
► careless, slapdash, slipshod, untidy, thoughtless

slow ADJECTIVE
1 *They walked on at a slow pace.*
► leisurely, unhurried, measured, moderate, steady, deliberate, plodding
OPPOSITES ARE fast, quick, rapid
2 *It was slow work.*
► lengthy, prolonged, protracted, tedious
OPPOSITES ARE rapid, speedy
3 *He could be extremely slow at times.*
► stupid, slow-witted, dim, obtuse, (more informal) dense
OPPOSITES ARE bright, quick, astute

slow VERB
The huge vehicle slowed to a halt.
► decelerate, go slower, slow down, reduce speed, brake
OPPOSITES ARE accelerate, speed up

sluggish ADJECTIVE
He woke up feeling sluggish after a sleepless night.
▶ lethargic, lifeless, listless, torpid, unresponsive, dull, idle, lazy, slothful
OPPOSITES ARE lively, vigorous

slump NOUN
a financial crisis and a slump in world trade
▶ decline, depression, downturn, collapse, drop, fall, tumble, crash, trough
AN OPPOSITE IS boom

slump VERB
1 *House values have slumped in the last few months.*
▶ decline, drop, fall off, collapse, plummet, plunge, sink, worsen
OPPOSITES ARE soar, rise
2 *Joanna slumped into a chair.*
▶ flop, loll, droop, sag, slouch, collapse
3 *He slumped to the ground, clutching his leg.*
▶ fall, sink, collapse, drop

slur NOUN
This is a slur on one of our great national heroes.
▶ insult, slight, slander, libel, defamation

sly ADJECTIVE
The master was a devious, sly man.
▶ cunning, crafty, clever, wily, foxy, canny, knowing, shifty, sneaky, furtive, scheming, conniving

smack VERB
She lost control and smacked him.
▶ slap, strike, hit, clout, whack, spank

smack NOUN
He frowned and gave her a smack.
▶ slap, clout, whack, blow, thump

small ADJECTIVE This word is often overused. Here are some alternatives:
1 *A small packet lay on the mat.*
▶ little, tiny, minute, compact, baby, diminutive, minuscule
AN OPPOSITE IS large
2 *His mother was a small woman.*
▶ short, little, slight, petite
OPPOSITES ARE big, large, tall
3 *We will need to make some small changes.*
▶ minor, trivial, trifling, insignificant, unimportant, negligible
OPPOSITES ARE major, substantial
4 *They wanted to complain about the small portions.*
▶ meagre, inadequate, paltry, insufficient
OPPOSITES ARE large, generous, ample

small-minded ADJECTIVE
a lot of small-minded chauvinists
▶ narrow-minded, intolerant, narrow, bigoted, conservative, illiberal, insular, parochial, short-sighted, hidebound
OPPOSITES ARE broad-minded, open-minded, tolerant

smarmy ADJECTIVE
His manner was over-polite and smarmy.
▶ smooth, oily, unctuous, obsequious, fawning

smart ADJECTIVE
1 *He looked smart in his new suit.*
▶ elegant, well dressed, stylish, spruce, trim, chic, fashionable
AN OPPOSITE IS scruffy
2 *Jenny had always been the smart member of the family.*
▶ clever, bright, intelligent, sharp, shrewd, astute
AN OPPOSITE IS stupid
3 *They would stay in a smart hotel and eat out every night.*
▶ fashionable, high-class, exclusive, fancy, (*more informal*) posh
AN OPPOSITE IS low-class
4 *They set off at a smart pace.*
▶ brisk, fast, quick, lively, spirited
AN OPPOSITE IS slow

smart VERB
The smoke made her eyes smart.
▶ sting, tingle, prickle, prick, hurt

smarten VERB
1 **smarten up** *The house had been smartened up before it was put on the market.*
▶ do up, refurbish, redecorate, renovate, improve
2 **smarten yourself up** *Eleanor went to smarten herself up for dinner.*
▶ dress, spruce yourself up, freshen yourself up, make yourself smart

smash VERB
1 *He dropped the glass and smashed it.*
▶ break, shatter, crack
2 **smash into** *A car had smashed into the lamppost.*
▶ crash into, collide with, smack into, bash into, thump into, hit

smashing ADJECTIVE
They had a smashing time.
▶ marvellous, excellent, wonderful, splendid, lovely, delightful, (*more informal*) terrific

smattering NOUN
She is fluent in French and has a smattering of German.
▶ bit, modicum, small amount, dash, rudiments, basics

smear VERB
1 *He smeared grease on the bearings.*
▶ daub, spread, wipe, plaster, rub, dab, smudge
2 *The canvas was smeared with paint*
▶ cover, coat, rub, streak
3 *The newspapers tried to smear his reputation*
▶ sully, besmirch, tarnish, blacken, defame, malign, vilify

smear NOUN
1 *a smear of paint*
▶ streak, smudge, daub, mark
2 *smears about them in the press*
▶ slander, libel, defamation, imputation, false report

s

smell NOUN

1 *the fresh smells of spring*
▶ fragrance, scent, perfume, aroma
2 *a smell of cooking*
▶ aroma, odour
3 *a bad smell*
▶ odour, stench, stink, reek, (*more informal*) pong, (*more informal*) niff
RELATED ADJECTIVE olfactory

smell VERB

1 *Smell the flowers.*
▶ scent, sniff
2 (*informal*) *The milk was starting to smell.*
▶ stink, whiff, pong, reek

smelly ADJECTIVE

The room was damp and smelly.
▶ smelling, stinking, malodorous, reeking, foul, putrid, (*more informal*) pongy

smile VERB

Jo smiled at her.
▶ beam, grin, simper, smirk, leer
USAGE Note that *smirk* and *leer* are unpleasant expressions.

smoke VERB

1 *The fire was smoking*
▶ smoulder, emit smoke, fume, reek
2 *He was smoking a cigar.*
▶ puff on, draw on, inhale

smooth ADJECTIVE

1 *a smooth road*
▶ even, level, flat, horizontal
OPPOSITES ARE uneven, rough
2 *a smooth surface*
▶ shiny, polished, glossy, silky
AN OPPOSITE IS dull
3 *a smooth sea*
▶ calm, still, tranquil, placid, serene, glassy
AN OPPOSITE IS rough
4 *a smooth talker*
▶ suave, articulate, glib, slick, smarmy, plausible, persuasive
AN OPPOSITE IS awkward
5 *the smooth running of the engine*
▶ regular, steady, rhythmic, flowing, fluent
OPPOSITES ARE irregular, jerky
6 *a smooth operation*
▶ straightforward, efficient, well-run, trouble-free, untroubled
OPPOSITES ARE troubled, fraught

smooth VERB

1 *He took his clothes out of the bag and smoothed them before putting them away.*
▶ flatten, press, iron
2 *Use sandpaper to smooth the surface.*
▶ plane, sand, polish, level
3 *Extra support would smooth their progress.*
▶ ease, facilitate, help, assist, expedite

smother VERB

1 *He tried to smother the flames with his coat.*
▶ put out, extinguish, snuff out, damp down, dampen, douse
2 *A young mother was accused of smothering her baby.*
▶ suffocate, stifle, asphyxiate, strangle, choke

smoulder VERB

1 *The fire was still smouldering a week later.*
▶ smoke, glow, burn slowly
2 *He was smouldering with rage.*
▶ fume, seethe, burn, boil

smudge NOUN

His thumb left a smudge on the paper.
▶ smear, mark, stain, blot, streak

smudge VERB

1 *Her hand slipped and she smudged the writing.*
▶ blur, smear, streak
2 *The wall was smudged with heavy drops of rain.*
▶ mark, stain, blot, dirty

smug ADJECTIVE

He tried not to look smug when the results were announced.
▶ self-satisfied, conceited, superior, self-righteous, complacent, priggish
AN OPPOSITE IS humble

smutty ADJECTIVE

They had been telling each other smutty jokes.
▶ dirty, rude, filthy, crude, indecent, coarse, obscene

snack NOUN

They had a quick snack before leaving.
▶ bite, bite to eat, light meal, refreshments, (*more informal*) nibble

snag NOUN

The snag was that nobody wanted to make the first move.
▶ problem, disadvantage, catch, hitch, obstacle, setback, complication, hindrance, difficulty, (*informal*) stumbling-block

---

snake NOUN

TYPES OF SNAKE

poisonous snakes: adder, asp (small viper), boomslang, cobra, copperhead, coral snake, flying snake, grass snake, king cobra (or hamadryad), mamba, pit viper, puff adder, rattlesnake, sea snake, sidewinder (type of rattlesnake), tree snake, viper.

snakes that crush their prey: anaconda, boa constrictor, python.

harmless snakes: grass snake, green snake, racer.

---

snap VERB

1 *The rope snapped and the trailer slipped backwards.*
▶ break, split, separate
2 *The dogs were snapping at them.*
▶ snarl, growl, bark, bite

snap

3 *'I wasn't there,' Ginny snapped.*
▸ bark, retort, snarl, say angrily, rejoin
4 *After years of suffering she finally snapped.*
▸ crack, lose control, go to pieces, (*more informal*) lose your cool, (*more informal*) freak out

snap NOUN
1 *He closed the case with a snap.*
▸ click, crack
2 *There is often a cold snap just after Christmas.*
▸ spell, period, interval, stretch
3 *She showed us her holiday snaps.*
▸ photo, photograph, picture, image

snap ADJECTIVE
a snap decision
▸ instant, on-the-spot, off-the-cuff, abrupt

snappy ADJECTIVE
1 *We need a snappy answer*
▸ quick, prompt, brisk
2 *a snappy dresser*
▸ smart, stylish, fashionable, chic, (*more informal*) trendy
3 *The campaign needs a slogan that's snappy.*
▸ pithy, crisp, memorable

snare NOUN
1 *A rabbit was caught in a snare.*
▸ trap, noose, (*old-fashioned*) gin
2 *Try to avoid the snare of overspending in the sales.*
▸ pitfall, trap, danger, hazard, catch

snare VERB
The smaller traps can snare dogs out for walks.
▸ ensnare, trap, net, catch

snarl VERB
'Leave me alone,' he snarled.
▸ growl, snap, bark, say angrily

snatch VERB
Thieves had snatched her handbag near the station.
▸ steal, seize, grab, take, grasp, pluck, wrench away, wrest away

sneak VERB
1 *The boys sneaked in when nobody was about.*
▸ creep, steal, slink, slip, sidle
2 **sneak on** (*informal*) *Someone must have sneaked on me.*
▸ inform on or against, report, tell tales about, (*informal*) grass on

sneaking ADJECTIVE
1 *She has a sneaking fondness for Turkish delight.*
▸ secret, private, hidden, concealed, inward, unexpressed
2 *Claudia had a sneaking feeling that Myra could be right.*
▸ nagging, niggling, lingering, lurking

sneaky ADJECTIVE
(*informal*) *a sneaky trick*
▸ sly, cunning, crafty, clever, wily, foxy, canny, knowing, shifty, sneaky, furtive, scheming, conniving
OPPOSITES ARE honest, open

sneer VERB
sneer at *It is easy to sneer at their first efforts.*
▸ scoff at, mock, scorn, ridicule, deride, jeer at, laugh at, look down on

snide ADJECTIVE
His snide remarks became irritating.
▸ disparaging, deprecating, sarcastic, scornful, sneering, spiteful, sneering, mocking, nasty
AN OPPOSITE IS complimentary

snigger VERB
They might snigger at him behind his back.
▸ laugh, snicker, giggle, titter, chuckle, sneer

snip VERB
1 *She snipped the ends off the stalks.*
▸ cut, clip, trim, crop, chop, dock
2 *The inspector snipped our tickets.*
▸ clip, nick, notch, snick

snippet NOUN
snippets of information
▸ piece, scrap, bit, morsel, fragment, particle, shred, snatch

snivel VERB
If you get caught, don't snivel about the consequences.
▸ complain, grizzle, moan, grouse, whine, make a fuss, (*more informal*) whinge

snobbery NOUN
Forget the snobbery and mystique that is associated with choosing wine.
▸ snobbishness, snootiness, arrogance, affectation, pretension, superciliousness

snobbish ADJECTIVE
She dislikes the snobbish and materialistic attitudes of many people.
▸ snooty, snobby, pretentious, superior, condescending, (*more informal*) stuck up, (*more informal*) toffee-nosed
AN OPPOSITE IS unpretentious

snoop VERB
You shouldn't snoop into our affairs.
▸ pry, meddle (in or with), nose, sneak, (*informal*) stick your nose (in or into)

snooze VERB
(*informal*) *There he was snoozing by the fire.*
▸ sleep, doze, rest, nap, take a nap, catnap

snub VERB
They snubbed the hosts by leaving the party early.
▸ insult, affront, offend, rebuff, reject, scorn, (*more informal*) put down

snug ADJECTIVE
1 *The cottage was warm and snug.*
▸ cosy, comfortable, homely, cheerful, welcome, reassuring, (*more informal*) comfy
OPPOSITES ARE forbidding, unwelcoming
2 *She wore a snug long dress.*
▸ close-fitting, tight, figure-hugging

soak VERB
1 *You need to soak the beans overnight in liquid.*
▶ immerse, steep, wet, submerge
2 *Days of rain had soaked the ground.*
▶ drench, saturate, swamp, inundate
soak into *Ink had soaked into the paper*
▶ permeate, penetrate, saturate
soak up *A sponge soaks up water*
▶ absorb, take up, draw up, suck up

soaking ADJECTIVES
By the time they returned their clothes were soaking.
▶ drenched, soaked, wet through, dripping, wringing, sodden, sopping
AN OPPOSITE IS dry

soar VERB
1 *Birds soared overhead.*
▶ climb, ascend, wing, glide, drift
2 *Prices have continued to soar.*
▶ rise, escalate, rocket

sob VERB
He turned his face to the wall and began to sob.
▶ cry, weep, shed tears, blubber, snivel

sober ADJECTIVE
1 *Matt craved a drink but knew he had to stay sober.*
▶ temperate, abstemious, not drunk
AN OPPOSITE IS drunk
2 *After sober reflection I decided to stay the way I was.*
▶ serious, thoughtful, calm, level-headed, sensible, sombre, grave, earnest, down-to-earth, commonsensical
AN OPPOSITE IS light-hearted
3 *She dressed in a sober style.*
▶ subdued, sombre, austere, severe, staid
AN OPPOSITE IS flamboyant

sociable ADJECTIVE
She had been a lively, bright, and sociable girl before the accident.
▶ friendly, outgoing, companionable, convivial, gregarious, clubbable, cordial, affable, amicable
OPPOSITES ARE unsociable, unfriendly

social ADJECTIVE
1 *Ants are social creatures.*
▶ gregarious, organized, civilized, collaborative
AN OPPOSITE IS solitary
2 *a range of cultural and social interests*
▶ communal, community, public, group
AN OPPOSITE IS individual

social NOUN
The club has a social every month.
▶ party, gathering, function

socialize VERB
Students tend to socialize in the evenings.
▶ associate, be sociable, entertain, fraternize, get together, join in, mix, relate

society NOUN
1 *In our society, men historically have occupied the positions of power.*
▶ civilization, nation, culture, community
2 *We must remember our position in society.*
▶ the community, the population, the public
3 *They enjoy the society of their friends*
▶ company, fellowship, friendship, companionship, camaraderie
4 *He joined a local history society.*
▶ association, club, group, organization, circle, fraternity

soft ADJECTIVE
1 *a soft pillow*
▶ supple, pliable, springy, yielding, flexible, malleable, squashy
AN OPPOSITE IS hard
2 *soft ground*
▶ squelchy, swampy, marshy, boggy, heavy
AN OPPOSITE IS firm
3 *soft music*
▶ gentle, soothing, melodious
AN OPPOSITE IS harsh
4 *a soft voice*
▶ quiet, low, faint, muted, subdued
AN OPPOSITE IS loud
5 *soft colours*
▶ pale, pastel, muted, subtle
OPPOSITES ARE bright, lurid
6 *a soft fabric*
▶ velvety, silky, smooth, downy, fleecy
7 *Some teachers are too soft with their pupils.*
▶ lenient, easygoing, indulgent, permissive, forbearing
OPPOSITES ARE strict, severe

soften VERB
1 *Lower interest rates might soften the effect of the tax increases.*
▶ moderate, temper, alleviate, ease, relieve, assuage
AN OPPOSITE IS intensify
2 *The butter softened in the warmth of the kitchen.*
▶ melt, liquefy, go soft
AN OPPOSITE IS harden

soft-hearted ADJECTIVE
You were always too soft-hearted to tell them what you thought.
▶ kind, kind-hearted, gentle, easygoing, generous, charitable

soggy ADJECTIVE
a pile of soggy clothes
▶ sodden, sopping, saturated, soaked, drenched, wet through
AN OPPOSITE IS dry

soil NOUN
1 *The tiny eggs can also be picked up in garden soil.*
▶ earth, loam, ground, humus, topsoil
2 *English troops withdrew from Scottish soil.*
▶ territory, land, space, jurisdiction

soil VERB
Try not to soil your clothes.
▶ dirty, make dirty, stain, tarnish, contaminate, defile, pollute

soiled ADJECTIVE
Lightly soiled surfaces can be cleaned with a good detergent.
▶ dirty, stained, grubby

soldier NOUN
The town was surrounded by enemy soldiers.
▶ serviceman or servicewoman, fighting man or woman, trooper
RELATED ADJECTIVE military

sole ADJECTIVE
The sole intention is to raise money.
▶ one, only, single, solitary, exclusive, singular, individual, unique

solemn ADJECTIVE
1 *He was tall with a thin, solemn face.*
▶ serious, earnest, sombre, staid, sober, thoughtful, reverential, glum, grave, grim
AN OPPOSITE IS cheerful
2 *The ceremony was a solemn occasion.*
▶ dignified, formal, grand, stately, majestic, impressive, pompous, awe-inspiring, ceremonious, imposing
AN OPPOSITE IS frivolous

solid ADJECTIVE
1 *The floor was of solid concrete. The metal below him was quite solid.*
▶ hard, firm, dense, rigid, fixed, unyielding
OPPOSITES ARE liquid, gaseous, hollow
2 *a solid sort of person*
▶ reliable, dependable, trustworthy, honest, upright, level-headed
OPPOSITES ARE unreliable, dishonest
3 *The police needed solid evidence.*
▶ real, genuine, substantial
4 *a ring of solid gold*
▶ pure, genuine, unalloyed
AN OPPOSITE IS alloyed
5 *He can expect solid support from a third of the delegates.*
▶ firm, united, unanimous
AN OPPOSITE IS divided

solidarity NOUN
feelings of solidarity in the workforce
▶ unity, harmony, unanimity, agreement, cohesion, concord, like-mindedness
AN OPPOSITE IS disunity

solidify VERB
As the liquid cools it rapidly solidifies.
▶ harden, set, thicken, stiffen, congeal, clot, coagulate
AN OPPOSITE IS liquefy

solitary ADJECTIVE
1 *He leads a solitary existence.*
▶ lonely, unsociable, friendless, isolated, cloistered, companionless
AN OPPOSITE IS sociable
2 *a solitary survivor*
▶ single, sole, one, only

3 *a few solitary villages dotted on the landscape*
▶ isolated, out-of-the-way, remote, secluded, hidden, sequestered, unfrequented, desolate

solitude NOUN
She craved a few hours of peace and solitude.
▶ privacy, seclusion, isolation, loneliness, remoteness, retirement
AN OPPOSITE IS companionship

solo ADJECTIVE
a solo performance
▶ unaccompanied, unattended
AN OPPOSITE IS accompanied

solution NOUN
1 *There is no easy solution to the problem.*
▶ answer, resolution, key, solving (of), explanation (of)
2 *a solution of ammonia in water*
▶ mixture, mix, blend, compound

solve VERB
This will solve our immediate problem.
▶ resolve, answer, settle, sort out, put right, deal with

sombre ADJECTIVE
1 *sombre colours*
▶ dark, dull, sober, drab, dreary, gloomy
AN OPPOSITE IS cheerful
2 *His face bore a sombre expression*
▶ serious, solemn, thoughtful, reverential, glum, grave

sometimes ADVERB
He sometimes seems preoccupied.
▶ occasionally, from time to time, at times, now and then, now and again

song NOUN
She sang an old song.
▶ tune, melody, air, strain, number
NAMES FOR TYPES OF SONG
songs telling a story: ballad, lay, calypso (West Indian).
popular songs: folk song, love song, pop song, golden oldie (old song still popular).
religious songs: hymn, psalm, spiritual, carol (associated with Christmas), bhajan, qawwali.
childrens' songs: lullaby, nursery rhyme, ditty (short simple song).
special songs: shanty (sea song), barcarolle (sung by gondoliers), chanson (French song), Lied (German song); dirge (mournful song), lament (sad song), paean (song of praise).
songs for several singers: chorus, round, duet, trio, quartet, madrigal (early song for several voices), part song.

soon ADVERB
We'll be there soon.
▶ shortly, presently, quickly, before long, in a while, in a moment or minute

sooner ADVERB

1 *I wish you'd said something sooner.*
▶ earlier, before, already

2 *I'd sooner stay and wait for them.*
▶ rather, preferably

soothe VERB

She patted him gently to soothe him.
▶ calm, comfort, console, pacify, mollify, settle, subdue, quiet, still
OPPOSITES ARE agitate, disturb

soothing ADJECTIVE

1 *a soothing ointment*
▶ healing, palliative, comforting, emollient, balmy, mild

2 *soothing words*
▶ calming, relaxing, restful, gentle, peaceful, pleasant

sophisticated ADJECTIVE

1 *sophisticated techniques for crime detection*
▶ advanced, developed, complex, elaborate

2 *a sophisticated person*
▶ worldly, experienced, cultivated, refined, urbane

soporific ADJECTIVE

soporific drugs   soporific music
▶ sedative, sleep-inducing, calmative, tranquillizing, hypnotic
OPPOSITES ARE stimulating, invigorating

soppy ADJECTIVE

(*informal*)

1 *a soppy story*
▶ sentimental, mawkish, maudlin, sugary, corny

2 *a soppy child*
▶ silly, daft, feeble, soft, foolish

sorcerer, sorceress NOUN

Come and see the sorcerer's workshop.
▶ wizard or witch, magician, conjuror, enchanter or enchantress, warlock, witch doctor

sorcery NOUN

She was charged with sorcery by his successor, Richard III, and made to do public penance.
▶ magic or black magic, charms, witchcraft, wizardry, conjuring, magic, voodoo

sordid ADJECTIVE

1 *He had a series of sordid affairs with older women.*
▶ sleazy, seamy, seedy, tawdry, cheap

2 *a sordid little eating-place off the motorway*
▶ dirty, squalid, shabby, run-down, rough

sore ADJECTIVE

1 *a sore arm*
▶ painful, hurting, aching, smarting, tender, stinging, burning, injured, wounded

2 (*informal*) *They were sore at us for leaving them like that.*
▶ annoyed, angry, upset, aggrieved, peeved (with), (*more informal*) miffed (with)

sore NOUN

There were sores all down his leg.
▶ swelling, inflammation, abscess, laceration, contusion, lesion, boil, carbuncle, ulcer

sorrow NOUN

1 *The loss caused him great sorrow.*
▶ sadness, unhappiness, regret, misery, grief, distress, anguish, heartbreak, tribulation
AN OPPOSITE IS joy

2 *He related all the sorrows of his life.*
▶ trouble, difficulty, affliction, problem

sorrowful ADJECTIVE

She gave a sorrowful smile.
▶ sad, unhappy, dejected, miserable, despondent, disconsolate
OPPOSITES ARE happy, cheerful

sorry ADJECTIVE

1 *He called his parents to say he was sorry for what he had done.*
▶ apologetic, ashamed (of), penitent, regretful, remorseful, repentant, conscience-stricken, contrite

2 *He felt rather sorry for his father.*
▶ sympathetic, compassionate, full of pity, pitying, understanding

3 *The house was in a sorry state*
▶ pitiful, pitiable, wretched, unfortunate, pathetic, dismal

sort NOUN

What sort of films do you like to see?
▶ type, kind, variety, category, class, genre, style, nature

sort VERB

The eggs are sorted by size and colour.
▶ class, grade, group, categorize, classify, divide
sort out *It took a long time to sort out the difficulties.*
▶ settle, resolve, put right, deal with

soul NOUN

1 *the immortality of the soul*
▶ psyche, spirit, inner being

2 (*informal*) *The poor soul had to wait for hours to be seen.*
▶ person, individual, creature

soulful ADJECTIVE

She gave him a soulful look
▶ emotional, expressive, heartfelt, deeply felt, passionate
AN OPPOSITE IS soulless

---

sound NOUN

They could hear the sound of traffic in the street.
▶ noise, din, hubbub, racket, tone
RELATED ADJECTIVES aural, acoustic, sonic

NAMES FOR TYPES OF SOUND

crying and shouting sounds: bawl, bellow, boo, cry, groan, howl, moan, scream, screech, shout, shriek, sigh, snarl, sniff, snore, snort, sob, splutter, squawk, squeak, squeal, wail, whimper, whine, whoop, yell, yelp. ▶▶

animal sounds: bark, bay, bleat, bray, buzz, cackle, caw, chirp, chirrup, cluck, coo, croak, grate, grizzle, growl, grunt, gurgle, low, miaow, moo, neigh, purr, quack, roar, snort, tweet, twitter, warble, whinny, woof, yap, yowl.

heavy sounds: bang, boom, chug, crunch, drone, plop, rumble, throb, thud.

sharp sounds: bleep, chime, chink, clack, clap, clash, clatter, click, clink, crack, crackle, creak, fizz, hiss, jangle, jingle, ping, pop, rattle, ring, snap, squelch, tick, ting, tinkle, toot, twang, whistle.

loud sounds: blare, clamour, clang, clank, crash, honk, hoot, peal (of bells), roar, slam, smash, thunder, trumpet.

gentle sounds: hum, murmur, patter, rustle, sizzle, swish, whir.

sound VERB

1 *A signal sounded*
► be heard, become audible, resound, resonate, reverberate, make a noise
2 *Opening a door or window will sound the alarm.*
► set off, operate, blast
3 *He sounded angry.*
► seem, appear, give the impression of being
4 *You can sound the depth of a river with a pole.*
► measure, gauge, plumb, determine, probe, test, try
sound out *The survey will sound out public opinion.*
► measure, gauge, canvass, test, investigate

sound ADJECTIVE

1 *sound advice*
► good, sensible, valid, well-founded, reasonable, dependable
AN OPPOSITE IS unsound
2 *The foundations seem sound.*
► firm, sturdy, solid, well built, substantial, stable
AN OPPOSITE IS unsafe
3 *a sound investment*
► wise, judicious, well chosen
AN OPPOSITE IS unwise
4 *She fell into a sound sleep.*
► deep, prolonged, unbroken, uninterrupted
OPPOSITES ARE light, shallow

sour ADJECTIVE

1 *a sour taste*
► sharp, acid, tart, bitter
2 *a sour look*
► embittered, resentful, peevish, acrimonious, disagreeable

source NOUN

1 *the source of the problem*
► cause, origin, originator, initiator, author, fount, root, derivation, starting point
2 *the source of the river*
► start, beginning, spring, origin, head

souvenir NOUN

They issued a recording of the concert as a souvenir.
► memento, keepsake, reminder, token

sovereign NOUN

The Act reduced the powers of the sovereign.
► ruler, monarch, king or queen, emperor or empress
RELATED ADJECTIVES regal, royal

sovereign ADJECTIVE

1 *Sovereign power should belong to the people.*
► supreme, absolute, principal, dominant
2 *a sovereign state*
► autonomous, independent, self-governing

sow VERB

Sow the seeds in parallel rows.
► plant, scatter, spread, distribute, put in the ground

space NOUN

1 *A minibus would have space for ten people.*
► room, capacity, accommodation, seating, seats, volume
2 *The city has very few green spaces left.*
► area, stretch, expanse
3 *There are spaces between the houses.*
► gap, interval, opening, aperture

spacious ADJECTIVE

A spacious hallway leads to the living rooms.
► roomy, sizeable, ample, capacious, commodious, extensive, generous, large, big
OPPOSITES ARE cramped, poky

span NOUN

1 *It can be achieved within the span of a week.*
► space, period, course, duration, extent
2 *a large bird with a six-foot wing span*
► width, length, reach, stretch, spread

span VERB

An old iron bridge spans the river.
► cross, straddle, bridge, pass over, reach over, stretch over, extend across, traverse, arch over

spank VERB

She warned him that next time she would spank him.
► smack, slap, chastise, give someone a spanking

spare ADJECTIVE

1 *Our neighbours have a spare set of our house keys.*
► extra, additional, supplementary, alternative, backup
2 *Do you have any spare paper?*
► leftover, surplus, odd, unwanted, superfluous, unused, unnecessary
3 *a spare figure*
► slender, slim, lean, slight, thin
AN OPPOSITE IS fat

go spare (*informal*) *They'll go spare if they find out.*
► lose your temper, be or become angry, go wild, (*informal*) hit the roof, (*informal*) go bananas, (*informal*) go ballistic

s

spare VERB
1 *We can't spare all that money.*
▶ afford, manage, part with, do without
2 *The captors would not spare any of the hostages.*
▶ pardon, show mercy to, let off, be lenient with, leave unharmed or unhurt

sparing ADJECTIVE
He was always sparing with his praise.
▶ careful, economical, frugal, mean, miserly, niggardly, prudent, stingy, thrifty, close
OPPOSITES ARE lavish, generous

spark NOUN
a spark of light
▶ flash, gleam, glint, flicker, sparkle, twinkle

spark VERB
The comments sparked a furious row.
▶ cause, give rise to, bring about, occasion, set off, stir up, provoke, stimulate, precipitate

sparkle VERB
Lights sparkled in the distance.
▶ glitter, glint, glisten, glimmer, twinkle, gleam, shimmer

sparkle NOUN
1 *a sparkle of light*
▶ flash, gleam, glint, flicker, spark, twinkle
2 *Life had lost its sparkle.*
▶ excitement, vitality, vivacity, verve, exuberance

sparkling ADJECTIVE
1 *sparkling jewellery*
▶ glittering, glinting, glistening, twinkling, flashing, scintillating, brilliant, shining, shiny
AN OPPOSITE IS dull
2 *a sparkling drink*
▶ fizzy, effervescent, bubbly, bubbling, aerated, carbonated, foaming
OPPOSITES ARE still, flat

sparse ADJECTIVE
an area of sparse vegetation
▶ meagre, sparse, scarce, scant, paltry, minimal, negligible
AN OPPOSITE IS dense

spartan ADJECTIVE
They led a spartan life.
▶ harsh, austere, frugal, ascetic, arduous, stringent, strict, stern
OPPOSITES ARE luxurious, opulent

spasm NOUN
1 *a spasm of coughing*
▶ fit, attack, outbreak, eruption, seizure
2 *a muscular spasm*
▶ convulsion, contraction, twitch

spasmodic ADJECTIVE
The night was interrupted by spasmodic gunfire.
▶ intermittent, fitful, sporadic, occasional, irregular, erratic
OPPOSITES ARE regular, continuous

spate NOUN
a spate of burglaries
▶ series, succession, run, string, outbreak, wave
AN OPPOSITE IS trickle

spatter VERB
He spattered water all over the bathroom.
▶ splash, splatter, spray, sprinkle

speak VERB
1 *She left before anyone could speak. He refused to speak about the incident.*
▶ talk, say anything, converse, communicate
2 *We must speak the truth.*
▶ tell, utter, express, declare, voice
3 *The chairman spoke for an hour.*
▶ lecture, give a speech, hold forth, declaim
4 **speak to** *She promised to speak to them soon. He did not speak to her for six months after that.*
▶ communicate with, say something or anything, converse with, contact

special ADJECTIVE
1 *a special occasion*
▶ important, exceptional, significant, particular, remarkable, extraordinary
2 *a perfume with a special smell*
▶ distinct, distinctive, characteristic, peculiar, unique, exclusive

specialist NOUN
a specialist in gynaecology
▶ expert, authority (on), consultant, connoisseur (of)

speciality NOUN
Her speciality is interior design.
▶ expertise, forte, strong point, special interest, strength, line

specific ADJECTIVE
There is no specific evidence to support the allegations.
▶ definite, particular, explicit, precise, special, clear-cut, detailed, exact
AN OPPOSITE IS general

specify VERB
He would not specify the source of his information.
▶ name, identify, state, mention, spell out, indicate, designate, detail, be specific about

specimen NOUN
They asked for a specimen of his handwriting.
▶ sample, illustration, example, demonstration, instance, model, pattern, copy

speck NOUN
a speck of dust
▶ particle, bit, fleck, grain, speckle, spot, trace, dot

speckled ADJECTIVE
a speckled brown egg
▶ flecked, speckly, spotted, freckly, freckled, mottled

spectacle NOUN
1 *The parade proved quite a spectacle*
▶ display, show, performance, pageant, extravaganza, exhibition

2 *The group did look quite an odd spectacle*
► sight, scene, vision, picture

3 *I think we're making a spectacle of ourselves.*
► exhibition, laughing stock, fool

spectacular ADJECTIVE
a spectacular display
► magnificent, splendid, impressive, sensational, dazzling, showy, stunning, outstanding

spectator NOUN
Spectators lined the streets.
► onlooker, watcher, viewer, observer, bystander, looker-on

speculate VERB
1 *His colleagues tended to speculate about his private life.*
► conjecture, theorize, wonder, hypothesize, make guesses, meditate, reflect, muse

2 *People have been speculating on the stock exchange.*
► gamble, venture, hazard

speculative ADJECTIVE
1 *Their conclusions are merely speculative.*
► conjectural, theoretical, hypothetical, notional, tentative

2 *a series of speculative investments*
► risky, hazardous, unpredictable, unsafe, unsound

speech NOUN
1 *the power of speech*
► speaking, talking, verbal communication
RELATED ADJECTIVES oral, phonetic

2 *His speech was slurred.*
► diction, articulation, enunciation, utterance, elocution, delivery

3 *an after-dinner speech*
► talk, address, lecture, oration, discourse

speechless ADJECTIVE
She was speechless with rage.
► dumbfounded, dumbstruck, thunderstruck, aghast, tongue-tied
OPPOSITES ARE talkative, verbose

speed NOUN
1 *It's important to check your speed on this piece of road.*
► velocity, pace, rate, tempo

2 *They completed the work with amazing speed.*
► rapidity, swiftness, alacrity, celerity, quickness, expeditiousness, promptness, fleetness, dispatch

speed VERB
1 *We sped back home*
► hurry, hasten, rush, dash, chase, hurtle, hustle, move quickly, (*more informal*) belt
OPPOSITES ARE go slowly, amble

2 *He was over the limit and speeding.*
► break the speed limit, go or drive too fast

speed up *He called to them to speed up.*
► hurry up, go faster, increase speed, get a move on, quicken, accelerate

speedy ADJECTIVE
We got a speedy response.
► quick, rapid, swift, fast, prompt, immediate, brisk

spell NOUN
1 *a magic spell*
► charm, incantation, magic formula, bewitchment, sorcery, witchcraft, conjuration, conjuring, enchantment

2 *She cast her spell on all around her.*
► magic, allure, charm, fascination, influence, glamour

3 *a spell of dry weather*
► period, interval, stretch, run, patch, turn, stint

spell VERB
Lack of rain has spelt disaster for the natural life of the region.
► mean, lead to, result in, signal, signify, presage, herald, foretell, indicate, suggest

spell out *Let me spell out what I plan to do.*
► explain, elucidate, clarify, make plain, set out, specify, detail

spellbound ADJECTIVE
The audience was spellbound by the performance.
► enthralled, entranced, captivated, enchanted, transfixed, mesmerized, gripped, bewitched, charmed, fascinated, hypnotized, transported

spend VERB
1 *You needn't spend more than £50 on it.*
► pay, pay out, expend, disburse, fritter, squander, (*more informal*) fork out, (*more informal*) shell out

2 *They spent all their time arguing.*
► pass, occupy, fill, while away

spendthrift NOUN
He was a spendthrift and lived luxuriously.
► big spender, profligate, prodigal, wastrel, squanderer
OPPOSITES ARE miser, scrooge, skinflint

sphere NOUN
1 *A glass sphere hung from the ceiling.*
► ball, globe, orb, spheroid, globule

2 *She has a lot of experience in this sphere*
► field, area, domain, milieu, department, scope, subject, province, range, territory

spherical ADJECTIVE
a spherical paper lantern
► round, globular, ball-shaped, rotund, spheroidal

spice NOUN
1 *Add some spices to liven up your dish.*
► herb, seasoning, flavouring

2 *The risk of getting caught added spice to the adventure.*
► excitement, interest, zest, colour

spicy ADJECTIVE
a spicy casserole
► highly flavoured, hot, piquant, tangy, pungent, seasoned

a
b
c
d
e
f
g
h
i
j
k
l
m
n
o
p
q
r
s
t
u
v
w
x
y
z

spiel NOUN
(informal) He gave the usual spiel about raising standards.
▶ speech, monologue, rigmarole, patter, line

spike NOUN
She tore her dress on a spike.
▶ prong, point, barb, stake, skewer, spit

spike VERB
He spiked another pea with his fork.
▶ pierce, spear, skewer, impale

spill VERB
1 *Keith slipped and spilled his drink.*
▶ knock over, tip over, upset, slop, overturn, splash about
2 *Water spilled over the top of the bath.*
▶ overflow, flow, brim, run, pour
3 *A lorry had spilled its load.*
▶ shed, tip, scatter, discharge, drop
4 *People spilled into the streets.*
▶ stream, pour, surge, swarm, throng

spin VERB
1 *A wheel spins on an axle.*
▶ turn, rotate, revolve, gyrate, whirl, twirl
2 *My head was spinning.*
▶ reel, swim, whirl, go round

spindle NOUN
The yarn is spun on a spindle.
▶ axle, rod, shaft

spine NOUN
1 *The posture puts an unnecessary stress on the spine.*
▶ backbone, spinal column, vertebrae
2 *the spines of a hedgehog*
▶ needle, quill, spike, bristle, point

spine-chilling ADJECTIVE
Head for the roller-coasters for a spine-chilling ride.
▶ frightening, terrifying, hair-raising, scaring, chilling, (more informal) scary

spineless ADJECTIVE
He is depicted as sly, drunken, and spineless.
▶ weak, feeble, ineffective, ineffectual, cowardly, faint-hearted, timid, irresolute, helpless
AN OPPOSITE IS brave

spin-off NOUN
The project is a spin-off from the work done last year.
▶ by-product, consequence, result, complement, corollary

spiral ADJECTIVE
a spiral column of smoke
▶ coiled, curling, winging, corkscrew, turning

spiral NOUN
a spiral of smoke
▶ coil, twist, whorl, corkscrew, screw

spiral VERB
1 *Costs continued to spiral.*
▶ soar, rise, mount, escalate, shoot up
OPPOSITES ARE tumble, fall

2 *Feelings of anger and jealousy can spiral violently out of control.*
▶ deteriorate, decline, degenerate, worsen, nosedive

spire NOUN
The spire of a church was just visible.
▶ steeple, spike, pinnacle, point

spirit NOUN
1 *a philosophy of reconciling the body and the spirit*
▶ soul, psyche, inner self, inner being
2 *They went about their task with a good deal of spirit.*
▶ enthusiasm, vigour, energy, vivacity, ardour, zest, keenness, eagerness, liveliness, animation, resolution
3 *There is a legend of spirits haunting the place.*
▶ ghost, spectre, phantom, apparition, wraith, shadow
4 *We need to approach this challenge with a positive spirit.*
▶ attitude, frame of mind, outlook
5 *My spirit was dampened by these setbacks.*
▶ mood, morale, temperament, disposition, humour
6 *an action that breaks the spirit of the law if not the letter*
▶ substance, essence, true meaning

spirited ADJECTIVE
The team gave a spirited performance   an attractive and spirited young person
▶ lively, vivacious, vibrant, animated, energetic, high-spirited, vigorous, dynamic, sparkling, vital
OPPOSITES ARE timid, lifeless

spiritual ADJECTIVE
1 *a spiritual existence*
▶ non-material, incorporeal, unworldly, other-worldly, metaphysical
OPPOSITES ARE physical, material
2 *spiritual music*
▶ religious, sacred, holy, divine, devotional

spit VERB
Don't spit in public.
▶ expectorate, hawk
spit out *He spat out a lemon pip.*
▶ eject, spew

spit NOUN
He wiped the spit from his face.
▶ spittle, saliva, dribble, sputum

spite NOUN
He publicly criticized her out of spite.
▶ malice, maliciousness, spitefulness, animosity, vindictiveness, rancour, ill will, ill feeling, resentment, malevolence

spiteful ADJECTIVE
The speech contained many spiteful remarks.
▶ malicious, malevolent, ill-natured, hostile, hurtful, vicious, venomous, wounding, unkind, snide, cruel, nasty

splash VERB
1 *A passing van splashed water over us.*
▶ splatter, spray, shower, spatter, slosh, slop, sprinkle, squirt, wash
2 *Children splashed about in the water.*
▶ paddle, wade, dabble, wallow, slosh
3 *The newspapers splashed the story across their front pages.*
▶ blazon, plaster, display, spread, flaunt, trumpet, publicize
splash out (*informal*) *He was tempted to splash out on a Porsche.*
▶ spend money, splurge, be extravagant

splash NOUN
1 *a splash of colour*
▶ spot, patch, splodge, speck, burst, touch, dash
2 *The scandal made quite a splash.*
▶ effect, impact, display

splendid ADJECTIVE
1 *The roses can be enjoyed in a splendid park setting.*
▶ magnificent, impressive, imposing, noble, glorious, spectacular, gorgeous, sumptuous
2 *He is a splendid police officer.*
▶ distinguished, outstanding, remarkable, exceptional, celebrated, acclaimed
3 *He had clearly had a splendid day out.*
▶ wonderful, marvellous, excellent, lovely, delightful

splendour NOUN
the classical splendour of the viceroy's palace
▶ magnificence, grandeur, sumptuousness, brilliance, resplendence, majesty, richness, pomp, spectacle, stateliness

splice VERB
The cables were spliced in mid-ocean.
▶ join, unite, connect, interweave, mesh, entwine

splinter NOUN
a splinter of wood   small splinters of glass
▶ sliver, chip, flake, shard, fragment, shaving, shiver

splinter VERB
She had a voice that could splinter a glass.
▶ shatter, shiver, crack, fracture, chip, smash, split

split NOUN
1 *There was a large split in the rock.*
▶ crack, fissure, crevice, breach, break, cleft
2 *Her dress was stained and has a split in the side.*
▶ tear, rip, cut, slash, slit
3 *The policy might produce a split in the party.*
▶ division, schism, rift, breach
AN OPPOSITE IS union
4 *After the split with her partner she moved to London.*
▶ break-up, separation (from), parting, estrangement (from)

split VERB
1 *The child had pulled the curtain and split it.*
▶ tear, rip, slash, slit
2 *He split the log with an axe.*
▶ chop, cut, hew, break, cleave

3 *They worked out a system for splitting the proceeds.*
▶ divide, share, distribute, allocate, apportion
4 *Further on the paths split.*
▶ fork, divide, diverge, branch
AN OPPOSITE IS merge
5 *The proposal would split the Party.*
▶ divide, disunite
split up *Her parents had split up when she was small.*
▶ separate, break up, part, divorce

spoil VERB
1 *She stayed off the beach because she didn't want to spoil her shoes.*
▶ damage, harm, mar, hurt, blemish, disfigure, deface
OPPOSITES ARE improve, enhance
2 *An emergency at a time like this could spoil everything.*
▶ ruin, wreck, upset, mess up, destroy, undo, scupper, sabotage, scotch
AN OPPOSITE IS further
3 *She decided to spoil herself with a vintage champagne.*
▶ indulge, pamper, cosset
AN OPPOSITE IS neglect

spoils NOUN
Looters were filmed carrying off their spoils.
▶ booty, loot, plunder, stolen goods, pickings

sponge VERB
1 *He asked his nephew to sponge the windows.*
▶ wash, clean, swab, mop, rinse, swill, wipe
2 **sponge on** *He didn't want to be sponging on his parents any longer.*
▶ live off, impose on, cadge from, scrounge from

spongy ADJECTIVE
The material was light and spongy.
▶ soft, springy, squashy, cushioned, absorbent, porous
OPPOSITES ARE solid, hard

sponsor NOUN
To raise enough funds they would need more than one sponsor.
▶ backer, patron, benefactor, promoter, donor

sponsor VERB
A local firm agreed to sponsor the championship.
▶ back, promote, subsidize, support, be a sponsor of, finance, fund, help

sponsorship NOUN
Private sponsorship generated an additional ten million.
▶ backing, promotion, support, benefaction, patronage, subsidy

spontaneous ADJECTIVE
1 *The March Revolution was a spontaneous uprising.*
▶ unplanned, unpremeditated, unprepared, unrehearsed, voluntary, impromptu, impulsive, unconstrained, unforced
AN OPPOSITE IS premeditated
2 *The verdict was announced to cheers and spontaneous applause.*
▶ involuntary, automatic, natural, reflex, instinctive

3 *She always seems so friendly and spontaneous.*
► natural, uninhibited, unaffected, open, genuine
AN OPPOSITE IS inhibited

spoof NOUN
The movie was a spoof of his own career.
► parody, skit, take-off, burlesque, satire

spooky ADJECTIVE
I bet this place is really spooky late at night.
► eerie, sinister, creepy, frightening, ghostly, weird, (*more informal*) scary

spool NOUN
a spool of cotton
► reel, bobbin

spoon-feed VERB
She was surprised at how much she had to spoon-feed them.
► indulge, spoil, cosset, mollycoddle, pamper, help

sporadic ADJECTIVE
There had been sporadic outbreaks of heavy rain
► occasional, intermittent, periodic, infrequent, irregular

---

sport NOUN
They showed a lot of interest in sport.
► games, competitive games, physical recreation, physical exercise

NAMES FOR TYPES OF SPORT

team sports: football, soccer (Association football), rugby, American football, hockey; baseball, basketball, volleyball, lacrosse, netball, rounders, cricket, bowls, croquet; polo (on horseback).

individual sports: tennis, badminton, squash; gymnastics, trampolining; boxing, wrestling; billiards, snooker, pool, table tennis; darts; roller skating, rollerblading, skateboarding, cycling, free running.

athletic sports: track events, field events; running, sprint, long-distance race, marathon, cross-country; hurdles; relay race; pentathlon (five events), decathlon (ten events), discus, javelin, shot put, long jump, high jump, triple jump, pole vault.

cross-country sports: cross-country running, orienteering, mountaineering, climbing, potholing, rock-climbing, skydiving.

sports with animals and machines: horse racing, show jumping, dog racing; motor racing; gliding.

water sports: swimming, diving, rowing, surfing, windsurfing, sailing, yachting, canoeing, waterskiing, water polo, kayaking.

winter sports: bobsleigh, ice hockey, skating, skiing, tobogganing, snowboarding.

blood sports: hunting, beagling (hunting hares with beagles), shooting, fishing.

---

sporting ADJECTIVE
It was sporting of them to pay the bill.
► generous, considerate, decent, sportsmanlike
AN OPPOSITE IS unsporting

sporty ADJECTIVE
They look sporty in their jogging suits.
► athletic, fit, healthy, energetic

spot NOUN
1 *There was a dirty spot in the middle of the carpet.*
► stain, mark, smudge, blotch, smear
2 *He had a small spot on the side of his nose.*
► pimple, freckle, mole, blemish
3 *a bright fabric with small spots*
► dot, speck, fleck
4 *We stopped at a quiet spot near the sea.*
► place, position, location, locality, setting, site
5 *Money problems left them in a bit of a spot.*
► predicament, difficulty, plight, mess, corner, trouble, awkward situation, quandary, dilemma, (*more informal*) jam, (*more informal*) fix

spot VERB
1 *My apron was spotted with splashes of grease.*
► stain, mark, smudge, spatter, speckle, streak, blot, discolour, fleck, mottle
2 *She spotted Jack weeding in the garden.*
► notice, observe, glimpse, spy, see, make out, discern, detect

spotless ADJECTIVE
1 *He could wear a white shirt if it was spotless.*
► unmarked, perfectly clean, immaculate, gleaming
2 *They had a spotless reputation for fair dealing.*
► unblemished, unsullied, untarnished, blameless, faultless, pure, immaculate, irreproachable, pure, (*more informal*) whiter than white

spotty ADJECTIVE
a spotty face
► pimply, pimpled, potmarked, spotted, blotchy, freckled

spouse NOUN
Spouses were also invited to the office party.
► husband or wife, partner

spout NOUN
Water poured from the spout.
► nozzle, outlet, jet, sprinkler

spout VERB
1 *Molten lava was spouting from the crater.*
► spurt, gush, spew, pour, stream, shoot, surge, discharge, issue
2 *He spouted endlessly about how much better life used to be.*
► hold forth, sound off, go on, pontificate, declaim, (*more informal*) mouth off, (*more informal*) rabbit on

sprawl VERB

1 *He sprawled on a huge armchair.*
▶ stretch out, lounge, recline, slump, slouch, flop
2 *The woods sprawled across the hillside.*
▶ spread, stretch, straggle, be scattered

spray NOUN

1 *a fine spray of water*
▶ shower, sprinkling, fountain, splash, mist
2 *a spray of flowers*
▶ bouquet, bunch, posy, nosegay, garland
3 *a paint spray*
▶ aerosol, atomizer, spray gun, sprinkler

spray VERB

1 *A sprinkler was spraying water over the grass.*
▶ sprinkle, spread, shower, disperse, diffuse
2 *Water sprayed into the air.*
▶ spout, gush, spurt, shoot

spread NOUN

1 *the spread of civilization*
▶ expansion, extension, growth, proliferation, diffusion, advance
2 *a vast spread of open country*
▶ stretch, expanse, extent, sweep, span
3 *(informal) There was a good spread on the table.*
▶ meal, feast

spread VERB

1 *He sat back and spread his arms*
▶ extend, stretch
2 *I found a map and spread it on the table.*
▶ open out, unfurl, unroll, display
3 *She spread seeds along the edge of the flower bed.*
▶ scatter, strew, diffuse
4 *new ways of spreading information*
▶ communicate, diffuse, propagate, broadcast, transmit, circulate, advertise
5 *These feelings of resentment were beginning to spread.*
▶ grow, increase, proliferate, escalate, develop, broaden

spree NOUN

a shopping spree
▶ bout, fling, orgy, revel, (*more informal*) binge

sprightly ADJECTIVE

He's very sprightly for his age.
▶ lively, active, spry, agile, nimble, spirited, vivacious, vigorous
OPPOSITES ARE doddering, lethargic

spring NOUN

1 *With a sudden spring he was out of the door.*
▶ leap, jump, bound, vault
2 *The cushion had lost its spring.*
▶ bounce, springiness, resilience, elasticity, flexibility

spring VERB

1 *Steve sprang to his feet.*
▶ leap, jump, bound, bounce
2 *Some of these ideas spring from earlier research.*
▶ originate, derive, arise, develop, come
spring up *New hotels are springing up all along the coast.*
▶ appear, develop, emerge, shoot up

springy ADJECTIVE

1 *The floor felt springy under their feet.*
▶ elastic, stretchy, pliable, resilient, spongy, supple, bendy, flexible
AN OPPOSITE IS rigid
2 *He walked on with a springy step.*
▶ jaunty, bouncy, buoyant, lively, light

sprinkle VERB

1 *He sprinkled sugar over his cereal.*
▶ scatter, strew, shower
2 *Sprinkle the grass with seed.*
▶ dust, powder, pepper

sprint VERB

She sprinted up the road.
▶ run, dash, tear, shoot, dart, (*more informal*) belt

sprout VERB

The seeds began to sprout.
▶ grow, germinate, shoot up, spring up, bud, develop, emerge

spruce ADJECTIVE

He looked spruce in his new uniform.
▶ smart, neat, well-groomed, well-dressed, dapper, elegant, (*more informal*) natty
OPPOSITES ARE scruffy, dishevelled

spruce VERB

spruce up *They would have to spruce up the house for the visit.*
▶ smarten up, tidy up, clean up, put in order, (*more informal*) do up

spry ADJECTIVE

She looks spry despite her age.
▶ lively, active, sprightly, agile, nimble, spirited, vivacious, vigorous
OPPOSITES ARE doddering, lethargic

spur NOUN

Music can become a spur to our imaginations.
▶ stimulus, incentive, impetus, encouragement, enticement, filip
on the spur of the moment *He decided to go with her on the spur of the moment.*
▶ on impulse, impulsively, impetuously, spontaneously, all of a sudden

spur VERB

The boy's frantic calls spurred her to action.
▶ stimulate, encourage, drive, prompt, goad, incite

spurious ADJECTIVE
The hotel may well bump up the bill with all sorts of spurious charges.
▶ false, bogus, fake, specious, fraudulent, trumped up

spurn VERB
Many visitors spurn the use of public transport.
▶ reject, refuse, decline, scorn, turn down, disdain, disregard
OPPOSITES ARE welcome, accept

spurt VERB
Blood spurted from his finger and he swore.
▶ squirt, gush, shoot, stream, pour, spew, erupt, surge

spy NOUN
He had never thought of himself as a traitor, or a spy.
▶ secret agent, undercover agent, double agent, (*more informal*) plant, (*more informal*) mole

spy VERB
1 **spy on** *She sent you to spy on me.*
▶ snoop on, keep a watch on, watch, shadow, trail
2 *We heard a rustle and spied a baby adder slithering away.*
▶ notice, observe, glimpse, spot, see, make out, discern, detect

squabble VERB
Every evening a crowd gathered to squabble over politics.
▶ argue, quarrel, bicker, wrangle, dispute, clash, fight

squalid ADJECTIVE
1 *a depressing mixture of cheap housing and squalid surroundings*
▶ dirty, filthy, grimy, grubby, sordid, seedy, dingy
AN OPPOSITE IS clean
2 *squalid attempts to rig the election*
▶ improper, shameful, sordid, dishonest, corrupt
AN OPPOSITE IS honourable

squander VERB
The servant girl he married squandered every penny of his.
▶ waste, misspend, fritter away, dissipate, (*more informal*) blow
AN OPPOSITE IS save

square ADJECTIVE
1 *They sat at a square table.*
▶ rectangular, right-angled, quadrilateral
2 *The sides were still square at full time.*
▶ level, even, neck and neck
3 *All they wanted was a square deal.*
▶ fair, honest, just, equitable, genuine, above-board, (*more informal*) on-the-level

square NOUN
1 *They arranged to meet in the town square.*
▶ piazza, plaza

2 (*informal*) *He must have seemed such a square to them.*
▶ old fogy, conservative, traditionalist, conformist, conventional person, (*informal*) stick-in-the-mud

square VERB
1 *He went in to square his bill.*
▶ settle, pay, clear, discharge
2 *He needed to square a few things with his dad.*
▶ resolve, settle, sort out, clear up, put right, remedy, reconcile
3 *These facts don't quite square with the accepted version of what happened.*
▶ agree, tally, accord, harmonize

squash VERB
1 *Someone had squashed the flowers in the garden.*
▶ crush, flatten, press, mangle, trample on, compress
2 *He squashed a few things into his case.*
▶ stuff, force, cram, ram, pack
3 *The uprising was ruthlessly squashed.*
▶ suppress, quash, quell, put down
4 *He meanly squashed them in front of everyone.*
▶ humiliate, humble, show up, put down, mortify, snub

squashy ADJECTIVE
a squashy pudding
▶ spongy, squelchy, mushy, pulpy, soft, yielding
AN OPPOSITE IS firm

squat ADJECTIVE
a cathedral with two squat towers
▶ short, dumpy, stocky, chunky, stubby, stunted, low
AN OPPOSITE IS tall

squat VERB
The children squatted on the floor to listen.
▶ crouch, stoop, sit

squawk VERB
A bird squawked overhead.
▶ screech, shriek, squeal, cry, call

squeak VERB
1 *The door squeaked.*
▶ creak, grate, rasp
2 *The bird squeaked in its cage.*
▶ chirp, peep, cheep

squeal VERB
She squealed with pain.
▶ cry, yell, yelp, screech, scream, shriek

squeamish ADJECTIVE
Her father had always been squeamish about changing nappies.
▶ queasy, nauseated, fastidious, finicky, fussy, choosy, particular, prim, prissy

squeeze VERB
1 *Katherine squeezed her daughter's hand affectionately.*
▶ press, clasp, grip, hug, squash, wring, compress, crush, embrace, enfold

2 *She put her arm round him and squeezed him.*
▶ hug, embrace, cuddle, hold, clasp
3 *They squeezed the audience into a room that was obviously too small. She squeezed herself into a bright red minidress.*
▶ cram, push, ram, shove, stuff, thrust, crowd, wedge
4 *Two elderly Americans squeezed past her chair.*
▶ push, force your way
5 *The government seems determined to squeeze as much money out of the motorist as it can.*
▶ wring, wrest, extort, extract, force, milk

squeeze NOUN
1 *He gave her hand a squeeze.*
▶ press, pinch, grip, grasp, clasp
2 *Three of us in the back of the car was quite a squeeze.*
▶ crush, jam, huddle, crowd

squint VERB
I saw him squint across at her.
▶ peer, peek, peep, glance, glimpse, look

squint NOUN
(informal) Kate had time for a bacon sandwich and a squint at the papers.
▶ look, glance, peek, peep

squirm VERB
Some scenes in the film make you squirm in your seat.
▶ wriggle, writhe, twist, fidget, twitch

squirt VERB
1 *The first bite made jam squirt down my chin.*
▶ spurt, shoot, gush, spout, spray, erupt, surge
2 *She squirted me with water.*
▶ splash, spray, shower, spatter, splatter, sprinkle

stab NOUN
1 *He got a stab in the leg.*
▶ wound, wounding, blow, jab, cut, prick, thrust
2 *She felt a brief stab of pain.*
▶ twinge, pang, sting, throb, spasm
3 *(informal) I'll have a stab at it.*
▶ try, go, attempt, (informal) bash, (informal) shot

stab VERB
1 *One of the gang stabbed him in the arm.*
▶ knife, spear, pierce, jab, stick, thrust, wound
2 *She stabbed at the ground with a spade.*
▶ thrust, jab, prod, lunge, poke

stability NOUN
1 *It is important to check the stability of the equipment.*
▶ firmness, solidity, steadiness, security, safety
2 *The refugee problem was affecting the stability of the region.*
▶ equilibrium, balance, permanence, soundness, strength
AN OPPOSITE IS instability

stabilize VERB
An increase in interest rates would stabilize the currency.
▶ settle, balance, strengthen, support, make secure
OPPOSITES ARE destabilize, upset

stable ADJECTIVE
1 *Make sure the equipment is stable.*
▶ steady, firm, secure, balanced, fixed, solid
OPPOSITES ARE unstable, flimsy
2 *Their power and authority depend on a stable regime.*
▶ well-founded, well-established, secure, firm, enduring, durable, lasting, sound, strong
OPPOSITES ARE unstable, changeable

stack NOUN
1 *The publisher had a stack of unsold copies on his hands.*
▶ heap, pile, mound, mass, load, accumulation, stockpile, mountain
2 *a stack of hay*
▶ rick, stook, haycock

stack VERB
The boxes were stacked on desks and tables.
▶ pile, heap, load, mass, assemble, collect, accumulate, build up, gather

stadium NOUN
a sports stadium
▶ arena, ground, field, pitch

staff NOUN
1 *We have extra staff on duty over the busy period.*
▶ personnel, assistants, employees, workers, workforce, crew, officers, team
2 *Magistrates carried a staff as a sign of their authority*
▶ cane, crosier, pole, rod, sceptre, stave, stick

staff VERB
The shop is staffed by volunteers.
▶ man, people, crew, operate, run

stage NOUN
1 *They faced the long last stage of their journey.*
▶ part, section, phase, portion, stretch, lap
2 *The treaty marks a new stage in relations between the two countries.*
▶ point, phase, step, juncture

stage VERB
1 *They even staged an opera.*
▶ mount, put on, present, perform, arrange
2 *Workers staged a two-hour strike on 5 November.*
▶ organize, mount, set up, go through with

stagger VERB
1 *He staggered up the stairs to bed.*
▶ totter, stumble, lurch, reel, sway, falter, walk unsteadily, waver, wobble
2 *Rory was staggered by his answer.*
▶ astonish, amaze, astound, surprise, dumbfound, flabbergast, shock, startle, stun, stupefy

stagnant ADJECTIVE
a mass of marshy grass and stagnant water
▶ still, motionless, standing, stale, brackish, static, foul, putrid
OPPOSITES ARE flowing, fresh

stagnate VERB
While revenues stagnate, expenditure has soared.
▶ stand still, stay still, languish, achieve nothing, vegetate, become stale, deteriorate, idle
OPPOSITES ARE rise, boom

staid ADJECTIVE
Surely she's too flamboyant for marriage to such a staid man.
▶ sedate, respectable, conventional, serious, demure, solemn

stain NOUN
1 *Her eyes alighted on a milk stain on the tablecloth.*
▶ mark, spot, smear, blemish, smudge, blot, blotch, discoloration
2 *It was not seen as a stain on their character.*
▶ blemish, taint, blot, slur, disgrace, discredit

stain VERB
1 *Sweat had stained his shirt.*
▶ discolour, mark, blemish, dirty, sully, spoil, blacken
2 *There is a product that will stain and varnish in one go.*
▶ dye, colour, tinge, tint, paint

stake NOUN
1 *The soldier had been speared with a wooden stake.*
▶ pole, post, spike, stave, stick, paling, pile
2 *The multinational has bought a 40% stake in the company.*
▶ share, interest, involvement
3 *If you win, you get your stake back plus ten times its value*
▶ bet, pledge, wager

stale ADJECTIVE
1 *You can make the pudding with stale bread and milk.*
▶ dry, hard, old, musty, mouldy
2 *The war had already become stale news.*
▶ worn out, jaded, hackneyed, out-of-date, uninteresting, unoriginal, overused
AN OPPOSITE IS fresh

stalemate NOUN
The negotiations ended in a stalemate.
▶ deadlock, impasse, standstill

stalk NOUN
the stalk of a plant
▶ stem, shoot, branch, trunk, twig

stalk VERB
1 *The cat began to stalk her through the long grass.*
▶ track, trail, hunt, pursue, shadow, tail, follow
2 *He rose and stalked out of the door.*
▶ stride, strut, march, flounce, sweep

stall NOUN
The school will have a stall at Fun in the Parks.
▶ stand, booth, kiosk

stall VERB
He clearly believed she was only stalling.
▶ play for time, delay, procrastinate, prevaricate, temporize, hang back

stalwart ADJECTIVE
a stalwart supporter of the new democracy
▶ staunch, faithful, loyal, devoted, reliable, resolute, robust, strong, dependable, sturdy, trustworthy, tough, valiant
AN OPPOSITE IS weak

stamina NOUN
The soft ground will make the event a real test of stamina.
▶ endurance, resilience, staying-power, energy

stammer VERB
He always began to stammer when he was under pressure.
▶ stutter, falter, splutter, stumble, hesitate

stamp NOUN
1 *The licence needs an official stamp to be valid.*
▶ mark, seal, brand, imprint
2 *She left her stamp on history as an inspired visionary.*
▶ mark, impression
3 *The new head was of a different stamp from her predecessor.*
▶ type, kind, sort, brand, character

stamp VERB
1 *'Bad girl,' she said and stamped her foot.*
▶ strike, bring down, thump
2 *Sir George had stamped his authority firmly on the subject.*
▶ imprint, mark, print, brand, engrave, impress
stamp on *Ellie moved forward and stamped on the creature.*
▶ tread on, crush, trample
stamp out *The police are trying to stamp out racism.*
▶ eliminate, eradicate, extinguish, end, put an end to, suppress

stampede NOUN
In the stampede that follows, the young elephants can easily get trampled.
▶ charge, rush, dash, rout, panic

stampede VERB
The audience panicked and stampeded for the exit.
▶ dash, bolt, charge, rush, flee

stance NOUN
The country has moved away from the neutral stance it previously took.
▶ attitude, stand, viewpoint, position, policy, posture

stand VERB
1 *The choir stood for the final chorus.*
▶ rise, get to your feet, get up
2 *A house once stood on this spot.*
▶ be situated, be located, be sited, exist, sit, be
3 *She stood the packet on the table.*
▶ put, place, set, deposit, position, situate, station, locate, (more informal) plonk
4 *The offer still stands*
▶ remain in force, remain valid, be unchanged, stay, continue
5 *Her heart could not stand the strain.*
▶ withstand, endure, handle, cope with

6 *I can't stand noise.*
▶ bear, abide, endure, tolerate, put up with, suffer, (*more informal*) stick, (*more informal*) stomach, (*more informal*) wear

stand by *He was determined to stand by his friends.*
▶ support, defend, stand or stick up for, be faithful to, be loyal to, adhere to, stay with, stick to
OPPOSITES ARE betray, let down

stand down *He would have to accept responsibility and stand down.*
▶ resign, step down, retire, (*more informal*) quit

stand for *What do the initials stand for?*
▶ mean, represent, signify, denote, indicate, symbolize, be a sign for

stand in for *She stood in for the lead singer who was unwell.*
▶ replace, substitute for, take over from, be a substitute for, deputize for, cover for, understudy

stand out *He stands out in that suit.*
▶ be prominent, be obvious, catch the eye, show, stick out

stand up for *It is important to stand up for our principles.*
▶ support, defend, champion, stand or stick by, be faithful to, be loyal to, adhere to, stay with, stick to
AN OPPOSITE IS betray

stand up to *The little band stood up bravely to the attack.*
▶ resist, withstand, confront, face up to, defy, oppose
OPPOSITES ARE give in to, succumb to

stand NOUN
1 *a large vase on a stand*
▶ base, pedestal, support, tripod, trivet, rack
2 *a newspaper stand*
▶ stall, booth, kiosk
3 *They are taking a bold stand.*
▶ attitude, stance, viewpoint, position, policy, posture

standard ADJECTIVE
The fee is subject to VAT at the standard rate. The council said the letter was part of their standard procedure.
▶ normal, usual, typical, customary, conventional

standard NOUN
1 *The standard of music-making can be very high indeed.*
▶ quality, level, calibre, grade, excellence
2 *a standard of behaviour*
▶ norm, principle, yardstick, criterion, benchmark, example
3 *Next day at dawn they raised the regimental standard for the last time.*
▶ flag, banner, pennant, colours, ensign

standardize VERB
Some attempt has been made to standardize the menus.
▶ average out, conform to a standard, equalize, normalize, regiment, stereotype

stand-in NOUN
They needed a stand-in for the injured goalkeeper.
▶ substitute, replacement, reserve

standing NOUN
The superintendent has to be a medical practitioner of high standing.
▶ reputation, distinction, status, repute, rank, stature, seniority, eminence

standoffish ADJECTIVE
I kept telling myself to relax and not be so standoffish.
▶ aloof, detached, reserved, uncommunicative

standpoint NOUN
From the consumer standpoint there are two main hazards.
▶ point of view, viewpoint, perspective, position, outlook, slant, view, angle

standstill NOUN
Traffic is forced to a standstill until visibility improves.
▶ stop, halt, dead stop

staple ADJECTIVE
a staple diet
▶ basic, standard , fundamental, principal, chief, main

star NOUN
1 *a sky full of stars*
▶ celestial body, heavenly body
RELATED ADJECTIVES astral, stellar
2 *She was an international star by the age of nineteen.*
▶ celebrity, famous person, public figure, big name, idol

stare VERB
1 *She seemed stunned and sat staring in front of her.*
▶ gaze, gape, glare, goggle, look fixedly, peer
2 **stare at** *Simon was staring at him.*
▶ gaze at, eye, scrutinize, study, watch, contemplate, examine

stark ADJECTIVE
1 *Those who survived had the stark choice of submitting or fleeing into exile.*
▶ grim, blunt, harsh, plain, bald
2 *Their barracks are a stark contrast to the brightness elsewhere.*
▶ absolute, complete, utter, total, sheer

start VERB
1 *The film starts at 8.*
▶ begin, (*more formal*) commence
2 *She wants to start a reading group.*
▶ set up, establish, found, launch, begin, institute, originate, activate, create, embark on, inaugurate, initiate, instigate, introduce, open
AN OPPOSITE IS finish
3 *The bus was ready to start*
▶ depart, leave, move off, set off, set out, (*more informal*) get going
AN OPPOSITE IS stop
4 *We'd better start if we are going to finish in time.*
▶ make a start, begin, (*more informal*) get going, (*more informal*) get cracking

5 *A crash in the kitchen made us start.*
▶ jump, recoil, flinch, spring up, blench, jerk, twitch, wince

start out *They would have to start out before breakfast.*
▶ set off, set out, set forth, make a start, depart, leave, (*more informal*) get going, (*more informal*) hit the road

start NOUN

1 *It was the start of a long process.*
▶ beginning, outset, inception, birth, dawn, initiation, inauguration
OPPOSITES ARE end, conclusion

2 *A good education gives you a start in life.*
▶ advantage, opportunity, encouragement, helping hand

3 *This was the start of all our problems.*
▶ origin, cause, source, starting point
OPPOSITES ARE end, culmination

4 *The doorbell rang, giving me a start*
▶ shock, jump, surprise

startle VERB
Some caterpillars manage to startle their attackers by raising themselves up like small snakes.
▶ alarm, frighten, scare, surprise, give you a start, take by surprise, catch unawares, make you start, shake, shock
AN OPPOSITE IS calm

startling ADJECTIVE
It was startling to see hundreds of people toiling up and down the hill. The letter contained some startling news.
▶ surprising, astonishing, amazing, staggering, disconcerting, unsettling

starvation NOUN
The civil war left most of the population facing starvation.
▶ hunger, malnutrition, undernourishment, malnourishment, deprivation, famine

starve VERB
Many starved in the famine.
▶ die of starvation, go hungry, go without, perish

starving ADJECTIVE

1 *She devoted her energies to helping the starving children of the world.*
▶ starved, underfed, undernourished, emaciated

2 *Let's go and eat, I'm starving.*
▶ very hungry, famished, ravenous

state NOUN

1 *The closure reflects the state of the town's economy.*
▶ condition, situation, shape, circumstances, predicament, position, health

2 *a sovereign state*
▶ country, nation, land, (*more formal*) polity

in a state *Try not to get in a state.*
▶ agitated, flustered, anxious, panicky, frenzied, (*more informal*) uptight

state VERB
In the speech she stated her company's objectives.
▶ declare, express, communicate, voice, utter, tell, say, affirm, make known, reveal, disclose, divulge

stately ADJECTIVE
a stately procession through the town
▶ dignified, majestic, ceremonious, grand, splendid, imposing, noble

statement NOUN
The minister issued a brief statement.
▶ announcement, declaration, account, report, communication, utterance

statesman NOUN
a distinguished banker and statesman who amassed a huge art collection
▶ senior politician, politician

static ADJECTIVE

1 *a static display of work and photographs*
▶ stationary, immobile, motionless, fixed, still, unmoving
AN OPPOSITE IS mobile

2 *Prices have remained static for several years.*
▶ unchanged, steady, stable, constant, invariable, stagnant
AN OPPOSITE IS variable

station NOUN

1 *a nuclear power station in Armenia   a research station funded by the EU*
▶ establishment, facility, base, depot, post, plant, headquarters, office

2 *a radio station*
▶ channel, transmitter, wavelength, company

3 *It's one of the busiest railway stations in the world*
▶ stopping place, terminus, halt, platform

4 *a grand station in life*
▶ standing, status, position, rank, situation, calling

station VERB
She used to date John when he was stationed in Berlin.
▶ post, base, assign (to), deploy, locate, establish

stationary ADJECTIVE
One moment we were stationary, the next moving forward smoothly.
▶ still, at a standstill, motionless, standing, immobile, at rest, halted, static
AN OPPOSITE IS moving

stationery NOUN
a shop selling cards and stationery
▶ paper, writing materials

statistics NOUN
a comprehensive volume of facts, records, and statistics
▶ data, figures, information, numbers

statue NOUN
a bronze statue of a Roman emperor
▶ figure, sculpture, effigy, carving, bronze

stature NOUN

1 *a family who were all of small stature*
▶ build, size, height, tallness

2 *His stature as a war-chief grew.*
▶ reputation, status, standing, esteem, distinction, importance, prominence, recognition, greatness, significance

status NOUN
1 *people who enjoy money and status*
▶ prestige, standing, position or social position, stature, rank
2 *The money is paid to every individual regardless of marital status.*
▶ position, standing

staunch ADJECTIVE
My grandfather was a miner and a staunch socialist.
▶ faithful, firm, loyal, steadfast, strong, reliable, dependable, constant, stalwart, unswerving, true, trustworthy
OPPOSITES ARE disloyal, unreliable

stave VERB
stave off *The government is anxious to stave off a back-bench rebellion.*
▶ prevent, avert, avoid, forestall, nip in the bud

stay VERB
1 *The officer told him to stay where he was.*
▶ wait, remain, continue, (*more informal*) hang on
OPPOSITES ARE leave, depart
2 *It was vital to stay calm.*
▶ remain, keep, continue, carry on being
3 *He said it would be better to stay in a hotel.*
▶ live, lodge, reside, settle, board, dwell, be accommodated, be a guest, be housed, sojourn, stop, visit

stay NOUN
I had several suitcases, in preparation for a long stay.
▶ visit, stop, stopover, break, holiday, sojourn

steadfast ADJECTIVE
She is among the most steadfast opponents of electoral reform.
▶ faithful, firm, loyal, staunch, strong, reliable, dependable, constant, stalwart, unswerving, true, trustworthy
OPPOSITES ARE disloyal, unreliable

steady ADJECTIVE
1 *The ladder doesn't look steady.*
▶ secure, stable, settled, fixed, balanced, fast, firm, solid, safe
AN OPPOSITE IS unsteady.
2 *The Middle East has provided Wimpey with a steady stream of work.*
▶ continuous, regular, constant, even, reliable, uninterrupted, consistent, dependable, ceaseless, non-stop
AN OPPOSITE IS intermittent
3 *Talk in a firm steady voice without shouting.*
▶ regular, even, invariable, rhythmic, smooth, uniform
4 *He didn't then have a steady girlfriend.*
▶ regular, habitual, settled, established, devoted, faithful, loyal, serious, steadfast

steady VERB
1 *Alec steadied himself as the ground shook again.*
▶ stabilize, balance, brace, make steady, secure
2 *I needed something to steady my nerves.*
▶ calm, soothe, settle, quieten, quell, control

steal VERB
1 *He rushed in to help when a mugger tried to steal a fan's camera. He had been caught stealing from a friend.*
▶ thieve, pilfer, purloin, appropriate, rob, run off with, (*more informal*) filch, (*more informal*) pinch, (*more informal*) nick, (*more informal*) swipe, (*more informal*) snaffle
2 *I stole quietly out of the room.*
▶ creep, slink, sneak, move stealthily, tiptoe
3 *Carson stole sideways glances at his passenger.*
▶ snatch, sneak, take

stealing NOUN
They were convicted of stealing.
▶ theft, thieving, robbery, burglary, pilfering, shoplifting

stealthy ADJECTIVE
a lot of stealthy movement from one room to another
▶ furtive, secretive, covert, secret, surreptitious, sneaking, sly, slinky, clandestine
AN OPPOSITE IS blatant

steam NOUN
The kitchen was full of steam.
▶ vapour, condensation, moisture, haze, mist

steamy ADJECTIVE
1 *The windows were steamy.*
▶ misty, cloudy, hazy
2 *the hot steamy jungle*
▶ humid, muggy, sticky, close, sultry, sweaty, damp, moist

steel VERB
She steeled herself for bad news.
▶ brace, stiffen, harden, prepare, nerve

steep ADJECTIVE
1 *steep cliffs overlooking the sea*
▶ sheer, precipitous, abrupt, perpendicular, vertical, sudden, sharp
AN OPPOSITE IS gentle
2 *The costs seem rather steep.*
▶ expensive, dear, costly, exorbitant, extortionate, (*more informal*) pricey, (*more informal*) stiff
OPPOSITES ARE reasonable, moderate

steer VERB
She steered the huge vehicle into the garage.
▶ drive, direct, guide, navigate, control, pilot
steer clear of *The rickety old barn was a place to steer clear of.*
▶ avoid, keep away from, give a wide berth to

stem NOUN
The plants are nourished by water drawn up the stem.
▶ trunk, stalk, stock

stem VERB
The important thing is to stem the spread of the disease. She could no longer stem the flow of tears.
▶ stop, check, restrain, restrict, hold back, control, curb

stench NOUN
The stench of rotting flesh is enough to make you vomit.
▶ stink, reek, foul smell, bad smell

step NOUN
1 *She took a step backwards*
▶ pace, stride, footstep
2 *Anyone seeking political asylum is taking a major step.*
▶ decision, move, action, course, measure
3 *This was a good first step towards retaining her title.*
▶ phase, stage, action, measure, manuvre
4 *an important step towards achieving peace*
▶ advance, movement, progress, progression
5 **steps** *I climbed the steps and knocked on the door.*
▶ stairs, staircase

step VERB
I stepped over several mounds of brick and rubble.
▶ tread, put your foot, walk , stamp, trample
step down *The minister would step down at the next election.*
▶ resign, stand down, retire, (*more informal*) quit
step up *The army stepped up the attack.*
▶ increase, intensify, escalate, augment, boost

stereotype NOUN
man's stereotype of how a woman should look
▶ conventional image, cliché, received idea, pattern, model, formula

sterile ADJECTIVE
1 *sterile soil*
▶ infertile, barren, unproductive, arid, dry, lifeless
AN OPPOSITE IS fertile
2 *a sterile bandage*
▶ sterilized, antiseptic, aseptic, clean, disinfected, germ-free, hygienic, uninfected
AN OPPOSITE IS unsterilized
3 *a sterile discussion*
▶ useless, fruitless, unfruitful, pointless, unprofitable, abortive, hopeless
AN OPPOSITE IS fruitful

sterilize VERB
1 *The room should be clean but you don't have to sterilize everything.*
▶ disinfect, fumigate, decontaminate, make sterile, pasteurize, purify, clean, cleanse
OPPOSITES ARE contaminate, infect
2 *In the poorest families both husband and wife have been sterilized.*
▶ make infertile, give a hysterectomy or vasectomy to

stern ADJECTIVE
1 *Their father looked stern for a while, but soon went to them.*
▶ strict, severe, harsh, grim, grave, serious, austere, authoritarian, dour
OPPOSITES ARE genial, kindly
2 *Stern measures were needed.*
▶ strict, severe, stringent, rigorous, harsh, drastic, tough
OPPOSITES ARE lenient, lax

stew NOUN
stew for dinner
▶ casserole, hot-pot, ragout, goulash, hash

stew VERB
The meat should be stewed slowly.
▶ braise, casserole, boil, simmer

stick NOUN
1 *a pile of dry sticks*
▶ twig, branch, stalk
2 *She threatened him with a stick.*
▶ rod, cane

stick VERB
1 *Iris stuck her fork in the earth.*
▶ poke, prod, dig, jab, stab, thrust
2 *He stuck a message on her computer screen.*
▶ attach, affix, fasten, fix, glue, paste, pin
3 *The plastic seats stuck to her skin.*
▶ cling, adhere, bond, fuse
4 (*informal*) *I've got some stewed fruit I stuck in the freezer.*
▶ put, place, leave, deposit, drop, (*informal*) bung, (*informal*) dump
5 *The wheels stuck in the soft mud.*
▶ become trapped, jam
6 *A particular memory stuck in his mind.*
▶ remain, linger, persist, stay
7 (*informal*) *I couldn't stick it any longer.*
▶ tolerate, put up with
stick at (*informal*) *If you want to learn a language, you'll have to stick at it.*
▶ persevere with, persist with, keep at, work hard at
stick out *He had his hands on his hips and his chin stuck out.*
▶ jut out, protrude, project
stick to *She advises her staff to stick to six basic safety guidelines.*
▶ abide by, adhere to, keep, hold to, fulfil
stick up *The monument sticks up above the trees.*
▶ rise, stand out, loom, tower
stick up for *I was born here and I try to stick up for Britain.*
▶ support, defend, stand up for

sticky ADJECTIVE
1 *She tied up the package with sticky tape.*
▶ adhesive, gummed, self-adhesive, glued
2 *There was a patch of sticky fluid on the carpet.*
▶ gluey, tacky, gummy, treacly, (*more informal*) gooey
AN OPPOSITE IS dry

3 *It was a hot sticky afternoon.*
▶ humid, muggy, sultry, clammy, close
OPPOSITES ARE fresh, cool

stiff ADJECTIVE

1 *You'll need a sheet of stiff cardboard.*
▶ rigid, firm, hard
OPPOSITES ARE limp, flexible

2 *Make a stiff paste.*
▶ thick, firm, semi-solid, viscous

3 *Her muscles were stiff. I was so stiff it was difficult to climb upstairs.*
▶ achy, aching, arthritic, painful, immovable, rheumatic, taut, tight
AN OPPOSITE IS supple

4 *a long stiff climb up the hillside*
▶ difficult, arduous, strenuous, tough, exacting, hard, tiring
AN OPPOSITE IS easy

5 *We will face some stiff competition later this year.*
▶ strong, powerful, severe

6 *His manner was stiff and aloof.*
▶ formal, reserved, unfriendly, cool, awkward
AN OPPOSITE IS relaxed

7 *The judge handed out stiff sentences.*
▶ harsh, severe, punitive, strict, hard, swingeing
AN OPPOSITE IS lenient

8 *A stiff breeze made it hard going.*
▶ fresh, strong, brisk
AN OPPOSITE IS gentle

9 *They all needed a stiff drink.*
▶ strong, potent, alcoholic
AN OPPOSITE IS weak

stiffen VERB

Stir until the mixture stiffens.
▶ become stiff, harden, set, solidify, thicken

stifle VERB

1 *The heat can stifle you.*
▶ suffocate, choke, smother

2 *Margaret stifled a cough. The policy has stifled realistic thinking.*
▶ suppress, check, smother, restrain, muffle, curb

stifling ADJECTIVE

a stifling June afternoon
▶ stuffy, sweltering, oppressive

stigma NOUN

the stigma of being branded a cheat
▶ disgrace, shame, taint, dishonour, reproach, slur, stain, blot

still ADJECTIVE

1 *Paul stood still and looked around.*
▶ motionless, immobile, stationary, unmoving, static, inert, lifeless
AN OPPOSITE IS moving

2 *The evening was warm and still*
▶ quiet, calm, silent, soundless, noiseless, wind-free
OPPOSITES ARE windy, stormy

still VERB

The wind had stilled.
▶ die down, abate, weaken, slacken

stimulate VERB

1 *The literature course stimulated their interest in modern fiction.*
▶ trigger, activate, kindle, rouse, arouse, stir, increase, enhance
AN OPPOSITE IS discourage

2 *The right words from you might stimulate them to keep trying.*
▶ encourage, prompt, motivate, inspire, provoke

stimulating ADJECTIVE

a stimulating lecture by Professor Smithers
▶ interesting, thought-provoking, entertaining, challenging, exciting, rousing, stirring, exhilarating, inspiring, invigorating, provoking
OPPOSITES ARE boring, dull

stimulus NOUN

Cash is the best stimulus to economic development in the region.
▶ spur, stimulant, encouragement, incentive, inducement, impetus, fillip
AN OPPOSITE IS deterrent

sting NOUN

1 *an ointment to soothe a wasp sting*
▶ bite, prick, wound

2 *He felt the sting of the wound still.*
▶ smarting, stinging, pain, burn, pricking

sting VERB

1 *an insect that stings*
▶ bite, nip, prick

2 *The salt water began to sting*
▶ smart, tingle, hurt, burn

stingy ADJECTIVE

Derek was notoriously stingy.
▶ mean, miserly, niggardly, penny-pinching, parsimonious, (*more informal*) tight-fisted
AN OPPOSITE IS generous

stink VERB

1 *The room stank of smoke.*
▶ reek, smell, (*more informal*) pong

2 *The whole idea stinks.*
▶ be unpleasant, be abhorrent, be repellent

stink NOUN

The stink hits you as soon as you open the door.
▶ stench, reek, foul smell, odour, (*more informal*) pong, (*more informal*) niff

stint NOUN

a three-month stint on night duty
▶ spell, stretch, period, term, turn, shift, run, session

stipulate VERB

The will stipulated certain conditions.
▶ specify, lay down, set down, demand, require, insist on

stipulation NOUN

The only stipulation was that the house should not be sold.
▶ condition, proviso, provision, demand, requirement, qualification

stir NOUN

The arrival of the royal car caused quite a stir.
▶ commotion, fuss, excitement, disturbance, sensation, to-do

stir VERB

1 *Use a wooden spoon to stir the mixture.*
▶ mix, blend, beat, agitate, whisk, fold in
2 *Mary stirred in her sleep.*
▶ move slightly, quiver, tremble, twitch
3 *A gentle breeze stirred.*
▶ rustle, shake, flutter
4 *a thought to stir our imaginations*
▶ kindle, rouse, arouse, stimulate, excite, inspire, trigger, activate
stir up *These remarks stirred up considerable anger.*
▶ whip up, work up, rouse, arouse, trigger, spark off, provoke

stirring ADJECTIVE

a stirring piece of music
▶ exciting, rousing, stimulating, thrilling, gripping, riveting, dramatic
AN OPPOSITE IS boring

stitch VERB

He stitched a patch on his jeans.
▶ sew, tack, darn, mend, repair

stock ADJECTIVE

a stock response to an old question
▶ standard, routine, customary, conventional, familiar
AN OPPOSITE IS unexpected

stock NOUN

1 *a stock of fuel   a stock of jokes*
▶ supply, store, hoard, reserve, quantity, cache, fund
2 *During winter the stock is kept in sheds*
▶ livestock, farm animals, cattle, beasts
3 *The shop will be closed for a day to review its stock.*
▶ goods, merchandise, wares, commodities
4 *He is descended from Italian stock.*
▶ descent, ancestry, origins, parentage, pedigree, heritage

stock VERB

The corner shop stocks cat food.
▶ sell, supply, keep, keep in stock, have, market, handle, provide

stocky ADJECTIVE

a short stocky man
▶ sturdy, thickset, heavily built, solid, squat, dumpy
AN OPPOSITE IS skinny

stodgy ADJECTIVE

1 *a rich stodgy pudding*
▶ starchy, indigestible, heavy, lumpy, soggy, solid, filling
AN OPPOSITE IS light
2 *a stodgy story about his childhood*
▶ boring, dull, tedious, turgid, unexciting, unimaginative, uninteresting, stuffy
OPPOSITES ARE lively, exciting

stoical ADJECTIVE

Her mother had been stoical all through these troubled years.
▶ patient, long-suffering, uncomplaining, philosophical, resigned, calm, dispassionate
OPPOSITES ARE excitable, anxious

stolid ADJECTIVE

a stolid, red-faced clergyman
▶ impassive, unemotional, calm, placid, dull, tedious
OPPOSITES ARE lively, emotional

stomach NOUN

I was hungry and my stomach started to rumble.
▶ gut, belly, abdomen, (*more informal*) tummy
RELATED ADJECTIVE gastric

stomach VERB

He had taken all the criticism he could stomach for one day.
▶ stand, bear, take, tolerate, endure

stone NOUN

1 *A gang threw stones.*
▶ rock, pebble, boulder
2 *a ring with a bright red stone*
▶ gem, gemstone, jewel
3 *A memorial stone stood by the grave.*
▶ gravestone, headstone, tombstone, tablet

stony ADJECTIVE

1 *a stony path*
▶ rocky, pebbly, rough, shingly
2 *a stony silence*
▶ unfriendly, cold, chilly, frosty, icy, hostile, stern, severe, unfeeling, heartless
AN OPPOSITE IS friendly

stoop VERB

1 *Fred stooped to pick up the dog.*
▶ crouch, bend, kneel, lean, squat, bow, duck
2 *I would never stoop to accepting such an idea.*
▶ lower yourself, sink, descend, condescend, deign

stop VERB

1 *measures taken to stop tax fraud*
▶ check, prevent, thwart, frustrate, reduce, put and end to, put a stop to
OPPOSITES ARE start, encourage

2 *He wanted to stop smoking.*
▶ give up, discontinue, cease, desist from, refrain from, quit
OPPOSITES ARE begin, start, resume

3 *The bus stopped near the corner.*
▶ halt, come to a stop, come to a halt, pull up, draw up, pull in, come to rest

4 *He tried to stop her leaving the house.*
▶ prevent, intercept, hinder, obstruct, bar

5 *a special dressing to stop the escape of blood*
▶ stem, staunch, check, restrict, block, arrest

stop NOUN

1 *Business came to a stop for the day.*
▶ halt, end, finish, standstill, conclusion, stoppage, cessation

2 *They had a short stop at the motorway services.*
▶ break, pause, stopover, rest

stoppage NOUN

1 *the stoppage of livestock exports*
▶ stopping, halting, cessation, termination, discontinuation, interruption

2 *a three-day stoppage by baggage handlers*
▶ strike, shutdown, walkout, closure

stopper NOUN

a bottle with a stopper
▶ cork, plug, bung

store NOUN

1 *a store of food*
▶ supply, stock, hoard, reserve, quantity, cache, fund

2 *the coal store*
▶ storeroom, storehouse, repository, depository

3 *a DIY store*
▶ shop, outlet, retail business, retailers, supermarket, mart

store VERB

a place to store food for the winter
▶ stow, keep, save, put aside, hoard, accumulate, amass, lay by, deposit, (*more informal*) stash

storey NOUN

an apartment on the third storey
▶ floor, level, stage, tier

storm NOUN

1 *A storm blew up out at sea.*
▶ tempest, gale, squall, hurricane, typhoon, deluge

2 *a storm of protest*
▶ outburst, outcry, uproar, clamour, commotion, furore

storm VERB

1 *Police decided to storm the building.*
▶ attack, assault, rush, charge

2 *He stormed out in a rage.*
▶ march, stomp, stalk, flounce

stormy ADJECTIVE

1 *The weather was wet and stormy.*
▶ blustery, squally, tempestuous, turbulent, gusty, wild
AN OPPOSITE IS calm

2 *a stormy relationship*
▶ volatile, passionate, violent, intense

story NOUN

1 *the dramatic story of a rescue at sea* *What happened that night turned out to be a long story.*
▶ tale, account, narrative, history, yarn, (*more informal*) spiel

2 *a novel with a gripping story*
▶ plot, storyline, scenario

3 *She read the newspaper stories.*
▶ news item, report, article, feature, piece

NAMES FOR TYPES OF STORY

adventure story, bedtime story, children's story, cliffhanger (exciting end to each part), crime story, detective story, epic, fable, fairy story or fairy tale, fantasy, folk story or folk tale, ghost story, gothic novel (with horror and mystery), historical novel (set in the past), legend, mystery, myth, novel, parable, romance, saga, science fiction, short story, thriller, (*informal*) whodunnit.

stout ADJECTIVE

1 *You'll need a stout pair of boots.*
▶ strong, sturdy, substantial, robust, solid, thick, tough, reliable, sound
AN OPPOSITE IS flimsy

2 *The small stout man marched on ahead.*
▶ fat, plump, stocky, portly, beefy, bulky, burly, chubby, heavy, tubby, well-built
OPPOSITES ARE thin, slender

3 *The defenders put up a stout resistance.*
▶ brave, courageous, determined, spirited, valiant, strong, forceful, staunch, resolute, firm
AN OPPOSITE IS feeble

stow VERB

He left her to stow the shopping in the fridge.
▶ store, load, put, stack, (*more informal*) stuff, (*more informal*) stash

straight ADJECTIVE

1 *They were driving along a straight stretch of road*
▶ direct, smooth, undeviating, unswerving
OPPOSITES ARE winding, crooked

2 *I'll make the room straight for our visitors.*
▶ tidy, neat, orderly, shipshape, organized, right
AN OPPOSITE IS untidy

3 *They have staged something of a comeback with three straight victories.*
▶ consecutive, continuous, unbroken, uninterrupted, non-stop

4 *John is a straight character and very much his own man.* *I'll give you a straight answer if I can.*
▶ honest, direct, frank, straightforward
AN OPPOSITE IS evasive

straight ADVERB

We would be walking straight into a trap, She looked straight into his face.
▶ directly, squarely, plumb, *(more informal)* slap bang

straight away *He went to see her straight away when he got the news.*
▶ at once, directly, immediately, instantly, now, without delay

straighten VERB

Rick straightened his tie.
▶ adjust, arrange, put straight, neaten, order

straighten out *It will take a while to straighten out all the confusion.*
▶ sort out, put right, settle, disentangle, make straight, clear up, tidy, unbend, untwist

straightforward ADJECTIVE

1 *It is hard to resist one straightforward conclusion.*
▶ plain, simple, direct, easy, intelligible, lucid, open, straight, uncomplicated
2 *These people seem straightforward enough.*
▶ honest, genuine, sincere, forthright, truthful, frank, candid
AN OPPOSITE IS devious

strain VERB

1 *The dog strained at its leash.*
▶ tug, pull, stretch, haul, tighten
2 *Martha strained to hear but heard only faint sounds.*
▶ struggle, strive, make an effort, endeavour, exert yourself, attempt, try
3 *Try not to strain yourself.*
▶ weaken, wear out, exhaust, tire out, weary
4 *She had strained a muscle in the last race.*
▶ pull, sprain, twist, wrench, rick, damage, hurt, injure
5 *Strain the liquid to remove impurities.*
▶ sieve, sift, filter, separate

strain NOUN

the strain of doing jobs for which they are unsuited
▶ stress, pressure, tension, worry, anxiety, burden, difficulty, effort

strained ADJECTIVE

the strained relations between Russia and Japan, Her strained face.
▶ tense, awkward, uneasy, fraught, uncomfortable, troubled
AN OPPOSITE IS relaxed

strand NOUN

Sibyl frowned, absent-mindedly twirling a strand of hair round her fingers.
▶ fibre, filament, string, thread, wire

stranded ADJECTIVE

1 *marks left by jellyfish stranded on the beach*
▶ grounded, run aground, marooned, beached
2 *The waiting rooms were filled with stranded passengers.*
▶ helpless, abandoned, deserted, forsaken, lost

strange ADJECTIVE

1 *I heard a strange noise outside.*
▶ funny, odd, unusual, weird, peculiar, curious, extraordinary, unexplained
AN OPPOSITE IS ordinary
2 *They wear strange clothes.*
▶ weird, eccentric, bizarre, unconventional, idiosyncratic, *(more informal)* oddball, *(more informal)* wacky
AN OPPOSITE IS normal
3 *He found it hard to get to sleep in a strange house.*
▶ unfamiliar, unknown, new, alien
AN OPPOSITE IS familiar
4 *She began to feel a little strange and went to the bathroom.*
▶ unwell, ill, sick, poorly, indisposed, *(more informal)* funny
AN OPPOSITE IS well

stranger NOUN

They were strangers in the town.
▶ newcomer, outsider, visitor, alien, foreigner, guest

strangle VERB

1 *The victim had been strangled and left in a ditch.*
▶ throttle, asphyxiate, choke, suffocate, strangulate
2 *She strangled a cry of alarm.*
▶ suppress, smother, stifle, restrain, choke back

strap NOUN

The package was tied with straps.
▶ thong, tie, belt, cord

strap VERB

He strapped the bag to his bicycle.
▶ fasten, secure, tie, bind, lash

strapping ADJECTIVE

Three strapping men arrived to help.
▶ strong, sturdy, big, brawny, well-built, muscular

strategy NOUN

a highly effective political strategy
▶ plan, policy, scheme, approach, programme, procedure, design

stray VERB

1 *The aircraft had strayed into unauthorized airspace*
▶ wander, drift, roam, meander
2 *We are rather straying from the main point.*
▶ digress, diverge, drift, wander, deviate, be sidetracked

stray ADJECTIVE

1 *A stray cat came into the kitchen.*
▶ lost, strayed, homeless, abandoned
2 *Stray images wandered into her mind.*
▶ random, chance, haphazard, casual, odd, freak

streak NOUN

1 *His hair had several streaks of white.*
▶ strip, stripe, vein, band, line, smear, stain
2 *She admits to having a competitive streak in her.*
▶ element, trace, component

streak VERB

1 *Their dirty faces were streaked with tears.*
▶ stain, smear, smudge, daub
2 *Huge lorries streaked past him.*
▶ rush, speed, tear, hurtle, flash, zoom, whistle

streaky ADJECTIVE

The windows were streaky from the rain
▶ smeary, smudged, streaked, lined, stripy, veined

stream NOUN

1 *a mountain stream*
▶ brook, burn, beck, rill, river, rivulet, watercourse, channel
2 *a stream of water*
▶ jet, flow, rush, gush, surge, spurt, spout
3 *a steady stream of visitors*
▶ series, succession, string, flood, torrent

stream VERB

Rain streamed through the hole
▶ flow, pour, gush, surge, spurt, flood

streamer NOUN

Streamers hung from the buildings.
▶ pennant, pennon, ribbon, banner, flag

streamlined ADJECTIVE

1 *a streamlined car*
▶ aerodynamic, sleek, smooth, graceful
AN OPPOSITE IS air-resistant
2 *the streamlined image of the organization*
▶ smooth-running, efficient, slick, well-organized

street NOUN

The streets are deserted at this time of night.
▶ road, avenue, boulevard, thoroughfare

strength NOUN

1 *Physical strength is important.*
▶ power, brawn, muscle, toughness, sturdiness, robustness, vigour, might
AN OPPOSITE IS weakness
2 *She has enormous strength of character.*
▶ courage, firmness, resolution, spirit, commitment
AN OPPOSITE IS feebleness

strengthen VERB

1 *The exercises will help strengthen your back.*
▶ build up, fortify, toughen, make stronger, harden, tone up
AN OPPOSITE IS weaken
2 *Stone columns strengthen the massive walls.*
▶ support, reinforce, bolster, brace, buttress, prop up
3 *The police want to strengthen their links with the local communities.*
▶ reinforce, consolidate, substantiate, bolster, fortify, enhance, back up, increase, invigorate
AN OPPOSITE IS undermine

strenuous ADJECTIVE

1 *Success was the result of three years' strenuous work.*
▶ hard, tough, demanding, arduous, taxing, gruelling, exhausting
2 *He has made strenuous efforts to get to know the area.*
▶ determined, vigorous, resolute, energetic, active, forceful

stress NOUN

1 *She was obviously under a lot of stress.*
▶ anxiety, difficulty, hardship, pressure, strain, tension, trauma, worry
2 *We need to lay greater stress on accuracy.*
▶ emphasis, accent, beat, importance, weight

stress VERB

I stressed the importance of a balanced diet.
▶ emphasize, accentuate, assert, insist on, lay stress on, put the stress on, repeat, underline

stressful ADJECTIVE

She'd had an extremely stressful day.
▶ anxious, difficult, tense, traumatic, worrying
AN OPPOSITE IS easy

stretch NOUN

1 *a five-hour stretch on duty*
▶ spell, stint, period, run, term, time
2 *a fine stretch of moorland*
▶ expanse, sweep, spread, tract, area

stretch VERB

1 *He stretched the rubber until it snapped.*
▶ pull, strain, tighten, extend, lengthen
AN OPPOSITE IS compress
2 *The road stretched into the distance*
▶ extend, continue, spread
3 **stretch to** *My money won't stretch to a two-week holiday.*
▶ be enough for, cover, reach to
stretch out *She stretched out on a couch.*
▶ recline, lean back, lie down, sprawl, relax

strict ADJECTIVE

1 *Their parents could be too strict at times.*
▶ severe, stern, harsh, authoritarian, rigid, austere
AN OPPOSITE IS lenient
2 *strict controls on public spending*
▶ tough, stringent, rigorous, severe, extreme
AN OPPOSITE IS liberal
3 *a strict interpretation of the rule*
▶ exact, precise, scrupulous, rigid, rigorous
AN OPPOSITE IS loose

strident ADJECTIVE

a strident voice
▶ harsh, shrill, jarring, grating, raucous, rasping, screeching, loud
OPPOSITES ARE soft, quiet

strife NOUN
years of strife in the manufacturing industries
▶ conflict, discord, friction, dissension, wrangling, controversy

strike NOUN
The dispute ended in a prolonged strike.
▶ stoppage, withdrawal of labour, industrial action, work-to-rule, walkout

strike VERB
1 *I struck my head on the low ceiling.*
▶ hit, knock, bump, smack, thump
2 *The commandos struck without warning*
▶ attack, raid, pounce
3 *The two sides struck a deal at the last moment.*
▶ agree, agree on, reach, endorse, settle on, sign
4 (*informal*) *The workforce threatened to strike.*
▶ down tools, stop work, come out, take industrial action, withdraw your labour

striking ADJECTIVE
She has a striking resemblance to her sister.
▶ noticeable, conspicuous, outstanding, prominent, distinctive, impressive, memorable, obvious, stunning, telling, unmistakable
AN OPPOSITE IS inconspicuous

string NOUN
1 *a piece of string*
▶ twine, cord, line, rope
2 *a string of vehicles*
▶ row, file, line, series, succession, procession, queue
3 *a string of misfortunes*
▶ series, sequence, chain, progression

string VERB
Lights had been strung across the road.
▶ hang, link, thread, connect, join, line up

stringent ADJECTIVE
stringent rules
▶ strict, firm, severe, harsh, rigorous, binding
AN OPPOSITE IS lenient

strip NOUN
1 *a strip of paper   a narrow strip of land*
▶ slip, band, ribbon, belt, sliver, narrow piece, stripe, swathe, lath, line, shred, slat
2 *The team were sporting a new strip.*
▶ outfit, kit

strip VERB
1 *He stripped and climbed into the shower.*
▶ undress, take off your clothes, remove your clothes, (*more informal*) peel off
2 *Thieves had completely stripped the house.*
▶ empty, clear out, ransack, loot, pillage, burgle
strip down *Mechanics were busy stripping down the engine*
▶ dismantle, take to pieces, take apart, disassemble
strip off *First you must strip off the old paint.*
▶ peel off, remove, take off, scrape off, flake off

stripe NOUN
tracksuit bottoms with a stripe down the side
▶ line, strip, band, bar, flash

striped ADJECTIVE
a striped blue and white shirt
▶ lined, banded, stripy, barred, streaky

strive VERB
We strive to please.
▶ try, attempt, endeavour, aim, aspire, struggle, strain

stroke NOUN
1 *a swift stroke of the axe*
▶ blow, swipe, hit, knock
2 *a stroke of genius*
▶ feat, accomplishment, achievement, attainment
3 *She gave the cat a gentle stroke.*
▶ pat, rub, caress

stroke VERB
You can stroke the dog if you like.
▶ pat, caress, fondle, touch, brush, pass your hand over, pet

stroll VERB
They strolled together round the grounds.
▶ wander, saunter, amble, meander, ramble, dawdle

stroll NOUN
There was time for a stroll in the woods.
▶ walk, saunter, amble, ramble, turn

---

strong ADJECTIVE This word is often overused. Here are some alternatives:
1 *a strong lad of nineteen*
▶ tough, muscular, powerful, brawny, well built, strapping, burly
OPPOSITES ARE weak, puny
2 *The door needs a strong lock*
▶ robust, sturdy, firm, durable, sound, secure
AN OPPOSITE IS weak
3 *She had a strong interest in what they were doing.*
▶ keen, eager, deep, dedicated, passionate, fervent, zealous
AN OPPOSITE IS feeble
4 *a cup of strong coffee*
▶ highly flavoured, pungent, piquant
AN OPPOSITE IS weak
5 *We have a strong case to make.*
▶ convincing, forceful, persuasive, cogent, effective
OPPOSITES ARE weak, unconvincing

---

stronghold NOUN
The army advanced on the enemy stronghold.
▶ fortress, fort, castle, citadel, keep, bastion

stroppy ADJECTIVE
(*informal*) *I hope he doesn't get stroppy with us.*
▶ bad-tempered, irritable, grumpy, cross, peevish, truculent, sulky

structure NOUN
a tall structure of five storeys
▶ construction, edifice, building, erection, pile

structure VERB
The classes are carefully structured to cater for all levels of ability.
▶ organize, arrange, design, shape, construct, put together

struggle VERB
1 *We struggled to get free.*
▶ work hard, strive, strain, toil, try, endeavour, exert yourself, labour, wrestle, make an effort, move violently, wriggle about, writhe about
2 *They had to struggle with a determined enemy.*
▶ fight, contend, battle, grapple, wrestle, vie
3 *She struggled over the wet rocks.*
▶ scramble, flounder, stumble, labour

struggle NOUN
1 *It was a struggle to finish the work in time.*
▶ effort, challenge, difficulty, endeavour, exertion, labour, problem
2 *The police arrested the gang without a struggle*
▶ fight, scuffle, brawl, fracas, affray

stub NOUN
1 *a cigarette stub*
▶ butt, end, (*more informal*) dog-end
2 *the stub of a ticket*
▶ counterfoil, slip

stubborn ADJECTIVE
He was too stubborn to admit he was wrong.
▶ obstinate, obdurate, strong-willed, headstrong, wilful, pig-headed
OPPOSITES ARE compliant, yielding

stuck ADJECTIVE
1 *The door was stuck and wouldn't open.*
▶ jammed, fixed, fast, immovable
2 *He admitted he was stuck and needed help.*
▶ baffled, beaten, at a loss, bewildered, (*more informal*) stumped

stuck-up ADJECTIVE
a bunch of stuck-up businessmen
▶ arrogant, conceited, snobbish, snobby, haughty, supercilious, overweening, (*more informal*) snooty, (*more informal*) uppish, (*more informal*) toffee-nosed

student NOUN
1 *a student at the university*
▶ undergraduate, postgraduate, scholar
2 *a student at the local school*
▶ pupil, schoolboy or schoolgirl, schoolchild, scholar
3 *a nursing student*
▶ learner, novice, trainee

studio NOUN
the artist's studio
▶ workroom, workshop, atelier

studious ADJECTIVE
a studious young pupil
▶ scholarly, serious-minded, hard-working, diligent, industrious, thoughtful, intellectual, academic, bookish, brainy, earnest

study NOUN
1 *two years of study in the sixth form*
▶ learning, education, schooling, reading, academic work, (*informal*) cramming
2 *a study of the causes of conflict*
▶ investigation (into), inquiry (into), survey, examination, research (into)
3 *The study deals with all aspects of the subject.*
▶ essay, article, report, review

study VERB
1 *She studied the information carefully.*
▶ examine, analyse, survey, consider, investigate, inspect, scrutinize, look into, peruse
2 *They both wanted to study languages.*
▶ learn, work at, be taught, read
3 *Alan had studied hard at school.*
▶ work, apply yourself

stuff NOUN
1 *There was some wet stuff on the floor.*
▶ matter, substance
2 *The skirt was made of a tough lightweight stuff.*
▶ material, fabric, cloth, textile
3 *I'll put all my stuff in a suitcase.*
▶ belongings, effects, possessions, things, (*more informal*) gear

stuff VERB
1 *I stuffed everything in a drawer.*
▶ pack, push, cram, ram, shove, squeeze, force, jam
2 *Use foam to stuff the cushions.*
▶ fill, pad, pack
stuff yourself *They had been stuffing themselves all day and were no longer hungry.*
▶ gorge, guzzle, cram, overindulge, eat

stuffing NOUN
The stuffing was coming out of the chair.
▶ padding, filling, wadding, quilting

stuffy ADJECTIVE
1 *a stuffy atmosphere*
▶ airless, close, muggy, sultry, musty, stifling, oppressive, unventilated
AN OPPOSITE IS airy
2 *a stuffy lecture on citizenship*
▶ dull, boring, staid, prim, strait-laced, pompous, conventional, stodgy
AN OPPOSITE IS informal

a b c d e f g h i j k l m n o p q r **s** t u v w x y z

stumble VERB

1 *She stumbled on a loose paving stone.*
▶ trip, totter, tumble, lose your balance

2 *He stumbled back to his house.*
▶ stagger, totter, lumber, lurch, blunder, bumble, hobble

3 *The speaker stumbled through the rest of the speech.*
▶ stammer, stutter, falter, flounder, hesitate

stump VERB

One of the questions stumped us.
▶ baffle, puzzle, perplex, mystify, bewilder, outwit, confound, confuse, defeat, (*more informal*) flummox

stun VERB

1 *A hard blow had stunned him.*
▶ daze, knock out, knock senseless, make unconscious

2 *The election results stunned everyone.*
▶ amaze, astonish, astound, stagger, stupefy, shock, dumbfound, flabbergast, bewilder, confound

stunning ADJECTIVE

1 *a stunning victory*
▶ remarkable, sensational, spectacular, extraordinary, staggering, incredible

2 *She looked stunning in a red dress.*
▶ beautiful, dazzling, gorgeous, ravishing, sensational, lovely
AN OPPOSITE IS unattractive

stunt NOUN

a circus stunt
▶ trick, exploit, feat, turn, performance

stunt VERB

a disease that can stunt growth
▶ inhibit, hamper, impede, retard, restrict

stupendous ADJECTIVE

a stupendous achievement
▶ amazing, astounding, astonishing, extraordinary, remarkable, wonderful, staggering, breathtaking, (*more informal*) mind-boggling
AN OPPOSITE IS ordinary

stupid ADJECTIVE

1 *They are not as stupid as they seem.*
▶ foolish, silly, foolhardy, unintelligent, dim-witted, half-witted, empty-headed, vacuous, dim, dumb, thick
OPPOSITES ARE intelligent, wise

2 *It was a stupid thing to do.*
▶ foolish, silly, unwise, senseless, mindless, idiotic, crass, absurd, ridiculous, ludicrous
AN OPPOSITE IS sensible

stupidity NOUN

Their stupidity had been breathtaking.
▶ foolishness, folly, silliness, irresponsibility, ineptitude, idiocy
OPPOSITES ARE wisdom, intelligence

stupor NOUN

He lay slumped in a drunken stupor
▶ daze, lethargy, coma, trance, state of insensibility, torpor, shock, oblivion

sturdy ADJECTIVE

1 *a sturdy and handsome young man*
▶ strong, strapping, big, brawny, well-built, muscular
AN OPPOSITE IS weak

2 *He packed a sturdy pair of shoes for the walk.*
▶ stout, strong, substantial, robust, solid, thick, tough, reliable, sound
AN OPPOSITE IS flimsy

stutter VERB

He stuttered over the next word.
▶ stammer, stumble, falter, hesitate

style NOUN

1 *an old-fashioned style of writing*
▶ manner, technique, mode, method, fashion, tone, way

2 *the latest styles in the fashion magazines*
▶ design, pattern, fashion, mode, vogue, cut, taste

3 *She always dresses with style.*
▶ elegance, refinement, flair, panache, stylishness, smartness, sophistication, refinement, taste

stylish ADJECTIVE

stylish clothes
▶ fashionable, elegant, chic, modish, trendy, snappy, smart, (*more informal*) snazzy
OPPOSITES ARE unfashionable, dowdy

suave ADJECTIVE

a suave man of about forty
▶ charming, sophisticated, urbane, debonair, refined, polished, civilized
OPPOSITES ARE unsophisticated, crude

subconscious ADJECTIVE

Dreams reflect a person's subconscious desires
▶ subliminal, unacknowledged, unconscious, inner, hidden, intuitive, repressed
AN OPPOSITE IS conscious

subdue VERB

1 *The army quickly subdued all opposition.*
▶ overcome, defeat, quell, suppress, crush, overpower

2 *It was difficult to subdue their excitement.*
▶ restrain, suppress, check, curb, repress, hold back, keep under, quieten

subdued ADJECTIVE

1 *Sylvie was in a subdued mood.*
▶ serious, sombre, downcast, restrained, silent, sober, solemn, depressed, grave, reflective, thoughtful
AN OPPOSITE IS lively

2 *They spoke in subdued tones.*
▶ hushed, muted, quiet, soft, low, faint, calm
AN OPPOSITE IS loud

subject NOUN

1 *a British subject*
▶ citizen, national, passport-holder
2 *a subject for discussion*
▶ theme, topic, affair, business, issue, matter, point, question
3 *a subject of study*
▶ discipline, field, branch, course, area

subject ADJECTIVE

1 *subject nations*
▶ dependent, subjugated, subservient, tributary
AN OPPOSITE IS independent
2 *The trains are subject to constant delays.*
▶ liable, prone, disposed, vulnerable
3 **subject to** *The decision is subject to approval by the board.*
▶ dependent on, contingent on, conditional on

subject VERB

subject to *Thye have been subjected to a lot of verbal abuse.*
▶ expose to, lay open, put through

subjective ADJECTIVE

It is difficult to build a theory on such subjective criteria.
▶ biased, prejudiced, personal, individual, intuitive, idiosyncratic
OPPOSITES ARE objective, unbiased

sublime ADJECTIVE

Mozart's sublime masterpiece
▶ exalted, elevated, noble, awesome, majestic, supreme, lofty, spiritual, transcendent
OPPOSITES ARE ordinary, lowly

submerge VERB

1 *The utter darkness submerged them.*
▶ inundate, overwhelm, immerse, engulf, flood, swamp, cover, drown
2 *Submerge the vegetables in cold water.*
▶ dip, plunge, immerse, dunk
3 *The submarine had no time to submerge*
▶ dive, go down

submission NOUN

1 *Complete submission was the key point of women in the eighteen-forties.*
▶ compliance, submissiveness, acquiescence, passivity, docility, meekness
2 *The enemy's submission was only a matter of time.*
▶ surrender, capitulation, defeat
3 *There was an alternative submission that the money had been paid under duress.*
▶ claim, contention, proposal, argument, suggestion, theory

submissive ADJECTIVE

Be polite, but not submissive.
▶ meek, passive, acquiescent, compliant, servile, deferential, ingratiating, subservient, docile, uncomplaining, humble
OPPOSITES ARE domineering, assertive

submit VERB

1 *She had only submitted under duress.*
▶ give in, yield, accede, back down, surrender, capitulate, relent, succumb, comply, (more informal) knuckle under
2 *They submitted a revised version of their plan. The union agreed to submit their disagreement to arbitration.*
▶ present, offer, tender, put forward, suggest, propose
3 **submit to** *We refuse to submit to political pressure. Applicants have to submit to a full medical examination.*
▶ accept, agree to, succumb to, undergo, tolerate, endure, comply with, conform to, defer to, bow to, keep to, obey

subordinate ADJECTIVE

It would not be easy to accept a subordinate role.
▶ inferior, lower, lesser, secondary, subservient, subsidiary, minor, junior

subordinate NOUN

There stood the manager with her three subordinates.
▶ assistant, junior, inferior, dependant, employee, (more informal) underling
AN OPPOSITE IS superior

subscribe VERB

1 **subscribe to** *There are so many good causes to subscribe to.*
▶ contribute to, support, donate to, give to
2 **subscribe to** *How many magazines do they subscribe to?*
▶ buy regularly, pay a subscription to, take, read
3 **subscribe to** *I don't subscribe to that view at all.*
▶ agree with, accept, endorse, support, approve of, believe in, advocate, give your blessing to

subsequent ADJECTIVE

She needed a lot of help during the subsequent months.
▶ following, ensuing, succeeding, later, next
AN OPPOSITE IS previous

subside VERB

1 *We'd better wait for the storm to subside.*
▶ die down, abate, diminish, moderate, slacken, quieten, ease up, let up
AN OPPOSITE IS intensify
2 *The flood waters had begun to subside.*
▶ recede, fall back, ebb
3 *Paul subsided into a chair.*
▶ collapse, sink, settle, drop
AN OPPOSITE IS rise

subsidiary ADJECTIVE

Money should be of subsidiary importance.
▶ secondary, subordinate, lesser, minor, ancillary, supplementary

subsidize VERB
We do not believe that we should subsidize international rail services.
▶ finance, fund, sponsor, support, back, promote, underwrite

subsidy NOUN
The corporation needed an even bigger subsidy from public funds.
▶ grant, backing, financial help, sponsorship, support

subsistence NOUN
1 *people living on the margins of subsistence*
▶ survival, existence, livelihood, sustenance, nourishment
2 *The grant was to cover travel and subsistence*
▶ maintenance, upkeep, livelihood

substance NOUN
1 *a strange sticky substance*
▶ material, matter, stuff, chemical
2 *The substance of the story is not hard to follow.*
▶ essence, gist, theme, meaning, content, subject-matter
3 *We may wonder how much substance there was in many of the accusations.*
▶ meaning, force, weight, significance

substandard ADJECTIVE
low income, substandard housing, and high crime rates
▶ inferior, poor, inadequate, shoddy, below par, disappointing, unworthy
AN OPPOSITE IS superior

substantial ADJECTIVE
1 *a substantial building*
▶ strong, sturdy, hefty, solid, well-made, durable, sound
AN OPPOSITE IS flimsy
2 *If you make substantial improvements to your home they might increase its value.*
▶ significant, sizeable, worthwhile, big, considerable, generous, large
AN OPPOSITE IS trivial

substitute ADJECTIVE
a substitute teacher
▶ acting, replacement, deputy, relief, reserve, standby, surrogate, temporary

substitute NOUN
1 *There is no substitute for practical experience.*
▶ replacement, alternative (to)
2 *Nurses can often be effective substitutes for doctors.*
▶ alternative, replacement, stand-in, proxy, surrogate

substitute VERB
1 *You can substitute yoghurt for cream cheese in this recipe.*
▶ change, exchange, interchange, swop, switch, replace
USAGE If you use *replace*, you have to say *You can replace cream cheese with yoghurt.*

2 *Maggie agreed to substitute for her boss for a few days.*
▶ deputize, stand in, act as a substitute

subterfuge NOUN
Journalists should not use subterfuge to gain admission to hospitals.
▶ trickery, deception, deviousness, duplicity, evasion, dishonesty

subtle ADJECTIVE
1 *Add a subtle yet striking change to your hair*
▶ mild, slight, faint, delicate, elusive, unobtrusive
2 *a subtle hint*
▶ gentle, tactful, indirect, understated
AN OPPOSITE IS tactless
3 *subtle colours*
▶ muted, subdued, delicate, faint, pale
AN OPPOSITE IS lurid
4 *a subtle distinction*
▶ fine, nice, precise, tenuous
AN OPPOSITE IS crude

subtract VERB
Half a pint of skimmed milk supplies 100 calories, which must be subtracted from your daily total.
▶ deduct, take away, remove, debit
AN OPPOSITE IS add

suburban ADJECTIVE
The couple disappeared from their suburban house about two weeks ago.
▶ residential, outlying, provincial, outer

suburbs NOUN
an apartment in the southern suburbs of Rome
▶ residential area, outskirts, fringes, outer areas, suburbia

subversive ADJECTIVE
Why isn't she in prison for her subversive activities?
▶ revolutionary, seditious, disruptive, treacherous, inflammatory, traitorous, undermining, unsettling
AN OPPOSITE IS loyal

subvert VERB
The country saw him as a liberal subverting the president's conservative instincts.
▶ undermine, destabilize, disrupt, corrupt, destroy, overthrow, challenge, pervert

succeed VERB
1 *For some people, happiness is to compete and succeed no matter how.*
▶ be successful, do well, prosper, thrive, flourish, triumph, be victorious, accomplish your objective, (*more informal*) get on, (*more informal*) make it
2 *The scheme might still succeed.*
▶ be effective, produce results, work, (*more informal*) catch on
AN OPPOSITE IS fail
3 *Kim's ambition to succeed Roh as President*
▶ replace, take the place of, take over from, supersede, come after, follow
AN OPPOSITE IS precede

succeeding ADJECTIVE
This trend continued in succeeding years.
▶ subsequent, successive, following, ensuing, later, future, coming, next

success NOUN
1 *The criteria for judging success would not be the same for all pupils.*
▶ achievement, accomplishment, attainment, fame, prosperity
AN OPPOSITE IS failure
2 *Links with industry are essential for the success of the programme.*
▶ effectiveness, successful outcome, completion
OPPOSITES ARE failure, collapse
3 *(informal) Her first novel was an instant success.*
▶ triumph, hit, sensation, victory, *(more informal)* winner
OPPOSITES ARE failure, disaster
4 *This performance alone might well have made him a success.*
▶ celebrity, star, big name, household name, sensation

successful ADJECTIVE
1 *Blazer, the successful menswear chain*
▶ thriving, flourishing, prosperous, effective, profitable, fruitful, lucrative, productive, profit-making
OPPOSITES ARE unsuccessful, unprofitable
2 *He had been a successful prize fighter at the time. This wooden aeroplane was one of the most successful aircraft of all time.*
▶ victorious, triumphant, winning, effective
OPPOSITES ARE unsuccessful, ineffective

succession NOUN
He drifted into a succession of menial jobs.
▶ series, sequence, string, chain, run, line, cycle, course, progression

successive ADJECTIVE
Thousands were forced into exile by successive military governments.
▶ consecutive, succeeding, following

succinct ADJECTIVE
He gave a succinct judgement about what had happened.
▶ concise, short, brief, compact, condensed, terse, pithy

succulent ADJECTIVE
a vine that produces succulent black grapes
▶ juicy, fleshy, luscious, moist, mouth-watering, rich

succumb VERB
We may succumb to flattery because it makes us feel good.
▶ yield, surrender, capitulate, submit, give way, give in
OPPOSITES ARE resist, overcome

suck VERB
1 *The boys sat sucking their drinks.*
▶ sip, sup, slurp, drink
2 *Extra roads can suck people away from buses and trains.*
▶ draw, entice, attract, pull
suck up *He fetched a cloth to suck up the water.*
▶ soak up, absorb, draw up, pull up
suck up to *(informal) They suck up to him, hanging on his every word.*
▶ flatter, grovel to, kowtow to, behave obsequiously towards

sudden ADJECTIVE
Lydia emitted a sudden giggle. a sudden increase in student numbers
▶ unexpected, startling, abrupt, sharp, unforeseen, unlooked for, impulsive, quick, rash
OPPOSITES ARE expected, gradual

suds NOUN
The basin was full of suds.
▶ lather, foam, froth, bubbles, soapsuds

sue VERB
He could sue the railway company for negligence.
▶ take to court, take legal action against, persecute

suffer VERB
1 *She loved him too much to see him suffer.*
▶ feel pain, hurt, be in pain, be in distress
2 *England suffered a humiliating defeat.*
▶ experience, undergo, meet with, receive, be subjected to, sustain, encounter
3 *Dustin's relationship with Anne did suffer.*
▶ deteriorate, decline, be damaged, be impaired

suffering NOUN
Damage and suffering are inflicted on the population.
▶ hardship, distress, misery, anguish, pain, unhappiness, sorrow, grief

suffice VERB
Whatever you have in the freezer will suffice.
▶ be enough, be sufficient, be adequate, do, serve, satisfy

sufficient ADJECTIVE
There should be sufficient staff day and night.
▶ enough, adequate, satisfactory
OPPOSITES ARE insufficient, inadequate

suffocate VERB
She reacted violently, as if he was trying to suffocate her.
▶ asphyxiate, strangle, throttle, smother, stifle, choke

suggest VERB
1 *Connie suggested an outing to the lake.*
▶ propose, recommend, advise, propound, put forward, raise, advocate, moot, move
2 *The evidence suggests we could be right.*
▶ imply, indicate, hint, intimate, mean, signal

suggestion NOUN

1 *We have a few suggestions to consider.*
▶ recommendation, proposal, proposition, idea, plan
2 *There has been no suggestion of dishonesty.*
▶ hint, trace, suspicion, sign, implication, insinuation

suggestive ADJECTIVE

1 *a view suggestive of Tuscany*
▶ evocative, reminiscent, characteristic, expressive, typical
2 *suggestive remarks*
▶ indecent, improper, indelicate, immodest, unseemly, risqué

suit NOUN

He wore a dark suit with a cream shirt.
▶ outfit, set of clothes, ensemble, clothing

suit VERB

1 *credit terms to suit all pockets*
▶ satisfy, accommodate, be suitable for, please, gratify, fit
2 *Black doesn't really suit me.*
▶ look attractive on, look right on, become, flatter

suitable ADJECTIVE

1 *Would tomorrow afternoon be a suitable time?*
▶ convenient, appropriate, fitting, acceptable, satisfactory, apposite
AN OPPOSITE IS unsuitable
2 *a film that is considered suitable for all age groups*
▶ appropriate (to), suited (to), right, relevant (to)

sulk VERB

Dave was sulking in his room.
▶ mope, brood, be sullen, pout

sulky ADJECTIVE

A row of sulky faces greeted him.
▶ moody, sullen, surly, morose, glum, moping, pouting, disgruntled
AN OPPOSITE IS cheerful

sullen ADJECTIVE

1 *a sullen expression*
▶ sulky, moody, morose, glum, gloomy, surly, sour
AN OPPOSITE IS cheerful
2 *a sullen sky*
▶ dark, dull, gloomy, leaden, dismal, grey, sombre
OPPOSITES ARE bright, fine

sully VERB

He would not sully the family name with such behaviour.
▶ taint, defile, dirty, soil, tarnish, blemish, dishonour, disgrace

sultry ADJECTIVE

a hot sultry day in July
▶ humid, close, airless, muggy, stifling, stuffy, sticky, sweltering, oppressive
AN OPPOSITE IS cool

sum NOUN

1 *a large sum of money*
▶ amount, quantity

2 *a sum you can do in your head*
▶ calculation, problem
3 *These books were the sum of her life's work.*
▶ total, entirety, totality, sum total, whole, aggregate

sum up VERB

It took two days to present the case and ten minutes to sum it up.
▶ summarize, review, recapitulate, outline

summarize VERB

The ideas can be summarized very easily.
▶ sum up, outline, review, precis

summary NOUN

1 *There is a summary of the main arguments at the end of the article.*
▶ resumé, review, summing-up, summation, outline, recapitulation, abstract, digest
2 *a summary of a story*
▶ synopsis, precis, abridgement

summit NOUN

1 *This year thirty-two people reached the summit of Everest.*
▶ top, peak, crest, crown, apex, pinnacle
OPPOSITES ARE foot, bottom
2 *the summit of their success*
▶ high point, acme, culmination, apogee, zenith
AN OPPOSITE IS nadir

summon VERB

1 *Coleman was summoned to Washington for a final briefing.*
▶ send for, call, order, command, demand, invite
2 *The lawyers then summon a meeting.*
▶ call, convene, assemble, convoke, gather together, announce

sumptuous ADJECTIVE

Emily thought ruefully of the sumptuous meals she used to eat.
▶ lavish, luxurious, extravagant, splendid, magnificent, grand, gorgeous
AN OPPOSITE IS humble

sun NOUN

Enjoy the sun while you can.
▶ sunlight, sunshine
RELATED ADJECTIVE solar

sunbathe VERB

Jill was sunbathing on the beach.
▶ sun yourself, bask, get a tan

sunburnt ADJECTIVE

His neck and shoulders were sunburnt.
▶ burnt, inflamed, peeling, red, blistered
AN OPPOSITE IS pale

sundry ADJECTIVE

In London yesterday he addressed sundry gatherings.
▶ various, varied, assorted, miscellaneous, mixed, diverse, motley

sunken ADJECTIVE

1 *The Palace has a sunken garden and an orangery.*
▶ submerged, recessed

2 *He was tall and gaunt, with sunken eyes.*
▶ hollowed, haggard

sunny ADJECTIVE
1 *It will be a day of sunny spells and showers.*
▶ bright, clear, fine, cloudless, summery, sunlit
AN OPPOSITE IS dull
2 *There was rage beneath the sunny smile.*
▶ cheerful, happy, joyful, joyous, smiling, beaming, bright, jolly
OPPOSITES ARE miserable, gloomy

sunrise NOUN
A farmer's day begins at sunrise.
▶ dawn, daybreak, daylight, crack of dawn

sunset NOUN
Walk along the beach at sunset.
▶ dusk, twilight, sundown, evening, close of day, half-light, (*literary*) gloaming

super ADJECTIVE
There is a super kitchen with a traditional tiled stove.
▶ excellent, superb, superlative, first-class, first-rate, marvellous, magnificent, wonderful, splendid, fine, remarkable, (*more informal*) brilliant, (*more informal*) fantastic, (*more informal*) terrific, (*more informal*) awesome

superb ADJECTIVE
The large bay has a superb backdrop of mountains.
▶ excellent, superlative, marvellous, magnificent, wonderful, splendid, fine, remarkable, (*more informal*) fantastic, (*more informal*) awesome

supercilious ADJECTIVE
His manner was supercilious and he had a way of making you feel silly.
▶ arrogant, superior, condescending, patronizing, overbearing, haughty, pretentious, (*more informal*) snooty, (*more informal*) hoity-toity

superficial ADJECTIVE
1 *He sustained superficial injuries which soon disappeared. Time spent on repairing superficial damage is well worthwhile.*
▶ surface, exterior, external, slight, moderate
OPPOSITES ARE severe, deep
2 *These similarities are purely superficial.*
▶ apparent, cosmetic, slight, shallow, specious
OPPOSITES ARE significant, meaningful
3 *At a superficial level these categories appear to be the same.*
▶ shallow, surface
AN OPPOSITE IS deep
4 *It was no more than a superficial examination of the subject.*
▶ cursory, casual, perfunctory, desultory, hurried, lightweight
OPPOSITES ARE thorough, rigorous

superfluous ADJECTIVE
1 *Superfluous material can be trimmed from around the edges.*
▶ excess, surplus, spare, redundant, unwanted

2 *This is so obvious that at first sight it might seem superfluous to state it.*
▶ unnecessary, needless, pointless, gratuitous, redundant

superhuman ADJECTIVE
1 *Their madness gives them superhuman strength.*
▶ extraordinary, phenomenal, exceptional, immense, prodigious, herculean, heroic
AN OPPOSITE IS average
2 *The myths describe encounters with superhuman beings of all kinds.*
▶ divine, higher, metaphysical, supernatural
OPPOSITES ARE earthly, mundane

superior ADJECTIVE
1 *Lewis watched, aware of his superior status.*
▶ senior, higher, higher-level, higher-ranking, greater, more important
OPPOSITES ARE inferior, lower
2 *Superior rooms are all recently renovated. The Americans have superior technology.*
▶ first-class, first-rate, high-quality, top-quality, better, exclusive, choice, fine, select, surpassing
OPPOSITES ARE inferior, low-quality
3 *He found her cold and superior.*
▶ haughty, arrogant, disdainful, condescending, patronizing, supercilious, self-important, stuck-up, (*informal*) snooty, (*informal*) hoity-toity
OPPOSITES ARE modest, approachable

superiority NOUN
The professional troops soon proved their technical superiority over the poorly trained local forces.
▶ advantage, supremacy, dominance, predominance, ascendancy, pre-eminence, edge, lead
AN OPPOSITE IS inferiority

superlative ADJECTIVE
The mountains offer superlative climbing and trekking.
▶ excellent, magnificent, wonderful, marvellous, unsurpassed, unbeatable, unrivalled
OPPOSITES ARE poor, average

supernatural ADJECTIVE
Certain animals were thought to have supernatural powers
▶ paranormal, preternatural, unearthly, unnatural, abnormal, inexplicable, magical, metaphysical, miraculous, mysterious, mystic, occult, psychic
OPPOSITES ARE natural, normal

supersede VERB
Steel began to supersede iron in the 1880s.
▶ replace, supplant, take the place of, displace, oust, succeed

superstition NOUN
the old superstition that seagulls were the souls of dead sailors
▶ myth, superstitious belief, delusion, illusion, old wives' tale

s

superstitious ADJECTIVE
a haze of superstitious beliefs and practices
▶ irrational, mythical, traditional, unfounded, unprovable, groundless, illusory
OPPOSITES ARE rational, factual, scientific

supervise VERB
People are needed during the summer to supervise children and organize activities.
▶ oversee, watch over, superintend, be in charge of, be responsible for, direct, manage

supervision NOUN
These tasks should be carried out under the supervision of a senior member of staff.
▶ control, direction, oversight, surveillance, care, charge, oversight, management

supervisor NOUN
The housewife is her own supervisor.
▶ manager, director, overseer, superintendent, controller, boss

supplant VERB
the society which Marx believed would eventually supplant capitalism
▶ replace, supersede, take the place of, displace, oust, succeed

supple ADJECTIVE
1 *Regular exercise keeps the body supple.*
▶ lithe, nimble, agile, graceful, limber, lissom
OPPOSITES ARE stiff, unfit
2 *a strip of supple leather*
▶ flexible, pliable, pliant, soft
AN OPPOSITE IS rigid

supplement NOUN
1 *A supplement is payable for rooms with a sea view.*
▶ surcharge, additional payment, excess
2 *the newspaper's new travel supplement*
▶ insert, pull-out, addendum, addition

supplement VERB
the need to supplement the family income
▶ add to, top up, augment, increase, boost, enlarge, swell, complement, reinforce

supplementary ADJECTIVE
The answers may be followed up by supplementary questions.
▶ extra, additional, complementary, auxiliary, accompanying

supplier NOUN
This kit can be ordered from your usual supplier.
▶ dealer, retailer, seller, shopkeeper, vendor, wholesaler, provider

supply NOUN
1 *As a breeder, I give one week's supply of food with each puppy.*
▶ stock, store, quantity, amount, stockpile, reserve
2 **supplies** *Many people use their cars to buy a whole week's supplies.*
▶ provisions, stores, rations, materials, shopping, food, necessities

supply VERB
1 *studios set up to supply cheaply-made films*
▶ provide, produce, purvey, sell, contribute
2 *The reservoir supplies water to an area of about five hundred square miles.*
▶ serve, provide, furnish
3 *They were unable to supply us with what we needed.*
▶ equip, provide, furnish
4 *A supermarket that supplies all your needs.*
▶ provide, fulfil, fill

support NOUN
1 *The group offers emotional support to members in times of stress.*
▶ encouragement, solace, comfort, succour, relief, strength, friendship, protection
2 *The Arts Council eventually withdrew all financial support.*
▶ backing, funding, funds, aid, subsidy, donations, money
3 *The shelf was resting on three supports.*
▶ prop, brace, bracket, pillar, foundation

support VERB
1 *The walls were too weak to support the weight of the roof. He supported the old man over to his bed.*
▶ carry, bear, sustain, hold up, prop up, provide a support for, underpin
2 *She was determined to support Alice during these difficult weeks.*
▶ comfort, be a support to, sustain, encourage, hearten, console, fortify, reassure, succour
AN OPPOSITE IS abandon
3 *His land was not fertile enough to support his family.*
▶ maintain, nourish, provide for, sustain, feed, keep
AN OPPOSITE IS neglect
4 *The company supports research into the causes of back pain.*
▶ sponsor, subsidize, fund, patronize, contribute to, encourage
AN OPPOSITE IS discourage
5 *They both support some sort of fees. The Socialist Party agreed to support the bill. There is no evidence to support such a notion.*
▶ agree with, argue for, advocate, endorse, promote, substantiate, uphold, confirm, corroborate, defend, justify
AN OPPOSITE IS oppose

supporter NOUN
1 *The perpetrators were unlikely to be genuine rugby supporters.*
▶ enthusiast, follower, devotee, fan
2 *The United States became an important supporter of the project.*
▶ champion, advocate, adherent, defender, seconder, upholder, apologist (for)
3 *Labour's supporters in business*
▶ backer, adherent, ally, sponsor, henchman

supportive ADJECTIVE
Alan and Ian were the most supportive friends in her life.
▶ encouraging, helpful, caring, concerned,

reassuring, sympathetic, understanding, protective, interested, kind, loyal, positive
OPPOSITES ARE unhelpful, discouraging

suppose VERB

1 *I suppose it would be nice for you to earn a little pin money.*
► assume, expect, guess, infer, dare say, presume, imagine, fancy, surmise, suspect, think, conclude, conjecture, judge
2 *Just suppose I saw her again.*
► imagine, pretend, hypothesize, fancy, assume

supposed ADJECTIVE

Where is this supposed cousin of yours?
► alleged, assumed, presumed, rumoured, reputed, imagined, conjectural, hypothetical, reported, putative
be supposed to *You are supposed to read the whole book.*
► be meant to, be expected to, be required to, be obliged to, have to, need to, ought to

supposition NOUN

Terry had gone to bed happy in the supposition that he would get revenge.
► belief, assumption, presumption, notion, suspicion, expectation, conjecture, idea, hunch, feeling

suppress VERB

1 *The National Guard was established to suppress anti-government demonstrations.*
► quash, quell, crush, subdue, overcome, overthrow, conquer, put an end to, put down, stamp out, stop
2 *She had been advised to suppress all critical remarks. McGuire made a conscious effort to suppress his emotions.*
► hide , conceal, restrain, stifle, repress, control, contain, hold back, smother, silence, cover up, bottle up, choke back

supremacy NOUN

the doctrine of the supremacy of parliament
► dominance, predominance, sovereignty, ascendancy, primacy, pre-eminence, domination, lead

supreme ADJECTIVE

1 *He was on course to carry off skiing's supreme prize*
► greatest, highest, top, foremost, principal, chief
OPPOSITES ARE lowest, least
2 *the supreme achievement of God's creation*
► greatest, superlative, crowning, ultimate, pre-eminent, unsurpassed, matchless, incomparable, extraordinary, remarkable
OPPOSITES ARE unremarkable, insignificant

sure ADJECTIVE

1 *I'm sure Dan will be perfectly safe.*
► certain, convinced, confident, positive, assured, definite, persuaded, satisfied, decided, resolute
OPPOSITES ARE doubtful, uncertain

2 *He's sure to ask us what we were doing.*
► bound, certain, likely, destined, compelled, obliged, required
AN OPPOSITE IS unlikely
3 *He left in the sure knowledge that he would be returning. He was pacing the floor, a sure sign of anxiety.*
► clear, undoubted, indisputable, inescapable, undeniable, undisputed, guaranteed, convincing, precise, proven, inevitable, accurate, true
OPPOSITES ARE uncertain, doubtful, unsure
4 *James was always a sure friend.*
► reliable, faithful, dependable, steadfast, steady, firm, solid, trusty, trustworthy, effective, loyal, safe, secure, unfailing, unswerving
OPPOSITES ARE fickle, unreliable.

surf VERB

surfing the Internet
► browse, explore, search, probe, research, survey, scrutinize

surface NOUN

1 *The surface of the door had become rotten.*
► outside, exterior, facade, veneer, covering, face
AN OPPOSITE IS inside
2 *A cube has six surfaces.*
► face, side, facet, plane

surface VERB

A submarine surfaced in the loch. A new idea has surfaced
► come up, rise, appear, emerge, materialize, come to light, (*informal*) pop up
AN OPPOSITE IS dive

surge NOUN

1 *a surge of water*
► gush, rush, sweep, flow, wave
2 *a surge of excitement*
► outburst, upsurge, outpouring, rush, gush, increase, onrush

surge VERB

1 *Water surged into people's houses.*
► gush, rush, stream, flow, swirl, roll
2 *The crowd surged forward*
► rush, sweep, push, stampede

surly ADJECTIVE

A surly parking attendant had spoken to him.
► bad-tempered, unfriendly, churlish, ungracious, morose, sullen, sulky
AN OPPOSITE IS friendly

surpass VERB

The television adaptation far surpassed the film version.
► outclass, outdo, eclipse, excel over, outshine, outstrip, better, do better than, beat, exceed, overshadow

surplus NOUN

a fruit surplus
► excess, surfeit, glut, superfluity, oversupply, oversufficiency, superabundance, profusion

a
b
c
d
e
f
g
h
i
j
k
l
m
n
o
p
q
r
s
t
u
v
w
x
y
z

surplus ADJECTIVE
Wipe off any surplus paint.
▶ excess, superfluous, spare, redundant, unwanted

surprise NOUN
1 *Alice looked at him in surprise.*
▶ amazement, astonishment, incredulity, wonder, alarm, consternation, bewilderment, dismay
2 *This might come as a surprise to you.*
▶ shock, revelation, bolt from the blue, (*more informal*) bombshell, (*more informal*) eye-opener

surprise VERB
1 *Here's a piece of information that will surprise you.*
▶ astonish, amaze, astound, shock, stupefy, dumbfound, stagger, disconcert, flabbergast, nonplus, take your breath away, take aback, (*more informal*) bowl over, (*more informal*) gobsmack
2 *He surprised an intruder, who ran off.*
▶ discover, take unawares, take by surprise, come upon, catch out, catch in the act, catch red-handed, detect

surprised ADJECTIVE
I was surprised to see Lisa sitting up in bed reading.
▶ astonished, amazed, astounded, dumbfounded, flabbergasted, nonplussed, shocked, speechless, staggered, disconcerted, incredulous, startled, stunned, taken aback, taken by surprise, thunderstruck, (*more informal*) gobsmacked

surprising ADJECTIVE
They completed the task with surprising speed.
▶ astonishing, amazing, astounding, unexpected, extraordinary, remarkable, incredible, staggering, startling, stunning
OPPOSITES ARE predictable, unsurprising

surrender VERB
1 *The rebels surrendered after months of fierce fighting.*
▶ give up, capitulate, submit, yield, succumb, resign, (*more informal*) throw in the towel
2 *We are being asked to surrender personal freedoms in the national interest.*
▶ give up, forgo, relinquish, cede, abandon, renounce, waive

surreptitious ADJECTIVE
Stacey sneaked a surreptitious look at her watch.
▶ secret, furtive, discreet, stealthy, clandestine, sneaky, sly, covert
AN OPPOSITE IS blatant

surround VERB
1 *The garden surrounds the ruins of a fourteenth-century castle.*
▶ encircle, ring, skirt, encompass
2 *Anabelle found herself surrounded by angry faces.*
▶ besiege, beset, engulf, girdle, hedge in, hem in

surroundings NOUN
The hotel is set in the beautiful surroundings of a country park.
▶ environment, location, setting, vicinity, neighbourhood, background, ambience, milieu

surveillance NOUN
Police surveillance prevented us from contacting your sister-in-law.
▶ check, observation, scrutiny, supervision, vigilance, watch

survey NOUN
1 *In our main survey, people were asked where they would go for a loan.*
▶ poll, investigation, appraisal, inquiry, census, count, evaluation, study, assessment, examination
2 *a survey of recent work on the subject*
▶ review, overview, synopsis, summary
3 *Be sure to get a survey of the house before making an offer.*
▶ inspection, assessment, appraisal, examination, valuation

survey VERB
1 *Those who wish can survey the scene from a panoramic tower.*
▶ observe, view, look at, look over
2 *The artist stood back to survey his work.*
▶ examine, inspect, study, scrutinize, consider, review
3 *Engineers arrived to survey the area.*
▶ do a survey of, reconnoitre, plot, map out, plan out, measure, (*technical*) triangulate

survival NOUN
longer-term threats to the survival of capitalism
▶ continuance, continued existence

survive VERB
1 *They had enough water to survive until help came.*
▶ remain alive, live, last, carry on, keep going, sustain yourself, continue, endure
AN OPPOSITE IS perish
2 *Some of the workers' cottages still survive.*
▶ remain, exist
3 *Six people survived the crash.*
▶ live through, withstand, come through, weather
AN OPPOSITE IS succumb to
4 *She is survived by her husband and three sons.*
▶ outlast, outlive

susceptible ADJECTIVE
Network cables are susceptible to electrical interference.
▶ liable, vulnerable, prone, subject, sensitive, inclined, predisposed
OPPOSITES ARE resistant, immune

suspect ADJECTIVE
Two suspect packages stood by the door.
▶ suspicious, doubtful, dubious, questionable, (*more informal*) fishy, (*more informal*) dodgy

suspect VERB
1 *The plan's only going to be successful if they don't suspect anything.*
▶ distrust, mistrust, call into question, have doubts about, doubt
2 *I suspect another visit may not be possible.*
▶ expect, surmise, presume, assume, imagine, dare say, think, fancy, guess, infer, conclude, conjecture, judge

suspend VERB

1 *Long sacks were suspended from hooks on the wall.*
▶ hang, sling, swing, dangle, drape
2 *The Stock Exchange decided to suspend trading.*
▶ interrupt, break off, adjourn, discontinue, postpone, put off, defer, delay
3 *Two directors were suspended for a year.*
▶ exclude, debar, remove, dismiss, expel

suspense NOUN

There is an art to building up suspense.
▶ tension, uncertainty, doubt, anticipation, expectation, expectancy, excitement, apprehension, drama

suspicion NOUN

1 *The KGB did not need proof; suspicion was more than enough.*
▶ intuition, conjecture, speculation, supposition, belief, caution, wariness
2 *As we drank our coffee I outlined my suspicions about Martinez.*
▶ doubt, misgiving, qualm, uncertainty, reservation
3 *A suspicion of a grin appeared on her face.*
▶ trace, hint, glimmer, shadow, suggestion, tinge, touch

suspicious ADJECTIVE

1 *It was clear that he was increasingly suspicious of his visitor.*
▶ doubtful, distrustful, mistrustful, unsure, sceptical, apprehensive, wary, chary, disbelieving, incredulous, unconvinced (about), uneasy (about)
OPPOSITES ARE trusting, credulous
2 *He's a highly suspicious character and we haven't spoken for years. At first the police treated the case as a suspicious death.*
▶ questionable, suspect, dubious, disreputable, unreliable, untrustworthy, peculiar, irregular, (more informal) fishy, (more informal) shady
OPPOSITES ARE straightforward, innocent

sustain VERB

1 *The country would have to sustain a large population.*
▶ maintain, keep, continue, preserve, provide for, nurture
2 *She had some bread and cheese to sustain her.*
▶ nourish, feed
3 *They were sustained by these happy memories.*
▶ comfort, support, encourage, succour, hearten, (more informal) buck up
4 *It was doubtful whether the structure could sustain the increased weight.*
▶ support, bear, carry

sustained ADJECTIVE

They might succeed with a sustained effort.
▶ continuous, prolonged, protracted, determined, unremitting, steady
OPPOSITES ARE intermittent, sporadic

sustenance NOUN

Without sustenance the animals will die.
▶ nourishment, food, nutriment, nutrition, provisions

swagger VERB

He swaggered into the room, looking for Susan.
▶ strut, prance, parade

swagger NOUN

1 *She walked with a slight swagger.*
▶ strut, prance
2 *His behaviour was full of swagger now.*
▶ boasting, bluster, ostentation, brashness

swallow VERB

1 *He was finding it hard to swallow food*
▶ eat, drink, consume, devour, gulp down, guzzle
2 *I was a little surprised when they swallowed my story.*
▶ accept, believe, (more informal) buy
swallow up *The darkness swallowed them up.*
▶ engulf, enfold, envelop, absorb, enclose

swamp NOUN

The rains had turned the fields into a huge swamp.
▶ marsh, bog, quagmire, mire, fen, marshland, morass, wetland, slough

swamp VERB

1 *A tidal wave swamped the coastal regions.*
▶ flood, inundate, overwhelm, engulf, drench, saturate, submerge, waterlog
2 *Journalists had swamped the unfortunate village.*
▶ overrun, overwhelm, besiege, beset

swampy ADJECTIVE

swampy ground
▶ marshy, boggy, soggy, waterlogged, miry, muddy, soft
AN OPPOSITE IS firm

swap VERB

Helen swapped her Spanish stamps for some Belgian ones she didn't have.
▶ exchange, barter, bargain, switch

swap NOUN

They had arranged a house swap for July.
▶ exchange, switch, interchange

swarm NOUN

There were swarms of police everywhere.
▶ crowd, horde, mass, throng, multitude, host

swarm VERB

Reporters were swarming all over the place.
▶ crowd, throng, flock, mass, cluster, congregate
be swarming with *The beaches were swarming with tourists.*
▶ be overrun with, be crawling with, be teeming, be full of, be infested with, be invaded by, abound in

swarthy ADJECTIVE

a swarthy complexion
▶ dark, dark-skinned, dusky, tanned, brown

sway VERB

1 *The branches swayed in the breeze.*
▶ swing, bend, rock, wave, lurch, lean from side to side, move to and fro, oscillate
2 *Many people are swayed by what they read in the newspapers.*
▶ influence, persuade, affect, govern

s

swear VERB

1 *He swore he had told the truth.*
▶ promise, give your word, pledge, vow, affirm, attest, declare, state on oath, take an oath, testify
2 *She spilled her drink and swore.*
▶ blaspheme, curse, use bad language

swear word NOUN

1 *In those days you never heard a swear word on television.*
▶ expletive, obscenity, profanity, curse, oath, four-letter word
2 swear words
▶ bad language, foul language, profanity, swearing

sweat VERB

He had begun to sweat in the heat.
▶ perspire, swelter, exude

sweat NOUN

1 *By now he was drenched in sweat.*
▶ perspiration, moisture, dampness
2 *(informal) We were in a sweat to get away.*
▶ panic, fluster, state of agitation, state of anxiety

sweaty ADJECTIVE

He shook Karl's sweaty hand.
▶ sweating, perspiring, sticky, clammy, damp, moist

sweep VERB

1 *It was time to sweep the kitchen floor.*
▶ brush, clean, scrub, wipe, hoover
2 *Another bus swept past them.*
▶ sail, glide, streak, tear, hurtle, whizz

sweeping ADJECTIVE

1 *We are expecting sweeping changes.*
▶ far-reaching, wide-ranging, extensive, comprehensive, wholesale, thoroughgoing, radical, indiscriminate
AN OPPOSITE IS limited
2 *Avoid sweeping statements.*
▶ broad, general, over-general, oversimplified, unqualified, simplistic
OPPOSITES ARE precise, specific

sweet ADJECTIVE

1 *The tea was too sweet.*
▶ sweetened, sugary, saccharine, honeyed, cloying
2 *the sweet perfume of roses*
▶ fragrant, aromatic, sweet-smelling, balmy, scented
3 *She sang a sweet song.*
▶ melodious, lyrical, mellifluous, sweet-toned
4 *Life can be sweet.*
▶ pleasant, pleasing, enjoyable, satisfying, delightful, agreeable
5 *the sweet air of the mountains*
▶ fresh, pure, wholesome, clear, clean
6 *a sweet little baby*
▶ cute, pretty, delightful
7 *Dora has a sweet nature.*
▶ loving, appealing, affectionate, adorable, lovely, charming

sweeten VERB

1 *You may need to sweeten the juice a little.*
▶ make sweeter, sugar
2 *She was furious and he had no idea how to sweeten her.*
▶ pacify, calm, mollify, soothe, appease, mellow

sweetheart NOUN

Maureen was my school sweetheart.
▶ girlfriend or boyfriend, darling, admirer, lover

swell VERB

1 *He could almost feel his stomach swelling.*
▶ expand, dilate, distend, enlarge, bloat, bulge, balloon, inflate, puff up, billow
OPPOSITES ARE contract, shrink
2 *The droning in her head swelled and faded.*
▶ increase, intensify, heighten, surge
AN OPPOSITE IS subside
3 *The population swelled with immigration after the war.*
▶ increase, enlarge, expand, grow or get bigger, build up, extend
OPPOSITES ARE decrease, decline

swell NOUN

a heavy swell in the Channel
▶ surge, roll, billow, undulation

swelling NOUN

There was redness and a swelling in his throat.
▶ inflammation, protuberance, puffiness, lump, bump, excrescence, tumour

sweltering ADJECTIVE

a sweltering day in July
▶ stifling, baking, scorching, sultry, oppressive, hot, sticky, humid

swerve VERB

The car swerved to avoid a squirrel.
▶ turn aside, deviate, swing, weave, change direction, veer, take avoiding action

swift ADJECTIVE

1 *Her letter brought a swift reply.*
▶ quick, rapid, prompt, immediate, instant, speedy, fast, instantaneous, punctual
AN OPPOSITE IS slow
2 *They all made swift progress.*
▶ rapid, quick, speedy, fast, brisk, lively

swindle VERB

The company had been swindled out of a large sum of money.
▶ cheat, defraud, trick, fleece, dupe, deceive, (more informal) con, (more informal) diddle, (more informal) do, (more informal) bamboozle

swindle NOUN

an insurance swindle
▶ fraud, fiddle, racket, deception, sham, (more informal) con

swindler NOUN
Thousands of pensioners had fallen victim to the swindlers.
▸ fraudster, confidence trickster, confidence man, trickster, imposter, cheat, charlatan, (*more informal*) con man

swing VERB
1 *The inn sign swung in the wind.*
▸ sway, flap, dangle, hang loose, rock, swivel, oscillate, turn, wave about
2 *The van swung across the carriageway.*
▸ swerve, veer, turn aside, deviate, weave
3 *Public opinion was swinging in favour of the war.*
▸ shift, change, fluctuate, waver, move, alter, oscillate

swing NOUN
1 *a huge swing in public opinion*
▸ shift, change, fluctuation, movement, oscillation, variation
2 *a swing of the pendulum*
▸ oscillation

swingeing ADJECTIVE
a swingeing increase in taxes
▸ drastic, severe, extreme, harsh, draconian, exorbitant

swipe VERB
1 *He threatened to swipe at her with the bottle.*
▸ hit, strike
2 (*informal*) *Someone swiped my pen.*
▸ steal, take, filch, snatch, (*informal*) nick, (*informal*) pinch

swipe NOUN
She took a playful swipe at his face.
▸ blow, strike, swing, slap, smack, clout, hit

swirl VERB
The water swirled round their feet.
▸ surge, whirl, churn, eddy, spin, twirl, twist

switch NOUN
Whitlock activated the switch on the dashboard.
▸ button, control, key, lever, handle

switch VERB
She managed to switch places so she was sitting next to Neil.
▸ change, swap, exchange, replace, shift, substitute
switch on or **off** *The user must not switch off the computer before this option is chosen.*
▸ turn on or off, put on or off, activate or deactivate, power up or down

swivel VERB
I had to swivel round to see her.
▸ turn, swing, spin, twirl, gyrate, pivot, revolve, rotate, wheel

swollen ADJECTIVE
I climbed the ladder despite my swollen foot.
▸ inflamed, distended, bloated, enlarged, puffed up, puffy, tumescent
OPPOSITES ARE shrunken, shrivelled

swoop VERB
1 *Wagtails swooped across my path.*
▸ dive, sweep, plunge, plummet, drop, descend, fly down, lunge
2 **swoop on** *Fifty police officers swooped on a group of farm buildings.*
▸ descend on, pounce on, raid, besiege, search

sword NOUN
James had armed himself with the sword of Robert the Bruce.
▸ blade, foil, rapier, sabre, broadsword, cutlass, scimitar

swot VERB
swot up on (*informal*) *Choose a topical issue each week and swot up on it from newspapers and magazines.*
▸ study, work on, research, (*informal*) mug up, (*informal*) bone up on

syllabus NOUN
They must begin teaching the syllabus this September.
▸ curriculum, course, course of study, programme of study, schedule

symbol NOUN
1 *Snakes were seen as symbols of sexuality.*
▸ emblem, token, sign, image, figure, representation, mark
2 *Too many symbols make the timetable difficult to use if you are in a hurry.*
▸ sign, character, hieroglyph
3 *The Red Cross symbol was painted on the roof of the vehicle.*
▸ logo, badge, mark, crest, insignia

symbolic ADJECTIVE
1 *John Wayne was held up as being symbolic of everything that was good and right about America.*
▸ representative, suggestive, typical, characteristic, emblematic, figurative, meaningful, significant
2 *The treaty is more than a symbolic milestone.*
▸ allegorical, metaphorical, representative, token

symbolize VERB
The beaver was chosen to symbolize the school because it was an industrious as well as a social animal.
▸ represent, epitomize, encapsulate, stand for, be a sign of, be a symbol of, embody, signify, exemplify, betoken, denote

symmetrical ADJECTIVE
Note the symmetrical design of the building.
▸ balanced, regular, uniform, harmonious, even
AN OPPOSITE IS asymmetrical

sympathetic ADJECTIVE
1 *She managed a sympathetic smile.*
▸ commiserating, comforting, supportive, understanding, appreciative, consoling, caring, compassionate, considerate, tender
OPPOSITES ARE unsympathetic, unfeeling

a b c d e f g h i j k l m n o p q r **s** t u v w x y z

2 sympathetic to *All the parents felt very sympathetic to what their daughters were going through.*
▶ understanding of, appreciative of, concerned about, well-disposed towards

3 sympathetic to *Some of the republics seem to have been sympathetic to this idea.*
▶ in favour of, in sympathy with, in agreement with, supportive of, receptive to

sympathize VERB

1 sympathize with *We sympathize with the views of the people living in the area.*
▶ understand, agree with, approve of, support, commend, appreciate

2 sympathize with *Many trade unionists instinctively sympathized with the plight of the miners.*
▶ commiserate with, show sympathy for, be sympathetic towards, be sorry for, identify with, empathize with, feel for, side with, pity

sympathy NOUN

Friends expressed sympathy for those who died or were injured. Don't waste your sympathy on them.
▶ commiseration, pity, compassion, condolences, feeling, fellow-feeling, tenderness, understanding, consideration, empathy

symptom NOUN

1 *Several patients suffered from symptoms such as nausea and vomiting.*
▶ manifestation, indicator, indication, feature

2 *The first symptom of a frozen waste pipe is that the water won't flow out.*
▶ sign, evidence, indication, warning, testimony

symptomatic ADJECTIVE

The town's poverty is symptomatic of chronic unemployment.
▶ indicative, characteristic, suggestive, typical, representative

synopsis NOUN

a short synopsis of last week's episode
▶ resumé, summary, precis, outline

synthetic ADJECTIVE

The whole pitch has been replaced by a synthetic surface
▶ artificial, imitation, manufactured, simulated, substitute, man-made, unnatural, concocted, mock, ersatz, fabricated, fake
OPPOSITES ARE natural, real, genuine

system NOUN

1 *a reform of the criminal justice system*
▶ organization, structure, framework, network, institution, (*informal*) set-up

2 *a system for recording accidents at work*
▶ procedure, process, routine, scheme, arrangement, means (of), method, methodology, plan, structure, set of rules

3 *a system of government that commands the confidence of all the people*
▶ regime, philosophy, science, constitution, principles

systematic ADJECTIVE

Citizenship should be taught in every school in a systematic way.
▶ methodical, ordered, orderly, organized, structured, planned, systematized, coherent, scientific, logical
AN OPPOSITE IS unsystematic

Tt

table NOUN

1 *He put the glasses on the table.*
▶ dining table, kitchen table, worktop, working surface, coffee table

2 *The table on page three shows monthly rainfall in the region.*
▶ chart, diagram, graph, list

tablet NOUN

1 *There is a stone tablet over the doorway.*
▶ plaque, slab, plate, sign

2 *She rang reception and asked for another tablet of soap.*
▶ bar, piece, block, chunk, slab

3 *He went to his room and took a headache tablet.*
▶ pill, capsule, caplet

taboo NOUN

There is a taboo against doing business on the sabbath.
▶ ban, prohibition, proscription, veto, restriction, anathema

taboo ADJECTIVE

Politics were a taboo subject at the dinner table.
▶ forbidden, prohibited, banned, proscribed, unacceptable, disapproved of, unmentionable

tacit ADJECTIVE

The deal continued with their tacit agreement.
▶ implicit, unspoken, silent, implied, understood, unvoiced

tack NOUN

1 *The carpet was held down with a row of tacks.*
▶ pin, drawing-pin, nail, tin tack

2 *We ought to change tack and speak out more.*
▶ approach, policy, tactic, method, technique, direction

tack VERB

1 *He tacked a photo to the notice board.*
▶ pin, nail, fix

2 *She tacked the hem and tried it on for length.*
▶ stitch, sew

tack on *A few maps and plans are tacked on at the back of the book.*
▶ attach, add, append

tackle NOUN
1 *He wanted to buy new fishing tackle.*
▶ gear, equipment, apparatus, implements, kit, outfit, paraphernalia, rig, tools
2 *The referee penalized him for a late tackle.*
▶ challenge, interception, attack, block

tackle VERB
1 *The Government is determined to tackle the issue of tax avoidance.*
▶ deal with, grapple with, address yourself to, confront, cope with, face up to, sort out, handle, manage, attend to, combat, set about, undertake
2 *An opposing player tackled him near the touchline.*
▶ challenge, intercept, stop, confront, attack, take on
3 *Lettie decided to tackle him directly about her pay.*
▶ confront, approach, challenge, address

tacky ADJECTIVE
1 *The paint was still tacky.*
▶ sticky, wet, gluey
AN OPPOSITE IS dry
2 *tacky quizzes and game shows*
▶ vulgar, coarse, crude, tawdry, garish, trashy
AN OPPOSITE IS tasteful

tact NOUN
A police officer told her the news with great tact.
▶ discretion, consideration, sensitivity, tactfulness, delicacy, diplomacy, thoughtfulness, understanding
OPPOSITES ARE indiscretion, tactlessness

tactful ADJECTIVE
Molly gave them a tactful reminder about the rent.
▶ discreet, judicious, considerate, polite, delicate, diplomatic, sensitive, thoughtful
OPPOSITES ARE tactless, indiscreet

tactical ADJECTIVE
a tactical move to force the authorities to act
▶ calculated, planned, deliberate, strategic, politic

tactics NOUN
The enemy drove them back by superior tactics.
▶ planning, battle plans, logistics, moves, manoeuvres, strategy
USAGE There is a difference between *tactics* and *strategy*: a *strategy* is an overall plan, whereas *tactics* are the way in which you carry out the plan.

tactless ADJECTIVE
She was plainly upset by his tactless remark.
▶ indiscreet, insensitive, thoughtless, unthinking, indelicate, clumsy
OPPOSITES ARE tactful, discreet

tag NOUN
His jacket still had a price tag on it.
▶ label, ticket, tab, sticker

tag VERB
Each bottle was tagged with a different coloured label.
▶ label, mark, identify, ticket
tag along *Sometimes he let me tag along.*
▶ follow, go along, accompany

tag on *A note was tagged on at the end of the letter.*
▶ add, attach, append, tack on

tail NOUN
They waited at the tail of the queue.
▶ back, end, rear, extremity, tail end

tail VERB
A squad of reporters had tailed him for five years.
▶ follow, shadow, stalk, pursue, track, trail
tail off *Her words tailed off at the expression in his eyes.*
▶ fade, wane, ebb, peter out, drop away, subside, dwindle, decline, decrease, lessen, reduce, slacken

taint NOUN
free from the taint of corruption
▶ stain, smear, hint, trace, blight, contamination

taint VERB
1 *an area tainted by pollution*
▶ contaminate, pollute, poison, soil, adulterate, dirty, infect
2 *These unhappy events tainted their reputation for ever.*
▶ tarnish, stain, sully, besmirch, blacken, dishonour, smear, ruin, slander

take VERB
1 *Many prisoners were taken.*
▶ catch, seize, capture, take captive, arrest
2 *He took her hand gently.*
▶ clasp, clutch, grasp, grab, grip, take hold of, lay hold of
3 *Someone had taken his car.*
▶ steal, remove, make off with, appropriate, (*more informal*) pinch, (*more informal*) nick, (*more informal*) filch, (*more informal*) swipe
4 *Take ten percent from the total.*
▶ subtract, deduct, knock off, discount
5 *It takes a long time to recover from an illness like this.*
▶ need, require, call for, necessitate
6 *The pain was more than he could take.*
▶ bear, put up with, endure, tolerate, suffer, stomach
7 *I'll take you home.*
▶ accompany, drive, bring, convey, conduct, escort, guide, transport, carry
be taken with *Tanya was rather taken with the idea.*
▶ be interested in, be attracted by, be captivated by, be fascinated by, be delighted by, be enchanted by
take aback *This suggestion took us aback.*
▶ surprise, astonish, astound
take apart *a cot that can be easily taken apart*
▶ dismantle, take to pieces, disassemble
take back *I took back everything I had said.*
▶ withdraw, retract, disown, recant, repudiate, deny
take down *A police officer took down the details.*
▶ write down, note, jot down, record
take in
1 *a confidence trick that took everyone in*
▶ fool, deceive, mislead, dupe, trick, hoodwink, cheat

2 *It was too much information to take in at once.*
▶ understand, comprehend, grasp, absorb, assimilate, digest
3 *a cruise that takes in the main Greek islands*
▶ include, incorporate, encompass, comprise, cover
take it *I take it you want to stay.*
▶ assume, infer, deduce
take off
1 *I took off my shoes before going in.*
▶ remove, shed, throw off, discard
2 *a plan that might never take off*
▶ succeed, do well, catch on
3 *The man took off at a run.*
▶ run off, run away, leave, escape, depart, disappear
take on *She took on more responsibilities that year.*
▶ accept, assume, undertake, acquire, shoulder
take up
1 *She took up painting in her forties.*
▶ engage in, practise, become interested in
2 *a cupboard that takes up a lot of space*
▶ occupy, absorb, use up, fill

take-off NOUN
1 *The flight was bumpy for a while after take-off.*
▶ lift-off, departure, ascent
2 *The sketch is a take-off of the American President.*
▶ parody, imitation, pastiche, satire, lampoon

takeover NOUN
a plan for the takeover of a British bank
▶ acquisition, purchase, buyout, gaining of control

takings NOUN
She took the day's takings to the bank.
▶ proceeds, returns, receipts, earnings, income, profits, revenue, gains

tale NOUN
a tale about dragons and heroes
▶ story, narrative, narration, history, account, yarn

talent NOUN
a talent for playing the violin
▶ gift, aptitude, ability, accomplishment, flair, genius, skill, capacity, expertise, knack, prowess

talented ADJECTIVE
a talented young player
▶ gifted, able, accomplished, skilful, skilled, artistic, brilliant, clever, distinguished, expert
OPPOSITES ARE inept, unskilful

talk VERB
1 *I was talking to a friend.*
▶ speak, chat, converse (with)
2 *They were talking complete rubbish.*
▶ speak, utter, express, articulate, communicate
3 *They looked for a quiet spot to talk.*
▶ have a talk, have a chat, converse, confer, speak to one another, communicate with one another
4 *He refused to talk.*
▶ give information, confess, admit anything
5 *People were beginning to talk.*
▶ gossip, spread rumours, make remarks, pass comments

6 **talk of** *She talked of leaving and settling abroad.*
▶ speak about, mention, refer to
7 **talk to** *He talked to an eager audience.*
▶ speak to, address, lecture

talk NOUN
1 *too much talk and not enough action*
▶ conversation, speaking, chatter, discussion, dialogue, (*more informal*) yakking
2 *There was talk of an affair.*
▶ rumour, gossip (about), (*more informal*) tittle-tattle
3 *a talk in the village hall*
▶ lecture, address, speech, presentation, discourse
4 **talks** *Peace talks will resume next week.*
▶ negotiations, discussions, consultations

talkative ADJECTIVE
He had chanced on an unusually talkative taxi driver
▶ chatty, loquacious, garrulous, voluble, effusive, vocal, communicative, forthcoming, articulate
OPPOSITES ARE taciturn, unforthcoming

talking-to NOUN
(*informal*) *He was given a severe talking-to and told not to come back.*
▶ reprimand, lecture, scolding, (*informal*) telling-off, (*informal*) dressing-down

tall ADJECTIVE
1 *a tall man*
▶ large, big
2 *a tall building*
▶ high, lofty, towering, soaring, elevated

tally NOUN
a final tally of twenty goals scored during the season
▶ total, count, reckoning, account

tally VERB
Her explanation did not tally with the evidence before their eyes.
▶ agree, accord, correspond (with or to), concur, fit

tame ADJECTIVE
1 *The animal was so tame that it shinned up his leg and dived into a deep pocket.*
▶ domesticated, gentle, manageable, disciplined, trained, meek, obedient, safe, subdued, submissive, tractable
AN OPPOSITE IS wild
2 *Aren't you Joe's tame reporter?*
▶ cooperative, willing, amenable, biddable
AN OPPOSITE IS uncooperative
3 *It turned out to be a tame evening after all.*
▶ dull, tedious, boring, unexciting, uninteresting, humdrum, bland, feeble, flat, lifeless, uninspiring, unadventurous
AN OPPOSITE IS exciting

tame VERB
1 *Wild rabbits can be tamed in captivity.*
▶ domesticate, break in, train, discipline, house-train, master
2 *She made strenuous efforts to tame her behaviour.*
▶ control, subdue, curb, conquer, master, moderate, mitigate, quell, repress, subjugate, suppress, temper

tamper VERB

tamper with *A student was able to enter the cockpit of an empty aircraft and tamper with the controls.*
▶ interfere with, meddle with, tinker with, alter, change, adjust, play about with, fiddle about with, make adjustments to

tan ADJECTIVE

a tan overcoat
▶ light brown, pale brown, tawny

tan VERB

Be careful not to overdo it when tanning in the sun.
▶ get a tan, bronze, brown

tang NOUN

1 *Olives will add a special tang to your stews.*
▶ flavour, taste, zest, savour, piquancy, spice
2 *We could already smell the tang of the sea.*
▶ smell, odour, fragrance

tangible ADJECTIVE

The experiment brought no tangible results.
▶ definite, solid, substantial, concrete, actual, real, material, positive, discernible
AN OPPOSITE IS intangible

tangle NOUN

a tangle of wires and cables
▶ mass, muddle, jumble, confusion, maze, jungle, knot, twist

tangle VERB

1 *She had managed to tangle her hair.*
▶ entangle, knot, twist, ravel
OPPOSITES ARE untangle, disentangle
2 *A dolphin had become tangled in the net.*
▶ trap, ensnare, entrap, catch, enmesh
3 *Better not to tangle with people like that.*
▶ become involved with, come into conflict with, confront, quarrel with, cross swords with

tangled ADJECTIVE

1 *Later they emigrated, but could never escape their tangled past.*
▶ complicated, complex, confused, convoluted, involved, entangled, intricate
AN OPPOSITE IS straightforward
2 *an undergrowth of tangled bushes and trees*
▶ knotted, matted, convoluted, dishevelled, tousled, unkempt, untidy
AN OPPOSITE IS tidy

tangy ADJECTIVE

Citrus adds a tangy taste to all sorts of savoury dishes.
▶ sharp, pungent, piquant, appetizing, spicy, strong, tart, fresh, refreshing
OPPOSITES ARE insipid, bland

tank NOUN

1 *a hot water tank*
▶ container, cistern, reservoir, basin
2 *a tank of fish*
▶ aquarium, bowl

tantalize VERB

Selina's cool aloofness has tantalized her audience for years.
▶ tease, frustrate, titillate, intrigue, fascinate, provoke

tantamount ADJECTIVE

tantamount to *Killing a dolphin was tantamount to killing a person.*
▶ equivalent to, comparable to, commensurate with, the same as

tantrum NOUN

He threw a tantrum and rolled on the floor, kicking and screaming.
▶ fit of rage, fit of temper, scene, outburst, (more informal) paddy, (more informal) wobbly

tap NOUN

1 *a water tap*
▶ faucet, stopcock, valve
2 *There was a tap at the window.*
▶ knock, rap, knocking, touch

tap VERB

1 *She tapped on the door.*
▶ knock, rap, strike
2 *I leaned forward to tap her shoulder.*
▶ pat, touch, poke, nudge

tape NOUN

1 *The parcel was bound with tape.*
▶ band, binding, strip, braid, ribbon
2 *They listened to music on tapes.*
▶ cassette, tape recording

tape VERB

I'll tape up the parcel.
▶ bind, tie, seal

taper VERB

1 *The leaves taper to a point.*
▶ narrow, thin, become narrower
2 *Their enthusiasm soon tapered off.*
▶ decrease, lessen, dwindle, wane, diminish, die down, peter out

target NOUN

1 *a target of £100,000*
▶ goal, objective, aim, ambition, end, intention
2 *the target of attacks*
▶ victim, butt, object, quarry, prey

tariff NOUN

1 *the hotel's high-season tariff*
▶ price list, list of charges, schedule
2 *the reduction of import tariffs*
▶ tax, duty, toll, excise, levy

tarnish VERB

1 *Constant use of abrasives has tarnished the metal.*
▶ dull, discolour, stain, blacken, corrode
2 *The accusations will tarnish his reputation.*
▶ taint, stain, sully, besmirch, blacken, dishonour, smear

tart ADJECTIVE

1 *the tart taste of cooked apples*
▶ sharp, sour, acid, tangy, piquant, pungent
OPPOSITES ARE sweet, bland

2 *He regretted his rather tart response.*
▶ acerbic, sharp, biting, cutting, caustic, scathing

tart NOUN

a jam tart
▶ pastry, flan, tartlet, pie, quiche

task NOUN

Finishing the book in time proved a daunting task.
▶ job, undertaking, enterprise, exercise, chore, duty, charge, burden, labour, work, mission, requirement

take to task *He took his advisers to task for misleading him.*
▶ criticize, rebuke, reproach, reprove, upbraid, censure, admonish

taste NOUN

1 *I don't much like the taste of raisins.*
▶ flavour, savour, character

2 *Would you like a taste of my pudding?*
▶ mouthful, bite, morsel, nibble, bit, piece, sample

3 *a millionaire with a taste for travel*
▶ liking, appreciation, fondness, desire, inclination, preference

4 *Hilary is a person of taste. The decoration was done with taste.*
▶ judgement, discernment, discretion, discrimination, perception, refinement, sensitivity, style

taste VERB

Anna tasted her drink and smiled.
▶ sample, test, try, sip, check

tasteful ADJECTIVE

a plain and tasteful decor
▶ discriminating, refined, restrained, sensitive, smart, stylish, well-judged, elegant, fashionable, in good taste, judicious, fastidious, proper
AN OPPOSITE IS tasteless

tasteless ADJECTIVE

1 *The vegetables were overcooked and tasteless.*
▶ flavourless, bland, insipid, weak, watery, characterless, mild, uninteresting
AN OPPOSITE IS tasty

2 *a tasteless remark*
▶ crude, indelicate, uncouth, vulgar, tactless, crass, injudicious, unseemly
OPPOSITES ARE tasteful, delicate

tasty ADJECTIVE

a tasty meal
▶ delicious, appetizing, luscious, mouth-watering, (*more informal*) yummy, (*more informal*) scrumptious

tattered ADJECTIVE

When he arrived his clothes were tattered.
▶ ragged, ripped, frayed, tatty, shabby, threadbare, torn
AN OPPOSITE IS smart

tatters PLURAL NOUN

The paintwork had peeled and the curtains were in tatters.
▶ shreds, rags, ribbons, pieces

taunt VERB

People taunted him about his marriage.
▶ tease, torment, jeer at, mock, ridicule, bait

taut ADJECTIVE

The rope should be taut.
▶ tight, tense, firm, rigid, stretched
AN OPPOSITE IS slack

tawdry ADJECTIVE

She wore tawdry ornaments on her arms.
▶ cheap, vulgar, tasteless, gaudy, showy, fancy, flashy, garish, inferior, worthless, (*more informal*) tatty, (*more informal*) tacky
AN OPPOSITE IS superior

tax NOUN

The new government immediately imposed a tax on imports.
▶ duty, tariff, charge, imposition, levy
RELATED ADJECTIVE fiscal

tax VERB

1 *It seems unfair to many people to tax pensions.*
▶ impose a tax on, levy a tax on

2 *The long walk taxed them severely.*
▶ tire, strain, exhaust, burden, make heavy demands on

teach VERB

1 *He taught me to swim in the holidays.*
▶ instruct, train, coach

2 *She teaches children with special needs.*
▶ educate, tutor, instruct, coach

teacher NOUN

He had been a teacher all his working life.
▶ educator, tutor, instructor, schoolteacher, schoolmaster or schoolmistress, pedagogue, academic
RELATED ADJECTIVE pedagogic or pedagogical

teaching NOUN

1 *Languages need experience in the country as well as rigorous teaching.*
▶ instruction, tuition, schooling, grounding, coaching

2 *the Church's teaching on marriage*
▶ doctrine, dogma, tenet

team NOUN

1 *the local cricket team*
▶ squad, side, line-up

2 *the BBC's production team*
▶ group, crew, company, body, gang

team VERB
team up *She teamed up with her fellow artists for a joint exhibition.*
▶ join forces, collaborate, cooperate, get together, band together, work together, combine, unite

SOME TEAM SPORTS
American football, Association football or soccer, Australian Rules football, baseball (chiefly American and Canadian), basketball, beach ball, cricket, curling (played on ice, chiefly Scottish and Canadian), football, goalball (for visually handicapped players), hurling, ice hockey, lacrosse, netball, polo (played with on horseback with long-handled mallets), punchball (American), rounders, Rugby League, Rugby Union, shinty (Scottish), stoolball (simple form of cricket with a stool or board for a wicket), volleyball, water polo.

tear NOUN (rhymes with *fear*)
1 *There was a tear in his eyes.*
▶ teardrop, droplet
2 **tears** *She was so upset she was close to tears.*
▶ crying, weeping, sobbing, blubbering

tear VERB (rhymes with *bear*)
1 *Take care you don't tear your clothes.*
▶ rip, slit, snag, split
2 *She tore the packet open.*
▶ rip, pull
3 *He tore the book from my hands.*
▶ snatch, grab, seize, wrench, wrest
4 (*informal*) *James tore round to the shop.*
▶ rush, hurry, race, speed, sprint, shoot, bolt
AN OPPOSITE IS stroll

tear NOUN (rhymes with *bear*)
There's a tear in my jeans.
▶ rip, hole, split, slit, rent, gash

tearaway NOUN
a young tearaway
▶ hooligan, hoodlum, ruffian, roughneck, (*more informal*) yob

tearful ADJECTIVE
1 *Glenda was tearful.*
▶ in tears, crying, weeping, close to tears, upset
OPPOSITES ARE cheerful, happy
2 *a tearful farewell*
▶ emotional, distressing, upsetting, sorrowful, sad, heartbreaking

tease VERB
His friends teased him about his hair.
▶ make fun of, poke fun at, laugh at, mock, taunt, provoke, torment

technical ADJECTIVE
1 *The information is fairly technical.*
▶ specialized, specialist, esoteric, professional
2 *an important technical advance*
▶ scientific, practical

technique NOUN
1 *There are various techniques for dealing with this problem.*
▶ method, procedure, approach, system
2 *She played the cello with a brilliant technique.*
▶ skill, ability, expertise, proficiency, facility

tedious ADJECTIVE
The work is tedious and time-consuming.
▶ dull, boring, monotonous, uninteresting, dreary, humdrum, laborious, irksome, tiresome, unexciting, wearisome
OPPOSITES ARE interesting, exciting

tedium NOUN
We played cards to relieve the tedium of the evening.
▶ monotony, boredom, tediousness, dreariness, dullness

teem VERB
teem with *The pond teemed with fish.*
▶ be full of, abound in, seethe with, swarm with, be infested with, be crawling with

teenager NOUN
a club for teenagers
▶ adolescent, youth, young person, juvenile, boy or girl, minor

tell VERB
1 *Tell me what happened.*
▶ inform, advise, notify (of), let know, acquaint (with)
2 *She told us there would be another train in an hour.*
▶ assure, promise, advise, inform
3 *I'll tell you a secret.*
▶ disclose, reveal, confess, admit
4 *He became more and more excited as he told his story.*
▶ recount, narrate, relate, describe, communicate, speak
5 *Colin told us to leave.*
▶ order, instruct, command, direct, call on
6 *It's not easy to tell them apart.*
▶ distinguish, differentiate, identify, recognize, discern
tell off (*informal*) *He told them off for being late.*
▶ reprimand, scold, rebuke, upbraid, censure, berate, (*informal*) tick off

telling ADJECTIVE
The argument is expressed in a few telling phrases.
▶ revealing, forceful, striking, persuasive, potent, compelling, effective
AN OPPOSITE IS insignificant

telling-off NOUN
(*informal*) *They were lucky to escape with a mild telling-off.*
▶ reprimand, scolding, rebuke, caution, admonishment, (*informal*) ticking-off

a b c d e f g h i j k l m n o p q r s **t** u v w x y z

temerity NOUN
(*usually disapproving*) *You have the temerity to refuse me, do you?*
▶ cheek, nerve, audacity, effrontery, boldness, impertinence, impudence, insolence, presumptuousness, shamelessness, (*more informal*) sauce

temper NOUN
1 *He walked out in a temper.*
▶ rage, fury, fit of rage, passion, tantrum
2 *Jenny's temper flared.*
▶ anger, fury, rage, annoyance, irritation, irritability, petulance
3 *Both children had a calm temper*
▶ temperament, disposition, nature, character, personality
lose your temper *Diana was capable of losing her temper.*
▶ become angry, fly into a rage, lose control, blow up, go berserk, (*more informal*) go mad, (*more informal*) go crazy, (*more informal*) go bananas, (*more informal*) fly off the handle, (*more informal*) go through the roof, (*more informal*) have a fit, (*more informal*) see red

temper VERB
William was a man who tempered sentiment with business sense.
▶ moderate, modify, modulate, mitigate, qualify, tone down

temperament NOUN
His main problem was an anxious temperament.
▶ disposition, nature, temper, character, personality

temperamental ADJECTIVE
1 *The new king proved to be a temperamental despot.*
▶ moody, excitable, emotional, volatile, unpredictable, highly-strung, sensitive, capricious, mercurial, touchy, neurotic
OPPOSITES ARE placid, phlegmatic
2 *He had a strong temperamental dislike of all conflict.*
▶ natural, inherent, innate, inborn, characteristic, congenital, constitutional

temperate ADJECTIVE
1 *Lizards and snakes bask in the sun in temperate climates.*
▶ mild, clement, warm, pleasant, balanced
AN OPPOSITE IS extreme
2 *He was patient and temperate in his habits.*
▶ moderate, restrained, self-restrained, self-controlled, disciplined, abstemious
AN OPPOSITE IS intemperate

tempestuous ADJECTIVE
1 *Not long after there arose a tempestuous wind.*
▶ stormy, blustery, squally, turbulent, wild, gusty, raging
AN OPPOSITE IS calm
2 *It was the first of many tempestuous scenes he was to be involved in.*
▶ passionate, emotional, temperamental
OPPOSITES ARE placid, phlegmatic

temporal ADJECTIVE
The bishops enjoyed considerable temporal authority.
▶ secular, earthly, terrestrial, worldly, mundane
AN OPPOSITE IS spiritual

temporary ADJECTIVE
The restrictions on imports were a temporary measure only.
▶ short-term, interim, provisional, stop-gap, short-lived, transitory, momentary, transient, ephemeral
AN OPPOSITE IS permanent

tempt VERB
Window displays tempt shoppers into their stores.
▶ entice, lure, allure, attract, persuade, coax, woo, inveigle, seduce
OPPOSITES ARE deter, repel, discourage

temptation NOUN
1 *She had to resist the temptation to call him from her mobile.*
▶ urge, desire, impulse, inclination
2 *I could see the dangers in the temptations of life in London.*
▶ attraction, appeal, lure, pull, fascination, seduction, allurement, draw, enticement

tempting ADJECTIVE
It was a tempting package, and I bought the whole deal.
▶ attractive, enticing, appealing, beguiling, tantalizing, irresistible

tenable ADJECTIVE
This theory is disproved by modern science and is no longer tenable.
▶ credible, defensible, plausible, reasonable, sensible, viable, sound, feasible, justifiable, arguable, legitimate, logical, rational
OPPOSITES ARE untenable, indefensible

tenacious ADJECTIVE
Nick was our tenacious, skilful, and hard-running midfield man.
▶ persevering, persistent, determined, resolute, dogged, pertinacious, strong-willed, single-minded, unwavering, unyielding
OPPOSITES ARE weak, feeble

tenant NOUN
The top floor was occupied by tenants.
▶ lodger, leaseholder, lessee, occupant, resident

tend VERB
1 *She spends many hours in the garden tending her flowers.*
▶ look after, attend to, manage, take care of, care for, cultivate, mind
2 *Nurses tend the sick and wounded in the field hospitals.*
▶ look after, attend to, care for, minister to, treat, nurse
3 **tend to** *At this time of year, our appetites tend to favour rich, stodgy puddings.*
▶ be inclined to, be apt to, be liable to, have a tendency to, be disposed to

tendency NOUN
John has a tendency to put his foot in it.
▶ propensity, proclivity, readiness, susceptibility, predilection, predisposition, disposition, inclination, liability, partiality, penchant, trend

tender ADJECTIVE
1 *She liked him tender, gentle like this.*
▶ kind, caring, compassionate, considerate, humane, affectionate, sensitive, warm-hearted
OPPOSITES ARE hard-hearted, callous, uncaring
2 *He pressed a tender loving kiss on her fingertips.*
▶ fond, loving, affectionate
3 *In my tender pre-teen years, I hadn't yet learned to be critical.*
▶ young, youthful, early, callow, immature, green, inexperienced, impressionable
OPPOSITES ARE advanced, mature
4 *Alan's voice cut into the tender little scene coldly. This is one of the author's most tender passages.*
▶ romantic, touching, moving, poignant
5 *Cook the rice in boiling salted water until tender.*
▶ soft, succulent, juicy, fleshy
OPPOSITES ARE hard, tough
6 *He lifted her up with tender care, holding her head to his cheek.*
▶ gentle, fond, loving
7 *Her ankle felt tender.*
▶ sore, painful, sensitive, inflamed, raw

tense ADJECTIVE
1 *The muscles in his neck were tense.*
▶ taut, tight, strained, stretched
AN OPPOSITE IS slack
2 *Angela was feeling tense and nervy.*
▶ anxious, nervous, edgy, on edge, strained, stressed, agitated, apprehensive, jittery, fidgety, ill at ease, jumpy, (*more informal*) uptight
OPPOSITES ARE calm, relaxed
3 *There was a tense atmosphere in the room.*
▶ fraught, uncomfortable, strained, charged
AN OPPOSITE IS relaxed

tension NOUN
1 *the tension of the ropes*
▶ tightness, tautness, strain, stretching
AN OPPOSITE IS slackness
2 *The tension was unbearable.*
▶ stress, strain, anxiety, suspense, apprehension, excitement, nervousness, unease, worry
AN OPPOSITE IS relaxation.

tentative ADJECTIVE
1 *This conclusion can only be tentative.*
▶ provisional, unconfirmed, cautious, diffident, doubtful, halfhearted
2 *a few tentative steps*
▶ hesitant, indecisive, indefinite, nervous, timid, uncertain
AN OPPOSITE IS decisive

tenuous ADJECTIVE
a tenuous argument
▶ slight, insubstantial, flimsy, thin, weak, unconvincing
AN OPPOSITE IS strong

tepid ADJECTIVE
1 *tepid water*
▶ warm, lukewarm
2 *The offer got a tepid response.*
▶ unenthusiastic, lukewarm, half-hearted, apathetic
AN OPPOSITE IS enthusiastic

term NOUN
1 *a technical term*
▶ word, expression, name, designation
2 *a five-year term of office*
▶ period, duration, interval, spell, session

terminal ADJECTIVE
a terminal illness
▶ incurable, untreatable, inoperable, fatal, mortal, lethal, deadly

terminate VERB
Doctors decided to terminate the treatment.
▶ end, cease, bring to an end, break off, cut short, abort, conclude, finish

terminology NOUN
scientific terminology
▶ language, phraseology, vocabulary, technical language, nomenclature, jargon

terms PLURAL NOUN
1 *She was on good terms with all her staff.*
▶ relations, standing, footing
2 *The two kings came to terms.*
▶ agreement, understanding, deal
3 *The terms of the contract prevented this.*
▶ conditions, provisos, stipulations, specifications
4 *The hotel offers good terms out of season.*
▶ rates, prices, tariff, charges

terrain NOUN
They were back on familiar terrain in the foothills.
▶ country, territory, ground, land, landscape, topography

terrestrial ADJECTIVE
one of the factors that give rise to intelligent terrestrial life
▶ earthly, worldly, mundane, earthbound, ordinary
OPPOSITES ARE heavenly, extraterrestrial
USAGE *Mundane* has the special meaning 'ordinary'. Also, be careful how you use the opposite word *heavenly*, which has a common second meaning 'wonderful'.

terrible ADJECTIVE
1 *I had a terrible fall which left me with two broken legs.*
▶ dreadful, frightful, horrible, awful, fearful, ghastly, hideous, shocking, frightening, terrifying
2 *There was a terrible smell in the kitchen.*
▶ disgusting, nasty, unpleasant, dreadful, horrible

terribly ADVERB

1 *This is terribly important.*
▶ very, extremely, exceptionally, exceedingly, dreadfully, awfully
2 *In the next game they played terribly.*
▶ badly, dreadfully, atrociously, awfully, appallingly, dismally

terrific ADJECTIVE

1 *We heard a terrific thud.*
▶ tremendous, huge, mighty, massive, colossal, enormous, gigantic
2 *The novel provides the basis for a terrific movie.*
▶ excellent, wonderful, marvellous, outstanding, magnificent, superb, splendid, first-class, first-rate

terrified ADJECTIVE

She gave them a terrified glance, and then bolted.
▶ petrified, frightened, scared, alarmed, terror-stricken, horror-stricken, panic-stricken

terrify VERB

The prospect of all that responsibility terrified him.
▶ frighten, petrify, scare, horrify, appal, dismay, shock, unnerve

terrifying ADJECTIVE

Water was pouring in with terrifying speed.
▶ frightening, horrifying, petrifying, dreadful, hair-raising, blood-curdling, spine-chilling, appalling, unnerving, (*more informal*) scary

territory NOUN

1 *France sought to locate the launching site on French territory.*
▶ land, country, terrain, ground
2 *a Dutch territory in the East*
▶ domain, state, dependency, dominion, colony, possession

terror NOUN

Men were driven to do these things by hunger and terror.
▶ fear , extreme fear, alarm, fright, horror, panic, shock, trepidation

terrorist NOUN

Security loopholes allowed the terrorists to plant the bomb.
▶ bomber, assassin, gunman, hijacker

terrorize VERB

In the 1820s, Romney Marsh was openly terrorized by armed gangs of smugglers.
▶ threaten, intimidate, torment, tyrannize, menace, persecute, victimize, oppress, terrify, frighten

terse ADJECTIVE

'Good,' came the terse reply.
▶ brief, curt, brusque, succinct, concise, abrupt, laconic
AN OPPOSITE IS verbose

test NOUN

1 *They will have to pass a test to continue to be paid for the work.*
▶ exam, examination, appraisal, assessment, evaluation
2 *We'll be conducting a series of scientific tests.*
▶ trial, experiment, study, evaluation, investigation, analysis, probe

test VERB

1 *Psychologists have developed experiments to test their ideas.*
▶ check, appraise, evaluate, validate, examine, analyse, assess, study, screen, try out
2 *Here's a chance to test your DIY skills.*
▶ try out, put to the test, explore, trial
3 *These demands tested his patience to breaking point.*
▶ strain, tax, put a strain on, stretch, make demands on, sap, drain

testify VERB

1 *I may be called on to testify in court.*
▶ give evidence, be a witness, go into the dock
2 *He testified that he had not been present at the time of the incident.*
▶ swear, state on oath, attest, declare, affirm, give evidence
3 **testify to** *The latest finds testify to the great wealth of the city in antiquity.*
▶ confirm, attest to, demonstrate, substantiate

testimonial NOUN

Jim received a glowing and thoroughly deserved testimonial.
▶ commendation, recommendation, reference, character reference

testimony NOUN

1 *The girls would not be subjected to the trauma of giving testimony in court.*
▶ evidence, statement, submission
2 **testimony to** *His survival was a testimony to his courage and spirit after horrific injuries.*
▶ evidence of, proof of, witness to, testament to, confirmation of

testy ADJECTIVE

I would get very testy if things weren't exactly right.
▶ irritable, bad-tempered, irascible, grumpy, grouchy, touchy, tetchy, crotchety, cantankerous, peevish, fractious, cross, (*more informal*) stroppy, (*more informal*) shirty
AN OPPOSITE IS good- humoured

tether NOUN

A goat was tangled up in its tether.
▶ rope, lead, leash, chain, cord

tether VERB

When they want to shoot a tiger, Sophie told him, they tether a goat near a tree.
▶ tie, tie up, chain, rope, secure, fasten

text NOUN

1 *Supplying material on disk saves having to retype the text.*
▶ words, wording, content
2 *a literary text*
▶ piece of writing, work, book, textbook
3 *a text from the Bible*
▶ passage, extract, reading, quotation

texture NOUN

The dough should have a soft spongy texture.
▶ consistency, composition, quality, feel, constitution, structure, touch

thank VERB

1 *I want to thank all those people who have supported us over the years.*
▶ acknowledge, express thanks to, show or express gratitude to, express appreciation of, recognize
2 *He only had himself to thank for the mess he was in.*
▶ blame, hold responsible

thankful ADJECTIVE

She was thankful for the moonlight, without which she would never have found her way.
▶ grateful, appreciative (of), pleased (about), relieved (about), happy (about)
OPPOSITES ARE disappointed, ungrateful
USAGE Note that *thankful* and *thankless* are not opposites: *thankful* is normally used about a person, whereas *thankless* is used about an activity.

thankless ADJECTIVE

America inherited Britain's thankless task of maintaining stability in the region.
▶ unenviable, unappreciated, unrecognized, unrewarding, fruitless
OPPOSITES ARE worthwhile, rewarding
USAGE See the note at *thankful*.

thanks NOUN

Julia smiled her thanks and then turned to accept David's invitation.
▶ gratitude, appreciation, acknowledgement, recognition, thanksgiving

thaw VERB

The snow was beginning to thaw.
▶ melt, unfreeze, soften, liquefy, defrost
AN OPPOSITE IS freeze

---

theatre NOUN

1 *This is a work that needs to be heard in a theatre.*
▶ playhouse, auditorium
2 *What made you take up the theatre?*
▶ acting, drama, theatricals, performing

PARTS OF A THEATRE

entrance area: box office, foyer, front of house.

audience area: auditorium, aisles; stalls, circle, dress circle, gallery, balcony, box, upper circle; house lights. ▶▶

---

stage area: stage, set (collection of scenery, stage furniture, and props), scenery, props (small portable items used on the set), apron or proscenium (part of stage in front of curtain), trap (on floor of stage, through which actors can come up); curtain, fire curtain, drop curtain (lowered on stage, forming part of the set); flies (space over the stage), wings (at side of the stage, from which actors come on stage); footlights, orchestra pit.

backstage area: backstage, dressing room, green room, stage door.

---

theatrical ADJECTIVE

1 *She wanted a theatrical career.*
▶ dramatic, acting, stage, thespian
2 *'My dear,' cried Ruby making a theatrical gesture.*
▶ affected, exaggerated, ostentatious, melodramatic, showy, stagy, stilted, unnatural
AN OPPOSITE IS natural
USAGE In the first meaning, be careful how you use *dramatic*, which has a common second meaning 'sudden and exciting'.

theft NOUN

a report of the theft of jewels from a hotel room
▶ robbery, stealing, thieving, pilfering, burglary

theme NOUN

1 *Public services have become the dominant theme of domestic politics.*
▶ topic, issue, subject, concern, question, matter
2 *The theme is played by the orchestra and then picked up by the soloist.*
▶ melody, motif, subject, tune, air

theoretical ADJECTIVE

1 *theoretical physics*
▶ conceptual, pure, abstract, academic
OPPOSITES ARE practical, applied
2 *a theoretical possibility*
▶ hypothetical, notional, conjectural, suppositional, speculative, postulated
OPPOSITES ARE concrete, actual, real

theorize VERB

We cannot theorize without data.
▶ form a theory, hypothesize, conjecture, postulate, speculate

theory NOUN

1 *His theories are based on observations and experiments.*
▶ argument, assumption, belief, conjecture, explanation, guess, hypothesis, idea, notion, speculation, supposition, surmise, thesis, view
2 *the theory of quantum physics*
▶ laws, principles, rules, science
AN OPPOSITE IS practice

therapeutic ADJECTIVE

the therapeutic effect of gardening
▶ beneficial, corrective, curative, healing, helpful, restorative
AN OPPOSITE IS harmful

therapy NOUN
They are still undergoing therapy following the accident.
▶ treatment, remedial treatment, healing, cure, remedy

therefore ADVERB
This is only a story and therefore you shouldn't believe a word of it.
▶ consequently, accordingly, for this or that reason, as a result, as a consequence, so, thus, hence

thesis NOUN
1 *The facts do not bear out his thesis.*
▶ theory, hypothesis, argument, premise or premiss, proposition, idea
2 *Her research was presented in her PhD thesis.*
▶ dissertation, monograph, paper, treatise

thick ADJECTIVE
1 *He was stuffing a thick wad of notes into his jacket pocket. The thick felt curtains were closely fastened.*
▶ fat, chunky, broad, wide, hefty, bulky, solid, stout, sturdy, substantial
AN OPPOSITE IS thin
2 *The lava deposit was no more than a few metres thick. He was a good-looking man with a head of thick black hair.*
▶ deep, heavy
3 *The collision occurred in thick fog. The path wound through thick oak and pine forests.*
▶ dense, solid, impenetrable
OPPOSITES ARE sparse, clear, open
4 *The shallow water was thick with paddling children.*
▶ crowded, filled, packed, swarming, teeming, covered
5 *Beat the mixture into a thick smooth paste.*
▶ stiff, heavy, concentrated, condensed, clotted, coagulated, viscous
OPPOSITES ARE thin, watery
6 (*informal*) *'Some of these councillors are so thick,' said the woman.*
▶ stupid, foolish, dull, slow, dim-witted, brainless
OPPOSITES ARE clever, bright

thicken VERB
Put a little flour in to thicken the sauce.
▶ stiffen, concentrate, condense, reduce, set
AN OPPOSITE IS thin out

thickness NOUN
1 *You can use paper of similar thickness.*
▶ breadth, width, bulk
2 *The thickness of the smoke made it impossible to see.*
▶ density, denseness, murkiness
3 *Great thicknesses of pumice and ash had piled up on the slopes of Vesuvius.*
▶ layer, coating, stratum, seam

thick-skinned ADJECTIVE
He was too thick-skinned to notice the insult.
▶ insensitive, unfeeling, hardened, tough, (*informal*) hard-boiled
OPPOSITES ARE sensitive, thin-skinned

thief NOUN
The 28-year-old thief was arrested when he returned to collect his dog.
▶ robber, burglar, housebreaker, shoplifter, pilferer, bandit

thieving NOUN
a life of thieving
▶ theft, robbery, stealing, pilfering, burglary

---

thin ADJECTIVE This word is often overused. Here are some alternatives:
1 *Frankie was small and thin for his age. He wore a silk shirt with a cravat tucked in round his thin neck.*
▶ slim, slender, lean, slight, skinny
AN OPPOSITE IS fat
2 *She was clad only in a thin nightgown. Thermal underwear keeps you warm by trapping a thin layer of air in its fibres.*
▶ fine, delicate, light, filmy, flimsy, diaphanous, insubstantial, wispy
OPPOSITES ARE thick, heavy
3 *When the paint is nearly dry, apply another thin coat.*
▶ light, runny, watery, dilute, flowing, fluid
OPPOSITES ARE thick, heavy
4 *a thin spread of butter*
▶ sparse, meagre, scanty, scarce
AN OPPOSITE IS thick
5 *The soft thin mist gave a mysterious air to the scene.*
▶ light, rarefied
AN OPPOSITE IS dense
6 *'Get on with it,' said a thin, peevish voice.*
▶ weak, faint, feeble
OPPOSITES ARE strong, loud
7 *a thin excuse*
▶ feeble, tenuous, unconvincing, implausible
AN OPPOSITE IS convincing

---

thin VERB
Thin the paint with water before use.
▶ dilute, water down, weaken

thin out *The crowds began to thin out.*
▶ decrease, diminish, dwindle, disperse, scatter

thing NOUN
1 *The cupboard was full of weird things.*
▶ object, item, artefact, article, body, device, entity, implement
2 *A strange thing happened today.*
▶ event, occurrence, incident, eventuality, happening, phenomenon, affair, circumstance, deed
3 *He didn't have a single thing to add.*
▶ idea, point, statement, thought, concept, detail, fact, factor
4 *There's a thing we have to do.*
▶ job, task, deed, act, action
5 (*informal*) *He's got this thing about wasps.*
▶ obsession, preoccupation, phobia, fear (of), terror (of), dislike (of), (*informal*) hang-up

6 things *Susan put her things in the back of the car*
▶ belongings, possessions, baggage, clothing, luggage, equipment, (*more informal*) gear, (*more informal*) stuff
7 things *Things improved once I had a job.*
▶ circumstances, conditions, life

think VERB

1 *Do you think Molly will come? We thought Rose must have gone home.*
▶ believe, expect, imagine, consider, surmise, conclude
2 *Jennifer thought hard for a few moments.*
▶ concentrate, ponder, contemplate, deliberate, cogitate, reflect, muse
think about *It was time to start thinking about the future.*
▶ consider, contemplate, weigh up, deliberate about
think of *He thought of all the good times they had had together.*
▶ recall, remember, recollect, call to mind
think over *Think over what we have said.*
▶ consider, reflect on, muse on, ponder, mull over, (*more informal*) chew over
think to be *She was thought to be worthy of high office.*
▶ consider, deem, judge, hold, reckon
think up *We tried to think up a convincing excuse.*
▶ concoct, invent, contrive, devise

thinker NOUN

Russell was one of the great thinkers of recent times.
▶ philosopher, intellect, scholar, theorist, ideologist, brain, innovator

thinking ADJECTIVE

He seems to be a thinking man.
▶ intelligent, sensible, rational, reasonable, thoughtful, educated
OPPOSITES ARE stupid, irrational
USAGE Note that *unthinking* is not a true opposite, as it normally means 'without proper consideration', as in *an unthinking remark.*

thinking NOUN

Their thinking on the matter has changed.
▶ opinion, view, reasoning, rationale, philosophy, outlook, judgement, policy

thin-skinned ADJECTIVE

He is thin-skinned and hates criticism.
▶ sensitive, touchy, defensive, paranoid
AN OPPOSITE IS insensitive

third-rate ADJECTIVE

a third-rate piece of work
▶ inferior, poor, poor-quality, substandard, inadequate, deplorable, dismal, atrocious

thirst NOUN

1 *We needed a drink to quench our raging thirst.*
▶ dehydration, thirstiness, dryness

2 *their thirst for knowledge*
▶ appetite, hunger, longing, love (of), yearning, craving, hankering, desire, eagerness, passion

thirst VERB

thirst for *They thirsted for power.*
▶ be thirsty for , crave, strive after, long for, have a thirst for, hunger after, yearn for

thirsty ADJECTIVE

1 *The boys were hot and thirsty after their run.*
▶ dehydrated, dry, parched, (*more informal*) gasping (for a drink), (*more informal*) panting
2 *They were thirsty for adventure.*
▶ eager, hungry, yearning, greedy, itching, longing, avid

thorny ADJECTIVE

1 *They had to scramble through thorny undergrowth.*
▶ prickly, bristly, sharp, spiky, spiny, scratchy, barbed
2 *the thorny question of who would pay*
▶ tricky, difficult, problematic, awkward, delicate

thorough ADJECTIVE

1 *a thorough inquiry*
▶ rigorous, exhaustive, thoroughgoing, detailed, in-depth
AN OPPOSITE IS superficial.
2 *He was slow but very thorough.*
▶ meticulous, scrupulous, conscientious, assiduous, methodical, diligent
3 *He's being a thorough nuisance.*
▶ utter, complete, downright, absolute, perfect, thoroughgoing, total

thought NOUN

1 *She appeared to be lost in thought. It only needs a moment's thought.*
▶ thinking, contemplation, deliberation, meditation, reflection, pondering, regard, consideration, introspection
2 *I had a sudden thought.*
▶ idea, notion, belief, concept, conception, perception, conjecture, conviction, opinion
3 *We've given up all thought of extending the project.*
▶ hope, expectation, intention, aspiration, aim, plan, purpose, design, objective
4 *They seem to have no thought for others.*
▶ consideration, sympathy, regard, concern, caring, understanding, compassion

thoughtful ADJECTIVE

1 *The thoughtful look on his face did not change.*
▶ pensive, reflective, contemplative, introspective, absorbed, preoccupied
OPPOSITES ARE blank, vacant
2 *Members of the audience added thoughtful comments after the lecture.*
▶ profound, studious, intelligent, scrupulous, thorough, diligent, meticulous
AN OPPOSITE IS superficial
3 *It was thoughtful of you to visit.*
▶ considerate, kind, caring, attentive, helpful, concerned, friendly, good-natured, unselfish
AN OPPOSITE IS thoughtless

thoughtless ADJECTIVE
1 *She realized it was thoughtless of her to rush off like that.*
▶ inconsiderate, insensitive, unthinking, unkind, unfeeling, uncaring
AN OPPOSITE IS considerate
2 *One thoughtless remark can prompt a feeling of depression.*
▶ unthinking, careless, unmindful, injudicious, ill-considered, unwise, rash
AN OPPOSITE IS thoughtful

thrash VERB
1 *The boy was thrashed by his exasperated mother.*
▶ punish, beat, whip, flog, spank, cane, strap, birch
2 *She thrashed her arms, attempting to swim towards him.*
▶ jerk, toss, flail
3 (*informal*) *They were thrashed by six wickets in the final.*
▶ defeat, beat, trounce, overwhelm

thrash out *I must thrash things out with him over the next few months.*
▶ resolve, settle, sort out, clarify

thread NOUN
1 *He sewed it up with a needle and thread in his girlfriend's flat.*
▶ cotton, yarn, fibre, strand, twine
2 *I lost the thread of the argument.*
▶ train of thought, line of thought, drift, tenor, continuity, course, direction, theme

threadbare ADJECTIVE
He inched his way along the threadbare strip of carpet.
▶ worn, frayed, ragged, shabby, tattered, tatty

threat NOUN
1 *We got bomb threats against our building.*
▶ warning, ultimatum, menace
2 *It is a brutal regime that poses a threat to world peace.*
▶ danger, risk, hazard, menace

threaten VERB
1 *When they came in they threatened us.*
▶ intimidate, menace, make threats against, browbeat, bully, terrorize, frighten, pressurize
2 *The freedom fighters threatened reprisals. A mass of rain clouds threatened a dramatic change in the weather.*
▶ warn of, forebode, foreshadow, forewarn of, give warning of, portend, presage, indicate
3 *Dumping waste here will threaten the safety and well-being of the region.*
▶ endanger, imperil, jeopardize, put at risk

threatening ADJECTIVE
The dog was baring its teeth in threatening snarls.
▶ ominous, menacing, sinister, forbidding, grim, minatory, stern, unfriendly
AN OPPOSITE IS comforting

threshold NOUN
1 *They stood on the threshold of the main entrance.*
▶ doorstep, doorway, entrance, sill
2 *These events marked the threshold of a new era.*
▶ brink, verge, dawn, beginning, start, outset, opening

thrift NOUN
He succeeded through thrift and business acumen.
▶ prudence, providence, economy, thriftiness, good management

thrifty ADJECTIVE
Students were expected to be hard-working and thrifty.
▶ careful, economical, frugal, prudent, provident, parsimonious, sparing
AN OPPOSITE IS extravagant

thrill NOUN
Just to work with him was a thrill.
▶ adventure, excitement, sensation, pleasure, tingle, tremor, (*more informal*) buzz, (*more informal*) kick

thrill VERB
She knew he was hers and it thrilled her.
▶ excite, delight, rouse, stimulate, exhilarate, stir, electrify, titillate
AN OPPOSITE IS bore

thrilling ADJECTIVE
a thrilling boat ride to the base of Niagara falls
▶ exciting, electrifying, riveting, gripping, stirring, rousing, sensational, spectacular, stimulating, (*more informal*) hair-raising
OPPOSITES ARE unexciting, boring

thrive VERB
Plants often thrive when the same species are massed together. Two-year-olds thrive on attention.
▶ flourish, burgeon, grow, prosper, succeed, be vigorous, develop strongly, do well
OPPOSITES ARE decline, wither

thriving ADJECTIVE
By Tudor times distilling was a thriving industry in Scotland.
▶ flourishing, growing, prosperous, booming, burgeoning, vigorous, developing, expanding, successful, healthy, affluent, lively, profitable
OPPOSITES ARE failing, dying

throaty ADJECTIVE
Lucinda's smile gave way to a throaty laugh.
▶ gruff, guttural, deep, hoarse, husky, croaky, gravelly, rasping, rough, thick

throb NOUN
the annoying dull throb of a neighbour's stereo
▶ beat, rhythm, pulsation, pounding, thud, thump, thrum, vibration

throb VERB
A vein started to throb in his forehead.
▶ pound, pulsate, pulse, beat, thump, palpitate

throng NOUN
Vehicles mingled with the throng of foot passengers.
▶ crowd, mass, horde, mob, crush

throng VERB
Tourists thronged the streets and canals.
▶ pack, cram, fill, press into, squeeze into

throttle VERB
You're lucky Lewis didn't throttle you.
▶ strangle, choke, stifle, smother, suffocate, asphyxiate

throw VERB
1 *They asked her to throw their ball back.*
▶ toss, fling, hurl, pitch, lob, cast, (more informal) chuck, (more informal) sling
2 *He threw a quick glance at them.*
▶ direct, cast, send, shoot, dart
3 *The horse threw its rider.*
▶ unseat, dislodge, upset, bring down
4 *The torch threw a beam of light across the passage.*
▶ cast, project, send, emit, radiate
throw away *He cleared out his room and threw lots of stuff away.*
▶ discard, throw out, dispose of, get rid of, (more informal) ditch
throw off *He hoped he had thrown off his pursuers.*
▶ shake off, escape, elude, give the slip to, get away from
throw out *He tried to get in the house but was thrown out. The government might be thrown out at the next election.*
▶ eject, expel, remove, force out, oust, get rid of
throw up *He was tempted to throw up his job and go abroad.*
▶ abandon, relinquish, give up, (more informal) quit, (more informal) chuck in

throw NOUN
With one mighty throw the ball went over the fence.
▶ heave, fling, toss, lob, pitch

throwaway ADJECTIVE
a throwaway remark
▶ casual, offhand, passing, unthinking, unimportant

thrust VERB
1 *He thrust a mug of tea into my hands.*
▶ push, shove, force, press, stick, poke
2 *His attacker thrust at him with a knife.*
▶ lunge, jab, prod, stab, plunge, poke, stick

thrust NOUN
1 *He gave the door a firm thrust.*
▶ shove, push, prod, poke
2 *I strongly support the thrust of your argument.*
▶ gist, substance, drift, burden, force

thud VERB
Heavy footsteps thudded across the front porch.
▶ thump, clump, stomp, crash

thud NOUN
He was hammering on the door, thud after thud.
▶ thump, bang, rap, clunk, clonk, crash

thug NOUN
(informal) A fight broke out between two armies of thugs.
▶ ruffian, hoodlum, tough, bully

thumb VERB
She thumbed through her notes.
▶ browse, flick, flip, leaf, riffle, scan

thump NOUN
1 *He sat down with a painful thump on the floor.*
▶ thud, bang, clunk, clonk, crash
2 *The heavy thump of acid house music was everywhere.*
▶ beat, rhythm, pulsation, pounding, throb, thud, thrum, vibration

thump VERB
The woman thumped the table with her fist.
▶ bang, hit, strike, pound, beat, rap, batter, wallop, knock

thunder NOUN
Her musings were interrupted by the thunder of hooves.
▶ rumble, rumbling, boom, booming, roar, roaring, thud, thump, ringing

thunder VERB
Fighter aircraft thundered overhead.
▶ roar, boom, rumble, blast

thunderous ADJECTIVE
The speech was greeted by thunderous applause and standing ovations.
▶ deafening, tumultuous, resounding, loud, booming

thwart VERB
He stayed in power as long as he could, just to thwart his main rival.
▶ frustrate, hinder, impede, foil, obstruct, prevent, stand in the way of, stop
OPPOSITES ARE help, further

tick NOUN
1 *Put a tick in the box marked 'no'.*
▶ mark, stroke, dash, line
2 *They heard the tick of a clock.*
▶ ticking, clicking
in a tick *(informal) I'll be back in a tick.*
▶ in a moment, in a minute, in a second, in a trice, very soon, very shortly, (informal) in a jiffy

tick VERB
1 *It was so quiet I could hear my watch ticking.*
▶ click, make a tick, beat
2 *Tick the box against your preferred method of payment.*
▶ mark, check off, indicate
tick off *(informal) She ticked off the children for making a noise.*
▶ tell off, scold, reprimand, admonish, rebuke

ticket NOUN
1 *a ticket to the game*
▶ pass, permit, token, voucher, coupon
2 *a price ticket*
▶ label, tag, sticker, marker, slip, tab

tickle VERB
1 *He tickled her toes until she gurgled happily.*
▶ touch, stroke, pet
2 *The little story tickled us.*
▶ amuse, entertain, delight, cheer

a b c d e f g h i j k l m n o p q r s **t** u v w x y z

ticklish ADJECTIVE

1 *'It's lucky I'm not ticklish,' she squealed.*
▶ giggly, wriggly, sensitive
2 *He had the ticklish problem of explaining where he had been all night.*
▶ tricky, awkward, delicate, thorny, difficult, hazardous, risky, touchy, (*more informal*) dodgy

tide NOUN

The tide of opinion was turning against the government.
▶ trend, tendency, current, course, drift, movement

tidy ADJECTIVE

1 *Each desk should be tidy and have a place card.*
▶ neat, orderly, uncluttered, shipshape, smart, spick and span
OPPOSITES ARE untidy, messy
2 *He tried to be tidy in his new apartment.*
▶ methodical, meticulous, organized, systematic, house-proud
OPPOSITES ARE untidy, disorganized
3 (*informal*) *All those books will cost a tidy sum.*
▶ sizeable, considerable, substantial, appreciable, large, (*informal*) hefty

tidy VERB

The girls started to wash up and tidy.
▶ clean up, put in order, set straight, arrange, smarten, spruce up, neaten, straighten
OPPOSITES ARE untidy, muddle

tie VERB

1 *The dog was tied to a lamppost.*
▶ fasten, secure, attach, tether, bind, hitch
AN OPPOSITE IS untie
2 *Her new job tied her to the office.*
▶ restrict, limit, confine, restrain
3 *The home side tied its next game.*
▶ draw, finish level

tie up

1 *He tied up the boat at the jetty.*
▶ moor, tether, fasten, attach
2 *We were keen to tie up the deal.*
▶ complete, finalize, conclude, settle
3 **be tied up** *The manager is still tied up I'm afraid.*
▶ be busy, be occupied, be engaged

tie NOUN

Family ties are important.
▶ bond, connection, link, attachment, relationship, association

tier NOUN

The seats are arranged in three tiers
▶ row, rank, line, level, stage, storey, terrace

tight ADJECTIVE

1 *The rope was pulled tight.*
▶ taut, stretched, rigid, stiff, tense
OPPOSITES ARE slack, loose
2 *Her grip was tight.*
▶ firm, fast, secure, clenched
AN OPPOSITE IS relaxed
3 *The joint was completely tight.*
▶ sealed, airtight, impervious
AN OPPOSITE IS leaking

4 *The bed had to fit into a tight space.*
▶ small, compact, constricted, snug, poky
5 *He can be very tight with his money.*
▶ mean, stingy, niggardly, miserly, parsimonious, (*more informal*) tight-fisted, (*more informal*) penny-pinching
AN OPPOSITE IS generous
6 *There is tight security at the airport.*
▶ strict, stringent, rigorous, severe, tough, scrupulous
AN OPPOSITE IS lax

tighten VERB

1 *Jane tightened her grip on the rail.*
▶ strengthen, squeeze, tense, stiffen, increase
OPPOSITES ARE loosen, relax
2 *You need to tighten your shoelaces.*
▶ make tight, pull tighter, tauten, stretch
AN OPPOSITE IS slacken
3 *Tighten all screws when the chair is assembled.*
▶ make tighter, screw up, give another turn to
AN OPPOSITE IS loosen

tighten up *Security will be tightened up during the peak season.*
▶ increase, heighten, strengthen, intensify, escalate

tight-fisted ADJECTIVE

We were too tight-fisted to pay a motorway toll.
▶ mean, stingy, niggardly, miserly, parsimonious, (*more informal*) penny-pinching

till VERB

country people who till the land
▶ cultivate, work, farm, plough, dig

tilt VERB

He tilted his hat to one side The wall tilted alarmingly.
▶ lean, slant, slope, tip, angle

tilt NOUN

The tray was on a tilt.
▶ slant, slope, incline, angle

at full tilt *They ran at full tilt down the bank.*
▶ headlong, pell-mell, at full speed, at full pelt, at a gallop, fast

timber NOUN

Houses built of timber and mud would be very damp.
▶ wood, planks, planking, beams, laths, boarding, boards, logs, lumber, trees

time NOUN

1 *in the time of Queen Mary*
▶ age, era, period, generation
2 *He lived here for a time.*
▶ while, period, spell
3 *It took a long time to fix the problem.*
▶ while, interval, duration
4 *When is the best time to come? I didn't know what to do at that time.*
▶ moment, point, juncture, stage, date, occasion
RELATED ADJECTIVES temporal, chronic, chronological

time VERB

1 *She had timed her arrival for half an hour after the party was due to start.*
▶ regulate, choose, fix, set, schedule
2 *The nurse timed ten minutes.*
▶ measure, count

timeless ADJECTIVE

the instant, timeless attraction of a good tune
▶ immortal, ageless, enduring, lasting, perennial, abiding

timely ADJECTIVE

The incident was a timely reminder of how dangerous these waters had become.
▶ opportune, fitting, suitable, appropriate, apt, prompt

timetable NOUN

They established a timetable for elections and political reform.
▶ schedule, agenda, programme, calendar, diary, roster, rota

timid ADJECTIVE

Elaine handed him her bag with a timid smile.
▶ shy, diffident, bashful, modest, timorous, faint-hearted, weak, fearful
OPPOSITES ARE bold, brazen

tinge NOUN

1 *The light took on a green tinge.*
▶ tint, shade, hue, colour
2 *There was a tinge of amusement on his face.*
▶ trace, touch, note, suggestion, flavour, streak

tingle NOUN

1 *There was a strange tingle in her fingers.*
▶ prickling, stinging, tickle, tickling, itch, itching, pins and needles
2 *Melissa felt a tingle of excitement.*
▶ quiver, tremor, thrill, sensation, shiver

tingle VERB

His shoes were so tight they made his feet tingle.
▶ itch, prickle, sting, tickle

tinker VERB

He watched Nathan tinkering with his bike.
▶ fiddle, play, meddle, tamper, dabble, trifle, interfere, (*more informal*) mess about, (*more informal*) play about

tinny ADJECTIVE

1 *She pressed a button and a tinny voice rang out.*
▶ jangling, jingly, metallic
OPPOSITES ARE full, deep
2 *He drove his tinny little car west out of Oxford.*
▶ cheap, inferior, poor-quality
AN OPPOSITE IS solid

tint NOUN

smooth glossy paper with a yellowish tint
▶ tinge, shade, hue, colour

tiny ADJECTIVE

1 *We've got a tiny pond in the front garden.*
▶ minute, miniature, diminutive, midget, mini, very small, (*more informal*) teeny, (*more informal*) titchy
AN OPPOSITE IS huge
2 *These man-made gases are present in the atmosphere only in tiny amounts.*
▶ minute, insignificant, negligible, paltry, meagre

tip NOUN

1 *He ran the tip of his finger along the handlebar. The tip of the arrow couldn't be far into the tree.*
▶ end, point, extremity, sharp end, nib
2 *The tip of a mountain was visible above the clouds.*
▶ summit, peak, pinnacle, top, apex, cap, crown, head
3 *He paid his bill, left a good tip, and walked home.*
▶ gratuity, gift
4 *My tip is to go for really good-quality ski pants.*
▶ hint, suggestion, advice, clue, information, warning
5 *To most people the rubbish tip is an eyesore.*
▶ dump, heap, pit

tip VERB

1 *He tipped his head back to look. The van was tipping to one side.*
▶ lean, incline, list, slant, slope, tilt, keel over
2 *She tipped the fish into the sink and began to clean them.*
▶ empty, dump, pour out, spill, unload
3 *He decided to tip the driver after all.*
▶ give a tip to, remunerate, reward

tip over *A whale is capable of tipping over a small boat.*
▶ overturn, capsize, topple, turn over, upset, knock over

tip-off NOUN

(*informal*) *The police received a tip-off about a shipment of cocaine.*
▶ alert, clue, prompt, piece of information

tire VERB

The long walk tired us.
▶ exhaust, fatigue, weary, tire out, wear out, drain
OPPOSITES ARE refresh, invigorate

tired ADJECTIVE

1 *He was tired from his hectic battle with the goblins.*
▶ exhausted, fatigued, wearied, worn out
OPPOSITES ARE energetic, refreshed
2 *tired old debates about nature and nurture*
▶ stale, hackneyed, overworked, banal
OPPOSITES ARE fresh, new

tired of *They grew tired of waiting.*
▶ bored with, fed up with, sick of, impatient with

tiredness NOUN

He felt good despite his tiredness.
▶ exhaustion, fatigue, weariness, lethargy, listlessness, sleepiness, drowsiness, inertia, lassitude
OPPOSITES ARE vigour, energy

tireless ADJECTIVE
a tireless campaigner on behalf of chimpanzees in the wild
▶ vigorous, energetic, determined, unflagging, untiring, indefatigable, persistent, zealous, diligent, sedulous, unceasing
AN OPPOSITE IS lazy
USAGE Note that *tireless* and *tiresome* are not opposites.

tiresome ADJECTIVE
Richard was back from work after a tiresome day.
▶ irritating, annoying, wearisome, troublesome, trying, irksome, bothersome, vexing, distracting, exasperating
OPPOSITES ARE stimulating, exciting
USAGE See the note at *tireless*.

tiring ADJECTIVE
Infant care can be tiring.
▶ exhausting, exacting, taxing, wearying, fatiguing, demanding, difficult, hard
AN OPPOSITE IS refreshing

tissue NOUN
1 *body tissue*
▶ substance, material, matter, structure, stuff
2 *a box of tissues*
▶ paper handkerchief, paper napkin
3 *a tissue of lies*
▶ web, network, tangle, maze, series

titbit NOUN
1 *She fed the dogs titbits.*
▶ scrap, bit, morsel, delicacy
2 *a titbit of information*
▶ piece, morsel, scrap

titillate VERB
sensational news articles to titillate readers
▶ stimulate, excite, thrill, intrigue, fascinate, stir, arouse

title NOUN
1 *The title of the picture was printed underneath.*
▶ caption, heading, name
2 *Specify the title you want to be known by.*
▶ form of address, designation, appellation, rank, status, office, position
3 *He sought to prove his title to the land.*
▶ right, entitlement, claim, ownership (of), tenure (of)

titter NOUN
The remark caused a few titters.
▶ giggle, snigger, chuckle, laugh

titter VERB
Some of the audience began to titter.
▶ giggle, snigger, chuckle, laugh

toast VERB
1 *They toasted bread by the fire.*
▶ grill, brown, heat, warm
2 *The guests then toasted their host.*
▶ drink a toast to, drink the health of, raise your glass to, salute, honour

together ADVERB
1 *They were all speaking together.*
▶ simultaneously, at the same time, at once, collectively, concurrently, in chorus, in unison, jointly
OPPOSITES ARE independently, separately
2 *Naim and I work together.*
▶ jointly, with each other, in concert, side by side
OPPOSITES ARE separately, alone
3 *Nothing happened for days together.*
▶ in a row, in succession, continuously, consecutively

toil NOUN
years of hardship and toil
▶ work, labour, donkey work, slaving, drudgery, effort, exertion, industry

toil VERB
The team needed to toil all day.
▶ work, labour, slave, sweat, struggle, (*more informal*) slog, (*more informal*) grind away

toilet NOUN
1 *There is a toilet on the first floor.*
▶ lavatory, WC, convenience, facilities, privy, (*more informal*) loo
2 *She was taking ages over her toilet.*
▶ washing, bathing

token NOUN
1 *Saladin's ring was sent as a token of good faith.*
▶ symbol, sign, mark, expression, testimony, evidence, indication, proof, reminder
2 *He had a cross tattooed on his chest as a token of this religious experience.*
▶ memento, souvenir, record, keepsake
3 *a book token*
▶ voucher, coupon, counter

token ADJECTIVE
1 *She did the work for a token fee.*
▶ nominal, minimal, trivial, slight
AN OPPOSITE IS substantial
2 *The garrison offered only token resistance.*
▶ perfunctory, insignificant, superficial, symbolic
AN OPPOSITE IS considerable

tolerable ADJECTIVE
1 *The pain was barely tolerable.*
▶ bearable, acceptable, endurable, sufferable, supportable
AN OPPOSITE IS intolerable
2 *He was fond of music and had a tolerable voice.*
▶ adequate, passable, middling, ordinary, satisfactory, fair, mediocre, indifferent

tolerance NOUN
1 *He has always preached tolerance for people of whatever religion.*
▶ toleration, forbearance, sufferance, acceptance, open-mindedness, broad-mindedness, liberalism, understanding, permissiveness
2 *Allow a slight tolerance in measurement.*
▶ variation, fluctuation, deviation, leeway

tolerant ADJECTIVE
He's a tolerant chap who didn't seem to mind if I got it wrong.
► understanding, open-minded, long-suffering, forbearing, sympathetic, fair, magnanimous, charitable
OPPOSITES ARE intolerant, unsympathetic

tolerate VERB
1 *At work she will not tolerate interference.*
► put up with, bear, endure, stand, abide, stomach, suffer, take, (*more informal*) stick
2 *This sort of behaviour is difficult to tolerate.*
► accept, condone, countenance, admit, brook, make allowances for, permit, sanction

toll NOUN
1 *a road toll*
► charge, fee, levy, tariff, payment, duty, tax
2 *the death toll from the accident*
► count, tally, total, reckoning

toll VERB
We heard a bell toll.
► ring, peal, chime, sound

tomb NOUN
the tomb of Ramesses II
► burial chamber, burial place, sepulchre, grave, catacomb, crypt, mausoleum
RELATED ADJECTIVE sepulchral

tone NOUN
1 *He objected to the arrogant tone of the letter.*
► manner, mood, spirit, attitude, tenor, quality
2 *She called out in an angry tone of voice.*
► expression, timbre, quality, sound, modulation, intonation
3 *emulsion paint with a rosy tone*
► tint, tinge, hue, shade, blush, colour

tone VERB
tone with *The pastel shades of the wallpaper tone beautifully with the light wood of the furniture.*
► harmonize with, coordinate with, match, go well with, suit
tone down *He was unwilling to tone down his criticisms of the management.*
► moderate, modify, temper, mitigate, soften, restrain, dampen, subdue, play down
AN OPPOSITE IS intensify

tongue NOUN
He spoke in a foreign tongue.
► language, vernacular, idiom, talk, speech, utterance

tongue-tied ADJECTIVE
He is often tongue-tied in company.
► lost for words, inarticulate, dumbstruck, speechless, mute, silent

tonic NOUN
A tonic will do you good.
► stimulant, restorative, refresher, cordial, (*more informal*) pick-me-up

tool NOUN
1 *a set of garden tools*
► implement, utensil, device, gadget, appliance, contraption
2 *The tabloid press became a tool of the government.*
► dupe, pawn, puppet, creature, stooge, minion, (*more informal*) poodle

VARIOUS TOOLS

tools for cutting and chopping: knife; saw, hacksaw; axe, chopper, cleaver, hatchet, mattock, pickaxe.

tools for drilling: brace and bit, bradawl, drill, gimlet.

tools for nails and screws: hammer, mallet, punch; screwdriver.

tools for gripping and forcing: clamp, vice, jack; crowbar; spanner; pincers, pliers, tweezers, wrench.

tools for shaping: chisel, plane, spokeshave, file, sander, sandpaper.

gardening and agricultural tools: fork, spade, shovel; dibble or dibber, hoe; rake, pitchfork; scythe, secateurs, shears, sickle.

top NOUN
1 *The top of the mountain was still covered in snow.*
► summit, peak, pinnacle, tip, apex, cap, crown, head
AN OPPOSITE IS foot
2 *The top of the jar was stuck.*
► lid, cap, cover, covering
AN OPPOSITE IS bottom

top ADJECTIVE
1 *an office on the top floor*
► highest, topmost, uppermost, upper
OPPOSITES ARE bottom, lowest
2 *some of the world's top golf professionals*
► leading, finest, foremost, principal, chief, pre-eminent, prime
3 *the top Paris restaurants*
► best, prime, superior, leading, foremost, finest
AN OPPOSITE IS inferior

top VERB
1 *The cake can be topped with chopped nuts.*
► cover, cap, decorate, finish off, garnish, crown
2 *Sales are expected to top the million mark.*
► exceed, beat, be higher than, outdo, surpass, better, cap, excel

topic NOUN
An article on this topic appeared last month.
► subject, theme, issue, matter, question, talking-point

topical ADJECTIVE
Choose a news item of topical interest each week.
► current, contemporary, recent, up-to-date, up-to-the-minute, newsworthy

a b c d e f g h i j k l m n o p q r s **t** u v w x y z

topple VERB

1 *The heavy winds toppled several pylons, causing power cuts.*
▶ knock down, overturn, tip over, throw down, upset
2 *She saw a man topple sideways into the gutter. If kangaroos had no tails, they would topple over.*
▶ fall, overbalance, tumble
3 *A party revolt had toppled the conservative leadership.*
▶ bring down, overthrow, oust, unseat, depose

topsy-turvy ADJECTIVE

The carts lay in a topsy-turvy heap at the bottom of the hill. My emotions are all topsy-turvy.
▶ disordered, confused, mixed up, muddled, jumbled, untidy, higgledy-piggledy
OPPOSITES ARE ordered, neat

torment NOUN

Jason never escaped the torment of self-doubt.
▶ agony, affliction, anguish, pain, ordeal, distress, misery, suffering, torture

torment VERB

1 *The urge to express her feelings tormented her. Sometimes, he was tormented by jealousy.*
▶ afflict, torture, distress, persecute, plague, bedevil, bother, be a torment to, pain, vex
2 *Marjory loved tormenting her younger brother.*
▶ tease, bait, pester, harass, annoy, bully, victimize

torrent NOUN

1 *The sky opened and a heavy torrent fell down.*
▶ downpour, deluge, flood, shower, flow
AN OPPOSITE IS trickle
2 *These points are lost to the reader in a torrent of words.*
▶ cascade, gush, rush, outburst, spate, stream, tide

torrential ADJECTIVE

They landed safely in torrential rain.
▶ heavy, violent, teeming, relentless, soaking

tortuous ADJECTIVE

They took a tortuous route through Dijon and Lyons. Acquiring skills can be a tortuous process.
▶ twisted, twisting, winding, circuitous, devious, meandering, roundabout, indirect
OPPOSITES ARE straight, direct

torture NOUN

1 *Human rights groups claimed that torture of prisoners had taken place.*
▶ maltreatment, persecution, cruelty, torment, humiliation, degradation, inquisition
2 *The rest of the journey was torture.*
▶ agony, torment, misery, affliction

torture VERB

1 *They were out to torture their victims.*
▶ persecute, inflict pain on, inflict suffering on, be cruel to, degrade, humiliate, hurt, torment
2 *I was having thoughts that tortured me.*
▶ afflict, torment, distress, persecute, plague, bedevil, bother, be a torment to, pain, vex

toss VERB

1 *He tossed a ball high in the air.*
▶ throw, fling, hurl, cast, pitch, heave
2 *The boat was tossing about in shallow water.*
▶ lurch, pitch, reel, rock, roll, bob, shake, wallow, welter, writhe
3 *Marion tossed restlessly in bed.*
▶ twist and turn, move restlessly, flail, thrash about, wriggle, fidget

toss NOUN

a toss of a coin
▶ flip, fling, throw, jerk, heave

tot VERB

tot up *He was totting up some figures.*
▶ add up, calculate, count, total, find the total of, reckon up, totalize, work out

total ADJECTIVE

1 *The total volume of sales reached five million.*
▶ complete, comprehensive, entire, full, gross, overall, whole
2 *A senior fire officer said it was total carnage.*
▶ sheer, utter, absolute, downright, thorough, unmitigated, unqualified, perfect, out-and-out

total NOUN

The airport will handle a total of a million passengers in the week before Christmas.
▶ sum, totality, aggregate, amount, whole

total VERB

1 *The cash bag totalled £1,200.*
▶ amount to, come to, add up to, make, reach
total up *Total up your scores.*
▶ add up, calculate, count, tot up, find the total of, reckon up, totalize, work out

totalitarian ADJECTIVE

In totalitarian societies, newspapers are wholly controlled by the state.
▶ authoritarian, autocratic, dictatorial, one-party, oppressive, repressive, tyrannical, undemocratic, unrepresentative
OPPOSITES ARE democratic, liberal

totter VERB

Lizzy held out her arms and the child tottered towards her.
▶ stagger, teeter, dodder, stumble, shuffle, waddle, shamble, stagger, falter, reel

touch NOUN

1 *Animals communicate by touch.*
▶ feeling, touching, contact
2 *She jumped under his touch.*
▶ pat, stroke, tap, caress, contact, dab
3 *Funny speeches need a bubbly, light touch.*
▶ manner, style, technique, flair, knack, feel, sensitivity
4 *There was a touch of genius in the way he talked that night.*
▶ hint, suggestion, suspicion, tinge, trace
5 *A gift of flowers can be a nice touch.*
▶ feature, detail, extra

6 *He and Carol kept in touch.*
▶ contact, communication, correspondence
RELATED ADJECTIVE tactile

touch VERB

1 *She touched his arm and he turned.*
▶ pat, brush, contact, feel, rub, stroke, tap, caress, dab

2 *Their sorrow touched him.*
▶ move, affect, concern, disturb, influence, inspire, stir, upset

3 *Their speed touched 100 m.p.h.*
▶ reach, rise to, attain

4 (*informal*) *Nothing could touch them for good value.*
▶ equal, match, compare with, rival, come up to, parallel

touch on *The programme touched on recent concerns.*
▶ refer to, deal with, mention, treat, raise, cover

touch up *The room had been touched up and given a new carpet.*
▶ improve, repaint, renovate, refurbish, redecorate

touched ADJECTIVE

1 *I was touched by their generosity.*
▶ moved, affected, impressed, stirred, responsive (to)

2 (*informal*) *You have to be a bit touched to do something like that.*
▶ mad, crazy, deranged, disturbed, insane, unbalanced, (*more informal*) barmy

touching ADJECTIVE

She was beautiful, her face crossed by a touching sadness.
▶ moving, affecting, poignant, emotional, tender

touchy ADJECTIVE

Like most tired children she was touchy and uncooperative.
▶ irritable, bad-tempered, irascible, grumpy, grouchy, testy, tetchy, crotchety, cantankerous, peevish, fractious, cross, (*more informal*) stroppy, (*more informal*) shirty
AN OPPOSITE IS good- humoured

tough ADJECTIVE

1 *It was my first outing in my tough new boots.*
▶ strong, stout, durable, hard-wearing, indestructible, lasting, unbreakable, well-made
OPPOSITES ARE flimsy, delicate

2 (*informal*) *He is tall with a tough physique.*
▶ sturdy, muscular, strong, beefy, brawny, burly, hardy, robust, stalwart
AN OPPOSITE IS weak

3 *They proved to be tough rivals. She's a tough, single-minded woman.*
▶ determined, tenacious, unyielding, resilient, resolute, resistant, stiff, stubborn
AN OPPOSITE IS weak

4 *The meat was overcooked and tough.*
▶ chewy, leathery, gristly, rubbery, hard, uneatable
AN OPPOSITE IS tender

5 *There was a tough climb ahead.*
▶ difficult, arduous, strenuous, exacting, exhausting, gruelling, stiff, hard, laborious
AN OPPOSITE IS easy

6 *They had some tough questions to answer.*
▶ difficult, baffling, intractable, puzzling, perplexing, (*more informal*) thorny, (*more informal*) knotty
AN OPPOSITE IS easy

toughen VERB

ways of toughening wood
▶ harden, strengthen, make tougher, reinforce
AN OPPOSITE IS weaken

tour NOUN

a tour round the castles of southern Bavaria
▶ journey, expedition, trip, ride, drive, outing, excursion

tour VERB

The town is well situated for touring the area.
▶ travel round, visit, explore, sightsee, go round, make a tour of

tourist NOUN

Tribal dances are performed for the tourists.
▶ sightseer, holidaymaker, visitor, tripper, traveller

tournament NOUN

He was due to take part in a celebrity golf tournament.
▶ competition, contest, championship, match, meeting, series

tow VERB

The rope seemed too slender to tow the forty-foot barge.
▶ pull, drag, tug, draw, haul, transport, trail

tower NOUN

We passed two abbeys, one with a tower and one without.
▶ steeple, turret, column, pillar, belfry

tower VERB

Clouds towered on every side. He stood up, and he towered above her.
▶ loom, rear, rise, dominate, stand out, stick up, ascend

towering ADJECTIVE

towering crags and cliffs
▶ tall, high, lofty, soaring, mighty, colossal, gigantic, imposing

town NOUN

The family moved to an industrial town.
▶ conurbation, urban area, borough, city, municipality, settlement
RELATED ADJECTIVE urban, civic, municipal

toxic ADJECTIVE

You have two minutes to get out before the heat and toxic fumes overcome you.
▶ poisonous, noxious, lethal, deadly, dangerous, harmful
OPPOSITES ARE harmless, safe

a b c d e f g h i j k l m n o p q r s t u v w x y z

toy ADJECTIVE

giant toy animals
▶ model, imitation, make-believe, simulation, (*more informal*) pretend

toy NOUN

The children can bring their favourite toy.
▶ plaything, game, doll

toy VERB

toy with

1 *She picked up her fork and toyed with her food.*
▶ play with, fiddle with, fidget with, tinker with, peck at, pick at

2 *He toyed with the idea of walking to the station to meet her.*
▶ think about, play with, consider

trace NOUN

1 *'No,' he said with a trace of irritation.*
▶ hint, touch, suggestion, suspicion

2 *The animal had left no trace.*
▶ trail, track, mark, sign, spoor, indication

3 *The investigators could find no trace of blood.*
▶ sign, remnant, remains, vestige

trace VERB

1 *Police are trying to trace the owner of the car.*
▶ track down, find, discover, uncover, unearth, detect

2 *It would be best to trace the map from an atlas.*
▶ copy, draw, outline, mark out, sketch, make a copy of

track NOUN

1 *An animal had left clear tracks.*
▶ trace, trail, mark, scent, spoor, footmark, footprint

2 *a track across the fields*
▶ path, way, pathway, footpath, route, lane, trail

3 *a racing track*
▶ course, circuit, dirt-track, race-track

4 *Passengers were seen walking along the tracks.*
▶ rail, line

track VERB

He tracked a bear all day.
▶ follow, trail, pursue, stalk, chase, hunt, dog, shadow, trace

track down *It took years to track everyone down.*
▶ discover, trace, find, detect, recover, retrieve

tract NOUN

large tracts of land
▶ area, expanse, region, stretch, extent, sweep, span, parcel

trade NOUN

1 *international trade*
▶ commerce, buying and selling, dealing, trading, traffic, transactions, barter, business, marketing
RELATED ADJECTIVE mercantile

2 *He wanted to be trained in a trade.*
▶ craft, occupation, job, career, profession, calling, pursuit, line of work

trade VERB

1 *The family traded in diamonds.*
▶ deal, traffic, buy and sell, do business

2 *She traded her old car for a new model.*
▶ exchange, part-exchange, barter, swap, switch

trader NOUNS

local high-street traders
▶ dealer, merchant, retailer, tradesman, shopkeeper, stockist, supplier, vendor

tradition NOUN

the old tradition of first-footing
▶ custom, practice, convention, institution, observance, habit, routine

traditional ADJECTIVE

1 *a traditional white wedding*
▶ conventional, customary, established, accustomed, familiar, time-honoured, typical, orthodox, regular, usual
AN OPPOSITE IS unconventional

2 *traditional beliefs*
▶ popular, folk, oral, unwritten, historical
OPPOSITES ARE modern, contemporary

traffic NOUN

1 *Road traffic is not allowed in the park.*
▶ vehicles, cars, transport

2 *goods traffic*
▶ transport, transportation, movement

3 *illegal traffic in antiquities*
▶ trade, trading, dealing, commerce, peddling

traffic VERB

He was arrested on suspicion of trafficking in illegal exports.
▶ trade, deal, buy and sell

tragedy NOUN

the tragedy of their son's death
▶ disaster, calamity, catastrophe, affliction, blow, misfortune, misadventure

tragic ADJECTIVE

1 *a tragic accident*
▶ disastrous, catastrophic, calamitous, dreadful, fatal, appalling, terrible, unfortunate
AN OPPOSITE IS fortunate

2 *a tragic expression on her face*
▶ sad, sorrowful, woeful, wretched, distressed, grief-stricken, hurt, pathetic, piteous, pitiful
AN OPPOSITE IS comic

trail NOUN

1 *The fox followed the trail of its prey.*
▶ track, footprints, mark, scent, signs, spoor, traces

2 *a nature trail*
▶ path, pathway, route, track, road

3 *They left a trail of clues.*
▶ series, string, stream, chain, line

trail VERB

1 *The car was trailing a large caravan.*
► draw, haul, drag, pull, tow
2 *His feet were trailing in the water.*
► dangle, hang
3 *She suspected someone was trailing her.*
► follow, pursue, shadow, stalk, track, trace, tail, chase
4 *The smaller children were trailing behind.*
► straggle, linger, lag, fall behind, dawdle, dally

train NOUN

1 *a strange train of events*
► chain, series, sequence, succession
2 *The minister had a train of attendants.*
► entourage, retinue, cortège, following, suite

train VERB

1 *Now she had three assistants to train.*
► teach, instruct, tutor, coach, educate, prepare
2 *The team was training hard.*
► practise, exercise, prepare yourself, get fit, *(more informal)* work out
3 *The guns were trained on a position in the hills.*
► aim (at), point (at), direct (at), level (at)

trainee NOUN

For half price you can have your hair done by a trainee.
► beginner, apprentice, novice, pupil, starter, cadet, student, tiro

trainer NOUN

a fitness trainer
► instructor, coach, teacher, tutor, mentor

training NOUN

Next week he would report for training.
► exercise, exercises, physical exercise, fitness routine, *(more informal)* working out

traipse VERB

She didn't want to traipse round town all afternoon.
► trudge, trek, tramp, trail, plod

trait NOUN

This was an unfortunate trait for a prime minister.
► characteristic, quality, attribute, peculiarity, idiosyncrasy, quirk

traitor NOUN

Thousands of students denounced Kim as a traitor.
► betrayer, defector, deserter, double-crosser, apostate, blackleg, turncoat, collaborator, informer, quisling, renegade

tramp NOUN

1 *the ritual tramp across Ilkley Moor*
► trek, trudge, march, walk, *(more informal)* slog
2 *He remembered an old tramp he used to see by the tube station.*
► beggar, vagrant, homeless person, destitute person, *(more informal)* dosser, *(more informal)* down and out

tramp VERB

We tramped across the wet grass and bracken.
► trudge, trek, traipse, hike, march, plod, stride, toil

trample VERB

trample on *Her dog had trampled on his tulips.*
► tread on, stamp on, walk over, crush, flatten, squash

trance NOUN

She was lost in a trance.
► daze, dream, hypnotic state, reverie, daydream, ecstasy, spell

tranquil ADJECTIVE

1 *the tranquil and pretty hamlet of Blore*
► peaceful, quiet, calm, restful, placid, serene, still, undisturbed, unruffled
OPPOSITES ARE noisy, busy
2 *He felt relaxed and tranquil.*
► calm, placid, sedate, sober, unemotional, unexcited, untroubled, collected, composed, dispassionate, *(more informal)* laid-back
AN OPPOSITE IS excited

transaction NOUN

The assets can be purchased or sold in a single transaction.
► deal, agreement, settlement, arrangement, proceeding, undertaking, deed

transcend VERB

events that transcended their worst fears
► exceed, surpass, outdo, go beyond, eclipse, outstrip

transcribe VERB

The recording had to be transcribed for circulation.
► copy out, write out, take down, put in writing, reproduce

transcript NOUN

a transcript of the tapes
► written version, printed version, record, text, reproduction

transfer VERB (with the stress on -*fer*)

The books will be transferred to the central library.
► move, remove, shift, relocate, take over, take across, convey, transmit

transfer NOUN (with the stress on *trans-*)

the transfer of rights to the new owner
► change, changeover, shift, shifting, handover, transferral, transmission

transform VERB

The new owners transformed the property into a lovely family house.
► convert, change, alter, develop, renovate, reorganize, *(more formal)* metamorphose

a b c d e f g h i j k l m n o p q r s t u v w x y z

transformation NOUN
There was a transformation in her attitude.
▶ change, conversion, alteration, improvement, revolution, transfiguration, transition, (*more formal*) metamorphosis, (*more informal*) turn-about

transient ADJECTIVE
a transient change in public opinion
▶ transitory, temporary, passing, brief, momentary, fleeting, impermanent, short-term
AN OPPOSITE IS permanent

transit NOUN
Some of the goods had been lost in transit.
▶ shipment, transportation, passage, conveyance, movement, shipment, travel

transition NOUN
the transition from childhood to adulthood
▶ change , alteration, changeover, evolution, progress, progression, shift, transformation

translate VERB
a poem by Goethe translated into English
▶ render, convert, interpret, express, paraphrase, transcribe

translation NOUN
an English translation of the Iliad
▶ version, rendering, transcription, interpretation, gloss, paraphrase

transmission NOUN
The programme was scheduled for transmission after 9 o'clock.
▶ broadcast, relaying, diffusion, dissemination, sending out

transmit VERB
1 *The broadcast will be transmitted next Saturday.*
▶ broadcast, relay, send out
2 *Short-wave radios are used to transmit messages.*
▶ communicate, convey, dispatch, disseminate, emit, pass on
AN OPPOSITE IS receive

transparent ADJECTIVE
a transparent fabric
▶ see-through, translucent, diaphanous, clear, sheer, filmy, gauzy, limpid, pellucid

transpire VERB
1 *The witnesses explained what had transpired.*
▶ happen, occur, take place, come about, ensue
2 *It transpired that Martha had been at home all the time.*
▶ become known, become evident, become apparent, be discovered, be revealed, be divulged

transplant VERB
Transplant the seedlings when they need spreading out.
▶ transfer, move, relocate, reposition, shift, uproot

transport VERB (with the stress on -*port*)
The larger components will be transported by rail.
▶ take, carry, convey, ship, transfer, bring, fetch, haul, move, shift

transport NOUN (with the stress on *trans*-)
The village has limited access to public transport.
▶ conveyance, haulage, shipping, transportation

NAMES FOR TYPES OF TRANSPORT

road transport: car, bus, minibus, coach, tram, taxi, lorry, van, bicycle or cycle.

rail transport: train, diesel, electric train, express, high-speed train, intercity train, sleeper, freight train or goods train; locomotive, rolling stock, coach, buffet car, dining car, goods van, guard's van, wagon; sleeping car; monorail; main line; branch line; metro, underground or (*informal*) tube; shuttle.

transport by water: boat, ship, liner, ferry; tanker, supertanker; barge, narrow boat, gondola; cabin cruiser; motor boat, launch, yacht; catamaran, hovercraft, hydrofoil, raft, dinghy, kayak, canoe, punt.

air transport: aircraft, aeroplane or plane, airliner, passenger aircraft, jump jet, jumbo jet, supersonic aircraft; biplane; STOL (short take-off and landing), shuttle (making short journeys back and forth); helicopter; airship; balloon.

transpose VERB
Two of the images had been transposed.
▶ interchange, switch, reverse, swap, change, exchange, move round, rearrange, substitute, transfer

transverse ADJECTIVE
a transverse bar
▶ crosswise, horizontal, oblique, diagonal

trap NOUN
1 *Some kinds of animal traps are illegal.*
▶ snare, noose, net, gin
2 *The cavalry rode straight into a trap.*
▶ ambush, lure, decoy, ambuscade
3 *The last question might be a trap.*
▶ trick, ploy, deception, artifice

trap VERB
1 *They had to find a way of trapping the fox before it did any more damage.*
▶ snare, capture, catch, ensnare, entrap, corner
2 *The question was designed to trap them.*
▶ trick, deceive, fool, dupe

trappings NOUN
Although a top executive, he spurns the visible trappings of success.
▶ finery, accoutrements, adornments, accessories, trimmings, accompaniments, decorations, equipment, fittings, ornaments, paraphernalia

trash NOUN
1 *The cleaners shake out your carpets and empty your trash.*
▶ rubbish, waste, refuse, garbage, litter
2 *He despised himself for having to write such trash.*
▶ rubbish, nonsense, drivel, gibberish, junk

trash VERB
He went to a phone box but it had been trashed.
▶ vandalize, wreck, ruin, destroy

trashy ADJECTIVE
(informal) a trashy horror movie from the sixties
▶ inferior, poor-quality, second-rate, rubbishy, worthless

trauma NOUN
the trauma of being snatched from her mother
▶ shock, distress, ordeal, suffering, stress, upset, anguish, upheaval, pain, grief

traumatic ADJECTIVE
She talked about her traumatic divorce from Ronnie.
▶ distressing, stressful, disturbing, shocking, upsetting, hurtful, painful
AN OPPOSITE IS soothing

travel NOUN
When he retired he had much more time for travel.
▶ travelling, touring, tourism, journeying, sightseeing, excursions, globetrotting

travel VERB
With this ticket you can travel as many miles as you wish.
▶ journey, go, ramble, wander, rove, tour, move, proceed, progress

traveller NOUN
1 *refreshments for the weary traveller*
▶ voyager, passenger, tourist, tripper, holidaymaker, sightseer
2 *ground set aside for travellers' camps*
▶ gypsy, itinerant, nomad

travelling ADJECTIVE
travelling tribes
▶ wandering, itinerant, migrant, vagrant, migratory, nomadic, roaming, roving

travesty NOUN
Their claim was a travesty of the facts.
▶ distortion, misrepresentation, perversion, corruption, parody, mockery, caricature

treacherous ADJECTIVE
1 *She did not believe him capable of such treacherous behaviour.*
▶ traitorous, disloyal, deceitful, faithless, false, unfaithful, perfidious, double-dealing, duplicitous
AN OPPOSITE IS loyal
2 *There was a mile of deep treacherous water separating him from the mainland.*
▶ dangerous, hazardous, perilous, unsafe, unreliable, deceptive, misleading, risky, shifting, unpredictable, unstable
OPPOSITES ARE safe, reliable

treachery NOUN
His resignation from the party would be seen as an act of treachery.
▶ betrayal, disloyalty, infidelity, perfidy, treason, dishonesty, double-dealing, duplicity, faithlessness, untrustworthiness
AN OPPOSITE IS loyalty

tread VERB
1 *There is erosion along the route and walkers should tread carefully.*
▶ step, walk, proceed, pace, stride
2 **tread on** *His father accidentally trod on a model boat he'd been making.*
▶ step on, walk on, trample, crush, squash, stamp on

tread NOUN
I heard the familiar tread of Dad's boots on the cobbles.
▶ footstep, footfall, step, tramp, trudge, plod, stomp

treason NOUN
In July 1540 he was beheaded for treason.
▶ treachery, betrayal, sedition, rebellion, mutiny
OPPOSITES ARE loyalty, allegiance

treasure NOUN
1 *The treasure sank to the bottom of the sea, along with the ship that held it.*
▶ hoard, cache, jewels, riches, fortune, gold, treasure trove, valuables, wealth
2 *Rosie was a treasure who had brought happiness to the house.*
▶ gem, paragon, angel, prize, star

treasure VERB
It's a very special photo and we'll treasure it for ever.
▶ prize, value, cherish, esteem, guard, keep safe, adore, appreciate, love

treat NOUN
1 *Add some prawns to the dish for a special treat.*
▶ indulgence, extravagance
2 *She would give the children a birthday treat next year.*
▶ celebration, surprise, entertainment, outing
3 *The ballet is a treat to the eye.*
▶ pleasure, delight, joy, thrill

treat VERB
1 *They didn't treat her badly, but she was made to feel a nuisance.*
▶ behave towards, deal with, look after, care for, use, serve, attend to
2 *The lectures treat all broad aspects of the subject.*
▶ deal with, discuss, cover, consider, tackle
3 *attempts to treat illness by radiation*
▶ cure, heal, medicate, dress, tend
4 *People tend to treat the videos as entertainment rather than information.*
▶ regard, consider, view
5 *If you like, I'll treat you to a film.*
▶ give, pay for, provide for, entertain

treatment NOUN
1 *She found it difficult to accept his treatment of her.*
▶ care, handling, management, behaviour (towards), conduct (towards), dealing (with), use
2 *He was responding well to the treatment.*
▶ therapy, medical care, medication, nursing, healing

a
b
c
d
e
f
g
h
i
j
k
l
m
n
o
p
q
r
s
t
u
v
w
x
y
z

3 *The book's treatment of this topic is extremely thorough.*
► coverage, handling, explanation, analysis, discussion

treaty NOUN
The two countries signed a treaty of mutual support.
► agreement, settlement, pact, deal, entente, alliance, compact, concordat, convention, protocol, understanding

trek NOUN
a long trek through the hills
► journey, trip, expedition, march, hike, slog, tramp, trudge, walk

trek VERB
They've trekked all over the Greek mainland.
► hike, tramp, march, journey, walk, slog

tremble VERB
1 *His hands were trembling.*
► shake, shiver, quake, quaver, quiver
2 *Heavy traffic outside makes the ornaments tremble.*
► vibrate, shake, wobble, shudder, waver

tremendous ADJECTIVE
1 *It had been a tremendous achievement.*
► great, wonderful, marvellous, sensational, stupendous, extraordinary, considerable, significant, immense
OPPOSITES ARE insignificant, trivial
2 *There was a tremendous crash.*
► terrible, terrific, frightful, awful, fearful, fearsome, alarming, appalling, frightening, horrifying, shocking
OPPOSITES ARE faint, slight

tremor NOUN
1 *There was a tremor in Susan's voice.*
► trembling, quiver, agitation, shaking, hesitation, quavering, vibration
2 *Tremors were recorded all afternoon.*
► shock, earthquake
RELATED ADJECTIVE seismic

trend NOUN
1 *a downward trend in unemployment*
► tendency, movement, shift, bias, leaning, direction, inclination
2 *the latest trend in rock music*
► fashion, vogue, craze, rage, mode, style, fad, way

trendy ADJECTIVE
(informal) trendy clothes
► fashionable, stylish, up-to-date, contemporary, latest, modern, (*more informal*) cool, (*more informal*) in
AN OPPOSITE IS unfashionable

trespasser NOUN
The high wall discouraged trespassers.
► intruder, interloper, poacher

trial NOUN
1 *The trial will last about a month.*
► lawsuit, court case, hearing, tribunal, proceedings, examination
2 *The latest model is undergoing trials.*
► test, testing, experiment, pilot, try-out
3 *Such a long meeting was a real trial.*
► ordeal, problem, tribulation, difficulty, trouble, burden, worry, affliction, hardship
4 *Joan can be a trial at times.*
► nuisance, pest, bother, (*more informal*) pain

tribe NOUN
nomadic tribes
► people, race, nation, group, horde, stock, clan

tribute NOUN
1 *Tributes came in from friends and colleagues.*
► praise, accolade, eulogy, testimonial, appreciation, commendation, recognition, compliment, panegyric
2 *Their eventual success was a tribute to their courage and determination.*
► testimony, evidence (of), proof (of)
3 *The city had to pay an annual tribute to the king.*
► tax, payment, levy, duty, contribution
pay tribute to *She paid tribute to her staff for their hard work.*
► praise, commend, applaud, celebrate, honour, pay homage to, respect

trick NOUN
1 *He entertained the children with conjuring tricks.*
► feat, stunt, illusion, magic
2 *He saw through every trick she used.*
► ruse, scheme, stratagem, deceit, deception, subterfuge, manœuvre, ploy, pretence, fraud, wile, cheat, (*more informal*) con
3 *My favourite trick was to hide above everyone and jump on them. Who else would play a trick like that on me?*
► joke, practical joke, prank, stunt, (*informal*) leg-pull
4 *The essential trick is to think backwards and write forwards.*
► knack, secret, skill, device, dodge, technique, art, craft, expertise, gimmick, (*informal*) know-how

trick VERB
He was furious with himself for being tricked so easily.
► fool, deceive, cheat, dupe, hoodwink, swindle, trap, outwit, hoax, bluff, mislead, catch out, defraud, (*informal*) con, (*informal*) bamboozle

trickery NOUN
The excuses he makes sound like the old trickery.
► deception, pretence, cheating, chicanery, deceit, mischief, dishonesty, bluffing, fraud, (*informal*) monkey business, (*informal*) jiggery-pokery, (*informal*) shenanigans

trickle VERB
Sweat trickled down his sides despite the cold.
▶ drip, dribble, seep, ooze, leak, flow slowly, percolate, run
OPPOSITES ARE pour, gush

trickle NOUN
She saw a trickle of blood flow over her fingers.
▶ dribble, seepage, thin stream
OPPOSITES ARE flood, gush

trickster NOUN
I shall reveal you for the sly trickster that you are.
▶ cheat, swindler, fraud, fraudster, impostor, charlatan, deceiver, dissembler

tricky ADJECTIVE
1 *Tony was a tricky individual.*
▶ cunning, crafty, wily, artful
2 *Tricky negotiations were taking place.*
▶ difficult, complicated, awkward, delicate, sensitive

trifle NOUN
1 *It cost a mere trifle.*
▶ small amount, next to nothing, pittance, (*more informal*) peanuts
2 **a trifle** *He looked a trifle embarrassed.*
▶ a little, a bit, somewhat, a touch, a spot

trifle VERB
trifle with *You should not trifle with people's feelings.*
▶ treat lightly, toy with, dally with, fool about with, play about with, behave frivolously towards

trifling ADJECTIVE
We shouldn't bother them with such a trifling matter.
▶ trivial, unimportant, insignificant, inconsequential, minor, petty

trigger VERB
The spending cuts triggered many protests.
▶ cause, provoke, stimulate, give rise to, lead to, spark off, set off

trim VERB
1 *He had trimmed his hair and beard.*
▶ cut, crop, clip, tidy, shape, shear
2 *The Chancellor will have either to increase taxes or trim his budget.*
▶ reduce, cut, prune, scale down
3 *The silk curtains were trimmed with gold.*
▶ decorate, embellish

trim ADJECTIVE
1 *a housing estate with trim gardens*
▶ neat, tidy, orderly, smart, spruce, well-groomed, well-kept
AN OPPOSITE IS untidy
2 *Trousers help to accentuate a trim figure.*
▶ slim, slender, lean

trip NOUN
He met the czar during a trip to Russia in 1908.
▶ journey, visit, voyage, excursion, expedition, holiday, jaunt, outing, tour

trip VERB
1 *Angela tripped along in her red mac and hood.*
▶ run, skip, walk
2 *She tripped over and gashed her knee.*
▶ stumble, totter, tumble, catch your foot, fall, stagger

trite ADJECTIVE
However trite it may sound, there is joy to be found in a spring day.
▶ banal, commonplace, ordinary, hackneyed, clichéd, stale

triumph NOUN
1 *He was a key figure in the party's election triumph.*
▶ victory, win, conquest, (*informal*) walkover
AN OPPOSITE IS defeat
2 *She smiled in triumph.*
▶ celebration, joy, exultation, jubilation, elation
3 *The visit to Wales had been a triumph.*
▶ success, accomplishment, achievement, master stroke, (*more informal*) hit

triumph VERB
triumph over *He had triumphed over disease and misfortune.*
▶ overcome, defeat, conquer, prevail over, succeed against, be victorious over, win over

triumphant ADJECTIVE
1 *The communists emerged triumphant from the revolution.*
▶ successful, victorious, dominant, conquering, winning
AN OPPOSITE IS unsuccessful
2 *He gave her a knowing, triumphant look.*
▶ exultant, jubilant, boastful, joyful, elated, gleeful, gloating, immodest, proud
OPPOSITES ARE modest, humble

trivial ADJECTIVE
The offence was regarded as trivial.
▶ insignificant, unimportant, inconsequential, minor, trifling, incidental
OPPOSITES ARE important, significant

troop NOUN
A troop of tourists crossed the square.
▶ group, party, band, body, company

troop VERB
Rod looked up as Sara and the others trooped in.
▶ march, file, flock, parade, straggle

trophy NOUN
1 *trophies of war*
▶ souvenir, memento, reward, spoils, booty, loot
2 *a sports trophy*
▶ award, cup, medal, prize

tropical ADJECTIVE
tropical areas such as East Africa
▶ equatorial, hot, humid, sultry, torrid

trot VERB
Danny trotted into the house.
▶ run, scurry, scamper, scuttle, hurry

trouble NOUN

1 *See what trouble you've caused.*
▶ difficulty, bother, problems, inconvenience, distress, anxiety

2 *He recounted his troubles and asked for advice.*
▶ problem, misfortune, difficulty, tribulation, trial, affliction, suffering, hardship

3 *We took some trouble to help them.*
▶ care, effort, bother, exertion, pains

4 *I hope I wasn't a trouble to you.*
▶ nuisance, bother, irritation

5 *The trouble with these machines is the lack of spare parts.*
▶ problem, difficulty, disadvantage, weakness, failing
OPPOSITES ARE advantage, benefit

6 *There was crowd trouble after the match.*
▶ disturbance, disorder, unrest, conflict, fighting, violence
OPPOSITES ARE order, peace

7 *She suffered from back trouble.*
▶ ailment, disorder, complaint, illness, disability

trouble VERB

1 *Something was troubling him.*
▶ bother, worry, distress, concern, pain, vex, torment, upset

2 *I'm very sorry to trouble you.*
▶ disturb, interrupt, bother, inconvenience

troubled ADJECTIVE

1 *Tara looked troubled.*
▶ anxious, worried, bothered, concerned, disturbed, perturbed, uneasy, unhappy, vexed, restless
OPPOSITES ARE untroubled, peaceful

2 *We live in troubled times.*
▶ difficult, unsettled, uncertain

troublemaker NOUN

She was branded a troublemaker for complaining about a colleague who harassed her.
▶ mischief-maker, agitator, rabble-rouser, ringleader, wrongdoer

troublesome ADJECTIVE

1 *Craig was recovering from a troublesome knee injury.*
▶ annoying, irritating, irksome, tiresome, trying, bothersome, vexing, distressing, inconvenient, upsetting
OPPOSITES ARE trouble-free, harmless

2 *The younger boy was being particularly troublesome.*
▶ badly behaved, naughty, unruly, disobedient, disorderly, uncooperative, rowdy

trounce VERB

Essex trounced Cambridgeshire in the final.
▶ defeat, beat, crush, rout, overwhelm, annihilate

trousers NOUN

He was wearing a pair of pale trousers.
▶ pants, slacks

truancy NOUN

We are determined to crack down on truancy.
▶ absenteeism, malingering, shirking, (*more informal*) skiving
AN OPPOSITE IS attendance

truant NOUN

I was a truant from a Youth Custody Centre.
▶ absentee, non-attender, runaway, malingerer, shirker, (*more informal*) skiver

play truant *52 percent admitted to playing truant for the odd lesson now and then.*
▶ be absent, stay away, desert, malinger, (*more informal*) skive off

truce NOUN

The enemy broke the truce and resumed the war.
▶ ceasefire, armistice, moratorium, pact, peace, suspension of hostilities, treaty

truck NOUN

The truck was skidding all over the motorway.
▶ lorry, heavy goods vehicle, juggernaut

trudge VERB

Tony and I were trudging through deep snow.
▶ plod, slog, tramp, clump

true ADJECTIVE

1 *The story turned out to be true.*
▶ correct, right, accurate, factual, authentic, confirmed, proper, veracious, veritable
OPPOSITES ARE untrue, false

2 *The document was certified as a true copy.*
▶ exact, faithful, genuine, real, actual
AN OPPOSITE IS false

3 *Anne, true friend though she was, would never give in to him.*
▶ loyal, faithful, devoted, firm, constant, sincere, steady, trustworthy, dependable, honest, honourable
OPPOSITES ARE false, unfaithful

4 *He was acting under the authority of the property's true owner.*
▶ legal, legitimate, rightful, authorized, valid

5 *Such studies do not give a true reflection of people's needs.*
▶ accurate, precise, exact, perfect, unerring
AN OPPOSITE IS inaccurate

truly ADVERB

1 *a truly remarkable woman*
▶ really, absolutely, extremely, very

2 *I'm truly glad for you.*
▶ sincerely, genuinely, honestly

3 *Tell us truly what you think.*
▶ truthfully, frankly, candidly, honestly

trumpet NOUN

a part for solo trumpet
▶ bugle, clarion, cornet
blow your own trumpet *He was blowing his own trumpet and promoting his new show.*
▶ boast, brag, sing your own praises, congratulate yourself, show off, swank

trunk NOUN

1 *A squirrel leapt on a branch and ran up the trunk.*
▶ stem, bole, stock
2 *A slit in his shirt revealed his powerful trunk.*
▶ torso, frame, body
3 *He locked the trunk and stored it in a shed.*
▶ chest, case, coffer, box, crate, suitcase

trust NOUN

1 *I am grateful to you for your trust.*
▶ confidence, faith, belief, reliance, certainty, credence
2 *She enjoyed a position of trust in the City.*
▶ responsibility, obligation

trust VERB

1 *He doesn't trust me not to do it again.*
▶ believe in, have confidence in, have faith in, rely on, be sure of, bank on, count on, depend on
2 *We trust they will be here soon.*
▶ hope, expect, presume, suppose, assume, imagine, surmise
AN OPPOSITE IS doubt

trusting ADJECTIVE

The trouble with me is I'm too trusting.
▶ trustful, credulous, gullible, unquestioning, unsuspecting, ingenuous, innocent
OPPOSITES ARE suspicious, cynical

trustworthy ADJECTIVE

Harriet was always trustworthy and hard-working.
▶ reliable, dependable, responsible, honest, upright, steadfast
OPPOSITES ARE untrustworthy, deceitful

truth NOUN

1 *He doubted the truth of some of these statements.*
▶ veracity, accuracy, validity, truthfulness, correctness, candour, honesty, authenticity, reliability
AN OPPOSITE IS falseness
2 *Elizabeth had been telling the truth.*
▶ fact or facts, reality, actuality
3 *an acknowledged truth*
▶ fact, axiom, maxim, certitude, truism
AN OPPOSITE IS lie

truthful ADJECTIVE

1 *Clive had been less than truthful.*
▶ honest, sincere, candid, frank, reliable, straight, forthright, credible, straightforward, trustworthy, veracious
2 *The truthful answer has to be 'no'.*
▶ proper, right, accurate, correct, true, valid
AN OPPOSITE IS dishonest

try VERB

1 *Always try to respond positively.*
▶ aim, attempt, endeavour, essay, exert yourself, make an effort, strain, strive, struggle, venture
2 *(informal) Why not try another school?*
▶ check out, evaluate, examine, experiment with, investigate, test, try out, undertake

try NOUN

I'll have another try.
▶ attempt, endeavour, effort, experiment, test, trial, (*more informal*) bash, (*more informal*) go, (*more informal*) shot

trying ADJECTIVE

1 *This could be quite a trying evening.*
▶ difficult, stressful, taxing, frustrating, troublesome, vexatious
2 *Clare can be very trying.*
▶ annoying, irritating, tiresome, exasperating, infuriating

tub NOUN

1 *Corbett bathed in the guest house's one and only tub.*
▶ bath, bathtub
2 *a plastic tub of sandwiches*
▶ pot, barrel, drum, cask, keg, vat

tubby ADJECTIVE

(informal) A short tubby man was waiting at the front door.
▶ chubby, podgy, plump, fat, dumpy, rotund, round, overweight, stout, portly, pudgy
OPPOSITES ARE thin, slim, skinny

tuck VERB

1 *He tucked his shirt into his jeans.*
▶ push, ease, insert, stuff, shove, cram, (*more informal*) pop
2 **tuck into** *We tucked into plates of fish and chips.*
▶ eat up, consume, devour, gobble up, wolf down

tuft NOUN

tufts of grass and weeds
▶ clump, cluster, bunch, knot, tuffet, tussock

tug VERB

1 *Lee tugged the rope.*
▶ pull, heave, drag, draw, haul, lug, tow
2 **tug at** *A litte boy tugged at her skirt.*
▶ jerk, pluck, twitch, wrench, yank

tumble VERB

1 *He let out a yell as he tumbled into the water.*
▶ topple, collapse, pitch, stumble, plummet, drop, fall, flop, trip up
2 *Most of the audience then tumbled out of the room.*
▶ hurry, rush, pile, scramble
3 *Interest rates were set to tumble.*
▶ plunge, fall, drop, dive, slump
OPPOSITES ARE soar, rise
4 *Her long dark hair tumbled down her back.*
▶ flow, fall, cascade

tumbledown ADJECTIVE

I demolished a tumbledown shed at the bottom of the garden.
▶ ramshackle, dilapidated, rickety, crumbling, decrepit, derelict, ruined

tumult NOUN

His voice could not be heard above the tumult.
▶ noise, din, commotion, hubbub, clamour, racket, rumpus, uproar

tumultuous ADJECTIVE

John Knox returned to a tumultuous welcome.
▶ loud, excited, uproarious, boisterous, unrestrained, deafening, passionate, tempestuous, hectic, turbulent, wild
AN OPPOSITE IS restrained

tune NOUN

She sang a tune to the baby.
▶ melody, song, air, strain, theme

tune VERB

A mechanic tuned the engine.
▶ adjust, regulate, set, temper

tuneful ADJECTIVE

She spoke in a quiet, tuneful voice.
▶ musical, melodious, mellifluous, pleasant, sweet, rhythmical, catchy
OPPOSITES ARE tuneless, discordant

tunnel NOUN

a tunnel under the Thames
▶ underpass, passage, passageway, subway, shaft, gallery

tunnel VERB

A dog had tunnelled under the fence.
▶ burrow, dig, excavate, mine, penetrate

turbulent ADJECTIVE

1 *Her turbulent feelings got the better of her.*
▶ passionate, excited, violent, volatile, seething, unrestrained
2 *an increasingly turbulent part of the world*
▶ unstable, unsettled, troubled, restless, explosive, anarchic
AN OPPOSITE IS peaceful
3 *The ship was in turbulent waters.*
▶ rough, stormy, tempestuous, choppy, violent, wild
AN OPPOSITE IS calm

turgid ADJECTIVE

A violent episode livened up this otherwise turgid prose.
▶ pompous, pretentious, stilted, wordy, affected, bombastic, flowery, fulsome, grandiose, high-flown, overblown
OPPOSITES ARE clear, simple

turmoil NOUN

(informal) Her mind was in a state of turmoil.
▶ confusion, chaos, disorder, upheaval, turbulence, agitation, disruption, disturbance, mayhem, unrest, upset
OPPOSITES ARE calm, peace

turn VERB

1 *The big wheel started to turn.*
▶ go round, revolve, rotate, whirl, roll
2 *The gates turned on a set of massive hinges.*
▶ swivel, hinge
3 *She turned to return home.*
▶ change direction, change course, turn round
4 *The van turned the corner and disappeared.*
▶ go round, negotiate, take
5 *The path turned to the right.*
▶ bend, curve, twist, loop, snake
6 *Ellie turned pale.*
▶ become, go, grow
7 *The house will be turned into luxury apartments.*
▶ convert, adapt, transform, modify, change, rebuild
8 *The milk had turned.*
▶ go off, go sour, curdle
9 **turn to** *She turned to her neighbour for help.*
▶ resort to, appeal to, approach, have recourse to, apply to

turn away *Reporters were turned away from the house.*
▶ send away, dismiss, rebuff, reject
AN OPPOSITE IS admit (to)

turn down *The panel turned down her application.*
▶ reject, refuse, decline, dismiss, spurn
AN OPPOSITE IS approve

turn in
1 *I decided to turn in early.*
▶ go to bed, retire
2 *He was ordered to turn in his passport.*
▶ hand in, hand over, surrender, submit

turn off
1 *They had to turn off the motorway.*
▶ leave, branch off, deviate from
AN OPPOSITE IS join
2 *She turned off the lights and left the building.*
▶ switch off, turn out, put out, extinguish
OPPOSITES ARE turn on, switch on
3 *The violence in the film turned many people off.*
▶ deter, put off, discourage, disconcert, unnerve, repel, distract
OPPOSITES ARE appeal to, attract

turn on
1 *She turned on the radio.*
▶ switch on, put on
AN OPPOSITE IS turn off
2 *Rick always turned her on.*
▶ excite, arouse, stimulate, titillate
AN OPPOSITE IS turn off

turn out
1 *Her father might well turn her out of the house.*
▶ throw out, expel, evict, eject, drive out
OPPOSITES ARE admit (to), welcome (to)
2 *It was a relief that things turned out so well.*
▶ occur, happen, evolve, develop, end up, come out, work out

3 *Don't forget to turn out the light.*
▶ switch off, turn off, put out, extinguish
OPPOSITES ARE turn on, switch on
turn over
1 *The car skidded and turned over.*
▶ overturn, roll over, keel over, capsize
2 *I've been turning it over in my mind.*
▶ consider, ponder, deliberate, think about, weigh up, mull over, chew over
turn up
1 *Several guests failed to turn up.*
▶ arrive, appear, put in an appearance
2 *A gardener in Oxfordshire has turned up a hoard of ancient coins.*
▶ discover, unearth, uncover, bring to light, dig up, find
3 *The voices are inaudible unless you turn the sound up.*
▶ increase, raise, amplify

turn NOUN
1 *hot water at the turn of a tap*
▶ twist, spin, twirl, whirl, rotation, revolution, circle, cycle
2 *The car came to a turn in the road*
▶ bend, corner, curve, angle, deviation, hairpin bend, junction, loop, twist
3 *an unexpected turn of events*
▶ reversal, shift, change of direction, turning point
4 *It's your turn to speak.*
▶ chance, opportunity, occasion, time, stint, spell
5 *She was trying to do James a good turn.*
▶ favour, support
6 *a comic turn in a concert*
▶ act, performance, show
7 *His sudden appearance gave her quite a turn.*
▶ shock, start, surprise, fright, scare, jolt
in turn *The Eastern capital in turn influenced the culture of Venice.*
▶ in succession, successively

turning NOUN
Take the second turning on the right.
▶ turn-off, turn, exit

turning point NOUN
Their meeting was a turning point in his life.
▶ watershed, critical moment, landmark, crisis, crossroads, new direction

turnout NOUN
The game attracted a good turnout.
▶ crowd, attendance, audience, assembly, gate

turnover NOUN
a company with a turnover of over three million
▶ revenue, throughput, income

tussle NOUN
His glasses were broken in the tussle.
▶ fight, scuffle, fracas, brawl, struggle, scrap, rumpus, commotion, argument

tussle NOUN
Some of the crowd tussled with police.
▶ fight, scuffle, brawl, struggle, scrap, come to blows

tutor NOUN
Mr Groves was looking for a tutor for his children.
▶ teacher, instructor, mentor, coach, educator

tutor VERB
Until two years ago, he had been tutored at home.
▶ teach, instruct, educate, coach

tweak VERB
1 *She tweaked Peter's ear.*
▶ twist, pinch, nip, pull, squeeze
2 *They know how to tweak gadgets.*
▶ adjust, modify, alter, adapt, refine, improve

tweak NOUN
The controls needed a few gentle tweaks.
▶ adjustment, alteration, modification, refinement

twee ADJECTIVE
(informal) twee little harbours with neat fishing boats
▶ quaint, sweet, cute, (informal) cutesy

twiddle VERB
Link your fingers in your lap so you're not tempted to twiddle them.
▶ fiddle with, fidget with, twirl, twist

twig VERB
(informal) I finally twigged where they had come from.
▶ realize, understand, grasp, comprehend

twin ADJECTIVE
twin towers on the French pattern
▶ identical, matching, balancing, corresponding, duplicate, paired, similar, symmetrical, indistinguishable

twin NOUN
Fiona drove her own car, the twin of Harry's.
▶ double, duplicate, clone, match, (more informal) lookalike

twine NOUN
He slowly unrolled the ball of twine.
▶ string, cord, thread, yarn

twine VERB
All she could do was twine her arms round him.
▶ wind, wrap, twist, coil

twinge NOUN
1 *I was getting sharp twinges in one knee.*
▶ pain, stab, spasm
2 *She felt a twinge of sadness.*
▶ pang, prick, qualm

twinkle VERB
I could see Beverly Hills twinkling in the distance.
▶ glimmer, glitter, glint, glow, shine, flash, glisten, gleam, sparkle, shimmer

twinkle NOUN
the twinkle of a thousand lights
▶ sparkle, glimmer, glitter, glint, glow, shimmer

twirl VERB
1 *They twirled round the room arm in arm.*
▶ spin, turn, twist, whirl, wheel, gyrate, pirouette, revolve, rotate
2 *He twirled his empty glass in his hands.*
▶ twiddle, twist, play with

twist VERB
1 *Huge girders had been twisted in the explosion.*
▶ crush, buckle, mangle, misshape, deform
2 *He twisted a strand of her hair round his fingers.*
▶ coil, curl, wind, entwine, twine
3 *Twist the cork slowly as you pull it.*
▶ turn, screw, revolve
4 *She fell off her bike and twisted her ankle.*
▶ sprain, wrench, rick
5 *He accused the newspaper of twisting his words.*
▶ distort, change, alter, misrepresent, garble, contort, pervert

twist NOUN
1 *Give the lid a firm twist.*
▶ turn, screw, jerk, spin
2 *a twist in the rope*
▶ coil, curl, loop, kink, tangle, knot
3 *a twist in the road*
▶ bend, turn, zigzag
4 *There was an unexpected twist to the story.*
▶ development, surprise, quirk, oddity

twisted ADJECTIVE
1 *A mass of twisted metal barred the way.*
▶ crumpled, buckled, crushed, mangled, distorted, misshapen, deformed, warped
2 *It seemed to be the product of a twisted mind.*
▶ perverted, depraved, warped, deviant, corrupt

twit NOUN
(*informal*) *You're an ignorant little twit.*
▶ fool, idiot, clot, ass, halfwit, dimwit, blockhead, dunderhead, nincompoop

twitch NOUN
She suppressed an involuntary twitch of her lip.
▶ spasm, jerk, tremor, tic, blink, convulsion, flutter, jump

twitch VERB
The bushes twitched again.
▶ start, tremble, jerk, jump, fidget, flutter

two-faced ADJECTIVE
I consider you have been a two-faced liar.
▶ deceitful, insincere, double-dealing, dishonest, duplicitous, hypocritical
OPPOSITES ARE sincere, honest

tycoon NOUN
a newspaper advertisement sponsored by an oil tycoon
▶ magnate, mogul, industrialist, baron, supremo, big businessman

type NOUN
1 *This type of injury could happen to any player at any time.*
▶ kind, sort, category, class, form, variety, classification, description, designation, genre, group, species
2 *Footnotes are printed in small type.*
▶ print, characters, typeface, font, letters

typhoon NOUN
aid for victims of the typhoon
▶ cyclone, tornado, hurricane, whirlwind

typical ADJECTIVE
1 *Decorative carving is a typical feature of late Gothic architecture.*
▶ characteristic, distinctive, particular, representative, special
OPPOSITES ARE untypical, uncharacteristic
2 *It had been a fairly typical week.*
▶ average, ordinary, normal, usual, conventional, orthodox, predictable, standard, unsurprising
OPPOSITES ARE untypical, unusual
USAGE There is a slight difference in meaning between *untypical* and *atypical*: *untypical* means 'not typical, unusual', whereas *atypical* means 'not belonging to this type'.

typify VERB
The village typifies the beauty of the Lake District.
▶ epitomize, exemplify, characterize, embody, represent

tyrannical ADJECTIVE
His father is portrayed as a stern, tyrannical disciplinarian.
▶ authoritarian, autocratic, despotic, dictatorial, domineering, oppressive, overbearing, cruel, brutal, harsh, imperious, ruthless, severe, tyrannous, unjust
OPPOSITES ARE liberal, tolerant, easygoing

tyrannize VERB
He tyrannized his family.
▶ dominate, domineer over, oppress, bully, intimidate

tyranny NOUN
the injustice, cruelty, and tyranny in the world
▶ despotism, autocracy, dictatorship, oppression

tyrant NOUN
She was a tyrant to the girls.
▶ despot, autocrat, dictator, oppressor, slave-driver

Uu

ubiquitous ADJECTIVE
You can store them in a shoebox or the ubiquitous plastic bag.
▶ ever-present, universal, pervasive, widespread
OPPOSITES ARE scarce, rare

ugly ADJECTIVE
1 *He may be ugly, but at least he writes good songs.*
▶ unattractive, unsightly, deformed, repulsive, hideous, plain, grisly, unpleasant, monstrous
AN OPPOSITE IS attractive
2 *an ugly iron bedstead*
▶ unsightly, hideous, inelegant, tasteless, unattractive, unpleasant, displeasing, inartistic, plain
AN OPPOSITE IS beautiful

3 *There were a number of ugly scenes behind the goalposts.*
▶ angry, dangerous, threatening, ominous, unpleasant, sinister, unfriendly, forbidding, hostile, menacing
AN OPPOSITE IS pleasant

ulterior ADJECTIVE
They assumed she had some ulterior motive in coming here.
▶ hidden, personal, private, covert, concealed, secondary, secret, undeclared, undisclosed
AN OPPOSITE IS overt

ultimate ADJECTIVE
the decline and ultimate disappearance of the city-state
▶ eventual, final, consequent

ultimately ADVERB
Perhaps these problems will ultimately prove too great.
▶ eventually, finally, in the end, in the long run, in time

ultimatum NOUN
The ultimatum contained the threat of military force.
▶ final demand

umbrage NOUN
take umbrage *He amused them without taking umbrage when they laughed at him.*
▶ take offence, take exception, be offended, be annoyed, be aggrieved, be insulted, bridle

umpire NOUN
They all abided by the umpire's decision.
▶ referee, adjudicator, arbiter, judge, linesman, arbitrator, moderator, (*more informal*) ref

umpteen ADJECTIVE
(*informal*) *He had to tell the story umpteen times.*
▶ many, numerous, plenty of, countless, innumerable

unacceptable ADJECTIVE
Public opinion has rejected this strategy as shortsighted and unacceptable.
▶ intolerable, unsatisfactory, inadmissible, inappropriate, unsuitable, inadequate
OPPOSITES ARE acceptable, satisfactory

unaccountable ADJECTIVE
He could hear an unaccountable noise in front of him.
▶ inexplicable, unexplainable, incomprehensible, bewildering, puzzling, mystifying
AN OPPOSITE IS explicable

unaided ADJECTIVE
by your own unaided efforts
▶ single-handed, alone, by yourself, without help, independently

unambiguous ADJECTIVE
an unambiguous response
▶ definite, categorical, unequivocal, explicit, clear
OPPOSITES ARE ambiguous, unclear

unanimous ADJECTIVE
The resulting decision was unanimous.
▶ united, harmonious, of one mind

unarmed ADJECTIVE
Troops shot at unarmed civilians.
▶ defenceless, undefended, weaponless, unprotected, exposed, vulnerable
AN OPPOSITE IS armed

unassuming ADJECTIVE
Sparks was an unassuming and kindly man.
▶ modest, retiring, humble, self-effacing, unobtrusive

unattractive ADJECTIVE
The existing unattractive shop front would be replaced by a timber one.
▶ ugly, unsightly, plain, unappealing, uninviting, repulsive, unprepossessing
OPPOSITES ARE attractive, beautiful

unauthorized ADJECTIVE
The train made an unauthorized stop.
▶ unofficial, irregular, unapproved, abnormal, unsanctioned, illegal, unlawful, unusual
AN OPPOSITE IS authorized

unavoidable ADJECTIVE
Job losses are unavoidable.
▶ inevitable, inescapable, certain, necessary, obligatory, mandatory
OPPOSITES ARE avoidable, unnecessary

unaware ADJECTIVE
They seemed to be unaware of everything that had happened.
▶ ignorant, oblivious, unconscious, unmindful, heedless
OPPOSITES ARE aware, conscious

unbalanced ADJECTIVE
1 *We must not give an unbalanced picture.*
▶ unfair, unjust, biased, one-sided, partial, partisan, prejudiced
OPPOSITES ARE balanced, fair
2 *She said her husband had become unbalanced and capable of doing nasty things.*
▶ unstable, disturbed, deranged, demented, crazy, insane
3 *The wallpaper pattern looked unbalanced.*
▶ asymmetrical, irregular, uneven, lopsided, off-centre
OPPOSITES ARE balanced, symmetrical

unbearable ADJECTIVE
The pain was unbearable.
▶ unendurable, intolerable, excruciating, agonizing, insufferable, unmanageable
OPPOSITES ARE bearable, tolerable

unbeatable ADJECTIVE
1 *When in good form the side is unbeatable.*
▶ invincible, unassailable, indestructible, indomitable, unconquerable, matchless, supreme
2 *As a flavour enhancer, lemon is unbeatable.*
▶ incomparable, unrivalled, unsurpassed, matchless, supreme

a
b
c
d
e
f
g
h
i
j
k
l
m
n
o
p
q
r
s
t
u
v
w
x
y
z

unbelievable ADJECTIVE

1 *You may find the story bizarre, even unbelievable.*
▶ incredible, improbable, implausible, far-fetched, unconvincing, preposterous

2 *He acted with unbelievable recklessness.*
▶ incredible, unimaginable, inconceivable, unthinkable

unbend VERB

1 *Michael tried to unbend the damaged rail.*
▶ straighten, uncurl, untwist
AN OPPOSITE IS bend

2 *We have a few days to unbend and enjoy ourselves.*
▶ relax, rest, unwind, loosen up, (*more informal*) let your hair down

unbiased ADJECTIVE

Every effort is made to obtain an unbiased opinion.
▶ impartial, objective, dispassionate, neutral, independent
OPPOSITES ARE biased, partial

unbreakable ADJECTIVE

a sheet of unbreakable glass
▶ toughened, shatter-proof, indestructible, non-breakable, resistant

unbroken ADJECTIVE

1 *an unbroken night's sleep*
▶ continuous, uninterrupted, constant

2 *a world record that remains unbroken*
▶ unbeaten, unsurpassed, unequalled, unrivalled

uncalled-for ADJECTIVE

Such strict rules are totally uncalled-for.
▶ unnecessary, gratuitous, needless, inappropriate, unwarranted, unjustified, unreasonable, unwelcome
OPPOSITES ARE opportune, appropriate

uncanny ADJECTIVE

1 *The silence was uncanny.*
▶ eerie, unnatural, weird, creepy, unreal, ghostly, unaccountable
AN OPPOSITE IS normal

2 *He has an uncanny eye for spotting talent.*
▶ unusual, extraordinary, remarkable, exceptional, striking
AN OPPOSITE IS unremarkable

uncertain ADJECTIVE

1 *The side effects of the treatment are uncertain.*
▶ unknown, unclear, indefinite, undetermined, unforeseeable, unresolved, undecided, inconclusive, ambiguous, imprecise, indeterminate, speculative
OPPOSITES ARE known, definite

2 *I was uncertain what to say.*
▶ unsure, undecided, doubtful, unconvinced (about), ambivalent (about), dubious (about), hazy (about), wavering (about), in two minds (about)

3 *Workers in the industry face an uncertain future.*
▶ changeable, variable, erratic, unpredictable, unreliable, precarious
AN OPPOSITE IS certain

uncertainty NOUN

1 *He tried to disguise his uncertainty.*
▶ doubt, misgiving, apprehension, qualm, hesitation, scruple
OPPOSITES ARE certainty, positiveness

2 *Some degree of uncertainty is bound to ensue.*
▶ unpredictability, unreliability, changeability, risk, danger
OPPOSITES ARE certainty, assurance

uncivilized ADJECTIVE

I am sorry to see such uncivilized behaviour.
▶ uncouth, primitive, barbaric, rough, boorish, antisocial, barbarous, uncultured, uneducated, unenlightened, unsophisticated, wild
OPPOSITES ARE civilized, respectable

unclear ADJECTIVE

1 *The answers are all very unclear.*
▶ vague, obscure, ambiguous, equivocal, puzzling, opaque, cryptic, hazy, imprecise
OPPOSITES ARE clear, straightforward, unambiguous

2 *It was unclear whether the move was backed by the government.*
▶ uncertain, debatable, unsure, unsettled, doubtful, dubious
OPPOSITES ARE clear , obvious

uncomfortable ADJECTIVE

1 *The lecture room had uncomfortable plastic chairs.*
▶ hard, cramped, restrictive, stiff, tight, ill-fitting, tight-fitting, lumpy
AN OPPOSITE IS comfortable

2 *Carrying the bike over your shoulder is uncomfortable in the extreme.*
▶ painful, disagreeable, excruciating, inconvenient

3 *British workers felt uncomfortable about the slogans common in Japanese factories.*
▶ uneasy, embarrassed, awkward, troubled, worried, distressed, nervous, restless

uncommon ADJECTIVE

Two or three nights without sleep were not uncommon.
▶ unusual, infrequent, rare, exceptional, abnormal
OPPOSITES ARE common, usual

uncomplimentary ADJECTIVE

some very uncomplimentary remarks
▶ disapproving, disparaging, unfavourable, unflattering, depreciatory, censorious, critical, derogatory, pejorative, scathing
AN OPPOSITE IS complimentary

unconcerned ADJECTIVE

1 *They seemed unconcerned by our presence.*
▶ unaffected, unmoved, unruffled, indifferent (about), relaxed (about)

2 *She didn't want to appear unconcerned.*
▶ uninterested, indifferent, apathetic, complacent, uncaring

unconditional ADJECTIVE

All four offered their unconditional support.
▶ unqualified, unrestricted, unlimited, unreserved, unquestioning, total, outright, absolute, complete
AN OPPOSITE IS conditional

U

unconnected ADJECTIVE
The two events were unconnected. She has since died from causes unconnected with the incident.
▶ unrelated (to), distinct (from), irrelevant (to), independent, discrete, disparate

unconscious ADJECTIVE
1 *My mother was still unconscious in hospital.*
▶ concussed, knocked out, insensible, senseless, comatose
2 **unconscious of** *He ranted on, unconscious of the danger.*
▶ unaware of, heedless, ignorant of, disregardful of, disregarding, ignoring, impervious to
3 *He carries with him an unconscious guilt for his little sister's death.*
▶ subconscious, repressed, suppressed, involuntary, latent, subliminal, instinctive

unconventional ADJECTIVE
A wide range of colours can be used to create unconventional patterns.
▶ unusual, unorthodox, unfamiliar, innovative, original, experimental, individual
OPPOSITES ARE conventional, orthodox

unconvincing ADJECTIVE
They found that an unconvincing explanation. She put on a smile, but it was unconvincing.
▶ dubious, doubtful, implausible, incredible, strained, forced, feeble, weak

uncooperative ADJECTIVE
The lawyers were proving to be uncooperative.
▶ unhelpful, disobliging, awkward, obstructive, unaccommodating, inflexible, unwilling
AN OPPOSITE IS cooperative

uncoordinated ADJECTIVE
If the body is used in an uncoordinated fashion, some of the reflexes are not triggered.
▶ clumsy, awkward, disjointed, lumbering, ungainly
OPPOSITES ARE coordinated, dextrous

uncouth ADJECTIVE
They were rough uncouth men with the air of outcasts.
▶ coarse, rude, ill-mannered, uncivilized, unrefined
AN OPPOSITE IS refined

uncover VERB
1 *The earth had to be scraped away to uncover a trap door.*
▶ reveal, disclose, expose, lay bare, exhibit, show, strip, unmask, unveil, unwrap
OPPOSITES ARE cover, conceal
2 *The intention was to uncover the causes of human social behaviour.*
▶ detect, discover, locate, unearth, expose, make known, come across, make public, dig up
OPPOSITES ARE conceal, cover up

undaunted ADJECTIVE
They were undaunted, despite the huge amount of work needed to restore the house.
▶ undeterred, unbowed, unafraid, resolute, steadfast, intrepid, determined, positive

undecided ADJECTIVE
1 *The question of where to hold the trial remained undecided.*
▶ uncertain, unresolved, undetermined, unsettled, unclear, indefinite
OPPOSITES ARE decided, settled
2 *She stood undecided in the rain, wanting to find Simon but not daring to step inside.*
▶ hesitant, wavering, indecisive, unsure, uncertain, dithering, in two minds
AN OPPOSITE IS certain

undeniable ADJECTIVE
The undeniable fact is that chlorine is building up in the atmosphere.
▶ indisputable, irrefutable, unquestionable, incontrovertible, undoubted, proven, certain
OPPOSITES ARE questionable, debatable

undercover ADJECTIVE
Undercover agents are suspected of the assassination.
▶ secret, covert, clandestine, underground, surreptitious, hidden, furtive

undercurrent NOUN
There was an undercurrent of curiosity surrounding the visit.
▶ undertone, overtone, suggestion, atmosphere, sense, feeling, trace, hint

underestimate VERB
1 *Radiation fallout was underestimated by 40 times.*
▶ misjudge, miscalculate, set too low
OPPOSITES ARE overestimate, exaggerate
2 *Sara puzzled him; he had underestimated her.*
▶ underrate, undervalue, misjudge, belittle, disparage, minimize, dismiss
OPPOSITES ARE overestimate, overrate

undergo VERB
He may have to undergo more surgery.
▶ experience, endure, go through, submit to, be subjected to, put up with, face, bear, suffer, withstand

underground ADJECTIVE
1 *the waters of an underground river*
▶ subterranean, buried, sunken
AN OPPOSITE IS surface
2 *The two main underground opposition groups have decided to unite.*
▶ secret, clandestine, covert, surreptitious, undercover, unofficial

undergrowth NOUN
There were rustling noises in the undergrowth.
▶ brush, shrubbery, vegetation, scrub, bushes

underhand ADJECTIVE
He had behaved in a thoroughly sneaky, underhand way.
▶ deceitful, dishonest, dishonourable, unethical, improper, sly
OPPOSITES ARE honest, open

a
b
c
d
e
f
g
h
i
j
k
l
m
n
o
p
q
r
s
t
u
v
w
x
y
z

underline VERB
The killings underlined the need for political talks to resume.
▶ emphasize, highlight, stress, accentuate, point up
OPPOSITES ARE minimize, play down

underling NOUN
They reckoned the underlings could be trusted to deal with the pudding and dessert.
▶ subordinate, inferior, junior, minion, menial, flunkey

underlying ADJECTIVE
He took issue with their underlying aims.
▶ basic, fundamental, essential, intrinsic, principal

undermine VERB
He denied that the change would undermine local democracy.
▶ weaken, subvert, threaten, compromise, enfeeble, sap, wear away, destroy, ruin
OPPOSITES ARE support, enhance, boost

underprivileged ADJECTIVE
Many children from underprivileged families have been able to join youth clubs.
▶ needy, deprived, disadvantaged, impoverished, destitute, poor
OPPOSITES ARE privileged, wealthy

underrate VERB
Most of us have a tendency to underrate our own skills.
▶ underestimate, undervalue, belittle, disparage, minimize, dismiss, misjudge
OPPOSITES ARE overrate, exaggerate

understand VERB
1 *They were unusually quiet, and I could not understand why. He began to understand the story in its full horror.*
▶ comprehend, grasp, perceive, discern, apprehend, fathom, follow, take in
2 *Do they not understand how much people like me love Morrissey?*
▶ appreciate, realize, recognize, acknowledge
3 *We understand that the university doesn't have a science park.*
▶ believe, think, suppose, conclude, surmise, fancy

understanding NOUN
1 *Coins can contribute to our understanding of the past.*
▶ knowledge, comprehension, perception, grasp
AN OPPOSITE IS ignorance
2 *We should look on them with deep understanding.*
▶ compassion, sympathy, feeling, consideration
AN OPPOSITE IS indifference
3 *My understanding was that there is a three-year guarantee.*
▶ belief, perception, conviction, notion, idea, conclusion
4 *She is a woman of acute understanding.*
▶ intelligence, intellect, intuition, discernment, judgement
5 *The various groups had come to an understanding.*
▶ agreement, arrangement, deal, settlement, pact, treaty, entente

understate VERB
The level of complaints received may well understate the scale of the problem.
▶ play down, underplay, minimize, belittle, make light of, soft-pedal
OPPOSITES ARE overstate, exaggerate

undertake VERB
1 *He undertook to guarantee her son's safety.*
▶ agree, promise, guarantee, pledge, consent
2 *Some students undertake an industrial placement in their third year.*
▶ begin, commence, embark on, take on, take up, engage in, take responsibility for, manage, handle

undertaking NOUN
1 *Finding a suitable site is a difficult undertaking.*
▶ enterprise, venture, project, operation, endeavour, business, task, affair, scheme
2 *Booksellers agreed to sign an undertaking not to sell the book.*
▶ agreement, commitment, pledge, assurance

undertone NOUN
Meredith caught a sinister undertone in his words.
▶ undercurrent, overtone, connotation, association, implication, reverberation, suggestion

undervalue VERB
He seemed to undervalue his own work.
▶ underestimate, underrate, misjudge, belittle, disparage, minimize, dismiss
OPPOSITES ARE overestimate, overrate

underwater ADJECTIVE
Underwater sonar equipment was used to test for the presence of Nessie.
▶ undersea, subaquatic, submarine, submerged, immersed

undesirable ADJECTIVE
1 *These undesirable side effects cannot be disregarded.*
▶ unpleasant, unwelcome, unwanted, disagreeable
OPPOSITES ARE desirable, pleasant
2 *Adam had allowed some undesirable people access to the place.*
▶ nasty, repellent, objectionable, disagreeable, distasteful
OPPOSITES ARE pleasant, agreeable

undignified ADJECTIVE
Getting off the boats was often an undignified scramble.
▶ unseemly, indecorous, ungainly, inelegant, unbecoming, ignominious
AN OPPOSITE IS dignified

undisciplined ADJECTIVE
An undisciplined cheer went up from the crew members. The Byzantine Greeks were regarded as a brilliant but undisciplined people.
▶ disorganized, disorderly, chaotic, unruly, intractable, rebellious, uncontrolled, wild, wilful, anarchic, disobedient, unsystematic, untrained
OPPOSITES ARE disciplined, controlled

undisputed ADJECTIVE
A few years earlier he had been the undisputed master of the empire.
▶ undoubted, unchallenged, unquestioned, indubitable, indisputable, incontrovertible
OPPOSITES ARE disputed, doubtful

undivided ADJECTIVE
Be prepared to give your undivided attention and listen carefully.
▶ complete, unqualified, unreserved, unbroken, full, total, whole, absolute
OPPOSITES ARE divided, partial

undo VERB
1 *She hardly had time to undo her safety belt and get out of the car.*
▶ unfasten, release, untie, unbutton, unlock, unhitch, loosen
OPPOSITES ARE fasten, tie up
2 *Human error undid years of endeavour in a few seconds.*
▶ undermine, subvert, overturn, nullify, scupper, sabotage
3 *A higher court might undo this decision.*
▶ reverse, overturn, revoke, overrule, disallow, rescind, annul

undoing NOUN
At this point fear was his undoing.
▶ ruin, downfall, ruination, destruction, overthrow, weakness, failing

undoubted ADJECTIVE
The one undoubted gain has been improved health.
▶ indisputable, unquestionable, indubitable, incontrovertible, unchallenged

undoubtedly ADVERB
There will undoubtedly be things you do well already.
▶ definitely, doubtless, indubitably, certainly, of course, surely, undeniably, unquestionably
AN OPPOSITE IS possibly

undress VERB
The patient has to undress slowly and carefully.
▶ take off your clothes, strip, disrobe, (*more informal*) peel off
AN OPPOSITE IS dress

undressed ADJECTIVE
She was half undressed when the doorbell rang.
▶ naked, unclothed, disrobed, nude, stripped, bare

undue ADJECTIVE
If people are under undue stress, they make mistakes.
▶ excessive, extreme, unwarranted, unreasonable, disproportionate, unnecessary
OPPOSITES ARE due, appropriate

unduly ADVERB
Perhaps you think me unduly harsh to express these things so openly.
▶ excessively, unreasonably, inordinately, immoderately, unnecessarily

unearth VERB
They have done all they can to unearth the truth.
▶ uncover, detect, discover, expose, make known, make public, dig up
OPPOSITES ARE conceal, cover up

unearthly ADJECTIVE
1 *She was a lady of unearthly beauty.*
▶ eerie, uncanny, strange, supernatural, otherworldly, weird
OPPOSITES ARE ordinary, mundane
2 (*informal*) *I had a job that involved getting up at an unearthly hour.*
▶ unreasonable, abnormal, unusual, (*informal*) ungodly
OPPOSITES ARE reasonable, comfortable

uneasy ADJECTIVE
1 *The uneasy peace lasted a few months.*
▶ precarious, insecure, unsettled
AN OPPOSITE IS comfortable
2 *Moore was uneasy about the coat.*
▶ anxious, nervous, apprehensive, troubled, worried, concerned, fearful, jittery
AN OPPOSITE IS confident
3 *There was an uneasy atmosphere in the room.*
▶ tense, awkward, fraught, strained, edgy, uncomfortable

uneducated ADJECTIVE
The superstition was by no means confined to uneducated people.
▶ ill-educated, untaught, ignorant, ill-informed, uninformed, uncultured, unsophisticated
OPPOSITES ARE educated, learned

unemployed ADJECTIVE
I don't know what his job is; is he unemployed at the moment?
▶ out of work, jobless, on the dole, not working, redundant
OPPOSITES ARE employed, working, in work

unending ADJECTIVE
Her work seemed to be unending.
▶ endless, interminable, never-ending, everlasting, unceasing, incessant

unenthusiastic ADJECTIVE
He was distinctly unenthusiastic about the idea.
▶ indifferent, apathetic, half-hearted, lukewarm

unenviable ADJECTIVE
The job of being a project leader is an unenviable one.
▶ unpleasant, disagreeable, undesirable, unwelcome, thankless

unequal ADJECTIVE
1 *The chair had four legs of unequal length.*
▶ different, differing, varying, uneven, dissimilar, disparate
AN OPPOSITE IS equal
2 *the unequal distribution of power and resources in society*
▶ unfair, unjust, inequitable, disproportionate
OPPOSITES ARE fair, equitable

3 *Should I give up the unequal struggle?*
▶ unbalanced, uneven, unfair, ill-matched, one-sided
OPPOSITES ARE equal, well-balanced

4 unequal to *Melanie felt unequal to the task she had been given.*
▶ inadequate for, incapable of, unqualified for, not up to, (*more informal*) not cut out for

unequalled ADJECTIVE
Gregory of Tours provides evidence of unequalled richness.
▶ incomparable, unmatched, unparalleled, unrivalled, unsurpassed, inimitable, supreme, matchless, peerless

unequivocal ADJECTIVE
His answer was a swift and unequivocal 'no'.
▶ definite, clear, unambiguous, categorical, explicit
OPPOSITES ARE ambiguous, unclear

uneven ADJECTIVE
1 *Be careful when wheeling a trolley over uneven ground.*
▶ bumpy, rough, rutted, undulating, bent, broken, crooked, irregular, jagged, jerky, pitted, wavy
AN OPPOSITE IS smooth

2 *The demand for electricity is uneven throughout the day.*
▶ inconsistent, variable, spasmodic, unpredictable, varying, erratic, fitful, fluctuating
AN OPPOSITE IS consistent.

3 *Uneven steps led down to a rocky cove.*
▶ irregular, unsteady, lopsided, unbalanced

4 *He soon gave up the uneven contest.*
▶ unequal, unfair, ill-matched, one-sided, unbalanced
AN OPPOSITE IS balanced

uneventful ADJECTIVE
Annie led a quiet, uneventful life.
▶ dull, monotonous, unexciting, uninteresting, tedious, humdrum
OPPOSITES ARE eventful, exciting

unexceptional ADJECTIVE
Most of the music is functional and unexceptional.
▶ ordinary, routine, average, typical, undistinguished, unremarkable, uninteresting
OPPOSITES ARE exceptional, remarkable

unexpected ADJECTIVE
An unexpected error had occurred.
▶ unforeseen, accidental, unpredictable, chance, fortuitous, sudden, surprising, unhoped for, unlooked for, unplanned, unusual
OPPOSITES ARE expected, predictable

unfair ADJECTIVE
1 *It was so unfair that she could never see him.*
▶ unjust, unreasonable, inequitable
OPPOSITES ARE fair, just

2 *It seemed to Watson a cruel, unfair remark. He claims I have unfair advantages.*
▶ undeserved, unwarranted, uncalled-for, unreasonable, unjustified
OPPOSITES ARE fair, justified

3 *The law was placing an unfair burden on small businesses.*
▶ unreasonable, discriminatory
OPPOSITES ARE reasonable, legitimate

4 *The rules relating to unfair play need to be tightened up.*
▶ illegal, unsporting, dishonourable, illegitimate
OPPOSITES ARE fair, honourable

unfaithful ADJECTIVE
He could not deny that he had been an unfaithful husband.
▶ adulterous, disloyal, untrustworthy, deceitful, duplicitous, faithless
OPPOSITES ARE faithful, loyal

unfamiliar ADJECTIVE
An unfamiliar smell was drifting from the flat.
▶ strange, unusual, curious, novel, different

unfashionable ADJECTIVE
Now they were unfashionable, maybe it would be OK to get a personal organizer.
▶ old-fashioned, outmoded, out of date, passé, obsolete
OPPOSITES ARE fashionable, trendy

unfavourable ADJECTIVE
1 *A new head would face unfavourable comparison with his predecessor.*
▶ critical, hostile, unfriendly, adverse, negative, uncomplimentary, unsympathetic
OPPOSITES ARE favourable, positive

2 *A high cost of living and unfavourable exchange rates ate into their holiday funds.*
▶ bad, adverse, unsatisfactory, undesirable, unenviable
OPPOSITES ARE favourable, advantageous

unfeeling ADJECTIVE
He smiled, but it was a cool, unfeeling smile.
▶ insensitive, heartless, hard-hearted, callous, uncaring
OPPOSITES ARE sensitive, sympathetic

unfinished ADJECTIVE
The work remained unfinished on his death.
▶ incomplete, uncompleted, imperfect, rough, sketchy, unpolished
AN OPPOSITE IS complete

unfit ADJECTIVE
1 *The house was rapidly becoming unfit for habitation. They were unfit to pass judgement on modern architecture.*
▶ unsuited, ill-equipped, inadequate, unsatisfactory, useless, incapable (of)

2 *Kevin was also unfit, leaving the defence weakened.*
▶ out of condition, out of shape, unhealthy, feeble
OPPOSITES ARE fit, healthy

unfold VERB

1 *Mick unfolded the space blanket.*
▶ open out, spread out, straighten out, unfurl
AN OPPOSITE IS fold up

2 *Come and see history unfold before your eyes.*
▶ happen, evolve, develop, take place, progress, emerge

unforeseen ADJECTIVE

Many of the long-term results were unforeseen.
▶ unexpected, unpredicted, unthought of, surprising, unanticipated
OPPOSITES ARE foreseen, predictable

unforgettable ADJECTIVE

The recreation park will provide hours of fun and an unforgettable experience.
▶ memorable, striking, noteworthy, remarkable, impressive, distinctive
OPPOSITES ARE forgettable, unexceptional

unforgivable ADJECTIVE

Losing your temper with him was unforgivable.
▶ inexcusable, reprehensible, shameful, unjustifiable, unpardonable, unwarrantable
AN OPPOSITE IS forgivable

unfortunate ADJECTIVE

1 *Some of these unfortunate prisoners were later found to be innocent.*
▶ unlucky, hapless, wretched, poor, unhappy, ill-fated, luckless

2 *The incident led to the most unfortunate disagreement between the Allies.*
▶ disastrous, disadvantageous, unwelcome, inopportune, harmful, regrettable, lamentable, deplorable

3 *He said it would be most unfortunate if one year's results were regarded as typical.*
▶ regrettable, inappropriate, unsuitable

unfounded ADJECTIVE

We now realize that these claims are totally unfounded.
▶ groundless, baseless, unsupported, unsubstantiated, unjustified, spurious

unfriendly ADJECTIVE

He glowered back in an unfriendly manner.
▶ hostile, aggressive, disagreeable, unpleasant, antagonistic, unsociable, standoffish, aloof
OPPOSITES ARE friendly, amiable

ungainly ADJECTIVE

A kangaroo must use a lot of energy in its lopsided and ungainly walk.
▶ awkward, clumsy, ungraceful, graceless, inelegant
OPPOSITES ARE elegant, graceful

ungrateful ADJECTIVE

I'm going to seem so ungrateful if I refuse the offer.
▶ unappreciative, unthankful, ungracious, ill-mannered, selfish
OPPOSITES ARE grateful, thankful

unhappy ADJECTIVE

1 *Her absence made Thomas unhappy.*
▶ sad, sorrowful, melancholy, miserable, dejected, despondent, dispirited, depressed
OPPOSITES ARE happy, pleased

2 *One person at least had benefited from these unhappy events.*
▶ unlucky, unfortunate, luckless, ill-fated
AN OPPOSITE IS fortunate

3 *Clearly it has been an unhappy compromise.*
▶ inappropriate, unsuitable, inapt, unsatisfactory, unfortunate
OPPOSITES ARE happy, satisfactory

4 *Graham was very unhappy with his performance.*
▶ dissatisfied, disappointed, displeased, discontented

unharmed ADJECTIVE

Almost all the population seem to have escaped unharmed.
▶ safe, safe and sound, uninjured, unhurt, unscathed, intact
OPPOSITES ARE harmed, injured

unhealthy ADJECTIVE

1 *He was looking tired and unhealthy.*
▶ sickly, ill-looking, ailing, unwell, poorly, frail, weak
OPPOSITES ARE healthy, well

2 *They lived in an unhealthy environment.*
▶ insalubrious, dirty, insanitary, polluted, unhygienic, unwholesome
OPPOSITES ARE healthy, salubrious

3 *As a nurse I knew it was unhealthy to be so overweight.*
▶ harmful, unnatural, deleterious
AN OPPOSITE IS healthy

unheard of ADJECTIVE

It was unheard of in those days for anyone to get so much money.
▶ unprecedented, inconceivable, unimaginable, exceptional, extraordinary, unusual, uncommon
AN OPPOSITE IS common

unhelpful ADJECTIVE

The bank cashier had been unhelpful.
▶ uncooperative, disobliging, inconsiderate, uncivil, unwilling, negative, slow
OPPOSITES ARE helpful, obliging

unidentified ADJECTIVE

An unidentified vandal drew a Hitler moustache on the portrait.
▶ unknown, unnamed, nameless, unrecognized, unspecified, anonymous, incognito, unfamiliar
OPPOSITES ARE identified, known, named

uniform ADJECTIVE

A thermostat will maintain a uniform temperature.
▶ regular, consistent, unvarying, homogeneous, identical, indistinguishable, similar, single
OPPOSITES ARE varying, inconsistent

a b c d e f g h i j k l m n o p q r s t **u** v w x y z

uniform NOUN

He had never worn a uniform in his life.
▶ outfit, livery, regalia, costume

unify VERB

He was concerned to unify the country.
▶ unite, integrate, harmonize, bring together, combine, consolidate, amalgamate, bind, fuse, join, merge, weld together
OPPOSITES ARE divide, separate, split

unimaginable ADJECTIVE

He was motivated by the promise of unimaginable rewards.
▶ inconceivable, unbelievable, incredible, unthinkable, unheard of, untold, mind-boggling

unimaginative ADJECTIVE

The drawings were flat and unimaginative.
▶ boring, dull, uninspired, uncreative, uninventive, uninteresting, unexciting, unoriginal, pedestrian, prosaic, stale, trite, banal, derivative, ordinary
OPPOSITES ARE imaginative, creative

unimportant ADJECTIVE

The size of the power supply is unimportant.
▶ insignificant, inconsequential, immaterial, irrelevant, trivial, trifling, minor, of no account, of no consequence, of no moment
AN OPPOSITE IS important

uninhabited ADJECTIVE

The centre of the island is vast and uninhabited.
▶ empty, unoccupied, unpeopled, unsettled, deserted, depopulated, uncolonized, vacant
AN OPPOSITE IS inhabited

uninhibited ADJECTIVE

1 *He shared her uninhibited sense of humour and fun.*
▶ unrestrained, unconstrained, spontaneous, unrepressed, abandoned, impetuous, carefree, reckless
AN OPPOSITE IS inhibited

2 *She's a lively and uninhibited girl.*
▶ unselfconscious, unreserved, unrestrained, liberated, relaxed, informal

unintelligible ADJECTIVE

The conversation was unintelligible to Gina.
▶ incomprehensible, incoherent, unfathomable, baffling, perplexing, obscure, cryptic, opaque, mysterious, confusing, inscrutable, enigmatic
OPPOSITES ARE intelligible, comprehensible

unintentional ADJECTIVE

Sometimes the harassment may be unintentional.
▶ unintended, inadvertent, accidental, involuntary, unconscious, unplanned, unwitting, fortuitous
AN OPPOSITE IS intentional

uninterested ADJECTIVE

uninterested in *He was uninterested in politics.*
▶ indifferent to, unconcerned about, uninvolved in, incurious about, apathetic about, bored by, unenthusiastic about, unresponsive to
AN OPPOSITE IS interested

uninteresting ADJECTIVE

She was struggling through an uninteresting article on cosmetics.
▶ dull, boring, unexciting, tedious, dreary, monotonous, humdrum, uninspiring, vapid, wearisome
AN OPPOSITE IS interesting

uninterrupted ADJECTIVE

A few extra hours of uninterrupted sleep can remedy the situation.
▶ continuous, unbroken, undisturbed, constant, sustained, consecutive
OPPOSITES ARE interrupted, intermittent, broken

union NOUN

1 *A union was formed to fight the war with Persia.*
▶ alliance, coalition, league, federation, confederation, confederacy

2 *The company was formed from the union of three smaller firms.*
▶ merger, merging, amalgamation, fusion, combination, unification, uniting, joining

unique ADJECTIVE

1 *Each file has got a unique name.*
▶ distinctive, special, individual, peculiar, single, singular, (*more informal*) one-off
AN OPPOSITE IS common

2 *The production was a unique opportunity to hear the music in its original form.*
▶ remarkable, outstanding, incomparable, extraordinary, unparalleled, unprecedented, unusual
AN OPPOSITE IS unremarkable

unit NOUN

The family is a fundamental unit of society.
▶ component, constituent, element, entity, item, portion, section, segment

unite VERB

1 *They tried to unite the population in a common war effort against the English.*
▶ unify, integrate, combine, bring together, bind, join
AN OPPOSITE IS divide

2 *Police and publicans united to solve the problem.*
▶ combine, join forces, cooperate, collaborate

3 *Mother and son were united after the war.*
▶ bring together, join

united ADJECTIVE

the potential power of a united Germany
▶ unified, integrated, merged, amalgamated, combined
AN OPPOSITE IS disunited

be united *They were united on this one issue.*
▶ agree, be in agreement, be in accord, be unanimous, be of the same mind, have the same opinion
OPPOSITES ARE be disunited, disagree

unity NOUN

1 *Creating national unity is a fundamental task for our people.*
▶ agreement, harmony, accord, consensus, concord
OPPOSITES ARE discord, disagreement
2 *the issue of European unity*
▶ union, unification, federation
OPPOSITES ARE division, disunity

universal ADJECTIVE

A sudden fall in house prices is a universal fear.
▶ common, general, ubiquitous, widespread, worldwide, global, all-embracing, all-round
OPPOSITES ARE restricted, local

unjust ADJECTIVE

1 *She was still smarting from her unjust dismissal.*
▶ unfair, unjustified, undeserved, unmerited, unreasonable, unwarranted, unlawful, wrong, wrongful, indefensible, inequitable
OPPOSITES ARE just, justified
2 *The report was widely criticized for being unjust.*
▶ unfair, biased, one-sided, partial, partisan, prejudiced, bigoted
OPPOSITES ARE just, fair, balanced

unjustifiable ADJECTIVE

Some might consider it an unjustifiable expense.
▶ unreasonable, unwarrantable, indefensible, inexcusable, unacceptable, unforgivable, excessive, immoderate
OPPOSITES ARE justifiable, acceptable

unkempt ADJECTIVE

He had long unkempt hair and several missing teeth.
▶ untidy, messy, scruffy, dishevelled, disordered, rumpled, bedraggled
OPPOSITES ARE tidy, neat, well-groomed

unkind ADJECTIVE

He says unkind things that cause her pain.
▶ cruel, thoughtless, unfeeling, callous, uncharitable, unpleasant, inconsiderate, unfriendly, malicious, malevolent, spiteful, harsh
OPPOSITES ARE kind, considerate

unknown ADJECTIVE

1 *Some of the civilians were transferred to unknown destinations. For some unknown reason, the blinds were always drawn. The date of their marriage is unknown.*
▶ unspecified, unidentified, unnamed, undisclosed, mysterious, strange, unrecognized, anonymous, nameless
AN OPPOSITE IS named
2 *Lowell began a search for this unknown planet.*
▶ undiscovered, unfamiliar, unexplored, unmapped, uncharted, alien, foreign
AN OPPOSITE IS familiar
3 *The part was taken by the then unknown Maria.*
▶ unheard of, obscure, little known, undistinguished, lowly, inconsequential, insignificant, unimportant
AN OPPOSITE IS famous

unlawful ADJECTIVE

It was unlawful for any foreigner to enter the temple.
▶ forbidden, prohibited, unauthorized, illegal, banned, outlawed
OPPOSITES ARE lawful, allowed

unlikely ADJECTIVE

1 *It is unlikely that they will attend, being so busy.*
▶ doubtful, improbable, dubious
AN OPPOSITE IS likely
2 *They would hardly believe such an unlikely explanation.*
▶ implausible, improbable, far-fetched, incredible, suspect, suspicious, dubious, questionable, unbelievable, unconvincing
AN OPPOSITE IS likely

unlimited ADJECTIVE

1 *The President emphasized that the USA did not have unlimited funds.*
▶ limitless, inexhaustible, infinite, unbounded, boundless, bottomless
OPPOSITES ARE limited, finite
2 *All parts carry a 12-month unlimited mileage warranty.*
▶ unrestricted, unqualified, unconditional, open, unhindered, clear
OPPOSITES ARE limited, restricted

unload VERB

1 *Unload the box of essential items first.*
▶ remove, take off, offload, drop off, unpack, discharge
AN OPPOSITE IS load
2 *About thirty men would be needed to unload the ship.*
▶ unpack, empty, unburden

unlock VERB

He took the keys from his pocket and unlocked the boot.
▶ open, release, unfasten, undo
OPPOSITES ARE lock, fasten

unloved ADJECTIVE

As a child I felt very unloved.
▶ uncared-for, unwanted, neglected, rejected, spurned, friendless, forsaken, unpopular, uncherished, unvalued
AN OPPOSITE IS loved

unlucky ADJECTIVE

1 *You could be ruined as a result of some unlucky accident.*
▶ chance, untimely, unfortunate, unintended, disastrous, dreadful, tragic, calamitous, unwelcome
OPPOSITES ARE lucky, timely, fortunate
2 *Miss Hill was unlucky not to get a medal. Phil was again unlucky with injuries.*
▶ unfortunate, hapless, luckless, unhappy, unsuccessful, wretched
OPPOSITES ARE lucky, fortunate
3 *The 13th proved to be unlucky for one American skier.*
▶ inauspicious, ominous, unfavourable, jinxed, cursed, ill-fated, ill-omened, ill-starred
OPPOSITES ARE lucky, auspicious

u

unmistakable ADJECTIVE

Then came the unmistakable sound of a shot.
▶ distinct, distinctive, clear, plain, obvious, unambiguous, telltale
OPPOSITES ARE uncertain, unclear

unmitigated ADJECTIVE

an unmitigated disaster
▶ absolute, complete, total, utter, unqualified, outright
OPPOSITES ARE qualified, partial

unnatural ADJECTIVE

1 *It was an unnatural crime: was the man mad? He was uneasy in this unnatural silence.*
▶ abnormal, unusual, uncanny, weird, bizarre, strange, odd, unaccountable, inexplicable, extraordinary
AN OPPOSITE IS normal

2 *Her voice sounded unnatural.*
▶ affected, self-conscious, mannered, stilted, theatrical, unspontaneous, feigned, (*more informal*) put on
OPPOSITES ARE natural, normal

3 *The white fur looked unnatural.*
▶ artificial, fabricated, imitation, man-made, manufactured, simulated, synthetic
OPPOSITES ARE natural, genuine

unnecessary ADJECTIVE

1 *Don't let's take any unnecessary risks.*
▶ inessential, non-essential, needless, uncalled-for, unjustified, unneeded, unwanted, excessive, extra
OPPOSITES ARE necessary, essential

2 *A deposit is unnecessary with this order.*
▶ superfluous, dispensable, redundant
OPPOSITES ARE necessary, obligatory

unofficial ADJECTIVE

1 *She acted as an unofficial bank, cashing cheques for customers.*
▶ informal, casual, private, personal, unauthorized
OPPOSITES ARE official, formal

2 *Unofficial figures put the dead and wounded at over 300.*
▶ unconfirmed, unauthenticated, unsubstantiated
OPPOSITES ARE official, confirmed

unorthodox ADJECTIVE

A former pupil remembers his unorthodox teaching methods.
▶ unconventional, unusual, radical, irregular, novel, idiosyncratic, bizarre
OPPOSITES ARE orthodox, conventional

unpaid ADJECTIVE

1 *There were unpaid bills spread all over the table.*
▶ outstanding, overdue, unsettled, owing, due
OPPOSITES ARE paid, settled

2 *Some staff also did unpaid charity work.*
▶ voluntary, unremunerative
OPPOSITES ARE paid, professional

unpleasant ADJECTIVE

1 *It reminded him of an earlier unpleasant experience.*
▶ disagreeable, distressing, distasteful, nasty, horrible, horrid, uncomfortable
OPPOSITES ARE pleasant, agreeable

2 *They were the most unpleasant people I had ever met.*
▶ unlikable, disagreeable, objectionable, unattractive, unfriendly, obnoxious, repugnant, repulsive, revolting, repellent, ill-natured
OPPOSITES ARE friendly, agreeable

3 *substances that give rise to unpleasant odours*
▶ repulsive, revolting, unappealing
OPPOSITES ARE pleasant, appealing

unpopular ADJECTIVE

1 *The tax proved deeply unpopular and was later abolished.*
▶ hated, disliked, detested, unwelcome, unwanted, rejected, despised
AN OPPOSITE IS popular

2 *He was unpopular at school.*
▶ disliked, friendless, unliked, shunned

unprecedented ADJECTIVE

an unprecedented growth in small businesses
▶ exceptional, extraordinary, abnormal, unequalled, unrivalled, extreme, unusual
AN OPPOSITE IS normal

unpredictable ADJECTIVE

1 *The weather is unpredictable in the hills.*
▶ changeable, variable, erratic, uncertain, unreliable, unforeseeable, unexpected
AN OPPOSITE IS predictable

2 *She was unpredictable and likely to say anything.*
▶ unreliable, fickle, erratic, volatile, capricious, moody, unstable
AN OPPOSITE IS predictable

unprepared ADJECTIVE

unprepared for *They were often inexperienced and unprepared for the demands of the work.*
▶ ill-equipped for, unqualified for, unready for, surprised by, caught out by

unpretentious ADJECTIVE

1 *The exterior of the house is very simple and unpretentious.*
▶ plain, simple, ordinary, unostentatious, straightforward
OPPOSITES ARE pretentious, elaborate

2 *He was a friendly and unpretentious man.*
▶ modest, unassuming, unaffected, humble
OPPOSITES ARE pretentious, vain

unproductive ADJECTIVE

1 *His lands were not encumbered by a costly and unproductive bureaucracy.*
▶ ineffective, worthless, unprofitable, useless, fruitless, futile, pointless, unrewarding, valueless
AN OPPOSITE IS productive

2 *The land is unproductive for much of the year. The rest of the week was equally unproductive.*
▶ unfruitful, barren, infertile, sterile, arid
AN OPPOSITE IS productive

unprofessional ADJECTIVE
1 *The work was sloppy and unprofessional.*
▶ amateurish, inexpert, unskilled, incompetent, inefficient, irresponsible
OPPOSITES ARE professional, skilful
2 *We wouldn't like to be accused of unprofessional conduct.*
▶ improper, unethical, unprincipled, unscrupulous, lax, incompetent, unworthy
AN OPPOSITE IS professional

unprofitable ADJECTIVE
Airlines will start pulling out of unprofitable routes.
▶ unproductive, uneconomic, loss-making, uncommercial, unremunerative, unrewarding
AN OPPOSITE IS profitable

unqualified ADJECTIVE
1 *Too many nursing lectures are given by unqualified lecturers.*
▶ untrained, inexperienced, incapable, incompetent, unsuitable, ineligible
OPPOSITES ARE qualified, competent
2 *The experiment was an unqualified success.*
▶ absolute, unreserved, complete, outright, total, utter, unmitigated
OPPOSITES ARE qualified, partial

unravel VERB
1 *He cut the climbing rope and started to unravel its strands.*
▶ disentangle, untangle, unwind, untwist, undo, separate
AN OPPOSITE IS entangle
2 *the sequence of events that archaeologists attempt to unravel*
▶ resolve, sort out, solve, puzzle out, interpret, explain, elucidate, clarify

unreal ADJECTIVE
It is a curiously unreal state of affairs.
▶ false, artificial, fake, sham, illusory, imaginary
OPPOSITES ARE real, genuine

unrealistic ADJECTIVE
It would be unrealistic to think of removing road congestion entirely.
▶ impractical, unreasonable, unworkable, fanciful, impracticable, over-ambitious, idealistic, impossible
OPPOSITES ARE realistic, practical, pragmatic

unreasonable ADJECTIVE
1 *I knew I was being unreasonable.*
▶ unfair, unjust, unhelpful, uncooperative, obstructive
OPPOSITES ARE reasonable, helpful, fair
2 *It was unreasonable of him to expect her to know the answer.*
▶ irrational, illogical, perverse, unwarranted, absurd
OPPOSITES ARE reasonable, sensible
3 *They were making unreasonable demands.*
▶ excessive, immoderate, exorbitant, extortionate
OPPOSITES ARE reasonable, moderate

unrecognizable ADJECTIVE
He's unrecognizable as the boy we once knew.
▶ unidentifiable, unknowable, changed (from), altered (from)
AN OPPOSITE IS recognizable

unrelated ADJECTIVE
1 *Two men had been charged after the match in unrelated incidents.*
▶ separate, distinct, unconnected
2 *He was assigned to a menial post unrelated to his abilities.*
▶ irrelevant, unconnected (with), dissimilar

unrelenting ADJECTIVE
Success came through unrelenting hard work.
▶ constant, continuous, relentless, remorseless, persistent, unremitting, unflagging, merciless, ruthless
AN OPPOSITE IS intermittent

unreliable ADJECTIVE
1 *The official figures are unreliable for gauging levels of unemployment.*
▶ inaccurate, misleading, deceptive, suspect, false, implausible, unconvincing
OPPOSITES ARE reliable, accurate
2 *The more he defended himself, the more unreliable he sounded.*
▶ untrustworthy, irresponsible, undependable, changeable, inconsistent, unpredictable, unsound, unstable, fallible, fickle
OPPOSITES ARE reliable, dependable

unrepentant ADJECTIVE
He remains unrepentant about his comments last week.
▶ unapologetic, unashamed, impenitent, unrepenting, unabashed, shameless, hardened
AN OPPOSITE IS repentant

unreserved ADJECTIVE
Clara admired the results with unreserved satisfaction.
▶ absolute, unqualified, complete, wholehearted, outright, total, utter, unmitigated
OPPOSITES ARE qualified, partial

unrest NOUN
There was Jacobite unrest throughout much of England.
▶ rebellion, disorder, agitation, disturbance, disruption, upheaval, tumult, insurrection
OPPOSITES ARE order, peace

unrestricted ADJECTIVE
The public has unrestricted access to the gardens during daylight hours.
▶ unlimited, open, unhindered, clear, unqualified, unconditional
OPPOSITES ARE limited, restricted

unrivalled ADJECTIVE
From the hotel you look out on unrivalled views of Venice.
▶ incomparable, unequalled, unmatched, unparalleled, unsurpassed, inimitable, supreme, matchless, peerless

a b c d e f g h i j k l m n o p q r s **u** v w x y z

unruffled ADJECTIVE

Matthew's unruffled manner had evidently soothed them.
▶ calm, composed, collected, self-possessed, cool, poised, unperturbed, unflustered, unbothered, untroubled, (*more informal*) unflappable, (*more informal*) laid-back
OPPOSITES ARE excited, anxious, upset

unruly ADJECTIVE

A military unit had been stoned by a hungry and unruly mob.
▶ disorderly, rowdy, wild, rebellious, disruptive, undisciplined, disobedient, boisterous, rough
OPPOSITES ARE orderly, disciplined

unsafe ADJECTIVE

1 *They agreed it would be unsafe to try to get a message to London.*
▶ dangerous, risky, hazardous, precarious, insecure
OPPOSITES ARE safe, harmless
2 *The verdicts were unsafe because they were based entirely on confessions.*
▶ unreliable, unsound, insecure, doubtful, unstable
OPPOSITES ARE safe, reliable, secure

unsatisfactory ADJECTIVE

It was an unsatisfactory conclusion to an otherwise useful visit.
▶ disappointing, dissatisfying, unacceptable, unhappy, displeasing, inadequate, unworthy, poor, unsatisfying
AN OPPOSITE IS satisfactory

unsavoury ADJECTIVE

There were too many unsavoury characters lurking about.
▶ unpleasant, disreputable, objectionable, unwholesome, obnoxious, repellent
AN OPPOSITE IS reputable

unscathed ADJECTIVE

Richard walked away unscathed from the wreckage of his car.
▶ unharmed, unhurt, uninjured, safe, intact
OPPOSITES ARE injured, hurt

unscrupulous ADJECTIVE

He showed himself to be a cunning and unscrupulous politician.
▶ dishonest, dishonourable, unprincipled, unethical, immoral, improper, self-interested, shameless
OPPOSITES ARE honest, principled

unseemly ADJECTIVE

There was another unseemly row that evening.
▶ undignified, unbecoming, embarrassing, indecorous, indelicate, discreditable, unsuitable
OPPOSITES ARE seemly, dignified

unseen ADJECTIVE

The practice was activated by some unseen hands.
▶ hidden, concealed, invisible, unnoticed, obscured, imperceptible
OPPOSITES ARE visible, seen

unselfish ADJECTIVE

They were motivated by entirely unselfish motives.
▶ kind, selfless, thoughtful, altruistic, disinterested, magnanimous, charitable, considerate, caring, generous, humanitarian, philanthropic
AN OPPOSITE IS selfish

unsettled ADJECTIVE

1 *Unsettled weather makes a long painting session impossible.*
▶ changeable, variable, changing, unreliable, unpredictable, unsteady
OPPOSITES ARE settled, calm
2 *He looked anxious and unsettled.*
▶ disturbed, upset, troubled, agitated, restless, uneasy, flustered
OPPOSITES ARE settled, composed

unsightly ADJECTIVE

There is already an unsightly quarry there.
▶ ugly, unattractive, hideous, inelegant, tasteless, unpleasant, displeasing
AN OPPOSITE IS beautiful

unskilled ADJECTIVE

For unskilled workers the death rate was 40% above average.
▶ unqualified, untrained, inexperienced, unskilful
AN OPPOSITE IS skilled

unsociable ADJECTIVE

He was grumpy and unsociable.
▶ unfriendly, aloof, distant, taciturn, reclusive, uncommunicative, uncongenial
OPPOSITES ARE sociable, friendly

unsolicited ADJECTIVE

You might get unsolicited mail every so often.
▶ unrequested, unsought, unwanted, uninvited, unasked-for
AN OPPOSITE IS requested

unsophisticated ADJECTIVE

She was unsophisticated and shy.
▶ innocent, naive, unworldly, artless, ingenuous, unpretentious, childlike
AN OPPOSITE IS sophisticated

unsound ADJECTIVE

1 *Many of the older buildings were structurally unsound.*
▶ unsafe, unstable, unsteady, flimsy, weak
OPPOSITES ARE sound, strong
2 *These arguments are obviously unsound.*
▶ untenable, flawed, erroneous, defective, ill-founded, fallacious
OPPOSITES ARE sound, cogent

unspeakable ADJECTIVE

The gang was guilty of the most unspeakable acts.
▶ indescribable, awful, dreadful, appalling, repellent, frightful, unutterable, inexpressible, monstrous

unstable ADJECTIVE

1 *The buildings are highly unstable.*
▶ unsteady, shaky, rickety, wobbly, flimsy, insecure, unsafe, precarious

2 *an emotionally unstable young student named Karl*
▶ unbalanced, disturbed, insecure, deranged, demented

The country has a history of unstable government.
▶ unreliable, changeable, erratic, unsettled, volatile

unsteady ADJECTIVE

1 *She balanced her cup on an unsteady iron table. He smelled of alcohol and was unsteady on his feet.*
▶ shaky, rickety, unstable, wobbly, insecure, unsafe, precarious
OPPOSITES ARE steady, firm

2 *She took a deep unsteady breath.*
▶ irregular, uneven, changeable, erratic, inconstant, intermittent, variable
OPPOSITES ARE steady, regular

3 *He read by the unsteady light of a candle*
▶ flickering, fluctuating, wavering, quavering, quivering, trembling, tremulous
AN OPPOSITE IS steady

unsuccessful ADJECTIVE

He was the leader of an unsuccessful military coup against the previous government.
▶ failed, abortive, fruitless, futile, ill-fated, vain, ineffective, ineffectual, unproductive, unsatisfactory, useless
OPPOSITES ARE successful, effective

unsuitable ADJECTIVE

I think the proposed new site is unsuitable.
▶ inappropriate, unsuited, ill-suited, inapt, unsatisfactory, unfitting, unfit, out of keeping, ill-chosen, ill-judged, mistaken, inapposite
OPPOSITES ARE suitable, appropriate

unsure ADJECTIVE

I was unsure of my welcome when I visited the cottage the next afternoon.
▶ uncertain, doubtful, dubious, sceptical, suspicious, mistrustful, distrustful
AN OPPOSITE IS confident

unsure of yourself *She was still a little unsure of herself in formal society.*
▶ unconfident, hesitant, diffident, timid, timorous
OPPOSITES ARE sure of yourself, self-confident

unsympathetic ADJECTIVE

1 *The planning authority showed an unsympathetic attitude to applications for new homes.*
▶ uncaring, unconcerned, unresponsive, indifferent, insensitive, unfeeling, hostile, antagonistic
AN OPPOSITE IS sympathetic

2 **unsympathetic to** *The new assembly was quite unsympathetic to these views.*
▶ opposed to, hostile to, unconcerned about, antagonistic towards, ill-disposed towards
OPPOSITES ARE sympathetic to, understanding of

unsystematic ADJECTIVE

Their use of data was unsystematic.
▶ disorganized, unmethodical, disorderly, haphazard, muddled, jumbled, unstructured, indiscriminate, inconsistent
AN OPPOSITE IS systematic

unthinkable ADJECTIVE

In a free society such a ban would be unthinkable.
▶ inconceivable, unimaginable, unbelievable, undreamed of, incredible, absurd, preposterous, implausible
OPPOSITES ARE conceivable, plausible

untidy ADJECTIVE

1 *He staggered out of his untidy bedroom. The handwriting was untidy.*
▶ disorganized, messy, cluttered, muddled, disordered, chaotic
OPPOSITES ARE tidy, orderly

2 *Her hair looked untidy.*
▶ dishevelled, scruffy, bedraggled, uncombed, ungroomed, unkempt, rumpled, shabby, tangled, tousled, uncared for
OPPOSITES ARE tidy, neat

untie VERB

She began to untie the string around the box.
▶ undo, loosen, unfasten, unknot, release, unbind, disentangle, free, untether
AN OPPOSITE IS tie up

untimely ADJECTIVE

Accounts vary as to how William met his untimely death.
▶ premature, unseasonable, unfortunate, inopportune, inauspicious
OPPOSITES ARE timely, opportune

untold ADJECTIVE

Vandals caused untold damage.
▶ incalculable, boundless, infinite, unlimited, countless
AN OPPOSITE IS limited

untrue ADJECTIVE

The claims were completely untrue.
▶ wrong, false, inaccurate, erroneous, incorrect, mistaken, unfounded, fallacious
OPPOSITES ARE true, correct

unusual ADJECTIVE

1 *The town had electric lighting, unusual in those days.*
▶ uncommon, rare, unfamiliar
OPPOSITES ARE usual, common

2 *It was an unusual story.*
▶ strange, odd, curious, weird, queer, bizarre, peculiar, exceptional, unconventional
OPPOSITES ARE normal, conventional

3 *Vera was a woman of unusual quality.*
▶ remarkable, exceptional, extraordinary, untypical
AN OPPOSITE IS typical

u

unwanted ADJECTIVE

1 *Lila kept guard dogs to ward off unwanted visitors.*
▶ unwelcome, undesirable, undesired, unsolicited, uninvited, rejected
OPPOSITES ARE welcome, wanted, desirable

2 *The ants will bring dead ants and unwanted rubbish from their nests.*
▶ superfluous, discarded, redundant, unused
OPPOSITES ARE needed, useful, wanted

unwary ADJECTIVE

Deep potholes can bring down an unwary rider and his horse.
▶ careless, unthinking, inattentive, absent-minded, thoughtless, unguarded, incautious
OPPOSITES ARE wary, attentive

unwelcome ADJECTIVE

1 *As she went downstairs, an unwelcome voice reached her ears.*
▶ disagreeable, unacceptable, undesirable, unwanted
AN OPPOSITE IS welcome

2 *He had been made to feel unwelcome.*
▶ unwanted, unpopular, excluded, spurned, uninvited

unwell ADJECTIVE

She told the ambulance service she was feeling unwell.
▶ ill, sick, poorly, indisposed, out of sorts, under the weather
OPPOSITES ARE well, in good health

unwieldy ADJECTIVE

He would also need to transport some unwieldy equipment.
▶ awkward, cumbersome, clumsy, bulky, unmanageable, ungainly, heavy, massive
OPPOSITES ARE manageable, handy

unwilling ADJECTIVE

1 *He called together his group of unwilling helpers.*
▶ unenthusiastic, grudging, reluctant, uncooperative, half-hearted, hesitant
OPPOSITES ARE willing, keen

2 *A spokesman was unwilling to give a precise date.*
▶ reluctant, disinclined, averse, loath
OPPOSITES ARE willing, ready

unwind VERB

1 *Kittie unwound balls of pink and blue wool.*
▶ unroll, unreel, unravel, untwist, undo, uncoil, untwine

2 *He found the farm a place to unwind and let himself go.*
▶ relax, ease up, loosen up

unwise ADJECTIVE

You would be unwise to ignore the warning signs.
▶ foolish, stupid, silly, ill-advised, crazy, mad, insane, (*more informal*) daft
OPPOSITES ARE wise, sensible

unworthy ADJECTIVE

1 *His was an unworthy remark.*
▶ shameful, discreditable, dishonourable, undeserving, unsuitable, despicable, disreputable, ignoble, inappropriate
AN OPPOSITE IS worthy

2 *Such claims are unworthy of consideration.*
▶ undeserving, unfit (for), ineligible (for)
OPPOSITES ARE worthy, deserving

upbringing NOUN

They knew all about his birth, upbringing, and police record.
▶ education, breeding, raising, rearing, teaching, training, bringing up, upkeep, care, instruction, nurture

update VERB

You should continually update your information.
▶ review, amend, upgrade, bring up to date, correct, revise, modernize

upgrade VERB

You can upgrade our system free of charge.
▶ improve, enhance, update, make better, renovate, expand

upheaval NOUN

Further changes could be made without major upheaval.
▶ disruption, commotion, disturbance, confusion, disorder, turmoil

uphill ADJECTIVE

We are all facing an uphill struggle.
▶ hard, arduous, strenuous, taxing, tough, difficult, exhausting, gruelling, laborious, stiff
AN OPPOSITE IS easy

uphold VERB

The courts robustly upheld the right of freedom of speech.
▶ support, endorse, confirm, defend, sustain, back, vindicate
AN OPPOSITE IS oppose

upkeep NOUN

Each owner is liable to contribute to the upkeep of the building as a whole.
▶ maintenance, running, repair, care, keep, conservation, preservation
AN OPPOSITE IS neglect

uplifting ADJECTIVE

It's an uplifting story about an English girl in India.
▶ inspiring, moving, touching, warming, cheering, enlightening, encouraging, edifying, enriching, humanizing, improving
AN OPPOSITE IS dispiriting

upper ADJECTIVE

There are lifts to the upper floors of the building.
▶ higher, upstairs, raised, elevated, superior

upright ADJECTIVE
1 *Crude figures are incised on upright stones.*
▶ perpendicular, vertical, erect
2 *upright Victorians with a strong sense of family pride*
▶ honourable, honest, respectable, reputable, righteous, upstanding, moral, principled, righteous, virtuous, trustworthy
OPPOSITES ARE dishonourable, corrupt

uprising NOUN
The uprising was soon suppressed by the army.
▶ rebellion, revolt, rising, insurrection, insurgence, revolution, mutiny
USAGE You use *mutiny* about members of the armed forces.

uproar NOUN
1 *There was an uproar when the council refused to hear the delegation.*
▶ outcry, clamour, protest, furore, rumpus
2 *They found the place in uproar.*
▶ turmoil, confusion, disorder, pandemonium, mayhem, commotion

uproot VERB
1 *He always imagined himself as some great monster uprooting trees.*
▶ pull up, tear up, rip out, root out, weed out, remove, destroy, (*more formal*) extirpate
AN OPPOSITE IS plant
2 *Building a dam would uproot over a million people.*
▶ displace, disrupt, remove

upset VERB
1 *I would never want to upset anyone.*
▶ distress, trouble, agitate, disturb, unsettle, disquiet, disconcert, unnerve, dismay, grieve, perturb, fluster, confuse
OPPOSITES ARE reassure, put at ease
2 *Grazing sheep is prohibited so as not to upset the natural balance.*
▶ disrupt, disturb, interfere with, affect, throw out, ruin
OPPOSITES ARE maintain, restore
3 *He upset a pot of soup.*
▶ tip over, knock over, spill, overturn

upset NOUN
The youngsters put the upset behind them.
▶ distress, worry, trouble, upheaval, bother, anxiety

upset ADJECTIVE
1 *She was upset about missing all the excitement.*
▶ distressed, dismayed, disturbed, troubled, unsettled, disconcerted, worried, anxious, grieved
2 *He rang in to say he had an upset stomach.*
▶ queasy, disordered, (*more informal*) gippy

upshot NOUN
The upshot was that George received a written apology.
▶ result, consequence, outcome, conclusion, effect, sequel

upside-down ADJECTIVE
1 *I could read the writing upside-down on his desk.*
▶ the wrong way up, inverted, topsy-turvy, upturned
OPPOSITES ARE upright, the right way up
2 *Somebody broke in and turned the place upside-down. It is traumatic having one's life turned upside-down like this.*
▶ into disarray, into chaos, into a muddle, untidy, chaotic
AN OPPOSITE IS tidy

uptight ADJECTIVE
(*informal*) *When Ian gets uptight it can affect his game.*
▶ tense, anxious, nervous, edgy, on edge, strained, stressed, agitated, apprehensive, jittery, fidgety, ill at ease, jumpy
OPPOSITES ARE calm, relaxed

up-to-date ADJECTIVE
1 *None of the disks contained up-to-date programs.*
▶ current, latest, recent, new, modern, present-day, advanced
AN OPPOSITE IS out-of-date
2 *Use the Internet to keep yourself up to date on this topic.*
▶ informed (about), in touch (with), conversant (with), (*more informal*) up to speed
AN OPPOSITE IS uninformed

upward ADJECTIVE
Take the upward path. an upward trend in prices
▶ rising, ascending, uphill

urban ADJECTIVE
greenfield sites on the edge of urban areas
▶ built-up, town, city, densely populated, metropolitan, suburban, municipal

urge VERB
1 *We would urge people to be aware and alert with fireworks.*
▶ encourage, entreat, exhort, advise, counsel, appeal to, entreat, beg, press, plead with, beseech, implore, recommend
OPPOSITES ARE deter, discourage
2 *The working group urged caution in implementing any changes.*
▶ advise, recommend, counsel, advocate, suggest
3 *He urged his crew on through the mountainous waves.*
▶ drive, spur, press, force, compel, impel, propel, push

urge NOUN
The urge to give him a hug was almost impossible to resist.
▶ desire, wish, need, impulse, inclination, eagerness, compulsion, craving, fancy, instinct, longing, yearning, (*more informal*) itch, (*more informal*) yen

urgent ADJECTIVE
1 *The buildings are in urgent need of renovation.*
▶ immediate, pressing, acute, grave, dire, desperate, critical, serious, essential, drastic, extreme, instant, top-priority

2 *He was roused from sleep by the urgent calls of his mother.*
▶ insistent, persistent, earnest, determined, eager, pleading
AN OPPOSITE IS casual

usable ADJECTIVE
1 *a thousand square metres of usable floor space*
▶ functional, working, available, practical, serviceable, fit for use, functioning, operating, operational
AN OPPOSITE IS unusable.
2 *The ticket is usable at all the country's museums and galleries.*
▶ valid, acceptable, current
AN OPPOSITE IS invalid

use NOUN
1 *What's the use of arguing?*
▶ point, advantage, purpose, benefit, value, sense, usefulness, reason (for)
2 *There isn't much use for mechanical calculators any more.*
▶ need, call, demand, necessity, reason, justification
3 *There was trial and error in the use of video equipment.*
▶ utilization, employment, operation, application, usage
4 *People have to make the best use of their time.*
▶ application, utilization, employment, exercise

use VERB
1 *They use the garden like an extra room.*
▶ utilize, make use of, employ, avail yourself of, put to use
2 *He learned to use a word processor.*
▶ work, operate, utilize, handle, manage, make use of
3 *You will need to use all your judgement.*
▶ exercise, apply, employ, draw on, make use of, implement
4 *How much milk did you use?*
▶ use up, consume, exhaust, waste
use up *By now Billy had used up all his money.*
▶ spend, get through, exhaust, deplete, squander, consume
USAGE You use *squander* when you are talking about wasting something or using it extravagantly. You use *consume* when you are talking about food.

used ADJECTIVE
1 *They always bought used cars.*
▶ second-hand, pre-owned, nearly new, old
OPPOSITES ARE unused, new
2 **used to** *He was used to being woken up in the middle of the night.*
▶ accustomed to, familiar with, in the habit of, no stranger to

useful ADJECTIVE
1 *These specialists can offer useful advice and practical support.*
▶ helpful, beneficial, worthwhile, valuable,

profitable, advantageous, positive, constructive, good, invaluable
OPPOSITES ARE useless, unhelpful
2 *This is a useful tool for working in tight spaces.*
▶ handy, practical, convenient, effective, efficient, powerful, productive, utilitarian
OPPOSITES ARE useless, awkward
3 *They had some useful players.*
▶ skilful, talented, competent, capable, proficient, effective, successful
OPPOSITES ARE useless, incompetent

useless ADJECTIVE
1 *I'm full of useless bits of knowledge like that. Further inquiries would be useless.*
▶ worthless, pointless, futile, fruitless, vain, hopeless, unavailing, unprofitable, unsuccessful
OPPOSITES ARE useful, helpful, practical
2 *It was a useless suggestion.*
▶ impractical, unusable, unworkable, ineffective, hopeless, (*more informal*) dud
OPPOSITES ARE useful, positive
3 *She's useless at spelling.*
▶ bad, inept, no good, incompetent, ineffective, untalented, incapable (of)
OPPOSITES ARE useful, competent

usual ADJECTIVE
Today he didn't take his usual route home.
▶ normal, customary, habitual, regular, routine, typical, familiar, accustomed, conventional, traditional, standard, orthodox
OPPOSITES ARE unusual, exceptional

usually ADVERB
Usually he lingered by the stream to throw in stones.
▶ normally, generally, habitually, as a rule, customarily, routinely, regularly, often
OPPOSITES ARE exceptionally, seldom, rarely

usurp VERB
The military had usurped the functions of the civil government.
▶ seize, appropriate, take over, assume, commandeer, steal

utensil NOUN
During the recession people were not buying kitchen utensils.
▶ implement, appliance, device, gadget, instrument, machine, tool

utility NOUN
The utility of teaching a foreign language should not be underestimated.
▶ usefulness, use, advantage, benefit, value, helpfulness, efficacy

utilize VERB
All combatants utilize armour and weapons of the period.
▶ use, make use of, employ, avail yourself of, deploy

utmost ADJECTIVE
1 *I was able to breathe only with the utmost difficulty.*
► greatest, maximum, enormous, extreme, supreme
OPPOSITES ARE minimum, least
2 *The house was at the utmost tip of the island.*
► furthest or farthest, extreme, outermost, ultimate

utter ADJECTIVE
Amy stared at him in utter disbelief.
► absolute, complete, total, sheer, positive, thorough, outright, downright, out-and-out, unmitigated

utter VERB
They were all too stunned to utter a word.
► say, speak, express, voice, articulate, enunciate

utterly ADVERB
The whole exercise seems utterly pointless.
► absolutely, completely, totally, perfectly, quite, unquestionably, unreservedly

U-turn NOUN
It had been the most dramatic U-turn of her political career.
► change of mind, reversal of policy, volte-face, about-face, about-turn, shift

Vv

vacancy NOUN
There was a vacancy for part-time work.
► opening, post, place, opportunity, position, situation

vacant ADJECTIVE
1 *There is a plan to build offices on a vacant site in the city centre.*
► unused, unoccupied, unfilled, empty, bare, blank, clear, free, available
AN OPPOSITE IS occupied
2 *Guns and ammunition were found in a planned search of a vacant house.*
► empty, unoccupied, deserted
AN OPPOSITE IS occupied
3 *She maintained a vacant expression.*
► blank, expressionless, deadpan, absent-minded, vacuous, abstracted, inattentive, dreamy, far away
OPPOSITES ARE attentive, alert

vacate VERB
They must vacate the premises by the end of the month.
► leave, evacuate, quit, withdraw from, abandon, depart from, give up
AN OPPOSITE IS occupy

vacation NOUN
Although I'm officially on vacation, I'm actually working.
► holiday, leave, time off

vacuous ADJECTIVE
He still wore his vacuous expression.
► blank, expressionless, deadpan, absent-minded, vacant, abstracted, inattentive, dreamy, far away
OPPOSITES ARE attentive, alert

vacuum NOUN
The fall of the president resulted in a brief power vacuum.
► gap, space, void, emptiness

vagrant NOUN
He lived as a vagrant for several months.
► tramp, beggar, drifter, destitute person, homeless person, itinerant, vagabond, (*more informal*) down-and-out

vague ADJECTIVE
1 *He was full of vague promises.*
► indefinite, imprecise, inexact, unspecific, ill-defined, generalized
OPPOSITES ARE specific, definite
2 *Vague shapes could be made out in the distance.*
► hazy, unclear, indistinct, indefinite, blurred
OPPOSITES ARE distinct, clear
3 *He always seemed vague about money.*
► uncertain, unclear, unsure, confused, indecisive, uninformed
OPPOSITES ARE certain, informed
4 *Our plans are fairly vague at this stage.*
► unsettled, uncertain, inexact, open, unsure, indefinite
OPPOSITES ARE firm, definite

vain ADJECTIVE
1 *They are vain and ostentatious by nature.*
► conceited, arrogant, self-satisfied, self-important, boastful, egotistical
AN OPPOSITE IS modest
2 *Dr Neil made vain attempts to stop the bleeding.*
► unsuccessful, ineffective, futile, abortive, fruitless, unavailing
OPPOSITES ARE successful, effective

valiant ADJECTIVE
Valiant efforts have been made to collect the backlog of refuse.
► brave, determined, resolute, courageous, gallant, bold, intrepid
OPPOSITES ARE weak, irresolute

valid ADJECTIVE
1 *This may be a valid conclusion.*
► legitimate, reasonable, rational, sound, cogent, convincing, acceptable
OPPOSITES ARE invalid, spurious
2 *Make sure you have a valid passport and a visa if necessary.*
► current, up-to-date, legal, certified, approved, authorized, official, suitable, bona fide, genuine
AN OPPOSITE IS invalid

a b c d e f g h i j k l m n o p q r s t **u** **v** w x y z

validate VERB

1 *There is no independent control that can validate the data.*
▶ support, substantiate, endorse, uphold, back up, vindicate, justify, prove
OPPOSITES ARE invalidate, disprove

2 *A witness is needed to validate the signature on the contract.*
▶ authenticate, authorize, certify, legitimize, make valid, ratify, legalize
AN OPPOSITE IS invalidate

valley NOUN

Pupils will be taught in the school across the valley.
▶ dale, glen, dell, vale, hollow, gorge, gulch

valour NOUN

The medals are awarded for acts of valour.
▶ bravery, courage, daring, gallantry, heroism
AN OPPOSITE IS cowardice

valuable ADJECTIVE

1 *You need separate insurance cover for the more valuable jewellery.*
▶ costly, high-priced, expensive, precious, priceless, dear
OPPOSITES ARE valueless, worthless

2 *The work provided them with valuable experience.*
▶ helpful, beneficial, advantageous, constructive, invaluable, positive, profitable, useful, valued, worthwhile, good
AN OPPOSITE IS worthless

USAGE Note that *invaluable* is not an opposite of *valuable*, but means 'too great to be valued', i.e. 'extremely valuable', as in *an invaluable member of the team.*

value NOUN

1 *Houses in the area have practically doubled in value.*
▶ price, cost, worth, market value

2 *The value of regular exercise cannot be overestimated.*
▶ importance, merit, benefit, advantage, significance, usefulness, use

value VERB

1 *The vineyard is valued at £160 million.*
▶ assess, evaluate, price, cost, estimate the value of, *(more informal)* put a figure on

2 *His honesty endeared him to many who valued his wise advice.*
▶ appreciate, prize, rate highly, esteem, hold in high regard, have a high opinion of, set store by
OPPOSITES ARE neglect, disregard

valueless ADJECTIVE

The shares had become completely valueless.
▶ worthless, of no value, trifling
AN OPPOSITE IS valuable

values PLURAL NOUN

Each generation has its special values.
▶ principles, standards, morality, morals, moral code, code of behaviour

vanish VERB

1 *Maria had vanished into the garden.*
▶ disappear, leave, withdraw, clear off
OPPOSITES ARE appear, reappear

2 *All thoughts of her vanished in the excitement.*
▶ evaporate, melt away, dissolve, end, come to an end, dwindle, fade, go away, disperse, pass
OPPOSITES ARE materialize, endure

vanity NOUN

A divorce would hit her vanity and her pocket.
▶ pride, self-regard, self-admiration, conceit, arrogance, egoism
AN OPPOSITE IS modesty

vapour NOUN

His breath formed a vapour on the air.
▶ mist, haze, fog, smoke, steam, fumes, gas, miasma

variable ADJECTIVE

The photos are of variable quality.
▶ changing, varying, changeable, fluctuating, irregular, inconsistent, unpredictable, vacillating, unstable, unsteady, temperamental
OPPOSITES ARE constant, uniform

variation NOUN

1 *There was considerable regional variation in these findings.*
▶ diversity, deviation, diversification, disparity, inequality, difference, discrepancy

2 *Prices are subject to variation.*
▶ change, alteration, adjustment, modification

varied ADJECTIVE

There is a varied choice of restaurants and tavernas.
▶ diverse, assorted, wide-ranging, miscellaneous, mixed, sundry, motley, *(more formal)* heterogeneous

variety NOUN

1 *It is hard work, but the variety makes it stimulating.*
▶ diversity, variation, diversification, change, many-sidedness, unpredictability

2 *one-day courses on a variety of cookery themes*
▶ assortment, array, miscellany, mixture, multiplicity, range, collection, medley

3 *The list offers sixteen varieties of drinking chocolate.*
▶ kind, sort, type, form, brand, category, class, strain, make, species, breed

various ADJECTIVE

1 *The job can be done in various ways.*
▶ different, differing, diverse, distinct, varying, varied, assorted, dissimilar, miscellaneous
AN OPPOSITE IS similar

2 *An uneasy truce existed between the various political parties.*
▶ numerous, many, several, innumerable, countless, multifarious, sundry

vary VERB

1 *Prices vary enormously for group holidays.*
▶ differ, fluctuate, range, change, shift, go up and down, *(more formal)* oscillate
OPPOSITES ARE be static, be fixed

2 *The routine never varies.*
▶ change, alter, differ, deviate, diverge, fluctuate
3 *You can vary the size of your pictures.*
▶ alter, adapt, adjust, modify, diversify
AN OPPOSITE IS fix

vast ADJECTIVE
1 *The birds fly over vast distances.*
▶ huge, great, extensive, enormous, immense, colossal, tremendous
OPPOSITES ARE small, short
2 *The vast majority of patients are elderly.*
▶ great, huge, large

vat NOUN
a vat of wine
▶ tank, tub, vessel, cask

vault NOUN
The treasures are locked in a vault.
▶ strongroom, repository, depository, basement, cellar, crypt

vault VERB
'That rock,' she pointed. 'Vault over it.'
▶ jump, leap, leapfrog, spring, bound, clear, hurdle
USAGE You can say either *vault over it* or *vault it*, and you can use *jump*, *leap*, and *leapfrog* in the same ways. If you use *spring* or *bound* you have to use *over* (e.g. *spring over it*); if you use *clear* or *hurdle* you do not use *over* (e.g. *clear it*).

veer VERB
She was about to veer in a different direction.
▶ turn, swerve, swing, shift, tack, change course, skew, dodge, wheel

---

vegetable NOUN
VARIOUS VEGETABLES
beans and peas: bean, broad bean, butter bean, pea, runner bean, sweetcorn.
root vegetables: beet, beetroot, carrot, onion, parsnip, potato, shallot (= small onion), swede, turnip.
leaf vegetables: broccoli, Brussels sprout, cabbage, calabrese, cauliflower, celeriac (type of celery), celery, chicory, fennel, kale (variety of cabbage), kohlrabi (variety of cabbage), spinach.
flesh vegetables (some are also regarded as fruits): asparagus, artichoke, aubergine, chicory, courgette (small variety of marrow), cucumber, eggplant (= aubergine), fennel, marrow, leek, okra, pepper, pumpkin, tomato, zucchini (= courgette).

---

vegetation NOUN
Here on the island there is lush vegetation.
▶ foliage, plant life, plants, growth, undergrowth, greenery

vehemence NOUN
We were surprised by the vehemence of their opposition.
▶ force, passion, intensity, ardour, vigour, violence, strength, urgency
OPPOSITES ARE mildness, apathy

vehement ADJECTIVE
We are quite vehement in our pursuit of safety procedures. Opposition to the whale hunt drew vehement criticism from the islanders.
▶ fierce, passionate, forceful, impassioned, intense, ardent, eager, fervent, vigorous, violent, enthusiastic, animated, excited, heated, strong, powerful, urgent
OPPOSITES ARE mild, apathetic

vehicle NOUN
Vehicles are not allowed in the town centre.
▶ motor vehicle, car, automobile, wheeled transport

veil NOUN
1 *The veil came from her head to her feet.*
▶ covering, cloak, mask
2 *The city lay under a veil of darkness.*
▶ cover, screen, layer, blanket, film, curtain

veil VERB
The mountain was veiled in mist.
▶ hide, cover, shroud, envelop, conceal, screen
AN OPPOSITE IS expose

vein NOUN
Sebastian went on in the same vein for several minutes.
▶ mood, tenor, tone, manner

vendetta NOUN
He was the victim of a personal vendetta.
▶ feud, quarrel, blood-feud, rivalry

veneer NOUN
1 *chipboard with a mahogany veneer*
▶ surface, finish, coating, covering, layer
2 *His veneer of good humour vanished instantly.*
▶ show, display, pretence, facade, front, appearance, guise

venerable ADJECTIVE
He was interviewed by three venerable gentlemen.
▶ respected, venerated, revered, esteemed, honoured, august, dignified
AN OPPOSITE IS disreputable

vengeance NOUN
He swore vengeance when he was banished four years ago.
▶ revenge, retribution, retaliation, reprisal

vengeful ADJECTIVE
He felt vengeful towards his attackers.
▶ revengeful, unforgiving, spiteful, bitter, avenging, vindictive, rancorous
AN OPPOSITE IS forgiving

a
b
c
d
e
f
g
h
i
j
k
l
m
n
o
p
q
r
s
t
u
v
w
x
y
z

venom NOUN

1 *Snake venom is usually clear yellow.*
▶ poison, toxin
2 *She was told to leave with such venom she recoiled.*
▶ malice, malevolence, rancour, ill-will, acrimony, animosity, bitterness, vitriol, virulence, hatred

venomous ADJECTIVE

1 *The only mammals with venomous bites are certain moles and shrews.*
▶ poisonous, toxic, noxious, deadly
AN OPPOSITE IS harmless
2 *He wrote a venomous criticism of their work.*
▶ vicious, spiteful, malicious, malevolent, vindictive, baleful, vitriolic, rancorous
AN OPPOSITE IS friendly

vent NOUN

Open the air vent to increase the rate of flow.
▶ opening, outlet, duct, aperture, hole, passage, slit

vent VERB

The crowd vented their fury on the police rather than one another.
▶ express, release, emit, pour out, give vent to

venture NOUN

This new venture holds great promise for the future.
▶ enterprise, undertaking, project, scheme, endeavour, operation, adventure

venture VERB

1 *Harry ventured an opinion.*
▶ put forward, suggest, offer, dare, risk, chance
2 *We venture to ask you for your permission.*
▶ dare, presume, be so bold as to
3 *When darkness came he ventured out.*
▶ journey, set forth, proceed, dare to go, risk going

verbal ADJECTIVE

A verbal exchange was recorded between two people.
▶ spoken, oral, word-of-mouth, unwritten
AN OPPOSITE IS written

verbatim ADJECTIVE

The article includes several verbatim quotations.
▶ word-for-word, exact, precise, direct, literal, close
AN OPPOSITE IS loose

verbatim ADVERB

He passed on the complaint verbatim.
▶ word for word, exactly, precisely, faithfully
AN OPPOSITE IS loosely

verbose ADJECTIVE

Parts of the speech were repetitive and verbose.
▶ wordy, loquacious, diffuse, effusive, garrulous, talkative, long-winded, rambling
AN OPPOSITE IS succinct

verdict NOUN

The verdict was suicide, but many people thought he was murdered.
▶ judgement, decision, finding, ruling, adjudication, assessment, conclusion, opinion

verge NOUN

1 *Cars were parked on the grass verge.*
▶ edge, bank, kerb, margin, border, roadside, shoulder, side, wayside
2 *The country was on the verge of bankruptcy.*
▶ brink, point, threshold

verge VERB

verge on *By this time the urgency verged on desperation.*
▶ border on, tend towards, approach, come close to

verifiable ADJECTIVE

The theory may be verifiable by means of experiments.
▶ demonstrable, provable
AN OPPOSITE IS unverifiable

verify VERB

There was no one around to verify what happened.
▶ prove, support, confirm, substantiate, establish, uphold, show the truth of, validate, authenticate, corroborate, check out, ascertain
AN OPPOSITE IS refute

versatile ADJECTIVE

1 *She was a gifted and versatile teacher.*
▶ adaptable, many-sided, all-round, flexible, resourceful, talented, skilful
2 *The property offers spacious and versatile accommodation.*
▶ flexible, adaptable, modifiable, all-purpose
AN OPPOSITE IS restricted

verse NOUN

a story written in verse
▶ rhyme, lines, lyrics, metre, stanza

version NOUN

1 *Would you like to tell us your version of the story?*
▶ account, record, explanation, interpretation, rendering
2 *a new version of the machine*
▶ form, type, model, design

vertical ADJECTIVE

1 *Pull the lever back to its vertical position.*
▶ upright, perpendicular, standing, erect
AN OPPOSITE IS horizontal
2 *The passageway ended with a vertical drop into darkness.*
▶ sheer, steep, precipitous

vertigo NOUN

A feeling of vertigo kept him from the edge.
▶ dizziness, giddiness, fear of heights, light-headedness

verve NOUN

He played the piano with great verve.
▶ enthusiasm, vigour, liveliness, spirit, energy, vitality, vivacity, gusto, relish

very ADVERB This word is often overused. Here are some alternatives:
He felt very ashamed.
▶ extremely, highly, deeply, exceedingly, acutely, truly, (*more informal*) terribly
AN OPPOSITE IS slightly

very ADJECTIVE
1 *The key on the floor was the very one he had lost the week before. Those were her very words.*
▶ actual, same, selfsame, identical, exact, precise
2 *The very thought of it made him tremble.*
▶ mere, sheer, simple

vessel NOUN
1 *Pour the liquid into a sterile vessel.*
▶ container, receptacle, flask, bottle, jar, jug, holder
2 *Small vessels were bobbing about in the harbour.*
▶ craft, boat, ship
USAGE Note that *craft* can be singular or plural (e.g. *a small craft was bobbing about* or *small craft were bobbing about*).

vet VERB
Peter vetted all the outfits and knew exactly what would suit Tara.
▶ inspect, examine, screen, assess, evaluate, appraise, scrutinize, investigate, check out

veteran ADJECTIVE
He handled it all like a veteran superstar.
▶ established, seasoned, mature, hardened, master, expert

veto NOUN
He had in effect acquired a right of veto over all sales of land.
▶ rejection, refusal, embargo, prohibition, ban, (*more informal*) thumbs down
AN OPPOSITE IS approval

veto VERB
The government had vetoed the proposal in late July.
▶ reject, turn down, overrule, rule out, throw out, disallow, refuse, dismiss, ban, bar, blackball, forbid, prohibit, say no to, vote against
AN OPPOSITE IS approve

vex VERB
His remarks had vexed her deeply.
▶ annoy, irritate, displease, anger, infuriate, enrage, exasperate, incense, madden, aggravate, nettle, antagonize, inflame, make angry, (*more informal*) needle, (*more informal*) rile, (*more informal*) bug, (*more informal*) rub up the wrong way
OPPOSITES ARE please, gratify

vexed ADJECTIVE
1 *She was still vexed with me for bringing Frankie.*
▶ annoyed, irritated, angry, cross, displeased, peeved, infuriated, incensed, enraged, (*more informal*) miffed, (*more informal*) put out
AN OPPOSITE IS pleased
2 *The note was about the vexed question of sexism.*
▶ controversial, difficult, contentious, disputed, thorny, knotty

viable ADJECTIVE
Pirate TV might become a viable possibility. It was not viable to work on a computer of that age.
▶ practical, realistic, feasible, workable, practicable, usable, achievable, operable, sustainable, possible
OPPOSITES ARE impractical, unworkable

vibrant ADJECTIVE
1 *Green plants provide splashes of vibrant colour.*
▶ bright, vivid, brilliant, intense, striking
OPPOSITES ARE dull, pale
2 *She made the most of her cheerful and vibrant personality.*
▶ vivacious, spirited, dynamic, alert, alive, energetic, electric
OPPOSITES ARE restrained, reserved

vibrate VERB
1 *The room was vibrating from the sounds of rock music.*
▶ reverberate, throb, pulsate, resonate, resound, thud, ring, boom
2 *The machinery began to vibrate alarmingly.*
▶ tremble, shake, shudder, judder, quiver, oscillate, rattle, shiver, wobble, quake

vibration NOUN
The special smoke detector produces a vibration as well as a flashing light.
▶ reverberation, oscillation, pulsation, throbbing, trembling, juddering, quivering, rattling, shaking, shivering, shuddering, tremor, wobbling

vice NOUN
1 *They are determined to put an end to vice and prostitution.*
▶ immorality, depravity, corruption, wickedness, wrongdoing, degeneracy, evil-doing, evil, sin, (*more formal*) venality, (*more formal*) iniquity
AN OPPOSITE IS virtue
2 *Cowardice isn't the worst vice.*
▶ failing, fault, weakness, shortcoming, bad habit, blemish, defect, deficiency, imperfection
OPPOSITES ARE virtue, strength

vicinity NOUN
There are several castles and abbeys in the vicinity.
▶ neighbourhood, area, district, locality, region, locale, environs, outskirts, proximity

vicious ADJECTIVE
1 *He was finally captured in the vicious street fighting in Berlin in 1945.*
▶ brutal, savage, fierce, ferocious, wild, barbaric
OPPOSITES ARE gentle, humane
2 *He hadn't the vicious streak that showed in his brother.*
▶ cruel, malicious, spiteful, malevolent, vindictive, sadistic, brutish, callous, heartless, cold-blooded, aggressive, pitiless, ruthless, merciless, inhuman, vile
OPPOSITES ARE kind, benevolent

victim NOUN

1 *It's thought she was the victim of a random attack by a thief. He is the third victim of this tough new policy.*
▶ target, casualty, sufferer, injury, fatality, scapegoat
USAGE You use *fatality* about someone who has died as a result of an incident.
2 *At their feet, a white-clad sacrificial victim, was the body.*
▶ offering, martyr, prey, sacrifice

victimize VERB

The company had been victimizing workers for reporting safety concerns.
▶ discriminate against, persecute, intimidate, oppress, mistreat, harass, treat unfairly, bully, terrorize, torment, (*more informal*) pick on

victor NOUN

The victors pressed on and captured the city.
▶ winner, conqueror, hero, champion
AN OPPOSITE IS loser

victorious ADJECTIVE

He emerged victorious in the second round of voting.
▶ triumphant, successful, first, top, winning, leading, prevailing, undefeated, unbeaten
OPPOSITES ARE defeated, unsuccessful

victory NOUN

Her well-deserved victory in this year's Olympics was a boost for the British team.
▶ win, success, triumph, conquest, knockout, mastery, superiority, achievement, (*more informal*) walkover
AN OPPOSITE IS defeat

vie VERB

A dozen teams vie for honours in a novelty sand-building competition.
▶ compete, contend, contest, struggle, grapple, jostle, strive, fight, cross swords, lock horns

view NOUN

1 *From the top floor you get a magnificent view across the city.*
▶ outlook, prospect, panorama, perspective, vista, scene, aspect, picture, landscape, scenery, spectacle
2 *She caught a brief view of her top half in the mirror.*
▶ look, sight, glance, peek, vision
3 *Luke came into view.*
▶ sight, vision, range of vision, perspective
4 *He declined to give any official view of the situation.*
▶ opinion, viewpoint, point of view, belief, judgement, notion, perception, idea, thought, attitude, conviction
in view of *In view of the length of time since the incident, no action was taken.*
▶ because of, on account of, considering, as a result of, as a consequence of, owing to, due to

view VERB

1 *He set out at ten and viewed as many houses as possible. A drop from a pond, viewed through a microscope, swarms with tiny organisms.*
▶ look at, inspect, survey, examine, observe, behold, eye, scan, gaze at, stare at
2 *She viewed him with dislike.*
▶ regard, contemplate, consider, perceive, behold
3 *Some of the guests were viewing a television programme.*
▶ watch, look at, see

viewer NOUN

The presenter has been asking viewers to write in.
▶ spectator, watcher, audience, observer

viewpoint NOUN

Parents are not altogether good from a child's viewpoint.
▶ point of view, standpoint, outlook, perspective, way of thinking, angle, position, stance, slant

vigilant ADJECTIVE

Everyone should be vigilant and report anything of a suspicious nature.
▶ watchful, observant, alert, attentive, awake, on the lookout, on your guard, on the watch, sharp-eyed, eagle-eyed, careful, wide-awake, (*more informal*) on your toes
AN OPPOSITE IS negligent

vigorous ADJECTIVE

1 *Regular vigorous exercise can help to reduce blood pressure.*
▶ strenuous, energetic, animated, brisk, full-blooded
AN OPPOSITE IS feeble
2 *The child is strong and vigorous.*
▶ healthy, in good health, energetic, vivacious, active, lively, lusty, virile, vital
3 *He made a vigorous case for controlling the money supply.*
▶ strong, spirited, forceful, effective, robust, energetic, dynamic, active

vigour NOUN

1 *Geoffrey supported his wife's cause with vigour.*
▶ energy, force, forcefulness, spirit, vitality, gusto, verve, animation, dynamism
2 *He recovered from the illness with renewed vigour.*
▶ energy, fitness, vitality, stamina, robustness, life, strength, health, resilience, potency

vile ADJECTIVE

1 *It's ironic that such a fine building should house so vile an organization.*
▶ wicked, evil, foul, contemptible, despicable, obnoxious, shameful, abhorrent, repellent, loathsome
AN OPPOSITE IS pleasant
2 *I drank three cups of vile, greyish coffee.*
▶ nasty, horrible, foul, unpleasant, disgusting, revolting, repulsive, repellent, dreadful, terrible
AN OPPOSITE IS pleasant

V

3 *The vile weather had emptied the streets.*
▶ unpleasant, bad, foul, disagreeable, inclement
AN OPPOSITE IS fine

villain NOUN
Did not two of history's greatest villains come from beautiful surroundings?
▶ wrongdoer, evil-doer, rogue, scoundrel, criminal, reprobate, (*more formal*) malefactor, (*more formal*) miscreant

vindicate VERB
1 *He left claiming that history would vindicate him.*
▶ clear, exonerate, absolve, acquit, excuse, endorse, support, rehabilitate
OPPOSITES ARE blame, censure
2 *She was desperate to vindicate her decision to be an artist.*
▶ justify, uphold, defend, sustain, maintain, assert
AN OPPOSITE IS compromise

vindictive ADJECTIVE
His eyes flashed vindictive rage.
▶ malicious, spiteful, malevolent, hostile, baleful, malign, malignant, pernicious, hurtful, offensive, venomous
AN OPPOSITE IS forgiving

vintage NOUN
They needed four aircraft of 1940s vintage.
▶ period, era, epoch, time, date, origin

vintage ADJECTIVE
He gave his usual vintage performance.
▶ high-quality, fine, classic, choice, good, mature

violate VERB
1 *Uses of these weapons against civilian targets violate international law.*
▶ breach, break, contravene, infringe, transgress, flout, defy, disobey, disregard, ignore
AN OPPOSITE IS comply with
2 *Several of the royal tombs had been violated.*
▶ desecrate, defile, vandalize, deface
3 *I did not like having my privacy violated.*
▶ invade, disturb, encroach on, interfere with, abuse
AN OPPOSITE IS respect
4 *He set out to trap and violate women.*
▶ rape, abuse, indecently assault, sexually assault, molest, interfere with

violation NOUN
the violation of human rights throughout the world
▶ contravention, breach, infringement, flouting, defiance, transgression, offence (against)

violence NOUN
1 *A whole generation had been brought up in violence.*
▶ brutality, brute force, savagery, cruelty, barbarity, destructiveness
2 *The violence of the blow made him reel.*
▶ force, forcefulness, strength, power, might, ferocity

violent ADJECTIVE
1 *There were violent clashes between police and demonstrators.*
▶ brutal, vicious, rough, aggressive, forceful
AN OPPOSITE IS mild
2 *Too often violent criminals do not get sent to prison as they should.*
▶ rough, brutal, wild, fierce, vicious, aggressive, bloodthirsty, headstrong
AN OPPOSITE IS gentle
3 *He felt a rush of violent jealousy.*
▶ intense, extreme, acute, forceful, devastating
AN OPPOSITE IS weak

VIP NOUN
Only visitors and VIPs get that special treatment.
▶ celebrity, dignitary, luminary, grandee, important person

virile ADJECTIVE
It pleases them to have a virile young man about the place.
▶ masculine, vigorous, manly, potent, (*more informal*) macho

virtual ADJECTIVE
The traffic was at a virtual standstill.
▶ effective, near, almost, practical, potential

virtually ADVERB
Once on, paint is virtually impossible to remove.
▶ effectively, in effect, practically, as good as, almost

virtue NOUN
1 *the virtue of a simple life*
▶ goodness, righteousness, virtuousness, rectitude, integrity, honesty, dignity, uprightness, worthiness, decency, morality, honour, nobility, principle, rectitude
AN OPPOSITE IS iniquity
2 *I can see no virtue in such an arrangement.*
▶ merit, advantage, benefit, point
AN OPPOSITE IS disadvantage
3 *Punctuality is not one of her virtues.*
▶ strength, quality, good point, redeeming feature
OPPOSITES ARE failing, weakness

virtuous ADJECTIVE
Sam's virtuous and superior tone was beginning to irritate him.
▶ moral, righteous, upright, worthy, honourable, exemplary, high-minded, right-minded, high-principled
OPPOSITES ARE wicked, sinful

visible ADJECTIVE
There is no visible pattern in the paper. Kim received the news without any visible signs of emotion.
▶ noticeable, perceptible, discernible, obvious, apparent, conspicuous, recognizable, evident, manifest, clear, detectable, distinct
AN OPPOSITE IS invisible

vision NOUN

1 *Symptoms include blurred vision and sensitivity to bright lights.*
▶ eyesight, sight, seeing

2 *The Great Society remained more a vision than a reality.*
▶ ideal, fantasy, apparition, illusion, mirage, phantasm, daydream, delusion, ghost, hallucination, phantom, spectre

3 *The plan made sense but lacked vision.*
▶ foresight, farsightedness, insight, imagination

visionary ADJECTIVE

It was one of the most powerful and visionary speeches I had heard.
▶ imaginative, farsighted, creative, inventive, idealistic, prophetic, speculative

visit NOUN

1 *Mrs Curdle paid her final visit to the place.*
▶ call, stay

2 *It was their first visit to Rome.*
▶ trip, outing, excursion, day out

visit VERB

1 *He was ten years old when he first started visiting the old woman.*
▶ call on, come to see, make a visit to, pay a call on, stay with, descend on, (more informal) drop in on, go to see, (more informal) look up

2 *The chairman of the airline recently visited Moscow.*
▶ travel to, make a trip to, spend time in, stay in

visitor NOUN

1 *Edward was a frequent and welcome visitor.*
▶ guest, caller

2 *The site will attract visitors during the festival.*
▶ tourist, holidaymaker, sightseer, tripper, globetrotter

visualize VERB

I like to visualize the mood of the song and take it from there.
▶ picture, imagine, envisage, conceive, dream up

vital ADJECTIVE

1 *It's vital to keep momentum going. The college is expected to play a vital role in promoting these languages.*
▶ essential, crucial, fundamental, imperative, important, necessary, indispensable
OPPOSITES ARE unimportant, inessential

2 *He was a vital force in British music.*
▶ dynamic, lively, energetic, vibrant, vigorous, vivacious, life-giving, invigorating, exuberant, sparkling, spirited, animated, sprightly, zestful
AN OPPOSITE IS lifeless

vitality NOUN

For all her vitality, Faye was only five feet four inches tall.
▶ energy, vivacity, vigour, spirit, gusto, verve, dynamism, exuberance, zest, (more informal) go
AN OPPOSITE IS lethargy

vivacious ADJECTIVE

She must once have been quite a vivacious woman.
▶ lively, high-spirited, exuberant, animated, alert, active, spirited, exciting, cheerful
OPPOSITES ARE lifeless, dull

vivid ADJECTIVE

1 *a bouquet with four vivid blue flowers*
▶ bright, brilliant, colourful, vibrant, showy, striking, gaudy
AN OPPOSITE IS dull

2 *Wilson's autobiography gives a vivid account of his experiences.*
▶ clear, graphic, dramatic, lively, powerful, evocative, lucid, memorable, imaginative, lifelike, realistic
AN OPPOSITE IS lifeless

vocabulary NOUN

1 *He was learning English and had a limited vocabulary.*
▶ word stock, lexicon, lexis

2 *There is a vocabulary at the back of the book.*
▶ glossary, word list, dictionary, lexicon

vocal ADJECTIVE

1 *animals capable of vocal sounds*
▶ voiced, spoken, oral, said, articulated

2 *The students were becoming the most vocal critics of reform.*
▶ outspoken, vociferous, forthright, plain-spoken, candid

vogue NOUN

Small-scale farming is enjoying a new vogue.
▶ fashion, mode, trend, style, craze, rage, taste
in vogue *Suddenly it was in vogue to have an all-over tan.*
▶ fashionable, in fashion, stylish, modish, smart, chic, (more informal) trendy, (more informal) all the rage, (more informal) cool, (more informal) hip

---

voice NOUN

1 *There was no emotion in his voice.*
▶ speaking, speech, utterance, tone, inflection

2 *They were able to have a voice in choosing the chairman.*
▶ opinion, view, say, input, vote

TYPES OF SINGING VOICE

male voices: basso profundo, bass, baritone, tenor, castrato, countertenor, falsetto, treble.

female voices: alto, contralto, mezzo or mezzo-soprano, soprano.

---

voice VERB

Right-thinking people have voiced their disgust.
▶ express, speak, utter, convey, communicate, articulate, give voice to, give vent to

void ADJECTIVE

The contract was declared void.
▶ invalid, null, cancelled, inoperative, worthless
AN OPPOSITE IS valid

volatile ADJECTIVE
She was headstrong and volatile.
▶ temperamental, unpredictable, variable, changeable, erratic, vacillating, inconstant, unsteady
OPPOSITES ARE stable, constant

volley NOUN
They maintained their composure under a volley of missiles
▶ barrage, bombardment, battery, blast, salvo, hail, storm, shower, deluge

volume NOUN
1 *I bought his Travels and read through all five volumes.*
▶ book, tome
2 *They expect an increased volume of traffic over the bridge this year.*
▶ amount, quantity, size, body, mass, capacity

voluntary ADJECTIVE
1 *Voluntary work tends to carry higher prestige than paid work.*
▶ optional, unpaid, willing
AN OPPOSITE IS paid
2 *The pay cuts will be voluntary.*
▶ optional, discretionary, unforced
OPPOSITES ARE obligatory, compulsory
3 *Her decision had been a voluntary act.*
▶ deliberate, conscious, intentional, intended, wilful
AN OPPOSITE IS involuntary
USAGE Note that *involuntary* is an opposite of *voluntary* only in the third meaning.

volunteer VERB
Having promised his help, he had better volunteer at least.
▶ offer your services, present yourself, step forward, make an offer, propose yourself, show willing

vomit VERB
He rushed towards the drain before the urge to vomit overcame him.
▶ be sick, regurgitate, retch, heave, bring up, spew up, (more informal) throw up, (more informal) puke

voracious ADJECTIVE
There is a voracious demand for holiday homes and weekend cottages.
▶ insatiable, unquenchable, unsatisfiable, uncontrollable, ravenous, immoderate, prodigious

vote NOUN
People suspected the vote of being rigged.
▶ ballot, poll, election, plebiscite, referendum, show of hands

vote VERB
1 *Less than a third of the electorate voted in the last election.*
▶ cast a vote, go to the polls, ballot
2 *I vote we play another round.*
▶ suggest, propose, recommend, move
3 **vote for** *You may vote for one candidate only.*
▶ choose, pick, select, opt for, nominate

vouch VERB
vouch for *I can vouch for the accuracy of these figures.*
▶ guarantee, verify, affirm, attest to, testify to, corroborate, endorse, confirm, support, speak for

voucher NOUN
You get a wallet of vouchers to pay for the various parts of your holiday.
▶ coupon, ticket, token, certificate

vow NOUN
The monks take a vow of silence.
▶ pledge, oath, promise, commitment, avowal, assurance, guarantee, undertaking, word of honour

vow VERB
She vowed to do better.
▶ promise, pledge, swear, take an oath, give an assurance, give your word, guarantee

voyage NOUN
The voyage lasted two weeks.
▶ journey, passage, crossing, trip, expedition, excursion

vulgar ADJECTIVE
1 *She sent him a postcard with a vulgar picture on the back.*
▶ rude, indecent, lewd, suggestive, racy, risqué
2 *The decor was new and vulgar.*
▶ tasteless, gaudy, garish, tawdry, flashy, (more informal) tacky
3 *He was a bit too vulgar for her taste. It was considered vulgar to smoke in public.*
▶ ill-mannered, unrefined, unseemly, impolite, indecorous, coarse, ill-bred

vulnerable ADJECTIVE
1 *We are most vulnerable when we are asleep.*
▶ defenceless, exposed, unguarded, unprotected, at risk, weak, wide open
AN OPPOSITE IS invulnerable
2 **vulnerable to** *More people are vulnerable to age discrimination.*
▶ in danger of, at risk of, exposed to, open to, liable to, prone to, susceptible to
AN OPPOSITE IS immune to

Ww

wad NOUN
1 *He took a wad of notes from his pocket and began to count them.*
▶ bundle, roll, pad, (more informal) wodge
2 *I needed a wad of cotton wool.*
▶ lump, mass, chunk, hunk

wadding NOUN
sleeping bags insulated with wadding
▶ padding, lining, packing, filling, stuffing

waddle VERB
He waddled across the garden to join Sylvia.
▶ totter, toddle, teeter, dodder, stumble, shuffle

waffle NOUN
(informal) My panic reduced the interview to waffle.
▶ blather, prattle, nonsense, verbosity, wordiness, evasiveness, padding, prevarication

waffle VERB
(informal) She waffled on for a while about things that didn't matter.
▶ blather, prattle, ramble, babble, chatter on, gibber, gabble

wag VERB
1 *The dog's tail began to wag frantically.*
▶ shake, swing, wave, waggle
2 *'You see what I mean,' Eleanor said, wagging her finger.*
▶ wave, shake, waggle, brandish

wage VERB
The country lacks any means to wage war.
▶ carry on, conduct, engage in, fight, undertake

wages PLURAL NOUN
He was pleased to be earning regular wages at last.
▶ earnings, income, pay, recompense

wail VERB
He was tearing at his hair and wailing 'Why me?'
▶ howl, bawl, weep, moan, sob, shriek, whimper, snivel, cry, lament, yowl

wail NOUN
Tom let out a wail.
▶ howl, bawl, moan, sob, shriek, cry, whimper, yowl

wait NOUN
The photos were ready after a short wait.
▶ interval, pause, delay, hold-up, break, hiatus, halt, hesitation, rest, stay

wait VERB
She left the room and waited outside. I can't wait for you any longer.
▶ remain, rest, linger, stay, stop, halt, delay, mark time, stand by, hold back, pause, hesitate, *(old-fashioned)* tarry, *(more informal)* hang about
AN OPPOSITE IS proceed

waive VERB
Some agencies might waive their fee if you register with them.
▶ give up, forgo, relinquish, renounce, cede, resign, disclaim, dispense with, surrender, abandon
AN OPPOSITE IS enforce

wake VERB
1 *Be careful not to wake the baby.*
▶ waken, rouse, disturb, stir, awaken, arouse
2 *Sara woke to find Rodney's arm round her. When I woke up I was in the back of a car.*
▶ awake, awaken, waken, become conscious, come round, stir, get up, rise

wake up to *Parliament finally woke up to the electronic age.*
▶ become aware of, appreciate, comprehend, realize
USAGE See the note at *awake* (verb).

wakeful ADJECTIVE
He had been wakeful all night.
▶ sleepless, restless, disturbed
OPPOSITES ARE sleepy, asleep

walk NOUN
1 *Go for short walks near your home.*
▶ stroll, ramble, saunter, march, hike, tramp, trek
2 *There is a pretty walk round the cathedral.*
▶ path, pathway, walkway, lane, alley, footway, promenade
3 *He observed her elegant walk.*
▶ gait, tread, carriage, stride

walk of life *There are cheats in every walk of life.*
▶ sphere, class, field, calling, profession, activity

walk VERB This word is often overused. Here are some alternatives:
1 *She decided to save her bus fare and walk to work.*
▶ go on foot, travel on foot, be a pedestrian
2 *They walked together along the sands, and talked.*
▶ stroll, amble, saunter, stride, pace, trudge, proceed, promenade
3 *I'll walk the children home.*
▶ accompany, escort, take, see, show

walk all over *(informal) You don't want to let the cops walk all over you.*
▶ take advantage of, make use of, exploit, impose on, manipulate

walk away or **off with** *(informal) Someone had walked off with his wallet.*
▶ steal, pilfer, purloin, filch, take

walk out on *(informal) He had just walked out on his girlfriend.*
▶ leave, abandon, desert, run out on, *(informal)* jilt

walker NOUN
Keen walkers will be spoilt for choice.
▶ rambler, hiker, wayfarer, pedestrian

walkout NOUN
The workers staged a walkout.
▶ strike, stoppage, withdrawal of labour, go-slow

walkover NOUN
The election will be no walkover.
▶ easy victory, rout, landslide, triumph, *(more informal)* piece of cake

wall NOUN

1 *There was a noticeboard on the wall.*
▶ partition, screen, room divider
2 *The east wall of the castle had been breached.*
▶ fortification, rampart, barricade, palisade, barrier, bulwark, stockade
RELATED ADJECTIVE mural

wallet NOUN

The wallet contained some money in euros.
▶ purse, notecase, pouch, pocketbook

wallop VERB

She walloped his back with her hand.
▶ thump, hit, strike, pound, beat, bang, rap, batter, knock

wallow VERB

1 *I was wallowing in a hot bath.*
▶ luxuriate, loll about, splash about, lie
2 *Jack loves to wallow in praise.*
▶ revel, glory, take delight, indulge yourself

wand NOUN

No magic wand can solve these problems.
▶ baton, stick, rod, staff, sceptre

wander VERB

1 *We spent the day wandering about the old town.*
▶ ramble, roam, meander, range, rove, stray, walk, wind
2 *She had wandered away from the main group.*
▶ stray, deviate, digress, drift, veer
3 **wander off** *I've told you not to wander off like that.*
▶ go away, drift off, leave, get lost

wane VERB

Support for their action was waning.
▶ diminish, decrease, subside, be reduced, dwindle, ebb, lessen, go down, drop away
AN OPPOSITE IS strengthen

want NOUN

1 *The client always has wants and feelings.*
▶ demand, desire, need, requirement, wish
2 *The bridge is decaying for want of repair.*
▶ absence, lack, need

want VERB

1 *A clever alien wants to steal the spaceship.*
▶ wish, desire, hope, long
2 *That is exactly what he wanted.*
▶ wish for, desire, long for, yearn for, hanker after, crave, covet, fancy, hunger for, thirst for
3 **want to** (*informal*) *You want to keep an eye on them.*
▶ need to, ought to, should

wanton ADJECTIVE

There are stories of wanton violence against civilians.
▶ wilful, malicious, malevolent, spiteful, vicious, shameless, unprovoked, needless, unnecessary, unrestrained

war NOUN

1 *During the war he joined the police force. They had been badly affected by the chaos of war.*
▶ conflict, fighting, hostilities, struggle, warfare, action, military action, strife
RELATED ADJECTIVES martial, belligerent
2 *a war against drugs*
▶ campaign, crusade, battle, fight, struggle

ward VERB

ward off
1 *Garlands of garlic are worn to ward off evil spirits.*
▶ fend off, drive away, beat off, repel, avert, stave off, thwart, turn aside, repulse
2 *He brought up his arm to ward off the blow.*
▶ deflect, parry, block, check

warden NOUN

The resident warden let us look over the apartments.
▶ caretaker, custodian, guardian, supervisor, superintendent, janitor

warder NOUN

Her husband was a warder at the local prison.
▶ prison officer, prison warden, guard, jailer, keeper

wardrobe NOUN

1 *Large areas of wardrobe doors can look plain.*
▶ cupboard, clothes cupboard, closet, cabinet
2 *Her mother organized her wedding and her wardrobe.*
▶ clothes, outfit, attire

warehouse NOUN

The goods were stored in a heated warehouse.
▶ store, storehouse, storeroom, depot, depository, repository

wares PLURAL NOUN

Luxury firms can sell their wares at high prices by keeping them 'exclusive'.
▶ merchandise, goods, products, commodities, stock, produce

warfare NOUN

thirty years of continuous warfare
▶ fighting, hostilities, war, conflict, combat, bloodshed, action, battle, arms
RELATED ADJECTIVES martial, belligerent

warlike ADJECTIVE

Tethlis was another warlike ruler.
▶ belligerent, aggressive, warmongering, warring, combative, pugnacious
AN OPPOSITE IS peaceable

warm ADJECTIVE

1 *She strolled in warm winter sunshine towards San Marco. The sun was already warm on their backs.*
▶ hot, balmy, summery, sultry, sunny, temperate, tropical, warmish
AN OPPOSITE IS cold
2 *the warm waters of the western Mediterranean*
▶ heated, lukewarm, tepid
3 *She was dressed in warm clothes.*
▶ thick, cosy, woolly, thermal, winter

a b c d e f g h i j k l m n o p q r s t u v w x y z

4 *He gave them a warm welcome.*
▶ friendly, cordial, amiable, enthusiastic, affable, genial, affectionate, loving, sympathetic, warm-hearted, pleasant
OPPOSITES ARE cool, unfriendly

warm VERB
1 *She was in the kitchen warming some soup.*
▶ heat (up), reheat, thaw
OPPOSITES ARE cool, chill
2 **warm to** *Anne was by now warming to her theme.*
▶ take to, become enthusiastic about, get on with, feel attracted by

warm-hearted ADJECTIVE
She is a generous, warm-hearted person.
▶ kind, caring, good, kind-hearted, kindly, considerate, sympathetic, thoughtful, obliging, tender-hearted, benevolent
OPPOSITES ARE unkind, unfriendly

warmth NOUN
1 *Despite the warmth of the fire, Isabel began to shiver.*
▶ heat, warmness, comfort
AN OPPOSITE IS coldness
2 *The warmth of their welcome took them by surprise.*
▶ friendliness, cordiality, geniality, enthusiasm
AN OPPOSITE IS hostility

warn VERB
The manufacturers had failed to warn doctors of the possible side effects.
▶ advise, alert, notify, inform, caution, remind, forewarn, give a warning about, (*more informal*) tip off

warning NOUN
1 *The changes were announced without warning.*
▶ notice, advance notice, forewarning, hint, indication, omen, premonition, presage, sign, signal, threat, augury, (*informal*) tip-off
2 *The remarks were a warning of what might be in store.*
▶ omen, sign, signal, presage, portent, premonition, foreboding, prediction, token
3 *The warning in his voice was clear.*
▶ caution, reservation, caveat, doubt
4 *England received their third and final warning.*
▶ caution, reprimand, admonition

warp VERB
A steel door won't rot, split, or warp.
▶ twist, bend, buckle, distort, deform, kink, contort, become deformed, curve

warrant NOUN
1 *They now had a warrant to search the building.*
▶ authorization, authority, permit, commission, document
2 *On leaving prison he was given a travel warrant.*
▶ voucher, permit, pass, licence

warrant VERB
This is another area that warrants attention.
▶ need, deserve, call for, justify, necessitate

warrior NOUN
a mighty warrior
▶ fighter, soldier, fighting man, combatant

wary ADJECTIVE
She had been wary of making known her name.
▶ cautious, chary, careful, circumspect, suspicious, apprehensive, vigilant (about), watchful (about), alert (to), distrustful, heedful
OPPOSITES ARE unwary, heedless

wash NOUN
1 *I said I needed to go for a wash.*
▶ bath, shower, rinse, shampoo
2 *They give all the cars a wash each morning.*
▶ clean, shampoo, hosing-down

wash VERB
1 *She took a couple of minutes to wash her face and comb her hair. Wash all fruit and vegetables thoroughly before use.*
▶ clean, cleanse, rinse, scrub, shampoo, mop, sluice, swill, wipe
OPPOSITES ARE dirty, soil
2 *It was time to wash the dog.*
▶ soap down, sponge down, swab down, hose down
3 *He found the soap and began to wash.*
▶ bath, bathe, shower
4 *She washed, dried, and ironed the clothes.*
▶ launder, clean, scrub, rinse, sponge
wash your hands of *They cannot wash their hands of social problems.*
▶ disown, renounce, have nothing to do with, disclaim, reject, abandon
AN OPPOSITE IS embrace

washing NOUN
Even the washing hanging from the windows seemed to be fluttering a welcome.
▶ laundry, clothes, wash

washout NOUN
(*informal*) *The summer had been a total washout.*
▶ flop, failure, disappointment, fiasco, disaster, debacle

waste ADJECTIVE
1 *Energy savings are achieved by recycling waste materials.*
▶ unwanted, discarded, superfluous, unused, extra
2 *There was a patch of waste ground for them to play on.*
▶ bare, wild, empty, overgrown, barren, derelict, undeveloped, run-down, uncared for, uncultivated

waste NOUN
1 *Sewage and industrial waste still enter the North Sea.*
▶ refuse, rubbish, debris, effluent, garbage, dross, detritus, trash, junk, litter, scraps
2 *The trip had been a waste of time and money.*
▶ squandering, misuse, frittering away, misspending, dissipation

W

waste VERB

He didn't want to waste money on a taxi fare.
► squander, fritter away, misspend, misuse, throw away, lavish, consume, exhaust, dissipate, use wastefully, use up
AN OPPOSITE IS conserve

waste away *Many people wasted away from disease and malnutrition.*
► wither, become emaciated, become weaker, decline, pine, weaken
AN OPPOSITE IS thrive

wasteful ADJECTIVE

a wasteful use of resources
► extravagant, prodigal, profligate, spendthrift, lavish, reckless, thriftless, excessive, improvident, imprudent, uneconomical, needless
AN OPPOSITE IS economical

watch NOUN

1 *David checked the time by his new watch.*
► wristwatch, pocket watch, timepiece, chronometer, clock, timer
2 *One of us should keep watch at the back of the house.*
► guard, vigil, lookout, surveillance, heed
on the watch *Be on the watch for jellyfish.*
► alert, vigilant, attentive

watch VERB

1 *She watched him as he cleaned the room.*
► look at, observe, keep your eyes on, contemplate, eye, gaze at, survey, heed, regard, see, stare at, take notice of, view, pay attention to, concentrate on, attend to, mark, note
2 *We need someone to watch the children for a few hours.*
► look after, mind, supervise, keep an eye on, keep watch on, care for, tend, guard, protect, safeguard, shield
watch out *Watch out for snakes.*
► look out for, be alert, be vigilant, be attentive, (*more informal*) keep an eye open for

watcher NOUN

There was a little group of watchers on the touchline.
► onlooker, spectator, viewer, observer, witness, looker-on

watchful ADJECTIVE

Their father kept a watchful eye on them.
► observant, alert, vigilant, careful, sharp, attentive, heedful, perceptive
AN OPPOSITE IS inattentive

water NOUN

1 *a glass of water*
► drinking water, tap water, mineral water
2 *a picnic by the water*
► river, lake, sea, ocean, loch, pond, pool
RELATED ADJECTIVES aquatic, hydraulic

water VERB

She went out to water the plants.
► sprinkle, wet, moisten, dampen, hose, soak, douse, drench, flood, irrigate, souse

water down

1 *He asked her to water down his drink.*
► dilute, add water to, weaken, thin
2 *The proposals had to be watered down to stand any chance of success.*
► moderate, tone down, soften, mitigate, temper, mellow, weaken

waterfall NOUN

They looked down from the top of the waterfall.
► cascade, cataract, shower, torrent, falls, rapids, chute

waterproof ADJECTIVE

a waterproof jacket
► water-repellent, water-resistant, weatherproof, watertight, damp-proof, impermeable, impervious

watertight ADJECTIVE

1 *Use a watertight container.*
► sealed, hermetic, sound, waterproof
AN OPPOSITE IS leaky
2 *a watertight excuse*
► foolproof, unassailable, flawless, conclusive, perfect
AN OPPOSITE IS flawed

watery ADJECTIVE

1 *a bowl of watery porridge*
► runny, sloppy, thin, watered down, weak, insipid, liquid, tasteless, (*more informal*) wishy-washy
2 *His eyes looked watery.*
► damp, moist, tear-filled, tearful, wet

wave NOUN

1 *Surfers were riding the waves.*
► breaker, roller, billow, crest, ridge, surf, white horse
2 *A wave of panic seemed to grip the crowd.*
► surge, upsurge, outbreak, current, flood, rash, sweep, stream, swell
3 *She gave a wave of her hand as he sped past.*
► gesture, shake, signal, flourish, gesticulation
4 *Her hair flowed in long waves.*
► curl, twist, kink

wave VERB

1 *Jill waved at us to go over.*
► beckon, gesture, signal, motion, indicate
2 *He waved his umbrella at them.*
► shake, brandish, flourish, waggle, wiggle, wag
3 *A flag waved in the breeze.*
► flap, flutter, ripple, quiver, move to and fro
wave aside *All these objections were waved aside.*
► dismiss, reject, disregard, ignore, discount, brush aside, shrug off

wavelength NOUN

Tune your radio to the right wavelength
▶ channel, station, waveband

waver VERB

1 *Her voice began to waver and she looked faint.*
▶ tremble, falter, quaver, quiver, become unsteady, change, quake, shake, shiver, shudder, sway, teeter, totter, wobble

2 *He could see I was wavering.*
▶ hesitate, be undecided, be indecisive, dither, equivocate, vacillate

3 *the wavering light from the candle*
▶ flicker, quiver, tremble, glimmer

wavy ADJECTIVE

She ran her hand through her wavy hair.
▶ curly, curling, curving, rippling, sinuous, undulating, winding, zigzag
AN OPPOSITE IS straight

way NOUN

1 *His engine overheated on the way home.*
▶ road, route, journey, direction

2 *There was a long way to go.*
▶ distance, length, measurement

3 *It was the best way of dealing with the problem.*
▶ method, means, manner, approach, mode, procedure, process, avenue, course, system, technique, mechanism

4 *He knew he had to change his ways.*
▶ habit, practice, routine, custom, fashion, style, tradition

5 *The arts benefit society in several ways.*
▶ respect, particular, aspect, circumstances, detail, feature

waylay VERB

1 *They were waylaid by bandits on the road to the coast.*
▶ ambush, hold up, attack, accost

2 *She waylaid me to chat as I was leaving.*
▶ catch, accost, intercept, buttonhole, detain, (*more informal*) get hold of, (*more informal*) nab

way-out ADJECTIVE

(*informal*) *He introduced some way-out visual ideas that no one had tried before.*
▶ unconventional, offbeat, eccentric, quirky, bizarre, weird, odd, (*informal*) wacky

wayward ADJECTIVE

Her husband treated her like a wayward child.
▶ disobedient, naughty, wilful, stubborn, headstrong, self-willed, perverse, obstinate, contrary, badly behaved, uncontrollable, uncooperative
OPPOSITES ARE cooperative, well-behaved

weak ADJECTIVE

1 *The bridge was weak as a result of metal fatigue.*
▶ unsafe, unsound, fragile, unsteady, rickety, shaky, flimsy, decrepit, substandard
AN OPPOSITE IS strong

2 *He was still too weak to get up by himself.*
▶ frail, feeble, poorly, ill, infirm, sickly, debilitated, helpless, delicate, enervated, exhausted, listless, puny
AN OPPOSITE IS strong

3 *A weak man, when provoked, is often more dangerous than a violent one.*
▶ timid, timorous, irresolute, spineless, ineffectual, pusillanimous, cowardly, fearful, impotent, indecisive, ineffective
OPPOSITES ARE strong, brave

4 *His mistakes had put him in a weak position.*
▶ vulnerable, exposed, defenceless, unguarded, unprotected
OPPOSITES ARE strong, powerful

5 *The weak joke fell hollowly.*
▶ feeble, lame, unconvincing, unsatisfactory

6 *She sipped the sweet, weak tea and began to feel better.*
▶ watery, diluted, watered down, insipid, bland, thin, tasteless
AN OPPOSITE IS strong

7 *The light was becoming weak.*
▶ dim, pale, faint, feeble
OPPOSITES ARE strong, bright

weaken VERB

1 *Their purpose was to weaken the unions' power.*
▶ reduce, sap, enfeeble, erode, impair, lessen, diminish, lower, debilitate, destroy, emasculate, enervate, make weaker, ruin, soften, undermine
OPPOSITES ARE strengthen, boost

2 *Our resolve had weakened.*
▶ dwindle, ebb, fade, flag, wane, abate, become weaker, decline, decrease, give way
OPPOSITES ARE strengthen, increase, intensify

weakness NOUN

1 *There is an obvious weakness in your argument.*
▶ fault, flaw, defect, imperfection, weak point, blemish, error, failing, mistake, shortcoming
OPPOSITES ARE strength, strong point

2 *The economy is showing signs of weakness.*
▶ fragility, frailty, flimsiness, inadequacy, softness

3 *Her illness left her with a permanent physical weakness.*
▶ infirmity, debility, feebleness, illness, impotence, lassitude, vulnerability
OPPOSITES ARE strength, vigour

4 *He has a weakness for chocolate cake.*
▶ liking, fondness, inclination, penchant, predilection, (*more informal*) soft spot

wealth NOUN

1 *We want to see wealth passed down from generation to generation.*
▶ affluence, assets, opulence, property, prosperity, capital, fortune, money, possessions, riches
AN OPPOSITE IS poverty

2 *You realize the wealth of information inside the government.*
▶ abundance, profusion, plethora, store, plenty

wealthy ADJECTIVE
Her mother was a very wealthy woman.
▶ rich, affluent, prosperous, well-off, well-to-do, moneyed, comfortable, (*more informal*) flush, (*more informal*) loaded
OPPOSITES ARE poor, impoverished

wear VERB
1 *Did you have to wear any special kind of clothing? Ruth wore a pale lavender cotton dress. He often wore dark glasses to hide the bags under his eyes.*
▶ dress in, be dressed in, clothe yourself in, put on, have on, present yourself in, wrap up in, don
2 *He wore his usual benign expression.*
▶ show, assume, present, exhibit
3 *Years of passing footsteps had badly worn the carpet.*
▶ damage, fray, scuff, mark, weaken
4 *The tyres have worn well.*
▶ last, endure, survive, hold up, (*more informal*) stand the test of time
wear away *Most of the grass had been worn away by the spectators.*
▶ rub away, erode, grind down, abrade, corrode, eat away
wear off *The effect of the tranquillizers was wearing off.*
▶ fade, subside, dwindle, reduce, lessen, diminish, peter out, disappear
wear out
1 *His shoes wear out twice as fast when he's working.*
▶ become worn, deteriorate, become damaged, become scuffed
2 *They cheered until their lungs were worn out.*
▶ exhaust, fatigue, tire out

wear NOUN
1 *Repairs were made necessary by heavy wear.*
▶ use, service, utility, wearing
2 *The brakes showed signs of wear.*
▶ damage, deterioration, friction, erosion, wear and tear
3 *The guests were dressed in formal wear.*
▶ dress, clothes, clothing, costume, outfit

wearing ADJECTIVE
The care of others can be a wearing business.
▶ tiring, exhausting, tiresome, fatiguing, wearying, wearisome, trying, taxing
AN OPPOSITE IS refreshing

wearisome ADJECTIVE
Waiting is the most wearisome of all activities.
▶ tedious, monotonous, boring, dreary, tiring, troublesome, exhausting
AN OPPOSITE IS stimulating

weary ADJECTIVE
I have been too sad and too weary to write anything.
▶ tired, exhausted, fatigued, wearied, worn out, sapped, drained, spent, (*more informal*) knackered

weary VERB
Gemma had not the heart to say how much they wearied her.
▶ tire, exhaust, fatigue, bore

wearying ADJECTIVE
The wearying journey lasted for three days.
▶ tiring, exhausting, tiresome, fatiguing, wearing, wearisome, trying, taxing
AN OPPOSITE IS refreshing

weather NOUN
She was tempted to use the weather as an excuse to postpone her visit. All farmers are exposed to the vagaries of the weather.
▶ climate, the elements, meteorological conditions, atmospheric conditions
under the weather *She felt under the weather and went to rest.*
▶ unwell, poorly, indisposed, out of sorts, ill, sick
OPPOSITES ARE well, in good health
RELATED ADJECTIVE meteorological

WORDS TO DO WITH WEATHER

general words to do with weather: climate, forecast, foul, lightning, meteorology, meteorologist, outlook, rough, thunder.

meteorological instruments: barometer, barograph; thermometer; anemometer (measuring the force of the wind); weathercock, weathervane.

words to do with air pressure: high, low; anticyclone, cyclone, depression.

words to do with rain and other precipitation: rain, sleet, slush, hail, snow; blizzard, deluge, downpour, drizzle, drought, flood, ice storm, shower, torrent; dew.

words to do with sky and clouds: cirrus, clear, cumulus, cumulo-nimbus, haze, mist, stratus, sunless, sunny, sunshine, thundercloud; thunder, lightning; blue, bright, brilliant; fair, fine, cloudless, cloudy; misty, overcast, dull, fog, foggy, grey, hazy.

words to do with temperature: cold, hot, freezing, frost, frosty, hoar-frost, ice, icy; oppressive, sultry, sweltering, wintry; heatwave.

words to do with wind: blustery, breeze, cyclone, gale, hurricane, monsoon, squall, storm, tempest, tornado, dust devil; typhoon, waterspout, whirlwind, willy-willy, wind-vane.

weather VERB
Many small businesses had managed to weather the recession.
▶ survive, endure, withstand, ride out, come through, live through, overcome

weave VERB
1 *The design had been woven into the carpet.*
▶ intertwine, interweave, knit, plait, sew, entwine, interlace
2 *Victorian novelists weave romances round great houses. She wove a spell over him, so that he slept for ever and never grew old.*
▶ create, compose, make, plot, put together

3 *He dragged himself out of bed and weaved his way to the bathroom.*
▶ thread, wind, work, dodge, zigzag

web NOUN
1 *The webs are built to a definite pattern.*
▶ mesh, net, netting, network, crisscross, lattice
2 *Their lives were caught up in a web of deception.*
▶ network, nexus, maze, complex

wedding NOUN
The wedding went ahead with two hundred guests.
▶ marriage, marriage ceremony, nuptials, union
RELATED ADJECTIVE nuptial, bridal

wedge NOUN
1 *He put a huge wedge of gleaming white pudding on her plate.*
▶ slice, segment, triangle, chunk, lump
2 *The window was held open with a wedge.*
▶ chock, block, door stop

wedge VERB
She wedged the string bag between her feet and took out a book. The children were wedged so tightly that it was difficult to move.
▶ squeeze, jam, cram, push, force, thrust, stick, push, fasten, (*more informal*) shove

weedy ADJECTIVE
1 *I walked up through the weedy garden.*
▶ untidy, unweeded, overgrown, unkempt, wild, rank
2 (*informal*) *He was short and physically weedy.*
▶ weak, puny, feeble, frail

weep VERB
I began to weep, burying my face in my hands.
▶ cry, sob, shed tears, whimper, blubber, snivel, wail

weepy ADJECTIVE
She was weepy and nervy, anxious about her baby.
▶ tearful, in tears, crying, weeping, sobbing, upset, emotional

weigh VERB
1 *The man weighed some vegetables and put them in a bag.*
▶ measure the weight of, measure out, put on the scales
2 *I weigh the same now as when I married.*
▶ have a weight of, tip the scales at
3 **weigh** or **weigh up** *These were considerations that she weighed carefully. I weighed up my chances and decided to go.*
▶ consider, evaluate, assess, examine, think about, give thought to, ponder, study, mull over, meditate on
4 *Two other matters weigh in their favour.*
▶ be important, count, have weight
weigh down
1 *No one wants to be weighed down with heavy gear.*
▶ burden, weight, saddle, load, overload
2 *She walked to her room, mentally weighed down by her thoughts.*
▶ depress, oppress, trouble, bother, beset, afflict, prey on

weight NOUN
1 *The supports could no longer sustain the weight of the bridge, and it collapsed.*
▶ heaviness, load, burden, mass, pressure, strain
2 *The Prime Minister has attached a lot of weight to the scheme.*
▶ importance, seriousness, significance, authority, emphasis, gravity, substance

weight VERB
1 *Driftwood can be sealed and weighted in the same way.*
▶ weigh down, make heavy, ballast, hold down, keep down, load
2 *The odds were weighted against them.*
▶ bias, load, slant, balance

weighty ADJECTIVE
1 *A pile of books can be very weighty.*
▶ heavy, bulky, cumbersome, massive, clumsy
2 *The weighty question, what is happiness?*
▶ serious, important, significant, momentous, far-reaching, consequential
3 *It is a weighty responsibility to be given.*
▶ demanding, onerous, exacting, taxing, troublesome

weird ADJECTIVE
1 *Some pretty weird things seemed to be happening.*
▶ uncanny, eerie, unearthly, unnatural, ghostly, mysterious, scary, supernatural, unaccountable, (*more informal*) spooky, (*more informal*) creepy
OPPOSITES ARE normal, ordinary
2 *They wouldn't make those weird garden ornaments if they'd ever seen a real gnome. The fridge made some really weird noises yesterday.*
▶ strange, peculiar, bizarre, grotesque, odd, curious, eccentric, outlandish, queer, unusual, abnormal, quirky, unconventional, (*more informal*) wacky, (*more informal*) freaky, (*more informal*) way-out
AN OPPOSITE IS conventional

welcome ADJECTIVE
We've received some welcome news.
▶ pleasant, pleasing, gratifying, encouraging, good, nice
OPPOSITES ARE unwelcome, disappointing

welcome NOUN
Make for the Visitors' Centre, where you can be sure of a warm welcome.
▶ reception, greeting, hospitality

welcome VERB
1 *Sophie welcomed her warmly and pulled out a chair.*
▶ greet, receive, hail, meet
2 *His colleagues welcomed his cheerfulness.*
▶ appreciate, approve of, delight in, like, want, accept

weld VERB
Steel spikes were welded on to the toecaps.
▶ fuse, join, attach, fasten, solder, bond, cement, unite

welfare NOUN
the safety and welfare of people at work
▶ well-being, good, security, prosperity, comfort, benefit, happiness, health, interests

well ADJECTIVE
Mary was looking well.
▶ healthy, in good health, fit, fine, sound, strong, thriving, flourishing, hearty, lively, robust, vigorous

well ADVERB
1 *They behaved well.*
▶ satisfactorily, correctly, nicely, properly
AN OPPOSITE IS badly
2 *She sings well.*
▶ ably, skilfully, expertly
OPPOSITES ARE badly, poorly
3 *Mix the ingredients well.*
▶ thoroughly, fully, completely, rigorously
AN OPPOSITE IS lightly
4 *You have been working well.*
▶ carefully, diligently, conscientiously, attentively
OPPOSITES ARE badly, poorly
5 *He has made enough money to live well.*
▶ comfortably, in comfort, prosperously

well VERB
The tears welled in her eyes.
▶ flow, stream, spring, course, surge, flood, gush, rise, run, trickle

well-behaved ADJECTIVE
You will have to be quiet and well-behaved.
▶ well-mannered, polite, obedient, respectful, courteous, cooperative, good, dutiful, nice
AN OPPOSITE IS naughty

well-being NOUN
The medical staff are responsible for the well-being of the patients.
▶ welfare, good, security, prosperity, comfort, benefit, happiness, health, interests

well-dressed ADJECTIVE
A well-dressed young woman came in.
▶ smart, stylish, elegant, fashionable, well-groomed, chic, trim

well-known ADJECTIVE
1 *They played well-known types such as the domineering wife and the henpecked husband.*
▶ familiar, widely known, popular, common, typical
2 *She came from a well-known North London family.*
▶ famous, notable, prominent, leading, distinguished, eminent

well-off ADJECTIVE
dream gardens of well-off homeowners
▶ rich, wealthy, well-to-do, affluent, moneyed, prosperous, opulent
AN OPPOSITE IS poor

wet ADJECTIVE
1 *Her jacket was soaking and clung to her like a wet tea towel.*
▶ damp, soaked, saturated, drenched, moistened, sopping, dripping
AN OPPOSITE IS dry
2 *The mowers could not be used because the ground was too wet.*
▶ waterlogged, sodden, boggy, soggy, spongy, swampy, squelchy
OPPOSITES ARE dry, firm
3 *They were unlucky enough to meet wet weather at harvest time.*
▶ rainy, raining, drizzly, showery, pouring, humid, misty
OPPOSITES ARE dry, fine
4 *The paint was still wet.*
▶ runny, sticky, tacky
OPPOSITES ARE dry, set
5 *(informal) Some of the trainees seemed a bit wet.*
▶ feeble, weak, silly, soft, (informal) weedy, (informal) wimpish
OPPOSITES ARE tough, strong

wet NOUN
The front wheels were prone to locking in the wet.
▶ rain, dampness, wet weather, damp weather, drizzle

wet VERB
There is no need to wet your hair first.
▶ dampen, damp, douse, drench, soak, spray, sprinkle, water, steep, irrigate, moisten, saturate
AN OPPOSITE IS dry

whack VERB
I saw him take a stick and whack his dog.
▶ hit, strike, smack, slap, thump, (more informal) slug

whack NOUN
She gave him a hefty whack across his shoulders.
▶ blow, hit, slap, punch, thump, knock, smack

wheel VERB
1 *He grabbed a trolley and began to wheel the luggage away.*
▶ push, trundle, roll
2 *A flock of birds wheeled above them.*
▶ circle, gyrate, turn, orbit
wheel round *Elinor wheeled round, a look of horror on her face.*
▶ turn, swing round, change direction, swerve, veer

wheeze VERB
He was wheezing now, as if in the grip of an asthma attack.
▶ gasp, breathe noisily, cough, pant, puff

whereabouts NOUN
Despite inquiries, his whereabouts remain unknown.
▶ location, position, situation, vicinity, address, site

whet VERB
1 *He whetted his knife on a stone.*
▶ sharpen, hone, put an edge on
2 *There are many new brews to whet the appetite.*
▶ stimulate, excite, arouse, rouse, kindle, awaken

a b c d e f g h i j k l m n o p q r s t u v w x y z

whiff NOUN

1 *He caught a whiff of expensive perfume.*
▶ scent, aroma, smell , breath, puff, odour
USAGE You normally use *odour* when you mean an unpleasant smell.
2 *At the slightest whiff of trouble he takes to his bed.*
▶ hint, trace, suggestion, suspicion, intimation

whim NOUN

It was silly to waste a whole morning on a foolish whim.
▶ impulse, notion, urge, fancy, caprice, desire, quirk

whimper VERB

He began to whimper with fear.
▶ snivel, wail, moan, cry, groan, weep, (*more informal*) grizzle

whimper NOUN

The dog made off with a whimper.
▶ whine, cry, snivel

whine NOUN

There was a whine from the engines.
▶ drone, whimper, hum

whine VERB

1 *Mosquitos whined in my ears.*
▶ drone, hum
2 (*informal*) *I'm sick of him whining to me about you.*
▶ grumble, complain, carp, grouch, moan, beef, (*informal*) whinge

whip NOUN

He threatened to use a whip on any intruders.
▶ lash, scourge, cat, cat-o'-nine-tails, horsewhip, riding-crop, switch

whip VERB

1 *He whipped the boys and sent them away.*
▶ thrash, beat, flog, lash, scourge
2 *Why can you whip cream but not milk?*
▶ whisk, beat, stir vigorously
3 (*informal*) *She whipped a piece of paper out of her pocket.*
▶ pull, whisk, pluck, tug, take
4 (*informal*) *I can always whip round to the corner shop.*
▶ dash, hurry, shoot, run, sprint, rush, race, tear

whirl NOUN

1 *His mind was in a whirl and he was worried.*
▶ daze, spin, muddle, stupor, state of confusion
2 (*informal*) *The only way to find out was to give it a whirl.*
▶ try, test, (*informal*) shot, (*informal*) bash

whirl VERB

The dancers appear to whirl round with their hands on their hips.
▶ circle, gyrate, twirl, spin, rotate, pirouette, reel, revolve, swivel, turn, twist, wheel

whisk VERB

1 *Whisk the sugar and eggs together.*
▶ beat, mix, stir, whip
2 *You will be whisked off to a studio for a photo session.*
▶ rush, speed, hurry, sweep, shoot, hurtle
3 *He whisked a blanket off the nearest trolley.*
▶ pull, pluck, tug, take, (*more informal*) whip

whisper VERB

Anne whispered something in his ear.
▶ murmur, breathe, mutter, mumble
AN OPPOSITE IS shout

whisper NOUN

1 *He spoke in a whisper.*
▶ murmur, mutter, undertone, hushed voice
2 *I heard a whisper that he's left the country.*
▶ rumour, report, piece of gossip, piece of hearsay

white ADJECTIVE

1 *He rested his fingers on the white keys.*
▶ ivory, snowy, chalky, pale , snow-white, cream
2 *Her face was white with fear.*
▶ pale, pallid, ashen, colourless, bloodless

whittle VERB

whittle away *The monarch's powers were gradually whittled away.*
▶ erode, wear away, reduce, undermine
whittle down *The original hundred contestants have been whittled down to six.*
▶ reduce, cut down, cut back, trim, scale down, pare down

whole ADJECTIVE

1 *I don't have time to read the whole book.*
▶ entire, complete, full, total, full-length, unabridged, uncut, unexpurgated
OPPOSITES ARE incomplete, partial
2 *The archaeologists uncovered a Greek vase that turned out to be whole.*
▶ intact, in one piece, unbroken, undamaged, unharmed, unscathed, perfect
OPPOSITES ARE broken, fragmentary

wholehearted ADJECTIVE

You have our wholehearted support.
▶ total, complete, unreserved, unqualified, committed, absolute, outright, utter
OPPOSITES ARE half- hearted, partial

wholesale ADJECTIVE

the wholesale destruction of sacred images
▶ total, comprehensive, extensive, large-scale, indiscriminate, widespread, mass, universal

wholesome ADJECTIVE

1 *wholesome food*
▶ nourishing, nutritious, healthy, good, health-giving, hygienic
AN OPPOSITE IS unhealthy
2 *a good wholesome story*
▶ decent, innocent, moral, edifying, improving
AN OPPOSITE IS unwholesome

wholly ADVERB

The money collected was wholly inadequate.
▶ completely, totally, utterly, absolutely, altogether, downright

whopping ADJECTIVE
The bill came to a whopping £500.
► huge, enormous, gigantic, mammoth, immense, massive, colossal

wicked ADJECTIVE
1 *a wicked person a wicked act*
► evil, bad, sinful, base, immoral, corrupt, depraved, heinous, iniquitous
OPPOSITES ARE moral, good, upright
2 *It was wicked of you to say such things.*
► naughty, wrong, nasty, mischievous, unkind
OPPOSITES ARE good, kind
3 *There was a wicked gleam in his eye.*
► mischievous, playful, rascally, impish, devilish, cheeky
4 *(informal) He makes a wicked fruit salad.*
► excellent, marvellous, wonderful, superb
AN OPPOSITE IS lousy

wickedness NOUN
the sheer wickedness of their plan
► evil , enormity, iniquity, vileness, baseness, foulness, heinousness, immorality, infamy, sinfulness, villainy, turpitude, wrong, wrongdoing
AN OPPOSITE IS goodness

wide ADJECTIVE
1 *The river was fast and wide. Players are spread over a wide area*
► broad, expansive, extensive, vast, large, spacious, spread out, outspread
AN OPPOSITE IS narrow
2 *There is a wide choice of dinner menu. The programmes reach a wide audience.*
► extensive, comprehensive, wide-ranging, inclusive, all-embracing, broad, ample, universal
OPPOSITES ARE narrow, limited
3 *Wide trousers became fashionable again.*
► baggy, loose, full, flared
OPPOSITES ARE narrow, tight
4 *The shot went wide.*
► off course, off target, off the mark
AN OPPOSITE IS on target

wide ADVERB
Her eyes opened wide.
► fully, completely

widen VERB
1 *There are plans to widen parts of the motorway.*
► broaden, make wider, expand, enlarge, extend, open out, spread, stretch
AN OPPOSITE IS narrow
2 *Her smile widened.*
► broaden, become wider, spread
AN OPPOSITE IS narrow
3 *They must widen the scope of the inquiry.*
► expand, extend, broaden, enlarge, increase
OPPOSITES ARE narrow, restrict, limit

widespread ADJECTIVE
1 *These incidents provoked widespread protest.*
► general, extensive, universal, wholesale, far-reaching, global
AN OPPOSITE IS uncommon
2 *Death and disease were widespread in these years.*
► rife, prevalent, endemic, pervasive, common

width NOUN
Two white lines should be drawn across the width of the pitch.
► breadth, span, girth, diameter

wield VERB
1 *He was wielding a piece of wood outside a pub.*
► brandish, flourish, wave, swing, ply, flaunt
2 *He did not wield the same influence as his father.*
► have, exercise, exert, command, possess

wife NOUN
His new wife is a Parisian.
► spouse, partner, (more formal) consort, (more informal) woman, (more informal) mate, (more informal) better half

wiggle VERB
He removed his shoes and wiggled his toes.
► wriggle, waggle, jiggle

wild ADJECTIVE
1 *He began attacking me like a wild animal.*
► fierce, feral, ferocious, untamed, undomesticated
AN OPPOSITE IS tame
2 *There are many wild flowers that can be legally picked.*
► natural, uncultivated, indigenous
AN OPPOSITE IS cultivated
3 *Even seemingly wild ideas may be aired at this point.*
► crazy, ridiculous, madcap, absurd, foolish, silly, outrageous, extravagant, impractical, rash, foolhardy
OPPOSITES ARE sensible, practical
4 *A wild urge rose up inside her to tell everything.*
► reckless, rash, intense, extreme
OPPOSITES ARE gentle, mild
5 *My father liked these wild people.*
► primitive, savage, barbarous, uncivilized, uncultured
AN OPPOSITE IS civilized
6 *She said she was sorry for her wild behaviour.*
► unruly, rowdy, violent, disorderly, uncontrolled, unrestrained, undisciplined, unconstrained, unbridled
OPPOSITES ARE calm, restrained
7 *The parties involve loud music and wild dancing.*
► lively, flamboyant, boisterous, exuberant, animated
AN OPPOSITE IS restrained
8 *Don't plan to go out in really wild weather.*
► rough, stormy, tempestuous, blustery, foul, inclement
AN OPPOSITE IS calm
9 *the beautiful wild scenery of the Highlands*
► rugged, rough, desolate, uncultivated, unpopulated, barren

a b c d e f g h i j k l m n o p q r s t u v w x y z

10 *His team mates were wild with joy.*
► excited, ecstatic, delirious, frantic, frenzied
11 *Without knowing the answer I decided to risk a wild guess.*
► arbitrary, random, haphazard, hit-or-miss
AN OPPOSITE IS considered
12 (*informal*) *Being disturbed at this time made him wild.*
► furious, angry, enraged, irate, cross, livid, (*more informal*) hopping mad
AN OPPOSITE IS pleased
13 wild about (*informal*) *I'm not wild about the music.*
► keen on, enthusiastic about, (*informal*) mad about, (*informal*) crazy about

wilful ADJECTIVE
1 *He was charged with wilful damage and assault.*
► deliberate, intentional, premeditated, intended, planned, calculated, conscious, voluntary
AN OPPOSITE IS accidental
2 *She checked her wilful and impulsive self.*
► headstrong, self-willed, strong-willed, obstinate, stubborn, perverse, determined, dogged, intransigent, obdurate
AN OPPOSITE IS amenable

will NOUN
1 *Corruption exists when politicians have lost the will to enforce the law.*
► determination, resolve, resolution, intention, purpose, aim, desire, inclination, volition, will-power, wish
2 *I don't think it's the will of the people.*
► desire, wish, choice, preference
3 *She had died without making a will.*
► testament, last wishes

will VERB
1 *He willed them not to panic.*
► encourage, inspire, influence, wish
2 *She willed her money equally to all her nephews and nieces.*
► bequeath, leave, pass on

willing ADJECTIVE
1 *Let us know if you are willing to make cakes or prepare sandwiches.*
► prepared, ready, disposed, agreeable, eager, inclined, content, pleased, (*more informal*) game
OPPOSITES ARE unwilling, reluctant, disinclined
2 *You'd be surprised what can be achieved by willing hands eager to do good turns.*
► enthusiastic, helpful, obliging, cooperative, amenable, compliant, consenting
OPPOSITES ARE unwilling, unhelpful

wilt VERB
1 *The flowers had begun to wilt.*
► droop, fade, shrivel, wither, become limp, flop, languish, sag
OPPOSITES ARE thrive, revive, perk up
2 *Their joy soon wilted.*
► fail, flag, wane, dwindle, evaporate, weaken, diminish, sink
AN OPPOSITE IS grow

wily ADJECTIVE
He was constantly in danger of being outwitted by his wily opponents.
► clever, crafty, shrewd, artful, astute, cunning, devious, guileful, knowing, scheming, shifty, foxy, sly, underhand
AN OPPOSITE IS naive

win VERB
1 *She had a good chance of winning.*
► be victorious, be the winner, succeed, triumph, come first, finish first, prevail, conquer, overcome
AN OPPOSITE IS lose
2 *Next year they would win first prize.*
► achieve, receive, acquire, (*more informal*) carry off, (*more informal*) come away with, (*more informal*) pick up, (*more informal*) walk away with
3 *Charles II managed to win the support of the Scots.*
► gain, secure, obtain, earn, deserve, get

win NOUN
His win ended eleven years of American domination of the championship.
► victory, triumph, success, conquest
AN OPPOSITE IS defeat

wind NOUN (rhymes with *pinned*)
She shivered in the chill wind.
► breeze, air current, gust, blast, puff, breath, draught, gale, squall

wind VERB (rhymes with *mind*)
1 *He wound the cord tightly.*
► coil, loop, twist, twine, curl, curve, furl, turn, roll
2 *The Saigon River begins to wind like a serpent.*
► twist, snake, bend, curve, meander, ramble, twist and turn, zigzag
wind up (*informal*) *We could wind up paying the whole lot.*
► end up, finish up, land up, find yourself
wind someone up (*informal*) *I'm sure he's just doing it to wind me up.*
► tease, annoy, disconcert, trick

winding ADJECTIVE
A winding road leads down to the village.
► bending, sinuous, snaking, meandering, tortuous, rambling, roundabout, serpentine, circuitous, (*more informal*) windy, (*more informal*) twisty, (*more informal*) bendy
AN OPPOSITE IS straight

windy ADJECTIVE
It was too cold and windy to sit and wait.
► blowy, breezy, blustery, gusty, squally, boisterous, draughty, stormy
AN OPPOSITE IS calm

wing NOUN
1 *The maternity department is in the north wing of the hospital.*
► section, annexe, end, extension
2 *the military wing of the organization*
► section, faction, branch, group

wink VERB
The red light winked.
▶ flash, gleam, flicker, sparkle, twinkle

wink NOUN
Then, in a wink, it all turned to dust.
▶ instant, moment, second, flash

winner NOUN
The points system produces an overall winner.
▶ victor, champion, conqueror, first, prizewinner
AN OPPOSITE IS loser

winning ADJECTIVE
1 *For the fourth time he was on the winning side.*
▶ victorious, successful, triumphant, champion, conquering, prevailing, leading, top-scoring
AN OPPOSITE IS losing
2 *The show lacks a really winning song.*
▶ appealing, attractive, fetching, charming, engaging

winnings PLURAL NOUN
She used part of her winnings to buy a new house.
▶ prize money, gains
AN OPPOSITE IS losses

wintry ADJECTIVE
He opened a window, letting in damp wintry air.
▶ chilly, frosty, cold, bleak, freezing, icy, biting, snowy

wipe VERB
She wiped the table with a damp cloth. Nathan wiped the crumbs from his mouth.
▶ rub, brush, clean, mop, sponge, swab, wash
wipe out *Two hurricanes almost wiped out the flourishing egg industry.*
▶ destroy, obliterate, annihilate, eradicate, exterminate, demolish

wisdom NOUN
He would persuade them of the wisdom of adopting this course.
▶ sense, prudence, common sense, good sense, intelligence, judgement, astuteness, sagacity, discernment, insight, reason

wise ADJECTIVE
1 *Wise parents are able to give support and advice.*
▶ sensible, prudent, shrewd, perceptive, intelligent, sagacious, sage, clever, astute, informed, judicious, discerning, enlightened
OPPOSITES ARE unwise, foolish
2 *The action they took seemed wise and reasonable.*
▶ sensible, prudent, advisable, appropriate, proper, fair, just, right, sound
OPPOSITES ARE unwise, foolish, ill-advised

wish NOUN
1 *It was her parents' dearest wish that she should be happy.*
▶ desire, ambition, objective, want, longing, inclination, aim, aspiration, craving, fancy, hankering, hope, yearning
2 *He had no wish to appear impolite.*
▶ desire, inclination

3 *We will respect your wishes.*
▶ request, bidding, direction, will, order

wish VERB
1 *If guests wish to eat out, there are several pubs in the village.*
▶ want, hope
2 **wish for** *I wish for a really good night's sleep.*
▶ desire, want, long for, yearn for, crave, fancy, hanker after

wisp NOUN
She brushed aside a wisp of hair.
▶ strand, lock, shred, streak

wispy ADJECTIVE
The sky was streaked with wispy white clouds.
▶ streaky, feathery, light, thin, flimsy, fragile, gossamer, insubstantial

wistful ADJECTIVE
His anger passed, and a wistful smile crossed his face.
▶ sad, melancholy, thoughtful, pensive, nostalgic, forlorn

wit NOUN
1 *The speech was improved by moments of great wit.*
▶ humour, wittiness, banter, repartee, drollery, badinage, facetiousness, ingenuity, comedy, jokes
2 *Jack was regarded as the club wit.*
▶ joker, comedian, wag, comic, humorist, jester
3 *She was a woman of great wit and wisdom.*
▶ intelligence, shrewdness, wisdom, cleverness, sense, understanding

witch NOUN
1 *She must look for the witch's hat.*
▶ sorceress, enchantress
2 *What are you talking about, you stupid witch?*
▶ hag, crone, harpy

withdraw VERB
1 *She withdrew the photo abruptly and returned it to the folder.*
▶ take back, remove, snatch
2 *All the objections were eventually withdrawn.*
▶ retract, rescind, revoke, take back, cancel, remove, disclaim, renounce, take away
AN OPPOSITE IS introduce
3 *The rebels were forced to withdraw into the hills.*
▶ retreat, retire, draw back, move back, fall back
AN OPPOSITE IS advance
4 *One of the representatives decided to withdraw from future discussions.*
▶ pull out, back out, drop out, secede, (*more informal*) cry off
AN OPPOSITE IS enter

withdrawn ADJECTIVE
Frank appeared even more withdrawn than usual.
▶ reserved, shy, retiring, introverted, uncommunicative, unsociable, unforthcoming
AN OPPOSITE IS outgoing

wither VERB

The flowers had withered in the strong sun.
▶ wilt, droop, become limp, dehydrate, dry up, sag, shrivel, waste away, flag, flop
AN OPPOSITE IS thrive

withhold VERB

He had deliberately withheld the fact that he couldn't sail.
▶ suppress, repress, conceal, hide, hold back, keep back, keep secret, retain

withstand VERB

The boat must be strong enough to withstand the roughest weather.
▶ resist, endure, hold out against, last out against, bear up against, stand up to, survive, tolerate, brave, cope with
AN OPPOSITE IS succumb to

witness NOUN

The only witness was the office cleaner.
▶ observer, bystander, onlooker, spectator, eyewitness, looker-on, watcher

witness VERB

He said he has witnessed several instances of police brutality.
▶ see, observe, be present at, be a witness to, notice, view, watch, attend, behold, look on

witty ADJECTIVE

Dolly is witty and entertaining.
▶ humorous, amusing, funny, quick-witted, sharp-witted, waggish, droll, comic, facetious, sparkling
AN OPPOSITE IS dull

wizard NOUN

1 *We were still under the wizard's spell.*
▶ magician, sorcerer, enchanter, warlock
2 *He's an absolute wizard with engines.*
▶ expert, genius, adept, master, (*more informal*) star

wobble VERB

1 *She reached out and caught it without so much as wobbling.*
▶ shake, sway, teeter, totter, be unsteady, oscillate, quake
2 *Once more the glass wobbled.*
▶ tremble, shake, quiver, vibrate, rock

wobbly ADJECTIVE

1 *The table had a wobbly leg.*
▶ unsteady, loose, rickety, rocky, unstable, shaky, insecure, unbalanced, unsafe
AN OPPOSITE IS steady
2 *He felt wobbly and had to sit down.*
▶ giddy, dizzy, faint, groggy, unsteady

woman NOUN

The car pulled up and a woman got out.
▶ female, lady, girl
RELATED ADJECTIVES female, feminine

wonder NOUN

1 *We were speechless with wonder.*
▶ awe, admiration, amazement, wonderment, astonishment, fascination, respect, reverence, surprise
2 *a wonder of nature*
▶ marvel, miracle, sensation, spectacle, prodigy
3 *It's a wonder there were no casualties.*
▶ marvel, miracle, extraordinary thing

wonder VERB

1 *I was beginning to wonder if they would ever come.*
▶ ponder, speculate, ask yourself, be curious about, reflect on
2 **wonder at** *We wondered at such bravery.*
▶ marvel at, admire, be amazed by, feel wonder at, stand in awe of

wonderful ADJECTIVE

We had a wonderful time.
▶ excellent, marvellous, fantastic, splendid, lovely, delightful, smashing, (*more informal*) terrific
OPPOSITES ARE awful, dreadful

---

wood NOUN

1 *There is a nature trail through the wood.*
▶ forest, woodland, woods, trees, coppice, copse, thicket, grove, spinney
RELATED ADJECTIVE sylvan
2 *a little cabin made from wood*
▶ timber, planks, planking, lumber
RELATED ADJECTIVE ligneous

KINDS OF WOOD USED IN BUILDING AND CARPENTRY

ash (hard pale wood), balsa (lightweight wood used for making models), beech (hard pale wood with fine grain), cedar (fragrant durable wood), chestnut, deal (fir or pine used as a building material), ebony (hard very dark wood), elm, mahogany (hard reddish-brown wood used for furniture), oak (hard durable wood), pine (soft wood), rosewood (used for furniture and musical instruments), sandalwood (fragrant wood), sapele (African hardwood like mahogany), teak (hard durable wood), walnut.

---

wooded ADJECTIVE

a wooded valley
▶ tree-covered, forested or afforested, woody, timbered, (*poetic*) sylvan

wooden ADJECTIVE

1 *wooden furniture*
▶ timber, wood
2 *The acting and production were wooden.*
▶ stiff, unnatural, stilted, lifeless, leaden, deadpan, emotionless, unemotional, expressionless, awkward, clumsy, graceless
AN OPPOSITE IS lively

woody ADJECTIVE

1 *a woody plant*
▶ tough, hard, fibrous, ligneous, wooden
2 *a woody hillside*
▶ wooded, tree-covered, forested or afforested, timbered, (*poetic*) sylvan

woolly ADJECTIVE

1 *a woolly hat*
▶ woollen, wool, fleecy
2 *a sheep's woolly coat*
▶ fleecy, furry, downy, fuzzy, hairy, shaggy, soft
3 *woolly thinking*
▶ vague, ill-defined, unfocused, unclear, imprecise, confused, muddled, blurry, hazy, foggy

word NOUN

1 *She wanted to find another word for 'chuckle'.*
▶ expression, term, locution
RELATED ADJECTIVES verbal, lexical
2 *Have you had any word from the hospital?*
▶ news, information, communication, report, comment, advice
3 *I'll have a word with them in private.*
▶ talk, conversation, chat, discussion, consultation, exchange of views, tête-à-tête
USAGE Note that tête-à-tête is normally used about a personal conversation between two people.
4 *I gave her my word.*
▶ promise, guarantee, pledge, assurance, word of honour, oath
word for word *He had copied it word for word from the Internet.*
▶ verbatim, exactly, precisely, faithfully
AN OPPOSITE IS loosely

word VERB

The book has advice on how to word your CV.
▶ phrase, express, construct, formulate, frame, couch, write, say, put

wording NOUN

The wording of the contract was unclear.
▶ phrasing, phraseology, language, choice of words, mode of expression, terminology, style, diction

wordy ADJECTIVE

a wordy essay   a wordy speaker
▶ long-winded, verbose, diffuse, rambling, repetitious, protracted, prolix, garrulous, loquacious, talkative
OPPOSITES ARE brief , succinct
USAGE You would normally use the last three synonyms about a person.

work NOUN

1 *The plastering will be several days' work.*
▶ labour, effort, exertion, toil, industry, (*more informal*) slog
2 *Stella's looking for work abroad.*
▶ employment, a job, an occupation, a career, business
3 *He had finished all his work by lunchtime.*
▶ tasks, jobs, assignments, projects, commissions

4 *He has written a new work for mixed choir.*
▶ composition, piece, opus, oeuvre, production
5 *It is a fine literary work.*
▶ creation, achievement, accomplishment

work VERB

1 *Some staff were still working at nine in the evening.*
▶ labour, toil, exert yourself, be at your desk, slave, (*more informal*) keep at it
AN OPPOSITE IS rest
2 *Margaret works in a bank.*
▶ have a job, be employed, earn a living
3 *The dishwasher was working again, thank goodness.*
▶ function, operate, perform, run, in working order, (*more informal*) behave
AN OPPOSITE IS break down
4 *He showed me how to work the coffee machine.*
▶ operate, use, manipulate
5 *The plan had worked.*
▶ succeed, be successful, work out, take effect, (*more informal*) pay off, (*more informal*) do the trick
AN OPPOSITE IS fail
6 *farmers who work the land*
▶ cultivate, till, dig, farm
7 *You can work miracles with the right ingredients.*
▶ achieve, accomplish, produce, perform, bring about, cause, (*more informal*) pull off
8 *Work the mixture into a thick dough.*
▶ knead, form, mould, mix, blend, stir, shape
work out
1 *The idea should work out.*
▶ succeed, be successful, work, (*more informal*) pay off, (*more informal*) do the trick
AN OPPOSITE IS fail
2 *Things didn't quite work out as expected.*
▶ turn out, occur, happen, evolve, develop, end up, come out
work out at *The cost worked out at over a million dollars.*
▶ amount to, add up to, come to, total, reach
work something out
1 *Let's work out a plan.*
▶ devise, draw up, formulate, prepare, put together
2 *I can't work out the answer.*
▶ calculate, determine, reckon up, resolve, solve
3 *We're trying to work out what all this means.*
▶ understand, comprehend, make sense of, puzzle out, figure out, clear up
work up *It's hard to work up any enthusiasm.*
▶ raise, rouse, generate, stimulate, stir up

workable ADJECTIVE

A law on such matters could be workable.
▶ practical, practicable, feasible, realistic, possible, sensible, practical
OPPOSITES ARE unworkable, impractical

worker NOUN

1 *A strike by clerical workers brought the system to a standstill.*
▶ employee, member of staff, operative, working person
2 *She was a tireless worker for the party.*
▶ labourer, campaigner, supporter

a b c d e f g h i j k l m n o p q r s t u v **w** x y z

workforce NOUN

The company will lay off 15% of its workforce.
► employees, workers, staff, labour force, personnel

working ADJECTIVE

1 *extra support for working mothers*
► employed, in work, salaried, waged
AN OPPOSITE IS unemployed

2 *a working model of a steam engine*
► functioning, operational, operating, running, usable, going, in use, in working order
AN OPPOSITE IS non- functioning

workmanship NOUN

The quality of workmanship is of a high standard.
► craftsmanship, artistry, handiwork, technique, expertise, skill

works PLURAL NOUN

1 *Visitors can explore the glass works and blacksmith's shop.*
► factory, workshop, foundry, plant, unit

2 *The works of the clock needed cleaning.*
► mechanism, movement, action, parts, machinery, insides

workshop NOUN

1 *Her husband had a workshop at the end of the garden.*
► workroom, studio

2 *The company organized a workshop on teleconferences.*
► seminar, discussion group, meeting, class

world NOUN

1 *The university has links with academic institutions around the world.*
► earth, globe, planet

2 *Representatives came from the world of high finance*
► sphere, domain, field, area, realm, circle, milieu

3 *The world knows that these people need help.*
► everyone, everybody, people, humankind, humanity

worldly ADJECTIVE

1 *He had no ambitions for worldly power.*
► earthly, terrestrial, temporal, physical, material, materialistic, mundane, avaricious, greedy, selfish
AN OPPOSITE IS spiritual

2 *She was worldly enough to understand what was going on.*
► sophisticated, experienced, worldly-wise, knowing
AN OPPOSITE IS naive

worn ADJECTIVE

His coat was old and worn.
► shabby, threadbare, tattered, frayed, worn out, moth-eaten, ragged, scruffy, (*more informal*) tatty
AN OPPOSITE IS smart

worn out *By the time they got home they were all worn out.*
► exhausted, tired out, weary, fatigued, shattered, (*more informal*) dead tired, (*more informal*) played out, (*more informal*) washed out

worried ADJECTIVE

1 *She had a worried look on her face. You seem worried about something.*
► anxious, troubled, disturbed, uneasy, distraught, apprehensive, bothered, tense, strained, nervous

2 *I was worried that our money would run out.*
► afraid, fearful, concerned, frightened, scared

worry VERB

1 *Try not to worry Dad while he's working.*
► bother, pester, disturb, annoy

2 *A dog had been worrying the sheep.*
► attack, torment, savage

3 *I was trying not to worry.*
► be anxious, be troubled, be disturbed, fret, panic
AN OPPOSITE IS be unconcerned

4 *Something was worrying her.*
► trouble, bother, disturb, distress, upset, concern

worry NOUN

1 *I was too affected by worry to concentrate on the work.*
► anxiety, agitation, apprehension, unease, distress, fear, misgiving, tension

2 *Each day seems to bring another worry.*
► problem, difficulty, trouble, concern, care, burden, misgiving

worrying ADJECTIVE

There was a worrying smell of gas.
► alarming, disturbing, worrisome, disquieting, distressing, perturbing, troublesome
AN OPPOSITE IS reassuring

worsen VERB

1 *Development of the site would worsen traffic problems.*
► aggravate, exacerbate, make worse, intensify, magnify, increase
AN OPPOSITE IS improve

2 *The economic situation was beginning to worsen.*
► get or become worse, deteriorate, decline, degenerate, weaken, slide
OPPOSITES ARE improve, recover

worship NOUN

Temples are places of worship.
► adoration, veneration, reverence (for), adulation, exaltation, devotion (to), idolatry

PLACES OF WORSHIP
abbey, church, cathedral, chapel, gurdwara, mandir, meeting house (for Quakers), minster, mosque, synagogue, tabernacle, temple, vihara.

worship VERB

1 *They worshipped the sun as the giver of life.*
► revere, reverence, venerate, glorify, exalt, laud, pray to

2 *a materialistic society that worships consumer goods*
► idolize, revere, adore, dote on, be devoted to, look up to, love
AN OPPOSITE IS despise

W

worth NOUN
1 *She knows her own worth.*
▶ value, merit, excellence, worthiness, quality, calibre, talents, strengths
2 *He was forced to sell the car for a fraction of its true worth.*
▶ value, cost, selling price

worthless ADJECTIVE
1 *The certificate turned out to be worthless.*
▶ valueless, of no value
AN OPPOSITE IS valuable
2 *Their advice proved worthless.*
▶ useless, futile, ineffective, ineffectual, pointless
OPPOSITES ARE useful, worthwhile
She regarded him as a worthless slob.
▶ good-for-nothing, useless, contemptible, despicable, miserable, wretched, vile, (*more informal*) no-good
AN OPPOSITE IS worthy

worthwhile ADJECTIVE
1 *I've never done anything worthwhile like writing a book.*
▶ useful, valuable, worthy, meaningful, significant, positive, productive, important, invaluable
OPPOSITES ARE worthless, useless
2 *It might be worthwhile to join a local archaeology society.*
▶ advantageous, beneficial, helpful, useful, profitable, rewarding
OPPOSITES ARE pointless, useless

worthy ADJECTIVE
1 *Our support extends to worthy causes around the country.*
▶ worthwhile, praiseworthy, deserving, creditable, honourable, reputable, commendable, respectable, admirable
OPPOSITES ARE unworthy, disreputable
2 *a worthy member of society*
▶ virtuous, honourable, honest, upright, moral, decent
OPPOSITES ARE unworthy, disreputable
3 **worthy of** *The site yielded pottery worthy of study and publication.*
▶ deserving, meriting, warranting, good enough for

would-be ADJECTIVE
Are we asking too much of would-be adoptive parents?
▶ aspiring, budding, intending, hopeful, prospective

wound NOUN
1 *There was a deep wound in the animal's forehead.*
▶ injury, scar, gash, cut, abrasion, disfigurement, hurt
2 *She survived these wounds inflicted by fate.*
▶ blow, insult, trauma, slight, affront, hurt

wound VERB
He was trying to rescue a colleague who had been wounded.
▶ injure, hurt, harm, maim, disable, damage, disfigure

wrangle VERB
I did not come here to wrangle with you.
▶ quarrel, argue, row, fight, squabble

wrangle NOUN
The courts rejected the appeal after a long legal wrangle.
▶ dispute, argument, disagreement, quarrel, row, fight, squabble

wrap VERB
1 *She wrapped a rug round her legs.*
▶ fold, swathe, wind, pack, place
2 *Harry wrapped himself in a towel.*
▶ cover, swathe, envelop, sheathe, enfold
3 *I'll wrap the sandwiches in foil.*
▶ cover, pack, fold, enclose

wrapper NOUN
The chocolate bar had 'extra value' printed on its wrapper.
▶ wrapping, cover, packaging

wreath NOUN
A wreath of artificial poppies was held down by a brick.
▶ garland, circlet, coronet, crown, ring

wreck NOUN
1 *The wreck of an ancient galley was discovered off Sicily.*
▶ wreckage, shipwreck, remains, hulk, skeleton
2 *It was the wreck of all their hopes.*
▶ ruin, destruction, undoing, demolition, devastation, overthrow, termination

wreck VERB
1 *The ship had been wrecked in a storm.*
▶ shipwreck, sink, destroy, break up
2 *He had wrecked his car when it skidded off the road.*
▶ crash, smash, demolish, shatter, crumple, crush, (*more informal*) write off
3 *A freak virus wrecked their holiday plans.*
▶ ruin, spoil, disrupt, undo, dash, put an end to

wreckage NOUN
1 *One person had to be cut from the wreckage by firemen.*
▶ wreck, debris, rubble, remains, ruin
2 *Wreckage from the aircraft was scattered for miles.*
▶ debris, fragments, remains, detritus, pieces, relics

wrench NOUN
1 *With a wrench he tore himself free.*
▶ jerk, jolt, pull, tug, twist, (*informal*) yank
2 *It was a wrench leaving the children behind with Polly.*
▶ trauma, painful experience

wrench VERB
Charlotte heard her wrench the door open.
▶ pull, jerk, tug, force, prise, lever, wrest, (*informal*) yank

a b c d e f g h i j k l m n o p q r s t u v w x y z

wretch NOUN

1 *He was a lonely, miserable wretch.*
▶ poor creature, down and out, beggar, pauper

2 *He had been mugged by some wretches in the park.*
▶ ruffian, scoundrel, rogue, villain, rascal, delinquent

wretched ADJECTIVE

1 *She had seldom felt so tired or so wretched.*
▶ miserable, unhappy, sad, despondent, melancholy, cast down, unwell, poorly

2 *The weather was wretched all week. The family had to endure wretched living conditions.*
▶ atrocious, appalling, dreadful, dismal, bleak

wriggle VERB

He wriggled further back on the bed till he was leaning up against the wall.
▶ twist, writhe, squirm, waggle, wiggle, worm

wriggle out of *He tried to wriggle out of work, as usual.*
▶ avoid, shirk, dodge, evade, escape from

wring VERB

1 *He went to the sink to wring out the socks.*
▶ squeeze, twist, compress, crush, press

2 *They managed to wring more money out of the government.*
▶ extract, coerce, force, wrest, exact, extort

3 *The look on his face wrung her heart.*
▶ stab, tear, pierce, rend, distress, pain, hurt

wrinkle NOUN

Despite being carefully ironed the shirt was full of wrinkles. The wrinkles on her neck moved when she swallowed.
▶ crease, fold, pucker, crinkle, ridge, furrow, dimple, gather, line, pleat

wrinkle VERB

You have to wrinkle your nose to break the spell.
▶ crease, crinkle, pucker up, crumple, fold, furrow, ridge, ruck up, rumple
AN OPPOSITE IS smooth

wrinkled ADJECTIVE

His hands were white and very wrinkled.
▶ creased, wrinkly, crinkly, crumpled, furrowed, shrivelled, lined, pleated, ridged, rumpled, wavy, wizened

write VERB

1 *He wrote the details in a notebook.*
▶ write down, jot down, take down, put down, record, transcribe, make a note of, note down, scribble, register

2 *After a while she stopped writing to him.*
▶ communicate (with), send letters, keep in touch

3 *The music was written one summer at the lakeside retreat.*
▶ compose, create, set down, compile, pen, draft

write off *He wrote off for a free voucher.*
▶ apply, send off, send away

write something off

1 *The Inland Revenue wrote off millions of pounds in unpaid taxes.*
▶ disregard, cancel, delete, annul

2 *(informal) He wrote off his car on a Belgian motorway.*
▶ crash, smash, wreck

---

writer NOUN

one of the great writers of the 20th century
▶ author, novelist, poet, dramatist, essayist, wordsmith

NAMES FOR WRITERS

books: author, novelist, biographer, essayist, ghostwriter (writes for another person named as author), fabulist (writer of fables).

newspapers: journalist, reporter, columnist, copywriter, correspondent, leader-writer, diarist, reviewer.

poetry and drama: poet; dramatist, playwright, comedian, tragedian; librettist (texts of operas), scriptwriter.

---

writhe VERB

I tossed and writhed on the hard bed.
▶ wriggle, squirm, thrash about, toss, flail, struggle, twist, contort

writing NOUN

1 *Her writing is neater than mine.*
▶ handwriting, penmanship, calligraphy, script, letters, longhand, scribble, scrawl

2 *She took up writing in old age.*
▶ composition, literature, letters

3 **writings** *His political views are clearly reflected in his writings.*
▶ literary texts, literature, texts, works

wrong ADJECTIVE

1 *It was wrong to take the books without asking.*
▶ bad, dishonest, blameworthy, reprehensible, sinful, wicked
AN OPPOSITE IS right

2 *The law lays down limits and it is wrong to exceed them.*
▶ unlawful, illegal, criminal, delinquent
OPPOSITES ARE lawful, legal

3 *She knew she had given a wrong answer. The visitor pressed the wrong buzzer.*
▶ incorrect, erroneous, inaccurate, mistaken
OPPOSITES ARE correct, right

4 *I must have said something wrong.*
▶ inappropriate, unsuitable, inapt, ill-advised, ill-judged, unfitting
AN OPPOSITE IS appropriate

5 *There's something wrong with the equipment.*
▶ faulty, defective, amiss, broken down, out of order, unusable
AN OPPOSITE IS right

wrong NOUN
1 *He had done many wrongs that needed putting right.*
▶ misdeed, bad deed, offence, crime, injury, injustice
AN OPPOSITE IS good deed
2 *We know the difference between right and wrong.*
▶ immorality, badness, sinfulness, wickedness, evil
OPPOSITES ARE goodness, virtue

wrong VERB
She was determined to forget the man who had wronged her.
▶ mistreat, abuse, be unfair to, maltreat, ill-treat, treat unfairly, cheat, do an injustice to, harm, hurt, misrepresent, traduce

wrongdoer NOUN
Wrongdoers will be punished.
▶ offender, transgressor, miscreant, lawbreaker, culprit, delinquent, malefactor, criminal, crook, evildoer, sinner

wrongdoing NOUN
The law prevents criminals profiting from their wrongdoings.
▶ lawbreaking, criminality, misbehaviour, delinquency, offence, crime, sinfulness, wickedness, immorality

wrongful ADJECTIVE
She is claiming damages for wrongful dismissal.
▶ unjust, unfair, unlawful, unjustified, unwarranted, undeserved, unreasonable, uncalled-for
OPPOSITES ARE rightful, fair

wry ADJECTIVE
1 *Robbie sipped his drink and pulled a wry face.*
▶ twisted, distorted, contorted, crooked, uneven, bent
2 *Lawrence allowed himself a wry smile.*
▶ mocking, sardonic, derisive, dry, ironic, droll

xenophobia NOUN
Feelings of xenophobia can so easily be whipped up.
▶ nationalism, jingoism, racism

xenophobic ADJECTIVE
the triumphs of xenophobic right-wing parties
▶ nationalistic, jingoistic, racist

yank VERB
(informal) He yanked the door open and stumbled inside.
▶ pull, force, jerk, tug, wrench, prise, wrest

yap VERB
A dog yapped frantically somewhere inside.
▶ yelp, bark, woof

yard NOUN
A pony stood in the middle of the yard.
▶ court, courtyard, enclosure, quadrangle, (more informal) quad

yardstick NOUN
They regard the family as the yardstick to measure values by.
▶ standard, criterion, benchmark, gauge, guideline, measure

yarn NOUN
1 *This is a lovely soft yarn.*
▶ thread, wool, fibre, strand, twine
2 *(informal) He rang with a yarn about problems at his hotel.*
▶ story, tale, rigmarole, anecdote, narrative

yearn VERB
They yearned to be home.
▶ long, crave, pine, desire, hanker, wish

yearning NOUN
She had always had a yearning to play the piano.
▶ longing, desire, craving, hankering, wish, (more informal) yen

yell VERB
He yelled at them to stop.
▶ shout, cry out, call, shriek, scream, bawl, exclaim

yell NOUN
She gave a yell of pain.
▶ cry, shriek, scream, screech

yelp VERB
He yelped with delight.
▶ squeal, squawk, shriek, scream, howl, yell

yelp NOUN
The dog let out a yelp.
▶ yap, bark, woof

yen NOUN
(informal) a yen for travel
▶ yearning, longing, desire, craving, hankering, wish

yield NOUN
1 *The farm has produced a good yield.*
▶ crop, harvest, produce, product
2 *I'm looking for a savings bond with a high yield.*
▶ return, interest, earnings, income, profit

yield VERB

1 *The contest continues until one side yields.*
▶ surrender, succumb, capitulate, submit, give in, give way, concede defeat, (*more informal*) cave in, (*informal*) throw in the towel, (*informal*) throw up the sponge

2 *The allotment yields a fine crop of root vegetables.*
▶ produce, grow, bear, supply

3 *an investment yielding a high interest*
▶ earn, generate, provide, return, pay, attract

yob NOUN

A gang of yobs were making a nuisance of themselves.
▶ hooligan, hoodlum, lout, ruffian, troublemaker, vandal, thug, bully, delinquent, tough, rough, tearaway

young ADJECTIVE

1 *She enjoyed working with young people.*
▶ youthful, juvenile, teenage, adolescent
OPPOSITES ARE old, elderly

2 *They seem young for their age.*
▶ immature, childish, babyish
AN OPPOSITE IS mature

---

young NOUN

1 *Parents have an instinct to protect their young.*
▶ offspring, family, progeny, brood, issue, litter
2 **the young** *They enjoyed talking to the young.*
▶ young people, youths, youngsters, juveniles, minors
RELATED ADJECTIVE juvenile

SOME NAMES FOR YOUNG ANIMALS

calf (cattle, elephant, seal, and other large animals), chick (chicken, hawk, pheasant), colt (horse), cub (badger, bear, fox, leopard, lion, tiger, walrus, wolf), cygnet (swan), duckling (duck), eaglet (eagle), elver (eel), fawn (deer), filly (horse), foal (horse, zebra), gosling (goose), joey (kangaroo, wallaby, possum), kid (antelope, goat), kitten (cat), lamb (sheep), leveret (hare), owlet (owl), parr (salmon), piglet (pig), pup (dog, wolf, seal), puppy (dog), smolt (salmon), tadpole (frog, toad), whelp (dog, wolf).

---

youth NOUN

1 *She had spent most of her youth abroad.*
▶ early life, early years, teenage years, adolescence, boyhood or girlhood, childhood, infancy, (*informal*) teens

2 *a group of youths*
▶ young person, teenager, youngster, adolescent, boy or girl, juvenile, (*more informal*) kid, (*more informal*) lad

youthful ADJECTIVE

1 *They sang before a youthful audience.*
▶ young

2 *He had a youthful appearance.*
▶ young-looking, fresh, lively, sprightly, vigorous, well-preserved

Zz

zany ADJECTIVE

a zany thriller about ecological disaster
▶ crazy, weird, bizarre, eccentric
OPPOSITES ARE serious, sensible

zeal NOUN

a zeal to improve society
▶ enthusiasm, fervour, ardour, zest, passion, devotion, keenness, eagerness, dedication

zealous ADJECTIVE

Brian was a zealous patriot and served his country well.
▶ keen, fervent, enthusiastic, fanatical, passionate, conscientious, committed, diligent, eager, earnest
AN OPPOSITE IS apathetic

zenith NOUN

The country was then at the zenith of its power.
▶ peak, pinnacle, height, top, acme, apex, climax
AN OPPOSITE IS nadir

zero NOUN

Opportunities for further education might be reduced to zero.
▶ nothing, nought, nil

zero VERB

zero in on *We need to zero in on being accurate and careful.*
▶ focus on, concentrate on, fix on, centre on, home in on

zest NOUN

After his recovery he had a renewed zest for life.
▶ eagerness, energy, enjoyment, enthusiasm, zeal, liveliness, pleasure

zigzag ADJECTIVE

Some escaping animals take a zigzag course.
▶ winding, meandering, serpentine, twisting, weaving, bendy, crooked

zigzag VERB

A narrow path zigzagged steeply down to the shore.
▶ wind, meander, snake, twist, weave, curve, bend

zone NOUN

He decided to leave the war zone and get back to his family.
▶ area, sector, section, region, sphere, district, vicinity, locality, neighbourhood, territory, tract

zoom VERB

(*informal*) *A motorbike zoomed across their path.*
▶ race, rush, speed, dash, hurry, hurtle, (*informal*) whiz, (*informal*) zip

Top 10 tips for story writing

1. Plan your story or description. Think of story hooks for the beginning—and perhaps a twist or surprise at the end.

2. You may find it helpful to discuss your writing with a friend before you write.

3. Keep to your plan when you write.

4. Focus on the character of the people in your story. Showing is better than telling.

5. Think about the setting; try to create a sense of atmosphere.

6. Think about the pace of the story. It is often better to use short sentences for dramatic moments and longer sentences for description.

7. Check over your use of dialogue. Does it move the story forward well?

8. Watch out for any overused words like the ones listed on page x. Instead of using these words, try to choose synonyms from the relevant entries.

9. Write in well-punctuated sentences.

10. Use a dictionary to check your spelling and this thesaurus to find the best words.

Top tips for non-fiction writing

1. Plan your writing. Think about the style of your writing—whether it is instructional, a report, persuasive writing, or letter writing.

2. The Topic panels will be particularly useful when you are writing non-fiction. For example, if you are writing about the human skeleton, you will find the panel at 'bone' informative. Look for other subject-specific panels—you will find a full list at the beginning of this thesaurus.

3. Be careful about the language you use—in non-fiction it is often more appropriate to use formal words and phrases, rather than informal ones.